Frommer's®
Caribbean 2005

The Baths, Virgin Gorda, where giant boulders form a series of pools and caves. A great spot for swimming and snorkeling. See chapter 8. © *M. Timothy O'Keefe Photography.*

Beach on the laid-back island of Cayman Brac. See chapter 9. © Stephen Frink/Waterhouse.

Aerial view of Little Bay on the small, secluded island of Anguilla. See chapter 3.
© Susan Pierres Photography.

The sheltered harbor of Gustavia, the capital of St. Barthélemy. See chapter 19.
© Susan Pierres Photography.

The Anse Chastanet reef off St. Lucia (see chapter 22). Other great dive sites are Bonaire (chapter 7), Virgin Gorda (chapter 8), Grand Cayman (chapter 9), Saba (chapter 18), and St. Croix (chapter 26). © M. Timothy O'Keefe Photography.

Grand Anse Beach in Grenada, with its clear, calm waters and pure white sand, is 2 miles of heaven. See chapter 13. © M. Timothy O'Keefe Photography.

The Buccaneer Golf Course in St. Croix offers scenic views and challenging play. See chapter 26. © M. Timothy O'Keefe Photography.

For a different side of Grenada, visit the market in St. George, especially lively on Saturday mornings, with everything from spices to sandals for sale. See chapter 13.
© M. Timothy O'Keefe Photography.

Carnival transforms Port-of-Spain, Trinidad, into one big colorful party, complete with dazzling costumes, calypso, and dancing. See chapter 25. © Robert Holmes Photography.

The lush rain forest in Morne Trois Pitons National Park, Dominica, is dotted with hot springs and waterfalls. See chapter 11. © Markham Johnson/Robert Holmes Photography.

A view of Antigua's historic English Harbour from Shirley Heights. The harbor is known for its sailing facilities. See chapter 4. © Susan Pierres Photography.

Nevis's reef-protected Pinney's Beach, a 3-mile strip of golden sand that culminates in a sleepy lagoon. See chapter 21. © Susan Pierres Photography.

Frommer's

Caribbean

2005

by Darwin Porter & Danforth Prince

Here's what the critics say about Frommer's:

"Amazingly easy to use. Very portable, very complete."
—Booklist

"Detailed, accurate, and easy-to-read information for all price ranges."
—Glamour Magazine

"Hotel information is close to encyclopedic."
—Des Moines Sunday Register

"Frommer's Guides have a way of giving you a real feel for a place."
—Knight Ridder Newspapers

WILEY
Wiley Publishing, Inc.

About the Authors

As a team of veteran travel writers, **Darwin Porter** and **Danforth Prince** have produced numerous titles for Frommer's, including best-selling guides to Italy, France, the Caribbean, England, and Germany. Porter, a former bureau chief of *The Miami Herald*, is also a Hollywood biographer, his most recent releases titled *The Secret Life of Humphrey Bogart* and *Katharine the Great*, the latter a close-up of the private life of the late Katharine Hepburn. Prince was formerly employed by the Paris bureau of the *New York Times*, and is today the president of Blood Moon Productions and other media-related firms.

Published by:

Wiley Publishing, Inc.

111 River St.
Hoboken, NJ 07030-5774

ISBN 0-7645-7063-3

Editor: Jennifer Moore
Production Editor: Blair J. Pottenger
Cartographer: Nicholas Trotter
Photo Editor: Richard Fox
Production by Wiley Indianapolis Composition Services

Front cover photo: Under an umbrella on a Caribbean beach
Back cover photo: Grand Anse Beach, Grenada

For information on our other products and services or to obtain technical support, please contact our Customer Care Department within the U.S. at 800/762-2974, outside the U.S. at 317/572-3993 or fax 317/572-4002.

Wiley also publishes its books in a variety of electronic formats. Some content that appears in print may not be available in electronic formats.

Manufactured in the United States of America

5 4 3 2 1

Contents

19 St. Barthélemy 512

20 St. Eustatius 532

21 St. Kitts & Nevis 540

22 St. Lucia 569

23 St. Maarten/St. Martin 593

List of Maps

An Invitation to the Reader

In researching this book, we discovered many wonderful places—hotels, restaurants, shops, and more. We're sure you'll find others. Please tell us about them, so we can share the information with your fellow travelers in upcoming editions. If you were disappointed with a recommendation, we'd love to know that, too. Please write to:

Frommer's Caribbean 2005
Wiley Publishing, Inc. • 111 River St. • Hoboken, NJ 07030-5774

An Additional Note

Please be advised that travel information is subject to change at any time—and this is especially true of prices. We therefore suggest that you write or call ahead for confirmation when making your travel plans. The authors, editors, and publisher cannot be held responsible for the experiences of readers while traveling. Your safety is important to us, however, so we encourage you to stay alert and be aware of your surroundings. Keep a close eye on cameras, purses, and wallets, all favorite targets of thieves and pickpockets.

Other Great Guides for Your Trip:

Frommer's Caribbean Cruises & Ports of Call
Frommer's Caribbean Ports of Call
Frommer's Puerto Rico
Frommer's Jamaica
Frommer's Virgin Islands
Frommer's Portable Aruba

Frommer's Star Ratings, Icons & Abbreviations

Every hotel, restaurant, and attraction listing in this guide has been ranked for quality, value, service, amenities, and special features using a **star-rating system.** In country, state, and regional guides, we also rate towns and regions to help you narrow down your choices and budget your time accordingly. Hotels and restaurants are rated on a scale of zero (recommended) to three stars (exceptional). Attractions, shopping, nightlife, towns, and regions are rated according to the following scale: zero stars (recommended), one star (highly recommended), two stars (very highly recommended), and three stars (must-see).

In addition to the star-rating system, we also use **eight feature icons** that point you to the great deals, in-the-know advice, and unique experiences that separate travelers from tourists. Throughout the book, look for:

Finds	Special finds—those places only insiders know about
Fun Fact	Fun facts—details that make travelers more informed and their trips more fun
Kids	Best bets for kids and advice for the whole family
Moments	Special moments—those experiences that memories are made of
Overrated	Places or experiences not worth your time or money
Tips	Insider tips—great ways to save time and money
Value	Great values—where to get the best deals
Warning	Warning—traveler's advisories are usually in effect

The following **abbreviations** are used for credit cards:

AE	American Express	DISC	Discover	V	Visa
DC	Diners Club	MC	MasterCard		

Frommers.com

Now that you have the guidebook to a great trip, visit our website at **www.frommers.com** for travel information on more than 3,000 destinations. With features updated regularly, we give you instant access to the most current trip-planning information available. At Frommers.com, you'll also find the best prices on airfares, accommodations, and car rentals—and you can even book travel online through our travel booking partners. At Frommers.com, you'll also find the following:

- Online updates to our most popular guidebooks
- Vacation sweepstakes and contest giveaways
- Newsletter highlighting the hottest travel trends
- Online travel message boards with featured travel discussions

THE DISAPPEARANCE OF CLAUDIA KIRSCHHOCH

Claudia Kirschhoch, an assistant editor for Frommer's Travel Guides, went on a Sandals Resort press trip with a group of journalists on May 24, 2000. The itinerary was originally New York City to Cuba by way of Montego Bay, Jamaica. The American journalists were unexpectedly denied entry into Cuba. Because all return flights to New York were full, Claudia stayed on in Jamaica, at Sandals' Beaches Resort in Negril, until her scheduled return flight to New York on June 1, 2000.

The last confirmed sighting of Claudia was at the resort on Saturday, May 27, 2000. Her luggage, purse, passport, cash, credit cards, and camera were found in her room. Claudia was 29 years old at the time of her disappearance. She is 5'2" tall and 105 pounds with long dark brown hair, brown eyes, and fair skin. If you have any information, call ℂ **888/967-9300.** For more information about Claudia and the latest media coverage of her disappearance, please visit the "Help Find Claudia" website at http://findclaudia. homestead.com.

Frommer's is fully supportive of the ongoing investigation. Because we do not know the full story of Claudia's disappearance, Frommer's is not currently advising travelers against visiting Jamaica. According to the Bureau of Consular Affairs, however, crime is a serious problem in Jamaica. Thus, we encourage you to consult the bureau's website (http://travel.state.gov) for Consular Information Sheets, travel advisories, and safety tips. Our readers' safety is important to us, and we will continue to provide you with pertinent information to assist your safe and happy travel experiences.

What's New in the Caribbean

ANGUILLA Overlooking Meads Bay, the aptly named **Meads Bay Hideaway,** Meads Bay (© 264/498-5555), is this chic island's latest resort property. A tropical oasis, it offers spacious one- or two-bedroom penthouses. Right off the beach, this is a pocket of posh. See p. 66.

ANTIGUA The only accommodation on island that would qualify as a little plantation inn, **Harmony Hall,** Brown's Bay Mill (© 268/460-4120), is also an art gallery and restaurant built around a ruined sugar mill. Secluded and tranquil, the hall rents out six large, high-ceilinged bedrooms. It's not on the beach, however, but some tempting sands are nearby. More and more resort guests are escaping their grounds at night to dine at local eateries, such as **Papa Zouk,** Hilda Davis Drive, St. Johns (© 268/464-7576), which serves some of the best and freshest seafood on island. If not that choice, you can sample the zesty cuisine at **Sticky Wicket,** Pavilion Drive, Coolidge (© 268/481-7000), featuring an international cuisine focusing on West Indian dishes. It's also the island's most frequented sports bar. See p. 86, 87, and 89.

ARUBA Those visitors wishing to escape the megaresorts and go "the inn way" are seeking out **The Boardwalk Vacation Retreat,** Bakval 20 (© 297/86-66654), a short walk from the high rises and casinos, but a world apart. Accommodations consist of well-furnished one- or two-bedroom casitas only 135m (450 ft.) from Palm Beach, a strip of white sand with the best

swimming. The island's hot new dining choice is **Hostaria da' Vittorio,** L. G. Smith Blvd. 380, Palm Beach (© 297/58-63838), across from the Hyatt Regency. Vittorio Muscariello dazzles palates with Mediterranean specialties cooked in his open-to-view kitchen. See p. 113 and 116.

BARBADOS Talk about recycling. **Lone Star Hotel,** Hwy. 1, Mount Stanfast, St. James (© 246/419-0599), is a chic new restaurant and hotel that was converted from a dreary 1940s garage. Four sumptuous suites—two opening right on the beach—are available for rent, and they're named after such vehicles as the Studebaker, Lincoln, or Buick. A real discovery, **Little Arches,** Enterprise Coast Road, Christ Church (© 800/860-8013), is a little charmer, a standout among boutique hotels on the island, with its individually styled bedrooms opening onto the ocean and containing four-poster beds. A hot dining ticket during the winter of 2004 was **Daphne's,** Paynes Bay, St. James (© 246/432-2731), serving a sublime Mediterranean and Caribbean cuisine in an intimate beach-bordering setting. In a former beachfront villa, **The Tides,** Holetown, St. James (© 246/432-8356), is introducing its take on a Caribbean and international cuisine—and doing so with charm and grace. The chef studied with England's fabled duet, the Roux brothers, who arguably are the best chefs in the British Isles. See p. 137, 140, 144, and 147.

BONAIRE A new airline, **BonairExel** (℃ **599/717-3471**), has begun flying 14 times a day between Bonaire and Curaçao and six times a day between Bonaire and Aruba. A popular new eatery on island is the oddly named **It Rains Fish,** Kaya Jan N. E. Craane 24 in Kralendijk (℃ **599/717-8780**). With a name like that, you know it specializes in seafood, and it does so exceedingly well. See p. 164 and 170.

DOMINICA If you're already in the Caribbean and would like to extend your vacation by adding the lush island of Dominica to your itinerary, you can fly an emerging airline, **Caribbean Star** (℃ **268/480-2561**), from such islands as St. Lucia, Antigua, Barbados, St. Kitts, Sint Maarten, St. Vincent, Tortola (B.V.I.), and Trinidad. For a close-up look at the exotic interior of Dominica, you can take the **Rain Forest Aerial Tram** (℃ **767/448-8775**), which takes you "over" the rainforest and through Morne Trois National Park. You're treated to exotic bird life, roaring waterfalls, and much tropical flora. See p. 256 and 266.

DOMINICAN REPUBLIC In the capital city of Santo Domingo, **Sofitel Nicolas de Ovando,** Calle Las Damas (℃ **809/685-9955**), a 16th-century mansion, has been restored and opened to the public in the heart of the colonial city. It is now one of the most atmospheric choices in town, with such features as a good restaurant with a terrace facing a courtyard and two bars with a view of the pool. All the modern amenities have been added but the classic architecture retained. See p. 295.

GRENADA In this spice island, a new and secluded hideaway, **Bel Air Plantation,** St. David's Point (℃ **473/ 444-6305**), has opened. In a jungle-like setting, it stands on 7.2 hectares (18 acres) of land at the southwestern end of the island. Guests stay in vibrantly colored gingerbread cottages overlooking St. David's Harbour. One of the greatest chefs of London, Gary Rhodes, has invaded Grenada, with the opening of **Rhodes** in the Calabash Hotel, L'Anse Aux Epines (℃ **473/444-4334**). The chic restaurant, which was inaugurated in the winter of 2004, immediately became the choice dining table on island. The chef brings "a taste of Grenada with a touch of Rhodes" to this fine dining enclave. See p. 308 and 315.

JAMAICA In August Jamaica comes alive with the pulsating sounds of reggae presented at weeklong music extravaganzas. The biggest and best of these has been relaunched as **Reggae Summerfest,** taking place in August (dates vary) at Montego Bay, the leading resort on island. During the same month an equally compelling festival, the **Reggae Sunfest,** also takes place at Mo Bay. Featured performers include some of the biggest names in reggae, especially Ziggy Marley, son of the late reggae king, Bob Marley. In the northern resort of Ocho Rios, the famous old all-inclusive, Ciboney, has renewed itself as the **Grand Sport Villa Golf Resort & Spa,** Main Street, St. Ann (℃ **876/974-1027**). Much improved, this lush resort stands on 18 hectares (44 acres) of tropical gardens, with its own white-sandy beach. See p. 368 and 394.

PUERTO RICO The colonial sector of San Juan continues to blossom out with some of the leading restaurants of the Caribbean. Chief among these is **Aquaviva,** Calle Fortaleza 364 (℃ **787/722-0665**), which serves the capital's finest Latino take on fresh seafood. A new competitor, although not quite as good, is the innovative **Barú,** Calle Sebastián 150 (℃ **787/ 977-7107**). One of Puerto Rico's most fashionable restaurants, this establishment serves some of the finest

Caribbean and Mediterranean-inspired cuisine in the city. See p. 466.

SABA On this remote volcanic island, the dining picture has improved considerably with the opening of **YIIK,** Windwardside (© **533/ 416-2539**), a rooftop restaurant that presents a savory international cuisine nightly. Just wait until you try the chicken strips grilled in a mandarin orange and ginger sauce and served with honey mustard. The views match the food. See p. 509.

ST. BARTS On the chic and pricey French-held island of St. Barts, **Baie des Anges,** Flamands (© **590/ 27-63-61**), has emerged as a secluded little hideaway of luxury and charm. Built right on the ocean and surrounded by gardens, the 10-room unit also shelters one of the island's finest dining rooms, La Langouste, serving a savory array of French specialties, including Caribbean lobsters selected from a tank. See p. 520.

ST. EUSTATIUS In this sleepy Dutch-held island, change comes slowly. But visitors in the winter of 2004 were delighted with the opening of a new restaurant, the aptly named **Ocean View Terrace** in Fort Oranje (© **599/318-2934**), serving a savory West Indian cuisine with the focus on fresh seafood. It's set within the courtyard of the government's guesthouse, part of the island's most historic fort. The chef makes the best curried goat on island. See p. 536.

ST. KITTS & NEVIS On the island of St. Kitts, the newest attraction is **The St. Kitts Scenic Railway** (© **869/ 465-7263**), which takes visitors in a double-decker railcar through some of the island's most spectacular scenery. The narrow gauge railway follows old sugar-cane train tracks. On the sister island of Nevis, the **Nevisian Heritage Village** (© **869/469-5521**) has opened at Fothergill's Estate. Historic structures such as a blacksmith's

workshop were moved to the site. The attraction affords a chance to wander into Nevis of yesterday. See p. 553 and 567.

ST. LUCIA In this island of megaresorts, **Ti Kaye Village Resort,** Anse Cochon (©**758/456-8101**), has opened as the most special, fun, and quirky place to stay. An elite retreat, it is spread across a cliff overlooking the Caribbean and evokes a small village standing in a lush setting of 6.4 hectares (16 acres). Accommodations are in individual gingerbread-trimmed cottages, and bedrooms contain four-posters and an open-air garden shower. See p. 579.

ST. VINCENT The launch pad for the Grenadines, St. Vincent is a stopover for yachties who dine at its new waterfront enclave of fine cuisine— **L'Aubergine des Grenadines,** Belmont Walkway, Belmont (© **784/458- 3201**), an expat operation with wood tables and a lobster tank. The couple who run the place make the best conch salad on island and flame their lobster with old dark rum. See p. 631.

TRINIDAD & TOBAGO The capital of this two-island nation, Port-of-Spain, is known for its varied population and exotic cuisine. Creating the biggest buzz in the winter of 2004 was **Battimamzelle,** in the Coblentz Inn, 44 Coblentz Ave., Cascade (© **868/621-0591**). Against a so-called Mexicanish decor, this "Dragonfly" (its English name) serves a savory cuisine inspired mainly by the West Indies but with international overtones. The barbecued kingfish brushed with fresh guava and served with pumpkin is an even better version than your mama made. In the adjoining island of Tobago, a once-famous inn, **Blue Haven Hotel,** Bacolet Bay, Scarborough (© **868/660- 7400**), has made a comeback. In the 1950s it was one of the most famous inns in the southern Caribbean, attracting such movie stars as Rita Hayworth and Robert Mitchum when they were on island making the forgettable *Fire Down Below.* The newly restored property opens onto a beach of white sands. See p. 657 and 666.

TURKS & CAICOS The island of Providenciales (nicknamed Provo) continues to attract the glitterati, and now features some of the most expensive beach resorts in the Caribbean. To combat that, **Comfort Suites,** Grace Bay (✆ 649/946-8888), has opened to bring a moderately priced alternative. It's hardly bare-boned living, though, as each of its accommodations is a well-furnished suite. The location is across the street from the fabled Grace Bay Beach. See p. 689.

U.S. VIRGIN ISLANDS On the most popular of the U.S. Virgin Islands, St. Thomas, new restaurants continue to create a sensation in and around the port city of Charlotte Amalie. The most recent attention focuses on the opening of the **Blue Moon Café,** 6280 Estate Nazareth Bay (✆ 340/779-2262), which has become known locally for its creative American cuisine. In a romantic open-air setting under the Caribbean stars, this beachfront restaurant appeals to a wide range of palates. In Frenchtown, right outside Charlotte Amalie, **Oceana,** in the Villa Olga, 8 Honduras (✆ 340/774-4262), is an upscale, hip, and stylish enclave that opened to rave reviews for its international cuisine that highlights fresh seafood. On the street level is a chic little wine bar and singles enclave; upstairs is the more formal dining room with flickering oil lamps and tantalizing dishes, including several preparations of Caribbean lobster. See p. 714 and 715.

1

Choosing the Perfect Island: The Best of the Caribbean

In the Caribbean, you can hike through national parks and scuba dive along underwater mountains. But perhaps your idea of the perfect island vacation is to plunk yourself down on the sands with a frosted drink in hand. Whether you want a veranda with a view of the sea or a plantation house set in a field of sugar cane, this chapter will help you choose the vacation that best suits your needs.

For a thumbnail portrait of each island, see "The Islands in Brief," in chapter 2.

1 The Best Beaches

Good beaches with soul-warming sun, crystal-clear waters, and fragrant sea air can be found on virtually every island of the Caribbean, with the possible exceptions of Saba (which has rocky shores) and Dominica (where the few beaches have dramatically black sands that absorb the hot sun).

- **Shoal Bay** (Anguilla): This luscious stretch of silvery sand helped put Anguilla on the world tourism map. Snorkelers are drawn to the schools of iridescent fish that dart among the coral gardens offshore. You can take the trail walk from Old Ta to little-known Katouche Beach, which offers perfect snorkeling and is also a prime site for a beach picnic under shade trees. See chapter 3.

- **The Beaches of Antigua:** Legend has it that there is a beach here for every day of the year, though we haven't bothered to count them. Antiguans claim, with justifiable pride, that their two best beaches are Dickenson Bay, in the northwest corner of the island, and Half Moon Bay, which stretches for a white-sandy mile along the

eastern coast. Chances are your hotel will be built directly on or near a strip of white sand, as nearly all major hotels open onto a good beach. See chapter 4.

- **Palm Beach** (Aruba): This superb strip of white sand put Aruba on the tourist map. Several publications, including *Condé Nast,* have hailed it as one of the 12 best beaches in the *world.* It's likely to be crowded in winter, but for swimming, sailing, or fishing, it's idyllic. See chapter 5.

- **The Gold Coast** (Barbados): Some of the finest beaches in the Caribbean lie along the so-called Gold Coast of Barbados, site of some of the swankiest deluxe hotels in the Northern Hemisphere. Our favorites include Paynes Bay, Brandon's Beach, Paradise Beach, and Brighton Beach, all open to the public. See chapter 6.

- **Cane Garden Bay** (Tortola, British Virgin Islands): One of the Caribbean's most spectacular stretches, Cane Garden Bay has 2km (1¼ miles) of white sand and is a jogger's favorite. It's a much

The Caribbean Islands

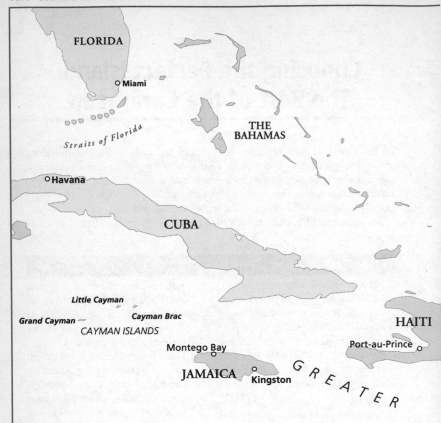

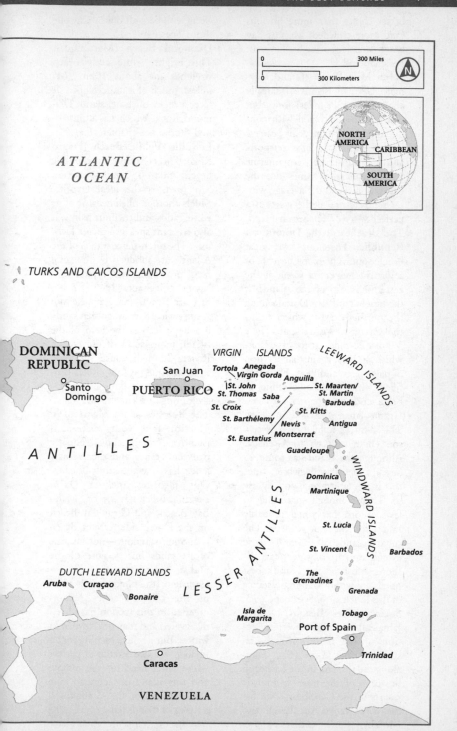

ATLANTIC
OCEAN

NORTH
AMERICA
CARIBBEAN
SOUTH
AMERICA

0   300 Miles
0   300 Kilometers

TURKS AND CAICOS ISLANDS

DOMINICAN
REPUBLIC
Santo
Domingo

VIRGIN   ISLANDS
San Juan   Tortola   Anegada
                        Virgin Gorda   Anguilla
PUERTO RICO   St. John   St. Maarten/
            St. Thomas   Saba   St. Martin
St. Croix   Barbuda
St. Barthélemy   St. Kitts
            Nevis   Antigua
St. Eustatius   Montserrat

LEEWARD ISLANDS

A N T I L L E S

Guadeloupe

Dominica
Martinique

WINDWARD ISLANDS

St. Lucia

St. Vincent   Barbados

DUTCH LEEWARD ISLANDS
Aruba   Curaçao
        Bonaire

L E S S E R   A N T I L L E S

The
Grenadines   Grenada

Isla de
Margarita   Tobago
Port of Spain

Caracas   Trinidad

VENEZUELA

better choice than more obvious (and more crowded) Magens Bay beach on neighboring St. Thomas. See chapter 8.

- **Seven Mile Beach** (Grand Cayman, Cayman Islands): It's really about 9km (5½ miles) long, but who's counting? Lined with condos and plush resorts, this beach is known for its array of watersports and its translucent aquamarine waters. Australian pines dot the background, and the average winter temperature of the water is a perfect 80°F (27°C). See chapter 9.

- **The Beaches of the Dominican Republic:** There are two great beach options here: the beaches of resort-riddled Punta Cana at the easternmost tip of the island, or the beaches at Playa Dorada along the northern coast, which fronts the Atlantic. Punta Cana is a 32km (20-mile) strip of oyster-white sands set against a backdrop of palm trees, and Playa Dorada is filled with beaches of white or beige sands. See chapter 12.

- **Grand Anse Beach** (Grenada): This 3km (2-mile) beach is reason enough to go to Grenada. Although the island has some 45 beaches, most with white sand, this is the fabled one, and rightly so. There's enough space and so few visitors that you'll probably find a spot just for yourself. The sugary sands of Grand Anse extend into deep waters far offshore. Most of the island's best hotels are within walking distance of this beach strip. See chapter 13.

- **Seven Mile Beach** (Negril, Jamaica): In the northwestern section of the island, this beach stretches for 11km (6¾ miles) along the sea, and in the backdrop lie some of the most hedonistic resorts in the Caribbean. Not for the conservative, the beach also contains some nudist patches

along with bare-all Booby Cay offshore. See chapter 15.

- **Diamond Beach** (Martinique): This bright, white-sandy beach stretches for about 10km (6¼ miles), much of it undeveloped. It faces a rocky offshore island, Diamond Rock, which has uninhabited shores. See chapter 16.

- **Luquillo Public Beach** (Puerto Rico): This crescent-shaped public beach, 48km (30 miles) east of San Juan, is the local favorite. Much photographed because of its white sands and coconut palms, it also has tent sites and picnic facilities. The often-fierce waters of the Atlantic are subdued by the coral reefs protecting the crystal-clear lagoon. See chapter 17.

- **St-Jean Beach** (St. Barthélemy): A somewhat narrow, golden sandy beach, St-Jean is the gem of the island, reminiscent of the French Riviera (though you're supposed to keep your top on). Reefs protect the beach, making it ideal for swimming. See chapter 19.

- **The Beaches of St. Maarten/St. Martin:** Take your pick. This island, divided about equally between France and the Netherlands, has 37 white-sandy beaches. Our favorites include Dawn Beach, Mullet Bay Beach, Maho Bay Beach, and Great Bay Beach on the Dutch side. Orient Beach is another standout—not because of its sands but because of the nudists. See chapter 23.

- **Canouan** (the Grenadines): Most of the other beaches recommended in this section have been discovered and may be crowded in winter. But if you're looking for an idyllic, secluded stretch of perfect white sand, head for the remote and tiny island of Canouan, one of the pearls of the Grenadines, a string of islands lying south of its parent, St. Vincent. You'll have the beaches and the crystal-clear waters to yourself, even in winter. See chapter 24.

- **The Beaches of Tobago:** For your Robinson Crusoe holiday in the southern Caribbean, head for the little island of Tobago. Even Trinidadians fly over here on weekends to enjoy the beach life. It doesn't get any better than a long coral beach called Pigeon Point on the northwestern coast. Other good beaches on Tobago include Back Bay (site of an old coconut plantation) and Man-O-War Bay, known for its beautiful natural harbor and long stretch of sand. See chapter 25.

- **Grace Bay Beach** (Providenciales, Turks and Caicos Islands): These 19km (12 miles) of pale sands are the pride of Provo; *Condé Nast* has called this one of the world's best beaches. It's such a spectacular setting that increasing numbers of resorts, including Club Med, have sprung up along the shore. A couple of miles out from the northern shore, the beach is fringed by a reef with fabulous snorkeling. Back on land, there are plenty of places where you can rent watersports equipment. See chapter 26.

- **Trunk Bay** (St. John): Protected by the U.S. National Park Service, this beach is one of the Caribbean's most popular. A favorite with cruise-ship passengers, it's known for its underwater snorkeling trail, where markers guide you along the reef just off the white sands; you're sure to see a gorgeous rainbow of tropical fish. See chapter 27.

2 The Best Snorkeling

The Virgin Islands offer some particularly outstanding sites, but there are many other great places for snorkeling in the Caribbean.

- **Antigua:** This is a snorkeler's dream. Most of its lovely beaches open onto clear, calm waters populated by rainbow-hued tropical fish. The marine life offshore is particularly dense, including gentle manta rays and colorful sea anemones. The rich types of different elk and brain coral make snorkeling particularly rewarding. See chapter 4.

- **Bonaire Marine Park** (Bonaire): All the attributes that make Bonaire a world-class diving destination apply to its snorkeling, too. Snorkelers can wade from the shores off their hotels to the reefs and view an array of coral and a range of colorful fish. The reefs just off Klein Bonaire and Washington-Slagbaai National Park receive especially rave reviews. See chapter 7.

- **Stingray City** (Grand Cayman): Stingray City is an easy 4m (13-ft.) diving site that can also be seen while snorkeling. It's an extraordinary experience to meet the dozens of tame, gentle stingrays that glide around you in the warm, crystal-clear waters. See chapter 9.

- **Curaçao Underwater Marine Park** (Curaçao): In contrast to Curaçao's arid terrain, the marine life that rings the island is rich and spectacular. The best-known snorkeling sites, in the Curaçao Underwater Marine Park, stretch for 20km (12 miles) along Curaçao's southern coastline, and there are many other highly desirable sites as well. Sunken ships, gardens of hard and soft coral, and millions of fish are a snorkeler's treat. See chapter 10.

- **St. Martin:** The best snorkeling on the island lies on the French side, where the government religiously protects the calm waters, which are populated with schools of brilliantly colored fish. Find a tiny cove and explore the shallow reefs along its shores, especially in the northeastern underwater nature reserve. See chapter 23.

- **The Grenadines:** Every island offers great snorkeling possibilities right off of magnificent white-sandy beaches. In most places you'll have the waters to yourself. A reef stretching for 1.6km (1 mile) along white sands on the island of Canouan invites snorkelers, and the waters are filled with beautiful brain coral and rainbow-hued fish. The snorkeling is also good at Palm Island and Petit St. Vincent. See chapter 24.

- **Tobago:** The shallow, sun-dappled waters off the Latin American coastline boast enormous colonies of marine life. Buccoo Reef on Tobago is especially noteworthy, and many local entrepreneurs offer snorkeling cruises. See chapter 25.

- **Coki Point Beach** (St. Thomas): On the north shore of St. Thomas, this beach offers year-round snorkeling, especially around the coral ledges near Coral World's underwater tower, a favorite with cruise-ship passengers. See chapter 27.

- **Provo** (Turks and Caicos): Although this island is known primarily as one of the world's best dive sites, it also offers a number of snorkeling possibilities. The government has established the best snorkel trails at Smith's Reef and Bight Reef, right off of Provo's spectacular Grace Bay Beach. These reefs are right off the shoreline, and they provide easy access into the fragile but stunningly

beautiful world of coral gardens, the most dramatic in the vast area immediately south of The Bahamas. See chapter 26.

- **Buck Island** (St. Croix): More than 250 species of fish, as well as a variety of sponges, corals, and crustaceans, have been found at this 340-hectare (840-acre) island and reef system, 3km (2 miles) off St. Croix's north shore. The reef is strictly protected by the National Park Service. See chapter 27.

- **Cane Bay** (St. Croix): One of the best diving and snorkeling sites on St. Croix is off this breezy north-shore beach. On a clear day, you can swim out 137m (449 ft.) and see the Cane Bay Wall that drops off dramatically to deep waters below. Multicolored fish and elkhorn and brain coral are in abundance here. See chapter 27.

- **Trunk Bay** (St. John): Trunk Bay's self-guided 205m-long (672-ft.) trail has large underwater signs that identify species of coral and other items of interest. The beach offers showers, changing rooms, equipment rentals, and a lifeguard. See chapter 27.

- **Leinster Bay** (St. John): With easy access from land and sea, Leinster Bay is filled with calm, clear, and uncrowded waters, with an abundance of sea life. See chapter 27.

- **Haulover Bay** (St. John): A favorite with locals, this small bay is rougher than Leinster and is often deserted. The snorkeling is dramatic, with ledges, walls, nooks, and sandy areas set close together. At this spot, only about 182m (597 ft.) of land separates the Atlantic Ocean from the Caribbean Sea. See chapter 27.

3 The Best Diving

All the major islands offer diving trips, lessons, and equipment, but here are the top picks.

- **Bonaire:** The highly accessible reefs that surround Bonaire have never suffered from poaching or pollution, and the island's environmentally conscious diving industry ensures they never will. Created from volcanic eruptions, the island is an underwater mountain, with fringe reefs right off the beach of every hotel on any part of the island. See chapter 7.

- **Virgin Gorda:** Many divers plan their entire vacations around exploring the famed wreck of the HMS *Rhone,* off Salt Island. This royal mail steamer, which went down in 1867, is the most celebrated diving site in the Caribbean. See chapter 8.
- **Grand Cayman:** This is a world-class diving destination. There are 34 dive operators on Grand Cayman (with five more on Little Cayman, plus three on Cayman Brac). A full range of professional diving services is available, including equipment sales, rentals, and repairs; instruction at all levels; underwater photography; and video schools. See chapter 9.
- **Saba:** Islanders can't brag about its beaches, but Saba is blessed with some of the Caribbean's richest marine life. It's one of the premier diving locations in the Caribbean, with 38 official diving sites. The unusual setting includes underwater lava flows, black sand, large strands of black coral, millions of fish, and underwater mountaintops submerged under 27m (89 ft.) of water. See chapter 18.

- **Turks and Caicos Islands:** These islands offer a rich assortment of relatively unexplored underwater sites, including sea lanes where boaters and divers often spot whales in April. A collection of unusual underwater wrecks includes the HMS *Endymion,* which sank during a storm in 1790. Miles of reefs house myriad kinds of colorful marine life. Right off Grand Turk, experienced divers love the many miles of "drop-off" diving, where the sea walls suddenly drop into the uncharted depths of blue holes more than 2,100m (6,888 ft.) below sea level. As you descend you'll see colonies of black coral, rare forms of anemone, purple sponges, stunning gorgonian, endless forms of coral, and thousands of fish. See chapter 26.
- **St. Croix:** Increasingly known as a top diving destination, St. Croix hasn't yet overtaken Grand Cayman, but it has a lot going for it. Beach dives, reef dives, wreck dives, nighttime dives, wall dives—they're all here. The highlight is the underwater trails of the national park at Buck Island, off St. Croix's mainland. Other desirable sites include the drop-offs and coral canyons at Cane Bay and Salt River. Davis Bay is the location of the 3,600m-deep (11,808-ft.) Puerto Rico Trench, the fifth-deepest body of water on earth. See chapter 27.

4 The Best Sailing

Virtually every large-scale hotel in the Caribbean provides small sailboats (especially Sunfish, Sailfish, and small, one-masted catamarans) for its guests. If you're looking for larger craft, the Virgin Islands and the Grenadines come instantly to mind for their almost-ideal sailing conditions. These two regions offer many options for dropping anchor at secluded coves surrounded by relatively calm waters. Both areas are spectacular, but whereas the Virgin Islands offer more dramatic, mountainous terrain, the Grenadines offer insights into island cultures little touched by the modern world.

Other places to sail in the Caribbean include Antigua, Barbados,

St. Martin, and the French-speaking islands. But if you plan on doing a lot of sailing, know in advance that the strongest currents and biggest waves are usually on the northern and eastern sides of most islands—the Atlantic (as opposed to the Caribbean) side.

- **The Grenadines:** Boating is a way of life in the Grenadines, partly because access to many of the tiny remote islands is difficult or impossible by airplane. One of the most prominent local charter agents is **Nicholson Yacht Charters** (© **800/662-6066** in the U.S., or 617/661-0555), headquartered in nearby St. Vincent. On Bequia, Mustique, Petit St. Vincent, and Union Island, all the hotels can put you in touch with local entrepreneurs who rent sailing craft. See chapters 2 and 24 for more details.
- **The Virgin Islands:** Perhaps because of their well-developed marina facilities (and those of the nearby United States), the Virgin Islands receive the lion's share of devoted yachties. The reigning capital for sailing is Tortola, the largest island of the British Virgins. On-site are about 300 well-maintained sailing craft available for bareboat rentals and perhaps 100 charter yachts.

  The largest of the Caribbean's yacht chartering services is **The Moorings** (© **888/535-7289** or 888/952-8420 in the U.S. and Canada, or 284/494-2332 in the British Virgin Islands). This yachting charter center is described more fully in chapter 8, as are the other outfits in this paragraph. If you'd like sailing lessons, consider Tortola's **Treasure Isle Hotel** (© **284/494-2501**), which offers courses in seamanship year-round. (One of Treasure Isle's programs is exclusively on how to sail catamarans.) On the island of Virgin Gorda, in the British Virgin Islands, the best bet for both boat rentals and accommodations, as well as for a range of instruction, is the **Bitter End Yacht Club** (© **800/872-2392** in the U.S., or 284/494-2746).

  Some of the biggest charter business in the Caribbean is conducted on St. Thomas, especially at **American Yacht Harbor,** Red Hook (© **340/775-6454**), which offers bareboat and fully crewed charters. Other reliable rental agents include **Charteryacht League,** at Flagship (© **800/524-2061** in the U.S., or 340/774-3944). The U.S. Virgin Islands are covered in chapter 27; look there for more information.

  On St. Croix, boating is less essential to the local economy than it is on St. Thomas or in the British Virgins, so if you're taking a Virgin Islands sailing trip, plan accordingly.

5 The Best Golf Courses

Some of the world's most famous golf architects, including Robert Trent Jones (both Junior and Senior), Pete Dye, and Gary Player, have designed challenging courses in the Caribbean.

- **Tierra del Sol Golf Course** (Aruba; © **297/58-67800**): Robert Trent Jones Jr. has designed an 18-hole, par-71, 6,811-yard course that is one of the grandest in the southern Caribbean. On the northwest coast of this arid, cactus-studded island, the course takes in Aruba's indigenous flora, including the divi-divi tree. See p. 122.
- **Teeth of the Dog** and **The Links,** both at Casa de Campo (Dominican Republic; © **809/523-3333**): Teeth of the Dog is one of

designer Pete Dye's masterpieces. Seven holes are set adjacent to the sea, whereas the other 11 are confoundedly labyrinthine. The resort also has a second golf course, The Links, which some claim is even more difficult. See p. 276.

- **Golf de St-François** (Guadeloupe; ✆ **590/88-41-87**): Six of its 18 holes are ringed with water traps, the winds are devilishly unpredictable, and the par is a sweat-inducing 71. This fearsome course displays the wit and skill of its designer, Robert Trent Jones Sr. Most of the staff is multilingual, and because it's owned by the local municipality, it's a lot less snobby than you might expect. See p 349.

- **The Tryall Club** (Montego Bay, Jamaica; ✆ **800/238-5290** in the U.S., or 876/956-5660): This is the finest golf course on an island known for its tricky breezes. The site occupied by The Tryall Club was once the home of one of Jamaica's best-known sugar plantations, the only remnant of which is a ruined waterwheel. The promoters of Johnnie Walker Scotch, who know a lot about golfing, selected this place for their most prestigious competition. In winter, the course is usually open only to guests of The Tryall Club. See p. 377.

- **Wyndham Rose Hall Resort & Country Club** (Rose Hill, Jamaica; ✆ **800/996-3426** in the U.S., or 876/953-2650): This is one of the top five courses in the world, even though it faces tough competition in Montego Bay. The signature hole is number 8, which doglegs onto a promontory and a green that thrusts about 183m (600 ft.) into the sea. The back nine, however, is the most scenic and most challenging, rising into steep slopes and deep ravines on Mount Zion. See p. 377.

- **Hyatt Dorado Beach Resort & Country Club** (Puerto Rico; ✆ **800/233-1234** in the U.S., or 787/796-1234): This resort maintains two golf courses, both set on what were originally citrus and coconut plantations. Robert Trent Jones Sr. designed both courses. No one can agree on which of the two courses is the more interesting, but the elegance of both is breathtaking. See p. 489.

- **Four Seasons Resort Nevis** (Nevis; ✆ **800/332-3442** in the U.S., 800/268-6282 in Canada, or 869/469-1111): We consider this our personal favorite in all of the Caribbean, and so do readers of *Caribbean Travel & Life*. It was carved out of a coconut plantation and tropical rainforest in the 1980s, and its undulating beauty is virtually unequaled. Designed by Robert Trent Jones Jr., the course begins at sea level, rises to a point midway up the slopes of Mount Nevis, and then slants gracefully back down near the beachfront clubhouse. Electric carts carry golfers through a labyrinth of well-groomed paths, some of which skirt steep ravines. See p. 565.

6 The Best Tennis Facilities

- **Curtain Bluff** (Antigua; ✆ **888/ 289-9898** in the U.S., or 268/462-8400): Small, select, and carefully run by people who love tennis, it's also the annual site of a well-known spring tournament. The courts are set in a low-lying valley. See p. 92.

- **Casa de Campo** (Dominican Republic; ✆ **800/877-3643** or

809/523-3333): The facilities here include 13 clay courts (10 are lit, and two are ringed with stadium seating), four all-weather Laykold courts, a resident pro, ball machines, and tennis pros who are usually available to play with guests. During midwinter, residents and clients of Casa de Campo have first crack at court times. See p. 277.

- **Half Moon Golf, Tennis & Beach Club** (Montego Bay, Jamaica; ✆ **876/953-2211**): This resort sprawls over hundreds of acres, with about a dozen tennis courts and at least four squash and/or racquetball courts. Jamaica has a strong, British-based affinity for tennis, and Half Moon keeps the tradition alive. See p. 378.

- **Wyndham El Conquistador Resort & Golden Door Spa** (Puerto Rico; ✆ **800/468-5228** in the U.S., or 787/863-1000): Facilities at this megaresort include seven Har-Tru tennis courts, a resident pro, and a clubhouse with its own bar. If you're looking for a partner, the hotel will find one for you. Only guests of the hotel can use the courts, some of which are illuminated for night play. See p. 500.

- **Hyatt Dorado Beach Resort & Country Club** (Puerto Rico; ✆ **787/796-1234**): This beachfront resort offers seven all-weather tennis courts, some lit, some ringed with stadium seats; all are administered by a tennis pro who gives lessons. If you want pointers on improving your serve or strokes, someone will be on hand to videotape you. These facilities are open only to resort guests. See p. 488.

- **Wyndham Sugar Bay Beach Club & Spa** (St. Thomas; ✆ **800/WYNDHAM** in the U.S., or 340/777-7100): The resort offers the first stadium tennis court in the U.S. Virgin Islands, with a capacity of 220 spectators. In addition, it has four Laykold courts, each of which is lit for night play. There's an on-site pro shop, and lessons are available. See p. 722.

- **The Buccaneer** (St. Croix; ✆ **800/255-3881** in the U.S., or 340/773-2100): Hailed as having the best tennis facilities in the Virgin Islands, this resort hosts several tournaments every year. There are eight all-weather Laykold courts, two of which are illuminated at night; there's also a pro shop. Nonguests can play here for a fee. See p. 743.

7 The Best Places to Honeymoon

More and more couples are exchanging their vows in the Caribbean. Many resorts will arrange everything from the preacher to the flowers, so we've included in the following list some outfits that provide wedding services. For more information about the various options and the legal requirements for marriages on some of the more popular Caribbean islands, see chapter 2.

- **Cap Juluca** (Anguilla; ✆ **888/858-5822** in the U.S., or 264/497-6779): This resort boasts a unique postmodern design, multimillion-dollar decor, and a thrillingly beautiful beach. The result: something like a Saharan Casbah whose domed villas seem to float against the scrubland and azure sky. It's an extremely stylish setting for romance. More than any other resort on Anguilla, Cap Juluca affords the most privacy on its 72 hectares (178 acres). In a private villa, honeymooners enjoy private pools and huge tubs for two. You can join other guests for meals and/or retreat into total seclusion. See p. 64.

- **St. James's Club** (Antigua; C **800/345-0356** in the U.S., or 268/460-5000): There are enough diversions at this very posh, British-style resort to keep a honeymoon couple up and about for weeks. Breakfast, lunch, and dinner are included, along with unlimited drinks. Among the perks is a private, candlelit dinner for two in a romantic setting. Honeymooners are greeted with a bottle of champagne and freshly cut bougainvillea in their rooms, which can be private villas, suites, or, for complete seclusion, a hillside home. Unlike Cap Juluca, which promotes seclusion, this is for honeymooners who prefer an active lifestyle, gambling at the casino, taking in the beach, or enjoying the widest array of dining and drinking options of any hotel on the island. See p. 82.

- **Biras Creek Estate** (Virgin Gorda, B.V.I.; C **800/223-1108** in the U.S., or 284/494-3555): If you're eager to escape your in-laws and bridesmaids after a wedding ceremony, this is the place. It's a quintessential mariner's hideaway that can be reached only via a several-mile boat ride across the open sea. Perched on a narrow promontory jutting into the Caribbean, it's an intensely private retreat set on 60 hectares (148 acres) with a crisscrossing network of signposted nature trails. Spacious, open-air, walled showers are provided in each bathroom. Honeymooners come here not to be pampered, but to be left alone to do their thing. Entertainment and dancing enliven some evenings, but for the most part you'll enjoy utter tranquillity. Its king-size beds are the best on the island.

Don't come here for a lot of activities. See p. 196.

- **Peter Island Resort** (Peter Island, B.V.I.; C **800/346-4451** or 284/ 495-2000): Romantics appreciate the isolation of this resort, on a 720-hectare (1,778-acre) private island south of Tortola and east of St. John. Reaching it requires a 30-minute waterborne transfer, which many urban refugees consider part of the fun. It's very laid-back—bring your new spouse and a good book, and enjoy the comings and goings of yachts at the island's private marina while you recover from the stress of your wedding. See p. 206.

- **Hyatt Regency Grand Cayman** (Grand Cayman; C **800/233-1234** or 345/949-1234): Hands down, this is the most glamorous and best-landscaped resort in the Cayman Islands. Honeymooners can buy a package that includes champagne and wine, a room with an oversize bed, a 1-day Jeep rental, a romantic sundowner sail on a 12m (39-ft.) catamaran, and discounts at clothing stores, the resort's restaurants, and a golf course. They'll even present you with a honeymoon memento for your home. See p. 213.

- **Sutton Place Hotel** (Dominica; C **767/449-8700**): If you want something completely different, head for the remote island of Dominica. It's an inexpensive destination, with a lush, tropical setting, although the beaches aren't great (there is river swimming instead). Start off your married life at this romantic old place, where Princess Margaret and Noël Coward retreated in days of yore (not together). Opt for one of the top-floor suites for a real romantic getaway, and relax in your four-poster bed. See p. 260.

- **Sandals Royal Caribbean** (Jamaica; © **800/SANDALS** in the U.S. or 876/953-2232): There are a handful of members of this resort chain in Jamaica alone (plus three others on St. Lucia, another luxe one at Cable Beach outside Nassau, and yet another one on the island of Antigua that is far less grand). Each prides itself on providing an all-inclusive (cash-free) environment where meals are provided in abundance. Enthusiastic members of the staff bring heroic amounts of community spirit to ceremonies celebrated on-site. Sandals provides everything from a preacher to petunias (as well as champagne, a cake, and all the legalities) for you to get hitched here. Any of these resorts can provide a suitable setting, but one of the most appealing is **Sandals Royal Caribbean,** outside Montego Bay, Jamaica. See p. 368.
- **The SuperClubs of Jamaica** (© **877/GO-SUPER** in the U.S., or 876/940-1150): These all-inclusive properties, including the Breezes and the Grand Lido hotels, are for honeymooners who can afford a little more elegance and luxury. They operate somewhat like Sandals, but have far more style and a higher price tag. Prices are high in winter, but when mid-April arrives, rates plummet. SuperClubs, such as Grand Lido and Grand Lido Sans Souci, are scattered between Ocho Rios and Negril. If you pay for the food and room packages, the hotel chain will throw in the wedding for free—providing the license, the witnesses, the minister, and even a two-tier cake. You can be married in the garden or on a white-sandy beach. See chapter 15.
- **Wyndham El Conquistador Resort & Golden Door Spa** (Puerto Rico; © **800/468-5228** in the U.S., or 787/863-1000): A complex of hotels set on a forested bluff overlooking the sea, this is one of the most lavish resorts ever built in the Caribbean. The architecture incorporates Moorish gardens and Andalusian fortresses. You'll find hammocks for two on the resort's offshore private island, as well as about a dozen private Jacuzzis artfully concealed by vegetation throughout the grounds. See p. 500.
- **The Horned Dorset Primavera** (Puerto Rico; © **800/633-1857** in the U.S., or 787/823-4030): This is the most elegant, intimate, secluded, romantic inn in Puerto Rico. It has private plunge pools; a cantilevered porch over the sea perfect for champagne at sunset; a fabulous candlelit restaurant; vast, well-equipped bathrooms with tubs big enough for two; seaview balconies; romantic four-poster beds; and a discreet, helpful staff that doesn't interfere with honeymooners who want to be alone. See p. 490.
- **Golden Lemon Inn & Villas** (St. Kitts; © **800/633-7411** in the U.S., or 869/465-7260): It started its life as a French manor house during the 17th century, but by the time its present owners began restoring it, the Golden Lemon was decidedly less glamorous. It required the refined tastes of Arthur Leaman, a former editor at *House & Garden,* to bring it to its full potential. Today the Golden Lemon is an authentic Antillean retreat—luxurious, laid-back, and romantic—set in an isolated fishing village loaded with charm. See p. 545.
- **Four Seasons Resort Nevis** (Nevis; © **800/332-3442** in the U.S., 800/268-6282 in Canada, or 869/469-1111): Though not as historic as some of the island's

plantation-style inns, the Four Seasons rules without peer as the most deluxe hotel on the island, with the most extensive facilities. Set in a palm grove adjacent to the island's finest beach, it has the atmosphere of a supremely indulgent country club. The Four Seasons offers a 4-day wedding package with a choice of ceremony styles (in a church or on a beach, with a judge or with a civil magistrate). The resort's pastry chef designs each wedding cake individually, and the staff can arrange music, photographs, flowers, legalities, and virtually anything else you want. See p. 557.

- **Anse Chastanet** (St. Lucia; ✆ **800/223-1108** in the U.S., or 758/459-7000): Offering panoramic views of mountains and jungle, this intimate hotel is a winner with romantics. With its small size, it offers a lot of privacy and rustic charm. See p. 573.

- **Petit St. Vincent Resort** (The Grenadines; ✆ **800/654-9326** in the U.S., or 784/458-8801): If your idea of a honeymoon is to run away from everybody except your new spouse, this is the place. It takes about three planes and a boat to reach it, but the effort to get here is worth it, if you want total isolation and privacy. Even the staff doesn't bother you unless you raise a flag for room service. If the honeymoon's going well, you may never have to leave your stone cottage by the beach. The artfully built clubhouses and bungalows were crafted from tropical woods

and local stone. The results are simultaneously rustic and lavish. See p. 646.

- **The Cotton House** (The Grenadines; ✆ **784/456-4777**): Cosmopolitan and stylish, this hotel was built as a cotton warehouse on the tiny island of Mustique during the 18th century. It's intimate, exclusive, and full of undeniable charm and romance. See p. 641.

- **Le Grand Courlan Resort & Spa** (Tobago; ✆ **868/639-9667**): This is the favorite honeymoon retreat on Tobago. If you want to be fussed over, you and your new spouse can attend the spa for "release massages," or you can be left entirely alone to enjoy the bay outside your window or the sandy beach at your doorstep. From Guyanan hardwood to Italian porcelain, the decor is refined and elegant. See p. 667.

- **The Buccaneer** (St. Croix; ✆ **800/255-3881** in the U.S., or 340/773-2100): Posh and discreet, this resort boasts some of the most extensive vacation facilities on St. Croix—three beaches, eight tennis courts, a spa and fitness center, an 18-hole golf course, and 3km (2 miles) of carefully maintained jogging trails. The accommodations include beachside rooms with fieldstone terraces leading toward the sea. The resort's stone sugar mill (originally built in 1658) is one of the most popular sites for weddings and visiting honeymooners on the island. See p. 730.

8 The Best Places to Get Away from It All

In addition to the choices below, see also the listings under "The Best Honeymoons" for additional information on Biras Creek Estate and Peter Island Resort, both in the British Virgin Islands, and the Petit St. Vincent Resort and the Cotton House, both in the Grenadines.

- **Biras Creek Estate** (Virgin Gorda, B.V.I.; ✆ **800/223-1108** in the U.S., or 284/494-3555):

The only access to this resort is by private launch. The sea air and the views over islets, cays, and deep blue waters will relax you in your charming guest room. The nautical atmosphere will quickly remove all thoughts of the 9-to-5 job you left behind. See p. 196.

- **Guana Island Club** (Guana Island, B.V.I.; ℭ **800/544-8262** in the U.S., or 284/494-2354): One of the most secluded hideaways in the entire Caribbean, this resort occupies a privately owned 340-hectare (840-acre) bird sanctuary with nature trails. Head here for views of rare plant and animal life and for several excellent uncrowded beaches. See p. 207.

- **Little Cayman Beach Resort** (Cayman Islands; ℭ **800/327-3835** in the U.S. and Canada, or 345/948-1033): The only practical way to reach the 26 sq. km (10-sq.-mile) island where this resort is located is by airplane. Snorkelers will marvel at some of the most spectacular and colorful marine life in the Caribbean. The resort has the most complete watersports facilities on the island, and bikes are available for exploring. See p. 230.

- **Rawlins Plantation Inn** (St. Kitts; ℭ **800/346-5358** in the U.S., or 869/465-6221): Surrounded by 5 hectares (12 acres) of carefully manicured lawns and tropical shrubbery, and set on a panoramic hillock about 105m (344 ft.) above sea level, this hotel evokes a 19th-century plantation with its rugs of locally woven rushes and carved four-poster beds. You'll be separated from the rest of the island by hundreds of acres of sugar cane, and there are few phones and no televisions. See p. 545.

9 The Best Family Vacations

- **Hyatt Regency Aruba Resort & Casino** (Aruba; ℭ **800/233-1234** in the U.S. and Canada, or 297/58-61234): Designed like a luxurious hacienda, with award-winning gardens, this resort is the most upscale on Aruba. Supervised activities for children age 3 to 12 include games and contests such as crab races and hula-hoop competitions. See p. 110.

- **Almond Beach Village** (Barbados; ℭ **800/4-ALMOND** in the U.S., or 246/422-4900): One of the best programs for kids in the southern Caribbean is found at this hotel set on the site of a 19th-century sugar plantation. There's a nursery, along with children's programs that encompass everything from lessons in Bajan culture to pool activities to computer games, even instruction in reggae. Family suites are available, and babysitting can be arranged at night. See p. 135.

- **Sandy Beach Island Resort** (Barbados; ℭ **800/448-8355** in the U.S., or 246/435-8000): Set amid lots of fast-food and family-style restaurants on the southwest coast, this family-oriented hotel offers one- and two-bedroom suites. Each unit has a kitchen, so you can cook for yourself and save money. The beach is a few steps away, and the ambience is informal. If you bring the kids, they'll have plenty of playmates. See p. 142.

- **Hyatt Regency Grand Cayman** (Grand Cayman Island; ℭ **800/233-1234** in the U.S., or 345/949-1234): Safe and serene, Grand Cayman Island, with its 11km (6¾-mile) sandy beach, seems designed for families with children. No one coddles children as much as the Hyatt people, who offer not only babysitting but also Camp Hyatt, with an activity-filled agenda, for children age 3 to 12. See p. 213.

- **Negril Cabins Resort** (Negril, Jamaica; ✆ **800/382-3444** in the U.S., or 876/957-5350): Rising on stilts, these wooden cottages with private decks add a sense of adventure to a beach vacation. Surrounded by tropical vegetation, families are only steps from the beach. Features for kids include a playground, computer games, arts and crafts lessons, and even storytelling sessions. Children under age 12 stay free if they share a room with their parents; children age 12 and over are $25 extra. See p. 386.

- **FDR** (Runaway Bay, Jamaica; ✆ **888/FDR-KIDS** in the U.S., or 876/973-4592): FDR gives you a suite with its own kitchen, and a "vacation nanny" whose duties include babysitting. Neither its beach nor its pool is the most appealing on Jamaica, but the price is right, and the babysitting is part of the all-inclusive deal. Programs for children include dress-up parties, donkey rides, basketball, tennis, and snorkeling. See p. 403.

- **Wyndham El Conquistador Resort & Golden Door Spa** (Puerto Rico; ✆ **800/468-5228** in the U.S., or 787/863-1000): Children aren't forgotten amid the glamour and hoopla of this fabulous resort. Camp Coquí provides day care daily from 9am to 3pm for children age 3 to 12, at a price of $40 per child per day. Activities include fishing, sailing, arts and crafts, and nature treks. Babysitting services are available, and children age 15 and under stay free in a room with their parents. See p. 500.

- **Four Seasons Resort Nevis** (Nevis; ✆ **800/332-3442** in the U.S., 800/268-6282 in Canada, or 869/469-1111): The staff of the Kids for All Seasons day camp are kindly, matronly souls who work well with children. During the adult cocktail hour, when parents might opt for a romantic sundowner, kids attend a supervised children's hour that resembles a really good birthday bash. Other kid-friendly activities include tennis lessons, watersports, and storytelling. See p. 557.

- **The Buccaneer** (St. Croix; ✆ **800/255-3881** in the U.S., or 340/773-2100): Posh, upscale, and offering extremely good service, this hotel is a longtime favorite that occupies a 96-hectare (237-acre) former sugar estate. Its kids' programs (ages 2–12) include a half-day sailing excursion to Buck Island Reef and guided nature walks that let kids touch, smell, and taste tropical fruit. See p. 730.

10 The Best Inns

- **Admiral's Inn** (Antigua; ✆ **800/223-5695** in the U.S., or 268/460-1027): The most historically evocative corner of Antigua is Nelson's Dockyard, which was originally built in the 1700s to repair His Majesty's ships. The brick-and-stone inn that flourishes here today was once a warehouse for turpentine and pitch. In the late 1960s it was transformed into a well-designed and very charming hotel. *Note:* If you're sensitive to noise, you might be bothered by the sometimes raucous bar and restaurant. See p. 85.

- **Avila Beach Hotel** (Curaçao; ✆ **800/77747-8162** or 599/9-461-4377): This hotel's historic core, built in 1780 as the "country house" of the island's governor, retains its dignity and simplicity.

Although it's been a hotel since the end of World War II, a new owner added 40 bedrooms in motel-like outbuildings and upgraded the sports and dining facilities in the early 1990s. Today the Avila provides a sandy beach and easy access to the shops and distractions of nearby Willemstad. See p. 239.

- **Spice Island Beach Resort** (Grenada; ℂ **800/742-4276** in the U.S., or 473/444-4258): Each of this hotel's 66 units is a suite (with Jacuzzi) either beside the beach (one of Grenada's best) or near a swimming pool. Friday night features live music from the island's most popular bands. See p. 309.

- **François Plantation** (St. Barthélemy; ℂ **590/29-80-22**): At this inn, about a dozen pastel-colored bungalows are scattered among the lushest gardens on St. Barts. The mood is discreet, permissive, and fun. The food is French-inspired and served on a wide veranda decorated in a whimsical colonial style. See p. 518.

- **Ottley's Plantation Inn** (St. Kitts; ℂ **800/772-3039** in the U.S., or 869/465-7234): As you approach, the inn's dignified verandas appear majestically at the crest of 14 hectares (35 acres) of impeccably maintained lawns and gardens. It's one of the most charming plantation-house inns anywhere in the world, maintained with style and humor by its expatriate U.S. owners. The food is the best on the island, and the setting will soothe your tired nerves within a few hours after you arrive. See p. 545.

- **Montpelier Plantation Inn** (Nevis; ℂ **869/469-3462**): Style

and grace are the hallmarks of this former 18th-century plantation, now converted to an inn and set on a 40-hectare (100-acre) estate. Guests have included the late Princess of Wales. Cottage rooms are spread across 4 hectares (10 acres) of ornamental gardens. Swimming, horseback riding, windsurfing, a private beach, and "eco-rambles" fill the agenda. See p. 558.

- **Hermitage Plantation** (Nevis; ℂ **800/682-4025** in the U.S., or 869/469-3477): Guests stay in clapboard-sided cottages separated by carefully maintained bougainvillea and grasslands. The beach is a short drive away, but this slice of 19th-century plantation life (complete with candlelit dinners amid the antiques and polished silver of the main house) is decidedly romantic. See p. 558.

- **The Frangipani** (Bequia, the Grenadines; ℂ **784/458-3255**): This is the century-old homestead of the Mitchell family, whose most famous scion later became prime minister of St. Vincent. Today, it's a small, very relaxed inn. It's fun to watch the yachts setting out to sea from the nearby marina. See p. 638.

- **Villa Madeleine** (St. Croix; ℂ **800/496-7379** in the U.S., or 340/778-8782): This recently built, almost perfect re-creation of a 19th-century great house occupies the summit of a scrub-covered ridge. The food is among the best on St. Croix. Accommodations include richly furnished hideaway suites with sweeping views over the coastline. See p. 732.

11 The Best Destinations for Serious Shoppers

Because the U.S. government allows its citizens to take (or send) home more duty-free goods from the U.S. Virgins than from other ports of call, the U.S. Virgin Islands remain the shopping bazaar of the Caribbean. U.S. citizens may carry home $1,200 worth of goods untaxed, as opposed to only $400 worth of goods from most other islands in the Caribbean. (The only exception to this rule is Puerto Rico, where any purchase, regardless of the amount, can be carried tax free back to the U.S. mainland.) St. Maarten/St. Martin, which is ruled jointly by France and the Netherlands, gives the Virgins some serious shopping competition. It is virtually a shopper's mall, especially on the Dutch side. Although the U.S. doesn't grant the generous customs allowances on St. Maarten/St. Martin that it does to its own islands, the island doesn't have duty so you still can find some lovely bargains.

- **Aruba:** The wisest shoppers on Aruba are cost-conscious souls who have carefully checked the prices of comparable goods before leaving home. Duty is relatively low (only 3.3%). Much of the European china, jewelry, perfumes, watches, and crystal has a disconcerting habit of reappearing in every shopping mall and hotel boutique on the island, so after you determine exactly which brand of watch or china you want, you can comparison shop. See chapter 5.
- **Barbados:** Local shops seem to specialize in all things English. Merchandise includes bone china from British and Irish manufacturers, watches, jewelry, and perfumes. Bridgetown's Broad Street is the shopping headquarters of the island, although some of the stores here maintain boutiques (with similar prices but a less extensive range of merchandise) at many of the island's hotels and in malls along the congested southwestern coast. Except for cigarettes and tobacco, duty-free items

can be hauled off by any buyer as soon as they're paid for. Duty-free status is extended to anyone showing a passport or ID and an airline ticket with a date of departure from Barbados. See chapter 6.

- **The Cayman Islands:** Goods are sold tax free from a daunting collection of malls and minimalls throughout Grand Cayman. Most of these are along the highway that parallels Seven Mile Beach; you'll need a car to shop around. There are also lots of stores in George Town, which you can explore on foot, poking in and out of some large emporiums in your search for bargains. See chapter 9.
- **Curaçao:** In the island's capital, tidy and prosperous Willemstad, hundreds of merchants are only too happy to cater to your needs. A handful of malls lie on Willemstad's outskirts, but most shops are clustered within a few blocks of the center of town. During seasonal sales, goods might be up to 50% less than comparable prices in the United States; most of the year, you'll find luxury items (porcelain, crystal, watches, and gemstones) priced at about 25% less than in the U.S. Technically, you'll pay import duties on virtually everything you buy, but rates are so low you may not even notice. See chapter 10.
- **The Dominican Republic:** The island's best buys include handcrafts, amber from Dominican mines, and the distinctive pale-blue semiprecious gemstone known as *larimar.* The amber sold by street vendors may be nothing more than orange-colored, transparent plastic; buy only from wellestablished shops if your investment is a large one. Other charming souvenirs might include a Dominican rocking chair (remember the one JFK used to sit in?), which is sold

boxed, in ready-to-assemble pieces. Malls and souvenir stands abound in Santo Domingo, in Puerto Plata, and along the country's northern coast. See chapter 12.

- **Jamaica:** The shopping was better in the good old days, before new taxes added a 10% surcharge. Despite that, Jamaica offers a wealth of desirable goods, including flavored rums, Jamaican coffees, handcrafts (such as wood-carvings, woven baskets, and sandals), original paintings and sculpture, and cameras, watches, and DVD players. Unless you're a glutton for handmade souvenirs (which are available on virtually every beach and street corner), you'd be wise to limit most of your purchases to bona fide merchants and stores. See chapter 15.

- **Puerto Rico:** For U.S. citizens, there's no duty on anything bought in Puerto Rico. That doesn't guarantee that prices will be particularly low, however. Jewelry and watches abound, often at competitive prices, especially in the island's best-stocked area, Old San Juan. Also of great interest are such Puerto Rican handcrafts as charming folkloric papier-mâché carnival masks and *santos,* carved wooden figures depicting saints. See chapter 17.

- **St. Maarten/St. Martin:** Because of the massive influx of cruise ships, shopping in Dutch St. Maarten is now about the finest in the Caribbean, though you may have to fight the crowds. Because there's no duty, prices can be 30% to 50% lower than in the U.S. Forget about local crafts and concentrate on leather goods, electronics, cameras, designer fashions, watches, and crystal, along with linens and jewelry. Philipsburg, capital of the island's Dutch side, is the best place to shop. Although it can't compete with Dutch St. Maarten, French St. Martin has been becoming a more popular shopping destination, especially for goods such as fashion or perfumes imported from France. See chapter 23.

- **St. Thomas:** Many of its busiest shops are in restored warehouses that were originally built in the 1700s. Charlotte Amalie, the capital, is a shopper's town, with a staggering number of stores stocked with more merchandise than anywhere else in the entire Caribbean. However, despite all the fanfare, real bargains are hard to come by. Regardless, the island attracts hordes of cruise-ship passengers on a sometimes frantic hunt for bargains, real or imagined. Look for two local publications, *This Week* and *Best Buys;* either might steer you to the type of merchandise you're seeking. If at all possible, try to avoid shopping when more than one cruise ship is in port—the shopping district is a madhouse on those days. See chapter 27.

- **St. Croix:** This island doesn't have the massive shopping development of St. Thomas, but its merchandise has never been more wide-ranging than it is today. Even though most cruise ships call at Frederiksted, with its urban mall, our favorite shops are in Christiansted, which boasts many one-of-a-kind boutiques and a lot of special finds. Prices are about the same here as on St. Thomas. See chapter 27.

12 The Best Nightlife

Nighttime is sleep time on the British Virgins, Montserrat, Nevis, Anguilla, St. Eustatius, Saba, St. Barts, Dominica, Bonaire, St. Vincent, and all of the Grenadines. The serious partyer will probably want to choose one of the following destinations.

- **Aruba:** This island has 10 casinos, each with its own unique decor and each with a following of devoted gamblers. Some offer their own cabarets and comedy shows, dance floors with live or recorded music, restaurants of all degrees of formality, and bars. The casinos are big, splashy, colorful, and, yes, people even occasionally win. Drinks are usually free while you play. The legal tender in most of Aruba's casinos is the U.S. dollar. See chapter 5.

- **Barbados:** Bridgetown is home to at least two boats (the *Bajan Queen* and the *Jolly Roger*) that embark at sundown for rum-and-reggae cruises, as well as oversize music bars like Harbour Lights. Otherwise, a host of bars, British-style pubs, dozens of restaurants, and discos (both within and outside large hotels) beckon from St. Lawrence Gap or the crowded southwest coast. See chapter 6.

- **Curaçao:** Although outdistanced by Aruba, the action spinning around the island's casinos make this one of the southern Caribbean's hot spots for gamblers. Salinja, a sector of Willemstad, has lively bars where locals and visitors drink and party until the wee hours, and live jazz often fills the air. See chapter 10.

- **The Dominican Republic:** Large resort hotels in the Dominican Republic evoke a Latino version of Las Vegas. If cabaret shows aren't your thing, there are enough discos in the major towns and resorts to keep nightclubbers busy for weeks. The tourist areas of Puerto Plata and Santo Domingo are sprinkled with casinos, and the island's ever-developing north shore contains its share of jingle-jangle, too. Our

favorite is the casino in the Renaissance Jaragua Hotel & Casino in Santo Domingo, which offers floor shows, live merengue concerts, a wraparound bar, and at least five different restaurants. See chapter 12.

- **Jamaica:** Many visitors are drawn here by a love for the island's distinct musical forms. Foremost among these are reggae and soca, both of which are performed at hotels, resorts, and raffish dives throughout the island. Hotels often stage folkloric shows that include entertainers who sing, dance, swallow torches, and walk on broken glass. There are also plenty of indoor/outdoor bars where you might actually be able to talk to people. Local tourist boards in Negril and Montego Bay sometimes organize weekly beach parties called "Boonoonoonoos." See chapter 15.

- **Puerto Rico:** Puerto Rico contains all the raw ingredients for great nightlife, including casinos, endless rows of bars and bodegas, cabaret shows with girls and glitter, and discos that feature everything from New York imports to some of the best salsa and merengue anywhere. The country's gaming headquarters lies along the Condado in San Juan, although there are also casinos in megaresorts scattered throughout the island. The casinos here are the most fun in the Caribbean, and they're also some of the most spectacular. Each contains lots of sideshows (restaurants, merengue bars, art galleries, piano bars, and shops) that can distract you from the roulette and slots. Puerto Ricans take pride in dressing well at their local casinos, which enhances an evening's glamour. *Note:* You can't drink at the tables. If you're a really serious partyer, you'll have lots of company in Puerto Rico. Be prepared to stay out very late; you can recover from your Bacardi hangover on a palm-fringed beach the next day. See chapter 17.

• **St. Maarten/St. Martin:** This island has a rather cosmopolitan nightlife and contains the densest concentration of restaurants in the Caribbean, each with its own bar. Discos are often indoor/outdoor affairs. Hotel casinos abound on the Dutch side, and if you're addicted to the jingle of slot machines and roulette wheels, you won't lack for company. The casinos tend to be low-key, which might appeal to you if you dislike high-stakes tables with lots of intensity. See chapter 23.

• **St. Thomas:** The Virgin Islands' most active nightlife is found here. Don't expect glitzy shows like those in San Juan's Condado area, and don't expect any kind of casino. But you'll find plenty of fun at the beach bars, restaurants, concerts, clubs, and folklore and reggae shows. See chapter 27.

2

Planning Your Trip to the Caribbean

Golden beaches shaded by palm trees and crystalline waters teeming with colorful tropical fish—it's all just a few hours' flight from the East Coast of the United States. Dubbed the "Eighth Continent of the World," the Caribbean islands have an amazing variety of terrain that ranges from thick rainforests to haunting volcanoes, from white- to black-sand beaches. Spicy food, spicier music, and the gentle, leisurely lifestyle of the islands draw millions of visitors each year, all hoping to find the perfect place in the sun. In this chapter, we'll help you choose the right destination, the right time to go, and the best strategies for getting a good package deal or airfare.

1 The Islands in Brief

ANGUILLA   Although it's developing rapidly as vacationers discover its 19km (12 miles) of arid but spectacular beaches, Anguilla (rhymes with *vanilla*) is still quiet, sleepy, and relatively free of racial tensions. A flat, coral island, it maintains a maritime tradition of proud fisherfolk, many of whom still make a living from the sea, catching lobsters and selling them at high prices to expensive resorts and restaurants. Although there's a handful of moderately priced accommodations, Anguilla is a very expensive destination, with small and rather exclusive resorts. It's as posh as St. Barts, but without all the snobbery. There are no casinos (and that's the way most of the locals want it). There's not much to do here except lie in the sun, bask in luxury, and enjoy fine dining.

ANTIGUA   Antigua is famous for having a different beach for each day of the year, but it lacks the lushness of such islands as Dominica and Jamaica. Some British traditions (including a passion for cricket) linger, even

though the nation became independent in 1981. The island has a population of 80,000, mostly descended from the African slaves of plantation owners. Antigua's resorts are isolated and conservative but very glamorous; its highways are horribly maintained; and its historic naval sites are interesting. Antigua is politically linked to the sparsely inhabited and largely undeveloped island of Barbuda, about 48km (30 miles) north. In spite of its small size, Barbuda has two posh, pricey resorts.

ARUBA   Until its beaches were "discovered" in the late 1970s, Aruba, with its desertlike terrain and lunarlike interior landscapes, was an almost-forgotten outpost of Holland, valued mostly for its oil refineries and salt factories. Today, vacationers come for the dependable sunshine (it rains less here than virtually anywhere else in the Caribbean), the spectacular beaches, and an almost total lack of racial tensions despite an amazingly culturally diverse population. The high-rise hotels of Aruba are within walking distance of each other along a strip of fabulous beach. You don't stay in old, converted, family-run sugar mills here, and you don't come for history. You come here if you're interested in gambling and splashy high-rise resorts.

BARBADOS Originally founded on a plantation economy that made its aristocracy rich (on the backs of slave laborers), this Atlantic outpost was a staunchly loyal member of the British Commonwealth for generations. Barbados is the Caribbean's easternmost island, floating in the mid-Atlantic like a great coral reef and ringed with glorious beige-sand beaches. Cosmopolitan Barbados has the densest population of any island in the Caribbean, with few racial tensions despite its history of slavery. A loyal group of return visitors appreciate its many stylish, medium-size hotels (many of which carry a hefty price tag). Service is usually extremely good, a byproduct of its British mores, which have flourished for a century. Topography varies from rolling hills and savage waves on the eastern (Atlantic) coast to densely populated flatlands, rows of hotels and apartments, and sheltered beaches in the southwest. If you're looking for a Las Vegas–type atmosphere and fine beaches, go to Aruba. If you want history (there are lots of great houses and old churches to explore), a quiet and conservative atmosphere, and fine beaches, come here.

BONAIRE Its strongest historical and cultural links are to Holland, and although it has always been a poor relation of nearby Curaçao, Bonaire boasts better scuba diving and better bird life than any of its larger and richer neighbors. The terrain is as dry and inhospitable as anything you'll find in the Caribbean, a sparse desert landscape offset by a wealth of marine life that thrives along miles of offshore reefs. Except for its scuba diving and snorkeling, the island isn't overly

blessed with natural resources. But those coral reefs around most of the island attract divers from all over the world. The casino and party crowd should head for Aruba instead.

THE BRITISH VIRGIN ISLANDS (B.V.I.) Still a British Crown Colony, this lushly forested chain consists of about 50 small, mountainous islands (depending on how many rocks, cays, and uninhabited islets you want to include). Superb for sailors, the B.V.I. are less populated, less developed, and have fewer social problems than the U.S. Virgin Islands. **Tortola** is the main island, followed by **Virgin Gorda,** which boasts some of the poshest hotels in the West Indies. **Anegada,** a coral atoll geologically different from the other members of the B.V.I., mainly attracts the yachting set. Come here for the laidback lifestyle, the lovely sandy beaches, the friendly people, and the small, intimate inns.

THE CAYMAN ISLANDS This is a trio of islands set near the southern coast of Cuba. This prosperous, tiny nation depends on Britain for its economic survival and attracts millionaire expatriates from all over because of its lenient tax and banking laws. Relatively flat and unattractive, these islands are covered with scrubland and swamp, but they boast more than their share of expensive private homes and condominiums. Until recently, **Grand Cayman** enjoyed one of the most closely knit societies in the Caribbean, although recent prosperity has created some socioeconomic divisions. The warm, crystal-clear waters and the colorful marine life in the offshore reefs surrounding the island attract scuba divers and snorkelers. Many hotels line the luscious sands of Seven Mile Beach.

CURAÇAO Because much of the island's surface is an arid desert that grows only cactus, its canny Dutch settlers ruled out farming and made Curaçao (Coo-ra-*sow*) into one of the Dutch Empire's busiest trading posts. Until the post–World War II collapse of the oil refineries, Curaçao was a thriving mercantile society with a capital (Willemstad) that somewhat resembled Amsterdam and a population with a curious mixture of bloodlines, including African, Dutch, Venezuelan, and Pakistani. The main language here is Papiamento, a mixture of African and European dialects, though Dutch, Spanish, and English are also spoken. Tourism began to develop during the 1980s, and many new hotels have been built since then. The island has a few interesting historic sights, and Willemstad is one of the most charming towns in the Caribbean. Go to Aruba for beaches and gambling, Bonaire for scuba diving, and Curaçao for little cove beaches, shopping, history, and its distinctive "Dutch-in-the-Caribbean" culture.

DOMINICA An English-speaking island set midway between Guadeloupe and Martinique, Dominica (Doh-mi-*nee*-kah), the largest and most mountainous island of the Windward Islands is not to be confused with the Dominican Republic (see below). A mysterious, little-visited land of waterfalls, rushing streams, and rainforests, it has only a few beaches, which are mainly lined with black volcanic sand. But if you like the offbeat and unusual, you may find this lush island the most fascinating in the Caribbean. Some 82,000 people live here, including 2,000 descendants of the Carib Indians. Roseau, one of the smallest capitals in the Caribbean, is more like an overgrown Creole village than a city. Dominica is one of the poorest islands in the Caribbean, and it has the misfortune of lying directly in the hurricane belt.

THE DOMINICAN REPUBLIC Occupying the eastern two-thirds of Hispaniola, the island it shares with Haiti, the mountainous Dominican Republic is the second-largest country of the Caribbean. Longtime victim of an endless series of military dictatorships, it now has a more favorable political climate and is one of the most affordable destinations in the entire Caribbean. Its crowded capital is Santo Domingo, with a population of two million. The island offers lots of Latin color, zesty merengue music, and many opportunities to dance, drink, and party. Unfortunately, the contrast between the wealth of foreign tourists and the poverty of locals is especially obvious here, and it's not the safest of the islands. For fun in the sun and good beaches, too, head for La Romana in the southeast, Punta Cana on the easternmost shore, Puerto Plata in the northwest, or any resorts along the Amber Coast in the north.

GRENADA The southernmost nation of the Windward Islands, Grenada (Gre-*nay*-dah) is one of the lushest islands in the Caribbean. With its gentle climate and extravagantly fertile volcanic soil, it's one of the largest producers of spices in the Western Hemisphere. There's a lot of very appealing local color on Grenada, particularly since the political troubles of the 1980s seem, at least for the moment, to have ended. There are beautiful white-sand beaches, and the populace (a mixture of English expatriates and islanders of African descent) is friendly. Once a British Crown Colony but now independent, the island nation also incorporates two smaller islands: Carriacou and Petit Martinique, neither of which has many tourist facilities. Grenada's capital, St. George's, is one of the most charming towns in the Caribbean.

GUADELOUPE Although it isn't as sophisticated or cosmopolitan as the two outlying islands over which it holds administrative authority—St. Barthélemy and the French section of

St. Martin—there's a lot of natural beauty in this *département* of mainland France. With a relatively low population density (only 440,000 people live here, mostly along the coast), butterfly-shaped Guadeloupe is actually two distinctly different volcanic islands separated by a narrow saltwater strait, the Rivière Salée. It's ideal for scenic drives and Creole color, offering an unusual insight into the French colonial world. The island has a lot of good beaches, each one different, and a vast national park (a huge tropical forest with everything from wild orchids to coffee and vanilla plants). It's life *à la française* in the Tropics, but we'd give the nod to Martinique (see below) if you can visit only one French island.

JAMAICA A favorite of North American honeymooners, Jamaica is a mountainous island that rises abruptly from the sea 145km (90 miles) south of Cuba and about 161km (100 miles) west of Haiti. One of the most densely populated nations in the Caribbean, with a vivid sense of its own identity, Jamaica has a history rooted in the plantation economy and some of the most turbulent and impassioned politics in the Western Hemisphere. In spite of its economic and social problems, Jamaica is one of the most successful black democracies in the world. The island is large enough to allow the more or less peaceful coexistence of all kinds of people within its beach-lined borders—everyone from expatriate English aristocrats to dyed-in-the-wool Rastafarians. Its tourist industry has been plagued by the island's reputation for aggressive vendors and racial tension, but it is taking steps to improve the situation. Overall, and despite its long history of social unrest, increasing crime, and poverty, Jamaica is a fascinating island. It offers excellent beaches, golf, eco-tourism adventures, and fine hotels in all price brackets, making it one of the most popular destinations in the Caribbean, especially since you can find package deals galore.

MARTINIQUE One of the most exotic French-speaking destinations in the Caribbean, Martinique was the site of a settlement demolished by volcanic activity (St. Pierre, now only a pale shadow of a once-thriving city). Like Guadeloupe and St. Barts, Martinique is legally and culturally French (certainly many islanders drive with a Gallic panache—read: very badly), although many Creole customs and traditions continue to flourish. The beaches are beautiful, the Creole cuisine is full of flavor and flair, and the island has lots of tropical charm. Even more than Guadeloupe, this is the social and cultural center of the French Antilles. If you'd like the chance to speak French on a charmingly beautiful island with elegant people, the Martiniquaise will wish you *bonjour.*

PUERTO RICO Home to 3.9 million people whose primary language is Spanish (though English is widely spoken, too), the Commonwealth of Puerto Rico is under the jurisdiction of the United States and has a more-or-less comfortable mix of Latin culture with imports from the U.S. mainland. It's the most urban island of the Caribbean, with lots of traffic and relatively high crime, though it compensates with great beaches, glittering casinos, a range of hotels in all price brackets, sports and eco-tourism offerings, good hearty food, and sizzling salsa clubs. The island's interior is filled with rainforests and ancient volcanic mountains; the coastline is ringed with gorgeous sandy beaches. The commonwealth also includes a trio of small offshore islands: Culebra, Mona, and Vieques (the last has the most tourist facilities). San Juan, the island's 16th-century capital, has some of the most extensive and best-preserved Spanish colonial neighborhoods in the

New World, with historic sites and lots of things to see and do, and a steady flow of cruise-ship passengers who keep the stores and casinos filled throughout much of the year. You can usually find great package deals through Puerto Rico's hotels and resorts.

SABA Saba is a cone-shaped extinct volcano that rises abruptly and steeply from the watery depths of the Caribbean. There are no beaches to speak of, and the local Dutch- and English-speaking populace has traditionally made a living from fishing, trade, and needlework, rather than tourism. Hotel choices are limited. Saba's thrifty, seafaring folk can offer insights into the old-fashioned lifestyle of the Netherlands Antilles. There's only one road on the island, and unless you opt to hike away from its edges, you'll have to follow the traffic along its narrow, winding route. Basically, you come here if you want to hang out at your hotel pool, climb up to a rainforest, go diving, and perhaps make a day trip to one of the nearby islands. It's a place to visit if you like to collect untouristy islands. You may want to come only for an afternoon—you can do this by plane or trimaran. You don't come for fabulous white-sand beaches, ocean swimming, or historic sights.

ST. BARTHÉLEMY (ALSO CALLED ST. BARTS OR ST. BARTHS) Part of the French *département* of Guadeloupe, lying 24km (15 miles) from St. Martin, St. Barts is a small, hilly island with a population of 6,500 people who live on 34 sq. km (13 sq. miles) of verdant terrain ringed by pleasant white-sand beaches. A small number of African descendants live harmoniously on this chic Caribbean island with descendants of Norman and Breton mariners and a colony of more recent expatriates from Europe. An expensive and exclusive stomping ground of the rich and famous, with a distinctive seafaring tradition and a decidedly French flavor, St. Barts has a lovely "storybook" capital in Gustavia. For sophistication and luxury living, St. Barts is equaled in the Caribbean only by Anguilla, and the price tag isn't cheap. It's a place to come to if you want to wind down from a stressful life.

ST. EUSTATIUS (ALSO CALLED STATIA) Statia is part of the Netherlands Antilles and the Leeward Islands, lying to the west of Dutch Sint Maarten. During the 1700s, this Dutch-controlled island ("The Golden Rock") was one of the most important trading posts in the Caribbean. During the U.S. War of Independence, a brisk arms trade helped to bolster the local economy, but the glamour ended in 1781, when British Admiral Romney sacked the port, hauled off most of the island's wealth, and propelled St. Eustatius onto a path of obscurity—where it remained for almost 200 years, until the advent of tourism. Today, the island is among the poorest in the Caribbean, with 21 sq. km (8 sq. miles) of arid landscape, beaches with strong and sometimes dangerous undertows, a population of around 2,900 people, and a sleepy capital named Oranjestad. Out of desperation, the island is very committed to maintaining its political and fiscal links to the Netherlands. This is a destination for people who are interested in American Revolution–era history and who like hanging out around a pool at a friendly, informal local inn. Most people will want to make a day trip to see the historic sites, have lunch, and leave.

ST. KITTS & NEVIS The first English settlement in the Leeward Islands, St. Kitts has a rich sense of British maritime history. With 176 sq. km (69 sq. miles) of land, St. Kitts enjoyed one of the richest sugar-cane economies of the plantation age. This island lies somewhat off the beaten tourist track and has a very appealing, intimate charm. A lush, fertile mountain island with a rainforest and waterfalls, it is crowned by the 1,138m (3,733-ft.) Mount Liamuiga—a crater that thankfully has remained dormant (unlike the one at Montserrat). St. Kitts is home to some 38,000 people and Brimstone Hill, the Caribbean's most impressive fortress. Come here for the beaches and the history, for lush natural scenery, and to stay at a restored plantation home that's been turned into a charming inn. Lots of sporting activities, ranging from mountain climbing to horseback riding, are also available.

Now forging its own road to independence from St. Kitts, from which it is separated by 3km (2 miles) of water, Nevis was spotted by Columbus in 1493 on his second voyage to the New World. He called it Nieves—Spanish for snows—when he saw the cloud-crowned volcanic isle that evoked for him the snow-capped peaks of the Pyrenees. Known for its long beaches of both black and white sand, Nevis, more than any other island in the Caribbean, has turned its former great houses, built during the plantation era, into some of the most charming and atmospheric inns in the West Indies. It also boasts the Four Seasons Resort for those who want world-class elegance and service. The capital city of Charlestown looks like a real Caribbean backwater, though it is home to hundreds of worldwide businesses that are drawn to Nevis for its tax laws and bank secrecy.

ST. LUCIA St. Lucia (*Loo*-sha), 39km (24 miles) south of Martinique, is the second largest of the Windward Islands, with a population of around 162,000. Although in 1803 Britain eventually won control of the island, French influence is still evident in the Creole dialect spoken here. A volcanic

island with lots of rainfall and great natural beauty, it has white- and black-sand beaches, bubbling sulfur springs, and beautiful mountain scenery. Most tourism is concentrated on the island's northwestern tip, near the capital (Castries), but the arrival of up to 200,000 visitors a year has definitely altered the old agrarian lifestyle throughout the island. Come here for the posh resorts and the gorgeous beaches, the rainforests, and the lush tropical foliage.

ST. MAARTEN/ST. MARTIN Lying 232km (144 miles) east of Puerto Rico, this scrub-covered island has been divided between the Dutch (Sint Maarten) and the French (Saint Martin) since 1648. Regardless of how you spell its name, it's the same island on both sides of the unguarded border—though the two halves are quite different. The Dutch side contains the island's major airport, more shops, and more tourist facilities, and the French side has some of the poshest hotels and superior food. Both sides are modern, urbanized, and cosmopolitan. And both suffer from traffic jams, a lack of parking space in the capitals, tourist-industry burnout (especially on the Dutch side), and a disturbing increase in crime. In spite of the drawbacks, there's a lot to attract you here—great beaches, the shopping (some of the Caribbean's best), the gambling, the self-contained resorts, the nonstop flights from the U.S., nightlife, and some of the best restaurants in the Caribbean. From here, you can fly over for a day trip to St. Eustatius or Saba.

ST. VINCENT & THE GRENADINES Despite its natural beauty, visitors have only recently discovered this mini-archipelago, though it has always been known to divers and the yachting set, who consider its north-to-south string of cays and coral islets one of the most beautiful sailing regions in the world. The nation's population is only about 116,000 people (of mostly African descent). **St. Vincent** (29km/18 miles long and 18km/11 miles wide) is by far the largest and most fertile island in the country. Its capital is the sleepy, somewhat dilapidated town of Kingstown (not to be confused with Kingston, Jamaica). **The Grenadines,** some 32 neighboring islands, stretch like a pearl necklace to the south of St. Vincent. These include the charming boat-building communities of **Bequia** and **Mustique,** where the late Princess Margaret had a home. Less densely populated islands in the chain include the tiny outposts of **Mayreau, Canouan, Palm Island,** and **Petit St. Vincent,** which was mostly covered with scrub until hotel owners planted much-needed groves of palm and hardwood trees and opened resorts.

TRINIDAD & TOBAGO The southernmost of the West Indies, this two-island nation lies just 11km (6¾ miles) off the coast of Venezuela. Both islands once had sugar-plantation economies and enjoyed fantastic wealth during the 18th century. **Trinidad** is the most industrialized island in the Caribbean, with oil deposits and a polyglot population from India, Pakistan, Venezuela, Africa, and Europe. Known for its calypso music and carnival celebrations, Trinidad is one of the most culturally distinctive nations in the Caribbean, with a landmass of more than 4,662 sq. km (1,818 sq. miles), a rich artistic tradition, a bustling capital (Port-of-Spain), and an impressive variety of exotic flora and fauna. You don't come to Trinidad for the beaches; it has some excellent beaches, but they are far removed from the capital of Port-of-Spain and hard to locate. For beach life, head for Tobago and just pass through Trinidad, which makes a worthy stopover if you're visiting one of its wildlife sanctuaries.

About 32km (20 miles) northeast of Trinidad, tiny **Tobago** (14km/8¾ miles wide and 42km/26 miles long) is calmer and less heavily forested, with a rather dull capital (Scarborough) and an impressive array of white-sand beaches. While Trinidad seems to consider tourism only one of many viable industries, Tobago is absolutely dependent on it. Life is sleepy on Tobago, unlike bustling Trinidad. Tobago boasts coral reefs ideal for scuba diving, rainforests, luscious sands, shoreline drives, lanes of coconut palms, and a soothing getaway-from-it-all atmosphere—that is, until the developers ruin it.

TURKS & CAICOS Although these islands are actually part of the Bahamian archipelago—they are to the east of the southernmost islands of The Bahamas, directly north of Haiti and the Dominican Republic—they are governed separately.

Home of Cockburn Town, the capital of Turks and Caicos (*Kayk*-us), **Grand Turk** nevertheless has a small-town atmosphere. The farthest island from Florida, it totals 23 sq. km (9 sq. miles). Although Grand Turk is ringed by abundant marine life, most of the island's surface is flat, rocky, and dry. The diving here is world-class—the main draw for most visitors. Grand Turk has a relatively undeveloped tourist infrastructure, although it offers a scattering of inns and hotels.

Providenciales' (Provo) 19km (12-mile) beach and pristine coastline were a tourist development waiting to happen. In the late 1970s, hotel megaliths such as Club Med poured money into increasingly popular low-rise eco-conscious resorts. Now Provo's tourist infrastructure far surpasses anything on Grand Turk. One of the larger islands of the Turks and Caicos, Provo is green but arid, with miles of scrubland and stunted trees covering the island's low, undulating hills. Whatever the Turks and Caicos have to offer in organized sports is found here, including the nation's only golf course, boat tours, and diving excursions. The island also has the best cuisine and the finest entertainment in the Turks and Caicos, but it's still much, much sleepier than the big developments of Aruba.

THE U.S. VIRGIN ISLANDS Formerly Danish possessions, these islands became part of the United States in 1917. Originally based on a plantation economy, **St. Croix** is the largest and flattest of the U.S. Virgins, and St. Thomas and St. John are more mountainous. St. Thomas and, to a lesser degree, St. Croix have lots of diversions, facilities, bars, restaurants, and modern resort hotels. **St. Thomas,** which is overbuilt, is sometimes referred to as the shopping mall of the Caribbean, and cruise-ship passengers constantly pass through. Much of the surface of **St. John** is devoted to a national park, a gift from Laurance Rockefeller to the national park system. Crime is on the increase, however—an unfortunate fly in the ointment of this otherwise soothing corner of paradise. If you want great shopping, go to St. Thomas. St. Croix is more laid-back, a better place to escape for peace and quiet. St. John is most often visited on a day trip from St. Thomas. All three islands offer stunning beaches, great snorkeling, sailing, and lovely scenery, but they are, unfortunately, rather expensive destinations.

2 Visitor Information

All the major islands have tourist representatives who will supply information before you go; we list each one in the "Fast Facts" section of the individual island chapters.

The **Caribbean Tourism Organization,** 80 Broad St., 32nd Floor, New York, NY 10004 (© **212/ 635-9530;** www.doitcaribbean.com), can also provide general information.

SIGHTSEEING: INFO ON THE WEB The Internet is a great source of current travel information. **"Planning Your Trip Online,"** later in this chapter, is a detailed guide that will help you use the Web to its best advantage to research and perhaps even book your trip.

Whenever possible throughout this book, we've included Web addresses along with phone numbers and addresses for attractions, outfitters, and other companies. We've also given each hotel and resort's website, so you can see pictures of a property before you make your reservation.

TRAVEL AGENTS Travel agents can save you time and money by steering you toward the best package deals, hunting down the best airfares, and arranging cruises and rental cars. Most travel agents still charge nothing for their services—they're paid through commissions from the airlines and other agencies they book for you. However, airlines have begun to cut commissions, and increasingly agents are finding they have to charge a fee to hold the bottom line. In the worst instances, unscrupulous agents will only offer you travel options that bag them the juiciest commissions. Shop around and ask questions, and use this book to become an informed consumer. Don't be pushed into booking a vacation that's not right for you.

If you decide to use a travel agent, make sure the agent is a member of the **American Society of Travel Agents (ASTA),** 1101 King St., Alexandria, VA 22314 (© **703/739- 8739;** www.astanet.com). If you send a self-addressed, stamped envelope, ASTA will mail you the free booklet *Avoiding Travel Problems.*

3 Entry Requirements & Customs

ENTRY REQUIREMENTS

Even though most of the Caribbean islands are independent nations and, therefore, are classified as international destinations, passports may not be strictly required of Americans. We recommend carrying them nevertheless. You'll certainly need identification at some point, and a passport is the best form of ID for speeding through Customs and Immigration. Driver's licenses are not acceptable as a sole form of ID. Visas are usually not required, but some countries may require you to fill out a tourist card (see the individual island chapters for details).

FOR RESIDENTS OF THE UNITED STATES Whether you're applying in person or by mail, you can download passport applications from the U.S. State Department website at **http://travel.state.gov/passport_services.html.** To find your regional passport office, either check the U.S. State Department website or call the **National Passport Information Center** toll-free number (© **877/487-2778**) for automated information.

FOR RESIDENTS OF CANADA Passport applications are available at travel agencies throughout Canada or from the central **Passport Office,** Department of Foreign Affairs and International Trade, Ottawa, ON K1A 0G3 (© **800/567-6868;** www.dfait-maeci.gc.ca/passport).

FOR RESIDENTS OF THE UNITED KINGDOM To pick up an application for a standard 10-year passport (5-year passport for children under 16), visit your nearest passport office, major post office, or travel agency, or contact the United Kingdom Passport Service at © 0870/521-0410 or search its website at www.ukpa.gov.uk.

CUSTOMS

Each island has specific guidelines on what you can bring in with you; these are detailed in the destination chapters that follow. Generally, you're permitted to bring in items intended for your personal use, including tobacco, cameras, film, and a limited supply of liquor—usually 40 ounces.

Just before you leave home, check with your country's Customs or Foreign Affairs department for the latest guidelines—including information on items that are not allowed to be brought into your home country—since the rules are subject to change and often contain some surprising oddities.

U.S. Customs allows $1,200 worth of duty-free imports every 30 days from the U.S. Virgin Islands; if you go over this amount, you're taxed at 5% rather than the usual 10%. The duty-free limit is $800 for such international destinations as the French islands of Guadeloupe and Martinique, and $600 for many other

---

Tips Passport Savvy

Allow plenty of time before your trip to apply for a passport; processing normally takes 3 weeks but can take longer during busy periods (especially spring). And keep in mind that if you need a passport in a hurry, you'll pay a higher processing fee. When traveling, safeguard your passport in an inconspicuous, inaccessible place like a money belt and keep a copy of the critical pages with your passport number in a separate place. If you lose your passport, visit the nearest consulate of your native country as soon as possible for a replacement.

islands. If you visit only Puerto Rico, you don't have to go through Customs at all, since the island is a U.S. commonwealth.

Joint Customs declarations are possible for members of a family traveling together. For instance, if you are a husband and wife with two children, your purchases in the U.S. Virgin Islands become duty free up to $4,800! Unsolicited gifts can be sent to friends and relatives at the rate of $200 per day from the U.S. Virgin Islands and $50 a day from the other islands. U.S. citizens, or returning residents at least 21 years of age, traveling directly or indirectly from the U.S. Virgin Islands are allowed to bring in free of duty 1,000 cigarettes, 5 liters of alcohol, and 100 cigars (but not Cuban cigars). Duty-free limitations on articles from other countries are generally 1 liter of alcohol, 200 cigarettes, and 200 cigars.

You should collect receipts for all purchases made abroad. You must also declare on your Customs form the nature and value of all gifts received during your stay abroad. It's prudent to carry proof that you purchased expensive cameras or jewelry on the U.S. mainland. If you purchased such an item during an earlier trip abroad, you should carry proof that you have previously paid Customs duty on the item.

Sometimes merchants suggest a false receipt to undervalue your purchase. *Beware:* You could be involved in a sting operation—the merchant might be an informer to U.S. Customs.

If you use any medication that contains controlled substances or requires injection, carry an original prescription or note from your doctor.

For specifics on what you can bring back, download the invaluable free pamphlet *Know Before You Go* online at **www.customs.gov.** (Click "Know Before You Go!–Online Brochure.") Or contact the **U.S. Customs Service,** 1300 Pennsylvania Ave. NW, Washington, DC 20229 (© **877/287-8667**) and request the pamphlet.

U.K. citizens should contact **HM Customs & Excise** at © **0845/010-9000** (© 020/8929-0152 from outside the U.K.), or consult their website at www.hmce.gov.uk.

For a clear summary of **Canadian** rules, write for the booklet *I Declare,* issued by the **Canada Customs and Revenue Agency** (© **800/461-9999** in Canada, or 204/983-3500; www.ccra-adrc.gc.ca).

Citizens of **Australia** should request a helpful brochure available from Australian consulates or Customs offices, *Know Before You Go.* For more information, call the **Australian Customs Service** at © **1300/363-263,** or log on to www.customs.gov.au.

For **New Zealand** Customs information, contact the **New Zealand Customs Service** at (© **04/473-6099** or 0800/428-786; www.customs.govt.nz).

4 Money

CASH/CURRENCY Widely accepted on many of the islands, the U.S. dollar is the legal currency of the U.S. Virgin Islands, the British Virgin Islands, and Puerto Rico. Many islands use the Eastern Caribbean dollar, even though your hotel bill will most likely be presented in U.S. dollars. For details, see "Fast Facts" in the individual island chapters.

ATMs (automated teller machines) The easiest and best way to get cash away from home is from an ATM. The **Cirrus** (© **800/424-7787;** www.mastercard.com) and **PLUS** (© **800/843-7587;** www.visa.com) networks span the globe; look at the back of your bank card to see which network you're on, then call or check online for ATM locations at your destination.

The Euro, the U.S. Dollar, the Canadian Dollar & the British Pound

FOREIGN CURRENCIES VS. THE U.S. DOLLAR Conversion ratios between the U.S. dollar and other currencies fluctuate, and their differences could affect the relative costs of your holiday. The figures reflected in the currency chart below were valid at the time of this writing, but they might not be valid by the time of your departure. This chart would be useful for conversions of small amounts of money, but if you're planning on any major transactions, check for more updated rates prior to making any serious commitments.

The U.S. Dollar and the Euro. At the time of this writing US$1 was worth approximately .80€. (Inversely stated, that means that 1€ was worth approximately US$1.25.)

The British pound, the U.S. Dollar, and the Euro. At press time, £1 equaled approximately US$1.61 or approximately 1.29€.

The Canadian dollar, the U.S. dollar, and the Euro. At press time, C$1 equaled approximately 72¢ U.S. or approximately .58€.

US$	UK£	C$	Euro€	US$	UK£	C$	Euro€
1.00	0.62	1.40	0.80	75.00	46.50	105.00	60.00
2.00	1.24	2.80	1.60	100.00	62.00	140.00	80.00
3.00	1.86	4.20	2.40	125.00	77.50	175.00	100.00
4.00	2.48	5.60	3.20	150.00	93.00	210.00	120.00
5.00	3.10	7.00	4.00	175.00	108.50	245.00	140.00
6.00	3.72	8.40	4.80	200.00	124.00	280.00	160.00
7.00	4.34	9.80	5.60	225.00	139.50	315.00	180.00
8.00	4.96	11.20	6.40	250.00	155.00	350.00	200.00
9.00	5.58	12.60	7.20	275.00	170.50	385.00	220.00
10.00	6.20	14.00	8.00	300.00	186.00	420.00	240.00
15.00	9.30	21.00	12.00	350.00	217.00	490.00	280.00
20.00	12.40	28.00	16.00	400.00	248.00	560.00	320.00
25.00	15.50	35.00	20.00	500.00	310.00	700.00	400.00
50.00	31.00	70.00	40.00	1000.00	620.00	1400.00	800.00

Be sure you know your personal identification number (PIN) and your daily withdrawal limit before you leave home. Also keep in mind that many banks impose a fee every time a card is used at a different bank's ATM, and that fee can be higher for international transactions (up to $5 or more) than for domestic ones (where they're rarely more than $1.50). On top of this, the bank from which you withdraw cash may charge its own fee. To compare banks' ATM fees within the U.S., use **www.bankrate.com**. For international withdrawal fees, ask your bank.

TRAVELER'S CHECKS Traveler's checks are something of an anachronism from the days before the ATM made cash accessible at any time. Traveler's checks used to be the only sound alternative to traveling with dangerously large amounts of cash. They were as reliable as currency, but, unlike cash, could be replaced if lost or stolen.

These days, traveler's checks are less necessary because most cities have 24-hour ATMs that allow you to withdraw small amounts of cash as needed. However, keep in mind that you will likely be charged an ATM withdrawal fee if the bank is not your own, so if you're withdrawing money every day, you might be better off with traveler's checks—provided that you don't mind showing identification every time you want to cash one.

You can get traveler's checks at almost any bank. **American Express** offers denominations of $20, $50, $100, $500, and (for cardholders only) $1,000. You'll pay a service charge ranging from 1% to 4%. You can also get American Express traveler's checks over the phone by calling ⓒ **800/221-7282;** Amex gold and platinum cardholders who use this number are exempt from the 1% fee. **Visa** offers traveler's checks at Citibank locations nationwide, as well as at several other banks. The service charge ranges between 1.5% and 2%; checks come in denominations of $20, $50, $100, $500, and $1,000.

Call ⓒ **800/732-1322** for information. AAA members can obtain Visa checks without a fee at most AAA offices or by calling ⓒ **866/339-3378. MasterCard** also offers traveler's checks. Call ⓒ **800/223-9920** for a location near you.

If you choose to carry traveler's checks, be sure to keep a record of their serial numbers separate from your checks in the event that they are stolen or lost. You'll get a refund faster if you know the numbers.

CREDIT CARDS   Credit cards are a safe way to carry money, they provide a convenient record of all your expenses, and they generally offer good exchange rates. You can also withdraw cash advances from your credit cards at banks or ATMs, provided you know your PIN. If you've forgotten yours, or didn't even know you had one, call the number on the back of your credit card and ask the bank to send it to you. It usually takes 5 to 7 business days, though some banks will provide the number over the phone if you tell them your mother's maiden name or some other

---

ⓒ**Tips Dear Visa: I'm Off to Saba**

Some credit card companies recommend that you notify them of any impending trip abroad so that they don't become suspicious when the card is used numerous times in a foreign destination and block your charges. Even if you don't call your credit card company in advance, you can always call the card's toll-free emergency number if a charge is refused—a good reason to carry the phone number with you. But perhaps the most important lesson here is to carry more than one card with you on your trip; a card might not work for any number of reasons, so having a backup is the smart way to go.

Almost every credit card company has an emergency toll-free number that you can call if your wallet or purse is stolen. Credit card companies may be able to wire cash advances immediately, and in many places, they can deliver an emergency credit card in a day or two. **Citicorp Visa's** U.S. emergency number is ⓒ **800/336-8472. American Express** cardholders and traveler's check holders should call ⓒ **800/221-7282** for all money emergencies. **MasterCard** holders should call ⓒ **800/307-7309. Diners Card** users should call ⓒ **800/234-6377,** and **Discover Card** users should call ⓒ **800/347-2683.**

Tips **Small Change**

When you change money, ask for some small bills or loose change. Petty cash will come in handy for tipping and public transportation. Consider keeping the change separate from your larger bills, so that it's readily accessible and you'll be less of a target for theft. U.S. dollars are accepted nearly everywhere, and in some countries, such as Jamaica, most locals prefer their tips to be in U.S. dollars.

---

personal information. Your credit card company will likely charge a commission (1%–2%) on every foreign purchase you make, but don't worry; for most purchases, you'll still get the best deal with credit cards when you factor in things like ATM fees and higher traveler's check exchange rates.

Odds are that if your wallet is gone, the police won't be able to recover it for you. However, after you realize that it's gone and you cancel your credit cards, it is still worth informing them. Your credit card company or insurer may require a police report number.

5 When to Go

THE WEATHER

The temperature variations in the Caribbean are surprisingly slight, averaging between 75°F and 85°F (24°C–29°C) in both winter and summer. It can get really chilly, however, especially in the early morning and at night. The Caribbean winter is usually like a perpetual May. Overall, the mid-80s Fahrenheit (high 20s Celsius) prevail throughout most of the region, and trade winds make for comfortable days and nights, even without air-conditioning.

The humidity and bugs can be a problem here year-round. However, more mosquitoes come out during the rainy season, which traditionally occurs in the autumn.

If you come in the summer, be prepared for really broiling sun in the midafternoon.

Brochures make people feel that it's virtually always sunny in the Caribbean and that isn't always so. Different islands get different amounts of rain. On Aruba, it hardly ever rains; on other islands, you can have overcast skies your entire vacation. Winter is generally the driest season, but even then, it can be wet in mountainous

areas, and you can expect brief afternoon showers, especially in December and January, on Martinique, Guadeloupe, Dominica, St. Lucia, on the north coast of the Dominican Republic, and in northeast Jamaica.

If you want to know how to pack just before you go, check the Weather Channel's online 5-day forecast at **www.weather.com** for the latest information.

HURRICANES The curse of Caribbean weather, the hurricane season lasts—officially, at least—from June 1 to November 30. But there's no cause for panic: Satellite forecasts give enough warning that precautions can be taken.

To get a weather report before you go, call the nearest branch of the **National Weather Service,** listed in your phone directory under the "U.S. Department of Commerce." You can also check the **Weather Channel** on the Web at **www.weather.com**.

THE HIGH SEASON & THE OFF SEASON

The Caribbean has become a year-round destination. The "season" runs roughly from mid-December to mid-April, which is generally the driest time of year in the Caribbean and the most miserable time of year in the U.S. Northeast and Midwest and in Canada. Hotels charge their highest prices during the peak winter period, and you'll have to make your reservations well in advance—months in advance if you want to travel over Christmas or in the depths of February, especially around U.S. President's Day weekend.

The off season in the Caribbean—roughly from mid-April to mid-December (although this varies from hotel to hotel)—is one big summer sale, though it's become more popular in recent years. In most cases, hotels, inns, and condos slash 20% to 50% off their winter rates.

Dollar for dollar, you'll spend less money by renting a summer house or self-sufficient unit in the Caribbean than you would on Cape Cod, Fire Island, or Laguna Beach. You just have to be able to tolerate strong sun if you're considering coming in the summer.

Off season, the beaches are less crowded, and you can get good deals. But restaurants close and hotels offer fewer facilities and use the off season for construction—so make sure you ask what work is going on. If you decide to go anyway, make sure your room is far away from the noise. If you're single and going off season, ask for the hotel's occupancy rate. You want crowds!

Because there's such a drastic difference in high-season and off-season rates at most hotels, we've included both on every property we review. You'll see the incredible savings you can enjoy if your schedule allows you to wait a couple of months for your fun in the sun.

6 Travel Insurance

Check your existing insurance policies and credit card coverage before you buy travel insurance. You may already be covered for lost luggage, canceled tickets, or medical expenses. The cost of travel insurance varies widely, depending on the cost and length of your trip, your age, health, and the type of trip you're taking.

TRIP-CANCELLATION INSUR-ANCE Trip-cancellation insurance helps you get your money back if you have to back out of a trip, if you have to go home early, or if your travel supplier goes bankrupt. Allowed reasons for cancellation can range from sickness to natural disasters to the State Department declaring your destination unsafe for travel. (Insurers usually won't cover vague fears, though, as many travelers discovered who tried to cancel their trips in Oct 2001 because they were wary of flying.) In this unstable world, trip-cancellation insurance is a good buy if you're getting tickets well in advance—who knows what the state of the world, or of your airline, will be in nine months? Insurance policy details vary, so read the fine print—and especially make sure that your airline or cruise line is on the list of carriers covered in case of bankruptcy. For information, contact one of the following insurers: **Access America** (© 866/807-3982; www.accessamerica.com); **Travel Guard International** (© 800/826-4919; www.travelguard.com); **Travel Insured International** (© 800/243-3174; www.travelinsured.com); and **Travelex Insurance Services** (© 888/457-4602; www.travelex-insurance.com).

MEDICAL INSURANCE Most health insurance policies cover you if you get sick away from home—but check, particularly if you're insured by an HMO. With the exception of certain HMOs and Medicare/Medicaid, your medical insurance should cover medical treatment—even hospital care—overseas. However, most out-of-country hospitals make you pay your bills upfront, and send you a refund after you've returned home and filed the necessary paperwork. And in a worst-case scenario, there's the high cost of emergency evacuation. If you require additional medical insurance, try **MEDEX International** (*©* **800/ 527-0218** or 410/453-6300; www. medexassist.com) or **Travel Assistance International** (*©* **800/821- 2828;** www.travelassistance.com; for general information on services, call the company's Worldwide Assistance Services, Inc., at 800/777-8710).

LOST-LUGGAGE INSURANCE On domestic flights, checked baggage is covered up to $2,500 per ticketed passenger. On international flights (including U.S. portions of international trips), baggage coverage is limited to approximately $9.07 per pound, up to approximately $635 per checked bag. If you plan to check items more valuable than the standard liability, see if your valuables are covered by your homeowner's policy, get baggage insurance as part of your comprehensive travel-insurance package, or buy Travel Guard's "BagTrak" product. Don't buy insurance at the airport, as it's usually overpriced. Be sure to take any valuables or irreplaceable items with you in your carry-on luggage, as many valuables (including books, money, and electronics) aren't covered by airline policies.

If your luggage is lost, immediately file a lost-luggage claim at the airport, detailing the luggage contents. For most airlines, you must report delayed, damaged, or lost baggage within 4 hours of arrival. The airlines are required to deliver luggage, once found, directly to your house or destination free of charge.

7 Health & Safety

Keep the following suggestions in mind:

- On some islands, it's best to drink bottled water during your trip. (See "Fast Facts" in the individual island chapters for details.)
- If you experience diarrhea, moderate your eating habits and drink only bottled water until you recover. If symptoms persist, consult a doctor.
- The Caribbean sun can be brutal. Wear sunglasses and a hat and use sunscreen liberally. Limit your time on the beach the first day. If you do overexpose yourself, stay out of the sun until you recover. If your exposure is followed by fever or chills, a headache, or a feeling of nausea or dizziness, see a doctor.
- One of the biggest menaces is the "no-see-ums," which emerge mainly in the early evening. You can't see these gnats, but you sure can "feel-um." Window screens can't keep these critters out, so carry bug repellent.
- Mosquitoes are a nuisance. Malaria-carrying mosquitoes in the Caribbean are confined largely to Haiti and the Dominican Republic. If you're visiting either, consult your doctor for preventive medicine at least 8 weeks before you leave.
- Dengue fever is prevalent in the islands, most prominently on Antigua, St. Kitts, Dominica, and the Dominican Republic. To date, no satisfactory treatment has been developed; visitors are advised to avoid mosquito bites—as if that were possible. Infectious hepatitis has been reported on islands such as Dominica and Haiti. Unless you have been immunized for both hepatitis A and B, consult your doctor about the advisability of getting a gamma-globulin shot before you leave. The United

States **Centers for Disease Control and Prevention** (© **800/ 311-3435;** www.cdc.gov) provides up-to-date information on necessary vaccines and health hazards by region or country.

- Pack prescription medications in your carry-on luggage. Carry written prescriptions in generic, not brand-name, form, and dispense all prescription medications from their original labeled vials. Many people try to slip drugs such as cocaine into the Caribbean (or pick them up there). Drugs are often placed into a container for prescription medication after the legal medications have been removed. Customs officials are well aware of this type of smuggling and often check medications if they suspect a passenger is bringing illegal drugs into or out of a country.
- If you wear contact lenses, pack an extra pair in case you lose one.

WHAT TO DO IF YOU GET SICK AWAY FROM HOME

Finding a good doctor in the Caribbean is not a problem, and most speak English. See the "Fast Facts" section in each chapter for specific names and addresses on each individual island.

If you worry about getting sick away from home, you might want to consider medical travel insurance (see the section on travel insurance above). In most cases, however, your existing health plan will provide all the coverage you need. Be sure to carry your identification card in your wallet.

If you suffer from a chronic illness, consult your doctor before your departure. For conditions like epilepsy, diabetes, or heart problems, wear a **MedicAlert identification tag** (© **888/633-4298;** www.medicalert. org), which will immediately alert doctors to your condition and give them access to your records through MedicAlert's 24-hour hot line.

Contact the **International Association for Medical Assistance to Travelers (IAMAT)** (© **716/754-4883** or 416/652-0137; www.iamat.org) for tips on travel and health concerns on the islands you're visiting, and lists of local English-speaking doctors.

8 Specialized Travel Resources

TRAVELERS WITH DISABILITIES

In general, the Caribbean is not user friendly for persons with disabilities. Attractions and sights, for the most part, don't have elevators, ramps, or wheelchair-accessible toilets. Nor are most hotels constructed for accessibility. If you are contemplating a holiday in the sun, consider the islands of Puerto Rico or one of the U.S. Virgins—St. Thomas, St. Croix, or St. John. As part of U.S. territories, these islands must abide by the Americans with Disabilities Act. Even so, getting around can still be difficult. You should know that transportation is woefully inadequate and many Caribbean hotels lie in hilly or mountainous regions. However, some resorts have ground-floor bedrooms with wide doors and accessible bathrooms. We've indicated this in the amenities section of the hotel reviews. There are options and resources out there. Many travel agencies offer customized tours and itineraries for travelers with disabilities. **Flying Wheels Travel** (© **507/ 451-5005;** www.flyingwheelstravel. com) offers escorted tours and cruises that emphasize sports and private tours in minivans with lifts. **Accessible Journeys** (© **800/846-4537** or 610/521-0339; www.disabilitytravel. com) caters specifically to slow walkers and wheelchair travelers and their families and friends.

Organizations that offer assistance to disabled travelers include the **Moss-Rehab** (www.mossresourcenet.org), which provides a library of accessible-travel resources online; **SATH (Society for Accessible Travel and Hospitality);** © **212/447-7284;** www.sath.org; annual membership fees: $45 adults, $30 seniors and students), which offers a wealth of travel resources for all types of disabilities and informed recommendations on destinations, access guides, travel agents, tour operators, vehicle rentals, and companion services; and the **American Foundation for the Blind** (© **800/232-5463;** www.afb.org), which provides information on traveling with Seeing Eye dogs.

For more information specifically targeted to travelers with disabilities, the community website **iCan** (www.icanonline.net/channels/travel/index.cfm) has destination guides and several regular columns on accessible travel. Also check out the quarterly magazine *Emerging Horizons* ($15 per year, $20 outside the U.S.; www.emerginghorizons.com); **Twin Peaks Press** (© **360/694-2462;** http://home.pacifier.com/~twinpeak), offering travel-related books for travelers with special needs; and *Open World Magazine,* published by the Society for Accessible Travel and Hospitality (see above; subscription: $13 per year, $21 outside the U.S.).

FOR GAY & LESBIAN TRAVELERS

Some Caribbean islands are more gay friendly than others. The most gay-friendly islands are the U.S. possessions, and most notably Puerto Rico, which is hailed as the "gay capital of the Caribbean" and offers gay guesthouses, nightclubs, bars, and discos. To a lesser extent, the U.S. Virgin Islands are welcoming, too.

The French islands—St. Barts, St. Martin, Guadeloupe, and Martinique—are technically an extension of mainland France, and the French have always regarded homosexuality with a certain blasé tolerance.

The Dutch islands of Aruba, Bonaire, and Curaçao are quite conservative, so discretion is suggested.

Gay life is fairly secretive in many of the sleepy islands of the Caribbean. Some islands even have repressive antihomosexual laws. Homosexuality is actively discouraged in places like the Cayman Islands. Gay travelers might also note that the Cayman Islands refused to allow an all-gay cruise ship to dock on Grand Cayman, and several gay advocacy groups have even called for a boycott on travel to the Caymans in response. In Barbados, homosexuality is illegal, and there is often a lack of tolerance in spite of the large number of gay residents and visitors on the island.

Jamaica is the most homophobic island in the Caribbean, with harsh antigay laws, even though there is a large local gay population. Many all-inclusive resorts, notably the famous Sandals of Jamaica, have discriminatory policies, allowing only male-female couples; gay men and lesbians are definitely excluded from their love nests. However, not all the all-inclusives practice such blatant discrimination. **Hedonism II,** a rival of Sandals in Negril, is not a "couples-only" resort, though it will help you find a roommate so that you can travel on the lower double-occupancy rate. The **Grand Lido,** a more upscale all-inclusive in Negril, welcomes whatever combinations show up (even singles, for that matter). For more information on all these resorts, see chapter 15.

The **International Gay and Lesbian Travel Association (IGLTA)** (© **800/448-8550** or 954/776-2626; www.iglta.org) is the trade association for the gay and lesbian travel industry and offers an online directory of gay- and lesbian-friendly travel businesses.

Many agencies offer tours and travel itineraries specifically for gay and lesbian travelers. **Above and Beyond Tours** (© **800/397-2681;** www.abovebeyondtours.com) is the exclusive gay and lesbian tour operator for United Airlines. **Now, Voyager** (© **800/255-6951;** www.nowvoyager. com) is a well-known San Francisco– based gay-owned and -operated travel service. **Olivia Cruises & Resorts** (© **800-631-6277** or 510/655-0364; www.olivia.com) charters entire resorts and ships for exclusive lesbian vacations and offers smaller group experiences for both gay and lesbian travelers.

The following travel guides are available at most travel bookstores and gay and lesbian bookstores, or you can order them from **Giovanni's Room** bookstore, 1145 Pine St., Philadelphia, PA 19107 (© **215/923-2960;** www.giovannisroom.com): *Out and About* (© **800/929-2268** or 415/ 644-8044; www.outandabout.com), which offers guidebooks and a newsletter 10 times a year packed with solid information on the global gay and lesbian scene; *Spartacus International Gay Guide* and *Odysseus,* both good annual English-language guidebooks focused on gay men; the *Damron* guides, with separate annual books for gay men and lesbians; and *Gay Travel A to Z: The World of Gay & Lesbian Travel Options at Your Fingertips,* by Marianne Ferrari (Ferrari Publications; Box 35575, Phoenix, AZ 85069), a very good gay and lesbian guidebook series.

FOR SENIORS

Mention the fact that you're a senior citizen when you make your travel reservations. Although all of the major U.S. airlines except America West have canceled their senior-discount and coupon-book programs, many hotels still offer discounts for seniors. In most cities, people over the age of 60 qualify for reduced admission to theaters, museums, and other attractions, as well as discounted fares on public transportation.

Members of **AARP** (formerly known as the American Association of Retired Persons), 601 E St. NW, Washington, DC 20049 (© **888/ 687-2277** or 202/434-2277; www. aarp.org), get discounts on hotels, airfares, and car rentals. AARP offers members a wide range of benefits, including *AARP: The Magazine* and a monthly newsletter. Anyone over 50 can join.

Many reliable agencies and organizations target the 50-plus market. **Elderhostel** (© **877/426-8056;** www.elderhostel.org) arranges study programs for those aged 55 and over (and a spouse or companion of any age) in the U.S. and in more than 80 countries around the world. Most courses last 5 to 7 days in the U.S. (2–4 weeks abroad), and many include airfare, accommodations in university dormitories or modest inns, meals, and tuition. **ElderTreks** (© **800/741- 7956;** www.eldertreks.com) offers small-group tours to off-the-beaten- path or adventure-travel locations, restricted to travelers 50 and older.

Recommended publications offering travel resources and discounts for seniors include: the quarterly magazine *Travel 50 & Beyond* (www. travel50andbeyond.com); *Travel Unlimited: Uncommon Adventures for the Mature Traveler* (Avalon); *101 Tips for Mature Travelers,* available from Grand Circle Travel (© **800/221-2610** or 617/350-7500; www.gct.com); *The 50+ Traveler's Guidebook* (St. Martin's Press); and *Unbelievably Good Deals and Great Adventures That You Absolutely Can't Get Unless You're Over 50* (McGraw-Hill).

9 Planning Your Trip Online

SURFING FOR AIRFARES

The "big three" online travel agencies, **Expedia.com, Travelocity,** and **Orbitz,** sell most of the air tickets bought on the Internet. (Canadian travelers should try Expedia.ca and Travelocity.ca; U.K. residents can go for Expedia.co.uk and Opodo.) Each has different business deals with the airlines and may offer different fares on the same flights, so it's wise to shop around. Expedia.com and Travelocity will also send you **e-mail notification** when a cheap fare becomes available to your favorite destination. Of the smaller travel agency websites, **SideStep** (www.sidestep.com) has gotten the best reviews from Frommer's authors. It's a browser add-on that purports to "search 140 sites at once," but in reality only beats competitors' fares as often as other sites do.

Also remember to check **airline websites,** especially those for low-fare carriers such as Southwest, JetBlue, AirTran, WestJet, or Ryanair, whose fares are often misreported or simply missing from travel agency websites. Even with major airlines, you can often shave a few bucks from a fare by booking directly through the airline and avoiding a travel agency's transaction fee. But you'll get these discounts only by **booking online:** Most airlines now offer online-only fares that even their phone agents know nothing about. For the websites of airlines that fly to and from your destination, go to "Getting There," below.

Great **last-minute deals** are available through free weekly e-mail services provided directly by the airlines. Most of these are announced on Tuesday or Wednesday and must be purchased online. Most are only valid for travel that weekend, but some (such as Southwest's) can be booked weeks or months in advance. Sign up for weekly e-mail alerts at airline websites or check megasites that compile comprehensive lists of last-minute specials, such as **Smarter Living** (smarterliving.com). For last-minute trips, **Site59** in the U.S. and **lastminute.com** in Europe often have better deals than the major-label sites.

If you're willing to give up some control over your flight details, use an

---

Frommers.com: The Complete Travel Resource

For an excellent travel-planning resource, we highly recommend Frommers.com (www.frommers.com). We're a little biased, of course, but we guarantee that you'll find the travel tips, reviews, monthly vacation giveaways, and online-booking capabilities thoroughly indispensable. Among the special features are our popular **Message Boards,** where Frommer's readers post queries and share advice (sometimes even our authors show up to answer questions); **Frommers.com Newsletter,** for the latest travel bargains and insider travel secrets; and **Frommer's Destinations Section,** where you'll get expert travel tips, hotel and dining recommendations, and advice on the sights to see for more than 3,000 destinations around the globe. When your research is done, the **Online Reservations System** (www.frommers.com/book_a_trip) takes you to Frommer's preferred online partners for booking your vacation at affordable prices.

Online Traveler's Toolbox

Veteran travelers usually carry some essential items to make their trips easier. Following is a selection of online tools to bookmark and use.

- For general advice visit the **Caribbean Tourism Organization** (www. doitcaribbean.com) or the **Caribbean Homepage** (www.caribinfo. com).
- **Caribbean Hotel Association** (www.caribbeantravel.com) has information on hotels in the Caribbean.
- For information on cruises, check **Cruise Lines International Association** (www.cruising.org).
- **Visa ATM Locator** (www.visa.com) has locations of PLUS ATMs worldwide, and **MasterCard ATM Locator** (www.mastercard.com) has locations of Cirrus ATMs worldwide.
- **Intellicast** (www.intellicast.com) and **Weather.com** (www.weather. com) give weather forecasts for all 50 states and for cities around the world.
- **Mapquest** (www.mapquest.com), the best of the mapping sites, lets you choose a specific address or destination, and in seconds it will return a map and detailed directions.
- Check the **Universal Currency Converter** (www.xe.com) to see what your dollar or pound is worth in more than 100 other countries.
- **Travel Warnings** sites (http://travel.state.gov; www.fco.gov.uk/ travel; www.voyage.gc.ca; www.dfat.gov.au/consular/advice) report on places where health concerns or unrest might threaten American, British, Canadian, and Australian travelers respectively. Generally, U.S. warnings are the most paranoid; Australian warnings are the most relaxed.

opaque fare service like **Priceline** (www.priceline.com; www.priceline. co.uk for Europeans) or **Hotwire** (www.hotwire.com). Both offer rock-bottom prices in exchange for travel on a "mystery airline" at a mysterious time of day, often with a mysterious change of planes en route. The mystery airlines are all major, well-known carriers—and the possibility of being sent from Philadelphia to Chicago via Tampa is remote; the airlines' routing computers have gotten a lot better than they used to be. But your chances of getting a 6am or 11pm flight are pretty high. Hotwire tells you flight prices before you buy; Priceline usually has better deals than Hotwire, but you have to play their "name our price" game. If you're new at this, the helpful folks at **BiddingForTravel. com** (www.biddingfortravel.com) do a good job of demystifying Priceline's prices. Priceline and Hotwire are great for flights within North America and between the U.S. and Europe. But for flights to other parts of the world, consolidators will almost always beat their fares.

For much more about airfares and savvy air-travel tips and advice, pick up a copy of *Frommer's Fly Safe, Fly Smart* (Wiley Publishing, Inc.).

SURFING FOR HOTELS

Shopping online for hotels is not as easy in the Caribbean as it is, for example, in the United States or

Canada. You can, of course, book hotel rooms online, although the larger islands such as St. Thomas or Puerto Rico have better data than smaller destinations such as Dominica or St. Vincent. Also, many smaller hotels and B&Bs, especially in the Caribbean, don't show up on websites at all. There are specific island links, and you can also reach the Caribbean Hotel Association at www.caribbean travel.com. Of the "big three" sites, **Expedia.com** may be the best choice, thanks to its long list of special deals. **Travelocity** runs a close second. Hotel-specialist sites **hotels.com** and **hoteldiscounts.com** are also reliable. An excellent free program, **TravelAxe** (www.travelaxe.net), can help you search multiple hotel sites at once, even ones you may never have heard of.

When booking a Caribbean hotel online, it's important to be aware of hidden costs. You may reserve a double room for $85 a night online, only to discover when paying the bill that neither taxes nor service charges were included. Also ascertain if the transfer charge is included if you're met by a hotel van at the airport. Often it isn't unless you booked an all-inclusive package deal.

Priceline and Hotwire are even better for hotels than for airfares; with both, you're allowed to pick the neighborhood and quality level of your hotel before offering up your money. Priceline's hotel products cover certain islands of the Caribbean—but not all. Featured are such islands as the U.S. Virgin Islands, Curaçao, the Dominican Republic, Jamaica, and St. Lucia. *Note:* Hotwire overrates its hotels by one star—what Hotwire calls a four-star is a three-star anywhere else.

SURFING FOR RENTAL CARS

For booking rental cars online, the best deals are usually found at rental-car company websites, although all the major online travel agencies also offer rental-car reservations services. Priceline and Hotwire work well for rental cars, too; the only "mystery" is which major rental company you get, and for most travelers the difference between Hertz, Avis, and Budget is negligible.

10 Getting There

American Airlines (© 800/433-7300; www.aa.com) is the major carrier throughout the region. Other airlines serving the islands include **Air Canada** (© 888/247-2262 in the U.S. and Canada; www.aircanada.ca), **Air Jamaica** (© 800/523-5585; www.airjamaica.com), **British Airways** (© 800/247-9297 in U.S., 0870/850-9850 in the U.K.; www.britishairways.com), **BWIA** (© 800/538-2942; www.bwee.com), **Continental** (© 800/231-0856; www.continental.com), **Delta** (© 800/241-4141; www.delta.com), **LIAT** (© 888/844-5428 in most of the Caribbean, or 868/624-4727 elsewhere; www.liatairline.com), **Northwest/KLM** (© 800/447-4747; www.nwa.com), **United** (© 800/241-6522; www.united.com), and **US Airways** (© 800/428-4322; www.usairways.com), plus some smaller regional carriers. In each of the island chapters that follow, we'll list details on which airlines fly the various routes.

GETTING THROUGH THE AIRPORT

With the federalization of airport security, security procedures at U.S. airports are more stable and consistent than ever. Generally, you'll be fine if you arrive at the airport **1 hour** before a domestic flight and **2 hours** before an international flight; if you show up late, tell an airline employee, and he or she will probably whisk you to the front of the line.

Bring a **current government-issued photo ID** such as a driver's license or passport, and if you've got an e-ticket, print out the **official confirmation page;** you'll need to show your confirmation at the security checkpoint, and your ID at the ticket counter or the gate. (Children under 18 do not need photo IDs for domestic flights, but the adults checking in with them do.)

Speed up security by **not wearing metal objects** such as big belt buckles or clanky earrings. If you've got metallic body parts, a note from your doctor can prevent a long chat with the security screeners. Keep in mind that only **ticketed passengers** are allowed past security, except for folks escorting disabled passengers or children.

Federalization has stabilized **what you can carry on** and **what you can't.** The general rule is that sharp things are out, nail clippers are okay, and food and beverages must be passed through the X-ray machine—but security screeners can't make you drink from your coffee cup. Bring food in your carry-on rather than checking it, as explosive-detection machines used on checked luggage have been known to mistake food (especially chocolate, for some reason) for bombs. Travelers in the U.S. are allowed one carry-on bag, plus a "personal item" such as a purse, briefcase, or laptop bag. Carry-on hoarders can stuff all sorts of things into a laptop bag; as long as it has a laptop in it, it's still considered a personal item. The Transportation Security Administration (TSA) has issued a list of restricted items; check its website (www.tsa.gov) for details.

Passengers with E-tickets and without checked bags can beat the ticket-counter lines by using **electronic kiosks** or even **online check-in.** Ask your airline which alternatives are available, and if you're using a kiosk, bring the credit card you used to book the ticket. If you're checking bags, you will still be able to use most airlines' kiosks; again, call your airline for up-to-date information. **Curbside check-in** is also a good way to avoid lines, although a few airlines still ban curbside check-in entirely; call before you go.

TSA also recommends that you **not lock your checked luggage** so screeners can search it by hand if necessary. The agency says to use plastic "zip ties" instead, which can be bought at hardware stores and can be easily cut off.

FLYING FOR LESS: TIPS FOR GETTING THE BEST AIRFARE

Before you do anything else, read the section "Packages for the Independent Traveler," below. But if a package isn't for you, and you need to book your airfare on your own, keep in mind these money-saving tips:

- **When you fly makes all the difference.** If you fly in spring, summer, and fall, you're guaranteed substantial reductions on airfares to the Caribbean. Passengers who can book their tickets long in advance, who can stay over Saturday night, or who fly midweek or at less-trafficked hours will pay a fraction of the full fare. If your schedule is flexible, say so, and ask if you can secure a cheaper fare by changing your flight plans.

- **Keep an eye out for sales.** Check the newspaper for advertised discounts or call the airlines directly and ask if any promotional rates or special fares are available. You'll almost never see a sale during the peak winter vacation months of February and March, or during the Thanksgiving or Christmas seasons; but in periods of low-volume travel, you should find a discounted fare. If you already hold a ticket when a sale breaks, it may even pay to exchange your ticket, which usually incurs a $50 to $75 charge. *Note:* The lowest-priced fares are often nonrefundable, require advance purchase of 1 to 3 weeks and a certain length of stay, and carry penalties for changing dates of travel.

- **Consolidators,** also known as bucket shops, are great sources for international tickets, although they usually can't beat the Internet on fares within North America. Start by looking in Sunday newspaper travel sections; U.S. travelers should focus on the *New York Times, Los Angeles Times,* and *Miami Herald.* For less-developed destinations, small travel agents who cater to immigrant communities in large cities often have the best deals. *Beware:* Bucket-shop tickets are usually nonrefundable or rigged with stiff cancellation penalties, often as high as 50% to 75% of the ticket price, and some put you on charter airlines with questionable safety records. For flights to the Caribbean, check out **Airline Consolidators** (© 888/468-5385; ww.airline consolidator.com), **Cheap Tickets** (www.cheaptickets.com), or **Economy Travel** (© 888/222-2110; www.economytravel.com). Several reliable consolidators are worldwide and available on the Web. **STA Travel** is now the world's leader in student travel, thanks to their purchase of Council Travel.

It also offers good fares for travelers of all ages. **Eltexpress (Flights. com)** (© 800/TRAV-800; www. eltexpress.com) started in Europe and has excellent fares worldwide, but particularly to that continent. It also has "local" websites in 12 countries. **Air Tickets Direct** (© 800/778-3447; www.airtickets direct.com) is based in Montreal and leverages the currently weak Canadian dollar for low fares; it'll also book trips to places that U.S. travel agents won't touch, such as Cuba.

- Search **the Internet** for cheap fares (see "Planning Your Trip Online," above).
- Join **frequent-flier clubs.** Accrue enough miles, and you'll be rewarded with free flights and elite status. It's free, and you'll get the best choice of seats, faster response to phone inquiries, and prompter service if your luggage is stolen, your flight is canceled or delayed, or if you want to change your seat. You don't need to fly to build frequent-flier miles—**frequent-flier credit cards** can provide thousands of miles for doing your everyday shopping.
- For many more tips about air travel, including a rundown of the major frequent-flier credit cards, pick up a copy of *Frommer's Fly Safe, Fly Smart* (Wiley Publishing, Inc.).

11 Packages for the Independent Traveler

For value-conscious travelers, packages are often the smart way to go because they can save you a ton of money. Especially in the Caribbean, package tours are *not* the same thing as escorted tours. You'll be on your own, but in most cases, a package to the Caribbean will include airfare, hotel, and transportation to and from the airport—and it'll cost you less than just the hotel alone if you booked it

yourself. A package deal might not be for you if you want to stay in a more intimate inn or guesthouse, but if you like resorts, read on.

You'll find an amazing array of packages to popular Caribbean destinations. Some packages offer a better class of hotels than others. Some offer the same hotels for lower prices. Some offer flights on scheduled airlines, and others book charters. Remember to comparison shop among at least three different operators, and always compare apples to apples.

Many land-and-sea packages include meals, and you might find yourself locked into your hotel dining room every night if your meals are prepaid. If you're seeking a more varied dining experience, avoid **AP (American Plan)**, which means full board, and opt for **MAP (Modified American Plan)**, meaning breakfast and either lunch or dinner. That way, you'll at least be free for one main meal of the day and can sample a variety of an island's regional fare.

The best place to start your search is the travel section of your local Sunday newspaper. Also check the ads in national travel magazines like *Arthur Frommer's Budget Travel, National Geographic Traveler,* and *Travel Holiday.*

Liberty Travel (© 888/271-1584; www.libertytravel.com) is one of the biggest packagers in the Northeast, and it usually boasts a full-page ad in Sunday papers. **Vacations** (© 800/654-6559; www.deltavacations.com) is another option.

Another good resource is the airlines themselves, which often package their flights together with accommodations. Among the airline packagers, your options include **American Airlines Vacations** (© 800/321-2121; www.aavacations.com), **Delta Vacations** (© 800/221-6666; www.deltavacations.com), **US Airways Vacations** (© 800/455-0123; www.usairwaysvacations.com), **Continental Airlines Vacations** (© 800/301-3800; www.coolvacations.com), and **United Vacations** (© 888/854-3899; www.unitedvacations.com). Several big **online travel agencies**—Expedia.com, Travelocity, Orbitz, Site59, and lastminute.com—also do a brisk business in packages. If you're unsure about the pedigree of a smaller packager, check with the Better Business Bureau in the city where the company

is based or go online at www.bbb.org. If a packager won't tell you where it's based, don't fly with it. American usually has the widest variety of offerings since it's the major carrier to the region.

The biggest hotel chains, casinos, and resorts also offer package deals. If you already know where you want to stay, call the resort itself and ask if it offers land/air packages.

To save time comparing the prices and value of all the package tours out there, contact **TourScan, Inc.** (© 800/962-2080 or 203/655-8091; www.tourscan.com). Every season, the company computerizes the contents of travel brochures that contain about 10,000 different vacations at 1,600 hotels in the Caribbean, the Bahamas, and Bermuda. TourScan selects the best-value vacation at each hotel and condo. Two catalogs are printed each year, which list a choice of hotels on most of the Caribbean islands in all price ranges. The price of a catalog ($4) is credited toward any TourScan vacation.

Another source for one-stop shopping on the Web is **VacationPackager** (www.vacationpackager.com), a search engine that will link you to many different package-tour operators offering Caribbean vacations.

Other tour operators include the following:

- **Just-A-Vacation, Inc.** (© 301/559-0510; www.justavacation.com) specializes in good deals for all-inclusive resorts in Jamaica, Aruba, Puerto Rico, Antigua, and St. Lucia.
- **Club Med** (© 800/258-2633; www.clubmed.com) has various all-inclusive options throughout the Caribbean and the Bahamas, as does **Sandals** (© 800/SANDALS; www.sandals.com).
- **SuperClubs** (© 800/859-7873; www.superclubs.com) has a wide variety of all-inclusive resorts in Jamaica.

12 Organized Adventure Trips

BIKING The Dominican Republic is the best mountain bike destination in the Caribbean. *Bicycling Magazine* said the island, "with its towering mountains and miles of single track, defy(s) all stereotype." The best organized trips are offered by **Iguana Mama Mountain Bike,** Cabarete (© **800/ 849-4720** in the U.S., or 809/571-0908; www.iguanamama.com).

BIRD-WATCHING Victor Emanuel Nature Tours (© **800/ 328-8368** or 512/328-5221; www. ventbird.com) offers 10-day bird-watching trips led by a biologist in Trinidad and Tobago. Each trip costs approximately $2,500 per person, and trips are based at the **Asa Wright Nature Centre** (© **868/667-4655;** www.asawright.org), which has 150 of the more than 400 species of birds found in Trinidad. Field trips and discussions on the symbiosis between plant and bird life are offered.

ECO-TOURS Some of the best wildlife cruises are packaged by **Oceanic Society Expeditions** (© **800/326-7491** in the U.S., or 415/474-3385; www.oceanic-society. org). Whale-watching jaunts and some research-oriented trips are also featured. You can swim with humpback whales in the Dominican Republic, for example.

Puerto Rico's varied and often hard-to-reach natural treasures have been conveniently packaged into a series of affordable eco-tours. **Hillbilly Tours,** Route 181, km. 13.4, San Juan (© **787/760-5618**), specializes in nature-based and countryside tours in Puerto Rico's rainforest. **Adven-Tours,** Luquillo (© **787/889-0251**), features customized private tours with activities like bird-watching, hiking, camping, visits to coffee plantations, and kayaking. **Aventuras Tierra Adentro,** 268 Piñero Ave., San Juan (© **787/766-0470;** www.

aventurastierraadentro.com), specializes in rock climbing, body rafting, caving, and canyoning in Puerto Rico. **Eco Xcursion Aquatica,** Road 191, km. 1.7, Rio Grande, Fajardo (© **787/ 888-2887**), offers some of the best rainforest hikes and mountain bike tours.

Machias Adventures (© **888/427-3497** or 203/227-7337; www.machias adventures.com) offers adventure tours to St. Vincent, including hiking up a volcano, a day's sailing with a crew, seeking out the huge variety of bird life, and hiking up a river canyon to a dramatic water pool—a perfect pool for swimming. The cost of these 7-day jaunts is $2,450 per person, based on double occupancy.

The best eco-tours in lush Trinidad and Tobago are offered by **Wildways,** Ariapita Road, St. Ann's, Port-of-Spain (© **868/623-7332;** www.wildways. org). The most exciting is the 8-day Trinidad "Trek & Tour," following Amerindian trails through rainforests to watch turtle egg laying and other adventures.

HIKING Unlike many of its neighboring islands, Jamaica's mountain peaks climb to 2,220m (7,282 ft.). The flora, fauna, waterfalls, and panoramas of those peaks have attracted increasing numbers of hikers determined to experience the natural beauty of the island firsthand. Because of the dangers involved, it's often best to go on an organized tour. Good ones are offered by **Sunventure Tours,** 30 Balmoral Ave., Kingston 10, Jamaica, W.I. (© **876/960-6685;** www.sun venturetours.com). For more information, refer to the section "The Blue Mountains," in chapter 15.

SCUBA TRIPS A number of outfitters offer scuba packages and cruises. Into the Blue (© 800/6-GETWET or 610/642-1920; www.intotheblue. com) is a travel company specializing

---

Tips   Websites for Divers

For useful information on scuba diving in the Caribbean, check out the website of the **Professional Association of Diving Instructors (PADI)** at **www.padi.com**. This site provides descriptions of dive destinations throughout the Caribbean and a directory of PADI-certified dive operators. *Rodale's Scuba Diving Magazine* also has a helpful website at **www. scubadiving.com**. Both sites list dive package specials and display gorgeous color photos of some of the most beautiful dive spots in the world.

---

in diving trips throughout the Caribbean for individuals, couples, and families. Their destinations range from the British Virgin Islands to Bonaire. Island Dreams Tours & Travel (© 800/346-6116 or 713/973-9300; www.islandream.com) also offers trips, including itineraries in the Cayman Islands and Bonaire.

Explorer Ventures (© 800/322-3577 or 903/887-8521; www.explorer ventures.com) takes divers on its *Caribbean Explorer II* to excursions in the waters of St. Kitts and Saba. Trips usually last a week.

Another specialist in this field is **Caradonna Caribbean Tours**

(© 800/330-3322 or 407/774-9000; www.caradonna.com), which offers adventurous scuba-cruise packages to Bonaire, St. Croix, and St. Kitts, among other islands.

SEA KAYAKING The only outfitter in the Virgin Islands that offers sea-kayaking/island-camping excursions is **Arawak Expeditions,** based in Cruz Bay, St. John (© **800/238-8687** in the U.S., or 340/693-8312; www. arawakexp.com). It provides kayaking gear, healthy meals, camping equipment, and two experienced guides. Multiday excursions range from $1,125 to $2,500.

---

13 Getting Married in the Caribbean

See also "The Best Places to Honeymoon," in chapter 1, for information on specific resorts that offer wedding and honeymoon packages. **Club Med** (© 800/CLUB-MED), **Sandals** (© 800/SANDALS), and **Super-Clubs** (© 800/859-7873) are three chains that have married many couples.

If you yearn to take the plunge in the Caribbean, you need to know the requirements on the different islands.

ANGUILLA Couples need to file a license application on Anguilla, which takes approximately 48 hours to process. You'll need to present a passport, and, if applicable, proof of divorce or the death certificate of a deceased spouse. The fee for the license and stamp duty is $282. For further information, contact the

Registrar of Births, Deaths, and Marriages, Judicial Department, The Valley, Anguilla, B.W.I. (© **264/497-2377**).

ANTIGUA There's a 24-hour waiting period for marriages on Antigua. A couple appears at the Ministry of Justice in the capital of St. John to complete and sign a declaration before a marriage coordinator and pays a $200 license fee. The coordinator will arrange for a marriage officer to perform a civil ceremony at any of Antigua's hotels or another place the couple selects. The fee for the marriage officer is $50. Several hotels and resorts offer wedding/honeymoon packages. For more information on civil or religious wedding ceremonies, contact the **Antigua Department of**

Tourism, 610 Fifth Ave., Suite 311, New York, NY 10020 (© **888/ 268-4227** or 212/541-4117; www. antigua-barbuda.org).

ARUBA   Civil weddings are possible on Aruba only if one of the partners is an Aruban resident, which rules out most couples. Consider it for your honeymoon instead.

BARBADOS   Couples can now marry the same day they arrive on Barbados, but they must first obtain a marriage license from the **Ministry of Home Affairs** (© **246/228-8950**). Bring either a passport or a birth certificate and photo ID, $77 in fees, $26 for the revenue stamp which you can obtain at the local post office, a letter from the authorized officiant who will perform the service, plus proof, if applicable, of pertinent deaths or divorces from any former spouse(s). A Roman Catholic wedding on Barbados carries additional requirements. For more information, contact the **Barbados Tourism Authority,** 800 Second Ave., New York, NY 10017 (© **800/221-9831** in the U.S., or 212/986-6516; www.barbados.org).

BONAIRE   The bride and/or groom must have a temporary residency permit, obtained by writing a letter to the governor of the **Island Territory of Bonaire,** Wilhelminaplein no. 1, Kralendijk, Bonaire, N.A. (© **599/ 717-5330**). The letter, submitted at least 4 weeks in advance of departure for Bonaire, should request permission to marry on Bonaire and to apply for temporary residency. You'll also need to inform the governor of your arrival and departure dates and the date you wish to marry. The partner who applies for residency must be on the island for 7 days before the wedding. A special dispensation must be issued by the governor if there is less than a 10-day time period between the announcement of the marriage and the ceremony. In addition, send two

passport photos, copies of the bride's and groom's passports, birth certificates, and, if applicable, proof of divorce or the death certificate of a deceased spouse.

If you desire, you can arrange your wedding on Bonaire through **Multro Travel and Tours,** Attn: Mrs. Marvel Tromp, Muller Light House Beach Resort no. 22 (P.O. Box 237), Bonaire, N.A. (© **599/717-8334;** fax 599/ 717-8834; www.bonaireweddings. com), or check with the hotel where you're planning to stay. Some hotels arrange weddings on special request. For further information, contact the **Bonaire Tourist Office,** 10 Rockefeller Plaza, Suite 900, New York, NY 10020; (© **800/BONAIRE** or 212/ 956-5912; www.infobonaire.com).

THE BRITISH VIRGIN ISLANDS
Island residency is not required, but a couple must apply for a marriage license at the attorney general's office and must stay in the B.V.I. for 3 days while the application is processed. Present a passport or original birth certificate and photo identification, plus certified proof of your marital status and, if applicable, proof of divorce or the death certificate of a deceased spouse. Two witnesses must be present. The fee is $110. Marriages can be performed by the local registrar or by the officiant of your choice. Contact the **Registrar's Office,** P.O. Box 418, Road Town, Tortola, B.V.I. (© **284/ 494-3492** or 284/494-3701).

THE CAYMAN ISLANDS   Visitors have to call ahead and arrange for an authorized person to marry them. The name of the "marriage officer," as it is called, has to appear on the application for a marriage license. The application for a special marriage license costs $200 and can be obtained from the **Deputy Secretary's Office,** 3rd Floor, Government Administration Building, George Town (© **345/949-7900**). There is no waiting period. Present a birth certificate, the embarkation/disembarkation cards issued by the island's immigration authorities, and, if applicable, divorce decrees or proof of a spouse's death. Complete wedding services and packages are offered by **Cayman Weddings of Grand Cayman,** which is owned and operated by Caymanian marriage officers Vernon and Francine Jackson. For more information, contact them at P.O. Box 678, Grand Cayman (© **345/949-8677;** fax 345/949-8237; www.caymanweddings.com.ky). A brochure, *Getting Married in the Cayman Islands,* is available from **Government Information Services,** Broadcasting House, Grand Cayman (© **345/949-8092;** fax 345/949-5936).

CURAÇAO   Couples must be on island 3 days before applying for a marriage license, for which there is a 14-day waiting period. Passport, birth certificate, return ticket, and, if applicable, proof of divorce or the death certificate of a deceased spouse are required. The $216 fee is subject to change, so check in advance. For further information, call the **Curaçao Tourist Board,** 7951 SW 6th St., Suite 216, Plantation, FL 33324; (© **800/328-7222;** fax 954/723-7949; www.curacao-tourism.com).

JAMAICA   In high season, some Jamaican resorts witness several weddings a day. Many of the larger resorts have wedding coordinators on staff who can arrange for an officiant, a photographer, and even the wedding cake and champagne. Some resorts even throw in your wedding with the cost of your honeymoon at the hotel. Both the Jamaican Tourist Board and your hotel will assist you with the paperwork. Participants must reside on Jamaica for 24 hours before the ceremony. Bring birth certificates and affidavits saying you've never been married before. If you've been divorced or widowed, bring copies of your divorce papers or a copy of the

deceased spouse's death certificate. The license and stamp duty costs J$4,000 (US$64). Or you can apply in person at the **Ministry of National Security and Justice,** 12 Ocean Blvd., Kingston, Jamaica (© **876/906-4908**).

PUERTO RICO   There are no residency requirements for getting married in Puerto Rico. For U.S. citizens, blood tests are required, although a test conducted on the U.S. mainland within 10 days of the ceremony will suffice. A doctor in Puerto Rico must sign the license after conducting an examination of the bride and groom. For complete details, contact the **Commonwealth of Puerto Rico Health Department,** Demographic Register, P.O. Box 11854, Fernandez, Juncos Station, San Juan, PR 00910 (© **787/767-9120**).

ST. LUCIA   Both parties must be on the island for 48 hours before the ceremony. Present your passport or birth certificate, plus, if applicable, proof of divorce or the death certificate of a deceased spouse. It usually takes about 2 days before the ceremony to process all the paperwork. Fees run around $200 for a lawyer (one is usually needed for the application to the governor-general), $40 for the registrar to perform the ceremony, and $150 for the stamp duty, notary, certificates, and the license. Some resorts also offer wedding packages that include all the necessary arrangements for a single fee. For more information, contact the **St. Lucia Tourist Board,** 800 Second Ave., Suite 910, New York, NY 10017 (© **800/456-3984** or 212/867-2950; fax 212/867-2795; www.stlucia.org).

TURKS & CAICOS   You need the usual documents here, including passport, original birth certificate, proof of status (if single, a sworn affidavit), and a divorce decree, plus a $50 license fee. You must be on island for 24 hours to establish residency. For more details, contact **The Registrars of Marriages**

on Front Street at © **649/941-5123** in Provo.

THE U.S. VIRGIN ISLANDS No blood tests or physical examinations are necessary, but there is a $50 notarized application and license, and an 8-day waiting period, which is sometimes waived depending on circumstances. Civil ceremonies before a judge of the territorial court cost $250 each; religious ceremonies performed by clergy are equally valid. Fees and schedules for church weddings must be negotiated directly with the officiant. More information is available from the **U.S. Virgin Islands Division of Tourism,** 1270 Ave. of the Americas, New York, NY 10020 (© **800/372-USVI** or 212/332-2222; www.usvitourism.vi).

The U.S. Virgin Islands tourism offices distribute the guide *Getting Married in the U.S. Virgin Islands,* which gives information on all three islands, including wedding planners, places of worship, florists, and limousine services. The guide also provides a listing of island accommodations that offer in-house wedding services.

Couples can apply for a marriage license for **St. Thomas** or **St. John** by contacting the **Territorial Court of the Virgin Islands,** P.O. Box 70, St. Thomas, U.S.V.I. 00804 (© **340/774-6680**). You can apply for weddings on **St. Croix** by contacting the **Territorial Court of the Virgin Islands,** Family Division, P.O. Box 929, Christiansted, St. Croix, U.S.V.I. 00821 (© **340/778-9750**).

14 Chartering Your Own Boat

For detailed information on the cruise lines serving the Caribbean, pick up a copy of *Frommer's Caribbean Cruises & Ports of Call 2005.*

Experienced sailors and navigators can charter "bareboat," a fully equipped rental boat with no captain or crew. You're on your own, and you'll have to prove your qualifications before you're allowed to rent one. Even an experienced skipper may want to take along someone familiar with local waters, which may be tricky in some places.

You can also charter a boat with a skipper and crew. Charter yachts, ranging from 15m to 30m (49 ft.– 98 ft.), can accommodate 4 to 12 people.

Most yachts are rented on a weekly basis, with a fully stocked bar and equipment for fishing and watersports. The average charter carries four to six passengers, and usually is reserved for 1 week.

The Moorings (© **888/535-7289** or 888/952-8420 in the U.S. and Canada, or 284/494-2332 in the British Virgin Islands; www.moorings. com) operates the largest charter yacht fleet in the Caribbean. Its main branch is located in the British Virgin Islands, but it has outposts in St. Martin, Guadeloupe, Martinique, St. Lucia, and Grenada, to name a few. Each location has a regatta of yachts available for chartering. Depending on their size, yachts are rented to as many as four couples at a time. You can arrange to rent bareboat (for qualified sailors only) or rent yachts with a full crew and cook. Depending on circumstances, the vessels come equipped with a barbecue, snorkeling gear, a dinghy, and linens. The boats are serviced by an experienced staff of mechanics, electricians, riggers, and cleaners. If you're going out on your own, you'll get a thorough briefing on Caribbean waters, reefs, and anchorages. Seven-night combined hotel-and-crewed-yacht packages can run US$930 to US$1,640 per person in Tortola, and US$1,050 to US$1,360 in Grenada.

Nicholson Yacht Charters (© **800/662-6066** in the U.S., or 617/661-0555; fax 617/661-0554; www.yachtvacations.com) is one of the best in the business, handling charter yachts for use throughout the Caribbean basin, particularly the route between St. Maarten and Grenada and the routes around the U.S. Virgin Islands and British Virgin Islands and Puerto Rico. Featuring boats of all sizes, the company rents motorized vessels or sailing yachts up to 89m (292 ft.) long. Sometimes groups of friends rent two or more yachts (each sleeping eight guests in four double cabins) to race each other from island to island during the day and anchor near each other in secluded coves at night. The price for renting a yacht or motor yacht depends on the number in your party, the size of the vessel, and the time of the year. Weekly rates range from US$6,000 up to US$175,000 plus.

You can get a small but comfortable vessel for two starting at US$6,000. A 24m (79-ft.) yacht for six can go for US$60,000 and up.

Sunsail (© **800/327-2276** in the U.S., or 410/280-2553; fax 410/280-2406; www.sunsail.com) specializes in yacht chartering from its bases in the British Virgin Islands, Antigua, St. Vincent, and the French West Indies. More than 150 bareboat and crewed yachts, between 9m and 16m (30 ft.– 52 ft.), are available for cruising these waters. Programs include Caribbean racing and regattas, flotilla sailing, skippered sailing, and one-way or stay-and-sail bareboat cruises. Weekly rentals of bareboats begin at US$1,300, with yacht charters beginning at US$11,725 per week. The company usually requires a deposit of 25% of the total rental fee; arrangements should be made months in advance. Sunsail also offers charter flights from the United States to the Virgin Islands.

15 Tips on Accommodations

WATCH OUT FOR THOSE EXTRAS! Nearly all islands charge a government tax on hotel rooms, usually 7½%, but that rate varies from island to island. When booking a room, make sure you understand whether the price you've been quoted includes the tax. That will avoid an unpleasant surprise when it comes time to pay the bill. Sometimes the room tax depends on the quality of the hotel—it might be relatively low for a guesthouse but steeper for a first-class resort.

Furthermore, most hotels routinely add 10% to 12% for "service," even if you didn't see much evidence of it. That means that with tax and service, some bills are 17% or even 25% higher than the price that was originally quoted to you! Naturally, you need to determine just how much the hotel, guesthouse, or inn plans to add to your bill at the end of your stay, and

whether it's included in the initial price.

That's not all. Some hotels slip in little hidden extras that mount quickly. For example, it's common for many places to quote rates that include a continental breakfast. Should you prefer ham and eggs, you will pay extra charges. If you request special privileges, like extra towels for the beach or laundry done in a hurry, surcharges may mount. It pays to watch those extras and to ask questions before you commit.

WHAT THE ABBREVIATIONS MEAN Rate sheets often have these classifications:

- **MAP (Modified American Plan)** usually means room, breakfast, and dinner, unless the room rate has been quoted separately, and then it means only breakfast and dinner.

- **CP (Continental Plan)** includes room and a light breakfast.
- **EP (European Plan)** means room only.
- **AP (American Plan)** includes your room plus three meals a day.

HOTELS & RESORTS Many budget travelers assume they can't afford the big hotels and resorts. But there are so many packages out there (see the section "Packages for the Independent Traveler," earlier in this chapter) and so many frequent sales, even in winter, that you might be pleasantly surprised.

The rates given in this book are only "rack rates"—that is, the officially posted rate that you'd be given if you just walked in off the street. Almost no one actually pays them. Always ask about packages and discounts. Think of the rates in this book as guidelines to help you comparison shop.

A good travel agent can help save you serious money. Some hotels are often quite flexible about their rates, and many offer discounts and upgrades whenever they have a big block of rooms to fill and few reservations. The smaller hotels and inns are not as likely to be generous with discounts, much less upgrades.

ALL-INCLUSIVE RESORTS The promises are persuasive: "Forget your cash, put your plastic away." Presumably, everything's all paid for in advance at an "all-inclusive" resort. But is it?

The all-inclusives have a reputation for being expensive, and many of them are, especially the giant **Super-Clubs** of Jamaica or even the **Sandals** properties (unless you book in a slow period or off season).

In the 1990s, so many competitors entered the all-inclusive game that the term now means different things to the various resorts that use this marketing strategy. The ideal all-inclusive is just that—a place where everything, even drinks and watersports, is included. But in the most narrow sense, it means a room and three meals a day, with extra charges for drinks, sports, whatever. When you book, it's important to ask and to understand exactly what's included in your so-called all-inclusive. Watersports programs vary greatly at the various resorts. Extras might include horseback riding or sightseeing.

The all-inclusive market is geared to the active traveler who likes organized entertainment, a lot of sports, and workouts at fitness centers, and who also likes a lot of food and drink.

If you're single or gay, avoid Sandals. If you have children, stay away from Hedonism II in Negril, Jamaica, which lives up to its name. Even some Club Meds are targeted more for singles and couples, although many now aggressively pursue the family market. Some Club Meds have Mini Clubs, Baby Clubs, and Teen Clubs at some of their properties, at least during holiday and summer seasons.

The trick is to look for that special deal and to travel in off-peak periods, which doesn't always mean just from mid-April to mid-December. Discounts are often granted for hotels during certain slow periods, called "windows," most often after the New Year's holiday. If you want a winter vacation at an all-inclusive, choose the month of January—not February or the Christmas holidays, when prices are at their all-year high.

One good deal might be **Club Med's "Wild Card,"** geared to singles and couples. You must be 18 or over. Reservations must be made 2 or more weeks before departure. One week before departure, Club Med tells you which "village" on which island you're going to visit. If this uncertainty doesn't bother you, you can save $150 to $300 per weekly package. Deals like this can change constantly, so check to see exactly how "wild" this card is to play. Each package includes round-trip air transportation from New York, double-occupancy accommodations, all meals with complimentary wine and beer, use of all sports facilities except scuba gear (extra charges), nightly entertainment, and other recreational activities such as boat rides, snorkeling expeditions, and picnics. For more information, call ℂ **800/CLUB-MED.**

GUESTHOUSES An entirely different type of accommodation is the *guesthouse,* where most of the Antilleans themselves stay when they travel. In the Caribbean, the term *"guesthouse"* can mean anything. Sometimes so-called *guesthouses* are really like simple motels built around swimming pools. Others are small individual cottages, with their own kitchenettes, constructed around a main building in which you'll often find a bar and a restaurant that serves local food. Some are surprisingly comfortable, often with private baths and swimming pools. You may or may not have air-conditioning.

For value, the *guesthouse* can't be topped. You can always journey over to a big beach resort and use its seaside facilities for only a small charge, perhaps no more than $5. Although they don't have any frills, the guesthouses we've recommended are clean and safe for families or single women. The cheapest ones are not places where you'd want to spend a lot of time, because of their simple, modest furnishings.

RENTING A CONDO, VILLA, OR COTTAGE Particularly if you're a family or a group of friends, a "house-keeping holiday" can be one of the least expensive ways to vacation in the Caribbean, and if you like privacy and independence, it's a good way to go. Accommodations with kitchens are now available on nearly all the islands.

Some are individual cottages, others are condo complexes with swimming pools, and some are private homes that owners rent out while they're away. Many (though not all) places include maid service, and you're given fresh linen as well.

In the simpler rentals, doing your own cooking and laundry or even your own maid service may not be your idea of a good time in the sun, but it saves money—a lot of money. The savings, especially for a family of three to six people, or two or three couples, can range from 50% to 60% of what a hotel would cost. Groceries are sometimes priced 35% to 60% higher than on the U.S. mainland, as nearly all foodstuffs have to be imported, but even so, preparing your own food will be a lot cheaper than dining at restaurants.

There are also quite lavish homes for rent, where you can spend a lot and stay in the lap of luxury in a prime beachfront setting.

Many villas have a staff, or at least a maid who comes in a few days a week, and they also provide the essentials for home life, including linens and housewares. Condos usually come with a reception desk and are often comparable to a suite in a big resort hotel. Nearly all condo complexes have pools (some more than one). Like condos, villas range widely in price and may begin at $700 per week for a modest one and go over $50,000 a week for a luxurious one. More likely, the prices will be somewhere in between.

You'll have to approach these rental properties with a certain sense of independence. There may or may not be a front desk to answer your questions, and you'll have to plan your own watersports.

For a list of agencies that arrange rentals, refer to the accommodation sections of the individual island chapters. You can also ask each island's tourist office for good suggestions.

Make your reservations well in advance.

Here are a few agencies renting throughout the Caribbean:

- **Villas of Distinction** (© **800/ 289-0900** in the U.S., or 914/273-3331; www.villasofdistinction. com) offers upscale private villas with one to six bedrooms and a pool. Domestic help is often included. They have offerings on St. Martin, Anguilla, Mustique, Barbados, the U.S. and British Virgins, the Cayman Islands, St. Lucia, Nevis, Turks and Caicos, St. Barts, and Jamaica. Descriptions, rates, and photos are available online.

- **At Home Abroad** (© **212/421-9165;** fax 212/752-1591; www. athomeabroadinc.com) has private upscale homes for rent on Antigua, Barbados, Dominican Republic, Grenada, Jamaica, Mustique, St. John, St. Lucia, St. Martin, St. Thomas, Tortola, and Virgin Gorda, most with maid service included.

- **Caribbean Connection Plus Ltd.** (© **800/893-1100** or 203/ 261-8603; fax 203/261-8295; www.islandhoppingexperts.com) offers many apartments, cottages, and villas in the Caribbean, especially on St. Kitts and Nevis, but also on some of the more obscure islands such as St. Eustatius, Tobago, St. Vincent, and Dominica. Caribbean Connection specializes in island hopping with InterIsland Air, and offers especially attractive deals for U.S. West Coast travelers. This is one of the few reservations services staffed by people who have actually been on the islands, so patrons can talk to people who really know the Caribbean.

- **Hideaways International** (© **800/843-4433** in the U.S., or 603/430-4433; fax 603/430-4444; www.hideaways.com) publishes *Hideaways Guide,* a pictorial directory of home rentals throughout the world, including the Caribbean, especially the British Virgin Islands, the Cayman Islands, Jamaica, and St. Lucia, with full descriptions so you know what you're renting. Rentals range from cottages to staffed villas to whole islands! Other services include yacht charters, cruises, airline ticketing, car rentals, and hotel reservations. Annual membership is $145. Membership information, listings, and photos are available online.

- **Heart of the Caribbean Ltd.** (© **800/231-5303** or 262/783-5303; www.hotcarib.com) is a villa wholesale company offering travelers a wide range of private villas and condos on several islands, including St. Maarten/St. Martin, Barbados, and St. Lucia. Accommodations range from one to six bedrooms, and from modest villas and condos to palatial estates. Homes have complete kitchens and maid service. Catering and car rentals can also be provided. Rates, listings, and photos are available online.

LANDING THE BEST ROOM

Somebody has to get the best room in the house. It might as well be you. You can start by joining the hotel's frequent-guest program, which may make you eligible for upgrades. A hotel-branded credit card usually gives its owner "silver" or "gold" status in frequent-guest programs for free. Always ask about a corner room. They're often larger and quieter, with more windows and light, and they often cost the same as standard rooms. When you make your reservation, ask if the hotel is renovating; if it is, request a room away from the construction. Ask about nonsmoking rooms, rooms with views, and rooms with twin, queen- or king-size beds. If you're a light sleeper, request a quiet room away from vending machines, elevators, restaurants, bars, and discos. Ask for one of the rooms that have been most recently renovated or redecorated.

If you aren't happy with your room when you arrive, say so. If another room is available, most lodgings will be willing to accommodate you. Ask the following questions before you book a room:

- What's the view like? Cost-conscious travelers may be willing to pay less for a back room facing the parking lot, especially if they don't plan to spend much time in their room.

- Does the room have air-conditioning or ceiling fans? Do the windows open? If they do, and the nighttime entertainment takes place alfresco, you may want to find out when show time is over.

- What's included in the price? Your room may be moderately priced, but if you're charged for beach chairs, towels, sports equipment, and other amenities, you could end up spending more than you bargained for.

- How far is the room from the beach and other amenities? If it's far, is there transportation to and from the beach?

16 Recommended Reading

GENERAL *Pirates of the Virgin Islands* and *Mavericks in Paradise,* by Fritz Seyfarth (Spanish Main Press), two books bound in one volume, capture the daring exploits of the maritime gangsters who collected immense booty in the West Indies.

Caribbean Pirates, by Warren Alleyne (Macmillan-Caribbean), tries to separate fact from fiction using some published letters and documents as sources. *Caribbean Style,* the work of several authors (Crown Publishers), is a coffee-table book filled with Caribbean images, from decaying old plantation houses and balcony-fronted typical West Indian houses with peeling paint, to lush gardens and flowers.

Catch a Fire, The Life of Bob Marley, by Tim White (Guernsey Press), chronicles the musician's life and career. It's an insightful exploration of the historical, cultural, religious, and folkloric milieu that shaped Marley's spiritual and political beliefs.

FICTION Herman Wouk's *Don't Stop the Carnival* (in many editions) is a Caribbean classic, and we recommend that anyone contemplating a visit to the Caribbean read this book before going there. *Kiss the Hibiscus Goodnight* (Birch-Lane Press), by Carleton Varney, has been called the "first important novel about the U.S. Virgin Islands" since the publication of *Don't Stop the Carnival.*

Caribbean, by James A. Michener (Fawcett paperback), is a grand epic beginning with the 1310 conquest of the peaceful Arawaks by the cannibalistic Caribs and continuing 7 centuries to the rise of Castro.

Easy in the Islands (Viking Penguin), by Bob Shacochis, winner of the American Book Award in 1986, is a collection of short stories that giddily re-creates the flavor of the West Indies.

Green Cane and Juicy Flotsam: Short Stories by Caribbean Women (Rutgers University Press) represents authors ranging from Jean Rhys to Maryse Condé (the author of the 1993 novel, *Tree of Life,* set in the West Indies).

TRAVEL   *Love and the Caribbean: Tales, Characters and Scenes of the West Indies,* by Alec Waugh (Paragon House), is a vivid portrait of the Caribbean by a famous writer.

The Traveller's Tree: A Journey Through the Caribbean Islands, by Patrick Leigh Fermor (Quentin Crewe), is a classic account of Fermor's now-famous journey through the West Indies in the 1940s.

The Islands and the Sea: Five Centuries of Nature Writing from the Caribbean, edited by John A. Murray (Oxford University Press), is the first comprehensive anthology of writing in the West Indies from 1492 until the present.

HISTORY   In *From Columbus to Castro: The History of the Caribbean,* by Eric Williams (Vintage Books), the former prime minister of Trinidad and Tobago, takes you on a grand tour of a region dominated by slavery, sugar, and often sheer greed.

Columbus and the Age of Discovery, by Zvi Dor-Ner with William G. Scheller (William Morrow), is the best general survey of what is known about the voyages of Columbus.

The Caribbean People, by Reginald Honychurch (T. Nelson & Sons), in three volumes, is a well-balanced account by one of the so-called new historians of the Caribbean.

The Tainos: Rise and Decline of the People Who Greeted Columbus, by Irving Rouse (Yale University Press), is for those with a keen interest in the first people to inhabit the West Indies.

3

Anguilla

If you want a small, serene, secluded, and exclusive island, this is the place for you. Instead of high rises, one local commented, you get "low-rise dreams" here, referring to the posh inns. Anguilla (rhymes with *vanilla*) used to tout itself as the Caribbean's best-kept secret. Those days are gone: The news is out. But you still get tranquillity here. Exclusive St. Barts is a prettier island and just as luxurious as Anguilla. Anguilla's interior offers no waterfalls, rivers, or lush tropical foliage. Its scant rainfall makes for unproductive soil that supports mainly low foliage and sparse scrub vegetation. But its white-sand beaches are among the finest in the Caribbean; more than 30 of them dot the coastline, shaded by sea-grape trees. Come here to rest, unwind, and be pampered on the gorgeous sands or by your hotel pool.

You can enjoy the privacy of a small-island experience at Anguilla and still be close to St. Maarten/ St. Martin, with its gambling, shopping, and nightlife. You can also take a number of day trips if you get bored with the beach, including visits to Dutch-held St. Eustatius and Saba.

The northernmost of the British Leeward Islands in the eastern Caribbean, 8km (5 miles) north of St. Maarten, Anguilla is only 26km (16 miles) long, with 91 sq. km (35 sq. miles) in land area. The little island has a population of approximately 9,000 people. Most are of African descent, though many are European, predominantly Irish. The locals work primarily in the tourist industry or fish for lobster.

Once part of the federation with St. Kitts and Nevis, Anguilla gained its independence in 1980 and has since been a self-governing British possession. In 1996, however, London issued a policy statement that locals have viewed as a move to push them toward independence. Many Anguillians believe that Britain has now reduced its global ambitions and wants to relinquish colonies that have become too expensive to maintain. Many islanders fear going it alone as a nation. They know, however, that to retain Britain's protection, they would also have to abide by British laws— including its liberal position on gay rights. For the most part, islanders remain archly conservative and often homophobic.

With the opening of some superdeluxe (and superexpensive) hotels in the 1990s, Anguilla has become one of the Caribbean's most chic destinations, rivaling even St. Barts. Recently more moderately priced hotels have opened, too. Except for a handful of large-scale hotels, operations on Anguilla tend to be small and informal, as Anguilla has tried to control development and conserve natural beauty and resources.

1 Essentials

VISITOR INFORMATION

The **Anguilla Department of Tourism,** Old Factory Plaza, P.O. Box 1388, The Valley, Anguilla, B.W.I. (© **264/497-2759**), is open Monday to Friday from 8am to 5pm.

You can also log on to **www.anguilla-vacation.com.**

In the United Kingdom, contact the **Anguilla Tourism Office,** Oakwood House, 414 Hackney Rd., London E27SY (© **020/7729-8003**).

GETTING THERE

BY PLANE More than 50 flights into Anguilla are scheduled each week, not counting various charter flights. There are no nonstop flights from mainland North America, however, so visitors usually transfer through San Juan, Puerto Rico, or nearby St. Maarten. Some visitors also come from St. Kitts, Antigua, or St. Thomas.

Anguilla's most reliable carrier, **American Eagle** (© **800/433-7300** in the U.S.), the commuter partner of American Airlines, has two nonstop daily flights to Anguilla from American's hub in San Juan. In the off-season flights are reduced to one each day during the week and two on weekends. Flights leave at different times based on the seasons and carry 44 to 46 passengers. Schedules are subject to change, so check with the airline or your travel agent.

From Dutch St. Maarten, **Winair** (Windward Islands Airways International; © **800/634-4907**) has four daily flights to Anguilla. The small airline also has Anguilla links to the islands of Saba, St. Eustatius, St. Barts, St. Kitts, and Nevis.

LIAT (© **868/624-4727** or 888/844-5428 in Anguilla) offers daily flights daily to Anguilla from Antigua via St. Kitts. It's not the most punctual airline.

A small airline, **Caribbean Star/TransAnguilla** (© **866/864-6272** in the U.S., or 264/497-8690) wings in from St. Kitts and Antigua on Thursday, Friday, and Sunday. Schedules are likely to change, so it's always best to call and confirm before planning any trip.

BY FERRY Ferries run between the ports of Marigot Bay, French St. Martin, and Blowing Point, Anguilla, three times daily. The trip takes 20 to 30 minutes, making it easy for visitors on one island to do a day trip to the other. The first ferry leaves St. Martin at 11:20am and the last at 6pm; from Blowing Point, the first ferry leaves at 8:40am and the last at 5:30pm. The one-way fare is US$10 plus a US$3 departure tax. No reservations are necessary; schedules and fares, of course, are always subject to change. Ferries are small, and none take vehicles.

Fun Fact **A Special Celebration**

Anguilla's most colorful annual festival is **Carnival,** held jointly under the auspices of the Ministries of Culture and Tourism. Boat races are Anguilla's national sport, and they make up much of the Carnival celebration. The festival begins on Friday before the first Monday in August and lasts a week. Carnival harks back to Emancipation Day, or "August Monday," in 1834, when all enslaved Africans were freed.

Anguilla

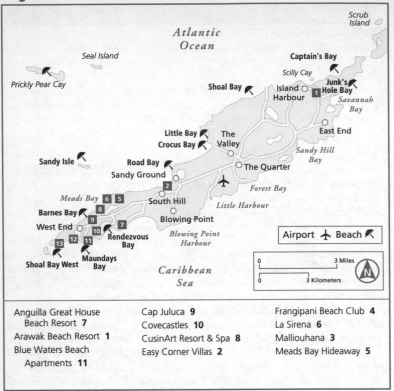

Anguilla Great House Beach Resort **7**
Arawak Beach Resort **1**
Blue Waters Beach Apartments **11**
Cap Juluca **9**
Covecastles **10**
CusinArt Resort & Spa **8**
Easy Corner Villas **2**
Frangipani Beach Club **4**
La Sirena **6**
Malliouhana **3**
Meads Bay Hideaway **5**

GETTING AROUND

BY RENTAL CAR   To explore the island in any depth, it's best to rent a car, though be prepared for badly paved roads. Four-wheel-drive vehicles aren't necessary, however. Several rental agencies on the island can issue the mandatory Anguillian driver's license, which is valid for 3 months. You can also get a license at police headquarters in the island's administrative center, The Valley, and at ports of entry. You'll need to present a valid driver's license from your home country and pay a one-time fee of US$20. *Remember:* Drive on the left side of the road!

Most visitors take a taxi from the airport to their hotel and arrange, at no extra charge, for a rental agency to deliver a car there the following day. All rental companies offer small discounts for rentals of 7 days or more.

There's a branch of **Avis** at The Quarter (✆ **800/331-1212** in the U.S., or 264/497-2642 in Anguilla; www.avis.com), which offers regular cars and some four-wheel-drive vehicles. Local firms include **Connor's Car Rental,** c/o Maurice Connor, South Hill (✆ **264/497-6433**), and **Triple K Car Rental,** Airport Road (✆ **264/497-5934**).

BY TAXI   Typical taxi fares are US$18 to US$22 from the airport to Cap Juluca; US$15 to the Fountain Beach Hotel; and US$17 to the Malliouhana hotel. Most rides take 15 to 20 minutes. For a cab, call ✆ **264/497-5054** or 264/497-4238.

FAST FACTS: Anguilla

Banks Banks are open Monday to Thursday from 8am to 3pm, Friday from 8am to 5pm. *Warning:* Do not count on ATMs to work. The most reliable is **Scotiabank,** The Valley, Fairplay Commercial Complex (© **264/497-3333**).

Currency The **Eastern Caribbean dollar (EC$)** is the official currency of Anguilla, although U.S. dollars are the actual "coin of the realm." The exchange rate is permanently fixed at about EC$2.70 to each US$1 (EC$1 = US37¢). *Rates in this chapter are quoted in U.S. dollars.*

Customs Even for tourists, duties are levied on imported goods at varying rates: from 5% on foodstuffs to 30% on luxury goods, wines, and liquors.

Documents All visitors must have an onward or return ticket. For U.S. and Canadian citizens, the preferred form of ID is a passport, even if it has expired within the past 5 years. In place of a passport, a photo ID with an original birth certificate is required (play it safe and bring a passport anyway). Citizens from the United Kingdom or other countries must have a valid passport.

Electricity The electricity is 110-volt AC (60 cycles), so no transformers or adapters are necessary to use U.S. appliances.

Hospitals For medical services, consult the **Princess Alexandra Hospital,** Stoney Ground (© **264/497-2551**), or one of several district clinics.

Language English is spoken here.

Liquor Laws Beer, wine, and liquor are sold 7 days a week during regular business hours. It's legal to have an open container on the beach.

Pharmacies Go to the **Government Pharmacy** at the Princess Alexandra Hospital, Stoney Ground (© **264/497-2551**), open Monday to Friday from 8am to 4pm and Saturday from 10am to noon. **Paramount Pharmacy,** Water Swamp (© **264/497-2366**), is open Monday through Saturday 8:30am to 7pm and Sunday (as needed).

Police You can reach the police at their headquarters in The Valley (© **264/497-2333**) or the substation at Sandy Ground (© **264/497-2354**). In an emergency, dial © **911.**

Post Office The main post office is on Wallblake Road, The Valley (© **264/497-2528**). Collectors consider Anguilla's stamps valuable, and the post office also operates a philatelic bureau, open Monday to Friday from 8am to 5pm. Airmail postcards and letters cost US$1.50 to the U.S., Canada, and the United Kingdom.

Safety Although crime is rare here, secure your valuables; never leave them in a parked car or unguarded on the beach. Anguilla is one of the safest destinations in the Caribbean, but you should still take standard precautions.

Taxes The government collects a 10% tax on rooms and a departure tax of US$20 if you leave the island by air, US$3 if you leave by boat.

Telephone Telephone, cable, and Telex services are offered by **Cable & Wireless Ltd.,** Wallblake Road, The Valley (© **264/497-3100**), open Monday to Friday from 8am to 5pm. To call the United States from Anguilla, dial **1,** the area code, and the seven-digit number. You can call **MCI** by dialing © **800/888-8000.**

Time Anguilla is on Atlantic Standard Time year-round, which means it's usually 1 hour ahead of the U.S. East Coast—except when the U.S. is on daylight savings time, when the clocks are the same.

Weather The hottest months in Anguilla are July to October; the coolest, December to February. The mean monthly temperature is about 80°F (27°C).

2 Accommodations

Instead of staying at a hotel, you might want to consider renting a private villa. Several rental agencies list villas in a vast range of prices. One of the best is **Anguilla Connection** (© 800/916-3336 in the U.S., or 264/497-9852; www. luxuryvillas.com). Choices range from luxurious, secluded houses to condos.

In addition to the choices below, the Ferryboat Inn (see "Dining," later in this chapter) also offers accommodations.

Don't forget that the government adds a 10% tax to your hotel bill, and you'll pay 10% for service. Be sure to read the section "Packages for the Independent Traveler" in chapter 2 before you book your hotel on your own!

VERY EXPENSIVE

Cap Juluca ✹✹✹ This is one of the most boldly conceived, luxurious oases in the Caribbean, fronting one of the island's best white-sand beaches. Overlooking Maundays Bay on a rolling 72-hectare (178-acre) site, Cap Juluca caters to Hollywood stars and financial barons and offers serious pampering. This is the only resort on the island to match the classy Malliouhana (see below). Cap Juluca is more fun loving and has a festive atmosphere, whereas Malliouhana is more subdued. Malliouhana has superior dining and service, but Cap Juluca fronts a better beach, and its accommodations are plusher.

Most of the villa-style accommodations have soaring domes, walled courtyards, labyrinthine staircases, and concealed swimming pools ringed with thick walls so you can take it all off. Inside, a mixture of elegantly comfortable wicker furniture is offset with Moroccan accessories. Rooms are spacious, with luxurious beds and Italian-tile floors. If money is no object, opt for the extravagant suites with their own plunge pools. Large marble and mirrored baths are luxuriously appointed, with shower/tub combinations. Although the cuisine at this hotel has never been better—the chefs have been called "the dream team"—it still doesn't equal Malliouhana. At the elegant Pimms (© **264/497-6666** for reservations) you can count on imaginative seafood-based dishes with Asian accents.

Maundays Bay (P.O. Box 240), Anguilla, B.W.I. © **888/858-5822** in the U.S., or 264/497-6779. Fax 264/497-6340. www.capjuluca.com. 98 units, 18 villas. Winter/spring US$445–US$780 double; from US$980 suite; off season US$345–US$420 double, from US$530 suite. MAP (breakfast and dinner) US$95 per person extra. AE, MC, V. Closed Sept–Oct. **Amenities:** 3 restaurants; 2 bars; outdoor pool; driving range; 3 tennis courts; fitness center; spa; kayaks; scuba diving; snorkeling; water-skiing; windsurfing; children's programs (in summer only); rental cars; business center; room service (7:30am–9:30pm); massage; babysitting; laundry service; dry cleaning. *In room:* A/C, dataport, minibar, hair dryer, safe.

Covecastles ✹✹ A cross between a collection of private homes and a monumental yet minimalist resort on a white-sand beach, this is a wonderful (if shockingly expensive) small resort, with an attentive staff. Designed by award-winning architect Myron Goldfinger in 1985 and enlarged in 1998, the structure combines elements from North Africa, the Caribbean, and the futuristic theories of Le Corbusier. The units include an interconnected row of town house–style beach structures that accommodate two to four persons, and a handful of larger, fully detached villas that house up to six. Large bedrooms have twin- or king-size beds with hand-embroidered linens and deluxe mattresses, and bathrooms are large and stylish with shower/tub combinations. This place offers even more privacy than Cap Juluca.

Each building has views of the sea, amid the dunes and scrublands of the southwestern coast. Guest rooms have louvered doors and windows crafted from Brazilian walnut; terra-cotta tiles; comfortably oversize rattan furniture; a fully equipped, state-of-the-art kitchen; and a hammock. The most spectacular place to stay is the five-bedroom grand villa that opens directly on the beach; this is one of the most fabulous accommodations in the Caribbean.

The resort's French chef pampers guests with candlelit dinners of impeccable quality, in an intimate private dining room that overlooks the beach or en suite.

Shoal Bay West (P.O. Box 248), Anguilla, B.W.I. © **800/223-1108** in the U.S., or 264/497-6801. Fax 264/497-6051. www.covecastles.com. 15 units. Winter US$795–US$1,195 beach house, US$1,095–US$1,595 villa; off season US$525–US$625 beach house, US$625–US$825 villa. AE, MC, V. Closed Sept to mid-Oct. **Amenities:** Restaurant; tennis court; aerobics; deep-sea fishing; glass-bottom boat excursions; kayaks; scuba diving; snorkeling; Sunfish sailboats; windsurfing; bicycles; car rental; secretarial service; room service (8am–10pm); massage; babysitting; laundry service; dry cleaning. *In room:* Ceiling fan, TV, dataport, full kitchen, beverage maker, hair dryer, iron/ironing board, safe.

CuisinArt Resort & Spa 🏝🏝🏝   Yes, it's owned by CuisinArt, and, yes, it fronts a powdery beach of white sand (assuming that this is your next question). Evoking the architecture of nearby Cap Juluca, this is Anguilla's latest word in luxury. For privacy and seclusion, CuisinArt challenges Covecastles. A complex of whitewashed villas crowned by blue domes and surrounded by lush tropical foliage, it seems straight out of Mykonos. The resort offers the first-ever hydroponic farm and the only full-service resort spa in Anguilla (their milk-and-honey-almond scrub is the most fantastic we've experienced). It also features an herb garden, an orchid solarium, and a rare plant house. Italian upholsteries, Haitian cottons, dark-wood furniture, and large shower/tub combination bathrooms in soft-toned Italian marble characterize the well-furnished accommodations.

The Hydroponic Café's daily lunch features the US$1 million, .6-hectare (1½-acre) hydroponic farm's fresh vegetables in salads and other light fare. The Santorini Restaurant is the fine-dining choice, with a French rotisserie on-site. Expect brawny, lusty dishes infused with the flamboyant flavors and spices of the Caribbean.

Rendezvous Bay (P.O. Box 2000), Anguilla, B.W.I. © **800/943-3210** or 264/498-2000. Fax 264/498-2010. www.cuisinartresort.com. 93 units. Winter US$525 double, US$625–US$1,625 suite; off season US$325 double, from US$375–US$1,025 suite. AE, MC, V. Closed Sept–Oct. **Amenities:** 2 restaurants; 2 bars; outdoor pool; 3 tennis courts; fitness center; spa; Jacuzzi; deep-sea fishing; kayaks; sailing; scuba diving; snorkeling; windsurfing; mountain bikes; salon; limited room service; babysitting; laundry service; dry cleaning; non-smoking rooms. *In room:* A/C, TV, dataport, minibar, hair dryer, iron/ironing board, safe.

Malliouhana 🏝🏝🏝 *Kids*   The Caribbean's ultrachic hotel, this cliff-side retreat conjures up images of Positano in the Tropics. It's even more spectacular than Cap Juluca—opulent and lavishly decorated, and situated on a rocky bluff between two white-sand beaches. In fact, it outdazzles Cap Juluca in every way except for that resort's fabulous beach and glitzier digs. Malliouhana's 10 hectares (25 acres) are lushly landscaped with terraces, banks of flowers, pools, and fountains. Thick walls and shrubbery provide seclusion. A 224-member staff attends to 55 units; their motto is "Your wish is my command."

Haitian art and decorations are so splendid that you might not spot Gwyneth Paltrow sitting among the palms. Spacious bedrooms and suites are distributed among the main buildings and outlying villas. Each room has tropical furnishings and wide private verandas; the villas can be rented as a single unit or subdivided into three. Three of the suites have private Jacuzzis, and one unit has a private pool. Some accommodations open onto garden views, and others front Meads Bay Beach or Turtle Cove. Many rooms have luxurious four-poster beds, plus spacious Italian marble bathrooms with tubs and shower stalls. If you're a wealthy parent with child, this is a kid-friendly oasis, complete with a water park and faux pirate ship.

Meads Bay (P.O. Box 173), Anguilla, B.W.I. ℂ 800/835-0796 in the U.S., or 264/497-6111. Fax 264/497-6011. www.malliouhana.com. 55 units. Winter US$590–US$815 double, from US$970 suite; off season US$380–US$530 double, from US$620 suite. AE, MC, V. Closed Sept–Oct. **Amenities:** Restaurant; bar; 3 outdoor pools; 4 tennis courts; exercise room; spa; Jacuzzi; boat trips; fishing; sailing; snorkeling; water-skiing; windsurfing; children's center; salon; room service (7:30am–10:30pm); massage (spa only); laundry service; dry cleaning; TV room; library. *In room:* A/C, ceiling fan, dataport, minibar, hair dryer, iron/ironing board, safe.

Meads Bay Hideaway   One of the island's newest properties, this small hideaway opens onto panoramic views over Meads Bay. In a classical tropical style, it offers 100 sq. m (1,076-sq. ft.) accommodations. These include your choice of one- or two-bedroom suites or, even more lavish, two-bedroom penthouses, the latter with their own private rooftop patios shaded by umbrellas. Right off Meads Bay beach, this modern three-story structure is built of concrete with wooden balconies. Bedrooms are simply but tastefully furnished with white-tile floors and light wicker or dark-wood pieces. Each unit contains a contemporary bathroom with walk-in shower. This is a retreat for adults and doesn't actually encourage the family trade. Units also come with kitchenettes and living and dining areas. Next door is the Coral's Restaurant, specializing in such dishes as Greek-style *mezedes* (appetizers), all under a mammoth thatched roof.

Meads Bay, Anguilla, B.W.I. ℂ 264/498-5555. Fax 264/498-5511. www.meadsbayhideaway.com. 12 units. Winter US$400–US$550 suite, US$500–US$650 penthouse; off season US$250–US$400 suite, US$300–US$450 penthouse. AE, MC, V. **Amenities:** Restaurant/bar next door; snorkel equipment; laundry service. *In room:* A/C, kitchenette, beverage maker, hair dryer, no phone.

EXPENSIVE

Frangipani Beach Club 🐾   Set on 1.6km (1 mile) of luscious white sand, this condo complex feels like a villa along the Spanish Mediterranean, with wrought-iron railings and red-tile roofs. Its major competitor is La Sirena, but La Sirena is more of a resort, with better facilities, including dining, whereas Frangipani attracts self-catering types who want to have their own condos in Anguilla. Accommodations are light and airy, done in soft pastels with natural rattan furnishings; they're very comfortable, with king-size beds. All units also have marble bathrooms with shower/tub combinations, along with private terraces or balconies. Many of the more expensive rooms have full kitchens, and two- or three-bedroom units work for families or friends traveling together.

Meads Bay (P.O. Box 1378), Anguilla, B.W.I. ℂ 800/892-4564 in the U.S., or 264/497-6442. Fax 264/497-6440. www.frangipani.ai. 18 units. Winter US$300–US$490 double, from US$600 suite; off season US$185–US$215 double, from US$270 suite. AE, MC, V. Closed Sept to mid-Oct. **Amenities:** Restaurant; 2 bars; outdoor pool; tennis court; fishing; snorkeling; limited room service; laundry service; dry cleaning. *In room:* TV dataport, beverage maker, hair dryer, iron/ironing board.

La Sirena 🐾   Built in 1989 on 1 hectare (2½ acres) of sandy soil, a 4-minute walk from a clean white beach, this Swiss-owned resort is inviting, intimate, and low key. At least 80% of its clientele comes from Switzerland or Germany.

Accommodations, arranged in two-story bougainvillea-draped wings, are large and airy, with fine rattan and wicker furnishings. Some have air-conditioning; all have ceiling fans. Rooms have large double, queen-, or king-size beds with fine linens. Bathrooms are spacious, with shower/tub combinations. To reach the beach, guests walk down through the garden and a sandy footpath. Beach hats, umbrellas, and lounge chairs await on the sand. If possible, request rooms away from the second-floor Top of the Palms restaurant, thereby avoiding the noise and kitchen fumes.

The Top of the Palms is open to cool ocean breezes and offers views over Meads Bay and the surrounding treetops. A well-trained local chef prepares specialties ranging from alpine fondues to West Indian favorites.

Meads Bay (P.O. Box 200), Anguilla, B.W.I. © 800/331-9358 in the U.S., or 264/497-6827. Fax 264/497-6829. www.la-sirena.com. 29 units. Winter US$260–US$330 double, US$400–US$560 villa; off season US$145–US$190 double, US$230–US$360 villa. MAP (breakfast and dinner) US$48 per person extra. AE, MC, V. **Amenities:** Restaurant; bar; 2 outdoor pools; tennis court (nearby); dive center; snorkeling; windsurfing; car rental; limited room service; babysitting; laundry service; dry cleaning. In room: A/C (in some), ceiling fan, dataport, minibar, hair dryer, safe.

MODERATE

Anguilla Great House Beach Resort   On Rendezvous Bay, with its 4km (2½ miles) of white sand, this bungalow colony is like those you often see on the fringes of Los Angeles. These cottages with their gingerbread trim sit in landscaped gardens. Each bungalow contains a number of well-furnished bedrooms, which can be rented in various configurations depending on your needs. You get an offering of different beds here, including both king- and queen-size, or else two double beds. We particularly like the private porches opening onto water views. Cooled by ceiling fans, rooms can also be opened to capture the trade winds unless you prefer to chill out with air-conditioning. Bathrooms are small, tidily kept, and contain showers. The beachside amenities are good and include lounge chairs, umbrellas, kayaks, Sunfish sailboats, windsurfers, and both snorkeling and fishing gear.

Rendezvous Bay, Anguilla, B.W.I. © 264/497-6061. Fax 264/497-6019. www.anguillagreathouse.com. 35 units. Winter US$250–US$280 double; off season US$140–US$170 double. AE, MC, V. **Amenities:** Restaurant; bar; outdoor pool; fishing; kayaks; snorkeling; Sunfish sailboats; windsurfing; laundry service; dry cleaning. In room: A/C, ceiling fan, dataport, hair dryer, iron/ironing board.

Arawak Beach Inn *Value*   Built on the site of an ancient Arawak village and only minutes from beautiful Shoal Bay Beach, this comfortable and inviting family-run hotel is a good value (for pricey Anguilla, anyway), especially during the summer months. It opens onto views of Scilly Cay and Captains Ridge. The property has been greatly improved. It offers studios and one-bedroom suites in octagonal-shaped buildings. Beachfront units are built in the style of a re-created Amerindian village and are equipped with wet bars and coffeemakers, plus large balconies or terraces. Furnishings are comfortable and include king-size beds, plus small bathrooms with a shower.

The rather formal restaurant features a good Continental and Caribbean menu.

Island Harbour (P.O. Box 1403, The Valley), Anguilla, B.W.I. © 877/427-2925 or 264/497-4888. Fax 264/497-4889. www.arawakbeach.com. 17 units. Winter US$175–US$225 double; off season US$95–US$125 double. Children under 12 stay free in parent's room. AE, MC, V. **Amenities:** Restaurant; cafe; beach bar; outdoor pool; canoeing; windsurfing; bike rental; car rental; 24-hr. room service; babysitting; laundry service; dry cleaning. In room: Ceiling fan, TV (in some), fridge, hair dryer, safe, no phone.

Blue Waters Beach Apartments *(Kids)* Fronting .8km (½ mile) of white-sand beachfront, this tranquil resort has a vaguely Moorish look. It offers well-designed and immaculately kept one-bedroom units and two-bedroom apartments, each opening directly on the beach and cooled by a ceiling fan. Family friendly, it's really a do-it-yourself kind of place, so plan to be self-sufficient; units have their own kitchens so you can do your own cooking. You'll find ample closets and comfortable furnishings such as king-size beds. Rollaway beds and baby cribs are available but must be requested at the time of booking. Bathrooms are immaculately white, very Calvin Klein, each with a shower stall. Rooms have terraces down below or balconies if on the second floor.

Shoal Bay West (P.O. Box 69), Anguilla, B.W.I. © **264/497-6292.** Fax 264/497-6982. www.caribbean concepts.com. 9 units. Winter US$275 1-bedroom apt, US$390 2-bedroom apt; off season US$140 1-bedroom apt, US$195 2-bedroom apt. AE, MC, V. **Amenities:** Bar. *In room:* Ceiling fan, TV, kitchen, safe.

INEXPENSIVE
Easy Corner Villas On a bluff overlooking Road Bay, this modest villa complex lies a 5-minute walk from a good beach. On the main road west of the airport, Easy Corner Villas is owned by Maurice E. Connor, the same entrepreneur who rents many of the cars on the island. His one-, two-, and three-bedroom apartments are simply furnished and set on landscaped grounds with beach views from their private porches. Each comes equipped with a kitchen, combination living and dining room, a ceiling fan and air-conditioning, good beds, and large, airy living areas, plus small bathrooms with shower stalls. Maid service is available for an extra charge, except on Sunday.

South Hill (P.O. Box 65), Anguilla, B.W.I. © **264/497-6433.** Fax 264/497-6410. www.caribbean-inns.com. 12 units. Winter US$160–US$240; off season US$125–US$195. AE, MC, V. **Amenities:** Laundry service; dry cleaning. *In room:* A/C, ceiling fan, TV, kitchen, beverage maker.

3 Dining
VERY EXPENSIVE
Malliouhana Restaurant 🏵🏵🏵 FRENCH/CARIBBEAN Even better than the restaurant at Cap Juluca, Malliouhana Restaurant, with the Caribbean's most ambitious French menu, offers fluidly choreographed service, fine food, a 25,000-bottle wine cellar, and a glamorous clientele. You'll dine in an open-sided pavilion on a rocky promontory over the sea. At night your candlelit table will be set with French crystal, Limoges china, and Christofle silver. There are well-spaced tables, an ocean view, and a splashing fountain.

The hors d'oeuvres selection is the finest on the island, including warm lobster medallions sautéed with spinach and baby corn in a citrus sauce, or crayfish *frita* (dried crayfish dipped in potato flakes) served with a spicy tomato chutney. This year you are likely to savor such main courses as marinated conch in lemon and olive oil, served with green asparagus tips, or filet of mahimahi seared skin side and served with an eggplant caviar and tomato-pulp vinaigrette, truly delectable.

Meads Bay. © **264/497-6111.** Reservations required. Main courses US$32–US$52. AE, MC, V. Daily 7–11am, 12:30–3pm, and 7:30–10:30pm.

EXPENSIVE
Blanchards 🏵🏵🏵 INTERNATIONAL Bob and Melinda Blanchard are the masterminds behind this elegantly casual, intensely fashionable restaurant on a garden-swathed pavilion beside the sea, next to the Malliouhana's beach. The

cuisine is the most creative and interesting on the island, and Blanchards has attracted a sprinkling of celebs (say hi to Robert de Niro or Janet Jackson if you see them). Blanchard's 3,000-bottle wine cellar is one of the finest in the Caribbean.

Behind tall teal shutters (which can be opened to the sea breezes), you'll enjoy sophisticated food with a Caribbean flair, enhanced with spices from Spain, Asia, California, and the American Southwest. Dishes change according to the inspiration of chef Melinda but are likely to include such delights as lobster cakes with mixed greens and a tomato-flavored tartar sauce. Here the famous Anguilla lobster is grilled with a honey glaze or a Cajun spicy sauce. Prepared with faultless technique is the tuna seared on the outside and served rare inside along with Israeli couscous. For a real island dessert, opt for the cracked coconut with coconut ice cream accompanied by a rum-custard sauce in a chocolate-crusted shell.

Meads Bay. *©* **264/497-6100.** Reservations recommended. Main courses US$36–US$48. AE, MC, V. Mon–Sat 6:30–9pm. Closed Mon in off season and also closed in Aug and Sept.

Hibernia *✿ Finds* FRENCH/INDOCHINESE   Following Blanchards's lead closely, this is another little stunner of creativity. Chef Raoul Rodriguez and his wife, hostess Mary Pat O'Hanlon, have converted a lovely West Indian cottage into a charming restaurant with a French- and Indonesian-inspired decor that's a nice change of pace. When you taste Chef Raoul's creative dishes, you'll know why he was voted chef of the year in 1997. He's as good now as he was then—maybe better. Start with Asian mushroom soup, or a selection of finely sliced, smoked West Indian fish. Main courses are likely to include Caribbean fish filets in a spicy Thai broth or crayfish sautéed with shiitake mushrooms and flavored with a tangy ginger sauce. French duck magret is a stunning choice, its light honey glaze the perfect touch.

Island Harbour. *©* **264/497-4290.** Reservations recommended. Main courses US$24–US$38. AE, MC, V. Tues–Sat noon–2pm; Tues–Sun 7–9pm. Closed Aug–Sept.

Straw Hat *✿* ASIAN/CARIBBEAN   Winning rave reviews from such magazines as *Gourmet,* chef James Hassell lives up to his hype. The panoramic setting by the sea and the distant vistas of French St. Martin more than match the superb cuisine. A plain wood-built structure, the restaurant stands on pilings overlooking a virtual aquarium of fish below. On a hot day, the cold cucumber-and-dill soup is refreshing, as is the cilantro-infused ceviche of local red snapper with plantain chips. Some dishes, like the jerk pork tenderloin, are traditional favorites; others are more eclectic, like the seared Anguillian red snapper with a lime, ginger, and saffron sauce or the grilled loin of tuna with Asian noodles and a compote of caramelized onions. A cilantro, lime, and pecan pesto pasta can be served with your choice of grilled chicken, tuna, or red snapper. For dessert, indulge in the chocolate indulgence (three types of chocolate in one cake).

Forest Bay. *©* **264/497-8300.** Reservations recommended. Main courses US$23–US$41. AE, DISC, MC, V. Mon–Sat 6–10pm. Closed Sept–Oct.

Trattoria Tramonto *✿ Finds* NORTHERN ITALIAN   One of the island's best, this breeze-swept restaurant lies between Blue Waters Beach Apartments and Covecastles. The chef, Valter Belli, hails from Emilia Romanga in central Italy. The tables lie near the water with distant views of St. Martin, the neighboring island. The "sundowners" here are the best on island, including a peachy Bellini as good as that served at Harry's Bar in Venice. Other champagne drinks are mixed with fruits like mango, passion fruit, or guava. The chef takes special care with his appetizers, including a *zuppa di pesce* (fish soup with porcini mushrooms) and spicy hot penne with a garlic, tomato, and red-pepper sauce. All the ingredients are superb and treated with care, including a delectable red snapper with a caper-laced fresh tomato sauce or, our favorite and the house specialty, lobster-filled ravioli in a truffle-cream sauce. "It's of the gods," we heard a diner at the next table say.

Shoal Bay West. ✆ 264/497-8819. Reservations required. Main courses US$8–US$22 lunch, US$22–US$38 dinner. MC, V. Tues–Sun noon–3pm and 6:30–9:30pm. Closed Sept–Oct.

MODERATE

Bistro Phil ✿ FRENCH/ITALIAN Perched on a cliff 15m (49 ft.) above the sea, this restaurant is a showcase for the talents of French-born Philippe Kim, the owner and chef, who draws a stylish crowd of diners to his restaurant. Many of them request a table on the terrace with its view of the sea. Kim is a master at flavoring, and he cooks with zest and spice, importing excellent ingredients into Anguilla. He also makes the best pizza on the island, and sometimes guests order a small one at the start of their meal. For starters, the house specialty is the French onion soup, or you can more daringly partake of the tuna tartar. The chef takes justifiable pride in his seafood kabob and his tender and succulent lamb shank cooked to perfection. For dessert, a classic chocolate mousse might be resting on your plate.

South Hill. ✆ 264/497-6810. Reservations recommended. Main courses US$20–US$30. AE, DC, MC, V. Mon–Sat 6:30–9:30pm. Closed mid-Aug to mid-Oct.

Cedar Grove ✿ CARIBBEAN In the olden days, if you wanted to eat at this beachfront, you had to dine with the chickens in someone's backyard. No more: Cedar Grove continues the volcanic restaurant explosion on Anguilla. It's one of the hottest dining tickets on island. In a setting evocative of *Casablanca,* you can enjoy a series of ever-changing specialties, based on the best and freshest ingredients. Signature dishes include lobster cakes with slivers of fresh ginger and a dash of curry-cream sauce. Try the coconut-crusted shrimp in a mango-ginger sauce, and the rice-paper red snapper is genuinely delicious.

Rendezvous Bay. ✆ 264/497-6549. Main courses US$16–US$28. AE, MC, V. Daily 7am–9pm. Closed Sept–Oct.

Mango's ✿ AMERICAN/CARIBBEAN In a pavilion a few steps from the edge of the sea, on the northwestern part of the island, Mango's serves healthier cuisine than the island's other top restaurants. The fresh fish, meat, and produce are grilled with a minimum of added fats or calories. All the breads and desserts, including ice cream and sorbet, are made fresh daily on the premises. You might start with delectable lobster cakes and homemade tartar sauce, or creamy conch chowder. Grilled local lobster and spicy whole snapper are featured main courses, but the best main dish is the simple grilled fish with lemon-and-herb butter.

Seaside Grill, Barnes Bay. ✆ 264/497-6479. Reservations required for dinner, as far in advance as possible. Main courses US$20–US$38. AE, MC, V. Wed–Mon 6:30–9pm. Closed Aug–Oct.

Zara's Restaurant ✿ ITALIAN/CARIBBEAN Award-winning master chef Shamash Brooks presides at this casually elegant place, which opened in 1996. Since then it has won many fans who visit every time they return to Anguilla. The chef uses excellent ingredients, which are prepared to order. He's known islandwide for his pasta dishes. His fish dishes, especially the crusted snapper, are delightful and he does veal, chicken, and steak equally well. Try his Bahamian cracked conch, and look for various daily specials. A few items are costly, but most dishes are in the moderate range.

Allamanda Beach Club, Upper Shoal Bay East. © 264/497-2120. Reservations required. Main courses US$16–US$38. AE, MC, V. Daily 6:30–9pm.

INEXPENSIVE

Good, affordable food is served in a festive atmosphere at **Johnno's Beach Bar,** Road Bay, Sandy Ground (© **264/497-2728**), and at **Pumphouse Bar & Grill,** Sandy Ground (© **264/497-5154**). See "Anguilla After Dark," below, for details. Johnno's is open for lunch and dinner; the Pumphouse is open only for dinner.

Cora's Pepperpot *Finds* WEST INDIAN/INTERNATIONAL   This, one of Anguilla's most charming and authentic restaurants, is run by Ms. Cora Richardson, a former local police officer. The concrete-sided building is adjacent to the island's secondary school. Cora cooks traditional island favorites like lip-smacking spare ribs, Anguillan pea soup, and red snapper grilled to your specification. When available, she offers grilled Anguillan lobster, but at a higher price than the main courses indicated below. Her most authentic local dish (try it at least once) is curried goat meat, an island favorite.

The Valley. © 264/497-2328. Reservations recommended for dinner. Main courses US$7–US$18. MC, V. Mon–Sat 7am–10pm.

Ferryboat Inn *Value* CARIBBEAN/FRENCH   Established by English-born John McClean and his Anguillan wife, Marjorie, this place is one of the best deals on the island. On the beach, a short walk from the Blowing Point ferry pier, it features French onion soup, black-bean soup, some of the best lobster thermidor on the island, and scallop of veal Savoyard. Unless you order expensive shellfish, most dishes are reasonably priced.

The McCleans also rent six one-bedroom apartments and a two-bedroom beach house. In winter, apartments cost US$160 to US$180, and the beach house is US$280. Off season, an apartment is US$90 to US$110, and the beach house is US$175.

Cul de Sac Rd., Blowing Point. © 264/497-6613. Reservations recommended. Main courses US$9–US$35. AE, MC, V. Mon and Wed–Sat noon–3pm and 7:30–10pm; Sun 7:30–10pm. Turn right just before the Blowing Point Ferry Terminal and travel 137m (449 ft.) before making a left turn.

Ripples CARIBBEAN/INTERNATIONAL   This restaurant is earthier and more British than most others in Sandy Ground, which has the biggest cluster of bars and restaurants on Anguilla. Its cheerful staff and long, busy bar will make you feel as though you're on the set of *Cheers*. Set in a restored clapboard house, it has a raised deck, a casual West Indian decor, and a crowd of regulars. Local fish—mahimahi, snapper, tuna, and grouper—are prepared any way you like. The coconut-shrimp house special, puffy Brie in beer batter, and Creole-style conch are the reasons we keep coming back. Only a few dishes are at the high end of the price scale.

Sandy Ground. © 264/497-3380. Reservations recommended. Main courses US$16–US$30. MC, V. Daily noon–3 or 4am.

4 Beaches

Superb beaches put Anguilla on the tourist map. There are dozens of them, plus another handful on the outer cays. The island's interior may be barren, but

---

(Moments   Grilled Lobster on a Remote Cay

At Island Harbor, just wave your arms, and a boatman will pick you up and transport you across the water to **Scilly Cay,** pronounced "silly key." You wouldn't really call this place an island; it's more like a spit of sand 155m (508 ft.) off the coast of the main island's northeastern shoreline. At a little cafe and bar here, you can select a fabulous fresh lobster. Grilled while you wait, the lobster is marinated in a sauce of honey-laced orange juice, orange marmalade, roasted peanuts, virgin olive oil, curry, and tarragon. Chicken is prepared here the same way. Lunch is daily Tuesday to Sunday from noon to 3pm.

---

there's no denying the beauty of its shores. Miles and miles of pristine, powdery-soft sands open onto crystal-clear waters. Many of the beaches are reached via bone-jarring dirt paths that ultimately give way to sand and sea. All the beaches are open to the public, but you may have to walk through the lobby of a deluxe hotel to reach one.

The best beaches are on the west end of the island, site of the most expensive hotels. **Rendezvous Bay** is the island's most famous, a long curving ribbon of pale gold sand that stretches along the bay for 4km (2½ miles). It's calmer, warmer, and shallower than Shoal Bay, which is on the Atlantic side. With an alfresco beach bar, it attracts all kinds, from families to romantic couples.

Our favorite is 3km (2-mile) **Shoal Bay** 𝕽𝕽 in the northeast, one of the best beaches in the Caribbean. With silver-white, powder-soft sands, it also boasts some of Anguilla's best coral gardens, home to hundreds of tiny iridescent fish, making it great for snorkeling. Umbrellas, beach chairs, and other equipment are available here so you can enjoy the backdrop of coconut palms and sea-grape trees. This beach is often called "Shoal Bay East" to distinguish it from "Shoal Bay West" (see below). The waters are usually luminous, transparent, and brilliant blue. At noon the sands are blindingly white, but at sunrise and sunset they turn a pink to rival any beach in Bermuda. You'll hear music from the terraces of the Hard Broke Café and Uncle Ernie's. The Upper Shoal Bar serves first-rate tropical drinks, and souvenir shops hawk T-shirts and suntan lotion on the beach. For a little more tranquillity, you can also take the trail walk from Old Ta to little-known **Katouche Beach,** which offers perfect snorkeling and is also a prime site for a beach picnic under shade trees.

Shoal Bay West, next to Maundays Bay, has pristine white sands opening onto the southwest coast. You'll find deluxe accommodations, including Covecastles, on these shores.

Adjoining Shoal Bay West, and site of Cap Juluca, is 1.6km-long (1 mile), white-sand **Maundays Bay Beach,** justifiably one of the island's most popular shorelines, with good snorkeling and swimming. Though the waters are luminescent and usually calm, sometimes the wind blows enough to attract windsurfers and sailboats. On a clear day you can see St. Martin across the way.

Sandy Isle, on the northwest coast, is a tiny islet with a few palms surrounded by a coral reef. It lies offshore from Road Bay. Once here, you'll find a beach bar and restaurant, and a place to rent snorkeling gear and buy underwater cameras. **Sandy Island Enterprises** (© 264/772-0787) has daily trips from the pier by Johnno's Beach Bar at Sandy Ground. The cost of a round-trip ticket is US$20, and the first boat leaves at 8:30am. The last boat back usually departs at 3pm.

Warning: There is no service from late August to September and only one trip weekly in October. You can also go farther out, to Prickly Pear Cay, which stretches like a sweeping arc all the way to a sand spit populated by sea birds and pelicans.

The northwest coast has a number of other beaches worth seeking out, notably **Barnes Bay Beach,** filled with powdery white sand and opening onto clear blue waters. You can relax in the shade of the chalky hillside or a beach umbrella or join the windsurfers and snorkelers. It's usually less crowded after lunch.

Almost never crowded, **Little Bay Beach** is one of the most dramatic in Anguilla, set against steep cliffs. Here the sands are grayish, but snorkelers and scuba divers don't seem to mind. The beach also attracts bird-watchers and picnickers. Local weddings are sometimes performed here.

Road Bay Beach, also on the northwest coast, is known for spectacular sunsets and clear blue waters, often filled with yachts coming from St. Martin. A watersports center here on the beach will set you up with gear. You can also watch lobstermen set out in their boats.

The beaches along the northeast coast are the stuff of fantasies—especially if you've got a four-wheel-drive. Calm and tranquil, the incredibly blue waters of **Island Harbour Beach** attract both locals and the odd visitor or two. For centuries Anguillians have set out from these shores to haul in Anguillan lobster. There are a few beach bars and alfresco dining rooms here, so you can make a day of it—or take a 3-minute boat ride over to Scilly Cay.

Chances are you'll have **Captain's Bay's Beach** all to yourself. Near Junk's Hole, it's better for enjoying the sun and sand than it is for swimming. The undertow is dangerous, though the setting is dramatic and appealing.

5 Sports & Other Outdoor Pursuits

CRUISES & BOATING   A great way to have fun on Anguilla is to cruise to a secluded beach on an offshore cay for a picnic and some snorkeling, whether on your own or with a group. Several outfitters on the island rent vessels, including **Anguillan Divers** (© 264/497-4750), offering a 10m (33-ft.) motorboat.

FISHING   Your hotel can arrange for you to cast your line with a local guide, but you should bring your own tackle. Agree on the cost before setting out, however, to avoid the "misunderstandings" that have been reported.

Malliouhana, Meads Bay (© 264/497-6111), has a 10m (33-ft.) fishing cruiser, *Kyra,* which holds up to eight passengers, and another 12-passenger cruiser, *Dakota.* You can charter it for fishing parties for US$400 for up to 4 hours, with a US$100 surcharge for each additional hour. All fishing gear is included, and they can pack a boxed lunch for an additional charge.

GOLF   By the time of your visit, a new 18-hole, par-72 Greg Norman–designed golf course may have been completed on an 111-hectare (274-acre) site

---

Tips Island Tours

The best way to get an overview of the island is on a **taxi tour.** In about 2½ hours, a local driver (all of them are guides) will show you everything for US$50. The driver will also arrange to let you off at your favorite beach after a look around, and then pick you up and return you to your hotel or the airport.

that in time will develop into a luxury spa and residential complex. Four holes will play to and from the ocean. Check with your hotel desk or the tourist office for the latest details on this development.

SCUBA DIVING & SNORKELING Most of the coastline of Anguilla is fringed by coral reefs, and the island's waters are rich in marine life, with sunken coral gardens, brilliantly colored fish, caves, and stingrays offshore. Conditions for scuba diving and snorkeling on the island are ideal. In addition, the government of Anguilla has artificially enlarged the existing reef system, a first for the Caribbean. Battered and outmoded ships, deliberately sunk in carefully designated places, act as nurseries for fish and lobster populations and provide new dive sites. At **Stoney Bay Marine Park** off the northeast coast, you can explore the ruins of a Spanish ship that sank in the 1700s.

Anguillan Divers, Meads Bay (© 264/497-4750), is a one-stop dive shop that answers most diving needs. PADI instructors are on hand, with a two-tank dive costing US$70, plus another US$10 for equipment. Another good choice is **Shoal Bay Scuba & Water Sports** (© 264/497-4371), with one of the best-designed dive boats in the area (it was custom built). A two-tank dive costs US$80.

It's easy to find places to rent snorkeling gear on the island's most popular beaches, if your hotel doesn't provide it. The snorkeling's great at Shoal Bay, Maundays Bay, Barnes Bay, Little Bay, and Road Bay.

TENNIS Most of the resorts have their own tennis courts (see "Accommodations," earlier in this chapter). **Malliouhana,** Meads Bay (© 264/497-6111), has a pro shop and four championship Laykold tennis courts. All courts are lit for night games.

6 Shopping

For serious shopping, it's best to take the ferry (see above) and visit the big stores in Marigot on French St. Martin. Little branch shops of some of the bigger stores are also found on Anguilla, but the better merchandise and the larger selection await you just a ferry boat ride away.

On Anguilla itself, the most fun shopping is at **World Art & Antiques Gallery,** Old Factory Plaza, The Valley (© 264/497-5950), where Nik and Christie Douglas have assembled a fascinating array of collectibles from around the world. Treasures include Chinese bronzes and jades, exotic jewelry, tribal and pre-Columbian sculptures and masks, and antiques and paintings.

What you can't get in St. Martin is local arts and crafts from Anguilla. The best of these are on display at the **Savannah Gallery,** Coronation Street, Lower Valley (© 264/497-2263), on the road to Crocus Bay, and the **Devonish Art Gallery,** West End Road (© 264/497-2949). Courtney Devonish is a well-known potter and sculptor. You can also preview original paintings by local artists at **Lobolly Gallery,** in Rose Cottage, Crocus Hill Road (© 264/497-6006).

7 Anguilla After Dark

Nightlife on Anguilla centers mainly on the various hotels, especially in winter, when they host barbecues, West Indian parties, and singers and other musicians. The hotels hire calypso combo groups and other bands, both local and imported.

Open-air **Johnno's Beach Bar,** Road Bay, Sandy Ground (© 264/497-2728), is a favorite of Hollywood types when they visit Anguilla. The club offers Beck's beer on the beach, barbecued spareribs, grilled chicken, and fresh fish for lunch and dinner. Live entertainment takes place Wednesday, Friday, and Saturday from 8pm to 1am. A weekly Sunday barbecue begins at noon, with live light jazz music starting mid-afternoon in winter. Try the Johnno special (similar to a piña colada, but made with rum and guava berries).

A restaurant-cum–beach bar, **Palm Grove Bar & Grill,** Junk's Hole Bay (© **264/497-4224**), offers a long stretch of uncrowded white sand and offshore reefs full of eels, squid, and manta rays. Nat Richardson, the owner, is waiting to boil or grill fresh-caught lobster, crayfish, or shrimp for you. *Bon Appétit* liked his johnnycakes so much it stole the recipe and published it. Hours are usually 11am to around 6:30pm daily, but can vary greatly depending on when the owner feels like getting there, and whenever clients decide to show up.

Pumphouse Bar & Grill, Sandy Ground (© 264/497-5154), is the island's latest hot spot, boasting 30 different rums. The food is good, too, served in a funky dining room with an uneven concrete slab floor that was originally designed as a repair station for heavy trucks. Standard but satisfying menu items include platters of fish or chicken, steaks, and a Caesar salad with slices of jerk chicken. Go any time from 5pm to 2am, except Sunday, when it's closed. Reggae lovers should show up on Wednesday, Friday, and Saturday nights; Thursday nights are often devoted to merengue.

There are some other little nighttime joints on island that seem to close with irritating irregularity. Most of these dives are active only on the weekend, including **Dune Preserve** at Rendezvous Bay (© **264/497-2660**), where the best known singer on island, "Bankie" Banx, performs. You might also check out another weekend hot spot, **Rafee's Back Street** at Sandy Ground (© **264/497-3918**), offering live music for dancing on Friday and Saturday nights, which are also the nights to hit **The Red Dragon Disco,** The Valley (© **264/497-2687**), a dance club where a DJ provides the music.

4

Antigua

Antiguans boast that they have a different beach for every day of the year. That may be an exaggeration, but the beaches here are certainly spectacular: Most are protected by coral reefs, and the sand is often sugar white.

Antigua, Barbuda, and Redonda form the independent nation of Antigua and Barbuda, within the Commonwealth of Nations. Redonda is an uninhabited rocky islet of less than a square mile, located 32km (20 miles) southwest of Antigua. Barbuda, which lies 42km (26 miles) to the north of Antigua, is covered at the end of this chapter.

Antigua (An-*tee*-gah) may be an independent nation, but it is still British in many of its traditions. Economically, it has transformed itself from a poverty-stricken island of sugar plantations to a modern-day vacation haven. The landscape of rolling, rustic Antigua is dotted with stone towers that were once sugar mills.

The inland scenery isn't as dramatic as what you'll find on St. Kitts, but, oh, those beaches! If you want high rises and glittering gambling and nightlife, head elsewhere, perhaps to Puerto Rico. Antigua does have some casinos, but they're hardly a reason to visit, and most of its hotels are intimate one- or two-story inns rather than glitzy, sprawling resorts. In general, the dining and shopping of Antigua are comparable to those of St. Kitts but don't hold up to those of St. Maarten or the U.S. Virgin Islands.

Most locals will treat you with respect if you show them respect, but Antigua is hardly the friendliest of islands in the Caribbean—too much unemployment, too great a gap between rich and poor.

Most hotels, restaurants, beach bars, and watersports facilities lie north of the capital of **St. John's,** in the northwest. St. John's is a large, neatly laid-out town 10km (6¼ miles) from the airport and less than a mile from Deep Water Harbour Terminal. This port city is the focal point of commerce and industry and the seat of government and shopping. Protected within a narrow bay, St. John's is charming, with cobblestone sidewalks and weather-beaten wooden houses with corrugated iron roofs and louvered Caribbean verandas. Trade winds keep the wide streets cool. Since all the major resorts are on good beaches, most visitors tend to stay put, going into St. John's for a day's shopping jaunt or to English Harbour for some history.

Before volcanic ash covered much of Antigua's neighbor, **Montserrat,** that little island was a destination in its own right. It was once a haven for many American expatriates, mostly retired couples, and at one time was the Caribbean island of choice for music stars like Paul McCartney, who came here to write and record songs.

Montserrat is slowly bouncing back, hoping to recapture the tourism it once enjoyed. Until the volcanic dust settles, however, it is most often visited as a day trip from Antigua, mainly by curiosity or adventure seekers.

1 Essentials

VISITOR INFORMATION

You can contact the **Antigua and Barbuda Department of Tourism** at 610 Fifth Ave., Suite 311, New York, NY 10020 (© 212/541-4117; www.antigua-barbuda.org); or 25 SE Second Ave., Suite 300, Miami, FL 33131 (© 305/381-6762). A toll-free number also gives information: © 888/268-4227. Operators are available Monday to Friday 9am to 5pm Eastern Standard Time.

In Canada, contact the **Antigua and Barbuda Department of Tourism and Trade,** 60 St. Clair Ave. E., Suite 304, Toronto, ON, M4T 1N5 (© 416/961-3085).

On the island, the **Antigua and Barbuda Department of Tourism,** on Friendly Alley in St. John's (© 268/462-0480), is open Monday to Thursday from 8am to 4:30pm and Friday from 8am to 3pm.

GETTING THERE

Before you book your airline ticket on your own, refer to the section "Packages for the Independent Traveler" in chapter 2. Even if you don't buy a package, take a look at the tips on getting the best airfare in the section "Getting There," in chapter 2.

The major airline that flies to Antigua's V. C. Bird Airport is **American Airlines** (© 800/433-7300 in the U.S.; www.aa.com), which offers four daily non-stop flights to Antigua from its hub in San Juan, Puerto Rico. A flight takes about 1½ hours, and each departs late enough in the day to allow easy transfers.

Continental (© 800/231-0856; www.continental.com) has daily flights out of Newark, New Jersey.

British Airways (© 800/247-9297 in the U.S.; www.britishairways.com) offers flights four times a week from London's Gatwick Airport.

Air Canada (© 888/247-2262; www.aircanada.ca) has regularly scheduled flights from Toronto to Antigua on Saturday or Sunday.

Air Jamaica (© 800/523-5585; www.airjamaica.com) offers three weekly direct flights from New York. For many people in the greater New York area, these are the most convenient flights.

BWIA (© 800/538-2942 in the U.S.; www.bwee.com) is increasingly popular. Each week, flights depart for Antigua—one from Toronto; three from Kingston, Jamaica; and two from London.

GETTING AROUND

BY TAXI Taxis meet every airplane, and drivers wait outside the major hotels. If you're going to spend a few days here, a particular driver may try to "adopt" you. The typical one-way fare from the airport to St. John's is US$15, but to English Harbour it's US$28 and up. The government of Antigua fixes rates, and taxis are meterless.

Fun Fact **Special Events**

The week before the first Tuesday in August, summer **Carnival** brings exotic costumes that recall Antiguans' African heritage. Festivities include a beauty competition, and calypso- and steel-band competitions. The big event in spring is **Sailing Week** in late April or early May.

Antigua

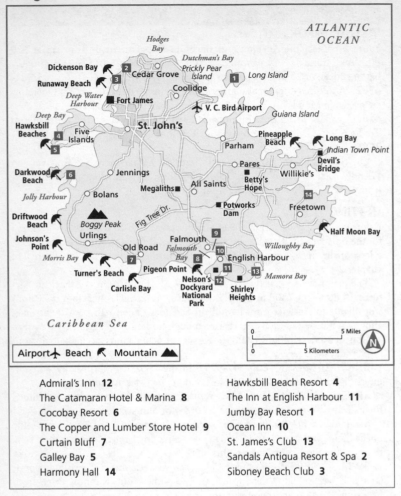

ATLANTIC OCEAN

Hodges Bay

Dutchman's Bay

Dickenson Bay **2** Cedar Grove Prickly Pear Island **1** Long Island

Runaway Beach **3** Coolidge

Deep Water Harbour Fort James

Deep Bay

Hawksbill Beaches **4** Five Islands

St. John's

V. C. Bird Airport

Guiana Island

Parham Pineapple Beach **Long Bay** Indian Town Point

Pares Devil's Bridge

Darkwood Beach **6** Jennings Betty's Hope Willikie's

Jolly Harbour Bolans Megaliths All Saints

Driftwood Beach

Johnson's Point

Boggy Peak Urlings

Fig Tree Dr.

Potworks Dam **14** Freetown

Half Moon Bay

Old Road Falmouth **9** Willoughby Bay

Morris Bay Falmouth Bay **10**

7 Pigeon Point **8** English Harbour

Turner's Beach **11**

Carlisle Bay Nelson's Dockyard National Park **12** Shirley Heights **13** Mamora Bay

Caribbean Sea

Airport ✈ Beach ⚓ Mountain ▲▲

0   5 Miles
0   5 Kilometers

N

Admiral's Inn **12**
The Catamaran Hotel & Marina **8**
Cocobay Resort **6**
The Copper and Lumber Store Hotel **9**
Curtain Bluff **7**
Galley Bay **5**
Harmony Hall **14**

Hawksbill Beach Resort **4**
The Inn at English Harbour **11**
Jumby Bay Resort **1**
Ocean Inn **10**
St. James's Club **13**
Sandals Antigua Resort & Spa **2**
Siboney Beach Club **3**

Taxis aren't cheap, but they're the best way to see Antigua, as the drivers also act as guides. Most taxi tours go from the St. John's area to English Harbour. Drivers generally charge US$45 for three or four passengers and often wait 30 minutes or more while you sightsee around English Harbour. If you split the cost with another couple, these tours become more affordable.

To call a taxi in St. John's, dial © **268/462-0711;** after 6pm, dial © **268/462-5190.**

BY RENTAL CAR   Renting a car on Antigua is not advisable. Newly arrived drivers quickly learn that the island's roads are terribly potholed and poorly signposted.

If you decide to drive despite these warnings, you must obtain an Antiguan license, which costs US$20 and requires a valid driver's license from home. Most car-rental firms can issue you an Antiguan license, which they usually do without a surcharge. *Remember:* Drive on the left.

It's best to stick with the major U.S. rental companies rather than use a local agency. **Avis** (© **800/331-1212** in the U.S., or 268/462-2840 in Antigua; www.avis.com) and **Hertz** (© **800/654-3131** in the U.S., or 268/462-6450 in Antigua; www.hertz.com) offer pickup service at the airport. Another agency to try is **Dollar** on Nevis Street, St. John's (© **800/800-4000** in the U.S., or 268/462-0362 in Antigua; www.dollarcar.com). **Budget** is also represented on Antigua with a kiosk at the airport (© **800/472-3325** in the U.S., or 268/462-3009 in Antigua; www.budgetrentacar.com).

BY BUS   Although buses are a cheap option, we don't recommend them for the average visitor. Service is erratic and undependable, and roads are impossibly bumpy. Buses are supposed to operate between St. John's and the villages daily from 5:30am to 6pm, but don't count on it. In St. John's, buses leave from two different "stations"—on Market Street, near the Central Market, and on Independence Avenue, adjacent to the Botanical Gardens. Most fares are US$1.

FAST FACTS: Antigua

Banks   Banks are usually open Monday to Thursday from 8am to 2pm and on Friday from 8am to 4pm. The best bank for visitors is Royal Bank at High and Market streets in St. John's (© **268/480-1150**). You'll find several ATMs here.

Currency   These islands use the **Eastern Caribbean dollar (EC$)**. Nearly all hotels bill in U.S. dollars, however, and only certain tiny restaurants present their prices in EC$. When you inquire about a price, make sure you know the type of dollars quoted. The EC dollar is worth about 37¢ in U.S. currency (EC$2.70 = US$1). *Unless otherwise specified, rates in this chapter are quoted in U.S. dollars.*

Customs   Arriving visitors are allowed to bring in 200 cigarettes, 1 quart of liquor, and 6 ounces of perfume.

Documents   A valid passport is preferred from U.S., British, and Canadian nationals. An original birth certificate accompanied by a photo ID that's issued by a government agency is also acceptable, but we recommend that you carry a passport when visiting a foreign country. All arriving visitors must have a departing ticket.

Electricity   Most of the island's electricity is 220-volt AC (60 cycles), which means that U.S. appliances require transformers. The Hodges Bay area and some hotels, however, are supplied with 110-volt AC (60 cycles).

Emergencies   In an emergency, contact the police (© **268/462-0125**), the fire department (© **268/462-0044**), or an ambulance (© **268/462-0251**). You can also call © **911** or © **999** for any type of emergency.

Hospital   The principal medical facility on Antigua is **Holberton Hospital,** on Hospital Road, St. John's (© **268/462-0251**).

Language   The official language is English.

Liquor Laws   Beer and liquor are sold in many stores, 7 days a week. It's legal to have an open container on the beach.

Safety Antigua is generally safe, but that doesn't mean you should wander alone at night on St. John's near-deserted streets. Don't leave valuables unguarded on the beach, either.

Taxes & Service Charges Visitors must pay a departure tax of US$20 and an 8.5% government tax on hotel bills. Most hotels also add a service charge of between 10% and 15%.

Telephone Telephone calls can be made from hotels or the office of Cable & Wireless, on Long Street, in St. John's (© 268/462-0840). You can also send faxes and telegrams from Cable & Wireless. To call Antigua from the United States, dial 1268, and then the number. To call the United States from Antigua, dial 1, the area code, and then the number. You might want to purchase a phone card, which you can use to connect with an American long-distance company. You can access **AT&T Direct** from some pay phones and some hotels by dialing © 800/872-2881. You can reach **MCI** at © 800/888-8000 and **Sprint** at © 800/366-4643.

Time Antigua is on Atlantic Standard Time year-round, so it's 1 hour ahead of U.S. Eastern Standard Time (EST). When daylight savings time takes over in the U.S., then Antigua's time is the same as the eastern United States.

Water Tap water is generally safe to drink here, but many visitors prefer to drink only bottled water.

Weather The average year-round temperature ranges from 75°F to 85°F (24°C–29°C).

2 Accommodations

Antigua's hotels are generally small, and many are closed during the summer. Owners may decide to shut down early if business isn't good. Air-conditioning is uncommon except in first-class hotels, so be warned: Antigua at midday can be quite steamy and uncomfortable.

An 8.5% government tax and a service charge of between 10% and 15%, depending on your hotel, are added to your hotel bill, which makes quite a difference in your final tab.

Antigua has lots of shockingly expensive hotels and resorts, but there are ways you can bring down the prices. Consider booking a package if you're interested in one of those pricey places. Refer to the section "Packages for the Independent Traveler," in chapter 2.

Because getting around the island is difficult, your choice of where to stay is crucial (the hotels are all plotted on the island map on p. 78). Those who prefer high winds, breaking waves, and dramatic scenery should stay on the northwest side, north of the capital of St. John's. This is an area of middle-bracket resorts such as Sandals. If you want to spend most of your vacation at one resort, venturing out only occasionally, and can afford it, try one of the superexclusives such as Curtain Bluff or St. James's Club in the remote southern coast. History buffs who like atmospheric B&Bs should try either Admiral's Inn or the Inn at English Harbour, unless a good beach is crucial. If it is, then head for one of the big resorts, all of which are on sandy beaches.

In addition to the choices listed in this section, Chez Pascal (see "Dining," later in this chapter) also offers accommodations.

VERY EXPENSIVE

Curtain Bluff ⭐⭐⭐   This serene oasis is the island's premier resort, with a price tag to match. The place has such ambience and class, it makes St. James's Club (see below) look like a glorified Holiday Inn. Twenty-four kilometers (15 miles) from the airport on the southwest shore, the hotel occupies the most lushly tropical section of the island, in the village of Old Road, and sits on two beautiful beaches (one turbulent, the other calm). This place is for a mature old-money crowd, who like the clubby feel and the good service.

The beautifully furnished accommodations include deluxe units with king-size beds; a terrace room with a king-size, four-poster bed; and spacious suites with two balconies. The roomy bathrooms have beautiful tiles, deluxe toiletries, tubs and showers, dual vanities, and bidets. Accommodations in the newer units are more spacious, with upgraded furnishings and two double beds. The two-story suites are among the most luxurious in the Caribbean. Although at times in the midday heat you may wish for air-conditioning, ceiling fans and trade winds generally keep the rooms cool. Some guests come primarily for the superb food. French-born Christophe Blatz keeps his Continental menu limited, so he can freshly prepare and artistically arrange everything. Curtain Bluff restaurant boasts the Caribbean's most extensive wine selection. Although it's not a requirement, men are encouraged to wear jackets during the dinner hour in high season.

Morris Bay (P.O. Box 288), Antigua, W.I. © 888/289-9898 in the U.S., or 268/462-8400. Fax 268/462-8409. www.curtainbluff.com. 72 units. Dec 19–Apr 14 US$850–US$925 double, from US$1,050 suite; Apr 15–May 14 and Oct 12–Dec 18 US$595–US$725 double, from US$795 suite; May 15 to mid-July US$495–US$595 double, from US$695 suite. Extra person US$180 Dec–Apr; US$160 Apr–May. Rates are all-inclusive. AE, DISC, MC, V. Closed mid-July to Oct 11. **Amenities:** 2 restaurants; 2 bars; outdoor pool; putting green; 4 tennis courts; squash court; fitness center; aerobics; yoga; sauna (in suites); deep-sea fishing; dive shop; kayaks; sailing; scuba diving; snorkeling; water-skiing; windsurfing; concierge; access to computer facilities; room service (8am–11pm); massage; babysitting; laundry service; dry cleaning. *In room:* Ceiling fan, dataport, safe.

Galley Bay ⭐⭐   This is still the best place to chill out in luxury, even after being taken over by Elite Island resorts and turned into an all-inclusive. It has none of that toga-party hysteria associated by such lesser all-inclusives as Sandals. Though Greta Garbo (or her modern-day equivalent) is no longer photographed topless on the hotel beach, the resort still has an aura of exclusivity. The Gauguin-inspired Tahitian-style rentals are laid back, but classically elegant. These intimate rooms open onto 16 secluded hectares (40 acres) of beachfront gardens, a bird sanctuary, and a lagoon, with the biggest draw, of course, being 1.2km (¾ mile) of white-sand beach. Choose among beachfront bungalows, the more romantic Gauguin rondavels (tiki-like huts) with thatch roofs, or deluxe accommodations and suites in the newer two-story wings. The Italian marble bathrooms with shower are part of the allure. Dining is among the best on the island either in the Sea Grape or the Gauguin Restaurant, the latter more intimate and casual, located at the beach.

Five Islands (P.O. Box 305), St. John's, Antigua, W.I. © 800/345-0356 or 268/462-0302. Fax 268/462-4551. www.eliteislandresorts.com. 70 units. Winter US$700–US$850 double, US$900 suite; off season US$600–US$750 double, US$800 suite. Rates are all-inclusive. AE, DISC, MC, V. Children under 16 not allowed. **Amenities:** 2 restaurants; 3 bars; outdoor pool; tennis court; gym; fitness center; kayaks; sailing; scuba diving; snorkeling; windsurfing; game room; limited room service; laundry service; dry cleaning; rooms for those with limited mobility. *In room:* A/C, TV, dataport, minifridge, beverage maker, hair dryer, safe.

Jumby Bay Resort ★★★   This sybaritic retreat of the rich and famous has a celebrity-and-CEO crowd that can afford its expensive rates. It occupies a 132-hectare (326-acre) offshore island. Boats depart from the Antiguan "mainland" every hour from 7am to midnight daily. You can preregister for the 3km (2-mile) ride on the Antiguan side. With secluded white-sand beaches along a coastline protected by coral reefs, the grounds have been handsomely planted with loblolly and white cedar.

Guests are coddled and pampered in a luxury topped only by Curtain Bluff. A haven for naturalists, the resort features Pasture Bay Beach on the island's windward side, home to endangered species of turtles, rare birds, and sheep. All the accommodations are recently refurbished, including a 12-unit Mediter-ranean-style complex, two- and three-bedroom luxury villas, and several spa-cious private manor houses. Beds are luxurious, as are the spacious marble-and-tile bathrooms with tubs. Only the bedrooms within the suites are air-conditioned. In light of the constant trade winds, no one seems to mind.

For breakfast and lunch, it's casual fare at the open-air Beach Pavilion. Din-ner 5 nights a week is at the Veranda Restaurant, the signature restaurant in the 230-year-old English plantation manor. Dinner Sunday night is an upscale beachfront barbecue. Imaginative and well-prepared dishes are inspired by Europe, America, and the Caribbean.

Long Island (P.O. Box 243), St. John's, Antigua, W.I. © 800/421-9016 or 268/462-6000. Fax 268/462-6020. www.jumbybayresort.com. 48 units. Winter US$1,050–US$1,250 junior suite, US$1,450 suite, US$2,800 2-bedroom villa, US$3,260 3-bedroom villa; off season US$700–US$950 junior suite, US$1,200 suite, US$1,500 2-bedroom villa, US$2,250 3-bedroom villa. AE, DC, MC, V. **Amenities:** 2 restaurants; 3 bars; golf arranged; 3 tennis courts; fitness center; snorkeling; Sunfish sailboats; water-skiing; windsurfing; bicycles; concierge; room service (7am–10pm). *In room:* A/C, ceiling fan, dataport, kitchenette, minibar, beverage maker, hair dryer, iron/ironing board, safe.

St. James's Club ★★   This remote, 40-hectare (99-acre) resort on Mamora Bay on two sand beaches tries for glamour, but it falls far behind Curtain Bluff and Jumby Bay, and it doesn't have the state-of-the-art maintenance of those properties, either. (To be fair, although it's very expensive, at least it hasn't jacked up its prices to the shocking levels of those two places.) Midrange package tours from Britain and America continue to fill many of the rooms on occasions. The sports facilities are among the Caribbean's best.

Some of the rooms are standard and medium-size, but others are spacious. The resort has never been able to escape the architectural curse of its former exis-tence as a somewhat banal-looking Holiday Inn. Despite that, all units have excellent beds, combination bathrooms (tub and shower), commodious vanities, dual basins, and sliding-glass doors that open onto private balconies or patios. Pricey two-bedroom villas and hillside homes are also available.

If you're looking into a package all-inclusive deal, be aware that the cuisine is merely average. You can relax in the Rainbow Garden Dining Room, or dine alfresco by candlelight at the Docksider Restaurant overlooking Mamora Bay. Piccolo Mondo serves Italian and international food, and simple lunches are available at the Coco Beach Barbecue. Sometimes the setting is more exciting than the cuisine. Guests can top off the evening at the Jacaranda nightclub. Many enjoy gambling in the glamorous but small European-style casino.

Mamora Bay (P.O. Box 63), St. John's, Antigua, W.I. © 800/345-0356 in the U.S., or 268/460-5000. Fax 268/460-3015. www.eliteislandresorts.com. 105 units, 73 villas. Winter US$330–US$370 double, US$540 suite, from US$740 villa for 2; off season US$250–US$290 double, US$460 suite, from US$660 villa for 2. Children age 2 and under stay free in parent's room. AE, DISC, MC, V. **Amenities:** 4 restaurants; 4 bars;

3 outdoor pools; casino; disco; 7 tennis courts; exercise room; spa facilities, Jacuzzi; sauna; aqua bikes; deep-sea fishing; marina; sailboards; scuba diving; snorkeling; water-skiing; playground and playhouse for children; salon; room service (7am–11pm); massage; babysitting; laundry service; dry cleaning; nonsmoking rooms; 1 room for those with limited mobility. *In room:* A/C, ceiling fan, TV, dataport, beverage maker, hair dryer, safe.

Sandals Antigua Resort & Spa $\mathcal{R}$ For straight couples—all others are denied admittance—this is the best all-inclusive on the island. If you like a resort where everything's paid in advance and you virtually live in a walled compound with lots of organized activities, this might be for you, providing you meet the sexual orientation criterion. On one of the island's best beaches, the resort offers eight different room categories, most of which are medium-size. Some of the more romantic ones offer four-poster beds and ocean views. Typical amenities include small patios and plush mattresses. If you want honeymoon privacy, opt for a cottage suite (because of its octagonal shape, the staff calls it a rondavel) opening directly onto Dickenson Beach.

A quintet of bars and restaurants serve everything from Tex-Mex to sushi. Il Palio's Italian specialties are particularly good, and the beachfront restaurant is another an excellent spot for meals.

Dickenson Bay (P.O. Box 147), St. John's, Antigua, W.I. $\mathcal{C}$ **888-SANDALS** or 268/462-0267. Fax 268/462-4135. www.sandals.com. 193 units. Winter US$650–US$750 double, from US$1,090 rondavel suite; off season US$610–US$720 double, from US$1,090 rondavel suite. Rates are all-inclusive. AE, DC, MC, V. **Amenities:** 4 restaurants; 5 bars; 5 outdoor pools; lit tennis courts; fitness center; spa (spa services not included in all-inclusive rate); 5 whirlpools; watersports. *In room:* A/C, TV, dataport, hair dryer, beverage maker, iron/ironing board, safe.

EXPENSIVE

Cocobay Resort $\mathcal{R}$ Set near three beaches, this hillside compound of color-ful wood-sided, tin-roofed cottages lies on 4 headland hectares (10 acres). When this all-inclusive opened in 2000, it gave Sandals some real competition. Under-stated elegance and West Indian charm combine in this cliffside setting on the "sunset side" of the island.

Accommodations are unpretentious, modeled on local architecture raised on stilts, with hand-carved furnishings and island art providing both comfort and color. It attracts a hip clientele who'd never patronize one of the stuffier resorts like Curtain Bluff. Guests stay in cottages or in one of four "plantation houses," suitable for up to four occupants, on the hill. Each cottage has a four-poster king-size bed, a private porch, and wooden louvered windows, plus a bathroom with a shower. Bathrooms in the plantation house have full-size tubs.

Valley Church (P.O. Box 431), St. John's, Antigua, W.I. $\mathcal{C}$ **800/816-7587** in the U.S., or 268/562-2400. Fax 268/562-2424. www.cocobayresort.com. 55 units. Winter US$160–US$190 per person double, US$820 plan-tation house for 4; off season US$130–US$160 per person double, US$690 plantation house for 4. Rates include all meals and watersports. AE, MC, V. **Amenities:** 2 restaurants; 2 bars; outdoor pool; gym; spa; kayaks; snorkeling; massage; babysitting; laundry service; dry cleaning; nonsmoking rooms. *In room:* Ceiling fan, dataport, fridge, beverage maker, hair dryer, safe, no phone.

The Copper and Lumber Store Hotel $\mathcal{R}$ Forget a pool. Forget a beach. This is the "museum hotel" of English Harbour, with more atmosphere than even The Inn at English Harbour and Admiral's Inn (see below). As its name suggests, this charming, 18th-century building was originally a store that sold wood and copper for repairing British sailing ships. The store and its adjacent harbor structures are built of brick that once was used as ships' ballast. Each of the period units is brick-lined, uniquely designed, and filled with fine Chippen-dale and Queen Anne reproductions, antiques, brass chandeliers, hardwood paneling, and hand-stenciled floors. The showers look as if they belong in a sailing vessel, with thick mahogany panels and polished brass fittings. All suites have kitchens with aging equipment, private bathrooms (with showers only), and ceiling fans. All the mattresses are first rate. The downside is the stream of visitors who view it as a museum rather than an inn. Although the English expatriates who founded the hotel in the 1980s did so with great imagination, today the Antiguan government runs it with less flair.

A traditional English pub serves standard food daily, and the Wardroom serves a stolid Continental dinner nightly. You may want to skip both of these for fish and chips and Bass on tap at the jumping **Mainbrace Pub** next door.

Nelson's Dockyard, English Harbour (P.O. Box 184), St. John's, Antigua, W.I. ℂ 268/460-1058. Fax 268/460-1529. www.copperlumberantigua.com. 14 units. Winter US$195–US$325 double, US$325 suite; off season US$135–US$195 double, US$275 suite. AE, MC, V. From St. John's, follow the signs southeast to English Harbour. **Amenities:** Restaurant; pub; ferry service to Galleon Beach; babysitting; laundry service; dry cleaning. In room: A/C, kitchen, beverage maker, hair dryer, iron/ironing board.

Hawksbill Beach Resort 🏖 *Kids*   Named after an offshore rock that resembles a hawksbill turtle, this 15-hectare (37-acre) all-inclusive resort is 16km (10 miles) west of the airport and 6km (3¾ miles) southwest of St. John's. Set on four beaches (one reserved for those who want to go home sans tan lines), it caters to active types and is popular for weddings and honeymoons. This resort caters to families and happy couples who like its informality and might feel uncomfortable in the atmosphere of pretension and social climbing that you get at Curtain Bluff. The hotel revolves around an open-air, breezy central core. Bedrooms are small and comfortably furnished, with tubs and showers. The least expensive accommodations open onto a garden; there are more secluded beachfront units available as well. The West Indian great house has three bedrooms for three to six occupants, with king-size beds and kitchenettes. *Note:* Rooms have neither TVs nor air-conditioning here. It's usually lively at this resort, with live music 3 nights a week in season.

Five Islands Village (P.O. Box 108), St. John's, Antigua, W.I. ℂ 800/223-6510 in the U.S., or 268/462-0301. Fax 268/462-1515. www.hawksbill.com. 111 units. Winter US$300–US$470 double, US$1,800 great house; off season US$265–US$345 double, US$1,300 great house. Rates are all-inclusive. AE, MC, V. **Amenities:** 2 restaurants; 2 bars; tennis court; snorkeling; Sunfish sailboats; water-skiing; windsurfing; nonsmoking rooms. In room: Ceiling fan, dataport, beverage maker, iron/ironing board, safe.

The Inn at English Harbour 🏖   This small, recently renovated inn occupies one of the finest sites on Antigua, 4 hectares (10 acres) that directly flank a beach, with views over Nelson's Dockyard and English Harbour. Better run than its closest competitor, the Copper and Lumber Store Hotel (see above), more elegant than nearby Admiral's Inn (see below), The Inn at English Harbour is tranquil and informal, very unpretentious. "We don't put on airs here," one staffer said, "unlike those other posh places." This charming old-fashioned resort has an historic feel that remains appealing despite the more glamorous places elsewhere on the island. The late actor Richard Burton liked it so well he spent two of his honeymoons here. You can take a free water taxi to finer beaches along English Harbour. White-tile floors, screened plantation shutters, balconies, and excellent beds invite you to linger. The least expensive units are farthest from the beach, on a hillside. In 2002, management added six suites decorated with a scattering of British and Caribbean antiques.

The inn is known for high-quality cooking. Lunch is served both at the beach house and in the main dining room. Have a drink before dinner in the old-style English Bar with stone walls and low overhead beams. Live entertainment is provided in winter.

English Harbour (P.O. Box 187), St. John's, Antigua, W.I. ℂ 268/460-1014 or 268/460-2602. Fax 268/460-1603. www.theinn.ag. 34 units. Nov–Jan 3 US$161–US$405 double, US$193–US$590 suite; Jan 4–Oct US$149–US$260 double, US$236–US$378 suite. MAP (breakfast and dinner) US$49 per person extra. AE, MC, V. From St. John's, head south, through All Saints and Liberta, until you reach the south coast. **Amenities:** 2 restaurants; 2 bars; pool; golf; tennis courts nearby; health club; day sailing; deep-sea fishing; scuba diving; water-skiing; bike rental; horseback riding; car rental; water taxi to Nelson's Dockyard; room service (7am–10pm); babysitting; laundry. *In room:* Ceiling fan, minibar, fridge, beverage maker, hair dryer, safe.

Siboney Beach Club ☆   Owned by Aussie Tony Johnson and his wife, Ann, the Siboney Beach Club is named for the Amerindian tribe who predated the Arawaks. Set north of St. John's on .4 hectares (1 acre) of thickly foliated land fronting the 1.6km-long (1 mile) white-sand beach of Dickenson Bay, the resort is shielded on the inland side by a tall, verdant hedge. The club's social center is the Coconut Grove restaurant (see "Dining," below). The comfortable suites are in a three-story balconied building draped with bougainvillea and other vines. The suites have louvered windows for natural ventilation, and TVs are available. All units have separate bedrooms, living rooms, and balconies or patios, plus tiny kitchens behind moveable shutters. Each comes with a small, immaculately kept private bathroom with shower. There's also a tree house: a single room with a king-size bed and jungle decor perched high in a *Ficus benjamina* tree.

Dickenson Bay (P.O. Box 222), St. John's, Antigua, W.I. ℂ 800/533-0234 in the U.S., or 268/462-0806. Fax 268/462-3356. www.siboneybeachclub.com. 12 suites. Winter US$170–US$310 double; off season US$130–US$180 double. AE, MC, V. **Amenities:** Restaurant; bar; outdoor pool; babysitting; laundry service; dry cleaning. *In room:* TV (on request), A/C, kitchenette, beverage maker, hair dryer, iron/ironing board, safe.

MODERATE

Admiral's Inn ☆☆   Though down in third position when stacked against its competitors, The Inn at English Harbour and the Copper and Lumber Store Hotel (see above), this place is full of character and atmosphere. Designed in 1785, the year Nelson sailed into the harbor as captain of the HMS *Boreas,* and completed in 1788, the building here once housed British officers stationed at the dockyards, with its ground floor devoted to the storage of tar and boat-repair supplies. Loaded with West Indian charm, this place in the heart of Nelson's Dockyard is constructed of weathered brick that was brought from England to be used as ships' ballast. Stay here if you want to experience Caribbean history, especially if you're an Anglophile and don't mind commuting to the beach.

There are three types of accommodations. The most expensive are the ground-floor rooms of a tiny brick building across the courtyard from the main structure. Each of these spacious units has a little patio, a garden entry, and air-conditioning. The front rooms on the first floor of the main building, with views of the lawn and harbor, are also more expensive. The back rooms on this floor are less pricey, and all have air-conditioning. With dormer-window views over the yacht-filled harbor, the least expensive rooms on the top floor are smaller and quiet, but they can get warm on summer afternoons. Not all rooms have air-conditioning.

For details on the inn's restaurant, see "Dining," below.

English Harbour (P.O. Box 713), St. John's, Antigua, W.I. ℂ 800/223-5695 in the U.S., or 268/460-1027. Fax 268/460-1534. www.admiralsantigua.com. 14 units. Winter US$130–US$160 double, US$400 apt for 4; off season US$90–US$110 double, US$250 apt for 4. US$25 per extra person. MAP (breakfast and dinner) US$48 per person extra. AE, MC, V. Closed Sept to mid-Oct. Take the road southeast from St. John's, following the signs to English Harbour. **Amenities:** Restaurant; bar; snorkeling; free transport to beaches; room service (7:30am–9pm); laundry service; dry cleaning. *In room:* A/C (in most), ceiling fan, phone (in some).

Harmony Hall ⬧ *Finds*   This is about the only accommodation in Antigua that could qualify as a little plantation inn so common on many other islands. This art gallery and restaurant cum hotel was constructed around a long-ago sugar mill. In addition to buying arts and crafts here, or stopping off for lunch, you can also spend the night. Standing on 2.6 hectares (6½ acres) of land, Harmony Hall opens onto Brown's Bay, part of the greater body of water, Nonsuch Bay. It is secluded and tranquil. Its Neapolitan owners have restored two separate villas, carving each into six large bedrooms with high ceilings and installing Italian marble and tiles for the bathrooms. It's not on the beach, but some good sands are just down the hill and there's also an on-site swimming pool. Complimentary boat trips are arranged to the uninhabited Green Island, with its lovely beaches and idyllic snorkeling conditions.

Brown's Bay Mill (P.O. Box 1558, St. John's), near Freetown, Antigua, W.I. ☏ 268/460-4120. Fax 268/460-4406. www.harmonyhall.com. 12 units. US$165 double. Rates include breakfast. AE, DISC, MC, V. Closed mid-May to Nov. **Amenities:** Restaurant (lunch daily, dinner Fri–Sat); bar; outdoor pool; tennis court; room service (dinner only, Fri–Sat); babysitting; laundry service. *In room:* Ceiling fan, minibar, beverage maker, safe.

INEXPENSIVE

The Catamaran Hotel & Marina   A favorite since the 1970s, the Catamaran opens onto a palm-lined beach at Falmouth Harbour, a 3km (2-mile) drive from English Harbour. When we first discovered the property years ago, a film crew had taken it over to make a movie about pirates of the West Indies. The management had to post a sign: TODAY'S "PIRATES" MUST WEAR BATHING SUITS ON THE BEACH. It's not as wild around here anymore, and peace, tranquillity, and lots of bougainvillea plants prevail. There's an Internet cafe inside the hotel where you can rent computers for US$30 for the first hour, US$10 each additional hour.

On the second floor, each of eight self-contained, motel-style rooms has a comfortable bed (in many cases, a four-poster), a queen-size mattress, and a balcony overlooking the water. The Captain's Cabin is the most luxurious. The ground-floor rooms are small but comfortable. Additional units are within a waterside annex. All but two of the units have kitchens, and each is furnished with a tiled, shower-only bathroom.

Boaters will like the hotel's location at the 30-slip Catamaran Marina. You can purchase supplies at a nearby grocery store.

Falmouth Harbour (P.O. Box 958), St. John's, Antigua, W.I. ☏ 268/460-1036. Fax 268/460-1339. www.catamaran-antigua.com. 14 units. Winter US$105–US$140 double, Captain's Cabin US$165; off season US$70–US$95 double, Captain's Cabin US$135. Extra person US$25. Children under 10 stay free in parent's room. DISC, MC, V. **Amenities:** 2 restaurants; bar; sport-fishing; Internet cafe; babysitting; laundry service; dry cleaning. *In room:* A/C (in 2 units), ceiling fan, kitchenette (in most), beverage maker, hair dryer, safe, no phone (but prepaid cellphones can be rented).

Ocean Inn ⬧⬧ *Finds*   This is Antigua's premier B&B, just a 10-minute walk from some golden sandy beaches. It's a special place, with the coziest and most homelike decor on the island, the ambience created by its friendly owners, Sandra and Eustace Potter, who are on-site to welcome you. Accommodations are divided between units in the main building or in one of the cottages on the grounds, each coming with a little deck opening onto the marina. Most rooms are equipped with a small, tiled bathroom with shower, and everything is beautifully kept. The garden of the hotel overlooks the historic dockyard. Guests share the communal swimming pool, or meet for drinks in the Tree Trunk Bar. The most popular night here is Thursday, when there's an open-air barbecue. This is a delightful place to stay in Antigua if you enjoy B&Bs.

P.O. Box 838, English Harbour, Antigua, W.I. © **888/686-8913** or 268/463-7950. Fax 268/460-1263. www. theoceaninn.com. 14 units, 10 with bathroom. Year-round US$60 double without bathroom, US$90–US$150 double in bungalow; winter US$95 cottage or suite, off season US$75 cottage or suite. Rates include continental breakfast. AE, MC, V. **Amenities:** Restaurant (lunch only); bar; outdoor pool; exercise room; babysitting; laundry service; dry cleaning. *In room:* A/C, TV (in most), beverage maker, hair dryer, iron/ironing board, safe, no phone.

3 Dining

Although the Eastern Caribbean dollar (EC$) is used on these islands, only certain tiny restaurants present their prices in the local currency. When you inquire about a price, make sure you know which type of dollars is being quoted. Unless otherwise specified, rates quoted in this section are given in U.S. dollars.

IN ST. JOHN'S

Big Banana-Pizzas in Paradise *✦* PIZZA/SUBS/SALADS   In former slave quarters, this place serves up some of the best pizza and grilled chicken sandwiches in the eastern Caribbean. It stands amid the most stylish shopping and dining emporiums in town, a few steps from the Heritage Quay Jetty. The frothy drinks, coconut or banana crush, are practically desserts. You can also order overstuffed baked potatoes and fresh-fruit or lobster salad. On Thursday a reggae band entertains from 9pm to 1am.

Redcliffe Quay, St. John's. © **268/480-6986.** Pizzas, sandwiches, and salads US$4–US$15. AE, MC, V. Mon–Sat 8am–11:30pm.

Papa Zouk *(Finds* SEAFOOD   If you like seafood, *zouk* (French Creole music), and rum, you've come to the right place. Run by two lively German brothers known only as Bert and Peter, this dive is known for its extensive collection of rums. Its signature tropical fruit drink is called Ti-punch, and is well worth a try. Against a backdrop of constantly playing *zouk* music, you can have a New Orleans–type Creole party in the Caribbean. To start with, try the stuffed clams baked with cheese or a selection of tapas. For dinner, you might try their savory bouillabaisse or a delectable pan-fried red snapper. The house special is the Carnival Platter, a medley of seafood such as mussels, scallops, and shrimp. The service is among the friendliest in town.

Hilda Davis Dr., St. John's. © **268/464-7576.** Reservations recommended. Main courses US$12–US$20. No credit cards. Mon–Sat 7–10pm.

ELSEWHERE AROUND THE ISLAND

Admiral's Inn *✦* AMERICAN/CREOLE   Enjoy lobster, seafood, and steaks in this 17th-century hotel (see "Accommodations," above), and make sure to try our favorite appetizer, the pumpkin soup. The chefs use quality ingredients to create four or five main courses daily. Though the atmosphere is sometimes more exciting than the cuisine, the service is agreeable. Before dinner, order a drink in the bar and read the names of sailors carved into the wood 100 years ago.

In Nelson's Dockyard, English Harbour. © **268/460-1027.** Reservations recommended, especially for dinner in high season. Lunch main courses US$10–US$20; dinner main courses US$20–US$33. AE, MC, V. Daily 7:30am–11pm. Closed Sept to mid-Oct.

Alberto's *✦* INTERNATIONAL   One of the most stylish and cosmopolitan restaurants on Antigua is Alberto's, the creative statement of Venice-born Alberto Ravanello and his English wife, Vanessa, who prepares much of the food herself. You'll find it close to the edge of the sea, near the St. James's Club, in an open-sided pavilion lavishly draped with bougainvillea. The owners' frequent travels have inspired the menu's satisfying medley of Italian, French, and Continental dishes. The best dishes include ravioli stuffed either with pulverized asparagus and shrimp, or with mascarpone cheese and sage-flavored butter; a zesty pasta with fresh local clams; savory stuffed crabs; and one of our favorites, fresh wahoo steak with a sautéed onion, garlic, and rosemary sauce. Lobster, a favorite here, is boiled in seawater, then grilled and served simply, usually with garlic-flavored butter. It's lip-smacking good, but pricey.

Willoughby Bay. ℂ 268/460-3007. Reservations recommended. Main courses US$20–US$35. AE, MC, V. Tues–Sun 7–10pm. Closed May–Nov.

Bay House INTERNATIONAL   This is the charming and intimate dining room associated with a 45-unit family-owned hotel set in a garden on a hillside, a 10-minute walk uphill from the beach at Dickenson Bay. Surrounded by lattices and potted plants in the open-sided dining room, you'll enjoy westward-facing views sweeping out over the hillside and down to the jagged coastline—genuinely fabulous at sunset. Lunch consists of simple salads, stuffed baguette sandwiches, and grills. The kitchen's culinary flair is more obvious at nighttime, when meals might begin with a salad of baby shrimp with grapefruit segments and truffle oil, or fresh chicken livers flambéed with brandy and served with shallots. Main dinner courses feature grilled fish; fresh local lobster that's either grilled and served with lime-and-garlic sauce, or prepared thermidor style. Steaks are served in a light soy sauce with braised Chinese cabbage. For vegetarians there's a platter piled high with grilled Provençal vegetables and served with mixed salads. The most popular dessert is an Antiguan pineapple flambéed in rum and served with rum-raisin ice cream.

In the Tradewinds Hotel, Dickenson Bay. ℂ 268/462-1223. Reservations recommended. Lunch main courses US$8–US$26; dinner main courses US$15–US$35. AE, MC, V. Daily noon–5pm and 7–11pm.

Chez Pascal ⓡ FRENCH   This Gallic-inspired bistro is like a small corner of France in Antigua—except here its gardens bloom with tropical vegetation. On the west coast of the island atop a hilly plateau, near the Royal Antiguan and Galley Bay Hotels, it features well-prepared cuisine, served on an open-air terrace around an illuminated swimming pool.

French colonial trappings include copper pots, rough-textured ceramics, dark-stained wicker and rattan, and tropically inspired fabric designs. The chef, Pascal Milliat, inherited generations of cooking skills in his former home, Lyon. Assisted by his Brittany-born wife, Florence, he prepares and serves classic French dishes with sublime sauces and seasonings. Fine cookery showcases a chicken-liver mousse with basil-flavored butter sauce, lobster bisque en croûte, sea scallops on a bed of leeks, roasted rack of lamb with *herbes de Provence* (prepared for only two diners at a time), and grouper with beurre blanc sauce.

On the premises are four very large bedrooms. Each unit has a whirlpool tub, air-conditioning, fridge, rattan furniture, sea views, and color schemes influenced by the sand and sky. With breakfast included, singles or doubles range from US$140 in low season and from US$210 in winter.

Galley Bay Hill, Five Islands. ℂ 268/462-3232. Reservations recommended. Main courses US$20–US$30. AE, DC, MC, V. Daily 11:30am–3pm and 6–11pm. Closed Sept.

Coconut Grove ⓡ INTERNATIONAL/SEAFOOD   North of St. John's in a coconut grove right on the beach, simple tables on a flagstone floor beneath a thatch roof are cooled by sea breezes. This is every visitor's dream of what a Caribbean restaurant should be. And it's one of the island's best. Soup is prepared fresh daily from local ingredients like ginger, carrot, and pumpkin. Lobster and shrimp dishes figure prominently, along with a catch of the day and a daily vegetarian special. Lunch fare is lighter. During happy hour at the bar (4–7pm), all drinks are half price.

In the Siboney Beach Club, Dickenson Bay. ✆ 268/462-1538. Reservations required for dinner. Lunch main courses US$12–US$23; dinner main courses US$20–US$30. AE, MC, V. Daily 7:30am–11:30pm.

Coco's CARIBBEAN/INTERNATIONAL   If you opt to dine here, the loudest noise you'll hear—other than the clinking of porcelain and glassware—is the sound of the splashing waves. That's because part of the restaurant is built on pilings sunk into the beachfront, granting diners an unimpeded view over the Caribbean and Antigua's westward-facing headlands, including Indian Mountain. Because it's within an all-inclusive resort, management urges diners who aren't staying within the hotel to phone in advance of their arrival. Once you get here, you'll dine at tables sheathed in azure-colored tiles. Lunches are simpler than dinners, focusing on salads, burgers, sandwiches, and pastas. The best dinner items are usually the grilled catch of the day, marinated and covered with butter. Also recommended is grilled mahimahi prepared in puff pastry like a beef Wellington and served with a slow-simmered Creole sauce of fresh tomatoes, sweet garden peppers, and onions.

Mount Prospect, Jolly Bay. ✆ 268/462-9700. Reservations required. Lunch main courses US$6–US$12; dinner main courses US$13–US$28. AE, DC, MC, V. Daily noon–2:30pm and 7–10:30pm.

Le Bistro ⚐ FRENCH   Less than a kilometer (½ mile) inland from the coast of Hodges Bay, this restaurant occupies a stone-sided structure built as a clubhouse for a now-defunct golf course. Sporting informal charm, it's Antigua's oldest continuously operated restaurant (since 1981). The owners are English-born Philippa Esposito and her husband, Raffaele, from Capri. Perfectly prepared with a dash of flair are such appetizers as grilled calamari salad with shrimp in a balsamic vinaigrette or spinach salad with sautéed portobello mushrooms with tomato and strips of mozzarella. The chef takes justifiable pride in such dishes as fresh blackened salmon in a tomato-and-pineapple sauce and the grilled mahimahi on a bed of spinach with glazed beets and a lime-and-butter sauce. Or else you might find comfort in the sea scallops with a glazed red-wine sauce.

Hodges Bay. ✆ 268/462-3881. Reservations recommended. Main courses US$24–US$37. AE, MC, V. Tues–Sun 6:30–10:30pm.

Sticky Wicket ⚐ INTERNATIONAL/CARIBBEAN   Lying next to a cricket field, this restaurant allows you to watch a match in progress as you feast on its good food. It is also one of the island's most popular sports-oriented gathering spots. There's a bit of posh here, with an elegant lounge decorated with cricket memorabilia and a courtyard overlooking the sports arena. The cuisine is far better than most sports bar you'll visit. You might launch your repast with a chile-flavored tomato dipping sauce or else tasty shrimp and seafood fritters with a rémoulade sauce. The soups and salads are always fresh and homemade, including Antiguan lobster bisque or an East Indian curried chicken salad mixed with toasted coconut and fresh fruit. The creations are sometimes simple, sometimes complex, but most always satisfying, as exemplified by the West Indian pork rib plate or the grilled lamb souvlakia. Nothing quite tops the Key lime cheesecake for dessert.

Pavilion Dr., Coolidge. ✆ 268/481-7000. Reservations recommended. Main courses EC$35–EC$68 (US$13–US$25). AE, MC, V. Daily 11am–midnight.

4 Beaches

There's a lovely white-sand beach on **Pigeon Point** at Falmouth Harbour, about a 4-minute drive from Admiral's Inn (p. 85). With calm waters and pristine sands, this is the best beach near English Harbour, but it's often crowded, especially when a cruise ship is in port. It's ideal for snorkelers and swimmers of most ages and abilities.

Dickenson Bay 𝕽𝕽 in the northwest, directly north of St. John's, is one of the island's finest beaches, with its wide strip of powder-soft sand and blissfully calm turquoise waters. This safe beach attracts families with small children. At the **Halcyon Cove Hotel** you can rent watersports equipment. Refreshments are available at the hotel, or mosey over to the casual bars and restaurants nearby.

On the north side of Dickenson Bay, you'll find more secluded beaches and some ideal snorkeling areas along the fan-shaped northern crown of Antigua. For a fee, locals will sometimes take beachcombers to one of the uninhabited offshore islets, such as **Prickly Pear Island,** surrounded by beautiful coral gardens. Glass-bottom excursion boats often visit one of the island's best snorkeling spots, **Paradise Reef,** a 1.6km-long (1 mile) coral garden of stunning beauty north of Dickenson Bay (see "Scuba Diving, Snorkeling & Other Watersports," in "Sports & Other Outdoor Pursuits," below).

If you're seeking solitude, flee to **Johnson's Point.** Between the hamlets of Johnson's Point and Urlings at Antigua's southwestern tip below Jolly Harbour, it opens onto the tranquil Caribbean Sea. There are no facilities, but the sand is dazzling white, and the waters, usually clear and calm, are populated with schools of rainbow-hued tropical fish.

Near Johnson's Point on the southwest coast, **Turner's Beach** is idyllic. This is one of the best places to lie out in the tropical sun, cooled by trade winds. The beach has fine white sand and gin-clear waters. If the day is clear (as it usually is), you can see the volcanic island of Montserrat.

If you head east of Urlings and go past the hamlet of Old Road, you'll reach **Carlisle Bay,** site of one of the island's most celebrated shores. Against a backdrop of coconut groves, two long beaches extend from the spot where Curtain Bluff, the island's most deluxe hotel, sits atop a bluff. Here, where the calm Caribbean meets the more turbulent Atlantic, the water is impossibly blue.

South of Jolly Harbour, **Driftwood Beach** is directly north of Johnson's Point, in the southwest. The white sands and calm, clear waters are delightful. It is close to all the villas at Jolly Harbour Beach Resort Marina, however, and can be overcrowded.

In the same vicinity is **Darkwood Beach,** a 5-minute drive south of Jolly Harbour Marina and the Jolly Harbour Golf Club. Here the shimmering waters are almost crystal blue. The snorkeling is great, and you can bet that gentle trade winds will keep you cool. Located in a tourist zone, it is likely to be crowded— almost unbearably so when cruise ships are in port.

If you continue north toward St. John's and cut west at the turnoff for Five Islands, you'll reach the four secluded **Hawksbill Beaches** on the Five Islands peninsula. The beaches here have white sands, dazzling blue-and-green waters, and coral reefs ideal for snorkeling. On one of them, you can sunbathe and swim in the buff. The Five Islands peninsula is the site of major hotel developments. Though it's secluded, the beaches are sometimes crowded.

Perhaps Antigua's most beautiful beach, **Half Moon Bay** 𝕽𝕽 stretches for nearly 1.6km (1 mile) on the southeastern coast, a 5-minute drive from Freetown village. The Atlantic surf is liable to be rough, but that doesn't stop a never-ending stream of windsurfers, who head out beyond the reef, which shelters protected waters for snorkeling. The beach is now a public park and ideal for a family outing. Half Moon Bay lies east of English Harbour near Mill Reef.

Directly north of Half Moon Bay, east of Willikie's, **Long Bay** fronts the Atlantic on the far eastern coast of Antigua. Guests of the Long Bay Hotel and the Pineapple Beach Club usually populate this sandy strip. The shallow waters are home to stunning coral reefs and offer great snorkeling.

In the same vicinity, **Pineapple Beach** is a 5-minute drive heading northeast from the village of Willikie's. It opens onto **Long Bay** and the west coast (Atlantic side) of Antigua. Crystal blue waters make it ideal for snorkeling. Most beach buffs come here just to sun on nearly perfect white sands.

5 Sports & Other Outdoor Pursuits

BOATING & YACHT CHARTERS   If you're contemplating serious yachting around Antigua, as many well-heeled visitors do, make arrangements through **Nicholson Yacht Charters** (© 800/662-6066) well in advance of your trip. They offer boats of all sizes.

Once on Antigua, if you plan only minor sailing such as in a Sunfish or small catamaran (i.e., Hobie Waves), or windsurfing, contact **Sea Sports,** on the beach in front of the Halcyon Cove Hotel at Dickenson Bay (© 268/462-3355). This outfitter also offers 3-hour eco-tours for US$40 per person.

CRUISES   All the major hotel desks can book a day cruise on the 32m (105-ft.) "pirate ship," the *Jolly Roger,* Redcliffe Quay. For information and reservations, call **Tropical Adventures** (© 268/462-2064). Outfitted like a Disney-inspired version of an early 18th-century schooner, it's the largest sailing ship in Antiguan waters. For US$60 for adults and US$30 for children under 12, you get a fun-filled day of sailing, with nonalcoholic drinks and barbecued steak, chicken, or perhaps lobster. After lunch, time is allowed for snorkeling. On the poop deck, members of the crew teach passengers how to dance calypso. Cruises last 4 hours and sail every Friday morning. A Saturday-night dinner cruise leaving Heritage Quay in St. John's at 6pm and returning at 11pm costs US$65. The same organization also offers day trips to remote Barbuda aboard a motorized catamaran, the *Excellence,* that's suitable for up to 70 passengers at a time. Departures are every Friday and Sunday at 9:30am, returning the same day around 4:30pm. The price is US$120 per person (no children under 8 allowed), which includes lunch, use of snorkeling equipment, and a visit to Barbuda's bird sanctuary. **Barbuda-bound cruises** depart from Tony's Water Sports at Dickenson Bay. For information and reservations, call © 268/480-1225.

FISHING   Many anglers visit Antigua just for the big-game fishing offshore, where wahoo, tuna, and marlin abound. The *Obsession* (© 268/464-3174) is a 15m (49-ft.) Hatteras Sportfisherman with excellent equipment. You can battle the big ones in a featured "fighting chair." For the day, the *Obsession* charges from US$800, a fee that is shared by all the passengers (usually at least nine). A competitor of similar size, the *Nimrod* (© 268/460-1568), is captained by Terry Bowen, who knows where the best catches are. You can arrange for the *Nimrod* to circle the island or go on sunset cruises. A full around-the-island tour costs US$1,000, with a half-day going for US$750. This price is usually divided among at least 10 passengers. The *Obsession* moors at the Catamaran Marina in the hamlet of Falmouth and the *Nimrod* anchors at the marina facilities of Nelson's Dockyard.

GOLF Antigua's golf facilities are not on par with some of the other islands', but its premier course is good. The 18-hole, par-69 **Cedar Valley Golf Club,** Friar's Hill Road (© **268/462-0161**), is 5km (3 miles) east of St. John's, near the airport, and has panoramic views of Antigua's northern coast. The late Richard Aldridge designed the island's most popular and largest course. Daily greens fees are US$45 for 18 holes. Cart rentals cost US$30 for 18 holes, and club rentals cost US$15 to US$20, depending on how many holes you play.

HIKING The best hiking tours in Antigua are offered by **Tropikelly Trails** (© **268/461-0383;** www.tropikellytrails.com). The trail leads from the hamlet of Wallens Estate, in the tropical rainforest on the south side of Antigua, and climbs to the top of Signal Hill. Tours cost US$20 per person, and last for about 3 hours each, but they're only conducted when a minimum of 10 participants can be assembled.

PARASAILING Parasailing is gaining popularity on Antigua. Facilities are available during the day, Monday to Saturday, on the beach at Dickenson Bay.

SCUBA DIVING, SNORKELING & OTHER WATERSPORTS The reefs that fringe Antigua are home to beautiful, brilliantly colored fish. Many of the island's beaches (see "Beaches," above) have clear, pure, calm waters that make for great snorkeling, and the most popular beaches, like Dickenson Bay, have concessions where you can rent snorkel gear and other equipment if it isn't available from your hotel.

Scuba diving is best arranged through **Dive Antigua,** at the Rex Halcyon Cove, Dickenson Bay (© **268/462-3483**), Antigua's most experienced dive operation. A resort course is US$88 (which also includes a shallow dive), and a two-tank dive costs US$72. A five-dive package goes for US$305, and open-water certification costs US$493. Prices do not include equipment, an additional US$21.

Splish Splash (© **268/462-3483**) regularly offers 2-hour snorkeling jaunts over to Paradise Reef.

Dolphin Fantaseas, Marina Bay (© **268/562-7946**), features an introductory Dolphin Encounter program and an interactive Dolphin Swim for US$125 per person. The Dolphin Swim involves a half-hour up close and personal playtime with dolphins. This outfitter also offers snorkeling and stingray adventures.

TENNIS True tennis buffs—well-heeled ones, that is—check into **Curtain Bluff** (see "Accommodations," earlier in this chapter). Its courts are the finest on the island. Most of the major hotels have courts as well, and some are lit for night games. (We don't recommend playing tennis at noon—it's just too hot!) Hotel guests usually play for free; if you're not a guest, you'll have to book a court and pay charges that vary from place to place.

WINDSURFING Most of the major resorts along the beach rent windsurfing equipment. The best outfitters are **Sea Sports** (© **268/462-3355**) at Dickenson Bay, charging US$30 per hour, or **Sunsail Club Colonna** (© **268/462-6263;** Hodges Bay), which rents equipment for US$25 per half day.

6 Exploring the Island

IN ST. JOHN'S

If you're staying outside St. John's (which is highly likely), you might consider visiting the city during the **Saturday morning market.** Many of the sellers get right on the bus with whatever they'll be peddling in town at the market: chickens, birds, luscious fruit, beautiful flowers, and certainly plenty of handcrafts. They'll probably start bargaining with you before you even get to the market. In the southern part of St. John's, the semi-open-air market, on the lower end of Market Street, is colorful and interesting, especially from 8am to noon.

St. John's Cathedral, the Anglican church between Long Street and Newgate Street at Church Lane (℃ **268/461-0082**), has resurrected itself time and again—it's been destroyed by earthquakes and rebuilt on the same site at least three times since it was first constructed in 1683. The present structure dates from 1845. Exhibits at the **Museum of Antigua & Barbuda,** at Market and Long streets (℃ **268/462-1469**), are within one of Antigua's oldest buildings, built by English colonials in 1750 as a courthouse. The museum covers the island's history, from prehistoric days up to its independence from Britain in 1981. Exhibitions include examples of each of the semiprecious stones (especially jade) you can find on Antigua, as well as models of sugar plantations, steam engines, paintings, and historical prints. It's open Monday through Friday from 8:30am to 4pm and on Saturday from 10am to 2pm. There is a US$2 suggested donation.

AROUND THE ISLAND
Eighteen kilometers (11 miles) southeast of St. John's is **Nelson's Dockyard National Park** 🎔🎔🎔 (℃ **268/460-1379**), one of the eastern Caribbean's biggest attractions. English ships took refuge from the hurricanes in this harbor as early as 1671. The park's centerpiece is the restored Georgian naval dockyard, which was used by admirals Nelson, Rodney, and Hood, and was the home of the British fleet during the Napoleonic Wars. From 1784 to 1787, Nelson commanded the British navy in the Leeward Islands and made his headquarters at English Harbour. The dockyard museum recaptures the 18th-century era of privateers, pirates, and battles at sea. Its colonial naval buildings remain as they were when Nelson was here. Although Nelson never lived at **Admiral House** (℃ **268/460-8181**)—it was built in 1855—his telescope and tea caddy are on display, along with other nautical memorabilia.

The park itself has sandy beaches and tropical vegetation, with various species of cactus and mangroves. A migrating colony of African cattle egrets shelters in the mangroves. Archaeological sites here predate Christ. Nature trails, with coastal views, lead you through the flora. Tours of the dockyard last 15 to 20 minutes; nature walks along the trails can last anywhere from 30 minutes to 5 hours. The dockyard and all the buildings noted in this section are open daily from 9am to 5pm. Children 12 and under are admitted free. The admission price of US$5 includes admission to Admiral House, Clarence House, and Dow's Hill Interpretation Center (see below).

The best **nature trail** on Antigua, a well-tended footpath, goes up the hill from English Harbour to **Shirley Heights** 🎔, beginning at the Galleon Beach Hotel. Follow the sign that points to the lookout. The trail is marked with tape on the branches of trees. Eventually you reach a summit of nearly 150m (492 ft.), where you're rewarded with a panoramic view. If you'd like to get more information about the walk, you can pick up a free brochure at the dockyard at the office of the National Parks Authority. This walk is easy; it takes less than an hour to reach the peak.

Another major attraction is the **Dow's Hill Interpretation Center** (℃ **268/ 481-5045**), just 4km (2½ miles) southeast of the dockyard. The only one of its kind in the Caribbean, it offers multimedia presentations that cover six periods

---

Tips   **Forts & Photo Ops**

Once, in the 1700s, the coastline of Antigua was ringed with British forts, though they're all in ruins today. Even if there isn't much left to see, the views from these former military strongholds are among the most panoramic in the Caribbean—and you can visit them for free. You can begin at St. John's harbor (the capital), which was once guarded by **Fort Barrington** on the south and **Fort James** on the north. Later you can head down to **Fort James Bay,** where you'll find a couple of bars right on the sand, including **Russell's Beach Bar,** which is most active on Sunday afternoon. It's an ideal place to unwind with a beer. In the south, near English Harbour, check out the view from **Shirley Heights.**

---

of the island's history, including the era of Amerindian hunters, the era of the British military, and the struggles connected with slavery. A belvedere opens onto a panoramic view of the park. Admission to the center, including the multimedia show, is included in the price of admission to the dockyards. Hours are daily from 9am to 5pm.

On the way back, take **Fig Tree Drive** ⚓, a 32km (20-mile) circular drive across the main mountain range. It passes through lush tropical hills and fishing villages along the southern coast. You can pick up the road just outside Liberta, north of Falmouth. Winding through a rainforest, it passes thatched villages, every one with a church and lots of goats and children running about. But don't expect fig trees: *Fig* is an Antiguan name for bananas.

Betty's Hope (no phone), a picturesque ruin just outside the village of Pares on the eastbound route to Long Bay, was Antigua's first sugar plantation (from 1650). You can tour it Tuesday to Saturday from 9am to 4pm (US$2 for adults, free for children). Exhibits in the visitor's center trace the sugar era, and you can also see the full restoration of one of the original plantation's two windmills. If you visit, you may see the local masons, who are sporadically involved in the restoration of the curing and boiling plant, where sugar cane used to be processed into sugar, rum, and molasses.

Indian Town is one of Antigua's national parks, on the island's northeastern point. Over the centuries, Atlantic breakers have lashed the rocks and carved a natural bridge known as **Devil's Bridge.** It's surrounded by numerous blowholes spouting surf, a dramatic sight. An environmentally protected area, Indian Town Point lies at the tip of a deep cove, Indian Town Creek. The park fronts the Atlantic at Long Bay, just west of Indian Town Creek at the eastern side of Antigua. Birders flock here to see some 36 different species. The park is blanketed mainly by the acacia tree, a dry shrub locally known as "cassie." A large, meadowy headland around Devil's Bridge makes a great spot for a **picnic.** Arm yourself with directions and a good map before you start out. The main highway ends at Long Bay, but several **hiking trails** lead to the coastline. Our favorite hike is to Indian Town Point at a distance of 2km (1½ miles). This is the most scenic walk in the park, passing through a protected area of great natural beauty. Long Bay is also great for snorkeling, if you bring along your gear.

7 Shopping

Most of Antigua's shops are clustered on **St. Mary's Street** or **High Street** in St. John's. Some stores are open Monday to Saturday from 8:30am to noon and 1 to

4pm, but this rule varies greatly from place to place—Antiguan shopkeepers are an independent lot. Many of them close at noon on Thursday.

Duty-free items include English woolens and linens. You can also purchase Antiguan goods: local pottery, straw work, rum, floppy foldable hats, shell curios, and hand-printed fabrics.

If you're in St. John's on a Saturday morning, visit the **fruit and vegetable market** at the south end of Market Street. The juicy Antiguan black pineapple alone is worth the trip.

One prime hunting ground in St. John's is the **Redcliffe Quay** waterfront on the southern edge of town, where nearly three dozen boutiques are housed in former warehouses set around tree-shaded, landscaped courtyards. Our favorite is **A Thousand Flowers** (© 268/462-4264), which sells linens, all natural fiber, rayon, and other fabrics.

At the **Gazebo** (© 268/460-2776), expect a little bit of everything, from a mass of south-of-the-border pottery to Indonesian wood items, and (our favorite) stunning blue-glaze plates. Additional Redcliffe Quay shops include **Isis** (© 268/462-4602) for unique Egyptian jewelry, cotton gowns, and handcrafts; and **The Goldsmitty** (© 268/462-4601), where precious stones are set in unique, exquisite creations of 14- and 18-karat gold.

Noreen Phillips, Redcliffe Quay (© 268/462-3127), is one of the island's major fashion outlets. Cruise-ship passengers beeline here for both casual wear and beaded glitzy dress clothes. **Exotic Antigua,** Radcliffe Quay, St. Mary's Street (© 268/462-2972), specializes in Caribbean-made gifts and clothing, including T-shirts and casual wear, and handcrafts.

At **Lipstick,** Heritage Quay (© 268/562-1133), you'll find a daunting array of cosmetics and perfumes, some of them locally made, many of the others imported from the U.S., Britain, and France. **Shoul's Chief Store,** St. Mary's Street at Market Street (© 268/462-1140), is an all-purpose department store selling fabric, appliances, souvenirs (more than 300 kinds), and general merchandise.

Heritage Quay, Antigua's first shopping-and-entertainment complex, features some 40 duty-free shops and an arcade for local artists and craftspeople. Its restaurants and food court offer a range of cuisines and views of St. John's Harbour. Many shops are open all day, Monday through Saturday.

At the foot of St. Mary's Street, stop in at **The Camera Shop** (© 268/462-3619), a Kodak distributor and photofinisher, selling film and brand-name cameras. **Fashiondock** (© 268/462-9672) is known for its duty-free Prada, Moshino, and Gucci accessories, plus other Italian styles. **Sunseekers** (© 268/462-4523) carries the largest collection of duty-free swimwear in the Caribbean. **Colombian Emeralds** (© 268/462-3462) is the world's largest retailer of these gemstones. **Albert's Jewelry** (© 268/462-3108) sells the best selection of watches on Antigua, plus china and crystal. **Island Arts,** upstairs at Heritage Quay (© 268/462-2787), was founded by Nick Maley, a makeup artist who worked on *Star Wars* and *The Empire Strikes Back*. You can purchase his own fine-art reproductions or browse through everything from low-cost prints to works by artists exhibited at the Museum of Modern Art in New York. You can also visit **Nick's home and studio** at Aiton Place, on Sandy Lane directly behind the Hodges Bay Club, 6km (3¾ miles) from St. John's. The residence is open Monday to Wednesday and on Friday, but call first (© 268/461-6324).

Rain Boutique, Lower St. Mary's (© 268/462-0118), offers casual clothes, formal wear, hats, scarves, shoes, jewelry, and handbags.

At Falmouth Harbour, **Seahorse Studios & Gift Shop** (© 268/460-1457) specializes in batiks, T-shirts, signs, and table linens. Their affiliated branch at English Harbour, **Seahorse Art Gallery** (© 268/460-1457), sells paintings, engravings, and watercolors, with lots of emphasis on seascapes.

The best for last: Head for **Harmony Hall** 🐾, in Brown's Bay Mill, near Freetown (© 268/460-4120), following the signs along the road to Freetown and Half Moon Bay. This restored 1843 plantation house and sugar mill overlooking Nonsuch Bay is ideal for a lunch stopover or a shopping expedition. It displays an excellent selection of Caribbean arts and crafts. Lunch is served daily from noon to 3:30pm, featuring Green Island lobster, flying fish, and other specialties. Sunday is barbecue day.

8 Antigua After Dark

Antigua has some of the best steel bands in the Caribbean. Most nightlife revolves around the hotels. If you want to roam Antigua at night looking for that hot local club, arrange to have a taxi pick you up, so you're not stranded in the wilds somewhere.

The **Royal Casino,** in the Royal Antiguan Hotel, Deep Bay (© 268/462-3733), has blackjack, baccarat, roulette, craps, and slot machines. It's open daily from 6pm until around midnight, and there's no cover. Far better and the most glamorous place to go if you have time for only one casino is the **St. James's Club** at Mamora Bay (© 268/460-5000), which has the island's most flamboyant gambling palace. Other action is found at **King's Casino** on Heritage Quay (© 268/462-1727), the only casino in St. John's proper. Entrance is free and no ID is required. You must be 18 to play.

Steel bands, limbo dancers, calypso singers, folkloric groups—there's always something happening by night on Antigua. Your hotel can probably tell you where to go on any given night. The following clubs are reliable hot spots.

18 Carat, Long Street at Market Street, St. Johns (© 268/562-1858), opened in 2002 and rose instantly to the status of most popular and sought-after dance club and night bar on the island. Expect a cover charge of less than US$3 per person, an indoor-outdoor format that's open to a view of the night air of downtown St. John's, and a barrage of music that includes lots of reggae and soca. It's open Friday to Sunday from around 8pm to 1am.

Stop in at the **Bay House,** Tradewinds Hotel, Marble Hill (© 268/462-1223), for the island's best mix of singles (both straight and—to a much lesser degree—gay). **Lashings,** Runaway Bay (© 268/462-4438), is the hangout of local cricketers, and always attracts a fun-loving bevy of patrons who dance the night away when not ordering Tex-Mex fare.

Live nightly entertainment takes place right on the beach at **Millers by the Sea,** at Runaway Beach (© 268/462-9414). Spilling over onto the sands, its happy hour is the best in town.

At English Harbour, action centers around the **Admiral's Inn** (© 268/460-1027), a barefoot-friendly kind of place. You can always play a game of darts and there's live music Thursday and Saturday nights, usually a local 14-piece steel band. Try one of Norman's daiquiris (the island's best), and ask the bartender about the famous guests he's served, from Richard Burton to Prince Charles. Another much-frequented English Harbour watering hole is **The Life Bar,** Nelson's Dockyard, VHF #68 (no phone), the most popular spot for visitors arriving aboard yachts. We like its real nautical atmosphere, the action centering on a wooden pier. On occasion, it's West Indian party time, with live groups performing. The most authentic British pub at Nelson's Dockyard is **Mainbrace** (© **268/460-1058**), with darts, of course, and fish and chips, and on some nights the jazz is live. The pub is part of the Copper and Lumber Store Hotel (see "Accommodations," earlier in this chapter).

9 Barbuda

Barbuda is part of the independent nation of Antigua and Barbuda. It's the Caribbean's last frontier, even though it is home to two of the region's most expensive and exclusive resorts. (See below for a review of the K-Club. The other property is the Coco Point Beach Resort, which we don't recommend because we think it has an exclusive, snobbish atmosphere.) Charted by Columbus in 1493, the island is 42km (26 miles) north of Antigua. Twenty-four kilometers (15 miles) long by 8km (5 miles) wide, it has a population of only 1,200 hardy souls, most of whom live around the unattractive village of Codrington. There's no lush tropical scenery, no paved roads, few hotels, and only a handful of restaurants.

So what's the attraction? The island's 27km (17 miles) of pink- and white-sand beaches—almost like those of Bermuda. (We prefer the sands north of Palmetto Point.) Barrier reefs protect the island and keep most of the waters tranquil. Beaches on the southwestern shore stretch uninterrupted for 16km (10 miles); these are the best for swimming. Fronting the Atlantic, the beaches on the island's eastern shore are somewhat rougher, but they're suitable for beachcombing and shell collecting. The temperature seldom falls below an average of 75°F (24°C).

Hunters and beachcombers gravitate to Barbuda to see fallow deer, guinea fowl, pigeons, and wild pigs. Anglers can also negotiate with small-boat owners to fish for bonefish and tarpon.

Day visitors usually head for **Wa'Omoni Beach Park** 🅐 to visit the frigate bird sanctuary, snorkel for lobster, and eat barbecue. A most impressive sight, the frigate bird sanctuary is one of the world's largest. Visitors can see the birds, *Fregata magnificens,* sitting on their eggs in the mangrove bushes, which stretch for miles in a long lagoon accessible only by small motorboat. At various hotels and resorts on Antigua, you can arrange tours to the sanctuary. The island attracts about 150 other species of birds, including pelicans, herons, and tropical mockingbirds.

While you're here, look into the **"Dividing Wall,"** which once separated the imperial Codrington family from the African islanders. Also visit the **Martello Tower,** which predates the known history of the island. Purportedly the Spanish erected it before the British occupied the island. Several tours explore interesting **underground caves** on Barbuda. Stamp collectors might want to stop in at the **Philatelic Bureau** in Codrington (no phone).

ESSENTIALS

GETTING THERE   The island is a 15-minute flight from Antigua's V. C. Byrd Airport. Barbuda has two airfields: one at Codrington, the other a private facility, the Coco Point Airstrip, which lies some 13km (8 miles) from Codrington at the Coco Point Lodge.

To reach Barbuda from Antigua, you can contact **Carib Aviation** (© **268/462-3147**), a carrier that's loosely associated the LIAT, the national airline of Antigua and Barbuda. It operates two daily flights from Antigua's Byrd airport to Barbuda's Codrington Airport. Planes hold 19 passengers each for a

Barbuda

Airport ✈ Beach ⚓ Reef ‖‖‖

Goat Point

ATLANTIC OCEAN

Cobb Cove

Cedar Tree Point

Hog Point

Wa'Omoni Beach Park

Two Foot Bay

Codrington Lagoon

Low Bay

○ Codrington
✈

■ Martello Tower

Palmetto Point

Pelican Bay

■ K-Club

Coco Point ⚓

Spanish Point

Gravener Bay

Caribbean Sea

0 ___ 3 Miles
0 ___ 3 Kilometers
N

ride that takes between 15 and 20 minutes, each way. Round-trip passage costs from EC$194 (US$72) per person, depending on restrictions.

GETTING AROUND   Many locals rent small four-wheel-drive Suzukis, which are the best way to get around the island. They meet incoming flights at Codrington Airport, and prices are negotiable. You'll need an Antiguan driver's license (p. 78) if you plan to drive.

ACCOMMODATIONS & DINING

K-Club 🐾🐾   The most interesting and costly hotel to open in the Caribbean in recent years, the beachfront K-Club brings a chic Italian panache to one of the most far-flung backwaters of the Antilles. The resort opened in 1990, when a planeload of glitterati headed for Barbuda en masse. The K-Club is the "temple in the desert" of Italy's Krizia Mariuccia Mandelli, whose sports and evening wear empire has grossed a fortune. On-site is a krizia boutique stocked with the designer's latest fashions. The resort is set on more than 80 hectares (198 acres), adjacent to the island's only other major hotel, a private club. Conceived by Italian architect Gianni Gamondi, the cottages and main clubhouse have roofs supported by a forest of white columns. Accommodations come in a huge range of styles and shapes; a hip island vibe predominates throughout. The Caribbean rattan furnishings include sumptuous beds. Bathrooms have two sinks, a bidet and adjacent shower, and a basket of deluxe toiletries. Rooms also have plenty of space for luggage.

The cuisine is Mediterranean, with an emphasis on Italian specialties and fresh pasta. The chef passionately believes in fresh ingredients, and his food is not only the finest on Barbuda but also tops anything on Antigua.

Barbuda, Antigua, W.I. © **268/460-0304**. Fax 268/460-0305. www.kclubbarbuda.com. 37 units. Winter US$1,200 cottage for 2, US$1,700 suite, US$2,800 villa; off season US$800 cottage for 2, US$1,150 suite, US$2,000 villa. Rates include all meals, but no drinks. AE, DC, MC, V. Closed mid-June to Thanksgiving. No children under 12. **Amenities:** Restaurant; bar; outdoor pool; 2 tennis courts; wellness center; Jacuzzi; deep-sea fishing; snorkeling; Sunfish sailing; water-skiing; windsurfing; transportation from Codrington Airport; limited room service; massage; laundry service; dry cleaning. *In room:* A/C, TV, ceiling fan, dataport, minibar, fridge, beverage maker, hair dryer, safe.

10 Montserrat

Adventurous visitors are returning to the partially destroyed island of Montserrat. Known as "the Emerald Isle of the Caribbean," partly because of its verdant vegetation, partly because of its historic links to Ireland, and partly because of the heroism of its populace in the face of recent disaster. Montserrat is 19km (12 miles) long and 11km (6¾ miles) wide, about the size of Manhattan. Two-thirds of the population of 12,000 had to be evacuated in 1995 and 1996 after the island's volcano, Chance's Peak, blew its top, smothering the southern two-thirds of the island with pyroclastic flows of hot gases and boiling hot ash, sometimes traveling downhill at hurricane velocity. In the aftermath, much of the island's southern tier—including the island's only airport—was burnt, buried, or rendered uninhabitable.

Although the biggest blast occurred on June 25, 1997, Mount Chance and other peaks in the Soufrière Hills had been rumbling for generations. Since the explosions, only about one-third of the island's original population has stayed on island, the others having been evacuated, or emigrating of their own volition, to the U.K. or, less frequently, to such neighboring islands as Antigua. Today, thanks to enormous investment of time and energy from local and international geologists, the path of future pyroclastic flows can more or less be predicted. That has allowed tourism to return, to a limited degree, to the island, albeit in very small volumes. In fact, the volcanic eruptions have defined Montserrat as one of the most haunting natural and geological spectacles in the Caribbean.

The most recent eruption at the time of this writing occurred on July 12, 2003, when almost two-thirds of the Soufrière Hills volcanic dome collapsed, sending ash and rocky debris as much as 50,000 feet into the sky over Montserrat. In the aftermath, some islanders found themselves shoveling 5-foot "drifts" of volcanic debris off their verandas and out from the bottom of their swimming pools.

Today, a visit to Montserrat can solicit hundreds of stories about heroism, endurance, sacrifice, and back-breaking labor. In a gesture of support, more than 1,500 native Montserratians returned from overseas in December 2002 for the island's 40th annual carnival celebration. A record number attended the carnival, which culminated in the Montserrat Calypso Festival on December 30.

Since the destruction of Plymouth, the island's historic and once-charming capital, Montserrat's new commercial center and gerrymandered capital is a rapidly growing strip of land between Brades and Little Bay, on the island's north coast. Overall, you'll get the sense of a small community galvanized into new forms of self-reliance and cooperation, with lots of emphasis on somewhat gritty business-related visits from construction crews and British and international relief agencies.

Pear-shaped and mountainous, and most definitely volcanic in origin, Montserrat lies 43km (27 miles) southwest of Antigua, about midway between Nevis and Guadeloupe. Before the volcanic eruptions, Montserrat was known as the place where such musicians as Elton John, Paul McCartney, Sting, and Stevie Wonder had studios. They, along with much of the rest of Montserrat's glitterati, moved long ago to safer, and more convenient, sites.

English is the island's official language, although it's spoken with a faint Irish brogue, a holdover from the island's early Irish settlers. The Eastern Caribbean dollar is the official unit of currency, although U.S. dollars are widely accepted. By international agreement each EC dollar is permanently fixed—at the time of this writing—at 37¢. There is no local representative of American Express (you'll have to go to Antigua for that), but the island's biggest and most comprehensive travel agency is **Runaway Travel,** P.O. Box 54, Brades, Montserrat, B.W.I. (© **664/491-2800**). They'll arrange access to Federal Express shipments, sell a limited roster of airline tickets, and perform a limited array of financial services, including foreign exchange.

Proof of citizenship is required for all visitors. A valid passport is recommended for everyone; however, U.S., Canadian, and British citizens may present a driver's license or official ID card with photo as proof of citizenship in lieu of a passport.

Information is available from the **Montserrat Tourist Board,** P.O. Box 7, Brades, Montserrat, B.W.I. (© **664/491-2230;** www.visitmontserrat.com). For up-to-the-minute information specifically related to the island's volcanic activity, check out www.mvo.ms.

ESSENTIALS

GETTING THERE   Montserrat is most easily reached from Antigua, but because its airport was destroyed by the volcano, it's accessible only by boat and by helicopter.

At least two, and sometimes three, helicopters depart every day except Wednesday and Saturday from Antigua's Byrd airport for Montserrat's newly built heliport in Gerald's, a hamlet on the still-intact north side of the island. With room for about 11 passengers, each helicopter charges EC$300 (US$111) round-trip for a ride that takes about 20 minutes each way. At the time of this writing, construction had already (slowly) begun on the expansion of the heliport into a full-fledged airport. Its completion was expected for sometime in the late autumn or winter of 2004.

Less expensive are the ferryboats that depart twice a day, every Monday to Saturday, from Antigua, carrying passengers who pay between EC$140 and EC$200 (US$52–US$74) round-trip each, depending on the day of the week they travel. In most cases, their departure point is Heritage Quay in St. John's, although whenever that port is clogged because of cruise-ship activities, they'll depart from Deepwater Harbour, a very short walk from Heritage Quay. It takes about an hour to reach Montserrat's Little Bay. One-way ferryboat passage costs EC$102 (US$38) per person.

Whereas reservations are required aboard the helicopter, ferryboat seats don't require advance bookings. For information about either mode of transport, contact **Montserrat Aviation** (© **664/491-2533** in Antigua, or 288/462-3147 in Montserrat).

GETTING AROUND   By Taxi & Bus   Although the island has about 24km (15 miles) of surfaced roads, only those within the island's northern tier are currently accessible, and most of the island's vehicular traffic is limited to the route between Jack Boy Hill, on the island's northeasterly tip, and the village of Fleming, incorporating the island's heliport and most points within the designated "northern safety zone" en route. The typical taxi fare from the heliport to any of the hotels in the northern tier, including Tropical Mansion Suites and the Vue Pointe Lodge, ranges from EC$19 to EC$59 (US$7.05–US$22). Sightseeing tours in a local taxi, when viable, cost between EC$80 and EC$120 (US$30–US$44) per hour, depending on how many hours you want to spend touring.

The only regular **buses** are those running from Salem near the island's southernmost tip to Lookout on the island's northern end, passing through hamlets that include Brades, Sweeney's, and St. John's en route. Sweeney's is the site of a newly built, government-funded residential community on the island's northern tip. The fare is EC$2 (US75¢) between any two points along this route. Don't expect the conventional buses you find in large North American cities. These are usually 15-seater minivans, each individually painted. If you want the bus to make a reasonable detour from the designated route, the driver will usually do it for an additional, negotiable fee, pending the approval of the other passengers.

By Rental Car None of the major U.S.-based car-rental companies operates on Montserrat, although you'll find a handful of privately owned agencies. You'll be required to buy a local Montserrat driver's license for EC$50 (US$19), which should accompany your own valid license. Rarely are these available directly from the rental agency. More often you'll need to purchase a license from the immigration office at either the heliport or the ferryboat terminal, or from the island's **Police Traffic Department** in Salem (© 664/491-2555), which is open 24 hours a day.

Most island car-rental agencies stock a battered roster of Toyota Corollas, Toyota RAV4s, Suzuki jeeps, or Mazdas, which rent for EC$94 (US$35) and up a day, or from EC$565 (US$209) per week, depending on their make, model, and the duration of your rental. A collision-damage waiver costs from EC$24 to EC$30 (US$8.90–US$11) per day. Even if you buy it, you'll still be liable for the cost of some of the repairs to your vehicle if you damage it, for any reason, during your tenure.

Be-Beeps Car Rentals (© 664/491-3787) is in the hamlet of Olveston, near Salem, close to the well-recommended Vue Pointe Hotel. **M.S. Osborne** (© 664/491-2494) has a virtual monopoly on supplying most of the Nissans and Suzukis, including some SUVs, on the island.

Before you begin driving here, be aware: You must drive on the left and you should be careful of the steep, winding roads, which can be treacherous. In addition, volcanic ash on the roads makes for slippery driving conditions. Finally, although a second gas station is presently under construction, at the time of this writing there's only one gasoline station on Montserrat, barely enough to serve all of the gas-related needs of an island that made do with five gas stations before the shutdown of Plymouth. Plan your refill stops accordingly, and remember its name and location: the **A&F Service Center,** on St. John's main road in the hamlet of Sweeney, immediately adjacent to the Tropical Mansions Suites.

ACCOMMODATIONS

Accommodations are extremely limited. The island's finest accommodations are within the **Vue Pointe Hotel** (© 664/491-5210; fax 664/491-4813; www. vuepointe.com) in the hamlet of Old Towne. In December of 2003, after

Herculean efforts at hauling away 2,500 truckloads of volcanic debris, a freshly repainted hotel opened for business. Once loaded with sun-loving tourists, it has, since the debut of the crisis, evolved into the island's premier lodging for scientists and volcanologists. With tennis courts, a restaurant and bar, an outdoor pool, and a brightly painted collection of cottages that dot the verdant hillside that rolls gently downhill to the sea, it's a charming and pleasant site that has become especially cost-effective since its owners, Carol and Cedric Osborne, lowered their rates for doubles to US$90 for units without kitchens and US$100 for units with kitchens. MasterCard and Visa are accepted.

Vue Pointe's direct competitor, catering mostly to business travels, is the well-conceived **Tropical Mansions** (© 664/491-8273), within the hamlet of Sweeney's and with its own outdoor pool and restaurant. At this 18-room inn, a double room with breakfast included costs US$106 to US$145 per night, although much cheaper packages are sometimes that include with breakfast, lunch, or dinner and transfers from either the heliport or the ferryboat dock for US$99 per person, double occupancy, per night. MasterCard and Visa are accepted.

RENTING A HOUSE ON MONTSERRAT

Montserrat real estate, thanks to the recent volcanic explosions, has disappointed more real estate investors than virtually any other island in the Caribbean. But what that means for you is that there is a pool of available buildings (at least 100) on island, of all sizes, shapes, and degrees of comfort and maintenance, that can be rented for anywhere from a few days to a season or more. We firmly believe that if you're tempted to rent a house for a Caribbean holiday, you should stay for the first time on island within a conventional hotel, and then—for a second- or third-time holiday—consider renting from a reputable agent. Three of the best agencies in Montserrat include **West Indies Real Estate, Ltd.,** P.O. Box 355, Olveston (© 664/491-8666; www.wirealest.com); **Trade Winds Real Estate,** P.O. Box 365, Old Towne (© 664/491-2004; www.tradewindsmontserrat.com); and **Montserrat Enterprises, Ltd.** P.O. Box 58, Old Towne (© 664/491-2431; melenter@candw.ag).

DINING

Although additional restaurants are likely to crop up soon, currently many of the island's eateries are simple takeaway stands. In addition to the restaurant (also recommended) that's within the Tropical Mansions hotel, there are the following noteworthy exceptions:

Tina's Restaurant (© 664/491-3538), on Brades Main Road, is set within a green-and-white Antillean house, less than a 5-minute drive uphill from the ferryboat terminal. This restaurant was established in 1998 by Tina Farrell, after she was evacuated from her home on Montserrat's southern tier. Expect a cozy, down-home Caribbean feel, with savory portions of chicken or beef, as well as grilled-chicken salads or lobster salads, and whatever type of fresh fish that was hauled in by local fishermen that day. Open Monday to Saturday from 8am to midnight, it charges EC$10 to EC$26 (US$3.70–US$9.60) for main courses at lunch, EC$45 (US$17) for a set menu at lunch, and EC$45 to EC$65 (US$17–US$24) for set menus at dinner. No credit cards are accepted; reservations are recommended.

JJ's Cuisine (© 664/491-9024), in Sweeney's Center, St. John's Main Road, is owned and operated by Dominica-born Zephrina Jnofinn. This popular restaurant lies within a building that's within a 5-minute drive from the heliport.

Inside the simple dining room you can order lobster, a worthy version of mountain chicken (frog's legs) sautéed in butter with garlic, sandwiches, and excellent burgers that Zephrina concocts herself with a few secret ingredients. Hours are Monday to Saturday from 8am to midnight. Burgers and sandwiches cost EC$6.50 to EC$15 (US$2.40–US$5.55); platters go for EC$16 to EC$65 (US$5.90–US$24). No credit cards are accepted; reservations are recommended.

Oriel Café (© 664/491-7144), in Brades, shares the blue-and-green building it occupies with the island's tourist board and several other government entities. Opened only since midsummer of 2003, it's open daily from 7am to 9pm, serving an ongoing roster of sandwiches, salads, and burgers for EC$13 to EC$18 (US$4.80–US$6.65). Between noon and 2pm, there's a selection of daily specials as well. These, priced at EC$20 to EC$25 (US$7.40–US$9.25), might include pork chop platters, grilled fish, and steaks. Gregarious and friendly, it employs a hardworking staff whose uniforms match the coloring (yellow and black) of Montserrat's national bird, the Oriel.

Since the volcano dumped 2,500 truckloads of ash and debris upon its premises, **The Restaurant at Vue Pointe Hotel** (© 664/491-5210) might have had more to cope with than any other on the island. But in December of 2003, it reopened on a limited (breakfast and lunch) basis that is almost certain to expand into the dinner hour during the lifetime of this edition. Expect well-prepared food that's supervised by the creative and hardworking owners, Carol and Cedric Osborne, and served by a young staff of enthusiastic trainees. Main courses cost from around EC$23 to EC$40 (US$8.50–US$15), and include a well-prepared roster of chicken, steak, fresh fish, frog's legs, and salads. More than most of its competitors, we expect this restaurant to continue its upwardly mobile ascent.

AROUND THE ISLAND

SCUBA DIVING   Montserrat offers 30 excellent dive sites, each with a rich assortment of marine life, including spotted drums and copper sweepers, and perhaps a large sea turtle. At the rim of the island's marine shelf, where relatively shallow waters suddenly drop off to great depths, divers can plunge into 21m-deep (69 ft.) waters to see mammoth sponges along with large star and brain coral reefs. German-born Wolf Krebs is the owner of the **Sea Wolf Diving School,** Woodlands (© 664/491-6859), and a noted expert on the island's marine botany and zoology. One-tank dives cost US$60, and two-tank dives cost US$80. Snorkeling equipment can be rented for US$10.

SIGHTS   Visiting an island with an active volcano is an attraction in itself. The **Soufrière Hills Volcano** in the still-restricted southern part of the island is eerily fascinating. Armed with clear instructions from geologists about where and where *not* to visit, taxi drivers and tour operators (see below) can sometimes show you the island's southern tier, but conditions, of course, are subject to change at any moment (and we mean that literally). You'll see mudslides, layers of volcanic ash, and from a safe distance, the ghostly remains of the partially destroyed former capital of Plymouth. (The only deaths suffered during the island's volcanic explosions occurred on June 25, 1997, when 19 people were farming in an area that had been declared an exclusion zone.)

The government aggressively discourages anyone to remain within the southern two-thirds of the island from 6pm until 6am the following morning, and appearing within some neighborhoods or districts, including the former capital of Plymouth, is out-and-out forbidden. Not only does the southern zone lack

---

Tips Beaches

Montserrat isn't known for its white-sand beaches. Most of its beaches are of volcanic black sand, and they lie on the northern rim of the island, the part not threatened by volcanic activity. And many observers have noted that the beaches have actually improved, becoming bigger, sandier, and wider since the volcano deposited millions of tons of sand, ash, and debris upon them. The best beach on the island—and the only one whose sands are white—is **Rendezvous Bay,** which is only accessible via water taxis that depart from both Little Bay and the nearly adjacent Carr's Bay, or after a half-hour's hike. If you want to walk, the routes to Rendezvous Bay are especially convenient from either Little Bay or from the hamlet of Drummond's, adjacent to the heliport. More readily accessible but less popular and hotter on bare feet are the dark-sand (a slate-gray color) beaches at **Carr's Bay, Woodlands Beach, Lime Kiln Bay, Little Bay** (near the arrival of the ferryboats from Antigua), and **Bunkum Bay.** The staff at **Tropical Mansions** (© 664/491-8273) or the **Vue Pointe Hotel** (© 664/491-5210) can arrange day sails to these beaches.

---

electricity and running water, but the government also wishes to prevent squatters from settling on land abandoned by the many homeowners who evacuated the island.

A good place to first learn about the volcanic catastrophe is the **Montserrat Volcano Observatory** ☆ (© 664/491-5647), which moved, in 2002, into premises in Flemings, above the village of Salem, on the island's north coast. The observatory is about a 25-minute drive from the ferry terminal and about a 30-minute drive from the heliport. Depending on how busy the staff is recording seismic phenomenon on the day of your arrival, tours may or may not be available (US$4 for adults, US$2 for children age 7–12, under 7 free). No reservations are necessary. The tour consists of a 30-minute talk about the observatory's goals and objectives, and an introduction to its activity over the past few years. There's an opportunity to look at a number of informative exhibits, including the instruments that constantly monitor the volcano's pulse and power.

TOURS By no means should any novice visitor to Montserrat venture into the island's southern tiers without a trained guide. One of the best tour operators, and especially appealing if you're based in Antigua, is **Jenny's Montserrat Day Tours** (© 268/461-9361 in Antigua, no local phone in Montserrat; www.jennietours.com). Operated by Montserrat native Jennifer Burke from a base in Antigua, it charges US$130 per person, depending on the day of the week. Advance reservations are necessary and there are no tours on Sunday. Tours begin and end at the Heritage Quay at St. John's in Antigua. The price includes ferryboat transit to Montserrat, breakfast and lunch, and a detailed tour of between 6 and 7 hours, with English-language commentary from a trained guide and driver.

5

Aruba

The most touristy island in the Dutch Caribbean, Aruba has a growing number of fans, from honeymooners and sun worshippers to snorkelers, sailors, and weekend gamblers. When you lie back along the 11km (6¾-mile) stretch of white-sand beach, you'll enjoy an average 82°F (28°C) daytime temperature, trade winds, and very low humidity. Moreover, you won't be harassed by peddlers on the beach; you'll find it relatively safe; and you won't feel racial tensions.

Don't come for local culture and history—you're here to enjoy that fantastic sandy beach and evenings of dining and drinking, moonlit strolls, and gambling. The main resort area is a row of comfortable but familiar high-rise hotels along a gorgeous shoreline, like a beach strip in Florida. The island's Palm Beach, one of the best beaches in the world, draws droves of tourists, as do its glittering casinos.

The smallest of the ABC Islands (Aruba, Bonaire, and Curaçao), Aruba is 32km-long (20 miles) and 10km-wide (6¼ miles), with a landmass of 298 sq. km (116 sq. miles). Its coastline on the leeward side is smooth and serene, with white-sand beaches; but on the eastern coast, the windward Atlantic side, it looks rugged and wild. Dry and sunny almost year-round, Aruba has clean, exhilarating air, like in the desert of Palm Springs, California. Forget lush vegetation. Aruba lies outside the hurricane belt and gets less rain than virtually any other popular island in the Caribbean.

Though it is still a Dutch protectorate, Aruba became a nation unto itself in 1986. Some visitors have called Oranjestad, Aruba's capital, a "Holland-meets-Disney fantasia" because of its step-gabled Dutch architecture painted with a Caribbean palette of bright pastels. With more than a dozen resort hotels populating its once-uninhabited beaches, it is now one of the Caribbean's most popular destinations. A recent moratorium on hotel construction, however, has halted the building of new resorts—so for now, Aruba remains safe from rampant overdeveloping.

1 Essentials

VISITOR INFORMATION

Before you leave home, contact the **Aruba Tourism Authority** at the following locations: 1000 Harbor Blvd., Weehawken, NJ 07087 (© **201/330-0800;** fax 201/330-8757; newjersey@aruba.com); One Financial Plaza, Suite 136, Fort Lauderdale, FL 33394 (© **954/767-6477;** fax 954/767-0432; ata.florida@aruba.com); 10655 Six Pines Dr., Suite 145, Woodland, TX 77380 (© **281/362-1616;** fax 281/362-1644; ata.houston@aruba.com); in Canada, 5875 Highway 7, Suite 201, Woodbridge, Ontario, L4L 1T9 (© **905/264-3434;** fax 905/264-3437; ata.canada@aruba.com); and in the U.K., The Copperfields, 25 Copperfield St., London SE1 0EN (© **020/7928-1600;** fax 020/7928-1700; geoff@saltmarshpr.co.uk).

Information is available on the Web at **www.aruba.com** or by calling ℭ **800-TOARUBA.**

Once on the island, you can go to the **Aruba Tourism Authority** at L. G. Smith Blvd. 172, Oranjestad (ℭ **297/58-23777**) for information.

GETTING THERE

Before you book your airline tickets, read the section "Packages for the Independent Traveler" in chapter 2—it could save you a bundle. Even if you don't book a package, you should see that chapter's tips on finding the best airfare.

On **American Airlines** (ℭ **800/433-7300;** www.aa.com), Aruba-bound passengers can catch a daily nonstop 4½-hour flight from New York's JFK airport. American also offers nonstop flights from Boston; Miami; and San Juan, Puerto Rico. American offers lots of great-value packages to Aruba, including a selection of several resorts. Ask for the tour department, or talk to a travel agent.

Air ALM (ℭ **800/327-7230**) has good connections into Aruba from Miami, but it offers no direct flights—all flights stop first in Curaçao.

US Airways (ℭ **800/428-4322;** www.usairways.com) offers nonstop flights from Charlotte, North Carolina, and Philadelphia several days a week.

Continental Airlines (ℭ **800/231-0856;** www.continental.com) flies to Aruba via nonstop flights from Newark, New Jersey, and also from Houston three times a week.

United Airlines (ℭ **800/538-2929;** www.united.com) has weekend service from Chicago.

Delta Air Lines (ℭ **800/241-4141;** www.delta.com) also flies to Aruba from its hub in Atlanta, taking 4¾ hours. The airline also offers Saturday-only flights from New York's JFK airport.

Air Canada (ℭ **888/247-2262** in the U.S. and Canada; www.aircanada.ca) has connections from Toronto and Quebec to Miami. Once in Miami, Canadians and other passengers can fly nonstop to the island (weekends only).

GETTING AROUND

BY RENTAL CAR   It's easy to rent a car in Aruba. Excellent roads connect major tourist attractions, and all the major rental companies accept valid U.S. or Canadian driver's licenses. Major U.S. car-rental companies maintain offices on Aruba at the airport and at major hotels. No taxes are imposed on car rentals on Aruba, but insurance can be tricky. Even when you purchase a collision-damage waiver, you are still responsible for the first $300 to $500 worth of damage. (Avis doesn't even offer this waiver. In the event of an accident, you would be liable for up to the full value of damage to your car unless you have private insurance.) Rental rates range between $40 and $90 per day.

Try **Budget Rent-a-Car,** at Tamarijn Aruba Beach Resort, J. E. Irausquin Blvd. 41 (ℭ **800/472-3325** in the U.S., or 297/58-24150, ext. 658, in Aruba; www.budgetrentacar.com); **Hertz,** Sabana Blanca 35 (ℭ **800/654-3131** in the U.S., or 297/58-21845 in Aruba; www.hertz.com); and **Avis,** Kolibristraat 14

⌒ Fun Fact Carnival

Many visitors come here for the annual pre-Lenten Carnival, a month-long festival held in February or March, with events day and night. The music, dancing, parades, costumes, and "jump-ups" (Caribbean hoedowns) make Carnival the highlight of Aruba's winter season.

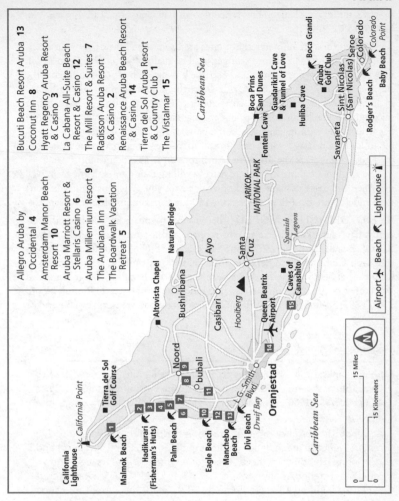

Bucuti Beach Resort Aruba **13**
Coconut Inn **8**
Hyatt Regency Aruba Resort & Casino **3**
La Cabana All-Suite Beach Resort & Casino **12**
The Mill Resort & Suites **7**
Radisson Aruba Resort & Casino **2**
Renaissance Aruba Beach Resort & Casino **14**
Tierra del Sol Aruba Resort & Country Club **1**
The Vistalmar **15**

Allegro Aruba by Occidental **4**
Amsterdam Manor Beach Resort **10**
Aruba Marriott Resort & Stellaris Casino **6**
Aruba Millennium Resort **9**
The Arubiana Inn **11**
The Boardwalk Vacation Retreat **5**

Airport ✈ Beach ⌅ Lighthouse ☼

(© **800/331-1212** in the U.S., or 297/58-28767 in Aruba; www.avis.com). Car rentals are also available at **Dollar Rent-a-Car** (© **800/800-4000** in the U.S.; www.dollar.com), whose branch is at the Queen Beatrix Airport (© **297/58-30101**). **National** (© **800/CAR-RENT** in the U.S.; www.nationalcar.com) has branches at Tanki Leendert 170 (© **297/58-71967**) and at the Queen Beatrix Airport (© **297/58-25451**).

For a better deal, consider **Hedwina Car Rental,** at the airport (© **297/58-30880**). If you rent for a week, you sometimes pay for only 5 days. Also consider **Thrifty Car Rental,** Balashi 65 (© **297/58-55300,** or 297/58-35335 at the airport), with rentals starting at $29 per day. Jeeps start at $59 per day.

BY BUS   Aruba has excellent bus service, with regular daily service from 6am to midnight. Round-trip fare between the beach hotels and Oranjestad is $2. Bus schedules are available at the **Arubus Office** at the central bus station on Zoutmanstraat. Your hotel reception desk will know when the buses pass by. Try to have the exact change. For schedules and information, call Arubus Co. (© **297/58-27089**).

BY TAXI   Taxis are unmetered but rates are fixed, so tell the driver your destination and ask the fare before you get in. The main office is near Palm Beach between Eagle Bowling Center and Taco Bell. A dispatch office is located at the Bosabao (© **297/58-22116**). A ride from the airport to most of the hotels, including those at Palm Beach, costs about $20 per car, with a four-passenger maximum. Some locals don't tip, but we suggest you do, especially if the driver has helped you with luggage. On some parts of the island, it's next to impossible to locate a taxi and you'll have to call. If you're going to a remote location, it's a good idea to ask the driver to return for you at a certain time.

The English-speaking drivers are usually willing tour guides. Most seem well informed and eager to share their knowledge with you. A 1-hour tour (you don't need much more than that) costs from $40 for a maximum of four passengers.

BY MOTORCYCLE & MOPED   Because Aruba's roads are good and the terrain is flat, many visitors like to rent mopeds and motorcycles. **Melchor Cycle Rental,** Bubali 106B (© **297/58-65648** or 297/58-65649), in front of Adventure Golf Club, rents scooters for $32 per day. You can also rent street bikes, beginning at $65 per day. These are cash prices; a 4% handling charge is assessed if you use a credit card. You can also find rentals at **Semver Cycle Rental,** Noord 22 (© **297/58-66851** or 297/58-66852), where scooters begin at $25 per day.

FAST FACTS: Aruba

Banks   Banks are open Monday to Friday from 8am to noon and 1:30 to 4pm. The most centrally located bank is **Aruba Bank** at Caya Betico Croes 41 (© **297/58-21550**). It's not hard to find an ATM (including one at the airport).

Currency   The currency is the **Aruba florin (AFl)**, which is divided into 100 cents. Silver coins are in denominations of 5¢, 10¢, 25¢, and 50¢, and 1 and 2½ florins. The 50-cent piece, the square *yotin,* is Aruba's best-known coin. The current exchange rate is 1.77 AFl to US$1 (1 AFl is worth about 56¢). (Just before you leave home, you can check the current exchange rates on the Web at **www.xe.com**.) U.S. dollars, traveler's checks, and major credit cards are widely accepted on the island. *Rates in this chapter are quoted in U.S. dollars.*

Documents   To enter Aruba, U.S. and Canadian citizens and British subjects may submit a valid passport or a birth certificate along with photo ID. We always recommend carrying your passport whenever you visit a foreign country.

Electricity   The electricity is 110-volt AC (60 cycles), the same as in the United States.

Emergencies   For the police, dial © **911**. For a medical emergency, dial © **58-74300**. For the fire department, call © **911**.

Hospital   For medical care, go to the **Horacio Oduber Hospital** on L. G. Smith Boulevard (© **297/58-74300**; this is also the number to call in case of a medical emergency). This modern building near Eagle Beach has excellent medical facilities. Hotels also have medical doctors on call, and there are good dental facilities as well (appointments can be made through your hotel).

Language The official language is Dutch, but nearly everybody speaks English. Spanish is also widely spoken, as is the local dialect, Papiamento.

Liquor Laws Liquor is sold on any day of the week throughout the island in most stores, including grocery stores and delis. By law (which doesn't seem to be heavily enforced), you can have an open container on the beach only if the liquor is purchased at one of the bars of the resort hotels lining the beachfront.

Safety Aruba is one of the Caribbean's safest destinations, in spite of its numerous hotels and casinos. Pickpockets and purse-snatchers are around, of course, but they're rare. Still, it's wise to guard your valuables. Never leave them unattended on the beach or even in a locked car.

Taxes & Service Charges The government of Aruba imposes a 6% room tax and a $37 airport departure tax. Your hotel will add a 15% to 20% service charge for room, food, and beverages.

Telephone To call Aruba from the United States, dial ℂ **011** (the international access code), then **297** (the country code for Aruba), then **58** (the area code) and the five-digit local number. Once you're in Aruba, dial only the five-digit local number for locations on the island. **AT&T** customers can dial ℂ **800-8000** from special phones at the cruise docks and at the airport to get service; from other phones, dial ℂ **121** to place a collect or AT&T calling card call. You can reach **MCI** at ℂ **800/888-8000**.

Time Aruba is on Atlantic Standard Time year-round, so most of the year, Aruba is 1 hour ahead of Eastern Standard Time (when it's 10am in Aruba, it's 9am in New York). When daylight savings time is in effect in the United States, clocks in New York and Aruba show the same time.

Water The water, which comes from the world's second-largest desalination plant, is pure.

Weather The island lies far outside the hurricane belt, so there is no threat of tropical storms. The average annual temperature is 82°F (28°C).

2 Accommodations

Most of Aruba's hotels are bustling, self-contained resorts. There's a dearth of family or budget hotels. Guesthouses are also rare and tend to fill up early in winter with faithful return visitors.

In season, it's imperative to make reservations well in advance; don't ever arrive expecting to find a room on the spot. You must give Immigration the address where you'll be staying when you arrive.

Don't forget to ask if the 6% room tax and 15% to 20% service charge (see above) are included in the rates quoted when you make your reservation.

Before you try to book your hotel on your own, read the section "Packages for the Independent Traveler" in chapter 2. Lots of the big resorts in Aruba are frequently featured in packages, which can bring their rates down dramatically.

In lieu of renting an actual house or villa, which you can do on some islands, your best bet here is to rent an apartment or condo. Amsterdam Manor Beach Resort is a good place for such rentals.

VERY EXPENSIVE

Allegro Aruba by Occidental ℛ (Kids)

Rising high above Palm Beach, this hotel, which calls itself "a cruise ship on land," underwent a $25 million renovation in 1998, and still looks in good shape. The Occidental chain, an outfit with many all-inclusive hotels in the Caribbean, acquired it a few years later. To stay at this all-inclusive is to feel part of an ongoing house party with a lot of action and organized activities. Guests have direct access to one of the island's best beaches. The hotel consists of a pair of nine-story interconnected towers in a landscaped garden with a lagoon-shaped swimming pool in the center. Bedrooms have carpeting, rattan furniture, comfortable beds, tub-shower combos, and very small balconies overlooking the beach. Well managed, the resort attracts families, repeat guests, and international tour groups.

The Caruso is the most upscale and formal restaurant, with sophisticated cuisine, and requires advance reservations. The food is fine, but unremarkable.

J. E. Irausquin Blvd. 83 (P.O. Box 218), Palm Beach, Aruba. © 800/858-2258 in the U.S., or 297/58-64500. Fax 297/58-63191. www.occidentalhotels.com. 417 units. Winter $248–$278 double, $417–$626 suite; off season $205–$251 double, $374–$598 suite. Rates are all-inclusive. AE, MC, V. **Amenities:** 3 restaurants; deli; 3 bars (1 swim-up); outdoor pool; casino; 2 lit tennis courts; fitness center; Jacuzzi; boating; dive shop; snorkeling; windsurfing; kids' club; drugstore; salon; room service (breakfast only); massage; babysitting; laundry service; dry cleaning. In room: A/C, hair dryer, iron/ironing board, safe.

Aruba Marriott Resort & Stellaris Casino ℛℛ (Kids)

Although it's no Hyatt (see below), this eight-story luxury high rise lies at a far extension of Palm Beach, forming a U around a large courtyard with lush landscaping. When you walk in, the waterfalls, streams, and fountains evoke a tropical garden. Known also for its casino and health spa, the hotel offers spacious and vividly decorated bedrooms, with large balconies opening onto prime views of the ocean. Each room is loaded with amenities, including a walk-in closet, dual sinks, and in-room movies.

Lunch can be poolside or else at Waves on the beach. La Vista offers Continental fare in a casual atmosphere. For more elegant dining, head for Tuscany's Ristorante, which has a northern Italian menu. The spa is state-of-the-art, with great massages and body wraps evocative of Indonesia.

L. G. Smith Blvd. 101, Palm Beach, Aruba. © 800/223-6388 in the U.S., or 297/58-69000. Fax 297/58-60649. www.marriott.com. 413 units. Winter $390–$470 double, $475–$713 suite; off season $179–$304 double, $274–$411 suite. AE, DC, MC, V. **Amenities:** 6 restaurants; 3 bars; outdoor pool; casino; 2 tennis courts; health club and deluxe Mandara Spa; Jacuzzi; sauna; dive shop; jet skis; kayaks; parasailing; sailing; snorkeling; water-skiing; children's programs; game room; business center; room service (7am–11pm); massage; babysitting; laundry service; dry cleaning; nonsmoking rooms; rooms for those with limited mobility. In room: A/C, TV, dataport, minibar, beverage maker, hair dryer, iron/ironing board, safe.

Hyatt Regency Aruba Resort & Casino ℛℛℛ (Kids)

The most glamorous resort on Aruba—even more so than the Radisson (see below)—lies on 5 landscaped beachfront hectares (12 acres) 3km (2 miles) north of Oranjestad. Built in the early 1990s for more than $57 million, the nine-story resort offers a series of public rooms reminiscent of a large-scale Latin American hacienda. Its gardens, Aruba's finest, are dotted with waterfalls and reflecting pools. The bedrooms are luxurious, with many extras, including original artworks commissioned from around the Americas. They are not as large, however, as those at the Marriott (see above). Room extras include a king or two double beds, and big bathrooms with combination tubs and showers and tile floors. Guests in the hotel's 29 Regency Club rooms enjoy a private concierge, upgraded linens, and other amenities.

In general, the Hyatt has better restaurants than any other hotel in Aruba. You can choose among four restaurants and lounges, including the lovely indoor/outdoor Ruinas del Mar restaurant, with Mediterranean food. The Casino Copacabana offers entertainment and gaming tables.

A $2.5 million multilevel pool complex and lagoon (with waterfalls, tropical gardens, and slides) is the showcase of the resort.

J. E. Irausquin Blvd. 85, Palm Beach, Aruba. (℃ **800/233-1234** in the U.S. and Canada, or 297/58-61234. Fax 297/58-61682. www.hyatt.com. 360 units. Winter $480–$630 double, from $650 suite; off season $240–$365 double, from $495 suite. MAP (breakfast and dinner) $70 per person extra. AE, DC, DISC, MC, V. **Amenities:** 4 restaurants; 4 bars; ice cream and coffee shop; outdoor pool; casino; 2 lit tennis courts; health club and spa; fitness center; Jacuzzi; canoes; dive shop; scuba diving; snorkeling; horseback riding; children's center and programs; game room; car rental; business center; salon; 24-hr. room service; massage; babysitting; laundry service; dry cleaning; nonsmoking rooms. *In room:* A/C, TV, dataport, minibar, beverage maker, hair dryer, iron/ironing board, safe.

Radisson Aruba Resort & Casino ⭐⭐⭐
One of the 10 most luxurious resorts in the Southern Caribbean, this eight-floor hotel occupies 6 choice hectares (15 acres) along Palm Beach. The restored property, Radisson's flagship, shows what a $55 million renovation can do, even though it's not as dramatic as the Hyatt (see above). Its high points are cascading waterfalls and the Aruba Tower, from whose rooms guests enjoy panoramic views of the Caribbean. Pampering sets the tone—everything from spacious balconies with teak patio furniture, full-size marble bathrooms with shower-tub combinations, to the most elaborate package of toiletries in the Caribbean. Spacious guest rooms are in a Colonial/West Indian style, with mahogany four-poster beds, oversize mirrors, and plantation shutters. The private accommodations here are even more stylishly inviting than those at Hyatt and Marriott, especially if you book the concierge floor, which has extra amenities.

J. E. Irausquin Blvd. 81, Palm Beach, Aruba. (℃ **800/333-3333** in the U.S., or 297/58-66555. Fax 297/58-63260. www.radisson.com. 358 units. Winter $360–$520 double, $525–$850 suite; off season $225–$370 double, from $425 suite. AE, DC, DISC, MC, V. **Amenities:** 3 restaurants; 2 bars; 2 outdoor pools; casino; golf privileges; tennis court; fitness center; spa; canoes; dive shop; sailing; water-skiing; windsurfing; children's center; business center; 24-hr. room service; babysitting; laundry service; dry cleaning. *In room:* A/C, TV, minibar, beverage maker, hair dryer, iron/ironing board, safe.

Tierra del Sol Aruba Resort & Country Club ⭐
This is the number-one choice for golfers in the southern Caribbean. Luxurious villa living is combined with a state-of-the-art fitness center and spa on 240 hectares (576 acres) of landscaping that includes one of the Caribbean's best 18-hole golf courses, the creation of Robert Trent Jones Jr. The vast complex sprawls across a cactus-studded landscape on the north coast, evocative of parts of Arizona. Your choice is two- or three-bedroom condos or free-standing villas that also come with two or three bedrooms, ideal for families or friends traveling together. A great deal of Aruba's "only planned community" is owned by "second homers," so expect a widely varied decor. We have, however, found the furnishings tasteful and tropical, very Caribbean in their breezy motif. Bedrooms come with kings, queens, or twins and private tiled bathrooms with tubs and showers. Accommodations open onto covered terraces with tables and chairs and a view of the golf course or ocean.

Malmokweg, Aruba. (℃ **800/992-2015** or 297/58-67800. Fax 297/58-64970. www.tierradelsol.com. 47 units. Winter $475 2-bedroom condo, $575 2-bedroom villa, $525 3-bedroom condo, $680 3-bedroom villa; off season $275 2-bedroom condo, $400 2-bedroom villa, $375 3-bedroom condo, $455 3-bedroom villa. $50 extra per day for villas with pool. AE, DISC, MC, V. **Amenities:** 2 restaurants; 2 bars; outdoor pool; golf; 2 tennis courts; fitness center; spa. *In room:* A/C, TV, kitchen, washer/dryer, wet bar (in some units), iron/ironing board, safe.

EXPENSIVE

Bucuti Beach Resort Aruba ☆☆ *(Finds* At little three-story Bucuti, you get personal service, European charm, and lush landscaping on a lovely 6-hectare (15-acre) stretch of one of the Caribbean's best beaches, the most secluded part of Eagle Beach. What this hotel has that those above don't is intimacy, a personal approach to innkeeping, and a sense of seclusion. An adult retreat, it's a top choice for honeymooners. Each spacious, well-furnished, bright bedroom is on the beach and has two queen-size beds or one king-size bed and sleeper sofa. The most expensive units have two queen-size beds and an oceanfront balcony or terrace. All rooms have well-maintained bathrooms with shower-tub combinations.

Across from the Alhambra Bazaar and Casino, the hotel operates the oceanfront Pirates' Nest Restaurant, a replica of a 17th-century Dutch galleon that specializes in good steaks, fresh seafood, and theme nights.

Eagle Beach, Aruba. © 297/58-31100. Fax 297/58-25272. www.bucuti.com. 102 units. Winter $240–$270 double, $330 bungalow or junior suite; off season $140–$160 double, $215 bungalow or junior suite. MAP (breakfast and dinner) $43 per person extra. AE, DISC, MC, V. **Amenities:** Restaurant; bar; outdoor pool; open-air health club; tour desk; 24-hr. business center; babysitting; laundry service; coin-operated laundry; dry cleaning. *In room:* A/C, TV, dataport, minibar, fridge, beverage maker, hair dryer, iron/ironing board, safe, microwave.

La Cabana All-Suite Beach Resort & Casino ☆☆ *(Kids* This is megaresort city, one of the Caribbean's largest hotel complexes and dwarfing anything else on the island. If an intimate West Indian inn is your dream, flee the premises. Otherwise join in the communal fun, which has been ongoing here since 1991. Couples of all ages and persuasions, honeymooners, and families with very active kids live harmoniously on acres of landscaped grounds in self-contained "villages" across the street from Eagle Beach. Spacious, well-furnished suites come in widely varied combinations, and range from studios for one or two adults, to one-, two-, or three-bedroom suites. Ground-floor rooms afford less privacy. Suites come with well-equipped kitchens, patios, or verandas.

J. E. Irausquin Blvd. 250, Oranjestad, Aruba. © 800/835-7193 in the U.S. or Canada, or 297/58-79000. Fax 297/58-75474. www.lacabana.com/resort. 811 units. Winter $244–$309 studio, $304–$390 1-bedroom, $595–$816 2-bedroom, $886–$998 3-bedroom; off season $138–$182 studio, $184–$214 1-bedroom, $345–$487 2-bedroom, $520–$602 3-bedroom. Children under 12 stay free in parent's room. Extra person $15 in winter, $12 in off season. Various packages offered. **Amenities:** 6 restaurants; 5 bars; 3 outdoor pools; casino; 5 tennis courts; health club and spa; children's center; business center; babysitting; coin-operated laundry. *In room:* A/C, TV, kitchenette, beverage maker, hair dryer, safe.

Renaissance Aruba Beach Resort & Casino ☆☆ Unlike the properties reviewed above, the Renaissance is not on Palm Beach; however, it has a lot of other attractions. This sprawling, bustling place is two resorts in one, located in the Seaport Village Complex (the island's largest shopping and entertainment facility). Next to two marinas and a recreational park, it's the only major resort at Oranjestad Harbor and the only resort on Aruba that boasts a 16-hectare (40-acre) private island, six beaches, and a round-the-clock casino. The first resort (with 299 units), is adjacent to the Seaport Mall and has an outdoor pool and terrace. The second resort (with 251 one-bedroom suites) is a timeshare resort that caters to yachties; rooms are rented out when timeshare owners are not present. Each of the one-bedroom suites opens onto the beach. Each unit has a kitchenette, blond rattan furniture with floral pastel prints, and a small balcony, plush carpeting, and either a king- or two queen-size beds. Bathrooms offer deluxe toiletries and a combination tub and shower.

The top restaurant, L'Escale, is reviewed later (see "Dining," below). If you don't like it, you'll have your choice of more than a dozen others spread out between the hotel and the mall complex.

L. G. Smith Blvd. 9, Oranjestad, Aruba. © 800/421-8188 in the U.S. and Canada, or 297/58-36000. Fax 297/58-25317. www.marriott.com. 560 units in 2 resorts. Winter $249–$265 double, $313–$345 suite; off season $175–$191 double, $239–$271 suite. Extra person $40. Children 12 and under stay free in parent's room. Breakfast and dinner plans available. AE, DC, DISC, MC, V. **Amenities:** 15 restaurants; 5 bars; 3 outdoor pools; 2 casinos; tennis court; exercise room; spa; fishing; scuba diving; water-skiing; windsurfing; children's programs; 24-hr. room service; babysitting; laundry service; coin-operated laundry; nonsmoking rooms; rooms for those with limited mobility. *In room:* A/C, TV, dataport, minibar, beverage maker, hair dryer, iron/ironing board, safe.

MODERATE

Amsterdam Manor Beach Resort ★★ (Kids)
Inspired by the canal-front row houses in Amsterdam, this hotel sports one of the most interesting facades on the island. In an arid landscape across the street from Eagle Beach, where there's good snorkeling and swimming, it has a series of inner courtyards.

Even the accommodations are Dutch colonial in style, with pine furniture, country-rustic blues, soft reds, and greens. In some cases, high ceilings lead to gable-capped peaks. Both studios and one- or two-bedroom apartments have fully equipped kitchens. This is a good choice for families, with babysitting, use of washer/dryers, and a children's playground. Units are small but well maintained and inviting, with ceiling fans, balconies or terraces (often with a sea view), white tile floors, and textured walls. The small bathrooms have tubs and showers.

J. E. Irausquin Blvd. 252 (P.O. Box 1302), Oranjestad, Aruba. © 800/932-6509 in the U.S., or 297/58-71492. Fax 297/58-71463. www.amsterdammanor.com. 72 units. Winter $199–$209 studio, from $269 suite; off season $130–$140 studio, from $170 suite. AE, DC, MC, V. **Amenities:** Restaurant; 2 bars; outdoor pool; kiddie pool; fitness center; playground; concierge; car rental; business center; laundry service; coin-operated laundry; dry cleaning; nonsmoking rooms; rooms for those with limited mobility. *In room:* A/C, TV, dataport, kitchenette, fridge, beverage maker, hair dryer, iron/ironing board, safe.

The Boardwalk Vacation Retreat
This charming island-style hotel is special, offering several one- or two-bedroom casitas, lying only 135m (443 ft.) from the island's best swimming and beach area, Palm Beach. Units are spacious, with large private patios situated amidst lush gardens and near a swimming pool. Personalized service and privacy are the hallmarks of this place. Bedrooms are decorated with floral paintings on the walls, tile floors, and tropical rattan pieces. The location is only a short walk from high-rise hotels, casinos, and watersports facilities. Private hammocks are a special feature, and each casita's living room adjoins a small kitchen.

Bakval 20, Aruba. © 297/58-66654. Fax 297/58-61836. www.arubaboardwalk.com. 13 units. Winter $206–$296 double; off season $106–$161 double. Children under 12 stay free in parent's room. Extra person $15. AE, DISC, MC, V. **Amenities:** Outdoor pool; sauna; babysitting; laundry service. *In room:* A/C, TV, dataport, kitchen, beverage maker, hair dryer.

The Mill Resort & Suites ★ (Finds)
This complex of two-story concrete buildings with red roofs is set in an arid, rather dusty location near the Wyndham. It's adjacent to a large, modern re-creation of a Dutch windmill, a kitschy Aruban landmark. Units ring a large swimming pool, and glorious Palm Beach lies across the highway, a 5-minute walk away. The room decor is tropical, with white rattan furniture and carpeting or white floor tiles; many units have king-size beds and Jacuzzi-style tubs. This hotel is best for independent travelers who don't mind venturing out to find their own dining and fun.

J. E. Irausquin Blvd. 330, Palm Beach, Aruba. ✆ **800/992-2015** or 297/58-67700. Fax 297/58-67271. www.millresort.com. 200 units. Winter $180–$256 double, $320–$450 suite; off season $85–$120 double, $170 suite. AE, DC, DISC, MC, V. **Amenities:** Restaurant; bar; 2 outdoor pools; 2 tennis courts; fitness center; sauna; children's programs; salon; massage; babysitting; laundry service; dry cleaning; nonsmoking rooms; rooms for those with limited mobility. *In room:* A/C, TV, dataport, beverage maker, hair dryer, safe.

INEXPENSIVE

Aruba Millennium Resort *(Value)*   This is a roadside motel evocative of Florida that is similar to The Arubiana Inn (see below), except it rises two stories and is a short walk from the white sands of Palm Beach and six casinos. Many of the island's best restaurants are also within a walk of the complex. Accommodations are studios or one-bedroom suites with complete kitchen facilities and a private balcony. Furnishings are very Caribbean, with pastel fabrics and walls and white wicker and bamboo furnishings. Rooms are coated in white tile, each with a small but efficiently organized private bathroom with shower.

Palm Beach 33, Palm Beach, Aruba. ✆ **297/58-63700.** Fax 297/58-62506. www.arubamillenniumresort. com. 22 units. Winter $130–$172 double; off season $60–$95 double. Children under 12 $10 extra. **Amenities:** Outdoor pool. *In room:* A/C, TV, dataport, kitchenette, fridge, beverage maker, iron/ironing board, safe.

The Arubiana Inn *(Value)*   Lying only a 12-minute stroll from Eagle Beach, one of the island's finest, this small and intimate inn is for those wishing to avoid the megaresorts along the beach. The place is really like a motel you might encounter along the Florida Keys, not dramatic or spectacular in any way, but offering decent, well-maintained accommodations. The cacti-studded landscape may make you think you've landed in Scottsdale. Built of coral stone with much use of a russet-brown terra cotta, the complex encloses a communal section with a pool and chaise longues. Rooms are comfortable but rather basic, very West Indian in motif with light pastels, tiles, wicker, and rattan, along with tiny bathrooms with shower/tub combinations. Each unit also comes with a small living room area.

Bubali 74, Noord, Aruba. ✆ **297/58-77700.** Fax 297/58-71770. www.arubianainn.com. 16 units. Winter $85 double; off season $55 double. Children under 12 stay free in parent's room. AE, MC, V. **Amenities:** Bar; outdoor pool; minimarket; babysitting; nonsmoking rooms. *In room:* A/C, TV, fridge, beverage maker, microwave.

Coconut Inn *(Value)*   Set inland from the sea, within a 7-minute walk from the village of Noord and a 20-minute walk to Palm Beach, this affordable hotel was built in five yellow-and-white sections between 1975 and 1996. Its rates are a steal. Though you won't be near the beach, the location is convenient to supermarkets and a public bus stop. The conventional rooms and one-bedroom suites contain almost the same amount of floor space; the studios are relatively cramped. All motel-style accommodations have a neatly-kept bathroom with a shower unit, a balcony or patio, and either a kitchenette or a microwave and refrigerator. There's no maid service on Sunday.

Noord 31, Aruba. ✆ **297/58-66288.** Fax 297/58-65433. www.coconutinn.com. 40 units. Winter $80 studio for 2, $95 double or 1-bedroom suite for 2; off season $65 studio for 2, $75 double or 1-bedroom suite for 2. Rates include breakfast. Extra person $20 in winter; $15 off season. MC, V. **Amenities:** Restaurant (breakfast only); bar; outdoor pool; coin-operated laundry; nonsmoking rooms; rooms for those with limited mobility. *In room:* A/C, TV, kitchenette or fridge/microwave, iron/ironing board.

The Vistalmar *(Value)*   An affordable and intimate place to stay on Aruba, this property is on a dead-end street in a residential neighborhood with a sun deck that's built directly over the water. The swimming is off a beach with a mix of sand and rocks. It's quite a bargain, however, for in addition to your accommodations you will have complimentary use of bikes, picnic coolers, snorkeling equipment, beach towels, and an outdoor grill. The complex of apartments is in two similar buildings, each with a balcony or courtyard offering water views. A little more stylish than some of the more bare-bones apartment units rented on the island, the accommodations here are spacious and furnished for comfort. Your hosts, among the island's more personable, have a wealth of island information. They even stock your refrigerator with food for your first night here.

Each apartment has a king-size bed with a good mattress, a well-maintained bathroom with a tub and shower, a separate dressing area, a fully equipped kitchen, and a living room with a sleeper sofa. There's also a second sleeping room and a sun porch.

Bucutiweg 28, Aruba. (C) **297/58-28579.** Fax 297/58-22200. www.arubavistalmar.com. 8 units. Winter $113–$124; off season $80. No credit cards. **Amenities:** Snorkeling; bicycles; laundry service; 1 room for those with limited mobility. *In room:* A/C, kitchenette, fridge, beverage maker, iron/ironing board, safe.

3 Dining

Sometimes—at least on off-season package deals—visitors on the Modified American Plan (breakfast and dinner) are allowed to dine around on an exchange plan with other hotels. Ask your hotel for details.

IN ORANJESTAD
EXPENSIVE

Chez Mathilde 🌾🌾 FRENCH   Oranjestad's French restaurant is expensive, but most satisfied customers agree that it's worth the price. The chef's savory kettle of bouillabaisse contains more than a dozen different sea creatures. We also recommend the delectable rack of lamb chops with fine French herbs and filet of red snapper prepared with a lightly peppered crust and lemon dressing. You get not only distinguished food and service, but an elegant setting as well. In this carefully preserved 19th-century building, dining rooms are intimate, tables are beautifully set, and the decor is restrained but romantic. Live piano music enhances the total experience. The restaurant is near the Renaissance hotel complex, a 5-minute drive north of the airport.

Havenstraat 23. (C) **297/58-34968.** Reservations recommended. Main courses $24–$38. AE, DC, DISC, MC, V. Mon–Sat noon–2:30pm; daily 6–11pm.

Gasparito 🌾 *Finds* ARUBAN/INTERNATIONAL   This bright, upbeat restaurant is set in a traditional Aruban-style house *(cunugu),* with yellow walls and local artwork. The atmosphere is lively and the food varied. Diners can enjoy baked chicken stuffed with a peach, filet mignon served with either sautéed mushrooms or black-pepper sauce, or *keshi yena*—Dutch cheese stuffed with a choice of beef, chicken, or seafood. The menu also features an array of fresh seafood, including lobster served with a garlic-butter sauce or sautéed with onions, green peppers, tomatoes, and a multitude of spices.

Gasparito 3. (C) **297/58-67144.** Reservations recommended. Main courses $15–$33. AE, DISC, MC, V. Daily 5–11pm.

L'Escale 🌾🌾 CARIBBEAN/INTERNATIONAL   Some locals claim L'Escale is Aruba's best restaurant, preferring it to Chez Mathilde (see above). We think it's a toss-up. L'Escale offers direct access to Oranjestad's bustling Crystal Casino, but remains calm and elegant, thanks to a raised bar area separating it from the action. Designed in French Empire style, it offers panoramic views of the harbor. Although the service is formal, formal attire is not required.

The meals rely on imported foodstuffs and are perfectly cooked. Try the Caribbean snapper or the award-winning lobster bisque. A 5-ounce portion of tenderloin steak transforms the seafood pasta into the Caribbean's most elegant surf and turf ("seafood mignon"). Some of the best desserts in town are served here, especially the Grand Marnier or chocolate soufflé.

In the Renaissance Aruba Beach Resort & Casino at Seaport Village, L. G. Smith Blvd. 82. © **297/58-36000.** Reservations recommended in winter. Main courses $25–$49; Sun brunch $31. AE, DC, DISC, MC, V. Daily 6–11pm; Sun brunch 10am–2pm.

MODERATE

Cuba's Cookin' 𝕉 *Finds* CUBAN　One of the oldest buildings on Aruba, constructed as a private home in 1877, is the setting for a restaurant where Batista-era Havana seems to come back to life. The most popular drink at its bar is a mint, rum, and sugar-laced *mojito*. There's a main dining room, plus three smaller areas, each lined with paintings inspired by the urban life in the Tropics and, in some cases, imported from Cuba. Lunch is simple, usually heaping platters of fish, chicken, or steak garnished with salad and vegetables. Dinners are more elaborate, and more representative of old-time Cuban cuisine. Try *ropa vieja* (shredded skirt steak fried with green peppers, tomatoes, and onions) or a succulent version of *picadillo de res* (ground beef garnished with olives and raisins). Cuban or Dominican cigars are available at the end of the meal. Every Monday to Saturday night this downtown Oranjested place is mobbed with islanders coming for the live merengue, salsa, and Cuban jazz that's produced by live bands, who play on those evenings from 10:30pm until at least 1am.

Wilhelminastraat 27 (across from the police station). © 297/58-80627. Reservations recommended. Lunch main courses $10; dinner main courses $15–$26. AE, DC, MC, V. Kitchen Mon–Sat noon–2:30pm and 5:30–11pm.

Driftwood 𝕉 *Finds* SEAFOOD　The married partners who run this restaurant have an unusual setup: He (Herbert Merryweather) spends the day on the high seas catching the fish served that night in the restaurant, while she (Francine Merryweather) stays on-site, directing the sometimes busy traffic in the dining room. The setting is an antique Aruban house in the center of Oranjestad, with interior walls covered with (guess what) irregular pieces of driftwood. The menu items that are always available include Argentine filet mignon served with a bacon-flavored mushroom sauce; boneless breast of chicken with Parmesan and linguine; stewed conch; and shrimp in Creole sauce. But the composition of the fish menu varies according to the day's catch. It might include mahimahi, wahoo, kingfish, grouper, and lobster. These will be prepared in ways that you'll discuss with a staff member, usually Francine, who will propose any of several methods of preparation, either blackened, meunière, fried, or baked, along with appropriate garnishes and sauces.

Klipstraat 12. © 297/58-32515. Reservations recommended. Main courses $16–$34. AE, MC, V. Wed–Mon 5:30–10:30pm (last order).

Hostaria da' Vittorio 𝕉 ITALIAN　Chef Vittorio Muscariello dazzles with specialties he learned cooking in the Mediterranean. His open kitchen exposes his secrets, which keeps some of his local fans returning again and again. There's a casual trattoria feel to the place, with bright linen tablecloths and the use of wood and earth tones. Even if the ingredients are imported, the chef seems to make everything taste fresh. The menu showcases the consistently well-prepared fare that might include such starters as a seafood soup swimming with grouper, shrimp, mussels, clams, squid, and baby octopus or baked fresh baby artichokes,

Travel Tip: He who finds the best hotel deal has more to spend on facials involving knobbly vegetables.

Hello, the Roaming Gnome here. I've been nabbed from the garden and taken round the world. The people who took me are so terribly clever. They find the best offerings on Travelocity. For very little cha-ching. And that means I get to be pampered and exfoliated till I'm pink as a bunny's doodah.

*** travelocity®

1-888-TRAVELOCITY / travelocity.com / America Online Keyword: Travel

tantalizingly flavored with garlic and herbs and served with black olives. The U.S. beef tenderloin is baked in puff pastry with porcini mushrooms, and the U.S. veal shank is delectably braised in a dry white wine with fresh herbs and spices. Our favorite pasta is the cheese ravioli cooked in a walnut sauce.

L. G. Smith Blvd. 380 (across from the Hyatt Regency), Palm Beach. © 297/58-63838. Reservations recommended. Main courses $19–$35; pizzas $9–$13. AE, DC, MC, V. Daily 11am–3pm and 6–11pm.

Kowloon CHINESE/INDONESIAN This elegant Asian restaurant offers two red-and-yellow dining rooms, accented with varnished hardwoods and Chinese lamps, that overlook one of the capital's thoroughfares. Skilled at preparing Hunan, Szechuan, and Shanghai cuisine, chefs here also offer Indonesian staples such as the classic *nasi goreng* and *bami goreng,* made with rice or noodles and tidbits of pork, vegetables, and shrimp. The elaborate *rijstafel* combines dozens of small curried vegetables and rice in one impressive display, and the house special seafood combines fish, scallops, lobster, shrimp, and Szechuan-style black-bean sauce.

Emmastraat 11. © 297/58-25959. Reservations recommended. Main courses $13–$24; set-price *rijstafel* (rice table) $38 for 2 diners. AE, MC, V. Daily 11am–10pm.

La Dolce Vita ✦ NORTHERN ITALIAN This restaurant is the most acclaimed Italian dining spot on Aruba, recognized by the food and wine critics at *Gourmet* magazine. It may not be as elegant as Valentino's (p. 119), but the food is better. The creative menu contains a few unusual dishes in addition to usual favorites. A meal might include slices of veal served either Parmesan style, cordon bleu style, with Marsala sauce, à la Florio (with artichokes), or à la Bartolucci (with ricotta, spinach, and mozzarella). Snapper comes four ways: simmered with clams and mussels, broiled with lemon or with wine, or stuffed with pulverized shrimp. We salivate over the stewpot of fish, served with linguine in red or white clam sauce.

Sasaky Hwy., Italiastraat 46, Eagle Beach. © 297/58-85592. Reservations recommended, especially in winter. Main courses $13–$39. AE, MC, V. Daily 5:30–11pm.

Le Dôme ✦ BELGIAN/FRENCH Belgian part-owner Peter Ballière runs this elegant restaurant on Eagle Beach. Some 12,000 bricks were shipped from Belgium to create an "Antwerp atmosphere." The menu is sumptuous and excellently prepared, including such appetizers as goose-liver pâté imported from France and, a most unusual dish for the Caribbean, creamy endive soup. From starters like escargots and frog legs, you can proceed to such tempting dishes as rack of lamb, Dover sole, or salmon with asparagus. You can order wine, or else wash it down with the island's best selection of Belgian beer. And don't forget the Belgian chocolates for dessert. The terrace, La Galerie, offers a view of Eagle Beach. The $35 Sunday brunch is an island tradition; you can order as often and as much from the a la carte menu as you want, and the price includes champagne or mimosas.

J. E. Irausquin Blvd. 224. © 297/58-71517. Reservations recommended. Main courses $15–$35; 7-course set menu $60. AE, DC, DISC, MC, V. Daily noon–3pm and 6–10pm.

INEXPENSIVE

The Paddock INTERNATIONAL In the heart of Oranjestad, this cafe and bistro overlooks the harbor, a short walk from virtually every shop in town. Much of the staff is hip and European. No one will mind whether you opt for a drink, a cup of tea or coffee, a snack of sliced sausage and Gouda cheese, or a full-fledged meal. The menu offers crab, salmon, shrimp, and tuna sandwiches;

salads; pita-bread sandwiches stuffed with chicken and a garlic sauce with plenty of tang; fresh poached or sautéed fish; and a glazed tenderloin of pork.

L. G. Smith Blvd. 13. ⓒ 297/58-32334. Sandwiches, snacks, and salads $3.50–$6; main courses $10–$16. MC, V. Mon–Thurs 10:30am–2am; Fri–Sun 10:30am–3am.

NEAR PALM BEACH
EXPENSIVE
Chalet Suisse ⚘ SWISS/INTERNATIONAL   Set beside the highway near La Cabana Hotel, this alpine-chalet restaurant feels like an old-fashioned Swiss dining room. In deliberate contrast to the arid scrublands that surround it, the restaurant is an air-conditioned refuge of thick plaster walls, pinewood panels, and a sense of *gemutlichkeit* (comfort). Tempting menu items include a lobster bisque, Dutch pea soup, beef stroganoff, a pasta of the day, wiener schnitzel, roast duckling with orange sauce, red snapper with Creole sauce, and an array of high-calorie desserts. The chefs boast that they serve the best rack of lamb in the Southern Hemisphere. We can't vouch for that, but it's really good. The hearty Swiss fare is good, if a bit heavy for the Tropics. Finish off with a smooth chocolate fondue or the eternal favorite, Swiss apple strudel. Most dishes are at the lower end of the price scale.

J. E. Irausquin Blvd. 246. ⓒ 297/58-75054. Reservations recommended. Main courses $19–$50. AE, DISC, MC, V. Mon–Sat 6–10:30pm.

Pago Pago ⚘⚘ POLYNESIAN   With their flaming torches and drinks crowned by pastel-colored umbrellas, many so-called Polynesian restaurants are more show than flavor. Not this one. You can begin with a South of Pago Pago drink while taking in nighttime views of the waters washing up on Palm Beach. Piano music and a small combo put you in the mood for some of the most tempting dishes you'll find in Aruba. The chef's signature dishes include grouper under a crust of macadamia nuts served with a coriander sauce made with fresh lime and papaya, and a Dover sole. The cooks do a superb roast duck and a perfectly prepared swordfish. Desserts change daily but a white-chocolate mousse in a chocolate shell is often the favorite.

In the Wyndham Aruba Beach Resort & Casino, J. E. Irausquin Blvd. 77. ⓒ 297/58-64466. Reservations required. Main courses $18–$39. Fixed-price menu $30. AE, MC, V. Mon–Sat 6–10:30pm.

MODERATE
Madame Janette ⚘ *(Finds* ARUBAN/CARIBBEAN/INTERNATIONAL   In a low-slung Aruban house, a short ride from Palm Beach, this local dive exudes island atmosphere, attracting windsurfers and a casual, laid-back crowd to its tables set in a "desert courtyard." Karsten Gesing, a European chef, has created a buzz among local foodies with his imaginative menu and clever blending of ingredients. We recommend "Madame's hot shrimps," succulent prawns baked in a well-flavored marinara sauce topped with Gouda and Gorgonzola. Even though the delicacy of the seafood is overpowered, the taste is still delightful. Or try the West Indian rock lobster in a velvety cream sauce laced with cognac, or the toasted almond grouper in a light cream sauce flavored with fresh spinach. The rack of lamb is the chef's masterpiece, but his marinade is "a secret I learned from my father." Finish off with such desserts as bourbon vanilla ice cream with blueberry sauce or a Swiss-chocolate truffle mousse. "Mama Jamaica" is a fresh pineapple marinated in old Appleton rum and served with vanilla ice cream topped with roasted coconut flakes.

Cunuco Abao 37 (next to the Blue Village Villas). ⓒ 297/58-70184. Reservations required. Main courses $13–$32. AE, MC, V. Wed–Mon 6–10pm.

IN OR NEAR NOORD

Buccaneer *SEAFOOD/INTERNATIONAL*   In a rustic building near the hamlet of Noord, close to many of the island's biggest high-rise hotels, the Buccaneer is one of Aruba's most popular seafood restaurants. Inside, you'll find a nautical decor and bubbling aquariums. There are a number of tempting appetizers, such as crabmeat cocktail or a savory plate of escargots with an infusion of Pernod. Lobster thermidor appears on the menu, or you can try the land-and-sea platter with fresh fish, shrimp, and tender beef tenderloin. The food is hearty and delicious. A spacious bar area is a good place to linger over drinks.

Gasparito 11-C, Noord. ℭ 297/58-66172. Reservations not accepted. Main courses $12–$23. AE, DC, DISC, MC, V. Mon–Sat 5:30–10pm.

Lekker Brasserie CHINESE/DUTCH   Set within a 10-minute drive north of Oranjestad, this is one of Aruba's most evocative restaurants. (*Lekker*, in Dutch, means tasty.) There's a semicircular bar area and a tropical dining room filled with rattan and bamboo furniture. The chefs prepare many Chinese favorites, along with the kind of Indonesian dishes that evoke nostalgia in Dutch visitors on holiday in Aruba. Dishes include *papapankan*, a Dutch version of slow-cooked pork; *nasi goreng* (fried rice with vegetables and meat); *bami goreng* (fried noodles with vegetables and meat); satay (skewers of grilled chicken or beef served with a peanut sauce); egg foo yong; chow mein, and curried chicken in the style of Bali.

Noord 39. ℭ 297/58-62770. Reservations recommended. Main courses $10–$25. MC, V. Mon–Fri 3pm–3am; Sat–Sun 3pm–5am.

The Old Cunucu House *ARUBAN/INTERNATIONAL*   When it was originally constructed as a private house in the 1920s, this was the only building in the neighborhood. Today it retains its original decor of very thick, plaster-coated walls, ultrasimple furniture, and tile floors. Many visitors start with a cocktail under a shed-style roof in front, where chairs and tables overlook a well-kept garden studded with desert plants. The restaurant maintains a warm, traditional feeling, and focuses on local and international recipes including fish soup, fried squid, and coconut fried shrimp. Several dishes are served with *funchi* (Caribbean polenta) and *pan bati* (a local pancake). The skilled chef knows how to embroider a traditional repertoire with first-class ingredients.

Palm Beach 150, Noord. ℭ 297/58-61666. Reservations recommended. Main courses $17–$33. AE, DISC, MC, V. Mon–Sat 5–10pm.

Valentino's *NORTHERN ITALIAN*   This is the most elegant Italian restaurant on Aruba, even if La Dolce Vita's (p. 117) food is somewhat better. In the central courtyard of an upscale condominium complex, guests enjoy cocktails near the entrance, and then climb a flight of stairs to the peak-ceilinged dining room. Here you can check out the glassed-in, well-designed kitchen, and bask in the attentions of the young but well-trained international staff. It's a cozy, comfortable place with views over the palms and pools of the condominium complex. The prices are somewhat high, but you'll forget that when you taste the food. The fish dishes are your best bet; also excellent are the chicken Parmesan, veal scaloppine, tenderloin pepper steak, and rack of lamb in rosemary sauce with mint jelly.

In the Caribbean Palm Village, Noord 43-E. ℭ 297/58-62700. Reservations recommended. Main courses $19–$35. AE, DC, MC, V. Mon–Sat 6–11pm.

AT TIERRA DEL SOL/NORTH ARUBA

La Trattoria "El Faro Blanco" ✺ ITALIAN   Charming and authentically Italian, this restaurant, built in 1914, was originally the local lighthouse keeper's home. It's now managed by the same people who maintain the nearby golf course. The staff is mostly European, and the head chef studied in Italy. Views sweep out over the sea, the island's northern coastline, and the island's largest golf course. The menu covers a full range of Italian cuisine, with a heavy dose of aromatic Neapolitan specialties. The best examples include heaping platters of fish and vegetable antipasti; linguine with shrimp, octopus, scallops, clams, and tomatoes (wins our vote for the island's best pasta); red snapper cooked in a potato crust with olive oil and rosemary; and *osso buco* (veal shank) served with Parmesan-laced risotto Milanese. The desserts are excellent; we recommend tiramisu or pears poached in red wine served with ice cream. The bar is a favorite stop for golfers.

At the California Lighthouse, North Aruba. ✆ 297/58-60787. Reservations required. Main courses $18–$35. AE, DC, DISC, MC, V. Daily noon–3pm and 6–11pm.

EAST OF ORANJESTAD

Brisas del Mar ✺ *Finds* SEAFOOD/ARUBAN   A 15-minute drive east of Oranjestad, near Savaneta's police station, Brisas del Mar is a little hut at the water's edge with an air-conditioned bar where locals gather to drink the day away. It's often jammed on weekends with many of the same locals, who come here to drink and dance. In back the tables are open to sea breezes, and nearby you can see the catch of the day, perhaps wahoo, being sliced and sold to local buyers. Specialties include a mixed seafood platter and broiled lobster; you can order meat and poultry dishes as well, including tenderloin steak, filet mignon, and broiled chicken. It's all solid, traditional fare, nothing too subtle or fancy.

Savaneta 222A. ✆ 297/58-47718. Reservations required. Main courses $12–$26. AE, MC, V. Tues–Sun noon–2:30pm; daily 6–9:30pm.

Charlie's Bar and Restaurant SEAFOOD/ARUBAN   Charlie's is the best reason to visit San Nicolas—come for the good times and the brew, not the food. The bar dates from 1941 and is the most overly decorated joint in the West Indies, sporting an array of memorabilia and local souvenirs. Where roustabouts and roughnecks once brawled, you'll now find tables filled with visitors admiring thousands of pennants, banners, and trophies dangling from the high ceiling. Two-fisted drinks are still served, but the menu has improved since the good old days, when San Nicolas was one of the toughest towns in the Caribbean. You can now enjoy freshly made soup, grilled scampi, Creole-style squid, and churrasco. Sirloin steak and red snapper are usually featured.

Main St., San Nicolas (a 25-min. drive east of Oranjestad). ✆ 297/58-45086. Daily soup $7; main courses $19–$31. AE, DISC, MC, V. Mon–Sat noon–9:30pm (bar open until 10pm).

4 Beaches

The western and southern shores of Aruba are called the Turquoise Coast. Along this stretch, Palm Beach and Eagle Beach (the latter closer to Oranjestad) are the best. No hotel along the strip owns these beaches, all of which are open to the public (if you use any of the hotel's facilities, however, you'll be charged).

The major resort hotels are built on the southwestern and more tranquil strip of Aruba. These beaches open onto calm waters, ideal for swimming. The beaches on the northern side of Aruba, although quite beautiful, face choppy waters with stronger waves.

Palm Beach ⟨⟨⟨⟨ is a superb stretch of wide white sand that fronts hotels. It's great for swimming, sunbathing, sailing, fishing, and snorkeling. Unfortunately, it's crowded in the winter. The waters off this beach are incredibly blue and teeming with neon-yellow fish and flame-bright coral reefs. Billowing rainbow-colored sails complete the picture. Along Palm Beach, all the resorts are set in flowering gardens. Of course, a river of water keeps these gardens blooming in this otherwise arid landscape, but the gardens take on a special beauty precisely because the island is so dry. As you walk along the beach, you can wander through garden after garden, watching the native bird life. The tropical mockingbird feeds on juicy local fruits, and the black-faced grassquit or the green-throated carib hover around the flowers and flowering shrubs. If you stop to have a drink at one of the hotels' open-air bars, chances are you'll be joined by a bananaquit hoping to steal some sugar from you.

Also worth seeking out is **Hadikurari (Fisherman's Huts),** where swimming conditions, in very shallow water, are excellent. The only drawback to this white powder-sand beach is some pebbles and stones at the water's edge. This beach is known for some of the finest windsurfing on island and is the site of the annual **Hi-Winds Pro-Am Windsurfing Competition.** Facilities include picnic tables.

Quite similar to Palm Beach, **Eagle Beach** ⟨⟨ is next door on the west coast, fronting a number of timeshare units. With gentle surf along miles of white-powder sand, swimming conditions here are excellent. Hotels along the strip organize watersports and beach activities.

The white-powder sands of **Punta Brabo,** also called **Manchebo Beach,** are a favorite among topless sunbathers. Actually, Manchebo is part of the greater Eagle Beach (see above), and the Manchebo Beach Resort is a good place to stop, as it offers a dive shop and rents snorkeling gear. It's also set amid 40 hectares (99 acres) of gardens, filled with everything from cacti to bougainvillea.

Practically every visitor winds up on Eagle Beach and Palm Beach. If you'd like something more private, head for **Baby Beach** ⟨⟨ on the eastern end of Aruba. The beach has white-powder sand and tranquil, shallow waters, making it ideal for swimming, and it's the best place on the island for beach-based snorkeling. There are no facilities other than a refreshment stand and shaded areas. You'll spot the Arubans themselves here on weekends. (Our local friends love this beach and may be furious at us for telling you about it!) Baby Beach opens onto a vast lagoon shielded by coral rocks that rise from the water. Bring your own towels and snorkeling gear.

Next to Baby Beach on the eastern tip of the island, **Rodger's Beach** also has white-powder sand and excellent swimming conditions. The backdrop, however, is an oil refinery at the far side of the bay. But the waters remain unpolluted, and

---

Moments Sunset at Bubali Pond

The **Bubali Pond** bird sanctuary lies on the north side of Eagle Beach at Post Chikito, south of De Olde Molen (a 19th-century windmill-turned-restaurant, Aruba's most famous landmark). Flocks of birds cluster at this freshwater pond, particularly at sunset, which makes for a memorable sight. You can see pelicans galore, black olivaceous cormorants, the black-crowned night herons, great egrets with long, black legs and yellow bills, and spotted sandpipers. Even the large wood stork and the glossy scarlet ibis sometimes fly in from Venezuela.

you can admire large and small multicolored fish here and strange coral formations. The trade winds will keep you cool.

5 Sports & Other Outdoor Pursuits

CRUISES   For a boat ride and a few hours of snorkeling, contact **De Palm Tours,** which has offices in eight of the island's hotels. Its main office is at L. G. Smith Blvd. 142, in Oranjestad (© **800/766-6016** or 297/58-24400). De Palm Tours offers a 1½-hour glass-bottom-boat cruise that visits two coral reefs and the German shipwreck *Antilla* on Tuesday through Thursday (the schedule varies). The cost is $25 per person.

DEEP-SEA FISHING   In the deep waters off the coast of Aruba you can test your skill and wits against the big ones—wahoo, marlin, tuna, bonito, and sailfish. **De Palm Tours,** L. G. Smith Blvd. 142, in Oranjestad (© **800/766-6016** or 297/58-24400), takes a maximum of six people (four can fish at the same time) on one of its five boats, which range in length from 8m to 12m (26 ft.–39 ft.). Half-day tours, with all equipment included, begin at $275 for up to four people. Extra persons are $20 each. The price for a full-day trip is $550. Boats leave from the docks in Oranjestad. De Palm maintains 13 branches, most of which are located in Aruba's major hotels.

GOLF   Aruba's **Tierra del Sol Golf Course** (© **297/58-67800**), designed by Robert Trent Jones Jr., is on the northwest coast near the California Lighthouse. The 18-hole, par-71, 6,811-yard course was designed to combine lush greens with the beauty of the island's indigenous flora, such as the swaying divi-divi tree. Facilities include a restaurant and lounge in the clubhouse, plus a swimming pool. Golf Hyatt manages the course. In winter, greens fees are a whopping $137, including golf cart, or $80 after 3pm. Off-season greens fees are $88, or $68 after 2pm. The course is open daily from 7am to 7pm.

A less pricey alternative is the **Aruba Golf Club,** Golfweg 82 (© **297/58-42006**), near San Nicolas on the southeastern end of the island. Although it has only 10 greens, you play them from different tees to simulate 18-hole play. Twenty-five different sand traps add an extra challenge. Greens fees are $10 for nine holes. The course is open daily from 7am to 5pm. You can rent golf carts and clubs in the on-site pro shop. On the premises, you'll find an airconditioned restaurant and changing rooms with showers.

HORSEBACK RIDING   De Palm Tours, L. G. Smith Blvd. 142 (© **800/766-6016** or 297/58-24400), will make arrangements for you to ride at **Rancho Del Campo** (© **297/58-50290**). Two daily rides last 3 hours each and cut through a park to a natural pool, where you can dismount and cool off with a swim. The price is $50 to $75 per person, and the minimum age is 10 years.

TENNIS   Most of the island's beachfront hotels have tennis courts, often swept by trade winds, and some have top pros on hand to give instruction. Many of the courts can also be lit for night games. We don't advise playing in Aruba's hot noonday sun. Some hotels allow only guests on their courts.

The best tennis is at the **Aruba Racket Club** (© **297/58-60215**), the island's first world-class tennis facility, which has eight courts, an exhibition center court, a swimming pool, a bar, a small restaurant, an aerobics center, and a fitness center. The club is open Monday through Friday from 6am to 9pm and on Sunday from 10am to 5pm. Rates are $10 per hour per court, and lessons are available by appointment only. The location is Rooisanto 21 on Aruba's northwest coast, near the California Lighthouse.

WATERSPORTS   You can snorkel in shallow waters, and scuba divers find stunning marine life with endless varieties of coral and tropical fish in myriad hues; at some points visibility extends up to 27m (89 ft.). Most divers set out for the German freighter *Antilla,* which was scuttled in the early years of World War II off the northwestern tip of Aruba, not too far from Palm Beach.

Red Sail Sports, Palm Beach (© **297/58-61603**), is the island's best watersports center. The activities include sailing and scuba diving. Red Sail dive packages include shipwreck dives and marine-reef explorations. Guests first receive a poolside dive-safety course from Red Sail's certified instructors. Those who wish to become certified can achieve full PADI certification in 4 days for $350. One-tank dives cost $40, and two-tank dives are $65. Night dives are $53.

6 Seeing the Sights

IN ORANJESTAD ✿

Aruba's capital, Oranjestad, attracts more shoppers than sightseers. The bustling city has a very Caribbean flavor, with part-Spanish, part-Dutch architecture. The main thoroughfare, Lloyd G. Smith Boulevard, cuts in from the airport along the waterfront and on to Palm Beach, changing its name along the way to J. E. Irausquin Boulevard. Most visitors cross it to head for **Caya G. F. Betico Croes** and the best duty-free shopping.

After a shopping trip, you might return to the harbor where fishing boats and schooners, many from Venezuela, are moored. Nearly all newcomers to Aruba like to photograph the **Schooner Harbor.** Colorful boats dock along the quay, and boat people display their wares in open stalls. The local patois predominates. A little farther along, at the **fish market,** fresh fish is sold directly from the boats. **Wilhelmina Park,** named after Queen Wilhelmina of the Netherlands, is also on the sea side of Oranjestad. The park features a tropical garden along the water and a sculpture of the Queen Mother.

AN UNDERWATER JOURNEY

One of the island's most fun activities is an underwater journey on one of the world's few passenger submarines, operated by **Atlantis Submarines** ✿, Seaport Village Marina (opposite the Sonesta), Oranjestad (© **800/253-0493** or 297/58-36090). Even nondivers can witness a coral reef firsthand without risking the obstacles and dangers of a scuba expedition. Carrying 46 passengers to a depth of up to 45m (148 ft.), the ride provides all the thrills of an underwater dive—but keeps you dry. In 1995 an old Danish fishing vessel was sunk to create a fascinating view for divers and submariners.

There are four departures from the Oranjestad harbor front Monday to Sunday from 10am to 1pm. Each tour includes a 15-minute catamaran ride to Barcadera Reef, 3km (2 miles) southeast of Aruba—a site chosen for the huge variety of its underwater flora and fauna. At the reef, participants are transferred to the submarine for a 1-hour underwater lecture and tour.

Allow 2 hours for the complete experience. The cost is $84 for adults and $35 for children age 4 to 16 (children under age 4 are not admitted). Advance reservations are essential. A staff member will ask for a credit card number (and give you a confirmation number) to hold the booking for you.

IN THE COUNTRYSIDE

If you can lift yourself from the sands for an afternoon, you might enjoy driving into the *cunucu,* which in Papiamento means "the countryside." Here Arubans live in modest, colorful, pastel-washed houses, decorated with tropical plants that require expensive desalinated water. Visitors who venture into the center of Aruba will want to see the strange **divi-divi tree,** with its trade wind–blown coiffure.

You probably will want to visit Aruba's most outstanding landmark, **Hooiberg,** affectionately known as "The Haystack." From Oranjestad, take Caya G. F. Croes (7A) toward Santa Cruz. Anybody with the stamina can climb steps to the top of this 162m-high (531-ft.) hill. On a clear day, you can see Venezuela from here.

Aruba is studded with massive boulders. You'll find the most impressive ones at **Ayo** and **Casibari,** northeast of Hooiberg. Diorite boulders stack up as high as urban buildings. The rocks weigh several thousand tons and puzzle geologists. Ancient Amerindian drawings appear on the rocks at Ayo. At Casibari, you can climb to the top for a panoramic view of the island or a close look at rocks that nature has carved into seats or prehistoric birds and animals. Pay special attention to the island's unusual species of lizards and cacti. Casibari is open daily from 9am to 5pm, with no admission charge. There's a lodge at Casibari where you can buy souvenirs, snacks, soft drinks, and beer.

Guides can also point out drawings on the walls and ceiling of the **Caves of Canashito,** south of Hooiberg. You may see some giant green parakeets here, too.

On the jagged, windswept northern coast of Aruba, the unrelenting surf carved the **Natural Bridge** out of coral rock. You can order snacks in a little cafe overlooking the coast. You'll also find a souvenir shop with trinkets, T-shirts, and wall hangings for reasonable prices.

NEAR SAN NICOLAS

As you drive along the highway toward the island's southernmost section, you may want to stop at the **Spaans Lagoen (Spanish Lagoon),** where pirates hid and waited to plunder rich cargo ships in the Caribbean. Today it's an ideal place for snorkeling, and you can picnic at tables under the mangrove trees.

To the east, you'll pass an area called **Savaneta,** where some of the oldest traces of human habitation on Aruba have been unearthed. You'll also find the oil tanks that marked the position of the **El Paso Oil & Transport Company,** the Exxon subsidiary around which the town of San Nicolas developed. San Nicolas was a company town until 1985, when the refinery curtailed operations. Nineteen kilometers (12 miles) from Oranjestad, it is now called the Aruba Sunrise Side, and tourism has become its main economic engine.

Boca Grandi, on the windward side of the island, is a favorite windsurfing location; if you prefer quieter waters, you'll find them at Baby Beach and Rodgers Beach, on Aruba's leeward side. Seroe Colorado (Colorado Point) overlooks the two beaches. From here, you can see the Venezuelan coastline and the pounding surf on the windward side. If you climb down the cliffs, you're likely to spot an iguana; protected by law, the once-endangered saurians now proliferate in peace.

You can see cave-wall drawings at the **Guadarikiri Cave** and **Fontein Cave.** At the **Huliba** and **Tunnel of Love** caves, guides and refreshment stands await visitors. The Tunnel of Love cave requires some physical stamina to explore. It is filled with steep climbs, and its steps are illuminated only by hand-held lamps. Wear sturdy shoes and watch your step.

7 Shopping

Aruba manages to offer goods from six continents along the .8km-long (¼-mile) **Caya G. F. Betico Croes,** Oranjestad's main shopping street. Technically this is not a free port, but the duty is so low (3.3%) that prices are attractive—and Aruba has no sales tax. You'll find the usual array of Swiss watches; German and Japanese cameras; jewelry; liquor; English bone china and porcelain; Dutch, Swedish, and Danish silver and pewter; French perfume; British woolens; Indonesian specialties; and Madeira embroidery. Delft blue pottery is an especially good buy. Other good buys include Dutch cheese (Edam and Gouda), Dutch chocolate, and English cigarettes in the airport departure area.

Alhambra, J. E. Irausquin Blvd. 47 (*C* **297/58-35000**), is a complex of buildings and courtyards designed like an 18th-century Dutch village. About a dozen shops here sell souvenirs, leather goods, jewelry, and beachwear. From the outside, the complex looks Moorish, with serpentine mahogany columns, arches, and domes.

8 Aruba After Dark

CASINOS: LET THE GOOD TIMES ROLL *RR*

The casinos in the big hotels along Palm Beach are the liveliest nighttime destinations. Most stay open into the wee hours. In plush gaming parlors, guests try their luck at roulette, craps, blackjack, and, of course, the one-armed bandits. Limits and odds are about the same as in the United States.

Excelsior Casino, J. E. Irausquin Blvd. 230 (*C* **297/58-67777**), wins the prize for all-around action. Its casino doors are open from 9am to 4am. The **Aruba Grand,** J. E. Irausquin Blvd. 79 (*C* **297/58-63900**), is open from noon to 2:30am. **Casino Masquerade,** at the Radisson Aruba Resort & Casino, J. E. Irausquin Blvd. 81, Palm Beach (*C* **297/58-66555**), is one of the newer casinos on Aruba. On the lower-level lobby of the hotel, it's open from noon to 3am daily. Table games start at 6pm. It offers blackjack, single deck, roulette, Caribbean stud, craps, and Let It Ride.

One of the island's best is the **Crystal Casino** at the Renaissance Aruba Beach Resort & Casino at Seaport Village (*C* **297/58-36000**), open daily 24 hours. The 1,260 sq. m (13,563 sq. ft.) casino offers 10 blackjack tables, 405 slot machines, five roulette tables, four Caribbean stud-poker tables, one craps table, and one minibaccarat table. New games of chance are added regularly. This place has luxurious furnishings, ornate moldings, marble, and crystal chandeliers.

Some of the largest, splashiest, and most visually interesting casinos include the one at the **Wyndham Aruba Beach Resort,** J. E. Irausquin Blvd. 77 (*C* **297/ 58-64466**), or the **Hyatt Regency Aruba,** J. E. Irausquin Blvd. 85 (*C* **297/58-61234**). The **Royal Cabana Casino,** at the **La Cabana All-Suite Beach Resort & Casino,** J. E. Irausquin Blvd. 250 (*C* **297/58-75001**), outdraws them all. It's known for its multitheme three-in-one restaurant and its showcase cabaret theater and nightclub, with Las Vegas–style revues, female impersonators, and comedy series on the weekend. The largest casino on Aruba, it offers 33 tables and games, plus 320 slot machines. It's open from 11am to 3am; tables open at 2pm.

A busy casino on the premises of **Alhambra,** J. E. Irausquin Blvd. 47 (*C* **297/ 58-35000**), is open from 10am until very early in the morning, usually 3am. **Aladdin Theatre** adjoins the casino. Shows feature gymnasts, dancers, singers, and magicians, but don't have the professionalism and appeal of the big hotel revues recommended below.

At the Allegro Aruba by Occidental, the **Royal Palm Casino,** J. E. Irausquin Blvd. 83, (*C* **297/58-69039**), is known for its Caribbean stud poker at the tables, and also for games of blackjack, roulette, baccarat, and craps. Its slot machines open for action at noon, and tables and other games open at 7pm.

Another choice, the **Stellaris Casino,** at Marriott's Aruba Ocean Club, L. G. Smith Blvd. 1012, Palm Beach (© 297/58-69000), is a large casino that starts to get busy daily at 4pm, when gamblers arrive to play roulette, craps, and Caribbean stud poker.

BIG STAGE REVUES

Aruba stages more Las Vegas–type spectacles than any other island in the Caribbean. These shows are most often at hotels but are open to nonguests who reserve a table. Some of the best shows are staged at the **Seaport's Crystal Theatre,** in the Renaissance Aruba Beach Resort & Casino, L. G. Smith Blvd. 82, in Oranjestad (© 297/58-36000). "Let's Go Latin," its current and long-running revue, has been attracting audiences from Oregon to Venezuela with its lavish costumes, nearly 200 in all, and some two dozen performers. Exquisite bods strut the stage in this ooh lah-lah extravaganza. The talent comes from Cuba where, as one performer told us, "rhythm is in our blood."

Tickets for just the show cost $39 or $19 for children under 12. A dinner show package costs $68 per person. Show times are Monday to Saturday at 9pm.

The biggest stage shows in Aruba are at **Las Palmas Showroom,** in the Allegro Aruba by Occidental, J. E. Irausquin Blvd. 83, Palm Beach (© 297/58-64500). Six different spectacles a week are offered every Monday to Saturday, starting at 9pm. The cost is $53 per person, including dinner and one show. The show is different every night—a revue of Latino rhythms one night, Broadway tunes the next night, or a "fantasy" on another night.

You'll think you've arrived in Havana when you attend performances at the **Cabaret Royal Showroom,** Wyndham Aruba Beach Resort & Casino, J. E. Irausquin Blvd. 77, Palm Beach (© 297/58-64466). It stages hot Cuban revues, with dancing and salsa music. Nearly all of the performers—music makers, dancers, and singers—come from Cuba. It's a high-energy revue with Latino and American classic songs, ballads, and Broadway favorites. The dinner show includes a three-course menu for $48 per person, but for only $28 you can enjoy the "cocktail show." Dinner show seatings are at 7pm, with cocktail show seatings at 8:15pm, and the revue beginning at 8:30pm. No shows Monday and Sunday.

THE CLUB & BAR SCENE

We like to begin our Aruban nights at **Salt 'n Pepper,** J. E. Irausquin Blvd. 368A (© 297/58-63280), where we can order the island's best tapas. Three or four of these appetizers are large enough to make a meal. If you bring in a set of original salt and pepper shakers for the owners to keep, you get your first glass of wine free with your dinner. *Note:* Sets can't be "borrowed" from local restaurants and hotels. Sangria, consumed in an alfresco courtyard, is the usual drink of choice, and the bar stays open until 1 am.

Mambo Jumbo, in the Royal Plaza Mall, L. G. Smith Boulevard (© 297/58-33632), is sultry and relaxing. Expect a cosmopolitan blend of Dutch and Latino visitors, and lots of Latin rhythms. The volume is kept at a tolerable level for anyone who wants to have a conversation. There's an array of specialty drinks; imagine coconut shells, very colorful straws, and large fruit. Hours are from 10pm to 3am, depending on the night of the week.

Iguana Joe's Caribbean Bar & Grill, Royal Plaza Mall, L. G. Smith Boulevard (© 297/58-39373), enjoys an equal vogue among visitors and islanders. It's known for its huge array of specialty drinks, including Pink Iguana, Grandma Joe's Pink Lemonade, and the aptly named Lethal Lizard, the latter packing four shots of liquor in a half-liter carafe. Line your stomach with fresh salads, pastas, fresh mahimahi, sizzling fajitas, and rich homemade desserts. Hours are from 11am to 11pm.

Other nightlife venues include the **Sirocco Lounge** at the Wyndham Aruba Beach Resort & Casino, J. E. Irausquin Blvd. 77 on Palm Beach (© **297/58-64466**), which presents life jazz nightly Thursday to Saturday.

Aruba's most popular nighttime attraction is a 1957 Chevy bus, **Kukoo Kunuku** (© **297/586-2010**), a psychedelically painted party bus that hits half a dozen of the island's hottest bars. The carousing begins at "sundowner" time at 6pm and goes on until around midnight Monday to Saturday. Every reveler gets maracas for this pub crawl on wheels. The cost of $55 per person includes dinner, champagne toast on the beach, a free drink at the three bars, and a pickup at your hotel.

Barbados

Endless pink- and white-sand beaches and a rich West Indian tradition are what put Barbados (Bar-*bay*-dose) on the map. Barbados is easily reached from the United States and has a grand array of hotels (many of them super-expensive). Although it doesn't offer casinos, it has more than just beach life. It's a terrific destination for travelers interested in learning about West Indian culture, and it offers more sightseeing attractions than most Caribbean islands.

After morning mists burn off to expose panoramas of valley and ocean, the Bajan landscape is one of the most majestic in the southern Caribbean. It's an ideal place to go on lovely driving tours to take in all the little seaside villages, plantations, gardens, and English country churches, some dating from the 17th century.

Barbados is known as "Little England" in the Caribbean. Afternoon tea remains a tradition in many places, cricket is still the national sport, and many Bajans speak with a British accent. Despite this legacy, islanders are weighing the possibility of a divorce from the mother country.

Don't rule out Barbados if you're seeking a peaceful island getaway. Although the south coast is known for its nightlife and the west-coast beach strip is completely built up, some of the island remains undeveloped. The east coast is fairly tranquil, and you can often be alone here (but because it faces the Atlantic, the waters aren't as calm as they are on the Caribbean side). Many escapists, especially Canadians seeking a low-cost place to stay in winter, don't seem to mind the Atlantic waters at all. Not only does the Atlantic Coast have Bathsheba Beach going for it, but it is also home to some of the most visited attractions on the island. These include Andromeda Botanical Garden, Farley Hill National Park, Barbados Wildlife Reserve, and Harrison's Cave.

Although crime has been on the rise in recent years, Barbados is still a relatively safe destination. The difference between the haves and the have-nots doesn't result in the violence seen on other islands like Jamaica. Bajans have a long history of welcoming foreign visitors, and that tradition of hospitality is still ingrained in most locals.

1 Essentials

VISITOR INFORMATION

In the United States, you can contact the following offices of the **Barbados Tourism Authority:** 800 Second Ave., New York, NY 10017 (© **800/221-9831**); 3440 Wilshire Blvd., Suite 1215, Los Angeles, CA 90010 (© **213/380-2198**); or 150 Alhambra Circle, Suite 1000, Miami, FL 33134 (© **305/442-7471**).

The Canadian office is at 105 Adelaide St. West, Suite 1010, Toronto, Ontario M5H 1P9 (© **800/268-9122**). In the United Kingdom, contact the

Barbados Tourism Authority at 263 Tottenham Court Rd., London W1T 7LA (© **020/7636-9448** or 020/7636-9449).

On the Internet, go to **www.barbados.org**. The tourism office may be able to help you track down condo and villa rentals.

On the island, the local **Barbados Tourism Authority** office is located on Harbour Road (P.O. Box 242), Bridgetown (© **246/427-2623**).

GETTING THERE

Before you book your flight, be sure to read the section "Packages for the Independent Traveler" in chapter 2; it can save you a bundle. Even if you don't book a package, see that chapter's tips on finding the best airfare.

More than 20 flights arrive on Barbados from all over the world every day. **Grantley Adams International Airport** is on Highway 7, on the southern tip of the island at Long Bay, between Oistins and a village called The Crane. From North America, the four major gateways to Barbados are New York, Miami, Toronto, and San Juan. Flying time to Barbados is 4½ hours from New York, 3½ hours from Miami, 5 hours from Toronto, and 1½ hours from San Juan.

Virgin Atlantic Airways (© **800/862-8621**) flies three times weekly from London's Gatwick Airport to Barbados.

American Airlines (© **800/433-7300**; www.aa.com) has dozens of connections passing through San Juan, plus daily nonstop flights to Barbados from Miami. **BWIA** (© **800/538-2942**; www.bwee.com), the national airline of Trinidad and Tobago, also offers daily flights from New York and Miami, plus many flights from Trinidad. **US Airways** (© **800/428-4322**) flies daily from New York's LaGuardia to Philadelphia, then on to Barbados. There are no direct flights on US Airways from New York to Barbados.

All flights are nonstop from Toronto to Barbados. **Air Canada** (© **888/247-2262** in the U.S., or 800/268-7240 in Canada; www.aircanada.ca) has daily flights from Toronto in winter. From Montreal connections are made through Toronto. In summer, when demand wanes, fewer flights are available.

Barbados is a major hub of the Caribbean-based airline **LIAT** (© **868/624-4727**, 888/844-5428 in most of the Caribbean, 246/434-5428 for reservations, or 246/428-0986 at the Barbados airport; www.liatairline.com), which provides generally poor service to Barbados from a handful of neighboring islands, including St. Vincent and the Grenadines, Antigua, and Dominica.

Air Jamaica (© **800/523-5585**; www.airjamaica.com) offers daily flights that link Barbados to Atlanta, Baltimore, and Miami through the airline's Montego Bay hub. Air Jamaica offers service between Los Angeles and Barbados on Friday and Sunday (but it requires an overnight stay in Montego Bay). Nonstop flights from New York to Barbados are available at least three days a week (Tues, Wed, and Sun).

Cayman Airways and **Air Jamaica** have joined forces to provide an air link from Grand Cayman to Barbados and Trinidad, going via Kingston in Jamaica. Flights wing out of Grand Cayman on Monday, Tuesday, Saturday, and Sunday, linking up in Kingston with continuing flights to Barbados and Port-of-Spain, with daily return flights. For reservations and information, call Air Jamaica at © **800/523-5585**.

British Airways (© **800/247-9297**; www.britishairways.com) flies nonstop service to Barbados from London's Gatwick Airport. **Virgin Atlantic** (© **800/862-8621** in the U.S.; www.virgin.com) also has one daily direct flight from London to Barbados.

Barbados

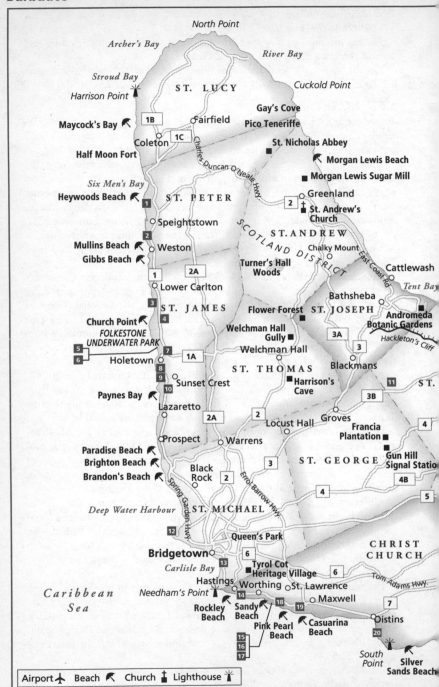

North Point

Archer's Bay

River Bay

Stroud Bay

ST. LUCY

Cuckold Point

Harrison Point

Maycock's Bay

1B

Fairfield

Gay's Cove

Pico Teneriffe

Coleton

1C

St. Nicholas Abbey

Half Moon Fort

Morgan Lewis Beach

Morgan Lewis Sugar Mill

Six Men's Bay

ST. PETER

Greenland

Heywoods Beach

1

2

St. Andrew's Church

Speightstown

ST. ANDREW

Mullins Beach

2

Weston

Chalky Mount

SCOTLAND DISTRICT

Gibbs Beach

Turner's Hall Woods

Cattlewash

1

2A

East Coast Rd.

Tent Bay

Lower Carlton

Bathsheba

3

Flower Forest

ST. JOSEPH

ST. JAMES

Andromeda Botanic Gardens

Church Point

4

Welchman Hall Gully

FOLKESTONE UNDERWATER PARK

3A

Hackleton's Cliff

5

Welchman Hall

3

6

Holetown

7

1A

ST. THOMAS

Blackmans

8

11

ST.

Sunset Crest

9

Harrison's Cave

3B

Paynes Bay

10

4

Lazaretto

Groves

Francia Plantation

2A

Warrens

2

Locust Hall

Prospect

Gun Hill Signal Station

Paradise Beach

ST. GEORGE

Brighton Beach

3

Brandon's Beach

Black Rock

4B

2

Errol Barrow Hwy.

4

Deep Water Harbour

5

ST. MICHAEL

Spring Garden Hwy.

CHRIST CHURCH

12

Queen's Park

Bridgetown

6

Carlisle Bay

13

Tyrol Cot Heritage Village

6

Hastings

14

Worthing

St. Lawrence

Tom Adams Hwy.

Needham's Point

18

Maxwell

Caribbean Sea

Rockley Beach

Sandy Beach

19

7

Pink Pearl Beach

Casuarina Beach

Distins

15

20

16

17

South Point

Silver Sands Beach

Airport ✈ Beach ☚ Church ✝ Lighthouse ☀

130

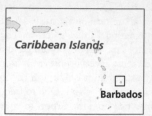

Caribbean Islands

Barbados

Accra Beach Hotel & Resort **14**
Allamanda Beach Hotel **12**
Almond Beach Village **1**
Cobblers Cove Hotel **2**
Coral Reef Club **3**
The Crane **21**
Divi Southwinds Beach Resort **18**
Fairholme **19**
The House **10**
Little Arches **20**
Lone Star Hotel **4**
Mango Bay Hotel & Beach Club **6**
Sandpiper **5**
Sandy Beach Island Resort **15**
Sandy Lane Hotel & Golf Club **8**
The Savannah **13**
Southern Palms **16**
Tamarind Cove **9**
Traveller's Palm **7**
Turtle Beach Resort **17**
Villa Nova **11**

ATLANTIC OCEAN

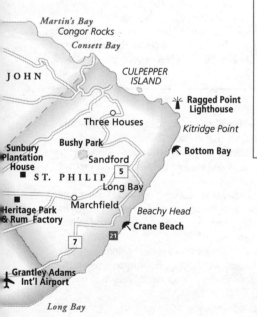

Martin's Bay
Congor Rocks
Consett Bay

J O H N

CULPEPPER ISLAND

Ragged Point Lighthouse

Three Houses

Kitridge Point

Bushy Park

Bottom Bay

Sunbury Plantation House

Sandford

ST. PHILIP

5

Long Bay

Heritage Park & Rum Factory

Marchfield

Beachy Head

Crane Beach

7

21

Grantley Adams Int'l Airport

Long Bay

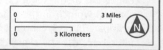

0   3 Miles
0   3 Kilometers

N

GETTING AROUND

BY RENTAL CAR   If you don't mind *driving on the left,* you may find a rental car ideal on Barbados. You'll need a temporary permit if you don't have an international driver's license. The rental agencies listed below can all issue this visitor's permit, or you can go to the police desk upon your arrival at the airport. You must have a license from home and pay a registration fee of BD$10 (US$5). The speed limit is 32kmph (20 mph) inside city limits, 72kmph (45 mph) else-where on the island. Due to frequent delays at airport counters, we suggest tak-ing a taxi from the airport to your hotel, and then calling to have your rental car delivered. No taxes apply to car rentals on Barbados.

None of the major U.S.-based car-rental agencies operates on Barbados, but a host of local companies rent vehicles. Except in the peak midwinter season, cars are usually readily available without prior reservations. Be forewarned that many local companies continue to draw serious complaints from readers, both for overcharging and for the poor conditions of their vehicles. Proceed very care-fully with rentals on this island. Check the insurance and liability issues carefully when you rent.

The island's most frequently recommended agency is **National Car Rentals,** Lower Carlton, St. James (© **246/426-0603**), which offers a wide selection of Japanese cars (note that it's *not* affiliated with the U.S. chain of the same name). National is 16km (10 miles) north of Bridgetown, near the main highway (Hwy. 1); it delivers cars to almost any location on the island, and the driver who deliv-ers it will carry the necessary forms for the Bajan driver's license.

Other comparable companies include **Sunny Isle Motors,** Dayton, Worthing Main Road, Christ Church (© **246/435-7979**), and **P&S Car Rentals,** Pleasant View, Cave Hill, St. Michael (© **246/424-2052**). One company conveniently

---

Finds Special Events

One of the hottest "cool" jazz festivals in the Caribbean is the **Barbados Jazz Festival.** The next scheduled festival is called "Paint It Jazz" and will take place in mid-January 2005. International artists appear, along with the best in local jazz talent. For tickets and further details, contact festival organizers at www.barbadosjazzfestival.com.

In mid-February, the **Holetown Festival** at St. James is a weeklong event commemorating the landing of the first European settlers at Holetown in 1627. Highlights include street fairs, police band concerts, a music festival in the parish church, and a road race.

During the first week of April, the **Oistins Fish Festival** commemorates the signing of the charter of Barbados with fishing, boat racing, fish-bon-ing competitions, a Coast Guard exhibition, food stalls, arts and crafts, dancing, singing, and road races.

Beginning in mid-July and lasting until the first week of August, the **Crop Over Festival** is the island's major national festival, celebrating the completion of the sugar-cane harvest and recognizing the hardworking men and women in the sugar industry. Communities all over the island participate in fairs, concerts, calypso competitions, car parades, and other cultural events. The climax of the festival occurs at **Kadooment Day,** a national holiday on the first Monday in August, which becomes the biggest party of the year in Barbados.

close to hotels on the remote southeastern end of Barbados is **Stoutes Car Rentals,** Kirtons, St. Philip (© **246/435-4456**). Because it's closer to the airport than its competitors, it can theoretically deliver a car there within 10 minutes of a call placed when you arrive.

BY TAXI   Taxis aren't metered, but rates are fixed by the government; one cab can carry up to four passengers for the same fare. Taxis are plentiful and easily identifiable by the letter Z on their license plates. Drivers will produce a list of standard rates (US$25–US$30 per hr., subject to change). To call a taxi, contact one of the following services: **Paramount Taxi Service** (© **246/429-3718**), **Royal Pavilion Taxi Service** (© **246/422-5555**), or **Lyndhurst Taxi Service** (© **246/436-2639**). A typical taxi ride from the airport to Bridgetown costs US$35; to Holetown along the western Gold Coast, US$40; and to St. Lawrence Gap, site of many of the less expensive hotels, US$30.

BY BUS   Take a bus only as a last resort, as the service is unreliable, in spite of the fact that many Bajans depend on this service to get to and from work. The nationally owned **buses** of Barbados are blue with yellow stripes. They're not numbered, but their destinations are marked on the front. On most major routes, buses run every 30 minutes or so. Wherever you go, the fare is BD$1.50 (US75¢), exact Barbados change required. Departures are from Bridgetown, leaving from Fairchild Street for the south and east, and from Lower Green and the Princess Alice Highway for the north going along the west coast. Call the **Barbados Tourism Authority** (© **246/427-2623**) for schedules and information.

Privately operated **minibuses** run shorter distances and travel more frequently. They are bright yellow with blue stripes, with their destinations displayed on the bottom-left corner of the windshield. Minibuses in Bridgetown are boarded at River Road, Temple Yard, and Probyn Street. The fare is BD$1.50 (US75¢).

FAST FACTS: Barbados

American Express   The island's affiliate is **Going Places Travel,** Suite 27, Becklith Mall, Nile Street (© **246/431-2423**), in Bridgetown.

Banks   Most banks are open Monday through Thursday from 8am to 3pm, and Friday from 8am to 5pm. The major banks of Barbados, **all with ATMs,** are found along Broad Street in Bridgetown, including branches of First Caribbean Bank (formerly Barclays), the Barbados National Bank, and the Bank of Nova Scotia. These banks also have branch offices in Holetown, Speightstown, and along the St. Lawrence Gap south of Bridgetown. There are ATMs at the airport as well, plus at bank branches throughout the island.

Consulates & High Commissions   The **Embassy of the United States** is on Broad Street, Bridgetown (© **246/436-4950**), and the **Canadian High Commission** at Lower Bishop's Court, Pine Road, Bridgetown (© **246/429-3550**). The **British High Commission** is found at Lower Collymore Rock, St. Michael (© **246/430-7880**).

Currency   The **Barbados dollar (BD$)** is the official currency, available in $5, $10, $20, and $100 notes, as well as 10¢, 25¢, and $1 silver coins, plus 1¢ and 5¢ copper coins. The Barbados dollar is permanently fixed because of an international agreement at the rate of approximately 50¢ in U.S. currency. Most stores take traveler's checks or U.S. dollars. However, it's best to convert your money at banks and pay in Barbados dollars. *Unless otherwise specified, rates in this chapter are quoted in U.S. dollars.*

Customs Most items for personal use (within reason, of course) are allowed into Barbados, except agricultural products and firearms. You can bring in perfume for your use if it's not for sale. You're also allowed a carton of cigarettes and a liter of liquor.

Dentists **Dr. Derek Golding,** with two other colleagues, maintains one of the busiest practices on Barbados, at 5 Stafford House, The Garrison, St. Michael (© 246/228-2201). They will accept any emergency (they treat most of the cruise-ship passengers' emergencies) and often stay open late. Otherwise, hours are Monday through Friday from 8:30am to 3:30pm, and Saturday 8:30 to 11am.

Documents U.S. or Canadian citizens coming directly from North America to Barbados for a period not exceeding 3 months must have a passport. An ongoing or return ticket is also necessary. British and Australian subjects need a valid passport.

Electricity The electricity is 110-volt AC (50 cycles), so at most places you can use your U.S.-made appliances.

Emergencies In an emergency, dial the police at © **211,** the fire department at © **311,** and an ambulance at © **511.**

Hospitals The **Queen Elizabeth Hospital** is located on Martinsdale Road in St. Michael (© **246/436-6450**). Of the several private clinics, one of the most expensive and best recommended is the **Bayview Hospital,** St. Paul's Avenue, Bayville, St. Michael (© **246/436-5446**).

Language The Bajans speak English, but with their own island lilt.

Liquor Laws Liquor, beer, and wine are sold throughout the island at every outlet from grocery stores to convenience stores on any day the stores are open. Be discreet with open containers on the beach, as legally they are not allowed.

Safety Crimes against visitors used to be rare, but there are today reports of pickpocketing, armed robbery, and even sexual assault. Avoid leaving cash or valuables in your hotel room, beware of purse snatchers when walking, exercise caution on the beach or at attractions, and be wary of driving in isolated areas.

Taxes A 7.5% government sales tax is tacked on to hotel bills. A 15% VAT (value-added tax) is levied on all meals. (For example, if your hotel costs US$200 per night, and you are charged US$50 per person for a MAP, you'll have to pay a 7.5% government tax plus the 10% additional service charge for the US$200 room rate, then an additional 15% VAT on the MAP rate.) Some visitors view these additional charges as "larcenous." They certainly won't make you happy when you go to pay your final bill. There's a departure tax of BD$25 (US$13) which is payable in either U.S. dollars or Barbadian currency.

Telephone To call Barbados from the United States, dial **1,** then **246** (the area code for Barbados) and the local number. Once on Barbados, to call another number on the island, only the local number is necessary. You can reach **MCI** at © **800/888-8000.**

Time Barbados is on Atlantic Standard Time year-round, so it's 1 hour ahead of New York except during daylight savings time, when Barbados's time is the same as the eastern United States.

Tipping Most hotels and restaurants add at least a 10% service charge to your bill. If service is extremely good, you may want to supplement that. If it has not been included, you may want to tip your waiter 10% to 15%. Taxi drivers expect a 10% tip.

Water Barbados has a pure water supply. It's pumped from underground sources in the coral rock that covers most of the island, and it's safe to drink.

Weather Daytime temperatures are in the 75°F to 85°F (24°C–29°C) range throughout the year.

2 Accommodations

Barbados has some of the best hotels in the Caribbean, many of which are small and personally run.

Most of our recommendations are on fashionable St. James Beach, which is the entire strip of beachfront bordering the parish of St. James. Although hotels are scattered around Barbados, most of them lie on the tranquil west coast as opposed to opening onto the turbulent Atlantic in the east. If you're into the grand life, head for one of the fashionable resorts north of Bridgetown, all opening onto sandy beaches. If you're in Barbados on business, you may want a hotel in Bridgetown, the capital. Otherwise, if you like more informality and cheaper prices, go to the lower south coast, especially around the busy strip of St. Lawrence Gap, where you'll find the most reasonably priced nightlife, restaurants, and local bars. This area also has beaches, although they're not as fabulous as those claimed by the pricey resorts north of Bridgetown.

To rent your own villa, cottage, or house on Barbados, contact **Property Management Services Ltd.,** The Cays, Greenridge Drive, Paynes Bay, St. James (© **246/432-6562;** property@sunbeach.net), which has properties in a wide range of prices.

ON THE WEST COAST
VERY EXPENSIVE

Almond Beach Village ✺✺ *Kids* This is our favorite of the island's all-inclusive resorts, and it's a good choice for (wealthy) families. Set near a string of even more expensive hotels (referred to as the island's Gold Coast), the Almond Beach Village occupies the site of a 19th-century sugar-cane plantation. In 1994, it underwent a US$13 million renovation, and since then renovations have been conducted at 2-year intervals. All meals, drinks, and most sports are included in one net price.

One section of the hotel is specifically set aside for families with kids (separate from all the honeymooning couples); it comes complete with a kids' club and lots of family suites.

The resort stands on 12 hectares (30 acres) of tropically landscaped gardens and 2km (1¼ miles) of prime beachfront. Accommodations are clustered into seven different compounds to create something akin to a miniature, self-contained village. Rooms, though not large, are well appointed, with ceiling fans, well-upholstered chairs, and small bathrooms with combination tub/showers. Exchange privileges are available with the hotel's all-inclusive twin, the Almond Beach Club in St. James Parish.

La Smaritta, the most formal restaurant, is Italian and serves excellent seafood pastas. Horizons, the largest restaurant and the resort's main dining room, offers two lavish buffet dinners per week and international food. The Reef focuses on fresh seafood. Least formal and funkiest of the lot is Enid's, with spicy Bajan food.

Hwy. 1B, Heywoods, St. Peter, Barbados, W.I. © 800/4-ALMOND in the U.S., or 246/422-4900. Fax 246/422-0617. www.almondresorts.com. 330 units. Winter US$535–US$800 double; off season US$350–US$500 double. Rates are all-inclusive. AE, DC, MC, V. 24km (15 miles) north of Bridgetown along Hwy. 2A. **Amenities:** 4 restaurants; 5 bars; 9 pools; 9-hole golf course; 5 tennis courts; 2 squash courts; fitness center; boating; water-skiing; windsurfing; children's program; room service (noon–9:30pm); babysitting; laundry service; dry cleaning; nonsmoking rooms; rooms for those with limited mobility. *In room:* A/C, TV, beverage maker, hair dryer, iron/ironing board, safe.

Cobblers Cove Hotel ★★★
This former mansion on a white-sand beach is built in a mock-medieval style on the site of a former British fort. A member of Relais & Châteaux, the hotel is a favorite honeymoon retreat. Elegant suites are housed in 10 Iberian-style villas, situated throughout lush gardens. Each unit has a spacious living room, a private balcony or patio, and a wet bar. Each year nine bedrooms are completely redecorated, so the property is always in top-notch condition. The spacious bathrooms come with combination shower/tubs. Two of the most exclusive accommodations on the entire island are the Camelot and Colleton suites, on the rooftop of the original mansion; they're beautifully decorated and offer panoramic views of both the beach and the garden. Both have their own pool. For their lethal prices, refer to the high end of the prices given below; other units are at the low end of the price scale.

The Terrace Restaurant is generally lighter and more refined than the heavier French food offered at some of its competitors along the Gold Coast. The open-air dining room overlooks the sea.

Road View, Speightstown, St. Peter, Barbados, W.I. © 800/890-6060 in the U.S., 020/8350-1000 in London, or 246/422-2291. Fax 246/422-1460. www.cobblerscove.com. 40 suites. Winter US$590–US$1,995 suite for 2; off season US$300–US$1,055 suite for 2. Rates include breakfast. AE, MC, V. Closed Sept to mid-Oct. No children Jan–Mar. **Amenities:** Restaurant; bar; outdoor pool; lit tennis court; snorkeling; Sunfish sailboats; water-skiing; windsurfing; tour desk; car rental; room service (8am–9:30pm); babysitting; laundry service; dry cleaning. *In room:* A/C, minibar, beverage maker, hair dryer, iron/ironing board, safe.

Coral Reef Club ★★
This family-owned and -managed luxury hotel is one of the best and most respected establishments on the island, set on elegantly landscaped grounds beside a white-sand beach that's ideal for swimming. A collection of veranda-fronted private units is scattered about the main building and clubhouse on a 5 landscaped hectares (12 acres), fronting the ocean. Rental units, housed in cottages, the main building, or in small, coral-stone wings in the gardens, can vary greatly, but each has a luxurious bed (a king, twins, or a four-poster) and a tiled bathroom, with a combination shower/tub. All units have private patios, and some have separate dressing rooms.

You can lunch in an open-air area, take afternoon tea, and then enjoy a first-rate dinner in a room with three sides open to ocean views. There's a folklore show and barbecue every Thursday, plus a Monday Bajan buffet featuring an array of food (including whole baked fish) and local entertainment.

Hwy. 1, St. James Beach, Barbados, W.I. ℂ 800/223-1108 or 246/422-2372. Fax 246/422-1776. www.coral reefbarbados.com. 88 units. Winter US$600 double, from US$740 suite; off season US$290 double, from US$320 suite. AE, MC, V. Drive 5 min. north of Holetown on Hwy. 1. No children under age 12 in Feb. **Amenities:** Restaurant; bar; 2 outdoor pools; 3 tennis courts; dive shop; salon; room service (8am–9pm); massage; babysitting; laundry service; dry cleaning; nonsmoking rooms; 1 room for those with limited mobility. *In room:* A/C, dataport, fridge, hair dryer, safe.

The House ✸✸✸ *Finds*   The House is a sanctuary of tranquillity and privacy, with the most personal service in Barbados. This exclusive retreat doesn't even call itself a hotel but "a concept." From the moment you arrive an "ambassador," clad in white linen, appears to serve you during your stay. As your luggage is taken to your room, you're invited for a complimentary massage on the beach to "de-stress" after your plane ride. The approach to the complex sets the tone, as you go over a wooden bridge across a lake studded with water lilies, passing along blossoming bougainvillea. Each unit is a luxuriously furnished suite containing many thoughtful extras such as Evian water and fresh fruit. All the bedrooms contain tubs and showers, and the most desirable accommodations overlook the golden sands at Paynes Bay, a 35-minute drive north of the airport. Two suites even have their own indoor pools.

Next door is Daphne's, the ultimate in island dining with an eclectic Italian menu inspired by its famous London counterpart. What's the food like? Ever had a delectable dish like marinated white anchovies with roast beets and linguine with spicy crab?

Hwy. 1, Paynes Bay, St. James, Barbados, W.I. ℂ 246/432-5525. Fax 246/432-5255. www.thehousebarbados. com. 31 suites. Winter US$1,143–US$2,058 double; off season US$550–US$1,065 double. Rates include full breakfast. AE, DC, MC, V. No children under 12 allowed. **Amenities:** Restaurant; bar; outdoor pool; Jacuzzi; kayaks; sailing; snorkeling; windsurfing; airport limousine; room service (8am–8pm); massage; laundry service; dry cleaning. *In room:* A/C, TV, dataport, beverage maker, hair dryer, iron/ironing board, safe.

Lone Star Hotel ✸ *Finds*   Talk about recycling old buildings. This chic new restaurant and hotel was converted from a dreary garage built in the 1940s. Today you are likely to see Monaco's Princess Caroline or Prince Albert running around the joint—perhaps one of the Spice Girls (remember them?). The gas jockeys and grease monkeys are long gone, and today the Lone Star offers four sumptuous suites—two on a good beach and the others on the upper level. Each is individually named to commemorate the building's former function. You can book into the Buick, Lincoln, Cord, or Studebaker suites, where you will find spacious bedrooms, beautiful furnishings, and opulent modern bathrooms with Philip Starck fittings. Upper suites open onto large furnished balconies. The building has had a long and colorful history, and during World War II a coral stone cave was carved out as a hideaway in case German bombs rained down. Today it is the wine cellar for the restaurant.

Hwy. 1, Mount Standfast, St. James. ℂ 246/419-0599. Fax 246/419-0597. www.thelonestar.com. 4 suites. Winter US$600–US$725 double; off season US$350 double. Extra person US$60. Rates include full breakfast. Children under 14 stay free in parent's room. AE, MC, V. **Amenities:** Restaurant; bar; room service (7am–11pm); babysitting; laundry service; dry cleaning; 1 unit for those with limited mobility. *In room:* A/C, TV, dataport, beverage maker, hair dryer, iron/ironing board, safe.

Mango Bay Hotel & Beach Club ✸   This all-inclusive resort offers barefoot elegance on a white-sand beach. The complex's several whitewashed buildings are set in tropical gardens. You get a lot for your money here: accommodations; three meals a day; afternoon tea; all drinks, including house wine with meals; watersports such as Sunfish sailing, kayaking, snorkeling, and windsurfing;

tennis; one catamaran cruise; one in-pool scuba lesson; glass-bottom boat rides; nightly entertainment; and walking tours.

Guest rooms range from standard to pool view to beachfront, though most units face the gardens. Decorated in tropical pastels, each has one king or two double beds, wicker furnishings, and a private terrace or balcony. Bathrooms are a bit small, and they contain shower/tub combinations.

Tasty grilled steaks, fresh seafood (including flying fish), and island fruits are just some of the delightful offerings in the resort's beachside restaurant. Nightly entertainment is presented in the piano lounge.

Second St., Holetown, St. James, Barbados, W.I. ℭ **246/432-1384.** Fax 246/432-5297. www.mangobay barbados.com. 64 units. Winter US$381–US$488 double; off season US$310–US$405 double. Extra person from US$110. Children under 4 stay free in parent's room. Rates are all-inclusive. AE, MC, V. **Amenities:** Restaurant; bar; piano bar; 2 outdoor pools; 2 tennis courts (nearby); kayaks; snorkeling; Sunfish sailboats; windsurfing; laundry service; dry cleaning. In room: A/C, TV, hair dryer, safe.

Sandpiper ℱ

The Coral Reef Club (see above) does it better, but if it's full, try this South Seas resort on a white-sand beach. It's a self-contained, intimate resort, set in a small grove of coconut palms and flowering trees. A cluster of rustic-chic units surrounds the pool; some have fine sea views. The rooms open onto little terraces that stretch along the second story, where you can order drinks or have breakfast. Accommodations are large, consisting of superior rooms and one- or two-bedroom suites beautifully furnished with tropical pieces. Each has a private terrace, luxurious bed, and small fridge. The medium-size bathrooms are equipped with combination tub/showers.

The refined cuisine is both Continental and West Indian; weekly buffets are offered in winter. The menu is varied and based on the best of seasonal products, so you can dine here every night without getting bored.

Holetown (a 3-min. walk north of town), St. James, Barbados, W.I. ℭ **800/223-1108** in the U.S., 800/567-5327 in Canada, or 246/422-2251. Fax 246/422-0900. www.sandpiperbarbados.com. 45 units. Winter US$495–US$725 double, from US$895 suite; off season US$395–US$440 double, from US$490 suite. Rates include breakfast and dinner. AE, MC, V. Children under 12 not accepted in Feb. **Amenities:** Restaurant; 2 bars; outdoor pool; 2 tennis courts; fitness center; children's programs; 24-hr. room service; babysitting; laundry service. In room: A/C, dataport, fridge, minibar, beverage maker, hair dryer, safe.

Sandy Lane Hotel & Golf Club ℱℱℱ

Sandy Lane is one of the most luxurious places to stay in the southern Caribbean, as its horrifying prices will attest. When Ronald Tree, an heir to the Marshall Field's department store fortune, constructed it in the 1960s, Sandy Lane enjoyed a celebrity-haunted heyday. After falling into neglect, it was rescued in 1997 by Irish investors, who poured US$350 million into its reconstruction. Fortunately, its pristine beach set against a backdrop of swaying palms needed no such rehabilitation.

The Palladian-style Sandy Lane is practically identical to its first incarnation, with the addition of a mammoth spa, better restaurants, and a trio of golf courses. You'll feel like royalty when checking in—especially when your valet unpacks your suitcase. On request, guests arrive in style—you'll be picked up at the airport in the hotel's Bentley.

The rooms are furnished grandly, with lots of extras not found at any of its competitors—such as a motion-sensor alarm to alert maids you're in the room, and a marble shower with seven adjustable nozzles. Accommodations are decorated mostly with redwood furnishings, each with a king-size bed or two twins. The bathrooms are the most luxurious on the island, and in addition to the shower, also contain oversize tubs and a bidet.

Four on-site restaurants offer the finest hotel dining on Barbados and serve mostly a French or Mediterranean cuisine. There's also the Spa Cafe for the weight conscious.

Hwy. 1, Paynes Bay, St. James. ℂ **246/444-2000**. Fax 246/444-2222. www.sandylane.com. Winter US$950–US$1,800 double, US$1,700–US$4,000 suite; off season US$700–US$1,000 double, US$1,200–US$3,200 suite. AE, DC, MC, V. **Amenities:** 4 restaurants; 4 bars; outdoor pool; 3 golf courses; 9 tennis courts; fitness center; health spa; kayaks; sailing; water-skiing; children's program; concierge; salon; 24-hr. room service; massage; nonsmoking rooms. *In room:* A/C, TV/DVD, dataport, minibar, beverage maker (on request), hair dryer, safe.

Tamarind Cove ⟨ℛ⟩ On 240m (787 ft.) of prime beachfront, this flagship of a British-based hotel chain (St. James Properties) is a major challenger to the Coral Reef Club/Sandpiper properties (see above), attracting the same upscale clientele. An US$8 million restoration in the 1990s made this one of the most noteworthy hotels on Barbados.

Designed in an Iberian style, with pale pink walls and red terra-cotta roofs, the hotel occupies a desirable location on St. James Beach, 2km (1¼ miles) south of Holetown. The chic and comfortable rooms are in a series of hacienda-style buildings interspersed with vegetation. Many units have a patio or balcony overlooking the gardens or ocean. The well-appointed bathrooms boast dual basins, spacious Roman tubs, stall showers, and long marble counters.

The Caribbean and international food here is among the finest of the resorts along the Gold Coast. There's some kind of musical entertainment every night.

Hwy. 1, Paynes Bay, St. James Beach (P.O. Box 429), Bridgetown, Barbados, W.I. ℂ **800/326-6898** in the U.S. or Canada, or 246/432-1332. Fax 246/432-6317. www.tamarindcovehotel.com. 105 units. Winter US$440–US$620 double, US$640–US$680 suite; off season US$250–US$430 double, US$450–US$490 suite. MAP (breakfast and dinner) US$96 per person extra. AE, DC, MC, V. **Amenities:** 3 restaurants; 4 bars; 3 outdoor pools; golf privileges; 2 tennis courts; fitness center; water-skiing; windsurfing; horseback riding; children's programs; concierge; business center; 3 boutiques; salon; 24-hr. room service; babysitting; massage; laundry service. *In room:* A/C, TV, minibar, hair dryer, iron/ironing board, safe.

INEXPENSIVE

Allamanda Beach Hotel ⟨Kids⟩ These apartments, last renovated in 1995, are one of the best bargains on Barbados and are ideal for families. Directly on a rocky shoreline 4km (2½ miles) southeast of Bridgetown, the hotel is in the heart of the village of Hastings. The U-shaped complex is built around a pool terrace overlooking the sea. Functional and minimalist in decor, the apartments are clean and comfortable, with tiny but fully equipped kitchenettes. All have balconies or decks, and some units have air-conditioning. Each unit has a small bathroom with a shower stall. Only three occupants are allowed in a double room.

Although some athletic guests attempt to swim off the nearby rocks, most walk 5 minutes to the white sands of nearby Rockley (Accra) Beach. A small restaurant on the property serves very average American and Bajan fare.

Hastings, Christ Church, Barbados, W.I. ℂ **246/435-6694**. Fax 246/435-9211. www.allamandabeach.com. 48 units. US$145 studio apt, US$185 1-bedroom apt; off season US$99 studio apt, US$125 1-bedroom apt. Extra person US$25. AE, MC, V. **Amenities:** Restaurant; bar; outdoor pool; babysitting; laundry service; dry cleaning; rooms for those with limited mobility. *In room:* A/C (in some), ceiling fan, TV, dataport, kitchenette, fridge, beverage maker, hair dryer, iron/ironing board.

Traveller's Palm Within a 10-minute walk of a good beach, this is for self-sufficient types who are not too demanding and want to save money. There's a choice of simply furnished, one-bedroom apartments with fully equipped kitchens and well-maintained bathrooms with shower units. They're simple,

slightly worn apartments, with bright but fading colors, but they're quite a deal in this high-rent district. The apartments have living and dining areas, as well as patios where you can have breakfast or a candlelit dinner you've prepared yourself (no meals are served here). To run the in-room air conditioners you must purchase tokens.

265 Palm Ave., Sunset Crest, St. James, Barbados, W.I. © 246/432-6750. Fax 246/432-7229. 16 units. Winter US$105 apt for 2; off season US$80 apt for 2. MC, V. **Amenities:** Outdoor pool; babysitting; laundry service; dry cleaning; nonsmoking rooms; rooms for those with limited mobility. *In room:* Token-operated A/C, kitchenette, safe.

SOUTH OF BRIDGETOWN/THE SOUTH COAST
VERY EXPENSIVE

Little Arches 🎀🎀 *Finds*   A real discovery, this family-owned boutique hotel overlooks white-sand Enterprise Beach on the south coast. It's a little charmer for those who seek out personalized hotels. The oceanview bedrooms are individually styled with four-poster king beds, along with such extras as private Jacuzzi sun decks. Italian fabrics and well-chosen furnishings grace the bedrooms. The colorful rooms look like an arranged set waiting for the *House & Garden* photographers. The extras make this place really thrive: a roof-deck swimming pool, a holistic massage therapist, an alfresco restaurant run by an international chef, and free use of mountain bikes. The hotel's own private 13m (43-ft.) yacht is available for charter. The location is a short walk from the village of Oistins at a point 6.5km (4 miles) from St. Lawrence Gap and 13km (8 miles) from the airport.

Enterprise Coast Rd., Christ Church, Barbados. © 800/860-8013 or 246/420-4689. Fax 246/435-6483. www.littlearches.com. 10 units. Winter US$220–US$384; off season US$154–US$269. AE, MC, V. **Amenities:** Restaurant; bar; outdoor pool; yacht; mountain bikes; room service (7am–10pm); massage; babysitting; laundry service. *In room:* A/C, TV, dataport, kitchenette (in 3 units), beverage maker, hair dryer, safe.

The Savannah 🎀 *Finds*   Blending traditional with the contemporary, this hotel on the beach offers some of the most luxurious bedrooms on the South Coast, lying a 10-minute drive from Bridgetown and about a 25-minute ride from the airport. Some part of this complex, especially the original plantation house, has been standing here for two centuries (it's a reincarnation of the old Sea View Hotel). Today, two newly built extensions reach toward the sea on the well-landscaped grounds of tropical foliage. Things have never looked so good around here, especially the waterfalls cascading into the lagoon-style pool.

Opening onto views of the pool, garden, or ocean, bedrooms are elegantly furnished with mahogany four-poster beds and all the modern amenities, such as high-speed Internet access. Rooms also open onto spacious patios or balconies. Extras range from nightly entertainment to beauty treatments, including a Swedish massage.

Garrison Main Rd., Hastings, Christ Church, Barbados. © 800/868-9429 or 246/228-3800. Fax 246/228-4385. www.gemsbarados.com. 100 units. Winter US$283–US$313 double; off season US$261–US$279 double. Children under 12 stay free in parent's room. AE, MC, V. **Amenities:** 2 restaurants; 3 bars (1 swimup); 2 outdoor pools; fitness center; spa services; children's programs; business center; salon; room service (7am–11pm); babysitting; laundry service; dry cleaning; nonsmoking rooms; rooms for those with limited mobility. *In room:* A/C, TV, dataport, beverage maker, hair dryer, iron/ironing board, safe.

Turtle Beach Resort 🎀🎀 *Kids*   Opening onto 450m (1,475 ft.) of white-sand beach, this is the only real "pocket of posh" on the south coast. A member of the Elegant Hotels Group, a swanky group of Bajan hotels, the resort opened in 1998 and was named after the turtles who sometimes nest on the nearby sands.

It's an all-inclusive property, drawing families, couples, and honeymooners. An open-air lobby opens onto the beach. All midsize rooms have ocean views, wicker furniture, ceiling fans, and voice mail. Beds have fine linens, and each one-bedroom suite offers both a queen-size bed and a sofa bed. If needed, free rollaway beds are provided. Bathrooms are luxurious, with tubs and showers.

The open-air restaurant, Chelonia, serves international, nouvelle dishes that are—especially for Barbados—rather artfully experimental. The casually elegant Waterfront offers informal food such as design-your-own pizzas. Casual Asiago serves pleasant Italian fare. For diversity, Turtle Beach offers a dine-around program with its other tony properties, including Crystal Cove and Coconut Creek. There's also nightly entertainment—calypso, jazz, cabaret, and more.

Dover, near St. Lawrence Gap, Barbados, W.I. ✆ **800/326-6898** in the U.S., or 246/428-7131. Fax 246/428-6089. www.turtlebeachresortbarbados.com. 161 units. Winter US$735–US$960 suite for 2; off season US$372–US$721 suite for 2. Rates are all-inclusive. AE, DC, MC, V. **Amenities:** 3 restaurants; 3 bars; 3 outdoor pools; golf privileges; 2 tennis courts; fitness center; Jacuzzi; kayaks; sailing; snorkeling; windsurfing; children's club and playground; tour desk; car rental; limited room service; massage (in room); babysitting; laundry service; dry cleaning. *In room:* A/C, ceiling fan, TV, dataport, fridge, beverage maker, hair dryer, iron/ironing board, safe.

EXPENSIVE

Accra Beach Hotel & Resort 🏖 This hotel, totally rebuilt in 1996, lies on the prettiest beach on the south coast. These manicured grounds lie in the center of the south strip, only 10 minutes from the airport, with Bridgetown about 3km (2 miles) to the west.

In a West Indian "megastyle," the three-story property is tastefully laid out, and it offers spacious rooms opening onto a view of the pool or ocean. The units have large balconies and wooden shutters, plus full-size bathrooms with showers and tubs. The look is a bit sterile, more corporate hotel than island escape. Steer clear of units marked "island view," as the panorama is of the parking lot. *One drawback:* Much of the hotel is open air (including a dance floor), and the mosquitoes appreciate that fact.

Hwy. 7, Accra Beach, Rockley, Christ Church, Barbados. ✆ 246/435-8920. Fax 246/435-6794. www.accrabeachhotel.com. 146 units. Winter US$184–US$230 for double, from US$240 suite; off season US$148–US$180 double, from US$200 suite. AE, MC, V. **Amenities:** 3 restaurants; 2 bars (1 swim-up); outdoor pool; open-air dance floor; squash court; fitness center; snorkeling; car rental; business center; limited room service; babysitting; laundry service; dry cleaning. *In room:* A/C, ceiling fan, TV, dataport (in some), beverage maker, hair dryer.

Divi Southwinds Beach Resort 🏖 *Kids* Midway between Bridgetown and Oistins on a .8km (½ mile) sandy beach, this resort was created when two distinctly different complexes were combined. The present resort consists of buildings scattered over 20 hectares (49 acres) of sandy flatlands. The showpiece is the newer (inland) complex, housing one- and two-bedroom suites with full kitchens—perfect for small families. These units look like a connected series of town houses, with wooden balconies and views of a large L-shaped pool. From here, you need only cross through two groves of palm trees and a narrow lane to reach the beach. The more modestly furnished older units lie directly on the beachfront, ringed with palm trees, near an oval pool. Each unit contains a full-size bathroom with tub and shower.

The Aquarius Restaurant serves decent food, and there's another casual spot for drinks and snacks by the beach.

St. Lawrence Gap, Christ Church, Barbados, W.I. ✆ **800/367-3484** or 246/428-7181. Fax 246/420-2673. www.diviresorts.com. 160 units. Winter US$208–US$220 double, US$307 suite; off season US$156–US$165 double, US$230 suite. Children under 16 stay free in parent's room. AE, DC, MC, V. **Amenities:** Restaurant; 2 bars; beach snack bar; 3 outdoor pools; 2 tennis courts; fitness room; dive shop; sailboat rentals; snorkeling; poolside activities for kids; salon; laundry. *In room:* A/C, TV, kitchen, beverage maker, safe.

Southern Palms   A seafront club on 304m (997 ft.) of sand, with a distinct personality, Southern Palms lies on the Pink Pearl Beach of Barbados, midway between the airport and Bridgetown. The core of the resort is a pink-and-white manor house built in the Dutch style, with a garden-level colonnade of arches. Spread along the sands are arched two- and three-story buildings, with Italian fountains and statues creating a Mediterranean feel. In its more modern block, an eclectic mixture of rooms includes some with kitchenettes, some facing the ocean, others opening onto the garden, and some with penthouse luxury. The suites have small kitchenettes. Each unit has a small bathroom containing a shower stall. A cluster of straw-roofed buildings, housing the drinking and dining facilities, links the accommodations.

The Garden Terrace Restaurant serves both West Indian and Continental cuisine. The Khus-Khus bar provides burgers, fish cakes, and light snacks. In general, the local Bajan dishes are the best. A local band often entertains with merengue and steel-band music.

St. Lawrence, Christ Church, Barbados, W.I. © **800/223-6510** in the U.S., or 246/428-7171. Fax 246/428-7175. www.southernpalms.net. 92 units. Winter US$206–US$242 double, US$293 suite; off season US$130–US$159 double, US$187 suite. MAP (breakfast and dinner) US$40 per person extra in winter, US$25 per person extra off season. AE, DC, DISC, MC, V. **Amenities:** Restaurant; bar; 2 outdoor pools; 2 tennis courts; exercise room; scuba lessons; windsurfing; salon; limited room service; babysitting; laundry service; dry cleaning; coin-operated laundry. *In room:* A/C, TV, dataport, kitchenette (in suites), fridge, beverage maker, hair dryer, safe.

INEXPENSIVE

Fairholme   Lying a 5-minute walk from a good beach, this converted plantation house has been enlarged over the past 20 years or so with a handful of connected annexes. The main house and its original gardens are just off a major road, 10km (6¼ miles) southeast of Bridgetown. The older section has 11 double rooms, each with a living-room area and a patio overlooking an orchard and a pool. The best units are the 20 Spanish-style studio apartments, which have cathedral ceilings, dark beams, traditional furnishings, and balconies or patios. All units have neatly kept bathrooms with shower units. Air-conditioning is available only in the studios; the reception desk sells US$3 brass tokens that you insert into your air-conditioning unit in exchange for around 8 hours of cooling-off time.

The restaurant here has a reputation for home cooking—wholesome and nothing fancy, but the ingredients are fresh. Guests may also use the waterfront cafe and bar at Fairholme's neighbor, the Sea Breeze.

Maxwell, Christ Church, Barbados, W.I. © **246/428-9425.** Fax 246/420-2389. 31 units. Winter US$35 double, US$65 studio apt; off season US$32 double, US$45 studio apt. MC, V. **Amenities:** Restaurant; outdoor pool; limited room service; coin-operated laundry. *In room:* Token-operated A/C, ceiling fan.

Sandy Beach Island Resort 🏖️🏖️ *Kids*   Definitely not to be confused with Sandy Lane, this hotel, originally established in 1980 and renovated in 2001, is a simple but thoroughly reliable choice, resting on .8 hectares (2 acres) of beachfront land, 6km (3¾ miles) southeast of Bridgetown. The Bajan-owned property rises around its architectural centerpiece, a soaring, cone-shaped structure known as a *palapa*. Great for families, the resort contains standard motel-like double rooms, and one- and two-bedroom suites. All the simply decorated and spacious units have fully equipped kitchenettes, private balconies or patios, and locally made furniture, plus small bathrooms containing shower units. Facilities for travelers with disabilities are available in some of the ground-floor suites.

Kolors, serving average seafood and steaks, is situated under the *palapa* and opens onto a view of the sea and pool. Every Monday, when nonguests are welcome, the resort sponsors a rum-punch party and a Bajan buffet. Entertainment is offered 3 nights a week.

Worthing, Christ Church, Barbados, W.I. © **800/448-8355** in the U.S., or 246/435-8000. Fax 246/435-8053. www.sandybeachbarbados.com. 128 units. Winter US$143 double, US$254 1-bedroom suite, US$372 2-bedroom suite; off season US$100–US$106 double, US$152–US$157 1-bedroom suite, US$206–US$242 2-bedroom suite. Extra person US$28. MAP (breakfast and dinner) US$45 per person extra. Children under 13 stay free in parent's room. AE, DC, DISC, MC, V. **Amenities:** Restaurant; bar; outdoor pool; boating; scuba lessons; snorkeling; windsurfing; children's center; babysitting; laundry service; dry cleaning; rooms for those with limited mobility. *In room:* A/C, TV, dataport, kitchenettes (in suites), hair dryer, safe.

ON THE EAST COAST
VERY EXPENSIVE

The Crane ⚘ It's so old it's new again. Opened in 1887, this is arguably the Caribbean's first resort hotel. Near the easternmost end of the island, 23 km (14 miles) east of Bridgetown, the hotel has bounced back for a new lease on life. What hasn't changed is Crane Beach, called by many the most beautiful spot on earth, or more accurately labeled one of the 10 best beaches in the world in *Lifestyles of the Rich and Famous.* It's spectacular with powder-soft white sand that can look pink in certain lights.

In the main house are 18 rooms with hardwood floors, resting under 3.5m (11-ft.) ceilings. These are graced with antiques and four-posters. Some of these accommodations offer wraparound balconies. We prefer these units, but you can also book into a trio of modern buildings in a series of one-, two-, and three-bedroom rooms. These, too, have been given great style with such lovely features as Jacuzzis, Asian carpets, plunge pools, and handcrafted furnishings. All bathrooms are newly restored and tiled.

Crane Bay, St. Philip, Barbados, W.I. © **246/423-6220.** Fax 246/423-5343. www.thecrane.com. 70 units. Winter US$330–US$350 double, from US$410 suite; off season US$155 double, from US$235 suite. MAP (breakfast and dinner) US$70 per person extra. AE, DC, MC, V. **Amenities:** Restaurant; bar; outdoor pool; limited room service; babysitting; laundry facilities; rooms for those with limited mobility. *In room:* A/C, TV, kitchenette in 1 suite, minibar, beverage maker, hair dryer, iron/ironing board, safe, dataport.

Villa Nova ⚘⚘⚘ *Finds* This is one of the last of the island's great houses. Once it was a sightseeing attraction open to the public. Built in 1834 as a sugar plantation, it's furnished with period antiques and Barbadian mahogany and surrounded by 6 walled hectares (15 acres) of tropical forest and lush gardens. Its most famous association was with Sir Anthony Eden, former prime minister of Great Britain, who purchased the estate from the government in 1965. In 1966, Eden, the earl of Avon, and his wife, the countess, entertained Queen Elizabeth II and Prince Philip at Villa Nova. Sir Winston Churchill also holidayed here.

Today, in the midst of sugar, banana, and mango plantations, it's been turned into an exclusive hotel, following a multimillion dollar refurbishment. Although the hotel has a very large swimming pool and terraces, you'll have to drive about 20 minutes to dip your toes into the surf. Rooms are beautifully furnished and spacious, each with its own private terrace. Every suite comes with a spacious bathroom with Victorian claw-footed tubs and walk-in showers. Nina Campbell designed each of the suites individually. Its food is among the finest of all the hotels, using regional organic produce whenever possible. Nearby are the golf courses of Sandy Lane and Royal Westmoreland.

Villa Nova, St. John, Barbados, W.I. © 246/433-1524. Fax 246/433-6363. www.villanovabarbados.com. 28 units. Winter US$650 double; from US$800 suite; off season US$450 double, from US$600 suite. Rates include continental or a la carte breakfast. AE, MC, V. No children under 12. **Amenities:** Restaurant; 2 bars; pool; golf privileges; 2 tennis courts; gym; spa; room service (7am–11pm); laundry service; nonsmoking rooms. *In room:* A/C, TV/DVD, dataport, hair dryer, safe.

3 Dining

ON THE WEST COAST
EXPENSIVE

Carambola 🍀🍀 FRENCH/CARIBBEAN/ASIAN   Built beside the road that runs along the island's western coastline, this restaurant sits atop a 6m (20-ft.) seaside cliff and offers one of the most panoramic dining terraces in the Caribbean. But you'll have to go early for dinner to see the view because lunch isn't served. This is the only restaurant in Barbados in the same league as The Cliff (see below); what sets Carambola apart are its Asian offerings. For sheer romantic dining, however, Carambola has all competitors beat. The prize-winning cuisine is creative, with modern, French-nouvelle touches, but Caribbean flair and flavor. Try the chef's rich, frothy lobster cappuccino, or his stir-fry of shrimp and scallops in roasted peanut sauce. Another spectacular dish is rack of lamb cooked under a honey-mustard crust, or you might try a favorite of ours, oven-roasted breast of duckling with anise seed and a bitter-orange marmalade. Save room for one of the luscious desserts, such as lime mousse. The impressive wine list features mostly French vintages.

Hwy. 1, Derricks, St. James. © 246/432-0832. Reservations recommended. Main courses US$21–US$40. AE, MC, V. Mon–Sat 6:30–9pm. Closed Aug. 2km (1¼ miles) south of Holetown on Hwy. 1.

The Cliff 🍀🍀 INTERNATIONAL/CARIBBEAN   Built atop a 3m (10-ft.) coral cliff adjacent to the Coconut Creek Hotel, this open-air restaurant features a four-level dining room crafted with terra-cotta tiles and coral stone. Though it's not exclusive or even particularly formal, it has attracted Prince Andrew and other titled and bejeweled guests of the nearby upscale hotels. The culinary technique is impeccably sharp, and the chefs here select only the finest cuts of beef, the freshest seafood, and the choicest vegetables. The best items are grilled snapper drizzled with three types of coriander sauce (cream-based, oil-based, and vinaigrette style), accompanied with garlic mashed potatoes and Thai-style curried shrimp. For sheer innovation, dishes such as this put The Cliff near the top. Also try the fresh sushi. As you dine, watch for stingrays, which glide through the illuminated waters below; a sighting is considered a sign of good luck.

Hwy. 1, Derrick, St. James. © 246/432-1922. Reservations required in winter. Set menu US$70. AE, MC, V. May–Nov Mon–Sat 6:30–10pm; Dec–Apr daily 6:30–10pm.

Daphne's 🍀🍀 MEDITERRANEAN/CARIBBEAN   The owners of The House hotel operate this sexy, intimate, and glitterati-styled restaurant which is an outpost of the fabled London eatery. The service is flawless, and the setting on the beach idyllic for dining in the Tropics. The interior evokes Bali with its coconut-shell lamp shades and Indonesian batiks. For greater privacy, tables are surrounded by silk curtains. Chef Nick Bell is a whiz, turning out memorable dishes based on fresh ingredients, either local or imported. The pasta dishes rate a rave, especially the linguine with spicy crab and the *pappardella* (wide ribbon noodles) with braised duck in a red-wine sauce. The chef's most successful main dishes, on a recent visit, were grilled mahimahi with Marsala, *peperonata,* and zucchini, or the chargrilled tuna with arugula. We've also enjoyed the spicy mussels with chickpea broth.

Paynes Bay, St. James. © **246/432-2731.** Reservations required. Lunch main courses US$16–US$28; dinner main courses US$24–US$45. AE, MC, V. Daily 12:30–2pm and 6:30–10:30pm. Closed Mon off season.

The Emerald Palm ✿ FRENCH/INTERNATIONAL   This stucco-and-tile

house is 3km (2 miles) north of Holetown in a tropical garden dotted with a trio of gazebos. After passing under an arbor, you'll be invited to order a drink, served on one of the banquettes that fill various parts of the French-inspired restaurant. You can then enjoy an alfresco, candlelit meal on the rear terrace. Come here for zesty dishes packed with international and island flavors. New menu items include portions of marinated, raw *(tartare),* and smoked salmon appearing on your plate with an orange-and-lime-flavored dressing; baked goat cheese salad served with mixed greens, roasted peppers, pine nuts, and balsamic dressing; sautéed Caribbean shrimp with coconut and lemon-grass sauce; and roasted rack of lamb with a mustard-flavored herb crust and gratin potatoes, served with rosemary sauce.

Porters, St. James. © **246/422-4116.** Reservations required. Main courses US$18–US$36. AE, MC, V. Tues–Sun 6:30–9:30pm (last seating). Closed Sept.

The Fish Pot ✿ *Finds* SEAFOOD/INTERNATIONAL   Just minutes north of

the port of St. Charles, this restaurant lies in a little fishing community called Shermans. The restaurant is in a family-run oceanfront hotel and is so special that even nonguests should visit. The complex was constructed on the site of a fort from the 17th century that later was used to store sugar. The food is intensely flavored and produced with finesse. The appetizers are among the most imaginative on the coast, everything from seared Canadian scallops on a truffle green-pea purée with toasted pine-nut dressing to fried *goujons* (small strips) of alligator in a spicy jalapeño-tartar-and-ginger vinaigrette. For a main course, try the herb-crusted filet of barracuda with a bell-pepper coulis or the grilled Atlantic shark with tomato aioli and basil oil. You can also enjoy tamer fare such as grilled beef tenderloin with a chicken-liver pâté and caramelized onion sauce. Lighter fare, like sandwiches and pastas, is featured at lunch.

You may fall in love with the place and want to stay here in its one-, two-, or three-bedroom chattel-styled cottages, each furnished to a high standard with a living room and a spacious covered dining terrace off a fully equipped kitchen. Winter rates for two begin at US$302 to US$413 for a double, but are lowered to US$226 to US$301 off season.

In Little Good Harbour, Shermans, St. Peter. © **246/439-3000.** Fax 246/439-2020. www.littlegoodharbour-barbados.com. Lunch main courses US$14–US$23; dinner main courses US$21–US$35. MC, V. Daily 8:30–11am, noon–3pm, and 6:30–9:30pm.

La Mer ✿✿ INTERNATIONAL   Intricately associated, architecturally and

socially, with the upscale Port St. Charles Condo and Marina complex in which it's located, this is a stylish and breezy restaurant with a prominent bar, a terrace that overlooks some of the most expensive yachts in the Caribbean, and a clientele that's composed of local homeowners and well-heeled foreign visitors. After dark, powerful spotlights illuminate the schools of fish swimming around the moored boats nearby. The decor features big glass windows with a view of the lagoon, lots of flowers and flickering candles, and artfully designed lighting from overhead spotlights. Menu items include the kind of hearty mariners' fare that goes beautifully with the fresh salt air. Begin with duck-liver pâté or shrimp in a sweet-and-sour rum sauce. Main courses include grilled fish of the day—usually mahimahi, and often grilled and served with a lime-flavored butter sauce; veal kidneys in a light mustard sauce; and Angus steak. Dessert usually includes caramelized banana crepes with rum-raisin ice cream—the kind of thing that's worth ruining your diet for. The bar is stylish but rarely raucous, with closing hours that rarely extend past 11pm.

In the Port St. Charles Condo and Marina complex, Speightstown, St. Peter. (© 246/419-2000. Reservations required. Main courses US$22–US$47; Sun lunch buffet US$62 per person. MC, V. Sun noon–2pm; Tues–Sat 7–9pm.

LaTerra 🎔🎔 BAJAN/INTERNATIONAL   This kitchen offers an exciting medley of flavors that roam the world for inspiration but come home to the Caribbean for spicing. In the open air, it's a romantic setting—an orchid spray on each of the 24 tables, and the sounds of taped jazz from New Orleans competing with the tree-frog symphony and the soothing surf.

The chef uses quality ingredients and searches for local produce whenever available. Each dish has a kind of harmonious simplicity; flavors maintain their integrity without being buried in heavy sauces. Our appetizer of risotto primavera with white-truffle oil set the tone of the meal. That was followed by baked barracuda flavored with tarragon and served with caper-studded red-wine sauce on a bed of fettuccine with fresh greens. Although many of the meat dishes are made with imported frozen meat, they don't taste that way. We recommend the grilled black Angus tenderloin on baked polenta with a zesty touch of roasted shallots and béarnaise sauce.

Royal Westmoreland. (© 246/432-1099. Reservations required. Main courses US$25–US$40. AE, MC, V. Daily 11am–3pm and 6:30–10pm.

Lone Star Restaurant 🎔 *Finds* BAJAN/INTERNATIONAL   This previously recommended hotel converted from a former 1940s garage is for elegant dining without stiff formality. In spite of its former role, it is today a pocket of posh—for example, offering the island's widest selection of pure Iranian caviar. Elegantly appointed, it is decorated with muslin curtains, polished wood floors, and an open-to-view kitchen. The main restaurant fronts the beach with a casual atmosphere during the day, which becomes more elegant in the evening. Top chefs cooking for a discerning international clientele turn out Caribbean fish pie (especially delectable with its cheesy mashed potatoes), blackened dolphin, and such fusion dishes as a Thai green king-prawn curry. Downstairs Mediterranean and modern European dishes, along with Barbadian specialties, are the focus, whereas the culinary delights of Southeast Asia are served upstairs—mainly Thai, Vietnamese, and Chinese dishes. You can even get Japanese dishes such as sushi and sashimi. Such *fruits de mer* as king prawns, crab legs, and fresh oysters add to the utterly delightful but frighteningly expensive seafood selections.

Hwy. 1, Mount Standfast, St. James. (© 246/419-0599. Reservations required. Lunch main courses US$23–US$33; dinner main courses US$23–US$90. AE, MC. V. Daily 7:30am–11pm (closing hours vary).

Starfish Restaurant 🎔 FRENCH/SEAFOOD   Located north of Holetown and 13km (8 miles) north of Bridgetown, this restaurant offers classic seafood in a charming, traditional atmosphere. Ingredients are obtained fresh on Barbados. Most diners begin with the Starfish seafood cocktail in a cucumber-mint sauce or fish cooked with plantain in a creamy ginger sauce. From there you can dig into such delights as the day's catch, which is grilled to perfection and served with breadfruit and fresh vegetables. Also reliable is the barbecue jumbo shrimp and the pan-fried and pepper-crusted scallops with a tri-color Bajan purée.

In the Settlers' Beach Hotel, Holetown, St. James. (C) **246/422-3245**. Reservations recommended. Main courses US$18–US$37. AE, MC, V. Daily 7:30–10:30am, 11:30am–3pm, and 6:30–9:30pm.

The Tides ⋊ INTERNATIONAL/CARIBBEAN   This former beachfront villa is now occupied by a restaurant of charm and grace, with a fine cuisine. The chef and owner, Guy Beasley, fine-tuned his culinary skills with the native Roux brothers in England—arguably the finest chefs in that land. Today, he's moved to Barbados, attracting such notables as Andrew Lloyd Weber or Tommy Hilfiger to his elegant precincts, where trees grow right through the ceiling.

Nearly 100 people can be fed here at any given time, each enjoying a sea view. The atmosphere at night is romantically candlelit, the restaurant set in the midst of lush gardens. The chef specializes in seafood but also offers finely honed meat, poultry, and vegetarian dishes. When not appreciating the art collection displayed on the wall, you can partake of such delectable food as crab cakes with a Thai sauce or the homemade Caribbean seafood chowder for starters. Follow with the fresh catch of the day—grilled, blackened, pan-fried, or poached. Other dishes to which we'd award a star include honey-and-mustard-coated roast of lamb with bacon-scented scalloped potatoes or the chargrilled filet of pork with Mexican rice, citrus juice, and a tangy orange salsa.

Holetown, St. James. (C) **246/432-8356**. Reservations required. Lunch main courses US$12–US$23; dinner main courses US$30–US$38. MC, V. Mon–Fri noon–2:30pm; Mon–Sat 6:30–10:30pm.

MODERATE

Angry Annie's Restaurant & Bar ⋊ *Value* INTERNATIONAL   Don't ask Annie why she's angry—she might tell you! Annie and Paul Matthews, both from the United Kingdom, run this friendly, cozy, 34-seat joint. It's decorated in tropical colors with a circular bar, and rock classics play on the excellent sound system. The dishes are tasty with lots of local flavor. The place is known for its "famous" ribs, the most savory on the island. We like the garlic-cream potatoes and the fresh local vegetables. Annie also turns out fresh fish and excellent pasta dishes. Take advantage of the takeout service if you'd like to dine back in your room.

First St., Holetown, St. James. (C) **246/432-2119**. Main courses US$15–US$38. MC, V. Daily 6–10pm (sometimes until midnight).

Il Tempio ⋊⋊ ITALIAN   Even gourmet/gourmand opera singer, the great Luciano Pavarotti, agrees: This restaurant serves the best Italian food in Barbados. At the southern end of the western coast, you are greeted by the owner, Anna Pirrelli, and welcomed into her citadel of fine cuisine. Many of the specialties are evocative of her hometown in Bari, whereas other dishes are inspired by Sardinia, home of her chef, Cristian Cadeddu. The chef's light touch with cuisine is ideal for tropical dining. The homemade pastas are a delight, including his fettuccine Alfredo with shrimp. The lasagna *a la Vesuvio* comes with a tantalizing meat sauce, and the main dishes are equally delectable, especially the *piccatina Marsala* (veal in wine sauce) or another veal dish, veal *piccatina agli agrumi* (with orange and grapefruit sauce). Mouthwatering desserts are prepared fresh nightly.

Fitts Village, St. James. (C) **246/432-2054**. Reservations required. Main courses US$18–US$24. MC, V. Tues–Sun noon–2pm and 6:30–10pm.

Finds   The Island's Freshest Fish

Savvy locals can guide you to the **Oistins Fish Market,** a historic fish market southeast of Bridgetown and past the settlements of Hastings and Worthing. This is where Bajan fishermen unload their catch of the day and sell it directly to the customer—ideal if you have an accommodation with a kitchen. If not, you'll find nearly a dozen shacks selling fresh-cooked fish: Flying fish is in the fryer and fish steaks like wahoo are on the grill.

Mango's by the Sea ✿ INTERNATIONAL/SEAFOOD   This restaurant and bar overlooking the water is best known for its seafood: The owners, Montreal natives Gail and Pierre Spenard, buy the catch of the day directly from the fishermen's boats. The food is exceedingly good, and the seasonings aren't as overpowering as they are at many Bajan restaurants. Appetizers might be anything from smoked salmon to pumpkin soup. If you don't want fish, opt for the 8-ounce U.S. tenderloin steak cooked to perfection or the fall-off-the-bone barbecued baby back ribs. Top off your meal with passion fruit cheesecake or star fruit torte. There's live entertainment on some nights. Next door is an art gallery under the same management, which features the silk screen prints of artist Michael Adams.

2 West End, Queen St., Speightstown, St. Peter. ✆ 246/422-0704. Reservations recommended. Main courses US$25–US$28. AE, MC, V. Daily 6–9:30pm.

Ragamuffin's ✿ *Value* CARIBBEAN   This is a real discovery: an affordable, lively place that serves authentic island cuisine. It's the only restaurant in Barbados in an authentic chattel house. The broiled T-bones are juicy and perfectly flavored; there's always an offering of fresh fish; and vegetarians can enjoy stir-fried vegetables with noodles. Other highlights include blackened fish, the local version of a spicy West Indian curry, and a zesty jerk chicken salad.

First St., Holetown, St. James. ✆ 246/432-1295. Main courses US$18–US$30. AE, MC, V. Sun–Fri 6:30–9:30pm.

BRIDGETOWN

Waterfront Café INTERNATIONAL/BAJAN   This is your best bet if you're in Bridgetown shopping or sightseeing. In a turn-of-the-century warehouse originally built to store bananas and freeze fish, this cafe serves international fare with a strong emphasis on Bajan specialties. Try the fresh catch of the day prepared Creole style, or peppered steak. For vegetarians the menu features such dishes as three-mushroom pasta, vegetable soup, and usually a special of the day. Both diners and drinkers are welcome here for Creole food with lots of stir-fried dishes, including a version made with fish. Tuesday nights bring live steel-band music and a Bajan buffet. To see the Thursday night Dixieland bands, reserve about a week in advance. There's jazz on Friday and Saturday.

Cavans Lane, the Carenage, Bridgetown. ✆ 246/427-0093. Reservations required. Main courses US$17–US$38. AE, DC, MC, V. Mon–Sat 10am–10pm.

SOUTH OF BRIDGETOWN

Brown Sugar ✿ BAJAN   Brown Sugar serves the tastiest Bajan specialties on the island. The alfresco restaurant is hidden behind lush foliage in a turn-of-the-century coral limestone bungalow. The ceiling is latticed, with slow-turning fans, and there's an open veranda for dining by candlelight beneath hanging plants. We suggest starting with black-bean soup. Creole pork is the best main dish, followed closely by stuffed crab backs. A selection of locally grown vegetables is also offered. Only the lobster is expensive; most of the other dishes are reasonably priced. The restaurant is known for its buffet-style lunches, popular with local businesspeople for their good value.

Aquatic Gap, St. Michael. ℂ 246/426-7684. Reservations recommended. Main courses US$16–US$36; fixed-price buffet lunch US$20, or US$23 on Sun. AE, DC, DISC, MC, V. Sun–Fri noon–2:30pm and 6–9:30pm (last order); Sat 6–9:30pm (last order).

ON THE SOUTH COAST
David's Place ✿ BAJAN   Owner/operators David and Darla Trotman promise you'll sample "Barbadian dining at its best"—and they deliver on that promise at a reasonable price. The cuisine may not be as exotic as Brown Sugar's (see above), but it's tasty nonetheless. The restaurant is on top of the St. Lawrence Water Gap, in an old-fashioned seaside house on St. Lawrence Bay. The tables are positioned so that diners enjoy a view of the Caribbean. Pumpkin or cucumber soup or the pickled chicken wings are good starters. For a main course fish steaks (mahimahi, kingfish, barracuda, shark, or red snapper) served in a white-wine sauce or deep-fried Bajan style are the best choice on the menu. Also recommended are the Baxters Road chicken marinated in lime, salt, and herbs, then deep-fried, and the hot-and-spicy pepper pot, with beef, salt pork, chicken, and lamb. Top off your meal with one of the old-fashioned desserts: a banana split, coconut cream pie, or carrot cake in rum sauce.

St. Lawrence Main Rd., Worthing, Christ Church. ℂ **246/435-9755.** Reservations recommended. Main courses US$16–US$43. AE, DISC, MC, V. Tues–Sun 6–10pm.

Pisces ✿ BAJAN/SEAFOOD   This beautiful restaurant with a tropical decor offers alfresco dining at the water's edge. Begin with one of the soups, perhaps Pisces fish chowder or lobster bisque, or a savory appetizer like flying fish Florentine. Seafood fanciers enjoy such dishes as pan-fried filet of salmon with a crisp herb crust and a light passion fruit sauce laced with citrus juice, or else the potato-crusted filet of Atlantic salmon, a seared filet with a crisp potato crust served with a champagne beurre blanc. You might also be drawn to the seasonal Caribbean fish, which can be broiled, blackened, or pan-fried, and then served with lime-herb butter. A limited but good selection of poultry and meat is offered, including roast pork Barbados with a traditional Bajan stuffing.

St. Lawrence Gap, Christ Church. ℂ **246/435-6564.** Reservations recommended. Main courses US$19–US$37. AE, DC, MC, V. Daily 6–10pm (last order). From Bridgetown, take Coast Rd. south about 6km (3¾ miles); turn right at the sign toward St. Lawrence Gap.

ON THE EAST COAST
Atlantis Hotel ✿ Finds BAJAN   Harking back to the Barbados of many years ago, the slightly run-down Atlantis Hotel is often filled with both Bajans and visitors. It's located between Cattlewash-on-Sea and Tent Bay on the east (Atlantic) coast. This sunny, breeze-filled restaurant, with its sweeping view of the turbulent ocean, has welcomed visitors since 1945. The copious buffets are one of the best values on the island. You can sample such Bajan foods as pumpkin fritters, peas and rice, macaroni and cheese, *souse* (pigs' feet marinated in lime juice), and Bajan pepperpot. No one ever leaves hungry.

Bathsheba, St. Joseph. ℂ 246/433-9445. Reservations required for Sun buffet and 7pm dinner, recommended at all other times. 2-course fixed-price lunch US$17; fixed-price dinner US$18; Sun buffet US$25. AE, MC, V. Daily 9am–8pm.

Round House Inn Restaurant & Bar   Built in 1832, this restaurant lies on the rugged east coast of Barbados with its dramatic view of the Atlantic Ocean. The owners, Robert and Gail Manley, will usher you to a table perched atop a rocky ledge opening onto the Bathsheba "Soup Bowl," the best surfing beach in Barbados. You can also come here for dinner under the moonlight, as the place lies only a half-hour drive from Bridgetown.

The freshest of ingredients go into the wholesome, good-tasting food, which is made all the more delightful by a reggae band at night. Tuck into such appetizers as flying fish pâté or brie baked in a light-rum-and-walnut sauce. For your main course, you'd do well with either the oven-baked dolphin steak or the blackened catch of the day resting on your plate. The chef will always whip you up a traditional grilled sirloin with sautéed onions as well.

Bathsheba, St. Joseph. (C) **246/433-9678.** Reservations required on Sun, recommended otherwise. Main courses US$20–US$35. MC, V. Mon–Sat 8–10am, 11:30am–3:30pm, and 6:30–9:30pm; Sun 11:30am–5pm.

4 Beaches

The island's beaches are all open to the public—even those in front of the big resort hotels and private homes—and the government requires that there be access to all beaches, via roads along the property line or through hotel entrances. The beaches on the west coast, the **Gold Coast** 𝒜𝒜, are the most popular.

ON THE WEST COAST   The waters are calm here. Major beaches include **Paynes Bay,** which is accessed from the Coach House, south of Holetown, and has a parking area. This is a good choice for watersports, especially snorkeling. The beach can get rather crowded, but the beautiful bay is worth the effort. Directly south of Payne's Bay, at Fresh Water Bay, are three of the best west-coast beaches: **Brighton Beach, Brandon's Beach,** and **Paradise Beach.**

We also recommend **Mullins Beach,** where the glassy blue waters attract snorkelers. There's parking on the main road and some shady areas. At the Mullins Beach Bar, you can order that rum drink you've been craving.

ON THE SOUTH COAST   **Casuarina Beach** is accessed from Maxwell Coast Road, going across the property of the Casuarina Beach Hotel. This is one of the wider beaches of Barbados, and it's cooled by trade winds even on the hottest days of August. Windsurfers are especially fond of this one. Food and drinks can be ordered at the hotel.

Silver Sands Beach, to the east of Oistins, is near the southernmost point of Barbados, directly east of South Point Lighthouse and near the Silver Rock Hotel. This white-sand beach is a favorite with many Bajans (who probably want to keep it a secret from as many tourists as possible). The Silver Rock Bar sells drinks.

Sandy Beach, accessible via the parking lot on the Worthing main road, has tranquil waters opening onto a lagoon. It's a family favorite, and especially boisterous on weekends. Food and drinks are available.

ON THE SOUTHEAST COAST   The southeast coast is the site of big waves, especially at **Crane Beach,** the white-sand strip set against a backdrop of palms that you've probably seen in travel magazines. The beach is spectacular, and Prince Andrew, who has a house overlooking it, might agree. It offers excellent bodysurfing, but at times the waters may be too rough for all but the strongest swimmers; take appropriate precautions. The beach is set against cliffs, with the Crane Beach Hotel towering above.

Bottom Bay ⚘, north of Sam Lord's Castle Resort, is one of our all-time Bajan favorites. Park on the top of a cliff, then walk down the steps to this much-photographed tropical beach with its grove of coconut palms; there's even a cave. The sand is brilliantly white against the aquamarine sea, a picture-postcard perfect beach paradise.

ON THE EAST (ATLANTIC) COAST   The miles and miles of uncrowded beaches on the rougher Atlantic side are ideal for strolling, but swimming can be dangerous. Waves are extremely high, and the bottom tends to be rocky. The currents are also unpredictable. Many travelers enjoy the rugged grandeur of these beaches, especially those in the **Bathsheba/Cattlewash** areas.

5 Sports & Other Outdoor Pursuits

GOLF   Open to all is the Tom Fazio 18-hole championship golf course of the **Sandy Lane Hotel,** St. James (© **246/444-2000**), on the west coast. Greens fees for 18 holes are $200 for non-guests and $150 for guests in winter and $160 for non-guests and $110 for guests in summer, or $85 for non-guests and $75 for guests year-round for its famed "Old Nine" holes, which winds through the estate grounds. Carts and caddies are available.

The **Royal Westmoreland Golf and Country Club,** Westmoreland, St. James (© **246/422-4653**), has become the island's premier golf course. Designed by Robert Trent Jones, Jr., this $30 million, 18-hole course is spread across 200 hectares (500 acres) overlooking the Gold Coast. It is part of a private residential community and can be played only by guests of the Royal Pavilion, Glitter Bay, Colony Club, Tamarind Cove, Coral Reef, Crystal Cove, Cobblers Cove, Sandpiper Inn, and Sandy Lane. It costs $75 for 9 holes for guests year-round, or $200 for 18 holes for nonguests and $150 for guests in winter, including a cart. Fees in off season are $125 for guests and $75 for nonguests.

Barbados Golf Club, Durants, Christ Church (© **246/434-2121;** Fax 256/418-3131; www.barbadosgolfclub.com) on the south coast opened as Barbados's first public championship golf course in 2000. The 6,905-yard, par-72 course, designed by Ron Kirby, hosted the PGA Seniors Tournament in 2002. Greens fees for 18 holes are $119 in the high season ($79 low season) plus $13 for a cart and $20 for Cobra club rentals. A three-day unlimited golf pass during high season is $270 ($189 low season).

HIKING   The **Barbados National Trust** (© 246/426-2421) offers popular Sunday morning hikes throughout the year. Led by young Bajans and members of the National Trust, the hikes cover a different area of the island each week, giving you an opportunity to learn about Barbados's natural beauty. The guides give brief talks on subjects such as geography, history, geology, and agriculture. The hikes, free and open to participants of all ages, are divided into fast, medium, and slow categories, with groups of no more than 10. Hikes leave promptly at 6am, and take about 3 hours to complete. There are also hikes at 3:30 and 5:30pm, the latter conducted only on moonlit nights. For more information, contact the Barbados National Trust.

In 1998, Barbados created a nature trail that explores the natural history and heritage of Speightstown, once a major sugar port and even today a fishing town with old houses and a bustling waterfront. The **Arbib Nature & Heritage Trail** takes you through town, the mysterious gully known as "the Whim," and the surrounding districts. The first marked trail is a 8km (5-mile) trek which begins outside St. Peter's Church in Speightstown, traverses the Whim, crosses one of the last working plantations in Barbados (Warleight), and leads to the historic 18th-century Dover Fort, following along white-sand beaches at Heywoods before ending up back in town. Guided hikes are offered on Wednesday, Thursday, and Saturday. For information and reservations, call the Barbados National Trust, and ask for a trail map at the tourist office.

The rugged, dramatic **east coast** stretches about 26km (16 miles) from the lighthouse at Ragged Point, the easternmost point of Barbados, north along the Atlantic coast to Bathsheba and Pico Teneriffe. This is the island's most panoramic hiking area. Some hardy souls do the entire coast; if your time is limited, hike our favorite walk, the 6km (3¾-mile) stretch from Ragged Point to Consett Bay, along a rough, stony trail that requires only moderate endurance. Allow at least 2½ hours. A small picnic facility just north of Bathsheba is a popular spot for Bajan families, especially on Sundays. As for information, you're pretty much on your own, although if you stick to the coastline, you won't get lost.

HORSEBACK RIDING A different view of Barbados is offered by the **Caribbean International Riding Centre,** St. Andrew, Sarely Hill (© **246/422-7433**). With nearly 40 horses, Mrs. Roachford and her daughters offer a variety of trail rides for all levels of experience, ranging from a 1½-hour jaunt for US$60 to a 2½-hour trek for US$90. You'll ride through some of the most panoramic parts of Barbados, including the hilly terrain of the Scotland district. Along the way, you can see wild ducks and water lilies, with the rhythm of the Atlantic as background music.

SCUBA DIVING & SNORKELING The clear waters off Barbados have a visibility of more than 30m (98 ft.) most of the year. More than 50 varieties of fish are found on the shallow inside reefs, and there's an unusually high concentration of hawksbill turtles. On night dives, you can spot sleeping fish, night anemones, lobsters, moray eels, and octopuses. Diving is concentrated on the leeward west and south coasts, where hard corals grow thick along the crest of the reef, and orange elephant ear, barrel sponge, and rope sponge cascade down the drop-off of the outer reef.

On a 2km-long (1¼-mile) coral reef 2 minutes by boat from **Sandy Beach,** sea fans, corals, gorgonians, and reef fish are plentiful. *J.R.,* a dredge barge sunk as an artificial reef in 1983, is popular with beginners for its coral, fish life, and 6m (20-ft.) depth. The *Berwyn,* a coral-encrusted tugboat that sank in Carlisle Bay in 1916, attracts photographers for its variety of reef fish, shallow depth, good light, and visibility.

Asta Reef, with a drop of 24m (79 ft.), has coral, sea fans, and reef fish in abundance. It's the site of a Barbados wreck that was sunk in 1986 as an artificial reef. **Dottins,** the most beautiful reef on the west coast, stretches 8km (5 miles) from Holetown to Bridgetown and has numerous dive sites at an average depth of 12m (39 ft.) and drop-offs of 30m (98 ft.). The SS *Stavronikita,* a Greek freighter, is a popular site for advanced divers. Crippled by fire in 1976, the 108m (354-ft.) freighter was sunk .4km (¼ mile) off the west coast to become an artificial reef in **Folkestone Underwater Park,** north of Holetown. The mast is at 12m (39 ft.), the deck at 24m (79 ft.), and the keel at 36m (118 ft.). While you explore the site, you might spot barracuda, moray eels, and a vibrant coat of bright yellow tube sponge, delicate pink rope sponge, and crimson encrusting sponge. The park has an underwater snorkel trail, plus glass-bottom boat rides, making it a family favorite.

The **Dive Shop,** Pebbles Beach, Aquatic Gap, St. Michael (© **246/426-9947**), offers some of the best scuba diving on Barbados, charging US$55 for a one-tank dive and US$80 for a two-tank dive, including equipment. Every day, three dive trips go out to the nearby reefs and wrecks; snorkeling trips and equipment rentals are also available. Visitors with reasonable swimming skills who have never dived before can sign up for a resort course. Priced at US$70, it includes pool training, safety instructions, and a one-tank open-water dive. The establishment is NAUI- and PADI-certified, and is open Sunday to Friday from 8:30am to 4:30pm. Some other dive shops in Barbados that rent or sell snorkeling equipment include **Hazel's Water World,** Bridgetown, St. Michael (© **246/426-4043**); and **Explore Sub,** Christ Church, near Bridgetown (no phone).

Several companies also operate snorkeling cruises that take you to particularly picturesque areas; see "Tours & Cruises" under "Seeing the Sights," below.

TENNIS   The big hotels have tennis courts that can be reserved even if you're not a guest. In Barbados, most tennis players still wear traditional whites. **Folkestone Park,** Holetown (© **246/422-2314**), is a free public tennis court. Courts at the **Barbados Squash Club,** Marine House, Christ Church (© **246/427-7913**), can be reserved for US$17 for 45 minutes.

WINDSURFING   Experts say the windsurfing off Barbados is as good as any this side of Hawaii. Windsurfing on Barbados has turned into a very big business between November and April, attracting thousands of windsurfers from as far away as Finland, Argentina, and Japan. The shifting of the trade winds between November and May and the shallow offshore reef of **Silver Sands** create unique conditions of wind and wave swells. This allows windsurfers to reach speeds of up to 50 knots and do complete loops off the waves. Silver Sands is rated the best spot in the Caribbean for advanced windsurfing (skill rating of 5–6).

Club Mistral Windsurfing Club, with two branches on the island, can get you started. Beginners and intermediates usually opt for the branch in Oistins (© **246/428-7277**), where winds are constant but the sea is generally flat and calm. Advanced intermediates and experts usually go to the branch adjacent to the Silver Sands Hotel, in Christ Church (© **246/428-6001**), where stronger winds and higher waves allow surfers to combine aspects of windsurfing and conventional Hawaiian-style surfing. Both branches use boards and equipment provided by the Germany-based Club Mistral. Equipment rents for US$50 per half-day or US$90 for a full day, depending on where and what you rent; rates are less expensive at the Oistins branch.

6 Seeing the Sights

TOURS & CRUISES

Barbados is worth exploring, either in a rental car or with a taxi-driver guide. Unlike many Caribbean islands, Barbados has fair roads. They are, however, poorly signposted, and newcomers invariably get lost—not only once, but several times. If you lose your way, you'll generally find people in the countryside helpful.

ORGANIZED TOURS   **Bajan Tours,** Shak-Shak Complex, no. 4 Frere Pilgrim, Christ Church (© **246/228-6000**), is a locally owned and operated company. The best bet for the first-timer is the Exclusive Island Tour, departing Monday to Friday between 8 and 8:30am and returning between 2:30 and 3pm.

It covers all the island's highlights, including the Barbados Wildlife Reserve, the Chalky Mount Potteries, and the rugged east coast. All tours cost US$58 per person and include a full buffet lunch.

CRUISES   Most popular and fun are the *Jolly Roger* **"Pirate" Cruises** run by Jolly Roger Cruises (© **246/228-8142**), operating either from Bridgetown Harbour or from the Boatyard Beach Bar. *Jolly Roger* is an ersatz, Disney-esque replica of an 18th-century pirate galleon. Departures are from one of two distinctly different berths within Bridgetown Harbour; ask at the time of your reservation which it will be. Passengers can rope swing, swim, snorkel, and suntan on the top deck. Even mock weddings are staged. A buffet lunch with rum punch is available Thursday and Saturday from 11am to 3pm. Lunch cruises cost US$65 per person. You can also sail on a catamaran lunch cruise, a 4-hour cruise offered daily from 10am to 3pm, costing US$65 per person. Children 12 and under are half price.

Part cruise ship, part nightclub, the **MV *Harbour Master Blockbuster*** (© **246/430-0900**) is a 30m (98-ft.), four-story vessel with theme decks, a modern galley, and three bars. It boasts a dance floor and a sit-down restaurant, and also offers formal buffets on its Calypso Deck. On the Harbour Master Deck, there's a bank of TVs for sports buffs. The showpiece of the vessel is an onboard semisubmersible, which is lowered hydraulically to 2m (6½ ft.) beneath the ship. This is, in effect, a "boat in a boat," with 30 seats. Lunch and dinner cruises cost US$62 and US$65 per person; the semisubmersible experience costs another US$10.

SUBMERGED SIGHTSEEING   You no longer have to be an experienced diver to see what lives 45m (148 ft.) below the surface of the sea. Now anybody can view the sea's wonders on sightseeing submarines. The air-conditioned submersibles seat 28 to 48 passengers and make several dives daily from 9am to 1pm, Monday, Tuesday, Thursday, and Friday, and 9am to 4pm on Wednesday. Passengers are transported aboard a ferryboat from the Carenage in downtown Bridgetown to the submarine site, about 2km (1¼ miles) from the west coast of Barbados. The ride offers a view of the west coast of the island.

The submarine, *Atlantic III,* features viewing ports that allow you to see a rainbow of colors, tropical fish, plants, and even a shipwreck that lies upright and intact below the surface. The cost is US$83 for adults, US$40 for children. For reservations, contact **Atlantis Submarines** (Barbados), Shallow Draught, Bridgetown (© **246/436-8929**). In addition, you can take a tour aboard a Rhino Rider, an inflatable motorized craft that goes up the West Coast on a tour lasting 2 hours. There's a 30-minute stop for a snorkeling adventure at a nearby shipwreck where you can feed the fish, and also a beach stop. The cost is US$57 for adults and US$40 for children age 4 to 12. No children under .9m (3 ft.) tall permitted. Tours are run Monday, Tuesday, Thursday, and Friday from 9am to 1pm, and on Wednesday from 9am to 4pm.

EXPLORING BRIDGETOWN

Often hot and clogged with traffic, the capital, Bridgetown, merits a morning's shopping jaunt (see "Shopping," later in this chapter), plus a visit to some of its major sights.

Since about half a million visitors arrive on Barbados by cruise ship each year, the government has opened a US$6 million **cruise-ship terminal** with 20 duty-free shops, 13 local retail stores, and scads of vendors. Cruise passengers can choose from a range of products, including the arts and crafts of Barbados,

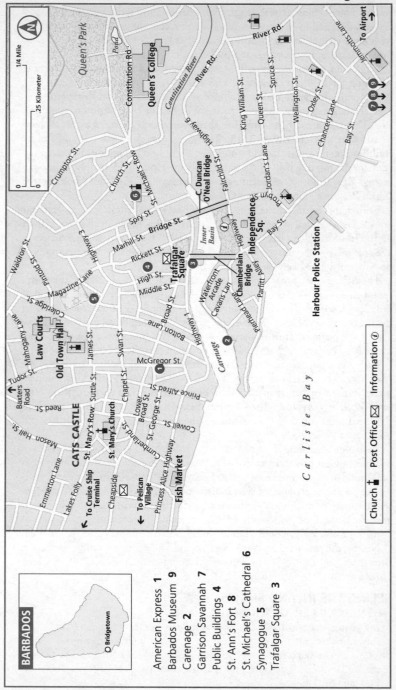

Bridgetown

Church †   Post Office ⊠   Information ⓘ

BARBADOS

○ Bridgetown

American Express **1**
Barbados Museum **9**
Carenage **2**
Garrison Savannah **7**
Public Buildings **4**
St. Ann's Fort **8**
St. Michael's Cathedral **6**
Synagogue **5**
Trafalgar Square **3**

jewelry, liquor, china, crystal, electronics, perfume, and leather goods. The interior was designed to re-create an island street scene; some storefronts appear as traditional chattel houses in brilliant island colors, complete with streetlights, tropical landscaping, benches, and pushcarts.

Begin your tour at the waterfront, called the **Carenage** (French for "turning vessels on their side for cleaning"). This was a haven for clipper ships, and even though today it doesn't have the color of yesteryear, it's still worth exploring.

At **Trafalgar Square,** the long tradition of British colonization is immortalized. The monument here, honoring Lord Nelson, was executed by Sir Richard Westmacott and erected in 1813. The great gray Victorian/Gothic **Public Buildings** on the square look like ones you might find in London. The east wing contains the meeting halls of the Senate and the House of Assembly, with some stained-glass windows representing the sovereigns of England. Look for the "Great Protector" himself, Oliver Cromwell.

Behind the Financial Building, **St. Michael's Cathedral,** east of Trafalgar Square, is the symbol of the Church of England. This Anglican church was built in 1655 but was completely destroyed in a 1780 hurricane. Reconstructed in 1789, it was again damaged by a hurricane in 1831. George Washington supposedly worshiped here on his visit to Barbados.

The **Synagogue,** Synagogue Lane (℡ 246/426-5792), is one of the oldest synagogues in the Western Hemisphere and is surrounded by a burial ground of early Jewish settlers. The present building dates from 1833. It was constructed on the site of an even older synagogue, erected by Jews from Brazil in 1654. It's now part of the National Trust of Barbados—and a synagogue once again. It's open Monday to Friday from 9am to 4pm; a donation is requested for admission.

First made popular in 1870, **cricket** is the national pastime on Barbados. Matches can last from 1 to 5 days. If you'd like to see one, watch for announcements in the newspapers or ask at the **Barbados Tourism Authority,** on Harbour Road (℡ 246/427-2623). From Bridgetown, take a taxi to **Garrison Savannah,** just south of the capital, a venue for frequent cricket matches and horse races.

Barbados Museum, St. Ann's Garrison, St. Michael (℡ 246/427-0201), is in a former military prison. Extensive collections show the island's development from prehistoric to modern times, as well as fascinating glimpses into the natural environment and fine examples of West Indian maps and decorative arts. The museum sells a variety of quality publications, reproductions, and handcrafts. Its cafe is good for a snack or light lunch. Hours are Monday to Saturday from 9am to 5pm, Sunday from 2 to 6pm. Admission is US$6 for adults, US$3 for children.

Nearby, the russet-red **St. Ann's Fort,** on the fringe of the savanna, garrisoned British soldiers in 1694. The fort wasn't completed until 1703. The **Clock House** survived the hurricane of 1831.

SEEING THE INLAND SIGHTS
IN THE CENTER OF THE ISLAND ✦✦

Many visitors stay on those fabulous west-coast beaches, but the island's true beauty is its lush interior. If you have the time, we highly recommend a hike, drive, or tour through such rarely visited parishes as St. Thomas and St. George (both are landlocked) and the wild Atlantic coast parishes of St. Andrews, St. Joseph, and St. John.

Flower Forest ✦ This former sugar plantation stands 255m (836 ft.) above sea level near the western edge of the Scotland district, 2km (1¼ miles) from

Harrison's Cave. Set in one of the most scenic parts of Barbados, it's more than just a botanical garden; it's where people and nature came together to create something beautiful. After viewing the grounds, visitors can purchase handcrafts at Best of Barbados.

Richmond Plantation, St. Joseph. ✆ 246/433-8152. Admission US$7.50 adults, US$4 children age 5–16, free for children age 4 and under. Daily 9am–5pm.

Francia Plantation ✦   A fine family home, the Francia Plantation stands on a wooded hillside overlooking the St. George Valley and is still owned and occupied by descendants of the original owner. Built in 1913, the house blends West Indian and European architectural influences. You can explore several rooms, including the dining room with its family silver and an 18th-century James McCabe bracket clock. On the walls are antique maps and prints, including a map of the West Indies printed in 1522.

St. George, Barbados. ✆ 246/429-0474. Admission US$6. Mon–Fri 10am–4pm. On the ABC Hwy., turn east onto Hwy. 4 at the Norman Niles Roundabout (follow the signs to Gun Hill); after going .8km (½ mile), turn left onto Hwy. X (follow the signs to Gun Hill); after 2km (1¼ miles), turn right at the Shell gas station and follow Hwy. X past St. George's Parish Church and up the hill for 2km (1¼ miles), turning left at the sign to Francia.

Harrison's Cave ✦✦ *Kids*   The underground world here, the number-one tourist attraction of Barbados, is viewed from aboard an electric tram and trailer. You'll see bubbling streams, tumbling cascades, and subtly lit deep pools, while all around stalactites hang overhead like icicles, and stalagmites rise from the floor. Visitors may disembark and get a closer look at this natural phenomenon at the Rotunda Room and the Cascade Pool. Although it's interesting, it may not impress those who have been to the far more spectacular Carlsbad or Luray Caverns.

Welchman Hall, St. Thomas. ✆ 246/438-6640. Tour reservations recommended. Admission US$15 adults, US$6 children 3–12 years old. Daily 9am–4pm. Closed Good Friday, Easter Sunday, and Christmas.

Welchman Hall Gully ✦   The Barbados National Trust owns this lush tropical garden, which contains specimens of plants—many of them labeled—that were here before the English settlers landed in 1627, and later imports that include cocoa bushes, exotic orchids, and trees from which both cloves and nutmeg are produced. Occasionally you'll spot a wild monkey amidst the flora. You can also see breadfruit trees that are supposedly descendants of the seedlings brought ashore by Captain Bligh, of *Bounty* fame.

Welchman Hall, St. Thomas. ✆ 246/438-6671. Admission US$6 adults, US$3 children age 6–12, free for children age 5 and under. Daily 9am–5pm. Take Hwy. 2 from Bridgetown.

SIGHTS ALONG THE WEST COAST

Folkestone Marine Park & Visitor Centre *Kids*   Set beside a shimmering stretch of coral sand beach, this is a "water park," lying just north of Holetown.

Tips **The Great Tour**

From mid-January through the first week of April, you can tour a different great house every Wednesday afternoon, many rarely seen by the public. You'll see a great array of plantation antiques and get a feeling for the elegant colonial lifestyle once commonplace on Barbados. For more information, call ✆ 246/426-2421.

It combines a museum and aquarium to illustrate the rich marine life of Barbados. An underwater snorkeling trail goes around a reef, and you can see the same sights in a glass-bottom boat. A number of beachfront restaurants and bars are nearby, and there is an on-site gift shop open Monday to Friday 9am to 5pm.

Church Point, Holetown, St. James. © 246/422-2314. Free admission. Snorkeling with equipment US$10. Daily 9am–5pm.

The Malibu Beach Club & Visitor Center   Lying to the north of Bridgetown, this manufacturer of white rum has been going strong since 1897. The distillery is known for producing a very popular island drink, coconut rum. To make this tour even more enticing, the center is constructed on an idyllic stretch of white-sand beach set against a backdrop of sea-grape and almond trees. Also on-site is a beachside grill where lunch and rum punches are served. The price of the tour includes a rum drink and the use of a beach chair. In contrast to the sunny beach, the distillery is dark with a lot of old equipment, including a century-old copper-pot still.

Black Rock, Brighton, St. Michael. © 246/425-9393. Admission US$33 with lunch and transportation from your hotel. Basic tour US$9. Day pass US$38. Mon–Fri 9am–3:45pm.

The Mount Gay Rum Tour & Gift Shop   On the northern edge of Bridgetown, you learn the story of island rum, produced here virtually since the British first settled on the island in 1627. By 1655 Barbados was producing some 900,000 gallons of rum annually. The actual distillery is in St. Lucy Parish to the north, but at this center you can see both old and contemporary equipment used in rum-making, along with rows and rows of barrels. First you view a video about Mount Gay's history, followed by a 15-minute crash course in rum making. The tour concludes with a rum tasting. Rum, along with gift items, is for sale in the on-site shop. You can also make a reservation for an admission-free tour of the actual Mount Gay refinery by calling © **246/439-8812.**

Spring Garden Hwy., Brandons, St. Michael. © 246/425-8757. Admission US$6, or US$28 including lunch and transportation from your hotel. Mon–Fri 9am–3:45pm.

IN THE SOUTHEAST (ST. PHILIP)

Heritage Park & Rum Factory   After driving through cane fields, you'll arrive at the first rum distillery to be launched on the island since the 19th century. Inaugurated in 1996, this factory is located on a former molasses and sugar plantation dating back some 350 years. Produced on-site is ESA Field, a white rum praised by connoisseurs. Adjacent is an admission-free park where Barbadian handcrafts are displayed. You'll also find an array of shops and carts selling global foods, handcrafts, and products.

Foursquare Plantation, St. Philip. © 246/420-1977. Free admission. Mon–Fri 9am–5pm.

Sunbury Plantation House ℛ   If you have time to visit only one plantation or great house in Barbados, make it this one. It's the only great house on Barbados where all the rooms are open for viewing. The 300-year-old plantation house is steeped in history, featuring mahogany antiques, old prints, and a unique collection of horse-drawn carriages. Take the informative tour, then stop in the Courtyard Restaurant and Bar for a meal or drinks; there's also a gift shop. A candlelight dinner is offered at least once a week; this five-course meal, served at a 200-year-old mahogany table, costs US$75 per person.

6 Cross Rd., St. Philip. © 246/423-6270. Admission US$7.50 adults, US$3.75 children. Daily 9:30am–4:30pm (last tour).

(Moments **A Beautiful Picnic Spot**

Farley Hill National Park surrounds what used to be one of the greatest houses of Barbados, Farley Hill, a mansion in ruins. The park lies to the north of the parish of St. Peter, directly across the road leading into the Barbados Wildlife Reserve. You can bring in a picnic and wander in the park, over-looking the turbulent waters of the Atlantic. You can enter the park for free if you're walking, but it costs US$2 to bring a car in. Hours are daily 8:30am to 5pm.

IN THE NORTHEAST

Andromeda Botanic Gardens ⭐ On a cliff overlooking the town of Bathsheba on the rugged east coast, limestone boulders make for a natural 3-hectare (7½-acre) rock-garden setting. Thousands of orchids, hundreds of hibiscus and heliconia, and many varieties of ferns, begonias, palms, and other species grow here in splendid profusion. You'll occasionally see frogs, herons, lizards, hummingbirds, and sometimes a mongoose or a monkey.

Bathsheba, St. Joseph. © 246/433-9384. Admission US$7.60 adults, US$3.80 children, free for children 5 and under. Daily 9am–5pm.

St. Nicholas Abbey Surrounded by sugar-cane fields, this Jacobean plantation great house has been around since about 1650. It was never actually an abbey—around 1820 an ambitious owner simply christened it as such. More than 80 hectares (198 acres) are still cultivated each year. The house, characterized by its curved gables, is believed to be one of three Jacobean houses in the Western Hemisphere. At least the ground floor of the structure is open to the public.

On Cherry Tree Hill, Hwy. 1, St. Peter. © 246/422-8725. Admission US$5 adults; US$1 children 11 and under. Mon–Fri 10am–3:30pm.

7 Shopping

You may find duty-free merchandise here at prices 20% to 40% lower than in the United States and Canada—but you've got to be a smart shopper to spot bargains, and you should be familiar with prices back in your hometown. Duty-free shops have two prices listed on items of merchandise: the local retail price and the local retail price less the government-imposed tax.

Some of the best duty-free buys include cameras, watches, crystal, gold jewelry, bone china, cosmetics and perfumes, and liquor (including locally produced Barbados rum and liqueurs), along with tobacco products and cashmere sweaters, tweeds, and sportswear from Britain. If you purchase items made on Barbados, you don't have to pay duty.

The quintessential Barbados handcrafts are black-coral jewelry and clay pottery. The latter originates at **Highland Pottery, Inc.** (© 246/431-0747), which is worth a visit. Potters turn out different products, some based on designs that are centuries old. The potteries (which are signposted) are north of Bathsheba on the east coast, in St. Joseph Parish near Barclay's Park. In shops across the island, you'll also find a selection of locally made vases, pots, pottery mugs, glazed plates, and ornaments.

Island craftspeople weave wall hangings from local grasses and dried flowers, and also turn out straw mats, baskets, and bags with raffia embroidery. Leatherwork, particularly handbags, belts, and sandals, is also found on Barbados.

IN BRIDGETOWN   Cruise passengers generally head for the **cruise-ship terminal** at Bridgetown Harbour, which has some 20 duty-free shops, 13 local shops, and many vendors (see "Exploring Bridgetown" under "Seeing the Sights," above).

At **Articrafts,** Norman Center Mall, Broad Street (✆ **246/427-5767**), John and Roslyn Watson have assembled an impressive display of Bajan arts and crafts. Roslyn's distinctive wall hangings are decorated with objects from the island, including sea fans and coral. The unique **Colours of De Caribbean,** the Waterfront Marina (next to the Waterfront Café, on the Carenage; ✆ **246/436-8522**), carries a limited selection of original hand-painted and batik clothing, all made in the West Indies, plus jewelry and decorative objects.

Cave Shepherd, Broad Street (✆ **246/431-2121**), is the largest department store on the island and the best place for duty-free merchandise. There are branches at Sunset Crest in Holetown, Da Costas Mall, Grantley Adams Airport, and the Bridgetown cruise-ship terminal, but if your time is limited, try this outlet, as it has the widest selection. The store sells perfumes, cosmetics, fine crystal and bone china, cameras, jewelry, swimwear, leather goods, men's designer clothing, handcrafts, liquor, and souvenirs. You can take a break in the cool comfort of the Balcony, overlooking Broad Street, which serves vegetarian dishes and has a salad bar and beer garden.

Harrison's, 1 Broad St. (✆ **246/431-5500**), has six branch stores, all selling a wide variety of duty-free merchandise, including china, crystal, jewelry, leather goods, and perfumes—all at fair prices. Also for sale are some fine leather products handcrafted in Colombia.

Little Switzerland, in the Da Costas Mall, Broad Street (✆ **246/431-0030**), offers a wide selection of watches, fine jewelry, Mont Blanc pens, and an array of goodies from Waterford, Lalique, Swarovski, Baccarat, and others.

Pelican Crafts Center, Harbour Road (✆ **246/426-4391**), is rather an overpriced tourist trap, hawking craft items. In Bridgetown, go down Princess Alice Highway to the city's Deep Water Harbour, where you'll find this tiny colony of thatch-roofed shops. Most of the shops here are gimmicky, but a few interesting items can be found if you search hard enough. Sometimes you can see craftspeople at work.

ELSEWHERE ON THE ISLAND The Watering Hole, Hwy. 7, St. Lawrence Gap (✆ **245/435-6375**), is not only the best place to purchase bottles of Bajan rum at duty-free prices, but is also a great dive to hang out. A small bottle of rum (about 6 oz.) sells for around US$4, and you can also order fish and chips dinners here, or else fried chicken meals, for about US$8. Some locals as well as savvy visitors come here and make an evening of it, sampling the various rum drinks. Of course, you'll need someone to carry you back to your hotel, as these punches are lethal. Opening times vary—call to be sure—but we've seen this place going strong at 3am. One of the most interesting shopping jaunts in Barbados is to **Tyrol Cot Heritage Village,** Codrington Hill, St. Michael (✆ **246/424-2074**), the former home of the Bajan national hero, Sir Grantley Adams. On the grounds of the former prime minister's estate is a colony of artisans, who turn out an array of articles for sale ranging from paintings to pottery, from baskets to handmade figurines.

Earthworks Pottery/The Potter's House Gallery, Edgehill Heights 2, St. Thomas (✆ **246/425-0223**), is one of the artistic highlights of Barbados. Deep in the island's central highlands, Canadian-born Goldie Spieler and her son, David, create whimsical ceramics in the colors of the sea and sky; many objects are decorated with Antillean-inspired swirls and zigzags. On the premises are a studio and a showroom that sells the output of at least half a dozen other island potters. Purchases can be shipped.

The **Shell Gallery,** Gibbes Hill, St. Peter (© **246/422-2593**), has the best collection of shells in the West Indies. Also offered are shell jewelry, local pottery and ceramics, and batik.

Greenwich House Antiques, Greenwich Village, Trents Hill, St. James (© **246/432-1169**), a 25-minute drive from Bridgetown, feels like a genteel private home where the objects for sale seem to have come from the attic of your slightly dotty great aunt. Dozens of objects fill every available inch of display space.

8 Barbados After Dark

ON THE WEST COAST   A lot of the evening entertainment around here revolves around the big resorts, many of which have lovely bars and many of which host bands and beach parties in the evening. See "Accommodations," earlier in this chapter.

Some say the green-and-white **Coach House,** Paynes Bay (on the main Bridgetown-Holetown road, just south of Sandy Lane, about 10km/6¼ miles north of Bridgetown), St. James (© **246/432-1163**), is 200 years old. Attracting mostly visitors, this is a Bajan version of an English pub, with an outdoor garden bar. From 6 to 10:30pm you can order bar meals, including flying-fish burgers, priced at US$5 and up. Starting at 9pm on most nights, there's live music—everything from steel bands to jazz, pop, and rock. The lunchtime buffet, offered Monday through Friday (US$15), is popular.

John Moore Bar, on the waterfront, Weston, St. James (© **246/422-2258**), is the most atmospheric and least pretentious bar on Barbados. Open to the sea breezes, and much weather-beaten, it's the nerve center of this waterfront town, filled day and night with a congenial group of neighborhood residents, and a scattering of tourists. Most visitors opt for a rum punch or beer, but you can order up a plate of local fish or chicken if you don't mind waiting.

One of our favorite bars in Barbados is **Olives Bar & Bistro,** Second Street at the corner of Hwy. 1, in Holetown (© **246/432-2112**). Not only is it a fine restaurant but it's also a good place to spend 2 or 3 hours before or after dinner—maybe both. Found upstairs in a *Casablanca*-like setting of potted palms and whirling fans, it draws a convivial international crowd, mostly expats, Americans, and English visitors in their 30s and 40s.

IN BRIDGETOWN   For the most authentic Bajan evening possible, head for **Baxters Road** in Bridgetown, where there's always something cooking on Friday and Saturday after 11pm. In fact, if you stick around until dawn, you'll find the party's still going strong. Some old-time visitors have compared Baxters Road to the back streets of New Orleans in the 1930s. If you fall in love with the place, you can "caf crawl" up and down the street, where nearly every bar is run by a Bajan mama.

The most popular "caf" on Baxters Road is **Enid's** (she has a phone, "but it doesn't work"), a little ramshackle establishment where Bajans come to devour fried chicken at 3 in the morning. This place is open daily from 8:30pm to 8:30am, when the last satisfied customer departs into the blazing morning sun and the employees go home to get some sleep. Stop in for a Banks beer.

Boatyard Bar & South Deck Grill, Bay Street in Bridgetown (© **246/436-2622**), is one of the busiest and most animated of the youth-oriented bars in Bridgetown occupying an outdoor, beach-fronting building whose interior is lavishly decorated in Creole colors of bright yellow, blue, and pink. If you want food, the menu contains simple platters of fish, chicken, or burgers. If you want to go swimming, the beach lies almost directly adjacent to the foundations of this place. Expect a 5-minute trek from central Bridgetown, hordes of dancers jiving to the DJ every Tuesday, Wednesday, Friday, and Saturday, and lots of local gossip. Open daily 9am to 1 or 3am, depending on business.

Harbour Lights, Marine's Villa, Lower Bay Street, about 2km (1¼ miles) southeast of Bridgetown (© **246/436-7225**), is the most popular weekend spot for dancing, drinking, and flirting on all of Barbados. In a modern seafront building with an oceanfront patio (which gives dancers a chance to cool off), the place plays reggae, soca, and whatever else is popular until the wee hours nightly. The barbecue pit/kiosk serves up grilled meats and hamburgers on Monday, Wednesday, and Friday. Monday is beach party night; the US$49 charge includes transportation to and from your hotel, a barbecue buffet, drinks, and a live band. On Wednesday and Friday, the cover is US$18. The place attracts a large local following, with a few foreign visitors showing up.

ON THE SOUTH COAST   The bustling activity at **Cafe Sol,** St. Lawrence Gap, Christ Church (© **246/435-9531**), attracts a very convivial crowd. As a specialty of the house, the bartender rubs the margarita glasses with Bajan sugar instead of the usual salt.

Plantation Restaurant and Garden Theatre, Main Road (Hwy. 7), St. Lawrence, Christ Church (© **246/428-5048**), is the island's main showcase for evening dinner theater and Caribbean cabaret. It's completely touristy, but enjoyable nonetheless. Every Wednesday and Friday, dinner is served at 6:30pm, followed by a show, *Basan Roots and Rhythm,* at 8pm. Expect elaborate costumes and lots of reggae, calypso, and limbo. For US$74, you get dinner, the show, and transportation to and from your hotel; the show alone costs US$41. Reserve in advance.

The Ship Inn, St. Lawrence Gap, Christ Church (© **246/435-6961**), is among the leading entertainment centers on the south coast. The pub is the hot spot: Top local bands perform most nights, offering reggae, calypso, and pop music. The entrance fee ranges from free to US$10; free if you're eating dinner. The place draws an equal number of visitors and locals.

The best sports bar, without equal, is **Bubba's Sports Bar,** Rockley Main Road, Christ Church (© **246/435-6217**), which offers a couple of satellite dishes, a 3m (10-ft.) video screen, and a dozen TVs. Wash a Bubba burger down with a Banks beer. The longest bar on the island is at **After Dark,** St. Lawrence Gap, Christ Church (© **246/435-6547**), where you can often hear live reggae, soca, Bajan calypso, and jazz.

Bonaire

Unspoiled Bonaire is only gently touched by development. Although your options range from bird-watching to doing nothing, Bonaire is foremost a scuba diver's delight and also offers some of the Caribbean's best snorkeling. This sleepy island doesn't attract crowds and has none of Aruba's glitzy diversions except for a few small casinos with minor action. Instead, turquoise waters beckon travelers to discover colorful clouds of tropical fish.

Bonaire is also a bird-watcher's haven, where flamingos nearly outnumber the sparse human population. There are more than 190 different species of birds—not only the flamingo, but also the big-billed pelican, parrots, snipes, terns, parakeets, herons, and hummingbirds. A pair of binoculars is an absolute necessity.

Bonaireans zealously protect their precious environment. Even though they eagerly seek tourism, they aren't interested in creating another Aruba, with its high-rise hotel blocks. Spearfishing isn't allowed in its waters, nor is the taking or destruction of any coral or other living animal from the sea. Unlike some islands, Bonaire isn't just surrounded by coral reefs—it *is* the reef, sitting on the dry, sunny top of an underwater mountain. Its shores are thick with rainbow-hued fish.

Boomerang-shaped Bonaire is close to the coast of Latin America, just 81km (50 miles) north of Venezuela. Part of the Netherlands Antilles (an autonomous part of the Netherlands), Bonaire has a population of about 10,000 and an area of about 290 sq. km (113 sq. miles). The capital is **Kralendijk** (*Kroll*-en-dike). It's most often reached from its neighbor island of Curaçao, 48km (30 miles) to the west; like Curaçao, Bonaire is desertlike, with a dry and brilliant atmosphere. Often it's visited by day-trippers, who rush through in pursuit of the shy, elusive flamingo. Its northern sector is hilly, tapering up to Mount Brandaris, all of 236m (774 ft.). However, the southern half, flat as a pancake, is given over to bays, reefs, beaches, and a salt lake that attracts the flamingos.

1 Essentials

VISITOR INFORMATION

Before you go, you can contact the **Bonaire Government Tourist Office** at Adams Unlimited, 10 Rockefeller Plaza, Suite 900, New York, NY 10020 (© **800/-BONAIR** or 212/956-5911). There's also information on the Web at **www.bonaire.org**.

On the island, you can go to the **Bonaire Government Tourist Bureau,** Kaya Grandid 2 (© **599/717-8322**), open Monday to Friday from 7:30am to noon and 1:30 to 5pm.

GETTING THERE

Before you book your flight, be sure to read the section "Packages for the Independent Traveler" in chapter 2; it can save you a bundle. Even if you don't book a package, see that chapter's tips on finding the best airfare.

Air DCA (© **800/327-7230;** www.flydca.net) is one of your best bets for flying to Bonaire. It offers daily flights from Miami to Curaçao and Bonaire.

American Airlines (© **800/433-7300;** www.aa.com) offers one daily nonstop flight to Curaçao from its hub in Miami. These depart late enough in the day (11am) to allow easy connections from cities all over the Northeast, and they reach Curaçao early enough to allow transfers to Bonaire. Passengers in Curaçao can book a connecting flight to Bonaire on Air DCA (see above).

In 2003, a new airline based in Bonaire, **BonairExel** (© **599/717-3471**), began offering 14 flights per day between Bonaire and Curaçao and six flights per day between Bonaire and Aruba. On these flights, BonairExel uses 46-seat ATR42 turboprop planes.

Air Jamaica (© **800/523-5585**) also flies to Bonaire on Wednesday, Saturday, and Sunday from its hub in Montego Bay.

Other routes to Bonaire are possible on any of American's daily nonstop flights to Aruba through hubs in New York, Miami, and San Juan. Although these transfers are somewhat complicated, American will set up any of them, and will also offer reduced rates at some Bonairean hotels if you book your reservation simultaneously with your air passage.

GETTING AROUND

Even though most of the island is flat and renting a moped or motor scooter is fun, you'll have to be prepared for some unpaved, pitted, and rocky roads.

BY RENTAL CAR You might want to rent a four-wheel-drive vehicle, especially from October to January, when it can be muddy.

It pays to shop around: Sometimes—but not always—you can make a better deal with a local agency. Among local agencies is **Island Rentals,** Kaya Industria 31 (© **599/717-2100**), offering soft-top jeeps for $40 a day.

Avis (© **800/331-1212** in the U.S.; www.avis.com) is at Flamingo Airport. Weekly arrangements are cheaper, but daily rates range from $56 to $80, with unlimited mileage. At the airport, **Total Car Rental** (© **599/717-7424**) rents such vehicles as four-wheel drives and Suzuki minivans. Some automatic, air-conditioned four-door sedans are available.

Your valid U.S., British, or Canadian driver's license is acceptable for driving on Bonaire. Drive on the right on Bonaire.

BY TAXI Taxis are unmetered, but the government has established rates. All taxis carry a license plate with the letters *TX*. Each driver should have a price list to be produced upon request. As many as four passengers can go along for the ride, unless there's too much luggage. A trip from the airport to your hotel should cost about $12 to $15. From 8pm to midnight, fares are increased by 25%; from midnight to 6am, they go up by 50%.

Most taxi drivers can take you on a tour of the island, but you'll have to negotiate a price according to how long a trip you want and what you want to see. For more information, call **Taxi Central Dispatch** (© **599/717-8100**).

BY BICYCLE If you're in good shape, you might consider renting a bike, although you'll have to contend with the hot sun and powerful trade winds. Nevertheless, much of the island is flat, and if you follow the main road, you'll

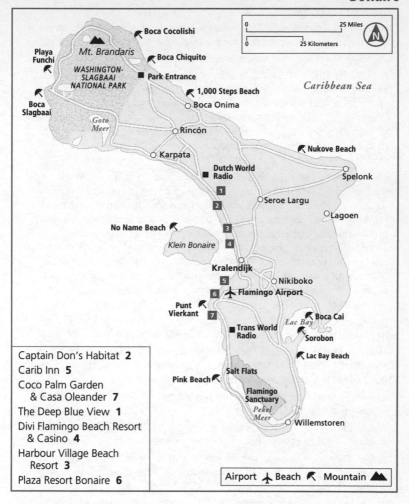

Bonaire

0 — 25 Miles
0 — 25 Kilometers

Boca Cocolishi

Playa Funchi

Mt. Brandaris

Boca Chiquito

WASHINGTON-SLAGBAAI NATIONAL PARK

Park Entrance

Caribbean Sea

1,000 Steps Beach

Boca Slagbaai

Boca Onima

Goto Meer

Rincón

Nukove Beach

Karpata

Dutch World Radio

Spelonk

1

2

Seroe Largu

Lagoen

No Name Beach

Klein Bonaire

3

4

Kralendijk

5

Nikiboko

6 ✈ Flamingo Airport

Punt Vierkant

7

Boca Cai

Lac Bay

Trans World Radio

Sorobon

Lac Bay Beach

Salt Flats

Pink Beach

Flamingo Sanctuary

Pekel Meer

Willemstoren

Captain Don's Habitat **2**

Carib Inn **5**

Coco Palm Garden
& Casa Oleander **7**

The Deep Blue View **1**

Divi Flamingo Beach Resort
& Casino **4**

Harbour Village Beach
Resort **3**

Plaza Resort Bonaire **6**

Airport ✈ Beach ↟ Mountain ▲▲

go along the water's edge. The best deals are at **Cycle Bonaire,** Kaya L. D. Gerjharts (ⓒ **599/717-7558**), where you can rent a 21-speed 830 Trek for $15 to $20 per day. Rental includes a water bottle, lock, helmet, repair kit, and pump. A map is provided for free.

FAST FACTS: Bonaire

Banks Banks are usually open Monday to Friday from 8am to noon and 2 to 3:30pm. **RBTT Bank,** Kaya Korona 15 (ⓒ **599/717-4500**), is the most convenient facility for visitors, and it has an ATM. There's also an ATM at the airport.

Currency Bonaire's coin of the realm is the **Netherlands Antillean florin (NAf),** sometimes called a guilder. The official rate is 1.77 NAf to US$1

(1 Naf = US56¢). However, U.S. dollars are widely accepted. *Unless otherwise specified, rates in this chapter are quoted in U.S. dollars.*

Customs There are no Customs requirements for Bonaire.

Documents U.S. and Canadian citizens don't need a passport to enter Bonaire, although an original birth or naturalization certificate or an alien registration card is required, plus a return ticket and photo ID. (We suggest carrying your passport anyway.) British subjects may carry a British Visitor's Passport, obtainable at post offices on Bonaire, although a valid passport issued in the United Kingdom is preferred, especially if you plan to visit other countries in the area.

Electricity The electricity on Bonaire is slightly different from that used in North America (110–130 volts/50 cycles), as opposed to U.S. and Canadian voltages of 110 volts (60 cycles). Adapters and transformers are necessary for North American appliances, but because of the erratic current, you should still proceed with caution when using any appliance and try to avoid usage if at all possible. Be warned, further, that electrical current used to feed or recharge finely calibrated diving equipment should be stabilized with a specially engineered electrical stabilizer. Every diving operation on the island has one of these as part of its standard equipment for visiting divers.

Emergencies Call ℂ **911** for the police or ambulance. Bonaire will soon have separate numbers to call for ambulance (ℂ **912**) and for fire (ℂ **919**).

Hospital The **St. Franciscus Hospital** is located at Kaya Soeur Bartola 2 in Kralendijk (ℂ **599/717-8900**). A plane on standby at the airport takes seriously ill patients to Curaçao for treatment.

Language English is widely spoken, but you'll hear Dutch, Spanish, and Papiamento, the local dialect, as well.

Liquor Laws Beer, wine, and liquor are sold in all kinds of stores 7 days a week. It's legal to have an open container on the beach.

Safety Bonaire is quite a safe haven in this crime-infested world. But remember, any place that attracts tourists also attracts people who prey on them. Safeguard your valuables.

Taxes The government requires a $6.50-per-person daily room tax on all hotel rooms. Upon leaving Bonaire, you'll be charged an airport departure tax of $20, so don't spend every penny. There's also an inter-island departure tax of $10 if you are flying to Curaçao.

Telephone To call Bonaire from the United States, dial **011** (the international access code), then **599** (the area code for Bonaire), and then **717** (the exchange) and the four-digit local number. Once on Bonaire, to call another number on the island, only the four-digit local number is necessary. You can access **AT&T Direct** on the island by dialing ℂ **001-800/872-2881**. It's often difficult to make international calls from Bonaire; phone service here lags far behind that on Aruba and Curaçao. Once you're connected to your party, the line isn't always crystal clear. Many hotel rooms don't have private phones. If you want to place an important international call, it's better to go to **TELBO,** the central phone company for the island. It's at Kaya Libertador Simon Bolivar, next to the tourist office.

Time Bonaire is on Atlantic Standard Time year-round, 1 hour ahead of Eastern Standard Time (when it's noon on Bonaire, it's 11am in Miami). When daylight savings time is in effect in the United States, clocks in Miami and Bonaire show the same time.

Tipping Most hotels and guesthouses add a 10% service charge in lieu of tipping. Restaurants generally add a service charge of 15% to the bill. Taxi drivers expect a 10% tip.

Water Drinking water comes from distilled seawater and is safe.

Weather Bonaire is known for its warm climate, with temperatures hovering around 82°F (28°C). The water temperature averages 80°F (27°C). It's warmest in August and September, coolest in January and February. The average rainfall is 22 inches, and December to March are the rainiest months. Like all the Dutch ABC (Aruba, Bonaire, and Curaçao) islands, Bonaire lies outside the hurricane belt, which comes as a relief to many visitors planning to visit the Caribbean during the hurricane season.

2 Accommodations

Hotels, all facing the sea, and in many cases opening onto beaches, are low-key, personally run operations where everybody gets to know everybody else in no time. They are concentrated on the west coast of the island immediately north or immediately south of the capital of Kralendijk.

Remember that taxes and service charges are seldom included in the prices you're quoted, so ask about them when making your reservations. Be sure to read the section "Packages for the Independent Traveler" in chapter 2 before you book a hotel on your own.

Your best deal at one of the dive resorts, such as Captain Don's Habitat, is to book a package deal, often for a week. Depending on the house count, more limited bookings can be accommodated if rooms are available.

VERY EXPENSIVE

Harbour Village Beach Resort ☆☆☆   Conceived by one of the largest land developers in Venezuela, this exclusive and newly renovated complex, the most stylish on the island, is designed like an Iberian village, opening onto a sandy beach. It's upscale and well managed, offering services and resort amenities to well-heeled divers who don't want the more laid-back atmosphere of Captain Don's Habitat (see below). Accommodations are in a cluster of Dutch Caribbean–style villas painted in pastels, with red-tile roofs and terraced balconies. Guest rooms have tropical decor, four-poster beds, white-tile floors, natural-wood furniture, island-style ceiling fans as well as air-conditioning, and marble bathrooms, with deluxe toiletries, shower stalls, and robes.

A wide array of very good food awaits you. Our favorite restaurant is **La Balandra Bar and Grill,** a gazebolike structure set beside a massive pier; an octagonal bar area flanked by an open grill and salad bar is open to the sea view and breezes. The marina-front Lighthouse Restaurant at Harbour Village offers seafood specialties in a cozy nautical decor.

Kaya Gobernador N. Debrot, Playa Lechi (P.O. Box 312), Bonaire, N.A. © 800/424-0004 in the U.S. and Canada, or 599/717-7500. Fax 599/717-7507. www.harbourvillage.com. 70 units. Winter $375–$554 double, from $640 suite; off season $318–$439 double, from $525 suite. Children under 16 stay free in parent's room.

Rates include continental buffet. AE, DC, DISC, MC, V. **Amenities:** 2 restaurants; 2 bars; outdoor pool; 4 tennis courts; health club and spa; aerobics; dive shop; marina; bikes; airport pickup; room service (8am–7pm); babysitting; laundry service. *In room:* A/C, ceiling fan, TV, kitchenette (in suites), hair dryer, safe.

EXPENSIVE

Captain Don's Habitat ☆ Built on a coral bluff overlooking the sea and a tiny beach about 5 minutes north of Kralendijk, this divers' resort, with an air of congenial informality, is for those whose souls belong to the sea. Habitat and its accompanying dive shop are the creation of Captain Don Stewart, Caribbean pioneer and "caretaker of the reefs," a former Californian who sailed his schooner from San Francisco through the Panama Canal, arriving on a reef in Bonaire in 1962—he's been here ever since. Known on the island as the "godfather of diving," Captain Don was instrumental in the formation of the Bonaire Marine Park, whereby the entire island became a protected reef.

More than 90% of the guests here opt for a package, which incorporates a variable number of dives with accommodations in settings ranging from standard double rooms to oceanfront villas, each with a bathroom with shower/tub combinations. The most popular is the 8-day/7-night package. Noteworthy expansions within the past several years have included some relatively upscale junior suites, plus villas with full kitchens and oceanview verandas.

This resort has an oceanfront restaurant and two seaside bars. A casual, laid-back crowd gathers for meals at Rum Runners, the social hub. Theme nights are staged weekly, which divert guests from the rather standard fare served here.

Kaya Gobernador N. Debrot 103, Pier 7, Bonaire, N.A. © **599/717-8290.** Fax 599/717-8240. For reservations and business arrangements, contact Captain Don's Habitat, 4500 Biscaye Blvd., Suite 320, Miami, FL 33127 (© **800/327-6709;** fax 305/438-4220). www.habitatdiveresorts.com. 84 units. Winter $1,566–$2,293 per person; off season $934–$1,373 per person. Rates are for 8-day/7-night stays and include breakfast, airport transfers, tax, service, equipment, 6 boat dives, and unlimited 24-hr. shore dives. AE, MC, V. **Amenities:** Restaurant; 2 bars; outdoor pool; dive program; babysitting; laundry service; dry cleaning; rooms for those with limited mobility. *In room:* A/C, TV, kitchenette (in some), fridge, beverage maker, safe, no phone in some units.

The Deep Blue View ☆☆ *Finds* Staying here is like being in your own private villa. This small, intimate retreat in the Santa Barbara Heights district is informally luxurious, and our favorite on the island. Luxuriant foliage envelops the villa, which attracts honeymooners, families, and romantic couples, among others. Each of the beautifully furnished guest rooms comes with a large patio and pool area. All accommodations have vaulted ceilings and tiled floors. The little extras make the difference here. The staff will even "brown bag" your breakfast if you've got an early flight, and when you head to the beach they give you thick towels, packed lunches, and cold drinks in coolers for an additional charge. From the villa's tiled patio, you experience an 180-degree vista of the Caribbean, whose color—deep blue—led to the name of the villa. As the sun goes down, you can enjoy happy hour or barbecue by the pool. Menneo de Bree, a dive instructor, will give you valuable diving tips.

Santa Barbara Heights, Kaya Diamanta 50, Bonaire, N.A. © **599/717-8073.** Fax 599/717-7826. www. deepblueview.com. 4 units. Year-round $1,085–$1,295 per week double; 3 nights $595 double. Rates include breakfast. AE, MC, V. No children under 10. **Amenities:** Laundry service; dry cleaning. *In room:* A/C, ceiling fan, hair dryer, iron/ironing board, no phone.

Plaza Resort Bonaire ☆ This luxury resort lies a short drive from the airport, on a strip of land midway between a saltwater lagoon and a sandy stretch of Caribbean beachfront. Designed in 1995 by a team of Italian architects, it resembles a white-sided village along the coast of southern Portugal, thanks to terra-cotta roofs and a pair of bridges that traverse the lagoon for easy access to the 5 hectares (12 acres) of grounds. It's an extremely large property for Bonaire, where most hotels are more intimate, and it contains a freshly renovated casino. Some units are privately owned. Rooms are quite large, though be aware that what management here refers to as suites are actually very large bedrooms, without interior dividers. The one- and two-bedroom villas contain a kitchenette, ceiling fans, and simple, summery furnishings. Most units are large and airy, with private balconies, and queen-size beds. Bathrooms are roomy and luxurious, with showers and deep tubs.

J. A. Abraham Blvd. 80, Bonaire, N.A. © 800/766-6016 in the U.S., or 599/717-2500. Fax 599/717-7133. www.plazaresortbonaire.com. 224 units. Winter $220–$250 suite, $280–$310 1-bedroom villa, $350–$380 2-bedroom villa; off season $170–$200 suite, $210–$240 1-bedroom villa, $280–$310 2-bedroom villa. Extra person $30. AE, MC, V. **Amenities:** 3 restaurants; 2 bars; outdoor pool; casino; 4 tennis courts; health club and spa; boats; dive shop; marina; sailing; windsurfing; bikes; children's programs; salon; limited room service; babysitting; laundry service; dry cleaning. *In room:* A/C, TV, dataport, fridge, beverage maker, hair dryer, safe.

MODERATE

Divi Flamingo Beach Resort & Casino
Divi is the comeback kid, having reinvented itself after a massive restoration. New furnishings, paint, tiles, and rejuvenated air-conditioning have made this once-tired waterfront hostelry more comfortable than it's been in years. Originally a seedy cluster of flimsy wooden bungalows used to intern German prisoners in World War II, today the resort consists of individual cottages and seafront rooms with private balconies. These accommodations rest on piers above the surf so you can stand on your balcony and watch rainbow-hued tropical fish in the waters below. This hotel was fully renovated in 2002.

The resort's original rooms were supplemented in 1986 with the addition of timeshare units, forming Club Flamingo. These are the newest and best rooms, and each can be rented by the day or the week. The accommodations in both sections are spacious and sunny, with ceiling fans and Mexican accents. The newer units are clustered into a green-and-white neo-Victorian pavilion facing its own curving pool. Each contains a kitchenette with carved cupboards and cabinets of pickled hardwoods. All units have well-kept bathrooms with shower/tub combinations.

Chibi-Chibi and Calabase provide satisfying, straightforward meals.

J. A. Abraham Blvd., Bonaire, N.A. © 800/367-3484 in the U.S., or 599/717-8285. Fax 599/717-8238. www.diviresorts.com. 130 units. Winter $140–$184 double, from $139 studio; off season $105–$138 double, from $95 studio. Rates about 10% higher between Christmas and New Year's. MAP (breakfast and dinner) $45 per person extra. Several inclusive packages offered. AE, DC, MC, V. **Amenities:** 2 restaurants; 3 bars; 2 outdoor pools; casino; fitness center; spa services; dive shop; snorkeling; car rental; salon; limited room service; babysitting; laundry service; rooms for those with limited mobility. *In room:* A/C, TV, beverage maker, iron/ironing board, safe, no phone.

INEXPENSIVE

Carib Inn ✦ Value
On a sliver of a beach, this inn, owned and managed by American diver Bruce Bowker, is occupied by dedicated scuba divers drawn to its five-star PADI dive facility. This is the most intimate little diving resort on Bonaire and remains one of the island's best values. All rooms have kitchenettes; larger units have a full kitchen, and maid service is provided daily. The accommodations are furnished with tropical rattan and every year, management devotes time and money to paint, repair, and spruce them up. Each of the bathrooms has a shower stall, but not a bathtub, although the many repeat guests,

who book this place far in advance every winter, don't seem to care. The hotel will not book through travel agents.

J. A. Abraham Blvd. (P.O. Box 68), Kralendijk, Bonaire, N.A. ☎ 599/717-8819. Fax 599/717-5295. www.carib inn.com. 10 units. Year-round $109 studio efficiency apt (max. 2 people); $129 1-bedroom apt (max. 2 people); $149 2-bedroom apt (up to 4 people); $159 3-bedroom house. Extra person $10. DISC, MC, V. **Amenities:** Outdoor pool; scuba diving. *In room:* A/C, TV, kitchenette, no phone.

Coco Palm Garden & Casa Oleander ⊀ *Value*   In the tranquil residential area of Belnem, south of the airport and Kralendijk, these vacation homes are a real discovery. Two friendly neighbors, Brigitte and Marin, combined their two properties into a cohesive whole and opened their affordable guesthouses to the world, drawing divers and windsurfers among their clients or anyone wanting to get away from the bigger resort hotels. Their accommodations consist of a series of little houses, studios, and apartments. A typical studio comes with one queen-size bed, a kitchen, a porch with tables and chairs, and a small garden with hammock and sun bed. Rooms are well furnished and have small bathrooms with showers. Even though each accommodation is self-sufficient, there are public areas, including a terrace for sunning, a pool, and a restaurant and bar for guests only.

The cuisine consists mainly of seafood and some tangy South American dishes.

Kaya van Eps 9, Belnem, Bonaire, N.A. ☎ 599/717-2108. Fax 599/717-8193. www.cocopalmgarden.org. 20 units. Year-round $59–$79 double; $89–$109 house for 2. Extra person $14. Children under 12 $8 extra in parent's room. MC, V. **Amenities:** Restaurant; bar; outdoor pool; babysitting; laundry service; dry cleaning. *In room:* A/C, kitchen, beverage maker, no phone.

3 Dining

EXPENSIVE

Capriccio ⊀ NORTHERN ITALIAN   One of the most charming (and most consistently booked) restaurants on Bonaire is run by Andrea Scandeletti and his wife, Lola, experienced Italian restaurateurs whose efforts were well received before their exodus from Italy to Bonaire. In a small, pink-and-green dining room with room for 50 diners, they prepare skillful interpretations of modern Italian cuisine using more olive oil than cream and butter. Pizzas emerge from a brick oven in at least 10 different variations, and can make a light meal for two with a salad. More filling is the set-price menu, which includes carpaccio, seafood pasta, filet mignon, and tiramisu. A la carte items include a platter of smoked fish, savory pastas, prosciutto with hearts-of-palm salad, and pumpkin ravioli with Parmesan cheese and sage. The wine list is mostly Italian, with a few French choices. Dining options include an alfresco area, set across the coastal road from the sea (it can get very hot in midsummer), and a more comfortable air-conditioned interior studded with flickering candles in the evening.

Kaya Isla Riba 1, Kralendijk. ☎ 599/717-7230. Reservations required. Pizzas and pastas $9–$21; main courses $22–$23; fixed-price menu $40. AE, MC, V. Mon and Wed–Sat noon–2pm; Wed–Mon 6:30–10:30pm.

It Rains Fish SEAFOOD/INTERNATIONAL   Set across the busy boulevard from the sands of the beach, within a breezy building whose big sides open directly onto the ocean breezes, this pleasant restaurant combines relatively formal food with a tropical, laid-back, and decidedly casual ambience. The mostly Dutch and South American staff are likely to be clad in workaday jeans, shorts, or T-shirts, and look a lot like the fit, hip, and urbanized clientele this place tends to attract. There's a small bar area where diners wait for the availability of their tables while ordering a sunset-colored cocktail. Delectable appetizers include roasted seaweed stuffed with fresh fish mousse and smoked salmon or snails swimming in a special mix of spices and garlic butter. For your main course, we'd recommend the catch of the day, served either with a creamy mustard or pesto sauce. If you don't like any of the fish dishes offered nightly, opt for their locally celebrated marinated pork loin ribs, so tender the meat just falls off the bone.

Kaya Jan N. E. Craane 24, Kralendijk. ℂ **599/717-8780.** Reservations required. Main courses $26–$39. DC, DISC, MC, V. Mon–Sat 5:30–10pm.

MODERATE

Blue Moon INTERNATIONAL   This seafront bistro near the Divi Flamingo is in one of the island's oldest houses. Intimate tables and candlelight create a romantic ambience in the main restaurant, although you can dine less formally outside on the terrace overlooking the harbor. The menu always features the catch of the day as well as steak dishes. Sample a delectable stuffed chicken breast with mango, or jumbo shrimp hollandaise, followed by one of the home-made desserts. Finish off with one of their rich, Cuban-style coffees. Flavors are precisely defined, although nearly all ingredients have to be imported. Specials change daily.

Kaya Hellmund 5. ℂ **599/717-8617.** Reservations recommended. Main courses $16–$21. AE, MC, V. Thurs–Tues 5–10pm.

Mona Lisa ✦ FRENCH/INTERNATIONAL   A local favorite on the main street of town, this is one of the best places for food that tastes homemade. The prices are more than reasonable, considering the quality of the food and the generous portions. Although many regulars come just to patronize the Dutch bar and catch up on the latest gossip, the old-fashioned dining room deserves serious attention. Guests enjoy the fresh fish of the day (often wahoo) or such meat dishes as a leg of lamb filet, tournedos, and sirloin steak. The most popular appetizers are onion soup, Bonairean fish and vegetable soup, and shrimp cocktail. Mona Lisa is known for serving fresh vegetables on an island where nearly everything is imported.

Kaya Grandi 15. ℂ **599/717-8718.** Reservations recommended. Main courses $17–$27; fixed-price menu $34. AE, MC, V. Mon–Fri 6–10pm.

The Old Inn DUTCH/ENGLISH   Set inland from the sea, in a prominent location a short walk from Kralendijk and very close to the Plaza Hotel, this is a casual and unpretentious open-air restaurant that's outfitted mostly in tones of dark blue. Come here for simple but well-prepared specialties that you might have expected either in England or Holland. One of the enduring favorites here is a succulent version of *rijstafel*, composed of rice that's accompanied by as many as 30 exotic side dishes that include curried chicken and beef, flaky coconut, cashews, raisins, and chives—a cultural legacy of the Dutch colonies in faraway Indonesia. Other, less exotic dishes might include thin-sliced carpaccio of beef or a creamy version of lobster bisque. Any of these might be followed by beef tenderloin served with stroganoff sauce; roasted pork with tomato sauce; and a wide selection of very fresh fish.

J. A. Abraham Blvd. ℂ **599/717-6666.** Reservations recommended. Main courses $15–$27; *rijstafel* $35 per person. MC, V. Mon–Sat 8am–10pm; Sun 9am–10pm.

Rendez-Vous Restaurant ✦ EUROPEAN/CARIBBEAN   Even Queen Beatrix of the Netherlands has dined here. You can dine indoors surrounded by paintings from an island-born artist or in the courtyard outdoors if the weather is right. Drop in for a drink in the bar, which has an amazing collection of hundreds of cigarette lighters from around the globe. The cuisine never rises to the sublime, but it features the freshest ingredients on island thoughtfully prepared and well flavored. We always opt for the catch of the day, which can be prepared in a number of ways, including with a dill sauce, or else Creole style with peppers, onions, and tomatoes. Quite delectable is the garlic shrimp. You can also order a number of other steak and seafood dishes. There's even something for vegetarians.

Kaya L.D. Gerharts 3, Kralendijk. © 599/717-8454. Main courses 28 NAf–35 NAf ($16–$20). AE, MC, V. Wed noon–2pm; Mon–Sat 6–10:30pm.

Richard's Waterfront Dining ⋆⋆ STEAK/SEAFOOD We've had some of our best meals on Bonaire here. On the airport side of Kralendijk, within walking distance of the Divi Flamingo Beach Resort, this restaurant, with its large covered terrace, was once a private home. Reasonable in price, it's the favorite of many locals who have sampled every restaurant on the island. Boston-born Richard Beady and his Aruban partner, Mario, operate a welcoming oasis with a happy hour at 5:30pm. Gathered around the coral bar, guests consider the chalkboard menu listing the offerings for the night: grilled wahoo or the fresh catch of the day, filet mignon béarnaise, U.S. sirloin with green-peppercorn sauce, scampi, or pasta. If it's on the menu, start with the fish soup. The menu is wisely kept small so that each night's entrees can be given the attention they deserve. The kitchen focuses on bringing out the natural flavors of a dish without overwhelming it with sauces or too many seasonings. You'll be welcomed warmly.

J. A. Abraham Blvd. 60. © 599/717-5263. Reservations recommended for groups of 6 or more. Main courses $15–$23. AE, MC, V. Daily 6–10pm.

Zeezicht Restaurant INTERNATIONAL This is the best place in the capital to see the sunset. Join the old salts or the people who live on boats to watch the sun go down, and try to see the "green flash" that Hemingway wrote about. Zeezicht (pronounced *zay*-zict and meaning "sea view") has long been popular for its excellent local cooking. It serves a small Indonesian *rijstafel* (rice served with numerous accompaniments), as well as fresh fish from the nearby fish market, plus lobster and steak.

Kaya Cachi-Craane 12. © 599/717-8434. Main courses $12–$23. AE, MC, V. Daily 8am–10:30pm.

4 Beaches

Come to Bonaire for the diving (see below), not the beaches. For the most part, the beaches are full of coral and feel gritty to bare feet. Those on the leeward side (the more tranquil side of the island) are often narrow strips. To compensate, some hotels have shipped in extra sand for their guests.

Pink Beach, south of Kralendijk, out past Salt Pier, is the best, despite its narrow strip of sand, shallow water, and lack of shade. It's aptly named: The beach really is a deep pink color, from the corals that have been pulverized into sand by the waves. Bring your own cooler and towels, as there are no refreshment stands or equipment rentals to mar the panoramic setting. It's also wise to bring along some sun protection, as the few palm trees bordering the dunes offer little shade. Enter the water at the southern end of this beach, as the northern tier has some exposed rock. Many Bonaireans flock here on weekends, but during the week you'll have the beach to yourself.

Bonaire's offshore island, tiny, uninhabited **Klein Bonaire,** just 1.6km (1 mile) offshore, has some of the most pristine beaches. Popular for snorkeling, scuba diving, and picnicking, **No Name Beach,** on the north side of Klein Bonaire, features a 273m (895-ft.) white-sand beach. Snorkelers can see a rainbow of colorful fish darting through stunning formations of elkhorn coral. Accessible only by boat, Klein Bonaire is home to sea turtles and other indigenous wildlife. Ask at your hotel if arrangements can be made for a trip to the island.

Playa Funchi, within Washington Slagbaai National Park, is good for snorkeling. Regrettably, it has almost no sand, there are no facilities, and the area surrounding the beach is a bit smelly. On one side of the beach, there's a lagoon where flamingos nest; snorkelers find the water most desirable on the other side. Also within the park, the more desirable **Boca Slagbaai** draws snorkelers and picnickers. You can spot flamingos nearby. A 19th-century building houses decent toilets and showers; drinks and snacks are also available. Don't venture into the waters barefoot, as the coral beach can be quite rough. A final beach at the national park is **Boca Cocolishi,** a black-sand strip on the northern coast. This is the windiest beach on Bonaire; you'll certainly stay cool as the trade winds whip the surf up. The waters are too rough for swimming, but it's a good picnic spot.

Many of Bonaire's beaches are situated along the east coast. The best spot for windsurfers is **Lac Bay Beach,** on the southern shore of Lac Bay. There are mangroves at the north end of the bay. A couple of windsurfing concessions usually operate here, and food and drink are available. One of the more unusual is **Nukove Beach,** a minicave in a limestone cliff with a small white-sand channel, which cuts through the dense wall of elkhorn coral near the shore, giving divers and snorkelers easy access to the water. Further north is **1,000 Steps Beach,** where 67 steps (although it can feel like 1,000 on the way back up) carved out of the limestone cliff lead to the white-sand beach. This beach offers good snorkeling and diving, a unique location and view, and nearly perfect solitude.

5 Diving & Snorkeling (★★★

The true beauty on Bonaire is under the sea, where visibility is 30m (98 ft.), 365 days of the year, and the water temperatures range from 78°F to 82°F (26°C–28°C). One of the richest reef communities in the entire West Indies, Bonaire has plunging walls that descend to a sand bottom at 39m or so (128 ft.). The reefs are home to various coral formations that grow at different depths, ranging from the knobby brain coral at .9m (3 ft.) to staghorn and elkhorn up to about 3m (10 ft.) deeper, and gorgonians, giant brain, and others. Swarms of rainbow-hued tropical fish inhabit the reefs, and the deep reef slope is home to a range of basket sponges, groupers, and moray eels. Most of the diving is done on the leeward side, where the ocean is lake flat. There are more than 40 dive sites on sharply sloping reefs.

Bonaire Marine Park ★★ was created to protect the coral-reef ecosystem off Bonaire. The park incorporates the entire coastline of Bonaire and neighboring **Klein Bonaire.** The park is policed, and services and facilities include a visitor information center at the **Karpata Ecological Center,** lectures, slide presentations, films, and permanent dive-site moorings.

Visitors are asked to respect the marine environment and to refrain from activities that may damage it, including sitting or walking on the coral. All

---

Fun Fact   *The Hooker*

The waters off the coast of Bonaire received an additional attraction in 1984. A rust-bottomed general cargo ship, 24m-long (79-ft.), was confiscated by the police, along with its contraband cargo, about 25,000 pounds of marijuana. Known as the *Hilma Hooker* (familiarly dubbed "The Hooker" by everyone on the island), it sank unclaimed (obviously) and without fanfare one calm day, in 27m (89 ft.) of water. Lying just off the southern shore near the capital, its wreck is now a popular dive site.

---

marine life is completely protected. This means there's no fishing or collecting fish, shells, or corals—dead or alive. Spearfishing is forbidden, as is anchoring; all craft must use permanent moorings, except for emergency stops (boats shorter than 4m/13 ft. may use a stone anchor). Most recreational activity in the marine park takes place on the island's leeward side and among the reefs surrounding Klein Bonaire.

Much of Bonaire's allure is based on its teeming offshore reefs and dive sites. Divers from around the world leave with a sense of awe about how good the diving really is. The major hotels offer personalized, close-up encounters with the island's fish and other marine life under the expertise of Bonaire's dive guides.

Dive II, on the beachfront of the Divi Flamingo Beach Resort & Casino, J. A. Abraham Boulevard (© **599/717-8285**), north of Kralendijk, is among the island's most complete scuba facilities. It's open daily from 8am to 12:30pm and 1:30 to 5pm. It operates out of a well-stocked beachfront building, renting diving equipment and offering expeditions. A resort course for first-time divers costs $90; for experienced divers, a one-tank dive goes for $35, a two-tank dive for $50.

Captain Don's Habitat Dive Shop, Kaya Gobernador N. Debrot 103 (© **599/717-8290**), is a PADI five-star training facility. The open-air, full-service dive shop includes a classroom, photo/video lab, camera-rental facility, equipment repair, and compressor rooms. Habitat's slogan is "Diving Freedom": Divers can take their tanks and dive anywhere, day or night. Most head for "The Pike," .8km (½ mile) of protected reef right in front of the property. The highly qualified staff is here to assist and advise, but not to police or dictate dive plans. Diving packages include boat dives, unlimited offshore diving (24 hr. a day), unlimited air, tanks, weights, and belts. Some dive packages also include accommodations and meals (see "Accommodations," earlier in this chapter). If you're not staying at the hotel as part of a dive package, you can visit for a beach dive, costing $24. If you want to rent snorkeling equipment, the charge is $9 a day. A boat dive, with all equipment, goes for $47.

Bonaire Dive and Adventures, adjacent to the Sand Dollar Condominium Retreat, Kaya Gobernador N. Debrot (© **599/717-2229**), is open daily from 8:30am to 4:30pm. It offers dive packages, PADI and NAUI (National Association of Underwater Instructors) instruction, and equipment rental and repairs; boat and shore trips with an instructor are available by appointment. A beginning course, including two dives, costs $105 per person. The photo shop offers underwater photo and video shoots, PADI specialty courses by appointment, E-6 slide processing, print developing, and equipment rental and repair.

Bonaire's coral reefs are also an underwater paradise for snorkelers. They start in just inches of water and therefore have dense coral formations in very shallow surf. Most snorkeling on the island is conducted in 5m (16 ft.) of water or less, and there's plenty to see even at this depth. As you travel around the island, particularly in the northern area, you'll see evidence of prehistoric reefs now 12m to 30m (39 ft.–98 ft.) above sea level, having lived submerged for hundreds of thousands of years and then uplifted as the island slowly rose.

Snorkeling equipment can be rented at the **Carib Inn,** J. A. Abraham Boulevard (© **599/717-8819**); **Bonaire Dive and Adventure,** Kaya Gobernador N. Debrot (© **599/717-2229**); and **Captain Don's Habitat Dive Shop,** Kaya Gobernador N. Debrot (© **599/717-8290**). A full day's rental of mask, fins, and snorkel costs $9 per day. Most snorkelers swim out to reefs from points directly offshore, but most of the dive operators will also allow snorkelers to ride out to dive sites with scuba divers for $14, plus the equipment rental cost.

6 Sports & Other Outdoor Pursuits

Bonaire is most striking underwater, but the sailing and birding are great, too.

BIRD-WATCHING   Bonaire is home to over 200 species of birds, 80 of which are indigenous to the island. Most famous are its flamingos, which can number 10,000 during the mating season. For great places to bring your binoculars, see "Exploring the Island," below.

FISHING   Fishing from shore is not permitted as the Bonaire Marine Park protects the waters surrounding the island, but Bonaire's offshore fishing grounds offer some of the best fishing in the Caribbean. A good day's catch might include mackerel, tuna, wahoo, dolphin (mahimahi), blue marlin, amberjack, grouper, sailfish, or snapper. Bonaire is also one of the best-kept secrets of bonefishing enthusiasts.

Your best bet is Chris Morkos of **Piscatur Fishing Supplies,** Kaya Herman 4, Playa Pabao (© **599/717-8774;** www.piscatur.com). A native Bonairean, he has been fishing all his life. A maximum of six people are taken out on a 13m (43-ft.) boat with a guide and captain, at a cost of $350 for a half-day or $500 for a whole day, including all tackle and bait. Reef fishing is another popular sport, in boats averaging 5m and 6m (16 ft. and 20 ft.). A maximum of six people can go out for a half-day at $350 or a whole day at $500. A maximum of two people can fish for bonefish and tarpon on the island's large salt flats for $225 for a half-day.

HIKING   Washington Slagbaai National Park (see "Exploring the Island," below) has a varied terrain; those ambitious enough to climb some of its steep hills are rewarded with panoramic views. The hiking possibilities are seemingly endless. Small hidden beaches with crashing waters by the cliffs provide ideal spots for picnics.

MOUNTAIN BIKING   Biking is an ideal way to see Bonaire's hidden beauty; you can explore more than 299km (185 miles) of trails and dirt roads, venturing off the beaten path to enjoy the scenery. Ask at the tourist office for a trail map that outlines the most scenic routes. You can check with your hotel about arranging a trip, or call **Cycle Bonaire,** Kaya Gobernador N. DeBrot no. 79 (© **599/717-2229**), an outfit that maintains an inventory of 24-speed mountain bikes, each of which rent for a price of $15 per day.

SAILING   Bonaire Boating (© **599/790-1228**), at the Divi Flamingo Beach Resort & Casino, features both half- and full-day charters on various luxury yachts, most of them under 18m (59 ft.). Prices vary, but expect to spend around

$400 for a half-day charter, with the services of a crewmember included. You can rent smaller boats for between $70 for a half-day, and $100 for a full day, without crew, but you'll first have to demonstrate that you're versed in sailing techniques.

SEA KAYAKING Paddle the protected waters of Lac Bay, or head for the miles of flats and mangroves in the south (the island's nursery), where you can see baby fish and wildlife. Kayak rentals are available at **Jibe City,** Lac Bay (© 599/717-5233), for $25 per half-day or $35 for a full day.

TENNIS There are two courts, lit for night play, at the **Sand Dollar Condominium Retreat,** Kaya Gobernador N. Debrot 79 (© 800/288-4773). If the courts aren't in use by residents, nonresidents pay a fee of $11 per hour (fee is subject to change).

WINDSURFING Consistent conditions, enjoyed by windsurfers with a wide range of skill levels, make the shallow, calm waters of Lac Bay the island's home to the sport. Call **Bonaire Windsurfing** (© 599/717-2288) for details. A half-day costs $40.

7 Exploring the Island

Bonaire Sightseeing Tours (© 599/717-8778) will show you the island, both north and south, taking in the flamingos, slave huts, conch shells, Goto Lake, the Amerindian inscriptions, and other sights. Each of these tours lasts 2 hours and costs $18 per person. You can also take a half-day City and Country Tour, lasting 3 hours and costing from $24 per person, which allows you to see the entire northern section and the southern part as far as the slave huts.

KRALENDIJK

Kralendijk is often referred to by locals as *Playa,* Spanish for "beach." A dollhouse town of some 2,500 residents, Kralendijk is small, neat, pretty, Dutch-clean, and just a bit dull. Its stucco buildings are painted pink and orange, with an occasional lime green. The capital's jetty is lined with island sloops and fishing boats.

Kralendijk nestles in a bay on the west coast, opposite **Klein Bonaire,** or Little Bonaire, an uninhabited, low-lying islet that's a 10-minute boat ride away.

The main street of town leads along the beachfront on the harbor. A Protestant church was built in 1834, and **St. Bernard's Roman Catholic Church** has some interesting stained-glass windows.

At **Fort Oranje,** you'll see a lone cannon dating from the days of Napoleon.

THE TOUR NORTH

The road north is one of the most beautiful stretches in the Antilles, with turquoise waters on your left and coral cliffs on your right. You can stop at several points along this road, where there are paved paths for strolling or bicycling.

After leaving Kralendijk and passing the Sunset Beach Hotel and the desalination plant, you'll come to **Radio Nederland Wereld Omroep (Dutch World Radio).** It's a 13-tower, 300,000-watter. Opposite the transmitting station is a lovers' promenade. Built by nature, it's an ideal spot for a picnic.

Continuing, you'll pass the storage tanks of the Bonaire Petroleum Corporation, the road heading to **Goto Meer,** the island's inland sector, with a saltwater lake. Several flamingos prefer this spot to the salt flats in the south.

Down the hill, the road leads to a section called **Dos Pos ("two wells");** the palm trees and vegetation here are a contrast to the rest of the island, where only the drought-resistant kibraacha and divi-divi trees, tilted before the constant wind, can grow, along with forests of cacti.

Bonaire's oldest village is **Rincón.** Slaves who used to work in the salt flats in the south once lived here. The Rincón Ice Cream Parlour makes homemade ice cream in a variety of interesting flavors; there are also a couple of bars here. Above the bright roofs of the village is the crest of a hill called Para Mira, which means "stop and look."

A side path outside Rincón takes you to some **Arawak inscriptions** supposedly 500 years old. The petroglyph designs are in pink-red dye. At nearby **Boca Onima,** you'll find grotesque grottoes of coral.

Before going back to the capital, you might take a short bypass to **Seroe Largu,** which has a good view of Kralendijk and the sea. Lovers frequent the spot at night.

THE NATIONAL PARK

Washington Slagbaai National Park ⭐⭐ (© 599/717-8444; www.washington parkbonaire.org) has a varied terrain that includes desertlike areas, secluded beaches, caverns, a visitor's center, and a bird sanctuary. Occupying 6,000 hectares (14,820 acres) of Bonaire's northwesternmost territory, the park was once plantation land, producing divi-divi, aloe, and charcoal, and now it exists as a wildlife preserve.

You can see the park in a few hours, although it takes days to appreciate it fully. If you want to drive through the park, you must use a four-wheel-drive vehicle. Even so, consider not going if it's rained recently as the roads quickly become deeply mired in mud and difficult to navigate—even in a four-wheel drive. There are two routes: a 24km (15-mile) "short" route, marked by green arrows, and a 35km (22-mile) "long" route, marked by yellow arrows. The roads are well marked and safe, but somewhat rugged, although they're gradually being improved. For those wanting a closer look, the hiking possibilities are nearly endless. The entrance fee is $10 for adults and $5 for children age 12 and under. The park is open daily except holidays from 8am to 5pm. You must enter before 3pm.

Whichever route you take, there are a few important stops you shouldn't miss. Just past the gate is **Salina Mathijs,** a salt flat that's home to flamingos during the rainy season. Beyond the salt flat on the road to the right is **Boca Chiquito,** a white-sand beach and bay. A few miles up the beach lies **Boca Cocolishi,** a two-part black-sand beach. Many a couple has raved about their romantic memories of this beach, perfect for a secluded picnic. Its deep, rough seaward side and calm, shallow basin are separated by a ridge of calcareous algae. The basin and the beach were formed by small pieces of coral and mollusk shells (*cocolishi* means "shells"), thus the black sand. The basin itself has no current, so it's perfect for snorkeling close to shore.

The main road leads to **Boca Bartol,** a bay full of living and dead elkhorn coral, sea fans, and reef fish. A popular watering hole good for bird-watching is **Poosdi Mangel. Wajaca** is a remote reef, perfect for divers and home to the island's most exciting sea creatures, including turtles, octopuses, and triggerfish. Immediately inland towers 236m (774-ft.) **Mount Brandaris,** Bonaire's highest peak, at whose foot is **Bronswinkel Well,** a watering spot for pigeons and parakeets. More than 200 species of birds live in the park, many with such exotic names as bananaquit and black-faced grassquit. Bonaire has few mammals, but you'll see goats and donkeys, perhaps even a wild bull.

HEADING SOUTH

Leaving the capital again, you pass the **Trans World Radio antennae,** towering 150m (492 ft.) in the air, transmitting with 810,000 watts. This is one of the hemisphere's most powerful medium-wave radio stations, the loudest voice in Christendom, and the most powerful nongovernmental broadcast station in the world. It sends out interdenominational Gospel messages and hymns in 20 languages to places as far away as Eastern Europe and the Middle East.

You then come to the **salt flats** ⚓, where the brilliantly colored pink flamingos live. Bonaire shelters the largest accessible nesting and breeding grounds in the world. The flamingos build high mud mounds to hold their eggs. The best time to see the birds is in spring, when they're nesting and tending their young. The salt flats were once worked by slaves, and the government has rebuilt some primitive stone huts, bare shelters little more than waist high. The slaves slept in these huts, and returned to their homes in Rincón in the north on weekends. The centuries-old salt pans have been reactivated by the International Salt Company. Near the salt pans, you'll see some 9m (30-ft.) obelisks in white, blue, and orange, built in 1838 to help mariners locate their proper anchorages.

Farther down the coast is the island's oldest lighthouse, **Willemstoren,** built in 1837. Still farther along, **Sorobon Beach, Lac Bay Beach,** and **Boca Cai** come into view. They're at landlocked Lac Bay, which is ideal for swimming and snorkeling. Conch shells are stacked up on the beach. The water here is so vivid and clear, you can see coral 20m to 36m (66 ft.–118 ft.) down in the reef-protected waters.

8 Shopping

Walk along Kaya Grandi in Kralendijk to see an assortment of goods, including gemstone jewelry, wood, leather, sterling, ceramics, liquors, and tobacco, priced 25% to 50% less than in the United States and Canada. Prices are often quoted in U.S. dollars, and major credit cards and traveler's checks are usually accepted.

Benetton, Kaya Grandi 29 (© 599/717-5107), has invaded the island and claims to offer its brightly colored merchandise at prices about one-quarter less than most U.S. outlets.

Littman Jewelers, Kaya Grandi 33 (© 599/717-8160), sells Tag Heuer dive watches and also carries Daum French crystal and Lladró Spanish porcelain. Next door is **Littman's Gifts,** selling standard and hand-painted T-shirts, plus sandals, hats, Gottex swimsuits, gift items, costume jewelry, and toys.

Although hardly great, other stores you might want to visit include **Best Buddies,** Kaya Grandi 32 (© 599/717-7570), which is known for its *pareos* or beach wraps and its batiks from Indonesia. Nearby at **Island Fashions,** Kaya Grandi 5 (© 599/717-7565), you can pick up the latest clothes and gifts.

9 Bonaire After Dark

Underwater **slide shows** provide entertainment for both divers and nondivers. The best shows are at **Captain Don's Habitat** (© 599/717-8290; see "Accommodations," earlier in this chapter). Shows are presented in the hotel bar, Rum Runners, Thursday night from 7 to 9pm.

Plaza Resort Bonaire Casino, J. A. Abraham Blvd. 80 (© 599/717-2500) is the larger of Bonaire's two casinos—and usually the noisier and more animated. Slot machines cover entire walls, and gaming tables offer all the games of chance you want. It is open daily from 8pm to 4am (sometimes until 6am in winter). Jackets and ties aren't required, but shorts after dark are frowned upon.

Divi Flamingo Beach Resort & Casino, J. A. Abraham Boulevard (© 599/ 717-8285), promoted as "The World's First Barefoot Casino," offers blackjack, roulette, poker, wheel of fortune, video games, and slot machines. Gambling on the island is regulated by the government. Entrance is free; hours are Monday to Saturday from 8pm to 2am.

Karel's Beach Bar, on the waterfront (© 599/717-8434), is almost Tahitian in its high-ceilinged, Tiki hut design. This popular place perches above the sea on stilts. You can sit at the long rectangular bar with many of the island's dive and boating professionals, or select a table near the balustrades overlooking the illuminated surf. Local bands entertain on weekends. Drink prices are reduced during happy hour, from 5:30 to 7pm.

We nominate the **City Cafe,** Kaya Grandi 7 (© 599/717-8286), the island's funkiest bar. Painted in screaming shades of electric blue, scarlet magenta, and banana, this bar is a popular local hangout with a no-holds-barred vibe.

8

The British Virgin Islands

With their small bays and hidden coves, the British Virgin Islands (B.V.I.) are among the world's loveliest sailing grounds. Strung over the northeastern corner of the Caribbean, about 97km (60 miles) east of Puerto Rico, are some 40 islands (although that's including some small, uninhabited cays or spits of land). Only three of the British Virgins are of any significant size: Tortola (which means "Dove of Peace"), Virgin Gorda ("Fat Virgin"), and Jost Van Dyke. Remote Norman Island is said to have been the inspiration for Robert Louis Stevenson's *Treasure Island.* On Deadman Bay, a rocky cay, Blackbeard marooned 15 pirates and a bottle of rum, which gave rise to the ditty.

Columbus came this way in 1493, but the British Virgins apparently made little impression on him. Although the Spanish and Dutch protested, the English officially annexed Tortola in 1672. Today these islands are a British colony, with their own elected government and a population of about 17,000.

The vegetation is varied and depends on the rainfall. In some parts, palms and mangos grow in profusion, whereas other places are arid and studded with cactus.

There are predictions that mass tourism is on the way, but so far the British Virgins are still a paradise for those who want to get away from it all in a peaceful, stunningly beautiful setting.

The British Virgins are among the most laid-back islands in the Caribbean. Except for a few deluxe hotels on Virgin Gorda, the inns of the B.V.I. represent life the way the Caribbean used to be before the advent of high-rise condos, McDonald's, and fleets of cruise ships. If you want an array of shops, restaurants, hotels, and nightlife, head for the U.S.V.I. But if you want an unhurried way of life, where you often provide your own amusement, seek the peace and tranquillity of the B.V.I.

1 British Virgin Islands Essentials

VISITOR INFORMATION

Before you go, contact the **British Virgin Islands Tourist Board,** 370 Lexington Ave., Suite 1605, New York, NY 10017 (© 212/696-0400). Other branches of the **British Virgin Islands Information Office** are located at 3450 Wilshire Blvd., Suite 1202, Los Angeles, CA 90010 (© 213/736-8931), and at 3390 Peachtree Rd. NE, Suite 1000, Lenox Towers, Atlanta, GA 30326 (© 404/240-8018). In the United Kingdom, contact the **B.V.I. Information Office,** 55 Newman St., London W1P 3PG (© 020/7947-8200).

The tourist board's official website is **www.bviwelcome.com.**

The British Virgin Islands

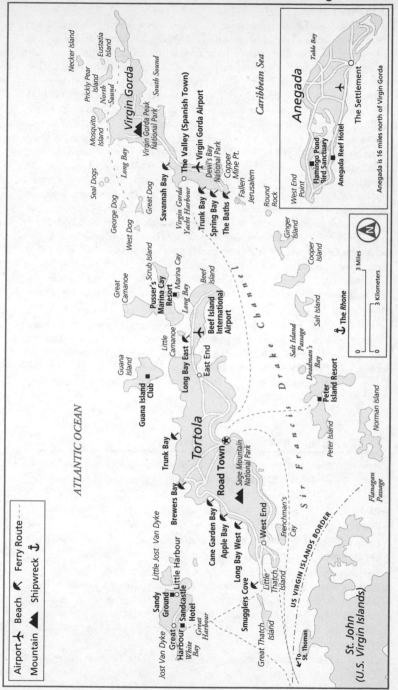

Legend:
Airport ✈ Beach 🏖 Ferry Route ---
Mountain ▲ Shipwreck ⚓

ATLANTIC OCEAN

Caribbean Sea

Anegada
Table Bay
The Settlement
✈
Flamingo Pond Bird Sanctuary ■
Anegada Reef Hotel ■
West End Point

Anegada is 16 miles north of Virgin Gorda

Necker Island
Prickly Pear Island
North Sound
Eustatia Island
Mosquito Island
South Sound
Long Bay
Seal Dogs
George Dog
Great Dog
West Dog

Virgin Gorda
Virgin Gorda Peak National Park ▲
The Valley (Spanish Town) ○
✈ Virgin Gorda Airport
Savannah Bay 🏖
Devil's Bay National Park
Virgin Gorda Yacht Harbour
Trunk Bay 🏖
Spring Bay 🏖
The Baths 🏖
Copper Mine Pt.
Fallen Jerusalem
Round Rock

Ginger Island

Cooper Island

⚓ The Rhone

Salt Island
Salt Island Passage

3 Miles
3 Kilometers
0

Great Camanoe
Marina Cay
Pusser's Marina Cay Resort ■
Long Bay
Beef Island
Beef Island International Airport ✈
Little Camanoe

D r a k e   C h a n n e l

Deadman's Bay
Peter Island Resort ■
Peter Island

Norman Island

S i r   F r a n c i s

Guana Island
Guana Island Club ■

Long Bay East
East End ○

Tortola
Trunk Bay 🏖
Brewers Bay 🏖
Road Town ★
Sage Mountain National Park ▲
Cane Garden Bay 🏖
Apple Bay 🏖
West End ○
Long Bay West 🏖
Smugglers Cove 🏖

Flanagan Passage

Frenchman's Cay

US VIRGIN ISLANDS BORDER

Little Thatch Island

St. John (U.S. Virgin Islands)

Jost Van Dyke
Little Jost Van Dyke
Sandy Ground ■
Little Harbour ○
Sandcastle Hotel ■
Great Harbour
White Bay

Great Thatch Island

← To St. Thomas

181

GETTING THERE

BY PLANE   Beef Island, the site of the major airport serving the British Virgins, is connected to Tortola by the one-lane **Queen Elizabeth Bridge.**

There are no direct flights from New York to the British Virgin Islands, but you can make connections from San Juan and St. Thomas to Beef Island/Tortola (see chapters 17 and 27 for information on flying to these islands).

Your best bet to reach Beef Island/Tortola is to take **American Eagle** (© 800/433-7300 in the U.S.; www.aa.com), which has dozens of flights to its hub in San Juan, and then at least four daily trips from San Juan to Beef Island/Tortola.

Another choice, if you're on one of Tortola's neighboring islands, is the much less reliable **LIAT** (© 868/624-4727 or 284/495-1187 locally). This Caribbean carrier makes the short hop to Tortola from St. Kitts, Antigua, St. Maarten, St. Thomas, and San Juan in small planes not known for their frequency or careful scheduling. Reservations are made through travel agents or through the larger U.S.-based airlines that connect with LIAT hubs.

Two minor airlines winging in include **Air Sunshine** (© 800/327-8900 or 284/495-8900), flying between San Juan or St. Thomas to Beef Island/Tortola and Virgin Gorda, and **Air St. Thomas** (© 800/522-3084 or 340/776-2722), going between St. Thomas and Virgin Gorda.

Clair Aero (© 284/495-2271) flies from St. Thomas to Tortola on Monday, Wednesday, and Friday, with flights continuing to Virgin Gorda and Anegada.

BY FERRY   You can travel from Charlotte Amalie (St. Thomas) by public ferry to West End and Road Town on Tortola, a 45-minute voyage along Drake's Channel through the islands. The trip costs $25 one-way, and $40 round-trip. Boats making this run include **Native Son** (© 284/495-4617), **Smith's Ferry Service** (© 284/495-4495), and **Inter-Island Boat Services** (© 284/495-4166). The latter specializes in a somewhat obscure routing—that is, from St. John to the West End on Tortola.

FAST FACTS: The British Virgin Islands

American Express There are local representatives on Tortola and Virgin Gorda. See individual island "Fast Facts" later in this chapter for information.

Banks Banks are generally open Monday through Thursday from 9am to 3pm, Friday from 9am to 5pm. Most banks have ATMs.

Currency The **U.S. dollar** is the legal currency, much to the surprise of British travelers. *Rates in this chapter are quoted in U.S. dollars.*

Customs You can bring items intended for your personal use into the British Virgin Islands. For U.S. residents, the duty-free allowance is only $600, providing you have been out of the country for 48 hours. You can send unsolicited gifts home if they total less than $100 per day to any single address. You don't have to pay duty on items classified as handcrafts, art, or antiques.

Electricity The electrical current is 110-volt AC (60 cycles), as in the United States.

Emergencies Dial © 999 in the event of an emergency.

Entry Requirements U.S. citizens and Canadians need a valid passport or a birth certificate with a raised seal along with a government-issued photo ID (we recommend that you carry a passport). U.K. residents need a valid passport.

Language The official language is English.

Liquor Laws Alcoholic beverages can be sold any day of the week, including Sunday. You can have an open container on the beach, but be careful not to litter, or you will be fined.

Mail Postal rates in the British Virgin Islands are 35¢ for a postcard (airmail) to the United States or Canada, 55¢ for a first-class airmail letter (½ oz.) to the United States or Canada.

Maps The best map of the British Virgin Islands is published by Vigilate and is sold at most bookstores in Road Town.

Medical Assistance The B.V.I.'s major hospital is Peebles Hospital in Road Town on Tortola; the island has more than a dozen doctors. If you need medical help, your hotel will put you in touch with the islands' medical staff.

Newspapers & Magazines The B.V.I. has no daily newspaper, but the *Island Sun,* published Wednesday and Friday, is a good source of information on local entertainment, as is the *BVI Beacon,* published on Thursday.

Safety Crime is rare here; in fact, the British Virgin Islands are among the safest places in the Caribbean. Still, you should take all the usual precautions you would anywhere, and don't leave items unattended on the beach.

Taxes There is no sales tax. A government tax of 7% is imposed on all hotel rooms. A $10 departure tax is collected from everyone leaving by air, $5 for those departing by sea.

Telephone You can call the British Virgins from the United States by just dialing **1**, the area code **284**, and the number. From all public phones and from some hotels, you can access **MCI** by dialing ✆ **800/888-8000.** You can reach **Sprint** at ✆ **800/877-4646** and **AT&T** at ✆ **800/225-5288.**

Time The islands operate on Atlantic Standard Time year-round. In the peak winter season, when it's 10am in the British Virgins, it's 9am in Florida. However, when Florida and the rest of the U.S. East Coast go on daylight savings time, Florida springs ahead to B.V.I. time.

Tipping & Service Charges Most hotels add on a 5% to 15% service charge; ask if it's already included when you're initially quoted a price. A 10% service charge is often (but not always) added on to restaurant bills; you can leave another 5% if you thought the service was unusually good. You usually don't need to tip taxi drivers, since most own their own cabs, but you can tip 10% if they've been unusually helpful.

Water The tap water in the British Virgin Islands is safe to drink.

Weather During the winter, temperatures in the British Virgin Islands range between 72°F (22°C) and 82°F (28°C). September is the warmest month, with temperatures averaging 90°F (32°C). Temperatures rarely drop below 77°F (25°C) in winter or rise above 90°F (32°C) in summer.

2 Tortola (★(★

Most visitors head to Virgin Gorda if they want to check into one of the posh, secluded inns and stay there, and they barely leave the grounds. Tortola, on the other hand, offers a larger selection of accommodations, many at more moderate prices. Here you'll sample more of the local life, ranging from visiting colorful markets to sailing. Tortola has more shopping, restaurants, attractions, nightlife, and diversions than Virgin Gorda. It also boasts one of the great beaches of the Caribbean, **Cane Garden Bay.**

On the southern shore of this 62-sq.-km (24-sq.-mile) island is **Road Town,** the capital of the British Virgin Islands. It's the seat of Government House and other administrative buildings, but it feels more like a small village than a town. The landfill at Wickhams Cay, a 28-hectare (69-acre) town center development and marina in the harbor, has lured a massive yacht-chartering business here and has transformed the sleepy capital into more of a bustling center.

Rugged mountain peaks characterize the entire southern coast, including Road Town. On the northern coast are white-sand beaches, banana trees, mangos, and clusters of palms.

Close to Tortola's eastern end, **Beef Island** is the site of the main airport for passengers arriving in the British Virgins. The tiny island is connected to Tortola by the one-lane Queen Elizabeth Bridge, which the queen dedicated in 1966. On the north shore of Beef Island is Long Bay Beach.

ESSENTIALS

VISITOR INFORMATION   A **B.V.I. Tourist Board Office,** at the center of Road Town near the ferry dock (✆ **284/494-3134**), has information about hotels, restaurants, tours, and more. Pick up a copy of *The Welcome Tourist Guide,* which has a useful map of the island.

GETTING THERE   Because Tortola is the gateway to the British Virgin Islands, the information on how to get here is covered above in "British Virgin Island Essentials."

GETTING AROUND   Taxis meet every arriving flight. Government regulations prohibit anyone from renting a car at the airport, so you'll have to take a taxi to your hotel. Fares are set by the government, and taxis are unmetered. The fare from the Beef Island airport to Road Town is $18 for one to three passengers. A **taxi tour** lasting 2½ hours costs $50 for one to three people. To call a taxi in Road Town, dial ✆ **284/494-2322;** on Beef Island, ✆ **284/495-1982.**

A handful of local companies and U.S.-based chains rent cars. **Itgo** (✆ **284/494-5150**) is located at 1 Wickhams Cay, Road Town; **Avis** (✆ **800/331-1212** in the U.S., or 284/494-3322 on Tortola; www.avis.com) maintains offices opposite police headquarters in Road Town; and **Hertz** (✆ **800/654-3131** in the U.S., or 284/495-4405 on Tortola; www.hertz.com) has offices outside Road Town, on the island's West End, near the ferryboat landing dock. Rental companies will usually deliver your car to your hotel. All three companies require a valid driver's license and a temporary B.V.I. driver's license, which the car-rental agency can sell you for $10; it's valid for 3 months. Because of the volume of tourism to Tortola, you should reserve a car in advance, especially in winter.

Remember: Drive on the left. Roads are pretty well paved, but they're often narrow, windy, and poorly lit, and they have few, if any, lines, so driving at night can be tricky. It's a good idea to rent a taxi to take you to that difficult-to-find beach, restaurant, or bar.

Tortola

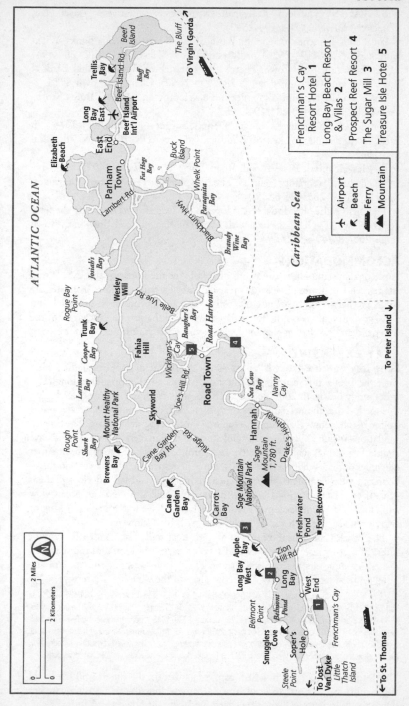

Frenchman's Cay Resort Hotel **1**
Long Bay Beach Resort & Villas **2**
Prospect Reef Resort **4**
The Sugar Mill **3**
Treasure Isle Hotel **5**

✈ Airport
↙ Beach
⛴ Ferry
▲ Mountain

Caribbean Sea

ATLANTIC OCEAN

The Bluff
To Virgin Gorda

Beef Island
Bluff Bay
Trellis Bay
Beef Island Rd.
Long Bay East
Beef Island Int'l Airport
East End
Parham Town
Fat Hog Bay
Buck Island
Whelk Point
Elizabeth Beach
Lambert Rd.
Paraquita Bay
Brandy Wine Bay
Blackburn Hwy.
Josiah's Bay
Rogue Bay Point
Wesley Will
Belle Vue Rd.
Trunk Bay
Cooper Bay
Larimers Bay
Fahia Hill
Baugher's Bay
Wickham's Cay
Joe's Hill Rd.
Road Town
Road Harbour
Rough Point
Shark Bay
Mount Healthy National Park
Skyworld
Ridge Rd.
Cane Garden Bay Rd.
Sea Cow Bay
Nanny Cay
Brewers Bay
Cane Garden Bay
Carrot Bay
Sage Mountain National Park
Hannah
Sage Mountain 1,780 ft.
Drake's Highway
Freshwater Pond
Fort Recovery
Apple Bay
Long Bay West
Zion Hill Rd.
Long Bay
West End
Frenchman's Cay
Belmont Point
Belmont Pond
Smugglers Cove
Soper's Hole
Steele Point
Little Thatch Island
To Jost Van Dyke
To St. Thomas
To Peter Island

N
2 Miles
2 Kilometers

185

FAST FACTS   The local **American Express** representative is Travel Plan, Waterfront Drive (© **284/494-2347**).

Local bank branches include the **Bank of Nova Scotia** (Scotia Bank), Wickhams Cay (© **284/494-2526**), or **Barclays Bank,** Wickhams Cay (© **284/494-2171**), both near Road Town. There's also a branch of **First National Bank** at Road Town on Wickhams Cay (© **284/494-2662**). Each has its own ATM.

The best place for camera supplies and developing on Tortola is **Bolos Brothers,** Wickhams Cay (© **284/494-2867**).

For dental emergencies, contact **Dental Surgery** (© **284/494-3474**), in Road Town, behind the Skeleton Building and next to the *BVI Beacon,* the local newspaper.

Peebles Hospital, Porter Road, Road Town (© **284/494-3497**), has X-ray emergency, and laboratory facilities. The best pharmacy is **Medicure Pharmacy,** Road Town (© **284/494-6189**).

The main **police headquarters** is located on Waterfront Drive near the ferry docks on Sir Olva Georges Plaza, with a branch office in Road Town in the town center (© **284/494-3822**).

ACCOMMODATIONS

None of the island's hotels is as big or splashy as the hotels in the U.S. Virgin Islands, and that's just fine with most of Tortola's repeat visitors. All rates are subject to between a 10% and 16% service charge, depending on the hotel, and a 7% government tax on the room. Be sure to read the section "Packages for the Independent Traveler" in chapter 2 before you book your hotel on your own.

VERY EXPENSIVE

Long Bay Beach Resort & Villas ⽊⽊   A favorite of sophisticated travelers since the 1960s, this resort is the finest on Tortola and lies on a 2km-long (1¼-mile) sandy beach. In 2001, it added 18 poolside studios. In a lovely setting on the north shore, about 10 minutes from West End, it's the only full-service resort on the island, a low-rise complex set in a 21-hectare (52-acre) estate. The accommodations include hillside rooms and studios; the smallest and most basic have simple furnishings while the deluxe beachfront rooms and cabanas have either balconies or patios that overlook the ocean. The resort also offers two- and three-bedroom villas complete with a kitchen, living area, and large deck with a gas grill. If you're not staying right on the beach, you'll still enjoy an ocean view from any of the other accommodations. All units have one four-poster king or two queen-size beds, plus large bathrooms with tiled showers.

The Beach Café is in the ruins of an old sugar mill. The Garden Restaurant offers dinner by reservation only and serves a variety of local and international dishes in a more elegant, alfresco setting. The cuisine is among the finest of any hotel on the island, especially the fresh fish, and the wine list is extensive.

P.O. Box 433, Road Town, Tortola, B.V.I. © **800/934-4699** in the U.S. and Canada, or 284/495-4252. Fax 914/833-3318. www.longbay.com. 155 units. Winter $275–$425 double, $625–$650 2-bedroom villa, $890–$925 3-bedroom villa; off season $155–$225 double, $320–$345 2-bedroom villa, $450–$475 3-bedroom villa. MAP (breakfast and dinner) $48 per person extra. AE, MC, V. **Amenities:** 2 restaurants; 3 bars; 2 outdoor pools; 3 tennis courts; health club; spa; sauna; snorkeling; car-rental desk; babysitting; laundry service; dry cleaning. *In room:* A/C, TV, dataport, kitchen (in villas), wet bar, beverage maker, hair dryer, safe.

The Sugar Mill ⽊   Set in a lush tropical garden on the site of a 300-year-old sugar mill on the north side of Tortola, this secluded cottage colony sweeps down the hillside to its own little beach, with vibrant flowers and fruits brightening the grounds. The accommodations are contemporary and well designed, ranging from suites and cottages to studios, all self-contained with kitchenettes and private terraces with views. Rooms have twin or king-size beds, plus well-maintained private bathrooms with showers. Four of the units are suitable for families of four. The latest addition, the Plantation House suites, evokes traditional Caribbean architecture, with fine stone work, breezy porches, and lacy gingerbread. Just steps from the beach, a pair of two-bedroom air-conditioned suites have tropical decor and sea views. Each has a king-size bed and a large bathroom with double sinks. About half of the rooms were renovated in 2002.

Lunch is served down by the beach at Islands, which features Caribbean specialties like jerk ribs or stuffed crab, plus burgers and salads. Dinner is offered at the Sugar Mill Restaurant (see "Dining," below).

Apple Bay (P.O. Box 425), Road Town, Tortola, B.V.I. © 800/462-8834 in the U.S., or 284/495-4355. Fax 284/495-4696. www.sugarmillhotel.com. 24 units. Winter $310 double, $325 triple, $340 quad, $650 2-bedroom villa; off season $225 double, $240 triple, $255 quad, $505 2-bedroom villa. AE, MC, V. Closed Aug–Sept. From Road Town, drive west 11km (6¾ miles), turn right (north) over Zion Hill, and turn right at the T-junction opposite Sebastians; Sugar Mill is .8km (½ mile) down the road. Children 11 and under not accepted in winter. **Amenities:** 2 restaurants; 2 bars; outdoor pool; snorkeling; concierge; car rental; babysitting; laundry service; dry cleaning; 1 room for those with limited mobility. *In room:* A/C, ceiling fan, TV (in villa and master suite), dataport, kitchenette, fridge, beverage maker, hair dryer, iron/ironing board.

EXPENSIVE

Frenchman's Cay Resort Hotel ⚶   This intimate resort is tucked away at the windward side of Frenchman's Cay, a little island connected by bridge to Tortola. The 5-hectare (12-acre) estate enjoys delightful year-round breezes and views of Sir Francis Drake Channel and the outer Virgins. The individual one- and two-bedroom villas (actually a cluster of condos) are well furnished, each with a shady terrace, full kitchen, dining room, and sitting room. Each two-bedroom villa has two full bathrooms—a vacation in and of itself for families looking to escape the morning bathroom line. Pastel colors and tropical styling make for inviting accommodations, and each unit has good linen and shower/tub combinations. There's a small beach with rocks offshore; it's best for snorkeling. The Clubhouse Restaurant and lounge bar are in the main pavilion, with a good Continental and Caribbean menu.

West End (P.O. Box 1054), Tortola, B.V.I. (U.S. address: Box 11156, St. Thomas, VI 00801). © 800/235-4077 in the U.S., 800/463-0199 in Canada, or 284/495-4844. Fax 284/495-4056. www.frenchmans.com. 9 units. Winter $260–$290 1-bedroom villa, $375–$420 2-bedroom villa; off season $170–$190 1-bedroom villa, $245–$275 2-bedroom villa. MAP (breakfast and dinner) $50 per person extra. AE, DISC, MC, V. Closed Sept. From Tortola, cross the bridge to Frenchman's Cay, turn left, and follow the road to the eastern tip of the cay. **Amenities:** Restaurant; bar; outdoor pool; tennis court; kayaks; sailing; snorkeling; windsurfing; horseback riding; island tours; car rental; babysitting. *In room:* Ceiling fan, dataport, kitchen, beverage maker.

Prospect Reef Resort ⚶   This is the largest resort in the British Virgin Islands. It rises above a small, private harbor in a sprawling series of two-story concrete buildings scattered over 18 hectares (44 acres) of steeply sloping, landscaped terrain. The panoramic view of Sir Francis Drake Channel from the bedrooms is one of the best anywhere, but there's no beach to speak of.

Each of the resort's buildings contains up to 10 individual accommodations and is painted in hibiscus-inspired shades. Initially designed as condominiums, there are unique studios, town houses, and villas, in addition to guest rooms. All include private balconies or patios; larger units, which are perfect for families, have kitchenettes, living and dining areas, and separate bedrooms or sleeping lofts. Eighty percent of the rooms are air-conditioned; ceiling fans and the trade winds cool the reef rooms. Bathrooms are well maintained, and come with showers.

The food at the hotel's Callaloo restaurant (see "Dining," below), offering a combination of Continental specialties and island favorites, was praised by *Gourmet* magazine.

Drake's Hwy. (P.O. Box 104), Road Town, Tortola, B.V.I. © **800/356-8937** in the U.S., 800/463-3608 in Canada, or 284/494-3311. Fax 284/494-5595. www.prospectreef.com. 120 units. Winter $155–$315 double, $480 2-bedroom villa for 4; off season $109–$250 double, $320 2-bedroom villa for 4. Ask about packages. AE, MC, V. **Amenities:** 2 restaurants; bar; outdoor pool; 5 tennis courts; fitness center; spa; Jacuzzi; dive shop; kayaks; sailing; scuba diving; snorkeling; sport-fishing; car rental; shuttle to beaches; room service (7am–10:30pm); massage; babysitting; laundry service; dry cleaning; nonsmoking rooms; 1 room for those with limited mobility. *In room:* A/C, TV, dataport, kitchenette (in villas), beverage maker, iron/ironing board.

MODERATE

Treasure Isle Hotel ⭐ Tortola's most centrally located resort is at the edge of the capital on 6 hectares (15 acres) of hillside overlooking a marina (not on the beach). The core of this attractive hotel is a rather splashy and colorful open-air bar boasting lovely views. The motel-like, midsize rooms are on two levels along the hillside terraces; a third level is occupied by more elegantly decorated suites at the crest of a hill. Details like local art, tile floors, white stucco walls, floral upholstery, and white rattan make for an inviting atmosphere. Bathrooms are small and only one has a tub, the rest have showers.

Adjoining the lounge and pool area is a covered open-air dining room overlooking the harbor. The cuisine is respected here, with barbecue on Saturday nights and full a la carte menus offered at dinner.

Pasea Estate (P.O. Box 68), Road Town, Tortola, B.V.I. © **284/494-2501.** Fax 284/494-2507. www.treasure islehotel.net. 43 units. Winter $187 double; off season $104 double. MAP (breakfast and dinner) $41 per person extra. Extra person $25. AE, DISC, MC, V. **Amenities:** Restaurant; bar; outdoor pool; limited room service; laundry service; dry cleaning; nonsmoking rooms. *In room:* A/C, TV, dataport (in some), kitchenette (in suites), beverage maker (in suites).

DINING
EXPENSIVE

Brandywine Bay Restaurant ⭐⭐ ITALIAN/INTERNATIONAL   Set on a cobblestone garden terrace along the south shore overlooking Sir Francis Drake Channel, this is one of Tortola's most elegant, romantic restaurants. Davide Pugliese, the chef, and his wife, Cele, have earned a reputation for their outstanding Florentine fare. Davide changes his menu daily, based on the availability of fresh produce. The best dishes include beef carpaccio, roast duck, homemade pasta, his own special calf-liver dish (the recipe is a secret), and homemade mozzarella with fresh basil and tomatoes. The skillful cooking ranges from classic to inspired.

Brandywine Estate, Sir Francis Drake Hwy. © **284/495-2301.** Reservations required. Appropriate dress required. Main courses $25–$30. AE, MC, V. Mon–Sat 6:30–9:30pm. Closed Aug–Oct. Drive 5km (3 miles) east of Road Town (toward the airport) on South Shore Rd.

Callaloo ⭐ INTERNATIONAL   One of the best hotel restaurants on Tortola, this place is rather romantic at night, especially if it's a balmy evening and the tropical breezes are blowing. It's the kind of cliché Caribbean setting that always works, and the food is quite good, too. The menu is hardly imaginative, but the chefs do well with their limited repertoire. Begin with the coconut prawns or steamed mussels, and don't pass on the house salad, which has a zesty papaya dressing. The best dishes are fresh lobster when available (not as good as the Maine variety, though) and pan-fried duck breast with a citrus-flavored spinach sauce, as well as fresh fish such as tuna, swordfish, or mahimahi. One heavenly special dish is Virgin Gorda swordfish with a tropical fruit salsa and red-pepper essence. For dessert, make it the coconut bread pudding or the Key lime pie. Downstairs is the less expensive Scuttlebutt Pub, open for lunch and dinner daily.

In Prospect Reef Resort, Drake's Hwy., Road Town. (✆ **284/494-3311.** Reservations recommended. Main courses $13–$28. AE, MC, V. Daily 7am–10pm.

Mrs. Scatliffe's Restaurant ✶ *Finds* WEST INDIAN   This Tortola mama offers home-cooked meals on the deck of her island home, and some of the vegetables come right from her garden, although others might be from a can. You'll enjoy excellent authentic West Indian dishes: perhaps spicy conch soup, followed by curried goat, "old wife" fish (triggerfish, in this case filleted, boiled, and served with onion sauce), or possibly chicken in a coconut shell. Service, usually from an inexperienced teenager, is not exactly efficient.

You may also be exposed to Mrs. Scatliffe's gentle and often humorous form of Christian fundamentalism. A Bible reading and a heartfelt rendition of a gospel song sometimes accompany a soft custard dessert.

Carrot Bay. (✆ **284/495-4556.** Reservations required by 5pm. Fixed-price meal $25–$32. No credit cards. One seating daily begins 7–8pm.

Skyworld ✶✶ INTERNATIONAL   Skyworld continues to be all the rage, one of the best restaurants on the island. On one of Tortola's loftiest peaks, at a breezy 400m (1,312 ft.), it offers views of both the U.S. Virgin Islands and the British Virgin Islands. The restaurant is divided into two sections—a main dining room and a bar. Both sections offer the same menu.

The fresh fish chowder is an island favorite, as are other, oft-changing soups, including one with peaches and coconuts, and another of champagne, coconut, and melons. The fresh fish of the day is your best bet. Recently we enjoyed the oven-baked yellow-fin tuna with a tantalizing pistachio and sesame-seed crust. Try the island's best Key lime pie or the heavenly cheesecake for dessert.

Ridge Rd., Road Town. (✆ **284/494-3567.** Reservations recommended. Main courses $24–$30. AE, MC, V. Daily 10am–2:30pm and 6–11pm.

Sugar Mill Restaurant ✶ CALIFORNIA/CARIBBEAN   Transformed from a 3-century-old sugar mill (see "Accommodations," above), this is a romantic spot for dining, and some of its recipes have been printed in *Gourmet*. Colorful works by Haitian painters hang on the old stone walls, and big copper basins have been planted with tropical flowers. Before going to the dining room, once part of the old boiling house, visit the open-air bar on a deck that overlooks the sea.

Your hosts, the Morgans, know a lot about food and wine. One of their most popular creations, published in *Bon Appétit*, is curried banana soup. You might also begin with the smoked conch pâté or the especially tasty pumpkin soup. Good choices for dinner are the scallops in puff pastry with roasted-red-pepper sauce or the almond-crusted loin of lamb with spinach, goat cheese, and roasted peppers.

Apple Bay. (✆ **284/495-4355.** Reservations required. Main courses $22–$35. AE, MC, V. Daily 7–8:30pm. Closed Aug–Sept. From Road Town, drive west 11km (6¾ miles), turn right (north) over Zion Hill, and turn right at the T-junction opposite Sebastians; Sugar Mill is .8km (½ mile) down the road.

MODERATE

Gourmet picnic, anyone? **Gourmet Chandler,** Nanny Cay (✆ **284/494-2894**), offers fabulous fixings, including cheeses, snacks, groceries, wines, beer, breads, and fine chocolates.

Capriccio di Mare ⊛ ITALIAN   Created in a moment of whimsy by the more upscale Brandywine Bay Restaurant (see above), this place is small, casual, laid-back, and a local favorite. It's the most authentic-looking Italian cafe in the Virgin Islands. At breakfast time, many locals stop in for a refreshing Italian pastry along with a cup of cappuccino, or else a full breakfast. If it's evening, you might try the mango Bellini, a variation of the famous cocktail served at Harry's Bar in Venice. Begin with such appetizers as *piedini* (flour tortillas with various toppings), then move on to fresh pastas with succulent sauces, the best pizza on the island, or even well-stuffed sandwiches. We prefer the pizza topped with grilled eggplant. If you arrive on the right night, you might even be treated to stuffed Cornish hen with scalloped potatoes. Also try one of the freshly made salads: We like the *insalata mista* with large, leafy greens and slices of fresh Parmesan.

Waterfront Dr., Road Town. ⓒ 284/494-5369. Reservations not needed. Main courses $9–$15. MC, V. Mon–Sat 8am–9pm.

Pusser's Landing CARIBBEAN   This Pusser's location is more desirably located in West End, opening onto the water, than the original Pusser's Road Town Pub on the waterfront across from the ferry dock. In this nautical setting, you can enjoy fresh grilled fish of the day cooked to your requirements. Begin with a hearty soup, perhaps pumpkin or a freshly made seafood chowder. Many of the main courses have real island flavor, the most justifiably popular being jerk chicken Jamaican style, or the grilled chicken breast with fresh pineapple salsa. A classic is the curried shrimp over rice. Mud pie remains the choice dessert here, but the Key lime pie and mango soufflé beckon as well. Happy hour is daily from 5 to 7pm.

Frenchman's Cay, West End. ⓒ 284/495-4554. Reservations needed. Main courses $15–$45. AE, DISC, MC, V. Daily 11am–10pm.

HITTING THE BEACH

Beaches are rarely crowded on Tortola unless a cruise ship is in port. You can rent a car or a jeep to reach them, or take a taxi (but arrange for a time to be picked up).

Tortola's finest beach is **Cane Garden Bay** ⊛⊛⊛, on Cane Garden Bay Road directly west of Road Town. You'll have to navigate some roller-coaster hills to get there, but these fine white sands, with sheltering palm trees, are among the most popular in the B.V.I., and the lovely bay is beloved by yachties. Outfitters here rent Hobie Cats, kayaks, and sailboards. Windsurfing is possible as well. This is one beach that may get crowded, at least in high season. There are about seven places to eat, along with a handful of bars. **Rhymer's** (ⓒ **284/495-4639**) is our favorite, offering cold beer and refreshing rum drinks. If you're hungry, try the conch or lobster, black-bean gazpacho, or barbecued spareribs. The beach bar and restaurant is open daily from 8am to 9pm. Ice and freshwater showers are available (and you can rent towels). Ask about renting Sunfish sailboats and windsurfers next door.

Surfers like **Apple Bay,** west of Cane Garden Bay, along North Shore Road. The beach isn't very big, but that doesn't diminish activity when the surf's up. Conditions are best in January and February. After enjoying the white sands here, you can have a drink at the Bomba Shack, a classic dive of a beach bar at the water's edge (see "Tortola After Dark," below).

Smugglers Cove, known for its tranquillity and beautiful sands, lies at the extreme western end of Tortola, opposite the offshore island of Great Thatch and just north of St. John. It's a lovely crescent of white sand, with calm turquoise waters. A favorite local beach, it's at the end of bumpy Belmont Road. Once you get here, a little worse for wear, you'll think the crystal-clear water and the beautiful palm trees are worth the effort. Snorkelers like this beach, which is sometimes called "Lower Belmont Bay." It's especially good for beginning snorkelers, since the reef is close to shore and easily reached. You'll see parrot fish, sea fans, sponges, and elkhorn and brain corals.

East of Cane Garden Bay and site of a campground, **Brewers Bay,** accessed from long, steep Brewers Bay Road, is ideal for snorkelers and surfers. This clean, white-sand beach is a great place to enjoy walks in the early morning or at sunset. Sip a rum punch from the beach bar, and watch the world go by.

The 2km-long (1¼-mile) white-sand beach at **Long Bay West,** reached along Long Bay Road, is one of the most beautiful in the B.V.I. Joggers run along the water's edge, and spectacular sunsets make it perfect for romantic strolls. The Long Bay Beach Resort stands on the northeast side of the beach; many visitors like to book a table at the resort's restaurant overlooking the water.

At the very east end of the island, **Long Bay East,** reached along Beef Island Road, is a great spot for swimming. Cross Queen Elizabeth Bridge to reach this 2km-long (1¼-mile) beach with great views and white sands.

EXPLORING THE ISLAND

Travel Plan Tours, Romasco Place, Harbour House (P.O. Box 437), Road Town (© **284/494-2347**), offers a 3½-hour tour that touches on the panoramic highlights of Tortola (a minimum of four participants is required). The cost is $30 per person, with a supplement of $5 per person if you want to extend the tour with hill climbing in the rainforest. The company also offers 2½-hour **snorkeling tours** for $58 per person (with snacks included). A full-day **sailing tour** aboard a catamaran that goes from Tortola to either Peter Island or Norman Island costs $81 per person; a full-day tour, which goes as far afield as The Baths at Virgin Gorda and includes lunch, costs $117 per person. And if **deep-sea fishing** appeals to you, you can go for a half-day excursion, with equipment, for four fishermen and up to two "nonfishing observers" for $780 or the full day for $1,080.

A **taxi tour** costs $45 for two passengers for 2 hours, or $60 for 3 hours. To call a taxi in Road Town, dial © **284/494-2322;** on Beef Island, © **284/495-1982.**

J. R. O'Neal Botanic Gardens ⚑, Botanic Station, Road Town (no phone), fills up a 1.6-hectare (4-acre) site of lush tropical growth. Wander at leisure, taking in the pergola walk, a waterfall, a lily pond, tropical birdhouses, and miniature "rainforests." Of course, you can also enjoy the rich plant life that ranges here from exotic orchids to gardens of medicinal herbs. Admission is free; the gardens are open Monday to Saturday 9am to 4:30pm.

No visit to Tortola is complete without a trip to **Sage Mountain National Park** ⚑, rising to an elevation of 534m (1,751 ft.). Here you'll find traces of a primeval rainforest, and you can enjoy a picnic while overlooking neighboring islets and cays. Go west from Road Town to reach the mountain. Before you head out, stop by the tourist office and pick up the brochure *Sage Mountain National Park.* It has a location map, directions to the forest and parking, and an outline of the main trails through the park. Covering 37 hectares (91 acres), the park protects the remnants of Tortola's original forests not burned or cleared during the island's plantation era. From the parking lot, a trail leads to the main park entrance. The two main trails are the Rainforest Trail and the Mahogany Forest Trail.

Shadow's Ranch, Todman's Estate (© **284/494-2262**), offers horseback rides through the national park or down to the shores of Cane Garden Bay. Call for details, daily from 9am to 4pm. The cost is from $50 per hour.

THE WRECK OF THE *RHONE* & OTHER TOP DIVE SITES

The one site in the British Virgin Islands that lures divers over from St. Thomas is **the wreck of the HMS *Rhone*** ⚓⚓, which sank in 1867 near the western point of Salt Island. *Skin Diver* magazine called it "the world's most fantastic shipwreck dive." It teems with marine life and coral formations and was featured in the 1977 movie *The Deep*.

Although it's no *Rhone, **Chikuzen*** is another intriguing dive site off Tortola. It's an 81m (266 ft.) steel-hulled refrigerator ship, which sank off the island's east end in 1981. The hull, still intact under about 24m (79 ft.) of water, is now home to a vast array of tropical fish, including yellowtail, barracuda, black-tip sharks, octopus, and drum fish.

South of Ginger Island, **Alice in Wonderland** is a deep-dive site with a wall that begins at around 3.6m (12 ft.) and slopes gently to 30m (98 ft.). It abounds with marine life such as lobsters, crabs, rainbow-hued fan coral and mammoth mushroom-shaped coral. **Spyglass Wall** is another offshore dive site dropping to a sandy bottom and filled with seafans and large coral heads. The drop is from 3m (10 ft.) to 18m (60 ft.). Divers here seek out tarpon, eagle rays, and stingrays.

Underwater Safaris (© **284/494-3235**) takes you to all the best sites, including the HMS *Rhone,* Spyglass Wall, and Alice in Wonderland. It has one office: Safari Base in Road Town. Get specific directions and information when you call. The center, connected with The Moorings (see "Yacht Charters," below), offers a complete PADI training facility. An introductory resort course and three dives costs $168, while an open-water certification, with 4 days of instruction and four open-water dives, goes for $410, plus $40 for the instruction manual.

YACHT CHARTERS

Tortola boasts the largest fleet of bareboat sailing charters in the world. The best place to get outfitted is **The Moorings,** Wickhams Cay (© **888/535-7289** or 888/952-8420 in the U.S. and Canada; or 284/494-2332 in the British Virgin Islands; www.moorings.com). This outfit, along with a handful of others, makes the British Virgins the cruising capital of the world. You can choose from a fleet of sailing yachts, which can accommodate up to five couples in comfort and style. Depending on your nautical knowledge and skills, you can arrange a bareboat rental (with no crew) or a fully crewed rental with a skipper, a staff, and a cook. Boats come equipped with a portable barbecue, snorkeling gear, dinghy, linens, and galley equipment. The Moorings has an experienced staff of mechanics, electricians, riggers, and cleaners. If you're going out on your own, you'll get a thorough briefing session on Virgin Island waters and anchorages.

If you'd like sailing lessons, consider **Steve Colgate's Offshore Sailing School** (© **800/221-4326**), which offer courses in seamanship year-round.

SHOPPING

Most of Tortola's shops are on Road Town's Main Street. Unfortunately, the British Virgins have no duty-free shopping. British goods are imported without duty, and you can find some good buys among these imported items, especially in English china. In general, store hours are Monday to Saturday from 9am to 4pm.

You might start your shopping expedition at **Crafts Alive,** an open-air market lying in the center of Road Town and impossible to miss. It consists of a series of old-fashioned West Indian–style buildings that are stocked with local crafts and locally made goods, ranging from Caribbean dolls to straw hats, from crocheted doilies to pottery, plus, of course, the inevitable B.V.I. T-shirts.

Sunny Caribbee Herb and Spice Company, Main Street, Road Town (© 284/494-2178), in an old West Indian building, was the first hotel on Tortola. It's now a shop specializing in Caribbean spices, seasonings, teas, condiments, and handcrafts. With an aroma of spices permeating the air, this factory is an attraction in itself. You can buy two famous specialties here: the West Indian hangover cure and the Arawak love potion. A Caribbean cosmetics collection, Sunsations, includes herbal bath gels, island perfume, and sunscreens. There's a daily sampling of island products—perhaps tea, coffee, sauces, or dips.

Caribbean Fine Arts Ltd., Main Street, Road Town (© 284/494-4240), sells original watercolors and oils, limited-edition serigraphs and sepia photographs, and pottery and primitives.

Samarkand, Main Street, Road Town (© 284/494-6415), evokes an exotic land, but is actually an unusually good bet for jewelry and other items. Look for an intriguing selection of bracelets, pins, pendants in both silver and gold, and pierced earrings. Caribbean motifs such as palms and sea birds often appear in the designs of the jewelry.

Bargain hunters gravitate to **Sea Urchin,** Mill Mall, Road Town (© 284/494-4108), for print shirts and shorts, T-shirts, bathing suits, and sandals.

Pusser's Company Store, Main Street and Waterfront Road, Road Town (© 284/494-2467), has gourmet food items including meats, spices, fish, and a nice selection of wines. Pusser's Rum is one of the best-selling items here.

Arawak, on the dock at Nanny Cay (© 284/494-5240), is known for its household furnishings such as placemats and candleholders, but it also sells sporty clothing for adults and kids, along with a selection of gifts and souvenirs.

Flamboyance, Waterfront Drive (© 284/494-4099), is the best place to shop for perfume and upscale cosmetics.

If you've rented a villa or condo, or even if your accommodation has a kitchenette, consider a visit to **Ample Hamper,** Villa Cay Marina, Wickham's Cay I, Road Town (© 284/494-2494). This outlet stocks some of the best-packaged food and bottled wines on the island. It also offers fresh fruit and a tasty selection of cheeses.

Philatelists from all over the world flock to the **British Virgin Islands Post office,** Main Street, Road Town (© 284/494-3701), for its exquisite and unusual stamps in beautiful designs. Even though the stamps carry U.S. monetary designations, they can only be used in the B.V.I. Most stamp collectors, however, only collect the stamps instead of actually using them.

TORTOLA AFTER DARK

Ask around to find out which hotel might have entertainment on any given evening. Steel bands and fungi or scratch bands (African Caribbean musicians who improvise on locally available instruments) appear regularly, and nonresidents are usually welcome. Pick up a copy of *Limin' Times,* an entertainment magazine listing what's happening locally; it's usually available at hotels.

Bomba's Surfside Shack, Cappoon's Bay (© 284/495-4148), is the oldest, most memorable, and most uninhibited hangout on the island, sitting on the beach near the West End. It's covered with Day-Glo graffiti and odds and ends of plywood, driftwood, and abandoned rubber tires. Despite its makeshift appearance, the shack has the sound system to create a really great party. Every month (dates vary), Bomba's stages a full-moon party, with free house tea spiked with hallucinogenic mushrooms. (The tea is free because it's illegal to sell it.) The place is also wild on Wednesday and Sunday nights, when there's live music and an $8 all-you-can-eat barbecue. It's open daily from 10am to midnight (or later, depending on business).

The bar at **The Moorings/Mariner Inn,** Wickhams Cay (© **888/535-7289** or 888/952-8420 in the U.S. and Canada, or 284/494-2332 in the British Virgin Islands), is the preferred watering hole for upscale yacht owners, but drink prices are low. Open to a view of its own marina, and bathed in a dim and flattering light, the place is relaxed. Another popular choice is the **Spyglass Bar,** in the Treasure Isle Hotel, Road Town (© **284/494-2501**), where a sunken bar on a terrace overlooks the pool and faraway marina facilities of this popular hotel.

Other places worth a stop on a bar-hopping jaunt include the **Jolly Roger,** West End (© **284/495-4559**), where you can hear local or sometimes American bands playing everything from reggae to blues. In the same area, visit **Stanley's Welcome Bar,** Cane Garden Bay (© **284/495-9424**), where a rowdy frat-boy crowd gathers to drink, talk, and drink some more. Finally, check out **Sebastians,** Apple Bay (© **284/495-4212**), especially on Sunday, when you can dance to live music under the stars, at least in winter.

Rhymer's, on the popular stretch of beach at Cane Garden Bay (© **284/495-4639**), serves up cold beer or tropical rum concoctions, along with a casual menu of ribs, conch chowder, and more. The beach bar and restaurant is open daily from 8am to 9pm.

The joint is jumping at **The Road House,** West End (© **284/494-1667**), on Friday to Sunday nights. The place is packed with locals and a scattering of visitors who come to listen to a DJ, but there's often live salsa and reggae as well.

3 Virgin Gorda ★★★

In 1493, on his second voyage to the New World, Columbus named this island Virgin Gorda, or "fat virgin" (from a distance, the island looks like a reclining woman with a protruding stomach). The second largest island in the cluster of British Virgin Islands, Virgin Gorda is 16km (10 miles) long and 3km (2 miles) wide, with a population of some 1,400. It's 19km (12 miles) east of Road Town and 42km (26 miles) from St. Thomas.

The island was a fairly desolate agricultural community until Laurance S. Rockefeller established the Little Dix Bay Hotel in the early 1960s, following his success with the Caneel Bay resort on St. John in the 1950s. He envisioned a "wilderness beach," where privacy and solitude would reign. In 1971, the Virgin Gorda Yacht Harbour opened. Operated by the Little Dix Bay Hotel, it accommodates 120 yachts today.

Come to Virgin Gorda to relax and escape at some of the poshest and most self-contained inns in the Caribbean, if you can afford them. Life here is much slower paced than on Tortola, without much shopping or nightlife. The island gets far less rain, making some sections of it quite arid. Goats wander among a landscape of cactus and scrub brush.

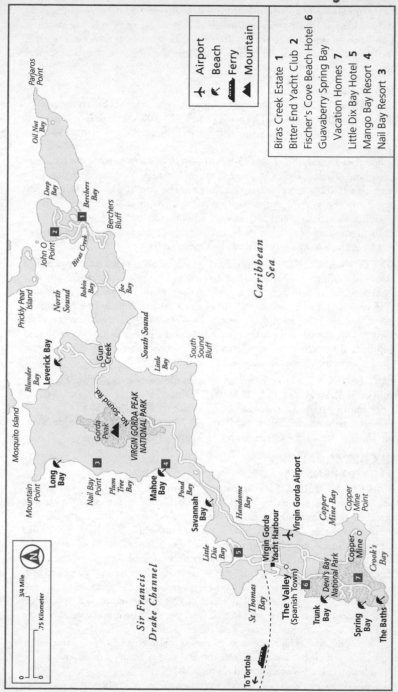

Virgin Gorda

Legend:
- ✈ Airport
- ⤵ Beach
- Ferry
- ▲ Mountain

Biras Creek Estate **1**
Bitter End Yacht Club **2**
Fischer's Cove Beach Hotel **6**
Guavaberry Spring Bay
Vacation Homes **7**
Little Dix Bay Hotel **5**
Mango Bay Resort **4**
Nail Bay Resort **3**

Parjaros Point
Oil Nut Bay
Deep Bay
Berchers Bay
Berchers Bluff
John O Point
Biras Creek

Caribbean Sea

Prickly Pear Island
North Sound
Robin Bay
Joe Bay
South Sound

Mosquito Island
Blunder Bay
Leverick Bay
Gun Creek
Little Bay
South Sound Bluff

No. Sound Rd.
Gorda Peak
VIRGIN GORDA PEAK NATIONAL PARK

Mountain Point
Long Bay
Nail Bay Point
Plum Tree Bay
Mahoe Bay
Pond Bay
Savannah Bay
Handsome Bay

Virgin Gorda Airport
Copper Mine Bay
Copper Mine Point

Little Dix Bay
Virgin Gorda Yacht Harbour
The Valley (Spanish Town)
Devil's Bay National Park
Copper Mine
Crook's Bay

Sir Francis Drake Channel

St Thomas Bay
Trunk Bay
Spring Bay
The Baths

To Tortola

N

3/4 Mile
.75 Kilometer

Try to visit Virgin Gorda, if only for the day, to see **The Baths,** gigantic rocks and boulders shaped by volcanic pressures millions of years ago. The beach at The Baths is simply spectacular. Virgin Gorda is also quite mountainous; if you're tired of flat Caribbean islands, you'll love the gorgeous, dramatic scenery here.

ESSENTIALS

GETTING THERE   You can get to Virgin Gorda by air via St. Thomas in the U.S. Virgin Islands. **Air St. Thomas** (② 800/522-3084 or 340/776-2722) flies to Virgin Gorda Monday to Saturday from St. Thomas. A one-way trip (40 min.) costs $81.

Speedy's Fantasy (② 284/495-5240) operates a ferry service between Road Town and Virgin Gorda. Monday through Saturday, four ferries a day leave from Road Town, three per day on Sunday. The cost is $15 one-way or $20 round-trip. From St. Thomas to Virgin Gorda, it offers service three times a week (on Tues, Thurs, and Sat), costing $35 one-way or $60 round-trip.

You'll also find that the more luxurious resorts have their own boats to take you from the airport on Beef Island to Virgin Gorda.

GETTING AROUND   Independently operated open-sided **safari buses** run along the main road. Holding up to 14 passengers, these buses charge upwards from $3 per person to transport a passenger, say, from The Valley to The Baths.

If you'd like to rent a car, try one of the local firms, including **Mahogany Rentals,** The Valley, Spanish Town (② 284/495-5469), across from the yacht harbor. This company is the least expensive on the island, beginning at around $45 daily for a Suzuki Samurai. Road conditions on Virgin Gorda range from good to extremely poor. *Remember:* Drive on the left.

FAST FACTS   The local **American Express** representative is **Travel Plan,** Virgin Gorda Yacht Harbour (② 284/495-5586).

The **police station** can be reached by calling ② 284/495-7584.

First Caribbean International Bank (② 284/495-5217) is located in Spanish Town at the Virgin Gorda Shopping Centre. It has an ATM.

ACCOMMODATIONS
VERY EXPENSIVE

Biras Creek Estate ⟨★★★⟩   Stay at this sophisticated and relaxing hideaway if you want to retreat from the world. This private, romantic resort is the classiest place on the island—Bitter End is more family-oriented, and Little Dix Bay more of a conventional resort. It stands at the northern end of Virgin Gorda like a hilltop fortress, opening onto the ocean. On a 60-hectare (148-acre) estate with its own marina, it occupies a narrow neck of land flanked by the sea on three sides. All the attractive, tropically decorated units have well-furnished bedrooms and private patios. Some have king-size beds, plus spacious bathrooms with inviting garden showers. There are no TVs in the rooms, but you do get such luxuries as oceanview verandas. Guests get their own bikes for their stay, and there are lots of hiking trails near the property.

The food has won high praise; the wine list is also excellent. The hotel restaurant and open-air bar are quietly elegant, and there's always a table with a view. A barbecued lunch is often served on the beach.

North Sound (P.O. Box 54), Virgin Gorda, B.V.I. ② 800/223-1108 in the U.S., or 284/494-3555. Fax 284/494-3557. www.biras.com. 34 units. Winter $750–$1,050 double, $1,650 suite for 4; off season $525–$825 double, $1,125 suite for 4. Rates include all meals. Ask about packages. AE, MC, V. Take the private motor launch from the Beef Island airport, $160 per person round-trip. No children under age 8. **Amenities:** Restaurant;

2 bars; outdoor pool; 2 tennis courts; kayaks; snorkeling; Sunfish sailboats; bikes; free beach trips; taxi service to launch; babysitting; laundry service; dry cleaning. *In room:* A/C, fridge, minibar, beverage maker, hair dryer, iron/ironing board, safe.

Bitter End Yacht Club ★★★
This is the liveliest of the B.V.I. resorts and even better equipped than the more exclusive Biras Creek. It's the best sailing and diving complex in the British chain. It opens onto one of the most unspoiled and secluded deep-water harbors in the Caribbean. Guests have unlimited use of the resort's million-dollar fleet and a complimentary introductory course at the Nick Trotter Sailing and Windsurfing School. The Bitter End offers an informal yet elegant experience in either a hillside chalet or a well-appointed beachfront or hillside villa overlooking the sound. Most units have varnished hardwood floors, sliding-glass doors, and wicker furnishings. All villas have two twins, two queens, or a king-size bed, plus a large dressing area and a shower with sea views.

For something novel, you can stay aboard one of the 9m (30-ft.) yachts, yours to sail, with dockage and daily maid service, meals in the Yacht Club dining room, and overnight provisions. Each yacht has a shower with pressure water and can accommodate four comfortably.

First-rate meals are available in the Clubhouse Steak and Seafood Grille, the English Carvery, or the Pub, with entertainment by a steel drum or reggae band.

John O Point, North Sound (P.O. Box 46), Virgin Gorda, B.V.I. (© 800/872-2392 in the U.S. for reservations, or 284/494-2746. Fax 284/494-4756. www.beyc.com. 85 units, 4 yachts. Winter (double occupancy) $585–$770 beachfront villa, suite, yacht, or hillside villa; off season (double occupancy) $430–$525 all units. Rates include all meals. AE, MC, V. Take the private ferry from the Beef Island airport, $25 per person one-way. **Amenities:** 3 restaurants; pub; outdoor pool; Boston whalers; scuba diving; snorkeling; sport-fishing; Sunfish sailing; windsurfing; boat trips to nearby cays; babysitting; laundry service; dry cleaning. *In room:* A/C (in some), ceiling fan (in some), TV (available upon request), dataport, fridge, beverage maker.

Little Dix Bay Hotel ★★
Full of low-key luxury, along a curving white-sand beach, Little Dix Bay Hotel is a resort discreetly scattered along a .8km (½-mile), crescent-shaped, private bay on a 200-hectare (494-acre) preserve. Many guests find this resort too pricey and stuffy; we ourselves prefer the more casual elegance of Biras Creek Estate and the Bitter End Yacht Club, though Little Dix Bay does have an undeniably lovely setting, fine service, and a quiet elegance.

All rooms, built in the woods, have private terraces with views of the sea or gardens. Trade winds come through louvers and screens, and units also have ceiling fans and air-conditioning. Some units are two-story rondavels (like tiki huts) raised on stilts to form their own breezeways. Accommodations are roomy, airy, and decorated with tropical flair, each with a smart private bathroom with shower stall. All guest rooms have been renovated with new furnishings and fabrics, evoking a Southeast Asian style with beautiful wicker or reed furniture, bamboo beds, Balinese boxes and baskets, and ceramic *objets d'art*.

1km (⅔ mile) north of Spanish Town (P.O. Box 70), Virgin Gorda, B.V.I. (© 888/767-3966 in the U.S., or 284/495-5555. Fax 284/495-5661. www.littledixbay.com. 100 units. Winter $575–$875 double, $1,800 suite; off season $295–$550 double, from $900 suite. MAP (breakfast and dinner) $90 per person extra. Extra person $75. AE, DC, MC, V. Take the private ferry from the Beef Island airport; $75 per person round-trip. **Amenities:** 3 restaurants; 2 bars; 7 tennis courts; fitness center; deep-sea fishing; kayaks; scuba diving; snorkeling; Sunfish sailboats; water-skiing; children's programs; teenage programs; island tours; jeep rental; limited room service; massage; babysitting; laundry service. *In room:* A/C, ceiling fan, fridge, beverage maker, hair dryer, iron/ironing board, safe.

EXPENSIVE
Guavaberry Spring Bay Vacation Homes ★
Staying in one of these hexagonal, white-roofed redwood houses built on stilts is like living in a tree

house. Screened and louvered walls let in sea breezes and The Baths, with its excellent sandy beach, is nearby. Each unique home, available for daily or weekly rental, has one or two bedrooms; all have private bathrooms with showers, small kitchenettes, and dining areas. Each also has an elevated sun deck overlooking Sir Francis Drake Passage. Within a few minutes of the cottage colony is the beach at Spring Bay, and the Yacht Harbour Shopping Centre is 2km (1¼ miles) away.

Spring Bay (P.O. Box 20), Virgin Gorda, B.V.I. ℭ 284/495-5227. Fax 284/495-5283. www.guavaberryspring bay.com. 18 units. Winter $195 1-bedroom house, $265 2-bedroom house; off season $130 1-bedroom house, $185 2-bedroom house. Extra person $17–$22. No credit cards. **Amenities:** Fishing; sailing; scuba diving; jeep rental; commissary; babysitting. *In room:* Ceiling fan, kitchenette, fridge, beverage maker, safe, no phone.

Nail Bay Resort ⭐ Near Gorda Peak National Park, and a short walk from a trio of usually deserted beaches, this resort enjoys an idyllic position. From its 59-hectare (146-acre) site, you can enjoy some of the best sunset views of Sir Francis Drake Channel and the Dog Islands. All the well-furnished units, each of which has a bathroom containing a shower stall, are comfortable and tasteful. Accommodations are wide ranging, including deluxe bedrooms, suites, apartments, and villas. This villa community has a core of a dozen units in two structures on a hillside, with sitting areas amid old sugar mill ruins. The most modest units are hotel-style bedrooms in the main building. The best accommodations are the four estate villas—Sunset Watch, Mystic Water, Island Spice, and Island Dream.

At night Nail Bay evokes a luxury property in Asia, its landscaping highlighted by circuitous stone walkways. One devotee told us that when she found the resort, it had the "terra-ultima exclusivity of Mustique, without that island's elitism."

Nail Bay (P.O. Box 69), Virgin Gorda, B.V.I. ℭ 800/871-3551 in the U.S., 800/487-1839 in Canada, or 284/494-8000. Fax 284/495-5875. www.nailbay.com. Winter $125–$250 double; off season $99–$175 double. AE, DISC, MC, V. **Amenities:** Restaurant; swim-up bar; outdoor pool; lit tennis court; Jacuzzi; kayaks; snorkeling; babysitting; laundry service; dry cleaning; nonsmoking rooms. *In room:* A/C, TV, dataport, kitchenette, beverage maker, hair dryer, iron/ironing board, safe.

MODERATE

Fischer's Cove Beach Hotel Swim from your doorstep in this group of units nestled near the sandy beach of St. Thomas Bay. Erected of native stone, each of the eight cottages is self-contained, with one or two bedrooms and a combination living/dining room with a kitchenette, plus a small bathroom with shower stall. You can stock up on provisions at a food store near the grounds. There are also 12 pleasant but simple rooms with views of Drake Channel. Each has its own private shower-only bathroom and private balcony.

The Valley (P.O. Box 60), Virgin Gorda, B.V.I. ℭ 284/495-5252. Fax 284/495-5820. www.fischerscove.com. 20 units. Winter $140–$165 double, $190–$315 studio cottage; off season $88 double, $125–$205 studio cottage. MAP (breakfast and dinner) $40 per person extra. AE, MC, V. **Amenities:** Restaurant; bar; bike rental; children's playground; jeep rental; babysitting. *In room:* A/C (in some), ceiling fans (in some), TV, dataport (in some), kitchenettes (in cottages), fridge, beverage maker, no phone in cottages.

Mango Bay Resort ⭐ *Value* This well-designed compound of eight white-sided villas is set on lushly landscaped grounds overlooking the scattered islets of Drake's Channel on the island's western shore. You get good value for your money here. The accommodations are the most adaptable on the island—doors can be locked or unlocked to divide each villa into as many as four independent units. Costs vary with the proximity of your unit to the nearby beach. Interiors are stylish yet simple, often dominated by the same turquoise as that of the seascape in front of you. Daily maid service is included. You can cook in, or dine on-site at Giorgio's Table (see "Dining," below), which is quite good and serves three meals a day.

Mahoe Bay (P.O. Box 1062), Virgin Gorda, B.V.I. © 800/223-6510 in the U.S., 800/424-5500 in Canada, or 284/495-5672. Fax 284/495-5674. www.mangobayresort.com. 11 units. Winter $132–$185 studio, $275 1-bedroom unit, $363 2-bedroom unit, $275 beachfront suite, $700 2-bedroom beachfront villa; off season $109–$143 studio, $195 1-bedroom unit, $259 2-bedroom unit, $197 beachfront suite, $510 2-bedroom beachfront villa. Extra person on foldaway couch $30–$50. MC, V. **Amenities:** Restaurant; bar; kayaks; sailing; snorkeling. In room: A/C, kitchen, no phone.

DINING
EXPENSIVE
Biras Creek Estate 🐾🐾 INTERNATIONAL   With even better cuisine than that of Little Dix Bay Pavilion (see below), this hilltop restaurant is our longtime island favorite, and for good reason. The resort hires the island's finest chefs, who turn out superb cuisine based on quality ingredients. The menu changes every night, but the panoramic view of North Sound doesn't. A recent sampling of the appetizers turned up such delights as five-spice duck salad for starters, followed by such well-prepared main courses as pan-seared salmon wrapped in Parma ham in a lentil-cream sauce or grilled grouper with an herby couscous. The chef's special grilled lobster is a daily creation of the chef. Desserts are prepared fresh daily here, and are likely to range from a chilled green apple parfait to a choice of sorbets served with a chilled cantaloupe soup.

In Biras Creek, North Sound. © 284/494-3555. Reservations required. Fixed-price dinner $65. AE, MC, V. Seatings daily 7–8:30pm.

Chez Bamboo 🐾 *(Finds* CAJUN/CREOLE   The closest approximation to a New Orleans supper club you're likely to find in Virgin Gorda is here, in a building with a big veranda and a location that's within a 5-minute walk north of the yacht club. Inside, there's a wraparound mural showing a jazz band playing within a forest of bamboo, as well as bamboo artifacts. Owner Rose Giacinto and Chef Joyce Rodriguez concoct superb versions of dishes—such as conch gumbo, Nassau grouper *en papillote,* and New Orleans–style strip steak that's covered with creamy Worcestershire sauce. Desserts such as apple *crostini* and crème brûlée are among the very best of their ilk on the island. Live music, usually blues or jazz, is presented every Friday night on the terrace.

Next to the Virgin Gorda Yacht Harbour, Spanish Town. © 284/495-5752. Reservations recommended. Main courses $20–$40. AE, MC, V. Daily 5–10pm.

Little Dix Bay Pavilion 🐾 INTERNATIONAL   The most romantic of the dining spots on Virgin Gorda, this pavilion is our preferred choice at this deluxe resort, which also operates Sugar Mill Restaurant. At the Pavilion the guests (most middle-aged and well-heeled) sit under a large thatched roof with the doors open to the trade winds. The chefs change the menu daily. Although many of the ingredients are shipped in frozen, especially meats and some seafood, there is much that is fresh and good. The most expensive items on the menu are the rack of lamb and grilled salmon. Many vegetables evoke the Pacific Rim, and the seafood keeps us returning again and again.

In the Little Dix Bay Hotel, 1km (²/₃ mile) north of Spanish Town. © 284/495-5555. Reservations recommended. Main courses $19–$40. AE, MC, V. Daily 12:30–2:30pm and 7–9pm.

MODERATE
The Flying Iguana MEDITERRANEAN/FRENCH/WEST INDIAN   The owner of this place, Puck (aka Orlington Baptiste), studied his craft in Kansas

City, with the Hilton Group, before setting up this amiable restaurant over-looking the airport's landing strip and the sea. Potted hibiscus and lots of effigies of iguanas, stuffed and carved, ornament a room that's a celebration of West Indian mystique. The house drink is the Iguana Sunset, a concoction whose secret ingredients change according to the whim of the bartender. Whatever the recipe, it usually produces a lightheaded effect that goes well with the carefully conceived cuisine. The finest examples include fresh fish and all kinds of shellfish, including calamari, shrimp, scallops, and conch, often served in combination. You'll also find steak, chicken, and lamb, seasoned in a way that evokes both the Caribbean and the Mediterranean. Happy hour is from 4 to 6pm daily.

The Valley, at the airport. ✆ 284/495-5277. Reservations recommended. Main courses $8–$15 lunch, $15–$32 dinner. MC, V. Daily 7am–9pm (last order).

Giorgio's Table ✦ *Finds* ITALIAN   This is the only authentic Italian restaurant on the island. Their chefs are flown in for the season from Venice, Milan, and Florence. Lying a 15-minute drive north of Spanish Town, it opens onto a big covered terrace, although its varnished interior evokes a yacht. We like to sit out here at night, "star-struck," gazing up at the heavens with the sounds of the surf nearby. The chef says he cooks Italian instead of "American Italian," and the food is good, despite its reliance on a lot of imported ingredients. Fresh locally caught fish is generally the best bet, although you can order an array of succulent pastas and such standard Italian staples as veal scaloppine. Pizzas and sandwiches will fill you at lunch. Looking at this place, we decided its owner, Giorgio, has an appropriate last name—Paradisio.

Mahoe Bay. ✆ 284/495-5684. Reservations recommended. Main courses $14–$18 lunch, $25–$35 dinner. AE, DISC, MC, V. Daily noon–3pm and 6:30–9pm.

Rock Café CARIBBEAN/ITALIAN   Unlike the name suggests, this is not some island clone of the ubiquitous Hard Rock Cafe. It's even better in our view than that overrated international chain. You can stop for a drink in the special tequila bar upstairs before heading for a table later. The setting is amidst boulders like the ones at The Baths, the number-one sightseeing attraction on Virgin Gorda. The recessed lighting and boardwalks add to the theatrical allure at night. Fortunately, the chefs don't depend just on the setting. The menu is wisely balanced, the dishes well prepared and consumed with affordable wine from a respectable list whose vintages range from Italy to California. Freshly caught red snapper comes in a tangy marinade, and we're especially fond of the chicken piccata.

The Valley. ✆ 284/495-5482. Reservations recommended. Main courses $15–$28. MC, V. Daily 4pm–midnight.

INEXPENSIVE

The Bath & Turtle INTERNATIONAL   At the end of the waterfront shopping plaza in Spanish Town sits the most popular pub on Virgin Gorda, packed with locals during happy hour, from 4 to 6pm. Even if you don't care about food, you might join the regulars over midmorning mango coladas or peach daiquiris. There's live music every Wednesday and Sunday night, in summer only (no cover). From its handful of indoor and courtyard tables, you can order fried fish fingers, tamarind-ginger wings, very spicy chili, pizzas, fresh pasta, barbecue chicken, steak, lobster, and daily seafood specials such as conch fritters from the simple menu here.

Virgin Gorda Yacht Harbour, Spanish Town. ✆ 284/495-5239. Reservations recommended. Breakfast $4–$10; main courses $7–$15 lunch, $7–$25 dinner. AE, MC, V. Daily 7:30am–11pm.

The Restaurant at Leverick Bay CONTINENTAL A combined restaurant and beach bar, this is today's version of the old Pusser's, which now operates only a store here. During the day, you can enjoy all sorts of light meals, including croissant sandwiches, burgers, fried snapper, and pizza. There's also a children's menu. At night, the menu is more ambitious, featuring such intriguing appetizers as roasted pumpkin soup made with island-grown pumpkins and a splash of truffle oil. The chicken satay served with a spicy peanut dipping sauce is also enticing. The chef's main dish specialty is a tender and slow-roasted prime rib of beef with mashed potatoes and fresh vegetables. The fresh Ahi tuna with a tangy wasabi and sweet soy sauce is full of aromatic flavor. If featured, you might also opt for the grilled wahoo, caught in local waters and marinated in lime and served with West Indian rice and fresh vegetables.

Leverick Bay, North Sound. ℂ 284/495-7154. Reservations recommended. Main courses $19–$28; lunch $8–$16; pizzas from $8. MC, V. Daily 11am–10pm. Closed Sept–Oct.

Top of The Baths CARIBBEAN This aptly named green-and-white restaurant has a patio with a swimming pool. Locals gather here to enjoy the food they grew up on. At lunch, you can order an array of appetizers, sandwiches, and salad plates. You're invited to swim in the pool either before or after dining. At night, the kitchen turns out good home-style cookery, including fresh fish, lobster, chicken, and steaks. Look for one of the daily specials. And save room for a piece of that rum cake! Live steel bands perform on Sunday.

The Valley. ℂ 284/495-5497. Dinner $16–$31; sandwiches and salads $6.50–$10. AE, MC, V. Daily 8am–10pm.

EXPLORING THE ISLAND

The northern side of Virgin Gorda is mountainous, with Gorda Peak reaching 411m (1,348 ft.), the highest spot on the island. However, the southern half of the island is flat, with large boulders at every turn.

The best way to see the island if you're over for a day trip is to call **Andy Flax** at the Fischers Cove Beach Hotel. He runs the **Virgin Gorda Tours Association** (ℂ **284/495-5252**), which will give you a tour of the island for $23 per person. The tour leaves twice daily, or more often if there's demand. You can be picked up at the ferry dock if you give 24 hours' notice.

HITTING THE BEACH The best beaches are at **The Baths** 𝕽𝕽, where giant boulders form a series of tranquil pools and grottoes flooded with seawater (nearby snorkeling is excellent, and you can rent gear on the beach). Scientists think volcanic activity brought the boulders to the surface eons ago.

Devil's Bay National Park can be reached by a trail from The Baths. The walk to the secluded coral-sand beach takes about 15 minutes through boulders and dry coastal vegetation.

The Baths and surrounding areas are part of a proposed system of parks and protected areas in the B.V.I. The protected area encompasses 273 hectares (674 acres) of land and includes sites at Little Fort, Spring Bay, The Baths, and Devil's Bay on the east coast.

Neighboring The Baths is **Spring Bay,** one of the best of the island's beaches, with white sand, clear water, and good snorkeling. **Trunk Bay** is a wide sandy beach reachable by boat or along a rough path from Spring Bay.

Savannah Bay is a sandy beach north of the yacht harbor, and **Mahoe Bay,** at the Mango Bay Resort, has a gently curving beach with neon-blue water.

DIVING **Kilbrides Sunchaser Scuba** is located at the Bitter End Resort at North Sound (ℂ **800/932-4286** in the U.S., or 284/495-9638). Kilbrides offers the best diving in the British Virgin Islands, at 15 to 20 dive sites, including the wreck of the ill-fated HMS *Rhone*. Prices range from $75 to $90 for a two-tank dive on one of the coral reefs. A one-tank dive in the afternoon costs $60. Equipment, except wet suits, is supplied at no charge. Hours are 7:45am to 5pm daily.

HIKING   Consider a trek up the stairs and hiking paths that crisscross Virgin Gorda's largest stretch of undeveloped land, **Virgin Gorda Peak National Park.** To reach the best departure point for your uphill trek, drive north of The Valley on the only road leading to North Sound for about 15 very hilly minutes (using a 4WD vehicle is a good idea). Stop at the base of the stairway leading steeply uphill. There's a sign pointing to Virgin Gorda Peak National Park.

Depending on your climbing speed, it takes between 25 and 40 minutes to reach the summit of Gorda Peak, the highest point on the island; you'll be rewarded with sweeping views of the many scattered islets of the Virgin archipelago. There's a tower at the summit, which you can climb for enhanced views. Admire the flora and the fauna (birds, lizards, nonpoisonous snakes) that you're likely to run across en route. Be sure to bring sunscreen, and consider bringing a picnic, as tables are scattered along the hiking trails.

VIRGIN GORDA AFTER DARK

There isn't a lot of action at night, unless you want to make some of your own. **The Bath & Turtle** pub, at Yacht Harbour (© **284/495-5239**), brings in local bands for dancing in the summer on Wednesday and Sunday at 8pm. The **Bitter End Yacht Club** (© **284/494-2746**) has live music on Fridays. Reached only by boat, this is the best bar on the island. With its dark wood, it evokes an English pub and even serves British brews. Call to see what's happening at the time of your visit.

Andy's Chateau de Pirate, at the Fischer's Cove Beach Hotel, The Valley (© **284/495-5252**), is a sprawling, sparsely furnished local hangout. It has a simple stage, a very long bar, and huge oceanfront windows which almost never close. The complex also houses the Buccaneer Bar and the nightclub Neuso.

4 Jost Van Dyke

This rugged island off the west side of Tortola was named for a Dutch settler. In the 1700s, a Quaker colony settled here to develop sugar-cane plantations. One of the colonists, William Thornton, won the worldwide competition to design the U.S. Capitol in Washington, D.C. Smaller islands surround the place, including Little Jost Van Dyke, the birthplace of Dr. John Lettsome, founder of the London Medical Society.

About 150 people live on the 10 sq. km (4 sq. miles) of this mountainous island. On the south shore, **White Bay** and **Great Harbour** are good beaches. Although there are only a handful of places to stay, there are several dining choices, as the island is a popular stop for the yachting set and many cruise ships, including Cunard (and often some all-gay cruises). The peace and tranquillity often disappear unless you're here when the cruise ships aren't.

ESSENTIALS

GETTING THERE   Take the ferry to White Bay on Jost van Dyke from either St. Thomas or Tortola. (*Be warned:* Departure times can vary widely throughout the year, and often don't adhere very closely to the printed timetables.) Ferries from St. Thomas depart from Red Hook 3 days a week (Fri, Sat, and Sun), usually twice daily. More convenient (and more frequent) are the daily ferryboat shuttles from Tortola's isolated West End. The latter departs five times a day for the 25-minute trip, and costs $12 one-way. Call the **Paradise New Horizons Ferry Service** (✆ 284/495-9278) for information about departures from any of the above-mentioned points. If all else fails, carefully negotiate a transportation fee with one of the handful of privately operated water taxis.

EMERGENCIES In the unlikely event that you need the police, call ✆ 284/495-9345.

ACCOMMODATIONS

Sandcastle Hotel A retreat for escapists who want few neighbors and absolutely nothing to do, these six cottages are surrounded by flowering shrubbery and bougainvillea and have panoramic views, opening onto a white-sand beach. Bedrooms are spacious, light, and airy, furnished in a tropical motif, with tile floors, local art, rattan furnishings, day beds, and king-size beds. Two units are air-conditioned. There are large, tiled bathrooms, with heated showers outside. Children under 10 are not welcome. You mix your own drinks at the beachside bar, the Soggy Dollar, and keep your own tab. Visiting boaters often drop in to enjoy the beachside informality and order a drink called The Painkiller. A line in the guest book proclaims, "I thought places like this only existed in the movies."

White Bay, Jost Van Dyke, B.V.I. ✆ 284/495-9888. Fax 284/495-9999. www.sandcastle-bvi.com. 6 units. Winter $200–$250 double; off season $125–$175 double. Extra person $35–$45. 3-night minimum. MC, V. **Amenities:** Restaurant; bar; diving; fishing trips; sailing. *In room:* A/C (in 2 rooms), ceiling fan, no phone.

Sandy Ground These self-sufficient apartments are along the edge of a beach on a 7-hectare (17-acre) hill site on the eastern part of Jost Van Dyke. The complex rents two- and three-bedroom villas. One of our favorites was constructed on a cliff that seems to hang about 24m (79 ft.) over the beach. The rates are quoted by the week. The airy villas, each privately owned, are fully equipped with refrigerators and stoves. The interiors vary widely, from rather fashionable to bare bones. The living space is generous, and extras include private balconies or terraces. Most rooms have showers only.

The managers help guests with boat rentals and watersports. Diving, day sails, and other activities can also be arranged, and there are dinghies available. Snorkeling and hiking are among the more popular pastimes.

P.O. Box 594, West End, Tortola, B.V.I. ✆ 284/494-3391. Fax 284/495-9379. www.sandyground.com. 8 units. Weekly rates: winter $1,950 villa for 2; off season $1,400 villa for 2. Extra person $300 per week in winter, $200 off season. MC, V. Take a private water taxi from Tortola or St. Thomas. **Amenities:** Day sails; dinghies; diving; snorkeling. *In room:* Ceiling fan, fridge, beverage maker, no phone.

DINING

Abe's by the Sea WEST INDIAN In this local bar and restaurant, sailors are satisfied with a menu of fish, lobster, conch, ribs, and chicken. Prices are low, too, and it's money well spent. With each main course you also get peas, rice, and coleslaw. Abe's will host a festive pig roast on request.

Little Harbour. ✆ 284/495-9329. Reservations recommended for groups of 5 or more. Dinner $18–$40; nightly barbecue $22. MC, V. Daily 9–11am, noon–3pm, and 7–10pm.

Foxy's Tamarind Bar 🐾🐾 WEST INDIAN Arguably the most famous bar in the B.V.I., this mecca of yachties and other boat people is built entirely around sixth-generation Jost Van Dyke native, Philicianno "Foxy" Callwood. He opened the place in the late 1960s, and guests have been coming back ever since.

A songwriter and entertainer, Foxy is part of the draw. He creates impromptu calypso—almost in the Jamaican tradition—around his guests. If you're singled out, he'll embarrass you, but it's all in good fun. He also plays the guitar and takes a profound interest in preserving the environment of his native island.

Thursday through Saturday nights, a live band entertains. On other evenings, it's rock 'n' roll, reggae, or soca. The food and drink aren't neglected, either—try Foxy's Painkiller Punch. During the day, flying-fish sandwiches, *rotis* (Caribbean burritos), and the usual burgers are served, but evenings might bring freshly caught lobster, spicy steamed shrimp, or even grilled fish, depending on the catch of the day.

Great Harbour. ℭ 284/495-9258. Reservations recommended. Dinner $16–$26; lunch $8–$12. Daily 9am "until."

Sandcastle INTERNATIONAL/CARIBBEAN This hotel restaurant often serves food that has been frozen, but, even so, the flavors remain consistently good. Lunch is served in the open-air dining room, while lighter fare and snacks are available at the Soggy Dollar Bar. Dinner is by candlelight, featuring four courses, including such dishes as mahimahi Martinique (marinated in orange-lemon-lime juice and cooked with fennel, onions, and dill). Sandcastle hen is another specialty likely to appear on the menu: It's a grilled Cornish hen that's been marinated in rum, honey, lime, and garlic. But we'd skip all that for the sesame snapper, if available. Meals are served with seasonal vegetables and fresh pasta, along with a variety of salads and homemade desserts. Those desserts are luscious, and include piña colada cheesecake, Key lime pie, Irish whiskey cheesecake, and mango mousse.

At the Sandcastle Hotel, White Bay. ℭ 284/495-9888. Reservations required for dinner by 4pm. Lunch main courses $6–$12; fixed-price dinner $32. MC, V. Daily 9:30am–3pm and 1 seating at 7pm.

5 Anegada

The most northerly and isolated of the British Virgins, 48km (30 miles) east of Tortola, Anegada has a population of about 250, none of whom has found the legendary treasure from the more than 500 wrecks lying off its notorious Horseshoe Reef. It's different from the other British Virgins in that it's a coral-and-limestone atoll, flat, with a 750m (2,460-ft.) airstrip. Its highest point reaches 8m (26 ft.), and it hardly appears on the horizon if you're sailing to it.

At the northern and western ends of the island are some good white-sand beaches, which might be your only reason for coming here. This is a remote little corner of the Caribbean: Don't expect a single frill, and be prepared to put up with some hardships, such as mosquitoes.

Most of the island has been declared off-limits to settlement and reserved for birds and other wildlife. The B.V.I. National Parks Trust has established a flamingo colony in a bird sanctuary, which is also the protected home of several different varieties of heron as well as ospreys and terns. It has also designated much of the interior of the island as a preserved habitat for Anegada's animal population of some 2,000 wild goats, donkeys, and cattle. Among the endangered species being given a new lease on life here is the rock iguana, a fierce-looking but quite harmless reptile that can grow to a length of 2m (6½ ft.). Although rarely seen, these creatures have called Anegada home for thousands of years.

ESSENTIALS

GETTING THERE The only carrier flying from Tortola to Anegada, **Clair Aero Service** (ℭ 284/495-2271), uses seven- to nine-passenger prop planes. It operates four times a week, on Monday, Wednesday, Friday, and Sunday, charging $66 per person round-trip. In addition, **Fly BVI** (© 284/495-1747) operates a charter/sightseeing service between Anegada and Beef Island off Tortola. The one-way cost is $171 for two to three passengers.

GETTING AROUND   Limited taxi service is available on the island—not that you'll have many places to go. **Tony's Taxis,** which you'll easily spot when you arrive, will take you around the island. It's also possible to rent **bicycles;** ask around.

ACCOMMODATIONS

The Anegada Reef Hotel is the only major accommodation on the island. Neptune's Treasure (see "Dining," below) rents tents and basic rooms.

Anegada Reef Hotel ★   The only major hotel on the island is 5km (3 miles) west of the airport, right on the beachfront. It's one of the most remote places covered in this guide—guests who stay here are, in effect, hiding out. It's a favorite of the yachting set, who enjoy the hospitality. The hotel offers motel-like, very basic rooms with private porches, with either a garden or ocean view. Bathrooms are cramped with shower stalls. Come here for tranquillity, not for pampering.

You can arrange to go inshore fishing, deep-sea fishing, or bonefishing (there's also a tackle shop); you can also set up snorkeling excursions and secure taxi service and jeep rentals.

There's a beach barbecue nightly; the house specialty is lobster, and many attendees arrive by boat. Reservations for the 7:30pm dinner must be made by 4pm. If you're visiting just for the day, you can use the hotel as a base. Call and they'll have a van meet you at the airport.

Setting Point, Anegada, B.V.I. © 284/495-8002. Fax 284/495-9362. www.anegadareef.com. 16 units. Winter $250–$275 double; off season $215–$250 double. Rates include all meals. MC, V. **Amenities:** Restaurant; bar; babysitting. *In room:* A/C, beverage maker, no phone.

DINING

Cow Wreck Beach Bar & Grill ★ *(Finds* WEST INDIAN   This laid-back, family-run, and definitely funky joint is a coveted address among yachties anchoring at Anegada. Ice-cold beer and the best lobster in the B.V.I. keep the patrons coming back. The crustaceans are kept in a cage under the water, waiting their "death summons" to the grill. Under a straw roof, diners sit at rough-hewn wooden tables placed outside on a terrace with a view of the water. If you go for lunch you can tie in a visit with a snorkel trip. At night this is the most popular place on the island for a sundowner. Other standard dishes appear on the menu, but we've never known a guest to order anything but lobster for a main course.

Lower Cow Wreck Beach. © 284/495-8047. Reservations required for dinner. Main courses $15–$40. MC, V. Daily 10:30am–3pm, dinner seatings 6–7pm. Closing time for bar "when the last customer departs."

Neptune's Treasure *(Finds* INTERNATIONAL   Set near its own 24-slip marina, near the southern tip of the island in the same cluster of buildings that includes the more high-priced Anegada Reef Hotel, this funky bar and restaurant usually hosts a mix of yacht owners and local residents. Dining is in a spacious indoor area whose focal point is a bar and lots of nautical memorabilia. The drink of choice is a Dark and Stormy, composed of ginger beer and rum. The Soares family and their staff serve platters of swordfish, lobster, fish fingers, chicken, steaks, and ribs; dispense information about local snorkeling sites; and generally maintain order and something approaching a (low-key) party atmosphere.

They also offer nine simple bedrooms with air-conditioning. Depending on the season, rooms with a private bathroom rent for $80 to $105 double. Discounts are offered for stays of a week or more.

Between Pomato and Saltheap points, Anegada, B.V.I. © 284/495-9439, or short-wave channel 16. www.islandsonline.com. Reservations for dinner must be made by 4pm. Breakfast $8; lunch main courses $4–$9; fixed-price meals $20–$40 MC, V. Daily 8am–10pm.

6 Peter Island (★

Half of this island, boasting a good marina and docking facilities, is devoted to the yacht club. The other part is deserted. Beach facilities are found at palm-fringed Deadman's Bay, which faces the Atlantic but is protected by a reef. All goods and services are at the one resort (see below).

The island is so private that except for an occasional mason at work, about the only company you'll encounter will be an iguana or a feral cat whose ancestors were abandoned generations ago by shippers (the cats are said to have virtually eliminated the island's rodent population).

A hotel-operated ferry, **Peter Island Boat** (© 284/495-2000), departs Tortola from the pier at Trellis Bay, near the airport. A round-trip costs $15. Other boats depart six or seven times a day from Baugher's Bay in Road Town. Passengers must notify the hotel 2 weeks before their arrival so transportation can be arranged.

ACCOMMODATIONS

Peter Island Resort ★★★   This 720-hectare (1,778-acre) tropical island is solely dedicated to Peter Island Resort guests and yacht owners who moor their crafts here. The island's tropical gardens and hillside are bordered by five gorgeous private beaches, including Deadman's Beach (in spite of its name, it's often voted one of the world's most romantic beaches in travel-magazine reader polls).

The resort contains 32 rooms facing Sprat Bay and Sir Francis Drake Channel (oceanview or garden rooms) and 20 larger rooms on Deadman's Bay Beach (beachfront). Designed with a casual elegance, each has a balcony or terrace. The least desirable rooms are also the smallest and housed in two-story, A-frame structures next to the harbor. Bathrooms with shower/tub combinations range from standard motel-unit types to spectacular luxurious ones, depending on your room assignment. The Crow's Nest, a luxurious four-bedroom villa, overlooks the harbor and Deadman Bay and features a private swimming pool. The Hawk's Nest villas are three-bedroom villas situated on a tropical hillside.

Peter Island (P.O. Box 211), Road Town, Tortola, B.V.I. © 800/346-4451 in the U.S., or 284/495-2000. Fax 284/495-2500. www.peterisland.com. 54 units. Winter $865–$1,115 double, $4,000 2-bedroom villa, $8,000 4-bedroom villa; off season $530–$775 double, $1,300–$1,630 2-bedroom villa, $5,000 4-bedroom villa. Rates include all meals and transportation from the Tortola airport. AE, MC, V. **Amenities:** 2 restaurants; 2 bars; outdoor pool; 4 tennis courts; fitness center; gym; spa; deep-sea fishing; sea kayaks; scuba diving; snorkeling gear; Sunfish sailboats; water-skiing; windsurfing; limited room service; massage; babysitting; laundry service; dry cleaning. In room: A/C, minibar, hair dryer, iron/ironing board, safe.

7 Guana Island (★

This 340-hectare (840-acre) island, a nature preserve and wildlife sanctuary, is one of the most private hideaways in the Caribbean. Don't come here looking for action; rather, consider vacationing here if you want to retreat from the world. This small island right off the coast of Tortola offers seven virgin beaches and nature trails ideal for hiking; it abounds in unusual species of plant and animal life. Arawak relics have been found here. You can climb 242m (794-ft.)

Sugarloaf Mountain for a panoramic view. It's said that the name of the island came from a jutting rock that resembled the head of an iguana.

The Guana Island Club will send a boat to meet arriving guests at the Beef Island airport (trip time is 10 min.).

ACCOMMODATIONS & DINING

Guana Island Club ★★   The sixth or seventh largest of the British Virgin Islands, Guana Island was bought in 1974 by Henry and Gloria Jarecki, dedicated conservationists who run this resort as a nature preserve and wildlife sanctuary. Upon your arrival on the island, a Land Rover will meet you and transport you up one of the most scenic hills in the region, in the northeast of Guana.

The cluster of white cottages was built as a private club in the 1930s on the foundations of a Quaker homestead. The stone cottages never hold more than 30 guests (and have only two phones), and because the dwellings are staggered along a flower-dotted ridge overlooking the Caribbean and the Atlantic, the sense of privacy is almost absolute. The entire island can be rented by groups of up to 30. Although water is scarce on the island, each airy accommodation has a shower. The decor is rattan and wicker, and each unit has a ceiling fan. Renting North Beach cottage, the most luxurious of the accommodations, is like renting a private home. The panoramic sweep from the terraces is spectacular, particularly at sunset. There are seven beaches, some of which require a boat to reach.

Guests will find a convivial atmosphere at the rattan-furnished clubhouse. Casually elegant dinners by candlelight are served on the veranda, with menus that include homegrown vegetables and Continental and U.S. specialties.

P.O. Box 32, Road Town, Tortola, B.V.I. (© 800/544-8262 in the U.S., or 284/494-2354. (For reservations, write or call the Guana Island Club Reservations Office, 10 Timber Trail, Rye, NY 10580; (© 800/544-8262 in the U.S., or 914/967-6050; fax 914/967-8048.) www.guana.com. 15 units. Winter $850 double, $1,500 cottage; off season $640 double, $1,200 cottage. Rent the island for $11,500–$15,000. Transport fees $35 per person. Rates include all meals and drinks served with meals. MC, V. Closed Sept–Oct. **Amenities:** Restaurant; self-service bar; 2 tennis courts; fishing; kayaks; sailboats; snorkeling; water-skiing; windsurfing; massage; babysitting; laundry service; dry cleaning; nonsmoking rooms. *In room:* Ceiling fan, hair dryer, no phone.

9

The Cayman Islands

Despite the emergence of Grand Cayman as a major tourism destination in the 1990s, don't go to the Cayman Islands expecting fast-paced excitement. Island life focuses on the sea. Snorkelers will find a paradise, beach lovers will relish the powdery sands of Seven Mile Beach, but party-hungry travelers in search of urban thrills might be disappointed. Come to slow down and relax.

The Caymans, 773km (479 miles) due south of Miami, consist of three islands: **Grand Cayman, Cayman Brac,** and **Little Cayman.** Despite its name, Grand Cayman is only 35km (22 miles) long and 13km (8 miles) across at its widest point. The other islands are considerably smaller, of course, and contain very limited tourist facilities, in contrast to well-developed Grand Cayman. George Town on Grand Cayman is the capital and is therefore the hub of government, banking, and shopping.

English is the official language of the islands, although it's often spoken with an English slur mixed with an American southern drawl and a lilting Welsh accent.

1 Cayman Islands Essentials

VISITOR INFORMATION

The **Cayman Islands Department of Tourism** has the following offices in the United States: Doral Centre, 8300 NW 53rd St., Suite 103, Miami, FL 33166 (© 305/599-9033); One Lincoln Centre, 18 W. 140 Butterfield Rd., Suite 9200, Oakbrook Terrace, IL 60181 (© 630/705-0650; fax 630/705-1383); Two Memorial City Plaza, 820 Gessner, Suite 1335, Houston, TX 77024 (© 713/461-1317); and 3 Park Ave., 39th Floor, New York, NY 10016 (© 212/889-9009).

In Canada, contact Earl B. Smith, **Travel Marketing Consultants,** 234 Eglinton Ave. E., Suite 306, Toronto, ON M4P 1K5 (© 800/263-5805 or 416/485-1550; fax 416/485-7578).

In the United Kingdom, the contact is **Cayman Islands,** 6 Arlington St., London SW1 1RE (© 020/7491-7771).

The website for the Cayman Islands is **www.caymanislands.ky.**

Fun Fact **Ahoy, Matey!**

Cayman Islands Pirates' Week is held in late October. It's a national festival in which cutlass-bearing pirates and sassy wenches storm George Town, capture the governor, throng the streets, and stage a costume parade. The celebration, which is held throughout the Caymans, pays tribute to the nation's past and its cultural heritage. For the exact dates, contact the **Pirates' Week Festival Administration** (© 345/949-5078).

GETTING THERE

The Cayman Islands are easily accessible. Flying time from Miami is 1 hour and 20 minutes; from Houston, 2 hours and 45 minutes; from Tampa, 1 hour and 40 minutes; and from Atlanta, 3 hours and 35 minutes. Only a handful of non-stop flights are available from the U.S. Midwest, so most visitors use Miami as their gateway.

Cayman Airways (© 800/422-9626 in the U.S. and Canada, or 345/949-2311; www.caymanairways.com) offers the most frequent service to Grand Cayman, with three daily flights from Miami, five flights a week from Tampa, two flights a week from Orlando, and three nonstop flights a week from Houston.

Many visitors also fly to Grand Cayman on **American Airlines** (© 800/433-7300; www.aa.com), which offers three daily nonstop flights from Miami. **Northwest Airlines** (© 800/447-4747; www.nwa.com) flies to Grand Cayman from Detroit. **US Airways** (© 800/428-4322; www.usairways.com) offers daily nonstop flights from Charlotte, N.C. **Delta** (© 800/241-4141; www.delta.com) flies daily into Grand Cayman from its hub in Atlanta. The newest carrier to fly to the Caymans is **Continental Airlines** (© 800/231-0856; www.continental.com), which offers service between its Houston hub and Grand Cayman on Wednesday, Friday, Saturday, and Sunday. In addition, **Air Canada** (© 888/247-2262; www.aircanada.ca) offers direct twice weekly service from Toronto on Sunday and Wednesday, and **British Airways** (© 0870/850-9850; www.british airways.com) offer twice weekly service from London's Gatwick Airport with a stopover in Nassau.

FAST FACTS: The Cayman Islands

Business Hours Normally, banks are open Monday through Thursday from 9am to 4pm, and Friday from 9am to 4:30pm. Shops are usually open Monday through Saturday from 9am to 5pm.

Currency The legal tender is the **Cayman Islands dollar (CI$)**, currently valued at US$1.25 (CI80¢ equal US$1). Canadian, U.S., and British currencies are accepted throughout the Cayman Islands, but you'll save money if you exchange your U.S. dollars for Cayman Islands dollars. The Cayman dollar breaks down into 100 cents. Coins come in 1¢, 5¢, 10¢, and 25¢ denominations. Bills come in denominations of $1, $5, $10, $25, $50, and $100 (there is no CI$20 bill). Most hotels quote rates in U.S. dollars. However, many restaurants quote prices in Cayman Islands dollars, which might lead you to think that food is much cheaper than it is. *Unless otherwise specified, rates in this chapter are quoted in U.S. dollars.*

The cost of living in the Cayman Islands is about 20% higher than in the United States.

Documents Citizens of the United States and Canada should carry a valid passport or a birth certificate with a raised seal along with a government-issued photo ID (we always recommend that you bring a passport). Citizens of the United Kingdom should have a valid passport. All visitors need a return or ongoing ticket.

Electricity It's 110-volt AC (60 cycles), so U.S. and Canadian appliances will not need adapters or transformers.

Emergencies For medical or police emergencies, dial © **911.**

Hospital There's a hospital on Grand Cayman and another small one on Cayman Brac. Seriously ill cases on Little Cayman must be taken to Grand Cayman.

Language English is the official language of the islands.

Liquor Laws Beer, wine, and liquor are sold at most grocery and convenience stores Monday to Saturday (not on Sun). It is legal to have an open container on the beach.

Taxes A government tourist tax of 10% is added to your hotel bill. A departure tax of CI$20 (US$25) is collected when you leave the Caymans. There is no tax on goods and services.

Telephone To call the Cayman Islands from home, dial **1,** then the **345** area code, and the local number. Once you're on the island, to charge a long-distance call to a calling card, here are some access numbers: **AT&T** at ℭ **800/225-5288, Sprint** at ℭ **800/877-4646,** and **MCI** at ℭ **800/888-8000.**

Time U.S. Eastern Standard Time is in effect year-round; daylight savings time is not observed.

Tipping Most restaurants add a 10% to 15% charge in lieu of tipping, so check your bill carefully. Hotels also often add a 10% service charge to your bill. Taxi drivers expect a 10% to 15% tip.

Water The water in the Cayman Islands is safe to drink.

Weather The temperature in the Cayman Islands seldom goes lower than 70°F (21°C) or higher than 90°F (32°C). The daily average is between 77°F (25°C) and 84°F (29°C).

2 Grand Cayman ★★

The largest of the three islands and a real diving mecca, Grand Cayman has become one of the hottest tourist destinations in the Caribbean in recent years. With more than 500 banks, its capital, George Town, is the offshore banking center of the Caribbean (no problems finding an ATM here!). Retirees are drawn to the peace and tranquillity of this British Crown colony, site of a major condominium development. Almost all the Cayman Islands' population of 32,000 live on Grand Cayman. The civil manners of the locals reflect their British heritage.

ESSENTIALS

GETTING THERE   See the information at the beginning of this chapter.

VISITOR INFORMATION   The **Department of Tourism** is located in the Pavilion Building, Cricket Square (P.O. Box 67), George Town, Grand Cayman, B.W.I. (ℭ 345/949-0623). Hours are Monday to Friday 8:30am to 5pm.

GETTING AROUND   All arriving flights are met by taxis. The fares are fixed by the director of civil aviation (ℭ **345/949-7811**); typical one-way fares from the airport to Seven Mile Beach range from US$11 to US$20. Taxis (which can hold five people) will also take visitors on around-the-island tours. **Cayman Cab Team** (ℭ 345/947-1173) offers 24-hour service. You can also call **A.A. Transportation** at ℭ 345/949-7222.

Several car-rental companies operate on the island, including **Cico Avis** (ℭ **800/331-1212** in the U.S., or 345/949-2468 on Grand Cayman; www. avis.com), **Budget** (ℭ **800/472-3325** in the U.S., or 345/949-5605 on Grand

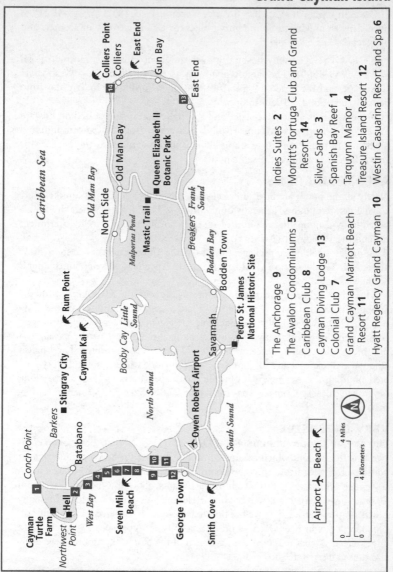

Caribbean Sea

Colliers Point
East End
Colliers
Gun Bay
East End

Old Man Bay
Old Man Bay
North Side
Queen Elizabeth II
Botanic Park
Malportas Pond
Mastic Trail
Breakers
Frank Sound
Bodden Bay
Bodden Town
Rum Point
Cayman Kai
Stingray City
Booby Cay
Little Sound
Savannah
Pedro St. James
National Historic Site
Barkers
Batabano
North Sound
Owen Roberts Airport
South Sound
Conch Point
Cayman Turtle Farm
Hell
West Bay
Seven Mile Beach
George Town
Smith Cove
Northwest Point

The Anchorage **9**
The Avalon Condominiums **5**
Caribbean Club **8**
Cayman Diving Lodge **13**
Colonial Club **7**
Grand Cayman Marriott Beach Resort **11**
Hyatt Regency Grand Cayman **10**

Indies Suites **2**
Morritt's Tortuga Club and Grand Resort **14**
Silver Sands **3**
Spanish Bay Reef **1**
Tarquynn Manor **4**
Treasure Island Resort **12**
Westin Casuarina Resort and Spa **6**

Airport ✈ Beach

4 Miles
4 Kilometers
0
0

Cayman; www.budgetrentacar.com), and **Ace Hertz** (✆ **800/654-3131** in the U.S., or 345/949-2280 on Grand Cayman; www.hertz.com). Each will issue the mandatory Cayman Islands driving permit for an additional US$7.50. All three require that reservations be made between 6 and 36 hours before pickup. At Avis drivers must be at least 21 and at Hertz, 25. Budget requires that drivers be between 25 and 70 years old. All three rental companies maintain kiosks within walking distance of the airport, although most visitors find it easier to take a taxi to their hotels and then arrange for the cars to be brought to them.

Remember: Drive on the left. And, reserve your car as far in advance as possible, especially in midwinter.

Cayman Cycle, at West Bay Road at Coconut Place (© **345/945-4021**), is open daily from 8am to 5pm, renting bikes for US$15 per day or scooters and motorcycles at US$40 per day.

FAST FACTS   The only hospital is **George Town Hospital,** Hospital Road (© **345/949-8600**). The largest pharmacy is **Island Pharmacy,** West Shore Centre, Seven Mile Beach (© **345/949-8987**), open Monday to Saturday from 9am to 7pm, Sunday 10am to 6pm.

In George Town, the **post office** and Philatelic Bureau are located on Edward Street (© **345/949-2474**), open Monday to Friday from 8:30am to 5pm and on Saturday from 8:30am to noon. There's also a counter at the Seven Mile Beach Post Office, open the same hours.

ACCOMMODATIONS

Nearly all the hotels are lined up along Seven Mile Beach. Hotels, unlike many Caymanian restaurants, generally quote prices in U.S. dollars. When choosing a hotel, keep in mind that the quoted rates do not include the 10% government tax and the 10% hotel service tax.

Consider booking a package tour to make those expensive resorts more affordable. See the section "Packages for the Independent Traveler" in chapter 2 before you book.

The Ritz-Carlton chain continues its invasion of the Caribbean with the announcement that it is opening a resort and a series of condos on Grand Cayman in December of 2004. A nine-hole Greg Norman–designed private golf course and the island's only full-service spa facility are part of the package. A 365-room resort will be integrated with a 71-unit condo complex. The English colonial architectural and interior design will include white roofs and ivory-covered buildings, all set on 58 tropically landscaped hectares (143 acres) along Seven Mile Beach. Contact Ritz-Carlton at © **800/241-3333** for more information.

VERY EXPENSIVE

The Avalon Condominiums 🌟🌟   One of Grand Cayman's best condo complexes is the Avalon, which occupies prime real estate on Seven Mile Beach. It consists of 27 oceanfront three-bedroom/three-bathroom units, 15 of which can be rented. Only a short distance from restaurants, about a 5-minute drive from George Town, it has an architectural style and grace that's lacking in many beachfront properties. The well-appointed, spacious units have a tropical motif, plus king or twin beds. Each condo has a fully equipped open kitchen and a large, screened lanai that overlooks a stretch of the beach. Bathrooms have oversize tubs and separate shower stalls.

West Bay Rd. (P.O. Box 31236), Grand Cayman, B.W.I. © **345/945-4171.** Fax 345/945-4189. www.cayman. org/avalon. 27 units. Winter US$710 apt for 4, US$785 apt for 6; off season US$495 apt for 4, US$560 apt for 6. AE, DISC, MC, V. Private garage. **Amenities:** Outdoor pool; tennis court; fitness center; Jacuzzi; sauna; non-smoking rooms. *In room:* A/C, TV, dataport, kitchen, washer/dryer, beverage maker, iron/ironing board, safe.

Colonial Club 🌟🌟   The pastel-pink Colonial Club occupies a highly desirable stretch of the famous Seven Mile Beach. Built in 1985, it's a three-story and rather standard condominium development about 6km (3¾ miles) north of George Town and some 10 minutes from the airport. First-class maintenance, service, and accommodations are provided in the apartments, all of which have kitchen fans, maid service, and laundry facilities. Usually only 8 of the 24 apartments are available for rent (the rest are privately owned and occupied but are sometimes rented out). You have a choice of units with two bedrooms and three bathrooms or units with three bedrooms and three bathrooms. The well-maintained bathrooms have showers, but no bathtubs.

West Bay Rd. (P.O. Box 320W), Grand Cayman, B.W.I. © 345/945-4660. Fax 345/945-4839. www.the colonialclub.com. 24 units. Winter US$470–US$530 apt for 2, US$520–US$590 apt for 3–4, US$570–US$650 apt for 5–6; off season US$260–US$340 apt for 2, US$310–US$390 apt for 3–4, US$360–US$440 apt for 5–6. Minimum stay 5 nights Dec 16–Apr 15. AE, MC, V. **Amenities:** Outdoor pool; lit tennis court. *In room:* A/C, TV, dataport, kitchen, washer/dryer, beverage maker, iron/ironing board, safe.

Hyatt Regency Grand Cayman ★★★ (Kids)   This US$80 million resort is the best managed, most luxurious, and most stylish hotel in the Cayman Islands. Lying on a lovely stretch of Seven Mile Beach 3km (2 miles) north of George Town, the hotel is a major component in the 36-hectare (89-acre) Britannia Resort community, which includes the Britannia Golf Course. The hotel has beautifully landscaped grounds. Dozens of Doric arcades are festooned with flowering vines that cascade beneath reflecting pools and comfortable teakwood settees. Low-rise buildings surround a large, landscaped courtyard that contains gardens, waterfalls, and the main swimming pool.

Rooms are luxurious and have private verandas but are only moderate in size. Each has a king-size or two double beds, and a spacious bathroom with a tub made of Italian marble. Two buildings and 44 rooms are devoted to the Exclusive Regency Club.

In the Hyatt's many restaurants and bars, you get the best hotel food and drink on the island. The Hyatt also offers the most complete watersports in the Caymans, with a beach club on the sands and the Red Sail Sports marina.

West Bay Rd. (P.O. Box 1588), Grand Cayman, B.W.I. © 800/233-1234 in the U.S., or 345/949-1234. Fax 345/949-8528. www.hyatt.com. 289 units. Winter US$415–US$540 double; off season US$220–US$285 double. Ask about packages. AE, DC, DISC, MC, V. **Amenities:** 5 restaurants; 4 bars (2 swim-up); 3 pools; golf; tennis courts; health club; spa; 2 Jacuzzis; room service (6:30am–11pm); babysitting; laundry service; nonsmoking rooms; rooms for those with limited mobility. *In room:* A/C, TV, dataport, minibar, beverage maker, iron/ironing board, hair dryer, safe.

Spanish Bay Reef ★   This is a small, intimate resort set in an isolated location amid the scrublands of the northwestern tip of Grand Cayman. Rather informally run, the pale-pink, two-story stucco units are favorites with divers. (There's great snorkeling and diving right offshore from the coral beach.) Don't expect a lot of comfort. If you're seeking resort-style accommodations and extras, this place may not appeal to you. The simply furnished accommodations have balconies or patios with garden or ocean views. Beds are comfortable, and bathrooms are a bit cramped, but contain shower/tub combinations. The casual furnishings are in a Caribbean motif.

Rates include all meals and beverages, island sightseeing, entertainment, use of bicycles, introductory scuba and snorkeling lessons, unlimited snorkeling or scuba diving from the shore (including tanks and weights), round-trip transfers, taxes, and service. If you're a diver, ask about certified divers packages when making your reservations. Guests lounge around Calico Jack's Poolside Bar, and later enjoy an array of food (with lots of fish) in the Spanish Main Restaurant.

West Bay Rd. (P.O. Box 9036T), Grand Cayman, B.W.I. © 800/482-3483 in the U.S., or 345/949-3765. Fax 345/949-1842. www.caymanresortsonline.com. 67 units. Winter US$190–US$255 per person double, US$250 per person condo, US$300 per person villa; off season US$160–US$205 per person double, US$250 per person condo or villa. Children under 12, US$50 each per night in parent's room. Rates are all-inclusive. Ask about dive packages. AE, MC, V. **Amenities:** Restaurant; 2 bars; outdoor pool; Jacuzzi; sauna; dive shop; scuba diving; snorkeling; bikes; island tours; laundry service; babysitting. *In room:* A/C, ceiling fan, TV, dataport.

Westin Casuarina Resort and Spa ✺✺✺   This resort runs a close second to the Hyatt (see above), which is more expensive and offers more facilities. The Westin lies right on the sands on Seven Mile Beach and has acres of landscaped grounds, a beautiful swimming pool, and lots of sports facilities. The bedrooms are in five-story wings; most have French doors leading onto balconies. Units are a bit small for such a luxury hotel but are well equipped with quality mattresses and bed linens. Bathrooms are very spacious, with oversize marble tubs. The best rooms have ocean views; the "island view" units simply look out on the parking lot and main highway, so ask carefully when you reserve. Wheelchair-accessible rooms are available.

The most upscale of the restaurants is Casa Havana, a dinner-only gourmet restaurant that evokes the glamour of pre-Castro Cuba. One of the largest pools and poolside decks (450 sq. m /4844 sq. ft.) in the Caymans is appealingly lined with palm and date trees. Swimming pools, designed as lazy ovals or lagoons, flank the north and south sides of the hotel, each with its own cascade/waterfall. An 18-hole championship golf course, The Links at Safehaven, is across the street.

West Bay Rd. (P.O. Box 30620), Grand Cayman, B.W.I. ℭ 800/WESTIN-1 in the U.S., or 345/945-3800. Fax 345/949-5825. www.westin.com. 343 units. Winter US$349–US$549 double, from US$1,050 suite; off season US$312–US$485 double, from US$735 suite. AE, MC, V. **Amenities:** 3 restaurants; 3 bars; outdoor pool; golf; exercise room; spa; sauna; dive shop; sailing; snorkeling; children's programs; car rental; 24-hr. room service; laundry service; dry cleaning; nonsmoking rooms; rooms for those with limited mobility. *In room:* A/C, TV, fax, dataport, kitchenette (in some), minibar, beverage maker, hair dryer, iron/ironing board, safe.

EXPENSIVE

Caribbean Club ✺✺   Located right at the midpoint of gorgeous Seven Mile Beach, the low-key Bermudan-looking Caribbean Club is an exclusive compound of well-furnished villas, each with a full-size living room, dining area, patio, and kitchen. (Its only serious competition is the Colonial Club.) When the owners are away, the units are rented to guests. Although it is hardly deluxe, the Caribbean Club has a long list of faithful repeat visitors who will stay nowhere else. The pink villas that make up the this resort are 5km (3 miles) north of George Town, either on or just off the beach; the six oceanfront units are more expensive than the others, of course. Accommodations are furnished in each owner's individual taste—which may not be yours. They contain attractive tropical furnishings, open verandas (often with barbecues), spacious closets, and combination bathrooms (tub and shower). At the core of the colony, the two-story club center, with tall, graceful arches, has picture windows that look out onto the grounds, which are planted with palm trees and flowering shrubs. The staff is one of the best and most helpful on the island.

Lantanas, the dining room, is open for lunch and dinner.

West Bay Rd. (P.O. Box 30499), Grand Cayman, B.W.I. ℭ 345/945-4099. Fax 345/945-4443. www.caribclub. com. 18 units. Winter US$286–US$506 1-bedroom villa, US$412–US$578 2-bedroom villa; off season US$198–US$368 1-bedroom villa, US$308–US$412 2-bedroom villa. AE, MC, V. **Amenities:** Tennis court; coin-operated laundry; rooms for those with limited mobility. *In room:* A/C, TV, dataport, kitchenette, beverage maker, hair dryer, iron/ironing board, safe.

Grand Cayman Marriott Beach Resort ✺   Way down in the pecking order from the Hyatt and Westin Casuarina, this five-story choice on Seven Mile Beach is still among the top-ranked hotels on the island. A favorite with large package-tour groups and conventions, it's a 5-minute drive north of George Town. The resort has good watersports facilities and there's good snorkeling 15m (49 ft.) offshore. Its red-roofed, vaguely colonial design resembles a cluster of balconied town houses. Accommodations open onto the ocean or the court-yard, and are decorated in cool Caribbean pastels. They have modern art, armoires, large closets, and private balconies. Bathrooms are spacious, with combination tubs and showers.

Come for the beach, not the cuisine.

West Bay Rd. (P.O. Box 30371), Grand Cayman, B.W.I. Ⓒ 800/228-9290 in the U.S., or 345/949-0088. Fax 345/949-0288. www.marriott.com. 309 units. Winter US$249–US$309 double, from US$679 suite; off season US$199–US$259 double, from US$629 suite. AE, DISC, MC, V. **Amenities:** 2 restaurants; 2 bars; outdoor pool; health club; Jacuzzi; sauna; dive shop; room service (6am–11pm); babysitting; laundry service; dry cleaning; nonsmoking rooms; rooms for those with limited mobility. *In room:* A/C, TV, dataport, minibar, beverage maker, hair dryer, iron/ironing board, safe.

Indies Suites 🏖 Indies Suites is for self-sufficient types who don't mind a lack of catering facilities or staying about two blocks from the beach. Built in 1990, this three-story resort offers some of the most comfortable accommodations on the island, though the design is cookie-cutter. The motel-like units surround a landscaped swimming pool. Each unit contains a kitchen and has a pastel decor, and some are sold as timeshare units. There's no hotel restaurant, although a wide choice of eateries lie within a short drive. Many of the long-term guests opt to cook in their own kitchens. On Wednesday night there's a barbecue with live music around the pool. Don't expect a lot of attention from the staff, though there is regular hotel-style maid service.

Raleigh Cay, off West Bay Rd., Grand Cayman, B.W.I. Ⓒ 345/945-5025. Fax 345/945-5024. info@indies suites.com. 38 suites. Winter US$299–US$360 double; off season US$180–US$215 double. Rates include continental breakfast. AE, MC, V. **Amenities:** Poolside bar; outdoor pool; sauna; babysitting; coin-operated laundry; dry cleaning; nonsmoking rooms. *In room:* A/C, TV, dataport, kitchen, washer/dryer, beverage maker.

Morritt's Tortuga Club and Grand Resort 🏖 On 3 beachfront hectares (7½ acres) on the east end of the island, this resort offers some of the island's best diving. Profiting from its position near offshore reefs teeming with marine life, it's the site of Cayman Windsurfing, which offers snorkeling and windsurfing, and rents sailboats and catamarans. Tortuga Divers, also on the premises, offers resort courses.

About a 42km (26-mile) drive from the airport, the club is composed of clusters of three-story beachfront condos opening onto the water. The condos were built in the Antillean plantation style from the wreckage of a former hotel. Many are rented as timeshare units. Some of the comfortably furnished apartments have a fully equipped kitchen, although many guests opt for meals in the complex's restaurant. Each unit has a small bathroom containing a shower.

East End (P.O. Box 496GT), Grand Cayman, B.W.I. Ⓒ 800/447-0309 in the U.S., or 345/947-7449. Fax 345/947-7669. www.morritt.com. 178 units. Winter US$185–US$195 studio, US$245–US$275 1-bedroom apt, US$325–US$375 2-bedroom apt; off season US$145–US$155 studio, US$185–US$220 1-bedroom apt, US$255–US$285 2-bedroom apt. AE, DISC, MC, V. **Amenities:** Restaurant; 3 bars; 4 pools (1 indoor, 3 outdoor); exercise room; sailing; scuba lessons; snorkeling; babysitting; laundry room; nonsmoking rooms; rooms for those with limited mobility. *In room:* A/C, TV, kitchenette (in some), beverage maker, iron/ironing board, safe (in some).

Silver Sands 🏖 *Kids* A good choice for families, this modern eight-building complex is arranged horseshoe-fashion on Seven Mile Beach, 11km (6¾ miles) north of George Town. The well-maintained apartments are grouped around a freshwater pool. The eight apartment blocks contain either two-bedroom/two-bathroom or three-bedroom/three-bathroom units. The two-bedroom units can hold up to six people, and the three-bedroom units can house up to eight. Each apartment has a balcony, a fully equipped kitchen, and a small bathroom with shower. In all, this is a smoothly run operation, which, in spite of its high costs, satisfies most guests.

West Bay Rd. (P.O. Box 205GT), Grand Cayman, B.W.I. ✆ 800/327-8777 in the U.S., or 345/949-3343. Fax 345/949-1223. www.silversandscondos.com. 42 units. Winter US$440–US$486 2-bedroom apt, US$534–US$582 3-bedroom apt; off season US$253–US$282 2-bedroom apt, US$352–US$384 3-bedroom apt. Additional person US$25 extra. Children 12 and under stay free in parent's room. Minimum stay 7 nights in winter, 3 nights in off season. AE, MC, V. **Amenities:** Outdoor pool; 2 tennis courts; laundry facilities; all nonsmoking rooms. *In room:* A/C, ceiling fans, TV, kitchen, beverage maker, iron/ironing board, safe.

Treasure Island Resort 🐕 (Kids)　It's not the prettiest architectural pile on the island, but this is a substantial and durable favorite lying at the southern tip of the golden sands of Seven Mile Beach, 1.6km (1 mile) from the center of George Town. Although both the building itself and the bedrooms have a somewhat functional feel, the artificial rock gardens and their waterfalls add a sense of fantasy. Since it's one of the largest hotels in the Caymans, expect lots of company. Bedrooms, though lacking style, are well-maintained and comfortable with king-size or two queen beds along with tiled bathrooms with shower. Many open onto a balcony or patio. The hotel maintains an active watersports program, with an on-site Bob Soto's outfitter with a full-service PADI dive center and watersports headquarters. The food is passable and affordable, though not a compelling reason to stay here.

269 West Bay Rd. (P.O. Box 1817 GT), Grand Cayman, B.W.I. ✆ 800/992-2015. Fax 345/949-8672. www. treasureislandresort.net. 277 units. Winter US$220–US$275 double; off season US$155–US$190 double. AE, DC, MC, V. **Amenities:** 2 restaurants; bar; 3 pools; kiddie pool; tennis court; sauna; 3 whirlpools; dive center; fishing; jet skis; sailing; bike rental; salon; limited room service; babysitting; nonsmoking rooms; rooms for those with limited mobility. *In room:* A/C, TV, dataport, fridge, beverage maker, iron/ironing board, safe.

MODERATE

The Anchorage　On a tranquil part of Seven Mile Beach, this villa complex offers a series of well-furnished privately owned and individually decorated accommodations. Each unit has two bedrooms and two baths and each garden view can accommodate up to four (great for two couples traveling together or for a family with kids). Units opening onto the garden are the least expensive; you pay more for oceanfront accommodations. Each villa has a screened porch or balcony overlooking the beach, where there's good snorkeling right offshore.

West Bay Rd. (P.O. Box 30986), Grand Cayman, B.W.I. ✆ 800/433-3483 in the U.S., or 345/945-4088. Fax 345/945-5001. www.theanchoragecayman.com. 15 units. Winter US$240–US$420 2-bedroom apt; off season US$170–US$290 2-bedroom apt. MC, V. **Amenities:** Outdoor pool; tennis court; arranged scuba expeditions; laundry facilities; rooms for those with limited mobility. *In room:* A/C, TV/VCR, dataport, kitchen, beverage maker, iron/ironing board.

Cayman Diving Lodge　This casual, laid-back place on a private coral sand beach in the southeast corner of the island, 32km (20 miles) east of George Town, offers good value to experienced divers. The horseshoe-shaped lodge is a two-story, half-timbered building set amid tropical trees, with a live coral barrier reef just offshore. Scuba trips include a daily two-tank morning dive of 3½ hours. The resort owns two 14m (46-ft.) Garcia dive boats that are very comfortable.

In the rooms, the view of the ocean is better than the somewhat plain decor and furnishings. Linoleum floors, shower-only bathrooms, and jalousies set the tone. A few units have balconies.

Chefs at the lodge's restaurant serve abundant meals and specialize in fish dishes; vegetarian food is also available.

East End (P.O. Box 11), Grand Cayman, B.W.I. ✆ 800/852-3483 in the U.S., or 345/947-7555. Fax 345/947-7560. www.divelodge.com. 12 units. Winter US$691 for 3 nights, US$888 4 nights, US$1,095 5 nights, US$1,292

6 nights, US$1,494 7 nights; off season US$620 for 3 nights, US$800 4 nights, US$985 5 nights, US$1,160 6 nights, US$1,340 7 nights. Rates are per person and all-inclusive featuring 2-tank dives. Nondiving plans are available. AE, MC, V. **Amenities:** Restaurant; bar; bikes; all nonsmoking rooms. *In room:* A/C, beverage maker, safe, no phone.

Tarquynn Manor   Opening onto one of the loveliest stretches of Seven Mile Beach, this condo complex is a breezy, airy Caribbean place. The compound consists of two- or three-bedroom air-conditioned apartments, all of which are roomy and well furnished, with fully equipped kitchens. Even when you fill a unit with the six-person maximum, you'll find the large living area spacious. Each unit has a small bathroom with a shower stall and master bath with shower/tub.

West Bay Rd. (P.O. Box 30435), Grand Cayman, B.W.I. (C) 866/596-8367 in the U.S., or 345/945-4038. Fax 345/945-5062. www.tarquynn.com. 19 units. Winter US$325 up to 4 persons, US$475 up to 6 persons; off season US$260 up to 4 persons, US$295 up to 6 persons. DISC, MC, V. **Amenities:** Outdoor pool; coin-operated laundry; nonsmoking rooms; rooms for those with limited mobility. *In room:* A/C, TV, kitchen, data-port, hair dryer, safe.

DINING

Make sure you understand which currency the menu is printed in. If it's not written on the menu, ask the waiter if the prices are in U.S. dollars or Cayman Island dollars. It will make a big difference when you get your final bill, as each Cayman Island dollar is worth US$1.25. *Note:* Because virtually everything must be shipped in, Cayman Islands restaurants are among the most expensive in the Caribbean—even so-called moderate restaurants can quickly push you into the expensive category if you order steak or lobster. For the best value, opt instead for West Indian fare like conch and grouper, which are invariably less expensive.

Fewer and fewer restaurants offer turtle steak these days, although traditionally it's been the culinary delight of the Caymans. Today, if served at all, it appears in soup or stews but most often as turtle steak.

EXPENSIVE

Grand Old House *&&* AMERICAN/CARIBBEAN/PACIFIC RIM   This former plantation house lies amid venerable trees 2km (1¼ miles) south of George Town, past Jackson Point. Built on bedrock near the edge of the sea, it stands on 129 ironwood posts that support the main house and a bevy of gazebos. Chef Tell Erhardt put this restaurant on the Cayman culinary map, and it's often called Chef Tell's. And though the former TV celebrity chef is long gone, the Grand Old House has suffered no fallout in either food or service. The same menu has been slightly updated by the current chef, Indian-born Kandaphil Matahi. Appetizers remain the most delectable on the island, including coconut beer-battered shrimp and home-smoked marlin and salmon. Later, dig into the fresh seafood and lobster prepared in a coconut-flavored curry sauce with tropical chutney, or the Cayman-style turtle steak in a spicy tomato sauce.

Petra Plantation, S. Church St., George Town. (C) 345/949-9333. Reservations required. Main courses CI$19–CI$33 (US$24–US$41). AE, DISC, MC, V. Mon–Fri 11:45am–2pm; daily 6–9pm.

Hemingway's *&&* SEAFOOD/INTERNATIONAL   The finest seafood on the island can be found 3km (2 miles) north of George Town at Hemingway's, which is named after the novelist and inspired by Key West, his one-time residence. You can dine in the open air, with a view of the sea. The menu is among the most imaginative on the island and has won acclaim from *Gourmet* magazine. Appetizers include a tasty coconut shrimp with a mango marmalade accent. The catch of the day, perhaps snapper or wahoo, is grilled to your specification. You can also order pistachio-crusted lamb with baby artichokes, white beans, and crispy eggplant. Want something more imaginative? Try potato-crusted sea bass with banana, light cheese, salsa, and fresh pineapple.

In the Hyatt Regency Grand Cayman, West Bay Rd. (C) **345/949-1234.** Reservations required. Main courses CI$22–CI$29 (US$28–US$36); lunch CI$9.75–CI$15 (US$12–US$19). AE, DC, DISC, MC, V. Daily 11:30am–2:30pm and 6–10pm.

Lighthouse at Breakers ♠ CARIBBEAN/ITALIAN/SEAFOOD   On the south shore of the island, this local landmark lies about a 25-minute drive from George Town. Its creative menu features mainly fresh local seafood. A well-trained chef, backed up by a skilled staff, offers well-prepared meals, attracting both locals and visitors. Ask for a table with an ocean view and sit back to enjoy such tempting appetizers as portobello mushroom carpaccio with Gorgonzola, or tuna sushi rolled in sesame seeds. For your main course, opt for the tender veal chop topped with Gorgonzola and pancetta, or else a mixed seafood grill in a lemon-butter sauce. The pastas are good; fettuccine Mediterranean with seasonal vegetables is a particular favorite. The restaurant has one of the best wine cellars on island.

Breakers. (C) **345/947-2047.** Reservations recommended. Main courses CI$15–CI$40 (US$19–US$50). AE, DISC, MC, V. Daily 11:30am–4pm and 5:30–10pm.

Lobster Pot ♠ SEAFOOD/INTERNATIONAL   Though not as good as Hemingway's (see above), Lobster Pot is still an island favorite. It overlooks the water from its second-floor perch at the western perimeter of George Town, near what used to be Fort George. True to its name, it offers lobster prepared in many different ways: Cayman style, bisque, and salad. Conch schnitzel, turtle steak, and seafood curry are on the menu. Sometimes the seafood is a bit overcooked, but most dishes are right on the mark. The place is also known for its prime beef steaks. For lunch, you might like the English fish and chips or perhaps seafood jambalaya or a pasta. The Lobster Pot's wine bar is a pleasant place for a drink.

N. Church St., George Town. (C) **345/949-2736.** Reservations required in winter. Main courses CI$16–CI$32 (US$20–US$40). AE, MC, V. Mon–Fri 11:30am–2:30pm; daily 5–10pm.

Ottmar's Restaurant and Lounge ♠♠ INTERNATIONAL/FRENCH/CARIBBEAN   One of the island's top restaurants, Ottmar's is outfitted in a French Empire motif with lots of paneling, rich upholstery, and plenty of space between tables. There's a formal bar/lounge area decorated with deep-sea fishing trophies. This is the domain of an Austrian expatriate, Ottmar Weber, who has long abandoned the kitchen of his youth to roam the world, taking culinary inspiration wherever he finds it. The results are usually pleasing. The Indonesian *rijstafel* with seafood in a mild curry sauce comes as a delightful surprise, as does a dish called mahimahi Chapultapez, which originated with the Aztecs. It is a tender filet of fish stuffed with avocado purée, spinach, red and green peppers, mushrooms, and onions and baked with Monterey cheese. You can also order a Swiss cheese fondue or jumbo shrimp lightly poached in white wine with lobster sauce. Ottmar's offers a professional welcome and attentive service. Every Friday from 5:30 to 9:30pm is happy hour on the waterfront terrace, with live entertainment and free hors d'oeuvres, in addition to raffles for various prizes.

West Bay Rd. (side entrance of Grand Pavilion Commercial Centre). (C) **345/945-5879.** Reservations recommended. Main courses CI$19–CI$32 (US$24–US$40). AE, MC, V. Daily 6–11pm.

The Reef Grill at Royal Palms ♠♠♠ SEAFOOD   In the heart of Seven Mile Beach, this is one of the island's finest restaurants. Prepared from quality

ingredients, the cuisine has a distinctive flavor and is imaginatively presented. You dine under the stars, listening to some of the most talented local musicians playing soca and calypso. One of the helpful, experienced staff members will guide you through one of the Cayman's best wine lists.

The seafood chowder is memorable, as are several Japanese-inspired treats such as sticky rice sushi or raw slices of tuna. For a main dish, we've found the jerk pork tenderloin in a black-bean sauce with garlic mashed potatoes seductive, as was the tender lamb shank braised to perfection and beautifully seasoned.

In the Royal Palms. West Bay Rd. © 345/945-6358. Reservations required. Main courses CI$19–CI$34 (US$24–US$43). AE, DC, MC, V. Daily 6:30–10pm.

Ristorante Pappagallo 🐾 NORTHERN ITALIAN/SEAFOOD   One of the island's most memorable restaurants lies on a 6-hectare (15-acre) bird sanctuary overlooking a natural lagoon, 15 minutes north of George Town. Its designers incorporated Caymanian and Aztec weaving techniques in its thatched roof. Glass doors, black marble, and polished brass mix a kind of Edwardian opulence with a Tahitian decor. Inside, you'll see some of the most beautiful (caged) parrots on the island, separated from the dining and drinking area (for sanitary reasons) by plate-glass windows. Soups as appetizers are appealing, especially the lobster-and-scallop bisque in coconut cream or the carpaccio of raw beef with arugula. Pastas are full of flavor, especially the fettuccine with lemon grilled chicken and sun-dried tomatoes or the penne with homemade sausage. Fish and shellfish are well prepared, as exemplified by the Chilean sea bass, or you can opt for peppered West Indian pork tenderloin in an apple-bourbon sauce.

At Villas Pappagallo, Conch Point, Barkers. © 345/949-1119. Reservations required. Main courses CI$7–CI$31 (US$8.75–US$39). AE, MC, V. Daily 6–10pm. Drive 13km (8 miles) north of George Town to the northern terminus of West Bay Rd. and Spanish Cove.

Smuggler's Cove 🐾 INTERNATIONAL   Part of the charm of a meal here derives from the colored lights that flank the adjacent shoreline. The venue is airy, breezy, and ultracomfortable, and hundreds of financial, sports-industry, and music-industry folk have enjoyed the generous portions here since the place opened in the late 1990s. Some of the island's most enticing and imaginative dishes as well as old favorites are served here. The mesquite-grilled jerk duck served with a wild-berry sauce is remarkable. Also mesquite grilled is the catch of the day, a combination of two fresh Caribbean fish with two matching sauces. The grilled and spicy pork tenderloin comes marinated with Cayman Scotch Bonnet peppers, and the seared Chilean salmon filet comes in a crispy and flavorful potato-and-leek shell with a ginger drizzle and a hint of lemon grass. You'll recognize the place by the rows of blue neon that ring its facade, its mustard-colored patio, and its location at the edge of George Town. Many diners like to come here early to sample the bartender's special drink, a pineapple martini.

North Church St., George Town. © 345/949-6003. Reservations required. Main courses CI$18–CI$29 (US$23–US$36). AE, MC, V. Mon–Fri 11:30am–3:30pm and 5:30–10:30pm; Sat–Sun 5:30–10:30pm.

The Wharf 🐾 CARIBBEAN/CONTINENTAL   About 3km (2 miles) north of George Town, the 375-seat Wharf has been everything from a dinner theater to a nightclub. Try to catch the traditional 9pm feeding of the tarpon, which are kept in a large tank on the premises; it's quite a show. The restaurant is decorated in soft pastels and offers dining inside, out on an elevated veranda, and on a beachside terrace. The sound of the surf mingles with music from the strolling Paraguayan harpist and pan flute player and chatter from the Ports of Call Bar, located on the premises. Many diners begin with the blue crab–and-shrimp salad with cucumber and mango, or the golden-fried Caribbean lobster cake with a roasted-corn relish. Main dishes are a delight, especially the basil-and-pistachio-crusted sea bass in a creamy champagne sauce or the grilled turtle-and-lobster pie with rice and vegetables. A local favorite is the pork tenderloin Tortuga baked between sugar cane and served with a dark-rum sauce. The kitchen makes a laudable effort to break away from typical, dull menu items, and for the most part they succeed.

West Bay Rd. ℂ 345/949-2231. Reservations recommended. Main courses CI$20–CI$33 (US$25–US$41). AE, MC, V. Daily 6–10pm.

MODERATE

Cracked Conch by the Sea SEAFOOD   Long a culinary landmark, this popular restaurant near the famous turtle farm in West Bay serves some of the island's freshest seafood and some of the most succulent turtle steak in the Caymans, along with burgers, chicken, steaks, and even a vegetarian pasta of the day. The menu is one of the largest on the island and, of course, conch appears in various combinations. Foods are freshly prepared—nothing frozen. The decor is a bit corny, including a cement floor made to look like "authentic" wood planking from a pirate ship. There's also a patio bar overlooking the sea.

West Bay Rd., near Turtle Bay Farm. ℂ 345/945-5217. Reservations recommended. Main courses CI$18–CI$34 (US$23–US$43); Sun brunch CI$13 (US$16). AE, MC, V. Daily 11am–10pm; Sun brunch 11am–3pm.

Crow's Nest Restaurant ✦ Value CARIBBEAN   With a boardwalk and terrace jutting onto the sands, this informal restaurant has a view of both Sand Cay and a nearby lighthouse. It's on the island's southwestern-most tip, a 4-minute drive from George Town. The restaurant is one of those places that evokes the Caribbean "the way it used to be." There's no pretense here—you get good, honest Caribbean cooking. Try a daily special or perhaps sweet, tender Caribbean lobster. Other dishes include grilled tuna steak with ackee and Jamaican chicken curry with roast coconut. For dessert, try the banana-toffee pie, if it's available.

South Sound. ℂ 345/949-9366. Reservations recommended. Main courses CI$15–CI$28 (US$19–US$35). AE, DISC, MC, V. Daily 11:30am–3pm and 5:30–10pm.

The Tree House ✦ SEAFOOD/INTERNATIONAL   Likable and unpretentious, this restaurant is supported by poles and branches and lined with reeds and thatch rising into a peak. The bar area is accented with Trader Vic's–style artifacts and the garden, where many guests prefer to dine, is lined with palmettos and flowering shrubs. The chefs prepare one of the best selections of appetizers in the area, including fried calamari with a Key lime–and-guava cocktail sauce or Maryland shrimp and crab cakes. The kitchen applies itself earnestly to turning out such main dishes as the almond snapper served with a pesto and chile capellini cake or the Cuban pork tenderloin marinated in orange, lime, garlic, and fresh oregano.

North Church St. (near the corner of Eastern Ave.), George Town. ℂ 345/945-0155. Reservations recommended. Main courses CI$17–CI$33 (US$21–US$41). AE, MC, V. Daily 11am–10pm.

INEXPENSIVE

Corita's Copper Kettle ✦ Value CARIBBEAN/AMERICAN   This place is generally packed in the mornings, when you can enjoy a full American breakfast or a wide selection of West Indian breakfast specialties, like green bananas served with fried dumplings, fried flying fish, and Corita's Special (ham, melted cheese, egg, and fruit jelly all presented on a fried fritter). For lunch, the menu varies from salads to chicken and beef along with conch, turtle, or lobster prepared as burgers or served up in a hearty stew.

In Dolphin Center, Eastern Ave., George Town. (C) **345/949-7078**. Reservations required. Main courses CI$7–CI$14 (US$8.75–US$18); lunch CI$7–CI$8.50 (US$8.75–US$11). No credit cards. Mon–Sat 7am–5pm.

Mezza's INTERNATIONAL   Hip, breezy, and urban, this restaurant sits one floor above a landmark liquor store and microbrewery (Big Daddy's and the Old Dutch Brewery). Much of the beer produced at the brewery is sold within Mezza's. This is the kind of place that you might expect to find in South Beach, Miami. Mugs of Old Dutch beer come in at least six colors ranging from pale to dark amber. Lunches are simple, featuring steak sandwiches, burgers, Caesar salads, and seafood linguines. The dinner menu is more artful, with dishes that include sautéed shrimp with wine sauce and asparagus, grilled swordfish with papaya salsa, sautéed lobster with curry-flavored cream sauce, marinated conch, and fettuccine with jerk chicken.

West Bay Rd. (above Big Daddy's Liquor Store, a few steps south of Treasure Island Resort). (C) **345/ 949-8511**. Reservations recommended on Fri and Sat nights. Main courses CI$16–CI$23 (US$20–US$29). Daily 11am–10pm.

HITTING THE BEACH

One of the finest beaches in the Caribbean, Grand Cayman's **Seven Mile Beach** ✦✦✦, which begins north of George Town, has sparkling white sands rimmed with Australian pines and palms. (Technically, it's called West Bay Beach, but everybody just says Seven Mile Beach.) Although it's not actually 7 miles (11km) long, it is still a honey: 9km (5½ miles) of white, white sands stretching all the way to West Bay. It tends to be crowded near the big resorts, but the beach is so big you can always find some room to spread out your towel. There are no peddlers to hassle you, and the beach is beautifully maintained.

Because the beach is on the more tranquil side of Grand Cayman, there is no great tide and the water is generally placid and inviting, ideal for families, even those with small children. A sandy bottom slopes gently to deep water. The water's so clear that you can generally see what's swimming in it. It's great for snorkelers and swimmers of most ages and abilities.

From one end of the beach to the other, there are hotels and condos, many with beachside bars that you can visit. All sorts of watersports concessions can be found along this beach, including places that rent snorkel gear, boats, wind-surfers, wave runners, paddlecats, and aqua trikes. Parasailing and water-skiing are also available.

Grand Cayman also has a number of minor beaches, although they pale in comparison to Seven Mile Beach. Visit these if you want to escape the crowds. Beaches on the east and north coasts of Grand Cayman are good, filled with white sand and protected by an offshore barrier reef, so waters are generally tranquil.

One of our favorites is on the north coast, bordering the **Cayman Kai Beach Resort.** This beach is a Caribbean cliché of charm, with palm trees and beautiful sands, along with changing facilities. You can snorkel along the reef to Rum Point. The beach is also ideal as a Sunday-afternoon picnic spot. **Red Sail Sports** at Rum Point offers windsurfers, wave runners, sailboats, water-skiing, and even glass-bottom boat tours to see the stingrays offshore. It also offers scuba diving.

SPORTS & OTHER OUTDOOR PURSUITS

What they lack in nightlife, the Caymans make up for in watersports—the fishing, swimming, water-skiing, snorkeling, and especially diving are among the finest in the Caribbean. Coral reefs and coral formations encircle the islands and are filled with lots of marine life (which scuba divers and snorkelers are forbidden to disturb, by the way).

Tips Into the Deep: Submarine Dives

So scuba diving's not enough for you? You want to see the real undiscovered depths of the ocean? On Grand Cayman, you can take the *Atlantis* reef dive. It's expensive, but it's a unique way to go underwater—and it might be the highlight of your trip.

One of the island's most popular attractions is the ***Atlantis XI***, Goring Avenue, George Town (© **345/949-7700**), a submersible that's 20m (66 ft.) long, weighs 80 tons, and was built at a cost of US$3 million to carry 48 passengers. You can view the reefs and colorful tropical fish through the 26 large viewpoints .6m (2 ft.) in diameter, as it cruises at a depth of 30m (98 ft.) through the maze of coral gardens at a speed of 1½ knots; a guide keeps you informed.

There are two types of dives. The premier dive, *Atlantis* Odyssey, features such high-tech extras as divers moving about on underwater scooters. This dive costs US$96. On the *Atlantis* Expedition dive, operated both day and night, you'll experience the reef and see the famous Cayman Wall; this dive lasts 55 minutes and costs US$84. Children age 4 to 12 are charged half price (no children under age 4 allowed). *Atlantis XI* dives daily, and reservations are recommended 2 days in advance.

It's easy to dive close to shore, so boats aren't necessary, but there are plenty of boats and scuba facilities available. On certain excursions, we recommend a trip with a qualified dive master. There are many dive rental shops, but they won't rent you scuba gear or supply air unless you have a card from one of the national diving schools, such as NAUI or PADI. Hotels also rent diving equipment to their guests, as well as arrange snorkeling and scuba-diving trips.

Universally regarded as the most up-to-date and best-equipped watersports facility in the Cayman Islands, **Red Sail Sports** maintains its headquarters at the Hyatt Regency Grand Cayman, West Bay Road (© **877/REDSAIL** in the U.S., or 345/949-8745; www.redsailcayman.com). Other locations are at the Westin Casuarina (© **345/949-8732**) and at Rum Point (© **345/947-9203**). Red Sail has a wide range of offerings, from deep-sea fishing to sailing, diving, and more. Red Sail can also arrange water-skiing for US$75 per half-hour (the cost can be divided among several people) and parasailing at US$60 per ride.

The following are the best options for a gamut of outdoor activities.

CRUISES   **Red Sail Sports** (see above) has a number of inexpensive ways you can go sailing in Cayman waters, including a glass-bottom boat ride costing US$30 without snorkeling equipment or US$35 with snorkeling equipment. It also offers sunset cruises for US$30, and a 10am to 2pm sail to Stingray City, with snorkeling equipment and lunch included, for US$50 per person; children under 12 pay half price.

FISHING   Grouper and snapper are most plentiful for those who bottom-fish along the reef. Deeper waters turn up barracuda and bonito. Sport-fishers from all over the world come to the Caymans for the big ones: tuna, wahoo, and marlin. Most hotels can make arrangements for charter boats; experienced guides are also available. **Red Sail Sports** (see above) offers deep-sea-fishing excursions in search of tuna, marlin, and wahoo on a variety of air-conditioned vessels with an experienced crew. Tours depart at 7am and 1pm, last half a day, and cost US$500 (a full day costs US$700). The fee can be split among four to six people.

GOLF   The best course on the island, the **Britannia Golf Club,** next to the Hyatt Regency on West Bay Road (© **345/949-8020**), was designed by Jack Nicklaus and incorporates two different courses in one: a 9-hole championship layout, an 18-hole executive setup, and a Cayman course. The last was designed for play with the Cayman ball, which goes about half the distance of a regulation ball. Greens fees are a pricey US$110 for 18 holes, or US$70 for 9 holes. Cart rentals are included, but club rentals cost US$20 for 9 holes or US$40 for 18 holes.

Constantly windswept, the **Link at Safe Haven** (© **345/949-5988**) is a par-71, 6,605-yard course designed by Roy Case and set in what is tantamount to a botanical garden. On-site are a clubhouse, pro shop, and restaurant. Greens fees are US$120 per person for 18 holes, with mandatory golf carts included. The golf course lies across Seven Mile Beach Road, opposite from the Westin Casuarina.

HIKING   The **Mastic Trail** is a restored 200-year-old footpath through a 2-million-year-old woodland area in the heart of the island. The trail lies west of Frank Sound Road, about a 45-minute drive from the heart of George Town, and showcases the reserve's natural attractions, including a native mangrove swamp, traditional agriculture, and an ancient woodland area—home to the largest variety of native plant and animal life found in the Cayman Islands. Guided tours, lasting 2½ to 3 hours and limited to eight participants, are offered Monday to Saturday at 8:30am. Reservations are required, and the cost is US$45 per person. The hike is not recommended for children under 6, the elderly, or persons with physical disabilities. Wear comfortable, sturdy shoes and carry water and insect repellent. For reservations, call © **345/945-6588.** Pick-ups are from Seven Mile Beach and the Georgetown area.

SCUBA DIVING & SNORKELING 🐠🐠   The leading dive operation in the Cayman Islands is **Bob Soto's Diving Ltd.** (© **800/262-7686** in the U.S., or 345/949-2871 to make reservations). Owned by Ron Kipp, the operation includes a full-service dive shop at Treasure Island, the SCUBA Centre on North Church Street. A full-day resort course, designed to teach the fundamentals of scuba to beginners who know how to swim, costs US$100: The morning is spent in the pool, and the afternoon involves a one-tank dive from a boat. All necessary equipment is included. Certified divers can choose from a wide range of one-tank (US$50) and two-tank (US$85) boat dives daily on the west, north, and south walls, plus shore diving from the SCUBA Centre. A one-tank night dive costs US$55. Nondivers can take advantage of daily snorkel trips (US$30–US$50), including Stingray City. The staff is helpful and highly professional.

Red Sail Sports (see the introduction to this section) offers beginners' scuba diving as well as excursions for the experienced. A two-tank morning dive includes exploration of two different dive sites at depths ranging from 15m to 30m (49 ft.–98 ft.), and costs US$100. Beginners can take a daily course that costs US$140 per person. See also "Cruises," above, for information on Red Sail Sports snorkel cruises.

The offshore waters of Grand Cayman are home to one of the most unusual underwater attractions in the world, **Stingray City** 🐠🐠. Set in the sun-flooded, 4m-deep (13-ft.) waters of North Sound, about 3km (2 miles) east of the island's northwestern tip, the site originated in the mid-1980s when local fishers cleaned their catch and dumped the offal overboard. They quickly noticed scores of stingrays (which usually eat marine crabs) feeding on the debris, a phenomenon that quickly attracted local divers and marine zoologists. Today, between 30 and 50 relatively tame stingrays hover in the waters around the site for daily hand-outs of squid and ballyhoo from increasing hordes of snorkelers and divers. To capitalize on the phenomenon, about half a dozen entrepreneurs lead expeditions from points along Seven Mile Beach, traveling around the landmass of Conch Point to the feeding grounds. One well-known outfit is **Treasure Island Divers** (© 345/949-4456), which charges divers US$60 per one tank. Trips are made daily at 1pm. (Be warned that stingrays possess deeply penetrating and viciously barbed stingers capable of inflicting painful damage to anyone who mistreats them. Above all, the divers say, never try to grab one by the tail. Despite the potential dangers, divers and snorkelers seem amazingly adept at feeding, petting, and stroking the velvet surfaces of these batlike creatures while avoiding unpleasant incidents.)

You'll find plenty of concessions offering snorkel gear for rent along Seven Mile Beach. The snorkeling is great in the clear, warm waters here. Other popular sites are Parrot's Reef and Smith's Cove, south of George Town. Lush reefs abound with parrot fish, coral, sea fans, and sponges. Also great for snorkelers is Turtle Farm Reef, a short swim from shore, with a miniwall rising from a sandy bottom.

Another good dive outfit, **Tortuga Divers** (© 345/947-2097), operates out of Morritt's Tortuga Club and Resort at East End. This outfitter caters to both experienced and novice divers, offering daily dives at 9am and 2pm. Half-day or full-day snorkeling adventures can also be arranged at the same time, and all types of gear are available for rent. The morning two-tank scuba dive costs US$100, the afternoon one-tank dive goes for US$60. A half-day's snorkeling costs US$50, going up to US$75 for a full day, the price including lunch.

TENNIS   Courts are available to the public at the **South Sound Squash Club,** South Sound Road, George Town (© 345/949-9469). Hours can vary, so call ahead before coming here.

WINDSURFING   The best place for windsurfing on the island is the beach-front resort of **Morritt's Tortuga Club & Resort** at the East End (© 345/947-7449). Surfing conditions here are ideal. The cost is US$35 for 1 hour, US$75 for 3 hours, and US$115 for 5 hours. Lessons are also available for US$45 for 1 hour. There's a large protected reef here opening onto a big lagoon.

EXPLORING THE ISLAND

The capital, **George Town,** can easily be explored in an afternoon; stop by for its restaurants and shops (and banks!)—not sights. The town does have a clock monument to King George V and the post office on Edward Street is the oldest government building in use in the Caymans. Stamps sold here are collected avidly.

The island's premier museum, the **Cayman Islands National Museum,** Harbor Drive, in George Town (© 345/949-8368), is in a much-restored clapboard-sided antique building directly on the water. (The veranda-fronted building served as the island's courthouse until recently.) The formal exhibits include a collection of Caymanian artifacts collected by Ira Thompson beginning in the 1930s. Today the museum incorporates a gift shop, theater, cafe, and more than 2,000 items portraying the natural, social, and cultural history of the Caymans. Admission is CI$4 (US$5) for adults and CI$2 (US$2.50) for children age 7 to 12 and seniors, free for children 6 and under. It's open Monday to

Friday from 9am to 5pm and on Saturday from 10am to 2pm (last admission is 30 min. before closing).

You might also go to **Hell!** At the north end of West Bay Beach is a jagged piece of rock named Hell by a former commissioner. There the postmistress will stamp "Hell, Grand Cayman" on your postcard to send back to the U.S.

Cayman Turtle Farm ⚘, Northwest Point (© **345/949-3893**), is the only green-sea-turtle farm of its kind in the world. Once the islands had a multitude of turtles in the surrounding waters (which is why Columbus called the islands "Las Tortugas"), but today these creatures are sadly few in number, and the green sea turtle has been designated an endangered species (you cannot bring turtle products into the United States). The turtle farm exists to provide the local market with edible turtle meat (preventing the need to hunt them in the wild) and to replenish the waters with hatchling and yearling turtles. Visitors today can observe 100 circular concrete tanks in which these sea creatures exist in every stage of development; the hope is that one day their population in the sea will regain its former status. Turtles here range in size from 6 ounces to 600 pounds. At a snack bar and restaurant, you can sample turtle dishes. The turtle farm is open daily from 8:30am to 5pm. Admission is CI$4.80 (US$6) for adults, CI$2.40 (US$3) for children 7 to 12, free for children 6 and under.

At **Batabano,** on the North Sound, fishers tie up with their catch, much to the delight of photographers. You can buy lobster (in season), fresh fish, and conch. A large barrier reef protects the sound, which is surrounded on three sides by the island and is a mecca for diving and sport-fishing.

If you're driving, you might want to go along **South Sound Road,** which is lined with pines and, in places, old wooden Caymanian houses. After leaving the houses behind, you'll find good spots for a picnic.

Pedro St. James National Historic Site, Savannah (© **345/947-3329**), is a restored great house dating from 1780, when only 400 people lived on the island. It lasted until 1970, when it was destroyed by fire. Now rebuilt, it is the centerpiece of a new heritage park with a visitor center and an audiovisual theater with a laser light show. Because of its size, the great house was called "the Castle" by generations of Caymanians. Its primary historic importance dates from December 5, 1831, when residents met here to elect Cayman's first legislative assembly. The great house sits atop a limestone bluff with a panoramic view of the sea. Guests enter via a US$1.5 million visitor center with a landscaped courtyard, a gift shop, and a cafe. Self-guided tours are possible. You can explore the house's wide verandas, rough-hewn timber beams, gabled framework, mahogany floors and staircases, and wide-beam wooden ceilings. Guides in 18th-century costumes are on hand to answer questions. Admission is CI$6.40 (US$8) for adults, CI$3.20 (US$4) for children, and free for those age 6 and under. Hours are daily from 9am to 5pm. Tours are from 10am to 4pm

On the road again, you reach **Bodden Town,** once the largest settlement on the island. At Gun Square, two cannons commanded the channel through the reef. They are now stuck muzzle-first into the ground.

On the way to **East End,** just before Old Isaac Village, you'll see the onshore sprays of water shooting up like geysers. These are called blowholes, and they sound like the roar of a lion.

Later, you'll spot the fluke of an anchor sticking up from the ocean floor. As the story goes, this is a relic of the famous "Wreck of the Ten Sails" in 1788. A more recent wreck can also be seen—the *Ridgefield,* a 7,500-ton Liberty ship from New England, which struck the reef in 1943.

Old Man Bay is reached by a road that opened in 1983. From here you can travel along the north shore of the island to **Rum Point,** which has a good beach and is a fine place to end your island tour. Rum Point got its name from barrels of rum that once washed ashore here after a shipwreck. Today, it is dreamy and quaint, surrounded by towering casuarina trees blowing in the trade winds. Hammocks hang from many of these trees' trunks, inviting you to enjoy the leisurely life. With its cays, reefs, mangroves, and shallows, Rum Point is a refuge that extends west and south for 11km (6¾ miles). It divides the two "arms" of Grand Cayman. The sound's many spits of land and its plentiful lagoons are ideal for snorkeling, swimming, wading, and birding. It you get hungry, drop in to the Wreck Bar for a juicy burger. After visiting Rum Point, you can head back toward **Old Man Village,** where you can go south along a cross-island road through savanna country that will eventually lead you west to George Town.

On 24 hectares (59 acres) of rugged wooded land off Frank Sound Road, North Side, the **Queen Elizabeth II Botanic Park** ✿ (© 345/947-3558) offers visitors a short walk through wetland, swamp, dry thicket, mahogany trees, orchids, and bromeliads. The trail is 1km (.6 mile) long. You'll probably see chickatees, which are freshwater turtles found only on the Caymans and in Cuba. Occasionally you'll spot the rare Grand Cayman parrot, or perhaps the anole lizard, with its cobalt-blue throat pouch. Even rarer is the endangered blue iguana. The park is open daily from 9am to 4:30pm. Admission is CI$6 (US$7.50) for adults, CI$4 (US$5) for children 6 and over, and free for children 5 and under. There's a visitor center with changing exhibitions, plus a canteen for food and refreshments. It's set in a botanic park adjacent to the woodland trail and includes a heritage garden with a re-creation of a traditional Cayman home, garden, and farm; a floral garden with .6 hectares (1½ acres) of flowering plants; and a .8-hectare (2-acre) lake with three islands, home to many native birds.

GRAND CAYMAN AFTER DARK

Lone Star Bar & Grill, West Bay Road (© 345/945-5175), is a transplanted corner of the Texas Panhandle. You can enjoy juicy burgers in the dining room or head immediately for the bar in back. Here, beneath murals of Lone Star beauties, you can sip lime and strawberry margaritas and watch several sports events simultaneously on 15 different TV screens. Monday and Thursday are fajita nights, all-you-can-eat affairs, at CI$13 (US$16), and Tuesday is all-you-can-eat lobster, at CI$38 (US$48).

Legendz, West Bay Road (© 345/945-1950), is a good lounge bar with mahogany paneling, polished brass, stiff drinks, and lots of good-looking and available clients of both genders. Another good spot is the **Royal Palms Beach Club,** West Bay Road (© 345/945-6358), offering a bar open to the trade winds where you can dance the night away in the moonlight. Local bands play here Thursday, Friday, and Saturday nights.

3 Cayman Brac ✦

The "middle" island of the Caymans was given the name *Brac* (Gaelic for "bluff") by 17th-century Scottish fishers who settled here. The bluff for which the 19km-long (12-mile) island was named is a towering limestone plateau rising 42m (138 ft.) above the sea, covering the eastern half of Cayman Brac. Caymanians refer to the island simply as Brac, and its 1,400 inhabitants, a hospitable bunch, are known as Brackers. In the early 18th century the Caymans were occupied by pirates, and Edward Teach, the infamous Blackbeard, is supposed

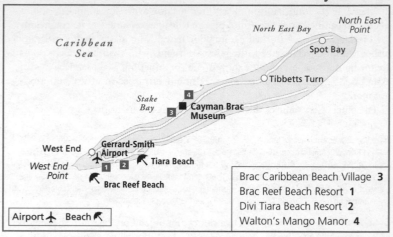

to have spent quite a bit of time around Cayman Brac. The island is about 143km (89 miles) east of Grand Cayman.

There are more than 170 caves honeycombing the limestone heights of the island. Some of the caves are at the bluff's foot; others can be reached only by climbing over jagged limestone rock. One of the biggest is Great Cave, which has a number of chambers. Harmless fruit bats cling to the roofs of the caverns.

On the south side of the bluff you won't see many people, and the only sounds are the sea crashing against the lavalike shore. The island's herons and wild green parrots are seen here. Most of the Brackers live on the north side, many in traditional wooden seaside cottages, some built by the island's pioneers. Given the variety of flowers, shrubs, and fruit trees in many of the yards, the islanders must all have green thumbs. You'll see poinciana trees, bougainvillea, Cayman orchids, croton, hibiscus, aloe, sea grapes, cactus, and coconut and cabbage palms. Gardeners grow cassava, pumpkins, breadfruit, yams, and sweet potatoes.

There are no actual towns, only settlements, such as Stake Bay (the "capital"), Spot Bay, the Creek, Tibbitts Turn, the Bight, and West End, where the airport is.

ESSENTIALS

GETTING THERE   Flights from Grand Cayman to Cayman Brac are operated by **Cayman Airways** (© **800/422-9626** in the U.S., or 345/949-2311; www.caymanairways.com). The airline uses relatively large 737 jets carrying 122 passengers each. On Friday through Monday there is an evening flight here leaving at 5:30pm, plus a morning return at 6:30am. The round-trip cost is US$107 to US$141 per person and requires a 3-day advance purchase.

VISITOR INFORMATION   A little office, the **Cayman Brac Tourist Office,** has opened at West End Community Park (© **345/948-1649**). If you're stopping in, call first to see if anybody's going to be there.

EMERGENCIES   There's a small hospital, the 18-bed **Faith Hospital** (© **345/ 948-2243**).

ACCOMMODATIONS

Brac Caribbean Beach Village ⍟   The largest condo project on the island offers 16 bright, spacious one-bedroom/two-bathroom or two-bedroom/three-bathroom condos on a white-sand beach, along with a pool and scuba-diving program. Each unit has a full-size refrigerator with an icemaker and a microwave, and 12 units open onto private balconies. A variety of items, including breakfast food, are stocked before your arrival. The master bedroom is furnished with a queen-size bed, the guest bedrooms with twin beds. Bathrooms are medium in size, each with a shower/tub combination. Maid service costs an extra US$35 per day. The units are rather simply furnished in a Caribbean tropical motif.

The hotel offers some of the best dining on the island, at the Captain's Table (see below).

Stake Bay (P.O. Box 4), Cayman Brac, B.W.I. © 800/866-THEBRAC in the U.S., or 345/948-2265. Fax 345/948-1111. www.866thebrac.com. 16 units. Winter US$185 apt for 2, US$245 apt for 4; weekly rates US$1,100 apt for 2, US$1,600 apt for 4. Off season US$139 apt for 2, US$149 apt for 4; weekly rates US$825 apt for 2, US$1,200 apt for 4. Dive packages from US$849 per person double occupancy, including 7 nights stay and 5 days of 2-tank dives. AE, MC, V. **Amenities:** Restaurant; bar; outdoor pool; snorkeling; coin-operated laundry; nonsmoking rooms. *In room:* A/C, ceiling fans, TV, kitchen, beverage maker.

Brac Reef Beach Resort 🐟
On a sandy plot of land on the south shore 3km (2 miles) east of the airport, near some of the best snorkeling in the region, this resort contains motel-style units comfortably furnished with carpeting, ceiling fans, air-conditioning, and shower/tub combination bathrooms. This is a durable resort, although frankly you'd be better housed at Walton's Mango Manor (see below) or Brac Caribbean Beach Village (see above). Once the location was little more than a maze of sea grapes, a few of whose venerable trunks still rise amid the picnic tables, hammocks, and boardwalks. There are still lots of nature trails surrounding the resort, good for bird-watching. On the premises are the rusted remains of a Russian lighthouse tower that was retrieved several years ago from a Cuban-made trawler.

Lunches are informal affairs, and dinners are most often served buffet style under the stars. The food is not quite as good as that at the Divi Tiara (see below).

P.O. Box 56, Cayman Brac, B.W.I. © 800/594-0843 in the U.S. and Canada, or 345/948-1323. www.bracreef.com. 40 units. Winter US$483 double for 3 nights; off season US$416 double for 3 nights. Rates include MAP (breakfast and dinner). Dive packages available. AE, MC, V. **Amenities:** Restaurant; bar; outdoor pool; tennis court; day spa; Jacuzzi; dive shop; kayaks; reef fishing; snorkeling; bikes; island tours; babysitting; laundry service; all nonsmoking rooms. *In room:* A/C, ceiling fans, TV, hair dryer.

Divi Tiara Beach Resort 🐟
Part of the Divi Divi hotel chain, the Tiara, about 4.8km (3 miles) east of the airport, has a white-sand beachfront. Its well-regarded dive operation makes it an excellent choice for divers. The striking landscaping incorporates croton, bougainvillea, and palms. All the rather basic accommodations are housed in motel-like outbuildings; 13 of the units are timeshares, each with an ocean view, Jacuzzi, and a king-size bed. Bathrooms, with combination tubs and showers, are well maintained.

At the bar, guests gaze out to sea while sipping their drinks. The Poseidon dining room serves good Caribbean and American cuisine. Most meals are buffet.

P.O. Box 238, Cayman Brac, B.W.I. © 800/367-3484 in the U.S. and Canada, or 345/948-1553. Fax 345/948-1657. www.divitiara.com. 71 units. Winter US$135–US$211 double; off season US$101–US$158 double. Children under 12 stay free in parent's room. MAP (breakfast and dinner) US$46 per person extra. AE, MC, V. **Amenities:** Restaurant; bar; outdoor pool; tennis court; sauna; dive shop; free bikes; limited room service; coin-operated laundry; nonsmoking rooms; rooms for those with limited mobility. *In room:* A/C, TV, dataport, beverage maker, hair dryer, safe.

Walton's Mango Manor 🐟🐟
Unique on Cayman Brac, this is a personalized, intimate B&B that's more richly decorated, more elegant, and more appealing

than you might have thought possible in such a remote place. Originally the home of a sea captain, it was moved to a less exposed location and rebuilt from salvaged materials shortly after the disastrous hurricane of 1932. Set on 1 hectare (2½ acres) on the island's north shore, within a lush garden, it contains intriguing touches such as a banister salvaged from the mast of a 19th-century schooner. The best accommodations are on the upper floor and have narrow balconies that offer views of the sea. Each room has a small bathroom equipped with a shower stall. Recently added is a two-bedroom, two-bathroom luxury villa, the perfect getaway for two to four guests. Your hosts are Brooklyn-born Lynne Walton and her husband, George, a former USAF major who retired to his native Cayman Brac.

Stake Bay (P.O. Box 56), Cayman Brac, B.W.I. ℂ and fax 345/948-0518. www.waltonsmangomanor.com. 6 units. Winter US$90–US$100 double; off season US$80–US$90 double. Year-round villa US$185 daily or US$1,200 weekly. Rates include full breakfast. AE, MC, V. *In room:* A/C, no phone.

DINING

With the exception of a handful of local eateries, there aren't any major restaurants outside of the hotels on Cayman Brac. Most guests dine at their hotels in the evening.

Captain's Table AMERICAN   The decor here is vaguely nautical, with oars over and around the bar and pieces of boats forming the restaurant's entryway. The restaurant offers both indoor air-conditioned seating and outdoor poolside dining. Begin with shrimp and lobster cocktail or a conch fritter, and then try one of the soups, such as black bean. Main dishes include everything from the catch of the day, often served pan-fried, to barbecue ribs. Lunch features burgers and sandwiches.

In Brac Caribbean Beach Village, Stake Bay. ℂ 345/948-1418. Reservations recommended. Main courses CI$15–CI$25 (US$19–US$31); lunch from CI$9 (US$11). AE, MC, V. Mon–Sat 11:30am–3pm and 6–10pm; Sun noon–3pm and 6–10pm.

FUN ON & OFF THE BEACH

The biggest lure to Cayman Brac is the variety of **watersports**—swimming, fishing, snorkeling, and some of the world's best diving. There are undersea walls on both the north and south sides of the island, with stunning specimens lining their sides. The big attraction for divers is the **MV *Tibbetts,*** a 99m-long (325-ft.) Russian frigate resting in 30m (98 ft.) of water, a relic of the Cold War sunk in September of 1996. Hatches into the ship have been barred off to ensure diver safety. Marine life is becoming more pronounced on this relic, which now rests in a watery grave far, far from its home. The best dive center is **Dive Tiara** at the Divi Tiara Beach Resort (ℂ **800/367-3484** in the U.S., or 345/948-1553).

History buffs might check out the **Cayman Brac Museum,** in the former Government Administration Building, Stake Bay (ℂ **345/948-2622**), which has an interesting collection of Caymanian antiques, including pieces rescued from shipwrecks and items from the 18th century. Hours are Monday to Friday from 9am to noon and 1 to 4pm, Saturday from 9am to noon, and Sunday from 1 to 4pm. Admission is free, but donations are accepted.

4 Little Cayman ⁂

The smallest of the Cayman Islands, cigar-shaped Little Cayman has only about 170 permanent inhabitants. About 16km (10 miles) long and 2km (1¼ miles) across at its widest point, it lies about 121km (75 miles) northeast of Grand

Cayman and some 8km (5 miles) from Cayman Brac. The entire island is coral and sand.

The islands of the Caymans are mountaintops of the long-submerged Sierra Maestra Range, which runs north and into Cuba. Coral formed layers over the underwater peaks, eventually creating the islands. Beneath Little Cayman's Bloody Bay is one of the mountain's walls—a stunning sight for snorkelers and divers.

This is a near-perfect place for diving and fishing. The late Jacques Cousteau hailed the waters around the little island as one of the three finest diving spots in the world. The flats on Little Cayman are said to offer the best bonefishing in the world, and a brackish inland pool can be fished for tarpon. Even if you don't dive or fish, you can row 182m (597 ft.) off Little Cayman to isolated and uninhabited Owen Island, where you can swim at the sandy beach and picnic by a blue lagoon.

There may still be pirate treasure buried on the island, but it's in the dense interior of what is now the largest bird sanctuary in the Caribbean. In addition to having the largest population of rock iguanas in the entire Caribbean, which you will easily see, Little Cayman is also home to one of the oldest species of reptiles in the New World—the tree-climbing *Anulis maynardi* (which is known by no other name). This rare lizard is difficult to spot, however, because the females are green, the males brown, and, as such, they blend into local vegetation.

Blossom Village, the island's "capital," is on the southwest coast.

Most visitors fly from Grand Cayman to Little Cayman via **Island Air** (© **345/949-5252** on Grand Cayman; www.islandaircayman.com), a charter company that charges US$170 per person round-trip. Flights leave Grand Cayman four times daily, at 7:45am, 9:45am, 2:35pm, and 4:35pm. The return flights are scheduled daily at 8:55am, 10:30am, 3:20pm, and 5:45pm.

ACCOMMODATIONS

Little Cayman Beach Resort 🎦🎦   Lying on the south coast, this resort is close to many of the island's diving and sporting attractions, including bonefishing in the South Hole Sound Lagoon. It's popular with anglers, divers, birdwatchers, and adventurous types. The hotel, owned by Dan Tibbetts, lies only .4km (¼ mile) from the Edward Bodden Airport (really a grass airstrip), and it has a white-sand beach fringing a shallow, reef-protected bay. The rooms occupy two pastel, coral, two-story buildings with gingerbread trim. The most desirable units are the four luxurious oceanfront rooms, which go fast, since they cost the same as the others despite their added comfort. Ceiling fans and tropical colors make for an inviting, airy atmosphere, and units have one king-size or two double beds, plus a combination bathroom (tub and shower).

Blossom Village, Little Cayman, B.W.I. © **800/327-3835** in the U.S. and Canada, or 345/948-1033. Fax 345/948-1040. www.littlecayman.com. 40 units. Winter US$169–US$243 double; off season US$133–US$206 double. MAP (breakfast and dinner) US$54 per person extra. 3-night dive packages: winter US$663–US$797 per person; off season US$596–US$730 per person. Package rates include MAP. Longer packages available. AE, DC, MC, V. **Amenities:** Restaurant; bar; outdoor pool; tennis court; health club; spa; Jacuzzi; sauna; fishing; scuba diving; snorkeling; bike rental; game room; babysitting; laundry service; all nonsmoking rooms. *In room:* A/C, ceiling fan, TV, kitchenette, beverage maker, hair dryer, safe, no phone.

Pirates Point Resort, Ltd. 🎦   For watersports or just relaxing, this resort near West End Point offers a family environment with gourmet cuisine, although it's a notch down from Little Cayman Beach Resort. The place has remodeled rooms with fresh paint and new linens, and a non-air-conditioned family cottage with two spacious bedrooms. In addition, it has four seaside

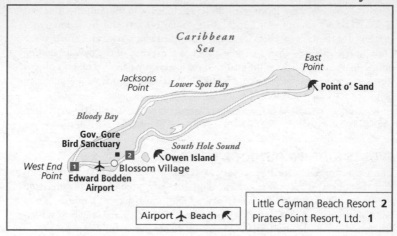

Airport ✈ Beach ⚓

Little Cayman Beach Resort **2**
Pirates Point Resort, Ltd. **1**

cottages, with balconies overlooking Preston Bay. The bathrooms are well maintained, with shower stalls.

The resort's packages include room, three excellent meals per day with appropriate wines and all alcoholic beverages, and two-tank boat dives daily, featuring tours of the Bloody Bay Wall and Jackson Reef. Other activities include snorkeling, bird-watching, off-island picnicking, and exploring.

Acclaimed as the island's finest chef, the owner and manager, Gladys Howard, is a graduate of Cordon Bleu in Paris and has studied with such stars as Julia Child and the late James Beard. She uses fresh fruits and vegetables grown locally, as well as local seafood. Her well-crafted menu changes daily.

Preston Bay, Little Cayman, B.W.I. (ℂ) **345/948-1010.** Fax 345/948-1011. www.piratespointresort.com. 11 units. Winter US$260 per person double (diver), US$195 per person double (nondiver); off season US$240 per person double (diver), US$180 per person double (nondiver). Rates are all-inclusive (nondiver rates do not include bar tab); triple rates are slightly lower. DISC, MC, V. No children under 5. **Amenities:** Restaurant; bar; outdoor pool; Jacuzzi; sauna; diving; fishing; snorkeling; coin-operated laundry; rooms for those with limited mobility. *In room:* A/C (in some), no phone.

DINING

Birds of Paradise AMERICAN/CONTINENTAL This spot caters primarily to Little Cayman Beach Resort guests but welcomes anyone. The specialty is buffet-style dinners—the kind your parents might have enjoyed back in the 1950s or '60s. Saturday night features the island's most generous barbecue spread—all the ribs, fish, and Jamaican-style jerk chicken you'd want. On other nights, try the prime rib, fresh fish Caribbean style (your best bet), or chicken either Russian style (Kiev) or French style (cordon bleu). There's a freshly made salad bar, and homemade desserts are yummy, especially the Key lime pie. At night, opt for an outdoor table under the stars.

At Little Cayman Beach Resort. (ℂ) **345/948-1033.** Reservations recommended for dinner. Dinner CI$34 (US$43); lunch CI$16 (US$20); breakfast CI$12 (US$15). AE, MC, V. Daily 7–8:30am, 12:30–1:30pm, and 6:30–8pm.

The Hungry Iguana AMERICAN/CARIBBEAN At the beach, you'll spot this place immediately with its mammoth iguana mural. The island's tastiest dishes are served here, a winning combination of standard American fare along with some zesty flavors from the islands south of here. It's the rowdiest place on the island, especially the sports bar with its satellite TV in the corner, with a sort of TGI Friday's atmosphere. Lunch is the usual burgers and fries along with some well-stuffed sandwiches. We prefer the grilled chicken salad. Dinner gets a little more elaborate—there's usually a special meat dish of the day, depending on the market (supplies are shipped in once a week by barge). The chef always seems willing to prepare a steak as you like it. Marinated conch with homemade chips is a tasty choice as well.

Paradise Resort. © 345/948-0007. Reservations recommended. Dinner CI$15–CI$25 (US$19–US$31); lunch CI$5–CI$13 (US$6.25–US$16). AE, MC, V. Daily noon–2:30pm and 5:30–9pm. Bar open Mon–Fri noon–1am, Sat–Sun noon–midnight.

SPORTS & OTHER OUTDOOR PURSUITS

The **Governor Gore Bird Sanctuary** 𝘈 is home to some 5,000 pairs of red-footed boobies. As far as it is known, this is the largest colony of such birds in the Western Hemisphere. The sanctuary, which is near the small airport, is also home to dramatic colonies of snowy egrets and black frigates. Many bird-watchers from the U.S. fly into Little Cayman just to see these bird colonies.

The best **fishing** is at Bloody Bay, lying off the island's north coast. It is especially noted for its bonefishing and tarpon catches. For fishing, contact **Sam McCoy's Diving and Fishing Lodge** (© 800/626-0496).

The **Bloody Bay Wall** 𝘈𝘈 is also the best dive site on island, lying just 20 minutes offshore and reached by boat. The drop here begins at only 6m (20 ft.) but plunges to more than 360m (1,181 ft.). This is one of the great dive spots in the Caymans. For more information about how to enjoy it, call **Paradise Divers** at © 877/322-9626 in the U.S., or 345/948-0001.

Curaçao

Curaçao (Coo-ra-*sow*), together with Bonaire, St. Eustatius, St. Maarten, and Saba, is in the Kingdom of the Netherlands as part of the Netherlands Antilles. Just 56km (35 miles) north of the coast of Venezuela, Curaçao, the "C" of the Caribbean's Dutch ABC (Aruba, Bonaire, and Curaçao) islands, is the most populous of the Netherlands Antilles. Visitors come for its distinctive culture, warm people, duty-free shopping, lively casinos, and watersports. Fleets of tankers head out from its harbor to bring refined oil to all parts of the world. If you want grand high-rise resorts on spectacular beaches, head for Aruba (see chapter 5). Curaçao has a few middle-bracket resorts on the beach, mostly along the island's southern coast, but we've always found the shopping and cultural experiences here more appealing than the beaches.

A self-governing part of the Netherlands, Curaçao was spotted not by Columbus, but by Alonso de Ojeda and Amerigo Vespucci, in 1499. The Spaniards exterminated all but 75 members of a branch of the peaceful Arawaks. However, they in turn were ousted by the Dutch in 1634, who also had to fight off French and English invasions.

The Dutch made the island a tropical Holland in miniature. Pieter Stuyvesant ruled Curaçao in 1644. The island was turned into a Dutch

Gibraltar, bristling with forts. Thick ramparts guarded the harbor's narrow entrance; the hilltop forts (many now converted into restaurants) protected the coastal approaches.

In the 20th century, Curaçao remained sleepy until 1915, when the Royal Dutch/Shell Company built one of the world's largest oil refineries here to process crude oil from Venezuela. Workers from some 50 countries poured onto the island, turning Curaçao into a multicultural, cosmopolitan community.

The largest of the Netherlands Antilles, Curaçao is 60km-long (37-miles) and 11km (6¾ miles) across at its widest point. Because of all that early Dutch building, Curaçao is the most important island architecturally in the entire West Indies, with more European flavor than anywhere else. After leaving the capital, **Willemstad,** you plunge into a strange, desertlike countryside that evokes the U.S. Southwest. The relatively arid landscape is studded with three-pronged cactus, spiny-leafed aloe, and divi-divi trees, with their windblown foliage. Classic Dutch-style windmills are scattered in and around Willemstad and in parts of the countryside. Curaçao has its own governmental authority, relying on the Netherlands only for defense and foreign affairs. Its population of 171,000 represents more than 50 nationalities.

1 Essentials

VISITOR INFORMATION
In the United States, contact the **Curaçao Tourist Board** at 7951 SW. 6th St., Suite 216, Plantation, FL 33324 (© **800/3-CURACAO**). You can also point your Web browser to **www.curacao-tourism.com**.

Once you're on the island, go to the **Curaçao Tourist Board,** Pietermaai 19 (© **599/9-434-8200**).

GETTING THERE
The air routes to **Curaçao International Airport,** Plaza Margareth Abraham (© **599/9-888-0101**), are firmly linked to those leading to nearby Aruba. In recent years, however, some airlines have initiated direct or nonstop routings into Curaçao from such international hubs as Miami.

American Airlines (© **800/433-7300** in the U.S.; www.aa.com) offers a daily nonstop flight to Curaçao from Miami; it departs late enough in the day to permit easy connections from cities all over the northeastern U.S. American also offers flights to Curaçao's neighbor, Aruba, from New York, Miami, and San Juan, Puerto Rico. Once on Aruba, many travelers transfer on to Curaçao on any of Antillean Airline's (ALM's) many shuttle flights. American Airlines also offers discounted hotel/airfare packages. The regional affiliate of American Airlines, **American Eagle,** flies from San Juan to Curaçao via Aruba.

Air DCA (© **800/327-7230** in the U.S.; www.flydca.net) flies several flights per week from Atlanta and Miami to Curaçao. Although some of these flights stop on Aruba, Bonaire, or Haiti, the others are nonstop. Some travelers take a British Airways flight to Amsterdam, where they connect on a daily KLM flight to Curaçao.

GETTING AROUND
BY RENTAL CAR   Because all points of interest on Curaçao are easily accessible via paved roads, you may want to rent a car. U.S., British, and Canadian visitors can use their own licenses, if valid. *Note:* Traffic moves on the right. International road signs are observed.

Avis (© **800/331-1212** in the U.S., or 800/228-0668 in Curaçao; www.avis.com) and **Budget** (© **800/472-3325;** www.budgetrentacar.com) offer some of the lowest rates. Budget usually offers the best deal if it has compact cars with manual transmissions in stock. **Hertz** (© **800/654-3131** in the U.S., or 599/9-868-1182 on Curaçao; www.hertz.com) is also on island. Rentals are cheaper if you reserve from North America at least a week before your departure, and rates vary depending on the various times of the year and seasonal promotions.

Fun Fact Special Events
The big event of the year is the **Curaçao Carnival,** which starts on New Year's Day, with various festivities extending until the day before Ash Wednesday. The schedule is available at the tourism office. The most fun events, similar to hoedowns, are called "jump-ups." The highlight of carnival is the **Festival di Tumba,** the second week in February, in which the island's musicians vie for prizes in a hot contest. Other carnival events include the crowning of a queen and king, street parades, concerts, and even a children's carnival.

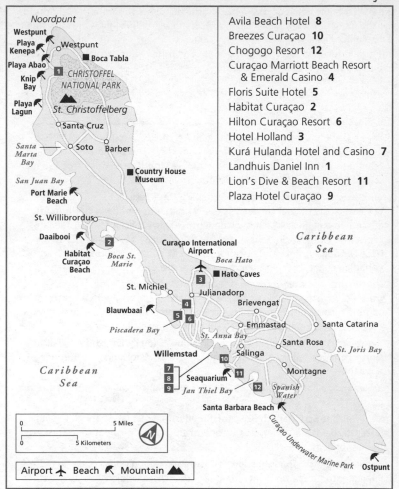

Noordpunt

Westpunt
Playa Kenepa
Westpunt
Boca Tabla
Playa Abao
Knip Bay
1 CHRISTOFFEL NATIONAL PARK
Playa Lagun
St. Christoffelberg
Santa Cruz
Santa Marta Bay
Soto
Barber
San Juan Bay
Country House Museum
Port Marie Beach
St. Willibrordus
Daaibooi
2
Habitat Curaçao Beach
Boca St. Marie
Curaçao International Airport
Boca Hato
Hato Caves
St. Michiel
3
Julianadorp
Brievengat
4
Blauwbaai
5 **6**
Piscadera Bay
Emmastad
Santa Catarina
St. Anna Bay
Santa Rosa
Santa Barbara Beach
Willemstad
Salinga
Montagne
St. Joris Bay
7
8
10
Seaquarium
11
9
Jan Thiel Bay
12
Spanish Water
Santa Barbara Beach
Curaçao Underwater Marine Park
Ostpunt

Caribbean Sea
Caribbean Sea

Avila Beach Hotel **8**
Breezes Curaçao **10**
Chogogo Resort **12**
Curaçao Marriott Beach Resort & Emerald Casino **4**
Floris Suite Hotel **5**
Habitat Curaçao **2**
Hilton Curaçao Resort **6**
Hotel Holland **3**
Kurá Hulanda Hotel and Casino **7**
Landhuis Daniel Inn **1**
Lion's Dive & Beach Resort **11**
Plaza Hotel Curaçao **9**

0 ————— 5 Miles
0 ————— 5 Kilometers

Airport ✈ Beach ☂ Mountain ▲▲

Local car-rental firms include **Rent a Yellow,** Cascoreweg 33 (℗ **599/9-767-3777**), whose cars are painted like a yellow cab. The lowest rates are for vehicles without air-conditioning, costing from $32 daily. Tariffs include tax and insurance.

BY TAXI Taxis are unmetered, so ask your driver to quote a price before you get in. Drivers are supposed to carry an official rate sheet, which they'll produce upon request. Charges go up by 25% after 11pm. Tipping isn't customary among islanders, but from tourists, drivers will appreciate a discretionary 10% tip, especially if they've helped with your luggage. The fare from the airport to Willemstad is about $20, and the cost can be split among four passengers. If a piece of luggage is so big that the trunk lid won't close, you'll be assessed a surcharge of $1.

In town, the best place to get a taxi is on the Otrabanda side of the floating bridge. To summon a cab, call ℗ **599/9-869-0747.** Cabbies will usually give you a tour of the island for around $30 per hour for up to four passengers.

BY BUS   Some hotels operate a free shuttle that takes you from the suburbs to the shopping district of Willemstad. A fleet of DAF yellow buses operates from Wilhelmina Plein, near the shopping center, to most parts of Curaçao. Some limousines function as C buses. If you see one listing your destination, you can hail it at any of the designated bus stops.

FAST FACTS: Curaçao

Banks   Bank hours are Monday to Friday from 8:30am to noon and 1:30 to 4:30pm. However, the Banco Popular and the Bank of America remain open during the lunch hour, doing business Monday to Friday from 9am to 3pm. Banks and ATMs can be found in Willemstad.

Currency   While Canadian and U.S. dollars are accepted for purchases on the island, the official currency is the **Netherlands Antillean florin (NAf),** also called a **guilder,** which is divided into 100 NA (Netherlands Antillean) cents. The exchange rate as of this writing is US$1 to 1.77 NAf (1 NAf = US56¢). Shops, hotels, and restaurants usually accept most major U.S. and Canadian credit cards. *Rates in this chapter are quoted in U.S. dollars.*

Documents   To enter Curaçao, U.S. or Canadian citizens need proof of citizenship, such as a birth certificate or a passport, along with a return or continuing airline ticket out of the country and photo ID. (We recommend that you bring a passport.) British subjects need a valid passport.

Electricity   The electricity is 110- to 130-volt AC (50 cycles), the same as in North America, although many hotels have transformers for European appliances.

Emergencies   For **police,** call ℂ 911. For **ambulance,** call ℂ 912. For **fire,** call ℂ 115.

Hospital   The **St. Elisabeth Hospital,** Breedestraat 193 (ℂ 599/9-462-4900), near Otrabanda in Willemstad, is one of the most up-to-date facilities in the Caribbean.

Language   Dutch, Spanish, and English are spoken on Curaçao, along with Papiamento, a patois that combines the three major tongues with Amerindian and African dialects. Most people in the tourism industry speak English, but you can always thank them by saying *masha danki* (*mas*-ha-dank).

Police   The police emergency number is ℂ 911.

Safety   Although Curaçao is not plagued with crime, it's wise to safeguard your valuables.

Taxes   Curaçao levies a room tax of 12% on accommodations and a $3 daily (per room) energy tax on all hotels. There's a departure tax of $22 for international flights, or $7 for flights to other islands in the Netherlands Antilles. You can pay it in U.S. dollars.

Telephone   To call Curaçao from the United States, dial **011** (the international access code), then **599** (the country code for Curaçao), and then **9** (the area code) and the local number. Once on Curaçao, to call another number on the island, only the local seven-digit number is necessary; to make calls to an off-island destination, dial **021** and then the area code and number. You can reach **AT&T Direct** on the island by dialing ℂ **800/ 225-5288.**

Time Curaçao is on Atlantic Standard Time year-round, 1 hour ahead of Eastern Standard Time and the same as eastern daylight savings time.

Water The water comes from a modern desalination plant and is safe to drink.

Weather Curaçao has an average temperature of 81°F (27°C); trade winds keep the island quite comfortable. It's flat and arid, with an average rainfall of only 22 inches per year.

2 Accommodations

Most hotels are in the capital of Willemstad or in one of the suburbs, which lie only 10 to 15 minutes from the shopping center. The bigger hotels often have free shuttle buses running into town, and most have their own beaches and pools.

Curaçao is a bustling commercial center, and the downtown hotels often fill up fast with business travelers as well as visitors from neighboring countries such as Venezuela. It's important to reserve well in advance.

When making reservations, ask if the 12% room tax and 12% service charge are included in the price you're quoted. There is also a $3 daily (per room) energy tax in all hotels. Be sure to take a look at the section "Packages for the Independent Traveler" in chapter 2 for money-saving tips.

EXPENSIVE

Breezes Curaçao 🏖🏖 *(Kids)*   This is the first of the superinclusive resorts of the southern Caribbean. Adjacent to both the Undersea National Park and Sea Aquarium, this big resort opens onto one of Curaçao's most beautiful and longest beaches, with good snorkeling offshore. Catering to both couples and singles, the resort also welcomes families, with its Camp Breezes offering the best kiddies program on island. For those who like to gamble, it also boasts the largest casino in Curaçao.

Bedrooms and suites come in a wide configuration of rooms, including the most desirable, those overlooking the ocean; others front the hotel's gardens. Bathrooms come with either shower or complete shower/tub combinations, and all open onto private patios or balconies. If the food isn't always gourmet, there is at least plenty of it. It's a real all-you-can-eat type of place, from breakfast buffets in the morning to lavish dinner feasts at night. Cuisine choices range from Italian to island specialties to Japanese, plus there's a beach grill. It also has an active entertainment program, complete with guest and staff talent shows.

Dr. Martin Luther King Blvd. 78, Willemstad, Curaçao, N.A. ℂ 599/9-736-7888. Fax 599/9-461-7205. www. breezes.com. 341 units. Winter $325 per person double, from $490 per person suite; off season $200 per person double, from $468 per person suite. Rates are all-inclusive. AE, DC, MC, V. **Amenities:** 3 restaurants; 5 bars; 3 outdoor pools; casino; disco; tennis court; fitness center; spa; Jacuzzi; deep-sea fishing; dive shop; snorkeling; windsurfing; children's program (kids' snack bar, playground); babysitting; laundry service; nonsmoking rooms; rooms for those with limited mobility. *In room:* A/C, TV, beverage maker, hair dryer, iron/ironing board, safe.

Curaçao Marriott Beach Resort & Emerald Casino 🏖🏖   This is the most glamorous and most prominent hotel on the island, set beside the largest and most popular beach on Curaçao. It's 10 minutes from both the airport and

Willemstad. The hotel is a cluster of three-story buildings whose distinctive shape and ocher color were adapted from traditional Dutch colonial architecture. The open-sided lobby was designed for optimum views of the beach and the hotel's many fountains. Scattered throughout the property are unusual, often monumental, artworks by local and international artists, and a collection of unfussy, overstuffed furniture.

Each of the colorful accommodations offers a view of the ocean and contains either one king-size or two double beds, plus a spacious bathroom with a combination shower/tub.

Although never rising to any great imagination or flair, the food here is consistently good, with quality ingredients. There's also a big casino.

Piscadera Bay (P.O. Box 6003), Willemstad, Curaçao, N.A. ℂ **800/223-6388** in the U.S., or 599/9-736-8800. Fax 599/9-462-7502. www.marriott.com. 257 units. Winter $229–$299 double, from $319 suite; off season $179–$229 double, from $269 suite. AE, DC, DISC, MC, V. **Amenities:** 5 restaurants; 2 bars; outdoor pool; casino; 2 tennis courts; Jacuzzi; sauna; diving; jet skis; kayaks; sailing; snorkeling; water-skiing; children's programs; car rental; business center; room service (7am–1am); massage; babysitting; laundry service; nonsmoking rooms; rooms for those with limited mobility. *In room:* A/C, TV, dataport, minibar, iron/ironing board, hair dryer, safe.

Floris Suite Hotel ℛℛℛ *Finds*

The Dutch millionaire philanthropist and architect Jacob Gelt Dekker created this gem of a boutique hotel in the vicinity of the Curaçao World Trade Center. Unlike any hotel on island, the all-suite hotel blends aspects of European colonial with West Indian architecture. Wedding natural stone tiles with solid mahogany doors and windows. The compound is enveloped by a beautiful tropical garden whose focus is a swimming pool. A good private sandy beach is just across the street.

The standard of luxury differs from suite to suite. For example, the Royal Suites offer a separate bedroom with one king-size bed and two singles. In the living area is yet another queen-size sleeper sofa, along with a fully equipped kitchen with a large covered porch or balcony. Everything is designed for comfort and convenience. A spa center is within walking distance, and a dive headquarters is just across from the hotel.

John F. Kennedy Blvd., Piscadera Bay, Curaçao, N.A. ℂ **599/9-462-6111.** Fax 599/9-462-6211. www.floris suitehotel.com. 72 units. Winter $202–$342 double; off season $157–$292 double. AE, MC, V. **Amenities:** 2 restaurants; 2 bars; outdoor pool; tennis court; fitness center; spa; room service (7am–11pm); babysitting; laundry service; coin-operated laundry; nonsmoking rooms. *In room:* A/C, TV, dataport, kitchenette, minibar, beverage maker, hair dryer, safe.

Hilton Curaçao Resort ℛ *Kids*

Although this hotel was built in 1965, it has a new lease on life following renovations and improvements when the people from Hilton took it over in 2003. Today, it rises five floors above the northern perimeter of Willemstad, amid rocky bluffs. Glass-enclosed elevators cling to the outside walls of the hotel, offering a panoramic view as you're whisked to your room. Each midsize accommodation has a view of either the ocean or the garden. Outfitted in bold tropical colors, each contains traditional furnishings, private balconies, and generously proportioned bathrooms, with tubs and showers. Rooms on the executive floor are somewhat better furnished and offer amenities like fax machines. The hotel opens onto two private sandy beaches.

The food isn't great, but it's varied—everything from Italian trattoria favorites to fresh seafood. A social director organizes theme nights based on Mexican or Antillean food and dance music. There's a casino on-site.

John F. Kennedy Blvd. (P.O. Box 2133), Piscadera Bay, Willemstad, Curaçao, N.A. ℂ **800/774-1500** in the U.S. and Canada, or 599/9-462-5000. Fax 599/9-462-5846. www.hilton.com. 196 units. Winter $115–$180 double, from $235 suite; off season $115–$160 double, from $165 suite. AE, DC, MC, V. **Amenities:** 2 restaurants; 2 bars; outdoor pool; children's pool; casino; tennis court; fitness center; spa; boating; dive shop; sailing; children's center; car rental; free shuttle to town; room service (7am–midnight); babysitting; laundry service; coinoperated laundry; nonsmoking rooms; rooms for those with limited mobility. *In room:* A/C, TV, dataport, beverage maker, hair dryer, iron/ironing board, safe.

Kurá Hulanda Hotel and Casino ★★ *Finds*   The island's most imaginative and unusual hotel opens onto St. Anna Bay in Otrabanda near the Queen Emma Bridge. If you'd like to escape impersonal modern hotel blocks, head here and immerse yourself in the Dutch colonial architecture of the 18th and 19th centuries. The property is the creation of Dr. Jacob Gelt Dekker, who also created the Kurá Hulanda Museum (see below), on the same grounds. Bedrooms are beautifully furnished with Indian marble bathrooms with tub and shower, all the modern amenities, and elegant beds and furnishings. Some accommodations also have kitchenettes. You're not on a beach, but if you're seeking West Indian inns or hotels with character, this is your best bet in the ABC islands.

Langestraat 8, Willemstad, Curaçao, N.A. © 599/9-434-7700. Fax 599/9-434-7701. www.kurahulanda.com. 80 units. Winter $219–$319 double, $369 suite; off season $189–$280 double, from $320 suite. AE, DC, MC, V. **Amenities:** 3 restaurants; 3 bars; 2 outdoor pools; casino; fitness center; limited room service; babysitting; laundry service; nonsmoking rooms. *In room:* A/C, ceiling fans, TV, dataport, kitchenette (in some), hair dryer, safe.

MODERATE

Avila Beach Hotel ★★   Set on a beach, this hotel has more charm, atmosphere, and personality than the resorts described above. It consists of a beautifully restored 200-year-old mansion and a large extension, called La Belle Alliance. The mansion was converted into a hotel in 1949, and today attracts the royals of the Netherlands. Each of the rooms in the newer Blues Wing has airconditioning, TV, private bathroom with tub, minifridge, and a balcony with an ocean view; some also contain kitchenettes. The rooms in the main mansion, though rather basic and small, still have charm. Most units have a king-size bed or full-size beds, each fitted with a good mattress. The newer units have combination tubs and showers, whereas some of the smaller rentals are shower only. The hotel lies on the shore road leading east out of the city from the shopping center.

The romantic, open-air Belle Terrace, shaded by huge trees, features a full a la carte menu of well-prepared international food. Blues, an elevated restaurant/ bar at the end of the pier, caters to small, informal parties with a taste for jazz, swing, and, of course, blues (see "Dining," below). Antillean nights feature local cuisine and live music, and there are barbecues Saturday night.

Penstraat 130–134 (P.O. Box 791), Willemstad, Curaçao, N.A. © 800/747-8162 or 599/9-461-4377. Fax 599/ 9-461-1493. www.avilahotel.com. 108 units. Winter $125–$270 double, $325 suite; off season $115–$200 double, $260 suite. Extra person $20. MAP (breakfast and dinner) $60 per person extra. AE, DC, MC, V. **Amenities:** 3 restaurants; 2 bars; tennis court; sauna; business center; limited room service; babysitting; laundry service. *In room:* A/C, TV, kitchenette (in some), minibar, beverage maker, hair dryer, safe, Jacuzzi (in some). From the airport, follow signs to Punda; turn left after the 2nd traffic light in town; stay on the right side of the Plaza Smeets rd. and go straight. The hotel is on the right.

Habitat Curaçao ★   Opening onto a private beach, this is Curaçao's best choice for divers. About 20 minutes from Willemstad, on the uncrowded southwest coast, this oceanfront resort provides environmentally sensitive diving vacations. Facilities include a PADI five-star instruction center offering diving courses from novice to instructor levels. The resort is set in manicured gardens. Accommodations include junior suites tastefully furnished with two queen-size beds, a fully equipped kitchenette, a large balcony or patio, and a full bathroom.

Villas each have two bedrooms, a living room, an outdoor kitchen, a bathroom, and a large patio. All bathrooms contain shower/tub combinations.

Rif St. Marie, Curaçao, N.A. © 800/327-6709 in the U.S., or 599/9-864-8800. Fax 599/9-864-8464. www. habitatdiveresorts.com. 70 units. $125–$165 double. 7-night dive packages $813–$1,084 double occupancy, including 6 2-tank boat dives and airport transfers. AE, MC, V. **Amenities:** Restaurant; bar; outdoor pool; exercise room; diving; sailing; snorkeling; windsurfing; babysitting; laundry service; nonsmoking rooms; rooms for those with limited mobility. *In room:* A/C, TV, kitchenette, hair dryer, iron/ironing board, safe.

Lions Dive & Beach Resort   On the island's largest white-sand beach, this hotel vies for the divers' trade with Habitat Curaçao (see above), which has better diving facilities. The hotel lies a 30-minute taxi ride southeast of the airport. This complete dive resort features programs supervised by the Underwater Curaçao staff. Each of its comfortable though standard accommodations has a sea and/or garden view, a balcony or terrace, two double beds, and a shower-only bath.

Bapor Kibrá, Willemstad, Curaçao, N.A. © 599/9-434-8888. Fax 599/9-434-8889. www.lionsdive.com. 72 units. Winter $267 per person for 3 nights; off season $237 per person for 3 nights. Dive packages available. AE, MC, V. **Amenities:** Restaurant; beach bar; outdoor pool; health club; dive shop; sailing; massage; babysitting; laundry service; rooms for those with limited mobility. *In room:* A/C, TV, dataport, kitchenettes (in some), fridge, safe.

Plaza Hotel Curaçao   Standing guard over the Punda side of St. Anna Bay, right in the heart of Willemstad, the Plaza is nestled in the ramparts of an 18th-century waterside fort on the eastern tip of the harbor entrance, a 30-minute drive south of the airport. In fact, it's one of the harbor's two "lighthouses." (The hotel has to carry marine collision insurance, the only accommodation in the Caribbean with that distinction.) The original part of the hotel was built in 1954, long before mass tourism swept the island, and followed the style of the arcaded fort. However, now there's a tower of rooms stacked 15 stories high. Each of the smallish bedrooms is comfortably furnished and contains a small combination bath.

The pool, with a bar and suntanning area, is inches away from the parapet of the fort. The Waterfort Restaurant serves standard American and Continental dishes.

Plaza Piar (P.O. Box 813), Willemstad, Curaçao, N.A. © 599/9-461-2500. Fax 599/9-461-6543. www.plaza hotelcuracao.com. 213 units. Winter $120–$150 double, $180–$325 suite; off season $80–$100 double, $120–$250 suite. All-inclusive plan $50 per person extra. AE, MC, V. **Amenities:** 2 restaurants; 3 bars; outdoor pool; casino; Sunset sails; car rental; business center; room service (6:30am–9:30pm); babysitting; laundry service; nonsmoking rooms; rooms for those with limited mobility. *In room:* A/C, TV, kitchenette (in some), hair dryer (in some), safe.

INEXPENSIVE

The Landhuis Daniel (see "Dining," below) also offers one of the best values in accommodations on the island.

Chogogo Resort   Lying on Curaçao's east end, a 2-minute walk from Jan Thiel Beach, this resort is for visitors seeking an apartment or a bungalow. It is named after a species of local flamingo and set within an arid landscape between the oceanfront beaches and a shallow saltwater bay southeast of Willemstad. One- and two-story buildings dot the grounds; these contain the guest bungalows, studios, and apartments, each with a kitchenette; airy, unpretentious furniture; and a compact shower-only bathroom.

Jan Thiel Bay, Curaçao, N.A. © 599/9-747-2844. Fax 599/9-747-2424. www.chogogo.com. 120 units. Winter $100 studio for 2, $110 apt for 2, $165 bungalow for 2, $195 bungalow for 4; off season $85 studio, $95 apt, $130 bungalow for 2, $155 bungalow for 4. AE, MC, V. **Amenities:** Restaurant; bar; outdoor pool; children's wading pool; babysitting; coin-operated laundry. *In room:* A/C, TV, kitchenette, beverage maker, safe.

Hotel Holland   A 2-minute drive from the airport, Hotel Holland contains the Flying Dutchman Bar, a popular gathering place, plus a casino. For a few brief minutes of every day, you can see airplanes landing from your perch at the edge of the poolside terrace, where well-prepared breakfasts, lunches, and dinners from The Cockpit restaurant are served in good weather (see "Dining," below).

This property is the domain of former Navy frogman Hans Vrolijk and his family. Hans still retains his interest in scuba and arranges dive packages for his guests. The comfortably furnished accommodations have VCRs, fridges, shower/tub combination bathrooms, and balconies. It's a 30-minute drive to the nearest good beach, so you definitely need a rental car if you stay here.

F. D. Rooseveltweg 524, Curaçao, N.A. © **599/9-868-8044** or 599/9-868-8114. 45 units. Year-round $79 double; from $117 suite. AE, DC, MC, V. **Amenities:** Restaurant; bar; outdoor pool; casino; laundry service. *In room:* A/C, TV/VCR, fridge, beverage maker (in some), hair dryer.

3 Dining

EXPENSIVE

Astrolab Observatory Restaurant ⊛⊛ CONTINENTAL/SEAFOOD   In the Kurá Hulanda compound (see above), this world-class restaurant is adjacent to the Indian Marble Garden, all part of the restored 18th-century village of Otrobanda. This is the best of the many restaurants located within this compound. The restaurant is named for the collection of astrolabs on display nearby. The chefs here create a finely honed modern continental cuisine, which is served both indoors or outdoors on a terrace under a mammoth ficus tree.

The best of fresh fish, based on the day's catch, is served here with well-prepared Caribbean lobster and beef dishes. Start with such delights as a lump crab cake with a caper rémoulade sauce or a pumpkin-cream soup with ground nutmeg. The best of the main dishes include a pan-fried filet of pompano in a lemon-butter sauce with red polenta or green seafood stew, the kettle brimming with lobster, shrimp, black mussels, and the fresh catch of the day. A perfect marriage is the duo of poached sea bass and sautéed salmon with a lentil ragout and pumpkin-flavored pesto sauce.

Kurá Hulanda, Langestraat 8, Otrobanda, Willemstad. © **599/9-434-7700.** Reservations suggested. Main courses $20–$38. AE, DC, MC, V. Mon–Sat 7–11pm.

Bistro Le Clochard ⊛ FRENCH/SWISS   This restaurant fits snugly into the northwestern corner of the grim ramparts of Fort Rif, at the gateway to the harbor. Fort Nassau (see below) is better, but Bistro Le Clochard finishes a close second in the culinary sweepstakes. Its entrance is marked with a canopy leading to a series of rooms, each built under the 19th-century vaulting of the old Dutch fort. This appealingly formal restaurant has several seating options, including a greenhouse-style glassed-in dining room near the entrance and an outdoor terrace. Appetizers like snails marinated in cognac or crepes stuffed with a seafood ragout with a hollandaise sauce might be more appropriate in a Paris bistro than on a tropical island. The kitchen staff is at its best when preparing beef dishes; the tenderloin with assorted mushrooms in a cream sauce is especially recommended. Another classic is the tender U.S. sirloin topped with herb butter. The catch of the day always appears on the menu with a lemon-butter sauce.

In Riffort Village (a condominium complex), on the Otrabanda side of the pontoon bridge. ⓒ 599/ 9-462-5666. Reservations recommended. Main courses $20–$30. AE, DC, DISC, MC, V. Daily noon–2:30pm and 6:30–10:45pm. Harborside Terrace, daily noon–11pm.

Fort Nassau 𝄢𝄢 INTERNATIONAL/SEAFOOD   This restored restaurant and bar is built on a hilltop overlooking Willemstad in the ruins of a buttressed fort dating from 1796. Inside, Fort Nassau has retained an 18th-century decor; outside, from the Battery Terrace, a 360-degree panorama of the sea, the harbor, and Willemstad unfolds. You can stop by the chic bar just to enjoy a drink and watch the sunset.

Queen Beatrix and Crown Prince Claus of the Netherlands have dined here, and rumor has it they were more captivated by the view than by the food. We are impressed with the perfectly prepared filet of grouper. The cream of mustard (yes, that's right) soup must be an acquired taste. Opt for the pan-fried filet of red snapper, or even a well-prepared steak with garlic-infused mashed potatoes. Also good are oven-roasted rack of lamb with pickled red onions and almond potatoes, and the caramelized filet of salmon on a bed of creamy leeks with fried polenta and plantain.

Near Point Juliana, a 5-min. drive from Willemstad. ⓒ 599/9-461-3086. Reservations recommended. Main courses $21–$28. AE, DC, MC, V. Mon–Fri noon–2pm; daily 6–11pm.

Landhuis Daniel 𝄢 *Finds* NOUVELLE CREOLE CUISINE   Surrounded by arid scrubland about 3.2km (2 miles) south of Westpunt, near the island's most northwesterly tip, this place was originally built in 1711 as an inn and tavern. Today, its mustard-colored facade, white columns, terra-cotta roof, and old-fashioned green-and-yellow dining room are carefully preserved and historically authentic. Menu items are cooked slowly, to order, in a setting of sea breezes and sunlight streaming in the big windows. Launch your repast with a spicy Caribbean bisque with fish and seafood. We generally opt for the main catch of the day, often requesting it with a basil-cream sauce and pine nuts, but you might prefer the Argentina beef tenderloin with spicy pumpkin sauce or the baked swordfish with shrimp sauce.

Renting for $60 a night year-round, eight very simple but comfortable bedrooms are located a floor above the restaurant. They are tidily maintained and have small private bathrooms with shower units. Only five rooms are air-conditioned, but all units have ceiling fans—or you can rely on the trade winds to keep cool.

In the Landhuis Daniel Inn, Wegnaar, Westpunt. ⓒ 599/9-864-8400. Reservations recommended. Lunch main courses $11–$18; dinner main courses $14–$23. AE, DC, MC, V. Daily 8am–2pm and 5–11pm.

La Pergola 𝄢 ITALIAN   This is one of the five restaurants nestled into the weather-beaten core of the island's oldest fort, and it's thrived here for more than a decade. As the name implies, the decor is enhanced by a replica of a Renaissance-style pergola. The kitchen and one of the three dining areas are in the cellar; two others benefit from streaming sunlight and a view over the seafront. Menu items change virtually every day, and all use truly authentic recipes. The best examples include gnocchi of chicken, fettuccine *Giulio Cesare* (with ham, cream, and mushrooms), a succulent version of *grigliata mista* (mixed grill), and a top-notch preparation of exotic mushrooms, in season, garnished with Parmesan cheese and parsley. The red snapper in extra virgin olive oil and garlic is always a palate pleaser. Looking for an unusual pasta? Ask for *maltagliata* (pasta cut at random angles and lengths) served with either Gorgonzola sauce or Genoan-style pesto. In addition, a dozen pizza options await you.

In the Waterfront Arches, Waterfort Straat, Willemstad. ℂ 599/9-461-3482. Reservations recommended. Main courses $18–$25. AE, MC, V. Mon–Sat noon–11pm; Sun 5–11pm.

The Wine Cellar ℛ INTERNATIONAL   Opposite the cathedral in the center of town is the domain of Nico and Angela Cornelisse and their son, Daniel, who offer one of the most extensive wine lists on the island. The Victorian atmosphere is reminiscent of an old-fashioned Dutch home. The kitchen turns out an excellent lobster salad and a sole meunière in a butter-and-herb sauce. You might also try fresh red snapper in garlic sauce, filet mignon from Argentina, or the rack of lamb with rosemary-port sauce. Game dishes, imported throughout the year from Holland, are likely to include venison roasted with mushrooms, hare, and roast goose. After years of dining here, we have found the food commendable in every way—dishes are hearty and full of flavor, and there are selections for lighter appetites as well. Of course, as good as the food is, it never matches the impressive wine list.

Intersection of Ooststraat and Concordiastraat, Willemstad. ℂ 599/9-461-2178. Reservations required. Main courses $20–$36. AE, MC, V. Mon–Fri noon–2:30pm and 7–10pm; Sat 7–11pm.

MODERATE

Belle Terrace ℛ INTERNATIONAL/DANISH   This open-air restaurant, in a 200-year-old mansion on the beachfront of Willemstad, offers superb dining in a relaxed and informal atmosphere. The beachfront Schooner Bar, where you can enjoy rum punch, is shaped like a weather-beaten ship's prow looking out to sea. The restaurant, sheltered by an arbor of flamboyant branches, features Scandinavian, Continental, and local cuisine, with such specialties as pickled herring, smoked salmon, and a Danish lunch platter. Local dishes, such as *keshi yena* (baked Gouda cheese with a spicy chicken filling), are also on the menu. On Saturday night there's a mixed grill and a serve-yourself salad bar all accompanied by live music. Fish is always fresh at Belle Terrace, and the chef prepares a seafood platter to perfection: grilled, poached, or meunière.

In the Avila Beach Hotel, Penstraat 130, Willemstad. ℂ 599/9-461-4377. Reservations required. Main courses $18–$28; 3-course fixed-price meal $34; Sat barbecue $29. AE, DC, MC, V. Daily 7–10am, noon–2:30pm, and 7–10pm. From the center of town, drive east along the Pieter Maai Weg (which becomes Pennstraat) for 1.6km (1 mile).

Blues SEAFOOD/INTERNATIONAL   As you dine here on a pier jutting far out from the beachfront of the Avila Beach Hotel, water ripples beneath your seat and heaping platters of fresh seafood challenge even the heartiest of appetites. You might enjoy blue mussels cooked in wine sauce with shallots and herbs, or lobster with a lime-and-orange beurre blanc. An especially impressive dish is the seafood special, compiled from three different types of fish, depending on the catch of the day. If after all this hearty fare from Neptune you still have room left, the chef makes great desserts, including a chocolate tart, one of our favorites.

In the Avila Beach Hotel, Penstraat 130, Willemstad. ℂ 599/9-461-4377. Reservations recommended. Main courses $20–$31; 3-course fixed-price menu $34. AE, MC, V. Tues–Sun 7pm–midnight. From the center of town, drive east along the Pieter Maai Weg (which becomes Pennstraat) for 1.6km (1 mile).

Rijsttafel Restaurant Indonesia and Holland Club Bar ℛ *Value* INDONESIAN   This is the best place on the island to sample Indonesian *rijstafel,* the traditional rice table with all the zesty side dishes. At lunchtime, the selection of dishes is more modest, but for dinner, Japanese cooks prepare the specialty of the house—a *rijstafel* consisting of 16, 20, or 25 dishes. There's even an all-vegetarian *rijstafel.* Warming trays are placed on your table; the service is buffet style. You can season your plate with peppers rated hot, very hot, and palate-melting. It's best to go with a party so that all of you can share in the feast. The spicy food is a good change of pace when you tire of seafood and steak.

Mercuriusstraat 13, Salinja. ℂ 599/9-461-2606. Reservations recommended. Main courses $17–$24; *rijstafel* $22 for 16 dishes, $27 for 20 dishes, $47 for 25 dishes; vegetarian *rijstafel* $22 for 16 dishes. AE, MC, V. Mon–Sat noon–2pm and 6–9:30pm. Take a taxi to this villa in the suburbs near Salinja, near Breezes Curaçao southeast of Willemstad.

Small World International Cuisine ℛ *(Finds* INTERNATIONAL   There is no more eclectic dining on the island than at Small World. The owner, Darryll Circkens, set out to open a restaurant that roamed the world for its culinary inspiration. He has succeeded admirably. The specialties are mainly Creole, Spanish, French, and Chinese. Dinner can be outside on the terrace overlooking the sea or inside, where the ideal table is a glass top over an aquarium. Some West Indian specialties will put hair on your chest, including *lengua* (tongue) in a savory sauce. We prefer the Spanish food, especially the paella and grilled seafood. Many French dishes rely heavily on beef, such as chateaubriand and filet mignon. We've also enjoyed a well-flavored Chinese chicken served with a medley of mushrooms. For us, nothing quite tops the shrimp in garlic sauce served with rice and fresh vegetables. There's a bar, so you can drop in early for a drink. Most dishes are at the lower end of the price scale.

Waterfortbogen 18–19, Punda, Willemstad. ℂ 599/9-465-5575. Reservations recommended. Main courses $9–$17. AE, DC, MC, V. Daily 5–11pm.

INEXPENSIVE

The Cockpit *(Value* DUTCH/INTERNATIONAL   The focal point of this restaurant's dining room is the nose of an airplane cockpit; for those preferring to dine outside, poolside seating is also available. Located on the scrub-bordered road leading to the airport, a few minutes from the landing strips, The Cockpit serves international cuisine with an emphasis on Dutch and Antillean specialties. Guests enjoy fresh fish in season served Curaçao style (with sweet peppers and onions), Dutch-style steak, Caribbean curried chicken, and split-pea soup. All dishes are accompanied by fresh vegetables and Dutch-style potatoes. No one pretends the food is gourmet fare—it's robust, hearty, and filled with good country flavor, at a terrific value to boot.

In the Hotel Holland, F. D. Rooseveltweg 524. ℂ 599/9-868-8044. Reservations required. Main courses $11–$25. AE, DC, MC, V. Daily 7am–11pm.

4 Beaches

Its beaches (called *playas* or *bocas*) aren't the best in the Dutch Leewards, but Curaçao does have nearly 40 of them, ranging from hotel sands to secluded coves. *Playas* are the larger, classic sandy beaches, and *bocas* are small inlets between two large rock formations. The northwest coast is generally rugged and difficult for swimming, but the more tranquil waters of the west coast are filled with sheltered bays, offering excellent swimming and snorkeling.

Seaquarium Beach, just to the east of the center of Willemstad, charges a fee of $2.50 for access to its complete facilities, including two bars, two restaurants, a watersports shop, beach-chair rentals, changing facilities, and showers. The calm waters make this beach ideal for swimming.

Just northwest of Willemstad, **Blauwbaai (Blue Bay)** is the largest and most popular beach on Curaçao, with enough white sand for everybody. Along with showers and changing facilities, there are plenty of shady places to retreat from

---

Warning   A Word of Caution to Swimmers

Beware of stepping on the spines of the sea urchins that sometimes abound in these waters. To give temporary first aid for an embedded urchin's spine, try the local remedies of vinegar or lime juice. Locals advise a burning match if you're tough. Although the urchin spines are not dangerous, they can give you several days of real discomfort.

---

the noonday sun. To get here, follow the road that goes past the Holiday Beach Hotel, heading in the direction of Juliandorp. Follow the sign that tells you to bear left for Blauwbaai and the fishing village of San Michiel.

Further up the west coast, about 30 minutes from Willemstad in the Willibrordus area on the west side of Curaçao, **Daaibooi** is a good beach, though there are no showers or changing rooms. Shade is provided by wooden umbrellas. Snorkelers are attracted to the sides of the bay, as the cliffs rise out of the surf. Small rainbow-hued fish are commonplace, and many varying corals cover the rocks. This beach gets very crowded with locals on Sunday.

A beach popular with families and a base for fishing boats, **Playa Lagun** lies well concealed in the corner of the village of Lagun as you approach from Santa Cruz. The narrow cove is excellent for swimming because of the tranquil, shallow water. Rainbow-hued fish appear everywhere, so the beach is also a favorite with snorkelers. Some concrete huts provide shelter from the scorching sun; a snack bar is open on weekends.

Knip Bay, just north of Playa Lagun, has white sands, rocky sides, and beautiful turquoise waters, making it suitable for snorkeling, swimming, and sunbathing. The beach tends to be crowded on weekends, often with locals. Manzanilla trees provide some shade, but their fruit is poisonous; never seek shelter under the trees when it rains, as drops falling off the leaves will cause major skin irritation. Changing facilities and refreshments are available.

Playa Abao, with crystal turquoise waters, is at the northern tip of the island. One of Curaçao's most popular strands, this is often called Playa Grandi ("Big Beach"). It can get very, very hot at midday, but thatched shade umbrellas provide some protection. A stairway and ramp lead down to the excellent white sands. There's a snack bar in the parking lot. Near the large cove at Playa Abao is **Playa Kenepa** ⚓, which is much smaller but gets our nod as one of the island's most beautiful strips. Partially shaded by trees, it's a good place for sunbathing, swimming, and shore diving. A 10-minute swim from the beach leads to a reef where visibility is often 30m (98 ft.). Baby sea turtles are often spotted here. A snack bar is open on weekends.

Westpunt, a public beach on the northwestern tip of the island, is known for the Sunday divers who jump from its gigantic cliffs into the ocean below. You can spot rainbow-hued little boats and fishermen's nets hanging out to dry here. There are no facilities at this beach, which tends to be exceptionally hot and has no shade trees (bring lots of sunscreen). The calm waters offer excellent swimming, though they're not good for snorkeling.

South of Willemstad is **Santa Barbara Beach.** It's between the open sea and the island's primary watersports and recreational area known as Spanish Water. A mining company owns this land, which also contains Table Mountain, a remarkable landmark, and an old phosphate mine. The natural beach has pure-white sand and calm water. A buoy line protects swimmers from boats. Facilities include restrooms, changing rooms, a snack bar, and a terrace; water bicycles and small motorboats are available for rent. The beach, open daily from 8am to 6pm, has access to the Curaçao Underwater Marine Park.

5 Sports & Other Outdoor Pursuits

CRUISES   **Taber Tours,** Dokweg (© **599/9-737-6637**), offers a handful of seagoing options, such as a 5-hour sunset and snorkeling cruise to a beach on Wednesday and Friday; the excursion costs $30 for adults including gear and one cocktail. Children pay half price. Charter cruises are also available.

Travelers looking for an experience similar to the sailing days of yore should book a trip on the *Insulinde,* Handelskade (© **599/9-560-1340** [note that this is a cellular phone and the connection may be poor]; fax 599/9-461-1538; www.insulinde.com). The 36km (118-ft.) traditionally rigged sail clipper is available for day trips and chartering. An afternoon tour on Wednesday and Friday leaves at 2:15pm, returning at 6:30pm, taking passengers to a sunken tugboat for snorkeling and a swim at Santa Barbara Beach. The cost is $42 per person (half price for kids), with free use of snorkel gear. Other tours, including some dinner buffets, are available, providing that a minimum of 20 people sign up. Call for more information about what might be offered at the time of your visit. Advance reservations are required for all trips.

Like a ghost ship from ancient times, a dual-masted, five-sailed wooden schooner cruises silently through the waters of Curaçao. It carries a name steeped in history—the *Bounty* (© **599/9-560-1887;** www.bountyadventures.com)— though it's not a replica of its famous namesake. Sailing and snorkeling trips depart Wednesday, Friday, and Sunday at 10am from Spanish Water, making a stop at Caracas Bay for great snorkeling before a return at 2:30pm. The price is $49 for adults or $30 for children ages 4 to 14. Prices include a barbecue buffet, salad bar, drinks, and use of snorkeling gear.

GOLF   The **Curaçao Golf and Squash Club,** Wilhelminalaan, in Emmastad (© **599/9-737-3590**), is your best bet. Greens fees are $30, and both clubs and trolleys can be rented upon demand. The nine-hole course (the only nine-hole course on the island) is open daily from 7:30am to sundown.

An 18-hole golf course lies at **Blue Bay Golf Course,** a par-3 course at Landhuis Blauw, on the road to Bullenbaai (© **599/9-868-1755**). This challenging course, designed by Rocky Roquemore, takes advantage of Curaçao's seaside terrain and views of the Caribbean. Some shots are over water. Depending on the time of year, greens fees range from $80 to $95, plus $11 to rent a cart. Hours are daily from 7am to 5pm.

HORSEBACK RIDING   At Christoffel National Park, **Rancho Alsin** (© **599/ 9-864-0535**) specializes in private trips along unspoiled trails, riding smooth-gaited "paseo" horses suitable even for nonriders. The ride, which lasts about 1½ hours, costs $35. Departures are Tuesday through Sunday at 8:30am. Call for reservations daily between 8am and 4pm.

TENNIS   Most of the deluxe hotels have tennis courts. Another option is the **Santa Catherine Sports Complex,** Koraal Tabac (© **599/9-767-7028**), where court costs are $9 to $20 per hour.

WATERSPORTS   Most hotels offer their own watersports programs. If your hotel isn't equipped, we suggest heading for one of the most complete watersports facilities on Curaçao, **Seascape Dive and Watersports,** at the Hilton Hotel Curaçao (© **599/9-462-5000;** www.seascapecuracao.com). Specializing in snorkeling and scuba diving to reefs and underwater wrecks, it operates from a hexagonal kiosk set on stilts above the water, just offshore from the hotel's beach.

Open from 8am to 5pm daily, the company offers snorkeling excursions for $25 per person in an underwater park offshore from the hotel, and jet-ski rentals for $40 per half-hour. An introductory scuba lesson, conducted by a competent dive instructor with PADI certification, goes for $45; four-dive packages cost $116.

Seascape can also arrange deep-sea fishing for $336 for a half-day tour carrying a maximum of six people, $560 for a full-day tour. Drinks and equipment are included, but you'll have to get your hotel to pack your lunch. The full-day tour does include lunch.

Ocean Encounters, in Bapor Kibrá (© **599/9-461-8131**), has a complete PADI-accredited underwater sports program. A fully stocked modern dive shop offers retail and rental equipment. Individual dives and dive packages are offered, costing $35 per dive for guided shore dives. An introductory dive for novices is priced at $75, and a snorkel trip costs $20 (only offered on Sun and Thurs), including equipment. Shop hours are daily 8am to 5pm.Scuba divers and snorkelers can expect spectacular scenery in waters with visibility often exceeding 30m (98 ft.) at the **Curaçao Underwater Marine Park** ★★, which stretches along 20km (12½ miles) of Curaçao's southern coastline. Although the park technically begins at Breezes Curaçao and extends all the way to East Point, the island's most southeasterly tip, some scuba aficionados and island dive operators are aware of other excellent dive sites outside the official boundaries of this park. Lying beneath the surface of the water are steep walls, at least two shallow wrecks, gardens of soft coral, and more than 30 species of hard coral. Although access from shore is possible at Jan Thiel Bay and Santa Barbara Beach, most people visit the park by boat. For easy and safe mooring, there are 16 mooring buoys, placed at the best dive and snorkel sites. A snorkeling trail with underwater interpretive markers is laid out just east of Breezes Curaçao and is accessible from shore. Spearfishing, anchoring in the coral, or taking anything from the reefs, except photographs, is strictly prohibited.

6 Exploring the Island

Most cruise-ship passengers see only Willemstad—or, more accurately, its shops—but you may want to get out into the *cunucu,* or countryside, and explore the towering cacti and rolling hills topped by *landhuizen* (plantation houses) built more than 3 centuries ago.

WILLEMSTAD ★★

Willemstad was originally founded as Santa Ana by the Spanish in the 1500s. Dutch traders found a vast natural harbor, a perfect hideaway along the Spanish Main, and they renamed it Willemstad in the 17th century. Not only is Willemstad the capital of Curaçao, but it's also the seat of government for the Netherlands Antilles. Today it boasts rows of pastel-colored, red-roofed town houses in the downtown area. After 10 years of restoration, the historic center of Willemstad and the island's natural harbor, Schottegat, have been inscribed on UNESCO's World Heritage List.

The easiest way to go exploring is to take a 1¼-hour **trolley tour,** visiting the highlights of the city. The open-sided cars, pulled by a silent "locomotive," make several trips each week. Tours leave at 10 or 11am. The tour begins at Fort Amsterdam near the Queen Emma Pontoon Bridge. The cost is $20 for adults, $10 for children age 2 to 12. Call © **599/9-461-0011** for more information.

The city grew up on both sides of the canal. It's divided into **Punda** (Old World Dutch ambience and the best shopping) and **Otrabanda** ("the other side," the contemporary side). Both sections are connected by the **Queen Emma Pontoon Bridge,** a pedestrian walkway. Powered by a diesel engine, it swings open many times a day to let ships from all over the globe pass in and out of the harbor.

From the bridge, there's a view of the old **gabled houses** in harmonized pastel shades. The bright colors, according to legend, are a holdover from the time when one of the island's early governors had eye trouble, and flat white gave him headaches. The colonial-style architecture, reflecting the Dutch influence, gives the town a storybook look. The houses, built three or four stories high, are crowned by steep gables and roofed with orange Spanish tiles. Hemmed in by the sea, a tiny canal, and an inlet, the streets are narrow, and they're crosshatched by still narrower alleyways.

Except for the pastel colors, Willemstad may remind you of old Amsterdam. It has one of the most intriguing townscapes in the Caribbean. But don't let the colors deceive you: The city can be rather dirty, in spite of its fairy-tale appearance.

A **statue of Pedro Luis Brion** dominates the square known as Brionplein right at the Otrabanda end of the pontoon bridge. Born in Curaçao in 1782, Brion became the island's favorite son and best-known war hero. Under Simon Bolivar, he was an admiral of the fleet and fought for the independence of Venezuela and Colombia.

In addition to the pontoon bridge, the **Queen Juliana Bridge** opened to vehicular traffic in 1973. Spanning the harbor, it rises 59m (194 ft.), which makes it the highest bridge in the Caribbean and one of the tallest in the world.

The Waterfront originally guarded the mouth of the canal on the eastern or Punda side, but now it has been incorporated into the Plaza Hotel. The task of standing guard has been taken over by **Fort Amsterdam,** site of the Governor's Palace and the 1769 Dutch Reformed church. The church still has a British cannonball embedded in it. The arches leading to the fort were tunneled under the official residence of the governor.

A corner of Fort Amsterdam stands at the intersection of Breedestraat and Handelskade, the starting point for a plunge into the island's major **shopping district.**

At some point, save time to visit the **Waterfort Arches,** stretching for .4km (¼ mile). They rise 9m (30-ft.) high and are built of barrel-vaulted 17th-century stone set against the sea. At Waterfort, you can explore boutiques, have film developed quickly, cash a traveler's check, or purchase fruit-flavored ice cream. You can walk through to a breezy terrace on the sea for a local Amstel beer or a

---

Moments The Floating Market

A few minutes' walk from the pontoon bridge, at the north end of Handelskade, is the **Floating Market** *☆*, where scores of schooners tie up alongside the canal, a few yards from the main shopping area. Boats arrive from Venezuela and Colombia, as well as other West Indian islands, to dock here and sell tropical fruits and vegetables—a little bit of everything, in fact, including handcrafts. The modern market under its vast concrete cap has not replaced this unique shopping expedition, which is fun to watch; arrive early or stay late.

choice of restaurants. The grand buildings and cobbled walkways are illuminated at night.

Between the I. H. (Sha) Capriles Kade and Fort Amsterdam, at Hanechi di Snoa 29, stands the **Mikve Israel-Emanuel Synagogue** (© **599/9-461-1067**), the oldest synagogue in the Western Hemisphere. Consecrated on the eve of Passover in 1732, it houses the oldest Jewish congregation in the New World. Joaño d'Illan led the first Jewish settlers (13 families) to the island in 1651, almost half a century after their expulsion from Portugal by the Inquisition. The settlers came via Amsterdam to Curaçao. This synagogue, a fine example of Dutch colonial architecture, covers about a square block in the heart of Willemstad; it was built in a Spanish-style walled courtyard, with four large portals. Following a Portuguese Sephardic custom, sand covers the sanctuary floor, representing the desert where Israelites camped when the Jews passed from slavery to freedom. The highlight of the east wall is the Holy Ark, rising 5m (16 ft.); a raised *banca* (balustraded dais), canopied in mahogany, is on the north wall.

Adjacent to the synagogue courtyard is the **Jewish Cultural Historical Museum,** Hanechi di Snoa 29 (© **599/9-461-1633**), housed in two buildings dating from 1728. They were originally the rabbi's residence and the bathhouse. The 250-year-old *mikvah* (a bath for religious purification purposes) was in constant use until around 1850, when this practice was discontinued and the buildings sold. They have since been reacquired through the Foundation for the Preservation of Historic Monuments and turned into the present museum. On display are ritual, ceremonial, and cultural objects, many of which date from the 17th and 18th centuries and are still in use by the congregation for holidays and events.

The synagogue and museum are open to visitors Monday through Friday from 9 to 11:45am and 2:30 to 4:45pm, and, if there's a cruise ship in port, Sunday from 9am to noon. Services are Friday at 6:30pm and Saturday at 10:30am. Visitors are welcome, with appropriate dress required. There's a $3.50 museum entrance fee for adults and $1.75 for children 5 to 13. Entrance to the synagogue is $2.

Museum Kurá Hulanda, Kipstraat 9 (© **599/9-434-7765**), is one of the most unusual—and one of the largest—museums in the Caribbean, housed in once-dilapidated 1800s buildings rescued from oblivion. The exhibits reflect the passion of Dr. Jacob Gelt Dekker, a Dutchman who resides next door. He has spent a great deal of his life devoted to the history and culture of Africa, and he has roamed that continent in search of cultural artifacts. At Otrabanda he has assembled his prize collection, including its most interesting exhibit, a life-size reconstruction of a slave ship that once sailed from the Ivory Coast carrying captured slaves into bondage and often death in the West. One exhibit, "Origin of Man," has a series of intriguing fossils. You can hear African music as you study the frightening wood masks, and look at everything from fertility dolls to sculptures from shona stone, along with such musical instruments as the djembe or the ballaphone. Much of the museum is devoted to objects that evoke the cultures of the former empires of West Africa. Hours are daily 10am to 5pm; admission is $6 for adults and $3 for children.

You can walk to the tiny **Curaçao Museum,** Van Leeuwenhoekstraat (© **599/9-462-3873**), from the Queen Emma Pontoon Bridge. Built in 1853 by the Royal Dutch Army Corps of Engineers as a military quarantine hospital, the building was carefully restored from 1946 to 1948 and is a fine example of 19th-century Dutch architecture, now housing paintings, objets d'art, and furniture crafted in the 19th century by local cabinetmakers. There's also a large collection from the Caiquetio tribes, the early inhabitants described by Amerigo Vespucci as 2m-tall (6½-ft.) giants, and a reconstruction of a traditional music pavilion in the garden, where Curaçao musicians give regular performances. It's open Monday to Friday from 9am to noon and 2 to 5pm, and Sunday from 10am to 4pm. Admission is $5 for adults, $3 for children age 13 and under.

Maritime Museum, Van De Brandhof Straat 7 (© **599/9-465-2327**), is in the historic Scharloo neighborhood of Willemstad, just off the old harbor of St. Anna Bay. More than 40 permanent displays trace the story of Curaçao, beginning with the arrival of the island's original inhabitants in 600 B.C. Video presentations cover the development of Curaçao's harbor and the role of the island as one of the largest slave depots in the Caribbean. There are also five oral histories (one from a 97-year-old Curaçaoan who served on the cargo vessel *Normandie*), antique miniatures, 17th-century ship models, and a collection of maps. Admission is $6 for adults, $4 for children age 12 to 16; free for children under 12. Hours are daily 10am to 5pm.

WEST OF WILLEMSTAD

On Schottegatweg West, northwest of Willemstad, past the oil refineries, lies the **Beth Haim Cemetery,** the oldest Caucasian burial site still in use in the Western Hemisphere. Meaning "House of Life," the cemetery was consecrated before 1659. There are some 2,500 graves on about 1 hectare (2½ acres) here. The carving on some of the 17th- and 18th-century tombstones is exceptional.

Country House Museum, 19km (12 miles) west of Willemstad at Doktorstuin 27 (© **599/9-864-2742**), is a small-scale restoration of a 19th-century manor house that boasts thick stone walls, a thatched roof, and artifacts that represent the old-fashioned methods of agriculture and fishing. It's open Monday to Friday from 9am to 5pm, Saturday and Sunday from 9am to 6pm. Admission is $2.

En route to Westpunt, you'll come across a seaside cavern known as **Boca Tabla,** one of many such grottoes on this rugged, uninhabited northwest coast. In the Westpunt area, a 45-minute ride from Punda in Willemstad, **Playa Forti** is a stark region characterized by soaring hills and towering cacti, along with 200-year-old Dutch land houses, the former mansions that housed slave owners.

Out toward the western tip of Curaçao, a high-wire fence surrounds the entrance to the 1,800-hectare (4,446-acre) **Christoffel National Park** 🦋🦋 in Savonet (© **599/9-864-0363**), about a 45-minute drive from the capital. A macadam road gives way to dirt, surrounded on all sides by abundant cactus and bromeliads. In the higher regions you can spot rare orchids. Rising from flat, arid countryside, 369m-high (1,210-ft.) **St. Christoffelberg** is the highest point in the Dutch Leewards. Donkeys, wild goats, iguanas, the Curaçao deer, and many species of birds thrive in this preserve, and there are some Arawak paintings on a coral cliff near the two caves. The park has 32km (20 miles) of one-way trail-like roads, with lots of flora and fauna along the way. The shortest trail is about 8km-long (5 miles) and, because of the rough terrain, takes about 40 minutes to drive through. There are also various walking trails; one takes you to the top of St. Christoffelberg in about 1½ hours. (Come early in the morning, when it isn't too hot.) The park is open Monday to Saturday from 7:30am to 4pm, Sunday from 6am to 3pm. The entrance fee is $10 per person and includes admission to the museum.

Next door, the park has opened the **National Park Shete Boka (Seven Inlets).** This turtle sanctuary contains a cave with pounding waves off the choppy north coast. Admission to this park is $2.50 per person.

NORTH & EAST OF WILLEMSTAD

Just northeast of the capital, **Fort Nassau** was completed in 1797 and christened Fort Republic by the Dutch. Built high on a hill overlooking the harbor entrance to the south and St. Anna Bay to the north, it was fortified as a second line of defense in case the waterfront gave way. When the British invaded in 1807, they renamed it Fort George in honor of their own king. Later, when the Dutch regained control, they renamed it Orange Nassau in honor of the Dutch royal family. Today, diners have replaced soldiers (see "Dining," earlier in this chapter).

Curaçao Liqueur Distillery, Landhuis Chobolobo, Saliña a Arriba (© **599/ 9-461-3526**), offers a chance to visit and taste at Chobolobo, the 17th-century *landhuis* where the famous Curaçao liqueur is made. The cordial is a distillate of dried peel of a particular strain of orange found only on Curaçao. Several herbs are added to give it an aromatic bouquet. One of the rewards of a visit here is a free snifter of the liqueur, offered Monday to Friday from 8am to noon and 1 to 5pm.

Curaçao Seaquarium, off Dr. Martin Luther King Boulevard at a site called Bapor Kibrá (© **599/9-461-6666;** www.curacao-sea-aquarium.com), has more than 400 species of fish, crabs, anemones, sponges, and coral on display in a natural environment. Located a few minutes' walk along the rocky coast from the Breezes Curaçao Resort, the Seaquarium is open daily from 8:30am to 3:30pm. Admission is $15 for adults, $7.50 for children age 12 and under.

A special feature of the aquarium is a "shark and animal encounter," which costs $39 for divers or $19 for snorkelers. Divers, snorkelers, and experienced swimmers can feed, film, and photograph sharks, which are separated from them by a large window with feeding holes. In the animal-encounters section, you can swim among stingrays, lobsters, tarpons, parrotfish, and other marine life, feeding and photographing these creatures in a controlled environment where safety is always a consideration. The Seaquarium is also the site of Curaçao's only full-facility, palm-shaded, white-sand beach. There is also a 3-D slide presentation in the minitheater.

Seaworld Explorer ✸ is a semisubmersible submarine that departs the Seaquarium daily in the mornings (times vary) on hour-long journeys into the deep. You're taken on a tour of submerged wrecks off the shores of Curaçao and treated to close encounters of coral reefs with rainbow-hued tropical fish. The *Explorer* has a barge top that submerges only 2 or so meters (6½ ft.) under the water, but the submerged section has wide glass windows allowing passengers underwater views, which can extend 33m (108 ft.). Reservations must be made a day in advance by calling © **599/9-461-0011.** It costs $30 for adults, $20 for children age 11 and under.

Curaçao Underwater Marine Park ✸✸ (© **599/9-462-4242**), established in 1983 with the financial aid of the World Wildlife Fund, stretches from the Breezes Curaçao Resort to the east point of the island, a strip of about 20km (12½ miles) of untouched coral reefs. For information on snorkeling, scuba diving, and trips in a glass-bottom boat to view the park, see "Sports & Other Outdoor Pursuits," earlier in this chapter.

The **Hato Caves,** F. D. Rooseveltweg (© **599/9-868-0379**), have been called mystical. Every hour, guides take visitors through this world of stalagmites and stalactites, found in the highest limestone terrace of the island. Actually, they were once old coral reefs, which were formed when the ocean water fell and the landmass was lifted up over the years. Over thousands of years, limestone formations were created, some mirrored in an underground lake. After crossing the lake, you enter the Cathedral, an underground cavern. The largest hall of the cave is called La Ventana ("The Window"). Also on display are samples of ancient Indian petroglyph drawings. The caves are open Tuesday to Sunday from 10am to 5pm; admission is $6.25 for adults and $4.75 for children age 4 to 12.

7 Shopping ★★

Curaçao is a shopper's paradise. Some 200 shops line the major shopping streets such as Heerenstraat and Breedestraat. Right in the heart of Willemstad is the 5-block **Punda** shopping district. Most stores are open Monday through Saturday from 8am to noon and 2 to 6pm (some 8am–6pm). When cruise ships are in port, stores are also open for a few hours on Sunday and holidays. To avoid the cruise-ship crowds, do your shopping in the morning.

Look for good buys on French perfumes, Dutch Delft blue souvenirs, finely woven Italian silks, Japanese and German cameras, jewelry, silver, Swiss watches, linens, leather goods, liquor, and island-made rum and liqueurs, especially Curaçao liqueur, some of which has a distinctive blue color. The island is famous for its 5-pound wheels of Gouda and Edam cheeses. You'll also see wooden shoes, although we're not sure what you'd do with them. Some of the stores also stock some deals on intricate lacework imported from Portugal, China, and everywhere in between. If you're a street shopper and want something colorful, consider one of the woodcarvings or flamboyant paintings from Haiti or the Dominican Republic. Both are hawked by street vendors at any of the main plazas.

Incidentally, Curaçao is not technically a free port, but its prices are often inexpensive because of its low import duty.

Every garment sold in **Bamali,** Breedestraat Punda 2 (© **599/9-461-2258**), is designed and, in many cases, crafted by the store owners. Influenced largely by Indonesian patterns, the airy attire includes V-neck cotton pullovers perfect for a casual, hot-weather climate, as well as linen shifts, often in batik prints, appropriate for a glamorous cocktail party. Most pieces here are for women; all are made from all-natural materials, such as cotton, silk, and linen, and there's also a limited array of sandals, hats, scarves, and leather bags. **Benetton,** Madurostraat 4 (© **599/9-461-4619**), has invaded Curaçao with all its many colors. Some items are marked down by about 20% below U.S. prices (this is done to get rid of surplus stock from the previous season); in-season clothing is available as well.

Bert Knubben Black Koral Art Studio, in the Breezes Curaçao Resort, Dr. Martin Luther King Boulevard (© **599/9-465-2122**), is synonymous with craftsmanship and quality. Although it's illegal to collect black coral here, an exception was made for Bert, a diver who has been harvesting corals and fashioning them into fine jewelry and objets d'art for more than 35 years. Collectors avidly seek out this type of coral, not only for the quality of its craftsmanship, but also because it's becoming increasingly rare and may one day not be offered for sale at all.

Gandelman Jewelers, Breedestraat 35, Punda (© **599/9-461-1854**), is the island's best and most reliable source for jewelry, often exquisitely designed and set with diamonds, rubies, emeralds, sapphires, and other gemstones. You'll also find watches and the unique line of Prima Classe leather goods embossed with the world map.

Little Holland, Braedestraat 37, Punda (© **599/9-461-1768**), specializes in silk neckties, Panama hats, Nautica shorts and shirts, Swiss Army knives, and, most important, a sophisticated array of cigars. Crafted in Cuba, the Dominican Republic, and Brazil, they include some of the most prestigious names in smoke, including Montecristos, Cohiba, and Churchills. *Remember:* It's still illegal to bring Cuban cigars into the United States; smoke them here.

Electronics are a good buy on Curaçao, as they can be sold duty free; we recommend the very reliable **Boolchand's,** Freedome Blokd 1, Punda (© **599/9-461-2262**), in business since 1930. If you can't find what you're looking for, try **Palais Hindu,** Heerenstraat 17 (© **599/9-461-6897**), which sells a wide range of video and cassette recorders, TVs, speakers, mini–disc players, photographic equipment, and watches.

Penha & Sons, Heerenstraat 1 (© **599/9-461-2266**), in the oldest building in town (1708), has a history dating from 1865. It has long been known for its fine selection of perfumes, cosmetics, and designer clothing (for both men and women). It distributes such names as Calvin Klein, Yves Saint Laurent, Elizabeth Arden, Clarins, and Estée Lauder, among others.

La Casa Amarilla (The Yellow House), Breedestraat 46 (© **599/9-461-3222**), operating since 1887 in a yellow-and-white 19th-century building, sells an intriguing collection of perfume and cosmetics from all over the world and is an agent of Christian Dior, Guerlain, Cartier, and Van Cleef & Arpels.

At **Landhuis Groot Santa Martha,** Santa Martha (© **599/9-864-1559**), craftspeople with disabilities fashion unusual handcrafts, some evoking those found in South America.

Should you, like many visitors from Venezuela, develop a shopping craze, there are a lot more stores to check out, including **New Amsterdam,** Gomerzpein 14 (© **599/9-461-2437**), a long-established store known for its Hummel figurines and hand-embroidered tablecloths, among other items. For novelties and souvenirs, head for **Warenhaus Van Der Ree,** Breedestraat 5, Punda (© **599/9-461-1645**).

8 Curaçao After Dark ★★

Most of the action spins around the island's **casinos:** the **Marriott Beach Resort,** Piscadera Bay (© **599/9-736-8800**); **Holiday Beach Hotel & Casino,** Otrabanda, Pater Euwensweg 31 (© **599/9-462-5400**); **Plaza Hotel & Casino,** Plaza Piar, in Willemstad (© **599/9-461-2500**); and **Breezes Curaçao Resort,** Dr. Martin Luther King Blvd. 8 (© **599/9-736-7888**).

Emerald Casino at the Marriott is especially popular, designed to resemble an open-air courtyard. It features 143 slot machines, six blackjack tables, two roulette wheels, two Caribbean stud poker tables, a craps table, a baccarat table, and a minibaccarat table. The casino at the Breezes Curaçao is the liveliest on the island. These hotel gaming houses usually start their action at 2pm, and some of them remain open until 4am.

The landlocked, flat, and somewhat dusty neighborhood of **Salinja** is now the nightlife capital of Curaçao. Among the best of them is **Blues,** in the Avila Beach Hotel, Penstraat 130 (© **599/9-461-4377**), a restaurant with a hopping bar that's packed every night except Mondays. Live jazz is offered Thursday from 7pm to 10pm and Saturday from 9pm to midnight. No cover.

Club Façade, Lindbergh 32 (© **599/9-461-4640**), in the Salinja district, is one of the most popular discos on the island. Spread over several different levels of a modern building, it has a huge bar, three dance floors, and live music nightly. It's open Thursday and Friday from 8pm to 3am. The cover is $5 to $10.

On Friday and Saturday nights the place to be is **Ole! Ole!,** Salinja (© **599/9-461-7707**), offering live music. If you like to party on the beach, head for **Hook's Hut,** Piscadera Bay (© **599/9-462-6575**). Jazz is a regular feature here, and it's also known to book the best local music on the island.

Dominica

The beaches aren't worth the effort to get here, but the landscape and rivers, as well as increasingly renowned scuba diving, are. Nature lovers who visit Dominica (Dom-in-*ee*-ka) experience a wild Caribbean setting, as well as the rural life that has largely disappeared on the more developed islands. Dominica is, after all, one of the poorest and least developed islands in the Caribbean. There are no casinos and no megaresorts—and hardly any road signs. It's one of the less expensive islands in the Caribbean, and probably the only one that Columbus would still recognize.

Hiking and mountain climbing are good reasons to visit Dominica; its flora is made unbelievably lush by frequent rainfall. Covered by a dense tropical rainforest that blankets its mountain slopes, including cloud-wreathed Morne Diablotin at 1,424m (4,670 ft.), it has vegetation unique in the West Indies and remains the most rugged of the Caribbean islands. The mountainous island is 47km (29 miles) long and 26km (16 miles) wide, with a total land area of 751 sq. km (291 sq. miles), much of which has never been seen by explorers. Should you visit, you'll find clear rivers, waterfalls, hot springs, and boiling lakes.

With a population of 71,000, Dominica lies in the eastern Caribbean, between Guadeloupe to the north and Martinique to the south. The Caribs, the indigenous people of the Caribbean whose numbers have dwindled to 3,000, live as a community on the northeast of the island, where the art of traditional basketry is still practiced.

Clothing is casual, including light summer wear for most of the year. However, take along walking shoes for those trips into the mountains and a sweater for cooler evenings. Locals, who are rather conservative, do not allow bikinis and swimwear to be worn on the streets of the capital city, Roseau, or in the villages.

1 Essentials

VISITOR INFORMATION

Before you go, you can contact the **Dominica Tourist Office** at 110-64 Queen Blvd. (Box 427), Forest Hills, NY 11375 (© **888/645-5637** or 212/949-1711).

In England, information is available from **Morris Kevan International,** Mitre House, 66 Abbey Rd., Bush Hill Park Enfield, Middlesex (© **0181/ 3500-1000**).

You can also get information on the Web at **www.dominica.dm**.

On the island, the **Dominica Tourist Information Office** is on the Old Market Plaza, Roseau, with administrative offices at the National Development Corporation offices, Valley Road (© **767/448-2045**); it's open Tuesday through Friday from 8am to 4pm, Monday from 8am to 5pm.

There are also information bureaus at **Melville Hall Airport** (© **767/445-7051**) and **Canefield Airport** (© **767/449-1242**).

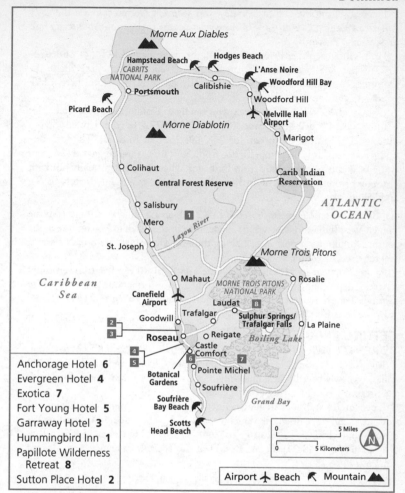

Anchorage Hotel **6**
Evergreen Hotel **4**
Exotica **7**
Fort Young Hotel **5**
Garraway Hotel **3**
Hummingbird Inn **1**
Papillote Wilderness Retreat **8**
Sutton Place Hotel **2**

GETTING THERE

BY PLANE Neither of the two airports on Dominica is large enough to handle a jet, so there are no direct flights from the U.S. or Canada. The **Melville Hall Airport** (© 767/445-7100) is on the northeastern coast, a 1½-hour taxi ride from Roseau on the southwestern coast. The drive takes you across the island through the forest and coastal villages; the fare is EC$43 (US$16) per person when there are four passengers. On your own, the fare could be EC$135 (US$50).

The more modern **Canefield Airport** (© 767/449-1199) is about a 15-minute taxi ride north of Roseau. The 600m (1,968-ft.) airstrip accommodates smaller planes than those that can land at Melville Hall. From here, the typical taxi fare into town is EC$46 (US$17). There's also a public bus (with an *H* that precedes the number on the license plate) that costs only EC$22 (US$8) per person; buses come every 20 minutes and hold between 15 and 18 passengers.

For many from the U.S., the easiest way to reach Dominica is via the daily **American Eagle** (© **800/433-7300;** www.aa.com) flight from American's hub in San Juan, Puerto Rico.

From Antigua, you can board one of the three daily **LIAT** (© **868/624-4727**in the U.S. and Canada, or 888/844-5428 in Dominica) flights to Dominica. Another possibility would be to fly via Barbados. From there, LIAT offers one nonstop flight daily.

If you're already in the Caribbean, you can fly to Dominica from several other islands aboard **Caribbean Star** (© **866/864-6272** in the United States, 800/744-7827 in the Caribbean, or 268/480-2561 in Antigua). The little airline offers two daily nonstop flights from St. Lucia, three flights daily from Antigua, and two flights daily from Barbados. There is one flight daily but with a stopover from the islands of St. Kitts, St. Maarten, St. Vincent, Tortola (BVI), and Trinidad.

BY BOAT   The *L'Express* (© **767/448-2181** on Dominica), sailing from the French West Indies, runs between Guadeloupe in the north to Martinique in the south; Dominica is a port of call along the way. Departures are 6 days a week; call for exact schedules.

In addition, car-ferries sail from Pointe-à-Pitre to Roseau five to seven times a week, depending on demand. For schedule information, contact **White Church Travel,** 5 Great Marlborough St., Roseau (© **767/448-2181**). A one-way fare costs EC$146 (US$54).

GETTING AROUND

BY RENTAL CAR   If you rent a car, there's a fee of EC$32 (US$12) to obtain a driver's license, which is available at the airports. The island has 499km (309 miles) of newly paved roads, and only in a few areas is a four-wheel-drive vehicle necessary. *Note:* Driving is on the left.

There are a handful of small, usually family-owned car-rental companies, the condition and price of whose vehicles vary widely. They include **Valley Rent-a-Car,** Goodwill Road, Roseau (© **767/448-3233**); **Wide Range,** 79 Bath Rd., Roseau (© **767/448-2198**); and **Best Deal Car Rental,** 15 Hanover St., Roseau (© **767/449-9204**).

BY TAXI   You can hire a taxi at either the Melville Hall or Canefield Airport. Prices are regulated by the government (see "Getting There," above, for airport fares). If you want to see the island by taxi, the driver will charge between EC$194 to EC$243 (US$72–US$90) for a tour that lasts between 4 and 5 hours. Rates are usually valid for between one and four passengers. After 6pm, taxis may be hard to find, so call ahead.

BY MINIBUS   The public transportation system consists of private minibus service between Roseau and the rest of Dominica. These flamboyantly painted minibuses are filled mainly with schoolchildren, workers, and country people

---

(*Fun Fact* **National Day**

National Day celebrations on November 3 commemorate both Columbus's discovery, in 1493, and independence, in 1978. Cultural celebrations of Dominica's traditional dance, music, song, and storytelling begin in mid-October and continue to Community Day, November 4, when people undertake community-based projects.

who need to come into Roseau. On most Caribbean islands, we don't recommend buses too zealously. But on Dominica, buses afford the best insight into local life. Taxis may be a more reliable means of transport for visitors, but there are hotels at which buses call during the course of the day. You can also just hail a bus when you see it, and tell the driver where you want to go. Fares range from EC$4 to EC$14 (US$1.50–US$5). Buses are identified by the letter *H* that precedes their license numbers.

FAST FACTS: Dominica

Banks Banks are open Monday to Thursday from 8am to 2pm, Friday from 8am to 5pm. There are several major bank branches in Roseau, complete with ATMs that dispense EC dollars.

Currency Dominica uses the **Eastern Caribbean dollar (EC$),** worth about EC$2.70 to US$1 (EC$1 = US37¢). U.S. dollars are readily accepted, though you'll usually get change in EC dollars. *Unless otherwise specified, rates in this chapter are quoted in U.S. dollars.*

Customs Dominica is lenient, allowing you to bring personal and household effects, plus 200 cigarettes, 50 cigars, and 40 ounces of liquor or wine per person.

Documents To enter, U.S. and Canadian citizens must have a passport. In addition, an ongoing or return ticket must be shown. British visitors should have a valid passport.

Electricity The electricity is 220- to 240-volt AC (50 cycles), so both adapters and transformers are necessary for U.S.-made appliances. It's smart to bring a flashlight with you, in case of power outages.

Emergencies To call the police, report a fire, or summon an ambulance, dial © **999.**

Hospital There's **Princess Margaret Hospital,** Federation Drive, Goodwill (© **767/448-2231**), but those with serious medical conditions may want to forego a visit to the hospital in Dominica, as island medical facilities are often inadequate.

Language English is the official language. Locals often speak a Creole-French patois.

Pharmacies The island's best-stocked drugstore is **Jolly's Pharmacy,** in Roseau at 37 Great George St., and 12 King George V St. Both branches share the same phone number and hours (© **767/448-3388**). They're open Monday to Friday from 8am to 5pm, and Saturday from 8am to 2pm.

Safety Although crime is rare here, you should still safeguard your valuables. Never leave them unattended on the beach or in a locked car.

Taxes A 10% government room tax is added on accommodations, and a 5% tax on alcoholic drinks and food items. Anyone who remains on Dominica for more than 24 hours must pay an EC$38 (US$14) departure tax.

Telephone To call Dominica from the United States, dial **1,** then **767** (the country code for Dominica) and the local number. To call Dominica from another island within the Caribbean, just dial **767,** plus the seven-digit local number. International direct dialing is available on Dominica, as well as U.S. direct service through AT&T. You can contact **AT&T** in Dominica by dialing ℂ **800/225-5288.** Most hotel telephone operators throw up their hands at even placing a long-distance call for a resident. Instead, they connect their clients to the island's long-distance phone operator, who dials the call for a client, and then calls are billed directly to a client's room.

Time Dominica is on Atlantic Standard Time, 1 hour ahead of Eastern Standard Time in the United States. Dominica does not observe daylight savings time, so when the United States changes to daylight saving time, clocks in Dominica and the U.S. East Coast tell the same time.

Tipping Most hotels and restaurants add a 10% service charge to bills; check carefully to see if it's been added. If this charge has not been included, tipping is up to you, though an additional 15% for particularly good service is always welcome.

Water Tap water is generally considered safe to drink, but because it's different from what you're used to, it still might cause a stomach disorder. Better stick to bottled water to be on the safe side.

Weather Daytime temperatures average between 70°F and 85°F (21°C–29°C). Nights are much cooler, especially in the mountains. The rainy season is June to October, when there can be hurricane activity. Dominica lies in the hurricane belt, and fierce storms have taken their toll on the island over the years.

2 Accommodations

The government imposes a 10% tax on hotel rooms and a 5% tax on beverages and food, which will be added to your hotel bill. On top of that most hotels add a 10% service charge.

If you don't want to rent a car, it's best to stay in Roseau, where you can get around better. But if you'd like to experience nature, head for one of the remote inns in exotic tropical settings.

IN ROSEAU & CASTLE COMFORT

Anchorage Hotel   The Anchorage, established in 1971, is at Castle Comfort, a .8km (½ mile) south of Roseau. For the active traveler, there is no better choice, as scuba diving, whale-watching, hiking, fishing, and bird-watching are emphasized. The Armour family provides small rooms with balconies overlooking a pool. The best open onto a view of the Caribbean and contain two double beds. The others are more standard, each with comfortable twins beds or one double. Bathrooms are adequate, with showers and decent shelf space. Although it's at the shore, there's little or no sandy beach available, so guests spend their days around the pool. However, the hotel has its own jetty, you can swim off a pebble beach, and there's a squash court.

The hotel's French and Caribbean cuisine is simple, with an emphasis on fresh fish and vegetables. A West Indian band plays music once a week for dancing.

Castle Comfort (P.O. Box 34), Roseau, Dominica, W.I. ℂ **767/448-2638.** Fax 767/448-5680. www.anchorage hotel.dm. 32 units. Year-round US$50–US$80 double. Children 11 and under granted 50% deduction on meals. AE, MC, V. **Amenities:** Restaurant; bar; outdoor pool; sailing; scuba diving; snorkeling; room service (7am–11pm); babysitting; laundry service; 1 room for those with limited mobility. *In room:* A/C, TV, fridge, beverage maker, hair dryer (in some).

Warning **Mosquito Alert**

At night you are likely to be plagued with mosquitoes. If that's a real problem for you, check into the Fort Young Hotel (see below), which is above the "mosquito line." Most hotels offer mosquito netting. Remember, you came to Dominica for unspoiled nature, right?

Evergreen Hotel This seafront, family-run hotel looks a bit like a Swiss chalet from the outside, but inside there's an open-air restaurant with bright jungle prints, crystal teardrop chandeliers, and an Art Deco bar. It lies 1.5 km (1 mile) south of Roseau. The newer annex, though sterile, has better rooms than the main building. A few units have wraparound tile-floored verandas; all have stone accents. Accommodations are bright and airy, with most rooms having two double beds and ample storage space; bathrooms have showers only. The most special accommodation is called the Honeymoon Hut, an exotic and charming retreat for either honeymooners or off-the-record weekenders. A stony beach is visible a few steps beyond the garden. Inside and out, the airy, comfortably modern place is trimmed with local gommier wood.

Castle Comfort (P.O. Box 309), Roseau, Dominica, W.I. 🕐 767/448-3288 or 3276. Fax 767/448-6800. www. avirtualdominica.com/evergreen.htm. 17 units. Year-round US$95–US$125 double. Extra person US$20. Children under 12 stay free in parent's room. Rates include full breakfast. AE, MC, V. **Amenities:** Restaurant; bar; pool; scuba diving; snorkeling; horseback riding; limited room service; babysitting; laundry service; 2 rooms for those with limited mobility. *In room:* A/C, TV, dataport.

Fort Young Hotel 🏵 Occupying a cliff-side setting, this modern hotel grew from the ruins of the 1770 Fort Young, once the island's major military installation. Traces of its former historic role remain, including cannons at the entrance. It's always attracted business travelers, but now more and more tourists are drawn to the comfortable bedrooms with ceiling fans and balconies. Here you are elevated far above the "mosquito line," so you can actually sit out and enjoy the balmy Caribbean air without being attacked. The hotel has 18 oceanfront guest rooms and three one-bedroom suites at the base of a cliff below the existing fort; ask for one of these suites, which have direct ocean views facing west, a sitting area, bathrooms with shower/whirlpool tub combinations, and two king-size beds. There's no beach, but there's a swimming pool.

Waterfront Restaurant is in a candlelit room with stone walls and wooden rafters. The Jamaican chef draws on his homeland for inspiration and is also an expert at regional dishes. Much of his repertoire has a Continental flair.

Victoria St. (P.O. Box 519), Roseau, Dominica, W.I. 🕐 767/448-5000. Fax 767/448-5006. www.fortyoung hotel.com. 53 units. Year-round US$125–US$155 double; US$230 suite. Extra person US$20. AE, MC, V. **Amenities:** 2 restaurants; 2 bars; outdoor pool; health club; spa; Jacuzzi; sauna; dive center; mooring facilities; whale-watching; island tours; room service (7am–10pm); babysitting; laundry service. *In room:* A/C, ceiling fan, TV, dataport, kitchenette (in some), beverage maker, hair dryer, safe (in some).

Garraway Hotel This is the best inn for those who want to be in the capital and plan to rely on public transportation. Of course, it's nowhere near a beach. This hotel opened in 1994, adjacent to the home of its owners, the Garraway family, who cater largely to business travelers, although it's a perfectly acceptable choice for vacationers, too. It's the closest thing to a Ramada Inn on the island. Most of the spacious guest rooms have vistas stretching all the way to Dominica's southernmost tip. Each unit is outfitted with rattan furniture and pastel floral-print fabrics, one king-size or two double beds, and a combination shower/tub bathroom. Public rooms are given an authentic island touch with artwork and locally made vetiver-grass mats. On the premises is the Balisier restaurant (see "Dining," below).

Place Heritage, The Bayfront (P.O. Box 789), Roseau, Dominica, W.I. ℂ 767/449-8800. Fax 767/449-8807. www.garrawayhotel.com. 31 units. Winter US$105 double, US$125–US$145 suite; off season US$88 double, US$102–US$125 suite. Children under 12 stay free in parent's room. AE, DC, MC, V. **Amenities:** Restaurant; 2 bars; room service (7am–11pm); laundry service; nonsmoking rooms. *In room:* A/C, TV, dataport, hair dryer, safe.

Sutton Place Hotel 🏝🏝   This small, historic property stands in the center of town and was once a 1930s guesthouse run by "Mother" Harris, a matriarch who became a local legend. Destroyed by Hurricane David in 1979, the new Sutton Place was rebuilt in a traditional Caribbean style by the same Harris family, which continues the old traditions but with far greater style. Rooms are tastefully furnished with antiques, including four-poster beds, brass desk lamps, and teak furnishings in the shower-only bathrooms. Suites contain fully equipped kitchenettes. The staircase and floors of the suites are laid with a fine hardwood, tauroniro, from South America. Stylized floral arrangements, exotic prints, and luxurious fabrics contribute to the upscale style.

The restaurant, The Sutton Grill, is now one of the choice places to dine in Roseau, with a Creole/international menu that also embraces some dishes from Italy, China, and India. The nearest beach is about 2km (1¼ mile) away.

25 Old St. (P.O. Box 2333), Roseau, Dominica, W.I. ℂ 767/449-8700. Fax 767/448-3045. www.avirtual dominica.com/sutton.htm. 8 units. Year-round US$95 double; US$135 suite. Extra person US$30. Rates include breakfast. AE, DISC, MC, V. **Amenities:** Restaurant; bar; room service (7am–10pm); laundry service; nonsmoking rooms. *In room:* A/C, ceiling fan, TV, dataport, kitchen (in suites), beverage maker, hair dryer.

IN THE RAINFOREST

Papillote Wilderness Retreat 🏝 *Finds*   This eco-inn is run by the Jean-Baptiste family: Cuthbert, who handles the restaurant, and his wife, Anne Grey, who was a marine scientist. Their unique resort, 6km (3¾ miles) east of Roseau, stands right in the middle of Papillote Forest, at the foothills of Morne Macaque. In this remote setting, you're surrounded by exotic fruits, flowers, and herb gardens. The rooms provide modern comforts like up-to-date bathrooms with plenty of hot water. They are most inviting with their hardwood floors, jungle-painted walls, floral quilts, and fresh flowers.

Don't expect constantly sunny weather, since this part of the jungle is known for its downpours, but that's what keeps the orchids, begonias, and brilliantly colored bromeliads lush. The 5 hectares (12 acres) of sloping and forested land have a labyrinth of stone walls and trails, beside which flow freshwater streams, a few of which come from hot mineral springs. Natural hot mineral baths are available, and you'll be directed to a secluded waterfall where you can swim in the river. The Jean-Baptistes also run a boutique that sells Dominican products, including appliquéd quilts made by local artisans. Even if you don't stay here, it's an experience to dine on the thatch-roofed terrace.

Trafalgar Falls Rd. (P.O. Box 2287), Roseau, Dominica, W.I. ℂ 767/448-2287. Fax 767/448-2285. www. papillote.dm. 7 units. Year-round US$95 double; US$105–US$150 suite. MAP (breakfast and dinner) US$35 per person extra. AE, MC, V. Closed Sept 1–Oct 15. **Amenities:** Restaurant; bar; 3 outdoor pools; room service (7am–10pm); laundry service; nonsmoking rooms. *In room:* Ceiling fan, beverage maker, hair dryer, safe, no phone.

AT MORNE ANGLAIS

Exotica 🏝 *Finds*   This tropical setting is home to what's called an "agro-eco" resort, with some 38 different flowers and fruit trees growing on the 2-hectare

(5-acre) organic farm. When you finally reach the place after a harrowing ride, you can enjoy the cool mountain breezes 480m (1,574 ft.) above sea level, at a point some 8km (5 miles) from Roseau. In 1995, Fae and Altherton Martin built this cluster of cottages on the western slope of Mount Anglais in the southern half of the island. The resort's cottages are constructed from hardwoods, cured pine, and stone. Accommodations are comfortable and tastefully furnished, each with a private porch, spacious living room, kitchen, large bedroom with two double beds, and private bathrooms with shower/tub combinations. You can go wading in a nearby stream, a 5-minute walk away.

Guests can prepare their own meals or dine at the Sugar Apple Cafe, enjoying such delights as steamed local fish or apricot-glazed chicken with savory rice.

Morne Anglais (P.O. Box 109), Roseau, Dominica, W.I. ℭ **767/448-8839.** Fax 767/448-8829. 6 units. Winter US$140 double; off season US$109 double. Extra person US$23. Children under 12 stay free in parent's room. MAP (breakfast and dinner) US$35 per person extra. AE, DISC, MC, V. **Amenities:** Cafe; bar; all nonsmoking rooms; rooms for those with limited mobility. *In room:* Ceiling fan, TV, dataport, kitchen, beverage maker, hair dryer, iron/ironing board.

AT MARIE DANIEL

Hummingbird Inn ⭐ *Value*   A short drive from Roseau and the Canefield Airport and a 2-minute walk to the beach, this hilltop retreat is a great little bargain. Opening onto panoramic views, the rooms are in two bungalows and have louvered windows and doors to capture the breezes in lieu of air-conditioning. Ceilings fans hum day and night, and you can also retreat to terraces with hammocks. Each accommodation has bedside tables and reading lamps (not always a guarantee on Dominica). The handmade quilts on the beds, which have excellent mattresses, add a homelike touch. One four-poster bed, a mammoth wooden affair, is 250 years old. Bathrooms are small but well maintained, and each has a shower. This is a friendly, family-style place, and there are lovely gardens with exotic plants that attract both hummingbirds and iguanas. The local cook is one of the best on the island, and she'll pack a picnic lunch for you.

Morne Daniel (P.O. Box 1901), Roseau, Dominica, W.I. ℭ and fax **767/449-1042.** www.thehummingbird inn.com. 10 units. Winter US$102 double, US$159 suite; off season US$86 double, US$126 suite. Extra person US$20. Children under 12 stay free in parent's room. AE, DC, DISC, MC, V. **Amenities:** Restaurant; bar; limited room service; laundry service; babysitting; all nonsmoking rooms; 1 room for those with limited mobility. *In room:* Ceiling fans.

3 Dining

If you're going out in the evening, always call to make sure your dining choice is actually open. You'll also have to arrange transportation there and back; you probably don't want to drive yourself because of the bad lighting, hairpin turns, and blind corners.

Dominica is a lush island like Grenada and grows a lot of its own foodstuff, but fish and meats are generally shipped in frozen.

IN ROSEAU

Balisier ⭐ CREOLE/INTERNATIONAL   Named after a small red flower that thrives in the jungles of Dominica, this restaurant was designed to maximize the views over Roseau's harbor. We highly recommend the food, which might include blackened tuna; chicken Garraway (breast of chicken stuffed with plantain and sweet corn); loin of pork with pineapple, mushrooms, and onions; and a choice of steak, vegetarian, or lobster entrees. Crab backs are a favorite local dish. End your meal with a slice of homemade coconut-cream pie. Lunches might feature West Indian curries, fish Creole, or several kinds of salads.

In the Garraway Hotel, Place Heritage, The Bayfront. ℂ **767/449-8800**. Reservations recommended. Main courses EC$35–EC$76 (US$13–US$28) lunch; EC$35–EC$84 (US$13–US$31) dinner; Fri lunch buffet EC$41 (US$15). AE, MC, V. Daily 7am–2:30pm and 7–10pm.

Guiyave CREOLE   This airy lunch-only restaurant occupies the second floor of a wood-frame West Indian house. Rows of tables almost completely fill the narrow balcony overlooking the street outside. You can enjoy a drink at the stand-up bar on the second floor. Specialties include different preparations of conch, octopus, lobster, spareribs, chicken, pork chops, and various Creole grills. On Saturday, *rotis* (Caribbean burritos) and "goat water" (a local goat stew) are available. The place is known for its juices, including refreshing glasses of soursop, tamarind, sorrel, cherry, and strawberry. There's also a patisserie specializing in local pastries.

15 Cork St. ℂ **767/448-2930**. Reservations recommended. Lunch buffet EC$26–EC$54 (US$9.50–US$20). AE, MC, V. Mon–Fri 9am–3pm; Sat 10am–2:30pm.

La Robe Creole WEST INDIAN/CREOLE   The best independent restaurant in the capital, La Robe Creole sits on the second floor of a colonial house, beside a sunny plaza on a slope above the sea. The staff, dressed in madras Creole costumes, serves food in a long, narrow dining room capped with heavy beams and filled with 19th-century relics. You can enjoy pumpkin-pimento soup, callaloo with cream of coconut soup, crab backs (in season), and shrimp in coconut with garlic sauce. For dessert, try banana or coconut cake or ice cream.

A street-level section of the restaurant, **The Mouse Hole,** is a good place for food on the run. You can buy freshly made sandwiches, salads, and light meals. They make good Trinidad-inspired *rotis*. On Dominica, these *rotis* are often flavored with curry.

3 Victoria St. ℂ **767/448-2896**. Main courses EC$27–EC$76 (US$10–US$28). MC, V. Mon–Sat 11am–9:30pm. The Mouse Hole, Mon–Sat 8am–4pm.

Pearl's Cuisine *Finds* CARIBBEAN   From this restored Creole house with a veranda, Chef Pearl enjoys a certain celebrity for her island delicacies. Come here for a true taste of Dominica. Begin with one of her tropical fruit juices, followed by perhaps freshly caught crayfish as an appetizer. Whenever lobster is available, it's served at dinner any way you want it. She also makes some mean pork chops, and her curried goat will make a man of you, even if you're a woman. Try the potato salad and spareribs or the codfish and plantains if you want to really go local.

50 King George V St. ℂ **767/448-8707**. Lunch EC$6–EC$35 (US$2.20–US$13); dinner EC$25–EC$59 (US$9.25–US$22). DC, MC, V. Mon–Fri 9:30am–8:30pm; Sat 9:30am–6:30pm.

World of Food Restaurant and Bar *Finds* CREOLE   This is one of the most charming Creole restaurants in town. In the 1930s the surrounding garden belonged to the novelist Jean Rhys, author of *Wide Sargasso Sea.* Some say that its owner, Vena McDougal, is the best Creole cook in town, and we more or less agree, though the competition is stiff. You can have a drink at the stone-walled building at the far end of the garden if you want, but many guests select one of the tables in the shadow of a large mango tree. Specialties include steamed fish or fish steak, pork chops, chicken-filled roti, black pudding, breadfruit puffs, conch, and *tee-tee-ree* (fried fish cakes). Vena also makes the best rum punches on the island.

In Vena's Hotel, 48 Cork St. (with another entrance on Field's Lane). ℂ **767/448-3286**. Main courses EC$25–EC$54 (US$9.25–US$20). MC. Daily 7:30am–10pm.

IN THE RAINFOREST

Papillote Wilderness Retreat *Finds* CREOLE/CARIBBEAN Even if you're not staying here, come by taxi for lunch; it's only 6km (3¾ miles) east of Roseau. For dinner, you'll need to make reservations. Amid exotic flowers, century-old trees, and filtered sunlight, you'll dine overlooking a gorgeous vista of rivers and mountains. The array of healthful food includes flying fish and truly delectable freshwater prawns known as *bookh*. Freshly caught kingfish is also a tasty treat. Breadfruit or dasheen puffs merit a taste if you've never tried them, and tropical salads are filled with flavor. Our favorite dishes include "the seafood symphony" and the green papaya chicken salad.

Trafalgar Falls Rd. (℃) 767/448-2287. Reservations recommended for lunch, required for dinner. Main courses EC$30–EC$59 (US$11–US$22). AE, DISC, MC, V. Daily 6:30am–10:30pm; dinner served at 7:30pm.

4 Sports & Other Outdoor Pursuits

BEACHES If you really want a great beach, you should choose another island. Dominica has some of the worst beaches in the Caribbean; most are rocky with gray-black volcanic sand. But some beaches, even though they don't have great sand or shade, are still good for diving or snorkeling in the turquoise waters.

The best beach on the island lies on the northwest coast. **Picard Beach** stretches for about 3km (2 miles), a strip of grayish sand with palm trees as a backdrop. It's ideal for snorkeling or windsurfing. You can drop in for food and drink at one of the hotels along the beach.

On the northeast coast, four beaches—**Hampstead Beach, Hodges Beach, L'Anse Noire,** and **Woodford Hill Bay**—are among the island's most beautiful, although none are great for swimming. Divers and snorkelers often come here, even though the water can be rough. Watch out for the strong currents.

The southwest coast also has some beaches, but the sand here is black and rock-studded. Nonetheless, snorkelers and scuba divers flock to **Soufrière Bay Beach** and **Scotts Head Beach** for the clear waters and the stunning underwater walls.

HIKING Wild and untamed Dominica offers hikers some of the most bizarre geological oddities in the Caribbean. Sights include scalding lava covered with a hot, thin, and not-very-stable crust; a boiling lake where mountain streams turn to vapor as they come into contact with superheated volcanic fissures; and a barren wasteland known as the "Valley of Desolation."

All these attractions are in the heavily forested 6,800 hectares (16,796 acres) of the **Morne Trois Pitons National Park** , in the island's south-central region. You should go with a guide—there are plenty of them waiting for your business in the village of Laudat. Few markers appear en route, but the trek, which includes a real assortment of geological oddities, stretches 10km (6¼ miles) in both directions from Laudat to the Boiling Lake. Ferns, orchids, trees, and epiphytes create a tangle of underbrush; insect, bird, and reptilian life is profuse.

The hill treks of Dominica have been described as "sometimes easy, sometimes hellish," and if it should happen to rain during your climb (and it rains very frequently on Dominica), the paths are likely to become very slippery. But botanists, geologists, and experienced hikers all agree that climbs through the jungles of Dominica are the most rewarding in the Caribbean. Hikers should walk cautiously, particularly in areas peppered with bubbling hot springs. Regardless of where you turn, you'll run into streams and waterfalls, the inevitable result of an island that receives up to 400 inches of rainfall a year. Winds on the summits are strong enough to have pushed one recreational climber to her death several years ago, so be careful.

An adventure only for the most serious and experienced hiker is to **Boiling Lake** and the Titou Gorge, a deep and very narrow ravine whose depths were created as lava flows cooled and contracted. En route, you might spot rare Sisserou and Jacquot parrots, monkeys, and vines whose growth seems to increase visibly on an hourly basis. The lake itself lies 10km (6¼ miles) east of Roseau, but reaching it requires about 4 hours, including some strenuous hiking. Go only with a guide, which can be arranged through the tourist office (see "Visitor Information," earlier in this chapter, and the "Tips" box below).

Taking the Wotton Waven Road, you branch off in the direction of **Sulphur Springs,** volcanic hot springs that are evidence of Dominica's turbulent past. Jeeps and Land Rovers can get quite close. This bubbling pool of gray mud sometimes belches smelly sulfurous fumes. The trail begins at the **Titou Gorge,** a narrow, deep gorge also formed by the island's volcanic past. At this gorge you can go for a cooling swim in a pool or enjoy the hot spring waters alongside the pool. A 5-minute swim will take you up the gorge to a small cave with a beautiful waterfall. After the gorge the marked trail goes through the appropriately named **"Valley of Desolation"** and comes out at Boiling Lake on the far side, a trek of 2 to 3 hours one-way. Sulfuric fumes in the area have destroyed much of the once-flourishing vegetation in the region.

Boiling Lake is the world's second-largest solfatara lake, measuring 63m (207 ft.) across. It is a bubbling cauldron with vapor clouds rising above blue-gray water. The depth of the lake is not known. The water temperature in the lake averages around 190°F (88°C). The lake is not the crater of a former volcano but a flooded fumarole. Getting here is extremely difficult and even hazardous. Some visitors have even stumbled and fallen to their deaths into the boiling waters. The trail is most often very slippery because of rainfall. You'll encounter few visitors along this trail and, if you do, will likely be glad for the company, especially if a hiker is returning from the area where you're heading. He or she can give you advance reports of the conditions ahead of you.

See also "Exploring the Island," below, for details on gorgeous **Cabrits National Park.**

KAYAKING 🐟🐟   Dominica is probably the best place in all the Caribbean for kayaking. You can rent a kayak for US$26 for a half-day, then go on a unique adventure around the rivers and coastline of the lushest island in the West

---

⌒Tips **Getting a Guide**

Locals warn that to proceed along the island's badly marked trails into dangerous areas is not a good idea; climbing alone or even in pairs is not advised. Guides should be used for all unmarked trails. You can arrange for a guide by going to the office of the **Dominica National Park,** in the Botanical Gardens in Roseau (ⓒ 767/448-2401), or the Dominica Tourist Board. Forestry officials recommend **Ken's Hinterland Adventure Tours & Taxi Service,** Fort Young Hotel on Victoria Street, Roseau (ⓒ 767/448-4850). Depending on the destination and the featured attractions, treks cost US$100 to US$220 per person for up to four participants and require 4 to 8 hours round-trip. Usually included in the price is minivan transportation from Roseau to the starting point of your hill climb.

Indies. **Nature Island Dive,** in Roseau (© 767/449-8181), offers rentals and gives the best advice. You can combine bird-watching, swimming, and snorkeling as you glide along. Consider Soufrière Bay, a marine reserve in southwest Dominica. Off the west coast, you will discover tranquil Caribbean waters with rainbow-hued fish along the beaches in Mero, Salisbury, and in the region of the Layou and Macoucherie rivers.

SCUBA DIVING   Diving has taken off on Dominica. The underwater terrain is spectacular. Most of the diving is on the southwestern end of the island, with its dramatic drop-offs, walls, and pinnacles. These volcanic formations are interwoven with cuts, arches, ledges, and overhangs, home to sponges, gorgonians, and corals. An abundance of invertebrates, reef fish, and unusual sea creatures such as sea horses, frogfish, batfish, and flying gunards attract the underwater photographer.

Dive Dominica, in the **Castle Comfort Diving Lodge** (P.O. Box 2253, Roseau), Castle Comfort, Dominica, W.I. (© 767/448-2188), gives open-water certification (both NAUI and PADI) and instruction. Two diving catamarans and a handful of smaller boats get you to the dive sites in relative comfort. The dive outfit is part of a hotel, a 15-room lodge where at least 90% of the clientele checks in as part of a dive package. A 7-night dive package, double occupancy, begins at US$995 per person, including breakfasts and dinners, five two-tank dives, and one night dive. A single tank dive goes for US$45, a two-tank dive for US$65, and a night dive for US$50. All rooms in the lodge are air-conditioned, and have TVs and phones. On the premises are a bar (for residents and their guests only) and a Jacuzzi.

Divers from all over the world come to the **Dive Centre,** at the Anchorage Hotel in Castle Comfort (© 767/448-2638). With a pool, classrooms, a private dock, a miniflotilla of dive boats, and a fully qualified PADI staff, this is the most complete dive resort on Dominica. A single-tank dive costs US$50; a double-tank dive, US$65; and a one-tank night dive, US$50. A whale- and dolphin-watch from 2pm to sunset is popular and costs US$50 per person. Rum punch is served.

SNORKELING   Snorkeling sites are never very far, regardless of where you are on Dominica. In all, there are some 30 separate and first-rate snorkeling areas immediately off the coast. The western side of the island, where nearly all of the snorkeling takes place, is the lee side, meaning the waters are tranquil. You can explore the underwater hot springs at Champagne and Toucari, the Coral Gardens off Salisbury, and the southern shoreline of Scotts Head Beach, with more than 190 species of flamboyantly colored fish. The closeness of the reefs to shore makes snorkeling here some of the best in the Caribbean. Your hotel or one of the dive shops can set you up with gear.

SWIMMING   The beaches may be lousy, but Dominica has some of the best river swimming in the Caribbean. Some say the little island has 365 rivers, one for every day of the year. The best places for swimming are under a waterfall, of which there are dozens on the island. Almost all waterfalls have a refreshing pond at the base, ideal for a dip. Your best bets are on the west coast at the **Picard** or the **Machoucherie Rivers.** On the east coast, the finest spot is **White River,** near the hamlet of La Plaine. Consider also the **Layou River** and its gorges. Layou is the island's largest river, ranging from tranquil beach-lined pools ideal for swimming to deep gorges and turbulent rapids. All the rivers are pristine and make nice spots for a little sunbathing or perhaps a picnic lunch along their banks.

The staff at the tourist office (see "Visitor Information," earlier in this chapter) knows the island intimately and will help you map out a place for a picnic and a swim during your tour of the island, depending on where you're going. They'll also arm you with a good map and directions if you're heading out on your own.

Our favorite place for a dip is the **Emerald Pool Trail** (see below), which lies in the Morne Trois Pitons National Park. You reach it northeast of Pont Casse, going for 6km (3¾ miles) along an unmarked road taking you north to Castle Bruce. Eventually you reach a sign pointing to the Emerald Pool Trail, the most accessible trail in this lush national park. A 30-minute hike takes you to a stunning cascade of water dropping 6m (20 ft.). This is Emerald Falls, where you can go for a cooling swim. Chances are, you'll have the place all to yourself.

5 Exploring the Island

Those making day trips to Dominica from other Caribbean islands will want to see the **Carib Indian Reservation** , in the northeast. In 1903, Britain got the surviving Caribs to agree to live on 1,480 hectares (3,656 acres) of land. Today, this reservation is the last remaining turf of the once-hostile tribe for whom the Caribbean was named. Their look is Mongolian, and they are no longer "pure-blooded," as they have married outside their tribe. Today they survive by fishing, growing food, and weaving baskets and vetiver-grass mats, which they sell to the outside world. The baskets sold at roadside stands make especially good buys. Once you get here there isn't a lot to do except look at the remains of this once-famous tribe that dominated the islands of the Caribbean. Of course, they'll be staring back at you with equal interest. One of the most interesting aspects is watching the Caribs making traditional dugout canoes.

It's like going back in time when you explore **Morne Trois Pitons National Park** , a primordial rainforest. Mists rise gently over lush, dark-green growth, drifting up to blue-green peaks that have earned Dominica the title "Switzerland of the Caribbean." Framed by banks of giant ferns, rivers rush and tumble. Trees sprout orchids, green sunlight filters down through trees, and roaring waterfalls create a blue mist. One of the best starting points for a visit to the park is the village of **Laudat,** 11km (6¾ miles) from Roseau. (See also "Hiking," above.)

The best tour is the **Rain Forest Aerial Tram,** at the corner of Old Street and Great George Street in Laudat (② **767/448-8775**), open daily from 8:30am to 4:30pm. For US$55 per person you're taken on a 70-minute tour that starts at the village of Laudat, "sailing" over the rainforest through the Morne Trois Pitons National Park. Along the way you're treated to exotic bird life, beautiful waterfalls, and much tropical flora.

Deep in the park is the **Emerald Pool Trail,** a .8km (½-mile) circuit loop that passes through the forest to a pool with a beautiful waterfall. Downpours are frequent in the rainforest, and at high elevations, cold winds blow. It lies 6km (3¼ miles) northeast of Pont Casse. See "Swimming," above, for more details.

Eight kilometers (5 miles) up from the **Roseau River Valley,** in the south-central sector of Dominica, **Trafalgar Falls** is reached after driving through the village of Trafalgar. Shortly beyond the hamlet of Trafalgar and up a short hill, there's a little kiosk where you can hire a guide to take you on the short walk to the actual falls. In all, allow about 1½ hours for the trip from Trafalgar to the falls. This is the only road or pathway into the falls, and you'll have to approach on foot, as the slopes are too steep for vehicles. After a 20-minute walk past

Moments **Searching for Moby Dick**

You'll see more sperm whales, pilot whales, killer whales, and dolphins during **whale- and dolphin-watching trips** 🐾 off Dominica than off any other island in the Caribbean. A pod of sperm whales can often be spotted just yards from your boat, since there are no laws here regarding the distance you must keep from the whales. The **Anchorage Hotel,** at Castle Comfort (℗ **767/448-2638**) offers the best tours. A 4-hour trip costs US$50 (children under age 12 pay half price). The vessels leave the dock every Wednesday and Sunday at 2pm (call ahead for availability).

ginger plants and vanilla orchids, you arrive at the base, where a trio of falls converge into a rock-strewn pool.

For another great way to spend half a day, head for the **Papillote Wilderness Retreat** (see previous recommendations in "Accommodations" and "Dining"). The botanical garden alone is worth the trip, as are the views of mountains and lush valleys. Near the main dining terrace is a Jacuzzi-size pool, which is constantly filled with the mineral-rich waters of a nearby hot spring. Nonguests can use the pool for EC$11 (US$4). Bring sturdy walking shoes in addition to a bathing suit.

On the northwestern coast, **Portsmouth** is Dominica's second-largest settlement. Once here, you can row up the Indian River in native canoes, visit the ruins of old Fort Shirley in Cabrits National Park, and bathe at Sandy Beach on Douglas Bay and Prince Rupert Bay.

Cabrits National Park 🐾🐾 (no phone), on Dominica's northwestern coast, immediately adjacent to Douglas Bay, is a 525-hectare (1,296-acre) protected site, only about 25% of which is devoted to dry land. Here you'll find low-rising hills, tropical forests, swampland, volcanic-sand beaches, coral reefs, and the sprawling ruins of a fortified, 18th-century garrison of British, then French, construction. This is one of the area's great natural attractions, and if your time is limited, you may want to head here even if you skip everything else in Dominica. The park's land extends over a panoramic promontory formed by the low-rising twin peaks of extinct volcanoes (known as East Cabrit and West Cabrit, respectively), overlooking beaches, with Douglas Bay on one side and Prince Rupert Bay across the headland. The marine section of the park extends over the teeming marine life of the shallow waters of Douglas Bay.

If you want to explore the park underwater, we strongly encourage you to take one of the scuba or snorkeling trips organized by the officially designated dive operator for the park, **Cabrit's Dive Center,** Picard Estate, Portsmouth (℗ **767/ 445-3010**). If you're interested in hiking, you'll find about 3km (2 miles) of trails, each clearly marked with brown and yellow signs, pointing out the geological and architectural highlights of the park. Foremost among these is **Fort Shirley,** a forbidding-looking hulk that was last used as a military post in 1854. The park's **Welcome Center** (no phone) contains a small on-site **museum** (open daily 9am–5pm, free admission) that highlights the natural and historic aspects of the park. The staff will make suggestions about the trails you might want to follow, but since the surface of the park is relatively limited in scope, it's hard to get lost. Signs point from the welcome center to the ruins of Fort Shirley, and to the low summits of the East and West Cabrit hills, neither of which rises more than about 150m (492 ft.) above sea level.

6 Shopping

Store hours are usually Monday to Friday from 8am to 5pm and Saturday from 9am to 1pm.

In Roseau, the **Old Market Plaza,** of historical significance as a former slave-trading market and more recently the site of a Wednesday-, Friday-, and Saturday-morning vegetable market, now houses three craft shops, each specializing in coconut, straw, and Carib craft products.

Tropicrafts Island Mats, 41 Queen Mary St. and Turkey Lane (© 767/448-2747), offers the well-known grass rugs handmade and woven in several intricate patterns at Tropicrafts' factory. They also sell handmade dolls, shopping bags, and place mats, all appliquéd by hand. The Dominican vetiver-grass mats are known throughout the world, and you can watch the weaving process during store hours.

Outlets for crafts include **Dominica Pottery,** Bayfront Street at Kennedy Avenue, Roseau (no phone), run by a local priest. An array of pottery made from local clays is on sale, as well as other handcrafts. **Ego Boutique,** 9 Hillsborough St. in Roseau (© 767/448-2336), has the best selection of clothing, much of it in the classic West Indian style, along with some crafts and home accessories, much of it made locally. At the Fort Young Hotel, **Mango Tango,** Victoria Street in Roseau (© 767/448-0342), offers one of the best selections of international clothing, including beautiful Indian silks.

Crazy Banana, 17 Castle St. in Roseau (© 767/449-8091), offers a little preview of some of the best items for which the Caribbean is known, including handcrafts, handmade jewelry, bottles of rum, cigars, and regional paintings.

7 Dominica After Dark

It's not very lively, but there is some evening activity. A couple of the major hotels, such as the **Fort Young Hotel,** Victoria Street (© 767/448-5000), and the **Reigate Hall Hotel,** Mountain Road (© 767/448-4032), have entertainment on weekends, usually a combo or "jing ping" (traditional local music). In the winter season, the Castaways Hotel sponsors a weekend barbecue on the beach with live music. The clubs and bars in these hotels attract mainly foreign visitors, so if you'd like to go where the locals go, head for one of the following.

The Warehouse, Checkhall Estate (© 767/448-5451), a 5-minute drive north of Roseau, adjacent to Canefield Airport, is the island's major dance club, and packed every Saturday. Recorded disco, reggae, and other music is played from 10pm to 5am in this 200-year-old stone building, once used to store rum. The cover is EC$12 (US$4.45).

Check out **Krazy Terrace,** Dame Euginia (© 767/448-8752), if late-night disco dancing is your thing.

Other hot spots include **QClub,** corner of Bath Road and High Street, Roseau (© 767/448-2995), the place to be on a Friday night. Records, both local and American, are played until dawn breaks. If you get bored here, head for **Symes Zee's,** 34 King George V St., Roseau (© 767/448-2494), the domain of Symes Zee, the island's best blues man. A local band entertains with blues, jazz, and reggae. Here's your chance to smoke a reasonably priced Cuban cigar.

12

The Dominican Republic

Sugar-white beaches, inexpensive resorts, and rich natural beauty have long drawn visitors to the Dominican Republic, while at the same time, a not-so-fair reputation for high crime, poverty, and social unrest has scared away many others. Which is it, a poverty-stricken country rife with pickpockets and muggers or a burgeoning destination of beautiful beach bargains?

The answer, of course, is a little of both. The people of the Dominican Republic are among the friendliest in the Caribbean, and the hospitality here seems more genuine than in more commercialized Puerto Rico. The weather is nearly perfect year-round. And the Dominican Republic's white-sand beaches are among the finest in the Caribbean. Punta Cana/Bávaro, for example, is the longest strip of white sand in the entire region.

Safety is still a concern in the Dominican Republic, but it shouldn't dissuade you from planning a vacation here. Crime consists primarily of theft, robberies, and muggings, and most of it is limited to Santo Domingo (although the north coast resorts around Puerto Plata and Playa Dorada are not as safe as they should be). There is a low incidence of violent crime against tourists, however. Follow some simple common-sense rules, and you'll be fine. (See "Fast Facts," below, for details.)

The combination of low prices and beautiful terrain has made the Dominican Republic one of the fastest-growing destinations in the Caribbean. Bargain-hunting Canadians, in particular,

flock here in droves. Don't expect the lavish, spectacular resorts that you'll find on Puerto Rico or Jamaica, but do expect your vacation to be that much less expensive.

Often mistakenly referred to as "just a poor man's Puerto Rico," the Dominican Republic has its own distinct cuisine and cultural heritage. Its Latin flavor is a sharp contrast to the character of many nearby islands, especially the British- and French-influenced ones.

Columbus sighted its coral-edged Caribbean coastline on his first voyage to the New World and pronounced: "There is no more beautiful island in the world." The first permanent European settlement in the New World was on November 7, 1493, and its ruins still remain near Montecristi in the northeast part of the island.

Nestled amid Cuba, Jamaica, and Puerto Rico in the heart of the Caribbean archipelago, the island of Hispaniola (Little Spain) is divided between Haiti, on the westernmost third of the island, and the Dominican Republic, which has a lush landmass about the size of Vermont and New Hampshire combined. In the Dominican interior, the fertile Valley of Cibao (rich sugar-cane country) ends its upward sweep at Pico Duarte, the highest mountain peak in the West Indies, which soars to 3,125m (10,250 ft.).

Much of what Columbus first sighted still remains in a natural, unspoiled condition. One-third of the Dominican Republic's 1,401km

(869-mile) coastline is devoted to beaches. The best are in Puerto Plata and La Romana, although Puerto Plata and other beaches on the Atlantic side of the island have dangerously strong currents at times.

Almost from its inception, the country was steeped in misery and bloodshed, climaxing with the infamous reign of dictator Rafael Trujillo (1930–61) and the ensuing civil wars (1960–66). But the country has been politically stable since then, and is building and expanding rapidly. The economic growth hasn't benefited everybody, though. The country is still poor, even by Caribbean standards.

The greatest threat to the Dominican Republic these days comes from hurricanes, which periodically flatten entire cities. The major resorts have become adept at getting back on their feet quickly after a hurricane, but if a hurricane hits the country before your trip, you might want to call ahead and make sure your room is still standing.

1 Essentials

VISITOR INFORMATION

In the United States, you can contact the **Dominican Republic Tourist Information Center** at 136 E. 57th St., Suite 803, New York, NY 10022 (© **888/374-6361** or 212/588-1012); or at 248 NW 42nd Ave., Miami, FL 33126 (© **888/358-9594** or 305/444-4592; fax 305/444-4845). In Canada, try the office at 2081 Crescent St., Montreal, PQ, H39 2B8 (© **800/563-1611** or 514/499-1918; fax 514/499-1393); or at 35 Church St., Unit 53, Toronto, Ontario M5E 1TE (© **888/494-5050;** fax 416/361-2130). Don't expect too many specifics.

In England, there's an office at 20 Hand Court, High Holborn, WC1 (© **020/7242-7778**).

On the Web, check out **www.dominicanrepublic.com**.

GETTING THERE

Before you book your airline tickets, read the section "Packages for the Independent Traveler" in chapter 2—it could save you a bundle. Even if you don't book a package, see that chapter's tips on finding the best airfare.

American Airlines (© **800/433-7300;** www.aa.com) offers the most frequent service, at least a dozen flights daily from cities throughout North America to either Santo Domingo or Puerto Plata. Flights from hubs like New York, Miami, or San Juan, Puerto Rico, are usually nonstop. American also offers some good package deals.

If you're heading to one of the Dominican Republic's smaller airports, your best bet is to catch a connecting flight with **American Eagle,** American's local commuter carrier. Its small planes depart every day from San Juan, Puerto Rico, for airports throughout the Dominican Republic, including Santo Domingo, Puerto Plata, La Romana, and Punta Cana.

Continental Airlines (© **800/231-0856** in the U.S.; www.continental.com) has a daily flight between Newark, New Jersey, and Santo Domingo.

Other airlines servicing the area include **Aeromar** (© **877/237-6672**), winging in daily nonstop from Miami to Santo Domingo. **Air DCE** (© **809/687-4569**) links Dutch St. Maarten and Curaçao with Santo Domingo. For Canadians, **Air Transat** (© **416/259-1118**) flies to Santo Domingo from Toronto, Vancouver, and Montreal. **Queen Air** (© **809/565-4041**) flies from New York to Santo Domingo four times weekly.

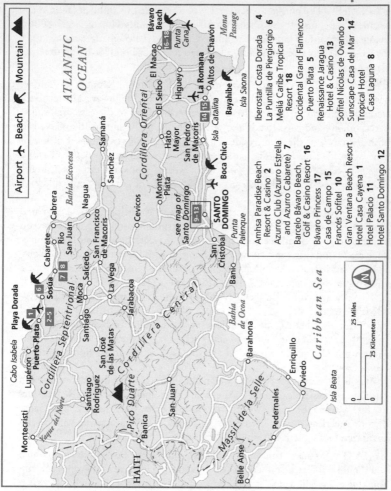

Airport ✈ Beach ↙ Mountain ◀

1 Amhsa Paradise Beach Resort & Casino 2
2 Azurro Club (Azurro Estrella and Azurro Cabarete) 7
3 Barcelo Bávaro Beach, Golf & Casino Resort 16
4 Bávaro Princess 17
5 Casa de Campo 15
6 Francés Sofitel 10
7 Gran Ventana Beach Resort 3
8 Hotel Casa Cayena 1
9 Hotel Palacio 11
10 Hotel Santo Domingo 12
11 Iberostar Costa Dorada 4
12 La Puntilla de Piergiorgio 6
13 Meliá Caribe Tropical Resort 18
14 Occidental Grand Flamenco Puerto Plata 5
15 Renaissance Jaragua Hotel & Casino 13
16 Sofitel Nicolas de Ovando 9
17 Sunscape Casa del Mar 14
18 Tropical Hotel
Casa Laguna 8

Iberia (© **800/772-4642** in the U.S.; www.iberia.com) offers daily flights from Madrid to Santo Domingo, making a brief stop in San Juan.

For information on flights into Casa de Campo/La Romana, see the section "La Romana & Altos de Chavón," below.

Be warned: Arriving at Santo Domingo's Las Américas International Airport is confusing and chaotic. Customs officials, who tend to be rude and overworked, may give you a very thorough check. Stolen luggage is not uncommon here; beware of "porters" who offer to help with your bags. Arrival at La Unión International Airport, 37km (23 miles) east of Puerto Plata on the north coast, is generally much smoother and safer, but you should still be cautious.

GETTING AROUND

Getting around the Dominican Republic is not always easy if your hotel is in a remote location. The most convenient modes of transport are shuttle flights, taxis, rental cars, *públicos* (multipassenger taxis), and *guaguas* (public buses).

BY PLANE   The quickest and easiest way to get across a difficult landscape is on one of the shuttle flights offered by **Air Santo Domingo** (✆ 809/683-8006), flying from Santo Domingo to Punta Cana and La Romana, among other towns. A one-way fare from Santo Domingo to Samaná is US$61, and to Punta Cana US$65.

BY RENTAL CAR   The best way to see the Dominican Republic is to drive. Motorists drive on the right here. Although major highways are relatively smooth, the country's secondary roads, especially those in the east, are riddled with potholes and ruts. Roads also tend to be badly lit and poorly marked in both the city and the countryside. Drive carefully and give yourself plenty of time when traveling between island destinations. Watch out for policemen who may flag you down and accuse you (often wrongly) of some infraction. Many locals give these low-paid policemen a US$5 *regalo*, or gift "for your children," and are then free to go.

The high accident and theft rate in recent years has helped to raise car-rental rates here. Prices vary, so call around for last-minute quotes. Make sure you understand your insurance coverage (or lack thereof) before you leave home. Your credit card issuer may already provide you with insurance; call to find out.

For reservations and more information, call the rental companies at least a week before your departure: **Avis** (✆ **800/331-1212** in the U.S., or 809/535-7191; www.avis.com), **Budget** (✆ **800/472-3325** in the U.S., or 809/549-0351; www.budget.com), and **Hertz** (✆ **800/654-3131** in the U.S., or 809/221-5333; www.hertz.com) all operate in the Dominican Republic. All three have offices at the Santo Domingo and Puerto Plata airports, as well as in downtown Santo Domingo. Avis and Hertz also have offices in La Romana and in Punta Cana.

Although the cars may be not as well maintained as the big three above, you can often get a cheaper deal at one of the local firms, notably **McAuto Rental Cars** (✆ **809/688-6518**). If you want a car with seat belts, you must ask. Your Canadian or American driver's license is suitable documentation, along with a valid credit card or a substantial cash deposit.

BY TAXI   Taxis aren't metered, and determining the fare in advance (which you should do) may be difficult if you and your driver have a language problem. You can easily hail a taxi at the airport and at most major hotels. *Warning:* Don't get into an unmarked street taxi. Many visitors, particularly in Santo Domingo, have been assaulted and robbed by doing just that. The minimum fare within Santo Domingo is RD$71 (US$1.70). In Santo Domingo, the most reliable taxi company is **Tecni-Taxi** (✆ **809/567-2010**). In Puerto Plata, call **Tecni-Taxi** at ✆ **809/320-7621**.

BY PUBLIC TRANSPORTATION   *Públicos* are unmetered multipassenger taxis that travel along main thoroughfares, stopping often to pick up people waving from the side of the street. A *público* is marked by a white seal on the front door. You must tell the driver your destination when you're picked up to make sure the *público* is going there. A ride is usually RD$4.20 (US10¢).

Public buses, often in the form of minivans or panel trucks, are called *guaguas* (pronounced *gwa-gwas*). For about the same price, they provide the same service as *públicos,* but they're generally more crowded. Larger buses provide service outside the towns. Beware of pickpockets on board.

FAST FACTS: The Dominican Republic

Banks Most banks are open Monday to Friday 8:30am to 4:30pm. **ATMs** are found at all branches of Banco Popular. Banks at the malls stay open until 6pm.

Currency The Dominican monetary unit is the **peso (RD$),** made up of 100 centavos. Coin denominations are 1, 5, 10, 25, and 50 centavos, 1 peso, and 5 pesos. Bill denominations are RD$5, RD$10, RD$20, RD$50, RD$100, RD$500, RD$1,000, and RD$2,000. Price quotations in this chapter sometimes appear in U.S. and sometimes in Dominican currency, depending on the policy of the establishment. *Unless otherwise specified, rates in this chapter are quoted in U.S. dollars.* The use of any currency other than Dominican pesos is technically illegal, but few seem to heed this mandate. At press time, the exchange rate was about RD$42 to US$1 (meaning that centavos are practically worthless). Bank booths at the international airports and major hotels will change your currency at the prevailing free-market rate.

Customs Visitors are allowed to bring in 200 cigarettes, 1 liter of alcohol, and gifts not exceeding a value of US$100. Anything over that will be subjected to import taxes.

Documents To enter the Dominican Republic, citizens of the United States and Canada need a valid passport or an original birth certificate with a raised seal and a photo ID. We always recommend carrying your passport. Citizens of the United Kingdom, Australia, and New Zealand need a valid passport. Upon your arrival at the airport in the Dominican Republic, you must purchase a tourist card for US$10. You can avoid waiting in line by purchasing this card when checking in for your flight to the island.

Electricity The country generally uses 110-volt AC (60 cycles), so adapters and transformers are usually not necessary for U.S. appliances. To be safe, ask when booking your hotel.

Embassies All embassies are in Santo Domingo, the capital. The **U.S. Embassy** is on Calle Cesar Nicholas Penson at the corner of Máximo Gomez (© **809/221-2171**). The embassy of the **United Kingdom** is located at Hotel Santo Domingo, Suite 1108 (© **809/472-7111**). The embassy of **Canada** is found at Calle Capitán Cugenio de Marchena 39 (© **809/685-1136**).

Emergencies Call © **911.**

Language The official language is Spanish; many people also speak some English.

Safety The Dominican Republic has more than its fair share of crime (see "Getting There," above, for a warning about crime at airports). Avoid unmarked street taxis, especially in Santo Domingo; you could be targeted for assault and robbery. While strolling around the city, beware of hustlers selling various wares; pickpockets and muggers are common here, and visitors are easy targets. Don't walk in Santo Domingo at night. Locals like to offer their services as guides, and it is often difficult to decline. Hiring an official guide from the tourist office is your best bet. Lock valuables in your hotel safe, carry only a reasonable amount of cash or (better yet) one or two credit cards, and avoid dark deserted places just like you would at home. (*One note:* The single male will find more solicitations from prosti-tutes [*putas* in Spanish] here than anywhere else in the Caribbean. *Putas* are at their most visible and aggressive in such relatively unmonitored tourist zones as Cabarete, and within the bars and lounges of most of the deluxe hotels of Santo Domingo, especially the Jaragua.)

Taxes A departure tax of US$10 is assessed and must be paid in U.S. cur-rency. The government imposes a 16% tax on hotel rooms, which is usu-ally topped by an automatic 10% service charge, bringing the total tax to staggering heights.

Telephone The area code for the Dominican Republic is **809.** You place calls to or from the Dominican Republic just as you would from any other area code in North America. You can access **AT&T Direct** by dialing ℭ **800/222-0300.** You can reach **MCI** at ℭ **800/888-8000** and **Sprint** at ℭ **800/877-7746.**

Time Atlantic Standard Time is observed year-round. Between November and March, when it's noon in New York and Miami, it's 1pm in Santo Domingo. However, during U.S. daylight savings time, it's the same time in the Dominican Republic and the U.S. East Coast.

Tipping Most restaurants and hotels add a 10% service charge to your check. Most people usually add 5% to 10% more, especially if the service has been good.

Water Stick to bottled water.

Weather The average temperature is 77°F (25°C). August is the warmest month, and January the coolest month, although even then it's warm enough to swim.

2 La Romana ⟨★ & Altos de Chavón ⟨★⟨★⟨★

On the southeast coast of the Dominican Republic, La Romana was once a sleepy sugar-cane town that specialized in cattle raising. Visitors didn't come near the place until Gulf + Western Industries opened a luxurious tropical par-adise resort, the Casa de Campo, about 2km (1½ mile) east of town. It's the finest resort in the Dominican Republic, and especially popular among golfers.

Just east of Casa de Campo is Altos de Chavón, a charming and whimsical copy of what might have been a fortified medieval village in Spain, southern France, or Italy. It's the country's leading attraction.

GETTING THERE

BY PLANE   American Airlines (ℭ **800/433-7300** in the U.S.; www.aa.com) offers daily service to Casa de Campo from Miami, with a travel time of about 2½ hours each way. (Yes, it's a slow plane.) **American Eagle** (same phone num-ber) operates at least two (and in busy seasons, at least three) daily nonstop flights to Casa de Campo/La Romana airport from San Juan, Puerto Rico (see "Getting There," in chapter 17). The flight takes about 45 minutes, and it departs late enough in the day to permit transfers from other flights.

BY CAR   You can drive here in about an hour and 20 minutes from the inter-national airport, along Las Américas Highway. (Allow another hour if you're in the center of the city.) Of course, everything depends on traffic conditions.

(Watch for speed traps—low-paid police officers openly solicit bribes, whether you're speeding or not.)

LA ROMANA
ACCOMMODATIONS

Casa de Campo ✪✪✪   Translated as "country house," Casa de Campo, on its own beach, is the leading resort in the Dominican Republic. In the 1960s, the former Gulf + Western corporation took a vast hunk of coastal land, more than 2,800 hectares (6,916 acres) in all, and carved out this chic resort. Tiles, Dominican crafts, mahogany furniture, louvered doors, and flamboyant fabrics decorate the interior of both the public areas and the accommodations.

Rooms are divided into red-roofed, two-story casitas, each with four units, radiating out from the main building, and more upscale villas that dot the edges of the golf courses, the gardens near the tennis courts, and the shoreline. (Ask for one near the water if you plan to spend most of your time on the beach, or one near the links if you're an avid golfer, since the grounds are massive.) Nineteen of the villas each have their own private pool. Some are clustered in a semi-private hilltop compound with views overlooking the meadows, the sugar cane, and the fairways down to the distant sea. Accommodations have either a shower only or a shower/tub combination.

La Romana, Dominican Republic. © 800/877-3643 or 809/523-3333. Fax 809/523-8548. www.casade campo.cc. 279 units. Winter US$190–US$299 casita for 2, US$580 suite; off season US$183–US$214 casita for 2, US$312 suite. Rates are all-inclusive. AE, MC, V. **Amenities:** 8 restaurants; 5 bars; 8 outdoor pools; 3 18-hole golf courses; 13 tennis courts (10 lit); health club; aerobics; sauna; fishing; snorkeling; bikes; horseback riding; polo; children's programs (ages 3–12); theater; room service (7am–midnight); massage; babysitting; laundry service. *In room:* A/C, TV, minibar, beverage maker, hair dryer, iron/ironing board, safe.

Sunscape Casa del Mar ✪   Casa de Campo dominates the southeast coast, but this newer contender on a spectacular beach is giving the grande dame a run for her money. The golf and tennis facilities here aren't as elaborate as those at Casa de Campo, and there are no polo grounds. But the resort is beautifully landscaped and the beach is palm fringed.

Casa del Mar was built in 1997 and virtually rebuilt after Hurricane Georges whacked it in 1998. Accommodations are within seven three-story buildings with yellow walls and blue-tiled roofs. Decor inside features lots of tile, varnished hardwood, wicker, and rattan, plus a neatly appointed shower-only bathroom. There's an overall cheerfulness about the place and lots of emphasis on merengue music that helps keep the good times rolling.

Everything served in all of the resort's restaurants is covered by the all-inclusive price. Michelangelo serves Italian food, Chinese is on the menu at Asia, and Saona does beachfront barbecues and grills, Dominican style. There's also a buffet restaurant and a disco.

Bayahibe Bay, La Romana, Dominican Republic. © 866/786-7227 in the U.S., or 809/221-8880. Fax 809 /221-2776. www.sunscaperesorts.com. 563 units. Winter US$130–US$145 per person double, US$160 per person suite; off season US$60–US$95 per person double, US$72–US$120 per person suite. Rates are all-inclusive. AE, MC, V. **Amenities:** 4 restaurants; 4 bars; outdoor pool; disco; 4 tennis courts; fitness center; Jacuzzi; sauna; banana-boat rides; dive shop; windsurfing; bikes; horseback riding; children's activities; room service (7am–midnight); babysitting. *In room:* A/C, TV, minibar, hair dryer, iron/ironing board, safe.

DINING

El Pescador ✪✪ SEAFOOD   The best and the freshest seafood in the area is served at one of the restaurants inside the Casa de Campo, which is not only the finest place to stay along the southern coast, but serves the grandest cuisine. In an elegant setting, you can dine inside or out on the alfresco terrace. The atmosphere is informal, but the service is first rate. The freshest fish, based on the catch of the day, is brought here for the chefs to concoct into a number of delectable dishes, including perfectly grilled fish, the most preferred method of cooking for most diners. A justifiably favorite dish is the deep-fry mix of calamari, shrimp, and the "catch of the day." For lunch many visitors prefer the fish salad with tropical fruit, or one of the best fish sandwiches in the area.

In Casa de Campo. (*) 809/523-3333. Reservations recommended. Main courses: dinner RD$630–RD$1,135 (US$15–US$27), lunch RD$405–RD$840 (US$9.60–US$20). AE, DC, MC, V. Daily noon–4pm and 7–11pm.

Lago Grill CARIBBEAN/AMERICAN With one of the best-stocked morning buffets in the country, Lago Grill is ideal for breakfast. At the fresh-juice bar, an employee in colonial costume will extract juices in any combination you prefer from 25 different tropical fruits. Then you can select your ingredients for an omelet and another staff member will whip it up while you wait. The lunchtime buffet includes sandwiches, burgers, *sancocho* (the famous Dominican stew), and fresh conch chowder. There's also an abundant salad bar.

In Casa de Campo. (*) 809/523-3333. Buffet RD$800 (US$19); breakfast buffet RD$670 (US$16). AE, DC, MC, V. Mon–Sat 7–11am and noon–3pm; Sun 6:30–11am and noon–4pm.

HITTING THE BEACH

La Minitas, Casa de Campo's main beach and site of a series of bars and restaurants, is a small but immaculate beach and lagoon that requires a 10-minute shuttle bus ride from the resort's central core. Bus transportation is provided, or you can rent an electric golf cart. A bit farther afield (a 30-min. bus ride, but only a 20-min. boat ride), **Bayahibe** is a large, palm-fringed sandy crescent on a point jutting out from the shoreline. Finally, **Catalina** is a fine beach on a deserted island, surrounded by turquoise waters; it's just 45 minutes away by motorboat. Unfortunately, many other visitors from Casa de Campo have learned of the glories of this latter retreat, so you're not likely to have the sands to yourself.

SPORTS & OTHER OUTDOOR PURSUITS

Casa de Campo is headquarters for just about any sporting activity or outdoor pursuit in the area. Call the resort's guest services staff at (*) **809/523-3333** for more information. Casa del Mar weighs in with a heavy array of outdoor activities ranging from horseback riding to banana boating. Call 809/221-8880 for more details.

FISHING You can arrange **freshwater river–fishing trips** through Casa de Campo. Some of the biggest snook ever recorded have been caught around here. A 3-hour tour costs US$31 per person, and includes tackle, bait, and soft drinks. A 4-hour deep-sea fishing trip costs US$549 to US$732 per boat, with 8 hours going for US$793 to US$1,098.

GOLF *Golf* magazine declared Casa de Campo ((*) **809/523-3333,** ext. 3187) "the finest golf resort in the world." The **Teeth of the Dog** course has been called "a thing of almighty beauty," and it is. The ruggedly natural terrain has seven holes skirting the ocean. Opened in 1977, **The Links** is an inland course modeled after some of the seaside courses of Scotland. In the late 1990s, the resort added a third golf course to its repertoire, **La Romana Country Club,** which tends to be used almost exclusively by residents of the surrounding countryside rather than by guests of Casa de Campo.

The cost for 18 holes of golf is US$140 at the Links and US$196 at Teeth of the Dog or the La Romana Country Club. (Some golf privileges may be included in packages to Casa de Campo.) You can also buy a 3-day membership, which lets you play all courses for US$252 per person (for Casa de Campo guests only). A 7-day membership costs US$502. You can hire caddies for US$25; electric golf-cart rentals cost US$20 per person per round. Each course is open 7:30am to 5:30pm daily. Call far in advance to reserve a tee time if you're not staying at the resort.

HORSEBACK RIDING Trail rides at Casa de Campo or Casa del Mar cost RD$1,220 (US$29) per person for 1 hour, RD$1,930 (US$46) for 2 hours. The stables shelter 250 horses, although only about 40 of them are available for trail rides. For more information, call **Casa de Campo** at © **809/523-3333,** ext. 5249, or **Casa del Mar** at © **809/221-8880.**

SNORKELING **Casa de Campo** has one of the most complete watersports facilities in the Dominican Republic. You can charter a boat for snorkeling. The resort maintains eight charter vessels, with a minimum of eight people. Full-day snorkeling trips to Isla Catalina cost US$39 per snorkeler. Rental of fins and masks cost US$5 per day, although they probably won't clock your time with a stopwatch; guests on all-inclusive plans use gear for free. Snorkeling is also included in the all-inclusive rates at Casa del Mar (©809/221-8880).

TENNIS **Casa de Campo**'s 13 clay courts are available from 7am to 9pm (they're lit at night). Charges are US$24 per court per hour during the day or US$30 at night. Lessons are US$61 per hour with a tennis pro, and US$49 with an assistant pro. Call far in advance to reserve a court if you're not staying at the resort. The four courts at Casa del Mar (© 809/221-8880) are reserved for the resorts all-inclusive guests.

ALTOS DE CHAVON: AN ARTISTS' COLONY

In 1976 a plateau 161km (100 miles) east of Santo Domingo was selected by Charles G. Bluhdorn, then chairman of Gulf + Western Industries, as the site for a remarkable project. Dominican stonecutters, woodworkers, and ironsmiths began the task that would produce **Altos de Chavón,** a flourishing Caribbean art center set above the canyon of the Río Chavón and the Caribbean Sea.

A walk down one of the cobblestone paths of Altos de Chavón reveals architecture reminiscent of another era at every turn. Coral block and terra-cotta brick buildings house artists' studios, craft workshops, galleries, stores, and restaurants. Mosaics of black river pebbles, sun-bleached coral, and red sandstone spread out to the plazas. The **Church of St. Stanislaus** is the central attraction on the main plaza, with its fountain of the four lions, colonnade of obelisks, and panoramic views. Mass is held every Saturday and Sunday at 5pm.

The **galleries** (© **809/523-8470**) at Altos de Chavón offer an engaging mix of exhibits. In three distinct spaces—the Principal Gallery, the Rincón Gallery, and the Loggia—the work of well-known and emerging Dominican and international artists is showcased. The gallery has a consignment space where finely crafted silk-screen and other works are sold. Exhibits change about every month.

Altos de Chavón's *talleres* are craft ateliers, where local artisans produce ceramic, silk-screen, and woven-fiber products. From the clay apothecary jars with carnival devil lids to the colored tapestries of Dominican houses, the rich island folklore is much in evidence. The posters, note cards, and printed T-shirts that come from the silk-screen workshops are among the most sophisticated in the Caribbean. All the products of Altos de Chavón's *talleres* are sold at **La Tienda** (© **809/523-3333,** ext. 5398), the foundation village store.

The Altos de Chavón **Regional Museum of Archaeology** (© 809/523-8554) houses the objects of Samuel Pion, an amateur archaeologist and collector of treasures from the vanished Taíno tribes, the island's first settlers. The timeless quality of some of the museum's objects makes them seem strangely contemporary in design—one discovers sculptural forms that recall the work of Brancusi or Arp. The museum is open daily from 9am to 8pm. Entrance is free.

At the heart of the village's performing-arts complex is the 5,000-seat open-air **amphitheater.** Since its inauguration by the late Frank Sinatra and Carlos Santana, the amphitheater has hosted concerts (by Julio Iglesias and Gloria Estefan, among others), symphonies, theater, and festivals. The annual Heineken Jazz Festival has brought together such diverse talents as Dizzy Gillespie, Toots Thielmans, Randy Brecker, Shakira, Carlos Ponce, Carlo Vives, and Jon Secada.

The creations at **Everett Designs** (© 809/523-8331) are so original that many visitors mistake this place for a museum. Each piece of jewelry is hand-crafted by Bill Everett in a minifactory at the rear of the shop.

Set amid the winding cobble-covered alleyways of this pseudo-medieval village, **Coco Point** (© 809/523-8656) sells hand-painted T-shirts, swimsuits, sportswear from Dolce & Gabbana, cigars, and amber and larimar jewelry. **Amber,** petrified tree resin that has fossilized over millions of years, is the national gem. Look for pieces with objects like insects trapped inside. Colors range from a bright yellow to black, but most of the gems are golden in hue. Fine-quality amber jewelry, along with lots of plastic fakes, is sold throughout the country. A semiprecious stone of light blue (and sometimes dark-blue) color, **larimar** is the Dominican turquoise. It often makes striking jewelry, and is sometimes mounted with wild boar's teeth.

DINING

Café del Sol ITALIAN   The pizzas at this stone-floored indoor/outdoor cafe, which is positioned one flight above the medieval-looking piazza outside, are the best on the south coast. The favorite seems to be *quattro stagioni,* topped with mushrooms, artichoke hearts, cooked ham, and olives. The chef makes a soothing minestrone served with freshly made bread. To reach the cafe, climb a flight of stone steps to the rooftop of a building whose ground floor houses a jewelry shop.

Altos de Chavón. © 809/523-3333, ext. 5346. Pizzas RD$355–RD$460 (US$8.45–US$11); salads RD$180–RD$245 (US$4.30–US$5.85). AE, MC, V. Daily noon–11pm.

El Sombrero MEXICAN   In this thick-walled, colonial-style building, the jutting timbers and roughly textured plaster evoke a corner of Old Mexico. There's a scattering of rattan furniture and an occasional example of Mexican weaving, but the main draw is the spicy cuisine. Red snapper in garlic sauce is usually very good. Most guests dine outside on the covered patio, within earshot of a group of wandering minstrels. Chances are you've had better versions of the standard nachos, enchiladas, black-bean soup, pork chops, grilled steaks, and brochettes served here, but a margarita or two will make it a fun night out anyway.

Altos de Chavón. © 809/523-3333. Reservations recommended. Main courses RD$415–RD$590 (US$9.85–US$14). AE, MC, V. Daily 6pm–midnight.

Giacosa ITALIAN/INTERNATIONAL   This is the only restaurant within Altos de Chavón that's not owned and operated by Casa de Campo. As such, its owners and staff tend to try a bit harder. It's a branch of a success story based in Coral Gables, Florida. Within a two-story stone Tuscan-style building you can try Mediterranean dishes like seafood soup studded with lobster and shrimp, risotto with shrimp and sun-dried tomatoes, or savory imported mussels with olive oil, garlic, white wine, parsley, and fresh tomatoes. Another superb dish is red snapper filet with fresh tomatoes, baked in a paper bag to seal in its aromatic flavors.

Altos de Chavón. ℂ **809/523-8466**. Reservations recommended. Main courses RD$330–RD$840 (US$7.90–US$20). AE, MC, V. Daily noon–midnight.

3 Punta Cana ⍟

On the easternmost tip of the island is Punta Cana, site of several major vacation developments with more scheduled to arrive in the near future. Known for its spectacular beaches and clear waters, Punta Cana is an escapist's dream. Its 32km (20 miles) of white sands, set against a backdrop of swaying palm trees, are unrivaled in the Caribbean, and that's the chief and perhaps only reason to come here.

Many Europeans (especially Spaniards) rushed to take advantage of Punta Cana's desirable climate—within one of the most arid landscapes in the Caribbean; it rarely rains during daylight hours. Capitalizing on cheap land and the virtually insatiable desire of Europeans for sunny holidays during the depths of winter, a half-dozen European hotel chains participated in something akin to a land rush, acquiring large tracts of sugar-cane plantations and pastureland. Today, at least a dozen megahotels, most with no fewer than 500 rooms, some with even more, attract a clientele that's about 70% European or Latin American. The hotel designs here range from the not particularly inspired to low-rise megacomplexes designed by the most prominent Spanish architects.

Some of them, particularly the Meliá Caribe Tropical Resort and the Barceló Bávaro complex (see below), boast some of the most lavish beach and pool facilities in the Caribbean, spectacular gardens, and relatively new concepts in architecture (focusing on postmodern interplays between indoor and outdoor spaces).

Don't expect a real town here. Although the mailing addresses for most hotels is the dusty and distinctly unmemorable Higüey, very few guests ever spend time there. Most remain on the premises of their all-inclusive hotels.

If you choose to vacation in Punta Cana, you won't be alone, as increasing numbers of Latino celebrities are making inroads, usually renting private villas within private compounds. Julio Iglesias has been a fixture here for a while. And one of the most widely publicized feuds in the Dominican Republic swirled a few years ago around celebrity designer Oscar de la Renta, who abandoned his familiar haunts at Casa de Campo for palm-studded new digs at Punta Cana.

Above all, don't expect a particularly North American vacation. The Europeans were here first, and many of them still have a sense of possessiveness about their secret hideaway. For the most part, the ambience is Europe in the Tropics, as seen through a Dominican filter. You'll find, for example, more formal dress codes, greater interest in soccer matches than in the big football game, and red wine rather than scotch and soda at dinner. Hotels are aware of the cultural differences between their North American and European guests, and sometimes strain to soften the differences that arise between them.

ESSENTIALS

GETTING THERE   American Eagle (ℂ **800/433-7300** in the U.S.; www. aa.com) offers two to six daily nonstop flights to Punta Cana from San Juan, Puerto Rico; flying time is about an hour. You can also opt for one of American Eagle's two or three (depending on the season) daily flights from San Juan to La Romana and then make the 90-minute drive to Punta Cana.

GETTING AROUND   Most **taxi fares,** including those connecting the airport with most of the major hotels, range from US$25 for up to four passengers. Your hotel can summon a cab for you. If you want to tour along the coast, you can **rent a car** on-site at the car-rental desks of all the major resorts.

ACCOMMODATIONS

Barcelo Bávaro Beach, Golf & Casino Resort ⚜

This huge complex of low-rise luxury hotels opens onto one of the most desirable of the many white-sand beaches along the 32km (20-mile) coast known as Bávaro Beach. This is the most ambitious resort colony in the Dominican Republic, a project whose scope hasn't been equaled since the early days of Casa de Campo, a resort Barcelo Bávaro strives to outdo but doesn't. Built in postmodern Spanish style, it occupies almost 12 sq. km (4¾ sq. miles) of land, including some of the best seafront property on the island. Developed by the Barcelos Group, a group of Spanish hotel investors, it consists of five separate hotels: Bávaro Beach Hotel, Bávaro Caribe Hotel, Bávaro Golf Hotel, Bávaro Casino Hotel, and the latest contender, the Bávaro Palace Hotel. Arranged within a massive park, and connected via a labyrinth of roadways and bike trails, all but one parallel the beachfront (the Bávaro Casino Hotel faces the golf course). Neither the decor nor the gardens are as well-conceived and stylish as those within the Meliá Caribe Tropical (see below), but the effect is nonetheless comfortable and pleasant. Accommodations in all five hotels are roughly equivalent and are outfitted in tropical furniture, with private verandas or terraces, plus an attractively tiled bathroom with tub and shower. (The Bávaro Palace's rooms are bigger and somewhat more comfortable than the others.) Bedrooms have tile floors, Dominican-made furniture, and colorful upholsteries and fabrics.

Each of the 15 restaurants within this megahotel is interconnected by mini-van service, and each will cheerfully accept diners from even the most far-flung corners of the compound. The most upscale and "gastronomic" of the lot is Chez Palace, serving French cuisine, some of whose main dishes require that all-inclusive guests pay a reasonable supplement for their meal. Other, slightly less pretentious eateries include Bohio and La Piña for Dominican food, Los Piños for Italian cuisine, the Coral Steakhouse for two-fisted slabs of grilled beef, chicken, and veal; Mexico Lindo, for Mexican food; and an absolutely vast buffet setup within the open-to-the-breezes Ambar.

Apdo. Postal 3177, Punta Cana, Higüey, Dominican Republic. (C) © 800/227-2356 in the U.S., or 809/686-5797. Fax 809/656-5859. www.barcelo.com. 1,957 units. Winter double in Palace US$250 per person, rooms in any of the other 4 hotels US$190 per person; off season double in Palace US$120 per person, doubles in any of the other 4 hotels US$95 per person. Prices are all-inclusive. Discounts of 45%–65% for children 2–12 staying parent's room. AE, DC, MC, V. **Amenities:** 15 restaurants; 18 bars; 5 outdoor pools; casino; 3 discos; 18-hole golf course; 9 tennis courts; aerobics; whirlpools big enough for 30 people; deep-sea fishing; parasailing; sailing; scuba diving; snorkeling; water-skiing; windsurfing; horseback riding; 3 theaters; salon; limited room service; massage; babysitting; laundry service; dry cleaning; nonsmoking rooms; rooms for those with limited mobility. *In room:* A/C, TV, minibar, beverage maker, hair dryer, iron/ironing board, safe.

Bávaro Princess ⚜

Drawing some of its architectural inspiration from Bali, this hotel opens onto a 2km-long (1¼-mile) white-sand private beach. The Spanish-born architect Alvaro Sanz retained most of the palms and mangrove clusters on the property and installed freshwater reservoirs, creating an oasis not only for vacationers, but also for the many species of birds that call the resort home.

All accommodations lie within 86 low-slung bungalows. The split-level suites contain refrigerators and king-size or twin beds, each fitted with comfortable furnishings. The small bathrooms have combination shower/tubs and marble counters.

Playa Arena Gorda, Punta Cana, Higüey, Dominican Republic. (✆ 809/221-2311. Fax 809/686-5427. www. princesshotelsandresorts.com. 750 units. Year-round US$170–US$200 double. Rates all-inclusive. AE, MC, V. **Amenities:** 7 restaurants; 5 bars; 2 outdoor pools; disco; 4 lit tennis courts; health club; kayaks; Sunfish sailboats; windsurfing; scooter rental; horseback riding; concierge; car rental; shopping arcade; 24-hr. room service; babysitting; laundry service; dry cleaning; nonsmoking rooms. *In room:* A/C, ceiling fans, TV, minibar, hair dryer, iron/ironing board, safe.

Meliá Caribe Tropical Resort 🎣 *(Kids*

The Meliá complex is less upscale than the Bávaro, but we prefer its innovative design. A series of bungalows is scattered within a spectacular garden, with palm trees, fountains, and real flamingos. When you tire of the grounds (if ever!), a little train will transport you over to the beach where topless sunbathing is commonplace. The lobby sets a fashionable tone with its lagoons, boardwalks, sculptures, and bubbling fountains. There's even a richly paneled, well-ventilated hideaway outfitted with poker tables, a bar, and an impressive inventory of Dominican cigars where patrons can puff away for hours. The spa is the best in the area, offering special features such as an aromatherapy massage.

Accommodations are clustered into four distinct parcels of land, two of them adjacent to the beach and the most dramatic swimming pools in the Dominican Republic. The other two lie about .2km (1/8 mile) inland, adjacent to lobby/reception areas and a cluster of discos, cabaret stages, gift shops, and restaurants. Spacious bedrooms are among the best in Punta Cana, with intricately crafted tile and stonework, private terraces or verandas, and roomy bathrooms with tiled showers.

On-site are 11 different eateries, including a trio of large-scale dining rooms (Los Atabales, El Turey, and La Alambra) with an ongoing roster of buffets; two restaurants with mostly a la carte French food (Le Gourmet and Ma Maison); a Mexican restaurant (Los Panchos) with a mixture of a la carte and buffet service; a pasta and pizza joint (Gondola); a Pan-Asian restaurant (Pagoda); a Japanese sushi bar (Hokkaido); and a seafood restaurant (Capri), which is open only for dinner. Know before you go that during periods when the hotel isn't fully booked, not all of these are likely to be open.

Punta Cana, Higüey, Dominican Republic. (✆ 800/336-3542 in the U.S., or 809/221-1290. Fax 809/221-4595. www.solmelia.com. 1,044 units. Year-round US$170–US$275 per person. Rates are all-inclusive. AE, DC, MC, V. **Amenities:** 11 restaurants; 6 bars; 2 outdoor pools; casino; disco; 27-hole golf course; 6 tennis courts; health club; spa; snorkeling; windsurfing; children's programs; business center; limited room service; launderette; nonsmoking rooms; rooms for those with limited mobility. *In room:* A/C, ceiling fans, TV, minibar, hair dryer, safe.

DINING

Given the wealth of restaurants in the hotels listed above, many guests never leave the premises for meals. But the following are worth a special trip.

Capitán Cook 🎣 SEAFOOD   Don't expect an elaborate food or fancy sauces; the allure here is the ultrafresh seafood that's simply but superbly grilled to order. A battery of smoldering outdoor grills lies near the entrance to a dining area whose tables are positioned beneath palm-frond gazebos overlooking a superb beach. Some guests don't bother to consult a menu, but order their meal based on whatever is sputtering over coals or displayed on ice as they enter. Platters of grilled fish or shellfish, chicken, pork chops, or steaks are accompanied by salad, baked potatoes, or french fries. As an alternative try a heaping platter of paella. The shrimp and grilled calamari are superb. Beer is the perfect accompaniment for anything served here, perhaps preceded by a rum-based cocktail.

Playa El Cortecito, Marina El Cortecito. ℂ 809/552-0645. Reservations recommended for dinner. Main courses US$12–US$45. AE, DC, MC, V. Daily noon–midnight.

Restaurant Palace ⭐ INTERNATIONAL   This is the showcase restaurant of one of the biggest resort complexes in the Dominican Republic. If you're not staying at one of the Barcelo hotels, you'll have to make reservations in advance. The decor is cool and stylish, as though it were imported from a chic resort in the south of Spain. A formally dressed staff serves superb dishes that include salmon mousse in a prawn sauce, tartar of tenderloin, grilled red snapper, grouper with mustard sauce, and filet mignon with truffles and foie gras.

In the Bávaro Palace Hotel, within the Barcelo Bávaro Beach, Golf & Casino Resort. ℂ 809/686-5797. Reservations required. Main courses US$8–US$36. Buffet lunch or dinner US$25. AE, DC, MC, V. Daily 7–10:30pm.

HORSEBACK RIDING & GOLF

Within Punta Cana, the guest services staff at your hotel can probably arrange horseback riding for you, but if they can't, consider an equestrian jaunt at the region's biggest stables. These are headquartered at **Rancho RN-23,** Arena Gorda (ℂ 809/221-6500). It supervises as many as 125 horses that are stabled at three separate "ranches," each within a reasonable distance of one another. For US$30 an hour, you'll be guided on equestrian tours through groves of coconut palms near the beach and, in most cases, onto the beach itself. To reach it, you'll follow some clearly marked signs 3km (2 miles) through some of the wildest terrain left in Punta Cana, down winding sandy paths to a series of palm groves, site of these stables.

The Bávaro Golf Course at **Barcelo Bávaro Beach, Golf & Casino Resort,** Bávaro Beach (ℂ 809/686-5797), isn't as great as the one at Casa de Campo, but it's the best on this end of the island. Greens fees are RD$965 (US$23) for 18 holes, with cart rentals going for RD$1,050 (US$25). Guests of the hotel pay only 50% of greens fees. Open daily 7am to 5pm.

PUNTA CANA AFTER DARK

Bávaro Disco, on the grounds of the Bávaro Barcelo Beach, Golf & Casino Resort (ℂ 809/686-5797), has emerged as the hottest, most popular, and sexiest disco in Punta Cana, thanks to a superb sound system. The venue is more European than North American, thanks to a heavy concentration of clients from Italy, Spain, and Holland. If you've been tempted to dress provocatively but never had the courage, the permissive and sexually charged ambience at this enormous club will give you the confidence to try. Painted black, with simulated stars overhead and lots of mirrors, the place is open nightly from 11pm to 5am. Entrance is free for residents of the Barcelo Hotel complex; nonresidents pay US$45.

4 Puerto Plata ⭐

Columbus wanted to establish a city at Puerto Plata and name it La Isabela. Unfortunately, a tempest detained him, so it wasn't until 1502 that Nicolás de Ovando founded Puerto Plata ("port of silver"), 209km (130 miles) northwest of Santo Domingo. The port became the last stop for ships going back to Europe, their holds laden with treasures taken from the New World.

Puerto Plata appeals to a mass-market crowd that prefers less expensive all-inclusives. More accommodations of this kind continue to pop up on this coast, and yet many are still booked solid almost year-round. An unfortunate byproduct of the all-inclusive trend is that several excellent restaurants have been forced to close; in fact, the most popular dining choice along the coast now is Pizza Hut.

Most of the hotels are not actually in Puerto Plata itself but in a tourist zone called Playa Dorada, which consists of major hotels, a scattering of secluded condominiums and villas, a Robert Trent Jones Jr.–designed golf course, and a riding stable.

Although this was the first custom-built tourist haven in the Dominican Republic, the beaches are not the greatest. They're relatively narrow, and subject— as most beaches are—to the vagaries of hurricane erosion. Don't expect Robinson Crusoe–style isolation either; you'll never be alone on a stretch of beach in Puerto Plata, since the beach is shared with the residents of at least nine hotels, all jostling for position. However, if you enjoy beige sand that's rarely too hot to walk on, and a never-ending array of watersports kiosks, chaises longues, and loudspeakers projecting merengue music, you'll be happy here. *One important note:* It rains a lot in Puerto Plata during the winter. If you want guaranteed sun, go to Punta Cana or the beaches on the southern coast.

ESSENTIALS

GETTING THERE   The international airport is east of Playa Dorado on the road to Sosúa. **American Eagle** (© 800/433-7300 in the U.S.; www.aa.com) has daily flights from San Juan, Puerto Rico, to Puerto Plata. The 2-hour flight costs between US$200 and US$370 round-trip. Most of the Puerto Plata resorts are about a 40-minute drive from the airport.

From Santo Domingo, the 3½-hour drive directly north on Autopista Duarte passes through the lush Cibao Valley, home of the tobacco industry and Bermudez rum, and through Santiago de los Caballeros, the second-largest city in the country, 145km (90 miles) north of Santo Domingo.

GETTING AROUND   **Avis** (© 800/331-1212 in the U.S., or 809/586-0214; www.avis.com), **Budget** (© 800/472-3325 in the U.S., or 809/586-0284; www.budgetrentacar.com), and **Hertz** (© 800/654-3131 in the U.S., or 809/586-0200; www.hertz.com) all have offices at the airport.

You probably won't need to rent a car, however, if you're staying at one of the all-inclusive resorts. You might just like to get around Puerto Plata by **motor scooter,** although the roads are potholed. You can rent a scooter at the guest services kiosk at just about any large hotel in Puerto Plata.

Minivans are another means of transport, especially if you're traveling outside town. They leave from Puerto Plata's Central Park and will take you all the way to Sosúa. Determine the fare before getting in. Usually a shared ride between Puerto Plata and Sosúa costs US$1.50 to US$2 per person. Service is daily from 6am to 9pm.

If you take a **taxi,** agree with the driver on the fare before your trip starts, as cabs are not metered. You'll find taxis on Central Park in Puerto Plata. At night, it's wise to rent your cab for a round-trip. If you go in the daytime by taxi to any of the other beach resorts or villages, check on reserving a vehicle for your return trip. A taxi from Puerto Plata to Sosúa will cost around RD$365 ($8.65) each way (for up to four occupants).

VISITOR INFORMATION   There's an **Office of Tourism** on Playa Long Beach (© 809/586-3676). Hours are Monday to Friday 8:30am to 3:30pm.

FAST FACTS   Round-the-clock **drugstore** service is offered by **Farmacia Deleyte,** Calle John F. Kennedy 89 (© 809/586-2583). Emergency medical service is provided by **Clínica Dr. Brugal,** Calle José del Carmen Ariza 15

(© 809/586-2519). To summon the **police** in Puerto Plata, call © 809/586-2331.

ACCOMMODATIONS

Amhsa Paradise Beach Club & Casino 🎯 *Kids*   This all-inclusive resort at the beach is the best-positioned of all the Playa Dorada hotels, with superior amenities and a well-trained staff. It also boasts an eco-friendly design: a cluster of Caribbean-Victorian low-rises with white-tile roofs and lattice-laced balconies. Brick paths cut through the well-manicured, tropical grounds, and kids have room to romp. Accommodations are neatly furnished with tile floors, twin or queen-size beds with excellent mattresses, refrigerators (in most cases), large closets, and tiled bathrooms with shower/tub combinations. Most rooms have French doors leading to private patios or balconies. Only the suites have views opening onto the water.

The resort has five restaurants, some of which are buffet style. The management also hosts poolside barbecues and weekly shows with singing and dancing acts.

Playa Dorada (Apdo. Postal 337), Puerto Plata, Dominican Republic. © 800/752-9236 in the U.S., or 809/320-3663. Fax 809/320-4858. www.amhsamarina.com. 436 units. Winter US$101–US$144 double, US$102–US$152 suite; off season US$81–US$111 double, US$120 suite. Rates are all-inclusive. AE, MC, V. **Amenities:** 3 restaurants; 4 bars; giant pool; casino; disco; lit tennis courts; aerobics; whirlpool; sailing; scuba diving; snorkeling; windsurfing; horseback riding; kids' club; limited room service; babysitting; laundry service; dry cleaning; nonsmoking rooms. *In room:* A/C, TV, safe.

Gran Ventana Beach Resort 🎯 *Kids*   Come here for the opulent style and glamour on the beach, everything set against a backdrop of 100 landscaped hectares (247 acres). If you like a hotel with some theatrical pizzazz, this is your baby. The three-story buildings are trimmed with ornate, Victorian-inspired gingerbread; each unit offers mahogany furniture, ceiling fans, a balcony or patio, and, in all but a few rooms, views of the sea. Bedrooms are compact but efficiently designed. Bathrooms are a bit small but have up-to-date plumbing with tub-and-shower combos. The gardens and lawns surrounding the site are dotted with gazebos, flowering shrubs, and tropical plants and palms.

The all-inclusive plan limits a guest to 1 hour per day for each of the following: snorkeling, windsurfing, sailing, horseback riding, kayaks, and scuba diving. It limits dining at the exclusive Octopus (the best cuisine at the resort) to once a week. Nightly entertainment is included.

Playa Dorada (Apdo. Postal 22), Puerto Plata, Dominican Republic. © 809/320-2111. Fax 809/320-4017. www.vhhr.com. 506 units. Year-round US$90–US$130 double; US$150–US$190 suite. Rates all-inclusive. AE, DC, MC, V. **Amenities:** 5 restaurants; 6 bars; 3 outdoor pools; tennis court; fitness center; sauna; kayaks; sailing; scuba diving; windsurfing; horseback riding; children's center; salon; limited room service; massage; babysitting/nursery; rooms for those with limited mobility. *In room:* A/C, TV, minibar (in suites), beverage maker (in suites), hair dryer, iron/ironing board, safe.

Iberostar Costa Dorada 🎯 *Kids*   With easy access to the beach, this hotel represents the new architectural ideas sweeping over Puerto Plata. It opened in 1999, outside the Zona Turistica, the gardenlike compound that until recently contained most of the resort's hotels. Owned and operated by a Madrid-based chain, it boasts one of the most exciting designs of any hotel in Puerto Plata, with some of the most intricate stone, tile, and mosaic work, and a rambling and sophisticated combination of Taíno, Andalusian, and Moorish architecture. Several roofs of this hotel are covered with woven palm fronds, amazing for a hotel of this scale, sheltering a design that opens onto views of arcades, hidden courtyards, and fountains. A day pass, which entitles you to a meal, a round of drinks, and a view of the unusual design, costs US$34 per adult (6pm–2am), US$29 (7am–6pm), or half price per child under age 12.

Rooms are cool and airy, with tilework floors, earth tones, brightly colored upholsteries, and wall weavings inspired by Taíno designs, and big windows. Each has a compact, shower-only bathroom.

Carretera Luperón, km. 4, Marapicá, Puerto Plata, Dominican Republic. ℰ 888/923-2722 or 809/320-1000. Fax 809/320-2023. www.iberostar.com. 516 units. Year-round US$80–US$160 per person double; US$90–US$170 per person junior suite. Rates are all-inclusive. AE, MC, V. **Amenities:** 3 restaurants; 3 bars; large pool; kayaks; sailing; windsurfing; kids' activities; limited room service. *In room:* A/C, TV, minibar, hair dryer, iron/ironing board, safe.

Occidental Grand Flamenco Puerto Plata 𝕽 *Kids* Opening onto a tran-
quil stretch of Las Papas Beach, this is one of the most upscale and consistently reliable hotels in Puerto Plata. The Occidental exudes a low-key classiness that some of its competitors lack. Operated by the Spain-based Occidental chain, it has a tasteful, discreetly elegant lobby outfitted with bouquets of flowers and reproductions of Taíno statues. Accommodations are set within clusters of three-story buildings with white walls and red terra-cotta roofs. Throughout the accommodations there's a sense of Iberian dignity, with strong contrasts of dark paneling with white walls, blue-and-white tilework, and plenty of space. More expensive rooms, in the Club Miguel Ange, are somewhat larger and have upgraded amenities and round-the-clock access to a concierge. Each bathroom has a tub-and-shower combo.

Dining options range from hot dogs, burgers, and pizza, to an array of international cuisine including seafood and a sampling of Mediterranean dishes. Our favorite is the grill restaurant, Las Reses.

Complejo Playa Dorada (P.O. Box 547), Puerto Plata, Dominican Republic. ℰ 809/320-5084. Fax 809/320-6319. www.occidental-hoteles.com. 582 units. Year-round US$62–US$87 per person double. Rates are all-inclusive. AE, MC, V. **Amenities:** 8 restaurants; 5 bars; 2 pools; disco; golf; tennis courts; aerobics; dive school; kayaks; snorkeling; windsurfing; horseback riding; children's center; travel agency; salon; limited room service; babysitting; laundry service. *In room:* A/C, TV, minibar (in suite), safe.

DINING

Aquaceros Bar & Grill INTERNATIONAL/MEXICAN This is one of our
favorite restaurants on the Malecón, just across the busy boulevard from the sea. The menu lists such tempting food items as Creole-style conch, two different preparations of lobster, burgers, barbecued fish, burritos, quesadillas, and fajitas. Of special note is the house version of Monterrey chicken, made with chicken breast, ham, salsa, sour cream, and cheese. Rum punch and banana mamas give diners a buzz. Adobe walls, a fountain, and merengue music complete the picture.

Malecón 32. ℰ 809/586-2796. Reservations recommended. Main courses RD$105–RD$355 (US$2.50–US$8.40). AE, MC, V. Daily 10am–2am.

Hemingway's Café INTERNATIONAL/MEXICAN The rough-hewn
character of this place stands in stark contrast to the manicured exterior of the shopping center that contains it. Inside, you'll find a dark and shadowy plank-sheathed bar and grill, dotted with accessories you might have found on a pier in Key West. We can just imagine Papa himself digging into the succulent pastas, fajitas, quesadillas, meal-size salads, burgers, and huge New York steaks, while downing one of the "Floridita" cocktails. After around 9pm, a karaoke machine cranks out romantic or rock 'n' roll favorites.

Playa Dorada Plaza. ℰ 809/320-2230. Sandwiches, salads, and pastas RD$120–RD$190 (US$2.90–US$4.55); main-course platters RD$330–RD$1,050 (US$7.80–US$25). AE, MC, V. Daily noon–2am.

Jardín Suizo INTERNATIONAL   This Swiss-run restaurant, a tradition here since 1990, resembles a European trattoria with its tiles, cloth-draped tables, and use of wood. Sliding windows are pulled back to take in views of the ocean. The food is fresh and well prepared, although some of the dishes might be a little heavy for the Tropics. You can order such dishes as filet of pork in a mushroom sauce, or three different medallions of meat in a wine sauce. The best item we recently enjoyed on the menu is the freshly caught fish filet of the day in garlic sauce. Many famous international dishes are offered as well, including tasty shish kabob, chicken curries, and a thick beef stroganoff.

Ave. Circunvalación Norte 13A. ℂ 809/586-9564. Main courses RD$90–RD$355 (US$2.15–US$8.40). AE, DC, MC, V. Daily 11am–11pm. Closed 3 weeks in July.

Le Papillon CARIBBEAN/CONTINENTAL   This is an unusual but charming restaurant set on a hillside in a residential neighborhood about 5km (3 miles) south of Puerto Plata. The expatriate German owner, Thomas Ackermann, manages to combine aspects of the Black Forest with merengue music. The best way to start a meal here is with a *caipirinha* (a Brazilian cocktail) at the bar beneath the cane-frond ceiling. Later, within an open-sided pavilion overlooking a forest, you'll be presented with a menu that's divided into categories that feature different preparations of pork, chicken, beef, seafood, rabbit, and even vegetarian offerings. Enduring favorites include fettuccine with lobster; "pirate" kabobs with shrimp, tenderloin of beef, and vegetables; an especially worthy chicken stuffed with shrimp and served with saffron sauce; and a four-fisted version of chateaubriand that's only prepared for two.

Villas Cofresi. ℂ 809/970-7640. Reservations recommended. Main courses RD$200–RD$460 (US$4.80–US$11). AE, MC, V. Tues–Sun 6–10:30pm. From downtown Puerto Plata, drive 5km (3 miles) south, following the signs to Santiago. Turn left at the signs to Villas Cofresi.

Sam's Bar & Grill STEAKHOUSE   The *gringo* and *gringa* expats have made Sam's their favorite dive since way back in 1970, when it was first established. In the center of town, only a block and a half from the central park and the Malecón, it lies in a Victorian building from 1896. Marilyn Monroe photographs and caricatures by local artists form the decor. Here is where you can order a plate of meatloaf like your mama made, or that eternal favorite, steak and eggs. The cook does a tasty filet of beefsteak or something more ambitious, like chicken cordon bleu. Come here for the memories, the good times, and, of course, the good-tasting food. You can start your day with fluffy pancakes, or later enjoy freshly made soups, salads, and sandwiches for lunch along with hot dishes.

Calle José del Carmen Ariza 34. ℂ 809/586-7267. Main courses RD$170–RD$290 (US$4.10–US$6.95). No credit cards. Daily 7am–11pm.

HITTING THE BEACH

Although they face the sometimes-turbulent waters of the Atlantic, and it rains a lot in winter, it's the beaches that put the north coast on the tourist map. The beaches at **Playa Dorada** are known collectively as the "Amber Coast" for the deposits of amber that have been discovered here. Playa Dorada has one of the highest concentrations of hotels on the north coast, so the beaches here, though good, are almost always crowded, both with tourists and locals. The beaches have lovely white or powdery beige sand and the waters are very popular with water-skiers and windsurfers. Many concession stands along the beach rent equipment.

Another good choice in the area, **Luperón Beach** lies about a 60-minute drive to the west of Puerto Plata. This is a wide stretch of powdery white sand, set amid palm trees that provide wonderful shade when the noonday sun grows too fierce. It's better for windsurfing, scuba diving, and snorkeling than swimming. Various watersports concessions are found here, along with several snack bars.

SPORTS & OTHER OUTDOOR PURSUITS

The north coast is a watersports scene, although the sea tends to be rough. Snorkeling is popular, and the windsurfing is among the best in the Caribbean.

GOLF Robert Trent Jones Jr. designed the 18-hole **Playa Dorada** championship golf course (© **809/320-4262**), which surrounds the resorts and runs along the coast. Even nongolfers can stop at the clubhouse for a drink or a snack to enjoy the views. Greens fees are US$55 for 18 holes; a caddy costs US$9. It's best to make arrangements at the activities desk of your hotel.

The 4,888-yard **Playa Grande Golf Course** at Playa Grande, km. 9, Carretera Rio San Juan-Cabrera (© **800/858-2258** or 809/582-0860), is generating a lot of excitement. Some pros have already hailed it as one of the best courses in the Caribbean. Its design consultant was Robert Trent Jones Jr. Ten of its holes border the Atlantic, and many of these are also set atop dramatic cliffs overlooking the turbulent waters of Playa Grande Beach. Greens fees are US$92 in winter, US$64 off season.

TENNIS Nearly all the major resort hotels have tennis courts.

WATERSPORTS Your watersports options in Puerto Plata are numerous. Most of the kiosks on the beach here are ultimately run by the same company, and prices don't vary among them. If there isn't one close to your hotel, try **Playa NACO Centro de Deportes Acuaticos** (© **809/320-2567**), a rustic clapboard-sided hut on the beachfront of the Dorado NACO Hotel. Prices are as follows: banana-boat rides, US$8 for a 10- to 12-minute ride; water-skiing, US$20 for a 10- to 15-minute ride; sea kayak and Sunfish sailboat rental, US$10 per hour; sailboards, US$20 a day; and paragliding, US$35 for a 10-minute ride.

There are watersports kiosks about every 100m along the beach, any of which will rent you snorkeling gear and tell you the best spots for seeing fish. Puerto Plata isn't great for snorkeling, but you can take a boat trip to some decent sites.

SEEING THE SIGHTS

Fort San Felipe, the oldest fort in the New World, is a popular attraction. Philip II of Spain ordered its construction in 1564, a task that took 33 years to complete. Built with 2m-thick (6½-ft.) walls, the fort was virtually impenetrable, and the moat surrounding it was treacherous—the Spaniards sharpened swords and embedded them in coral below the surface of the water. The doors of the fort are only 1m (3¼-ft.) high, another deterrent to swift passage. During Trujillo's rule, Fort San Felipe was used as a prison. Standing at the end of the Malecón, the fort was restored in the early 1970s. Admission is RD$11 (US25¢) (© **809/261-6043**). Open daily 8am to 6pm. Free for children under 12.

Isabel de Torres (© **809/970-0501**), an observation tower that was heavily fortified during the reign of Trujillo, affords a panoramic view of the Amber Coast from a point near the top, 779m (2,555 ft.) above sea level. You reach the observation point by cable car *(teleférico)*, a 10-minute ascent. Once here, you're also treated to 3 hectares (7½ acres) of botanical gardens. The round-trip costs RD$101 (US$2.40) for adults, RD$50 (US$1.20) for children age 12 and under. The aerial ride runs Thursday to Tuesday from 9am to 5pm. There's often a long wait in line for the cable car, and at certain times it's closed for repairs, so check at your hotel before you head out.

You can see a collection of rare amber specimens at the **Museo de Ambar Dominicano (Museum of Dominican Amber),** Calle Duarte 61 (© **809/586-2848**), near Puerto Plata's Central Park. It's open Monday to Friday 8am to 6pm, Saturday 9am to 5pm. Guided tours in English are offered. Admission is RD$25 (US60¢) for adults. Children under 10 are free.

SHOPPING

The neoclassical house sheltering the Museo de Ambar Dominicano (see above) also contains the densest collection of **boutiques** in Puerto Plata. Many of the paintings here are from neighboring Haiti, but the amber, larimar, and mahogany woodcarvings are local.

Plaza Turisol Complex, the largest shopping center on the north coast, has about 80 different outlets and the most upscale and tasteful merchandise. Make this your first stop if you want to get an idea of what's available in Puerto Plata—make it your only stop if you don't have time to visit all the shopping centers. It's about 5 minutes from Puerto Plata and Playa Dorada, on the main road heading east. Nearby is a smaller shopping center, **Playa Dorada Plaza,** with about 80 shops selling handcrafts, clothing, souvenirs, and gifts. Both it and the Plaza Turisol are open daily from 9am to 9pm.

Plaza Isabela, in Playa Dorada about 455m (1,492 ft.) from the entrance to the Playa Dorada Hotel complex, is a collection of small specialty shops constructed in Victorian gingerbread style, although much of its inventory has a Spanish inspiration or flair. Here you'll find the main branch of the Dominican Republic's premier jeweler, **Harrison's** (© **809/586-3933**), a specialist in platinum work. Madonna, Michael Jackson, and Keith Richards have all been spotted wearing Harrison's jewelry. The store has a special clearance area; tours are available. There's another branch in the Playa Dorada Plaza (© **809/320-2219**) in the Playa Dorada Hotel complex.

PUERTO PLATA AFTER DARK

If you have time to visit only one casino, make it **Playa Dorada Casino,** in the Playa Dorada Hotel (© **809/586-3988**). Its mahogany gaming tables are reflected in the silver ceiling. No shorts are permitted inside the premises after 7pm, and beach attire is usually discouraged. Access to the slot machines starts at 4pm, with full casino action after 6pm. **Amhsa Paradise Beach Casino** (© **809/320-3663**) has the most appealing design of Puerto Plata's three casinos. It is decorated in shades of hot pink, with a soaring ceiling and lots of mahogany trim and louvers. Open daily 4pm to 4am.

The Playa Dorada Hotel complex contains about 20 hotels, five of which have **discos** that welcome anyone, guest or not, into their confines. These after-dark diversions tend to be filled mainly with foreign visitors, although it occasionally attracts locals looking to hook up with tourists. None charge a cover, and the almost-universal drink of choice, Presidente Beer, costs RD$86 (US$2.05) a bottle. **Crazy Moon,** adjacent to the lobby of the AMHSA Paradise Hotel (© **809/320-3663**), is the hottest, hippest, and most sought-after nightclub in Puerto Plata. Fronted by an artful re-creation of a clapboard-sided Creole cottage, it's open Monday to Saturday 11pm to 4am. Admission charges range from RD$50 to RD$202 (US$1.20–US$4.80).

La Barrica, Avenida Manolo Tavares Justo 106 (© **809/586-6660**), lies behind an ochre-colored Spanish colonial facade on the dusty highway leading from Puerto Plata to Santiago, about 2km (1¼ mile) south of the town center. It's mobbed with locals every night after 11pm. They talk, smoke, drink, flirt, and often make out on any of the thousands of folding chairs. If you enjoy active, sometimes aggressive merengue bars where a man will positively never need to be alone, you might find it fascinating. Women should not come here alone. Entrance is free, and you might be frisked for weapons before you enter. Open Monday to Thursday from 6pm to 6am, Friday and Saturday 2pm to 6am.

5 Sosúa ⟨★

About 24km (15 miles) east of Puerto Plata is one of the finest beaches in the Dominican Republic, **Sosúa Beach.** A strip of soft, white sand more than a .8km (½ mile) wide, it's tucked in a cove sheltered by coral cliffs and has crystal-clear water. The beach connects two strikingly disparate communities, which together make up the town known as Sosúa. As increasing numbers of visitors flock to Sosúa, mainly for its beach life, it is beginning to rival Puerto Plata. You won't find the superdeluxe resorts that are commonplace in Puerto Plata, but prices in Sosúa are half what they are at the big resorts and the beaches are just as lovely.

At one end of the beach is **El Batey,** an area with residential streets, gardens, restaurants, shops, and hotels. Real-estate transactions have been booming in this area and many villas have been constructed, fronted by newly paved streets.

At the other end of Sosúa Beach lies the typical village community of **Los Charamicos,** a sharp contrast to El Batey. Here you'll find tin-roofed shacks, vegetable stands, chickens scrabbling in the rubbish, and warm, friendly people.

Sosúa was founded in 1940 by European Jews seeking refuge from Hitler. Trujillo invited 100,000 of them to settle in his country on a banana plantation, but only 600 or so Jews were actually allowed to immigrate, and of those, only about a dozen or so remained on the plantation. There are some 20 Jewish families living in Sosúa today, and for the most part they are engaged in the dairy and smoked-meat industries, which the refugees began during the war. Biweekly services are held in the local one-room synagogue. Many of the Jews intermarried with Dominicans, and the town has taken on an increasingly Spanish flavor; women of the town are often seen wearing both the Star of David and the Virgin de Altagracia, the patron saint of the Dominicans. Nowadays many German expatriates are also found in the town.

GETTING THERE   To get here from Puerto Plata, take the autopista (Rte. 5) east for about 30 minutes. If you venture off the main highway, anticipate enormous potholes. Taxis, charter buses, and *públicos* from Puerto Plata and Playa Dorada let passengers off at the stairs leading down from the highway to Sosúa beach.

ACCOMMODATIONS

Hotel Casa Cayena   Clean, decent, and well managed, this hotel, a short walk from the beach, gets its name from a native village. Inside, you'll find a two-story atrium illuminated by a skylight that's shaped like a Star of David, lots of exposed wood and stone, and a well-designed garden that rings a sheltered swimming pool. Each bedroom has more space than you might expect, with a decor that's based on varnished mahogany louvers and trim, terra-cotta tile floors, white walls, and a ceiling fan. Shower-only bathrooms are cramped but serviceable, the overall ambience is pleasant, and the prices are reasonable.

Calle Dr. Rosen 25, El Batey, Sosúa, Dominican Republic. © 809/571-2651. Fax 809/571-1314. 24 units. Year-round US$30–US$45 double. Rates include breakfast. AE, DC, MC, V. **Amenities:** Restaurant; bar; outdoor pool; scuba instruction; babysitting; laundry service; dry cleaning. *In room:* A/C, ceiling fan, TV, safe.

La Puntilla de Piergiorgio ★ Ⓥalue   This hotel lies in a quiet residential neighborhood, within a 10-minute walk from the bustling commercial center of Sosúa. Built on a rocky promontory high above the beach, it has a neo-Victorian design that includes lots of enticing gingerbread, lattices, and whimsical grace. Accommodations are bright, large, very clean, and outfitted with white-tile floors, flowered chintz upholsteries, and a semicircular veranda with views of either the garden or the ocean. Each accommodation comes with a small but neatly arranged tiled private bathroom with shower stalls.

Calle La Puntilla 1, El Batey, Sosúa, Dominican Republic. © 809/571-2215. Fax 809/571-2786. 51 units. Year-round US$75–US$110 double. Rates include breakfast. AE, MC, V. **Amenities:** Restaurant; bar; outdoor pool; limited room service; babysitting; laundry service; dry cleaning. *In room:* A/C, TV, hair dryer, safe.

DINING
La Puntilla de Piergiorgio ★ ITALIAN   A 10-minute walk west of Sosúa's center, this place serves the best Italian food in town, attracting an animated clientele of Europeans looking for a change from Creole and Dominican cuisine. The setting, located in the hotel of the same name, is a series of outdoor terraces, some of them covered, most of them open air, that cascade down to the edge of a sea cliff. There's enough space to allow conversational privacy for virtually any intimate dinner, and a pair of gazebo-style bars that provide an ongoing supply of mimosas and rum-based drinks. It's true we've had better versions of every dish served here, but for the area it is outstanding, especially the different preparations of fresh fish caught off local waters, which you can even order barbecued. Sometimes the chef gets fancy, as when he flames the prawns with cognac, or goes Continental with his filet steak in green-peppercorn sauce. The cannelloni Rossini (chopped meat and spinach) isn't bad at all.

Calle La Puntilla 1. © 809/571-2215. Main courses RD$290–RD$545 (US$6.95–US$13). AE, MC, V. Daily noon–midnight.

Morua Mai INTERNATIONAL   This is the most visible, and most deeply entrenched, restaurant in downtown Sosúa. Established by German entrepreneurs in the 1970s, and set at the town's busiest intersection, it incorporates the closest thing in town to a European cafe on the pavement in front. It was designed of timbers and palm thatch like an enormous Taíno teepee, under which ceiling fans slowly spin, and wicker and wooden furniture help create an ambience conducive to the leisurely consumption of tropical drinks and well-prepared food. Steaks and seafood are staples here. Depending on the arrival of fresh supplies that day, the menu might also include four different preparations of lobster; several kinds of shrimp, including a version with spicy tomato sauce and fresh vegetables; four different preparations of sea bass, including a version flavored with Chablis; orange-flavored chicken spiced with ginger; steak Diana, flavored with bacon; and pork in mustard-flavored cream sauce. An excellent version of paella contains chunks of lobster and fresh shrimp.

Pedro Clisante 5, El Batey. © 809/571-2966. Pizzas and pastas RD$85–RD$355 (US$2.05–US$8.40); main courses RD$90–RD$405 (US$2.15–US$9.60). AE, MC, V. Daily 8am–midnight.

SPORTS & OTHER OUTDOOR PURSUITS
There are **watersports** kiosks about every 100m along the beach, any of which will rent you snorkeling gear and tell you the best spots for seeing fish. You can also rent sailboats, windsurfers, and other watersports gear at any of the kiosks.

Tips **Serious Windsurfing**

Cabarete hosts an annual weeklong windsurfing tournament every June. Only amateurs are allowed to participate. For more information, contact the **Happy Surf School,** Hotel Villa Taina, Calle Principal ((*C* 809/571-0784), or any staff member at the **AMHSA Hotel Estrella del Mar** ((*C* 809/571-0808).

Gipsy Ranch, Carretera Sosua-Cabarete, opposite the Coconut Palm Resort (*C* 809/571-1373), is the region's largest and best-recommended **riding stable,** home to about 20 horses, which can be hired for equestrian treks of between 1 and 4 hours. You'll begin your experience at the stone corral about 7km (4½ miles) from Sosúa and 5km (3 miles) from Cabarete. A 1-hour jaunt goes for US$16; a 4-hour excursion through forests and along beaches costs US$57. Reservations are strongly recommended.

SHOPPING

Patrick's Silversmithy, Calle Pedro Clisante 3 (*C* 809/571-2121), was established by British expatriate Patrick Fagg in 1973 as a showcase for his unusual jewelry designs. At least half of the inventory here is made within his studios, and each incorporates such local stones as larimar, amber, and black coral. About 80% of the inventory is made from silver, making these one-of-a-kind creations affordable.

The best art gallery is **Viva,** Calle Dr. Alejo Martínez (*C* 809/571-2581), which sells local art and giftware. An excellent selection of Dominican masters is on sale; the giftware includes beautifully crafted wood sculptures in mahogany and *guayacán* (ironwood). Many ceramic "faceless" dolls are also for sale.

6 Cabarete

The winds that blow constantly southward off the Atlantic swept in a hip young crowd in the 1990s, as Cabarete emerged as the premier windsurfing site in the Caribbean. But only a small portion of the visitors who come here today are actually interested in the waves and jumping on a board. Many bask in the glory of the surfers by day and strut their stuff in the hyperhip town bars by night.

To service the needs of the growing number of visitors, the town has attracted some of the most aggressive prostitutes in the Dominican Republic; all ages, all skin tones, all degrees of blatancy. If you're a heterosexual male in Cabarete, you'll absolutely never, ever, lack for female companionship, paid or unpaid.

News of Cabarete's allure has spread among the 20-something populations of Europe. Especially prevalent are visitors from northern Europe, but there are fewer North Americans here than you'd think.

The big attraction is **Cabarete Beach,** with its white sands and ideal wind and surf conditions. Cabarete isn't particularly distinguished architecturally, consisting of a series of relatively small-scale hotels, restaurants, and gift shops lining either side of the highway that parallels the north coast. Virtually everything in town lies along this street (Calle Principal), with the exception of small-scale shops that are found on narrow alleyways that bisect the main street. But as word of the resort has spread, there have been increasing numbers of large all-inclusive hotels built on the outskirts of town.

GETTING THERE   To reach Cabarete from Sosúa, continue east along the autopista (Rte. 5) for about 13km (8 miles). Taxis and *públicos* from Sosúa will also take you here.

ACCOMMODATIONS

Azurro Club (Azurro Estrella and Azurro Cabarete)   One of Cabarete's more deeply entrenched resorts was built in the late 1990s in a stylish, avant-garde design. It has been bought, reconfigured, and expanded by the well-recommended Azurro chain of resorts. Today, you'll find slightly more upscale accommodations in the Azurro Cabarete, and lodgings that are just a notch less comfortable across the road, in the Azurro Estrella. With direct access to a wide sandy beach, on the outskirts of Cabarete's main commercial core, it's noted for a soaring network of steel girders, and an attempt on the part of the staff to keep its guests amused with a variety of organized although somewhat haphazard daily activities. Despite a slightly disorganized staff, this is one of our favorite large-scale hotels in Cabarete, thanks to its convenient location and sense of style. The respective buildings of this resort rise in four-story designs, usually around well-landscaped central courtyards. Bedrooms are well maintained, attractive, and airy, usually with white-tile floors and large bathrooms with tubs and showers. Expect many changes in this resort during the lifetime of this edition, and an ongoing improvement to both the physical plant and, in all probability, a possible discounting of the rates, depending on business.

Calle Principal, Cabarete, Dominican Republic. © 809/571-0808. Fax 809/571-0904. www.starzresorts.com. 274 units. Winter US$163–US$195 double; off season US$125–US$140 double. Rates are all-inclusive. AE, MC, V. **Amenities:** 2 restaurants; 2 bars; 3 outdoor pools; gym; 24-hr. room service; babysitting; laundry service; dry cleaning; units for those with limited mobility. *In room:* A/C, TV, hair dryer, iron/ironing board, safe.

Tropical Hotel Casa Laguna *Value*   One of the better lodging values in Cabarete is this 1980s hotel, just across the street from the beach, within a pleasant walled-in garden. Each of the rooms has a refrigerator, mahogany louvers, and lattices, plus functional furniture. Most have sparsely equipped kitchenettes, and each has a tiled bathroom with a combination tub and shower.

Calle Principal, Cabarete, Dominican Republic. © 809/571-0956. Fax 809/571-0709. www.tropicalclubs. com. 120 units. Year-round US$50–US$86 double; AP (full board) US$24 per person extra. DC, MC, V. **Amenities:** 3 restaurants; 4 bars; 3 outdoor pools; salon; massage; babysitting; laundry. *In room:* A/C, TV, kitchenette (in some), fridge, minibar, hair dryer, iron, safe.

DINING

Casa del Pescador SEAFOOD   Since 1988, Casa del Pescador has served sophisticated seafood in an engagingly hip environment. It's right on the beach, in the heart of town. To begin, sample the chef's flavor-filled fish consommé. He does very well with shrimp, too, either with pastis sauce or more zestily, with curry and fresh garlic. On a hot day, the seafood salads are a welcome relief and tasty, too, as are the grilled octopus in spicy Creole sauce and fresh lobster in garlic sauce (unless you love garlic, you might find the latter overpowering; ask for butter instead). Although there's a full wine list, Presidente beer seems the best accompaniment to the fish, especially on hot, sultry nights.

Calle Principal. © 809/571-0760. Reservations recommended for dinner. Main courses RD$380–RD$840 (US$9.10–US$20). AE, DC, MC, V. Daily 10am–11pm.

La Casita de Don Alfredo (Chez Papy) *♠* DOMINICAN/FRENCH   This quirky and durable bistro is one of our favorite restaurants in Cabarete. It's located on a battered pavilion directly on the sands of Cabarete's beachfront, and it's accessible from the town's Calle Principal. Don Alfredo himself, a French expatriate from Strasbourg, keeps a firm grip on things. Menu items sure to entice include spiny Caribbean lobster with garlic and saffron sauce or with pastis; filet mignon with peppercorn sauce; and an array of the local fishermen's daily catch. We nearly always go for the fresh fish, which can be prepared almost any way you like it. As you'd expect from an articulate Frenchman, the wines are well-chosen and urbane.

Playa de Cabarete (no phone). Reservations not accepted. Main courses RD$380–RD$630 (US$9–US$15). No credit cards. Bar and cafe daily 8:30am–midnight. Meals 8:30–10:30am, noon–2:30pm, and 6–10:30pm.

SPORTS & OTHER OUTDOOR PURSUITS

Not surprisingly, Cabarete is home to the Caribbean's best **windsurfing school, Carib Bic Center,** Playa Cabarete (© 809/571-0640). It's devoted to teaching proper techniques and to renting state-of-the-art equipment. Equipment rental costs US$45 a day, and instruction is US$35 an hour.

Iguana Mama at Cabarete (© 809/571-0908) offers the best **mountain biking** and hiking. Going strong since 1993, it features a trek to Mount Isabel de Torres with experienced guides that lasts a full day and costs US$65 per person. If enough people book, this tour is offered daily. Another trek involves a 900m (2,952-ft.) downhill cruise, costing US$40 per person and held only Monday, Wednesday, and Friday.

Finally, **Gipsy Ranch** (© 809/571-1373) is the most complete riding stable in the Dominican Republic; they'll take you **horseback riding** at a cost of US$16 per person for an hour or US$57 for a 4-hour ride. (For more information, see "Sports and Other Outdoor Pursuits" in section 5, above.)

CABARETE AFTER DARK

Las Brisas, Calle Principal Cabarete (© 809/571-0614), is the most popular nightlife venue in Cabarete, but arrive after 10:30pm when the disco action begins. From 8am to 10:30pm daily, food is served. The dance floor is illuminated with strobe lights and lasers, and the bar is always busy. Many patrons arrive with dates of their own, but if you're a man flying solo, never fear, as a bevy of attractive working women are invariably on hand to provide companionship.

Hip nightlife is also found at the little bars—shanties, really—along the beach. There's live music every night after sunset. Tuesday nights it's salsa and meringue at **Ohno's Bar. Café Pitú** has reggae parties on Thursday. **The Tiki Bar** is the place to be on Friday night, and on Saturday the new **Wave Bar** and **Tribal Café** draw the most patrons. (*Note:* These bars have no phone numbers and no addresses, although they are easy to spot as you walk up and down the beach.)

7 Santo Domingo ⋆⋆⋆

Santo Domingo is one of the Caribbean's most vibrant cities, with a 12-block Colonial Zone to rival that of Old San Juan in Puerto Rico. Come here to walk in the footsteps of Cortés, Ponce de León, and, of course, Columbus himself. Allow at least a day to capture some of the highlights of the old city such as its Alcazar and its Catedral Santa Maria la Menor.

Santo Domingo is also one of the grand shopping bazaars of the Caribbean, with such "hot" items as hand-wrapped cigars for sale virtually everywhere, along with local handcrafts. Jewelry made of larimar or amber is also much sought after. From gambling to merengue, Santo Domingo is also one of the liveliest cities in the Caribbean after dark. Be careful, however. Most of the Dominican Republic's crime is concentrated in Santo Domingo. Keep valuables in your hotel safe, carry a minimum of cash with you, don't wear flashy jewelry, and if in doubt, take a cab.

Bartholomeo Columbus, brother of Christopher, founded the city of New Isabella (later renamed Santo Domingo) on the southeastern Caribbean coast in 1496. It's the oldest city in the New World and the capital of the Dominican Republic. Santo Domingo has had a long, sometimes glorious, more often sad, history. At the peak of its power, Diego de Velázquez sailed from here to settle Cuba, Ponce de León went forth to conquer and settle Puerto Rico and Florida, and Cortés set out for Mexico. The city today still reflects its long history— French, Haitian, and especially Spanish.

ESSENTIALS

GETTING THERE   See the beginning of this chapter for details on the airlines serving Santo Domingo.

FAST FACTS   There's a **24-hour drugstore** called San Judas Tadeo, Ave. Independencia 57 (© **809/685-8165**). An emergency room operates at the **Centro Médico Universidad,** Ave. Máximo Gómez 68, on the corner of Pedro Enrique Urena (© **809/221-0171**). For the **police,** call © **911.**

VISITOR INFORMATION   The Tourist Office is located at Avenida Mexico, Esquina Calle 30 de Marzo (© **809/221-4660**), open Monday to Friday only from 8am to 3pm.

ACCOMMODATIONS

EXPENSIVE

Hotel Santo Domingo 🌟🌟🌟   Run by Premier Resorts & Hotels, the Hotel Santo Domingo is tastefully extravagant without having the glitzy overtones of the Jaragua (see below). Those seeking local character in a home-grown hotel should check in here. This waterfront hotel sits on 6 tropical hectares (15 acres), 15 minutes from the downtown area, in the La Feria district.

Oscar de la Renta helped design the interior. Most of the rooms have views of the sea, though some face the garden. Accommodations have bright floral carpets, tasteful Caribbean fabrics, and mirrored closets along with firm double beds. Bathrooms are tiled with shower/tub combinations and adequate shelf space. The superior Excel Club rooms offer seaview balconies and other amenities. Excel guests also have access to a private lounge.

The cuisine is among the finest hotel food in the capital.

Ave. Independencia (at the corner of Ave. Abraham Lincoln), Santo Domingo, Dominican Republic. © 800/ 877-3643 in the U.S., or 809/221-1511. Fax 809/535-4050. www.hotel.stodgo.com.do. 220 units. Year-round US$160 double; US$195 Excel Club double; US$300 executive suite. Rates include American breakfast. AE, MC, V. **Amenities:** Restaurant; 2 bars; Olympic-size outdoor pool; 3 lit tennis courts; gym; sauna; 24-hr. room service; babysitting; laundry service; dry cleaning; nonsmoking rooms; rooms for those with limited mobility. In room: A/C, TV, dataport, minibar, coffeemaker, hair dryer, iron/ironing board, safe.

Renaissance Jaragua Hotel & Casino 🌟🌟   A Las Vegas–style palace, this 10-story hotel lies on the 6-hectare (15-acre) site of the old Jaragua (ha-*ra*-gwa) Hotel, which was popular in Trujillo's day. Open since 1988, it's a splashy, pink-colored waterfront palace that doesn't have the dignity and class of the Hotel Santo Domingo. For example, the casino and bars are often rife with prostitutes plying their trade. Located off the Malecón and convenient to the city's major attractions and shops, the hotel consists of two separate buildings: the 10-story Jaragua Tower and the two-level Jaragua Gardens Estate. Jaragua boasts the largest casino in the Caribbean, a 1,000-seat Vegas-style showroom, a cabaret theater, and a disco. The luxurious rooms, the largest in Santo Domingo, feature

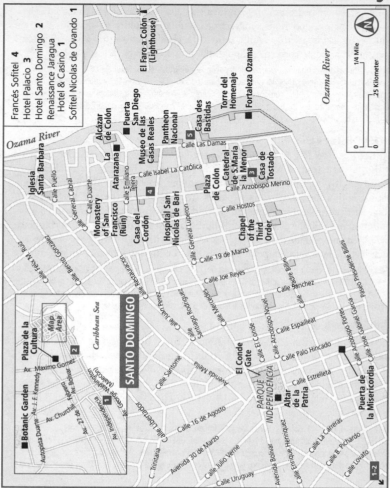

Francés Sofitel **4**
Hotel Palacio **3**
Hotel Santo Domingo **2**
Renaissance Jaragua Hotel & Casino **1**
Sofitel Nicolas de Ovando **1**

multiple phones, refrigerators, and marble bathrooms with large makeup mirrors and shower/tub combinations.

The Jaragua features some of the best hotel dining in the city. You can enjoy tasty Dominican barbecue and some of Santo Domingo's best steaks.

Ave. George Washington 367, Santo Domingo, Dominican Republic. ℂ **800/HOTELS-1** in the U.S. and Canada, or 809/221-2222. Fax 809/686-0528. www.renaissancehotels.com. 300 units. Year-round US$140–US$205 double; US$309 junior suite; US$500–US$750 suite. Valet parking US$2. AE, DC, MC, V. **Amenities:** 4 restaurants; 4 bars; outdoor pool; casino; disco; tennis center with 4 lit clay courts and a pro shop; health club and spa; salon; 24-hr. room service; babysitting; laundry service; dry cleaning; nonsmoking rooms. *In room:* A/C, TV, fridge, kitchenettes (in some), minibar, hair dryer, iron/ironing board, safe.

Sofitel Nicolas de Ovando ✦✦ In the heart of the colonial city, this 16th-century mansion has been restored and reopened as a hotel with all the modern amenities. For those seeking comfort among antiquity, this is an even better bet than the smaller Francés Sofitel (see below), another restoration. On the premises is a restaurant with a terrace facing a courtyard and two bars with a view of the pool. All the bedrooms are well furnished and handsomely maintained. The choice of accommodations ranges from standard doubles to spacious suites, which can also be used as family units. The classic architecture of the original mansion has been respected, although the property has been vastly enlarged.

Calle Las Damas, Santo Domingo, Dominican Republic. © **809/685-9955**. Fax 809/686-6590. www.sofitel. com. 104 units. Year-round US$244–US$390 double; US$390 junior suite; US$586 suite. AE, DC, MC, V. **Amenities:** Restaurant; 2 bars; outdoor pool; gym; sauna; 24-hr. room service; laundry service; dry cleaning; nonsmoking rooms; rooms for those with limited mobility. *In room:* A/C, TV, dataport, minibar, hair dryer, iron/ironing board, safe.

INEXPENSIVE

Francés Sofitel ♠   A favorite small hotel in the old city, this intimate inn lies within a stone-fronted town house dating from the 16th century. Arches surround an Iberian-style fountain, and columns reach up to the second-floor patios, with palms and tropical plants surrounding the rooms. You'll think you've arrived in Seville. A gracefully winding stone staircase leads to the high-ceilinged and thick-walled bedrooms outfitted in a somber, rather dark colonial style. Accommodations are simple but tasteful, with rugs resting on tile floors; each has a somewhat cramped but tidily kept bathroom with shower and tub.

Calle las Mercedes (corner of Calle Arzobispo Meriño), Santo Domingo, Dominican Republic. © **809/685-9331**. Fax 809/685-1289. www.sofitel.com. 19 units. Year-round US$170 double. Rates include breakfast. AE, MC, V. **Amenities:** Restaurant; bar; room service (7am–midnight); laundry service; dry cleaning; nonsmoking rooms. *In room:* A/C, TV, dataport, minibar, hair dryer, iron/ironing board, safe.

Hotel Palacio *(Value*   History buffs often opt to stay here, since the hotel is in the heart of the historic zone, only 2 blocks from the cathedral. The Palacio is also popular with business travelers. Built in the 1600s, it was the family home of a former president of the Dominican Republic, Buenaventura Báez, and still retains its original iron balconies and high ceilings. Not all rooms are the same size; if you want a more spacious unit, just ask. The shower-only bathrooms tend to be small.

Calle Duarte 106 (at Calle Solomé Ureña), Santo Domingo, Dominican Republic. © **809/682-4730**. Fax 809/687-5535. www.hotel-palacio.com. 34 units. Year-round US$80–US$95 double; US$120–US$125 suite. Children 12 and under stay free in parent's room. AE, MC, V. **Amenities:** Bar; small fitness center; rooftop Jacuzzi; limited room service; babysitting; laundry service; dry cleaning. *In room:* A/C, TV, dataport, minibar, hair dryer, safe.

DINING

Most of Santo Domingo's restaurants stretch along the seaside, bordering Avenida George Washington, popularly known as the Malecón. Some of the best restaurants are in hotels. It's safest to take a taxi when dining out at night.

In most restaurants, casual dress is fine, although shorts are frowned upon at the fancier, more expensive spots. Many Dominicans prefer to dress up when dining out, especially in the capital.

EXPENSIVE

El Mesón de la Cava ♠ DOMINICAN/INTERNATIONAL   At first we thought this was a gimmicky club—you descend a perilous iron stairway into an actual cave with stalactites and stalagmites—but the cuisine is among the finest in the capital. The quality ingredients are well prepared and beautifully flavored. Recorded merengue, Latin jazz, blues, and salsa give the place a festive ambience. Launch your repast with the small shrimp sautéed in a delicate sauce of garlic or white wine, perhaps a mixed seafood or "sexy" conch gratinée. The gazpacho is also an excellent beginning, as is the bubbling *sopa de pescado* (red snapper chowder). Follow it up with the grilled Caribbean rock lobster or the double French lamb chops, which are done to tender perfection.

Mirador del Sur 1. ✆ **809/533-2818.** Reservations required. Main courses RD$300–RD$925 (US$7.20–US$22). AE, DC, MC, V. Daily noon–midnight.

Lina Restaurant ★★ INTERNATIONAL/SPANISH This is one of the most prestigious restaurants in the Caribbean. Spanish-born Lina Aguado originally came to Santo Domingo as the personal chef of the dictator Trujillo, whom she served until opening her own restaurant. Today, four master chefs, whom Dona Lina entrusted with her secret recipes, rule the kitchen of this modern hotel restaurant. The cuisine is international, with an emphasis on Spanish dishes, and the service is first rate. Try the paella Valenciana, the finest in the Dominican Republic. We're equally enticed by the sea bass flambé with brandy, and few can resist the mixed seafood medley doused with Pernod (it's cooked casserole style). Lina's cuisine even wins the approval of some hard-to-please Madrileños we know, who are a bit contemptuous of Spanish food served outside Spain.

In the Barcelo Gran Hotel Lina. Máximo Gómez and 27 de Febrero aves. ✆ **809/563-5000,** ext. 7250. Reservations recommended. Main courses RD$265–RD$670 (US$6.25–US$16). AE, DC, DISC, MC, V. Daily noon–4pm and 6:30pm–midnight.

Vesuvio I ★ ITALIAN Along the Malecón, the most famous Italian restaurant in the Dominican Republic draws crowds of visitors and local businesspeople in spite of its fading decor. What to order? That's always a problem, as the Neapolitan owners, the Bonarelli family, have worked since 1954 to perfect and enlarge the menu. As they claim: "We like to catch it ourselves, cook it from scratch, or even grow it if that's possible." Their homemade soups are excellent. Fresh red snapper, sea bass, and oysters are prepared in enticing ways. Specialties include Dominican crayfish *a la Vesuvio* (topped with garlic and bacon). Recent menu additions feature *pappardelle al Bosque* (noodles with porcini mushrooms, rosemary, and garlic), and black tallarini with shrimp *a la crema.*

The owner claims to be the pioneer of pizza in the Dominican Republic. At **Pizzeria Vesuvio** next door (✆ **809/221-3000**), he makes a unique .9m-long (3-ft.) pizza! There's also **Vesuvio II** at Ave. Tiradentes 17 (✆ **809/562-6060**).

Ave. George Washington 521. ✆ **809/221-3333.** Reservations recommended Fri–Sat. Main courses RD$160–RD$630 (US$3.85–US$15). AE, MC, V. Daily noon–1am.

MODERATE

La Briciola ★★ ITALIAN/INTERNATIONAL This place has a touch of class, offering an elegant setting in two restored colonial palaces from the 16th century. Tables are romantically candlelit at night. In the Colonial Zone, it stands in front of Plazoleta Park. The menu reflects a commitment to prime ingredients and a determination not to let style overrule substance. The dishes here hardly test the creative culinary limits of the chefs but are tried-and-true favorites, beginning with many different pastas with various sauces—all made fresh daily. Our favorite is the delectable linguini with "fruits of the sea." Sometimes you're in the mood just for a good steak, and the chefs oblige with a perfectly grilled T-bone cooked to your specifications. This is also a good place at which to order fresh fish. Dominican rice accompanies all the meat and fish courses. A piano bar overlooks a courtyard.

Calle Arzobispo Meriño 152-A. ✆ **809/688-5055.** Reservations required. Main courses RD$180–RD$590 (US$4.30–US$14). AE, DC, DISC, MC, V. Mon–Sat 6pm–2am. Closed Dec 24, 25, 31, and Jan 1.

Paté Palo ⭐ INTERNATIONAL Part of Paté Palo's charm derives from its location, overlooking Plaza Colón, the graceful arcades of the Alcazar de Colón, where amiable clusters of Dominican families promenade every night at dusk. During the 1500s, the building was a bistro under the supervision of a mysterious Dutch buccaneer known as Peg-Leg (Paté Palo), who's credited with establishing the first tavern in the New World.

In the late 1990s, another Dutchman and his four partners transformed the place into a gregarious and engaging bistro that on weekends is one of the most crowded and popular singles bars in the country. Tables are thick-topped wooden affairs, set either on the plaza outside or within the antique walls of the dark and shadowy interior. The food is some of the best in the capital, and is usually accompanied by live guitar music every Thursday to Sunday from 6 to 10pm. Having dined here many times, we can highly recommend the sautéed shrimp in coconut-curry sauce. On festive occasions, ask for the brochette of mixed meats; the meat has been marinated in fresh spices and herbs and is artfully flambéed at your table. The sea bass with white-wine sauce is perfectly prepared, although the fancy Continental dishes such as charbroiled steak with onion sauce and a grilled rack of lamb might be more suited for the cold Alps.

La Atarazana 21, Zona Colonial. ℂ 809/687-8089. Burgers and salads RD$250–RD$355 (US$6–US$8.40). Main courses RD$250–RD$880 (US$6–US$21). AE, MC, V. Mon–Fri 4pm–1:30am, Sat–Sun noon–1:30am.

INEXPENSIVE

El Conuco ⭐ DOMINICAN Come to "the countryside" (its English name) for the best-tasting and most authentic Dominican dishes in the capital. La Bahía (see below) may have better seafood, but otherwise this place is superb, if a bit corny. The waiters in costume will even dance a wicked merengue with you. Few restaurants have been as successful at commercializing the charms of rural Dominican life, and as such, it has attracted many of the country's sports and pop-music stars. You'll find it within an upscale residential neighborhood near the Malecón, close to the Jaragua Resort. Inside, you'll find hammocks, domino tables, colorful weavings, and thatch-covered *bôhios* (beach huts). Familiar menu items here include six kinds of steak, and chicken *merengue,* prepared with red wine, onions, and mushrooms. Only the venturesome dare try cow's foot stew. A specialty here is the Dominican flag, a traditional platter whose various colors derive from artfully arranged portions of white rice, beans, meat, fried bananas, and salad.

Calle Casimiro de Moya 152, Gazcue. ℂ 809/686-0129. Reservations recommended. Main courses RD$140–RD$275 (US$3.35–US$6.60); lunch buffet RD$175 (US$4.20); dinner buffet RD$310 (US$7.45). AE, DC, MC, V. Daily noon–2am.

La Bahía ⭐ *Finds* SEAFOOD/INTERNATIONAL This unassuming place on the Malecón serves some of the best and freshest seafood in the Dominican Republic. One predawn morning as we passed by, fishermen were waiting outside to sell the chef their latest catch. Rarely in the Caribbean will you find a restaurant with such a wide range of seafood dishes. To start, you might try *ceviche* (seafood marinated in lime juice) or lobster cocktail. Soups usually contain big chunks of lobster as well as shrimp. Our favorite specialties include kingfish in coconut sauce, sea bass Ukrainian style, baked red snapper, and a savory kettle of seafood in the pot. The chef also works his magic with conch. Desserts are superfluous. The restaurant stays open until the last customer departs.

Ave. George Washington 1. ℂ 809/682-4022. Main courses RD$165–RD$420 (US$3.95–US$10). AE, MC, V. Daily 11am–2am.

SPORTS & OTHER OUTDOOR PURSUITS

BEACHES   The Dominican Republic has some great beaches, but they aren't in Santo Domingo. The principal beach resort near the capital is at **Boca Chica,** less than 3km (2 miles) east of the airport and about 31km (19 miles) from the center of Santo Domingo. Here you'll find clear, shallow blue water, a white-sand beach, and a natural coral reef. The east side of the beach, known as "St. Tropez," is popular with Europeans. In recent years, the backdrop of the beach has become rather tacky, with an array of pizza and fast-food stands, beach cottages, chaise longues, watersports concessions, and plastic beach tables.

Slightly better maintained is the narrow white-sand beach of **Playa Juan Dolio** or **Playa Esmeralda,** a 20-minute drive east of Boca Chica. Several resorts have recently located here. With all the hotels lining this beach, it's likely to be as crowded as Boca Chica any day of the week.

HORSE RACING   Santo Domingo's racetrack, **Hipódromo V Centenario,** on Avenida Las Américas, km. 14.5 (© **809/687-6060**), schedules races Tuesday, Thursday, and Saturday at 2pm. You can spend the day here and have lunch at the track's restaurant. Admission is free.

TENNIS   You can often play on the courts at the major resorts if you ask your hotel desk to call in advance for you and make arrangements.

SEEING THE SIGHTS

Prieto Tours, Ave. Francia 125 (© **809/685-0102**), one of the capital's leading tour operators, offers a 3-hour tour of the **Colonial Zone,** leaving most mornings at 9am and again at 3pm if there's sufficient demand; it costs US$25. A 6-hour tour visits the Colonial Zone, the **Columbus Lighthouse,** the **Aquarium,** and the city's modern neighborhoods; the US$50 fee includes lunch and entrance to several well-known museums and monuments. About an hour of the tour is devoted to shopping.

THE RELICS OF COLUMBUS & THE COLONIAL ERA

Santo Domingo—a treasure trove of historic, sometimes crumbling, buildings—is undergoing a major government-sponsored restoration. The old town is still partially enclosed by remnants of its original city wall. The narrow streets, old stone buildings, and forts are like nothing else in the Caribbean, except perhaps Old San Juan. The only thing missing is the clank of the conquistadors' armor.

Ancient and modern Santo Domingo meet at the **Parque Independencia,** a big city square whose most prominent feature is its **Altar de la Patria,** a national pantheon dedicated to the nation's heroes, Duarte, Sanchez, and Mella, who are all buried here. These men led the country's fight for freedom from Haiti in 1844. As in provincial Spanish cities, the square is a popular family gathering place on Sunday afternoon. At the entrance to the plaza is **El Conde Gate,** named for the count (El Conde) de Penalva, the governor who resisted the forces of Admiral Penn, the leader of a British invasion. It was also the site of the March for Independence in 1844, and holds a special place in the hearts of Dominicans.

In the shadow of the Alcázar, **La Atarazana** is a fully restored section of one of the New World's finest arsenals. It extends for a city block, holding within it a catacomb of shops, art galleries, boutiques, and some good regional and international restaurants.

Just behind river moorings is the oldest street in the New World, **Calle Las Damas (Street of the Ladies),** named not because it was the red-light district, but for the elegant ladies of the viceregal court who used to promenade here in the evening. It's lined with colonial buildings.

Moments   Uno, Dos, Tres Strikes You're Out

Dominicans were crazy about baseball long before their countryman Sammy Sosa set the United States on fire with his home run race against Mark McGwire. Almost every Major League baseball team has at least one player from the Dominican Republic on its roster these days. Pedro Martinez, Manny Ramirez, and Alphonso Soriano are just a few of the all-star team of players who hail from the Dominican Republic.

If you're here between October and January, you might want to catch a game in the Dominican Republic's Professional Winter League. The **Liga de Beisbol stadium** (© 809/567-6371) is in Santo Domingo; check local newspapers for game times, or ask at your hotel. There are also games at the Tetelo Vargas Stadium in San Pedro de Macoris, known to die-hard sports fans as the "land of shortstops" for the multitude of infielders that call this tiny town home.

Just north is the chapel of **Our Lady of Remedies,** where the first inhabitants of the city attended mass before the cathedral was erected.

Try to see the **Puerta de la Misericordia** (Calle Palo Hincado just north of Calle Arzobispo Portes). Part of the original city wall, this "Gate of Mercy" was once a refuge for colonists fleeing hurricanes and earthquakes.

The **Monastery of San Francisco** is a mere ruin, lit at night. That any part of it is still standing is a miracle; it was hit by earthquakes, pillaged by Drake, and bombarded by French artillery. To get here, go along Calle Hostos and across Calle Emiliano Tejera; continue up the hill, and about midway along you'll see the ruins.

You'll see a microcosm of Dominican life as you head east along **Calle El Conde** from Parque Independencia to **Columbus Square (Plaza de Colón),** which has a large bronze statue honoring the discoverer, made in 1882 by a French sculptor, and the **Catedral de Santa Maria la Menor** (see below).

Alcázar de Colón ⊛   The most outstanding structure in the old city is the Alcázar, a palace built for Columbus's son, Diego, and his wife, who was also niece to Ferdinand, king of Spain. Diego became the colony's governor in 1509, and Santo Domingo rose as the hub of Spanish commerce and culture in America. For more than 60 years, this coral limestone structure on the bluffs of the Ozama River was the center of the Spanish court, entertaining such distinguished visitors as Cortés, Ponce de León, and Balboa. The nearly two dozen rooms and open-air loggias are decorated with paintings, period tapestries, and 16th-century antiques.

Calle La Atarazana (at the foot of Calle Las Damas). © 809/686-8657, ext. 232. Admission RD$30 (US70¢). Mon–Sat 9am–5pm; Sun 9am–4pm.

Catedral de Santa Maria la Menor ⊛   The oldest cathedral in the Americas was begun in 1514 and completed in 1540. Fronted with a golden-tinted coral limestone facade, the church combines elements of both Gothic and baroque with some lavish plateresque styles as exemplified by the high altar chiseled out of silver. The treasury boasts an excellent art collection of ancient woodcarvings, furnishings, funerary monuments, silver, and jewelry.

Calle Arzobispo Meriño (on the south side of Columbus Sq.) © 809/689-1920. Free admission. Cathedral, Mon–Sat 9am–4pm, Sun masses begin at 6am; treasury, Mon–Sat 9am–4pm.

El Faro a Colón (Columbus Lighthouse)   Built in the shape of a cross, the towering 206m-tall (676-ft.) El Faro a Colón monument is both a sightseeing attraction and a cultural center. In the heart of the structure is a chapel containing the Columbus tomb, and, some say, his mortal remains. The "bones" of Columbus were moved here from the Cathedral of Santa María la Menor (see above). (Other locations, including the Cathedral of Seville, also claim to possess the explorer's remains.) The most outstanding and unique feature is the lighting system composed of 149 searchlights and a 70-kilowatt beam that circles out for nearly 71km (44 miles). When illuminated, the lights project a gigantic cross in the sky that can be seen as far away as Puerto Rico.

Although the concept of the memorial is 140 years old, the first stones were not laid until 1986, following the design submitted in 1929 by J. L. Gleave, the winner of the worldwide contest held to choose the architect. The monumental lighthouse was inaugurated on October 6, 1992, the day Columbus's "remains" were transferred from the cathedral.

Ave. España (on the water side of Los Tres Ojos, near the airport in the Sans Souci district). *(* 809/591-1492. Admission RD$21 (US50¢) adults, children 11 and under free. Tues–Sun 9am–5pm.

Museo de las Casas Reales (Museum of the Royal Houses)   Through artifacts, tapestries, maps, and re-created halls, including a courtroom, this museum traces Santo Domingo's history from 1492 to 1821. Gilded furniture, arms and armor, and other colonial artifacts make it the most interesting museum of Old Santo Domingo. It contains replicas of the *Niña,* the *Pinta,* and the *Santa Maria,* and one exhibit is said to hold some of Columbus's ashes. In addition to pre-Columbian art you can see the main artifacts of two galleons sunk in 1724 on their way from Spain to Mexico, along with remnants of another 18th-century Spanish ship, the *Concepción.*

Calle Las Damas (at corner Las Mercedes). *(* 809/682-4202. Admission RD$30 (US70¢), children under 12 RD$4.20 (US10¢). Daily 9am–5pm.

SHOPPING

The best buys in Santo Domingo are handcrafted native items, especially amber jewelry.

Ever since the Dominicans presented John F. Kennedy with what became his favorite rocker, visitors have wanted to take home a **rocking chair.** These rockers are often sold unassembled, for easy shipping. Other good buys include Dominican rum, hand-knit articles, macramé, ceramics, and crafts in native mahogany.

The best shopping streets are **El Conde,** the oldest and most traditional shop-flanked avenue, and **Avenida Mella.** In the colonial section, **La Atarazana** is filled with galleries and gift and jewelry stores, charging inflated prices. Duty-free shops are found at the airport, in the capital at the **Centro de los Héroes,** and at both the Hotel Santo Domingo and the Hotel Embajador. Shopping hours are generally Monday to Saturday from 9am to 12:30pm and 2 to 5pm.

Head first for the National Market, **El Mercado Modelo,** Avenida Mella, filled with stall after stall of crafts, spices, and produce; you can easily get lost in

---

Tips You Call That a Bargain?

Always haggle over the price of handcrafts, particularly in the open-air markets. No stall-keeper expects you to pay the first price asked. Remember the Spanish words for too expensive: *muy caro.*

the crush. The merchants are eager to sell, so remember to bargain. You'll see a lot of tortoiseshell work, but exercise caution, since many species, especially the hawksbill turtle, are on the endangered-species list and could be impounded by U.S. Customs if discovered in your luggage. Also for sale are rockers, mahogany, sandals, baskets, hats, and clay braziers for grilling fish.

Ambar Marie, Caonabo 9, Gazcue (© 809/682-7539), is a trustworthy source for amber. There are beautiful necklaces, as well as the earrings and pins; you can even design your own setting here. **Amber World Museum,** Arzobispo Meriño 452 (© 809/682-3309), lives up to its name. Many visitors flock here to see plants, insects, and even scorpions fossilized in resin millions of years ago. Although some of the displays are not for sale, in an adjoining salon you can watch craftspeople at work, polishing and shaping raw bits of ancient amber for sale. To visit the museum costs adults RD$25 (US60¢) and children up to age 12 are free. Open Monday to Saturday 8am to 6pm and Sunday 8am to noon.

Another reliable source for stunning amber, as well as coral, is **Ambar Nacional,** Calle Restauración 110 (© 809/686-5700). This is also the best source for purchasing larimar jewelry. In general, prices here are a bit less expensive than those at the more prestigious Amber World Museum nearby.

In the center of the most history-laden section of town is the well-known **Galería de Arte Nader,** Rafael Augusto Sanchez 22 (© 809/544-0878), which displays so many Latin paintings that they're sometimes stacked in rows against the walls. The works of the country's best-known painters and most promising newcomers are displayed here (though to be honest, the Dominican Republic is short on painters with international reputations). There is also a lot of tourist junk, shipped in by the truckload from Haiti. In the ancient courtyard in back, you can get a glimpse of how things looked in the Spanish colonies hundreds of years ago.

Nuebo, Fantino Falco 36, Naco (© 809/562-3333), is patronized by some of the capital's most upscale buyers. This shop sells a carefully chosen assortment of art objects, lamps, and furnishings. With some persuasion, anything you buy here can be shipped.

Columbus Plaza (Decla, S.A.), Calle Arzobispo Meriño 206 (© 809/689-0565), is one of the largest, supermarket-style gift and artifacts stores in the country. Well-organized and imaginative, with a helpful English-speaking staff, it sprawls over three floors of a modern building divided into boutiques specializing in amber, larimar, gold and silver jewelry, cigars, paintings and sculpture, plus craft items.

Cigars are big-sellers in Santo Domingo. The best selection is at **Cigar King,** Calle Conde 208, Baguero Building (© 809/686-4987), in the colonial city. Its selection of Dominican and Cuban cigars in a temperature-controlled room is wide-ranging.

SANTO DOMINGO AFTER DARK
DANCE CLUBS
Local young people flock to the dance clubs in droves after dinner. Even the hotel discos cater to locals as well as tourists. Great dancers abound, so go and watch even if you don't feel like dancing.

La Guácara Taína, Avenida Mirador del Sur, in Parque Mirador del Sur (© 809/533-1051), is the best *discoteca* in the country, drawing equal numbers of locals and visitors. Set in an underground cave within a verdant park, the specialty is merengue, salsa, and other forms of Latin music. There are three bars, two dance floors, and banquettes and chairs nestled into the rocky walls. The cover is RD$151 (US$3.60) (includes one drink). Open Tuesday to Sunday from 9pm; closing time varies.

Fantasy Disco, Avenida Heroes de Luperón 29, La Feria (© **809/535-5581**), is one of the capital's most popular discos, about a block inland from the Malecón. Once you get past the vigilant security staff, you'll find lots of intimate nooks and crannies, a small dance floor, and one of the country's best-chosen medleys of nonstop merengue music. Entrance is free, and beer costs RD$86 (US$2.05) a bottle. The place is open daily from 6pm 'til 4am.

Jet Set, Centro Comercial El Portal, Avenida Independencia (© **809/533-9707**), is one of the capital's most formal and elaborate nightclubs, admitting couples only, and nobody who is too rowdy. Most of the tables and chairs slope down toward an amphitheater-style dance floor, giving the place the feel of a bullfighting arena. The collection of live orchestras that play here are better than anywhere else in town. Entrance costs between RD$70 and RD$715 (US$1.70 to US$17), depending on the artist. The Jet Set takes off at 9pm and flies until the early morning.

In the Colonial Zone stands **Ataraza 9,** La Atarazana 9 (© **809/688-0969**). Currently, this is the island's best dance club, with action taking place on two floors. This club draws a heavier concentration of locals than visitors. Open daily 6pm to 4am.

Gay life (often gay for pay) flourishes in old Santo Domingo at such clubs as **Jay-Dee's,** 10 José Reyes (© **809/333-6905**). Your host is Jerry, the owner, who hails from Philadelphia. Gay Dominicans and visitors mingle to enjoy wet T-shirt contests, drink specials, drag shows, and male strippers. Another hot club is **Aire,** 313 Mercedes (© **809/689-4163**), also in the Colonial Zone. This is a cavernous club in a restored colonial mansion with an open-air courtyard. It's one of the best gay or gay-friendly clubs (some straights go here, too) in the Caribbean, and is best visited on Friday or Saturday nights.

ROLLING THE DICE

Santo Domingo has several major casinos, all of which are open nightly until 4 or 5am. Gambling here is a very minor attraction and the odds are pretty much against you. If gambling is your raison d'être, you'd do better to plan a holiday in Puerto Rico. The most glamorous casino in the Dominican Republic is fittingly housed in the capital's poshest hotel: the **Renaissance Jaragua Hotel & Casino,** Ave. George Washington 367 (© **809/221-2222**). You can't miss the brightly flashing sign; it's the most dazzling light along the Malecón. You can wager on blackjack, baccarat, roulette, and slot machines in either Dominican pesos or U.S. dollars. Open daily 4pm to 4am.

Another casino is at the **Hispaniola Hotel,** Avenida Independencia (© **809/535-9292**). One of the most stylish choices is the **Casino Diamante,** in the Meliá Santo Domingo Hotel & Casino, Ave. George Washington 361 (© **809/682-2102**). Its bilingual staff will help you play blackjack, craps, baccarat, and keno, among other games. There's also a piano bar. These casinos are open daily 4pm to 4am.

13

Grenada

This sleepy island has friendly people and the lovely and popular white sands of Grand Anse Beach. Exploring its lush interior, especially Grand Etang National Park, is also worthwhile. Crisscrossed by nature trails and filled with dozens of secluded coves and sandy beaches, Grenada has moved beyond the turbulence of the 1980s. It's not necessarily for the serious party person and definitely not for those seeking action at the casino. Instead, it attracts visitors who like snorkeling, sailing, fishing, and doing nothing more invigorating than lolling on a beach under the sun.

The "Spice Island," Grenada is an independent, three-island nation (the other two islands are Carriacou, the largest of the Grenadines, and Petite Martinique). Grenada has more spices per square mile than any other place in the world: cloves, cinnamon, mace, cocoa, tonka beans, ginger, and a third of the world's supply of nutmeg. "Drop a few seeds anywhere," the locals will tell you, "and you have an instant garden." The central area is like a jungle of palms, oleander, bougainvillea, purple and red hibiscus, crimson anthurium, bananas, breadfruit, ferns, and palms.

1 Essentials

VISITOR INFORMATION

In the United States, the **Grenada Tourist Office** is at 317 Madison Ave., Suite 1704, New York, NY 10017 (© **800/927-9554** or 212/687-9554).

In London, contact the **Grenada Board of Tourism,** Battersea Church Road, Earl's Court, London, SW11 3LY (© **020/771-7016**).

On the island, pick up maps, guides, and general information at the **Grenada Board of Tourism,** the Bums Point, in St. George's (© **473/440-2279**), open Monday to Friday from 8am to 4pm.

You can find information on the Web at **www.grenada.org**.

GETTING THERE

Point Salines International Airport lies at the southwestern toe of Grenada. The airport is a 5- to 15-minute taxi ride from most of the major hotels.

American Airlines (© **800/433-7300** in the U.S. or 473/444-2222 in Grenada; www.aa.com) offers daily flights to Grenada from New York and Miami.

British Airways (© **800/247-9297** in England or 473/440-2996 in Grenada; www.britishairways.com) flies to Grenada every Tuesday and Friday from London's Gatwick Airport, making a single stop at Antigua en route.

Air Jamaica (© **800/523-5585** or 473/444-5975; www.airjamaica.com) offers nonstop flights from New York to Grenada two to three times a week.

BWIA (© **800/538-2942**) flies to Grenada from New York; Washington, D.C.; and Miami. In Canada, it departs from Toronto. British citizens can make connections on BWIA from London or Manchester via Trinidad.

Allamanda Beach Resort **2**
Bel Air Plantation **14**
Blue Horizons Cottage Hotel **4**
Calabash **12**
Coyaba **5**
The Flamboyant Hotel **3**
Gem Holiday Resort **8**
Grenada Grand Beach Resort **6**
Laluna **9**
La Sagesse **15**
LaSource **11**
Rex Grenadian **10**
Spice Island Beach Resort **7**
True Blue Bay Resort **1**
Twelve Degrees North **13**

Airport ✈ Beach ↖ Mountain ▲

Levera Beach and
National Park
Sauteurs
Victoria
Mt. St. Catherine
Gouyave
(Charlottetown)
■ Douglaston Estate
Pearl's Beach
*Caribbean
Sea*
Grand Roy
*Grand Etang
National Park*
Grenville
Mt. Qua Qua
*Grand
Etang Lake*
*Grenville
Bay*
Marquis
Annandale Falls
▲ Mt. Sinai
Constantine
Beaulieu
St. David's
Grand Anse
Beach
St. George's
Morne Rouge Bay
Woburn
*ATLANTIC
OCEAN*
Point
Salines
L'Anse aux Epines
Pink Gin Beach
La Sagesse
Beach
0   5 Miles
0   5 Kilometers
N

Caribbean Star (© 866/864-6272 in the U.S., or 800/864-6272 in Grenada) offers daily flights from Antigua going via Dominica, St. Vincent, St. Lucia, and Trinidad. **SVG Air** (© 473/444-0328) offers flights between St. Vincent and Grenada, and **LIAT** (© 868/624-4727 or 473/440-5428 in Grenada), flies between Grenada and several neighboring islands in the southern Caribbean. Finally, **Virgin Atlantic** (© 800/662-8621 in the U.S., or 800/744-7477 in Grenada) flies nonstop once a week from London's Heathrow Airport.

GETTING AROUND

BY TAXI   Taxi rates are set by the government. Most arriving visitors take a cab at the airport to one of the hotels near St. George's, at a cost of US$15. Add 33% to the fare from 6pm to 6am. You can also use most taxi drivers as a guide for a day of sightseeing; negotiate a price beforehand.

BY RENTAL CAR   *First, remember:* Drive on the left. A U.S., British, or Canadian driver's license is valid on Grenada; however, you must obtain a local permit, costing EC$30 (US$11). These permits can be bought either from the car-rental company or from the traffic department at the Carenage in St. George's. The Carenage is both the walkway and the road that loops around the horseshoe-shaped St. George's Harbour. It is the capital's principal thoroughfare.

Avis (© 800/331-1212 in the U.S., or 473/440-3936; www.avis.com) operates out of a Shell station on Lagoon Road, on the southern outskirts of

---

Fun Fact Carnival on Grenada

The second weekend of August brings colorful Carnival parades, music, and dancing. The festivities begin on Friday, continuing practically non-stop through Tuesday. Steel bands and calypso groups perform at Queen's Park. **Jouvert,** one of the highlights of the festival, begins at 5am on Monday with a parade of Djab Djab/Djab Molassi, devil-costumed figures daubed with a black substance. (*Be warned:* Don't wear nice clothes to attend this event—you may get sticky from close body contact.) The Carnival finale, a gigantic "jump-up" (like a hoedown), ends with a parade of bands from Tanteen through the Carenage into town.

St. George's. Avis will meet you at the airport, but requires at least 24-hour notice to guarantee availability. You can also try **Dollar Rent-a-Car,** at the airport (© **800/800-4000** in the U.S., or 473/444-4786; www.dollar.com).

A word of warning about local drivers: There's such a thing as Grenadian driving machismo; the drivers take blind corners with abandon. An extraordinary number of accidents are reported in the lively local paper. Gird yourself with nerves of steel, and be on the lookout for children and pedestrians when driving at night. Many foreign visitors, in fact, find any night driving hazardous.

BY BUS Minivans, charging EC$1.50 to EC$6.50 (US55¢–US$2.40), are the cheapest way to get around. The most popular run is between St. George's and Grand Anse Beach. Most minivans depart from Market Square or from the Esplanade area of St. George's.

FAST FACTS: Grenada

Banks Banks in St. George's, the capital, include **First Caribbean International Bank,** at Church and Halifax streets (© 473/440-3232); **Scotiabank,** on Halifax Street (© 473/440-3274); the **National Commercial Bank (NCB),** at Halifax and Hillsborough streets (© 473/440-3566); the **Royal Bank of Trinidad & Tobago (RBTT),** at Halifax and Cross streets (© 473/440-3521); and the **Grenada Cooperative Bank,** on Church Street (© 473/440-2111). Most have ATMs. Hours are usually Monday through Thursday from 8am to 3pm and Friday from 8am to 5pm.

Currency The official currency is the **Eastern Caribbean dollar (EC$),** approximately EC$2.70 to US$1 (EC$1 = US37¢). Always determine which dollars, EC or U.S., you're talking about when someone on Grenada quotes you a price. *Unless otherwise specified, rates in this chapter are quoted in U.S. dollars.*

Documents A valid passport is required of U.S., British, and Canadian citizens entering Grenada, plus a return or ongoing ticket.

Electricity Electricity is 220- to 240-volt AC (50 cycles), so transformers and adapters will be needed for U.S.-made appliances.

Embassies & High Commissions The **U.S. Embassy** is located at L'Anse aux Epines Salines, St. George's (© 473/444-1173). The **British High Commission** is on Church Street, St. George's (© 473/440-3536).

Emergencies Dial 𝒞 **911** for police, fire, or an ambulance.

Hospital **St. George's General Hospital** located on Grandetang Road, St. George's (𝒞 **473/440-2051**), has an X-ray department and operating room. Private doctors and nurses are available on call.

Language English is commonly spoken. Creole English, a mixture of several African dialects, English, and French, is spoken informally by most.

Pharmacies Try **Gittens Pharmacy,** Halifax Street, St. George's (𝒞 **473/440-2165**), open weekdays from 8am to 6pm (they close at 5pm on Thurs), and Saturday from 8am to 3pm.

Post Office The general post office, at the Pier, St. George's, is open Monday to Friday from 8am to 3:30pm.

Safety Street crime occurs here, tourists have been victims of armed robbery in isolated areas, and thieves frequently steal U.S. passports and alien registration cards in addition to money. Muggings, purse-snatchings, and other robberies occur in areas near hotels, beaches, and restaurants, particularly after dark. Don't leave valuables unattended at the beach. Be cautious when walking after dark, or take a taxi. Report a stolen or lost passport immediately to the local police and the embassy.

Taxes A 10% VAT (value-added tax) is imposed on food and beverages, and there's an 8% room tax. You'll pay a departure tax of US$20 when you leave.

Telephone The area code for all of Grenada is **473**. You can call to or from Grenada as you would to or from any other area code in North America. Public phone and fax services are available at the Carenage offices of **Grenada Cable & Wireless** in St. George's (𝒞 **473/440-1000** for all Grentel offices). The office is open Monday to Thursday from 8am to 4:30pm, and Friday from 8am to 3:30pm.

Time Grenada is on Atlantic Standard Time year-round, which means it's usually 1 hour ahead of the U.S. East Coast—except during daylight savings time, when the clocks are the same.

Tipping A 10% service charge is added to most restaurant and hotel bills. No additional tip is expected.

Water Stick to bottled water.

Weather Grenada has two distinct seasons: dry and rainy. The dry season is from January to May; the rest of the year is the rainy season, although the rainfall doesn't last long. The average temperature is 80°F (27°C). Because of constant trade winds, there's little humidity.

2 Accommodations

Whether you're looking for a kitchenette apartment, a small, intimate inn, or a major resort, you'll find it waiting for you in Grenada, which has some of the best and most varied accommodations in the southern Caribbean. Unless you want to stay in an atmospheric inn tucked away somewhere, opt for a hotel lined up along Grand Anse Beach. All you'll have to do is walk out the door and head for the ocean.

Your hotel or inn will probably add a service charge of 10% to your bill—ask about this in advance, so you can accurately anticipate what your final bill will look like.

VERY EXPENSIVE

Bel Air Plantation 🌟🌟🌟 *Finds*　A secluded hideaway and one of the newest and most dramatic of the island accommodations stands on a 7.2-hectare (18-acre) tract of lush land on the southwestern side of the island. Beautifully integrated into the almost junglelike terraced waterfront landscape, this is a coterie of vibrantly colored gingerbread cottages built up and down the hillside overlooking St. David's Harbour. Surrounded by tropical gardens, each airy, spacious accommodation offers privacy and Old World charm, but also modern amenities. Each unit is furnished with its own character and personality, everything centered around a "waterfront village," complete with a restaurant, bar, grocery, deli, cafe, art gallery, and gift shop. Even the simplest accommodations here, the cottages, are handsomely furnished. You can live higher on the hog by renting one of the two-bedroom villas with spacious master bedrooms and living rooms furnished in wicker and teak.

St. David's Point, St. George's, Grenada, W.I. ⓒ 473/444-6305. www.belairplantation.com. 25 units. Winter US$295 cottage, US$425 1-bedroom villa, US$595 2-bedroom villa; off season US$250 cottage, US$360 1-bedroom villa, US$490 2-bedroom villa. AE, MC, V. No children under age 15. **Amenities:** Restaurant; cafe; bar; outdoor pool; kayaks; snorkeling; room service (8am–10:30pm); laundry service; dry cleaning. *In room:* Ceiling fans, TV, dataport, kitchens (in some), fridge, beverage maker, hair dryer, safe.

Calabash 🌟🌟🌟　On a landscaped 3-hectare (7½-acre) beach, the Calabash is today the leading hotel on Grenada. Of all the upmarket inns on the island, this is the smallest and most posh, drawing a devoted repeat clientele, especially among its English clients. Everything is refined and low key here—nothing splashy like LaSource (see below). Eight kilometers (5 miles) south of St. George's and only minutes from the airport, it occupies an isolated section of Prickly Bay (L'Anse aux Epines). Foremost among the multitude of shrubs here are the scores of beautiful *calabashes* (gourds) for which the resort was named. The eight private plunge-pool suites and 22 whirlpool-bath suites all have verandas and either one king-size bed or two double beds. Bathrooms are very spacious, with big stall showers, oversize tubs, and bidets.

The restaurant serves an excellent cuisine (see below), and entertainment, ranging from piano music to steel bands, is provided 4 or 5 nights a week.

L'Anse aux Epines (P.O. Box 382), St. George's, Grenada, W.I. ⓒ 800/528-5835 in the U.S. and Canada, or 473/444-4334. Fax 473/444-5050. www.calabashhotel.com. 30 units. Winter US$510–US$870 suite for 2; off season US$270–US$570 suite for 2. Extra person US$175–US$215 in winter; US$130 in off season. Children under 12 stay free in parent's room. Dinner US$50 per person extra. AE, MC, V. Children 12 and under not permitted in February. **Amenities:** Restaurant; 2 bars; outdoor pool; golf privileges; tennis court; exercise room; sailboat rentals; snorkeling; room service (10am–10pm); babysitting; laundry service; rooms for those with limited mobility. *In room:* A/C, ceiling fans, TV, minibar, beverage maker, hair dryer, iron/ironing board, safe.

Laluna 🌟🌟🌟　One of Grenada's newest hotel lies on an isolated, beautiful beach at Quarantine Point, near the extreme southern tip of the island. Designed along architectural lines you might expect in Indonesia, the resort consists of 16 thatch-covered, wood-and-stone sided cottages, each with a small pool, artwork, and fabric-swathed four-poster beds imported from Bali. Scattered up and down a hillside, about 1.6km (1 mile) north of the Port Salines airport, they lie within a 2-minute walk from the beach. The resort's social and architectural centerpiece is a clubhouse larger than the cottages, the site of big verandas, a restaurant, a good-looking bar area, and check-in facilities.

Laluna opened as the brainchild of Italian-born Bernardo Bertucci, who immigrated to Grenada after a successful career marketing fashion on New York's Seventh Avenue. With clients that have included members of the Eurythmics, *Sports Illustrated* swimsuit models, and Mick Jagger's ex-wife Jerry Hall, it seems headed for a glittery, hedonistic niche with a very appealing international kind of irony and worldliness. The restaurant, which is open to nonresidents who phone in advance, is artfully sited less than 12m (39 ft.) from the beach, and separated from the airy bar by a communal swimming pool. See "Dining," below.

Morne Rouge (P.O. Box 1500), St. George's, Grenada, W.I. (C) **473/439-0001.** Fax 473/439-0600. www. laluna.com. 16 cottages. Winter US$530–US$680 cottages and suites for 1–2 people, US$1,060 cottages for 1–4 people; off season US$290–US$390 cottages and suites for 1–2 people, US$580 cottages for 1–4 people. MAP (breakfast and dinner) US$65 per person extra. AE, MC, V. **Amenities:** Restaurant; bar; outdoor pool; exercise room; kayaks; sailing; snorkeling; windsurfing; bikes; car rental; shops; room service (breakfast only); massage facilities; babysitting; laundry service. *In room:* A/C, ceiling fan, TV/VCR, dataport, minibar, beverage maker, hair dryer, safe.

LaSource 𝄞𝄞𝄞
At the first completely all-inclusive hotel on Grenada, everything's laid out for you on a platter, from diving courses to limbo dancing. LaSource isn't as intimate as Calabash (see above), but if you want an all-inclusive with top spa facilities, you'll be happier here. It's spread across 16 hectares (40 acres) of a former cocoa and nutmeg plantation, with two white-sand beaches separated by a rocky knoll. LaSource stresses revitalization of the body and mind through spa treatments and experiences with nature. Meals, drinks, watersports, entertainment, and most spa treatments are included in the all-inclusive price.

Guest rooms are in a hillside compound of white-walled, terra cotta–roofed buildings. Rooms are furnished with mahogany four-poster beds, Italian marble floors, and ceiling fans, evoking a dignified colonial plantation house. The marble-clad shower/tub combination bathrooms are extremely roomy.

The plush great house serves some of the island's best cuisine; less formal is the open-sided Terrace Restaurant. Children under 16 are not welcome.

Pink Gin Beach (P.O. Box 852), St. George's, Grenada, W.I. (C) **473/444-2556.** Fax 473/444-2561. www. lasource.com.gd. 100 units. Winter US$530–US$580 double, US$640 suite for 2; off season US$440–US$490 double, US$530 suite for 2. Rates are all-inclusive. AE, MC, V. No children under 16. **Amenities:** 2 restaurants; 2 bars; piano bar; outdoor pool; 9-hole golf course; 2 tennis courts; health club and spa; Jacuzzi; sauna; dive shop; salon; room service (7am–10am); massage; laundry service. *In room:* A/C, beverage maker (in some), hair dryer, safe.

Spice Island Beach Resort 𝄞𝄞𝄞
This is *the* classic beach resort, where you can run from your bungalow onto the white sands of the island's most perfect beach. It's not the most romantic or atmospheric, and it has none of the array of facilities of LaSource (see above), but for the best location on Grand Anse there is no equal. On an estate overlooking the Caribbean, this inn is built along 360m (1,181 ft.) of Grand Anse Beach. The main house, reserved for dining and dancing, has a tropical feel and lots of tasteful touches. Of the accommodations, we prefer the beach suites for their location. Second-floor suites have terraces overlooking the ocean and the garden; 17 units have their own private plunge pools. Room furnishings are casual. The bathrooms are the largest and most luxurious on Grenada, with showers and Jacuzzis.

Well-crafted international cuisine is served at Oliver's Restaurant, an open-aired pavilion on the beach.

Grand Anse Beach (P.O. Box 6), St. George's, Grenada, W.I. (C) **800/742-4276** in the U.S., or 473/444-4258. Fax 473/444-4807. www.spicebeachresort.com. 66 units. Winter US$570–US$990 double; off season US$470–US$780 double. Rates are all-inclusive. AE, MC, V. **Amenities:** Restaurant; bar; outdoor pool;

complimentary greens fees at Grenada Golf Course; tennis court; fitness center; spa; Jacuzzi; sauna; kayaks; sailing; snorkeling; limited room service; laundry service. *In room:* A/C, TV, dataport, minibar, beverage maker, hair dryer, safe.

EXPENSIVE

Coyaba ⟨⟩   On a 2-hectare (5-acre) site on Grand Anse Beach, this resort, whose name means "heaven" in Arawak, is 10km (6¼ miles) from St. George's and 5km (3 miles) north of the airport. The hotel has views of town and of St. George's Harbour. All units have double beds, verandas or patios, and spacious bathrooms with tiled shower/tub combinations. For persons with disabilities, the widened doorways, ramps, and three wheelchair-accessible guest rooms here make it the best choice on the island.

Breakfast and lunch are served under the palm-thatch-covered roof of the Arawak Cabana, adjacent to the swimming pool. Dinners are served at the Pepper Pot and are usually based on themes that change nightly, including Italian night, steak and barbecue night, and seafood night.

Grand Anse Beach (P.O. Box 336), St. George's, Grenada, W.I. ⟨⟩ **473/444-4129.** Fax 473/444-4808. www. coyaba.com. 70 units. Winter US$215 double; off season US$135 double. Extra person US$50 in winter, US$25 off season. MAP (breakfast and dinner) US$42 per person extra. AE, DC, MC, V. **Amenities:** 2 open-air restaurants; 2 bars (1 swim-up); outdoor pool; tennis court; volleyball; canoes; sailing; snorkeling; limited room service; laundry service; nonsmoking rooms; rooms for those with limited mobility. *In room:* A/C, TV, hair dryer.

Grenada Grand Beach Resort ⟨⟩   On 8 hectares (20 acres) of lush ground, this hotel stands on a desirable stretch of white-sandy beachfront, across from the Grand Anse Shopping Centre. Guests are ushered between a pair of manicured formal gardens to their (often small) rooms, which are tiled and furnished with mahogany pieces. Each has a balcony or patio and a well-kept bathroom equipped with a shower/tub combination. The beachview rooms are the most desirable, naturally. You can dine indoors or out at the Waterfront Restaurant, which has passable international cuisine. Entertainment is offered.

Grand Anse Beach (P.O. Box 441), Grenada, W.I. ⟨⟩ **473/444-4371.** Fax 473/444-4800. www.grenada grand.com. 240 units. Winter US$160–US$299 double, US$599–US$799 suite; off season US$135–US$274 double, US$599–US$799 suite. Children 16 and under stay free in parent's room. AE, MC, V. **Amenities:** Restaurant; 2 bars (1 swim-up); 2 pools; 2 tennis courts; fitness center; 2 saunas; diving; snorkeling; salon; limited room service; babysitting; laundry service; nonsmoking rooms; rooms for those with limited mobility. *In room:* A/C, TV, dataport, beverage maker (in some), hair dryer.

Rex Grenadian ⟨⟩ *(Kids)*   This is the largest and most bustling hotel on the island, though not the best. It's a convention-group favorite, set on 14 rocky, partially forested hectares (35 acres) that slope steeply down to a pair of white-sand beaches. Each of the cream-and-pale-blue units is uniquely configured, and each is outfitted in rattan, wicker, and muted tropical fabrics. Eighty-four units offer ocean views and are all air-conditioned. The more expensive rooms contain shower/tub combinations. The bathrooms in other units are more compact with shower units. Adjacent to the accommodations is a .8-hectare (2-acre) artificial lake strewn with islands that are connected to the "mainland" with footbridges.

The International features buffets with foods from around the world, but The Oriental's Asian cuisine is far better. A bit more casual, Spicers serves local dishes for lunch. The Tamarind Lounge offers cabaret singing and disco music.

Point Salines (P.O. Box 893), St. George's, Grenada, W.I. ⟨⟩ **473/444-3333.** Fax 473/444-1111. www. rexcaribbean.com. 212 units. Winter US$263–US$364 double, US$474 suite; off season US$178–US$280 double, US$390 suite. AE, DC, MC, V. **Amenities:** 3 restaurants; 3 bars; 2 tennis courts; fitness center; dive shop; sailing; snorkeling; water-skiing; windsurfing; children's club; tour desk; limited room service; babysitting; laundry service; nonsmoking rooms; rooms for those with limited mobility. *In room:* A/C, minibar (in some), hair dryer (in some).

Twelve Degrees North ✿   On a very private beach, this cluster of spotlessly clean efficiency apartments is owned and operated by Joseph and Patricia Gaylord, who personally greets visitors on the front lawn. Many staff members have been with Mr. Gaylord since he opened the place many years ago. They'll cook breakfast, prepare lunch (perhaps pumpkin soup and flying fish), do the cleaning and laundry, and fix regional specialties for dinner (which you can heat up for yourself later). A housekeeper/cook, assigned to each unit, arrives at 8am to perform the thousand small kindnesses that make Twelve Degrees North a favorite lair for repeat guests. All units are equipped with efficiency kitchens, large beds, and shower-only bathrooms with robes.

L'Anse aux Epines (P.O. Box 241), St. George's, Grenada, W.I. ✆ and fax 473/444-4580 (call collect to make reservations). www.twelvedegreesnorth.com. 8 units. Winter US$225 1-bedroom apt for 2, US$350 2-bedroom apt for 4; off season US$150 1-bedroom apt for 2, US$265 2-bedroom apt for 4. Extra person US$60. No credit cards. No children under 15 accepted. **Amenities:** Beach bar; outdoor pool; tennis court; tandem kayak; snorkeling; Sunfish sailboats. *In room:* Ceiling fan, beverage maker, hair dryer, no phone.

MODERATE

Allamanda Beach Resort ✿   Opening onto a wide stretch of Grand Anse Beach, this is one of the best full-service operations on the island, with everything from a watersports center to a spa. Accommodations open onto views of the water. Units come with either a little terrace or a balcony, and some are suitable for persons with disabilities. The decor is light and airy in a Caribbean tropical motif, with tile floors, well-kept bathrooms with shower/tub combinations, and, in some cases, whirlpool baths in the tiled bathrooms.

The DeSoleil Restaurant, set within an open-sided pavilion directly on the beach, serves international and Caribbean cuisine.

Grand Anse Beach (P.O. Box 27), St. George's, Grenada W.I. ✆ **473/444-0095.** Fax 473/444-0126. www. allamandaresort.com. 50 units. Winter US$155–US$180 double, US$245–US$340 suite; off season US$115–US$140 double, US$190–US$235 suite. MC, V. **Amenities:** Restaurant; bar; tennis court; health club and spa; snorkeling; limited room service; massage; laundry service; rooms for those with limited mobility. *In room:* A/C, TV, kitchenettes (in some), fridge, hair dryer, iron/ironing board, safe.

Blue Horizons Cottage Hotel ✿   Co-owners Royston and Arnold Hopkin have transformed this once-neglected property into one of the finest on the island. Grand Anse Beach is only a 5-minute walk away. The medium-size units are strewn about a 2-hectare (5-acre) garden. Superior studios contain a small dining alcove and a king-size bed. The more expensive deluxe suites come with a separate living and dining area along with two king-size or double beds. Each room has an efficiency kitchen and comfortable, solid, mahogany furniture. Bathrooms, though small, are well maintained and equipped with shower/tub combinations.

Lunch is served around a pool bar, and guests who prefer to cook in their rooms can buy supplies from a food fair at Grand Anse, a 10-minute walk away. Its restaurant, La Belle Creole, is described in "Dining," below.

Grand Anse Beach (P.O. Box 41), Grenada, W.I. ✆ **800/223-9815** in the U.S., or 473/444-4316. Fax 473/444-2815. www.bluegrenada.com. 32 cottages. Winter US$175–US$195 double; off season US$120–US$130 double. Extra person US$50 winter, US$35 off season. AE, DC, DISC, MC, V. **Amenities:** Restaurant; 2 bars; outdoor pool; limited room service; babysitting; laundry service. *In room:* A/C, TV, kitchenette, beverage maker, hair dryer, iron/ironing board, safe.

The Flamboyant Hotel   This hotel is a well-established standby. It occupies a hillside that slopes down to Grand Anse Beach, in a neighborhood peppered with other resorts. It was designed as a complex of modern, red-roofed buildings punctuated with an outdoor swimming pool. The management arranges parties, crab races, barbecues, dinner dances, and live reggae music several nights a week. Each medium-size unit has a loggia-style balcony overlooking the beach, tile floors, good beds, and floral-patterned curtains and upholsteries. The apartments contain kitchenettes. The somewhat-cramped bathrooms have shower/tub combinations and are well-maintained.

The restaurant serves international and Caribbean meals and faces the sea.

Grand Anse Beach (P.O. Box 214), St. George's, Grenada, W.I. © 473/444-4247. Fax 473/444-1234. www. flamboyant.com. 60 units. Winter US$145–US$200 double, US$300–US$400 2-bedroom apt for 4; off season US$105–US$135 double, US$185–US$255 2-bedroom apt for 4. Extra person US$25–US$40. AE, DC, DISC, MC, V. **Amenities:** Restaurant; bar; outdoor pool; dive shop; snorkeling equipment; game room; car and jeep rental; minimart; limited room service; babysitting; laundry service; nonsmoking rooms. *In room:* A/C, TV, dataport, kitchenettes (in some), minibar, beverage maker (in some), hair dryer, iron/ironing board, safe.

True Blue Bay Resort This family-run resort takes its name from an old indigo plantation that once stood here, but panoramic views of Prickly Bay's blue waters make the name appropriate today as well. You can select one-bedroom apartments with verandas overlooking the bay, or two-bedroom cottages nestled in tropical gardens. The accommodations are tastefully furnished in pastels and tropical rattan pieces, with excellent beds, either king-size or twin. Each unit has a fully equipped kitchen and a tiled, shower-only bathroom.

Lunches and evening snacks are served in a raffish-looking beachfront grill called Stuart's Bar. Dinner at the True Blue Bay Restaurant is more formal. Also facing the water, it focuses on Caribbean and international dishes.

Old Mill Rd., True Blue (P.O. Box 1414), St. George's, Grenada, W.I. © 473/443-8783. Fax 473/444-5929. www.truebluebay.com. 26 units. Winter US$150–US$180 1-bedroom apt, US$220 2-bedroom cottage; off season US$120–US$130 1-bedroom apt, US$150 2-bedroom cottage. Extra person US$25–US$35. AE, MC, V. **Amenities:** Restaurant; 2 bars; 2 outdoor pools; exercise room; dive shop; yacht charter; limited room service; rooms for those with limited mobility. *In room:* A/C (in some), ceiling fans, TV, kitchenette, beverage maker, hair dryer, safe.

INEXPENSIVE

Gem Holiday Resort (*Kids*) Opening onto Morne Rouge Beach, this complex of self-catering apartments is family friendly. It's owned and operated by the Beadeau family, which welcomes guests to its one- and two-bedroom apartments. The units are a bit small, but they are fully equipped, with a kitchenette, good beds, mahogany furnishings, shower-only bathrooms, and a private terrace opening onto the beach.

If you don't prepare your own meals, you can patronize Sur La Mer at the beach, which offers fresh fish and Caribbean dishes at both lunch and dinner. There is an on-site dance club, Fantazia 2001 (see "Grenada After Dark," later in this chapter).

Morne Rouge Bay (P.O. Box 58), St. George's, Grenada, W.I. © 473/444-4224. Fax 473/444-1189. www.gem beachresort.com. 18 units. Winter US$126–US$135 double, US$180 quad; off season US$75–US$90 double, US$135 quad. Extra person US$20–US$30. AE, DC, DISC, MC, V. **Amenities:** Restaurant; bar; dance club; minimart; babysitting; laundry service; dry cleaning. *In room:* A/C, TV, kitchen, fridge, beverage maker, hair dryer, iron/ironing board.

La Sagesse (*Finds*) On a sandy, tree-lined beach 16km (10 miles) from the airport, La Sagesse consists of a seaside guesthouse, a simple, open-air restaurant serving Caribbean-style meals, a bar, and an art gallery, with watersports available. Nearby are trails for hiking and exploring, a haven for wading and shore birds, hummingbirds, hawks, and ducks. Rivers, mangroves, and a salt pond sanctuary enhance the natural beauty of the place. The original great house of what was once La Sagesse plantation contains two apartments, each with high ceilings and comfortable beds, plus shower-only bathrooms. Guests also have a choice of a two-bedroom beach cottage, with comfortable furnishings and a wraparound porch. The least desirable accommodations are two small, economy-priced bedrooms in back of the inn's patio restaurant.

St. David's (P.O. Box 44), St. George's, Grenada, W.I. ℂ 473/444-6458. Fax 473/444-6458. www.lasagesse. com. 12 units. Winter US$120–US$165 double; off season US$85–US$105 double. MC, V. **Amenities:** Restaurant; bar; snorkeling; 24-hr. room service; laundry; rooms for those with limited mobility. *In room:* Ceiling fan, beverage maker, hair dryer, no phone.

3 Dining

EXPENSIVE

The Boatyard ℛ INTERNATIONAL   This medical-student hangout overlooks the marina where the yachts are moored. It attracts a lot of visiting yachties, most of whom seem to prefer a liquid lunch. Lunch consists of a Caribbean daily special, and may include stewed pork or Creole *lambi* (conch). Some of the best featured dishes are stewed and barbecued chicken, seafood kabob, and grilled steak; most are served with rice, salad, and fresh vegetables. Mexican specialties and Italian pastas also appear on the menu, but they are not reason enough to come here. On Friday nights a steel drum band plays; when they're done the sound system is cranked up for indoor-outdoor dancing until the wee hours.

L'Anse aux Epines, Prickly Bay. ℂ 473/444-4662. Main courses EC$27–EC$81 (US$10–US$30). MC, V. Daily 8:30am–11pm.

Coconut Beach Restaurant ℛ FRENCH/CREOLE   This informal restaurant occupies a purple-and-green clapboard house set directly on the beach. From the dining room, you can watch the staff working in the exposed kitchen. They'll definitely be making callaloo soup, made with local herbs and blended to a creamy smoothness. The kitchen specializes in various kinds of lobster, including the classic served with garlic butter and an imaginative stir-fry with ginger chile. Almost anything prepared with fresh conch here is a taste sensation. Fish predominates, including a catch of the day served with mango chutney. Chicken and meats are also savory, especially breast of chicken cooked in local herbs and lime juice.

Warning: Because the restaurant is close to several major hotels, many people have opted to walk along the beach to reach it. Don't! Tourists have been robbed and had their lives threatened by machete-carrying thugs. Even if it's a short ride, take a taxi.

Grand Anse Beach (about .8km/½ mile north of St. George's). ℂ 473/444-4644. Reservations recommended. Lunch platters EC$15–EC$25 (US$5.55–US$9.25); main courses EC$20–EC$81 (US$7.40–US$30). AE, DISC, MC, V. Wed–Mon 12:30–10pm.

La Belle Creole ℛ CONTINENTAL/WEST INDIAN   This is one of the best restaurants on Grenada for West Indian specialties. The chefs' variety of continental recipes with West Indian touches result in one of the most creative cuisines on the island. To start, try the always delectable callaloo chicken fondue if it's featured. The lobster Creole is a classic, served in a shell, but even better are the spicy ginger pork chops with local seasonings, heightened with a touch of white wine. Another longtime favorite is the deviled fish with curry and local seasonings, or the Creole fish stew. Three local vegetables fresh from the lush countryside are served with each meal. Desserts, however, are nothing special.

At Blue Horizons, Grand Anse Beach. ℭ 473/444-4316. Reservations required for nonhotel guests. 5-course fixed-price dinner EC$111 (US$41), 3-course dinner EC$95 (US$35), 2-course dinner EC$81 (US$30). AE, DC, MC, V. Daily 7:30–10am and 7–10pm.

La Dolce Vita ITALIAN   Some of the island's best Italian cuisine is served in this open-air dining room. The view is one of the most scenic in the Caribbean. You enter tropical gardens and follow the aromas wafting from the kitchen of this well-run restaurant. We prefer the chef's homemade pasta dishes to all others on the island, although you may want to start with the constantly changing array of both hot and cold antipasti, often made with fresh vegetables. Our favorite dishes are the spaghetti La Dolce Vita with shrimp and conch and the beef tenderloin with Roquefort cheese or a green-peppercorn sauce.

Next to the Flamboyant Hotel, Grand Anse. ℭ 473/444-3456. Reservations required. Main courses EC$30–EC$68 (US$11–US$25). MC, V. Tues–Sun 3–10pm.

Laluna ITALIAN/INTERNATIONAL   This is the restaurant that feeds, nourishes, and entertains the sometimes hedonistic international clientele of one of Grenada's newest and quietly stylish cottage compounds. And it does so exceedingly well. You'll dine in a thatch-covered setting, adjacent to the sea and a swimming pool, enjoying the cooking of a Sicily-born chef with wide-ranging experience in Asia. The best dishes include seafood gnocchi; spice island sushi; pasta *a l'amatriciana* (with salami, ham, tomatoes, capers, and olives); and seafood Benedetto, a medley of wine-and-tomato-soaked seafood served over rice. A perfectly grilled steak or lobster almost invariably appear on the menu.

In the Laluna Resort, Morne Rouge (P.O. Box 1500). ℭ 473/439-0001. Reservations recommended. Main courses EC$76–EC$105 (US$28–US$39). AE, MC, V. Daily 7:30am–9:30pm.

Oliver's Restaurant ℛ CREOLE/SEAFOOD   Want to dine on an uncrowded beachfront protected from sudden tropical showers? The parapet here, built of imported pine and cedar, looks like a Le Corbusier rooftop. The view is of one of the finest beaches in the Caribbean—miles of white sand sprouting an occasional grove of sea-grape or almond trees. Some of the best hotel food on the island is served in this winning setting. You can even eat your lunch in a swimsuit. Local seafood is featured on the constantly changing menu. The most generous buffet on the island, a real Grenadian spread, is served on Friday, along with live entertainment. On Saturday seafood is the specialty.

Spice Island Beach Resort, Grand Anse Beach. ℭ 473/444-4258. Reservations required for nonguests. Fixed-price breakfast EC$68 (US$25); lunch EC$22–EC$41 (US$8–US$15); fixed-price dinner EC$135 (US$50). AE, DC, DISC, MC, V. Daily 7:30–10am, 12:30–3:00pm, and 7–9:30pm.

The Red Crab ℛ WEST INDIAN/INTERNATIONAL   The food at The Red Crab isn't as good as that at the restaurants recommended above, but it's a fun place to be at night. Your companions are likely to be the liveliest on island. Only a short taxi ride from the major hotels, The Red Crab attracts visitors and locals alike and is especially popular with students from the medical college. Patrons can dine inside or out under the starry sky. The beefsteaks, especially the pepper steak, are among Grenada's finest. Other fine offerings include local lobster tail; *lambi* (conch); and locally caught fish such as snapper, dolphin (mahimahi), and grouper, though other island chefs prepare better versions of these seafood dishes. If you weren't old enough to have dined in the '50s, you can relive those golden years by ordering beef stroganoff, veal cordon bleu, or lobster Newburg.

L'Anse aux Epines. ℭ 473/444-4424. Reservations required in winter. Main courses EC$49–EC$97 (US$18–US$36). AE, MC, V. Mon–Sat 11am–2pm and 6–11pm.

Rhodes *(star star star)* INTERNATIONAL   One of London's most exciting chefs, Gary Rhodes, has invaded Grenada, at least in the capacity of adviser. Opening in the winter of 2004, the chic restaurant of this fabled chef is bringing "a taste of Grenada with the touch of Rhodes" to this new enclave of fine cuisine. Rhodes has quickly secured his reputation as the finest place to eat on the island, and the atmosphere is so cozy you're wrapped in a "sybaritic cocoon," in the words of one satisfied diner. Rhodes himself came to the island to get acquainted with its local produce and especially its many spices such as mace and nutmeg. He also trained local chefs in his style of cuisine. He designed the whole menu to use local produce and flavors. The actual recipes change daily but feature seafood. In London Rhodes is known for presenting a menu with daring twists and flavors in his food, so expect some delightful surprises if you show up here.

In the Calabash Hotel, L'anse Aux Epines. *(C)* 473/444-4334. Reservations required. Main courses EC$59–EC$95 (US$22–US$35). AE, MC, V. Daily 7–9:30pm.

MODERATE

Aquarium Beach Club & Restaurant SEAFOOD   This beachfront club near the airport changes personalities between day and night. You can rent snorkeling equipment or ocean kayaks here in the morning and return in the afternoon for a good seafood lunch. There's always something happening around, including a "lobster barbecue" on Sunday afternoons, instead of the typical brunch. In the evening, the convivial bar fills up, often with locals.

At dinner the place becomes slightly more formal, and a full menu is offered. Your best bet is the fresh fish of the day, which can be prepared as you like it. Lots of other good dishes emerge from the kitchen as well, including two specialties: a tender and well-flavored pepper steak, and a spinachlike callaloo cannelloni, a uniquely Caribbean concoction. Most of the main courses are inexpensive; only the barbecued lobster will tax your wallet.

Point Salines. *(C)* 473/444-1410. Reservations required for dinner. Main courses EC$35–EC$89 (US$13–US$33). AE, MC, V. Tues–Sun 10am–midnight.

Little Dipper *(star)* *Finds* WEST INDIAN   This is a dining secret we're letting you in on, providing you agree to keep it to yourself. In the little fishing village of Woburn along the southern coast, lying to the west of La Sagesse nature center, you can dine on the terrace of a West Indian home with a panoramic view of the bay. Chef Joan Charles prepares some of the best and freshest tasting dishes we've ever enjoyed on island. Her pan-fried lobster in garlic butter makes you want to order a second one, and no one does curried conch quite as well—it's tender and served in a savory sauce of curry powder, saffron, and tomato. Her catch of the day is usually prepared with a Creole seasoning of paprika, onions, and tomatoes. The chef knows how to use locally grown foods like callaloo, breadfruit, *christophene* (Caribbean squash), or pumpkin to create something wonderful.

Woburn. *(C)* 473/444-5136. Reservations required. Main courses US$15–US$18. No credit cards. Daily 6pm–midnight.

The Nutmeg SEAFOOD/CREOLE   Right on the harbor, The Nutmeg is a rendezvous point for the yachting set. Its informal atmosphere is suitable for a snack or full-fledged dinner. The drinks are very good; try one of the Grenadian rum punches made with Angostura bitters, grated nutmeg, rum, lime juice, and syrup. There's always fresh fish, and usually callaloo or pumpkin soup. *Lambi* (that ubiquitous conch) is done very well here. A small wine list has some California, German, and Italian selections, and you can drop in just for a beer to enjoy the sea view. Sometimes, however, you'll be asked to share a table.

The Carenage, St. George's. ⓒ 473/440-2539. Main courses EC$16–EC$70 (US$5.90–US$26). AE, MC, V. Daily 8am–11pm; Sun 4–11pm.

Rudolf's ⓡ *Value* INTERNATIONAL   A longtime favorite and an excellent value for your money, Rudolf's is popular with the locals. It's a good spot for lethal rum drinks in the late afternoon. Austrian-born Rudolf is very charming, and he has a hardworking and genteel staff. The restaurant does a busy lunch business; ceiling fans cool patrons off at midday. The menu is the most extensive on the island, the food is well prepared, and the steaks are the best in the capital, especially the 16-ounce T-bone. Flying fish and mahimahi, prepared in several different ways, deserve the most praise. You can also order grilled swordfish in a mushroom sauce or roasted chicken. There's even a classic wiener schnitzel.

Cinnamon Hill, Morne Rouge, St. George's. ⓒ 473/440-2241. Reservations recommended. Main courses EC$27–EC$70 (US$10–US$26). MC, V. Mon–Sat 11am–2pm and 6–11pm; Sun 6–11pm.

Tout Bagay Restaurant & Bar ⓡ INTERNATIONAL   Facing the ocean at the northern fringe of the Carenage, this restaurant serves a flavorful range of nicely prepared dishes. Because of the inviting atmosphere and friendly service, it's a pleasure to cross the threshold. Its name translates as "everything is possible," and although the chefs don't go that far, they serve up a tasty brew with a lot of seafood. Fresh but simple starters are highlighted by a succulent shrimp cocktail or conch fritters. For a true taste of Grenada, opt for the spicy "pot soup," made with beef, pork, and chicken and served as a main course. More authentic island flavor emerges in their curried mutton or their blackened snapper. Even though it's a bit of a cliché, the most ordered item on the menu is the seafood platter, which can be served fried or blackened.

The Carenage, St. George's. ⓒ 473/440-1500. Reservations recommended. Main courses EC$20–EC$46 (US$7.40–US$17); lobster EC$76 (US$28). MC, V. Mon–Sat 8am–11pm; Sun 4–11pm.

INEXPENSIVE

Deyna's Tasty Food ⓡ *Finds* GRENADIAN   This little eatery is a closely guarded secret among locals. It's reached by heading up Melville Street to a modest three-story building overlooking the sea. The duenna of the stove, Deyna Hercules, resembles her namesake. Her savory stuffed crabs are the island's best, and you can check out her specialties scribbled on a countertop chalkboard. Her specialty is a "fix up"—a sampling of the best food of the day, perhaps "stew fish," green plantains, and curried goat. She also serves the national dish of Grenada, an "oil down," made with salted meat and breadfruit cooked in coconut milk. And where else could you get a tasty batch of *titiri,* those minnow-size fish just plucked from the Caribbean and wash them down with "bush tea" steeped from black sage leaves? Diners with hair on their chest can opt for one of the two gamey specialties—*manicou* (a cross between an opossum and a large rat) and *tatou,* akin to armadillo.

Melville St., St. George's. ⓒ 473/440-6795. Reservations recommended. Main courses EC$14–EC$20 (US$5.20–US$7.40). MC, V. Mon–Sat 8am–8pm; Sun 10am–4pm.

La Boulangerie FRENCH/ITALIAN   Don't be deterred by the shopping center location. This French coffee shop and bakery is an ideal spot for a good breakfast or light lunch (served throughout the afternoon). And prices at dinner are most reasonable. In the early morning, visitors throng here for the freshly brewed coffee, pastries, and croissants. The afternoon crowd devours well-stuffed baguettes, sandwiches, and pizzas. More substantial dishes are offered in the evening, including roast chicken and fresh fish.

Le Marquis Shopping Complex, Grand Anse Beach. ⓒ **473/444-1131.** Sandwiches and pizzas EC$23–EC$35 (US$8.50–US$13); dinner main courses EC$20–EC$59 (US$7.40–US$22). No credit cards. Daily 8:30am–9:30pm.

La Sagesse ⊛ CARIBBEAN/CONTINENTAL   Opening onto a sandy beach, this romantic open-air spot is one of the quirkiest places to dine on island. Although it is casually run, it serves good food based on fresh ingredients. The seafood served here is some of the island's finest—and freshest. You can order freshly made salads and well-stuffed sandwiches throughout the day. The conch *(lambi)* is an excellent choice, but on most nights, you can choose from a full range of fish, including dolphin (mahimahi) and grouper. In the evening several continental dishes appear. The restaurant also caters to vegetarians.

In the La Sagesse nature center, south of St. David's. ⓒ **473/444-6458.** Reservations recommended for dinner. Main courses EC$35–EC$59 (US$13–US$22). MC, V. Daily 8–10:30am, 11:30am–3:30pm, and 5:30–10:30pm.

Morne Fendue ⊛ *(Finds* CREOLE   This plantation house is the ancestral home of the late owner, Betty Mascoll. It was built in 1912 of carefully chiseled river rocks held together with a mixture of lime and molasses. Miss Mascoll died in 1998, but her loyal staff carries on her tradition. Of course, they need time to prepare food for your arrival, so it's imperative to give them a call to let them know you're coming by. Lunch is likely to include yam and sweet-potato casserole, curried chicken with lots of hot spices, and a hot pot of pork and oxtail. Because this is very much a private home, tipping should be done tactfully. Nonetheless, the hardworking cook and maid seem genuinely appreciative of a gratuity.

St. Patrick's (40km/25 miles north of St. George's). ⓒ **473/442-9330.** Reservations required. Fixed-price lunch EC$46 (US$17). No credit cards. Daily 12:30–2pm. Dinner served upon request. Follow the coastal road north out of St. George's. After you pass through Nonpareil, turn inland (east) and continue through Buguesng and follow the signs to Morne Fendue.

4 Beaches

The best of the 45 beaches on Grenada are in the southwestern part of the island. The granddaddy of them all is **Grand Anse Beach** ⊛⊛⊛, 3km (2 miles) of sugar-white sand fronting a sheltered bay. This beach is really the stuff of dreams—it's no surprise that many of the major resort hotels are here. Many visitors never leave this part of the island. Protected from strong winds and currents, the waters here are relatively safe, making Grand Anse a family favorite. The clear, gentle waters are populated with schools of rainbow-hued fish. Palms and sea-grape trees offer shade. Watersports concessions include water-skiing, parasailing, windsurfing, and scuba diving; vendors peddle coral jewelry, local crafts, and the inevitable T-shirts.

The beach at **Morne Rouge Bay** ⊛ is less frequented but just as desirable, with its white sands bordering clear waters. Morne Rouge is noted for its calm waters and some of the best snorkeling in Grenada. It's about 2km (1¼ mile) south of Grand Anse Bay.

Pink Gin Beach lies near the airport at Point Salinas, bordering two large resorts, LaSource and Rex Grenadian (see "Accommodations," earlier in this chapter). This is also a beach of white sand and clear waters, ideal for swimming and snorkeling. (No one seems to know why it's called Pink Gin Beach.) You'll find a restaurant and kayak rentals here.

Also on Grenada's southern coast, **La Sagesse Beach** is part of La Sagesse nature center. This especially powdery strip of white sand is a lovely, tranquil area; in between time spent on the beach, you can go for nature walks in most directions. A small restaurant opens onto the beach.

If you like your waters more turbulent, visit the dramatic **Pearl's Beach,** north of Grenville on the Atlantic coast. The light gray sand stretches for miles and is lined with palm trees. You'll practically have the beach to yourself.

Part of Levera National Park, **Levera Beach,** at the northeastern tip of the island, is one of the most beautiful on Grenada. Its sands front the Atlantic, which most often means rough waters. Many locals come here for Sunday picnics.

5 Sports & Other Outdoor Pursuits

DEEP-SEA FISHING Fishers visit from November to March in pursuit of both blue and white marlin, yellowfin tuna, wahoo, sailfish, and more. Most of the bigger hotels have a sports desk that arranges fishing trips. The **Annual Game Fishing Tournament,** held in January, attracts a number of regional and international participants. For more information, call Robert Miller at (© 473/ 444-2220).

GOLF At the **Grenada Golf Course and Country Club,** Woodlands (© 473/ 444-4128), you'll find a nine-hole course offering views of both the Caribbean Sea and the Atlantic. Greens fees are US$16 for nine holes, or US$23 if you want to play it twice (to get 18 holes). Hours are Monday 8am to 4pm, Tuesday to Thursday 8am to 7pm, Friday 8am to 4pm, Saturday 8am to 7pm, and Sunday from 8am to 1pm.

HIKING Grenada's lushness and beauty make it one of the best Caribbean islands for hiking. If you have time for only one hiking experience on Grenada, make it the **Grand Etang National Park and Forest Preserve** ℛ (© 473/440- 6160). It's sheer scenic beauty makes the **Lake Circle Trail** our number-one choice on the island. The trail makes a 30-minute circuit along Grand Etang Lake, the crater of an extinct volcano, amidst a forest preserve and bird sanctuary. You're likely to see the yellow-billed cuckoo and the emerald-throated hummingbird. The park is also a playground for Mona monkeys. Another easy hike, the **Morne LeBaye Trail,** begins at the park's forest center and affords a view of the 710m (2,329-ft.) Mount Sinai and the east coast. Of course, you can also take more elaborate hikes, perhaps to the peak of **Mount Qua Qua** at 712m (2,335 ft.). Trails can be slippery after a rainfall (especially June–Nov), so wear good hiking shoes and carry plenty of water with you. The park's **Grand Etang Interpretation (Nature) Centre** is open Monday to Friday from 8am to 4pm, featuring a video about the park. Admission is US$1.

You can hike the shorter trails independently, but you might wish to hire a guide for the ascent to Mount Qua Qua or the even more demanding hike to Mount Catherine, at 827m (2,712 ft.). The former costs US$25 per person for a 4-hour hike, while the latter is US$35. For information, call **Telfor Bedeau Hiking Tours** (© 473/442-6200). Good hiking trails can also be found at **Levera National Park** (see "A Spectacular Rainforest & More," below).

SAILING Two large party boats, designed for 120 and 250 passengers, operate out of St. George's Harbour. The **Rhum Runner** and **Rhum Runner II,** c/o Best of Grenada, P.O. Box 188, St. George's, Grenada, W.I. (© 473/440- 4FUN), make three trips daily, with lots of emphasis on strong liquor, steel-band music, and good times. Three-hour tours, conducted every morning and afternoon, coincide with the arrival of cruise ships, but will carry independent travelers if space is available. Evening tours on Friday and Saturday from 7:30 pm to midnight are much more frequently attended by island locals, and are more bare-boned, louder, and usually less restrained. The cost is US$12 to US$14.

SCUBA DIVING & SNORKELING   Grenada offers divers an underwater world rich in submarine gardens, exotic fish, and coral formations, sometimes with visibility stretching to 36m (118 ft.). Off the coast is the wreck of the ocean liner *Bianca C,* which is nearly 180m-long (590 ft.). Novice divers might want to stick to the west coast of Grenada, while more experienced divers might search out the sights along the rougher Atlantic side.

Aquanuts, in the Grenada Renaissance, Grand Anse Beach (© 473/444-4371, ext. 638), has night dives or two-tank dives for US$53 and US$70 respectively; PADI instructors offer an open-water certification program for US$394 per person. They also offer **snorkeling trips** for US$26 (1½-2 hr.). You can rent snorkel gear as well, even if you don't take the boat ride.

Giving Aquanuts serious competition is the affable **Eco-Dive,** at the Coyaba Beach Resort on Grand Anse Beach (© 473/444-7777). There's a PADI instructor on-site. The dive boat is well equipped with well-maintained gear. Both scuba diving and snorkeling jaunts to panoramic reefs and shipwrecks teeming with marine life are offered. A single dive costs US$35, a resort course US$75, and a night dive US$55. A **snorkeling trip** can be arranged for US$21. Diving instruction, including a resort course, is available.

> *Warning* **Divers Beware**
>
> Grenada doesn't have a decompression chamber. If you get the bends, you'll have to take an excruciatingly painful flight to Trinidad.

If you'd rather strike out on your own, take a drive to Woburn and negotiate with a fisher for a ride to **Glovers Island,** an old whaling station, and snorkel away. Glovers Island is an uninhabited rock spit a few hundred yards offshore from the hamlet of Woburn.

TENNIS   Most big resorts have tennis courts. There are public courts, as well, both at Grand Anse and in Tanteen in St. George's.

6 Exploring the Island

ST. GEORGE'S & VICINITY

The capital city of Grenada, **St. George's** is the prettiest harbor town in the West Indies. Its landlocked inner harbor is actually the deep crater of a long-dead volcano—or so one is told. In the town, you'll see some of the most charming Georgian colonial buildings in the Caribbean, still standing despite a devastating hurricane in 1955. The steep, narrow hillside streets are filled with houses of ballast bricks, wrought-iron balconies, and sloping, red-tile roofs. Many of the pastel warehouses date from the 18th century. Frangipani and flamboyant trees add to the palette of color.

The port, which some have compared to Portofino, Italy, is flanked by old forts and bold headlands. Among the town's attractions is an 18th-century pink **Anglican church,** on Church Street, and the **Market Square,** where colorfully attired farm women offer even more colorful produce for sale. **Fort George,** on Church Street, built by the French, stands at the entrance to the bay, with subterranean passageways and old guardrooms and cells.

Everyone strolls along the waterfront of the **Carenage** ⚓ on the inner harbor, or relaxes on its pedestrian plaza, with seats and hanging planters providing shade from the sun. The best place to sit and have a drink is **The Nutmeg** (see "Dining," earlier in this chapter). From its large open windows you'll have great views of the harbor activity. The hamburgers and rum drinks are great, too.

On this side of town, the **Grenada National Museum,** at the corner of Young and Monckton streets (© **473/440-3725**), is set in the foundations of an old French army barracks and prison built in 1704. Small but interesting, it houses finds from archaeological digs, including petroglyphs, native fauna, the first telegraph installed on the island, a rum still, and memorabilia depicting Grenada's history. The most comprehensive exhibit traces the native culture of Grenada. Hours are Monday through Friday from 9am to 4:30pm, Saturday from 10am to 1pm. Admission is US$2.

You can take a drive up to Richmond Hill and **Fort Frederick,** begun by the French in 1779 and completed by the English in 1791. From its battlements, you'll have a superb view of the harbor and of the yacht marina.

An afternoon tour of St. George's and its environs might take you into the mountains north of the capital. A 15-minute drive delivers you to **Annandale Falls** ⚓, a tropical wonderland, with a cascade about 15m (49 ft.) high. You can enjoy a picnic surrounded by liana vines, elephant ears, and other tropical flora and spices. The **Annandale Falls Centre** (© **473/440-2452**) offers gift items, handcrafts, and samples of the indigenous spices of Grenada. Nearby, an improved trail leads to the falls where you can enjoy a refreshing swim. Swimmers can use the changing cubicles at the falls for free. The center is open daily from 8am to 4pm.

A SPECTACULAR RAINFOREST & MORE

If you head north out of St. George's along the western coast, you can take in beaches, spice plantations, and the fishing villages that are so typical of Grenada.

You'll pass through **Gouyave,** a spice town, the center of the nutmeg and mace industry. At the **Grenada Cooperative Nutmeg Association** (© **473/444-8337**), near the entrance to Gouyave, huge quantities of the spice are aged, graded, and processed. This is the best place to see spices being readied for market. Workers sit on stools in the natural light from the open windows of the aging factory, and laboriously sort the raw nutmeg and its byproduct, mace, into different baskets for grinding, peeling, and aging. Jams, jellies, syrups, and more are sold. Hours are Monday to Friday 8am to 4pm; admission is US$1.

In the northeast corner of the island (just east of Sauteurs) is palm-lined **Levera Beach,** an idyll of sand where the Atlantic meets the Caribbean. This is a great spot for a picnic lunch, but swimming can sometimes be dangerous. On the distant horizon you'll see some of the Grenadines.

Opened in 1994, the 180-hectare (445-acre) **Levera National Park** ⚓ has several white-sand beaches for swimming and snorkeling, although the surf is rough here where the Atlantic meets the Caribbean. It's also a **hiker's paradise,** although you should go hiking here only after you've hiked Grand Etang National Park and Forest Preserve (see "Hiking," above), which is lusher and of far greater interest. Levera Park contains a mangrove swamp, a lake, and a bird sanctuary, where you might see a rare tropical parrot. Offshore are coral reefs and sea-grass beds. The park's interpretative center (© **473/442-1018**) is open Monday to Friday from 8am to 4pm, Saturday and Sunday from 8am to 4pm.

Heading down the east coast of Grenada, you reach **Grenville,** the island's second city. If you pass through on a Saturday morning, you can enjoy the hubbub of the native produce market. There's also a fish market along the waterfront. A nutmeg factory here welcomes visitors. From Grenville, you can cut inland into the heart of Grenada. Here you're in a world of luxuriant foliage, and you pass along nutmeg, banana, and cocoa plantations.

In the center of the island, reached along the major interior road between Grenville and St. George's, is **Grand Etang National Park** 🌲 (© **473/440-6160**), containing the island's spectacular rainforest. For information about hikes in the park, see "Hiking," above.

On your descent from the mountains, you'll pass hanging carpets of mountain ferns. Going through the tiny hamlets of Snug Corner and Beaulieu, you eventually come back to the capital.

7 Shopping

Everybody who visits Grenada goes home with a basket of **spices,** better than any you're likely to find in your local supermarket. Wherever you go, you'll be besieged by spice vendors. These hand-woven panniers of palm leaf or straw are full of items grown on the island, including the inevitable nutmeg, as well as mace, cloves, cinnamon, bay leaf, vanilla, and ginger. Grenada is no grand merchandise mart of the Caribbean like St. Thomas and St. Maarten, but you may locate some local handcrafts, gifts, and even art.

If you like to attend Caribbean markets as much as we do, head for **Market Square** at the foot of Young Street in St. George's. The market is at its liveliest on Saturday morning, but is also open Monday to Friday. It's best to go between 8am and noon. An array of handcrafts is for sale, but fresh spices are more plentiful.

For something really special, visit **Arawak Islands Ltd.,** Upper Belmont Road, in St. George's (© **473/444-3577**), founded in 1986 by Angelia Clements, a German woman. From the raw materials of Grenada, especially nutmeg and cinnamon, she manufactures delectable tropical perfumes and toiletries. The dedication here is to natural products and minimal processing, including products purchased from island companies and packaged here at the on-site workshop.

8 Grenada After Dark

Regular evening entertainment is provided by the resort hotels and includes steel bands, calypso, reggae, folk dancing, and limbo—even crab racing. Ask at your hotel desk to find out what's happening at the time of your visit.

The island's most popular nightspot is **Fantazia 2001,** Morne Rouge Beach (© **473/444-2288**). It's air-conditioned, with state-of-the-art equipment, good acoustics, and fantastic disco lights, and plays the best in regional and international sounds. There are live shows Friday and Saturday. The cover is EC$10 (US$3.70).

You can also try **Boatyard,** Prickly Bay, L'Anse aux Epines (© **473/444-4662**), down by the marina. Friday night after 11pm a local DJ spins dance music until dawn.

The **Beachside Terrace** at the Flamboyant Hotel, Grand Anse (© **473/444-4247**), is a laid-back spot featuring **crab races** on Monday, a steel band on Wednesday and Saturday, and, our favorite, a beach barbecue with live calypso music and limbo dancing on Sunday.

One of our favorite bars is **Aquarium Beach Club & Restaurant** at Point Salines (© **473/444-1410**), which also serves delectable food (see "Dining," earlier in this chapter). From the sprawl of decks open to the trade winds, you can enjoy the lights of St. George's Harbour here at night.

For those seeking culture, the 250-seat **Marryshow Folk Theatre,** Herbert Blaize Street near Bain Alley, St. George's (© **473/440-2451**), offers performances of Grenadian, American, and European folk music, drama, and West Indian interpretative folk dance. Check with the theater or the tourist office to see what's on. Tickets usually cost EC$20 to EC$41 (US$7.40–US$15).

14

Guadeloupe

Guadeloupe gives travelers a taste of France in the Tropics. In addition to its Gallic flair and fine Creole cuisine (among the best in the Caribbean), it offers some excellent beaches and mountainous, lush terrain full of gorgeous scenery. The resorts here are not as spectacular and plush as those on, say, Anguilla or Jamaica, though there are some large beachfront properties, but you can have a real island experience at small inns where locally prepared food and tranquillity are the specialties.

Guadeloupe is part of the Lesser Antilles, about 322km (200 miles) north of Martinique. It actually comprises two different islands, separated by a narrow seawater channel known as the Rivière Salée. **Grande-Terre,** the eastern island, is full of rolling hills and sugar plantations. **Basse-Terre,** to the west, is a rugged mountainous island, dominated by the 1,440m (4,723-ft.) volcano, La Soufrière, which is still alive and dotted with banana plantations. Guadeloupe's mountains are covered with tropical forests, impenetrable in many places. Beautiful white-sand beaches ring its islands. In the unlikely event that you should grow bored on Guadeloupe, you can hop over to really remote islands offshore, including **Iles des Saintes** and **Marie-Galante.**

1 Essentials

VISITOR INFORMATION

For information before you go, contact the **French Government Tourist Office** (© 202/659-7779; www.francetourism.com). There are offices at 444 Madison Ave., New York, NY 10022 (© 212/838-7800); 9454 Wilshire Blvd., Suite 715, Beverly Hills, CA 90212 (© 310/271-6665); or 676 N. Michigan Ave., Suite 3360, Chicago, IL 60611 (© 312/751-7800).

On the island, go to the **Office du Tourisme,** in the commercial heart of Gustavia, adjacent to La Capitanerie (the Port Authority Headquarters), quai du Général-de-Gaulle (© 590/27-87-27).

GETTING THERE

To get to Guadeloupe, most U.S. travelers will have to fly to another island and transfer. You can take an **American Airlines** (© 800/433-7300 in the U.S.; www.aa.com) flight to its hub in San Juan, Puerto Rico, and then get one of two American Eagle flights daily on to Guadeloupe. There are also connections available through Martinique (see chapter 16).

Air Canada (© 888/247-2262 in the U.S., or 590/21-12-77 in Guadeloupe; www.aircanada.ca) flies between Montreal and Guadeloupe every Saturday year-round. Passengers can also fly from Toronto on one of the daily nonstop flights to Barbados. From there, passengers can transfer onto other carriers (usually LIAT), making the ongoing journey to points within the French West Indies.

Air France (© 0820/820-820; www.airfrance.com) flies into Guadeloupe every day from Paris, with efficient connections from Britain and the rest of Europe. Air France also maintains direct service to Guadeloupe from Miami, via Port-au-Prince, Haiti.

If you're already on the islands, you can wing into Guadeloupe on **LIAT** (© 888/844-5428 in Guadeloupe, or 868/624-4727; www.liatairline.com), which flies here from Antigua, St. Maarten, St. Croix, St. Lucia, Martinique, Barbados, Grenada, Trinidad, and Dominica. **Air Caraïbes** (© 877/772-1005 in the U.S., or 590/82-47-00; www.aircaraibes.com) operates about a half-dozen flights a day into Guadeloupe from Martinique, as well as at least one flight a day, each, from St. Barts and French St. Martin.

Consider arriving in Guadeloupe as many of the locals do, on one of the daily ferryboats operated by **Express des Iles** (© 590/83-04-43), whose vessels originate every day in Martinique at 2pm, make a 30-minute stopover in Dominica en route (departing from Dominica around 4pm), and then dock at the quays of Pointe-à-Pitre sometime between 5:30 and 6pm, depending on weather, tides, and the vagaries of island life.

One-way passage to Pointe-à-Pitre from Dominica costs 55€ ($69) per person; one-way passage to Guadeloupe from Martinique is 55€ ($69) and round-trip 85€ ($106), partly the result of government subsidies within the French-controlled *departments d'outre-mer*. For timetables and more information in Guadeloupe, call **Agence Penchard** (the local representative of Express des Iles) at © 590/83-04-43. For timetables and information in Martinique, contact **Express des Iles** directly at © 590/91-69-68.

GETTING AROUND

BY RENTAL CAR You may want to rent a car on Guadeloupe so you can explore Basse-Terre; the loop around the island is one of the most scenic drives in the Caribbean. Car-rental kiosks at the airport are open to meet international flights. Rental rates at local companies might appear lower, but several readers have complained of mechanical problems, billing irregularities, and difficulties in resolving insurance disputes in the event of accidents. So we recommend reserving a car in advance through one of North America's largest car-rental companies: **Hertz** (© 800/654-3131 in the U.S., or 590/21-13-46 locally; www.hertz.com) or **Avis** (© 800/331-1212 in the U.S., or 590/21-13-54 locally; www.avis.com), each of which is headquartered at the airport. Many of the major hotels also have car-rental desks. You'll have to pay a one-time airport surcharge of 16€ ($20) and VAT (value-added tax) of 9.5%. Prices are usually 20% to 25% lower between March and early December, excepting July and August.

Driving is on the right-hand side of the road, and there are several gas stations along the island's main routes. Because of the distance between gas stations in outlying regions, try not to let your gas gauge fall below the halfway mark when driving outside of the capital.

BY TAXI You'll find taxis when you arrive at the airport, but no limousines or buses. From 9pm until 7am, cabbies are legally entitled to charge you 40% more. Some, but not all, taxis in Guadeloupe have meters, although the driver will either activate them or not, depending on a complicated set of parameters involving the time of day, your destination, and his or her whim, even though fares are technically regulated by the French government. If the taxi you're about to enter doesn't have a working meter, always agree on a price before getting in. Approximate fares are 18€ to 20€ ($23–$25) from the airport to the hotels of

Guadeloupe

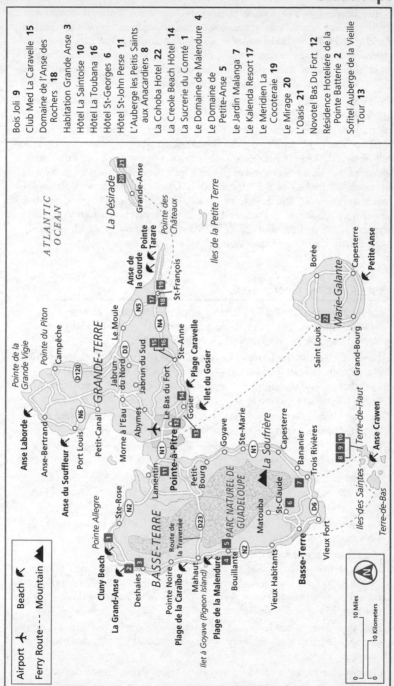

Gosier; or about 14€ ($18) from the airport to anywhere within Pointe-à-Pitre. Radio taxis can be contacted throughout Guadeloupe by calling **C.D.L. Taxi** at ℭ **590/20-74-74** or **Taxi Leader** at ℭ **590/82-26-26.** It's possible, but very expensive, to sightsee by taxi. Usually, the concierge at your hotel will help you make arrangements. Fares are usually negotiated at the rate of around 150€ ($188) for a 7-hour day for up to four passengers.

BY BUS Small buses link almost every hamlet to Pointe-à-Pitre. However, you may need to know some French to use the system. In Pointe-à-Pitre, you can catch a jitney van from the following departure points: If you're going anywhere in Basse-Terre you'll depart from the Gare Routière de Bergevin. If the northern half of Grande-Terre is your destination, catch a bus at the Gare Routière de Mortenol. For the southern end of Grande-Terre the buses depart from the *prolongement* (extension) of the Marché de la Darse. Infrequent and somewhat erratic service is available daily from 5:30am to 7:30pm. There is no direct bus service from the airport to Pointe-à-Pitre. To travel the entire island would cost between 3.50€ ($4.40) and 4€ ($5). Many visitors find it easier, especially when they first arrive on Guadeloupe, to take a taxi.

FAST FACTS: Guadeloupe

Banks Banks on Guadeloupe are usually open Monday through Friday from 9am to 3pm. There are about a dozen banks in Pointe-à-Pitre, most with ATMs (they're called *distributeurs des billets*).

Currency Because the territory of Guadeloupe falls under the same monetary system as mainland France, the island uses the **euro (€)** as its mode of exchange. The current rate of exchange is .80€ to the U.S. dollar. *Rates in this chapter are quoted in U.S. dollars.*

Customs Items for personal use, such as tobacco, cameras, and film, are admitted without formalities or tax if not in excessive quantity.

Documents U.S., British, or Canadian residents need a passport, plus a return or ongoing plane ticket.

Electricity The local electricity is 220-volt AC (50 cycles), which means that U.S.-made appliances will need a transformer and an adapter. Some of the big resorts lend these to guests, but don't count on it.

Emergencies Call the **police** at ℭ **17.** To report a **fire** or summon an **ambulance,** dial ℭ **18.**

Hospitals There are five modern hospitals on Guadeloupe, plus 23 clinics. Hotels and the Guadeloupe tourist office can assist in locating English-speaking doctors. There's a 24-hour emergency room at the **Centre Hôpitalier Universitaire de Pointe-à-Pitre,** Abymes (ℭ **590/89-10-10**), on the northern fringe of Pointe-à-Pitre.

Language The official language is French; Creole is the unofficial second language. English is spoken only in the major tourist centers, rarely in the countryside.

Liquor Laws Liquor is sold in grocery and liquor stores on any day of the week. It's legal to have an open container, though the authorities are very strict about any littering, disorderly behavior, and drunk driving.

Pharmacies The pharmacies carry French medicines, and most over-the-counter U.S. drugs have French equivalents. Prescribed medicines can be purchased if you have the prescription with you. At least one drugstore is always open; the tourist office can tell you what pharmacies are open at what time.

Police In an emergency, call ℭ **17**. Otherwise, call ℭ **590/82-99-86.**

Safety Guadeloupe is relatively free of serious crime. But don't go wandering alone at night on the streets of Pointe-à-Pitre; by nightfall they are relatively deserted and might be dangerous. Purse snatching by fast-riding motorcyclists has been reported, so exercise caution.

Taxes A departure tax, required on scheduled flights, is included in the airfares. Hotel taxes are included in all room rates.

Telephone To call Guadeloupe from the United States, dial **011** (the international access code), then **590** (the country code for Guadeloupe), then **590** again, and the rest of the local number, which will be six digits. If you want to call another island of the French Antilles, be aware that St. Barts, French St. Martin, and offshore dependencies of Guadeloupe such as Ile des Saints or La Désirade are all directly linked to the phone network of Guadeloupe. Consequently, no telephone prefix is required, and you can dial any of those islands simply by dialing the six-digit local phone number. But if you're on Guadeloupe and want to dial someone in Martinique, you'll have to punch in the prefix for Martinique **(0596)**, followed by the six-digit local number. To reach an **AT&T** operator on Guadeloupe, dial ℭ **00011;** to use **AT&T Direct,** dial ℭ **0800/99-00-11.** To reach **MCI,** dial ℭ **0800/99-00-19,** and to reach **Sprint,** dial ℭ **0800/99-00-87.** It looks like the island's phone technology will be improved soon.

Time Guadeloupe is on Atlantic Standard Time year-round, 1 hour ahead of Eastern Standard Time (when it's 6am in New York, it's 7am on Guadeloupe). When daylight savings time is in effect in the U.S., clocks in New York and Guadeloupe show the same time.

Tipping Hotels usually add a 10% to 15% service charge. Restaurants always add a 15% service charge, and no additional tip is needed. Most taxi drivers who own their own cars do not expect a tip; if they've been especially helpful with your luggage, you might give them an additional 10%.

Water While on Guadeloupe, stick to bottled water only.

Weather The average temperature in Guadeloupe is 82°F (28°C) in summer, dropping to an average of 76°F (24°C) in winter. The rainiest months are between June and October.

2 Pointe-à-Pitre

The port and chief city of Guadeloupe, Pointe-à-Pitre, lies on Grande-Terre. Unfortunately, it doesn't have the old-world charm of Fort-de-France on Martinique, and what beauty it does possess is often hidden behind closed doors.

Having been burned and rebuilt so many times, the port now lacks character. Modern apartments and condominiums form a high-rise backdrop over jerry-built shacks and industrial suburbs. The rather narrow streets are jammed during the day with a colorful crowd that creates a permanent traffic jam.

However, at sunset the town becomes quiet again and almost deserted. The only charm left is around the waterfront, where you half expect to see Bogie sipping rum at a cafe table.

Most visitors just drop in to Pointe-à-Pitre for **shopping.** It's best to visit the town in the morning (you can easily cover it in half a day), taking in the waterfront and outdoor market (the latter is livelier in the early hours).

The town center is **place de la Victoire,** a park shaded by palm trees and poincianas. Here you'll see some old sandbox trees said to have been planted by Victor Hugues, the mulatto who organized a revolutionary army of both whites and blacks to establish a dictatorship. In this square he kept a guillotine busy, and the death-dealing instrument stood here (unused) until modern times.

With the recent completion of the **Centre St-John-Perse,** a $20 million project that had been on the drawing boards for many years, the waterfront of Pointe-à-Pitre has been transformed from a bastion of old warehouses and cruise-terminal buildings into an architectural complex comprising a hotel, three restaurants, 80 shops and boutiques, a bank, and the expanded headquarters of Guadeloupe's Port Authority. Named for Saint-John Perse, the 20th-century poet and Nobel Laureate who was born just a few blocks away, the center is designed in contemporary French Caribbean style, which blends with the traditional architecture of Pointe-à-Pitre. For brochures and maps, the **Guadeloupe tourist office** is just minutes away, at Square de la Banque 5 (© **590/82-09-30**).

ACCOMMODATIONS

Hôtel St-John Perse   Stay here only if you have business in town or need to be here for an early morning flight (it's 15 min. from the airport). This hotel rises four stories above the harbor front, near the quays. The small rooms are clean, simple, and furnished with locally crafted mahogany pieces. Very few units have views of the sea. Bathrooms are small with no frills; about half have shower-tub combinations. Once you check in, the laissez-faire staff will probably leave you alone until the end of your stay.

There's a simple coffee shop/cafe on street level. To reach a beach, you'll have to travel 3km (2 miles) to the east to Le Bas du Fort and the Gosier area (see below).

Centre Saint-John-Perse, quai de Croisières (at the harbor front), 97110 Pointe-à-Pitre, Guadeloupe, F.W.I. © **590/82-51-57.** Fax 590/82-52-61. www.saint-john-perse.com. 44 units. Year-round 80€–90€ ($100–$113) double. Rates include continental breakfast. AE, MC, V. **Amenities:** Coffee shop; laundry service; dry cleaning. *In room:* A/C, TV, dataport, safe.

DINING

Côté Jardin 🏵 FRENCH   This is one of the finest, most upscale independent restaurants in Guadeloupe, with an allegiance to the tenets of French cuisine that you might expect on the French mainland. Because of its fine food and its sense of Gallic style, no one really cares that there isn't a water view. Surrounded by potted flowers and shrubs, with a view over palm trees and reproductions of paintings by Miró and Matisse, you'll dine in a red-and-green room with a hint of Provence. Menu items focus on fresh shellfish, much of which comes from fish tanks near the restaurant's entrance. Scallops with a subtle saffron sauce, and several different preparations of foie gras (including a succulent version that's fried and served with a reduction of sweet Banyuls wine) make a flavorful beginning. For an especially tasty treat, try grilled mahimahi served with teriyaki-flavored orange sauce.

La Marina, Pointe-à-Pitre. 𝒞 590/90-91-28. Reservations recommended. Main courses 23€–27€ ($29–$34); fixed-price menus 35€–37€ ($44–$46). AE, MC, V. Mon–Fri noon–2:30pm; Mon–Sat 7:30–11pm.

Restaurant Sucré-Salé TRADITIONAL FRENCH   In the heart of Pointe-à-Pitre, adjacent to an Air France office and near several banks, this restaurant is always filled at lunchtime with dealmakers and office workers. The decorative theme revolves around jazz, with portraits of Louis Armstrong, Billie Holliday, and Miles Davis. A covered terrace overlooking the busy boulevard serves as an animated singles bar on Friday and Saturday nights. The charming Marius Pheron, the Guadeloupe-born owner who did an 18-year stint in Paris, offers filets of snapper served with pommes soufflés and black pepper, meal-size salads, entrecôte steaks, and an impressive medley of grilled fish. The restaurant hosts a jazz concert 1 evening a month; posters announcing the event appear all over town.

Blvd. Légitimus, Pointe-à-Pitre. 𝒞 590/21-22-55. Reservations recommended. Main courses 7€–22€ ($8.75–$28). MC, V. Mon–Sat noon–3pm; Fri–Sat 7–9:30pm.

SHOPPING

We suggest that you skip a shopping tour of Pointe-à-Pitre if you're going to Fort-de-France on Martinique, as you'll find far more merchandise there, and perhaps friendlier service. If you're not, however, we recommend the following shops, some of which line rue Frébault.

Your best buys will be anything French—perfumes from Chanel, silk scarves from Hermès, cosmetics from Dior, crystal from Lalique and Baccarat. Though they're expensive, we've found some of these items discounted (but not often) as much as 30% below U.S. or Canadian prices. Most shops will accept U.S. dollars, but they'll give these discounts only for purchases made by traveler's check. Purchases are duty free if brought directly from store to plane. In addition to the places below, there are also two duty-free shops at **Raizet Airport** (𝒞 590/21-14-66) selling liquor, rums, perfumes, crystal, and cigarettes.

Most shops open at 8:30am, close at 1pm, and then reopen between 3 and 5:30pm. They're closed on Saturday afternoons, Sundays, and holidays. When the cruise ships are in port, many eager shopkeepers stay open longer and on weekends.

One of the best places to buy French perfumes, at prices often lower than those charged in Paris, is **Phoenicia,** 8 rue Frébault (𝒞 590/83-50-36), which has a good selection of imported cosmetics. Another leading perfume shop is **Au Bonheur des Dames,** 49 rue Frébault (𝒞 590/82-00-30), also known for its skin-care products.

If you're adventurous, you may want to seek out some native goods in little shops along the back streets of Pointe-à-Pitre. Look for the straw hats, or *sala-cos,* made in Les Saintes islands, usually created from split bamboo. Native **doudou dolls** are also popular gift items.

𝓜oments The Essence of Guadeloupe

At some point as you stroll through the market, order a glass of rum from one of the local vendors, and ask for *rhum agricole,* a pure form of the drink that's fermented from sugar-cane juice. Savvy locals claim that the rum (whose brand name is Rhum Damoiseau) is the only kind you can drink without a hangover the next morning.

Open-air stalls surround the **covered market (Marché Couvert)** at the corner of rue Frébault and rue Peynier. Here you can discover the many fruits, spices, and vegetables that are fun to look at as well as to taste. In madras turbans, local Creole women make deals over their strings of fire-red pimientos. The bright fabrics they wear compete with the rich colors of oranges, papayas, bananas, mangos, and pineapples. Best times to visit are Monday to Saturday 8am to 2pm.

3 Le Bas du Fort

Just 3km (2 miles) east of Pointe-à-Pitre is the tourist area of Le Bas du Fort, near Gosier. This is the best place to stay if you'd like to be near (but not in) the capital and if you'd like a location near the international airport. Although it has some good sandy beaches, there are far better ones further out from the center. One drawback is that the area is rather built up and you may not find the tranquillity here you'll enjoy in other parts of Guadeloupe.

Aquarium de la Guadeloupe, place Créole, Marina Gosier (© 590/90-92-38), is one of the largest and most modern aquariums in the Caribbean. Just off the highway near Le Bas du Fort Marina, the aquarium is home to tropical fish, coral, underwater plants, huge sharks, and other sea creatures. Hours are daily from 9am to 7pm. Admission is 6.50€ ($8.15) for adults, 3.50€ ($4.40) for children age 6 to 12; the aquarium is free for kids 5 and under.

ACCOMMODATIONS

Novotel Bas Du Fort   One of the island's biggest hotel complexes was formed in 2002 when two neighboring hotels (formerly known as the Novotel Fleur d'Epée and the Hotel Marissol) were combined into the same resort. The compound sits directly beside a coastline that's dotted with at least two crescent-shaped bays and short, white-sand beaches shaded with palms and sea-grape trees. Each of the somewhat small guest rooms is well kept and modern, with a tile-covered floor; a simple motel-style floor plan; a warm, summer-inspired color scheme; and, in most cases, either a private terrace or balcony. Other accommodations are configured into bungalows, set directly within a garden, a short walk from the sea. Prices of bungalows—rare for a Caribbean resort—are equivalent to those of a double room. The staff here is laid-back and cooperative, and the clientele includes a relatively young-ish group of mainland French who turn up here in bikini-clad droves, and who seem to appreciate the hotel's large size and holiday village format.

The resort has three separate eating options; two focus on French and Creole cuisine. For less formal meals, head for the snack bar (L'Alamanda) on the beach.

Le Bas du Fort, 97100 Gosier, Guadeloupe, F.W.I. © 800/221-4542 in the U.S., or 590/90-84-44. Fax 590/90-83-32. www.accordhotels.com. 385 units. Winter 193€–232€ ($241–$290) double; off season 140€–168€ ($175–$210) double. Rates include continental breakfast. AE, DC, MC, V. **Amenities:** 3 restaurants; 2 bars; 2 outdoor pools; disco; 2 tennis courts; fitness center; *hammam* (steam bath); boating; scuba diving; snorkeling; water-skiing; windsurfing; salon; massage; babysitting; laundry; nonsmoking rooms; rooms for those with limited mobility. *In room:* A/C, TV, dataport, hair dryer, safe.

DINING

Rosini ☆ NORTHERN ITALIAN   This is the best Italian restaurant in the French West Indies, thanks to the sophisticated father-in-law/son-in-law team of Venice-born Luciano Rosini and Christophe Giraud, from Provence. It's contained within two air-conditioned dining rooms on the ground floor of an upscale condo complex across from the Novotel in Le Bas du Fort. Recorded opera music sets the mood for succulent versions of tournedos layered with foie gras, *osso buco* (veal shanks), and freshwater prawns served *diavolo* style in a spicy tomato, garlic, and parsley sauce with freshly made fettuccine. Ravioli comes stuffed either with veal and herbs or with lobster. At least five types of pizza are available for the kids. English is readily understood here.

La Porte des Caraïbes, Le Bas du Fort. © 590/90-87-81. Reservations recommended. Main courses 10€–35€ ($13–$44). AE, DC, MC, V. Daily noon–2:30pm and 6:30–11pm.

4 Gosier

Gosier is where some of the best beachfront in Guadeloupe begins, and it has become one of the island's major resort centers, since it has nearly 8km (5 miles) of sandy but narrow beach, stretching east from Pointe-à-Pitre. All the hotels below are close to the sands. We like the funky charm of the town, which evokes a little resort along the French Riviera. Unlike many parts of the Caribbean, this area attracts mainly French visitors, so you'll feel like you're on a Mediterranean holiday. Gosier also has some of the island's best dining and nightlife, plus a casino.

You can take a 15-minute climb to the 18th-century ruins of **Fort Fleur-d'Epée.** Its dungeons and battlements are testaments to the ferocious fighting between the French and British armies in 1794. The ruins command the crown of a hill, which affords good views over the bay of Pointe-à-Pitre. If the visibility is good, you can see the neighboring offshore islands of Marie-Galante and Iles des Saintes.

ACCOMMODATIONS

La Creole Beach Hôtel ⋇ (Kids

This is the largest resort on Guadeloupe, but because it's divided into four distinct sections, you'll get a sense of isolation and privacy. It's alongside two beaches within a lush setting of lawns, trees, hibiscus, and bougainvillea, and it has a strong French Creole flavor.

The most upscale of the units is Les Palmes, a section completed in 2002 with the best furnishings and the most spacious accommodations, followed by Le Creole, a three-story building with verandas influenced by French colonial architecture. Slightly less desirable is Le Mahogany, a comfortable compound with oceanfront rooms (most without kitchens). The most basic, Le Yucca, houses the family units with kitchens. Most rooms are spacious and contain two queen-size beds. All units contain a private bathroom, most with a shower (one-fourth of them feature a shower/tub combination).

La Route des Epices serves excellent local specials and an international cuisine. Le Zawag lies just on the rocks by the sea, offering fresh fish and seafood.

Pointe de la Verdure, B.P. 61, 97190 Gosier, Guadeloupe, F.W.I. © 590/90-46-46. Fax 590/90-46-66. www.deshotelsetdesiles.com. 384 units. Winter 131€–220€ ($164–$275) double; off season 142€–192€ ($178–$240) double; year-round 250€ ($313) duplex for 1–4. Children under 12 stay free in parent's room. Rates include continental breakfast. AE, DC, MC, V. **Amenities:** 2 restaurants; bar; outdoor pool; tennis court; deep-sea fishing; sailboat rentals; scuba diving; water-skiing; windsurfing; room service (breakfast only); babysitting; laundry service; dry cleaning; nonsmoking rooms; rooms for those with limited mobility. *In room:* A/C, TV, fax, dataport, kitchenette (in some), minibar, fridge, hair dryer, safe.

Sofitel Auberge de la Vieille Tour ⋇

Though it's a Sofitel, this place was once a family inn built around the shadow of an old sugar mill. Set on a 2-hectare (5-acre) bluff, the property encompasses a small private beach.

The older guest rooms are relatively short on charm. The better maintained units are within La Résidence, a series of town house–style accommodations set near the pool. Their desirability is rivaled only by units referred to as "luxury-class," set close to the water near the beach. Rooms have comfortable furnishings and compact bathrooms with shower stalls or shower/tub combinations.

The restaurants La Vieille Tour and Le Zagaya serve excellent French and Creole food, respectively, in relatively elegant, semiformal settings. L'Ajoupa is a grill-style indoor-outdoor affair.

Montauban, 97190 Gosier, Guadeloupe, F.W.I. © 800/221-4542 in the U.S., or 590/84-23-23. Fax 590/84-33-43. www.sofitel.com. 180 units. Winter 320€–400€ ($400–$500) double, 480€ ($600) minisuite; off season 190€–240€ ($238–$300) double, 280€ ($350) minisuite. Rates include continental breakfast. AE, MC, V. **Amenities:** 3 restaurants; 2 bars; outdoor pool; 2 tennis courts; scuba diving; snorkeling; room service (6am–10pm); laundry service; dry cleaning; nonsmoking rooms. *In room:* A/C, TV, dataport, minibar, beverage maker, hair dryer, safe.

DINING

Le Bananier CREOLE   Locals flock to this restaurant where some of the most imaginative dishes in the Creole repertoire are handled with finesse and charm. Within an air-conditioned, 50-year-old clapboard-sided cottage, you'll enjoy old-fashioned staples, such as stuffed crab backs and *accras* (beignets) of codfish. Much more appealing, however, are dishes like filet mignon served with pulverized blood sausage, port wine, and a reduction of crayfish bisque; a *clafoutis* (gratinated medley) of shellfish; and a *tourtière d'oeufs aux crabes* (an omelet with breaded and baked crabmeat, fresh tomatoes, and reduction of callaloo leaves). The menu's most appealing dessert is banana flambéed in *Schrubb,* an obscure island liqueur made from fermented orange peels and prized by the owners' grandparents.

Rue Principale de Gosier, Montauban. © 590/84-34-85. Reservations recommended. Main courses 11€–27€ ($14–$34). AE, DC, MC, V. Tues–Sun 12:30–2pm and 7–10pm.

L'Hibiscus FRENCH/ANTILLEAN   The owner of this restaurant, Jocelyn Corvo, got his training thanks to years of association with the French hotel giant, ACCOR, eventually establishing this water-fronting restaurant as a well-earned expression of his personal freedom. It's about as close to the water as a building can reasonably get, with its foundation piers sunk directly into the sea, and with big-bayed windows overlooking the sun and storms that loom on the distant horizon. Menu items are firmly based on seafood and shellfish, with fare that celebrates the bounty of the sea. There's an elegant version of freshwater crayfish simmered in a coconut-and-saffron-cream sauce, stewed oysters in a Creole sauce, and many different types of very fresh grilled fish. The fanciful chef's specialty, *L'Océane du chef,* consists of a platter of cooked scallops, shellfish, and crayfish served in a luscious saffron-flavored cream sauce.

Bord de Mer, Gosier. © 0590/91-13-61. Reservations recommended. Main courses 10€–35€ ($13–$44); set-price menus 30€–70€ ($38–$88). AE, DC, MC, V. Tues–Fri noon–3pm; Tues–Sat 7–10pm. Closed Sept.

5 Ste-Anne

About 14km (8¾ miles) east of Gosier, little Ste-Anne is a sugar town and a resort offering many fine beaches and lodgings. In many ways, it's the most charming village of Guadeloupe, with its pastel-colored town hall, its church, and its principal square, **Place de la Victoire,** where a statue of Schoelcher commemorates the abolition of slavery in 1848.

ACCOMMODATIONS & DINING

Club Med La Caravelle ℛ   This all-inclusive chain resort, covering 18 hectares (44 acres) along a peninsula dotted with palm trees, opens onto one of the finest beaches in the French West Indies. The guest rooms tend to be small, but have good beds. (All but 10 units have twin beds; those 10 exceptions have queen-size beds.) Tiled and shower-only bathrooms are compact and short on amenities. The building known as Marie-Galante contains the resort's largest and most comfortable rooms (each with a terrace or veranda), costing about 25% more than the smaller, bland standard rooms. Children are welcome, but there are few, if any, programs catering to their needs, and no babysitting services. Consequently, this resort tends to attract couples and adult singles, with the occasional child rather awkwardly shoehorned in among the otherwise sybaritic adults.

In 2001, the resort added an annex ("La Fête") containing only single rooms, a boon for single holidaymakers. The meals here are nothing if not generous. The breakfast and lunch buffet tables groan with French, Continental, and Creole food. Dinner is served in the main dining room or in the candlelit, more romantic annex restaurant beside the sea. There's live entertainment several nights a week, sometimes a Brazil-inspired samba band, and at rare intervals, the Guadeloupe folklore ballet, Les Ballets Guadeloupéans.

97180 Ste-Anne, Guadeloupe, F.W.I. © **800/CLUB-MED** in the U.S., or 590/85-49-50. Fax 590/85-49-79. 329 units. www.clubmed.com. Nov–Apr 903€–1,250€ ($1,129–$1,563) weekly; May–Oct 605€–990€ ($756–$1,238) weekly. Rates are per person based on double occupancy. Rates are all-inclusive. Children age 4–12 are charged 70% of the adult rate. Single supplement 10%–50% above the per-person double rate. AE, MC, V. **Amenities:** 2 restaurants; 2 bars; outdoor pool; night club; 4 tennis courts; gym; aerobics; archery; basketball; volleyball; kayaks; snorkeling; windsurfing; children's programs; laundry service; dry cleaning; rooms for those with limited mobility. *In room:* A/C, TV, dataport, hair dryer, safe.

Hôtel La Toubana ⭑   Built on 2 hectares (5 acres) of sloping land close to the beach (a 5-min. walk on a path carved into the cliff side), La Toubana is centered around a low-lying stone building on a rocky cliff overlooking the bay and Ste-Anne Beach. Many guests come here just for the view, which on a clear day encompasses Marie-Galante, Dominica, La Désirade, and the Iles des Saintes, but you'll quickly learn that there's far more to this place than just a panorama. The red-roofed bungalows lie scattered among the tropical shrubs along the adjacent hillsides (*toubana* means "small house" in Arawak); there are 20 garden

---

(Moments   **Begin the Beguine**

The folkloric dance troupe **Les Ballets Guadeloupéans** makes frequent appearances at the big hotels, whirling and moving to the rhythms of island music in colorful costumes and well-choreographed routines. Some resorts, including the Club Med La Caravelle, use their visit to set the theme for the evening, serving up a banquet of traditional island dishes to accompany the dance, music, and costumes.

Ask at your hotel where the Ballets Guadeloupeans will be appearing during your stay, as their schedule tends to vary as they tour the island. You can catch them as they rotate through the hotels Arawak, Salako, L'Auberge de la Vieille Tour, and Novotel Coracia, as well as an occasional presentation at the Club Med La Caravelle. On the night of any of these performances, you can order a drink at the bar and catch the show, or join in the hotel buffet for a flat price. Buffets usually start around 8pm, with the show beginning at 8:30pm. The troupe also performs on some cruise ships.

units and 12 more upscale oceanview units. Each has a kitchenette, comfortable French furnishings, a terrace, a rather compact shower/tub combination bathroom, and either two twin beds or one king-size bed. Cots for kids are available on request.

Le Baobab offers both indoor and alfresco dining of fine quality in a site overlooking the pool. It serves the best lobster on the island. The beachfront bar serves tropical drinks and occasionally hosts live entertainment.

Durivage (B.P. 63), 97180 Ste-Anne, Guadeloupe, F.W.I. (Ⓒ) **800/451-3734** or 590/88-25-57. Fax 590/88-38-90. toubana@leaderhotels.gp. 32 units. Winter 180€–280€ ($225–$350) double; off season 100€–150€ ($125–$188) double. Rates include American breakfast. AE, MC, V. **Amenities:** Restaurant; bar; outdoor pool; tennis court; deep-sea fishing; snorkeling; scooters; babysitting; coin-operated laundry. *In room:* A/C, kitchenette, hair dryer.

6 St-François ⟨⋆⟩

Continuing east from Ste-Anne, you'll notice many old round towers named for Father Labat, the Dominican founder of the sugar-cane industry. These towers were once used as mills to grind the cane. St-François, 40km (25 miles) east of Pointe-à-Pitre, used to be a sleepy fishing village. Then Air France discovered it and opened a Méridien hotel with a casino. That was followed by the promotional activities of J. F. Rozan, a native who invested heavily to make St-François a jet-set resort. Now the once sleepy village has first-class accommodations, as well as an airport available to private jets, a golf course (it's the golfing center of the island), and a marina, where there's a casino (see "Guadeloupe After Dark," near the end of this chapter). It also has some good beaches and is known for its Creole restaurants.

ACCOMMODATIONS

Domaine de l'Anse des Rochers   The largest hotel on Guadeloupe sprawls across 8 hectares (20 acres) of sloping land in St-François and has a nice sandy beach. Accommodations are housed in either a half-dozen multileveled, hotel-style buildings, each of which contains 39 units, or 32 bungalows (four units per bungalow). The decor is airy, summery, and uncluttered. Bedrooms are fairly routine, usually small, each with a tiled, shower-only bathroom. Despite the size of the resort, guests still feel a sense of isolation and intimacy, thanks to the way the place is configured into smaller blocks. Expect lots of young families with children, honeymooners, and European package-tour groups.

There are four dining choices here, ranging from formal Le Sucrier, serving European cuisine to a deli-style outlet for takeout. You can catch live entertainment the resort's two bars.

Domaine de l'Anse des Rochers, 97118 St-François, Guadeloupe, F.W.I. (Ⓒ) **590/93-90-31.** Fax 590/88-43-21. www.anse-des-rochers.com. 356 units. Winter 140€–151€ ($175–$189) double, 169€–252€ ($211–$315) villa; off season 85€–96€ ($106–$120) double, 107€–121€ ($134–$151) villa. AE, MC, V. **Amenities:** 3 restaurants; 2 bars; outdoor pool; archery; beach volleyball; jet skis; scuba diving; snorkeling; car rental; laundry service; dry cleaning; rooms for those with limited mobility. *In room:* A/C, TV, dataport, kitchenette, hair dryer (in some), safe.

Le Kalenda Resort ⟨⋆⟩   At five stories, this is one of the tallest buildings in the area. It stands on one of the best beaches on Guadeloupe on 60 hectares (148 acres) of land at the most easterly tip of the island, a 10-minute walk from the village of St-François. This is a competent workhorse of a hotel, albeit without the glamour and architectural flair of Le Meridien La Cocoteraie (see below). Originally conceived as one of Air France's Meridien Hotels, it was bought in

2002 by a group of local investors, who immediately scheduled an overhaul and renovation of its bedrooms. The medium-size units are furnished comfortably and most contain twin beds. Each contains a small but tidily maintained bathroom with a shower-tub combination and overlooks either the sea or a Robert Trent Jones Sr.–designed golf course.

The more formal restaurant is La Casa Zomar, serving Continental and upscale Creole food. At lunch casual Le Balaou serves burgers, salads, and sandwiches.

97118 St-François, Guadeloupe, F.W.I. ℂ 800/543-4300 in the U.S., or 590/48-05-00. Fax 590/88-40-71. 263 units. Winter 216€–280€ ($270–$350) double, 285€–339€ ($356–$424) suite; off season 120€–190€ ($150–$238) double, 258€–285€ ($323–$356) suite. AE, DC, MC, V. **Amenities:** 2 restaurants; 2 bars; outdoor pool; golf available at course next door; 2 tennis courts; access to watersports; nearby marina; windsurfing; room service (breakfast only); massage; babysitting; laundry service. In room: A/C, TV, dataport, fridge, hair dryer.

Le Meridien La Cocoteraie 🐾🐾
This is a plush, suites-only resort, the island's finest choice for a luxury holiday. It opens onto a lagoon with two private but small white-sand beaches. The hotel hides behind a colonial plantation style facade, flanked by a series of buildings, also in the colonial style. Twenty of the units are more desirable because they open right onto the beach. Across from the hotel lies the Robert Trent Jones Sr. golf course. Each unit comes with a spacious patio or a balcony overlooking the water or else one of the largest hotel pools on Guadeloupe. Some of the accommodations are equipped with a duo of shower-only baths; others have tub-and-shower combination.

Meals are served in a well-designed, open-sided pavilion, La Varangue (see below). Lunch menus are relatively simple. Evenings are more romantic, with flickering candles and a wider choice of (mostly French) food.

Ave. De l'Europe, 97118 St-François, Guadeloupe, F.W.I. ℂ 800/322-2223 or 590/88-79-81. Fax 590/88-78-33. www.la-cocoteraie.com. 50 suites. Winter 419€–1,067€ ($524–$1,334) double; off season 229€–488€ ($286–$610) double. AE, DC, MC, V. Closed Aug 24–Oct 21. **Amenities:** Restaurant; bar; outdoor pool; 2 tennis courts; fitness center; car rental; limited room service; babysitting; laundry service; dry cleaning; rooms for those with limited mobility. In room: A/C, TV, dataport, minibar, hair dryer, safe.

DINING

La Varangue 🐾 FRENCH
Named after the figureheads that used to grace the prows of pirate ships, this is the culinary showcase (and the only restaurant) within Le Meridien La Cocoteraie hotel. In many ways, it functions as the social and decorative showcase of the hotel as well, positioned as it is adjacent to a low bridge that traverses the resort's swimming pool, near the reception desk of the hotel, within full view of the beach and the hotel gardens. Menu items at lunch revolve around fresh salads, pastas, and relatively simple versions of grilled fish and meats. Dinners are more elaborate, more leisurely, and more romantic, with flickering candles and such dishes as a crabmeat tart with exotic mushrooms; cream of shellfish soup; a confit of dorado (mahimahi) with tandoori spices and coconut milk; and an elegant version of lobster salad. And for any die-hard lover of all-Gallic food, there's even a version of foie gras like you'd have expected to find on the French mainland.

In Le Méridien La Cocoteraie, Ave. de l'Europe, St-François. ℂ 0590/88-79-81. Reservations recommended for nonresidents of the hotel. Lunch platters 19€–25€ ($24–$31); dinner main courses 20€–30€ ($25–$38). Note: Some shellfish dishes at both lunch and dinner can range up to 47€ ($59). AE, DC, MC, V. Daily 12:30–2:30pm and 7:30–10pm.

Les Oiseaux 🐾 FRENCH/CREOLE
This place feels like a Provençal farmhouse with views over the sea and the island of Marie-Galante. The walled-in

front garden frames a stone-sided, low-slung building that emits an aroma of southern French and Antillean cuisine. The antique furniture from Thailand and Burma are for sale. When not purchasing chairs and tables, you can order delectable Creole-style dishes, including such specialties as an entrecôte steak grilled and served with a green-peppercorn sauce and by now such famous dishes as couscous, paella, and *cassoulet* (a meat-and-bean dish famous in the southwest of France). Nothing is more popular than the freshly caught crayfish, which is grilled to perfection.

It's also possible to rent one of the four attractively furnished and comfortable bedrooms, costing from 45€ to 55€ ($56–$69) in a double, with breakfast included.

Anse des Rochers (6km/3¾ miles west of St-François). © 590/88-56-92. Reservations recommended. Main courses 15€–45€ ($19–$56). MC, V. Daily noon–2:30pm and 7–9:30pm. Closed Sept.

7 Pointe des Châteaux

Eleven kilometers (6¾ miles) east of St-François is the rocky headland of Pointe des Châteaux, the easternmost tip of Grand-Terre, where the Atlantic meets the Caribbean. Here, where crashing waves sound around you, you'll see a cliff sculpted by the sea into dramatic castlelike formations, the erosion typical of France's Brittany coast. The view from here is panoramic. At the top is a cross erected in the 19th century.

You might want to walk to **Pointe des Colibris,** the extreme end of Guadeloupe. From here you'll have a view of the northeastern sector of the island, and to the east a look at La Désirade, an island that has the appearance of a huge vessel anchored far away (see the section "Side Trips from Guadeloupe," later in this chapter).

Pointe des Châteaux has miles of coved white-sand beaches. Most of these are safe for swimming, except at the point where the waves of the turbulent Atlantic encounter the tranquil Caribbean Sea, churning up the waters.

Since there are no hotels here, you can come just for the day, to enjoy the beaches.

DINING

Iguane Café 𝒜 *Finds* FRENCH   This bistro/cafe is one of the best dining choices on the island, the equal of such stellar choices as Le Château de Feuilles (see below). Owners Marie and Sylvan Serrouart serve their creative cuisine at a point on the road connecting St.-François with Pointe du Châteaux. The restaurant has a colorful West Indian decor, an open-air kitchen, and English-language menus. Don't come here in a rush, as food is cooked to order and the service is,

---

Moments Nude Trysting

This part of Guadeloupe is studded with wind-carved coves. At **Anse Tarare,** the tranquil Caribbean meets the turbulent Atlantic. From the signposted parking lot along the Route de la Pointe des Château, you'll see a narrow pathway leading through scrub to the sea and Anse Tarare. Should it be your wish, you can strip down here and flaunt your charms. Of course, along with your loved one, it's wise to bring the makings of a French beachside picnic—a bottle of chilled rosé, a wheel of Brie, and a freshly baked baguette.

well, relaxed. Mellow out at the bar, with its selection of nearly two dozen rum punches, including one flavored with cinnamon. A novelty drink comes from a large jar of rum with several hibiscus flowers floating inside. On the creative and varied menu, begin with a delectable goat's cheese appetizer, battered in a crust with zesty Creole spices. You might also opt for the goose-liver pâté. We always gravitate to the fresh fish of the day, perhaps snapper, aromatically cooked in a puff pastry. Also good is caramelized chicken cooked in coconut milk and steamed fish flavored with five spices, the sweetbreads, and shrimp in saffron sauce. We avoid the rabbit or goat dishes, which are often a bit tough. For dessert, try the lemon-and-lime soufflé, or the coconut crisps served with chocolate sauce.

Route de la Pointe des Châteaux, St. François. ⓒ 590/88-61-37. Reservations recommended. Main courses 19€–28€ ($24–$35). AE, MC. Wed–Mon 7:30–10:30pm; Sun 12:30–2:30pm. Closed Sept 10–Oct 10.

A STOP IN LE MOULE

To go back to Pointe-à-Pitre from Pointe des Châteaux, you can use an alternative route, the N5 from St-François. After a 14km (8¾-mile) drive, you'll reach the village of **Le Moule,** which was founded at the end of the 17th century and known long before Pointe-à-Pitre. It used to be a major shipping port for sugar. Now a tiny coastal fishing village, it never regained its importance after it was devastated in the hurricane of 1928. Because it offers more than 16km (10 miles) of crescent-shaped beach, it's developing as a destination.

Specialties of this Guadeloupean village are *palourdes,* the clams that thrive in the semisalty mouths of freshwater rivers. Known for being more tender and less rubbery than saltwater clams, they often, even when fresh, have a distinct sulfur taste not unlike that of overpoached eggs. Local gastronomes prepare them with saffron and aged rum or cognac.

Five kilometers (3 miles) from Le Moule, heading toward Campêche, the **Musée Archéologique Edgar Clerc,** Parc de la Rosette, Le Moule (ⓒ **590/23-57-57**), shows a collection of both Carib and Arawak artifacts gathered from various islands of the Lesser Antilles. Hours are Monday 10am to 5pm and Wednesday to Sunday from 9am to 5pm. Admission is 5€ ($6.25), 2.50€ ($3.15) students, free for those under age 12.

To return to Pointe-à-Pitre, we suggest that you use Route D3 toward Abymes. The road winds around as you plunge deeply into Grand-Terre. About halfway along the way a road is signposted to **Jabrun du Nord** and **Jabrun du Sud.** These two villages are inhabited by Caucasians with blond hair, said to be survivors of aristocrats slaughtered during the Revolution. Those who escaped found safety by hiding out in Les Grands Fonds. The most important family here is named Matignon, and they gave their name to the colony known as "les Blancs Matignon." These citizens are said to be related to Prince Rainier of Monaco. Pointe-à-Pitre lies only 16km (10 miles) from Les Grand Fonds.

8 The North Coast of Grande-Terre ★★

From Pointe-à-Pitre, head northeast toward Abymes, passing next through Morne à l'Eau; you'll reach the small but not insignificant settlement of **Petit Canal** after 21km (13 miles). This is Guadeloupe's sugar-cane country, and a sweet smell fills the air.

PORT LOUIS

Continuing northwest along the coast from Petit Canal, you come to Port Louis, well known for its beautiful beach, **Anse du Souffleur,** which lacks facilities. We like it best in spring, when the brilliant white sand is effectively shown off against the flaming red poinciana. During the week, the beach is an especially quiet spot. The little port town has some good restaurants.

DINING

Le Poisson d'Or ✿ *(Finds)* CREOLE You enter this white-sided Antillean house by walking down a narrow corridor and emerging into a rustic dining room lined with varnished pine. Despite the simple setting, the food is well prepared and satisfying. You might begin with rillettes of marlin or stuffed crabs, followed by a heaping platter of raw shellfish; grilled lobster; or local fish, either grilled or prepared as a savory *court bouillon*. If you're in the mood for something inspired by the mainland of France, consider a wine-flavored boeuf bourguignon, or an *entrecôte maître d'hotel* (grilled steak with butter and fresh herbs). Dessert might be a flambéed banana or a scoop of coconut-flavored ice cream. Don't even think of coming here at night without an advance reservation—you might find the place locked up and empty.

2 rue Sadi-Carnot, Port Louis. ℂ 590/22-88-63. Reservations recommended. Main courses 10€–35€ ($13–$44); set-price menus 16€–20€ ($20–$25). AE, MC, V. Daily 11am–4pm and 7–10pm (with reservations only). Closed 3 weeks in Sept. Drive northwest from Petit-Canal along the coastal rd.

ANSE-BERTRAND

About 8km (5 miles) from Port Louis is Anse-Bertrand, the northernmost village of Guadeloupe. What is now a fishing village was the last refuge of the Carib tribes, and a reserve was once created here. Everything now, however, is sleepy.

DINING

Le Château de Feuilles ✿✿ FRENCH/CARIBBEAN We've had some of our finest meals on Guadeloupe here. Set inland from the sea, amid 3 rolling hectares (7½ acres) of greenery and blossoming flowers, this hideaway is owned and run by a Norman-born couple, Jean-Pierre and Martine Dubost, who moved here to escape civilization. To reach their place, which is 14km (8¾ miles) from Le Moule, near the eastern tip of Grande-Terre, you drive past the ruins of La Mahaudière, an 18th-century sugar mill. A gifted chef who makes maximum use of local ingredients, Monsieur Dubost prepares pâté of warm sea urchins, sautéed conch with Creole sauce, a cassoulet of land crabs, and a Caribbean adaptation of a classic French recipe, magret of duckling with fresh sugar cane. Two especially unusual dishes include a *pave de tazar* (a local fish), served with a garlic-flavored cream sauce, and a dish we've never seen anywhere else, green papaya stuffed with a fricassee of *lambi* (conch), scallops, and flying fish, all of it encased in puff pastry.

Campêche, Anse-Bertrand. ℂ 590/22-30-30. Reservations required, especially in summer when meals are prepared only in anticipation of your arrival. Main courses 18€–27€ ($23–$34). V. Oct–Aug Tues–Sun 11:30am–4pm; at night, at least 10 diners must reserve before they will open.

CONTINUING AROUND THE NORTHERN TIP

From Anse-Bertrand, you can drive along a gravel road heading for **Pointe de la Grande Vigie** ✿, the northernmost tip of the island, which you'll reach after 6km (3¾ miles) of what we hope will be cautious driving. Park your car and walk carefully along a narrow lane that will bring you to the northernmost rock of Guadeloupe. The view of the sweeping Atlantic from the top of rocky cliffs is remarkable—you stand about 84m (276 ft.) above the sea.

Afterward, a 6km (3¾-mile) drive south on a good road will bring you to the **Porte d'Enfer**, or "Gateway to Hell," where the sea rushes violently against two narrow cliffs.

After seeing this remote part of the island, you can head back, going either to **Morne à l'Eau** or **Le Moule** before connecting to the road taking you back to Pointe-à-Pitre.

9 Around Basse-Terre ⭑⭑⭑

Leaving Pointe-à-Pitre by Route N1, you can explore the western coast and the island of Basse-Terre. Here you'll find views as panoramic as those along the corniche along the French Riviera, but without the heavy traffic and crowds. After 2km (1¼ miles) you cross the Rivière Salée at Pont de la Gabarre. This narrow strait separates the two islands that form Guadeloupe. For the next 6km (3¾ miles) the road runs straight through sugar-cane fields.

At the sign, on a main crossing, turn right on Route N2 toward **Baie Mahault.** (Don't confuse this with the town of Mahault on Basse-Terre's westernmost coast.) Head northwest to **Lamentin,** a village settled by *corsairs* (pirates) at the beginning of the 18th century. Scattered about are some colonial mansions, but neither of these villages merit a stopover.

STE-ROSE

From Lamentin, you can drive for 10km (6½ miles) to Ste-Rose, where you'll find several good **beaches.** On your left, a small road leads in a few minutes to **Sofaia,** from which you'll have a panoramic view over the coast and forest preserve. You can easily skip this, however, if you're rushed for time.

Your main reason to stop here is La Sucrerie du Comté, one of the island's most atmospheric inns, set on the ruins of a sugar factory with gardens. The nearest beach is only a 10-minute stroll away. You might also stop in Ste-Rose for lunch at one of Basse-Terre's best restaurants, Restaurant Clara (see below).

ACCOMMODATIONS

La Sucrerie du Comté ⭑ Although you'll see the ruins of a 19th-century sugar factory (including a rusting locomotive) on this hotel's 3 hectares (7½ acres) of forested land overlooking the sea, most of the resort is modern. The medium-size accommodations are in 26 pink-toned bungalows. Each cozy bungalow has chunky and rustic handmade furniture and a bay window overlooking either the sea or a garden. (Each bungalow contains two units, both with ceiling fans; none have TVs or phones.) Shower-only bathrooms are tiny but tidy. The nearest major beach is La Grand-Anse, a 10- to 15-minute drive from the hotel. There's a small and narrow beach (Plage des Amandiers) within a 10-minute walk from the hotel, although the swimming here isn't very good.

Comté de Loheac, 97115 Ste-Rose, Guadeloupe, F.W.I. ℂ 590/28-60-17. Fax 590/28-65-63. www.prime-invest-hotels.com. 52 units. Winter 70€–90€ ($88–$113) double; off season 47€–58€ ($59–$73) double. Rates include breakfast. AE, MC, V. Closed Sept. **Amenities:** Restaurant; bar; outdoor pool; fishing; scuba diving; snorkeling; car rental; babysitting; laundry service; dry cleaning; rooms for those with limited mobility. *In room:* A/C, minibar, beverage maker, hair dryer, safe, no phone.

DINING

Restaurant Clara ⭑ CREOLE   On the waterfront near the center of town is the culinary statement of Clara Lesueur. Clara lived for 12 years in Paris as a member of an experimental jazz dance troupe, but years ago she returned to Guadeloupe, her home, to set up this breezy restaurant. Try for a table on the open patio, where palm trees complement the color scheme.

Clara artfully melds the classic French style of fine dining with authentic Creole flavors. Specialties include skate fish with rice and curry sauce, poached crayfish with Creole sauce and vegetables, brochette of swordfish, *palourdes* (small clams), several different preparations of conch, *salade de coffer* (made from a local fish whose name translates as "trunkfish"), and *crabes farcis* (red-orange crabs with a spicy filling). The "sauce chien" that's served with many of the dishes is a blend of hot peppers, garlic, lime juice, and "secret things." The house drink is made with six local fruits and ample quantities of rum.

Blvd. Maritime, Ste-Rose. ℂ 590/28-72-99. Reservations recommended. Main courses 9€–20€ ($11–$25). MC, V. Mon–Tues and Thurs–Sat noon–3pm and 7–10pm; Sun noon–3pm.

DESHAIES/LA GRAND-ANSE

A few miles farther along, you reach Pointe Allegre, the northernmost point of Basse-Terre. **Cluny Beach** is where the first settler landed on Guadeloupe, and it's a great place to break up your drive with a swim, although the waters are sometimes rough and there are no beach facilities.

Three kilometers (2 miles) farther will bring you to **La Grand-Anse** ⚜, one of the best beaches on Guadeloupe. It is very large and still secluded, sheltered by many tropical trees, especially palms. The place is ideal either for a swim or a picnic, although, again, there are no facilities.

At **Deshaies,** immediately to the south, snorkeling and fishing are popular, but you must bring your own equipment. The narrow road alongside the beach winds up and down and has a corniche look to it, with the blue sea underneath, and the view of green mountains studded with colorful villages.

Fourteen kilometers (8¾ miles) from Deshaies, **Pointe Noire** comes into view, its name comes from the black volcanic rocks. Look for the odd polychrome cenotaph in town, the only reason to stop over.

ACCOMMODATIONS

Habitation Grande Anse ⚜ Lying across the coastal road from one of the island's best beaches, Grande-Anse, this assemblage of bungalows and studio apartments, each with natural-grained wood trim, is evocative of a Mediterranean village. Studios and bungalows have kitchenettes, and all units—even the conventional bedrooms—contain rattan furniture, white walls, and a simple, summery decor that's well suited to life close to the beach. All the accommodations have small private bathrooms with shower. Don't expect too many activities here—the focus is on sunbathing surrounded by the tropical landscaping beside the beach. The on-site restaurant is often closed, due to the hotel's inability to attract and keep a full-time cook. Thus it may or may not be operational by the time of your visit, a fact that might tempt you to rent one of the units with a private kitchenette.

Localité Ziotte, 97126 Deshaies, Guadeloupe, F.W.I. ℂ 590/28-45-36. Fax 590/28-51-17. www.hotelhga. com. 50 units. Winter 88€–108€ ($110–$135) double, 103€–123€ ($129–$154) double occupancy of a studio with kitchen, 210€ ($263) 2-bedroom apt with kitchen for up to 6 occupants; off season 61€ ($76) double, 71€ ($89) double occupancy of a studio with kitchen, 149€ ($186) 2-bedroom apt with kitchen for up to 6 occupants. AE, DC, MC, V. **Amenities:** Bar; outdoor pool. *In room:* A/C, TV, minibar.

Résidence Hoteliére de la Pointe Batterie Built in 1996 on steeply sloping land near the edge of both the rainforest and the sea, these all-wood villas each contain a veranda, a kitchen, ceiling fans, good beds, and summery furniture made from rattan, local hardwoods, and wicker. All units have at least a shower/tub combination, the two-bedroom villas have an additional shower unit. The nearest beach, La Grand-Anse, is a 3-minute drive, or a long uphill walk, away. In addition to the communal pool, some of the villas have their own private pools.

Le Canon de la Baie specializes in Creole food from atop a wooden deck whose pilings are sunk directly into the seabed.

97126 Pointe Batterie, Deshaies, Guadeloupe, F.W.I. ℂ **800/322-2223** in the U.S., or 590/28-57-03. Fax 590/ 28-57-28. www.pointebatterie.com. 24 units. Winter 268€ ($335) 2-bedroom villa with pool (for up to 6), 216€ ($270) 1-bedroom villa with pool (for up to 4), 170€ ($213) 1-bedroom suite without pool (for up to 4); off season 160€ ($200) 2-bedroom villa with pool (for up to 6), 128€ ($160) 1-bedroom villa with pool (for up to 4), 100€ ($125) 1-bedroom suite without pool (for up to 4). MC, V. **Amenities:** Restaurant; bar; outdoor pool; tennis court (nearby); billiard tables; rooms for those with limited mobility. *In room:* A/C, ceiling fans, TV, dataport, kitchen.

DINING

Chez Jackye ❀ CREOLE/AFRICAN   Named after its owner, Creole matriarch Jacqueline Cabrion, this place enjoys a loyal following. In a French-colonial house about 9m (30 ft.) from the sea, it features lots of exposed wood, verdant plants, tropical furniture, and a bar. Some of the dishes and spices were inspired by Africa, and others are in the classic Creole repertoire. Our favorites are the *colombo* (curry) of conch and the fricassee of conch. If it's available, go for the freshwater crayfish, the grilled lobster, or several preparations of grilled fish based on the catch of the day. After all that, the bananas flambé are a bit much. Lighter fare includes a limited choice of sandwiches and salads, which tend to be offered only during daylight hours. The cuisine is somewhat zestier than Les Gommiers (see below), but both kitchens will feed you well with rather similar cuisine.

Anse Guyonneau, Pointe Noire. ℂ **590/98-06-98.** Reservations recommended at dinner. Main courses 9.15€–21€ ($11–$26); fixed-price menu 11€–21€ ($14–$26). AE, MC, V. Mon–Sat 8am–10pm; Sun 8am–4pm.

La Caféière Beausejour ❀ *Finds* CREOLE   In the green Pointe-Noire Valley on the site of a coffee plantation, you come upon one of the dining secrets of Guadeloupe: La Caféière Beausejour. This is the domain of Bernadette Hayot-Beauzelin, who grows the produce and herbs used in many of her nouvelle Creole dishes. Ms. Hayot-Beauzelin welcomes you into her home, which was constructed in 1764, years after Louis XIV sent the first coffee plant to Guadeloupe in 1721. (Ms. Hayot-Beauzelin is called a *bèkè*—that's a white Creole whose family came here from France some three centuries ago to colonize the French West Indies.)

Don't expect a menu—you'll be told what the kitchen prepared that day. Since early morning, your host has been gathering up the bounty of the day— everything from tomatoes and bananas to passion fruit and avocados. Chances are she'll have prepared your most memorable meal in the French West Indies. We still remember the quiche made with fresh leeks and papaya. She also makes papaya tarts. Your main course might be a delectable smoked duck served with some Pan-Asian sauce that tastes of ginger, with side dishes of fries (cut like french fries) from the breadfruit tree and pumpkin purée. Ms. Hayot-Beauzelin's coffee is the island's best. Always call for a reservation first, and get good directions.

Pointe Noire. ℂ **590/98-10-09.** Reservations required. Fixed-price menu 32€–41€ ($40–$51); set menu (Mon–Fri) 15€ ($19). MC, V. Tues–Sun noon–2:30pm. Dinner available for groups. Closed Sept 1–Oct 15.

Les Gommiers CREOLE   Named after the large rubber trees that grow nearby, this popular restaurant serves up well-flavored dishes in a dining room lined with plants. You can order such Creole staples as *accras de morue* (codfish beignets), *boudin Créole* (blood pudding), fricassee of freshwater crayfish, seafood paella, and a custardlike dessert known as *flan coco*. Dishes inspired by France include filet of beef with Roquefort sauce and veal scallops. We return year after year, and have never detected any slip-off in the quality. One chef told us, "We are not technically perfect, but we cook from the heart."

Rue Baudot, Pointe Noire. © 590/98-01-79. Main courses 11€–15€ ($14–$19). Fixed-price menus 11€–23€ ($14–$29). MC, V. Daily 11:30am–3pm; Tues–Sat 7–10pm.

PARC NATUREL DE GUADELOUPE: A TROPICAL FOREST ⋆⋆

Six kilometers (3¾ miles) from Pointe Noire, you reach **Mahault.** On your left is the **Route de la Traversée** ⋆⋆, the Transcoastal Highway. This is the best way to explore the scenic wonders of **Parc Naturel de Guadeloupe,** passing through a tropical forest as you travel between the capital, Basse-Terre, and Pointe-à-Pitre.

To preserve Parc Naturel, Guadeloupe has set aside 30,000 hectares (74,1000 acres), about one-fifth of its entire terrain. Easily accessible via modern roads, this is a huge tract of mountains, tropical forests, and gorgeous scenery, and one of the largest and most spectacular parks in the Caribbean.

The park is home to a variety of tame animals, including *titi* (a raccoon, adopted as the park's official mascot) and such birds as the wood pigeon, turtle-dove, and thrush. Small exhibition huts, devoted to the volcano, the forest, or to coffee, sugar cane, and rum, are scattered throughout the park. Parc Naturel has no gates, no opening or closing hours, and no admission fee.

You can hike for only 15 minutes or stretch out the adventure for an entire day, as there are 290km (180 miles) of trails here, taking in rainforests and the wooded slopes of the 1,444m-high (4,736-ft.) Soufrière volcano, passing by hot springs, rugged gorges, and rushing streams (see also "Hiking" under "Sports & Other Outdoor Pursuits," later in this chapter).

From Mahault, you drive slowly in a setting of giant ferns and luxuriant vegetation. Six kilometers (3¾ miles) after the fork, you reach **Les Deux Mamelles (The Two Breasts),** where you can park your car and go for a hike. Some of the trails are for experts only; others, such as the **Pigeon Trail,** will bring you to a summit of about 780m (2,558 ft.), where the view is impressive. Expect to spend at least 3 hours going each way. Halfway along the trail, you can stop at **Forest House;** from that point, many lanes, all signposted, branch off on trails that will take anywhere from 20 minutes to 2 hours.

The most enthralling walk in the park is to the **Chute de l'Ecrevisse** ⋆, the "Crayfish Waterfall," a little pond of very cold water at the end of a .4km (¼-mile) path. This spot in the tropical forest is one of the most beautiful spots on the island. The pool found at the base of the falls is an ideal place for a cooling swim. In just 10 minutes you can reach this signposted attraction from the Corossol River Picnic Area. To the left of the Route de la Traversée, a short trail parallels the Corossol River, ending at the crayfish falls.

After the hike, the main road descends toward **Versailles,** a village about 8km (5 miles) from Pointe-à-Pitre. However, before taking this route, while still traveling between Pointe Noire and Mahault on the west coast, you might consider the following lunch stop.

DINING

Chez Vaneau CREOLE   Set in an isolated pocket of forest about 29km (18 miles) north of Pointe Noire, far from any of its neighbors, Chez Vaneau has a wide, breezy veranda overlooking a gully. Neighbors often gather here to play cards, while steaming Creole specialties emerge from the kitchen. This is the domain of Vaneau Desbonnes, who is assisted by his wife, Marie-Gracieuse, and their children. Their best dishes include oysters with a piquant sauce, crayfish bisque, ragout of goat, fricassee of conch, different preparations of octopus, and roast pork. Lobsters are also featured. All these dishes bespeak admirable talents in the kitchen, and authenticity and personality go into what is served.

Mahault/Pointe Noire. © **590/98-01-71.** Main courses 10€–30€ ($13–$38); fixed-price menu 20€–25€ ($25–$31). AE, MC, V. Daily noon–4pm and 7–10:30pm.

BOUILLANTE

If you don't take the Route de la Traversée at this time but want to continue exploring the west coast, you can head south from Mahault until you reach the village of Bouillante, which is exciting for only one reason: You might encounter the former French film star and part-time resident, Brigitte Bardot.

ACCOMMODATIONS

Le Domaine de Malendure ♠ *(finds)*   Isolated within a scrub-and-forest-covered landscape, this hotel lies directly in front of the Reserve Jacques Cousteau, the underwater nature park beloved of scuba enthusiasts. Most of its accommodations are within a scattering of green-and-white bungalows (there are two units per bungalow), each with a private terrace a few steps from a beach (Malendure Plage) that's known for its nearly black (dark gray) sands. The decor of each accommodation includes contemporary-looking furniture imported from the French mainland, ceiling beams painted in pink, blue, or green, and tiled bathrooms (none with bathtub). A dozen units include an outside kitchenette set on the veranda. Expect a sports-oriented clientele that includes lots of scuba enthusiasts, many of whom sign up for extensive dive packages.

Morne Tarare Pigeon, 97132 Bouillante, Guadeloupe, F.W.I. © **590/98-92-12.** Fax 590/98-92-10. 50 units. Winter 128€ ($160) double; off season 109€ ($136) double. Rates include breakfast. Supplement for half-board 27€ ($34) per person. AE, MC, V. Closed Sept. **Amenities:** Restaurant; bar; outdoor pool; on-site scuba facility; laundry service; rooms for those with limited mobility. *In room:* A/C, TV, dataport, kitchenette (in some), fridge, safe (in some).

Le Domaine de Petite-Anse   This isolated holiday compound is composed of a central, three-story core that contains conventional bedrooms. Despite the appeal of the beach, many guests prefer the large swimming pool, with its surrounding sun terrace and scantily clad visitors, most of whom come from France. Decor within the simply furnished bedrooms includes white walls, dark-stained rattan furniture, and tile-sheathed bathrooms. Bathrooms in the regular doubles contain a shower; those in the bungalows have a shower/tub combo. Expect a sports-oriented, relatively youthful clientele, lots of emphasis on quiet relaxation beside the pool or beneath the sea-fronting palms and sea grapes, and an entertainment staff that tries to include hotel guests in any of the several activities that are planned during the course of any day here. Very few (only about eight) of the conventional bedrooms have a balcony or terrace.

Plage de Petite-Anse, Monchy, 97125 Bouillante, F.W.I. © **590/98-78-78.** Fax 590/98-80-28. hotelpetite anse@wanadoo.fr. 135 units. Winter 99€–155€ ($124–$194) double; off season 70€–90€ ($88–$113) double. Rates for doubles include breakfast. AE, DC, MC, V. Closed Sept. **Amenities:** Restaurant; bar; outdoor pool; disco; health club; scuba instruction; sea kayaks; babysitting; laundry service; dry cleaning; rooms for those with limited mobility. *In room:* A/C, TV, fridge, safe.

DINING

Chez Loulouse ♠ CREOLE   A good choice for lunch, this place offers plenty of offhanded charm, and it stands on the well-known beach opposite Pigeon Island. Many guests prefer their rum punches on the lovely veranda, overlooking loaded boats preparing to depart and merchants hawking their wares. The equally colorful dining room has a ceiling of palm fronds, wraparound Creole murals, and reggae music emanating from the bar. The charming Mme

Loulouse Paisley-Carbon holds court here, assisted by her children. She offers house-style Caribbean lobster, spicy versions of conch, octopus, *accras de morue* (codfish beignets), gratin of *christophene* (Caribbean squash), and savory *colombos* (curries) of chicken or pork.

Malendure Plage. ℂ 590/98-70-34. Reservations required for dinner. Main courses 10€–28€ ($13–$35); fixed-price menu 15€–40€ ($19–$50). AE, MC, V. Daily noon–3:30pm and 7–10pm.

Le Rocher de Malendure FRENCH/CREOLE   On a rocky peninsula 9m (30 ft.) above the rich offshore reefs near Pigeon Island, this restaurant offers gorgeous views. Each table is sheltered from direct sunlight (and rain) by a shed-style roof, which also affords a greater sense of privacy. Much of the cuisine served here is seafood caught in offshore waters: grilled red snapper, fondues of fish, marinated marlin steaks, and different preparations of crayfish and conch. There's a special emphasis here on marlin, with several creative adaptations that feature it as the main ingredient. Examples include rillettes of marlin, marlin sushi, brochettes of marlin, and fried scallops of marlin. There's also a well-prepared version of dorado (mahimahi) with vanilla sauce, and a mousse of wahoo that's usually an excellent starter. Meat dishes include veal in raspberry vinaigrette and filet of beef with any of three different sauces.

The restaurant also operates a small hotel on-site, Le Jardin Tropical, renting 11 bungalows, which cost 65€ ($81) per night, single or double occupancy. Each small unit has a sea view, a ceiling fan, a tiny bathroom with shower, and a simple kitchenette, where many visitors cook most of their meals. Amenities include a pool and laundry

Malendure Pigeon, 97125 Bouillante. ℂ 590/98-70-84. Fax 590/98-89-92. Reservations recommended. Main courses 13€–24€ ($16–$30). AE, V. Thurs–Tues 11am–4pm and 7–10pm. Closed Sept.

BASSE-TERRE ⊛

The winding coastal road brings you to **Vieux Habitants (Old Settlers),** one of the oldest villages on the island, founded in 1636. The name comes from the people who settled it: After serving in the employment of the West Indies Company, they retired here, but they preferred to call themselves inhabitants, so as not to be confused with slaves.

Another 16km (10 miles) of winding roads bring you to **Basse-Terre,** the capital of Guadeloupe. This sleepy town of some 15,000 inhabitants lies between the water and La Soufrière, the volcano. Founded in the 1640s, it's the oldest town on the island and still has a lot of charm. Tamarind and palm trees shade its market squares. Although there are many modern buildings, some grand old colonial structures are still standing.

The town suffered heavy destruction at the hands of British troops in 1691 and again in 1702. It was also the center of fierce fighting during the French Revolution, when the political changes that swept across Europe caused explosive tensions on Guadeloupe. As it did in France, the guillotine claimed many lives on the island during the infamous Reign of Terror.

In spite of the town's history, there isn't much to see in Basse-Terre except for a 17th-century **cathedral** and **Fort St-Charles,** which has guarded the city (not always well) since it was established. Much modernized and reconstructed over the years, the cathedral is only of passing interest. On the narrow streets, you can still see old clapboard buildings, upper floors of shingle-wood tiles, and wrought-iron balconies. For the most interesting views, seek out the **Place du Champ d'Arbaud** and the **Jardin Pichon.** At the harbor on the southern tier of town, you can see **Fort Delgrès,** which once protected the island from the English. There are acres of ramparts to be walked with panoramic vistas in all directions.

Originally selected as Guadeloupe's capital because of its prevailing breezes and location above the steaming lowlands of Pointe-à-Pitre, Basse-Terre is today a city that's curiously removed from the other parts of the French Antilles that it governs, and, when the business of the day is concluded, it's an oddly calm and quiet town. The neighboring municipality of **St-Claude,** in the cool heights above the capital, was always where the island's oldest families proudly maintained their ancestral homes and where they continue to live today. These families, direct descendants of the white, slave-owning former plantation owners who originally hailed from such major French Atlantic ports as Bordeaux and Nantes, tend to live quietly, discreetly, and separately from both the island's blacks and the French *métropolitains* whose tourist ventures have helped change the face of Guadeloupe.

ACCOMMODATIONS & DINING

Hotel St-Georges   This tastefully modern inn is set on a hill with sweeping views over the town, the gardens, and from the upper floors, the sea. A series of three-story buildings centers on a large swimming pool. The medium-size bedrooms are outfitted, Creole style, with dark-grained and rattan furniture, tiled floors, and small bathrooms trimmed with touches of marble. Most accommodations come with a shower/tub combination, the rest with showers. Overall, this place has the feel of a business hotel. Expect lots of amiable goodwill from the 20 or 30 students registered at the hotel training school that's associated with the St-Georges.

La Mazure specializes in French, Continental, and Creole cuisine. Views sweep out over the sea, the mountains, and La Soufrière volcano.

Rue Gratien, Parize, 97120 St-Claude, Guadeloupe, F.W.I. ℂ **590/80-10-10.** Fax 590/80-30-50. www.hotel-stgeorges.com. 40 units. Year-round 80€–105€ ($100–$131) double; 135€ ($169) suite. AE, DC, MC, V. **Amenities:** Restaurant; bar; outdoor pool; squash court; fitness center, laundry service; dry cleaning; rooms for those with limited mobility. *In room:* A/C, TV, dataport, minibar (in some).

Le Jardin Malanga ℛ *Finds*   Clandestine lovers, honeymooners, and those passionate about nature view this as their secret hideaway in Guadeloupe. In a secluded location in the midst of a banana plantation, it overlooks the Les Saintes archipelago. The nearest beach, La Plage de Trois Rivières, lies a 15-minute drive away. Wander in a secret garden of banana trees, birds of paradise flowers, rare orchids, hibiscus (the favorite food of iguanas), and flowering tropical foliage. Those who appreciate a place that looks like an outpost of French Guinea will gravitate to the main house of the inn, which was constructed in 1927 and contains a smattering of family antiques. Day trips can be made to Iles de Saintes, or to the nearby national park of Guadeloupe. You can also stay on-site, lounging at the swimming pool built into a cliff. Each of the bedrooms is comfortably and tastefully furnished, with bathrooms tiled in white. Some bathtubs open onto scenic views. The French-Creole meals are often made with produce from the hotel's own gardens and are worth a detour.

Route de Hermitage, Trois Rivières 97114, Guadeloupe, F.W.I. ℂ **590/92-67-57.** Fax 590/92-67-58. 9 units. Winter 240€ ($300) double; off season 172€ ($215) double. AE, MC, V. **Amenities:** Restaurant; bar; outdoor pool; laundry service; nonsmoking rooms. *In room:* A/C, hair dryer, no phone.

AROUND LA SOUFRIERE ℛℛ

The big attraction of Basse-Terre is the famous sulfur-puffing **La Soufrière** volcano, which is currently dormant. Rising to a height of some 1,444m (4,736 ft.), it's flanked by banana plantations and lush foliage.

After leaving the capital at Basse-Terre, you can drive to **St-Claude,** a suburb 6km (3¾ miles) up the mountainside at a height of 570m (1,870 ft.). It has a reputation for a perfect climate and various privately owned tropical gardens.

From St-Claude, you can begin the climb up the narrow, winding road the Guadeloupeans say leads to hell—that is, **La Soufrière.** The road ends at a parking area at La Savane à Mulets, at an altitude of 990m (3,247 ft.). At this point you have to leave your car and climb to the mouth of the volcano. Currently, the belching beast is quiet and it's presumed safe to climb to the summit at 1,444m (4,736 ft.), the tallest elevation in the Lesser Antilles. (Allow about 2 hr. for this climb.) In 1975, the appearance of ashes, mud, billowing smoke, and earthquakelike tremors proved that the old beast was still alive. In the resettlement process that followed the eruption, 75,000 inhabitants were relocated to safer terrain in Grande-Terre. No deaths were reported, but the inhabitants of Basse-Terre still keep a watchful eye on the smoking giant.

Even in the parking lot, you can feel the heat of the volcano merely by touching the ground. Steam emerges from fumaroles and sulfurous fumes from the volcano's "burps." Of course, fumes come from its pit and mud cauldrons as well. Esoteric and technical information is available only with advance reservations, Fridays between 4 and 5pm, at a government-funded laboratory, **Observatoire Volcanologique le Houëlmont,** 97113 Gourbeyre (© **590/99-11-33**). Conceived as an observation post for seismic and volcanic activities, and staffed with geologists and volcanologists from the French mainland, it can be toured without charge by anyone who's interested in the technical aspects of this science.

DINING

Chez Paul de Matouba CREOLE/INTERNATIONAL You'll find good food in this family-run restaurant, which sits beside the banks of the small Rivière Rouge (Red River). The dining room on the second floor is enclosed by windows, which allow you to take in the surrounding dark-green foliage of the mountains. The cooking is Creole, and the specialty is crayfish dishes, though well-prepared East Indian meals are also available. By all means, drink the mineral or spring water of Matouba. Hearty meals include perfectly executed stuffed crab, *colombo* (curry) of chicken, and an array of French, Creole, and Hindu specialties. You're likely to find the place overcrowded in winter with the tour-bus crowd.

Rivière Rouge. © 590/80-01-77. Main courses 12€–25€ ($15–$31); fixed-price menu 16€–18€ ($20–$23). No credit cards. Daily noon–3pm. Follow the clearly marked signs; it's beside a gully close to the center of the village.

THE WINDWARD COAST ⟡⟡

From Basse-Terre to Pointe-à-Pitre, the road N1 follows the east coast, called the Windward Coast. The country here is richer and greener than elsewhere on the island. There's no major sight or stopover along the way, so if your time is limited, you can simply savor the views along the coastal road, with the sea to your right and scenic landscapes to your left.

To reach the little town of **Trois Rivières** you have a choice of two routes: One goes along the coastline, coming eventually to Vieux Fort, from which you can see Les Saintes archipelago. The other heads across the hills, Monts Caraïbes.

Near the pier in Trois Rivières you'll see the pre-Columbian petroglyphs carved by the original inhabitants, the Arawaks. They're called merely **Roches Gravées,** or "carved rocks." In this **Parc Archéologique** at Bord de la Mer (© **590/92-91-88**), the rock engravings are of animal and human figures, probably dating from A.D. 300 or 400. You'll also see specimens of plants, including cocoa, pimento, and banana, that the Arawaks cultivated long before the Europeans set foot on Guadeloupe. Hours are daily 8:30am to 5pm; admission is 2€ ($2.50) for adults, free for children under age 12.

After leaving Trois Rivières, continue north on N1. Passing through the village of Bananier after a 15-minute drive, you turn to your left at Anse Saint-Sauveur to reach the famous **Les Chutes du Carbet** ✸, a trio of waterfalls that are wonderful to behold year-round. If you have time for only one stopover along the route, make it this one. The road to two of them is a narrow, winding one, along many steep hills, passing through banana plantations as you move deeper into a tropical forest.

Les Chutes du Carbet are the tallest falls in the Caribbean. The waters pour down from La Soufrière at 240m (787 ft.) in a trio of stages on the eastern slopes of Guadeloupe. The upper cascade falls 123m (403 ft.) through a steep crevice. Drawing the most visitors and the easiest to reach is the middle falls at 108m (354 ft.), dropping into a bigger canyon than the upper cascade. The second cascade in the falls is likely to be overrun with tour groups. The lower cascades drop only 20m (66 ft.) and are less interesting.

You can hike to each cascade. To reach the dramatic second stage from the little town of Saint-Sauveur, head inland via the village of Habituée, going to the end of the road. From here, follow the signs for a 30-minute walk along a marked trailway to the foot of the falls. There is a picnic area nearby.

If you have plenty of time and are in good shape, you can also reach the upper falls from here. Follow a signposted trail but note that this level of hiking takes about 1½ hours and is very steep, difficult, and often slippery.

After your hike, continue northeast on N1 to Capesterre. From there a 7km (4½-mile) drive brings you to **Ste-Marie.** In the town square, you can see the statue of the first visitor who landed on Guadeloupe: Christopher Columbus, who anchored .4km (¼ mile) from Ste-Marie on November 4, 1493. If you'd like to see the same view that greeted Columbus, you can stop off here. The statue and that view are the only reasons to take a look.

After Ste-Marie, you pass through Goyave, then Petit-Bourg, seeing on your left the route de la Traversée before reaching Pointe-à-Pitre.

10 Beaches

Chances are your hotel will be right on a beach, or no more than 20 minutes from a good one. Plenty of natural beaches dot the island, from the surf-brushed dark strands of western Basse-Terre to the long stretches of white sand encircling Grande-Terre. Public beaches are generally free, but some charge for parking. Unlike hotel beaches, they have few facilities. Hotels welcome nonguests, but charge for changing facilities, beach chairs, and towels.

Sunday is family day at the beach. Topless sunbathing is common at hotels, less so on village beaches.

Most of the best beaches lie between Gosier and St-François on Grande Terre. Visitors usually head for the hotel beaches at **Gosier.** Stone jetties were constructed here to protect the beaches from erosion. Since this area has the largest concentration of tourists, it's likely to be crowded.

These beaches are not peas in a pod. There's no shade at the **Creole Beach** fronting Creole Beach Hotel, although you can retreat to the bar there for a drink. A stone retaining wall blocks access to the water. Nearby, the **Salako Beach** has more sand and is set against a backdrop of palms that offer some shade. Part of this beach also leads up to a jetty. This is a fine sandy beach, although a little too crowded at times, and it also contains a snack bar.

Also nearby, **Arawak Beach** is a gorgeous spot, with plenty of swaying palm trees providing a bit of shade on the beige sands. It, too, is protected by jetties. Close at hand, **Callinago Beach** is smaller than Arawak, but still has a pleasant crescent of beige sand and palms.

Le Bas du Fort, 3km (2 miles) east of Pointe-à-Pitre and close to Gosier, is another popular area. Its beaches, also protected by jetties, are shared by guests at the Hotels Fleu d'Epée and Marissol. This is a picture-postcard tropical beach with tranquil waters, plenty of sand, and palms for shade. There are hotel bars as well as snack bars and vendors (some of whom are rather aggressive).

Some of Grande-Terre's best beaches are in the **Ste-Anne** area, site of a Club Med. **Plage Caravelle** is heaped with white sand, attracting crowds of sunbathers; snorkelers, too, are drawn to the beach's reef-protected waters.

The French visitors here often like to go nude, and there is no finer nude beach than **Pointe Tarare,** a 45-minute drive from Gosier. This beach lies east of St-François at Pointe des Chateaux. It's one of the island's most pristine, tranquil beaches, but there's no shade to protect you from the fierce noonday sun. You can snorkel here if the water's not kicking up. There's a good restaurant by the car park. *Warning:* The tourist office doesn't recommend that women come here unaccompanied.

If you're not a nudist, you can enjoy the lovely strip of white sand at **Anse de la Gourde,** lying between St-François and Pointe des Chateaux. It has good sand, but it tends to become crowded on weekends.

The eastern coast of Grande-Terre is less desirable for swimming, as it fronts the more turbulent Atlantic. Nonetheless, the sands at **Le Moule** make for an idyllic beach because a reef protects the shoreline. There are also beach bars here—and the inevitable crowds, especially on weekends. You'll find a more secluded strip of sand north of here at **La Porte d'Enfer.**

There are two other excellent beaches on the northwestern coast: one at **Anse Laborde** just outside the village of Anse-Bertrand, the other called **Anse du Souffleur** at Port-Louis. We especially like the beach at Souffleur for its brilliant, flamboyant trees that bloom in the summer. There are no facilities here, but you can pick up provisions in the shops in the little village, then enjoy a picnic on the beach.

In Basse-Terre, a highly desirable beach is **La Grande-Anse,** just outside Deshaies, reached by heading west from Sainte Rose along the N2. You won't find any facilities here, but we think you'll enjoy the powdery sands, tranquil waters, and palm trees. Another desirable beach is **Plage de la Malendure,** on the west coast (the more tranquil side) of Basse-Terre across from Pigeon Island. This is a major center for scuba diving, but the sand tends to be dark here.

If you want to escape the crowds, seek out the spurs and shoulders produced by the mountains of Basse-Terre. In the northwest is a string of fine sandy beaches. Although small, these are highly desirable enclaves for sunbathing. Favorites include **La Plage de Cluny** (near Pointe Allegre), **Plage de la Tillette,** and **Plage de la Perle.** *Warning:* The beaches on the north coast of Basse-Terre are exceedingly dangerous for swimming. **Plage de Cluny** is especially treacherous, and there have been several deaths by drowning.

South of Pointe Noire, also on the west coast, is **Plage des Caraïbes,** with its calm waters and sandy strip. This beach has picnic facilities, a shower, and toilets.

Other good beaches are found on the offshore islands, **Iles des Saintes** and **Marie-Galante** (p. 351 and p. 354, respectively).

11 Sports & Other Outdoor Pursuits

DEEP-SEA FISHING   Blue marlin, wahoo (known locally as *thazar*), and yellowfin tuna can be fished throughout the year; the season for dorado (mahimahi) is limited to November through May. Hotels can usually recommend a deep-sea outfitter or two, but one of the island's most consistently reliable is **Capitaine Valère** (© **590/95-67-26**), who moors his 11m (36-ft.) Bertram in the Le Bas du Fort Marina in Gosier. A full-day deep-sea fishing expedition for up to four fishermen at a time, with a picnic lunch and all equipment included, costs 800€ ($1,000).

GOLF   Guadeloupe's only public golf course is the well-known **Golf de St-François** ⭐⭐ (© **590/88-41-87**), opposite the Le Kalenda Resort. The course runs alongside a 320-hectare (790-acre) lagoon where windsurfing, water-skiing, and sailing prevail. Designed by Robert Trent Jones Sr., it's a challenging 6,755-yard, par-71 course, with water traps on six of the 18 holes, not to mention massive bunkers, prevailing trade winds, and a particularly fiendish 400-yard, par-4 ninth hole. The par-5 sixth is the toughest hole on the course; its 450 yards must be negotiated in the constant easterly winds. Greens fees are 38€ ($48) per day per person, which allows a full day of playing time. You can rent clubs for 15€ ($19) a day; an electric cart costs 34€ ($43) for 18 holes. Hours are daily from 7:30am to 6:30pm.

HIKING   The 30,000-hectare (74,100-acre) **Parc Naturel de Guadeloupe** contains some of the best hiking trails in the Caribbean (for our favorite trail, see the touring notes on Parc Naturel de Guadeloupe in the section "Around Basse-Terre," earlier in this chapter). The 290km (180 miles) of trails cut through the deep foliage of rainforest, passing waterfalls and cool mountain pools, hot springs, and rugged gorges along the way. The big excursion country, of course, is around the volcano, La Soufrière. Another highlight is Chutes du Carbet, one of the tallest waterfalls in the Caribbean, with a drop of 240m (787 ft.). More details are available in the touring notes on the Windward Coast near the end of the section "Around Basse-Terre," above.

Hiking brochures are available from the tourist office. Hotel tour desks can make arrangements. For information about this and other hikes in the national park, contact **Organisation des Guides de Montagne de la Caraïbe,** Maison Forestière, Matouba (© **590/94-29-11**).

Warning: Hikers may experience heavy downpours. The annual precipitation on the higher slopes is 6.3m (250 in.) per year, so be prepared with rain gear.

SCUBA DIVING   Guadeloupe is more popular for scuba diving than any of the other French-speaking islands. The allure is the relatively calm seas and **La Réserve Cousteau,** a kind of French national park with many intriguing dive sites, where the underwater environment is rigidly protected. Jacques Cousteau once described the waters off Guadeloupe's Pigeon Island as "one of the world's 10 best diving spots." Sergeant majors become visible at a depth of 9m (30 ft.), spiny sea urchins and green parrotfish at 18m (59 ft.), and magnificent stands of finger, black, brain, and star coral at 24m (79 ft.).

The most popular dive sites include Aquarium, Piscine, Jardin de Corail, Pointe Carrangue, Pointe Barracuda, and Jardin Japonais. Although scattered around the periphery of the island, many are in the bay of Petit Cul-de-Sac

Marin, south of Rivière Salée, the channel that separates the two halves of Guadeloupe. North of the Salée is another bay, Grand Cul-de-Sac Marin, where the small islets of Fajou and Caret also boast fine diving.

Reacting to the rich diversity of underwater flora and fauna, which thrive at relatively shallow, and relatively safe, depths, several entrepreneurs have set up shop. One of these is **Les Heures Saines,** Rocher de Malendure, Bouillante (© **590/98-86-63**), whose trio of dive boats departs four times a day at 8am, 10am, 12:30pm, and 3pm, for explorations of the waters within the reserve. With all equipment included, dives—depending on the level of expertise of the participants, and the intended destination—cost from 45€ ($56) each. Novices, at least for the very first time they engage in the sport, pay 50€ ($63) for what is referred to as a *baptême* (baptism).

Les Heures Saines maintains its own 12-unit hotel, **Le Paradis Creole** (© **590/98-71-62**). Here, simple, motel-style accommodations rent for 75€ ($94) in winter and 60€ ($75) off season. All have air-conditioning, but no TV or phone, and very few frills. Many of them are occupied almost exclusively by avid divers, and to a lesser degree, hill climbers, on tour-group holiday from the French mainland.

This outfit's slightly larger competitor, located a short distance away, is **Centre International de la Plongée (C.I.P.),** B.P. 4, Lieu-Dit Poirier, Malendure Plage, Pigeon, 97125 Bouillante (© **590/98-81-72**). It's acknowledged as the most professional dive operation on the island. In a wood-sided house on Malendure Plage, close to a well-known restaurant, Chez Loulouse, it's well positioned at the edge of the Cousteau Underwater Reserve. Certified divers pay 35€ ($44) for a one-tank dive. A "resort course" for first-time divers costs 44€ ($55) and is conducted one-on-one with an instructor. Packages of six or 10 dives are offered for 180€ ($225) and 275€ ($344), respectively.

TENNIS If you're a guest at a large-scale hotel with courts of its own, tennis will usually be free, although there might be a small fee for nighttime illumination if it's available. If your hotel doesn't have a court of its own, and if you've called nearby hotels without any luck about using—even for a fee—one of their courts, try either of the two tennis courts at the **Tennis Club de St-François,** Plage des Raisins Claires, St-François. Use of one of the courts costs around 7€ ($8.75) per hour. Call the local tourist office in St-François (© **590/88-75-61**) to reserve courts.

WINDSURFING If you want an intensive immersion in the sport, consider enrolling for a week-long course at the **Union Nationale des Centres de Sportifs,** 97118 St-François (© **590/88-64-80** or 590/88-54-84). Seven days lodging, double occupancy, with all meals, drinks, and windsurfing lessons included, costs 440€ to 540€ ($550–$675) per person. Lodgings are within simple bungalows, each built in 1986, arranged around a swimming pool, dining hall, and beachfront, each with ceiling fans, but without TV, phone, air-conditioning, or any other grace note. On the premises—in addition to windsurfing equipment—are extensive facilities for the teaching and enjoyment of golf and sailing. If you're just interested in renting equipment, the same organization can rent you a windsurfer for 25€ ($31) per half-day.

12 Guadeloupe After Dark

Guadeloupeans claim that the *beguine* was invented here, not on Martinique, and they dance it as if it truly were their own. Of course, there's also calypso, technically imported from points further south such as Trinidad, merengue sounds from the Dominican Republic, salsa from Puerto Rico, and fusion jazz from Cuba, too—the islanders are known for their dancing.

Ask at your hotel for details on the folkloric **Ballets Guadeloupéans** performances. This troupe makes frequent appearances at the big resorts.

An important casino, one of only two on the island, both administered by the same bureaucracy, is **Casino Gosier-les-Bains,** 43 Pointe de la Verdure, Gosier (© **590/84-79-68**). A casually elegant spot, it's open daily from 10am until 4am, although the most interesting activities—those associated with the roulette, chemin de fer, and blackjack—don't open till 8:30pm. There's no cover, and no ID requested, for admission to the area with the slot machines, but entrance to the gaming tables and roulette wheels costs 10€ ($13) per person, and requires the presentation of a photo ID or passport.

A smaller casino, with fewer slot machines but with the same opening hours and admission charge, is **Casino de la Marina,** avenue de l'Europe (© **590/ 48-05-00**), near the Le Kalenda Resort in St-François.

If you don't like casino action, you'll find other nighttime diversions in Guadeloupe, although these tend to be seasonal, with more offerings in the winter. Newer, and more closely linked to the nighttime esprit you might have expected in Paris, are the **Zoo Rock Café** at La Marina in Gosier (© **590/90-77-77**). Sheathed in wood, and open to the outdoor breezes, it offers a revolving series of theme parties ("Midnight in Rio," and "Carnival in New Orleans" that might remind you of something in St-Tropez).

Cuban salsa and Latin dancing draw patrons to **Lollapalooza,** 122 Montauban, Gosier (© **590/84-58-58**), where pictures of dictator Fidel and the long-dead Che Guevara decorate the walls. If you get tired of this joint, try **Fanzy Bar,** Mathurin Poucette (© **590/84-41-34**), where musical styles might include 1980s-style French disco, Bob Marley reggae, and in an occasional orgy of nostalgia, Edith Piaf singing songs from the 1940s and '50s. Other options include **Caraïbes 2,** Carrefour de Blanchard, Le Bas du Fort (© **590/90-97-16**), whose specialty is Brazilian music, or **Zenith,** Route de la Riviera (© **590/90-72-04**), which goes in and out of fashion as a sought-after island nightclub and disco. All these bars are free but the island's discos charge a uniform fee of about 22€ ($28), which includes the cost of a first drink. After that, most cocktails are a pricey 11€ ($14).

If you want to find some genuine local color, make it **Les Tortues,** off the N2 near Bouillante, signposted near the main road on Basse-Terre's western coast (© **590/98-82-83**). This bar is a local hangout, often filled with scuba divers downing Corsaire beer and telling tall tales of the deep. The bartender's rum specialty is ti-punch, cut with lime and cane syrup. You can also eat here. The catch of the day (marlin, kingfish, ray, snapper, or Caribbean lobster) is the best option.

13 Side Trips from Guadeloupe

ILES DES SAINTES ✧

A cluster of eight islands off the southern coast of Guadeloupe, the Iles des Saintes are certainly off the beaten track. The two main islands and six rocks are Terre-de-Haut, Terre-de-Bas, Ilet-à-Cabrit, La Coche, Les Augustins, Grand Ilet, Le Redonde, and Le Pâté. Only Terre-de-Haut ("land of high") and, to a lesser extent, Terre-de-Bas ("land below") attract visitors; **Terre-de-Haut** is the most interesting, and the only island with overnight accommodations.

Some claim that Les Saintes has one of the nicest bays in the world, a Lilliputian Rio de Janeiro with a sugarloaf. The isles, just 10km (6 miles) from the main island, were visited by Columbus on November 4, 1493, who named them "Los Santos."

The history of Iles des Saintes is very much the history of Guadeloupe itself. In years past, the islands have been heavily fortified, as they were Guadeloupe's Gibraltar. The climate is very dry, and until the desalination plant opened, water was often rationed.

The population of Terre-de-Haut is mainly Caucasian, all fisherfolk or sailors and their families who are descended from Breton *corsairs* (pirates). The very skilled sailors maneuver large boats called *saintois* and wear hats called *salacos,* which are shallow and white, with sun shades covered in cloth built on radiating ribs of thick bamboo. Frankly, the hats look like small parasols. If you want to take a photograph of these sailors, please make a polite request (in French, otherwise they won't know what you're talking about). Visitors often like to buy these hats (if they can find them) for use as beachwear.

Some visitors travel to the Iles des Saintes for the day just to go scuba diving. The island's two leading dive outfitters are **Dive-Bouteille** (℃ 590/99-54-25); and **Pisquettes** (℃ 590/99-88-80). Both charge competitive rates and have staffs well versed in the esoterica of the region's many dive sites.

ESSENTIALS

GETTING THERE   From Pointe-à-Pitre, **flights** depart via **Air Caraïbes** (℃ 590/82-47-00) three times a day for the 15-minute ride to Terre-de-Haut, on the Iles des Saintes. One-way passage costs 69€ ($86); round-trip passage costs 131€ ($164). The airport is a truncated landing strip that accommodates nothing larger than small propeller planes such as a 20-seat Twin Otter.

Most islanders reach Terre-de-Haut via one of the several **ferryboats** that travel from Guadeloupe every day. Two boats depart daily from **Pointe-à-Pitre's Gare Maritime de Bergevin,** on Centreville, across the street from the well-known open-air market. The trip is 60 minutes each way, and costs 34€ ($43) round-trip. The most popular departure time for Terre-de-Haut from Pointe-à-Pitre is daily at 8am, with returns scheduled every afternoon at 4pm. Be at the ferryboat terminal at least 15 minutes prior to the anticipated departure. Pointe-à-Pitre is not the only departure point for Terre-de-Haut: Other ferryboats depart daily at 8:30 and 9am and 4:30pm from **Trois Rivières,** and one additional boat leaves from **Basse-Terre** daily. The trip is 25 minutes each way from both of these towns, and costs 17€ ($21) round-trip. The waters are often rough, so you may want to take Dramamine before you set out. For more information and last-minute departure schedules, contact **Frères Brudey** (℃ 590/9004-48) or **Trans Antilles Express,** Gare Maritime de Bergevin, Pointe-à-Pitre (℃ 590/91-52-15).

VISITOR INFORMATION   In the center of town and easy to spot is the **Office du Tourisme,** 39 rue de la Grand Anse, Bourg, 97137 Terre-de-Haut (℃ 590/99-58-60). Its information, for the most part, is in French, but a map of the island might come in handy.

GETTING AROUND   On an island that doesn't have a single car-rental agency, you get about by walking or riding a bike or motor scooter, which can be rented at hotels and in town near the pier. **Localizé,** at Route Aerodrome in Terre-de-Haut (℃ 590/99-51-99), rents both motorboats and scooters, costing from 25€ ($31).

Finds An Escape to Pristine Beaches

There is no finer beach than **Plage de Pompierre,** which curves around the bay like a half moon, and is set against a backdrop of palms. The beach lies only a 15- to 20-minute walk from where the ferry from Guadeloupe docks. Unless a cruise ship is in port, the beach is generally uncrowded, filled with mainland French enjoying the powdery-white sand wearing next to nothing. If you want to bare all, head for **Anse Crawen** on the western coastline. It is the legal nudist beach, although visitors often go nude on the other beaches, too. The best snorkeling is on the southern coast at **Plage Figuier,** which, chances are, you'll have almost to yourself.

There are also minibuses called *taxis de l'Ile* (eight in all), which take six to eight passengers. A taxi from the airport to the port at Bourg costs 8€ to 10€ ($10–$13).

ACCOMMODATIONS ON TERRE-DE-HAUT

Bois Joli   Set on the western edge of the island, about 3km (2 miles) from the village of Bourg, this complex of pink-stucco buildings forms one of the most isolated resorts on the island. Known for housing families, some with children, from the French mainland, it offers both conventional bedrooms within the main house, plus eight outlying bungalows set into palm groves near the beach. Two of the bungalows have kitchenettes, but don't cost more than the other units. Decor includes bold-patterned fabrics, comfortable chairs, and modern but blandly international furnishings, plus small bathrooms with a shower. The food served in the dining room emphasizes simple Creole cuisine.

97137 Terre-de-Haut, Les Saintes, Guadeloupe, F.W.I. ⒸⒸ **590/99-50-38.** Fax 590/99-55-05. www.hotel-boisjoli.com. 31 units. Winter 184€ ($230) double, 240€ ($300) bungalow for 2; off season 77€ ($96) double, 134€ ($168) bungalow for 2. Rates include half-board (breakfast and dinner) in winter, only breakfast off season. MC, V. **Amenities:** Restaurant; bar; outdoor pool; sailing; snorkeling; water-skiing; boat trips to some of the islets or rocks that form Les Saintes; laundry service; dry cleaning. *In room:* A/C.

Hôtel La Saintoise   Originally built in the 1960s, La Saintoise is a modern two-story building set near the almond trees and widespread poinciana of the town's main square, near the ferryboat dock, across from the town hall. As in a small French village, the inn places tables and chairs on the sidewalk, where you can sit and observe what action there is. The owner will welcome you and show you through the uncluttered lobby to one of his modest, second-floor bedrooms, each outfitted with a small shower-only bathroom. Housekeeping is good, and the comfort level is fine for short stay. This is a friendly and unpretentious place.

Place de la Mairie, 97137 Terre-de-Haut, Les Saintes, Guadeloupe, F.W.I. ⒸⒸ or fax **590/99-52-50.** 8 units. Year-round 55€ ($69) double. Rates include continental breakfast. MC, V. **Amenities:** Bar; limited room service. *In room:* A/C, no phone.

L'Auberge les Petits Saints aux Anacardiers ⒶⒶ   The choice place to stay—and also to dine—is this antiques-filled former mayor's house set on a hillside site with a view of the turquoise bay and the adjacent beach. Surrounded by a tropical garden, a 5-minute walk north of Bourg, this is a tranquil retreat with much colonial charm. The owners, Didier Spindler and Jean-Paul Colas, have filled the house with their collection of furnishings and objects from around the world. All bedrooms, except a one-bedroom bungalow and a separate guest-house, have queen-size or twin beds. The guesthouse has five spacious rooms and is suitable for friends traveling together or families. All rooms have showers and toilets, but no bathtubs; corridor showers are also available.

The best food (French and Creole) on the island is served here. (The restaurant is open to the public but you should call for a reservation.)

La Savane, 97137 Terre-de-Haut, Les Saintes, Guadeloupe, F.W.I. © 590/99-50-99. Fax 590/99-54-51. www.petitssaints.com. 10 units. Winter 120€ ($150) double; off season 95€ ($119) double. Rates include breakfast. AE, MC, V. **Amenities:** Restaurant; bar; outdoor pool; sauna; limited room service; laundry service; nonsmoking rooms. *In room:* A/C, TV, dataport, minibar, hair dryer.

DINING ON TERRE-DE-HAUT

Le Génois *(R)* *(Finds)* INTERNATIONAL/FRENCH   Philippe and Chantal, refugees from the urban sprawl of mainland France, are the owners of this raffish green-and-white bistro that's set immediately adjacent to the quays where the ferryboats arrive from Guadeloupe. Views from the windows include the *génois* (mainsails) of the many sailing crafts that are moored a short distance from your table. The staff here is exceptionally cooperative, even charming. Look for mealsize salads, an array of both sweet (in other words, dessert) and salted (in other words, starter) *tartes,* each freshly made on-site and that might include versions with smoked fish, tomatoes and cheese, or fruits. Grilled fish, steaks, and confits of duckling add reminders of the cuisine of the faraway French mainland. Don't hesitate to drop in here just for drinks and tapas, and expect to overhear the dialogue of (or at least see) many of the yacht-owners whose craft are moored nearby.

On the harbor front, Terre-de-Haut. © 590/99-53-01. Main courses 13€–17€ ($16–$21). Set menu 19€–25€ ($24–$31). MC, V. Daily 10:30am–2pm and 7–9pm (until 10pm if there's a lot of business). Closed Sun nights.

Les Amandiers CREOLE   Across from the town hall on the main square of Bourg is the most traditional Creole bistro on Terre-de-Haut. Monsieur and Madame Charlot Brudey are your hosts in this blue-and-white building, with tables and chairs on the upper balconies for open-air dining. Conch *(lambi)* is prepared either in a fricassee or a *colombo,* a savory curry stew. Also offered are a court bouillon of fish, a *gâteau* (terrine) of fish, and a seemingly endless supply of grilled crayfish, a staple of the island. The catch of the day is also grilled the way you like it. You'll find an intriguing collection of stews, concocted from fish, bananas, and *christophene* (Caribbean squash). Knowledge of French is helpful around here.

Place de la Mairie. © 590/99-51-77. Reservations recommended. Main courses 6.80€–9.20€ ($8.50–$12). Fixed-price menu 10€–15€ ($13–$19). AE, MC, V. Daily noon–2:30pm and Sat–Thurs 7–9pm.

DIVING OFF TERRE-DE-HAUT

Scuba diving is not limited to mainland Guadeloupe. The underwater world off Les Saintes has attracted deep-sea divers as renowned as Jacques Cousteau, but even the less experienced may explore its challenging depths and multicolored reefs. Intriguing underwater grottoes can be found near Fort Napoléon on Terre-de-Haut. Two recommended outfitters include the **Centre Nautique de la Colline,** Fond-du-Curé (© 590/99-88-80) and **Club Pisquette,** Le Mouillage, in Bourg (© 590/99-88-80).

MARIE-GALANTE

Come to Marie-Galante to see the Caribbean the way it used to be before the advent of high-rise hotels and casinos. In just 1 hour from Pointe-à-Pitre you can be transported to a world that time seems to have forgotten. This offshore dependency of Guadeloupe is an almost-perfect circle of about 155 sq. km

(60 sq. miles). Almost exclusively French speaking, it lies 32km (20 miles) south of Guadeloupe's Grand-Terre and is full of rustic charm.

Today, some 30,000 inhabitants live here, making their living from sugar and rum, the latter said to be the best in the Caribbean. The best distillery to visit is **Distillerie Bielle,** Section Bielle, 97112 Grand-Bourg (© **590/97-93-62**). The island's climate is rather dry, and there are many good beaches, some of the best in Guadeloupe's archipelago. One of these stretches of brilliantly white sand covers at least 8km (5 miles). However, swimming can be dangerous in some places. The best beach is at **Petite Anse,** 10km (6¼ miles) from **Grand-Bourg,** the main town, with an 1845 baroque church.

ESSENTIALS

GETTING THERE **Antilles Trans Express (Exprès des Iles),** Gare Maritime, quai Gatine, Pointe-à-Pitre (© **590/91-52-15**), operates boat service to the island with three daily round-trips between Point-à-Pitre and Grand-Bourg. The round-trip costs 33€ ($41). Monday to Saturday, ferryboats depart from Pointe-à-Pitre for Grand-Bourg on Marie Galante, at 8am, 12:30pm, and 5pm, with Sunday departures occurring at 8am, 5pm, and 7pm. Monday to Saturday, ferryboats to Pointe-à-Pitre depart from Marie-Galante at 6am, 9am, and 3:45pm, and on Sunday, ferryboats leave from Marie-Galante at 6am, 3:45pm, and 6pm.

VISITOR INFORMATION The **Syndicate d'Initiatives,** or tourist office, is at rue du Fort, BP 15, 97112 Grand-Bourg, Marie-Galante (© **590/97-56-51;** fax 590/97-56-54).

GETTING AROUND A limited number of **taxis** are available at the airport, but be sure to negotiate the price before you drive off. Should you wish to rent a car, go to **Hertz** in Grand-Bourg (© **800/654-3001**), where rentals start at 40€ ($50) per day.

ACCOMMODATIONS

La Cohoba Hotel (Value On Folle Anse, an uncrowded white-sand beach, this hotel is a bargain and a comfortable nest. The beach is edged with sea-grape and mahogany trees. The hotel itself takes its name from the cohoba plant, known to the Caribs as a plant whose red pods have hallucinogenic powers. The hotel, the largest on Marie-Galante, has small, suitelike rooms decorated with white tile and ghost-white walls, along with bright Caribbean colors and tiny but efficient shower-only bathrooms. Thirty of the accommodations have kitchenettes.

Folle Anse, Marie Galante, Guadeloupe, F.W.I. © **800/322-2223** in the U.S., or 590/97-50-50. Fax 590/97-97-96. www.leader-hotels.gp. 100 units. Winter 132€–148€ ($165–$185) double; off season 104€–120€ ($130–$150) double. Rates include continental breakfast. AE, MC, V. **Amenities:** Restaurant; bar; outdoor pool; 2 tennis courts; rooms for those with limited mobility. *In room:* A/C, TV, dataport, kitchenette (in some), beverage maker (in some), hair dryer, safe.

DINING

Le Touloulou CREOLE Set adjacent to the beach, with a hardworking staff and a casual crowd, Le Touloulou specializes in shellfish and crayfish culled from local waters. If sea urchins or lobster are your passion, you'll find them here in abundance, prepared virtually any way you want. Other standbys include a savory, and highly ethnic, version of *bébelé* (cow tripe enhanced with breadfruit, dumplings, and plantains) and conch served either as fricassee or in puff pastry.

In the mid 1990s, the hotel added five very basic, bungalow-style accommodations, each with air-conditioning and a small private bathroom. In winter, double occupancy costs 50€ ($63), with or without a kitchenette. Off season, it goes for 40€ ($50). A two-bedroom bungalow, with kitchenette, suitable for up to four occupants, costs 70€ ($88) year-round. Staff here tends to be blasé, even terminally lethargic, so come here armed with a sense of humor.

Petite Anse, Marie-Galante, Guadeloupe, F.W.I. (℃) **590/97-32-63**. Fax 590/97-33-59. Main courses 10€–22€ ($13–$28); set menu 10€–28€ ($13–$35). MC, V. Tues–Sun noon–2:30pm and 7–9:30pm. Closed Sept 15–Oct 15.

LA DÉSIRADE

La Désirade is one of the few islands in the Caribbean that is not ruined or even touched by tourism of any significance. Most visitors come just for the day to enjoy the uncrowded white-sandy beach or perhaps to tour the island's barren expanses.

Columbus spotted this *terre désirée* or "sought-after land" after his Atlantic crossing in 1493. The island, just 8km (5 miles) off the eastern tip of Guadeloupe proper, is less than 11km (6¾ miles) long and about 2km (1½ miles) wide, and it has a single potholed road running along its length.

The island has fewer than 1,700 inhabitants, including the descendants of Europeans exiled here by royal command. There are a handful of exceptionally simple guesthouses charging from 66€ ($83) for overnight accommodations for two. Don't expect anything grand.

The main village is **Grande-Anse,** which has a small church with a presbytery and flower garden. **Le Souffleur** is a boat-building community, and at **Baie Mahault,** you'll see the ruins of the old leper colony (including a barely recognizable chapel) from the early 18th century.

The best **beaches** on the island's south side are **Souffleur,** a tranquil oasis near the boat-building center, and **Baie Mahault,** a small quintessentially Caribbean beach with white sand and palm trees.

ESSENTIALS

GETTING THERE   From Guadeloupe most passengers opt for transit to La Désirade by **ferry,** which leaves St-François every day at 8am and 5pm, with an additional boat departing every Saturday at 2pm, from the wharves at St-François, near Guadeloupe's eastern tip. Returns from La Désirade for St-François include a daily departure at 3pm, allowing convenient access for day-trippers. Trip time is around 50 minutes each way, depending on conditions at sea. Round-trip passage on the ferryboat costs 20€ ($25). Call (℃) **590/85-00-86** for schedules, but only from 4 to 7pm daily.

GETTING AROUND   On La Désirade, three or four **minibuses** run between the airport and the towns. To get around, you might negotiate with a local driver. **Bicycles** are also available at the hotels.

ACCOMMODATIONS

Accommodations are available at **L'Oasis** ((℃) **590/20-01-00**) and **Le Mirage** ((℃) **590/20-01-08;** fax 590/20-07-45). Both are at Beauséjour, .8km (½ mile) from the airport. L'Oasis has six plain rooms and charges 43€ ($54) for a double, including breakfast. Built in 1990 of concrete, it's simple and boxy, lying a short walk from a good beach. Le Mirage offers seven rather drab rooms and charges 40€ ($50) for a double, including breakfast. Built of concrete around the same time as L'Oasis, it offers a simple bar and restaurant, and it lies a bit closer to the sands than its competitor.

15

Jamaica

Most visitors have a mental image of Jamaica before they arrive, picturing its boisterous reggae and Rastafarianism; its white, sandy beaches; and its jungles, rivers, mountains, and clear waterfalls. However, this island nation's art and cuisine are also remarkable.

Jamaica lies 145km (90 miles) south of Cuba and is the third largest of the Caribbean islands, with some 11,396 sq. km (4,434 sq. miles) of lush green land, a mountain ridge peaking at 2,220m (7,282 ft.) above sea level, and, on the north coast, many white-sand beaches with clear blue waters.

It can be a tranquil and intriguing island, but there's no denying that it's plagued by crime, drugs, and muggings. There are also palpable racial tensions. But many visitors are untouched by these problems; they're escorted from the airport to their heavily patrolled hotel grounds and venture out only on expensive organized tours. These vacationers are largely sheltered from the more unpredictable and sometimes dangerous side of Jamaica, and this kind of trip can suit you just fine if all you want is to unwind on a beautiful beach. Those who want to see "the real Jamaica," or at least see the island in greater depth, had better be prepared for some hassle. Vendors on the beaches and in the markets can be particularly aggressive.

Should you go? Certainly. You'll want to be prudent and cautious, just as if you were visiting New York, Miami, or Los Angeles. But the island has fine hotels and cuisine. It's a good choice for couples getting married or honeymooning. As for sports, Jamaica boasts the best golf courses in the West Indies, and its landscape offers lots of outdoor activities, like rafting and serious hiking. The island has gorgeous beaches and some of the finest diving in the world.

CHOOSING WHERE TO STAY ON JAMAICA

Jamaica is such a large island that you have a wide range of choices.

The grand dame is **Montego Bay,** which has three of the leading and poshest resorts in the Caribbean (Half Moon, Round Hill, and Tryall), plus a very good selection of moderately priced hotels. The beaches are fabulous here, though often crowded in winter due to the hotel density. There are fine golf courses, and the shopping is excellent for Jamaica, but the nightlife is surprisingly lackluster.

Younger and hipper than Montego Bay, **Negril** is a sleepy town (with surprisingly little in the way of dining or nightlife) that has a freewheeling, sensual personality and a spectacular stretch of beach. A row of resorts, many of them lavish all-inclusives, has sprouted up along its shores. One visitor who flies in every year claims Negril is for "sand and sex," but not necessarily in that order.

To the west, **Ocho Rios** has some of the grandest and most traditional resorts in Jamaica as well as some of the leading Sandals properties. But it doesn't have the best beaches, shops, or scenic attractions, and it's frequently overrun with cruise-ship passengers. Nonetheless, if you like the sound of a particular resort there and just plan to stay put on your resort's beach, this might be for you.

Port Antonio is for the upscale traveler who wants to escape the mass package tours of Ocho Rios or even Montego Bay. Come here for some good beaches plus great river rafting, scuba diving, or snorkeling.

Most visitors go to **Kingston** for business reasons only. It does have interesting museums and historic sights, fine galleries, and a diverse nightlife scene. But all in all, it's a city with some serious urban problems, and probably not what you're looking for in an island vacation. You certainly wouldn't go to Kingston for beaches.

1 Essentials

VISITOR INFORMATION

Before you go, you can get information from the **Jamaica Tourist Board** at the following U.S. addresses: 500 N. Michigan Ave., Suite 1030, **Chicago, IL** 60611 (© **312/527-1296**); 1320 S. Dixie Hwy., Suite 1101, **Miami, FL** 33146 (© **305/665-0557**); 3440 Wilshire Blvd., Suite 805, **Los Angeles, CA** 90010 (© **213/384-1123**). In **Atlanta,** information can be obtained by phone (© **770/452-7799**).

In **Canada,** contact 303 Eglinton Ave. E., Suite 200, Toronto, ON M4P 1L3 (© **416/482-7850**). Brits can contact the **London** office: 1–2 Prince Consort Rd., London SW7 2BZ (© **020/7224-0505**).

The official website of the Jamaica Tourist Board is **www.visitjamaica.com**.

Once on the island, you'll find tourist offices at 64 Knutsford Blvd., **Kingston** (© **876/929-9200**); Cornwall Beach, St. James, **Montego Bay** (© **876/952-4425**); and in City Centre Plaza, **Port Antonio** (© **876/993-3051**).

GETTING THERE

Before you book your own airfare, read the section "Packages for the Independent Traveler" in chapter 2—you may save a bundle, because there are always lots of package deals available to Jamaica's resorts.

There are two **international airports** on Jamaica: **Donald Sangster Airport** in Montego Bay (© **876/952-3124**) and **Norman Manley Airport** in Kingston (© **876/924-8452**). The most popular flights to Jamaica are from New York and Miami. Flying time from Miami is 1¼ hours; from Atlanta, 2½ hours; from Dallas, 3 hours; from Chicago and New York, 3½ hours; from Toronto, 4 hours; and from Los Angeles, 5½ hours.

Some of the most convenient service to Jamaica is provided by **American Airlines** (© **800/433-7300** in the U.S.; www.aa.com) through its hubs in New York and Miami. Throughout the year, one daily nonstop flight departs from New York's JFK airport for Montego Bay, continuing on to Kingston. Return flights to New York usually depart from Montego Bay. From Miami, at least two daily flights depart for Kingston and two daily flights for Montego Bay.

US Airways (© **800/428-4322;** www.usairways.com) has two daily flights from New York, stopping in Charlotte or Philadelphia. One daily flight leaves out of Baltimore, stopping in either Charlotte or Philadelphia before continuing to Jamaica. **Northwest Airlines** (© **800/447-4747** in the U.S.; www.nwa.com) flies directly to Montego Bay from Detroit or Minneapolis.

Air Jamaica (© **800/523-5585** in the U.S.; www.airjamaica.com) operates about 14 flights per week from New York, most of which stop at both Montego Bay and Kingston, and even more frequent flights from Miami. There is also service from such cities as Atlanta, Baltimore, Boston, Chicago, Fort Lauderdale, Houston, Los Angeles, Orlando, Philadelphia, Phoenix, San Francisco, and

Washington, D.C. A minor airline, **Copa** (© 876/926-1762), also flies between Miami and Kingston. **Air Canada** (© 888/247-2262 in the U.S. or Canada; www.aircanada.ca) flies from Toronto, Montreal, and Winnipeg to Jamaica daily. **British Airways** (© 800/247-9297; www.britishairways.com) has three nonstop flights weekly to Montego Bay and Kingston from London's Gatwick Airport.

GETTING AROUND

Especially if you've booked a package at one of the big resorts, you're likely to have airport transfers from Montego Bay included. Many resorts from around the island send buses to pick up and drop off their arriving and departing guests.

BY PLANE   Most travelers enter the country via Montego Bay. If you want to fly elsewhere, you'll need to use the island's domestic air service, which is provided by **Air Jamaica Express** (© 800/523-5585), a subsidiary of Air Jamaica, whose planes usually hold between 10 and 37 passengers. Air Jamaica Express flies from the island's international airports at Montego Bay and Kingston to small airports around the island, including Boscobel (near Ocho Rios), and Tinson Pen (a tiny airport near Kingston for domestic flights only). For example, there are six flights a day between Kingston and Montego Bay. The only airports with car-rental facilities are the international airports at Kingston and Montego Bay.

The most convenient airline to Negril is on **International Air Link** (© 876/940-6660), which flies from Montego Bay.

BY TAXI   Not all of Jamaica's taxis are metered; if yours is not, negotiate the price before you get in. In Kingston and on the rest of the island, special taxis and buses for visitors are operated by **JUTA (Jamaica Union of Travellers Association)** and have the union's emblem on the side of the vehicle. All prices are controlled, and any local JUTA office will supply a list of rates. JUTA drivers handle nearly all the ground transportation, and some offer sightseeing tours. Rates are 25% higher after midnight.

BY RENTAL CAR   Jamaica is big enough, and public transportation is unreliable enough, that a car is a necessity if you plan to do much independent sightseeing. You can also take an organized tour or a taxi tour to the major sights and spend the rest of the time on the beaches near your hotel.

Depending on road conditions, driving time for the 81km (50 miles) from Montego Bay to Negril is 1½ hours; from Montego Bay to Ocho Rios, 1½ hours; from Ocho Rios to Port Antonio, 2½ hours; and from Ocho Rios to Kingston, 2 hours.

⌒Moments A True Taste of Jamaica

Wherever you go in Jamaica, you'll see ramshackle stands selling **jerk pork.** There is no more authentic local experience than to stop at one of these stands and order a lunch of jerk pork, preferably washed down with a Red Stripe beer. Jerk is a way of barbecuing spicy meats on slats of pimento wood, over a wood fire set in the ground. You can never be quite sure what goes into the seasoning, but the taste is definitely of peppers, pimento (allspice), and ginger. You can also order jerk chicken, sausage, fish, and even lobster. The cook will haul out a machete and chop the meat into bite-size pieces for you, then throw them into a paper bag.

Jamaica

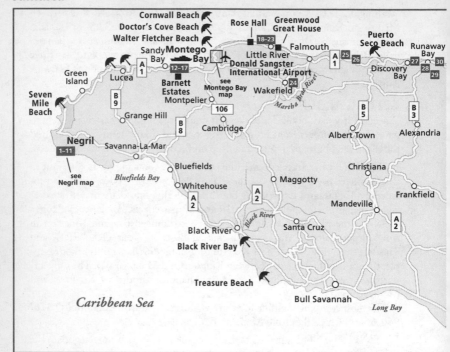

Breezes Montego Bay **15**	Doctors Cave Beach Hotel **15**	Hedonism III **27**
Breezes Runaway Bay **31**	FDR (Franklyn D. Resort) **29**	Hibiscus Lodge Hotel **34**
The Caves **10**	FDR Pebbles **25**	High Hope Estate **32**
Charela Inn **1**	Goblin Hill Villas at San San **51**	Holiday Inn SunSpree **16**
Coral Cliff Gaming Lounge	Goldeneye **41**	Hotel Mocking Bird Hill **47**
& Resort **19**	Grand Lido Braco **26**	Jamaica Heights Resort **48**
Country Country **3**	Grand Sport Villa Golf Resort	Jamaica Inn **38**
Couples Negril **6**	& Spa **37**	Jamaica Palace Hotel **46**
Couples Ocho Rios **40**	Half Moon Golf, Tennis,	The Jamaica Pegasus **43**
Couples Swept Away **4**	& Beach Club **20**	Morgans Harbour Hotel
Coyaba **21**	Hedonism II **7**	& Beach Club **42**

Unfortunately, car-rental rates on Jamaica have skyrocketed recently, making it one of the most expensive rental scenes in the Caribbean. There's also a 20% government tax on rentals. Equally unfortunate are the unfavorable insurance policies that apply to virtually every car-rental agency on Jamaica.

Try **Budget Rent-a-Car** (© 800/472-3325 in the U.S., 876/952-3838 at the Montego Bay Airport, or 876/759-2097 in Kingston; www.budgetrentacar.com); with Budget, a daily collision-damage waiver is mandatory at US$20 per day. **Hertz** (© 800/654-3131 in the U.S.; www.hertz.com) operates branches at the airports at both Montego Bay (876/979-0438) and Kingston (876/924-8028).

If you'd like to shop for a better deal with one of the local companies in Montego Bay, try **Jamaica Car Rental,** 23 Gloucester Ave. (© 876/952-5586; www.jamaicacar.net), with a branch at the Sangster International Airport at Montego Bay (© 876/952-9496). Daily rates begin at US$55. You can also try

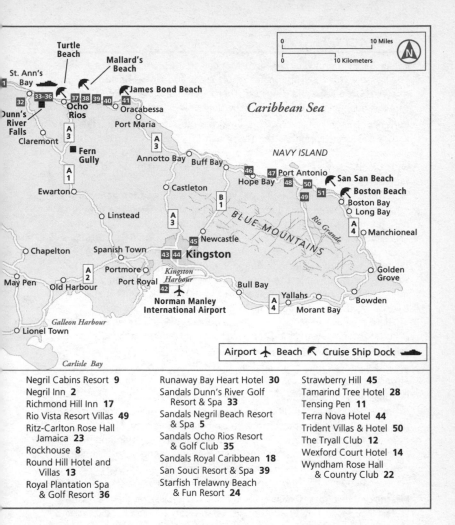

0 | 10 Miles
0 | 10 Kilometers

Turtle Beach
Mallard's Beach
St. Ann's Bay
1
James Bond Beach
32 **33–36** **37** **38** **39** **40** **41**
Ocho Rios
Oracabessa
Dunn's River Falls
Port Maria
Claremont
A 3
Caribbean Sea
A 3
■ Fern Gully
A 1
Annotto Bay
Buff Bay
NAVY ISLAND
Ewarton
46 **47** Port Antonio
Hope Bay **48** **50** San San Beach
Castleton **49** **51** Boston Beach
Linstead
B 1
Boston Bay
Long Bay
A 3
BLUE MOUNTAINS
Rio Grande
A 4 Manchioneal
45 Newcastle
Chapelton
Spanish Town
43 **44** Kingston
Portmore
A 2
Kingston Harbour
Golden Grove
May Pen
Old Harbour
Port Royal
42
Bull Bay
Galleon Harbour
Norman Manley International Airport
Yallahs
A 4
Bowden
Lionel Town
Morant Bay

Carlisle Bay

Airport ✈ Beach 🏖 Cruise Ship Dock ⛴

Negril Cabins Resort **9**
Negril Inn **2**
Richmond Hill Inn **17**
Rio Vista Resort Villas **49**
Ritz-Carlton Rose Hall Jamaica **23**
Rockhouse **8**
Round Hill Hotel and Villas **13**
Royal Plantation Spa & Golf Resort **36**

Runaway Bay Heart Hotel **30**
Sandals Dunn's River Golf Resort & Spa **33**
Sandals Negril Beach Resort & Spa **5**
Sandals Ocho Rios Resort & Golf Club **35**
Sandals Royal Caribbean **18**
San Souci Resort & Spa **39**
Starfish Trelawny Beach & Fun Resort **24**

Strawberry Hill **45**
Tamarind Tree Hotel **28**
Tensing Pen **11**
Terra Nova Hotel **44**
Trident Villas & Hotel **50**
The Tryall Club **12**
Wexford Court Hotel **14**
Wyndham Rose Hall & Country Club **22**

United Car Rentals, 49 Gloucester Ave. (© **876/952-3077**), which rents Toyotas and Hondas costing from US$48 per day for a four-door standard car with air-conditioning.

In Kingston, try **Island Car Rentals,** 17 Antigua Ave. (© **876/926-5991**), with a branch at Montego Bay's Sangster International Airport (© 876/952-7225). It rents Hondas and Jimmys with rates beginning at US$58 daily in winter, US$76 in the off season.

Remember: Drive on the left, and exercise more than your usual caution here because of the unfamiliar terrain. Be especially cautious at night. Speed limits in town are 48kmph (30 mph), and 80kmph (50 mph) outside towns. Gas is measured in liters, and the charge is officially payable only in Jamaican dollars; some stations accept credit cards. Your own valid driver's license from back home is acceptable for short-term visits to Jamaica.

FAST FACTS: Jamaica

Banks Banks islandwide are open Monday to Friday from 9am to 5pm. You'll find ATMs in all the major resort areas and towns, including Port Antonio, Ocho Rios, and Kingston. There are several in Montego Bay, of course, and even one or two in sleepy Negril.

Currency The unit of currency on Jamaica is the **Jamaican dollar (J$),** and it uses the same symbol as the U.S. dollar ($). There is no fixed rate of exchange. Visitors to Jamaica can pay for most goods in U.S. dollars or with credit cards. Always check if prices are listed in U.S. dollars or Jamaican dollars.

In this guide we've generally followed the price-quotation policy of the establishment, whether in Jamaican dollars or U.S. dollars. The symbol J$ denotes prices in Jamaican dollars; the conversion into U.S. dollars follows. *Unless otherwise specified, rates in this chapter are quoted in U.S. dollars.*

Jamaican currency is issued in banknotes of J$50, J$100, J$500, and J$1,000. Coins are available in denominations of J$1, J$5, J$10, and J$20. At press time, but subject to change, the exchange rate of Jamaican currency is J$60 to US$1 (J$1 equals about US1.6¢). As this will probably fluctuate a bit, use this rate for general guidance only.

There are Bank of Jamaica exchange bureaus at both international airports (Montego Bay and Kingston), at cruise-ship piers, and in most hotels.

Customs Do *not* bring in or take out illegal drugs from Jamaica. Your luggage will be searched; marijuana-sniffing police dogs are stationed at the airport. Otherwise, you can bring in most items intended for personal use.

Documents U.S. and Canadian residents need a passport and a return or an ongoing ticket. In lieu of a passport, an original birth certificate plus photo ID will do, but before you rely on this, always check in case document requirements have changed. We always recommend taking your passport. Other visitors, including Canadian and British subjects, need passports. Immigration cards, needed for bank transactions and currency exchange, are given to visitors at the airport arrival desks.

Electricity Most places have 110-volt AC (60 cycles), as in the United States. However, some establishments operate on 220-volt AC (50 cycles). If your hotel is on a different current from your U.S.-made appliance, ask for a transformer and an adapter.

Embassies, Consulates & High Commissions Calling embassies or consulates in Jamaica is a challenge. Phones will ring and ring before being picked up, if they are answered at all. Extreme patience is needed to reach a live voice on the other end. The embassy of the **United States** is located at the Jamaica Mutual Life Bldg., 2 Oxford Rd., Kingston 5 (© **876/929-4850**). The High Commission of **Canada** is situated at 3 Wet Kings House Rd., Kingston 10 (© **876/926-1500**), and there's a consulate at 29 Gloucester Ave., Montego Bay (© **876/952-6198**). The High Commission of the **United Kingdom** is found at 28 Trafalgar Rd., Kingston 10 (© **876/510-0700**).

Emergencies For the **police,** dial © **119;** to report a **fire** or call an **ambulance,** dial © **110.**

Language Jamaicans speak English with a lovely lilt. Among themselves, they also speak patois, a fast-spoken blend of French, English, and a number of other languages.

Safety Major resorts have security guards who protect the grounds, so most vacationers don't have any real problems. It's not wise to accept an invitation to see "the real Jamaica" from some stranger you meet on the beach. Exercise caution when traveling around Jamaica. Safeguard your valuables, and never leave them unattended on a beach. Likewise, never leave luggage or other valuables in a car, or even the trunk of a car. The U.S. State Department has issued a travel advisory about crime rates in Kingston, so don't walk around alone at night. Caution is also advisable in many north-coast tourist areas, especially remote houses and isolated villas that can't afford security.

Taxes The government imposes between 10% to 15% room tax, depending on your category of hotel. You'll be charged a J$1,000 (US$16) departure tax at the airport, payable in either Jamaican or U.S. dollars. There's also a 20% government tax on rental cars and a 20% tax on all overseas phone calls.

Time Jamaica is on Eastern Standard Time year-round and doesn't follow daylight savings time. When the United States is on daylight savings time, at 6am in Miami it's 5am in Kingston.

Tipping A general 15% or 20% is expected in hotels and restaurants on occasions when you would normally tip. Some places add a service charge to the bill, so make sure you know whether or not it's already included. Tipping is not allowed in the all-inclusive hotels. Taxi drivers expect about 15%.

Water It's usually safe to drink piped-in water, islandwide, as it's filtered and chlorinated. However, it's prudent to drink bottled water if it's available.

Weather Expect temperatures around 80°F to 90°F (27°C–32°C) on the coast. Winter is a little cooler. In the mountains it can get as low as 40°F (4°C). There is generally a breeze, which in winter is noticeably cool. The rainy periods generally are October and November (although it can extend into Dec), and May and June. Normally rain comes in short, sharp showers; then the sun shines.

⌐Warning A Word on Marijuana

You will almost certainly be approached by someone selling ganja (marijuana)—in fact, that's why many travelers come here. However, drugs, including marijuana, are illegal, and imprisonment is the penalty for possession. You don't want to experience the Jamaican penal system firsthand. Don't smoke pot openly in public. Of course, hundreds of visitors do and get away with it, but you may be the one who gets caught, and the person selling to you might even be a police informant. Above all, don't try to bring marijuana back into the United States. There are drug-sniffing dogs stationed at the Jamaican airports, and they will check your luggage. U.S. Customs agents, well aware of the drug situation on Jamaica, have arrested many tourists who have tried to bring some home.

2 Montego Bay ⟨★⟨★⟨★

Situated on the northwestern coast of the island, Montego Bay (MoBay) first attracted tourists in the 1940s, when Doctor's Cave Beach became popular with wealthy vacationers who bathed in the warm water fed by mineral springs. It's now Jamaica's second-largest city.

Despite the large influx of visitors, Montego Bay still retains its identity as a thriving business and commercial center, and it functions as the market town for most of western Jamaica. It has cruise-ship piers and a growing industrial center.

Montego Bay has its own airport, so those who vacation here have little need to visit the capital, Kingston. MoBay is the most cosmopolitan of Jamaica's resorts.

ESSENTIALS
MEDICAL FACILITIES The **Cornwall Regional Hospital** is at Mount Salem (© 876/952-5100). For medicines and prescriptions, try the **Overton Pharmacy,** 49 Union St., Overton Plaza (© 876/952-2699).

ACCOMMODATIONS
VERY EXPENSIVE

Breezes Montego Bay ⟨★⟨★ A five-story complex, this SuperClub—called "a sandbox for your inner child"—is the only major hotel directly on the sands of Montego Bay's most popular public beach, Doctor's Cave. It's adult and indulgent, but without the raucous partying of Hedonism II (a member of the same chain). Bedrooms are tastefully furnished and breezy, overlooking either the beach or the garden that separates the hotel from the traffic of Montego Bay's main commercial boulevard, Gloucester Avenue. Rooms range from intimate cabins to lavish suites. The cabin rooms, 31 in all, are similar to a ship's cabin, with a queen-size bed. Slightly larger are the deluxe rooms, with twins or a king-size bed. The best are the deluxe oceanfront rooms, with king-size beds, and the oceanfront suites. All units have bathrooms with shower/tub combinations.

Informal but good meals are served at Jimmy's Buffet, a terrace overlooking the pool and the beach. More formal meals, with a more refined cuisine, are dished out at the candlelit Martino's, an Italian rooftop restaurant.

Gloucester Ave., Montego Bay, Jamaica, W.I. © 800/417-5288 in the U.S., or 876/940-1150. Fax 876/940-1160. www.superclubs.com. 124 units. Rates for 3 nights: winter US$1,112 double; off season US$680 double. Rates include all meals, drinks, and most activities. AE, DC, DISC, MC, V. No children under 14 accepted. **Amenities:** 2 restaurants; 4 bars; outdoor pool; 2 tennis courts; fitness center; rooftop Jacuzzi; dive shop; kayaks; sailing; snorkeling; windsurfing. *In room:* A/C, TV, beverage maker, hair dryer, iron/ironing board, safe.

Half Moon Golf, Tennis & Beach Club ⟨★⟨★⟨★ Opening onto 160 hectares (400 acres) that take in a .8km (½-mile) of white-sand beach, this is one of the Caribbean's grand hotels, without the snobbery of Round Hill or Tryall (see below). It also has far more activities, excitement, amenities, restaurants, and a better beach. About 13km (8 miles) east of Montego Bay's city center and 10km (6¼ miles) from the international airport, this is a classic, and one of the 300 best hotels in the world, according to *Condé Nast Traveler.* It's a grand and appealing place, a true luxury hideaway with taste and style.

Accommodations include conventional hotel rooms, suites, and a collection of superbly accessorized private villas (most villas have private pools and a full-time staff). Each unit is comfortably furnished with an English colonial/Caribbean motif, with a private balcony or patio, plus a state-of-the-art bathroom with a shower/tub combo. Queen Anne–inspired furniture is set off by vibrant Jamaican paintings, and many units contain mahogany four-poster beds.

The Sugar Mill restaurant, our favorite in Montego Bay, is beside a working water wheel from a bygone sugar estate (see "Dining," later in this chapter). The Seagrape Terrace offers delightful meals alfresco. Il Giardino, set within a convincing replica of a Renaissance palazzo, serves savory Italian cuisine. The resort also has a Pan-Asian restaurant, a steakhouse, and an English pub.

Half Moon Post Office, Rose Hall, St. James, Montego Bay, Jamaica, W.I. (C) **800/626-0592** in the U.S., or 876/953-2211. Fax 876/953-2731. www.halfmoonclub.com. 419 units. Winter US$390–US$490 double, US$590–US$1,190 suite, US$1,170–US$2,940 villa; off season US$240–US$290 double, US$350–US$790 suite, US$720–US$1,740 villa. MAP (breakfast and dinner) US$70 per person extra. Ask about golf and spa packages. AE, DC, DISC, MC, V. **Amenities:** 7 restaurants; 6 bars; 3 outdoor pools; 18-hole golf course; 13 tennis courts (7 lit); croquet; spa; Jacuzzi; 2 saunas; deep-sea fishing; dive shop; bike rental; horseback riding; car rental; room service (7am–11:30pm); babysitting; laundry service. *In room:* A/C, TV, dataport, kitchenette (in some), minibar, beverage maker, hair dryer, iron/ironing board, safe.

Ritz-Carlton Rose Hall Jamaica 🏶🏶🏶 (Kids)

The most up-to-date and spectacular of the grand dames of MoBay (that includes Half Moon and Round Hill), this complex sprawls across a dazzling stretch of white-sand beach. The major draw is the White Witch golf course, a 10-minute shuttle ride away. This resort offers the ambience of a traditional Jamaican great house with all modern comforts, including a full-service spa. In the old plantation country of Jamaica, just a free 10-minute shuttle ride from the airport (departing every half-hour), the hotel is secluded, standing in carefully landscaped grounds. First-rate guest rooms, in tropical motifs, feature stoned-columned balconies and deluxe bathrooms with shower/tub combos. Those who can afford it live in even greater luxury in the executive suites. Among the top resorts of Jamaica, only Half Moon equals its cuisine. This resort has a good range of activities for kids, both indoor and outdoor, including arts and crafts, "making sandcastles," or hearing stories of old Jamaica, the latter usually reserved for a rainy day.

Rose Hall, Montego Bay, Jamaica, W.I. (C) **800/241-3333** in the U.S. or Canada, or 876/953-2800. Fax 876/953-8980. www.ritzcarlton.com. 427 units. Winter US$365–US$395 double, US$495–US$1,500 suite; off season US$195–US$225 double, US$325–US$1,500 suite. Children under 12 stay free in parent's room. AE, DISC, MC, V. **Amenities:** 6 restaurants; 2 bars; outdoor pool; 18-hole golf course; 2 tennis courts; health club and spa; Jacuzzi; nonmotorized watersports; children's activities; business center; 24-hr. room service; babysitting; laundry service; dry cleaning; nonsmoking rooms; rooms for those with limited mobility. *In room:* A/C, TV, dataport, minibar, beverage maker, hair dryer, iron/ironing board, safe.

Round Hill Hotel and Villas 🏶🏶🏶

Opened in 1953 on a small, private, white-sand beach, Round Hill is a legend and the most prestigious address in Jamaica, although it hasn't kept up with the times like Half Moon. Still, that doesn't stop the likes of Steven Spielberg and Harrison Ford from checking into villas on the 39-hectare (96-acre) estate. The guest rooms are in a richly appointed seaside building known as the Pineapple House, and each opens onto views of the water and beach. Each spacious, breezy unit has plantation-style decor with refinished antique furniture and a king-size or two twin beds, plus spacious bathrooms with shower/tub combinations. Privately owned villas dot the hillside, and each is individually decorated, sometimes lavishly. Rates for the villas include the services of a maid, a cook, and a gardener; 21 have their own private pools.

Breakfast is brought to your room or served on the dining terrace. Informal luncheons are held in an intimate straw hut with an open terrace in a little sandy bay. Standard Jamaican and Continental dishes are served on a candlelit terrace

Montego Bay

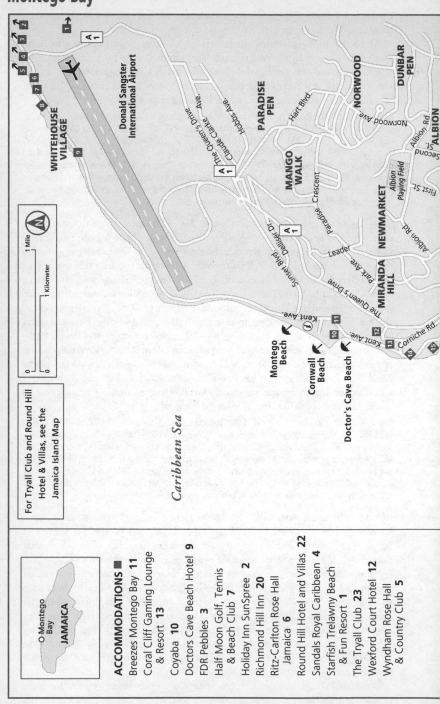

Caribbean Sea

Donald Sangster International Airport

WHITEHOUSE VILLAGE

PARADISE PEN

PASADISE PEN

MANGO WALK

NORWOOD

DUNBAR PEN

ALBION

Albion Playing Field

NEWMARKET

MIRANDA HILL

Montego Beach

Cornwall Beach

Doctor's Cave Beach

For Tryall Club and Round Hill Hotel & Villas, see the Jamaica Island Map

1 Mile

1 Kilometer

JAMAICA

Montego Bay

ACCOMMODATIONS ■

Breezes Montego Bay **11**
Coral Cliff Gaming Lounge & Resort **13**
Coyaba **10**
Doctors Cave Beach Hotel **9**
FDR Pebbles **3**
Half Moon Golf, Tennis & Beach Club **7**
Holiday Inn SunSpree **2**
Richmond Hill Inn **20**
Ritz-Carlton Rose Hall Jamaica **6**
Round Hill Hotel and Villas **22**
Sandals Royal Caribbean **4**
Starfish Trelawny Beach & Fun Resort **1**
The Tryall Club **23**
Wexford Court Hotel **12**
Wyndham Rose Hall & Country Club **5**

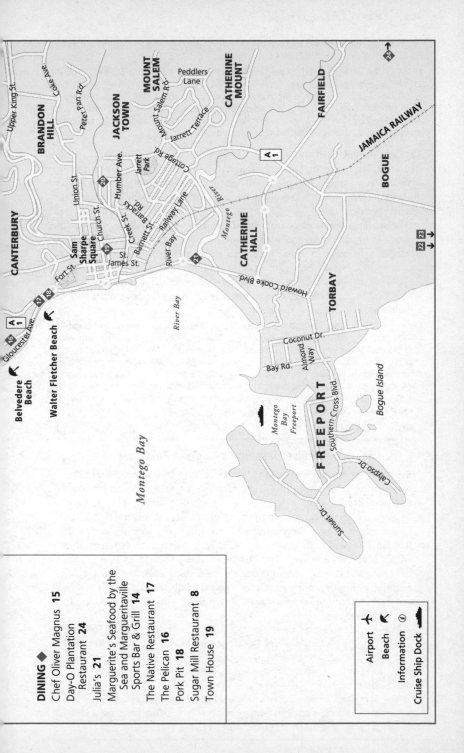

DINING ◆

Chef Oliver Magnus **15**
Day-O Plantation Restaurant **24**
Julia's **21**
Marguerite's Seafood by the Sea and Margueritaville Sports Bar & Grill **14**
The Native Restaurant **17**
The Pelican **16**
Pork Pit **18**
Sugar Mill Restaurant **8**
Town House **19**

Airport ✈
Beach ⚓
Information ⓘ
Cruise Ship Dock ⬛

CANTERBURY

BRANDON HILL

Coke Ave.
Upper King St.
Peter Pan Rd.

JACKSON TOWN

MOUNT SALEM

Peddlers Lane

CATHERINE MOUNT

FAIRFIELD

JAMAICA RAILWAY

BOGUE

Mount Salem Rd.
Jarrett Terrace
Cottage Rd.
Jarrett Park
Humber Ave.
Union St.

A 1

Montego River

CATHERINE HALL

Sam Sharpe Square
Fort St.
Church St.
Creek St.
Barracks Rd.
Barnett St.
St. James St.
Railway Lane
River Bay

Howard Cooke Blvd.

TORBAY

Coconut Dr.
Almond Way
Bay Rd.

FREEPORT

Montego Bay Freeport

Southern Cross Blvd.

Bogue Island

Calypso Dr.

Sunset Dr.

Montego Bay

River Bay

Gloucester Ave.
Belvedere Beach
Walter Fletcher Beach

A 1

367

or in the Georgian colonial room overlooking the sea. Ralph Lauren, a sometimes visitor, decorated the cocktail area.

Rte. A1 (P.O. Box 64), Montego Bay, Jamaica, W.I. © 800/972-2159 in the U.S., or 876/956-7050. Fax 876/956-7505. www.roundhilljamaica.com. 74 units. Winter US$420–US$510 double, US$600–US$850 villa; off season US$260–US$310 double, US$370–US$550 villa. Extra person US$70. MAP (breakfast and dinner) US$80 per person extra. AE, DC, DISC, MC, V. **Amenities:** Restaurant; 3 bars; outdoor pool; 5 tennis courts; health club and spa; dive shop; room service (7:30am–9:30pm); babysitting; laundry service; nonsmoking rooms. *In room:* A/C, dataport, kitchen, fridge, beverage maker, hair dryer, safe.

Sandals Royal Caribbean *☆☆* This all-inclusive, couples-only (male-female) resort, with a tranquil atmosphere, lies on its own private beach. Some of the British colonial atmosphere remains (the formal tea in the afternoon), but there are modern touches as well, including a private, clothing-optional island reached by boat.

The spacious rooms range from standard to superior to deluxe. Best are the grand luxe beachfront rooms, with private patios or balconies. Each unit has a small but well-equipped private bathroom with a shower/tub combination. The cuisine is more varied here than at other MoBay Sandals, with, for example, Royal Thai, an Indonesian restaurant on an offshore island. The Regency and The Pavilion serve a rather good Jamaican-inspired cuisine, among other options. Children are not allowed at this resort.

Mahoe Bay (P.O. Box 167), Montego Bay, Jamaica, W.I. © 800/SANDALS in the U.S. and Canada, or 876/953-2232. Fax 876/953-2788. www.sandals.com. 208 units. Rates for 4 days/3 nights: winter US$1,845–US$2,070 per couple, from US$3,360 suite for 2; off season US$1,125–US$1,733 per couple, from US$2,920 suite for 2. Rates include all meals, drinks, and activities. AE, DISC, MC, V. No one under 18 allowed. **Amenities:** 5 restaurants; 5 bars (1 swim-up); 4 outdoor pools; 3 lit tennis courts; fitness center; 5 Jacuzzis; sauna; canoes; kayaks; sailing; scuba diving; snorkeling; water-skiing; windsurfing; limited room service; massage; coin-operated laundry; nonsmoking rooms; rooms for those with limited mobility. *In room:* A/C, TV, beverage maker, hair dryer, iron/ironing board, safe.

⸢Fun Fact⸥ Catch a Fire: Jamaica's Reggae Festivals

Every August, during what might otherwise have been a slow tourist season, Montego Bay comes alive with the pulsating sounds of reggae when two well-known reggae festivals are presented almost back-to-back. Beginning in early August, and running for at least a week, the first of the two events is **Reggae Summerfest** (it was, until very recently, known as Reggae Sunsplash). Its events are usually presented at different sites within Montego Bay, usually at beach-fronting soundstages ringed with bars and food stands. Sometime during the second week in August, a different set of entrepreneurs produce **Reggae Sunfest** at Catharine Hall, a government-funded housing development beside the Roseway Bypass in Montego Freeport.

Performers at either of these festivals have included Ziggy Marley, Cocoa Tea, the Melody Makers, Barefoot Hammond, the Mystic Revelers, and some of the biggest names in reggae, both from Jamaica and abroad. Many local hotels are fully booked for the festival, so advance reservations are necessary.

The Jamaican Tourist Board's U.S. and Canadian offices can give you information about packages and group rates for the festivals and fill you in on other events held throughout the year on Jamaica.

The Tryall Club ☆☆☆ *(Kids)*   This is a top choice for vacationers who are serious about golf. With more spacious grounds than almost any other Jamaican hotel, this stylish and upscale resort sits 19km (12 miles) west of town on the site of a 880-hectare (2,174-acre) former sugar plantation. It has neither the fine beach of Half Moon, nor the elegant house-party atmosphere of Round Hill, but it's one of Jamaica's grandest resorts. The property lies along a 2km (1¼-mile) beachfront and is presided over by a 165-year-old Georgian-style great house.

The accommodations in luxurious villas are decorated in cool pastels with English colonial touches. All contain ceiling fans and some have air-conditioning, along with picture windows framing sea and mountain views. Bedrooms are exceedingly spacious, with luxurious beds, private patios or terraces, and tile floors. Bathrooms are roomy, with plenty of counter space and a shower/tub combination. The resort's villas are set amid lush foliage and are designed for privacy, each with a private pool. The most formal of the resort's dining areas is in the great house, but it's not the equal of the options available at Half Moon and the Ritz-Carlton. There's also a casual beach cafe, more for convenience than good food.

Many clients here are CEOs, so the hotel has opened an Internet room. On other fronts, Tryall is gaining recognition as one of the most eco-sensitive resorts in the Caribbean, winning acclaim as a "Green Globe Hotel."

St. James (P.O. Box 1206), Montego Bay, Jamaica, W.I. ℂ **800/238-5290** in the U.S., or 876/956-5660. Fax 876/956-5673. www.tryallclub.com. 69 villas. Winter US$400–US$1,700 villa; off season US$250–US$1,000 villa. MAP (breakfast and dinner) US$77 per person extra. AE, DC, DISC, MC, V. **Amenities:** 2 restaurants; 4 bars (1 swim-up); outdoor pool; championship 18-hole par-71 golf course; 9 Laykold tennis courts; fitness center; children's programs; deep-sea fishing; snorkeling; windsurfing; Internet room; salon; limited room service; massage; babysitting; laundry service; nonsmoking rooms; rooms for those with limited mobility. *In room:* A/C (in some), ceiling fan, TV, kitchen, fridge, beverage maker, hair dryer, safe.

EXPENSIVE

Coyaba ☆☆   On a lovely strip of private beachfront, this small all-inclusive resort evokes a British colonial atmosphere. It was established in 1994 by American/Jamaican/Chinese entrepreneurs, the Robertson family, and built from scratch at a cost of US$4 million. Set a 15-minute drive east of the center of Montego Bay, it's centered on an adaptation of an 18th-century great house.

Accommodations in the main building overlook the garden; those in the pair of three-story outbuildings lie closer to the beach and are somewhat more expensive. The decor is plantation style, with traditional prints, expensive chintz fabrics, French doors leading onto private patios or verandas, and mahogany furniture. Hand-carved bedsteads, often four-posters, are fitted with luxury coverings. The roomy bathrooms have combination shower/tubs. Its bedrooms are modern and well maintained, and some units have been upgraded to junior suites with small refrigerators and a sleeper sofa. The hotel's main and most formal restaurant, the Vineyard, serves first-rate Jamaican and Continental dinners. Less upscale is Docks Caribbean Bar & Grill.

Little River, Montego Bay, Jamaica, W.I. ℂ **877/232-3224** or 876/953-9150. Fax 876/953-2244. www.coyaba resortjamaica.com. 50 units. Winter US$300–US$400 double; off season US$200–US$350 double. All meals US$105 per person extra. Children 11 and under get a 50% discount on meals. AE, MC, V. **Amenities:** 3 restaurants; 3 bars; outdoor pool; lit tennis court with free tennis clinic; health club and spa; Jacuzzi; kayaks; snorkeling; Sunfish sailboat; tour desk; car rental; room service (7am–10pm); massage; nanny service; laundry service; nonsmoking rooms; rooms for those with limited mobility. *In room:* A/C, ceiling fan, TV/VCR, beverage maker, hair dryer, iron/ironing board, safe.

FDR Pebbles ☆ *(Kids)*   No, it's not named after the U.S. president. This resort, which pioneered at Runaway Bay, has invaded Montego Bay and almost overnight become the most family-friendly place in the area. It's even better than its parent outside Ocho Rios. FDR lies a 35-minute drive east of the airport, opening onto the waterfront and a beach. The resort is an all-inclusive property of cedarwood accommodations designed with real Jamaican flair, offering spacious living and bedroom areas, shower/tub combination bathrooms, plus generous balconies opening onto a view. It's most suited for families with two children, although a larger family can be very comfortable in adjoining units. Everything is geared towards family fun, with an array of activities including fishing and swimming in a nearby river and hiking along nature trails. Each family is assigned a "vacation nanny," who helps with housekeeping and babysitting.

First-rate ingredients are fashioned into a rather standard repertoire of both Jamaican and American dishes. Portions are exceedingly generous.

Main St., Trelawny (P.O. Box 1933), Jamaica, W.I. © **888/FDR-KIDS** in the U.S. or 876/617-2500. Fax 876/617-2512. www.fdrholidays.com. 96 units. Winter US$275–US$350 double; off season US$252–US$330 double. Children under 6 stay free in parent's room. Rates are per person per night and all-inclusive. AE, DISC, MC, V. **Amenities:** 2 restaurants; 3 bars; outdoor pool; dance club; lit tennis court; kayaks; scuba diving; snorkeling; Sunfish sailboats; kids' club; teen center; Internet cafe; babysitting; nonsmoking rooms; rooms for those with limited mobility. *In room:* A/C, TV, kitchenette, beverage maker, hair dryer, iron/ironing board.

Holiday Inn SunSpree *(Kids)* This is the only Holiday Inn resort in Jamaica that can be booked on all-inclusive terms. It opened in 1995 following a US$13 million renovation of another property and continues a tradition of catering to singles, couples, and honeymooners—but the resort also has a new emphasis on programs for families with children. The 4.8-hectare (12-acre) property fronts nearly .5m (⅓ mile) of white-sand beach on Jamaica's north shore. Accommodations are housed in eight free-standing buildings. Well-furnished, modern rooms and suites are for the most part spacious and all have a private balcony or patio. Of these, 76 are oceanfront units, and 27 suites come complete with indoor Jacuzzis. Each unit contains a midsize private bathroom with tub-and-shower combination. (*A tip:* If you turn in early, seek a room away from the dining, entertainment, and pool areas.) A wide range of dining options is available even though the resort is all-inclusive. Two nights each week are devoted to buffet theme nights, when guests dine on the beach and listen to Jamaican music. The Sports Bar with its big TV is a macho hangout; the Witches Disco attracts a younger crowd.

Rose Hall (P.O. Box 480), Montego Bay, Jamaica, W.I. © **800/HOLIDAY** or 876/953-2485. Fax 876/953-3274. www.sixcontinenthotels.com. 524 units. Winter US$290–US$390 double, from US$550 suite; off season US$249–US$290 double, from US$350 suite. Rates are all-inclusive. AE, MC, V. **Amenities:** 4 restaurants; 4 bars (1 swim-up); 3 outdoor pools; disco; 4 tennis courts; fitness center; basketball court; volleyball; dive shop; sailing; snorkeling; windsurfing; Kids Spree Vacation Club; salon; room service (breakfast only); babysitting. *In room:* A/C, TV, hair dryer, iron/ironing board.

Starfish Trelawny Beach & Fun Resort *(R) (Kids)* Following a US$5 million much-needed renovation, this all-inclusive is one of the best value vacations on the island. Opening onto a stretch of powder-white, soft, sandy beach, it offers activities for both children and adults. The location is 37km (23 miles) east of MoBay airport. The most spacious rooms are the cottages at the rear of the hotel, which can house three adults and two children. For those who must have an ocean view, the resort rents some "superior" rooms, suitable for three adults and one child, with a balcony overlooking the beach. The least expensive units have a mountain or garden view, with a balcony, which can also accommodate three adults and a child. The wide range of sports and amenities make this an alluring choice. The food is fairly standard but there's a sushi bar with Teppanyaki tables and a pasta and pizza restaurant. Four-course gourmet dinners are served in the Casablanca Restaurant.

North Coast Highway, Falmouth, Jamaica, W.I. © **800/659-5436** or 876/954-2451. Fax 876/954-2173. www. starfishresorts.com. 350 units. Winter US$416–US$480 double, US$540 cottage; off season US$364–US$416 double, US$510 cottage. Rates are all-inclusive. AE, DC, MC, V. **Amenities:** 5 restaurants; 4 bars; 4 pools; disco; 4 lit tennis courts; fitness center; badminton; sauna; dive shop; sailing; snorkeling; windsurfing; children's center; Internet cafe; babysitting; laundry service; nonsmoking rooms. *In room:* A/C, TV, minibar, beverage maker, hair dryer, iron/ironing board, safe.

Wyndham Rose Hall Resort & Country Club ⭐ *Kids*

If you have to be directly on a great beach, this place isn't for you, but if you want to escape the more impersonal all-inclusives, like the Sandals clones, in favor of a more authentic Jamaican experience, then check in. On a thin strip of white-sand beach, this 12-hectare (30-acre) resort stands along the north-coast highway 14km (8¾ miles) east of the airport. On a former sugar plantation, the hotel abuts the 200-year-old home of the legendary "White Witch of Rose Hall," now an historic site. The seven-story H-shaped structure features a large, attractive lobby on the ground floor; upstairs, guest rooms all have sea views and come with a small private balcony. The tiled bathrooms with tubs and showers are well-maintained.

Facing massive competition from the newly opened Ritz-Carlton (which is far superior), Wyndham has spent millions on renovations, improving and upgrading its accommodations with new designer furniture. Bathrooms have received a makeover with granite countertops, new plumbing fixtures, and Bath & Body Works amenities. The hotel's six restaurants are good but not sublime.

Rose Hall (P.O. Box 999), Montego Bay, Jamaica, W.I. © **800/996-3426** in the U.S., or 876/953-2650. Fax 876/ 518-0203. www.wyndham.com. 493 units. Winter US$410–US$440 double, from US$600 suite; off season US$355–US$415 double, from US$590 suite. Rates are all-inclusive. AE, DC, DISC, MC, V. **Amenities:** 6 restaurants; 4 bars (2 swim-up); 3 pools; 18-hole golf course; 6 lit all-weather Laykold tennis courts; fitness center; sailboats; children's programs; room service (7am–11pm); massage; babysitting; laundry service; nonsmoking rooms; rooms for those with limited mobility. *In room:* A/C, TV, dataport, hair dryer, beverage maker, iron/ironing board, safe.

MODERATE

Coral Cliff Gaming Lounge & Resort ⭐ *Value*

For good value, the Coral Cliff may be your best bet in Montego Bay, lying only a 2-minute walk from Doctor's Cave Beach. The hotel grew from a colonial-style building that was once the private home of Harry M. Doubleday (of the famous publishing family). It's located about 2km (1¼ miles) west of the center of town. Many of the light, airy, and spacious bedrooms open onto seaview balconies. The rooms, as befits a former private house, come in a wide variety of shapes and sizes, most of them containing old colonial furniture, wicker, and rattan. Most units have twin beds. The bathrooms are small in the older bedrooms, but more spacious in the newer wing out back. Each is tidily maintained and has a combination shower/tub.

Decent Jamaican and international dishes are served at Ma Loos restaurant.

165 Gloucester Ave. (P.O. Box 253), Montego Bay, Jamaica, W.I. © 876/952-4130. Fax 876/952-6532. www.coralcliffjamaica.com. 19 units. Winter US$100–US$180 double, US$120–US$160 triple, from US$180 suite; off season US$80–US$90 double, US$92–US$105 triple, from US$140 suite. MC, V. **Amenities:** 2 restaurants; bar; outdoor pool; casino; fitness center; spa; library; limited room service; babysitting; laundry service. *In room:* A/C, TV, dataport, safe.

Doctors Cave Beach Hotel ⭐ *Value*

This three-story hotel offers great value and lies in the bustle of the town's commercial zone. It's across from Doctor's

Cave Beach, the busiest and most crowded beach, but with the best sands, in the Montego Bay area. It has its own gardens on 2 hectares (5 acres) of tropical gardens. The well-maintained rooms are simply but comfortably furnished, and suites have kitchenettes. Rooms are rated standard or superior, the latter are more spacious and have balconies with a view. All units have tile floors, queen-size or twin beds (suites have king-size beds), and small but efficiently organized tiled bathrooms with combination shower/tubs. The food is more authentic than at the resorts recommended above.

Gloucester Ave. (P.O. Box 94), Montego Bay, Jamaica, W.I. ✆ 800/44-UTELL in the U.S., or 876/952-4355. Fax 876/952-5204. www.doctorscave.com. 90 units. Winter US$130–US$150 double, US$125 suite for 2; off season US$95–US$100 double, US$120 suite for 2. Extra person US$25. MAP (breakfast and dinner) US$29 per person extra. AE, DC, MC, V. **Amenities:** 3 restaurants; bar; outdoor pool; fitness center; Jacuzzi; limited room service; babysitting; nonsmoking rooms; rooms for those with limited mobility. *In room:* A/C, TV, kitchenette (in some), beverage maker, safe.

Richmond Hill Inn 🍸 *Finds* If you're an avid beach lover, you should know in advance that the nearest beach is a 15-minute drive away from this hotel. It was built as the homestead of the Dewar family (the scions of scotch). Very little of the original villa remains, but what you'll find is a hilltop aerie ringed with urn-shaped concrete balustrades, a pool terrace suitable for sundowner cocktails, and comfortable, slightly fussy bedrooms done up in lace-trimmed curtains, homey bric-a-brac, and pastel colors. Each accommodation comes with a midsize bathroom with tub-and-shower combination. Both the bar and restaurant look out over Montego Bay.

Union St. (P.O. Box 362), Montego Bay. ✆ 876/952-3859. Fax 876/952-6106. www.richmond-hill-inn.com. 20 units. Winter US$115 double, US$189 1-bedroom suite, US$300 3-bedroom suite; off season US$90 double, US$168 1-bedroom suite, US$250 3-bedroom suite. MC, V. **Amenities:** Restaurant; bar; outdoor pool; room service (7am–10pm); babysitting. *In room:* A/C, TV, fridge, beverage maker, iron/ironing board, safe.

INEXPENSIVE

Wexford Court Hotel *Kids* Especially good for families on a budget, this hotel lies within a 5-minute walk of Doctor's Cave Beach. This hotel has a small pool and a patio (where calypso is enjoyed in season). The apartments have living/dining areas and kitchenettes, so you can cook for yourself. All the rooms have patios shaded by gables and Swiss chalet–style roofs, and each has a tiled, shower-only bathroom. The restaurant serves some zesty Jamaican dishes in a setting that evokes a 1950s Howard Johnson.

39 Gloucester Ave. (P.O. Box 108), Montego Bay, Jamaica, W.I. ✆ 876/952-2854. Fax 876/952-3637. www. thewexfordhotel.com. 61 units. Winter US$105–US$110 double, US$120 apt; off season US$95–US$100 double, US$110 apt. MAP (breakfast and dinner) US$34 per person extra. AE, DISC, MC, V. **Amenities:** Restaurant; bar; outdoor pool; limited room service; laundry service; babysitting; rooms for those with limited mobility. *In room:* A/C, TV, kitchenettes (in some), safe.

DINING
EXPENSIVE

Day-O Plantation Restaurant 🍸 *Finds* INTERNATIONAL/JAMAICAN Here's your chance to wander back to Jamaica's plantation heyday. This place was originally built in the 1920s as the home of the overseer of one of the region's largest sugar producers, the Barnett Plantation. The restaurant occupies a long, indoor/outdoor dining room that's divided into two halves by a dance floor and a small stage. Here, owner Paul Hurlock performs as a one-man band, singing and entertaining the crowd while his wife, Jennifer, and their three children manage the dining room and kitchen.

Finds Going Native on the Street

MoBay has some of the finest and most expensive dining on the island. But if you're watching your wallet and have an adventurous streak, you'll find lots of terrific street food. The densest concentration of street food in Montego Bay is available at the junction of Gloucester Avenue and Kent Road. (The .8km/½-mile strip of beach-fronting boulevard stretching along both sides of that junction is also known as Bottom Road or, less formally, as "The Hip Strip.") The Hip Strip is lined with bars, food stands, and shops catering to the beach trade. At any of these stands, you might try authentic jerk pork or seasoned spareribs, grilled over charcoal fires and sold with extra-hot sauce. To complete the experience, order a Red Stripe beer to go with it. Cooked shrimp are also sold on the streets of downtown MoBay, especially along St. James Street; they don't look it, but they're very spicy, so be warned. And if you have an efficiency unit with a kitchenette, you can buy fresh lobster or the catch of the day and make your own dinner.

Every dish is permeated with Jamaican spices. Try the chicken plantation style, with red-wine sauce and herbs; filet of red snapper in Day-O style, with olives, white wine, tomatoes, and peppers; or, even better, one of the best versions of jerked snapper in Jamaica. We also like the grilled rock lobster with garlic butter.

Day-O Plantation, Lot 1, Fairfield. ℂ 876/952-1825. Reservations suggested. Main courses US$15–US$33. AE, MC, V. Tues–Sun 6–11pm. It's an 8-min. drive west of town off the A-1 hwy. toward Negril. Private van transportation provided; ask when you reserve.

Julia's ℛ CONTINENTAL   Julia's food, although competently prepared and using fresh ingredients whenever possible, can hardly compete with the view. The winding jungle road you take to get here is part of the before-dinner entertainment. After a jolting ride to a setting high above the city and its bay, you pass through a walled-in park that was the site of a private home built in 1840 for the Duke of Sutherland. The long, low-slung modern house boasts sweeping, open-sided views over the rolling hills and faraway coastline. Wills Green, the man running the place, draws on the styles of both the Caribbean and central Europe to prepare filet of fresh fish with lime juice and butter, lobster, shrimp, and many different kinds of pasta. Also look for such dishes as the mixed grilled seafood. Top off your meal with cheesecake of the day or their delicious raspberry tart.

Julia's Estate, Bogue Hill. ℂ 876/952-1772. Reservations required. Main courses US$18–US$36. AE, DISC, MC, V. Daily 5:30–11pm. Private van transportation provided; ask when you reserve.

Sugar Mill Restaurant ℛℛ INTERNATIONAL/CARIBBEAN   This restaurant, near the ruin of what used to be a water wheel for a sugar plantation, is reached after a drive through rolling landscape. The lovely setting and exquisite cuisine make this place a perennial favorite. Guests dine by candlelight either indoors or on an open terrace with a view of a pond, the water wheel, and plenty of greenery. Lunch can be a relatively simple affair, a daily a la carte offering, preceded by Mama's pumpkin soup and followed with homemade rum-and-raisin ice cream. For dinner, try one of the chef's zesty versions of jerk pork, fish, or chicken. He also prepares the day's catch with considerable flair. Smoked north-coast marlin is a specialty. On any given day, you can ask the waiter what's cooking in the curry pot. Chances are it will be a Jamaican specialty such as goat, full of flavor and served with island chutney.

At the Half Moon Golf, Tennis & Beach Club, Rose Hall. (€) 876/953-2314. Reservations required. Main courses US$27–US$42. AE, MC, V. Daily 7–9pm. Private van transportation provided; ask when you reserve.

Town House 🍴 JAMAICAN/INTERNATIONAL   Housed in a redbrick building dating from 1765, the Town House is a tranquil dining choice. It offers sandwiches and salads, or more elaborate fare if your appetite demands it. At night, it's floodlit, with outdoor dining on a veranda overlooking an 18th-century parish church. You can also dine in what used to be the cellars, where old ship lanterns provide a warm atmosphere. Pepperpot or pumpkin soup is a delectable start to a meal. The chef offers a wide selection of main courses, including the local favorite, red snapper *en papillote* (baked in parchment). We're fond of the large rack of barbecued spareribs, with the owners' special Tennessee sauce. The pasta and steak dishes are also good, especially the homemade fettuccine with whole shrimp and the perfectly aged New York strip steak.

16 Church St. (€) 876/952-2660. Reservations recommended. Main courses US$14–US$36. AE, DISC, MC, V. Mon–Fri noon–3pm; daily 6–10pm. Free limousine service to and from many area hotels if you eat dinner here.

MODERATE

Chef Oliver Magnus INTERNATIONAL   Set on a hill overlooking faraway cruise ships, this restaurant is housed in a tile-roofed villa. Chef Oliver Magnus dazzles with an array of appetizers ranging from gazpacho to smoked marlin; salads are also interesting, especially the marinated papaya with the tangy balsamic green-onion vinaigrette. Main dishes include a snapper Camembert with a ranch sauce topped with cheese and toasted almonds. We're also fond of the *misto di mare,* a medley of shrimp, crab, and other fish stewed in a tomato pesto ragout. The grilled lamb from New Zealand is given added Jamaican flair with the use of a mild jerk spice.

Corniche Rd. (€) 876/952-2988. Main courses J$465–J$1,200 (US$7.75–US$20). MC, V. Daily 6:30–10:30pm.

Marguerite's Seafood by the Sea and Margueritaville Sports Bar & Grill INTERNATIONAL/SEAFOOD   This two-in-one restaurant across from the Coral Cliff Hotel specializes in seafood served on a breeze-swept terrace overlooking the sea. There's also an air-conditioned lounge with an adjoining "Secret Garden." The chef specializes in exhibition cookery at a flambé grill. The menu is mainly devoted to seafood and fresh fish, but there are also numerous innovative pastas and rather standard meat dishes. The changing dessert options are homemade, and a reasonable selection of wines is served. The sports bar and grill features a 34m (112-ft.) waterslide, live music, satellite TV, watersports, a sun deck, and a straightforward menu of seafood, sandwiches, pasta, pizza, salads, and snacks—nothing fussy. Naturally, the bartenders specialize in margaritas.

Gloucester Ave. (€) 876/952-4777. Reservations recommended for Marguerite's Seafood by the Sea. Main courses US$12–US$42; snacks and platters from US$9. AE, MC, V. Restaurant daily 6–10:30pm; sports bar daily 10am–3am.

The Native Restaurant 🍴 *Finds* JAMAICAN/INTERNATIONAL   Open to the breezes, this casual restaurant with panoramic views serves some of the finest Jamaican dishes in the area. Appetizers include ackee and saltfish and jerk reggae chicken, or smoked marlin, which you can follow with steamed fish or jerk chicken. A more exotic specialty is Boonoonoonoos; billed as "A Taste of Jamaica," it's a big platter with a little bit of everything—meats, fish, and vegetables.

29 Gloucester Ave. ℂ 876/979-2769. Reservations recommended. Main courses US$12–US$32. AE, DISC, MC, V. Daily 7–10:30pm.

The Pelican JAMAICAN   A Montego Bay landmark, the family-friendly Pelican has been serving good food at reasonable prices for more than a quarter century. Most of the dishes are at the lower end of the price scale, unless you order shellfish. Many diners come here at lunch, for one of the well-stuffed sandwiches, juicy burgers, or barbecued chicken. You can also choose from a wide array of Jamaican dishes, including stewed peas and rice, curried goat, Caribbean fish, fried chicken, and curried lobster. A "meatless menu" is also featured. The soda fountain serves old-fashioned sundaes with real whipped cream.

Gloucester Ave. ℂ 876/952-3171. Reservations recommended. Main courses US$12–US$23. AE, MC, V. Daily 7am–11pm.

INEXPENSIVE
Pork Pit ⊛ JAMAICAN   This joint is the best place to go for the famous Jamaican jerk pork and jerk chicken, and the location is right in the heart of Montego Bay, near Walter Fletcher Beach. Many beachgoers desert their towels at noontime and head over here for a big, reasonably priced lunch. Picnic tables encircle the building, and everything is open-air and informal. A half-pound of jerk meat, served with a baked yam or baked potato and a bottle of Red Stripe, is usually enough for a meal. The menu also includes steamed roast fish.

27 Gloucester Ave. ℂ 876/952-3663. 1 lb. of jerk pork US$9.50. MC, V. Daily 11am–11pm.

HITTING THE BEACH
Cornwall Beach (ℂ 876/952-3463) is a long stretch of white sand with dressing rooms, a bar, and a cafeteria. The grainy sand and good swimming have made it a longtime favorite. Unlike some of Jamaica's remote, hard-to-get-to beaches, this one is near all the major hotels, especially the moderately priced ones. Unfortunately, it can be crowded in winter (mostly with tourists, not locals). This is a good beach for kids, with gentle waters and a gently sloping ocean bottom. The beach is open daily from 9am to 5pm. Admission is US$2.50 for adults, US$1.50 for children.

   Doctor's Cave Beach, on Gloucester Avenue (ℂ 876/952-2566 for the beach club), is arguably the loveliest stretch of sand bordering Montego Bay. Its gentle surf, golden sands, and fresh turquoise water make it an inviting place to swim, and there's always a beach-party atmosphere. Placid and popular with families, it's the best all-around beach in Montego Bay. Sometimes schools of tropical fish weave in and out of the waters, but usually the crowds of frolicking people scare them away. Since it's almost always packed, especially in winter, you have to get there early to stake out a beach blanket–size spot. Admission is US$5 for adults, US$2.50 for children age 12 and under. Open daily 8:30am to sunset. The beach club here has well-kept changing rooms, showers, restrooms, a food court, a bar, a cybercafe, and a sundries shop. Beach chairs and umbrellas can be rented daily.

   Walter Fletcher Beach (ℂ 876/979-9447), in the heart of MoBay, is noted for its tranquil waters, which makes it a favorite of families with children. It's one of the most beautiful beaches along Jamaica's southern coast. Easy to reach, it's generally crowded in winter and enjoyed by visitors and locals alike. If you bring a picnic be careful not to litter, as patrols will fine you. From December to March, there seems to be a long-running beach party here. Visitors show up in almost anything (or lack of anything), although actual nudity is prohibited. There are changing rooms, a restaurant, and lifeguards. Hours are daily from 10am to 10pm. Admission is J$200 (US$3.20) for adults, J$100 (US$1.60) for children.

Frankly, you may want to skip all these public beaches entirely and head instead for the **Rose Hall Beach Club** (© 876/680-0969 for the beach club), on the main road 18km (11 miles) east of Montego Bay. The club offers .8km (½ mile) of secluded white-sand beach with crystal-clear water, plus a restaurant, two bars, a covered pavilion, an open-air dance area, showers, restrooms, hammocks, changing rooms, beach volleyball courts, beach games, and a full watersports program. Admission is US$6 for adults, US$3 for children. Hours are daily from 9am to 5pm.

SPORTS & OTHER OUTDOOR PURSUITS

DEEP-SEA FISHING Seaworld Resorts, whose main office is at the Cariblue Hotel, Rose Hall Main Road (© 876/953-2180), operates flying-bridge cruisers, with deck lines and outriggers, for fishing expeditions. A half-day fishing trip costs US$380 for up to four participants.

DIVING, SNORKELING & OTHER WATERSPORTS Seaworld Resorts (see above) also operates scuba-diving excursions, plus sailing, windsurfing, and more. Its dives plunge to offshore coral reefs, among the most spectacular in the Caribbean. There are three certified dive guides, one dive boat, and all the necessary equipment for both inexperienced and already-certified divers. One-tank dives cost US$45; night dives are US$65.

Cool Aqua Sun Sport (© 876/953-2021), run by PADI-certified instructor Percival Plummer, offers everything from resort courses to specialty certification, with outings to a variety of sites, including the Basket Reef, where you'll see basket sponges, sea fans, parrot fish, and perhaps even a turtle or dolphin.

North Coast Marine Sports (© 876/953-2211), located at the Half Moon Golf, Tennis & Beach Club, offers everything from scuba diving to Sunfish sailboats, snorkel gear, kayaks, and more. They can arrange for deep-sea fishing trips and snorkel cruises, too.

Doctor's Cave Beach is part of the **Montego Bay Marine Park,** which was established to protect the wide variety of marine life among the coral reefs right offshore from the popular beaches. You can rent snorkel gear from the beach club at Doctor's Cave, or from the beach clubs at any of the local beaches.

You might also like to head across the channel to check out **Coyaba Reef, Seaworld Reef,** and **Royal Reef,** which are full of barjacks, blue and brown chromis, yellow-headed wrasses, and spotlight parrotfish. You must have a guide here, as the currents are strong and the wind picks up in the afternoon. If you're not staying at a resort offering snorkeling expeditions, then Seaworld is your best bet. For about US$30 per hour, a guide swims with you and points out various fish.

GOLF The **White Witch of Rose Hall Golf Course,** part of the Ritz-Carlton Rose Hall (© 876/953-2204), is one of the most spectacular courses in the Caribbean, situated on 80 hectares (198 acres) of lush greenery in Jamaica's old plantation country. The course is named after Annie Palmer, the notorious "White Witch" and mistress of Rose Hall nearby. Ten minutes from the deluxe resort by wheels, the course was created by Robert von Hagge, who designed the course to wind up and down the mountains, with panoramic vistas of the sea visible from 16 of the 18 holes. Greens fees are US$159 for hotel guests, US$179 for nonguests.

Wyndham Rose Hall Resort & Country Club 𝕲𝕲, Rose Hall (© 876/953-2650), has a noted course with an unusual and challenging seaside and mountain layout. Its eighth hole skirts the water, then doglegs onto a promontory and a green thrusting 182m (597 ft.) into the sea. The back nine are the most scenic and interesting, rising up steep slopes and falling into deep ravines on Mount Zion. The 10th fairway abuts the family burial grounds of the Barretts of Wimpole Street, and the 14th passes the vacation home of the late singer Johnny Cash. The 90m-high (295-ft.) 13th tee offers a rare panoramic view of the sea and the roof of the hotel, and the 15th green is next to a 12m (39-ft.) waterfall, once featured in a James Bond movie. Amenities include a fully stocked pro shop, a clubhouse, and a professional staff. Guests pay US$125 for 18 holes, or US$75 for nine holes; nonguests pay US$150 for 18 holes and US$105 for nine holes. Cart rental and the use of a caddy are included in the greens fees.

The excellent course at **The Tryall Club** 𝕲𝕲𝕲 (© 876/956-5660), 19km (12 miles) from Montego Bay, is so regal that it's often the site of major tournaments. For 18 holes, guests of Tryall are charged US$80 in winter, US$40 the rest of the year. In winter the course is usually closed to nonguests; the rest of the year, they pay US$115.

Half Moon, at Rose Hall (© 876/953-2560), features a championship course designed by Robert Trent Jones Sr., with manicured and diversely shaped greens. Half Moon hotel guests pay US$125 for 18 holes including caddy and cart. Nonguests pay US$130 for 18 holes; carts cost US$35, and caddies (which are mandatory) are hired for US$17.

The **Ironshore Golf & Country Club,** Ironshore, St. James, Montego Bay (© 876/953-3681), is another well-known 18-hole, par-72 course. Privately owned, it's open to all golfers. Greens fees for 18 holes are US$50, plus US$35 for a cart and US$16 for a caddy.

HORSEBACK RIDING A good program is offered at the **Rocky Point Riding Stables,** at the Half Moon Club, Rose Hall, Montego Bay (© 876/953-2286). Housed in the most beautiful barn and stables in Jamaica, it offers around 30 horses and a helpful staff. A 90-minute beach or mountain ride costs US$60.

RAFTING **Mountain Valley Rafting,** P.O. Box 23, Montego Bay (© 876/956-4920), offers somewhat tame and touristy excursions on the Great River, which depart from the Lethe Plantation, about 16km (10 miles) south of Montego Bay. Skip that, and head over to Falmouth, 45km (28 miles) to the east, where rafting on the **Martha Brae** is an adventure. To reach the starting point from Falmouth, drive approximately 5km (3 miles) inland to **Martha Brae's Rafters Village** (© 876/952-0889). The rafts are similar to those on the Rio Grande, near Port Antonio; you sit on a raised dais on bamboo logs. The cost is US$45, with two riders allowed on a raft, plus a small child if accompanied by an adult (but use caution). The trips last 1¼ hours and operate daily from 9am to 4pm. It's not necessary to wear swimsuits. Along the way, you can stop and order cool drinks or beer along the banks of the river. There's a bar, a restaurant, and two souvenir shops in the village.

TENNIS   Half Moon Golf, Tennis & Beach Club 🌟🌟🌟, outside Montego Bay (© 876/953-2211), has the finest courts in the area. Its 13 state-of-the-art courts, seven of which are lit for night games, attract tennis players from around the world. Lessons cost US$30 to US$35 per half-hour, US$50 to US$65 per hour. Residents play free, day or night. The pro shop, which accepts reservations for court times, is open daily from 7am to 9pm. If you want to play after those hours, you switch on the lights yourself. If you're not a hotel guest, you must purchase a day pass (US$40 per person) at the front desk; it allows access to the resort's courts, gym, sauna, Jacuzzi, pools, and beach facilities.

The Tryall Club, St. James (© 876/956-5660), offers nine hard-surface courts, three lit for night play. Day games are free for guests; nonguests pay US$30 per hour. There's a US$20 per hour charge to light the courts after dark. At least four on-site pros provide lessons for US$25 to US$35 per half-hour, or US$45 to US$60 per hour.

Wyndham Rose Hall Resort & Country Club, Rose Hall (© 876/953-2650), outside Montego Bay, is an outstanding tennis resort, though not the equal of Half Moon or Tryall. Wyndham offers six hard-surface courts, each lit for night play. The resident pro charges US$40 per hour for lessons, US$35 for 45 minutes; or US$30 for 30 minutes.

SEEING THE SIGHTS
TOURS & CRUISES

A **Hilton High Day Tour,** booked through Beach View Plaza (© 876/952-3343), includes round-trip transportation on a scenic drive through historic plantation areas. Your day starts with continental breakfast at an old plantation house. You can roam the 40 hectares (99 acres) of the plantation and visit the German village of Seaford Town or St. Leonards village nearby. Calypso music is played throughout the day, and a Jamaican lunch is served at 1pm. The cost is US$55 per person for the plantation tour, breakfast, lunch, and transportation. Tour days are Tuesday, Wednesday, Friday, and Sunday.

Day and evening cruises are offered aboard the *Calico,* a 17m (56-ft.) gaff-rigged wooden ketch that sails from Margaritaville on the Montego Bay waterfront. An additional vessel, *Calico B,* also carries another 40 passengers. You can be transported to and from your hotel for either cruise. The daily voyage departs at 10am and returns at 1pm and costs US$35; snorkeling (with equipment) is available. On the *Calico's* evening voyage, which goes for US$25 and is offered

---

(Kids A Waterworld for Families

The US$20 million **Aguasol Theme Park** (© 876/940-1344), Walter Fletcher Beach, lures with its array of watersports activities (including a giant water slide), a go-kart track, and a large sandy beach, plus planned amusements that cover everything from fashion shows to presentations of reggae. There's also an outdoor restaurant and a sports bar featuring 42 big-screen televisions, and at press time there was a health club under construction and some "go-buggy" electric carts. An upper deck is ideal for sunbathing, and there's also a picnic area. At night a dance club dominates the action. Open daily from 10am to 10pm, the attraction charges J$200 (US$3.20) adults, J$100 (US$1.60) for children age 12 and under. Rentals of beach chairs or umbrellas go for J$600 (US$9.60) each.

Moments **Meeting Some Feathered Friends**

At the **Rocklands Wildlife Station,** about 2km (1¼ miles) outside Anchovy on the road from Montego Bay, St. James (© **876/952-2009**), you can have a Jamaican doctor bird perch on your finger to drink syrup, feed small doves and finches millet from your hand, and watch dozens of other birds flying in for their evening meal. Don't take children age 5 and under to this sanctuary, as they tend to bother the birds. Admission is US$10; open daily from 9am to 5:30pm.

daily from 5 to 7pm, cocktails and wine are served as you sail through the sunset. For information and reservations, call **North Coast Cruises** (© **876/952-5860**) a few days in advance.

THE GREAT HOUSES

Occupied by plantation owners, each great house of Jamaica was always built on high ground so that it overlooked the plantation itself and was in sight of the next house in the distance. It was the custom for the owners to offer hospitality to travelers crossing the island by road. While these homes are intriguing and beautiful, it's important to remember that they represent the sad legacy of slavery—they were built by slaves, and the lavish lifestyle of the original owners was supported by the profits of slave labor. The two great houses below can be toured in the same day.

Greenwood Great House 🎔   Some people find the 15-room Greenwood even more interesting than Rose Hall (see below), because it's undergone less restoration and has more literary associations. Erected between 1780 and 1800, the Georgian-style building was the residence of Richard Barrett, cousin of poet Elizabeth Barrett Browning. Elizabeth herself never visited Jamaica, but her family was one of the largest landholders here. An absentee planter who lived in England, her father once owned 33,600 hectares (82,992 acres) and some 3,000 slaves. On display is the original library of the Barrett family, with rare books dating from 1697, along with oil paintings of the family, Wedgwood china, rare musical instruments, and a collection of antique furniture.

On Rte. A1, 23km (14 miles) east of Montego Bay. © 876/953-1077. Admission US$12 adults, US$6 children under 12. Daily 9am–6pm.

Rose Hall Great House 🎔   The legendary Rose Hall is the most famous great house on Jamaica. The subject of at least a dozen Gothic novels, it was immortalized in the H. G. deLisser book, *White Witch of Rose Hall.* The house was built from 1778 to 1790 by John Palmer, a wealthy British planter. At its peak, this was a 2,640-hectare (6,521-acre) plantation, with more than 2,000 slaves. However, it was Annie Palmer, wife of the builder's grandnephew, who became the focal point of fiction and fact. Called "Infamous Annie," she was said to have dabbled in witchcraft. She took slaves as lovers and then killed them off when they bored her. Servants called her "the Obeah woman" (*Obeah* is Jamaican for voodoo). Annie was said to have murdered several of her husbands while they slept and eventually suffered the same fate herself. Long in ruins, the house has now been restored. Annie's Pub is on the ground floor.

Rose Hall Hwy., 15km (9¼ miles) east of Montego Bay. © 876/953-2323. Admission US$15 adults, US$10 children. Daily 9am–6pm. Last tour at 5:15pm.

SHOPPING ☆☆

Be prepared for aggressive vendors in Montego Bay, as in all of Jamaica. There's a feverish attempt to peddle goods to tourists, all of whom are viewed as rich. Therefore, prepare yourself for being pursued persistently.

Some so-called "duty-free" prices are lower than stateside prices, until the government hits you with a 10% "general consumption tax" on all purchases. But you can still find good duty-free items here, including Swiss watches, Irish crystal, Italian handbags, Indian silks, and liquors and liqueurs. Appleton's rums are an excellent value. Tia Maria, laced with coffee, and rum-based Rumona are among the best of the traditional liqueurs. Increasingly popular recent introductions to the liquor inventories of Jamaica include Smirnoff Black Ice, a light version of Red Stripe Beer, and delicious (and incredibly fattening) mudslides that are sold as individual servings in short brown bottles. Khus Khus is the most famous of the local perfumes. Jamaican arts and crafts are available in daunting quantities throughout the resorts, from vendors hawking goods on the beaches, and at the Crafts Market (see below).

The main shopping areas are at **Montego Freeport,** within easy walking distance of the pier; **City Centre,** where most of the duty-free shops are, aside from those at the large hotels; and the **Holiday Village Shopping Centre,** located across from the Holiday Inn, on Rose Hall Road, heading from Montego Bay toward Ocho Rios.

If you have time for only one shopping complex, make it **Old Fort Craft Park,** as its handcrafts are more varied. It's grazing country for both souvenirs and more serious purchases. This shopping complex with 180 vendors (all licensed by the Jamaica Tourist Board) fronts Howard Cooke Boulevard (up from Gloucester Ave. in the heart of Montego Bay, on the site of Fort Montego). You'll see wall hangings, hand-woven straw items, and wood sculpture. You can even get your hair braided. Be aware that vendors can be very aggressive. If you want something, be prepared to bargain.

At the **Crafts Market,** near Harbour Street in downtown Montego Bay, you can find a good selection of handmade souvenirs of Jamaica, including straw hats and bags, wooden platters, straw baskets, musical instruments, beads, carved objects, and toys. That *jipijapa* (Panama-style) straw hat is important if you're out in the island sun.

One of the most intriguing places for shopping is an upscale minimall, **Half Moon Plaza,** on the coastal road about 13km (8 miles) east of the commercial center of Montego Bay. It caters to the guests of the Half Moon Club, and the carefully selected merchandise is upscale and expensive. On the premises are a bank, about 25 relatively upscale boutiques, and a private and well-respected prep school named in honor of the long-time manager of Half Moon, Heinz Simonowitz.

The best selection of native art is found at the **Gallery of West Indian Art,** 11 Fairfield Rd. (© **876/952-4547**), with a wide selection of paintings not only from Haiti and Jamaica, but Cuba as well, along with Jamaican hand-carved wooden animals—even some painted hand-turned pottery.

MONTEGO BAY AFTER DARK

Nightlife is not guaranteed at Montego Bay's top hotels. In winter, the restaurants and bars of the Ritz-Carlton or Half Moon have the most diverse amusements. After dark it's sleepy at Round Hill and Tryall.

The following clubs attract mainly a crowd in their 20s to their 40s.

Moments Rum & Reggae—& an Escape

When you want to escape, head for **Time 'n' Place,** just east of Falmouth (© **876/954-4371**). From Montego Bay, you'll spot the sign by the side of the road before you reach Falmouth: IF YOU GOT THE TIME, THEN WE GOT THE PLACE. On an almost deserted 3km (2-mile) beach sits this funky beach bar, built of driftwood. Sit back in this relaxed, friendly place and listen to the reggae from the local stations. You can order the island's best daiquiris, made from fresh local fruit, or stick around for peppery jerk chicken or lobster. Time 'n' Place isn't as completely undiscovered—somehow the fashion editors of *Vogue* have swooped down on the place, using it as a backdrop for beach fashion shots.

The number-one nightspot in MoBay is a two-in-one restaurant, **Marguerite's Seafood by the Sea** and **Margueritaville Sports Bar & Grill,** Gloucester Avenue (© **876/952-4777**), (p. 374 for full review).

Cricket Club, at Wyndham Rose Hall (© **876/953-2650**), is more than just a sports bar; it's where people go to meet and mingle with an international crowd. Televised sports, karaoke sing-alongs, tournament darts, and backgammon are all part of the fun. It's open daily from 8pm to 2am; there's no cover.

We enjoy the atmosphere at **Sunbaze Bar & Grill,** 39 Gloucester Ave. (© **876/952-9391**), which has an authentic Jamaican laid-back feel—complete with a constant flow of calypso and reggae music from as early as 10am daily (for the die-hards) until 2am.

The Brewery, Gloucester Avenue (© **876/940-2433**), is one of the city's most popular nightlife hangouts. It's a cross between an English pub and a Jamaican jerk-pork pit. There's a woodsy looking bar where everyone is into Red Stripe and reggae, lots of neomedieval memorabilia, and a covered veranda in back overlooking busy Gloucester Avenue.

3 Negril ★★★

This once-sleepy village has turned into a tourist mecca, with visitors drawn to its beaches along three well-protected bays: Long Bay, Bloody Bay (aka Negril Harbour), and Orange Bay. Negril became famous in the late 1960s, when it attracted American and Canadian hippies, who liked the idea of a place with no phones and no electricity; they rented modest digs in little houses on the West End where the local people extended their hospitality. But those days are long gone, and a strip of sophisticated hotels and all-inclusive resorts has sprouted along the sands of famous **Seven Mile Beach.**

Situated on the western tip of the island, Negril is 81km (50 miles) and about a 2-hour drive from Montego Bay's airport, along a winding road and past ruins of sugar estates and great houses.

There are really two Negrils: The West End is the site of many little local restaurants and funky cottages that still take in visitors. This is the area to head to if you want to recapture some of the charm and freewheeling spirit first publicized here in the '60s, though you can't expect a lot of creature comforts. The other Negril is on the east end, the first area you approach on the road from Montego Bay. Here are the upscale hotels and some of the most gorgeous beachfronts. Come here if you want to experience Negril from the confines of a luxury resort, particularly an all-inclusive.

GETTING THERE

BY PLANE   If you're going to Negril, you will fly into **Donald Sangster Airport** in Montego Bay. Some hotels, particularly the all-inclusive resorts, will arrange for airport transfers from that point. Be sure to ask when you book.

If your hotel doesn't provide transfers, you can fly to Negril's small airport, **International Air Link** (ⓒ **876/957-5924** in Negril, or 876/940-6660 in Montego Bay). The airfare is US$66 one-way from Montego Bay.

For a non-life-threatening emergency, try the **Negril Beach Medical Center,** Norman Manley Boulevard (ⓒ **876/957-4888**). **Negril Pharmacy,** Shop no. 14 in the Coral Seas Plaza (ⓒ **876/957-4076**), is open Monday to Saturday 9am to 7pm.

BY BUS   The 1¼-hour bus trip costs US$20. We recommend **Tour Wise** (ⓒ **876/952-4943** or 876/952-0019 in Montego Bay, or 876/974-2323 in Ocho Rios). The bus will drop you off at your final destination once you reach Negril.

ACCOMMODATIONS
VERY EXPENSIVE

The Caves ⊛   Although the nearest beach is a 12-minute ride away, Negril's most atmospheric and elegant small inn still attracts international celebrities. In spite of its fame, however, there are drawbacks. There's a sense of snobbishness at this member of Chris Blackwell's Outpost hotels, generally the finest in the Caribbean, and the prices are very high compared to the competition. The hotel is on 1 hectare (2½ acres) of land that's perched above a honeycombed network of cliffs, 10km (33 ft.) above the surf on a point near Negril's lighthouse, close to Jamaica's westernmost tip. The setting, though lavishly publicized, is difficult to negotiate with its stairwells and catwalks.

Accommodations, well suited for groups of friends traveling together, are in breezy units within five cement and wood-sided cottages, each with a thatched roof and sturdy furniture. Matisse could have designed them. None has air-conditioning, and the windows are without screens. A TV and VCR can be brought in if you request them. Many of the units contain alfresco showers.

Sumptuous meals are prepared only for guests and are included, along with domestic Jamaican drinks from the bar, as part of the all-inclusive price.

P.O. Box 313, Lighthouse Station, Negril, Jamaica, W.I. ⓒ 800/OUT-POST in the U.S. and Canada, or 876/957-0270. Fax 876/957-4930. www.islandoutpost.com. 10 units. Year-round US$445–US$575 double. Rates include all meals and self-service bar. AE, MC, V. No one under 18 allowed. **Amenities:** 2 restaurants; bar; outdoor saltwater pool; spa; Jacuzzi; sauna; snorkeling; bikes; airport transfers; laundry service; nonsmoking rooms. *In room:* Ceiling fan, TV/VCR (on request), dataport, minibar, beverage maker, hair dryer, iron/ironing board, safe.

EXPENSIVE

Couples Negril ⊛   If you're a man and a woman in love (others stay away!), you're welcomed at this romantic resort, lying on 300m (984 ft.) of white-sand beach, 8km (5 miles) from the center of Negril. The formula worked in Ocho Rios (see later in this chapter), so it was repeated here. A rival of Sandals properties, this love nest is the site of many weddings and honeymoons. On 7 hectares (17 acres) facing crescent-shaped Negril Harbour, this resort caters to those who want back-to-back scheduled activities, ranging from tennis tournaments to fashion shows. Each good-size unit has a king-size bed and a CD player (bring your own tunes), plus a balcony or patio with a view of the bay or of the lush gardens. Furnishings, though standard, are comfortable, and everything is

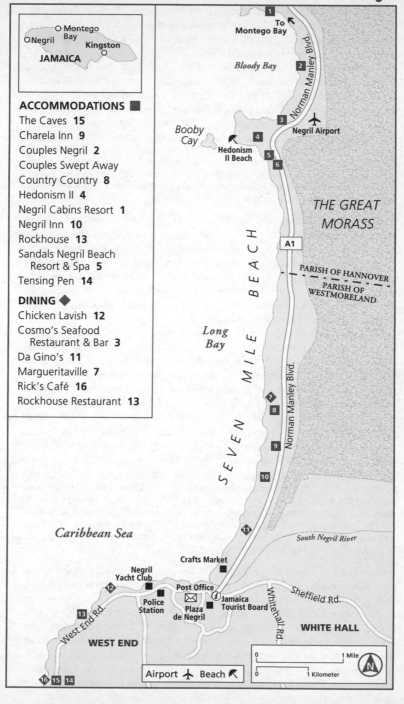

Negril

JAMAICA

O Montego Bay
O Negril
Kingston

ACCOMMODATIONS ■

The Caves **15**
Charela Inn **9**
Couples Negril **2**
Couples Swept Away
Country Country **8**
Hedonism II **4**
Negril Cabins Resort **1**
Negril Inn **10**
Rockhouse **13**
Sandals Negril Beach
Resort & Spa **5**
Tensing Pen **14**

DINING ◆

Chicken Lavish **12**
Cosmo's Seafood
Restaurant & Bar **3**
Da Gino's **11**
Margueritaville **7**
Rick's Café **16**
Rockhouse Restaurant **13**

To Montego Bay

Bloody Bay

Norman Manley Blvd.

Negril Airport

Booby Cay

Hedonism II Beach

THE GREAT MORASS

A1

PARISH OF HANNOVER
PARISH OF WESTMORELAND

Long Bay

SEVEN MILE BEACH

Norman Manley Blvd.

Caribbean Sea

South Negril River

Crafts Market

Negril Yacht Club

Post Office

Police Station

Plaza de Negril

Jamaica Tourist Board

Sheffield Rd.

Whitehall Rd.

WHITE HALL

West End Rd.

WEST END

Airport ✈ Beach 🏖

0   1 Mile
0   1 Kilometer

N

new, including the shower/tub combination bathrooms. The best doubles are the deluxe beachfront suites, which have Jacuzzis and hammocks. No building in the complex is higher than the tallest coconut tree. On the east side of the property, nude sunbathing is permitted.

The food is good, and you have a choice of three restaurants, including Otaheite, serving a Caribbean fusion cuisine. Mediterranean and Continental menus are also served. A resident band plays nightly and there's special entertainment planned throughout the week, including Caribbean dinner buffets with music.

Bloody Bay, Negril, Jamaica, WI. © 800/COUPLES in the U.S., or 876/957-5960. Fax 876/957-5858. www. couples.com. 234 units. Rates for 3 nights: winter US$1,590–US$2,780 double, from US$2,070 suite for 2; off season US$1,470–US$1,750 double, from US$1,590 suite for 2. Rates include all meals, drinks, and activities. AE, DC, MC, V. No one under 18 allowed. **Amenities:** 3 restaurants; 4 bars (1 swim-up); 2 outdoor pools; golf; 14 tennis courts; fitness room; aerobics; basketball court; dive shop; glass-bottom boat trips; Sunfish sailing; watersports; game room; tour desk; limited room service; laundry service. *In room:* A/C, TV, minibar (in some), beverage maker, hair dryer, iron/ironing board, safe.

Couples Swept Away 𝄞𝄞

This is one of the best beachside hotels in Negril—it's certainly the one of the most conscious of both sports and relaxation. All-inclusive, it caters to singles and couples eager for an ambience of all possible diversions available but absolutely no organized schedule and no pressure to participate if you just want to relax. As a staff member told us (privately, of course), "We get the health-and-fitness nuts, and Sandals or Hedonism get the sex crazed." The resort occupies 8 flat and sandy hectares (20 acres), which straddle both sides of the highway leading in from Montego Bay.

The accommodations (the hotel calls them "veranda suites" because of their large balconies) are in 26 two-story villas clustered together and accented with flowering shrubs and vines, a few steps from Seven Mile Beach. Each lovely, airy, and spacious unit has a ceiling fan, a king-size bed, and (unless the vegetation obscures it) sea views. Wooden shutters let sunlight and breezes in. Units contain showers only.

The cuisine here is more health conscious and of better quality than that served at Sandals and Hedonism II. The resort's social center is its international restaurant, Feathers, which lies inland, across the road from the sea. There's also an informal beachfront restaurant and bar, plus a veggie bar serving fresh fruit, juices, pita sandwiches, salads, and vegetarian dishes.

Norman Manley Blvd. (P.O. Box 3077), Negril, Jamaica, W.I. © 800/COUPLES in the U.S. and Canada, or 876/957-4061. Fax 876/957-4040. www.couples.com. 134 units. Winter US$530–US$665 double; off season US$485–US$620 double. Rates are all-inclusive. Ask about spa packages. AE, MC, V. No children under 18. **Amenities:** 3 restaurants; 4 bars; 2 outdoor pools; 10 tennis courts; racquetball; squash; health club and spa; 2 Jacuzzis; sauna; glass-bottom boat trips; sailing; scuba diving; sea kayaks; snorkeling; water-skiing; windsurfing; bikes; tour desk; airport transfers; room service (breakfast only); laundry service. *In room:* A/C, TV, beverage maker, hair dryer, iron/ironing board, safe.

Hedonism II 𝄞

Devoted to the pursuit of sophomoric pleasure, and with less class than Couples Negril, Hedonism II packs the works into a one-package deal, including all the drinks and partying anyone could want. The complex lies at the northern end of Negril Beach. Of all the members of the SuperClubs chain, this is the most raucous. It's a meat market, deliberately inviting its mainly single guests to go wild for a week. One manager boasted that the resort holds the record for the most people in a Jacuzzi at once.

The rooms are stacked in dull two-story clusters dotted around a sloping 9-hectare (22-acre) site about 3km (2 miles) east of the town center. This is not a couples-only resort; singles are both accepted and encouraged. The hotel will find you a roommate if you'd like to book on the double-occupancy rate.

> **Fun Fact The Naked Truth**
>
> Nude bathing is allowed at a number of hotels, clubs, and beaches (especially in Negril), but only where there are signs stating SWIMSUITS OPTIONAL. Elsewhere, the law prohibits even topless sunbathing.

Accommodations don't have balconies but are very spacious. Each has a king-size or twin beds, fitted with fine linen, with mirrors hanging over the beds. Each bathroom has a shower/tub combination.

On one section of this resort's beach, clothing is optional. It's called the "Nude" section; the other is known as "the Prude." The resort also has a secluded beach on nearby Booby Cay, where guests are taken twice a week for picnics.

There's nightly entertainment, along with a live band, a high-energy disco, and a piano bar. International cuisine, a bit bland, is served in daily buffets. There's also a clothing-optional bar, a "prude" bar, and a grill.

Negril Beach Rd. (P.O. Box 25), Negril, Jamaica, W.I. ℂ 800/859-7873 in the U.S., or 876/957-5070. Fax 876/957-5214. www.superclubs.com. 280 units. Winter US$362–US$581 double; off season US$379–US$487 double. Rates include all meals, drinks, and activities. AE, DC, DISC, MC, V. Children not accepted. **Amenities:** 4 restaurants; 6 bars (1 swim-up); 2 outdoor pools; dance club; 6 tennis courts; 2 indoor squash courts; fitness center; aerobics; badminton; basketball court; volleyball; Jacuzzi; sauna; dive shop; glass-bottom boat rides; sailing; scuba diving; snorkeling; water-skiing; windsurfing; airport transfers; Internet cafe; massage; nonsmoking rooms; 1 room for those with limited mobility. *In room:* A/C, beverage maker, hair dryer, safe.

Sandals Negril Beach Resort & Spa ⊛   On 5 hectares (12 acres) of prime beachfront land a short drive east of the center of Negril, Sandals Negril is an all-inclusive, couples-only (male-female) resort that attracts a basically young, convivial, and unsophisticated audience. It's far more active and freewheeling than the more formal Sandals properties in Ocho Rios and Montego Bay. The casual, well-furnished rooms have a tropical motif. Recently renovated, they come in a wide range of styles, but are generally spacious, each with a marble bathroom with a shower/tub combination. The best units open directly on the beach. Honeymooners usually end up in a Jamaican-built four-poster mahogany bed. For a balcony and sea view, you have to pay the top rates.

Rates include all meals; snacks; unlimited drinks, day and night, at one of four bars (including two swim-up pool bars); and nightly entertainment, including theme parties. Coconut Cove is the main dining room, but guests can also eat at one of the specialty rooms. The Sundowner offers white-glove service and Jamaican cuisine, and low-calorie health food is served beside the beach. Kimono features Japanese cuisine. In the typical Sandals style, the food is rather standard, but there is great variety and no one goes hungry.

Norman Manley Blvd., Negril, Jamaica, W.I. ℂ 800/SANDALS in the U.S. and Canada, or 876/957-5216. Fax 876/957-5338. www.sandals.com. 223 units. Winter US$335–US$415 double, US$430–US$650 suite; off season US$325–US$400 double, US$430–US$650 suite. Rates include all meals, drinks, and activities. AE, DISC, MC, V. Children under 16 not accepted. **Amenities:** 5 restaurants; 4 bars (2 swim-up); 2 outdoor pools; 4 tennis courts; fitness center with saunas, aerobics; canoeing; scuba diving; snorkeling; Sunfish sailboats; windsurfing; airport transfers; limited room service; massage; coin-operated laundry; nonsmoking rooms. *In room:* A/C, TV, minibar (in some), beverage maker, iron/ironing board, hair dryer, safe.

MODERATE

Charela Inn ⊛   Simplicity, quiet elegance, and good value are the hallmarks of this seafront inn reminiscent of a Spanish hacienda. This place sits on the main beach strip on 1 hectare (2½ acres) of landscaped grounds. The building's inner courtyard, with a tropical garden and a round, freshwater pool, opens onto one of the widest (75m/246 ft.) sandy beaches in Negril. Try for one of the 20 or so rooms with a view of the sea. Accommodations are generally spacious, often with a bit of Jamaican character with their wicker furnishings and ceiling fans. All have private patios or balconies. Most of the good-size bathrooms have shower/tub combinations, but some have showers only.

Le Vendôme, facing the sea and the garden, offers both an a la carte menu and a five-course fixed-price meal that changes daily. Thursday and Saturday nights, there's live entertainment.

Norman Manley Blvd. (P.O. Box 33), Negril, Jamaica, W.I. © 876/957-4648. Fax 876/957-4414. www. charela.com. 49 units. Winter US$158–US$210 double; off season US$108–US$148 double. MAP (breakfast and dinner) US$40 per person extra. 5-night minimum stay in winter. AE, MC, V. **Amenities:** Restaurant; bar; outdoor pool; kayaks; Sunfish sailboats; windsurfing; limited room service; laundry service; nonsmoking rooms; rooms for those with limited mobility. In room: A/C, TV, dataport, beverage maker (in some), hair dryer, safe.

Negril Cabins Resort *(Value) (Kids)*

This place appeals to travelers who want to get away from it all without spending a fortune; it's an especially good choice for families with kids. These wooden cabins (which have been featured in *Architectural Digest*) are in a forest, across the road from a beach called Bloody Bay. The 4 hectares (10 acres) of gardens are planted with royal palms, bull thatch, and a rare variety of mango tree.

The simple but stylish cabins are small timber cottages, none more than two stories high, rising on stilts. Each offers two spacious and comfortable bedrooms, plus a balcony and shower-only bathroom. Many units have been recently upgraded and improved, and all are brightened with vibrant Jamaican fabrics. The best are rented as "executive suites," with a sunken living and dining area, plus a pull-out queen-size sofa bed for small families. The executive units also come with air-conditioning and an iron and ironing board. Simple but tasty Jamaican and international dishes are served.

Norman Manley Blvd. (P.O. Box 118), Negril, Jamaica, W.I. © 800/382-3444 in the U.S., or 876/957-5350. Fax 876/957-5381. www.negril-cabins.com. 82 units. Winter US$240 cabin for 2; off season US$220 cabin for 2. Rates are all-inclusive. Children under age 12 stay free in parent's room; children age 12 and over are $25 extra. AE, MC, V. **Amenities:** 2 restaurants; bar; outdoor pool; tennis court; fitness center; Jacuzzi; scuba diving; snorkeling; bike rental; car rental; room service (7am–10pm); babysitting; laundry service; nonsmoking rooms; rooms for those with limited mobility. In room: A/C, TV (in some), hair dryer, iron/ironing board (in executive suites), safe.

Negril Inn *(★)*

About 5km (3 miles) east of the town center in the heart of the Seven Mile Beach stretch, this is one of the smallest and most reasonably priced all-inclusive resorts in Negril. Because of its size, it's very low-key. The resort, not confined to couples only, offers very simple but comfortably furnished guest rooms with private balconies, in a series of two-story structures in a garden setting. Each unit has a small tiled bathroom with a shower/tub combination.

Included in the package are all meals, all alcoholic drinks (except champagne), and nightly entertainment. The restaurant is rather good.

Norman Manley Blvd. (P.O. Box 59), Negril, Jamaica, W.I. © 876/957-4209. Fax 876/957-4365. www. negrilinn.com. 46 units. Winter US$240 double, US$300 triple; off season US$180 double, US$210 triple. Rates are all-inclusive, including airport transfers. AE, MC, V. Children not accepted in winter. **Amenities:** Restaurant; bar; outdoor pool; 2 tennis courts; fitness center; Jacuzzi; airport transfers; room service (breakfast only); laundry service; nonsmoking rooms. In room: A/C, hair dryer, iron/ironing board, no phone.

Tensing Pen *(★★) (Finds)*

Our favorite nest in Negril lies on the western tip and has grown and evolved since its hippie era in the early 1970s. On a cliff, a 10-minute stroll from the landmark lighthouse, it is 6km (3¾ miles) south of the center of Negril. Hidden away from the world, the place is a little gem. Those aggressive beach vendors will never find you here, tucked behind a high wall. On 1 hectare (2½ acres) of grounds, you're surrounded by tropical planting. Laze in the hammocks or sunbathe on the terraces hewn out of rock. Sleep in a rustic stone cottage covered in thatch in a four-poster draped in mosquito netting, plantation house–style. Some of the huts are elevated, evoking tree-house living. Local tiles, tropical woods, bamboo rockers, ceiling fans, and louvered windows set the tone. Bathrooms with shower/tub combinations are a bit cramped. There's a communal kitchen where guests sometimes cook for each other. The nearest beach is a 10- to 15-minute drive or a 30-minute walk.

Lighthouse Rd. (P.O. Box 13), Negril, Jamaica, W.I. ℂ **876/957-0387.** Fax 876/957-0161. www.tensingpen. com. 15 units. Winter US$128–US$279 double; off season US$87–US$180 double. AE, MC, V. **Amenities:** Restaurant; bar; laundry service; babysitting; communal kitchen; rooms for those with limited mobility. *In room:* Ceiling fan, fridge, no phone.

INEXPENSIVE

Another low-budget option for lodging is found at Da Gino's (see "Dining," below).

Country Country ⋆   The owners of this intimate hotel were determined to outclass their competitors, so they turned to celebrity decorator Ann Hodges, the creative force behind the gorgeous decor in many of the much-more-expensive Island Outpost properties. A narrow meandering path stretches from the coastal boulevard to the white-sand beach, where watersports await. Along the way is a collection of neo-Creole, clapboard-sided buildings that drip with elaborate gingerbread and cove moldings, each inspired by an idealized vision of vernacular Jamaican colonial architecture. The buildings are a rainbow of peacock hues highlighting the separate architectural features of each building. Inside, concrete floors keep the spacious interiors cool. Each unit has a vaguely Victorian feel, with comfortable furnishings, plus a shower-only bathroom. There's a beachfront bar and grill, plus the only Chinese restaurant in Negril, the Hunan Garden, offering good-tasting, moderately priced dishes in a setting that evokes Shanghai during the British colonial era.

Norman Manley Blvd. (P.O. Box 39), Negril, Jamaica, W.I. ℂ **876/957-4273.** Fax 876/957-4342. www.country negril.com. 14 units. Winter US$145–US$165 double; off season US$115–US$135 double. AE, MC, V. **Amenities:** Restaurant; bar; limited room service; nonsmoking rooms. *In room:* A/C, TV, fridge, beverage maker, hair dryer, safe.

Rockhouse ⋆   This funky boutique inn stands in stark contrast to hedonistic all-inclusive resorts like Sandals, and it offers very affordable rates. It's a cross between a South Seas island retreat and an African village, with thatched roofs capping stone-and-pine huts. A team of enterprising young Aussies restored and expanded this place, which was one of Negril's first hotels (the Rolling Stones hung out here in the 1970s). The rooms have ceiling fans, four-poster beds draped in mosquito netting, and open-air showers. All units contain queen-size beds; and four cottages have sleeping lofts with extra queen-size beds. Less than half a kilometer (¼ mile) from the beach, Rockhouse has a ladder down to a cove where you can swim and snorkel. After a refreshing dip in the cliffside pool, you can dine in the open-sided restaurant pavilion serving excellent, spicy local fare three times a day.

West End Rd. (P.O. Box 24), Negril, Jamaica, W.I. ℂ **876/957-4373.** Fax 876/957-0557. www.rockhousehotel. com. 26 units. Winter US$130 studio, US$250 villa; off season US$100 studio, US$175 villa. Children 11 and under stay free in parent's room. AE, MC, V. **Amenities:** Restaurant; 2 bars; outdoor pool; snorkeling; nonsmoking rooms; rooms for those with limited mobility. *In room:* A/C, minibar, hair dryer, iron/ironing board, safe.

DINING
EXPENSIVE

Rick's Café ⚡ SEAFOOD/STEAKS   At sundown, everybody in Negril heads toward the lighthouse along the West End strip to Rick's Café, whether they want a meal or not. Of course, the name was inspired by the old watering hole of Bogie's *Casablanca*. There was a real Rick (Richard Hershman), who first opened this bar back in 1974, but he's long gone. This laid-back cafe was made famous in the '70s as a hippie hangout, and ever since it's attracted the bronzed and the beautiful (and some who want to be). Management claims the sunset here is the most glorious in Negril, and after a few fresh-fruit daiquiris, you'll agree with them. (Actually, the sunset is just as spectacular at any of the waterfront hangouts in Negril, if nothing is blocking the view.) Casual dress is the order of the day, and the background music comprises reggae and rock. If you want dinner, you can order imported steaks along with a complete menu of blackened dishes, Cajun style. The fish (red snapper, fresh lobster, or grouper) is always fresh. The food is rather standard, and expensive for what you get, but that doesn't keep the touristy crowds away from the sunset party. You can also buy plastic bar tokens at the door, which you can use instead of money, a la Club Med. A bit tacky, we'd say. Bogie would never have tolerated this.

West End Rd. 🕿 876/957-0380. Reservations accepted for parties of 6 or more. Main courses US$19–US$28. AE, MC, V. Daily noon–10pm.

Rockhouse Restaurant ⚡ INTERNATIONAL   This is a gorgeous setting for enjoying some of the best food in Negril. Set on the premises of the previously recommended Rockhouse, it was developed by a team of Australian and Italian entrepreneurs who designed a bridgelike span, equivalent to a railway trestle, high above the surging tides of a rocky inlet on Negril's West End. You may get a touch of vertigo if you lean over the railing. This place attracts a hip international crowd. Enjoy a drink or two at the bar, which is built with glossy tropical hardwoods and coral stone, before your meal. Menu items, which are always supplemented with daily specials, might include a seasonal platter of smoked marlin or an upscale version of Jamaican peppered pork with yams.

In the Rockhouse, West End Rd. 🕿 876/957-4373. Reservations required for dinner in high season. Main courses US$9.50–US$27. AE, MC, V. Daily 7am–10:30pm.

MODERATE

Da Gino's ITALIAN   Four octagonal, open-sided dining pavilions, separated from Negril's beachfront by a strip of trees, evolved as the escapist dream of Gino Travaini, the Italy-born owner. Pastas and bread are made fresh daily. The best chef's specialties feature linguine with lobster, filet of beef with peppercorns, various forms of scaloppini, and huge platters of grilled seafood.

On the premises are a dozen very simple huts, each octagonal, rustic, and camplike, that rent for between US$60 and US$120 each, double occupancy, depending on the season. Each has a TV, a very basic kitchenette, and a ceiling fan, but no air-conditioning.

In the Hotel Mariposa Hideaway, Norman Manley Blvd. 🕿 876/957-4918. Reservations recommended. Main courses US$13–US$26. MC, V. Daily 8am–10pm.

Margueritaville AMERICAN/INTERNATIONAL   It's practically Disney gone Jamaican at this rowdy bar, restaurant, and entertainment complex. Thanks to the loaded buses that pull in for a field trip from some of Negril's all-inclusive hotels, it's a destination in its own right. People party here all day and night. There's an on-site art gallery where most of the works are by the very talented U.S.-born artist Geraldine Robbins, and at the gift shops you might actually be tempted to buy something. Every evening, beginning around 9pm, there's live music or perhaps karaoke. Permanently moored a few feet offshore is a pair of Jamaica's largest trampolines, whale-size floaters that feature high-jumping contests by any participant whose cocktails haven't affected them yet. Rock climbing is also available. Drinks are deceptively potent. In all this party atmosphere, you don't expect the food to be that good, but it might happily surprise, even though it consists of such fare as shrimp-and-tuna kabobs. You'll find Southern fried chicken, along with the standard club steaks and burgers.

Norman Manley Blvd. © **876/957-4467.** Burgers and sandwiches US$8.75–US$9.75. Main courses US$12–US$25. AE, MC, V. Daily 8am–11pm.

INEXPENSIVE
Chicken Lavish ⭐ *Finds* JAMAICAN We've found that Chicken Lavish, whose name we love, is the best of the low-budget eateries. Just show up on the doorstep of this place along the West End beach strip, and see what's cooking. Curried goat is a specialty, as is fresh fried fish. The red snapper is caught in local waters. But the big draw is the restaurant's namesake, the chef's special Jamaican chicken. It's amazingly consistent, fried or served with curry or sweet-and-sour sauce. The chef will tell you, and you may agree, that it's the best on the island. Ironically, this utterly unpretentious restaurant has achieved something like cult status among counterculture travelers who have eaten here since the 1970s. You can dine on the roofed veranda, or ask for takeout.

West End Rd. © **876/957-4410.** Main courses US$4.50–US$10. MC, V. Daily 10am–10pm.

Cosmo's Seafood Restaurant & Bar ⭐ *Finds* SEAFOOD/JAMAICAN One of the best places to go for local seafood enters on a Polynesian thatched *bohio* (beach hut) open to the sea and bordering the main beachfront. In this rustic setting, Cosmo Brown entertains locals and visitors. You can order his famous conch soup, or conch in a number of other ways, including steamed or curried. He's also known for his savory kettle of curried goat, or you might prefer freshly caught seafood or fish, depending on what the catch turned up. Unless you order shellfish, most dishes are rather inexpensive.

Norman Manley Blvd. © **876/957-4784.** Main courses US$5–US$15. AE, MC, V. Daily 9am–10pm.

FUN ON & OFF THE BEACH
BEACHES Beloved by the hippies of the 1960s, **Seven Mile Beach** ⭐⭐ is still going strong, but it's no longer the idyllic retreat it once was. Resorts attracting an international crowd now line this beach. Nudity, however, is just as prevalent as it's always been, especially along the stretch near Cosmo's. There's a carefree, laid-back vibe. On the western tip of the island, the white powdery sand stretches from Bloody Bay in Hanover to Negril Lighthouse in Westmoreland; clean, tranquil aquamarine waters, coral reefs, and a backdrop of palm trees add to the appeal. When you tire of the beach, you'll find all sorts of resorts, clubs, beach bars, open-air restaurants, and the like. Vendors will try to sell you everything from Red Stripe beer to ganja. Many of the big resorts have nude beaches as well. The hottest and most exotic is found at **Hedonism II,** although **Grand Lido** next door draws its fair share. Nude beaches at each of these resorts are in separate and "private" areas of the resort property. Total nudity is required for strolling the beach, and security guards keep peeping Toms at bay. Photography is not

permitted. Most of the resorts also have nude bars, nude hot tubs, and nude swimming pools.

GOLF **Negril Hills Golf Course,** Sheffield Road (© **876/957-4638**), is Negril's only golf course. Although it doesn't have the cachet of such Montego Bay courses as Tryall, it's the only golf course in western Jamaica. Greens fees for this 18-hole, par-72 course are US$68, and club rental is US$18. Carts and caddies, which are not obligatory, cost US$35 and US$14, respectively. Anyone can play, but advance reservations are recommended before 7am.

HORSEBACK RIDING Horseback riding, heretofore confined to the north shore, has come to Negril. For a close encounter with the natural beauty of this part of Jamaica, head for the local version of the OK Corral—**Rhodes Hall Plantation,** signposted at the eastern edge of the resort (© **876/957-6334**), which now offers guided excursions on horseback, a 2-hour ride across the most scenic beauty spots on the outskirts of Negril. Along the way you'll pass some of the richest vegetation in the Caribbean, including breadfruit, guava, and even wild tobacco plants. Costs average US$60 per rider. There is a free pick-up service.

WATERSPORTS **Watersports equipment** is easily available at any of at least seven associated kiosks that operate at strategic intervals along the sands. Each of the informal-looking outlets is operated under the umbrella of **Seatec Water Sports** (© **876/957-4401**). Each kiosk charges roughly the same rates, and in many cases, each of them has access to the same equipment. Jet skis cost US$40 to US$50 for a 30-minute ride; snorkeling is US$25 per person for a 90-minute excursion by boat to an offshore reef with equipment; parasailing is US$30 for a 12-minute ride; and water-skiing is US$30 for 15 minutes.

The best area for **snorkeling** is off the cliffs in the West End. The coral reef here is extremely lively, with marine life visible at a depth of about 3m to 5m (10 ft.–16 ft.). The waters are so clear and sparkling that just by wading in and looking down, you'll see lots of marine life. The fish are small but extremely colorful.

Negril has the best and most challenging **scuba diving** in Jamaica. Unusual dive sites within an easy boat ride of Negril include **Shallow Plane,** the site of a Cessna aircraft that crashed in 15m (49 ft.) of water, and which is a diving attraction today; an underwater cave, **Throne Room,** which allows divers to enter at one end and ascend into the open air at the other; and two separate sites, each about 20m (66 ft.) underwater, known as **Shark's Reef** and **Snapper Drop.** Each of these is loaded with flora and fauna whose species change as the elevations change.

Negril Scuba Centre, in the Negril Beach Club Hotel, Norman Manley Boulevard (© **800/818-2963** in the U.S., or 876/957-9641), is the most modern, best-equipped scuba facility in Negril. A professional staff of internationally certified scuba instructors and dive masters teach and guide divers through Negril's colorful coral reefs. Beginners' dive lessons are offered daily, as well as multiple-dive packages for certified divers. Full scuba certifications and specialty courses are also available.

A resort course, designed for first-time divers with basic swimming abilities, costs US$75 and includes all instruction and equipment, a lecture on water and diving safety, and one open-water dive. It begins daily at 10am and ends at 2pm. A one-tank dive costs US$30 plus US$20 for equipment rental (not necessary if divers bring their own gear). More economical is a two-tank dive, which must be completed in 1 day. It costs US$55, plus the (optional) US$20 rental of all equipment. This organization is PADI-registered, although it accepts all recognized certification cards.

NEGRIL AFTER DARK ⟨★⟩

Negril is not without nightspots, though you're likely to spend most evenings enjoying the entertainment in your own resort. Fun places are easy to find, as nearly *everything* is on Norman Manley Boulevard, the only major road in Negril.

See "Dining," above, for details on **Rick's Café** and **Margueritaville.**

Alfred's Ocean Palace, Norman Manley Boulevard (© 876/957-4735), draws mainly locals, but there's lots of intermingling and visitors are welcome. It attracts mainly a young party crowd, but if you're 80, you'll still be warmly embraced, your cold Red Stripe beer waiting. There's no cover, and in addition to grabbing a drink, you can order a bite to eat until midnight. Particularly interesting is the beach-party area, with a stage for live reggae and jazz acts. You can also boogie on the dance floor inside, shaking to hits you'll hear at clubs stateside.

Risky Business, Norman Manley Boulevard (© 876/957-3008), sits a few feet from the waves. It can be sleepy or manic, depending on the music. In season, you can order burgers and sandwiches, and the Red Stripe is cheap all year round. Basically, it's a young hangout with parties Monday, Thursday, and Saturday, beginning at 9pm. There's no cover. Saturday is "bottomless mug" night for US$10.

4 Ocho Rios ⟨★⟩

This north-coast resort is a 2-hour drive east of Montego Bay or west of Port Antonio. Ocho Rios was once a small banana and fishing port, but tourism became the leading industry long ago. Short on charm, it's now Jamaica's cruiseship capital. The bay is dominated on one side by a bauxite-loading terminal and on the other by a range of hotels with sandy beaches fringed by palm trees.

Ocho Rios and neighboring Port Antonio have long been associated with Sir Noël Coward (who invited the world to his doorstep) and Ian Fleming, creator of James Bond (see below for details about their homes here).

Frankly, unless you're a cruise passenger, you may want to stay away from the major attractions when a ship is in port. The duty-free markets are overrun then, and the hustlers become more strident in pushing their crafts and junk souvenirs. Dunn's River Falls becomes almost impossible to visit at those times.

However, Ocho Rios has its own unique flavor and offers the usual range of sports, including a major fishing tournament every fall, in addition to a wide variety of accommodations.

In our view, you go to overrun Ocho Rios only if you want to stay put at one of the resorts here: It is home to some of the leading inns of the Caribbean as well as two stellar Sandals properties. When in the area, we prefer to stay away from the center of Ocho Rios itself, perhaps at a resort in Runaway Bay or something really special like Ian Fleming's Goldeneye.

ESSENTIALS

GETTING THERE   If you're going to Ocho Rios, you'll fly into the **Donald Sangster Airport** in Montego Bay. Some hotels, particularly the larger resorts, will arrange for airport transfers from that point. Be sure to ask when you book.

By taxi, a typical one-way fare from Montego Bay to Ocho Rios is US$90. Always negotiate and agree on a fare *before* getting into the cab.

If your hotel does not provide transfers, you can go by bus for a US$20 one-way fare. We recommend **Tour Wise** (© 876/979-1027 in Montego Bay, or 876/974-2323 in Ocho Rios). The bus will drop you off at your hotel; the trip takes 1 hour and 45 minutes.

You can rent a car for the 108km (67-mile) drive east along Highway A1 (see "Getting Around" in the section "Essentials," at the beginning of this chapter).

MEDICAL SERVICES   The nearest hospital is St. Ann's Hospital (© 876/972-0150), 11km (6¾ miles) west. The most central pharmacy is **Ocho Rios Pharmacy,** Shop 27 in Ocean Village Plaza (© 876/974-2398), open Monday to Saturday 9am to 8pm and Sunday 9am to 7pm.

ACCOMMODATIONS
VERY EXPENSIVE

Goldeneye 🏨🏨   Few hotels in the world manage to be so luxurious and yet so appealingly informal as this intimate retreat. It's centered around the villa where the most famous secret agent in the world, James Bond (007), was created in 1952 by then-owner Ian Fleming. Fleming built the imposing but simple main house in 1946, and wrote each of the 13 original James Bond books there. In the early 1990s, music publisher–turned-hotelier Chris Blackwell bought and restored the by-then dilapidated property to its original modernist dignity. Fleming's original desk remains, and the oversize Indonesian furniture is enhanced with memorabilia from what became the most famous spy movies in the world. The main house is usually only rented as a three-bedroom whole for extended house parties, often to rock stars and other celebs.

You're more likely to rent one of the four additional villas that were built in harmony with nature, on the surrounding property. Each evokes a tropical version of a billionaire's summer camp in Maine, thanks to a juxtaposition of indoor and outdoor spaces, sofas, and well-chosen decorative pieces. Each unit has a fully equipped kitchen. All drinks, food, and most activities are included in the price. The cuisine features some Jamaican favorites as well as international dishes.

There's a pool on the premises, but it's reserved for occupants of the main house. Masonry paths lead to a nearby beach.

Oracabessa, St. Mary, Jamaica, W.I. © 800/688-7678 in the U.S. or 876/975-3354. Fax 876/975-3620. www.islandoutpost.com. 5 villas. Winter US$795 1-bedroom villa, US$995 2-bedroom villa, US$1,195 3-bedroom villa, US$3,500 Ian Fleming house; off season US$595 1-bedroom villa, US$795 2-bedroom villa, US$995 3-bedroom villa, US$2,500 Ian Fleming house. Rates include all meals, drinks, and activities. AE, DISC, MC, V. **Amenities:** Outdoor pool (for Ian Fleming house guests); lit tennis court; jet skis; kayaks; snorkeling; windsurfing; limited room service; babysitting; laundry service; nonsmoking rooms; rooms for those with limited mobility. *In room:* A/C, TV, dataport, kitchenette, minibar, coffeemaker, iron/ironing board, safe.

Jamaica Inn 🏨🏨   Built in 1950, the gracious beachfront Jamaica Inn is a series of long, low buildings set in a U shape near the sea, 2km (1¼ miles) east of town. Noël Coward, arriving with Katharine Hepburn or Claudette Colbert, was a regular, and Errol Flynn and Ian Fleming used to drop in from time to time. Today it's more likely to be Kate Moss. It's an elegant anachronism, a true retro hotel, and has remained little changed in 4 decades, avoiding the glitter of all-inclusives like Sandals.

Lovely patios open onto the lawns, and the bedrooms are reached along garden paths. Guest rooms are very spacious, with colonial two-poster beds, quality carved-wood period pieces, and balustraded balconies opening onto views. Bathrooms are elegant and roomy, gleaming with marble vanities, combination shower/tubs, robes, and deluxe toiletries. The beach is a wide, champagne-colored strip; close to the shore, the sea is almost too clear to make snorkeling an adventure, but farther out it's rewarding. The European-trained chef prepares both refined international and Jamaican dishes. The emphasis is on cuisine that uses fresh local produce. Men must wear a jacket and tie at night in winter.

Main St. (P.O. Box 1), Ocho Rios, Jamaica, W.I. © **877/470-6975** in the U.S., or 876/974-2514. Fax 876/974-2449. www.jamaicainn.com. 54 units. Winter including all meals US$440–US$715 double, from US$1,400 suite for 2; off season including MAP (breakfast and dinner) US$340–US$470 double, from US$500 suite for 2. AE, MC, V. Children age 11 and under not accepted. **Amenities:** Restaurant; 2 bars; outdoor pool; 4 tennis courts; exercise room; kayaks; Sunfish sailboats; 24-hr. room service; babysitting; laundry service; nonsmoking rooms; rooms for those with limited mobility. *In room:* A/C, ceiling fan, TV, dataport, iron/ironing board, safe.

Royal Plantation Spa & Golf Resort 🌴🌴

This stately inn, a rival of the Jamaica Inn, has fallen under the Sandals umbrella and become the chain's most upmarket property in Jamaica. The hotel entrance evokes the antebellum South. At any moment, you expect Scarlett O'Hara to rush out to greet Rhett. You drive up a sweeping driveway and enter through a colonnaded portico 2km (1¼ miles) east of the center. A complete renovation has brought major improvements to the rooms and public areas and added a full-service European spa. Accommodations are all suites, each opening onto the ocean views. Bedrooms are handsomely equipped with such extras as plush cotton robes, daily *New York Times,* fax service, Internet connections, CD players, and the like. Guests have full exchange privileges with the two other Sandals resorts in the area. The cuisine is far superior to that at the other Sandals properties, and the atmosphere less rowdy.

Main St., Ocho Rios, Jamaica, W.I. © **888/48ROYAL** or 876/974-5601. Fax 876/974-5912. www.royal plantation.com. Winter US$460–US$1,510 double; off season US$405–US$1,510 double. 77 units. No children under 18. **Amenities:** 3 restaurants; bar; golf at nearby Sandals; spa; glass-bottom boat; scuba diving; 24-hr. room service. *In room:* A/C, TV/VCR, dataport, minibar, beverage maker, hair dryer, safe.

Sans Souci Resort & Spa 🌴🌴🌴

If a cookie-cutter Sandals is the last thing you want, head for this classier beachfront joint. Winner of four diamonds from AAA, this pink, cliffside luxurious resort is 5km (3 miles) east of town on a forested plot of land abutting a good white-sand beach. There's a separate clothing-optional beach, a mineral bath big enough for an elephant, and a labyrinth of catwalks and bridges stretching over rocky chasms filled with surging water.

Each unit features a veranda or patio, copies of Chippendale furniture, plush upholstery, and subdued colonial elegance. Some contain Jacuzzis. Accommodations range from rather standard bedrooms to vast suites with large living and dining areas, plus kitchens. Deluxe touches include glazed-tile floors, luxurious beds, and marble bathrooms with whirlpool tubs. You'll enjoy the food at the elegant Casanova restaurant.

Rte. A3 (P.O. Box 103), Ocho Rios, Jamaica, W.I. © **800/448-7702** or 876/994-1206. Fax 876/994-1544. www.sanssoucijamaica.com. 146 units. All-inclusive rates: winter US$500–US$750 double; off season US$450–US$660 double. AE, DISC, MC, V. No children under 16. **Amenities:** 3 restaurants; 4 bars; 4 outdoor pools; 2 tennis courts; health club and spa; 2 Jacuzzis; sauna; kayaks; sailing; scuba diving; snorkeling; water-skiing; windsurfing; 24-hr. room service; laundry service; dry cleaning; nonsmoking rooms; rooms for those with limited mobility. *In room:* A/C, TV, minibar, beverage maker, hair dryer, iron/ironing board, safe.

EXPENSIVE

Couples Ocho Rios 🌴

This is a couples-only resort (and management defines couples as "any man and woman in love"). Most are married, and many are on their honeymoon. Everything is in pairs, even the chairs at night by the moon-drenched beach. Some guests slip away from the resort, which is an 18-minute drive (8km/5 miles) east of town, to Couples' private island to bask in the buff. (A shuttle boat transports visitors offshore to this beautiful little island with a fine sandy beach, a bar, and a pool. Security guards keep the gawkers from bothering guests here.)

In general, this is a classier operation than the more mass-market Sandals (at least the Dunn's River and the Ocho Rios versions). The bedrooms have either a king-size bed or two doubles, pleasantly traditional furnishings, and a patio fronting either the sea or the mountains. Good-size bathrooms have a shower/tub combination. For a chain that's all-inclusive, the cuisine is above average.

Tower Isle, Rte. A3 (P.O. Box 330), Ocho Rios, Jamaica, W.I. ℂ 800/268-7537 in the U.S., or 876/975-4271. Fax 876/975-4439. www.couples.com. 210 units. Winter US$500–US$540 double, US$650–US$750 suite; off season US$460–US$515 double, US$610–US$725 suite. Rates include all meals, drinks, and activities. AE, MC, V. The hotel usually accepts bookings for a minimum of any 3 nights of the week, though most guests book by the week. Children under 18 not accepted. **Amenities:** 5 restaurants; 3 bars; outdoor pool; golf; 4 tennis courts; squash courts; health club and spa; yoga; 5 Jacuzzis; sauna; sailing; scuba diving; snorkeling; water-skiing; windsurfing; bike rental; horseback riding; Internet room; room service (breakfast only); nonsmoking rooms; rooms for those with limited mobility. In room: A/C, TV, beverage maker, hair dryer, iron/ironing board, safe.

Grand Sport Villa Golf Resort & Spa 𝒢

This all-inclusive lies a 2km (1¼-mile) drive southeast of town, set on 18 hectares (44 acres) of tropical gardens on a private estate dotted with red-tile villas. A great house in the hills overlooks the Caribbean. Across from the imposing gate near the resort's entrance are the white sands of a private beach.

All but a handful of the accommodations are in one-, two-, or three-bedroom villas, each with a pool, a fully equipped kitchen, and a shaded terrace. Honeymoon villas have their own whirlpools. Thirty-six units are traditional single or double rooms on the third floor of the great house. Accommodations are high-ceilinged, roomy, and decorated in Caribbean colors. They're well furnished, with particularly fine beds, and the bathrooms with combination shower/tubs are well-maintained.

Main St. (P.O. Box 728), Ocho Rios, St. Ann, Jamaica, W.I. ℂ 800/BEACHES in the U.S. and Canada, or 876/974-1027. Fax 876/974-5838. www.beaches.com. 285 units. All-inclusive rates for 3 nights per couple: winter US$1,590–US$1,680 double, US$1,920 junior suite, US$2,400–US$2,640 1-bedroom villa suite, US$4,170 2-bedroom villa for 4; off season US$1,320–US$1,560 double, US$1,710 junior suite, US$1,890–US$2,370 1-bedroom villa suite, US$3,690 2-bedroom villa for 4. AE, MC, V. Children age 15 and under not accepted. **Amenities:** 4 restaurants; 5 bars; 9 outdoor pools; 6 tennis courts; spa; 5 Jacuzzis; 2 saunas; 2 steam rooms; scuba diving; laundry service; nonsmoking rooms; rooms for those with limited mobility. In room: A/C, TV, dataport, kitchenette, minibar, beverage maker, hair dryer, iron/ironing board, safe.

Sandals Dunn's River Golf Resort & Spa 𝒢

Located on a wide, sugary beach, this is the finest of the Sandals resorts, at least in the opinion of some guests who have sampled them all. As at all Sandals resorts, only adult male-female couples are allowed—no gays and no children. Set on the beachfront between Ocho Rios and St. Ann's Bay, the resort is very sports oriented. It occupies 10 well-landscaped hectares (25 acres), offering attractively furnished and often quite spacious accommodations. All the rooms have an Italianate/Mediterranean motif. The elegant guest rooms are scattered among the six-story main building, two lanai buildings, and a five-story west wing. Extras include spacious balconies, walk-in closets, king-size beds, and shower/tub combinations. Before retreating to the disco or enjoying the nightly entertainment, guests can choose among several dining options, selecting from an array of restaurants that attempt variety in lieu of first-rate cuisine. The International Room is elegant, with fabric-covered walls and rosewood furniture. The Windies Restaurant serves Caribbean specialties. D'Amoré offers Italian cuisine, and Restaurant Kimonos serves Chinese, Polynesian, and Japanese dishes.

Rte. A3 (P.O. Box 51), Ocho Rios, Jamaica, W.I. ℂ 800/SANDALS in the U.S. and Canada, or 876/972-1610. Fax 876/972-1611. www.sandals.com. 250 units. All-inclusive rates: winter US$930–US$1,100 double, from US$1,535 suite; off season US$510–US$785 double, from US$1,230 suite. Minimum stay of 4 days/3 nights. AE, DISC, MC, V. No one under 18 allowed. **Amenities:** 4 restaurants; 4 bars (2 swim-up); 2 outdoor pools; disco; shuttle to 18-hole golf course; pitch-and-putt golf course; 4 tennis courts; health club and spa; 3 Jacuzzis; saunas; steam rooms; canoes; kayaks; sailboats; scuba diving; snorkeling; water-skiing; windsurfing; laundry service; nonsmoking rooms; rooms for those with limited mobility. *In room:* A/C, TV, beverage maker, hair dryer, iron/ironing board, safe.

Sandals Ocho Rios Resort & Golf Club ⟨⟩

This resort opening onto a good sandy beach attracts a mix of unmarried and married (only male-female) couples, including honeymooners. At times the place seems like a summer camp for grown-ups (and some who didn't quite grow up). This is the most low-key of the Sandals properties. Is it romantic? Most guests think so, although we've encountered other couples whose relationship didn't survive the 3-night minimum stay.

On 5 well-landscaped hectares (12 acres) 2km (1¼ miles) west of the town center, it offers comfortably furnished but uninspired rooms with either ocean or garden views, plus some cottage units. All units are reasonably large, with king-size beds and good-size bathrooms with shower/tub combinations. You can sip drinks at an oceanside swim-up bar. Nightly theme parties and live entertainment take place in a modern amphitheater. A unique feature of the resort is an open-air disco. The resort's main dining room is Bayside; Valentino's serves standard Italian food, and the Reef Terrace Grill does above-average Jamaican cuisine and fresh seafood. A more recent addition is the Arizona Steakhouse, with some sizzling good steaks and Lone Star ribs.

Main St. (P.O. Box 771), Ocho Rios, Jamaica, W.I. ℂ 800/SANDALS in the U.S. and Canada, or 876/974-5691. Fax 876/974-5700. www.sandals.com. 237 units. All-inclusive rates per couple: winter US$520–US$730 double, from US$1,250 suite; off season US$490–US$660 double, from US$1,200 suite. AE, MC, V. No one under 18 allowed. **Amenities:** 4 restaurants; 5 bars (1 swim-up); 3 outdoor pools; disco; 2 tennis courts; fitness center; Jacuzzis; saunas; canoes; kayaks; sailboats; scuba diving; snorkeling; windsurfing; massage; babysitting; laundry service; nonsmoking rooms; rooms for those with limited mobility. *In room:* A/C, TV, beverage maker, hair dryer, iron/ironing board, safe.

MODERATE

Hibiscus Lodge Hotel ⟨Value⟩

This intimate little inn offers more value for your money than any other resort at Ocho Rios. Perched precariously on a cliff along the shore 3 blocks from the Ocho Rios Mall, the inn has character and charm. Mallards Bay Beach, shared by residents of some of the biggest hotels in Ocho Rios, lies within a 3- to 4-minute walk. All medium-size bedrooms, either doubles or triples, have small, shower-only bathrooms, ceiling fans, and verandas opening to the sea.

After a day spent in a pool suspended over the cliffs, or lounging on the large sun deck, guests can enjoy a drink in the unique swinging bar. The owners provide dining at the Almond Tree Restaurant (see "Dining," below).

83 Main St. (P.O. Box 52), Ocho Rios, St. Ann, Jamaica, W.I. ℂ 876/974-2676. Fax 876/974-1874. 26 units. Winter US$115–US$126 double, US$157 triple; off season US$103–US$115 double, US$140 triple. Rates include breakfast. AE, MC, V. **Amenities:** Restaurant; bar; outdoor pool; tennis court; Jacuzzi; limited room service; nonsmoking rooms. *In room:* A/C, ceiling fan, TV, hair dryer, iron/ironing board, no phone.

High Hope Estate ⟨⟩

Because this hotel is so intimate, whether you like it will depend on whether you click with the owner and the other guests. Basically, it's an upscale private home in the style of the British colonial world at its most rarefied that accepts paying guests. It was built for a socially prominent heiress, Kitty Spence, granddaughter of prairie-state populist William Jennings Bryan, and later served as the home and laboratory of a horticulturist who successfully bred 560 varieties of flowering hibiscus. The estate's 16 hectares (40 acres), set 165m (541 ft.) above the coast and 11km (6¾ miles) west of Ocho Rios, thrive with flowering plants as well as memories of such luminaries as Noël Coward, who used to play the grand piano that graces one of the public areas. There are absolutely no planned activities here. Bedrooms are a delight—spacious, well thought out, and exceedingly comfortable. The excellent bathrooms have shower/tub combinations. The staff is on hand to help supervise children, maintain the property, and prepare meals for anyone who gives advance notice.

The nearest beach is a 10-minute ride away. You could rent the entire villa with a group of friends, and you can purchase all-inclusive packages.

16 Top Rd. (P.O. Box 11), St. Ann's Bay, Jamaica, W.I. ℂ 876/972-2277. Fax 876/972-1607. www.highhope estate.com. 5 units. Year-round US$125–US$165. Rates include breakfast. MC, V. **Amenities:** Restaurant; outdoor pool; limited room service; babysitting; laundry service; nonsmoking rooms; rooms for those with limited mobility. *In room:* Ceiling fan, minibar, beverage maker, hair dryer.

DINING
MODERATE
Almond Tree Restaurant JAMAICAN/CONTINENTAL   The Almond Tree is a two-tiered patio restaurant with a tree growing through the roof. Lobster thermidor is the tastiest item on the menu, but we also like the bouillabaisse (made with conch and lobster). Other excellent choices are the roast suckling pig, medallions of beef, and a fondue bourguignon. Jamaican plantation rice is a local specialty. The wine list offers a variety of vintages, including Spanish and Jamaican. Have a cocktail in the unique "swinging bar"—with swinging chairs, that is.

In the Hibiscus Lodge Hotel, 83 Main St., St. Ann's Bay. ℂ 876/974-2813. Reservations recommended for dinner. Main courses US$15–US$26. AE, MC, V. Daily 7:30–10:30am, noon–2:30pm, and 6–9:30pm.

BiBiBips INTERNATIONAL/JAMAICAN   Set in the main tourist strip of Ocho Rios, this restaurant (whose name is the owner's nickname) occupies a sprawling open-air compound of porches and verandas. Lots of single folks come just to hang out at the bar. Drinks and flirtations sometimes segue into dinner at the adjacent restaurant, where well-prepared menu items include Red Stripe shrimp, which is deep-fried in a beer-based batter; coconut-curried chicken; vegetarian Rasta Pasta; and a combination Creole-style seafood platter. Lunches are a bit simpler, focusing mostly on sandwiches, salads, and an especially delicious jerk chicken burger. There's live entertainment, usually some kind of rap or reggae band, every Friday, Saturday, and Sunday beginning at 8pm.

93 Main St. ℂ 876/974-8759. Lunch main courses US$5.50–US$21; dinner main courses US$8.50–US$28. AE, MC, V. Daily 11am–5:30pm and 6pm–2am.

Evita's Italian Restaurant ✦ ITALIAN   A 5-minute drive south of the commercial heart of Ocho Rios, in a hillside residential neighborhood that enjoys a panoramic view over the harbor and beachfronts, this is one of the most fun restaurants along the north coast of Jamaica. Its soul and artistic flair come from Eva Myers, the convivial former owner of some of the most legendary bars of Montego Bay, who established her culinary headquarters in this green-and-white gingerbread Jamaican house in 1990. An outdoor terrace adds additional seating and enhanced views. More than half the menu is devoted to pastas, including almost every variety known to northern and southern Italy. The fish dishes are excellent—especially the snapper stuffed with crabmeat and the lobster and scampi in a buttery white cream sauce. Italian (or other) wines by the bottle might accompany your main course.

Eden Bower Rd. 𝄌 876/974-2333. Reservations recommended. Main courses US$12–US$23. AE, MC, V. Daily 11am–11pm.

Margaritaville at Ocho Rios *Kids* JAMAICAN Lying in the new Island Village, a shopping and entertainment complex, this is one of the largest restaurants ever constructed on the north coast, seating 450 diners and drinkers. A high-energy bar and grill, Margaritaville provides all-day family fun with the entertainment continuing late at night. Attractions include a rooftop whirlpool tub, a 30m-long (98-ft.) waterslide, a freshwater pool, along with three bars and a trading post. The decor is rustic West Indian, with an Afro-Cuban aura. Of course, being a Jimmy Buffett dive, expect the world-famous tropical margaritas and those delectable "Cheeseburgers in Paradise." There's dancing here—reggae-disco style—at night.

Turtle Beach Rd. (at the cruise-ship docks). 𝄌 876/675-8976. Main courses US$12–US$18; burgers and salads US$7–US$11. AE, MC, V. Daily 8:30am–11pm.

INEXPENSIVE

Little Pub Restaurant JAMAICAN/INTERNATIONAL Located in a red-brick courtyard with a fishpond and waterfall in the center of town, this pub is the town's most popular. No one will mind if you just drop in for a drink. If you want dinner, proceed to one of the linen-covered tables topped with cut flowers and candles. We're fond of the barbecued chicken and grilled kingfish, but you might like snapper or fresh lobster.

59 Main St. 𝄌 876/974-2324. Reservations recommended. Main courses US$12–US$28. MC, V. Daily 10am–midnight.

Ocho Rios Village Jerk Centre ✦ *Finds* JAMAICAN At this open-air restaurant, you can get the best jerk dishes along this part of the coast. When only a frosty Red Stripe beer can quench your thirst and your stomach is growling for the fiery taste of Jamaican jerk seasonings, head here—and don't dress up. Don't expect anything fancy: It's the food that counts, and you'll find fresh daily specials posted on a chalkboard menu on the wall. The dishes are hot and spicy, but not *too* hot; hot spices are presented on the side for those who want to go truly Jamaican. The barbecue ribs are especially good, and fresh fish is a delight, perfectly grilled—try the red snapper. Vegetarian dishes are also available on request, and if you don't drink beer you can wash it all down with natural fruit juices.

Da Costa Dr. 𝄌 876/974-2549. Jerk pork US$3 ¼ lb., US$10 1 lb.; whole jerk chicken US$12. MC, V. Daily 10am–11pm.

HITTING THE BEACH

The most idyllic sands are at the often-overcrowded **Mallards Beach,** in the center of Ocho Rios and shared by hotel guests and cruise-ship passengers. Locals may steer you to the white sands of **Turtle Beach,** between the Renaissance Jamaica Grande and Club Jamaica. It's smaller, more desirable, and not as over-crowded as Mallards.

The most popular spot (stay away when cruise ships are in port!) is **Dunn's River Beach,** located below the famous falls. Another great spot is **Jamaica Grande's Beach,** which is open to the public. Parasailing is a favorite sport here.

Our favorite beach is at Goldeneye, writer Ian Fleming's former home, now a hotel. Follow the trail of 007 and head for **James Bond Beach** (© **876/ 975-3663**), east of Ocho Rios at Oracabessa Beach. For J$150 (US$2.40) adults, J$50 (US80¢) children, nonguests can enjoy its sand strip any day except Monday. There's a watersports rental center here as well.

You might also escape the crowds at Ocho Rios and head to the lovely beach at nearby Runaway Bay (see the section "Runaway Bay," earlier in this chapter).

SPORTS & OTHER OUTDOOR PURSUITS

GOLF   SuperClub's Runaway Golf Club, at Runaway Bay near Ocho Rios on the north coast (© **876/973-7319**), charges no fee to guests who stay at any of Jamaica's affiliated SuperClubs. For nonguests, the price is US$80 year-round. Any player can rent carts for US$35 for 18 holes; clubs are US$14 for 18 holes.

Sandals Golf & Country Club (© **876/975-0119**), a 15-minute ride from the center of the resort, is a 6,500-yard course, known for its panoramic scenery some 210m (689 ft.) above sea level. (From the center of Ocho Rios, travel along the main bypass for 3km/2 miles until you reach Mile End Road. A Texaco station is located at the corner of Mile End Road. Turn right and drive for another 8km/5 miles until you come to the Sandals course on your right.) The 18-hole, par-71 course was designed by P. K. Saunders and opened in 1951 as the Upton Golf Club. Rolling terrain, lush vegetation, and flowers and fruit trees dominate the 48-hectare (119-acre) course. A putting green and driving range are available for those who wish to hone their skills first. Sandals guests play free; nonguests pay US$70 for nine holes or US$100 for 18 holes.

TENNIS   Grand Sport Villa Golf Resort & Spa, Main Street, Ocho Rios (© **876/974-1027**), focuses more on tennis than any other resort in the area. It offers three clay-surface and three hard-surface courts, all lit for night play. Guests play free, day or night, but nonguests must call and make arrangements with the manager. The resort also sponsors twice-a-day clinics for both beginners and advanced players. Frequent guest tournaments are also staged, including handicapped doubles and mixed doubles.

EXPLORING THE AREA

A scenic drive south of Ocho Rios along Route A3 will take you inland through **Fern Gully** 🎯, a lush gorge. This was originally a riverbed, but now the main road winds up some 210m (689 ft.) among a profusion of wild ferns, a tall rainforest, hardwood trees, and lianas. There are hundreds of varieties of ferns, and roadside stands offer fruits and vegetables, carved-wood souvenirs, and basketwork. The road runs for about 6km (3¾ miles). At Moneague, a small town, the A1 continues south into the interior of Jamaica, but it also heads back north along a route to the west of the southbound A3. If you take the A1 north, you'll come to the coast on the north shore at St. Ann's Bay.

Heading up A1 north, you'll pass the ruins of **Edinburgh Castle** lying 13km (8 miles) southwest of Claremont, the major town on the route back (but of no tourist interest). These ruins—not worth a detour but of passing interest if you're driving by—are a local curiosity.

This 1763 lair was the former abode of one of Jamaica's most famous murderers, a Scot named Lewis Hutchinson, who used to shoot passersby and toss their bodies into a deep pit. At his so-called "castle," really a two-story house, Hutchinson invited his victims inside. There he would wine and dine them before murdering and then robbing them.

The authorities got wind of his activities. Although he tried to escape by canoe, Hutchinson was captured and hanged at Spanish Town on March 16, 1773. Evidently proud of his achievements (evidence of at least 43 bodies was found), he left 100 British pounds and instructions for a memorial to be built in his honor. It never was.

These castle ruins can be viewed on the northern outskirts of the village of Bensonton, near the Bensonton Health Club.

In **St. Ann's Bay,** the site of the first Spanish settlement on the island, you can see the **statue of Christopher Columbus,** cast in his hometown of Genoa and erected near St. Ann's Hospital on the west side of town, close to the coast road. There are a number of Georgian buildings in the town—the **Court House** near the parish church, built in 1866, is the most interesting.

Brimmer Hall Estate   Some 34km (21 miles) east of Ocho Rios, in the hills 3km (2 miles) from Port Maria, this 1817 estate is an ideal place to spend a day. You can swim in the pool and sample a wide variety of brews and concoctions. The Plantation Tour Eating House offers typical Jamaican dishes for lunch, and there's a souvenir shop with a good selection of ceramics, art, straw goods, woodcarvings, rums, liqueurs, and cigars. All this is on a working plantation where you're driven around in a tractor-drawn jitney to see the tropical fruit trees and coffee plants; the knowledgeable guides will explain the various processes necessary to produce the fine fruits of the island. This is a far more interesting experience than the trip to Croydon Plantation in Montego Bay, so if you're visiting both resorts and have time for only one plantation, make it Brimmer Hall.

Port Maria, St. Mary's. ✆ 876/994-2309. Tours US$18. Tours Mon–Fri 9am–4pm.

Coyaba River Garden and Museum   Two kilometers (1¼ miles) from the center of Ocho Rios, at an elevation of 126m (413 ft.), this park and museum were built on the grounds of the former Shaw Park plantation. The word *coyaba* comes from the Arawak name for paradise. Coyaba is a Spanish-style museum with a river and gardens filled with native flora, a cut-stone courtyard, fountains, and a crafts shop and bar. The museum boasts a collection of artifacts from the Arawak, Spanish, and English settlements in the area.

Shaw Park Rd. ✆ 876/974-6235. Admission US$5, free for children 12 and under. Daily 8am–6pm. Take the Fern Gully–Kingston rd., turn left at St. John's Anglican Church, and follow the signs to Coyaba, just .4km (¼ mile) farther.

Dunn's River Falls *(Overrated)*   For a fee, you can relax on the beach or climb with a guide to the top of the 183m (600-ft.) falls. You can splash in the waters at the bottom of the falls or drop into the cool pools higher up between the cascades of water. A beach restaurant serves lackluster snacks and drinks, and dressing rooms are available. If you're planning to climb the falls, wear sneakers or sport sandals to protect your feet from the sharp rocks and to prevent slipping.

Climbing the falls with the crowds is a chance to experience some 183m (600 ft.) of cold but clear mountain water. In contrast to the heat swirling around you, the splashing water hitting your face and bare legs is cooling on a hot day. The problem here is slipping and falling, especially if you're joined to a chain of hands linking body to body. In spite of the slight danger, there seem to be few accidents. The falls aren't exactly a wilderness experience, with all the tour buses carrying cruise-ship passengers here. The place is always overrun.

Rte. A3. ✆ 876/974-2857. Admission US$10 adults, US$8 children age 2–11, free for children under 2. Daily 8:30am–5pm (7am–5pm on cruise-ship arrival days). From the center of Ocho Rios, head west along Route A3.

Firefly 🅐 This vacation retreat was the home of Sir Noël Coward and his long-time companion, Graham Payn, who, as executor of Coward's estate, donated it to the Jamaica National Heritage Trust. The recently restored house is more or less as it was on the day Sir Noël died in 1973. His Hawaiian-print shirts still hang in the closet of his austere bedroom, with its mahogany four-poster. The library contains a collection of his books, and the living room is warm and comfortable, with big armchairs and two grand pianos (where he composed several famous tunes). Guests stayed at Blue Harbour, a villa closer to Port Maria; they included Evelyn Waugh, Winston Churchill, Errol Flynn, Lord Laurence Olivier, Vivien Leigh, Claudette Colbert, Katharine Hepburn, Mary Martin, and the Queen Mother. Paintings by the noted playwright/actor/author/composer adorn the walls. An open patio looks out over the pool and the sea. Across the lawn, Sir Noël is buried under a simple white marble gravestone.

Grants Town, in St. Mary, 32km (20 miles) east of Ocho Rios above Port Maria. ⓒ 876/725-0920. Admission US$10. Children under 12 free. Mon–Thurs and Sat 9am–5pm.

Harmony Hall This was the centerpiece of a sugar plantation in the late 19th century. Today it has been restored and is the focal point of an art gallery and restaurant that showcases the painting and sculpture of Jamaican artists as well as a tasteful array of arts and crafts. Among the featured gift items are Sharon McConnell's Starfish Oils, which contain natural additives harvested in Jamaica. The gallery shop also carries the "Reggae to Wear" line of sportswear, designed and made on Jamaica, and Anabella boxes (for jewelry).

Tower Isles on Rte. A3, 6km (3¾ miles) east of Ocho Rios. ⓒ 876/975-4222. Free admission. Gallery daily 10am–6pm; restaurant Tues–Sun 10am–2:30pm and 6–11pm.

Island Village 🅐 The 2002 opening of this exotic-looking playland represents one of the largest private investments of the past decade within the tourism infrastructure of Ocho Rios. Scattered over 2 hectares (5 acres) on a beachfront within a few steps of the city's cruise-ship terminal is a replica of an idealized Jamaican village, complete with elaborate gingerbread, hundreds of feet of boardwalk, and a medley of psychedelic colors that glow, rainbow-style, in the streaming sunlight. It's not without its own Disney-ish theme-park overtones: They include **sound stages** strategically scattered within the sightlines of **bars** that serve the kind of high-octane cocktails that could fuel a heavily loaded jet-liner from here to Kingston. Music and hotel impresario Christopher Blackwell, who takes credit for the "discovery" and marketing of Bob Marley, is half-owner of this venture—thus you won't find any shame here about emphasizing reggae as both a lifestyle and an artistic venue.

Within the compound you'll find about 35 **shops** selling clothing, books, souvenirs, "reggae wear," and Bob Marley memorabilia; and four or five restaurants and bars.

Small-scale reggae presentations occur spontaneously, often when a cruise ship is in port, and large-scale **blockbuster concerts** are scheduled about once a month, and are usually attended by hundreds, or even thousands. Except when there's a world-class concert—usually when there's no cruise ship in port—there's no admission charged for entrance to the compound, but an alert security staff ensures that "panhandlers, pickpockets, and lowlifes" (at least those residing in Jamaica) are kept off the premises. Access to the beachfront—with its own floating trampoline—costs US$5 per person.

Island Village, Turtle Beach Rd. No central switchboard; each establishment has its own phone. Free admission. Daily 9am–midnight.

Prospect Plantation This working plantation adjoins the 18-hole Prospect Mini Golf Course. A visit to this property is an educational, relaxing, and enjoyable experience. On a leisurely tour by covered jitney through the scenic beauty of Prospect, you'll readily see why this section of Jamaica is called "the garden parish of the island." You can view the many trees planted by such visitors as Winston Churchill, Henry Kissinger, Charlie Chaplin, Pierre Trudeau, and Noël Coward. You'll learn about and see pimento (allspice), bananas, cassava, sugar cane, coffee, cocoa, coconut, pineapple, and the famous leucaena ("Tree of Life"). You'll see Jamaica's first hydroelectric plant and sample some of the exotic fruit and drinks.

Horseback riding is available on three scenic trails at Prospect. The rides are about 1 hour long. Advance booking of 1 hour is necessary.

Rte. A3, 5km (3 miles) east of Ocho Rios, in St. Ann. *©* 876/994-1058. Tours US$12 adults, US$6 for children 12 and under; 1-hr. horseback ride US$20. Tours Mon–Sat at 10:30am, 2pm, and 3:30pm.

SHOPPING

For many, Ocho Rios provides an introduction to Jamaica-style shopping. After surviving the ordeal, some visitors may vow never to go shopping again. Literally hundreds of Jamaicans pour into Ocho Rios to peddle items to cruise-ship passengers and other visitors. Be prepared for aggressive vendors. Pandemonium greets many an unwary shopper, who must also be prepared for some fierce haggling. Every vendor asks too much at first, which gives them the leeway to "negotiate" until the price reaches a more realistic level. Is shopping fun in Ocho Rios? A resounding no. Do cruise-ship passengers and land visitors indulge in it anyway? A decided yes.

In general, the shopping is better in Montego Bay. If you're not going there, wander the Ocho Rios crafts markets, although much of the merchandise is repetitive.

SHOPPING CENTERS & MALLS There are a number of shopping plazas in Ocho Rios. We've listed them because they're here, not because we heartily recommend them. Newer ones include the **New Ocho Rios Plaza,** in the center of town, with some 60 shops; opposite is the **Taj Mahal Mall,** with 26 duty-free stores. **Island Plaza** is another major shopping complex, as is the **Mutual Security Plaza** with some 30 shops.

Ocean Village Shopping Centre (*©* 876/974-2683) is one of the originals, with numerous boutiques, food stores, a bank, sundries purveyors, travel agencies, service facilities, and what have you. The **Ocho Rios Pharmacy** (*©* 876/974-2398) sells most proprietary brands, perfumes, and suntan lotions, among its many wares. Nearby is the major competitor of Ocean Village, the **Coconut Grove Shopping Plaza,** which is linked by walkways and shrubs. The merchandise here consists mainly of local craft items, and this center is often overrun with cruise-ship passengers. Ocean Village is slightly bigger and more upscale, and we prefer it.

Just east of Ocho Rios, the **Pineapple Place Shopping Centre** is a collection of shops in cedar shingle–roofed cottages set amid tropical flowers.

The **Ocho Rios Craft Park** has 135 stalls. A vendor will weave a hat or a basket while you wait, or you can buy a ready-made hat, hamper, handbag, place mats, or lampshade. Other stands stock hand-embroidered goods and will make small items while you wait. Woodcarvers work on bowls, ashtrays, statues, and cups.

Island Plaza, right in the heart of Ocho Rios, has some of the best Jamaican art, all paintings by local artists. You can also purchase local handmade crafts (be prepared to haggle), carvings, ceramics, kitchenware, and the inevitable T-shirts.

SPECIALTY SHOPS   Swiss Stores, in the Ocean Village Shopping Centre (© 876/974-2519), sells jewelry and all the big names in Swiss watches. The Rolex watches here are real, not those fakes touted by hustlers on the streets.

One of the best bets for shopping is **Soni's Plaza,** 50 Main St., the address of all the shops recommended below. **Casa de Oro** (© 876/974-5392) specializes in duty-free watches, fine jewelry, and classic perfumes. **Gem Palace** (© 876/974-2850) is the place to go for diamond solitaires, tennis bracelets, and 14-karat gold chains. **Mohan's** (© 876/974-9270) offers one of the best selections of 14-karat and 18-karat gold chains, rings, bracelets, and earrings. **Soni's** (© 876/974-2303) focuses strictly on souvenirs from coffee mugs to T-shirts. **Taj Gift Centre** (© 876/974-9268) has a little bit of everything: Blue Mountain coffee, film, cigars, and hand-embroidered linen tablecloths. For something different, look for Jamaican jewelry made from hematite, a mountain stone. **Diamonds Duty Free Fine Jewelry** (© 876/974-6455) beats most competition with its name-brand watches, and jewelry.

Jamaica Inn Gift Shop, in the Jamaica Inn, Main Street (© 876/974-2514), is better than most specialty shops here, selling everything from Blue Mountain coffee to Walkers Wood products, and even guava jelly and jerk seasoning. If you're lucky, you'll find marmalade from an old family recipe, plus Jamaican Reggae Rum. Local handcrafts include musical instruments for kids and brightly painted country cottages of tin. The store also sells antiques and fine old maps of the West Indies.

OCHO RIOS AFTER DARK

The **Sports Bar** is open daily from 10am to 3am, and Sunday is disco night. Most evenings are devoted to some form of entertainment, including karaoke. Also see "Dining," earlier in this chapter, for a review of **BiBiBips,** where there's a hopping bar and live bands on Friday, Saturday, and Sunday nights.

Jamaic'N Me Crazy, at the Renaissance Jamaica Grande (© 876/974-2201), has the best lighting and sound system in Ocho Rios (and perhaps Jamaica). The crowd includes everyone from the passing yachter to the curious tourist, who may be under the mistaken impression that he or she is seeing an authentic Jamaican nightclub. Hotel guests and foreign visitors can visit nightly from 10pm to 3am.

5 Runaway Bay

Once a mere satellite of Ocho Rios, Runaway Bay, 16km (10 miles) to the west, has become a destination in its own right, with white-sand beaches that are much less crowded than those in Ocho Rios.

Since you're so far removed from the action, such as it is, in Ocho Rios, you stay at Runaway Bay mainly if you're interested in hanging out at a particular resort. It is especially recommended for those who want to escape from the hordes descending on Ocho Rios, where cruise-ship crowds and aggressive vendors can intrude on your solitude.

This part of Jamaica's north coast has several distinctions: It was the first part of the island seen by Columbus, the site of the first Spanish settlement on the island, and the point of departure of the last Spaniards leaving Jamaica following their defeat by the British.

Fun Fact Nude Nuptials

At Hedonism III (p. 404), couples who want to see what they're getting before they tie the knot can be married in their birthday suits. Instead of a gown and a tuxedo, suntan lotion is recommended so that any body parts, already exposed, might not become overexposed, at least to the sun. After the "I do's" are said, the happy couple can head for the honeymoon suite at this adults-only all-inclusive resort.

Most people who stay at Runaway Bay stay at one of the all-inclusives, where meals are included. If you're not staying at such a resort, you can dine at Runaway Heart Country Club, which is open to nonguests; otherwise you can drive to Ocho Rios for meals.

ACCOMMODATIONS AND DINING

Breezes Runaway Bay 🦟 This stylish resort is an all-inclusive. Its clubhouse is approached by passing through a park filled with tropical trees and shrubbery. The lobby is the best re-creation of the South Seas on Jamaica, with hanging wicker chairs and totemic columns. There's a minijungle with hammocks and a nearby nude beach, in addition to the lovely stretch of sandy beach right out front. The resort lies 3km (2 miles) east of Paradise Beach and just next door to the town's second best beach, Cardiffall.

Guest rooms are spacious, with a light, tropical motif. They're fitted with local woods, cool tile floors, and private balconies or patios. The most elegant are the suites, with Jamaican-made four-poster beds. The good-size bathrooms have combination shower/tubs and generous marble counters.

Live music emanates from the stylish Terrace every evening at 7pm, and a nightclub offers live shows 6 nights a week at 10pm. Dine either in the beachside restaurant or in the more formal Italian restaurant, Martino's, which is the best. Breezes now has a bar on its *au naturel* beach. The resort's Starlight Grill has also expanded its menu to include a vegetarian cuisine. The club offers exchange and day-pass privileges with Hedonism III immediately next door.

P.O. Box 58 (10km/6¼ miles west of Ocho Rios), Runaway Bay, Jamaica, W.I. © 800/GO-SUPER in the U.S., or 876/973-4820. Fax 876/973-6390. www.superclubs.com. 234 units. Winter US$165–US$209 per person, per night double; off season US$153–US$159 per person, per night double. Rates include all meals, drinks, and activities. AE, DISC, MC, V. No children under age 14. **Amenities:** 4 restaurants; 4 bars; outdoor pool; 4 tennis courts; golf; tennis; fitness center; 3 Jacuzzis; dive shop; sailing; scuba diving; snorkeling; windsurfing; limited room service; laundry service; nonsmoking rooms; rooms for those with limited mobility. *In room:* A/C, TV, minibar (in some), beverage maker, hair dryer, iron/ironing board, safe.

FDR (Franklyn D. Resort) *Kids* Located on Route A1, 27km (17 miles) west of Ocho Rios, FDR is an all-inclusive that's the number-one choice if you're traveling with children. FDR lies 3km (2 miles) east of Paradise Beach and about .4km (¼ mile) east of Cardiffall. Its own no-name beach stretches for about 182m (597 ft.), a mixture of stone and sand. The resort, named after its Jamaican-born owner and developer, Franklyn David Rance, is on 2 hectares (5 acres) of flat, sandy land dotted with flowering shrubs and trees, on the main seaside highway. Each of the Mediterranean-inspired buildings has a terra-cotta roof, a loggia or an outdoor terrace, Spanish marble in the bathrooms, a kitchenette, and a personal attendant (called a vacation nanny), who cooks, cleans, and cares for children. Although neither the narrow beach nor the modest pools are the most desirable on the island, and most rooms lack a sea view, many visitors appreciate the spacious units and the resort's wholehearted concern for kids.

Two restaurants on the property serve free wine with lunch and dinner (and offer special children's meals), and a piano bar provides music every evening. There's live music nightly.

Main St. (P.O. Box 201), Runaway Bay, St. Ann, Jamaica, W.I. © **888/FDR-KIDS** in the U.S., or 876/973-4592. Fax 876/973-4600. www.fdrholidays.com. 76 units. Winter US$660–US$800; off season US$560–US$600. Rates are all-inclusive. Children age 5 and under stay free in parent's suite. Children 6–15 US$50 extra each. AE, MC, V. **Amenities:** 2 restaurants; 3 bars; outdoor pool; disco; tennis court; health club; dive shop; bikes; children's center; free babysitting (9:30am–4:45pm); laundry service; nonsmoking rooms. *In room:* A/C, ceiling fan, TV, kitchen.

Grand Lido Braco ✿

Established in 1995, this is one of the most historically evocative all-inclusive resorts in Jamaica, lying on a prime stretch of sandy, 319m (1046-ft.) beachfront. Set on 34 hectares (84 acres) of land near Buena Vista, a 15-minute drive west of Runaway Bay, it's a re-creation of a 19th-century Jamaican Victorian village, with charming gingerbread architecture. A copy of a courthouse hosts entertainment, and benches line the borders of the town square, where artisans display their handiwork. The old Jamaica that's portrayed here is a rather sanitized, Disney version. Yet this is not a place for children; it is a primarily adult retreat.

Accommodations are in 12 blocks of three-story buildings, each trimmed in colonial-style gingerbread and filled with wicker furniture. All the spacious units have private patios or verandas and face the ocean; blocks one through six are closer to the beachfront, and blocks five and six face a strip of sand designated as a "clothing-optional" area. Beds are very comfortable, with fine linen; all rooms are equipped with CD players and radios; the bathrooms are well maintained and have showers.

Separate dining areas serve tasty Jamaican cuisine, pizza and pasta, and blander international fare; the Piacere Restaurant offers upscale dinners and has a dress code. For variety, Munahana serves Japanese sushi and Teppanyaki cuisine.

Rio Bueno, Trelawny, Jamaica. © **877/GO-SUPER** in the U.S., or 876/954-0000. Fax 876/954-0020 or 876/954-0021. www.superclubs.com. 226 units. Winter US$512–US$967 double, US$930 suite for 2; off season US$493–US$729 double, US$885 suite for 2. Rates include all meals, drinks, and activities. AE, MC, V. Children under age 16 not accepted. **Amenities:** 5 restaurants; 8 bars; 2 outdoor pools; disco; 9-hole golf course; 3 tennis courts; health club and spa; 4 Jacuzzis; sauna; steam room; kayaks; scuba diving; snorkeling; Sunfish sailboats; water-skiing; windsurfing; bikes; business center; 24-hr. room service; laundry service. *In room:* A/C, TV, beverage maker, hair dryer, iron/ironing board, safe.

Hedonism III ✿

Following a chain format established in Negril, this latest beachfront Hedonism bills itself as a "truly active (and slightly wicked!) vacation." Though this branch of Hedonism isn't as rowdy and raunchy as the Negril branch—it's a little more serene and isolated from the action in town—it's still for the serious party person who likes to drink all night, hang out at the beach all day, and go wild at those toga parties. Set on 6 hectares (15 acres) of landscaped gardens on the eastern end of Runaway Bay, it features ocean views from all rooms and an all-inclusive package deal. Hedonism III has its own private, slightly rocky beach stretching for some 182m (597 ft.)—part of it is often nude. It lies a 15-minute drive east of Paradise Beach and a 10-minute walk west of Cardiffall.

Bedrooms are roomy and freshly decorated, with Jamaica's first-ever block of "swim-up" rooms. All swim-up rooms feature large marble tub-and-shower bathrooms with Jacuzzis and CD players. Single guests are paired up with a roommate of the same sex, or have to pay a single supplement.

Unique in Jamaica, the resort offers a circus workshop that features a flying trapeze, juggling, a trampoline "clinic," and various unicycle and bike-balancing acts. It's presented Monday to Saturday.

The food is quite decent—everything from Italian to Japanese to Jamaican. There is even a disco with a four-story water slide!

Runaway Bay, Jamaica, W.I. © 877/GO-SUPER in the U.S., or 876/973-4100. Fax 876/973-5402. www. superclubs.com. 225 units. Rates for 6 nights: winter US$2,220–US$4,029 double; off season US$1,740–US$3,714 double. Rates include all meals, drinks, and activities. AE, DC, DISC, MC, V. No children under age 18. **Amenities:** 5 restaurants; 6 bars; 3 large pools; disco; 3 tennis courts; fitness center; basketball court; volleyball; 3 Jacuzzis; sauna; kayaks; sailing; scuba diving; water-skiing; windsurfing; nonsmoking rooms; rooms for those with limited mobility. In room: A/C, TV, dataport, beverage maker, iron/ironing board, safe.

Runaway Bay Heart Hotel ✸ Value   This place wins hands-down as the bargain of the north coast. One of Jamaica's few training and service institutions, the club and its adjacent academy are operated by the government to provide a high level of training for young Jamaicans interested in the hotel trade. The helpful staff of both professionals and trainees offers the finest service of any hotel in the area. Runaway lies a 30-minute drive east of Paradise Beach and a 5-minute drive to Cardiffall. Free shuttles are offered only to Cardiffall.

The good-size rooms are bright and airy. Bathrooms have generous shelf space and shower stalls. The accommodations open onto private balconies with views of well-manicured tropical gardens or vistas of the bay and golf course. Guests enjoy having a drink in the piano bar (ever had a cucumber daiquiri?) before heading for the dining room, the Cardiff Hall Restaurant, which serves superb Jamaican and Continental dishes.

Ricketts Ave. (P.O. Box 98), Runaway Bay, St. Ann, Jamaica, W.I. © 876/973-2671. Fax 876/973-4704. www.runawayheart.com.jm. 56 units. Year-round US$110–US$135 double. Rates include MAP (breakfast and dinner). AE, DISC, MC, V. **Amenities:** Restaurant; bar; outdoor pool; gym; limited room service; babysitting; laundry service; nonsmoking rooms; rooms for those with limited mobility. In room: A/C, TV, kitchenette, hair dryer, iron/ironing board, safe.

Tamarind Tree Hotel ✸ Value   More and more frugal travelers are learning about this cozy enclave a short walk from a good sandy beach at Runaway Bay. Built in 1987, its white exterior with green accents is inviting. You're lodged either in the main building or in one of three cottages, all at very affordable prices. The bedrooms are simply but comfortably furnished. Five of the units are rather standard but the others are more attractively equipped and roomier. The cottages, which can accommodate up to six people, are the best deal of all. The rooms are carpeted, and 10 of them open onto their own private balconies. Each comes with a tiled bathroom with tub-and-shower combo. On-site is a little-known but good restaurant, The Bird Wing, serving international and Jamaican cuisine.

Runaway Bay, Jamaica, W.I. © 876/973-2678. Fax 876/973-5013. 25 units. Year-round US$55–US$65 double; US$150 cottage. MC, V. **Amenities:** Restaurant; bar; outdoor pool; limited room service; laundry service; nonsmoking rooms. In room: A/C, TV.

BEACHES & OUTDOOR ACTIVITIES

The two best beaches at Runaway Bay are **Paradise Beach** and **Cardiffall Lot Public Beach.** Both wide, white-sand strips are clean and well maintained—ideal spots for a picnic. If you're staying in Ocho Rios and want to escape the crowds, come here. There is a great natural beauty to this part of Jamaica, and many foreigners, especially Canadians, seek it out. You don't get a lot of facilities, however, so you'd better bring along whatever you need.

The waters are calm almost all year. Prevailing trade winds will keep you cool in the morning and late afternoon. Since there are no lifeguards, be careful, especially if you're with children.

Runaway Bay offers some of the best areas for **snorkeling** in Jamaica. The reefs are close to shore and swarming with marine life, including enormous schools of tropical fish such as blue chromis, triggerfish, small skate rays, and snapper. Since boats and fishing canoes can be a problem close to shore, go on a snorkeling excursion with the best diving facility at Runaway Bay: **Jamaica Dive Center,** at Club Ambience (© 876/973-4845), whose slogan is, "We Be Divin'." They take you to one of several protected reefs where the currents aren't dangerous, and where fishing boats are required to stay at least 183m (600 ft.) away from divers or snorkelers. The dive facility offers complete equipment rental and everything from one-tank dives to six-boat packages. A one-tank dive is US$42 and a two-tank dive costs US$75.

Jamaica's most complete **equestrian center** is the **Chukka Polo Club and Resort,** at Richmond Llandovery, St. Ann (© 876/972-2506), less than 6km (3¾ miles) east of Runaway Bay. A 1-hour trail ride costs US$30, while a 2-hour mountain ride goes for US$40. The most popular ride is a 3-hour beach jaunt that involves riding over trails to the sea, then swimming in the surf. The US$75 cost includes refreshments. A 6-hour beach ride, complete with picnic lunch, goes for US$130. Polo lessons are also available, costing US$50 for 30 minutes. A more recent feature is a mountain and sea adventure on a bike (90% of which is downhill). The 4-hour bike ride goes for US$50 and ends with a swim and some snorkeling.

SEEING THE SIGHTS

Columbus Park Museum, on Queens Highway, Discovery Bay (© 876/973-2135), is a large, open area between the main coast road and the sea at Discovery Bay. Just pull off the road and walk among the fantastic collection of exhibits; admission is free. There's everything from a canoe made from a solid piece of cottonwood (the way Arawaks did it more than 5 centuries ago) to a stone cross that was originally placed on the Barrett Estate (14km/8¾ miles east of Montego Bay) by Edward Barrett, brother of poet Elizabeth Barrett Browning. You'll see a tally, used to count bananas carried on men's heads from plantation to ship, as well as a planter's strongbox with a weighted lead base to prevent its theft. Other items are 18th-century cannons, a Spanish water cooler and calcifier, a fish pot made from bamboo, a corn husker, and a water wheel. Pimento trees, which produce allspice, dominate the park, which is open Monday to Friday 8am to 4pm, Saturday 8am to noon.

You can also visit the **Seville Great House,** Heritage Park (© 876/972-2191). Built in 1745 by the English, it contains a collection of artifacts once used by everybody from the Amerindians to African slaves. In all, you're treated to an exhibit of 5 centuries worth of Jamaican history. Modest for a great house, it has a wattle-and-daub construction. A small theater presents a 15-minute historical film about the house on request. It's open daily from 9am to 4pm; admission is US$4.

6 Port Antonio ⊙

Port Antonio, sometimes called the Jamaica of 100 years ago, is a verdant and sleepy seaport on the northeast coast, 101km (63 miles) northeast of Kingston. It's a mecca of the titled and the wealthy, including European royalty and stars like Whoopi Goldberg and Peter O'Toole.

This small, bustling town is like many on the island: clean but cluttered, with sidewalks around a market filled with vendors, and tin-roofed shacks competing with old Georgian and modern brick and concrete buildings. At the market, you can browse for local craftwork, spices, and fruits.

Travelers used to arrive by banana boat and stay at the Titchfield Hotel (which burned down). Captain Bligh landed here in 1793 with the first bread-fruit plants, and Port Antonio claims that the ones grown in this area are the best on the island. Visitors still arrive by water, but now it's in cruise ships that moor close to Navy Island, and the passengers come ashore just for the day.

Navy Island and the long-gone Titchfield Hotel were owned for a short time by Errol Flynn. The story is that after suffering damage to his yacht, he put into Kingston for repairs, visited Port Antonio by motorbike, fell in love with the area, and in due course acquired Navy Island (some say he won it in a bet). Later, he either lost or sold it and bought a nearby plantation, Comfort Castle, still owned by his widow, Patrice Wymore Flynn, who spends most of her time there. He was much loved and admired by the Jamaicans and was totally integrated into the community. They still talk of him in Port Antonio—his reputation for womanizing and drinking lives on.

We find Port Antonio one of the more relaxed retreats in Jamaica, certainly not as undiscovered as it was when William Randolph Hearst or J. P. Morgan visited, but a virtual Shangri-La compared to Ocho Rios or Montego Bay. It also has some of the finest beaches in Jamaica and has long been a center for some of the Caribbean's best deep-sea fishing. It's a good place to go to get away from it all.

ESSENTIALS

GETTING THERE   If you're going to Port Antonio, you will fly into the **Donald Sangster Airport** in Montego Bay or the **Norman Manley International Airport** in Kingston. Some hotels, particularly the larger resorts, will arrange for airport transfers from that point. Be sure to ask when you book. Port Antonio has its own small airfield. There are no regularly scheduled flights into the resort—only private charters.

You can rent a car for the 214km (133-mile) drive east along Route A1 (see "Getting Around" in the section "Essentials," at the beginning of this chapter), but we don't advise this 4-hour drive for safety's sake, regardless of which airport you fly into.

If you take a taxi, the typical one-way fare from Montego Bay is US$100, but always negotiate and agree upon a fare *before* you get into the cab.

MEDICAL FACILITIES   The **Port Antonio General Hospital** is at Naylor's Hill (© **876/993-2646**).

ACCOMMODATIONS

Despite its charms, Port Antonio is suffering increasingly from a lack of business as travelers are drawn to the more famous Negril, Ocho Rios, and Montego Bay. Many of the hotels are forced to fill up empty rooms with low-cost tour groups hailing from everywhere from Italy to Canada. Because of this, we've found that some of the hotels in the area are showing signs of wear and deterioration.

VERY EXPENSIVE

Trident Villas & Hotel 🌟🌟   This luxury hideaway is located on Allan Avenue, on the coast toward Frenchman's Cove. It sits regally above jagged coral cliffs with a seaside panorama. The hotel's main building is furnished with antiques and cooled by sea breezes. Your accommodations will be a studio cottage or tower, reached by a path through the gardens. In the cottages, a large bedroom with ample sitting area opens onto a private patio with a sea view. All units have ceiling fans, plenty of storage space, and tasteful Jamaican antiques and colorful chintzes. Beds are most comfortable, while bathrooms have combination shower/tubs. Trident has a horseshoe-shaped sandy beach cove at one end of its grounds, which is accessible by a path that meanders along a landscaped terrain. It's a strip of muddy-bottomed seafront that's not as appealing as a dip in the hotel pool. That pool is positioned near a graceful gazebo and sits above jagged rocks where the surf crashes and churns most of the day.

Men are required to wear jackets and ties at dinner, which is an excellent, multicourse, fixed-price meal; if you have dietary restrictions, make your requirements known early.

Rte. A4 (P.O. Box 119), Port Antonio, Jamaica, W.I. ℂ **800/330-8272** in the U.S., or 876/993-2602. Fax 876/993-2960. www.tridentjamaica.com. 26 units. Winter US$385 double, from US$620 suite; off season US$220 double, from US$340 suite. Rates include MAP (breakfast and dinner). AE, MC, V. **Amenities:** Restaurant; bar; outdoor pool; croquet; deep-sea fishing; scuba diving; snorkeling; limited room service; massage; babysitting; laundry service; rooms for those with limited mobility. *In room:* A/C, minibar, beverage maker, hair dryer, safe.

EXPENSIVE

Goblin Hill Villas at San San ℞   This green and sunny hillside—once said to shelter goblins—is now filled with Georgian-style vacation homes on San San Estate. The pool is surrounded by a vine-laced arbor, which lies just a stone's throw from an almost impenetrable forest. A long flight of steps leads down to the crescent-shaped sands of San San beach. This beach is now private, but guests of the hotel receive a pass. Everything has the aura of having last been fixed up in the 1970s, but the resort is still comfortable. The accommodations are town house–style; some have ceiling fans and king-size beds (some have twin beds), but none have phones. The generally roomy units are filled with handmade pine pieces, along with a split-level living and dining area with a fully equipped kitchen. All units have well-maintained bathrooms with shower/tub combinations. Housekeepers prepare and serve meals and attend to chores in the villas.

San San (P.O. Box 26), Port Antonio, Jamaica, W.I. ℂ **800/472-1148** or 876/925-8108. Fax 876/925-6248. www.goblinhill.com. 28 units. Winter US$110–US$195 1-bedroom villa, US$185–US$245 2-bedroom villa; off season US$90–US$165 1-bedroom villa, US$145–US$195 2-bedroom villa. AE, MC, V. **Amenities:** Bar; outdoor pool; 2 tennis courts; car rental; room service (8am–8pm); babysitting; laundry service; nonsmoking rooms; rooms for those with limited mobility. *In room:* A/C, TV, kitchenette, fridge, beverage maker (in some), no phone.

MODERATE

Jamaica Palace Hotel ℞   This stately mansion rises from a hillock surrounded by 2 tropically landscaped hectares (5 acres). It's not on the beach, but a free shuttle will take you to one of the best sandy beaches in the area, Frenchman Cove Beach. The public rooms are filled with furnishings and art from Europe, including a 2m (6½-ft.) Baccarat crystal candelabrum and a pair of Italian ebony-and-ivory chairs from the 15th century. Outside, the Palace offers white-marble columns, sun-filled patios and balconies, and an unusual 35m (115-ft.) pool shaped like Jamaica. Most accommodations are large, with 4m (13-ft.) ceilings and oversize marble bathrooms with tub and shower. Some, however, are rather small, though still comfortably appointed. Suites are individually furnished with crystal chandeliers, Persian rugs, and original works of art. All units have excellent beds, often sleigh beds. Both Continental and Jamaican food are served in the main dining room, with its lighted "water wall" sculpted from Jamaican cave stones. There is also a poolside cafe with barbecue, live dance and calypso bands, and a boutique.

Williamsfield (8km/5 miles east of Port Antonio; P.O. Box 277). (**876/993-7720.** Fax 876/993-7759. www.jamaicapalace.com. 80 units. Winter US$120–US$140 double, US$180–US$220 suite; off season US$100–US$120 double, US$160–US$200 suite. MAP (breakfast and dinner) for 2 people US$190. AE, MC, V. **Amenities:** 2 restaurants; bar; outdoor pool; beach shuttle; limited room service; babysitting; laundry service; nonsmoking rooms; rooms for those with limited mobility. *In room:* A/C, TV (US$6 extra per night), safe.

Rio Vista Resort Villas 🏝🏝 *Finds*   Featured in *Condé Nast Traveler,* this place is ideal for a luxurious vacation, a honeymoon, or even an off-the-record weekend. Six kilometers (3¾ miles) west of Port Antonio (most of the *luxe* properties lie to the east), Rio Vista is only 3km (2 miles) from the little local airstrip, nestled between the Rio Grande River and the Caribbean Sea. On a 4-hectare (10-acre) estate planted with tropical fruits, it offers handsomely furnished one- and two-bedroom cottages, plus a honeymoon villa with a river view. The setting is a garden of flowers, spices, and sweet-smelling herbs. Rooms have vaulted wooden ceilings and well-maintained tiled bathrooms, each with a shower. A housekeeper services each cottage and can assist with meals. Candlelit dinners can be arranged. Air-conditioning in summer costs US$10 extra.

St. Margarets Bay (P.O. Box 4). (**876/993-5444.** Fax 876/993-5445. www.riovistajamaica.com. 5 villas. Year-round US$110–US$120 for double; US$120–US$130 honeymoon villa; US$140–US$150 2-bedroom villa; US$1,200 5-night honeymoon package. MC, V. **Amenities:** Restaurant; bar; outdoor pool; rafting; limited room service; massage; laundry service; nonsmoking rooms. *In room:* A/C, TV, dataport, kitchenette, fridge, beverage maker, hair dryer, safe.

INEXPENSIVE

Hotel Mocking Bird Hill 🏝   A 10km (6¼-mile) drive east of Port Antonio, this inn lies a 5-minute drive from Frenchman's Cove Beach. In 1993, two imaginative women transformed the place into a blue-and-white enclave of good taste, reasonable prices, and ecological consciousness. Set about 180m (590 ft.) above the coastline on a hillside laden with tropical plants, the hotel attracts a clientele of mostly German and Dutch visitors, who revel in the artsy and ecologically conscious setting. The accommodations are simple but tasteful, with neatly kept shower-only bathrooms. Much of the establishment's interior, including its restaurant (Mille Fleurs—see below), is decorated with one of the owner's artworks. You can participate in rafting tours, day hikes, or classes in painting and papermaking, or you can just relax and enjoy a herbal massage or the sweeping views out over the Blue Mountains and the Jamaican coastline.

Mocking Bird Hill, North Coast Hwy. (east of Port Antonio), Port Antonio, Jamaica, W.I. (**876/993-7267.** Fax 876/993-7133. www.hotelmockingbirdhill.com. 10 units. Winter US$210–US$260 double; off season US$125–US$175. AE, MC, V. **Amenities:** Restaurant; bar; limited room service; laundry service; outdoor pool; nonsmoking rooms; rooms for those with limited mobility. *In room:* Ceiling fans, hair dryer, beverage maker, safe, no phone.

Jamaica Heights Resort 🏝 *Finds*   The funkiest, most amusing, and hippest guesthouse in town might be full of rock stars from Düsseldorf or up-and-coming filmmakers cranking out tomorrow's indie fave. The very worldly owner, Helmut Steiner, former professor of literature and philosophy in Berlin, and his wife, Charmaine, maintain this affordable but sophisticated retreat. It's set at the top of a rutted and very steep series of roads. The resort is not on a beach but provides transportation to two of the finest beach strips of sand at Port Antonio, Frenchman's Cove and San San.

Scattered amid the wedge-shaped 3-hectare (7½-acre) property are a half dozen buildings, each white-walled with shutters, gazebos, climbing vines, and a pavilion for meditating over views of the forested terrain that cascades down to Port Antonio's harbor. The garden sports exotic palms, a stream with its own waterfalls, the most elegant Ping-Pong pavilion in the world, and dozens of botanical oddities from around the world. The minimalist accommodations are spotlessly clean. Each has a four-poster bed and funky lighting fixtures, plus shower/tub combination bathrooms. Doors can be opened or closed to create suites with between two and four bedrooms.

Spring Bank Rd., Port Antonio, Jamaica, W.I. ⓒ 876/993-3305. Fax 876/993-3563. www.jamaicaheights.net. 8 units. US$60–US$75 double. No credit cards. **Amenities:** Restaurant; outdoor pool; watersports can be arranged; laundry service; nonsmoking rooms. *In room:* Ceiling fan, beverage maker, no phone.

DINING

All hotel restaurants welcome outside guests for dinner, but reservations are required.

Mille Fleurs 🏵🏵 CARIBBEAN   This restaurant is terraced into a verdant hillside about 180m (590 ft.) above sea level with sweeping views over the Jamaican coastline and the faraway harbor of Port Antonio. Sheltered from the frequent rains, but open on the side for maximum access to cooling breezes, it features candlelit dinners, well-prepared food, and lots of New Age charm. Lunches include sandwiches, salads, grilled fish platters, and soups. At night, you might feast on fresh lobster or tender lamb and beef dishes, even savory rabbit or smoked marlin. The restaurant has been praised by *Gourmet* magazine for its dishes. You may want to try the coconut-and-garlic soup, and the fish with spicy mango-shrimp sauce is a specialty. Breads and most jams are made on the premises. Two dishes are vegetarian.

In the Hotel Mocking Bird Hill, North Coast Hwy. ⓒ 876/993-7267. Reservations recommended. Lunch platters US$10–US$30; main courses US$19–US$40. AE, MC, V. Daily 8:30–10am, noon–2pm, and 7–9:30pm.

Panorama INTERNATIONAL/JAMAICAN   One of the finest dining spots in Port Antonio offers a sweeping view of the rugged coastline, with great sunsets. Specialties include jerk chicken, jerk pork, grilled lobster, and Creole fish. Depending on who's in the kitchen, the food here can be quite satisfactory, though once in a while, especially off season, the cuisine might be a bit of a letdown. The club also offers entertainment, with a calypso band during the week.

In the Fern Hill Club Hotel, Mile Gully Rd. ⓒ 876/993-7374. Reservations recommended. Main courses US$8–US$10 lunch, US$10–US$25 dinner. AE, DISC, MC, V. Daily 7:30am–10pm. Head east on Allan Ave.

Trident Hotel Restaurant 🏵 INTERNATIONAL/JAMAICAN   The elegant Trident Hotel Restaurant serves meals that evoke the Jamaica of the '50s. The cuisine is always prepared with first-class ingredients, though the setting and the white-glove service are generally more memorable than the food. The high-pitched wooden roof set on white stonewalls holds several ceiling fans that gently stir the air. The antique tables are set with old china, English silver, and Port Royal pewter. The formally dressed waiters will help you choose your wine and whisper the name of each course as they serve it. The five-course dinner menu changes daily but might include a Jamaican salad, mahimahi with mayonnaise-and-mustard sauce, steak with broccoli and sautéed potatoes, and for dessert, Peach Melba and Blue Mountain coffee with Tia Maria, a Jamaican liqueur.

In Trident Villas & Hotel, Rte. A4. ⓒ 876/993-2602. Reservations required. Jackets required for men. Fixed-price dinner US$44. AE, MC, V. Daily 7:30am–9:30pm. Head east on Allan Ave.

Moments **A Dip in the Blue Lagoon**

The young Brooke Shields made the film *The Blue Lagoon* in a calm, protected cove 16km (10 miles) east of Port Antonio. The water is so deep, nearly 6m (20 ft.) or so, that it turns a cobalt blue; there's almost no more scenic spot in all of Jamaica. The Blue Lagoon, with its small, intimate beach, is a great place for a picnic (you can pick up jerk pork at various shacks along the Boston Beach area).

HITTING THE BEACH

Port Antonio has several white-sand beaches, including the famous **San San Beach,** which has recently gone private. Guests of certain hotels are admitted with a pass; otherwise the fee is US$4.

Boston Beach is free, and it often has light surfing; there are picnic tables as well as a restaurant and snack bar. On your way here, stop and get the makings for a picnic lunch at the most famous area for peppery jerk pork and chicken on Jamaica. These rustic shacks also sell the much rarer jerk sausage. The beach is 18km (11 miles) east of Port Antonio and just east of the Blue Lagoon.

Also free is **Fairy Hill Beach** (Winnifred), with no changing rooms or showers. **Frenchman's Cove Beach** attracts a chic crowd to its white-sand beach combined with a freshwater stream. Nonguests are charged US$3.

SPORTS & OTHER OUTDOOR PURSUITS

DEEP-SEA FISHING   Northern Jamaican waters are world renowned for their game fish, including mahimahi, wahoo, blue and white marlin, sailfish, tarpon, barracuda, and bonito. The **Jamaica International Fishing Tournament** and **Jamaica International Blue Marlin Team Tournaments** run concurrently at Port Antonio every October. Most major hotels from Port Antonio to Montego Bay have deep-sea-fishing facilities, and there are many charter boats.

A 12m-long (39-ft.) **sport-fishing boat** (© 876/993-3209) with a tournament rig is available for charter rental. Taking out up to six passengers at a time, the charge is US$700 per half-day or US$1,200 per day, with crew, bait, tackle, and soft drinks included. It docks at Port Antonio's Marina, off West Palm Avenue, in the center of town. Call for bookings.

RAFTING   Although it's not exactly adventurous (it's a tame and safe outing), this is the best rafting experience on the island and the most fun. Rafting started on the Rio Grande as a means of transporting bananas from the plantations to the waiting freighters. In 1871, a Yankee skipper, Lorenzo Dow Baker, decided that a seat on one of the rafts was better than walking, but it was not until Errol Flynn arrived that the rafts became popular as a tourist attraction. Flynn used to hire the crafts for his friends, and he encouraged the rafters to race down the Rio Grande, betting on the winners. Now that bananas are transported by road, the raft skipper makes one or maybe two trips a day down the waterway. If you want to take a trip, contact **Rio Grande Tours,** Berrydale (© 876/913-5434).

The rafts, some 10m-long (33-ft.) and only 2m-wide (6½-ft.), are propelled by stout bamboo poles. There's a raised double seat about two-thirds of the way back. The skipper stands in the front, trousers rolled up to his knees, the water washing his feet, and guides the craft down the lively river, about 13km (8 miles) between steep hills covered with coconut palms, banana plantations, and flowers, through limestone cliffs pitted with caves, through the "Tunnel of Love," a narrow cleft in the rocks, then on to wider, gentler water.

Trips last 2 to 2½ hours and are offered from 9am to 5pm daily at a cost of US$45 per raft, which holds two passengers. A fully insured driver will take you in your rented car for a US$15 fee to the starting point at Berrydale or Grant's Level, where you board your raft. If you feel like it, take a picnic lunch, but bring enough for the skipper, too, who will regale you with lively stories of life on the river.

SNORKELING & SCUBA DIVING   The best outfitter is **Lady Godiva's Dive Shop** in Blue Lagoon (© 876/993-8988), 11km (6¾ miles) from Port Antonio. Full dive equipment is available. Technically, you can snorkel off most of the beaches in Port Antonio, but you're likely to see much more further offshore. The best spot is Winnifred on the other side of Dragon Bay. The reef is extremely active and full of a lot of exciting marine life. Lady Godiva offers two excursions daily to this spot for US$21 per person, including snorkeling equipment for the day.

EXPLORING THE AREA

Athenry Gardens and Cave of Nonsuch   It's an easy 20-minute drive from
Port Antonio and an easy walk to see the stalagmites, stalactites, fossilized marine life, and evidence of Arawak civilization in Nonsuch. The cave is 1.5 million years old, and you can explore its underground beauty by following railed stairways and concrete walkways on a 30-minute walk. The place is dramatically lit. Although the United States and Europe have far greater cave experiences, this is as good as it gets in Jamaica. From the Athenry Gardens, there are panoramic views over the island and the sea. The gardens are filled with coconut palms, flowers, and trees, and complete guided tours are given.

Portland. © 876/993-3740 or 876/779-7174. Admission (including guide for gardens and cave) US$6 adults, US$3 children 11 and under. Daily 10am–4pm. From Harbour St. in Port Antonio, turn south in front of the Anglican church onto Red Hassel Rd. and proceed approximately 2km (1¼ miles) to Breastworks community (fork in road); take the left fork, cross a narrow bridge, go immediately left after the bridge, and proceed approximately 6km (3¾ miles) to Anthenry Estates.

PORT ANTONIO AFTER DARK

The **Tree Bar** draws a fashionable crowd to the grounds of Goblin Hill Villas at San San (© 876/925-8108), high on a hill commanding a panoramic view of 5 hectares (12 acres). The aptly named bar is wrapped around huge ficus trees, whose mammoth aerial roots dangle over the drinking area. Giant-leafed pothos climb down the trunks. It's a sort of "Me Tarzan, You Jane" kind of place.

Go at your own risk to the infamous **Roof Club,** 11 West St. (no phone). The most crowded and animated nightclub in Port Antonio, it lies one floor above street level in a boxy-looking industrial building in the heart of town. Inside, the venue is earthy, raunchy, crowded, and boozy, with enough secondhand ganja smoke to get virtually anyone high. Recorded (and more rarely, live) reggae and soca music blares at high volumes. Expect a neopsychedelic decor of mirrors, UV lighting, and free-form Day-Glo artwork. A visit here is not for the squeamish or the faint-hearted, and it's a good idea to come with a friend and/or ally. Try to stay relatively sober, keep your wits about you, and enjoy the slow-moving gyrations of ordinary folks who—sometimes with the help of a spliff or two—get involved in the beat of the music and groove accordingly. Beers cost from US$2 each. It's open nightly from around 6pm, but most of the genuine hanging out and crowding happens after 11pm, especially from Thursday through Sunday.

7 Kingston & Vicinity

Kingston, the largest English-speaking city in the Caribbean, is the capital and cultural, industrial, and financial center of Jamaica. It's home to more than 750,000 people, including those living on the plains between Blue Mountain and the sea.

The buildings here are a mixture of the modern, graceful, old, and just plain ramshackle. It's a busy city, as you might expect, with a natural harbor that's the seventh largest in the world. The University of the West Indies has its campus on the edge of the city.

Few other cities in the Caribbean carry as many negative connotations for North American travelers as Kingston, thanks to widely publicized, and sometimes exaggerated, reports of violent crime. Marry that with urban congestion, potholed roads, and difficult-to-decipher road signs that make it hard to navigate, and you've got a bad reputation.

But if you're an urban dweller who copes with everyday life in, say, New York, Atlanta, or Los Angeles, you know how to deal with city life, and Kingston doesn't have to be that scary. It offers resources and charms that can't be found anywhere else. It is here that Jamaica is at its most urban and confident, its most witty, its most exciting, and its most challenging. No other place in Jamaica offers as many singles bars, dance clubs, and cultural outlets—it's the nation's creative cauldron. If you're truly interested in Jamaican culture, Kingston can be very stimulating, as it's very far removed from the tourist-oriented economies of Negril, Ocho Rios, and Montego Bay.

We've carefully screened the recommendations contained within this guidebook, eliminating any that lie within the most dangerous neighborhoods. So keep an open mind about Kingston—it can be a lot of fun and very exciting.

ESSENTIALS

GETTING THERE   See "Getting There," in section 1 of this chapter, for details on the airlines that serve Kingston's international airport.

GETTING AROUND   Because Kingston is a rather confusing place to negotiate, many visitors rely on taxis.

MEDICAL FACILITIES   The **University Hospital** is at Mona (© **876/927-1620**). **Moodie's Pharmacy** is in the New Kingston Shopping Centre (© **876/926-4174**).

ACCOMMODATIONS

The Jamaica Pegasus 𝒸 A favorite with business travelers, the Jamaica Pegasus barely outclasses its nearest rival, the Hilton, in a close race. It's located in the banking area of Kingston, which is also a fine residential area. After a major renovation, the hotel is now better than ever and is the site of many conventions and social events. The hotel combines British style with Jamaican warmth, arranging watersports and sightseeing. Each of the well-furnished bedrooms is of moderate size and contains bathrooms with combination tubs and showers and balconies opening onto mountain, sea, or cityscapes. The decorating, in dark tones, often brown, makes you yearn for the lighter pastel look of most Caribbean hotel bedrooms. Several floors of luxuriously appointed suites form the Knutsford Club, which offers special executive services.

The 4pm tea service is a bit of a social event among some residents. The premier restaurant is The Talk of the Town. The Brasserie is the hotel's informal restaurant that opens onto the swimming pool, where a splashing fountain cools the air. It adjoins a circular bar near the pool, at which occasional barbecues are prepared.

81 Knutsford Blvd., Kingston 5. ℂ **876/926-3690.** Fax 876/929-5855. www.jamaicapegasus.com. 300 units. Year-round US$140–US$220 double; US$250 junior suite; US$300 royal suite. AE, DC, MC, V. **Amenities:** 3 restaurants; 2 bars; outdoor pool; gym; business center; 24-hr. room service; laundry service; dry cleaning; nonsmoking rooms; rooms for those with limited mobility. *In room:* A/C, TV, dataport, minibar, hair dryer, safe.

Terra Nova Hotel 𝑅 *Finds*   This house is on the western edge of New Kingston, near West Kings House Road. Built in 1924 for a young bride, it was converted into a hotel in 1959. It was the birthplace of the well-known hotelier and Island Records mogul, Chris Blackwell. Set in 1 hectare (2½ acres) of gardens with a backdrop of greenery and mountains, it's now one of the best small Jamaican hotels, although the rooms are rather basic and not at all suited for those who want a resort ambience. Most of the bedrooms are in a new wing. All units have neatly kept bathrooms with shower units. The Spanish-style El Dorado Room, with a marble floor and wide windows, serves local and international food.

17 Waterloo Rd., Kingston 10, Jamaica, W.I. ℂ **876/926-2211.** Fax 876/929-4933. 35 units. Year-round US$120–US$135 double. AE, MC, V. **Amenities:** Restaurant; coffee shop; bar; outdoor pool; exercise room; limited room service; nonsmoking rooms; rooms for those with limited mobility. *In room:* A/C, TV, dataport, minibar (in some), beverage maker, hair dryer, iron/ironing board, safe.

IN NEARBY PORT ROYAL

Morgans Harbour Hotel   On the premises of this yachtie favorite is a 200-year-old redbrick building once used to melt pitch for His Majesty's navy, a swimming area defined by docks and buoys, and a series of wings whose eaves are accented with hints of gingerbread. Set on 9 hectares (22 acres) of flat and rocky seashore, the resort contains the largest marina in Kingston, plus a breezy waterfront restaurant and a popular bar (where ghost stories about the old Port Royal seem especially lurid as the liquor flows on Friday night). Longtime residents claim that the ghosts of soldiers killed by a long-ago earthquake are especially visible on hot and very calm days, when British formations seem to march out of the sea.

The well-furnished bedrooms are laid out in an 18th-century Chippendale-Jamaican style. Medium-size bathrooms are tidily maintained, each with a shower bath.

Port Royal, Kingston 1, Jamaica, W.I. ℂ **800/44-UTELL** in the U.S., or 876/967-8030. Fax 876/967-8073. www.hotelbook.com. 50 units. Year-round US$160 double; US$184 suite. AE, DISC, MC, V. Take the public ferryboat that departs every 2 hr. from near Victoria Pier on Ocean Blvd.; many visitors arrive by car or taxi. **Amenities:** Restaurant; bar; 2 outdoor pools; limited room service; laundry service; nonsmoking rooms; rooms for those with limited mobility. *In room:* A/C, TV, dataport, minibar, beverage maker, hair dryer, iron/ironing board, safe.

DINING

Norma's on the Terrace 𝑅𝑅 JAMAICAN   This is the creation of Jamaica's most famous businesswoman, Norma Shirley, purveyor of food to stylish audiences as far away as Miami. It's housed beneath the wide porticos of the gallery surrounding Kingston's most famous monument, Devon House. Ms. Shirley has taken the old, woefully dusty gardens and transformed them into something you'd find on a manicured English estate. Menus change with the season, but usually reflect Ms. Shirley's penchant for creative adaptations of her native Jamaican cuisine. Stellar examples include Jamaican chowder with crabmeat, shrimp, conch, and lobster; grilled whole red snapper encrusted with herbs and served with a thyme-and-caper sauce; and grilled smoked pork loin in a teriyaki/ginger sauce, served with caramelized apples.

In Devon House, 26 Hope Rd. ⓒ 876/968-5488. Reservations recommended. Main courses US$30–US$80. AE, DISC, MC, V. Mon–Sat 10am–10pm.

Redbones the Blues Café ★★ *Finds* JAMAICAN   The name alone lured us to this elegant place, which is the only restaurant in Kingston with cuisine as good as Norma's on the Terrace. All aglow in yellow and peach hues, Redbones is in a former Spanish colonial house. You're greeted with pictures of jazz greats on the wall, everybody from Billie Holiday to Louis Armstrong. A cozy bar, its ceiling studded with records, is installed in someone's former bedroom. Owners Evan and Betsy Williams give standard Jamaican dishes a new twist. Ask for *bammy,* a cassava dish crowned with sautéed shrimp, or a platter of stuffed crab backs, a delectable selection on a tri-color salad. A spinach callaloo with cream cheese is encased in a divine strudel. Seafood pasta is laden with shrimp, lobster, and salmon in a creamy coconut sauce. The best item on the menu is spicy lamb chops in a guava glaze. Live jazz or something is always going on.

21 Braemar Ave. ⓒ 876/978-6091. Reservations required. Main courses J$750–J$1,500 (US$12–US$24). AE, MC, V. Mon–Fri 1–11pm, Mon–Sat 6:30–10pm.

HITTING THE BEACH

You don't really come to Kingston for beaches, but there are some here. To the southwest of the sprawling city are black-sandy **Hellshire Beach** and **Fort Clarence.** Both of these beaches are very popular with the locals on weekends. Both have changing rooms, heavy security, and numerous food stands. The reggae concerts at Fort Clarence are legendary on the island.

Just past Fort Clarence, the fisherman's beach at **Naggo Head** is an even hipper destination, or so Kingston beach buffs claim. After a swim in the refreshing waters, try out one of the food stands selling "fry fish" and *bammy* (cassava bread). The closest beach to the city (although it's not very good) is **Lime Cay,** a little island on the outskirts of Kingston Harbour, reached after a short boat ride from Morgan's Harbour at Port Royal.

SEEING THE SIGHTS

Even if you're staying at Ocho Rios or Port Antonio, you may want to visit Kingston for the sights or to make a trip to nearby Port Royal and Spanish Town.

From Kingston, you can make excursions into the Blue Mountains. See the section "The Blue Mountains," below.

IN TOWN

One of the major attractions, **Devon House,** 26 Hope Rd. (ⓒ 876/929-6602), was built in 1881 by George Stiebel, a Jamaican who made his fortune mining in Latin America, becoming one of the first black millionaires in the Caribbean. A striking classical building, the house has been restored to its original beauty by the Jamaican National Trust. The grounds contain crafts shops, boutiques, two restaurants, shops that sell the best ice cream in Jamaica (in exotic fruit flavors), and a bakery and pastry shop with Jamaican puddings and desserts. The main house also displays furniture of various periods and styles. Admission to the main house is US$5; hours are Monday to Saturday from 9:30am to 4:30pm. Admission to the grounds (the shops and restaurants) is free.

Almost next door to Devon House are the sentried gates of **Jamaica House,** residence of the prime minister, a fine, white-columned building set well back from the road.

Continuing along Hope Road, at the crossroads of Lady Musgrave and King's House roads, turn left and you'll see a gate on the left with its own personal traffic light. This leads to **King's House,** the official residence of the governor-general of Jamaica, the queen's representative on the island. The outside and front lawn of the gracious residence, set in 80 hectares (198 acres) of well-tended parkland, is sometimes open for viewing Monday to Friday from 10am to 5pm. The secretarial offices are housed next door in an old wooden building set on brick arches. In front of the house is a gigantic banyan tree in whose roots, legend says, *duppies* (ghosts) take refuge when they're not living in the cotton trees.

National Library of Jamaica (formerly the West India Reference Library), Institute of Jamaica, 12 East St. (© **876/967-2494**), a storehouse of the history, culture, and traditions of Jamaica and the Caribbean, is the finest working library devoted to West Indian studies in the world. It has the most comprehensive, up-to-date, and balanced collection of materials on the region, including books, newspapers, photographs, maps, and prints. It's open Monday to Thursday from 9am to 5pm, Friday from 9am to 4pm.

Bob Marley Museum, 56 Hope Rd. (© **876/927-9152**), is the most-visited sight in Kingston, but if you're not a Marley fan, it may not mean much to you. The clapboard house with its garden and high surrounding wall was the famous reggae singer's home and recording studio until his death on May 11, 1981. You can tour the house and view assorted Marley memorabilia, and you may even catch a glimpse of his children, who often frequent the grounds. Hours are Monday to Saturday from 9:30am to 4pm. Admission is J$400 (US$6.40) for adults, J$300 (US$4.80) ages 13 to 18, J$200 (US$3.20) ages 4 to 12. It's reached by bus no. 70 or 75 from Halfway Tree, but take a cab to save yourself the hassle of dealing with Kingston public transport.

IN PORT ROYAL

From West Beach Dock in Kingston, a ferry ride of 20 to 30 minutes will take you to Port Royal, whose name in pirate lore conjures up visions of swashbuckling pirates led by Henry Morgan, swilling grog in harbor taverns. This was once one of the largest trading centers of the New World, with a reputation for being the wickedest city on earth. Blackbeard stopped here regularly on his Caribbean trips. But it all came to an end on June 7, 1692, when a third of the town disappeared underwater after a devastating earthquake. Nowadays, Port Royal, with its memories of the past, has been designated by the government for redevelopment as a tourist destination.

Today Port Royal is a small fishing village at the end of the Palisades strip. Some 2,000 residents live here with what many locals claim are a "lot of ghosts." Port Royal's seafaring traditions continue, and it's known for its seafood and ramshackle and much-battered architecture of yesterday. Once there were six forts here with a total of 145 guns, some of which can be seen today. Only Fort Charles still stands, however.

Fort Charles (© **876/967-8438**), the only remaining fort of Port Royal's original six, has withstood attack, earthquake, fire, and hurricane. Built in 1656 and later strengthened by Morgan for his own purposes, the fort was expanded and further armed in the 1700s, until its firepower boasted more than 100 cannons, covering both the land and the sea approaches. In 1779, Britain's naval hero, Horatio Lord Nelson, was commander of the fort and trod the wooden walkway inside the western parapet as he kept watch for the French invasion fleet. Scale models of the fort and ships of past eras are on display. The fort is open daily from 9am to 5pm; admission is J$100 (US$1.60) for adults, J$50 (US80¢) for visitors under age 19.

Part of the complex, **Giddy House,** once the Royal Artillery storehouse, is another example of what the earth's movements can do. Walking across the tilted floor is an eerie and strangely disorienting experience.

IN SPANISH TOWN

From 1662 to 1872, Spanish Town (19km/12 miles west of Kingston on A1) was the capital of the island. Originally founded by the Spaniards as Villa de la Vega, it was sacked by Cromwell's men in 1655, and all traces of Roman Catholicism were obliterated. The English cathedral, surprisingly retaining a Spanish name, **St. Jago de la Vega** (© **876/986-4405**), was built in 1666 and rebuilt after being destroyed by a hurricane in 1712. As you drive into the town from Kingston, the ancient cathedral catches your eye with its brick tower and two-tiered wooden steeple, which was not added until 1831. Since the cathedral was built on the foundation and remains of the old Spanish church, it is half English and half Spanish, and displays two distinct styles: Romanesque and Gothic. Of cruciform design and built mostly of brick, it's one of the most interesting buildings on the island. The black-and-white marble stones of the aisles are interspersed with ancient tombstones, and the walls are heavy with marble memorials that almost chronicle Jamaica's history, dating back as far as 1662.

After visiting the cathedral, walk 3 blocks north along White Church Street to Constitution Street and the **Town Square.** This little square is surrounded by towering royal palms. On the west side is old **King's House,** gutted by fire in 1925, although the facade has been restored. This was the residence of Jamaica's British governors until 1872, when the capital was transferred to Kingston.

Beyond the house is the **Jamaica People's Museum of Craft & Technology,** Old King's House, Constitution Square (© **876/907-0322**), open Monday to Thursday from 9:30am to 4:30pm and Friday 9:30am to 3:30pm. Admission is J$100 (US$1.60) for adults, J$40 (US65¢) for children under 18. The garden contains examples of old farm machinery, an old water-mill wheel, a hand-turned sugar mill, a fire engine, and more. An outbuilding houses a museum of crafts and technology, together with a number of smaller agricultural implements. In the small archaeological museum are old prints, models, and maps of the town's grid layout from the 1700s.

The streets around the old Town Square contain many fine Georgian town houses intermixed with tin-roofed shacks. Nearby is the **market,** so busy in the morning that you'll find it difficult, almost dangerous, to pass through. It provides, however, a bustling view of Jamaican life.

SHOPPING

Downtown Kingston, the old part of the town, is centered around **Sir William Grant Park,** formerly Victoria Park, a showpiece of lawns, lights, and fountains. Covered arcades lead off from King Street, and everywhere are teeming masses of people going about their business. There are some beggars and the inevitable hucksters who sidle up and offer "hot stuff, mon," frequently highly polished brass lightly dipped in gold and offered at as high prices as real gold.

For many years, the richly evocative paintings of Haiti were viewed as the most valuable contribution to Caribbean arts. There is on Jamaica, however, a rapidly growing perception of itself as one of the artistic leaders of the Third World. An articulate core of Caribbean critics is focusing the attention of the art world on the unusual, eclectic, and sometimes politically motivated paintings produced here.

Frame Centre Gallery, 10 Tangerine Place (© **876/926-4644**), is one of the most important art galleries on Jamaica. Its founder and guiding force, Guy McIntosh, is widely respected today as a patron of the Jamaican arts. There are three viewing areas and a varied collection of more than 300 works.

Kingston Crafts Market, at the west end of Harbour Street (reached via Straw Avenue, Drummer's Lane, or Cheapside), is a large, covered area of small stalls, selling all kinds of island crafts: wooden plates and bowls; pepper pots made from *mahoe* (the national wood of the island); straw hats, mats, and baskets; batik shirts; banners for wall decoration, inscribed with the Jamaican coat-of-arms; and wood masks with elaborately carved faces. You should bargain a bit, and vendors will take something off the price, but not very much.

The **Shops at Devon House,** 26 Hope Rd. (© **876/929-6602**), ring the borders of a 200-year-old courtyard once used by slaves and servants. It's associated with one of the most beautiful and historic mansions on Jamaica, a building owned by the Jamaican National Trust. On-site is a mellow old restaurant and pub, **The Grog Shop.** The most important shop is **Things Jamaican,** showcasing the crafts of the country and carrying a food section that features island-made sauces and spices. **Wessi Art** exhibits locally made ceramics, and **Jamaican Juice** sells natural and organic juices made from island-grown fruits. **Cooyaa** sells T-shirts and other memorabilia inspired by the career of Bob Marley and other reggae artists. The latest opening is an Internet cafe, which also offers a piano bar.

8 The Blue Mountains ★★★

Just a short drive north of Kingston is some of the most varied and unusual topography in the Caribbean, a beautiful mountain range laced with rough rivers, streams, and waterfalls. The 78,000-hectare (192,660-acre) **Blue Mountain–John Crow Mountain National Park** is maintained by the Jamaican government. The mountainsides are covered with coffee fields, producing a blended version that's among the leading exports of Jamaica. For the nature enthusiast, the mountains reveal a complex series of ecosystems that change radically as you climb from sea level into the fog-shrouded peaks.

The most popular, the most scenic, and our favorite climb begins at **Whitfield Hall** (© 876/927-0986), a high-altitude hostel and coffee estate about 10km (6¼ miles) north of the hamlet of Mavis Bank. Reaching the **summit of Blue Mountain Peak** (900m/2,952 ft. above sea level) requires about 3½ hours, each way. Of course, there are much shorter variations if you don't want to see "everything" (see below). En route, hikers pass through acres of coffee plantations and forest, where temperatures are cooler than you might expect, and where high humidity encourages thick vegetation. Along the way, watch for an amazing array of bird life, including hummingbirds, many species of warblers, rufous-throated solitaires, yellow-bellied sapsuckers, and Greater Antillean pewees.

Dress in layers and bring bottled water. If you opt for a 2am departure in anticipation of watching the sunrise from atop the peak, carry a flashlight as well. Sneakers are usually adequate, although many climbers bring their hiking boots. Be aware that even during the "dry" season (Dec–Mar), rainfall is common.

During the "rainy" season (the rest of the year), these peaks can get up to 3¾m (150 in.) of rainfall a year, and fogs and mists are frequent.

At no point do we recommend that you hike alone in the Blue Mountains, even if you're an experienced hiker. Weather conditions can change rapidly, and hiking maps are in general very poor. Since there are so few discernible landmarks, it is easy to lose your way.

Security is a major concern for an unaccompanied hiker, especially for those hiking on the Kingston side of the mountain. A guide will not only clear an overgrown path for you, but may keep you out of harm's way. Bandits might rob you and then disappear into the vast wilderness of the Blue Mountains, where they are hard, if not impossible, to track down. If you appeal to local authorities, you will probably face indifference and a belated suggestion that "you should have used a guide." A better bet involves engaging one of Kingston's best-known specialists in eco-sensitive tours, **Sunventure Tours,** 30 Balmoral Ave., Kingston 10 (© **876/960-6685**). The staff here can always arrange an individualized tour for you or your party, but offers a mainstream roster of choices as well. The **Blue Mountain Sunrise Tour** involves a camp-style overnight in one of the most remote and inaccessible areas of Jamaica. For US$100 per person, participants are picked up at their Kingston hotels, driven to an isolated ranger station, Wildflower Lodge, that's accessible only via four-wheel-drive vehicle, in anticipation of a two-stage hike that begins at 2pm. A simple mountaineer's supper is served at 6pm around a campfire at a ranger station near Portland Gap. At 3am, climbers hike by moonlight and flashlight to a mountaintop aerie that was selected for its view of the 5am sunrise over the Blue Mountains. Climbers stay aloft until around noon that day, then head back down the mountain and return to their hotels by 4pm. A 4-hour trek, costing from US$25 to US$30 per person, can also be arranged.

Another popular offering from the same company involves an excursion from Kingston **Y's Waterfall** on the Black River, in southern Jamaica's Elizabeth Parish. Participants meet in Kingston at 6:30am for a transfer to a raft and boating party near the hamlet of Lacovia, and an all-day waterborne excursion to a region of unusual ecological interest. Depending on the number of participants, fees range from US$75 to US$100 per person, including lunch.

Blue Mountain Bike Tours (© **876/974-7075**) offers all-downhill bike tours through the Blue Mountains—you peddle only about a half dozen times on this several-mile trip. Visitors are driven to the highest navigable point in the Blue Mountains, where they are provided bikes and protective gear. Breakfast, lunch, snacks, and lots of information about coffee, local foliage, and history are provided. The cost is about US$90 per person. The tours run Monday to Saturday.

ACCOMMODATIONS

Strawberry Hill 🌟🌟 *Finds*   Music-industry mogul turned hotelier extraordinaire Chris Blackwell worked here to re-create an idealized version of Jamaica that he remembered from his childhood. The setting is a former coffee plantation in the Blue Mountains, on precariously sloping rainforest terrain 930m (3,050 ft.) above the sea. Views from its terraces overlook the capital's twinkling lights. Eco-sensitive and fully contained, the resort has its own power and water-purification system, a small-scale spa, and elaborate botanical gardens. One former guest described this exclusive resort as a "home away from home for five-star Robinson Crusoes." Maps and/or guides are provided for tours of nearby coffee plantations, hiking and mountain biking through the Blue Mountains, and tours by night or by day of the urban attractions of nearby Kingston.

Accommodations are lavishly nostalgic, draped in bougainvillea and Victorian-inspired gingerbread, and outfitted with gracious mahogany furniture like that of a 19th-century Jamaican great house. Local craftspeople fashioned the cottages and furnished them with canopied four-poster beds and louvered mahogany windows. The elegant bathrooms, each designed in an artfully old-fashioned motif, come with shower/tub combinations. The food served in the hotel's glamorous restaurant is good enough to draw foodies from throughout eastern Jamaica.

Irish Town, Blue Mountains, Jamaica, W.I. ② **800/OUTPOST** in the U.S., or 876/944-8400. Fax 876/944-8408. www.strawberryhillresort.com. 12 units. Winter US$335 double, US$385 junior suite, US$675 1-bedroom villa, US$775 2-bedroom villa; off season US$275 double, US$355 junior suite, US$575 1-bedroom villa, US$675 2-bedroom villa. AE, DISC, MC, V. Guests are personally escorted to the hotel in a customized van or via a 7-min. helicopter ride. It's a 50-min. drive from the Kingston airport or 30 min. via mountain roads from the center of the city. **Amenities:** Restaurant; bar; outdoor pool; spa with hydrotherapy facilities and massage; sauna; bike rental; limited room service; babysitting; laundry service; nonsmoking rooms; rooms for those with limited mobility. *In room:* TV (on request), kitchenette, minibar, beverage maker, hair dryer, iron/ironing board, safe.

DINING

The Gap Café & Gift Shoppe ⓚ *Finds* JAMAICAN   The location is 1,260m (4,132 ft.) above sea level in the mountains overlooking Newcastle, with vistas of Kingston and the surrounding hills; Ian Fleming wrote parts of *Dr. No* in the house. The Blue Mountain coffee alone is worth the visit, as it's individually ground and brewed as you sit back taking in the scenery. You can also partake of curry or sautéed shrimp, and our favorite dish, pasta with jerk chicken. The chef is quite proud—and rightly so—of his crab backs, as well.

Main Rd., Harwar Gap in the Blue Mountains, John Crow Mountain National Park. ② **876/997-3032.** Main courses J$550–J$750 (US$8.80–US$12). MC, V. Mon–Fri 9am–5pm; Sat–Sun 10am–6pm.

Martinique

With beautiful white-sand beaches and a culture full of French flair, Martinique is part of the Lesser Antilles and lies in the semitropical zone; its western shore faces the Caribbean, and its eastern shore fronts the more turbulent Atlantic. The surface of the island is only 1,088 sq. km (424 sq. miles)—81km (50 miles) at its longest point and 34km (21 miles) at its widest point.

The terrain is mountainous, especially in the rainforested northern part, where the volcano Mount Pelée rises to a height of 1,397m (4,583 ft.). In the center of the island, the mountains are smaller, with Carbet Peak reaching a 1,188m (3,897-ft.) summit. The high hills rising among the peaks or mountains are called *mornes.* The southern part of Martinique has big hills that reach peaks of 350m (1,148 ft.) at Vauclin and 420m (1,378 ft.) at Diamant. The irregular coastline of the island has five bays, dozens of coves, and miles of sandy beaches. Almost a third of the island's year-round population of 360,000 lives in the capital and largest city, Fort-de-France.

The climate is relatively mild, with the average temperature in the 75°F to 85°F (24°C–29°C) range. At higher elevations, it's considerably cooler. The island is cooled by a wind the French called *alizé,* and rains are frequent but don't last very long. Late August to November is the rainy season. April through September are the hottest months.

The early Carib peoples, who gave Columbus such a hostile reception, called Martinique "the island of flowers," and indeed it has remained so. The lush vegetation includes hibiscus, poinsettias, bougainvillea, coconut palms, and mango trees. Almost any fruit can sprout from Martinique's soil, including pineapples, avocados, bananas, papayas, and custard apples.

Bird-watchers are often pleased at the number of hummingbirds, and visitors can also see mountain whistlers, blackbirds, and mongooses. Multicolored butterflies flit about, and after sunset, there's a concert of grasshoppers, frogs, and crickets.

1 Essentials

For advance information, contact the **French Government Tourist Office** in the U.S. at 444 Madison Ave., New York, NY 10022 (© 212/838-7800); 9454 Wilshire Blvd., Suite 715, Beverly Hills, CA 90212 (© 310/271-6665); or 676 N. Michigan Ave., Chicago, IL 60611 (© 312/751-7800). In Britain, contact 178 Piccadilly, London, W1V 9AL (© 020/7399-3500). In Canada, write to 1981 McGill College Ave., Suite 490, Montreal, Quebec H3A 2W9 (© 514/288-4264).

In **Canada,** contact the **Martinique Tourist Office,** 2159 rue Mackay, Montreal, Quebec H3G 2J2 (© 514/844-8566).

On the Web, go to **www.martinique.org**.

On the island, the **Office Départemental du Tourisme (tourist office)** is on Boulevard Alfassa in Fort-de-France, across the waterfront boulevard from the harbor (© **596/61-61-77**); it's open Monday to Friday from 8am to 5pm, Saturday from 8am to noon. The information desk at Lamentin Airport is open daily until the last flight comes in.

GETTING THERE

BY PLANE Before you book your own airfare, read the section "Packages for the Independent Traveler" in chapter 2.

Lamentin International Airport (© **596/42-16-00**) is outside the village of Lamentin, a 15-minute taxi ride east of Fort-de-France and a 40-minute taxi ride northeast of the island's densest concentration of resort hotels (Les Trois-Ilets peninsula). Most flights to Martinique require a transfer on a neighboring island—usually Puerto Rico, Antigua, or Barbados. From there another stopover or transfer in Guadeloupe is often required. Direct or nonstop flights to any of the French islands from the U.S. mainland are rare.

American Airlines (© **800/433-7300** in the U.S.; www.aa.com) flies into its busy hub in San Juan, Puerto Rico, from many points throughout North America. From here, passengers bound for Martinique transfer onto one or two daily **American Eagle** (same phone number) flights to Guadeloupe. From Guadeloupe, they transfer again onto one of up to 10 daily flights to Martinique on **Air Caraïbes** (formerly known as Air Guadeloupe). American can book all the legs of this complicated series of transfers.

Air France (© **800/237-2747** in the U.S.; www.airfrance.com) is the only airline with a direct connection with the United States and Martinique. Air France flies daily from Miami with a stopover in either Guadeloupe or Port-au-Prince. It operates separate nonstop flights from Paris to both Martinique and Guadeloupe. These depart at least once a day, and in some cases, depending on the season and the day of the week, twice a day. The airline also maintains three weekly flights from Port-au-Prince, Haiti, to Martinique, and three flights a week, depending on the season, between Cayenne, in French Guyana, and Martinique.

Antigua-based **LIAT** (© **868/624-4727;** www.liatairline.com; or through the reservations department of **American Airlines** © **800/433-7300** in the U.S.) flies from Antigua and Barbados to both Martinique and Guadeloupe several times a day. Depending on the season, flights to the two islands are either separate or combined into a single flight, with touchdowns en route. Both Antigua and Barbados are important air-terminus links for such larger carriers as American Airlines (see above).

Another option for reaching either Martinique or Guadeloupe involves flying **BWIA** (© **800/538-2942** in the U.S.; www.bwee.com), the national airline of Trinidad and Tobago, from either New York or Miami nonstop to both Barbados and Antigua, and from there transferring onto a LIAT flight to either of the French-speaking islands.

British Airways (© **800/247-9297** in the U.S., or 0870/850-9850 in England; www.britishairways.com) flies separately to both Antigua and Barbados three times a week from London. From either of those islands, LIAT connects to either Guadeloupe or Martinique.

BY FERRY One particularly evocative means of travel between Martinique and Guadeloupe involves taking one of the motorized catamarans that are maintained by a local operator, **Exprèss des Iles.** Carrying between 395 and 495 passengers,

Martinique

Airport ✈ Beach 🏝 Mountain 🔺

Martinique Passage

Macouba

Basse-Pointe

Grand-Rivière

Leyritz N1 Le Lorrain

Montagne Pelée 🔺

Ajoupa-Bouillon

Le Prêcheur

Morne Rouge

1 Le Marigot

N1

Ste-Marie

ATLANTIC OCEAN

Morne des Esses

St-Pierre

■ Musée Gaugin

Trinité 2

Gros-Morne

Tartane

Caravelle Nature Preserve ■

Caravelle Peninsula

Le Carbet

N2

N3

Balata

N4

Bellefontaine

🔺🔺 *Carbet Peak*

St-Joseph

Case-Pilote

N1

Schoelcher

N1 Lamentin

Fort-de-France 7 6

Lamentin International Airport ✈

Le François 5 4 3

Pointe du Bout 🏝

Anse Mitan 🏝

8–11

Anse-à-l'Ane 🏝

12

Les Trois-Ilets D7

N5

Mt. Vauclin 🔺 N6

Vauclin

Grande Anse

Anses-d'Arlets

D37

13 14

D7

Rivière-Pilote

Le Marin

Le Diamant

15

Ste-Luce

Caribbean Sea

■ Diamond Rock

Diamond Beach

16

Les Salines 🏝

17

Cap Chevalier 🏝

Ste-Anne

■ Petrified Forest

Pointe des Salines

St. Lucia Channel

0   5 Miles
0   5 Kilometers

N

Auberge de L'Anse Mitan **12**

Cap Est Lagoon Resort & Spa **5**

Frégate Bleue **4**

Habitation LaGrange **1**

Hotel Amyris **15**

Hotel Diamant Les Bains **13**

Hotel Diamant-Rock **14**

Hôtel L'Impératrice **7**

La Dunette **16**

La Pagerie **11**

Le Lafayette **6**

Le Kalenda Resort **9**

L'Habitation de L'Îlet Thierry **3**

Manoir de Beauregard **17**

Novotel Carayou **10**

Saint-Aubin Hôtel **2**

Sofitel Bakoua **8**

depending on the boat, they require 3¾ hours of waterborne transit, which includes an intermediate stopover on either Dominica or Terre-de-Haut, in the Iles des Saintes. The company operates one (and sometimes two) passage a day between the two largest islands of the French West Indies.

Morning departures from Pointe-à-Pitre for Fort-de-France are usually at 8am, and departures from Fort-de-France for Pointe-à-Pitre are usually at 2pm, although the schedule can vary unexpectedly according to the season and the day of the week. Fares are 80€ ($100) round-trip or 45€ ($56) one-way. For details and reservations, contact **Exprèss des Iles,** Gare Maritime, quai Gatine, 97110 Pointe-à-Pitre, Guadeloupe (© **0590-91-69-68**), or **Terminal Inter-Iles,** Bassin de Radoub, 97200 Fort-de-France, Martinique (© **0596-63-05-45**).

GETTING AROUND

BY RENTAL CAR   Unless you never plan to leave your hotel's beach, you probably want to rent a car to explore the island. Martinique has several local car-rental agencies, but clients have complained of mechanical difficulties and billing irregularities. We recommend renting from one of the U.S.-based firms. An international driver's license is required. Driving in Martinique is on the right side of the road.

Budget has an office at 31 rue Ernest-Desproges, Fort-de-France, in addition to an airport location (© **800/472-3325** in the U.S., or 596/63-69-00 locally; www.budgetrentacar.com). **Avis** is located at Lamentin Airport (© **800/331-1212** in the U.S., or 596/42-16-92 locally; www.avis.com), as is **Hertz** (© **800/654-3131** in the U.S., or 596/51-01-01 locally; www.hertz.com). Of the three outfitters, Hertz has more branches (about six) than either of its other competitors.

Regardless of which company you choose, you'll be hit with a value-added tax (VAT) of 8.5% on top of the final bill, plus either a charge of around 23€ ($29) if you ask the car to be delivered to your hotel, or an airport pickup charge of about 16€ ($20) if you retrieve your car at the airport. Collision damage waivers (CDWs), which eliminate some or all of your financial responsibility in the event of an accident, cost between 4.70€ ($5.90) and 10€ ($13) per day at Budget and Hertz, and usually a bit more at Avis. Of these three car-rental companies, the rates at Budget tend to be the least expensive, although that depends on a wide array of seasonal variations.

BY TAXI   Local laws demand that any bona-fide Martiniquais cab must contain a working meter. For specific itineraries—wherein a passenger tells the driver where he or she wants to go—the meter must be "on" and functioning. **Radio Taxi** (© **596/63-63-62**), the island's largest dispatcher, advises us that if a taxi driver quotes a flat rate to a passenger instead of activating the meter, that you're being robbed, and you should immediately get out and find another cab. For an idea of prices, a taxi ride for up to four passengers between Lamentin Airport and any of the hotels in Pointe du Bout will cost about 42€ ($53) during the day, and about 59€ ($74) between 7pm and 6am, when a 40% surcharge is added.

The rule about using a taxi's meter does not apply to passengers who want to hire a taxi for a **general tour** of the island. If that is your goal, expect to pay between 45€ ($56) and 48€ ($60) per hour for up to four passengers, depending on the itinerary and routing you negotiate with the driver. Frankly, we find touring the island with a taxi driver so expensive, and the venue so easily susceptible to the whims of the individual taxi driver, that we advise visitors to rent their own car for the day, driving themselves—armed with a good map—around the island's many rutted but often panoramic roads.

BY BUS & TAXI COLLECTIF   There are two types of buses operating on Martinique. Regular buses, called *grands busses,* hold about 40 passengers and cost 1€ to 1.50€ ($1.25–$1.90) anywhere within the city limits of Fort-de-France. To travel beyond the city limits, nine-passenger *taxis collectifs* are used. These are privately owned minivans that traverse the island and bear the sign TC. Their routes are flexible and depend on passenger need. A one-way fare from Fort-de-France to Ste-Anne is 5€ ($6.25). *Taxis collectifs* depart from the heart of Fort-de-France from the parking lot of Pointe Simon. There's no phone number to call for information about this unpredictable means of transport, and there are no set schedules. Traveling in a *taxi collectif* is for the adventurous visitor—these vehicles are crowded and not very comfortable.

BY FERRY   The least expensive—and most colorful—way to transfer between Fort-de-France and the hotel and tourist district of Pointe du Bout is via one of the ferryboats *(vedettes)* that depart from quai d'Esnambuc in Fort-de-France. Transit costs 3.80€ ($4.75) one-way or 6€ ($7.50) round-trip. Schedules for the ferryboats, at least 20 of which are scheduled at regular (usually 30-min.) intervals every day between 6:30am and midnight, are printed in the free visitor's guide *Choubouloute,* in French and English, which is distributed by the tourist office. Because they're so frequent, most visitors dispense with attempting to understand the schedule at all, and meander down to the waterfront to wait for the next boat.

There's a smaller ferryboat that runs between Fort-de-France and the unpretentious resorts of Anse Mitan and Anse-à-l'Ane, both across the bay and home to many two- and three-star hotels and modest Creole restaurants. The boat departs from quai d'Esnambuc in Fort-de-France at intervals of between 20 and 30 minutes every day from 7:30am to 6pm. The trip takes about 20 minutes. One-way and round-trip passage cost 3.80€ ($4.75) and 6€ ($7.50), respectively. If seas are

---

Fun Fact **Carnival**

If you like masquerades and dancing in the streets, you should be here to attend **Carnival,** or *Vaval,* as it's known here. Most of the celebrations associated with Carnival occur, depending on the calendar, for 5 days either in late February or early March, but there is also usually some form of celebration or contest conducted for the 6 Sundays prior. Most visible of these is the election of the **Carnival Queen,** a contest that's usually held the first Sunday before the actual week of Carnival itself. Each village prepares costumes and floats. Weekend after weekend, frenzied celebrations take place, reaching fever pitch just before Lent. Fort-de-France is the focal point for Carnival, but the spirit permeates the whole island. On Ash Wednesday, the streets of Fort-de-France are filled with *diablesses,* or she-devils (portrayed by members of both sexes). Costumed in black and white, they crowd the streets to form King Carnival's funeral procession. As devils cavort about and the rum flows, a funeral pyre is built at La Savane. When it's set on fire, the dancing of those she-devils becomes frantic (many are thoroughly drunk at this point). Long past dusk, the cortege takes the coffin to its burial, ending Carnival until next year.

extremely rough, or if there's a hurricane warning, all ferryboat services may be suspended.

For more information, call either **Somatour,** 14 rue Blenac, 97200 Fort-de-France (© **596/73-05-53**) or **Vedettes Madinina** (© **0596/63-06-46**).

BY BICYCLE & MOTORBIKE You can rent motor scooters from **Locabike,** 12 rue Pierre & Marie Curie, in Fort-de-France (© **0596/71-95-72**), upon presentation of a passport and a deposit of 762€ ($953), payable either in by cash or credit card. Scooters come in two sizes, including models with a not-very-powerful 50cc engine (for which no driver's license is required), and a faster, more aggressive 125cc engine (for which you'll have to show a valid automobile driver's license from your state or country of residence). Depending on their size and features, they rent for between 26€ and 34€ ($33–$43) per day. This outfit also rents a limited number of bicycles as well, but in hilly Martinique, where roads are narrow and traffic whizzes by at a sometimes terrifying speed, bike rentals are not particularly popular.

FAST FACTS: Martinique

Banks Most of the banks of Martinique maintain the following hours: Monday to Friday from 7:30am to noon, and from 2:30 to 4pm. In recent years a few of them have opted to close on Wednesday afternoon. Others maintain a policy of remaining closed all day Monday, but opening their doors every Saturday morning between 7:30am and noon. There are about 10 ATMs in Fort-de-France, at least 3 at Lamentin Airport, and a scattering of others throughout the island, usually in such touristed areas as Pointe du Bout, Le Diamant, and Ste-Anne.

Currency Because Martinique falls under the same monetary system as mainland France, the island uses the **euro** as its mode of exchange. The current rate of exchange is .80€ to the U.S. dollar. *Rates in this chapter are quoted in U.S. dollars.* Just before you leave home, you can check the current exchange rate on the Web at **www.x-rates.com**. **Change Caraïbes** maintains full-service foreign currency divisions, as well as ATMs, at both Lamentin Airport (© **596/42-17-11**) and at 4 rue Ernest Deproge, in the center of Fort-de-France (© **596/60-28-40**), across the street from the office of Air France. Banks give much better exchange rates than hotels.

Customs Items for personal use, such as tobacco, cameras, and film, are admitted without formalities or tax if not in excessive quantity.

Documents U.S. and Canadian citizens need a valid passport. A return or ongoing ticket is also necessary. British citizens need only an identity card.

Electricity Electricity is 220-volt AC (50 cycles), the same as that used on the French mainland. However, check with your hotel to see if it has converted the electrical voltage and outlets in the bathrooms (some have). If it hasn't, bring your own transformer and adapter for U.S. appliances.

Emergencies Call the **police** at © **17**, report a **fire** by dialing © **18**, and summon an **ambulance** at © **17** or **18**.

Hospitals There are 18 hospitals and clinics on the island, and there's a 24-hour emergency room at the island's largest, **Hôpital Pierre Zobda**

Quikman, Châteauboeuf, 5km (3 miles) south from Fort-de-France (© 596/55-20-00), on the road to Lamentin Airport.

Language French, the official language, is spoken by almost everyone. The local Creole patois uses words borrowed from France, England, Spain, and Africa. In the wake of increased tourism, English is occasionally spoken in the major hotels, restaurants, and tourist organizations—but don't count on driving around the countryside and asking for directions in English.

Liquor Laws Liquor is sold in grocery and liquor stores on any day of the week. It's legal to have an open container in public, though the authorities will be very strict with any littering, disorderly behavior, or drunk driving.

Pharmacies Try the **Pharmacie de la Paix,** at the corner of rue Perrinon and rue Victor-Schoelcher in Fort-de-France (© 596/71-94-83), open Monday to Friday from 7:15am to 6:15pm and on Saturday from 7:45am to 1pm.

Safety Crime is hardly rampant on Martinique, yet there are still those who prey on unsuspecting tourists. Follow the usual precautions, especially in Fort-de-France and in the tourist-hotel belt of Pointe du Bout. It's wise to protect your valuables and never leave them unguarded on the beach.

Taxes & Service Charges Most hotels include a 10% service charge in the bill; all restaurants include a 15% service charge. There's also a resort tax; this varies from place to place, but it never exceeds 2.25€ ($2.80) per person per day.

Telephone To call Martinique from the United States, dial **011** (the international access code), then **596** (the country code for Martinique), and then, if it's a conventional (i.e., noncellular) phone, dial 596 again, followed by the six-digit local number. If the number you're calling is a cellphone, dial 011, followed by 596, followed by 696, followed by the six-digit local number. To call the United States from Martinique, dial **19-1,** then the area code, then the seven-digit local number. You can reach **AT&T Direct** at © **0800/99-00-11.** To reach **MCI,** dial © **0800/99-00-19,** and to reach **Sprint,** dial © **0800/99-00-87.**

Time Martinique is on Atlantic Standard Time year-round, 1 hour later than Eastern Standard Time except when daylight savings time is in effect in the U.S. Then, Martinique time is the same as on the East Coast of the United States.

Tipping Restaurants generally add a 15% service charge to all bills, which you can supplement if you think the service is outstanding. Some hotels also add a 10% service charge to your bill. Tip taxi drivers at least 15% of the fare.

Water The water is safe to drink throughout the island.

Weather The climate is relatively mild—the average temperature is in the 75°F to 85°F (24°C–29°C) range.

2 Fort-de-France

With its iron-grille-work balconies overflowing with flowers, Fort-de-France, the largest town on Martinique, seems like a cross between New Orleans and a town on the French Riviera. It lies at the end of a large bay surrounded by green hills.

The proud people of Martinique are even more fascinating than the town of Fort-de-France, although today the Creole women are likely to be seen in jeans instead of their traditional turbans and Empress Joséphine–style gowns, and they rarely wear those massive earrings that used to jounce and sway as they sauntered along.

Narrow streets climb up the steep hills, where houses have been built to catch the overflow of the capital's more than 100,000 inhabitants.

ACCOMMODATIONS

Be sure to check out the "Packages for the Independent Traveler" section in chapter 2.

Don't stay in town if you want a hotel near a beach (see the hotels listed later in this chapter for beach resorts). If you do opt to stay in Fort-de-France, you'll have to take a ferryboat to reach the beaches at **Pointe du Bout** (see the section "Pointe du Bout & Les Trois-Ilets," later in this chapter). The one exception to this is the Hôtel La Bâtelière, which opens onto a small beach, but it's in the suburb of Schoelcher.

Hôtel L'Impératrice   Favored by businesspeople without unlimited expense accounts, this stucco-sided, five-story hotel faces a landscaped mall in the heart of town, near the water's edge. L'Impératrice was originally built in the 1950s and named in honor of one of Martinique's most famous exports, Joséphine. Its balconies overlook the traffic at the western edge of the sprawling promenade known as La Savane. The small- to medium-size guest rooms are modern and functional. The front rooms tend to be noisy, but they do offer a look into life along La Savane. Bathrooms are compact, with a combination shower/tub. Don't expect outstanding service. Almost no one speaks English, and they all seem a bit jaded. But despite the confusion in the very noisy lobby, and the unremarkable decor of the simple bedrooms, you might end up enjoying this hotel's unpretentiousness.

The hotel's restaurant, Le Joséphine, does a brisk business with local shoppers in town for the day.

Place de la Savane, 15 rue de la Liberté, 97200 Fort-de-France, Martinique, F.W.I. ⓒ 596/63-06-82. Fax 596/72-66-30. limperatrice@wanadoo.fr. 24 units. Winter 72€–85€ ($90–$106) double; off season 62€–80€ ($78–$100) double. Rates include breakfast. AE, MC, V. **Amenities:** Restaurant; bar; laundry service; dry cleaning; rooms for those with limited mobility. *In room:* A/C, TV, dataport, fridge.

Le Lafayette   After 10pm, you'll enter this modest downtown hotel through its entrance on the rue Victor-Hugo; during daylight hours, you'll use a larger entrance that opens onto the rue de la Liberté, and climb a short flight of terra-cotta steps to reach the simple lobby. Don't expect grandeur from this hotel, its snob appeal is almost nonexistent. The hotel was renovated in 2002, and its bedrooms are tidy and clean. Most units contain comfortable twin beds, with small, pure-white, shower-only bathrooms. The overall impression is neat but simple and unpretentious. The inn is the oldest continuously operating hotel on Martinique, originally built in the 1940s with quasi–Art Deco hints that are now slightly dowdy. There's no on-site restaurant, but several eateries are within a short walk.

5 rue de la Liberté, 97200 Fort-de-France, Martinique, F.W.I. ✆ 596/73-80-50. Fax 596/60-97-75. www. lelafayettehotel.com. 24 units. Winter 56€ ($70) double; off season 48€ ($60) double. AE, MC, V. **Amenities:** Restaurant; bar; laundry service; dry cleaning. *In room:* A/C, TV, dataport.

DINING
FORT-DE-FRANCE
La Belle Epoque ✶✶ FRENCH   In a turn-of-the-20th-century house, this elegant choice features a haute cuisine menu. In the affluent suburb of Didier, this colonial-style restaurant stands high above the capital of Fort-de-France. The dining room is filled with crystal, silver, white linens, and beautiful tiles, the room opening onto a terrace with a view of the garden. Guests savor the inventive, superbly prepared cuisine. A delicate salmon ravioli appears in a Breton crab spider's shell, puff pastry is stuffed with curried shrimp, and red snapper is flambéed in an antique rum. The fish dishes are the finest in the area, particularly filet of John Dory served with a lime butter or roasted scallops served with spice butter. Some classic beef dishes are also offered, cooked to order and appearing with sauces that often contain foie gras and truffles. The best of these is filet of beef Périgourdine with foie gras and truffles. Roasted stuffed pigeon is as good as anything this side of Morocco, and a rack of lamb is perfectly glazed in honey and lemon.

97 Route de Didier. ✆ 596/64-41-19. Reservations required. Main courses 22€–30€ ($28–$38); fixed-price lunch 27€ ($34). MC, V. Tues–Fri noon–1:30pm; Mon–Sat 7:45–9:30pm.

Le Dôme ✶✶ *Finds* FRENCH/ANTILLEAN   Set on the uppermost (eighth) floor of a hotel in the Valmenière district, midway between Fort-de-France's commercial center and the airport—and far from the neighborhoods and haunts visited by the leisure-industry crowd—this establishment caters almost exclusively to a clientele of business travelers, many of whom come from the French mainland. Outfitted with a contemporary-looking decor and pastel hues of beige and pink, it boasts large bay windows, through which diners enjoy a view that sweeps along the island's coastline. Menu items blend traditional French cuisine with Antillean ingredients, sometimes in very creative ways. The best examples include a cream of *christophene* (Caribbean squash) soup with crayfish; ground rack of lamb served with a sauce made from cocoa powder and red wine; seawolf with coconut sauce; filet of John Dory with yellow bananas and anise; and braised breast of duckling served with a sauce concocted from Caribbean cherries.

In the Hôtel Valmenière, Ave. des Arawaks. ✆ 0596/75-75-75. Reservations recommended. Main courses 14€–18€ ($18–$23); set-price menu 25€ ($31). AE, DC, MC, V. Daily 12:30–2pm and 7:30–10pm. Bus: 7.

OUTSIDE FORT-DE-FRANCE (LAMENTIN)
La Canne à Sucre ✶✶ FRENCH/CREOLE   Chef-owner Gerard Virginius brings sophisticated French style to this stellar choice. Foodies on the island appreciate his spicy specialties, a juxtaposition of traditional French cuisine and Antillean influences. They change with the seasons and the availability of ingredients, but are likely to include crayfish-stuffed ravioli with tarragon sauce; orange-flavored shrimp with shellfish sauce and sweet-potato pie; filet of lamb with wild mushrooms and star anise sauce; filet of beef with a rum-and–wild mushroom sauce, and red snapper served with a pastry case made from black

wheat with an island curry sauce. For dessert we have yet to see a better concoction on Martinique than the crème brûlée with passion fruit.

Patio de Cluny, route Schoelcher. ✆ 596/63-33-95. Reservations required. Main courses 19€–26€ ($24–$33), set-price lunch 26€ ($33). AE, DC, MC, V. Mon–Fri noon–2:30pm; Mon–Sat 7–10pm.

SPORTS & OTHER OUTDOOR PURSUITS

If it's a beach you're looking for, take the ferry to **Pointe du Bout** (see the section "Pointe du Bout & Les Trois-Ilets," below). The island's only **golf course** is located in Les Trois-Ilets, also discussed in the next section.

DEEP-SEA FISHING Most hotels maintain a list of the yachts and skippers who will take groups out for a day on the wide blue sea. If yours doesn't offer such arrangements, call the staff at **Caribtours,** B.P. 292, Lamentin (✆ **596/ 50-93-52**). The cost of renting such a boat, in which all equipment is usually included, is 130€ ($163) for a full-day charter for up to six anglers, with a brief stopover in St. Lucia. Most game fish tend to be most active very early in the morning, and many experienced fishermen claim that it's not worth going after 10am, so departures tend to leave before breakfast, around 6am. Caribtours's major competitor, charging roughly equivalent rates for its deep-sea fishing excursions, is **Peche Sportive Pelisson.** It maintains branches on a pier that's nearly adjacent to the Novotel Le Diamant, La Trinité (✆ **0596/76-24-20**), and in the hamlet of Ika Atas, La Trinité (✆ **0596/58-22-85**). Note, however, that this sport is in decline in waters around Martinique because of overfishing.

HIKING Inexpensive guided hikes, sometimes within the boundaries of the **Parc Naturel Régional de la Martinique,** are organized year-round by the **CRRPM (Centre Régional des Randonnés Pedestres de la Martinique).** This organization also gives out maps of recommended hikes within Martinique, and offers advice about routings and access to departure points for walks and hill treks. You can write or call the park's administrative headquarters (Domaine de Tivoli, BP 4037, 97200 Fort-de-France; ✆ **596/64-42-59**) for more information.

EXPLORING FORT-DE-FRANCE

At the heart of town is **La Savane,** a broad garden with many palms and mangos, playing fields, walks, and benches, plus shops and cafes lining its sides. In the middle of this grand square stands a statue of Joséphine, "Napoleon's little Creole," made of white marble by Vital Debray. The statue poses in a Regency gown and looks toward Les Trois-Ilets, where Joséphine was born. The statue was beheaded in 1991, probably because islanders felt she championed slavery. Near the harbor, at the edge of the park, you'll find vendors' stalls with handmade crafts, including baskets, beads, bangles, woodcarvings, and straw hats.

Your next stop could be the 1875 **Cathédrale St-Louis,** on rue Victor-Schoelcher. The religious centerpiece of the island, it's an extraordinary iron building, which someone once likened to "a sort of Catholic railway station." A number of the island's former governors are buried beneath the choir loft.

A statue in front of the Palais de Justice is of the island's second main historical figure, **Victor Schoelcher,** who worked to free the slaves more than a century ago. **Bibliothèque Schoelcher,** 1 rue de la Liberté (✆ **596/70-26-67**), also honors this popular hero. Functioning today as the island's central government-funded library, the elaborate structure was first displayed at the Paris Exposition of 1889. The Romanesque portal, the Egyptian lotus-petal columns, even the turquoise tiles were imported piece by piece from Paris and reassembled here. It's open Monday from 1 to 5:30pm, Tuesday through Thursday from 8:30am to 5:30pm, Friday from 8:30am to 6pm, and Saturday from 8:30am to noon.

Fort St-Louis, built in the Vauban style on a rocky promontory, guards the port. **Fort Tartenson** and **Fort Desaix** also stand on hills overlooking the port.

Musée Departemental d l'Archeologie et de Prehistoire de la Martinique, 9 rue de la Liberté (© **596/71-57-05**), the one place on Martinique that preserves its pre-Columbian past and has relics from the early settlers, the Arawaks and the Caribs. The museum preserves the years from 3000 B.C. to A.D. 1635. Everything here stops shortly after the arrival of the first French colonials on Martinique in the early 1600s. In other words, it's mostly an ethnological museum, which was enlarged and reorganized into a more dynamic and up-to-date place in 1997. The museum faces La Savane and is open Monday 1 to 5pm, Tuesday to Friday from 8am to 5pm, and on Saturday from 9am to noon; admission is 3.05€ ($3.80) for adults, 2.30€ ($2.90) for students, and 1.50€ ($1.90) for children ages 3 to 12.

The **Musée Régional d'Histoire et d'Ethnographie,** 10 Blvd. de Général-de-Gaulle, in Fort-de-France (© **596/72-81-87** or 596/63-85-55), is devoted to an illumination of the island's agrarian past (and the slave culture that made it possible). Expositions showcase the late 19th-century volcanic eruption that leveled St-Pierre, slavery and its effects on the island's society, and explorations of the sugar-cane industry. It's open Tuesday from 2 to 5pm, Saturday from 8:30am to noon, and Monday and Wednesday to Friday from 8:30am to 5pm. Entrance costs 3€ ($3.75) for adults, and .75€ (95¢) for children under 12. Entrance is free for anyone who presents a valid student ID.

Sacré-Coeur de Balata Cathedral, at Balata, overlooking Fort-de-France, is a copy of the one looking down from Montmartre upon Paris—and this one is just as incongruous, maybe more so. It's reached by going along route de la Trace (Route N3). Balata is 10km (6¼ miles) northwest of Fort-de-France.

A few minutes away on Route N3, **Jardin de Balata** (© **596/64-48-73**) is a tropical botanical park created by Jean-Philippe Thoze on land that the jungle was rapidly reclaiming around a Creole house that belonged to his grandmother. He has also restored the house, furnishing it with antiques and historic engravings. The garden contains a profusion of flowers, shrubs, and trees. It's open daily from 9am to 4pm from November to March and until 5pm from April to October. Admission is 6.50€ ($8.15) for adults, 2.50€ ($3.15) for children age 7 to 12, and free for children 6 and under.

SHOPPING

Your best buys on Martinique are French luxury imports, such as perfumes, fashions, Vuitton luggage, Lalique crystal, and Limogès dinnerware. Sometimes (but don't count on it) prices are as much as 30% to 40% below those in the United States.

You're usually better off shopping in the smaller stores, where prices are 8% to 12% lower on comparable items, and paying in euros that you have exchanged at a local bank.

FORT-DE-FRANCE AFTER DARK

The most exciting after-dark activity is seeing a performance of the folkloric troupe **Les Grands Ballets Martiniquais** (see "Begin the Beguine," above).

The popularity of individual bars and dance clubs in Martinique rises and falls almost monthly. Many of them charge a cover of 15€ ($19), although that's

Begin the Beguine

The sexy and rhythmic beguine was *not* an invention of Cole Porter. It's a dance of the islands—though exactly which island depends on whom you ask. Popular wisdom and the encyclopedia give the nod to Martinique, though Guadeloupeans claim it as their own, too.

Everybody who goes to Martinique wants to see the show performed by **Les Grands Ballets Martiniquais,** a troupe of about two dozen dancers, along with musicians, singers, and choreographers, who tour the island regularly. Their performances of the traditional dances of Martinique have been acclaimed in both Europe and the United States. With a swoosh of gaily striped skirts and clever acting, the dancers capture all the exuberance of the island's soul. The group has toured abroad with great success, but they perform best on their home ground, presenting tableaux that tell of jealous brides and faithless husbands, demanding overseers and toiling cane cutters. Dressed in traditional costumes, the island women and men dance the spirited mazurka, which was brought from the 18th- and 19th-century ballrooms of Europe, and, of course, the exotic beguine.

Les Grands Ballets Martiniquais usually perform Monday at the Hotel Diamant-Rock and Friday at the Sofitel Bakoua, but these schedules can vary, so check locally. In addition, the troupe gives miniperformances aboard visiting cruise ships. The cost of dinner and the show is usually 45€ ($56). Most performances are at 9pm, with dinners at the hotels beginning at 7:30pm.

often ignored if business is slow, and if you're a particularly appealing physical specimen. **Le Yucca Bar** (also known as Le Piano Bar), in the Fort de France suburb at Zac de Rivière Roche (② **596/60-48-36**), is also a restaurant that draws both locals and visitors from mainland France. A nightclub where anyone can be a star, at least for a few minutes, is **Le Karaoke Café California,** Immeuble Les Corneaux, Lamentin (② **596/50-07-71**).

If you're on the party circuit around Martinique, you are likely to find the most action at **Crazy Nights,** Ste-Luce (② **596/68-56-68**), a wild dance parlor that on a weekend can attract hundreds of patrons, each bent on having one "crazy night." Jazz is showcased at the **Calembesse Café,** 19 Blvd. Allegre Le Marin (② **596/74-69-27**), which sometimes features its own Billie Holiday clone. Meals are served, and the place is packed on Saturday nights. Live soirees on Wednesday and karaoke madness on Thursday are a regular feature at **Les Soirees de l'Amphore,** Anse-Mitan (② **596/66-03-03**), which is a small restaurant and minibar. Funk and soul music are featured, as is disco (yes, that was the Village People we recently heard). Pop music and *zouk* (rhythmic music tracing its roots to the Caribbean, Africa, and Europe) are regularly on the bill at the dive **Le Molokoi,** Le Diamant (② **596/76-48-63**).

And in downtown Fort-de-France, check out **La Cheyenne,** 8 rue Joseph Compère (② **596/70-31-19**), a cavernous disco where several bars and dance floors provide lots of visual distractions.

If you want to gamble, head for Martinique's major casino, **Casino Bâtelière Plaza,** at Schoelcher (© **596/61-73-23**), a 10-minute drive from the center of Fort-de-France. You'll need a passport and 11€ ($14) to enter the gaming rooms, where a jacket and necktie are not necessary for men. A special area reserved just for slot machines and their fans is open daily, without charge, from 10am to 4am. A more formal gambling area, with French baccarat, roulette, and blackjack, is open daily from 8pm to 4am. This is the larger, newer, and more crowded of the two casinos in Martinique, with 140 slot machines, compared to the 40 slots at the Casino des Trois-Ilets in Pointe du Bout, which is described in "Pointe du Bout After Dark," below. If you opt for an evening at the casino, you won't go hungry. On-site are two restaurants. On a cultural note, **L'Atrium,** Boulevard Général-de-Gaulle, Fort-de-France (© **596/70-79-29**), is the venue for major island cultural events, including dance and music. The theatrical presentations, of course, are in French. You can ask on island what might be happening at the time of your visit.

3 Pointe du Bout ⚹ & Les Trois-Ilets

Pointe du Bout is a narrow peninsula across the bay from the busy capital of Fort-de-France. It's the most developed resort area of Martinique, with at least four of the island's largest hotels, an impressive marina, about a dozen tennis courts, countless pools, facilities for horseback riding, and all kinds of watersports. There's also a handful of independent restaurants, a casino, boutiques, and in nearby Les Trois-Ilets, a Robert Trent Jones Sr.–designed golf course. Except for the hillside that contains the Sofitel Bakoua Caralia, most of the district is flat and verdant, with gardens and rigidly monitored parking zones. All the hotels listed below are near the clean white-sand beaches of Pointe du Bout. Some of the smaller properties are close to the white-sand beaches of Anse Mitan. Les Trois-Ilets, the birthplace of Joséphine, the empress of France and wife of Napoleon Bonaparte, lies at the base of the peninsula on the bay.

GETTING THERE
If you're driving from Fort-de-France, take Route 1, which crosses the plain of Lamentin—the industrial area of Fort-de-France and the site of the international airport. Often the air is filled with the fragrance of caramel, from the large sugar-cane factories in the surrounding area. After 32km (20 miles), you reach Les Trois-Ilets. Five kilometers (3 miles) farther on your right, take Route D38 to Pointe du Bout.

The **ferry service** runs all day long until midnight from the harbor front (quai d'Esnambuc) in downtown Fort-de-France. Round-trip fare is 6€ ($7.50). See "Getting Around" in section 1, earlier in this chapter, for details.

ACCOMMODATIONS
EXPENSIVE
Le Kalenda Resort ⚹   Originally built in the 1970s as a jazzy, then-trendy Meridien Hotel whose rooms and decor got a bit weary after many years of use, this hotel was bought late in 2002 by a local group of investors and renamed after a traditional Martiniquais dance, the Kalenda. With seven stories and a design that towers over the low-rise competitors that are clustered nearby, it's the second tallest building in Martinique, with more facilities and diversions than any other hotel in Pointe-du-Bout. Overall, expect a comfortable, well-accessorized hotel,

with a 1970s-era original design and lots of postmodern grace notes added since then. The reception area opens onto the palm-fringed swimming pool, the waters of the bay, and the faraway lights of Fort-de-France. The hotel is slightly angled to allow for the contours of the shoreline, so each of the bedrooms overlooks either the Caribbean or the bay. Each has a private balcony, conservatively modern furnishings, and tropical accents. Bathrooms are roomy and tile-sheathed, each with a bidet and a shower/tub combination.

Pointe du Bout, Trois-Ilets (B.P. 894, 97229 Fort-de-France), Martinique, F.W.I. ✆ **800/543-4300** in the U.S. and Canada, or 596/66-06-00. Fax 596/66-00-74. www.kalendaresort-hotels.com. 278 units. Dec–May 190€ ($238) double, 353€–453€ ($441–$566) suite; June–Nov 120€ ($150) double, 353€–453€ ($441–$566) suite. Rates include breakfast. AE, DC, MC, V. **Amenities:** 2 restaurants; 2 bars; outdoor pool; casino; 2 tennis courts; dive shop; marina; sailing; snorkeling; water-skiing; windsurfing; massage; laundry service; dry cleaning; nonsmoking rooms; rooms for those with limited mobility. *In room:* A/C, TV, dataport, hair dryer, safe.

Novotel Carayou ★ *Kids* A member of France's biggest hotel chain, the Accor Group, this hotel, popular with families because of its children's programs, has always prided itself on its lush gardens and glamorous garden setting opening onto a small beach. The accommodations aren't the most attractive in the area, but they are housed in a series of three-story outbuildings, each encircled by large lawns dotted with coconut or palm trees and flowering shrubs. The seaside rooms are the best, and some of the units are air-conditioned. Against a setting of wood trim and whitewashed walls, the rooms are generally small but well maintained. Each bathroom is equipped with a shower/tub combination, a bidet, toiletries, and large mirrors.

Creole dishes, especially the seafood items, are prepared with flair at Le Boucant.

Pointe du Bout, 97229 Trois-Ilets, Martinique, F.W.I. ✆ **800/221-4542** in the U.S., or 596/66-04-04. Fax 596/66-00-57. www.novotel.com. 201 units. Winter 220€–235€ ($275–$294) double; off season 140€–155€ ($175–$194) double. Rates include American buffet breakfast. AE, DC, MC, V. **Amenities:** 3 restaurants; bar; outdoor pool; tennis court; kayaks; sailing; windsurfing; children's programs; business service; laundry service; dry cleaning; nonsmoking rooms; rooms for those with limited mobility. *In room:* A/C (in some), TV, dataport, hair dryer, safe.

Sofitel Bakoua ★ Its reputation for French chic is a thing of the past, but this is still the only really upscale hotel in the area, even if airline crews fill up many of its rooms today. It's known for the beauty of its landscaping and its somewhat isolated hillside location. It consists of four low-rise buildings in the center of a garden. Built in 1967 and renovated several times since, accommodations come in a wide range of sizes, from small to spacious, and are comfortable albeit a little battered. Rooms have balconies or patios, extra comfortable beds, and small tiled bathrooms with showers.

There are two lunch restaurants, and evening meals are served in Le Châteaubriand, a formal but appealing French restaurant.

Pointe du Bout, 97229 Trois-Ilets, Martinique, F.W.I. ✆ **800/221-4542** in the U.S., or 596/66-02-02. Fax 596/66-00-41. www.sofitel.com. 139 units. Dec–Apr 320€–480€ ($400–$600) double, 610€–680€ ($763–$850) suite; May–Nov 200€–280€ ($250–$350) double, 550€–700€ ($688–$875) suite. Rates include breakfast. MAP (breakfast and dinner) 42€ ($53) per person extra. AE, DC, MC, V. **Amenities:** 3 restaurants; 2 bars; outdoor pool; shuttle to golf course; 2 tennis courts; deep-sea fishing; dive shop; snorkeling; water-skiing; business services; salon; limited room service; babysitting; laundry service; rooms for those with limited mobility. *In room:* A/C, TV, dataport, minibar, hair dryer, safe.

MODERATE

La Pagerie The facilities here are relatively modest compared to those in some of the larger and more expensive hotels of Pointe du Bout, but guests can compensate by visiting the many restaurants, bars, and sports facilities in the area. Set close to the gardens of the Sofitel Bakoua (see above) and a 26km (16-mile) drive from the airport, this hotel offers comfortably modern bedrooms. Although the walls are thin, the units are neat and uncomplicated, with tile floors, small fridges, and balconies with views opening onto the bay. About two-thirds of the units contain tiny kitchenettes, at no extra charge. The accommodations are outfitted with floral prints, low-slung furnishings, and louvered closets. The tiled bathrooms have combination shower/tubs, marble vanities, bidets, and wall-mounted showerheads. Guests usually walk 5 minutes to Novotel Carayou (see above) for watersports and access to the beach.

Pointe du Bout, 97229 Trois-Ilets, Martinique, F.W.I. ℂ 596/66-05-30. Fax 596/66-00-99. www.martinique-hotels.com. 94 units. Winter 126€–154€ ($158–$193) double; off season 73€–94€ ($91–$118) double. Rates include buffet breakfast. AE, MC, V. **Amenities:** 2 restaurants; bar; outdoor pool; laundry service; rooms for those with limited mobility. *In room:* A/C, TV, dataport, kitchenette (in some), fridge, hair dryer.

INEXPENSIVE

Auberge de L'Anse Mitan Many guests like this hotel's location at the isolated end of a road whose more commercial side is laden with restaurants and a bustling nighttime parade. The hotel was built in 1930, but it has been renovated several times, most recently in 2000, by the hospitable Athanase family. What you get today is a three-story concrete box-type structure. Six of the units are studios with kitchens and TVs; all have private showers. Rooms are boxy, but the beds are comfortable. Bathrooms are very small and cramped, but tidy. You don't get anything special here, but the price is right.

35 rue des Anthuriums, L'Anse Mitan, 97229 Trois-Ilets, Martinique, F.W.I. ℂ 596/66-01-12. Fax 596/66-01-05. www.aubergeansemitan.com. 20 units. Winter 65€ ($81) double, 61€ ($76) studio, 77€ ($96) 1-bedroom apt for 2, 84€ ($105) 2-bedroom apt for 4; off season 55€ ($69) double, 46€ ($58) studio, 65€ ($81) 1-bedroom apt for 2, 70€ ($88) 2-bedroom apt for 4. Room (but not studio or apt) rates include breakfast. *In room:* A/C, TV (in studios or apts), kitchenette (in studios), kitchen (in apts).

DINING

There isn't a great choice of restaurants, but here's the pick of the litter.

Au Poisson d'Or CREOLE   Its position near the entrance of the resort community of Pointe du Bout makes it easy to find. There's no view of the sea and the traffic runs close to the edge of the veranda and terrace, but the reasonable prices and the complete change of pace make up for that. The rustic dining room offers such classics as grilled fish, sometimes cooked in coconut milk; grilled conch scallops sautéed in white wine; poached local fish; and flan. These ordinary dishes are prepared with flair and served with style.

12 rue des Bougainvilliers, L'Anse Mitan. ℂ 596/66-01-80. Reservations recommended. Main courses 12€–22€ ($15–$28); fixed-price menu 12€–30€ ($15–$38). AE, MC, V. Tues–Sun noon–2pm and 7–9:30pm. Closed July.

La Villa Creole ✿ CREOLE/FRENCH   This restaurant, which lies a 3- or 4-minute drive from the hotels of Pointe du Bout, has thrived since the late 1970s, offering a colorful, small-scale respite from the island's high-rise resorts. Set within a simple but well-maintained Creole house, with no particular views other than the small garden that surrounds it, the restaurant serves fairly priced set-price menus of such staples as *accras de morue* (beignets of codfish), *boudin Créole* (blood sausage), and *feroce* (a local form of pâté concocted from fresh avocados, pulverized codfish, and manioc flour). A special delight is the red snapper prepared either with tomato sauce or grilled. If Creole food doesn't appeal to you, there's also a short list of dishes inspired by the traditional cuisine of mainland France, focusing on such Gallic staples as terrine of duck liver, a terrine of smoked salmon, and a confit of duckling with a purée of shallots. Owner Guy Bruère-Dawson, a singer and guitarist, entertains as you dine.

18 rue des Anthuriums, L'Anse Mitan. © 596/66-05-53. Reservations recommended. Main courses 12€–33€ ($15–$41); set menus 13€–38€ ($16–$48). AE, MC, V. Tues–Sat noon–2pm; Mon–Sat 7–10:30pm.

Pignon sur Mer CREOLE   Simple and unpretentious, this is an intimate Creole restaurant containing about 15 tables, set within a rustically dilapidated building beside the sea (it's a 12-min. drive from Pointe du Bout). Menu items are island-inspired, and might include *delices du Pignon,* a platter of shellfish, or whatever grilled fish or shellfish was hauled in that day. *Lambi* (conch), shrimp, and crayfish are usually available, and brochettes of chicken are flavorful. A specialty is a tender and well-flavored filet of beef with a choice of green-peppercorn sauce or Roquefort sauce.

Anse-a-l'Ane. © 596/68-38-37. Main courses 14€–22€ ($18–$28). MC, V. Tues–Sun 12:15–4pm; Tues–Sat 7–9:30pm.

Sapori d'Italia ★ *Finds* ITALIAN   In Creole Village in Les Trois-Ilets, this restaurant is worth the expense, as its dishes are well crafted and a refreshing change of pace from the typical French and Creole food. We like to open with Valentina, the best antipasti on the menu, with an assortment of bruschette, various types of salami and cheese, and olives. The house lasagna is excellent, and you can also take delight in the gnocchi or the tortellini *alle noce* (with nuts). There are, in fact, 18 types of pasta. If the night is right, opt for a table on the outdoor terrace. The Italian preferences and tastes of the owners are obvious in the decor, much of which was imported—tiles, ceramics, furniture—from Italy.

Village Créole, Pointe du Bout. © 596/66-15-85. Reservations required. Pastas 10€–15€ ($13–$19); main courses 9€–20€ ($11–$25). AE, MC, V. Thurs–Mon noon–2:30pm; daily 7–10:30pm. Closed June and 2 weeks in Oct.

HITTING THE BEACH

The clean white-sand beaches of **Pointe du Bout,** site of the major hotels of Martinique, were created by developers and tend to be rather small. Most of the tourists head here, so the narrow beaches are among the island's most crowded. It doesn't help that Pointe du Bout also has several marinas lining the shore and serves as the docking point for the ferry from Fort de France. Even if you don't find a lot of space on the beach, with its semiclear waters, you will find toilets, phones, restaurants, and cafes galore. The waters suffer from industrial usage, although apparently the pollution is not severe enough to prevent people from going in. You'll often see the French standing deep in the water, smoking cigarettes—perhaps not your idea of an idyllic beach vacation.

To the south, however, the golden-sand beaches at **Anse Mitan** are far less crowded and more inviting, with cleaner waters. However, the steepness of Martinique's shoreline leaves much to be desired by its swimmers and snorkelers. The water declines steeply into depths, no reefs ring the shores, and fish are rarely visible. Nonetheless, beaches here are ideal for sunbathing.

The neighboring beach is **Anse-à-l'Ane,** an ideal place for a picnic.

SPORTS & OTHER OUTDOOR PURSUITS

GOLF   Robert Trent Jones Sr. designed the 18-hole **Golf de l'Impératrice-Joséphine,** at Trois-Ilets (© 596/68-32-81), a 5-minute drive from Pointe du Bout and about 29km (18 miles) from Fort-de-France. The only golf course on Martinique, the greens slope from the birthplace of Empress Joséphine (for whom it's named) across rolling hills with scenic vistas down to the sea. Amenities include a pro shop, a bar, and a restaurant. Greens fees are 46€ ($58) for 18 holes. There are also three rather battered tennis courts, which cost 14€ ($18) per hour if you wish to play on them.

HORSEBACK RIDING   The premier riding facility on Martinique is **Ranch Jack,** Esperanze, Trois-Ilets (© **596/68-37-69**). It offers morning horseback rides for both experienced and novice riders, at a cost of 55€ to 60€ ($69–$75) for a 3-hour ride. Jacques and Marlene Guinchard make daily promenades across the beaches and fields of Martinique, with a running explanation of the history, fauna, and botany of the island. Cold drinks are included in the price, and transportation is usually free to and from the hotels of nearby Pointe du Bout. Four to 15 participants are needed to book a tour. This is an ideal way to discover both the botany and geography of Martinique.

SCUBA DIVING & SNORKELING   The beachfront of **Le Kalenda Resort** is the headquarters for the island's best-recommended dive outfit, **Espace Plongée Martinique** (© **596/66-06-00**), which welcomes anyone who shows up, regardless of where they happen to be staying. Daily dive trips, depending on demand, leave from Le Kalenda's pier every day at 9am, returning at noon, and departing again at 3pm, returning at 5pm. Popular dive sites within a reasonable boat ride, with enough diversity and variation in depth to appeal to divers of all levels of proficiency, include *La Baleine* (The Whale) and Cap Solomon. A dive shop stocks everything you'll need to take the plunge, from weight belts and tanks to wet suits and underwater cameras. Divers pay between 32€ and 40€ ($40–$50) per session. Instruction for novice divers, which is conducted in Le Méridien's pool every day from noon to 12:30pm, is free.

Coral, fish, and ferns abound in the semiclear waters around the Pointe du Bout hotels, and snorkeling equipment is usually available free to hotel guests.

TENNIS   Tennis pros at Bathy's Club at the **Le Kalenda Resort,** Pointe du Bout (© **596/66-06-00**), usually allow nonguests to play for free if the courts are otherwise unoccupied.

WINDSURFING   An enduringly popular sport in the French West Indies, windsurfing *(la planche à voile)* is available at most of the large-scale hotels. One of the best equipped (and long-lived) of Martinique's windsurfing centers is **Just in Fun,** which occupies a site directly on the beachfront of the Novotel Carayou (© **596/66-19-06**). Lessons cost 32€ ($40) per hour, and boards, depending on their make and model, rent for between 18€ and 20€ ($23–$25) per hour.

A VISIT TO LES TROIS-ILETS

Marie-Josephe-Rose Tascher de la Pagerie was born here in 1763. As Joséphine, she was to become the wife of Napoleon I and empress of France from 1804 to 1809. Six years older than Napoleon, she pretended that she'd lost her birth certificate so he wouldn't find out her true age. Although many historians call her ruthless and selfish, she is still revered by some on Martinique as an uncommonly gracious lady. Others have less kind words for her—Napoleon is said by some historians to have "reinvented" slavery and they blame Joséphine's influence.

Thirty-two kilometers (20 miles) south of Fort-de-France, you reach Les Trois-Ilets, a charming little village. Two kilometers (1¼ miles) outside the village, turn left to La Pagerie, where the small **Musée de la Pagerie** (© **596/68-34-55**) has been installed in the former estate kitchen, where Joséphine gossiped with her slaves and played the guitar. Along with her childhood bed, you'll see a passionate letter from Napoleon and other mementos. The collection was compiled by Dr. Robert Rose-Rosette. Still remaining are the partially restored ruins of the Pagerie sugar mill and the church (in the village itself) where she was christened in 1763. The plantation was destroyed in a hurricane. The museum is open Tuesday through Friday from 9am to 5:30pm, Saturday and Sunday from 9am to 12:30pm and 3 to 5pm. Admission is 5€ ($6.25) for adults, 2€ ($2.50) for children 5 to 13.

The museum and a botanical garden, the **Parc des Floralies,** are adjacent to Golf de l'Impératrice-Joséphine (see "Sports & Other Outdoor Pursuits" above).

Maison de la Canne, Pointe Vatable (© **596/68-32-04**), is on the road to Trois-Ilets. Located on the premises of an 18th-century distillery, its permanent exhibitions tell the story of sugar cane and the sweeping role it played in the economic and cultural development of Martinique. It's open Tuesday to Sunday from 8:30am to 5pm, charging an admission of 3€ ($3.75) for adults, .75€ (95¢) for children age 5 to 12, and free for children under 5.

The Marina complex has a number of interesting boutiques; several sell handcrafts and curios from Martinique. They're sometimes of good quality, but are quite expensive, particularly the enameled jewel boxes and some of the batiks of natural silk.

POINTE DU BOUT AFTER DARK

For such a popular resort area, night life is mostly confined to bars. Entertainment is sporadic, as it is at the **Havana Café,** Village Créole, Pointe du Bout (© **0596/66-15-93**), which occasionally presents guitarists. The entertainer and owner—known only as "Valentina"—at **Sapori d'Italia,** Village Créole, Pointe du Bout (© **9596/66-03-03**), is known as the best Creole singer on the island. Live entertainment featured on occasion at **La Casa de Da Paulette,** Village Créole, Pointe du Bout (© **0596/66-15-15**). This bar is set in a typical old Creole cottage and can be a lot of fun if the crowd is right. **L'Amphore,** a mellow piano bar, is found at in the rear of Sofitel Bakoua, Pointe du Bout (© **596/66-03-09**).

Martinique has one of the dullest casinos in the French West Indies, **Casino des Trois-Ilets,** Le Kalenda Resort, Trois-Ilets, Pointe du Bout (© **596/66-00-30**). Slot machines, for which entrance is free, are open daily from 10am to 3am. Roulette and blackjack *(les grands jeux),* for which there's an entrance charge of 11€ ($14) and for which a visitor must present ID or a passport, are open daily from 9pm to 3am.

4 The South Loop

South of Pointe du Bout you can find sun and beaches. Resort centers here include Le Diamant and Ste-Anne.

From Trois-Ilets, you can follow a small curved road that brings you to **Anse-à-l'Ane, Grande Anse,** and **Anses-d'Arlets.** At any of these places you'll find small beaches, which are quite safe and usually not crowded.

ANSES-D'ARLETS

The scenery is beautiful here. Brightly painted fishing boats *(gommiers)* draw up on the white-sand beach, and the nets are spread out to dry in the sun. Children swim and adults fish from the good-size pier. The waters off Anses-d'Arlets are a playground for divers, with a wide variety of small tropical fish and colorful corals.

The area itself has been a choice spot for weekend "second homes" for many years, and is now beginning to develop touristically. The little village features a pretty steepled church, a bandstand for holiday concerts, and a smattering of modest little dining spots. Aficionados of Martinique come here to see "the way it used to be" on the island. Unspoiled and folkloric, the hamlet still retains its *charm typique Martiniquaise.*

From Anses-d'Arlets, panoramic Route D37 takes you to Le Diamant.

LE DIAMANT

Set on the island's southwestern coast, this village offers a good beach, open to the prevailing southern winds. The village is named after one of Martinique's best-known geological oddities, **Le Rocher du Diamant (Diamond Rock),** a barren offshore island that juts upward from the sea to a height of 172m (564 ft.). Sometimes referred to as the Gibraltar of the Caribbean, it figured prominently in a daring British-led invasion in 1804, when British mariners carried a formidable amount of ammunition and 110 sailors to the top. Despite frequent artillery bombardments from the French-held coastline, the garrison held out for 18 months, completely dominating the passageway between the rock and the coast of Martinique. Intrepid foreigners sometimes visit Diamond Rock, but the access across the strong currents of the channel is risky.

Diamond Beach ⰓⰓⰓ, on the Martinique mainland, offers a sandy bottom, verdant groves of swaying palms, and many different surf and sunbathing possibilities. The entire district has developed in recent years into a resort, scattered with generally small hotels.

ACCOMMODATIONS

Hotel Diamant Les Bains   This is an unpretentious, family-style hotel with direct access to a sandy beach. From the edge of the resort's pool, you can enjoy a view of the offshore island of Diamond Rock. Twenty units are in outlying motel-style bungalows set either in a garden or beside the beach; the others are in the resort's main building, which also houses the restaurant and bar. Accommodations have furnished terraces or patios, white-tile floors, small fridges, and built-in furniture made from polished fruitwood. Most rooms are medium in size except for the small units on the second floor of the main building, which are often rented to business travelers from the French mainland. The best are the 10 rustic bungalows directly above the beach. Bathrooms, which are aging but still work just fine, are accented with blue tiles and equipped with such extras as bidets; each has a shower stall.

The cuisine at the hotel restaurant is for the most part Creole, with some French dishes thrown in.

97223 Le Diamant, Martinique, F.W.I. ⓒ **596/76-40-14.** Fax 596/76-27-00. www.martinique-hotels.com. 27 units. Winter 94€ ($118) double, 110€ ($138) bungalow; off season 60€ ($75) double, 70€ ($88) bungalow. Rates include continental breakfast. MAP (breakfast and dinner) 18€ ($23) per person extra. MC, V. Closed 10 days in June, and Sept 1 to early Oct. **Amenities:** Restaurant; bar; outdoor pool; laundry service; dry cleaning; rooms for those with limited mobility. *In room:* A/C, TV, dataport, fridge, safe.

Hotel Diamant-Rock   On 2 hectares (5 acres) of forested land, 3km (2 miles) outside the village and 29km (18 miles) south of Fort-de-France, this low-rise building is in one of the most beautiful districts on Martinique. It's the ultimate in laissez-faire management—guests, often tour groups from France, are basically left to fend for themselves. Guest rooms, housed in four three-story wings, face either the pool or the coast, with its view of Diamond Rock. From many of the rooms, the views are more evocative of the South Pacific than of the Caribbean. The inviting units have tropical decor, white-tile floors, whitewashed walls, roomy closets, and rattan furnishings, plus adequate desk space. Bathrooms have shower/tub combinations and full-length mirrors.

Outside the hotel, the neighboring beaches aren't too crowded. They consist of white sand but are rather narrow. The taxi ride from the airport should take about 40 minutes.

Two casual restaurants serve lunch, while more formal dinners are available at Le Boucaut, a French and Creole restaurant.

97223 Le Diamant, Martinique, F.W.I. © 800/221-4542 in the U.S., or 596/76-42-42. Fax 596/76-22-87. 181 units. Year-round 200€–250€ ($250–$313) double; 338€ ($423) suite. Rates include breakfast. AE, DC, MC, V. **Amenities:** 2 restaurants; 2 bars; large outdoor swimming pool; 2 tennis courts; diving; jet skis; snorkeling; water-skiing; windsurfing; limited room service; laundry service; dry cleaning; rooms for those with limited mobility. *In room:* A/C, TV, hair dryer, safe.

STE-LUCE

Between Le Diamant and Ste-Anne lies this sleepy fishing village, which is known for its fine beaches of white sand. Scuba divers flock to the waters at Pointe Figuier to the east of Ste-Luce. Most visitors come here to lodge at the hotel below or just to enjoy the beaches.

You can also visit **Ecomusée de Martinique,** Anse Figuier (© **596/62-79-14**), which exhibits artifacts unearthed from the days of the earliest settlers, the Carib and Arawak Indians. Entrance is 3€ ($3.75), and hours are Tuesday to Friday 9am to 5pm, Saturday to Sunday 9am to 1pm and 2 to 5pm.

ACCOMMODATIONS

Hotel Amyris ⭐ *Kids*   Opening right onto the sea and a beach, this winning choice is imbued with a tropical ambience and a welcoming staff. In the south, and a property of the Karibéa hoteliers, Amyris enjoys a scenic location on a natural cove with a beach. Accommodations are found in a quartet of buildings rising three floors, the upper levels reached by stairs in lieu of an elevator. The main feature of the hotel is its lovely pool, and the entire complex is set in well-landscaped tropical gardens. Many units open onto balconies, and are equipped with full kitchenettes. Cane furniture and West Indian decorative motifs are used throughout. Each room comes with two bathrooms with shower. The on-site restaurant's not bad, although not something you need to drive to if you're not a guest here.

Quartier Désert 97228 Ste-Luce, Martinique, F.W.I. © 596/62-12-00. Fax 596/62-12-10. www.martiniquehotels.com. 110 units. Winter 142€–157€ ($178–$196) double; off season 112€–127€ ($140–$159) double. Rates include breakfast. AE, MC, V. **Amenities:** Restaurant; bar; tennis court; outdoor pool; snorkeling; children's programs (age 4–12); car rentals; nonsmoking rooms; rooms for those with limited mobility. *In room:* A/C, TV, dataport, kitchenettes (in some), hair dryer, safe.

STE-ANNE

From Le Marin, an 8km (5-mile) drive brings you to Ste-Anne, at the extreme southern tip of Martinique. This sleepy little area is known for the white-sand beaches of Les Salines (those to the north are more grayish in color). In many ways, these are Martinique's finest. The climate is arid like parts of Arizona, and the beaches are almost always sunny, perhaps too much so at midday. The name comes from Etang des Salines, a large salt pond forming a backdrop to the strip of sand. Manchineel trees are found at the southeastern end of the beach. Under no circumstances should you go under these trees for protection in a rainfall. When it's sunny you can seek shade here, but when it rains, drops falling from the poisonous tree will be like acid on your tender skin.

Holidays and weekends tend to be crowded, as many islanders and their families flock to this beach. Unfortunately, it's not big enough to handle the hordes.

Les Salines is also the site of Martinique's only real **gay beach.** Drive to the far end of the parking lot, near the sign labeled PETITE ANSE DES SALINES. Here you'll find a trail leading through thick woods to a sun-flooded beach often populated by naked gay men, with an occasional lesbian couple or two. Technically, there are no legal nudist beaches on Martinique, so it's possible you could be arrested for going nude, although authorities don't seem to enforce this law. (Throughout the island, however, the European custom of topless bathing is not uncommon on any of the beaches or even around hotel pools.)

Ste-Anne opens onto views of the Sainte Lucia Canal, and nearby is the Petrified Savanna Forest, which the French call **Savane des Petrifications.** It's a field of petrified volcanic boulders in the shape of logs. The eerie, desertlike site is studded with cacti.

ACCOMMODATIONS

La Dunette *Value*   A three-story motel-like stucco structure directly beside the sea, this hotel appeals to guests who appreciate its simplicity and its isolation from the more built-up resort areas of other parts of Martinique. An unpretentious seaside inn with summery decor and basic bedrooms painted in bright tropical colors, the hotel is accented with a garden filled with flowers and tropical plants. The furnishings are casual and modern, although some rooms are quite small. The private shower-only bathrooms, though cramped, are well maintained. The in-house restaurant is better than you might expect, thanks to the culinary finesse of the Tanzania-born owner, Gerard Kambona.

97227 Ste-Anne, Martinique, F.W.I. ℂ **596/76-73-90.** Fax 596/76-76-05. www.ladunette.com. 18 units. Winter 78€ ($98) double; off season 60€ ($75) double. Rates include continental breakfast. AE, MC, V. **Amenities:** Restaurant; bar; laundry service; dry cleaning. *In room:* A/C, TV, hair dryer.

Manoir de Beauregard *★★*   One of the most venerable and historic hotels on Martinique lies within the massive walls of a manor house that once administered many acres of surrounding sugar-cane fields. It was originally built between 1720 and 1800 by a prominent French family, and almost resembles a medieval church. A fire in 1990 completely gutted the building's interior and led to 4 years of restoration. Today, there are three bedrooms on the upper floors of the original house, and another eight within a modern, less inspired one-story annex. Rooms within the annex, although not as dignified, have antique West Indian beds and direct views over the garden. Most units are roomy with double or twin beds, plus a compact tiled bathroom with a combination tub/shower. A truly superb beach, Plage des Salines, is a 5-minute drive to the south, and a slightly less appealing beach, Plage de Ste-Anne, is within a 15-minute walk.

Meals here are conservative, traditional, tried-and-true Creole cuisine, with dishes like codfish fritters, *boudin Créole* (blood sausage), grilled fish in Creole sauce, curries, and fresh lobster.

Chemin des Salines (a 10-min. walk south of Ste-Anne), 97227 Ste-Anne, Martinique, F.W.I. ℂ **596/76-73-40.** Fax 596/76-93-24. www.manoirdebeauregard.com. 11 units. Winter 120€–155€ ($150–$194) double; off season 98€–106€ ($123–$133) double. Rates include breakfast. AE, MC, V. **Amenities:** Restaurant; bar; outdoor pool. *In room:* A/C, TV, dataport, fridge.

5 The North Loop

As we swing north from Fort-de-France, our main targets are **Le Carbet, St-Pierre, Montagne Pelée,** and **Leyritz.** However, we'll sandwich in many stopovers along the way.

From Fort-de-France, there are three ways to head north to Montagne Pelée. The first is to follow Route N4 up to St-Joseph. From there take the left fork for 5km (3 miles)and then turn onto Route D15 toward Le Marigot.

Another option is to take Route N3 through the vegetation-rich *mornes* (hills) until you reach Le Morne Rouge. This road is known as "Route de la Trace" and is now the center of the Parc Naturel de la Martinique.

Yet a third route to Montagne Pelée is via Route N2 along the coast. This is the route we'll follow, and the order in which we'll list the towns along the way. Near Fort-de-France, the first town you reach is **Schoelcher.** Farther along Route N2 is **Case-Pilote,** and then Bellefontaine. This portion, along the most popular drive in Martinique—from Fort-de-France to St-Pierre—is very reminiscent of the way the French Riviera used to look. **Bellefontaine** is a small fishing village, with boats stretched along the beach. Note the many houses also built in the shape of boats.

LE CARBET

Leaving Bellefontaine, an 8km (5-mile) drive north will deliver you to Le Carbet. Columbus landed here in 1502, and the first French settlers arrived in 1635. In 1887, Gauguin lived here for 4 months before going to Tahiti. You can stop for a swim at an Olympic-size pool set into the hills, or watch the locals scrubbing clothes in a stream. The town lies on the bus route from Fort-de-France to St-Pierre.

Centre d'Art Musée Paul-Gauguin, Anse Turin, Le Carbet (© **596/ 78-22-66**), is near the beach represented in the artist's *Bord de Mer.* The landscape hasn't changed in 100 years. The museum, housed in a five-room building, commemorates the French artist's stay on Martinique in 1887, with books, prints, letters, and other memorabilia. There are also paintings by René Corail, sculpture by Hector Charpentier, and examples of the work of Zaffanella. Of special interest are faience mosaics made of once-white pieces that turned pink, maroon, blue, and black in 1902 when the fires of Montagne Pelée devastated St-Pierre. There are also changing exhibits of works by local artists. Hours are daily from 9am to 5:30pm; admission is 4€ ($5) for adults, 2€ ($2.50) for students, and 1€ ($1.25) children under age 8.

ST-PIERRE ✿

At the beginning of this century, St-Pierre was known as the "Little Paris of the West Indies." Home to 30,000 inhabitants, it was the cultural and economic capital of Martinique. On May 7, 1902, the citizens read in their daily newspaper that "Montagne Pelée does not present any more risk to the population than Vesuvius does to the Neapolitans."

However, on May 8, at 8am, the southwest side of Montagne Pelée exploded into fire and lava. At 8:02am, all 30,000 inhabitants were dead—that is, all except one. A convict in his underground cell was saved by the thickness of the walls. When islanders reached the site, the convict was paroled and left Martinique to tour in Barnum and Bailey's circus.

St-Pierre never recovered its past splendor. It could now be called the Pompeii of the West Indies. Ruins of the church, the theater, and some other buildings can be seen along the coast.

One of the best ways to get an overview of St-Pierre involves riding a rubber-wheeled "train," the **Cyparis Exprès** (© **596/55-50-92**), which departs on tours from the base at the Musée Volcanologique. Tours cost 8€ ($10) for adults and 4€ ($5) for children 5 to 13, and run Monday through Friday departing at

---

Fun Fact **Photo Ops**

Martinique is a photographer's dream—certainly the French fashion magazines know it, because crews are always around on shoots. The most picturesque sites are **La Savane,** in Fort-de-France; **St-Pierre,** the best place to photograph towering Mount Pelée; **La Pagerie,** with its decaying ruins of a sugar factory; and from the panoramic overlooks along **La Trace,** the serpentine road winding through the entire rainforest.

11am. Tours last about an hour. In winter or during periods of high demand, additional tours might be added, usually at 2:30pm, if at all.

Musée Volcanologique, rue Victor-Hugo, St-Pierre (© **596/78-15-16**), was created by the American volcanologist Franck Alvard Perret, who turned the museum over to the city in 1933. Here, in pictures and relics dug from the debris, you can trace the story of what happened to St-Pierre. Dug from the lava is a clock that stopped at the moment the volcano erupted. The museum is open daily from 9am to 5pm; admission is 2.50€ ($3.15), free for children age 7 and under.

DINING

Le Fromager ✿ *(Finds* CREOLE/FRENCH   Set about .8km (½ mile) uphill (east) of the center of St-Pierre, this indoor-outdoor villa, owned by the René Dement family, here since 1990, welcomes luncheon guests with a humor and charm that's half French, half Martiniquais. The restaurant, which resembles a covered open-air pavilion, has a sweeping view of the town. Good dishes include marinated octopus, grilled conch or lobster, curried goat or chicken, and whatever grilled fish is available that day. This is a good lunch stopover during your tour of the island.

Route de Fonds–St-Denis, Quartier St. James, St-Pierre. © **596/78-19-07**. Reservations recommended. Fixed-price Sun menu 24€ ($30); main courses 15€–24€ ($19–$30). V. Daily noon–2:30pm.

LE PRECHEUR

From St-Pierre, you can continue along the coast north to Le Prêcheur. Once the home of Madame de Maintenon, the mistress of Louis XIV, it's the last village along the northern coast of Martinique. Here you can see hot springs of volcanic origin and the *Tombeau des Caraïbes* (**Tomb of the Caribs**), where, according to legend, the collective suicide of many West Indian natives took place after they returned from a fishing expedition and found their homes pillaged by the French.

MONTAGNE PELEE ✿

A panoramic and winding road (Route N2) takes you through a tropical rainforest. The curves are of the hairpin variety, and the road is not always kept in good shape. However, you're rewarded with tropical flowers, baby ferns, plumed bamboo, and valleys so deeply green you'll think you're wearing cheap sunglasses.

The village of **Morne Rouge,** right at the foot of Montagne Pelée, is a popular vacation spot for Martiniquais. From here on, a narrow and unreliable road brings you to a level of 750m (2,460 ft.) above sea level, 480m (1,574 ft.) under the round summit of the volcano that destroyed St-Pierre. Montagne Pelée itself rises 1,373m (4,503 ft.) above sea level.

If you're a serious mountain climber and you don't mind 4 or 5 hours of hiking, you can scale the peak, though you should hire an experienced guide to accompany you. Realize that this is a real mountain, that rain is frequent, and that temperatures drop very low. Tropical growth often hides deep crevices in the earth, and there are other dangers. The park service maintains more than 161km (100 miles) of trails. Although the hikes up from Grand-Rivière or Le Prêcheur are generally the less arduous of the three options leading to the top, most visitors opt for departures from Morne Rouge because it doesn't take as long to finish the trip. It's steeper, rockier, and more exhausting, but you can make it in just 2½ hours versus the 5 hours it takes from the other two towns. There are no facilities other than these villages, so it's vital to bring water and food with you. Your arduous journey will be rewarded at the summit with sweeping views over the sea and panoramas that sometimes stretch as far as mountainous Dominica to the south. As for the volcano, its deathly eruption in 1902 apparently satisfied it—for the time being.

Upon your descent from Montagne Pelée, drive down to **Ajoupa-Bouillon,** one of the most beautiful towns on Martinique. Abounding in flowers and shrubbery with bright yellow and red leaves, this little village is the site of the remarkable **Gorges de la Falaise.** These are minicanyons on the Falaise River, up which you can travel to reach a waterfall. Ajoupa-Bouillon also makes a good lunch stop.

LEYRITZ

If you continue east toward the coast, near the town of Basse-Pointe in northeastern Martinique turn left 1.6km (1 mile) before Basse-Pointe and follow a road that goes deep into sugar-cane country to Leyritz, where you'll find one of the best-restored plantations on Martinique, **Leyritz Plantation** (② 596/78-53-92).

GRAND-RIVIERE

After Basse-Pointe, the town you reach on your northward trek is Grand-Rivière. From here you must turn back, but before doing so, you may want to stop at Yva Chez Vava, a good restaurant right at the entrance to the town.

DINING

Yva Chez Vava (ʁ (Finds) FRENCH/CREOLE   Directly west of Basse-Pointe, in a low-slung building painted the peachy-orange of a paw-paw fruit, Yva Chez Vava is a combination private home and restaurant. It represents the hard labor of three generations of Creole women. Infused with a simple country-inn style, it was established in 1979 by a well-remembered, long-departed matron, Vava, whose daughter, Yva, is now assisted by her own daughter, Rosy. Family recipes are the mainstay of this modest and very ethnic bistro. A la carte items include Creole soup, lobster, and various *colombos* (curries). Local delicacies used in the kitchen include *z'habitants* (crayfish), *vivaneau* (red snapper), *tazard* (kingfish), and *accras de morue* (codfish beignets), roasted or curried goat, and court bouillon of fish.

Before or after their meal, clients can bathe in the nearby river, or walk to an unnamed strip of sand, the nearest beach, which lies about .4km (¼ mile) from the restaurant.

Blvd. Charles-de-Gaulle. ② 596/55-72-72. Reservations recommended. Main courses 12€–29€ ($15–$36); fixed-price menu 14€ ($18). AE, DC, MC, V. Daily noon–5pm.

LE MARIGOT

After passing back through Basse-Pointe and Le Lorrain, you come to a small village that was relatively ignored by tourists until hotelier Jean-Louis de Lucy used France's tax-shelter laws to restore a landmark plantation and turn it into one of the finest hotels on the island. True, the nearest good beach is at Trinité, a 30-minute drive, but guests of the Habitation LaGrange don't seem to mind.

ACCOMMODATIONS & DINING

Habitation LaGrange 🐢🐢🐢   One of the most unusual and historic properties of Martinique, this hotel lies in isolation about 2km (1¼ miles) north of the village of Le Marigot. It's set on 2 hectares (5 acres) of land whose edges are engulfed by acres of banana fields. About 2km (1¼ miles) inland from the coast, it was originally built in 1928 as part of the last sugar plantation and rum distillery on Martinique. Today, the ruins of that distillery rise a short distance from the Louisiana-style main house. This hotel is the *ne plus ultra* of Martinique, superior in style and class to Leyritz, to which it bears some resemblance.

Rooms are either in the main house or in a comfortable annex, which was erected in 1990. In addition to that, another two very large rooms are in what used to be the stables. We actually prefer these rooms, photographs of which have appeared in architectural magazines. Each unit is different, and contains antique or reproduction furniture crafted from mahogany, baldachin-style (canopy) beds, and French colonial–style accessories. All units have verandas or patios, with views over a tropical landscape of gardens and banana groves. As part of an effort to preserve the quiet, units contain no TVs or radios. Bathrooms are among the island's finest, with wood paneling, four-footed tubs equipped with showers, and pedestal sinks. Meals are prepared in the Creole style by local chefs, then served in the Ajoupa, an open-sided pavilion.

97225 Le Marigot, Martinique, F.W.I. 📞 **596/53-60-60.** Fax 596/53-50-58. (For reservations, contact Caribbean Inns, P.O. Box 7411, Hilton Head Island, SC 29938; 📞 **800/633-7411** in the U.S.) www. habitationlagrange.com. 12 units. Winter 190€–294€ ($238–$368) double, 267€–352€ ($334–$440) suite; off season 186€–244€ ($233–$305) double, 267€–320€ ($334–$400) suite. Rates include breakfast. AE, MC, V. **Amenities:** Daytime restaurant at poolside; dining room; bar; outdoor pool; tennis court; library. *In room:* A/C, minibar, safe.

STE-MARIE

Heading south along the coastal road, you'll pass Le Marigot en route to the little town of Ste-Marie. **Musée du Rhum Saint-James,** route de l'Union at the Saint James Distillery (📞 **596/69-30-02**), displays engravings, antique tools and machines, and other exhibits tracing the history of sugar cane and rum from 1765 to the present. When inventories of rum are low and the distillery is functioning (only 4 months of the year, from early Mar to late June or mid-July), guided tours of the distillery are offered daily, whenever clients show up, between 9am and 5pm. Tours cost 5€ ($6.25) per person. Admission to the museum (open daily, year-round, from 9am–5pm, regardless of whether the distillery is functioning) is free. Rum is available for purchase on-site.

From here you can head out the north end of town and loop inland a bit for a stop at Morne des Esses, or continue heading south straight to Trinité.

TRINITE

Passing through Morne des Esses, continue south, then turn east, or from Ste-Marie head south along the coastal route (N1), to reach Trinité. The town is the gateway to the Caravelle peninsula, where the **Caravelle Nature Preserve,** a well-protected peninsula jutting into the Atlantic Ocean from the town of Trinité, has safe beaches and well-marked trails through tropical wetlands and to the ruins of historic Chateau Debuc. It offers excellent hiking and one of the only safe beaches for swimming on the Atlantic coast. It would hardly merit an actual stop were it not for the Saint Aubin Hotel.

ACCOMMODATIONS

Saint Aubin Hôtel ⚘ *Finds*   This restored three-story Victorian house is architecturally one of the loveliest inns in the Caribbean. With fancy gingerbread, the hotel was originally built in 1920 of brick and poured concrete as a replacement for a much older wood-sided house, which served as the seat of a large plantation. It sits on a hillside above sugar-cane fields and the bay, 3km (2 miles) from the village of Trinité itself. The nearest beach is Plage Cosmy, lying 1.6km (1 mile) from the hotel. The bedrooms are spacious and modern, with wall-to-wall carpeting and contemporary (not antique) furniture; views are of either the garden or the sea. There are some family rooms as well. All but two of the bedrooms have shower/tub combinations, the remaining two with shower. Other than breakfast, no meals are served, making a car absolutely necessary.

97220 Trinité, Martinique, F.W.I. ⓒ 596/69-34-77. Fax 596/69-41-14. 15 units. Winter 100€ ($125) double; off season 75€ ($94) double. Rates include continental breakfast. AE, DC, MC, V. **Amenities:** Outdoor pool; laundry. *In room:* A/C, no phone.

DINING

La Table de Mamy Nounou FRENCH/ANTILLEAN   Set about .8km (½ mile) east of the fishing village of Tartane, this is the most easterly restaurant in the most easterly hotel on La Caravelle peninsula. The setting, as created and maintained by a team of English-speaking expatriates from the French mainland, is a blue-and-white, recently renovated complex perched within a hill-hugging compound of veranda-fronted buildings overlooking the sea. The restaurant, which was rechristened La Table de Mamy Nounou in 2004, is the main allure of the well-managed and carefully maintained Hotel Caravelle.

Lunches are faster, and less elaborately orchestrated, than the candlelit dinners, where guests linger longer within an ambience that falls midway between what you'd expect on the French mainland and what's available in Fort-de-France. Menu items change frequently, but might include a *colombo* (spicy Creole stew) concocted from shark meat, fish, shellfish, or chicken; callaloo soup with crabmeat; braised filets of red mullet with tropical fruits; or, depending on the mood of the chef, classic dishes such as boeuf bourguignon. Desserts might feature a semimoist version of chocolate cake, or perhaps a rum-and-orange-flavored soufflé. There's dining on the veranda, easy access to a garden, and from virtually all points, a sweeping view of the sea.

On-site are 15 studio apartments, each with telephone, air-conditioning, ceiling fans, and a kitchenette. Accommodations rent for between 56€ and 76€ ($70–$95) per day for one to three occupants, and from 72€ to 98€ ($90–$123) for three to five occupants. Breakfast and dinner can be arranged for an additional 27€ ($34) per person per day.

In the Hotel Caravelle, Route du Château Dubuc, L'Anse l'Etang, 97720 Tartane (Trinité). ⓒ 596/58-07-32. Fax 596/58-07-90. http://perso.wanadoo.fr/hotelcaravelle. Reservations recommended for nonresidents of the hotel. Lunch platters and salads 5€–13€ ($6.25–$16); dinner main courses 14€–27€ ($18–$34). DC, MC, V. Daily noon–2:30pm and 7–9:30pm.

LE FRANÇOIS

Continuing your exploration of the east coast of Martinique, you can stop over in Le François to visit the **Musée Rhum Clement** at the Domaine de l'Acajou (ⓒ **596/54-62-07**), about 2km (1¼ miles) south of the village center. The setting for this museum is an outmoded distillery in the cellar of an 18th-century mansion with period furnishings that the Clement Rum Company closed in the early 1990s, when it shifted its production to a newer plant nearby (which cannot be visited). A Columbus exhibit is set up in caves, and other exhibits trace the institution of slavery in the islands. Products of the Clement rum distillery are prominently displayed for purchase, and tastings of some of the rums are available. The museum is in a botanic park; you could easily spend 2 or 3 hours exploring the exhibits and grounds. It's open daily from 8:30am to 5:30pm. Admission is 7€ ($8.75), free for age 11 and under.

ACCOMMODATIONS

Cap Est Lagoon Resort & Spa *Finds* Set on the island's east coast between the fishing hamlets of Vauclin and Le François—5km (3 miles) from either of them—this is the newest, poshest, and most cutting-edge hotel on Martinique. Scattered across 3.4 hectares (8½ acres) of gently sloping palm-studded beach-front, it's composed of 18 veranda-fronted, one- and two-story buildings housing 50 well-designed suites. This is as top of the line as you'll find in the French West Indies outside of St. Barts. It's the only government-rated five-star hotel on Martinique, and the only Relais & Château in either Martinique or Guadeloupe. Clients include a string of celebrities, the most impressive of which was the Queen of Denmark.

The venue that's encouraged here is very French, artfully permissive, and luxurious, where no one will mind if you simply vegetate, recovering from the stresses of urban life. Topless sunbathing for women is permitted on the beach or beside any of the pools, but not in the other public areas. Views throughout the resort extend outward over a coral reef to the wide blue seas. Construction and design emulates Creole models elsewhere, making full use of open access to sea breezes, with ample use of louvered doors, exotic tropical hardwoods, and exterior color schemes of blue, salmon, and pale pink. Public areas contain unusual artwork, including a large-scale triptych titled *Serenity*. It's all choreographed by designer Didier Lefort, who's well known within Gallic circles for his award-winning designs of hotels in French-speaking Tahiti and Mauritius. Each unit has a landscaped terrace or balcony, and separate bathtubs and showers. Besides the showpiece public pool, there are 36 plunge pools, some of them specifically associated with individual suites. Live music emanates many evenings from one of the two in-house bars throughout the dinner hour, and overall, the ambience is lighthearted, agreeable, and fun. The restaurants, Le Belém and Le Campêche, are recommended in "Dining," below.

Quartier Cap Est, 97240 Le François. ⓒ 800/633-7411 or 596/54-80-80. Fax 596/54-96-00. www.capest.com. 50 suites. Winter 500€–1,100€ ($625–$1,375) double; off season 400€–1,000€ ($500–$1,250) double. Rates include American breakfast. AE, DC, MC, V. **Amenities:** 2 restaurants; 2 bars; 1 outdoor pool; 36 plunge pools; lit tennis court; health club; spa; dock for mooring of private yachts and sailboats; fishing; kayaks; snorkeling; windsurfing; car rental; room service (7am–10pm); helipad. *In room:* A/C, plasma TV/DVD, dataport, minibar, beverage maker, hair dryer, safe.

Frégate Bleue *Finds* This is the closest thing to a European B&B on the island. It's a calm and quiet choice with touches of personal, old-fashioned charm. It's not the place for vacationers looking for nightlife and lots of activities—it's for escapists who don't mind the 10-minute drive to the beaches of St-François or the prevailing sense of isolation. Much of this ambience is the work of owner Yveline de Lucy de Fossarieu, an experienced veteran of the hotel industry. Her house is a 5-minute drive inland from the sea, and it overlooks several chains of deserted offshore islands (including Les Ilets de St-François and Les Ilets de l'Impératrice). Bedrooms are small but cozy, each with a compact bathroom with a shower. The site is perched in a quiet residential neighborhood high on a hill. Each room has either a terrace or a balcony with sweeping views over the coast.

Route de Vauclin, 97240 Le François, Martinique, F.W.I. © 800/633-7411 in the U.S., or 596/54-54-66. Fax 596/54-78-48. www.fregatebleue.com. 7 units. Winter 183€ ($229) double; off season 84€ ($105) double. Rates include breakfast. AE, MC, V. **Amenities:** Outdoor pool; laundry. *In room:* A/C, TV, kitchenette.

L'Habitation de L'Îlet Thierry ✹ *(Finds* On a remote, offshore island, this hotel has the most offbeat location in Martinique. The island's only beach is a sandy cove about a .8km (½ mile) from the inn. Around 1900, a Martinique-based merchant and planter from *la France metropolitaine* decided to build a clapboard- and stucco-covered, veranda-ringed second home on an isolated island off the southeastern coast of Martinique. In 1989, a trio of investors from the French mainland transformed it into one of the most isolated hotels in the French-speaking Caribbean. In 1999, it was renovated into a mostly white, somewhat spartan temple for rest, contemplation, and relaxation. Accommodations are large, with high-ceilings, and filled with rustic furniture. Each has direct access to one of the building's two levels of wraparound verandas, and none has any electronic amenities. Each has a sink and a toilet, but showers are in shared facilities off each hallway. You can swim and snorkel off the nearby pier or at any of several gravel-covered bays closer to home. If you want to kayak, sail, or windsurf, you can inform your hosts in advance, and they'll arrange to have a suitable craft (for a fee) delivered in advance of your arrival. The island itself, a scrub-covered expanse of about 15 hectares (37 acres), is the most distant of the seven islands of the Le François archipelago, and lies within a 12-minute boat ride from the Le François marina. It's there that—upon prior reservation—an employee of the hotel will fetch you and up to five other passengers in a motorboat.

L'Îlet Thierry, B.P. 26, 97240 Le François, Martinique, F.W.I. © 596/65-88-54 or 696/40-18-57. www. ilet-thierry.com. 4 units. Year-round 200€ ($250) double. Rates include round-trip transport from Martinique and breakfast. MAP (breakfast and dinner) 40€ ($50) per person per day. Full board 70€ ($88) per person per day. No credit cards. Closed Aug. **Amenities:** Restaurant; bar; bike and scooter rental; room service (7am–10pm); massage; babysitting; laundry service; dry cleaning. *In room:* A/C, TV (on request).

DINING
La Maison de L'Îlet Oscar ✹ *(Finds* INTERNATIONAL/FRENCH There are many similarities between this establishment and the one we also recommend on L'Ilet Thierry (directly above). Both lie on nearly adjacent islands off the southeast coast of Martinique; both are accessed by motorboat from the marina at Le François; both are centered around antique Creole houses, and both offer overnight accommodations in charming but somewhat spartan settings that appeal to offbeat adventurers. Less imposing than its sibling hotel on Îlet Thierry, this one is more amenable to day-trippers who want a meal, but not a night, on the island.

If you make advance reservations, you'll be taken on a 12-minute boat ride to the island, stopping at an emerald-colored tidal pool where legend says that Joséphine, wife of Napoleon I, once went swimming. You'll then head to the island's only dwelling, a one-story wood-sided house that was originally built in 1898 on nearby Îlet Thierry, and disassembled and floated, beam by beam, across to Îlet Oscar and reassembled there in 1935. Menu items focus on Creole specialties like an all-fish menu, an all-shrimp menu, or an all-lobster menu, but if you desire food inspired by the traditions of mainland France, Brittany-born Jean-Louis de Lussy and his staff will whip you up avocados stuffed with cray-fish, magret of duckling, or whatever else happens to be in the larder. If you want to overnight, the four bedrooms (all with shower, toilet, and double sinks) rent for 155€ ($194) per person, per day, with full board included. None has TV, phone, or air-conditioning.

L'Îlet Oscar, B.P. 12, 97240 Le François, Martinique. ⓒ 596/65-82-30 or 696/45-33-30. Reservations essential 1 day in advance. Set-price menu 40€–55€ ($50–$69). Round-trip transport from Le Marina du François 45€ ($56) for up to 6 passengers. AE, MC, V. Daily 11am–3pm and 6–9:30pm.

Le Bélem/Le Campêche ⭐⭐ FRENCH/ANTILLEAN   Two of the best-recommended dining spots in Martinique lie on the Atlantic coastline. If you arrive for lunch, you'll be steered toward the less expensive, and less formal, of the two restaurants, Le Campêche, an ocean-fronting outdoor bistro where good-looking people clad in minimalist bathing suits are not at all out of the ordinary. Menu items focus on tried-and-true Creole specialties, as well as sal-ads, pastas, and well-prepared versions of grilled fish and meats.

Dinners are more elaborate and more formal, served within Le Bélem, a romantic eatery noted for its wine list and its "gastronomic" interpretation of all things French and Antillean. Begin with a tarte tatin of foie gras with caramelized yellow bananas, shallots, and a confit of limes; or perhaps ravioli stuffed with conch and served with sautéed morels and a julienne of leeks; or a succulent version of foie gras of duckling with a vanilla-flavored mango sauce and banana jelly. Main courses include a filet of red snapper served with a fon-due of leeks and truffled fava beans.

In the Cap Est Lagoon Resort & Spa, Quartier Cap Est. ⓒ 596/54-80-80. Reservations strongly recommended for nonresidents. Main courses in Le Bélem 25€–45€ ($31–$56); main courses in Le Campêche 15€–30€ ($19–$38). AE, DC, MC, V. Le Bélem daily 7:30–10:30pm. Le Campêche daily noon–2:30pm.

Le Plein Soleil ⭐ (Finds) INTERNATIONAL   Meals here are taken on the wide veranda of a 1980s French colonial–style house that sits on a hillside about 90m (295 ft.) from the seafront. Your hosts are a trio of France- and Martinique-born entrepreneurs (Frank Cherere, José, and Jean-Christophe) who will welcome you, organize your meal (only if you phone in your intentions a day in advance), and cook sublime food. Menu items combine the aesthetics of France and the Antilles. Among the best examples are a terrine of foie gras with a compote of apples; an herb-enriched combination of scallops and dorado (mahimahi) in puff pastry; and a well-prepared filet of beef served with red-butter sauce.

There are also 12 bedrooms, each with private bathroom (shower only, no tubs) and telephone, but without TV or any other amenities. (A few of them are air-conditioned.) Depending on the season and their layouts, rooms rent for 81€ to 161€ ($101–$201) each, double occupancy. There's a beach within a walk of about 274m (899 ft.), and a formal-looking, rectangular swimming pool, but in most cases, whatever distractions and diversions appeal to you, you'll have to organize on your own.

Villa Lagon S.A.R.L., Pointe Thalemont, 97240 Le François. ⓒ 596/38-07-77. Reservations recommended. Set-price lunches 29€ ($36); set-price dinners 35€ ($44). MC, V. Daily 12:30–3pm; Mon–Sat 7:30–9pm. Lies 5km (3 miles) north from Le François, following signs first to Le Robert, then veering eastward when you see the signs to Thalemont, Mansarde, and Plein Soleil.

Puerto Rico

No one has ever suffered from boredom on Puerto Rico. It has hundreds of beaches, a mind-boggling array of watersports, miles of golf courses, acres of tennis courts, a huge variety of resorts, and casinos galore. It has more discos than any other place in the Caribbean, and shopping bargains to equal St. Thomas. And all this fun and variety comes with a much more reasonable price tag than it does on many of the other islands.

Lush, verdant Puerto Rico is half the size of New Jersey and is located some 1,000 miles southeast of the tip of Florida. With 272 miles of Atlantic and Caribbean coastline and a culture some 2,000 years old, Puerto Rico is packed with attractions. Old San Juan is its greatest historic center, with 500 years of history, as reflected in its restored Spanish colonial architecture.

It's also a land of contrasts. There are 79 cities and towns on Puerto Rico, each with a unique charm and flavor. The countryside is dotted with centuries-old coffee plantations, working sugar estates, a fascinating tropical rainforest, and forbidding caves and enormous boulders with mysterious petroglyphs carved by the Taíno peoples, the original settlers.

Dorado Beach, Cerromar Beach, and Palmas del Mar are the chief centers for those who have come for golf, tennis, and beaches. San Juan's hotels on the Condado/Isla Verde coast have, for the most part, a complete array of watersports. The continental shelf, which surrounds Puerto Rico on three sides, contributes to an abundance of coral reefs, caves, sea walls, and trenches for scuba diving and snorkeling.

San Juan is the world's second-largest home port for cruise ships, and the old port of San Juan recently underwent a $90 million restoration.

You can base yourself at one resort and still do a lot of exploring elsewhere, if you don't mind driving for a couple hours. It's possible to branch out and see a lot of the island even if you're staying in San Juan.

For even more comprehensive coverage, consider getting yourself a copy of *Frommer's Puerto Rico.*

1 Essentials

VISITOR INFORMATION

For information before you leave home, contact one of the following **Puerto Rico Tourism Company** offices: 666 Fifth Ave., **New York, NY** 10103 (© **800/223-6530** in the U.S. or 212/586-6262); 3575 W. Cahuenga Blvd., Suite 405, **Los Angeles, CA** 90068 (© **800/874-1230**); or 901 Ponce de León Blvd., Suite 101, **Coral Gables, FL** 33134 (© **800/815-7391** or 305/445-9112). In **Canada** you can stop by 230 Richmond St. W, Suite 902, Toronto, ON M5V 1V6 (© **416/368-2680**), for information. The official website is **www.prtourism.com.**

On the island, it's best to go to the local city hall for tourist information. Ask for a copy of *Qué Pasa,* the official visitors' guide.

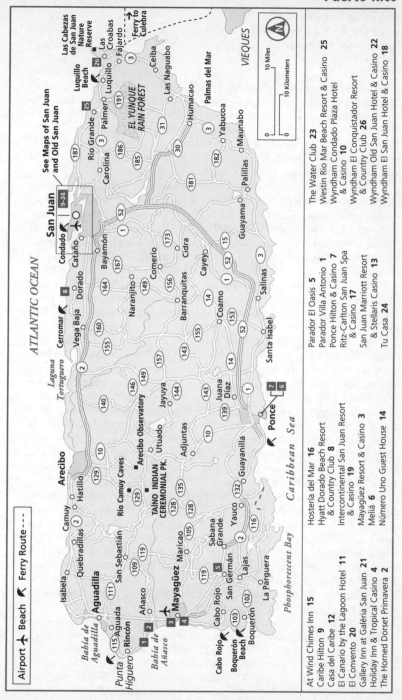

Puerto Rico

See Maps of San Juan and Old San Juan

ATLANTIC OCEAN

VIEQUES

Caribbean Sea

Phosphorescent Bay

Laguna Tortuguero

Bahía de Aguadilla

Bahía de Añasco

Punta Higuero

Airport ✈ **Beach** ⚓ **Ferry Route** - - -

N

10 Miles
10 Kilometers

EL YUNQUE RAIN FOREST

Las Cabezas de San Juan Nature Reserve

Ferry to Culebra

TAÍNO INDIAN CEREMONIAL PK.

At Wind Chimes Inn **15**
Caribe Hilton **9**
Casa del Caribe **12**
El Canario by the Lagoon Hotel **11**
El Convento **20**
Gallery Inn at Galéria San Juan **21**
Holiday Inn & Tropical Casino **4**
The Horned Dorset Primavera **2**

Hostería del Mar **16**
Hyatt Dorado Beach Resort & Country Club **8**
Intercontinental San Juan Resort & Casino **19**
Mayagüez Resort & Casino **3**
Melía **6**
Número Uno Guest House **14**

Parador El Oasis **5**
Parador Villa Antonio **1**
Ponce Hilton & Casino **7**
Ritz-Carlton San Juan Spa & Casino **17**
San Juan Marriott Resort & Stellaris Casino **13**
Tu Casa **24**

The Water Club **23**
Westin Rio Mar Beach Resort & Casino **25**
Wyndham Condado Plaza Hotel & Casino **10**
Wyndham El Conquistador Resort & Country Club **26**
Wyndham Old San Juan Hotel & Casino **22**
Wyndham El San Juan Hotel & Casino **18**

451

GETTING THERE

Before you book your own airfare, read the section "Packages for the Independent Traveler" in chapter 2—it can save you a bundle. There are more package deals to Puerto Rico than almost any other island except for Jamaica.

Puerto Rico is by far the most accessible of the Caribbean islands, with frequent airline service. **American Airlines** (© 800/433-7300 in the U.S.; www.aa.com) has designated San Juan as its hub for the entire Caribbean. American offers nonstop daily flights to San Juan from Baltimore; Boston; Chicago; Dallas–Fort Worth; Hartford, Connecticut; Miami; Newark, New Jersey; New York (JFK); Orlando; Philadelphia; Tampa; Fort Lauderdale; and Washington (Dulles), plus flights from both Montreal and Toronto with changes in Chicago or Miami. There are also at least two daily flights from Los Angeles to San Juan that stop in Dallas or Miami.

American also offers many money-saving packages that include your hotel or resort; contact **American Airlines FlyAway Vacations** (© 800/321-2121 in the U.S.; www.aavacations.com) to learn about their current offerings.

American Eagle (© 800/433-7300 in the U.S.) is the undisputed leader among the short-haul local commuter flights of the Caribbean. Collectively, American Eagle, along with its larger associate, American Airlines, flies to dozens of destinations on more than 30 islands of the Caribbean and the Bahamas.

Delta (© 800/221-1212 in the U.S.; www.delta.com) has four daily nonstop flights on weekdays and five on weekends from its international hub in Atlanta. Ask about their packages by calling **Delta Vacations** at © 800/872-7786 in the U.S. (www.deltavacations.com).

United Airlines (© 800/241-6522 in the U.S.; www.ual.com) offers daily nonstop flights from Chicago to San Juan. **Northwest** (© 800/225-2525 in the U.S.; www.nwa.com) has one daily nonstop to San Juan from Detroit, as well as at least one (and sometimes more) connecting flights to San Juan from Detroit. **Northwest** (© 800/225-2525 in the U.S.; www.nwa.com) also offers flights to San Juan, some of them nonstop, from both Memphis and Minneapolis, with a schedule that varies according to the season and the day of the week. **US Airways** (© 800/428-4322 in the U.S.; www.usairways.com) also competes, with daily flights between Charlotte, North Carolina, and San Juan. The airline also offers two daily nonstop flights from Philadelphia, and one from Pittsburgh. You can also ask about packages offered by **US Airways Vacations** (© 800/455-0123 in the U.S.).

Continental Airlines (© 800/231-0856) flies nonstop daily from Newark, New Jersey; Houston; and Cleveland. The airline also flies five times a week direct to the northwestern airport outside Aguadilla should you wish to begin your tour of Puerto Rico in the west. In winter, service is increased to daily flights. **Jet Blue** (© 800/538-2583) flies two times a day from New York's JFK airport to San Juan. **Spirit Air** (© 787/772-7117) offers two daily nonstop flights from Fort Lauderdale to San Juan.

Canadians can fly **Air Canada** (© 888/247-2262) from either Montreal or Toronto to San Juan.

Puerto Rico is the major transportation hub of the Caribbean, with the best connections for getting anywhere in the island. In addition to American Eagle (see above), **Cape Air** (© 787/253-1121) links the two major islands in the U.S. Virgins, both St. Croix and St. Thomas, with San Juan.

Seaborne Airlines (© 888/FLY-TOUR) offers daily links between St. Croix and St. Thomas with San Juan. The one-way cost from the U.S. Virgin Islands to Puerto Rico is a reasonable $65 per person. The planes are small, carrying 15 to 19 passengers. Often there are more than 50 flights a day.

⌒Value⌒ Great Discounts Through the LeLoLai VIP Program

To join Puerto Rico's **LeLoLai VIP (Value in Puerto Rico)** program, there is no charge, and you can enjoy the equivalent of up to $250 in travel benefits. Of course, most of the experiences linked to LeLoLai are of the rather touristy type, but it can still be a good investment. You'll get discounts on admission to folklore shows, guided tours of historic sites and natural attractions, lodgings, meals, shopping, activities, and more.

Paradores Puertorriqueños, the island's modestly priced network of country inns, give cardholders 10% to 20% discounts on room rates Monday to Thursday. Discounts of 10% to 20% are offered at many restaurants, from San Juan's toniest hotels to several *mesones gastronómicos:* government-sanctioned restaurants serving Puerto Rican fare. Shopping discounts are offered at many stores and boutiques, and cardholders get 10% to 20% discounts at many island attractions. The card also entitles you to free admission to some of the island's folklore shows.

For more information about this card, call ⓒ **787/722-1709** or go to the Centro de Información Turística located at Plaza Darsenas, Old San Juan. Although you can call for details before you leave home, you can only sign up for this program when you reach Puerto Rico. Many hotel packages include participation in this program as part of their offerings.

LIAT (ⓒ **888/844-5428** in Puerto Rico or 868/624-4727 in the U.S.) provides an air link to the Lesser Antilles islands.

British travelers can take a **British Airways** (ⓒ **0870/850-9850** in the U.K., 800/247-9297 in the U.S.) daily flight to New York and then a connection to San Juan.

GETTING AROUND

BY PLANE   American Eagle (ⓒ **787/791-5050**) flies from Luís Muñoz Marín International Airport in San Juan to Mayagüez, the gateway to western Puerto Rico. The flight takes 40 minutes. Fares vary widely, but expect to pay between $202 and $212 round-trip, per person, and try to book your passage as early as possible.

BY RENTAL CAR   We do not recommend renting a car in San Juan because of heavy traffic and difficult parking. To really explore the island, however, a car is necessary. Some local car-rental agencies may tempt you with slashed prices, but you won't find any local branches to help you should you run into car trouble elsewhere on the island. Plus, some of the agencies advertising low-cost deals don't take credit cards and want cash in advance. You also have to watch out for hidden extras and insurance problems with smaller and not-very-well-known firms.

The old reliables include **Avis** (ⓒ **800/331-1212** in the U.S., or 787/791-2500; www.avis.com), **Budget** (ⓒ **800/472-3325**in the U.S., or 787/791-3685; www.budgetrentacar.com), or **Hertz** (ⓒ **800/654-3131** in the U.S., or 787/791-0840; www.hertz.com). Each offers minivan transport to its office from the San Juan airport. Another alternative is **Kemwel Holiday Auto**

(© **800/678-0678** in the U.S.; www.kemwel.com). None of these companies rents jeeps, four-wheel-drive vehicles, or convertibles. *Note:* Theft is high on Puerto Rico, so extra precaution is always a good idea.

Distances in Puerto Rico are often posted in kilometers rather than miles (a kilometer is .62 miles), but speed limits are in miles per hour (mph).

BY PUBLIC TRANSPORTATION   *Públicos* are cars or minibuses that provide low-cost transportation and are designated with the letters *P* or *PD* following the numbers on their license plates. They usually operate only during daylight hours, carry up to six passengers at a time, and charge rates that are loosely governed by the Public Service Commission. Although prices are low, this option is slow and inconvenient, with frequent stops, and often erratic routing.

Locals are adept at figuring out their routes along rural highways, and in some cases, they simply wave at a moving *público* that they suspect might be headed in their direction. Unless you're fluent in Spanish and feeling adventurous, we suggest that you phone either of the numbers below, describe where and when you want to go, and agree to the prearranged price between specific points. Then, be prepared to wait. Although, at least in theory, a *público* might be arranged between most of the towns and villages of Puerto Rico, by far the most popular routes are between San Juan and Ponce and San Juan and Mayagüez. Fares vary according to whether a *público* will make a detour to pick up or drop off a passenger at a specific locale. If you want to deviate from the predetermined routes, you'll pay more than if you wait for a *público* at vaguely designated points beside the main highway, or at predefined points that include airports and, in some cases, the main plaza (central square) of a town.

Information about *público* routes between San Juan and Mayagüez is available from **Lineas Sultana,** Calle Esteban González 898, Urbanización Santa Rita, Rio Piedras (© **787/765-9377**). Information about *público* routes between San Juan and Ponce is available from **Choferes Unidos de Ponce,** terminal de carros públicos, Calle Vive in Ponce (© **787/721-2400** or 787/764-0540). Fares from San Juan to Ponce cost $30 to $50, or $30 from San Juan to Mayagüez.

SIGHTSEEING TOURS   If you want to see more of the island but don't want to rent a car or deal with public transportation, perhaps an organized tour is for you. **Castillo Sightseeing Tours & Travel Services,** Calle Laurel 2413, Punta La Marias, Santurce (© **787/726-5752** or 787/791-6195), maintains offices at some of San Juan's major hotels. They can also arrange pickup at other accommodations in one of their six air-conditioned buses. One of the most popular half-day tours runs from San Juan to El Yunque Rainforest; it departs in the morning, lasts 4 to 5 hours, and costs $40 per person. The company also offers a 4-hour city tour of San Juan that costs $35 and includes a stopover at the Bacardi rum factory. Full-day snorkeling tours to the reefs near the coast of a deserted island off Puerto Rico's eastern edge aboard one of two sail- and motor-driven catamarans go for $79, with lunch, snorkeling gear, and piña coladas included.

The best tours of Old San Juan itself are offered by **Legends** (© **787/605-9060**). In a personally conducted 3-hour walking tour, Wednesday to Monday from 10am to 1pm, you're conducted to the most intriguing sights in the old city, as you listen to pirate stories, legends, and historical facts. The rate is $38 per person (children under 5 free). Another intriguing tour is a night walk into Spanish colonial times. This 2-hour tour, costing $30 per person, is conducted from 6 to 8pm Sunday, Monday, Wednesday, and Thursday. When calling for information, ask about other tours that might be available.

(Fun Fact Special Events

The annual **Casals Festival,** February 28 to March 13 in 2005 (subject to change), is the Caribbean's most celebrated cultural event. The bill at San Juan's Performing Arts Center includes an array of international guest conductors, orchestras, and soloists who come to honor the memory of Pablo Casals, the renowned cellist who was born in Spain to a Puerto Rican mother, and who died in Puerto Rico in 1973. Tickets range from $27 to $36; a 50% discount is offered to students, seniors, and persons with disabilities. Call © 787/721-7727 for tickets.

The island's **Carnival** celebrations feature float parades, dancing, and street parties in the week leading up to Ash Wednesday. The festivities in **Ponce** are marked by masqueraders wearing brightly painted horned masks, the crowning of a Carnival queen, and the closing "burial of the sardine." Hotel rates go up at this time of year, sometimes considerably. For more information, call © **787/284-4141.** Ash Wednesday falls on February 9 in 2005.

FAST FACTS: Puerto Rico

Banks Most major U.S. banks have branches with ATMs in San Juan, and are open Monday to Friday from 8:30am to 4pm. Bank branches in malls are also open on Saturday from 8am to 5pm and Sunday from 9am to 3pm.

Currency The **U.S. dollar** is the coin of the realm. Canadian currency is accepted by some big hotels in San Juan, although reluctantly. *Rates in this chapter are quoted in U.S. dollars.*

Documents Since Puerto Rico is part of the United States, American citizens do not need a passport or visa. Canadians, however, should carry some form of identification, such as a birth certificate and photo ID, though we always recommend carrying your passport. Citizens of the United Kingdom should have a passport.

Electricity The electricity is 110-volt AC (60 cycles), the same as in the United States and Canada.

Emergencies Call © **911.**

Language English is understood at the big resorts and in most of San Juan, though it's polite to at least greet people in Spanish and ask if they speak English before you make assumptions. Out in the island, Spanish is still *número uno.*

Safety Use common sense and take precautions. Muggings are commonly reported on the Condado and Isla Verde beaches in San Juan, so you might want to confine your moonlit-beach nights to the fenced-in and guarded areas around some of the major hotels. The countryside of Puerto Rico is safer than San Juan, but caution is always the rule. Avoid narrow little country roads and isolated beaches day or night.

Taxes There's a government tax of 9% in regular hotels or 11% in hotels with casinos. The airport departure tax is included in the price of your ticket.

Telephone Puerto Rico is on the North American telephone system; the area code is **787**. Place a call to or from Puerto Rico just as you would from within the United States or Canada.

Time Puerto Rico is on Atlantic Standard Time year-round, putting it 1 hour ahead of U.S. Eastern Standard Time. In winter, when it's noon in Miami, it's 1pm in San Juan. But from April until late October (during daylight savings time on the U.S. East Coast), Puerto Rico and the East Coast keep the same time.

Tipping Some hotels add a 10% service charge to your bill. If they don't, you're expected to tip for services rendered. Tip as you would in the United States (15%–20%).

Water The water in Puerto Rico is generally safe to drink, although you may prefer bottled water.

Weather Puerto Rico is cooler than most of the other Caribbean islands because of its northeast trade winds. Sea, land, and mountain breezes also help keep the temperatures at a comfortable level. The climate is fairly stable all year, with an average temperature of 76°F (24°C). The only variants are found in the mountain regions, where the temperature fluctuates between 66°F and 76°F (19°C–24°C), and on the north coast, where the temperature ranges from 70°F to 80°F (21°C–27°C). There is no real rainy season, but August is the wettest month.

2 San Juan ★★★

Puerto Rico's capital is a major city—actually an urban sprawl of several municipalities that lies along the island's north coast. Its architecture ranges from classic colonial buildings that recall the Spanish empire to modern beachfront hotels reminiscent of Miami Beach.

SAN JUAN ESSENTIALS

ARRIVING   Dozens of taxis line up outside the airport to meet arriving flights, so you rarely have to wait. The island's **Public Service Commission** (© 787/756-1401) sets flat rates between the Luís Muñoz Marín Airport and major tourist zones as follows: From the airport to any hotel in Isla Verde, $10; to any hotel in the Condado district, $13; and to any hotel in Old San Juan, $16. Tips of between 10% and 15% of that fare are expected.

Airport Limousine Service (© 787/791-4745) offers minivan transport from the airport to various neighborhoods of San Juan for prices that are lower than taxis. You'll have to wait until they get a minimum of eight to 10 passengers to fill the van, however. The fare is $70 to $80 per van to any hotel in Isla Verde, $90 to $100 per van to the Condado or Old San Juan. The sign-up desk is near the American Airlines arrival facilities.

For conventional limousine service, **Bracero Limousine** (© 787/253-1133) will send a car and driver to meet you at the arrivals terminal for luxurious and strictly private transport to your hotel or anywhere you specify in Puerto Rico. This luxury and convenience will cost you, though. Three persons can rent a sedan for $55 per hour or a limousine for $75 per hour.

VISITOR INFORMATION   Tourist information is available at the **Luís Muñoz Marín Airport** (© 800/866-5829 or 787/791-1014), open daily from

9am to 8pm. From December 15 to April 15 the office closes at 10pm. Another office is at **La Casita,** Pier 1, Old San Juan (© 787/722-1709). Open Saturday to Wednesday 9am to 8pm, Thursday and Friday 9am to 5:30pm.

ORIENTATION   The city center is on **San Juan Island,** connected to the rest of the metropolitan area by causeways. The western half of San Juan Island contains the walled city of **Old San Juan.** The eastern half is known as **Puerto de Tierra,** and contains many government buildings. Across the causeways is the neighborhood of **Miramar,** which fronts the Laguna del Condado. **Condado** is the narrow peninsula that loops around the top of Miramar almost all the way back to San Juan Island. It's where you'll find many of the best beaches. Just east of Condado is the residential neighborhood of **Ocean Park.** South of Condado and Ocean Park is **Santurce.** To the east is the International Airport, and even further east is **Isla Verde,** home of some of the Caribbean's most upscale resort hotels, connected to the rest of San Juan by an isthmus.

GETTING AROUND   Walking is the best way to get around Old San Juan. The historic core of the old city is very compact. If your feet tire of the old cobblestone streets, board one of the free open-air trolleys that slowly make their way through the old city. You can board a trolley at any point along its route (either side of the Calle Fortaleza or Calle San José are good bets), or you can go to either the Marina or La Puntilla for departures.

The rest of the city is not so pedestrian-friendly. You'll want to take buses, taxis, or your own car to get around the rest of San Juan, including Condado and Isla Verde. The **Metropolitan Bus Authority** (© 787/767-7979) operates buses in the greater San Juan area. Bus stops are marked by upright metal signs or yellow posts that say *parada.* Bus terminals in San Juan are in the dock area and at Plaza de Colón. A typical fare is 25¢ to 50¢. The higher fee is for the faster buses that make fewer stops; call for more information about routes and schedules.

Taxis are metered; tips between 10% and 15% are customary. The initial charge for destinations in the city is $1, plus 10¢ for each $\frac{1}{16}$ mile and 50¢ for every suitcase, with a minimum fare of $3. Taxis are invariably lined up outside the entrance to most of the island's hotels, and if not, a staff member can almost always call one for you. If you want to arrange a taxi on your own, call the **Mejor Cab Company** (© 787/723-2460). If you want to take a cab to a destination outside the city, you must negotiate a flat fee with the driver. For complaints or questions, contact the **Public Service Commission** (© 787/791-2550), which regulates cabs.

Tren Urbano: The Way to Go

Perhaps by the time you read this, San Juan will be linked to its major suburbs such as Santurce, Bayamón, and Guaynabo by a $1.55 billion urban train called *Tren Urbano.* So far, three openings have been announced, only to face delays. This will be the first mass transit project in the history of Puerto Rico. The new train system is designed to bring a fast and easy mode of transportation to the most congested areas of metropolitan San Juan. Trains will run every 4 minutes during peak hours in morning and afternoon. The line is expected to carry some 115,000 passengers daily. For more information, call © 787/765-0927.

San Juan

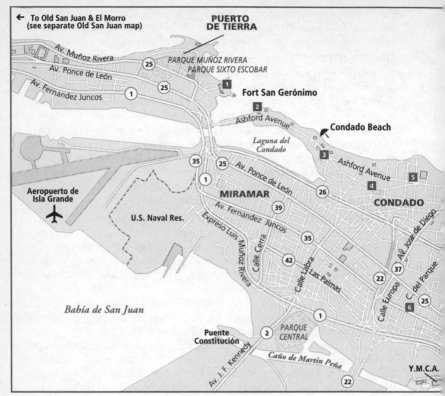

FAST FACTS One of the most centrally located **pharmacies** is the **Puerto Rico Drug Co.,** Calle San Francisco 157 (© **787/725-2202**), in Old San Juan; open Monday to Friday from 7am to 9:30pm, Saturday from 8am to 9:30pm, and Sunday from 8:30am to 7:30pm. **Walgreens,** 1130 Ashford Ave., Condado (© **787/725-1510**), is a 24-hour pharmacy.

In a **medical emergency,** call © **787/721-2116.** Ashford Memorial Community Hospital, 1451 Ashford Ave. (© **787/723-6430**), maintains a 24-hour emergency room.

American Express services are handled by the **Vithorn Travel,** 1035 Ashford Ave., Condado (© **787/723-9320**). The office is open Monday to Friday from 9am to 5pm and on Saturday from 9 to 11am.

ACCOMMODATIONS

All hotel rooms on Puerto Rico are subject to a 9% to 11% tax, which is not included in the rates listed in this chapter. Most hotels also impose a 10% service charge. Before you book a hotel, refer back to the section "Packages for the Independent Traveler" in chapter 2. Packages can save you a lot of money, especially if you want to stay at one of the big resorts.

IN OLD SAN JUAN

El Convento ⋆ The landmark is back. El Convento offers some of the most charming and historic hotel experiences anywhere in the Caribbean. Built in 1651, this hotel in the heart of the old city was once the New World's

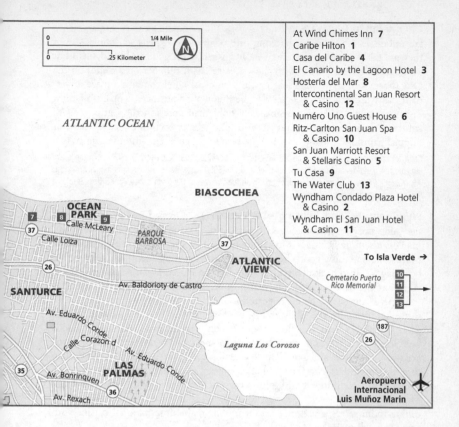

first Carmelite convent. Over the years El Convento was everything from a flop-house to a parking lot. It opened as a hotel in 1962, thanks to backing by the Woolworth family.

Furnishings are in traditional Spanish style, with mahogany beams, elaborate dark-stained paneling, and handmade Andalusian-styled terra-cotta tile floors. Each unit contains extras like VCRs, stereos, and comfortable robes and slippers. The small marble-floored bathrooms have scales, second phones, and shower/tub combinations. The interior courtyard is the focal point of the hotel. Of course, you won't have the same resort facilities here that you'd find in a blockbuster hotel on the Condado or in Isla Verde. The lower two floors house shops, bars, and restaurants.

The restaurants and bars are among the best in town. Delightful El Picoteo has terrific tapas, Patio del Nispero serves elegant alfresco meals, and hip Café Bohemio has great homemade desserts. The so-called pool here is accessible via the 4th floor, and it measures only about 6 feet by 10 feet—very small, but personalized, charming, and endearing because of its view over the facade of the nearby cathedral. There's a Jacuzzi immediately adjacent to the pool, and a big sun terrace.

Calle de Cristo 100, San Juan, PR 00901. ©️ 800/468-2779 or 787/723-9020. Fax 787/721-2877. www.
elconvento.com. 67 units. Winter $295–$400 double; off season $185–$275 double; year-round from
$500 suite. Rates include continental breakfast. AE, DC, DISC, MC, V. Parking $10. Bus: Old Town Trolley.
Amenities: 3 restaurants; 3 bars; tiny rooftop plunge pool; fitness center; Jacuzzi; massage; laundry service;
dry cleaning; all nonsmoking rooms; rooms for those with limited mobility. *In room:* A/C, TV/VCR, dataport,
fridge, beverage maker, hair dryer, iron/ironing board, safe.

Gallery Inn at Galería San Juan ★ *Finds*   This hotel's location and ambience are unbeatable. We suggest booking one of the least expensive doubles—even they are fairly roomy and attractively furnished, with good beds and small but adequate bathrooms, some with shower, some with tub. Set on a hilltop in the Old Town, with a sweeping sea view, this unusual hotel contains a maze of verdant courtyards. In the 1700s, it was the home of an aristocratic Spanish family. Today, it's one of the most whimsically bohemian hotels in the Caribbean. All courtyards and rooms are adorned with hundreds of sculptures, silk-screens, or original paintings, usually for sale. The nearest beach is a 15-minute ride away.

Calle Norzagaray 204–206, San Juan, PR 00901. ℭ **787/722-1808.** Fax 787/977-2909. www.thegallery inn.com. 24 units. Year-round $145–$350 double; $270–$350 suite. Rates include continental breakfast. AE, DC, MC, V. 6 free parking spaces, plus parking on the street. Bus: Old Town Trolley. **Amenities:** Breakfast dining room; bar. *In room:* A/C, hair dryer, safe.

Wyndham Old San Juan Hotel & Casino ★   Opened in 1997, this dignified nine-story waterfront hotel is part of a $100 million renovation of San Juan's cruise-port facilities. Most (but not all) of the major cruise ships dock nearby, making this a good choice if you want to spend time in San Juan before boarding a ship. Think of a typical Holiday Inn geared for business travelers. If you want Old Town character and atmosphere, head for the El Convento.

Upper floors of this hotel are geared to hotel guests. But on days when cruise ships pull into port, the lobby and its bars are likely to be jammed with passengers. The hotel's triangular floor plan surrounds an inner courtyard that floods light into the tasteful and comfortable beige-and-white bedrooms, each of which has two phone lines and a modem connection for laptop computers. Other than that, the rooms lack character and are a bit bandboxy and small, although each comes with a comfortable bed, plus a compact bathroom with shower and tub. Most of the lobby level is devoted to a 10,000-square-foot casino. The upscale dining room serves a perfectly fine if unremarkable international cuisine with some regional specialties.

100 Calle Brumbaugh, San Juan, PR 00902. ℭ **800/996-3426** or 787/721-5100. Fax 787/721-1111. www. wyndham.com. 240 units. Winter $230–$340 double, $290–$390 suite; off season $135–$200 double, $185–$290 suite. AE, DC, DISC, MC, V. Parking $12; valet parking $15. Bus: A7. **Amenities:** 2 restaurants; 2 bars; 2 outdoor pools; casino; fitness center; Jacuzzi; car-rental desk; business center; room service (6:30am–11:30pm); laundry service; dry cleaning; nonsmoking rooms; rooms for those with limited mobility. *In room:* A/C, TV, minibar, beverage maker, hair dryer, iron/ironing board.

IN PUERTO DE TIERRA

Caribe Hilton ★★★   This is one of the most up-to-date spa and convention hotels in San Juan. Thanks to an unusual configuration of natural barriers and legal maneuverings, the hotel has the only private beach on the island (and the only garden incorporating an antique naval installation, the semiruined colonial Fort San Gerónimo). The Caribe's size (17 acres of parks and gardens) and sprawling facilities often attract conventions and tour groups. Only the Wyndham Condado Plaza and the Hotel El San Juan rival it for nonstop activity.

Prices vary according to the views outside and the amenities within. Each room has a larger-than-expected bathroom with a shower/tub combination, and comfortable tropical-inspired furniture. An oceanfront spa and fitness center is the only beachside spa in Puerto Rico, featuring such delights as body wraps, hydrotherapy tub treatments, and soothing cucumber sun therapies.

The restaurants are so good that many locals visit for special events. Il Giardino serves northern Italian, Morton's of Chicago is the area's premier steakhouse, and Madrid-San Juan is one of Puerto Rico's best tapas restaurants. In the Caribe

Terrace Bar, you can order the bartender's celebrated piña colada, once enjoyed by movie legends like Joan Crawford and Errol Flynn.

As a preview of coming attractions, look for the development next door of the **Paseo Caribe,** which will add a roster of 264 luxurious Condado Lagoon Villas to the complex. Phase one will be completed in December of 2004, with Phase two following a year later. When it's all completed, the Hilton will have the largest conglomerate of bedrooms on the island. The new villas being added will boast a master bedroom, a kitchen, a dining room, and lots of storage space. New additions on the way include several new restaurants, boutiques, and even a cinema lounge.

Look for the opening, within a separate building from the hotel itself, of a casino on the grounds by early 2005. It will be the biggest in the Caribbean Basin.

Calle Los Rosales, San Juan, PR 00901. ℂ **800/HILTONS** or 787/721-0303. Fax 787/725-8849. www.hilton caribbean.com/sanjuan. 646 units. Winter $325–$365 double, $400–$1,400 suite; off season $265–$280 double; $301–$1,275 suite. Children 16 and under stay free in parent's room (maximum 4 people per room). AE, DC, DISC, MC, V. Self-parking $10; valet parking $20. Bus: B21. **Amenities:** 6 restaurants; 3 bars; outdoor pool; 3 tennis courts; health club and spa; playground; business center; limited room service; babysitting; laundry service; dry cleaning; nonsmoking rooms; rooms for those with limited mobility. *In room:* A/C, TV, dataport, minibar, beverage maker, hair dryer, safe.

IN CONDADO

Once this was a wealthy residential area, but with the construction of El Centro, the Puerto Rico Convention Center, all that has changed. Private villas were torn down to make way for high-rise hotels, restaurants, and nightclubs. The Condado shopping area, along Ashford and Magdalena avenues, became the center of a huge number of boutiques. There are bus connections into Old San Juan, or you can take a taxi.

Very Expensive

San Juan Marriott Resort & Stellaris Casino ✦   It's the tallest building on the Condado, a 21-story landmark that Marriott spent staggering sums to renovate after a tragic fire gutted the premises in 1989. The current building packs lots of postmodern style, and one of the best beaches on the Condado is right outside. Furnishings in the soaring lobby were inspired by Chippendale. If there's a flaw, it's the decor of the comfortable but bland bedrooms, with pastel colors that look washed out when compared to the rich mahoganies and jewel tones of the rooms in the rival Wyndham Condado Plaza (see below). The units are generally spacious, with good views of the water, and each comes with a tiled bathroom with a shower/tub combination.

1309 Ashford Ave., San Juan, PR 00907. ℂ **800/228-9290** or 787/722-7000. Fax 787/722-6800. www. marriottpr.com. 525 units. Winter $380–$580 double, $730 suite; off season $205–$255 double, $330 suite. Suite rate includes breakfast. AE, DC, DISC, MC, V. Parking $10; valet parking $15. Bus: B21. **Amenities:** 2 restaurants; 2 bars; 2 pools; casino; 2 tennis courts; health club; Jacuzzi; sauna; concierge; tour desk; car rental; business center; 24-hr. room service; babysitting; laundry service; dry cleaning; nonsmoking rooms; rooms for those with limited mobility. *In room:* A/C, TV, dataport, minibar, beverage maker, hair dryer, iron/ironing board, safe.

Wyndham Condado Plaza Hotel & Casino ✦ *Kids*   This is one of the busiest hotels on Puerto Rico, with enough facilities and restaurants to keep a visitor occupied for weeks. It's a favorite of business travelers, tour groups, and conventions, but it also attracts independent travelers. Families appreciate the extensive children's programs, some of the best on the island. The Caribe Hilton at Puerto de Tierra is its major rival, and we prefer that hotel's style and flair. Of

the three chain-related properties on island, the Wyndham Condado Plaza has revolved into the most middle-brow. It has two minor and rather unattractive swimming pools, and lots of security-related tension between the sunbathing area around those two pools and the narrow sands of not-so-great beach that the hotel shares with the public. Because the beach is small the pools tend to be overcrowded with hotel guests. The rooms, however, all have private terraces and are spacious, bright, and airy, fitted with deluxe beds and mattresses, either king-size or doubles, but most often twins. The good-size bathrooms contain shower/tub combinations. The complex's best section, the Plaza Club, has 80 units (including five duplex suites), a VIP lounge for guests, and private check-in/check-out.

Only Hotel El San Juan has a larger choice of dining options. This place is known for creating restaurants with culinary diversity. The hotel's premier restaurant, a hot ticket on San Juan's dining scene, is Cobia, winner of several culinary awards.

999 Ashford Ave., San Juan, PR 00907. ✆ 800/468-8588 in the U.S., or 787/721-1000. Fax 787/721-4613. www.wyndham.com. 570 units. Winter $350–$520 double, $635–$1,150 suite; off season $230–$400 double, $450–$1,400 suite. AE, DC, DISC, MC, V. Valet parking $15; self-parking $10. Bus: C10 or B21. **Amenities:** 6 restaurants; 3 bars; 2 outdoor pools; casino; 2 tennis courts; health club and spa; 3 Jacuzzis; fishing; scuba diving; snorkeling; children's programs; business center; salon; 24-hr. room service; laundry service; dry cleaning. *In room:* A/C, TV, dataport, minibar, beverage maker, hair dryer, iron/ironing board, safe.

Moderate

El Canario by the Lagoon Hotel
A relaxing, informal European-style hotel, El Canario is in a quiet residential neighborhood just a short block from Condado Beach. This is one of the better B&Bs in the area. The hotel is very much in the Condado styling, which evokes Miami Beach in the 1960s. The bedrooms are generous in size and have balconies. Most of them have twin beds and their bathrooms are sleek and contemporary, with shower stalls and enough space to spread out your stuff. If the hotel doesn't have room for you, it can book you into its sibling properties, either El Canario Inn or El Canario by the Sea.

Calle Clemenceau 4, Condado, San Juan, PR 00907. ✆ 800/533-2649 in the U.S., or 787/722-5058. Fax 787/723-8590. www.canariohotels.com. 40 units. Winter $115–$130 double; off season $90–$100 double. Rates include continental breakfast and morning newspaper. AE, DISC, MC, V. Bus: B21 or C10. **Amenities:** Tour desk; coin-operated laundry; all nonsmoking rooms. *In room:* A/C, TV, safe.

Inexpensive

At Wind Chimes Inn ✦
This restored and renovated Spanish manor, one short block from the beach and 3½ miles from the airport, is one of the best guesthouses on the Condado. Upon entering a tropical patio, you'll find tile tables surrounded by palm trees and bougainvillea. There's plenty of space on the deck and a covered lounge for relaxing, socializing, and eating breakfast. Dozens of decorative wind chimes add melody to the daily breezes. The good-size rooms offer a choice of size, beds, and kitchens; all contain ceiling fans and air-conditioning. Beds are comfortable and range from twin to king-size. The shower-only bathrooms, though small, are efficiently laid out.

1750 McLeary Ave., Condado, San Juan, PR 00911. ✆ 800/946-3244 or 787/727-4153. Fax 787/728-0671. www.atwindchimesinn.com. 22 units. Winter $99–$140 double, $125–$150 suite; off season $75–$125 double, $135 suite. AE, DISC, MC, V. Parking $5. Bus: B21 or A5. **Amenities:** Bar; outdoor pool; room service (7:30am–11pm); all nonsmoking rooms; 1 room for those with limited mobility. *In room:* A/C, ceiling fan, TV, dataport, kitchen (in some).

Casa del Caribe *Value*
It's not the Ritz, but if you're looking for a bargain on the Condado, this is it. This 1940s guesthouse has a very Puerto Rican ambience,

emphasizing Latin hospitality and comfort. On a shady side street just off Ashford Avenue, behind a wall and garden, you'll discover Casa del Caribe's wraparound veranda. The small but cozy guest rooms have ceiling fans and air-conditioners, and most feature original Puerto Rican art. The bedrooms are most inviting, with comfortable furnishings and efficiently organized shower-only bathrooms. The front porch is a social center for guests, and you can also cook out at a barbecue area. The beach is a 2-minute walk away, and the hotel is within walking distance of some megaresorts and their glittering casinos.

Calle Caribe 57, El Condado, San Juan, PR 00907. © 787/722-7139. Fax 787/723-2575. www.casadel caribe.net. 13 units. Winter $75–$125 double; off season $55–$110 double. Rates include continental breakfast. AE, DISC, MC, V. Parking $5. Bus: B21. **Amenities:** All nonsmoking rooms; 1 room for those with limited mobility. *In room:* A/C, ceiling fan, TV, safe.

IN OCEAN PARK

Hostería del Mar 🖈   Lying a few blocks from the Condado casinos are the white walls of this distinctive landmark. It's in a residential seaside community that's popular with locals looking for beach action on weekends. The hotel boasts medium-size oceanview rooms. Those on the second floor have balconies; those on the first floor open onto patios. The guest room decor is invitingly tropical, with wicker furniture, good beds, pastel prints, and ceiling fans, plus small but efficient bathrooms, some with shower, some with tub. The most popular unit is no. 201, with a king-size bed, private balcony, kitchenette, and a view of the beach, idyllic for a honeymoon. There's no pool, but a full-service restaurant here is known for its vegetarian, macrobiotic, and Puerto Rican plates, all freshly made. The place is simple, yet with its own elegance, and the hospitality is warm.

Calle Tapía 1, Ocean Park, San Juan, PR 00911. © 877/727-3302 or 787/727-3302. Fax 787/268-0772. hosteria@caribe.net. 27 units. Winter $75–$125 double without ocean view, $165–$195 double with ocean view, $230–$250 apt; off season $55–$100 double without ocean view, $120–$165 double with ocean view, $185–$195 apt. Children 11 and under stay free in parent's room. AE, DC, DISC, MC, V. Bus: A5. **Amenities:** Restaurant; limited room service; laundry service; dry cleaning. *In room:* A/C, TV, dataport, kitchenette (in 3 units), beverage maker (in some), safe.

Número Uno Guest House 🖈   As its name implies, this is the best of the small-scale, low-rise guesthouses in Ocean Park. It was originally built in the 1950s as a private beach house in a prestigious residential neighborhood adjacent to the wide sands of Ocean Park Beach, on a knoll that avoids the occasional flooding that's the curse of other homes nearby. The owner, Ester Feliciano, cultivates a garden within her walled compound, replete with fountains, a small swimming pool, and manicured shrubbery and palms.

Stylish-looking bedrooms contain white-tile floors, wicker furniture, and comfortable beds, plus tiled, shower-only bathrooms. Two of the units are apartments, suitable for families. Some repeat guests, many of whom are gay, refer to it as their fantasy of a private villa beside a superb and usually convivial beach.

Calle Santa Ana 1, Ocean Park, San Juan PR 00911. © 787/726-5010. Fax 787/727-5482. www.numero1 guesthouse.com. 14 units. Winter $125–$255 double, $265 apt; off season $80–$165 double, $165 apt; $165–$205 junior suite. $20 each additional occupant of a double room. Rates include continental breakfast. AE, MC, V. Bus: A5. **Amenities:** Restaurant; bar; outdoor pool; limited room service; babysitting. *In room:* A/C, ceiling fans, TV, dataport, minibar, hair dryer, iron/ironing board, safe.

Tu Casa 🖈 *(Finds)*   This discovery lies in the beach-fronted gate sector of Ocean Park. It's one of the most delightful places to stay in the area, with works of local and international artists exhibited throughout. The aura is Mediterranean, with small kitchenettes in the suites, walk-in showers, and an attractive decor. Some accommodations are decorated in a frilly, feminine style with half-tester netting over the beds. On-site is one of the best restaurants in Ocean Park, which you might want to visit even if you're not a guest. Parties are often staged in the courtyard, ranging from belly dancing to Hawaiian feasts.

Calle Cacique 2071, Ocean Park, San Juan, PR 00911. (C) **787/727-5100.** Fax 787/982-3349. www. tucasaguest.com. 20 units. Winter $125 double, $175 suite; off season $99 double, $125 suite. Rates include continental breakfast. AE, DC, DISC, MC, V. Bus: A5 or B6. **Amenities:** Restaurant; bar; outdoor pool; all nonsmoking rooms; 1 room for those with limited mobility. In room: A/C, TV, kitchenette (in some).

IN ISLA VERDE

Isla Verde, right on the beach, is closer to the airport than the other sections of San Juan, but it's farther from Old Town. Some of the Caribbean's most upscale hotels are here. If you plan to spend most of your time on the beach rather than exploring the city, consider one of the following hotels.

Very Expensive

Intercontinental San Juan Resort & Casino 𝕽 This resort competes with Wyndham El San Juan Hotel & Casino (see below) next door, but doesn't better it. It's more of a sophisticated beach resort than a hotel casino that focuses on the whims of high-rolling gamblers.

Most of the comfortable, medium-size rooms have balconies and terraces and tastefully conservative furnishings. Top-floor rooms are the most expensive, even though they lack balconies. Bathrooms have power showerheads, deep tubs, and scales. The most desirable units are in the Plaza Club, a minihotel within the hotel that sports a private entrance, concierge service, complimentary food and beverage buffets, and suite/spa and beach facilities. Dining within any of this hotel's five restaurants merits attention, although the choice is greater at the neighboring El San Juan Hotel.

5961 Isla Verde Ave., Isla Verde, PR 00937. (C) **800/468-9076** in the U.S., or 787/791-6100. Fax 787/ 253-2510. www.intercontinental.com. 400 units. Winter $399–$539 double, $559–$879 suite; off season $209–$289 double, $360–$690 suite. AE, DC, DISC, MC, V. Self-parking $10; valet parking $16. Bus: A7, M7, or T1. **Amenities:** 5 restaurants; 3 bars; the Caribbean's largest free-form pool; gym; sauna; whirlpool; scuba diving; limousine service; business center; 24-hr. room service; massage; babysitting; laundry service; dry cleaning, nonsmoking rooms; rooms for those with limited mobility. In room: A/C, TV, dataport, beverage maker, minibar, hair dryer, iron/ironing board, safe.

Ritz-Carlton San Juan Spa & Casino 𝕽𝕽𝕽 The Ritz-Carlton is one of the most spectacular deluxe hotels in the Caribbean. Set on 8 acres of prime beachfront, within a 5-minute drive from the airport, it appeals to both business travelers and vacationers. The hotel decor reflects Caribbean flavor and the Hispanic culture of the island, with artwork by prominent local artists. More visible, however, is an emphasis on continental elegance. Some of the most opulent public areas feature wrought-iron balustrades and crystal chandeliers.

Beautifully furnished guest rooms open onto ocean views or the gardens of nearby condos. Rooms are very large, with excellent furnishings, fine linen, and dataports. The bathrooms are exceptionally plush, with shower/tub combinations, scales, bathrobes, and deluxe toiletries. Preferred accommodations are in the ninth-floor Ritz-Carlton Club, which has a private lounge and personal concierge staff.

The scope and diversity of dining here is second only to the Wyndham El San Juan Hotel & Casino (see below), and as for top-shelf dining venues, the Ritz-Carlton has no equal. The Vineyard Room is one of the finest restaurants in San Juan. The hotel also houses the Caribbean's largest casino (see "Casinos" later in this chapter).

6961 Ave. of the Governors, Isla Verde, Carolina, PR 00979. ⓒ 800/241-3333 or 787/253-1700. Fax 787/ 253-1111. www.ritzcarlton.com. 414 units. Winter $319–$439 double; off season $215–$399 double; year-round from $575 suite. AE, DC, DISC, MC, V. Valet parking $16. Bus: A5, B40, or C45. **Amenities:** 3 restaurants; 5 bars; large pool; casino; nightclub; 2 tennis courts; gym; spa; children's programs; salon; 24-hr. room service; babysitting; laundry service; dry cleaning; nonsmoking rooms; rooms for those with limited mobility. *In room:* A/C, TV, dataport, minibar, hair dryer, iron/ironing board, safe.

The Water Club ★★★   A refreshing change from the megachain resorts of San Juan, this ultrachic hotel is hip and contemporary. It's the city's only "boutique hotel" on a beach. We find much to praise at this small and exclusive hotel because of its highly personalized and well-trained staff. Although avant-garde, the design is not daringly provocative. Behind glass are "waterfalls," even on the elevators, and inventive theatrical-style lighting is used to bring the outdoors inside. The one-of-a-kind glass art doors are from Murano, the famed center of glassmaking outside Venice. Overlooking Isla Verde's best beach area, all the bedrooms are spacious and contain custom-designed beds positioned to face the ocean. Bathrooms are tiled and elegant, with shower/tub combinations. Unique features are the open-air 11th-floor exotic bar with the Caribbean's only rooftop fireplace. The pool is a level above; it's like swimming in an ocean in the sky.

Tartak St. 2, Isla Verde, Puerto Rico 00979. ⓒ 888/265-6699 or 787/728-3666. Fax 787/728-3610. www.waterclubsanjuan.com. 84 units. Winter $180–$360 double, $680 suite; off season $140–$260 double, $580 suite. AE, DC, DISC, MC, V. Bus: T1 or A5. **Amenities:** Restaurant; 2 bars; outdoor pool; Jacuzzi; fitness center; limited room service; laundry service; dry cleaning. *In room:* A/C, TV, dataport, minibar, hair dryer, safe.

Wyndham El San Juan Hotel & Casino ★ *Kids*   Under Wyndham management, this hotel is no longer the dazzler it once was. The Ritz-Carlton has taken the truly elite business, and The Water Club is even more sophisticated. Nonetheless, El San Juan Hotel is still a good choice for well-to-do families, with lots of activities for children. The beachfront hotel is surrounded by 350 palms, century-old banyans, and gardens. Its 700-yard-long sandy beach is the finest in the San Juan area. The hotel's river pool, with its currents, cascades, and lagoons, evokes a jungle stream, and the lobby is the most opulent in the Caribbean. Entirely sheathed in red marble and hand-carved mahogany paneling, the public rooms stretch on almost endlessly.

The large, well-decorated guest rooms are imbued with honey-hued woods and rattans and king-size or double beds. Bathrooms have all the amenities and shower/tub combinations; a few feature Jacuzzis. About 150 of the units, designed as comfortable bungalows, are in the outer reaches of the garden. Known as casitas, they include Roman tubs, atrium showers, and access to the fern-lined paths of a tropical jungle a few steps away.

No other hotel in the Caribbean offers such a rich diversity of dining options and such high-quality food. Japanese, Italian, Mexican, and 24-hour American/Caribbean restaurants are just a few of the choices.

6063 Isla Verde Ave., San Juan, PR 00979. ⓒ 800/468-2818 or 787/791-1000. Fax 787/791-0390. www.wyndham.com. 385 units. Winter $255–$395 double, from $1,300 suite; off season $190–$335 double, from $1,100 suite. AE, DC, DISC, MC, V. Self-parking $8; valet parking $13. Bus: A5. **Amenities:** 8 restaurants; 15 bars; 2 outdoor pools; casino; tennis courts; health club and spa; sauna; steam room; children's club; business center; 24-hr. room service; massage; babysitting; laundry service; dry cleaning; nonsmoking rooms; rooms for those with limited mobility. *In room:* A/C, TV/VCR, dataport, minibar, beverage maker, hair dryer, iron/ironing board, safe.

DINING
IN OLD SAN JUAN
Expensive

Aquaviva ⭐⭐ LATINO/SEAFOOD   This is the third and final addition to a trio of restaurants, each within a few steps of each other, and each dauntingly stylish, that are owned by the same investors. The location is at the bottom of Calle Fortaleza, in Old San Juan, within a cool, turquoise-colored environment that is a welcome contrast to the saffron-and-fire-colored decor of the other members (Dragonfly and the Parrot Club, both also recommended). Presiding above the sometimes frenetic bar action and dining room hubbub of this place are replicas of three *aquaviva* (jellyfish), quivering with illumination, each painstakingly manufactured from stained glass specifically for this site. Don't come here expecting calm or respite from the madding crowds. Its owners spend a small fortune on publicity and promotion, making it one of the hottest restaurant tickets in Old San Juan.

The result verges on the chaotic, albeit in the most stylish of ways. Just when you think the bar area is packed to the point where no further clients will possibly be admitted, *boom,* a new carload of hopefuls, either with or—unfortunately for them—without dining reservations will cram themselves in among the stylish and scantily dressed crowd. Oysters and stiff drinks are served at the bar. Flowing from the open-to-view kitchens come dishes whose ingredients derive from the watery turquoise world which inspired this restaurant's color scheme. The best examples include six different ceviches, including one made with mahimahi, mango juice, and lemons; and another from marlin and garlic. You might opt for a heaping "tower" composed of fried oysters, coco-flavored shrimp, fried octopus and calamari. The best main courses include grilled fresh mahimahi with smoky shrimp, salsa, and coconut-poached yucca; seared medallions of halibut with a fondue of spinach and crabmeat; and a succulent version of paella garnished with seafood and pork sausage.

Calle Fortaleza 364. © **787/722-0665.** Reservations required. Main courses $16–$42. AE, DC, MC, V. Mon–Wed 6–11pm; Thurs–Sat 6pm–midnight; Sun 4–10pm. Bus: Old Town Trolley.

Barú ⭐ CARIBBEAN/MEDITERRANEAN   This might be one of the most fashionable and popular of the imaginative new restaurants of Old San Juan, with an attractive and hard-playing clientele, some of whom might effectively compete for roles on the Hispanic soap operas. Named after an unspoiled island off the north coast of Colombia, a personal favorite of its Colombian-born owner, it occupies a stately looking high-ceilinged space capped with massive timbers, fronted with a hyper-convivial mahogany bar, and decorated with paintings by such Colombia-born artistic luminaries as Botéro.

Many dishes are deliberately conceived as something midway between an appetizer and a main-course platter, so it's hard to know how much, or how many courses, to order. Hopefully, your waitperson will guide you. Menu items include an unusual choice of five different kinds of carpaccio (tuna, halibut, salmon, beef, or Serrano ham), presented in paper-thin and very small portions that are spread out like a few sheets of tissue paper on a pretentiously large plate. Ceviche of mahimahi is appropriately tart, appealingly permeated with citrus; and the marinated lamb chops with a paprika and pineapple mojo sauce is flavorful. Other culinary creations include almond-encrusted goat cheese with Jamaican jerk mango dip and yucca chips, and sliced filet mignon. Regrettably, the place is not cheap, and service is well-intentioned but disorganized as the youthful staff maneuvers as best it can through the packed-in crowd.

Calle San Sebastián 150. © 787/977-7107. Reservations required. Main courses $15–$28. AE, MC, V. Mon–Sat 6pm–midnight; Sun 6–10pm. Bus: M2, M3, or A5.

Carli Café Concierto ⭐ INTERNATIONAL   This stylish restaurant at the base of the Banco Popular building in Old San Juan is the arena for the music of owner Carli Muñoz. The gold disc hanging on the wall attests to Carli's success in his previous role as a pianist for the Beach Boys. Nowadays, he entertains his dinner guests with a combination of standards, romantic jazz, and original material on his grand piano. Diners can choose to sit outside on the Plazoleta, where they can enjoy a panoramic view of the bay, or they can eat inside against a backdrop of a tasteful decor of terra-cotta walls, black marble tables, and a black-and-white-tiled floor. The chef tempts visitors with an imaginative menu including such delights as quail rockettes stuffed with dried fruits and sage, and a classic filet mignon with wild mushrooms. The filet of salmon and a mouth-watering rack of lamb are among the finest main dishes. Carli plays Wednesday to Saturday. The bar, with its mahogany and brass fittings, is an ideal spot to kick back and chill out.

Edificio Banco Popular, Plazoleta Rafael Carrion, Calle Recinto Sur. © 787/725-4927. Reservations recommended. Main courses $17–$36. AE, MC, V. Mon–Sat 11:30am–3pm and 5–11:30pm. Bus: M2 or M3.

Parrot Club ⭐⭐ NUEVO LATINO/CARIBBEAN   Serving a Nuevo Latino cuisine that blends traditional Puerto Rican cookery with Spanish, Taíno, and African influences, this bistro and bar is one of Old San Juan's most popular. It's set in a stately building dating back to 1902 that was originally a hair-tonic factory. Today, you'll find a cheerful-looking dining room where San Juan's mayor and the governor of Puerto Rico are sometimes spotted, and a verdantly landscaped courtyard where tables for at least 200 diners are scattered amid potted ferns, palms, and orchids. Live music, either Brazilian, salsa, or Latino jazz, is offered nightly, as well as during the popular Sunday brunches.

Menu items include ceviche of halibut, salmon, tuna, and mahimahi; delicious crab cakes; *criolla*-style (Creole) flank steak; and pan-seared tuna served with a sauce made from dark rum and essence of oranges. Everybody's favorite drink is a "parrot passion," made from lemon-flavored rum, triple sec, oranges, and passion fruit.

Calle Fortaleza 363. © 787/725-7370. Reservations not accepted. Main courses $18–$36 dinner, $12–$20 lunch. AE, DC, MC, V. Mon–Fri noon–3pm and 6–11pm; Sat–Sun noon–4pm and 6–11pm. Closed 2 weeks in Sept. Bus: Old Town Trolley.

Trois Cent Onze (311) ⭐⭐ FRENCH   When the French and Puerto Rican owners renovated this place in 1999, they discovered some of the most beautiful Moorish-Andalusian tile work in San Juan's Old Town buried beneath layers of later coverings. Because of those tiles, and because of the delicate Andalusian-style iron rosette above the door, they wisely decided to retain the area's Moorish embellishments during the reconfiguration of their restaurant's decor. What you'll get today is the premier French restaurant of San Juan, replete with a zinc bar near the entrance, a soaring and richly beamed ceiling, and a decor like what you might have expected in the Casbah of old Tangiers. Your hosts are Christophe Gourdain and Zylma Perez, who are proud to recite the building's former use as the photography studio that developed many of Puerto Rico's earliest movies.

Colors, textures, and flavors combine here to produce an irresistible array of dishes. Menu items include a carpaccio of salmon marinated in citrus; sautéed sea scallops served with an almond-flavored butter sauce; mango and crabmeat salad; magret of duckling roasted with honey; and pork medallions served with caramelized onions, stewed white beans, and spicy *merguez* sausage.

Calle Fortaleza 311. © 787/725-7959. Reservations recommended. Main courses $19–$30. AE, DC, MC, V. Tues–Thurs noon–3pm and 6:30–10:30pm; Fri–Sat noon–3pm and 6:30–11:30pm; Sun noon–10pm. Bus: Old Town Trolley, T2, or 2.

Moderate

Amadeus *🎯* CARIBBEAN Housed in a brick-and-stone building that was constructed in the 18th century by a wealthy merchant, Amadeus offers Caribbean ingredients with a nouvelle twist. The appetizers alone are worth the trip here, especially the Amadeus dumplings with guava sauce and arrowroot fritters. One zesty specialty is pork scaloppini with sweet-and-sour sauce. The chef will even prepare a smoked-salmon-and-caviar pizza.

Calle San Sebastián 106 (across from the Iglesia de San José). © 787/722-8635. Reservations recommended. Main courses $7.75–$25. AE, DISC, MC, V. Mon 6pm–midnight; Tues–Sun noon–midnight. Bus: M2, M3, or A5.

Dragonfly *🎯🎯🎯* LATIN/ASIAN It's hip and in great demand. The decor looks like that of a bordello in old San Francisco: beaded curtains, red ceilings, fringed lamps, and gilded mirrors. The restaurant lies right across the street from the Parrot Club, and next to Aquaviva. These three restaurants have put the SoFo district (south of Calle Fortaleza in Old Town) on the culinary map. A dizzy array of sexy dishes includes a seafood ceviche served with yucca and plantain chips, *chicharrónes* (pork rinds), spicy crab cakes, and a host of other dishes, such as marinated grilled meats. The red snapper and grouper are excellent, and we love all the pumpkin and bean dishes. The barbecued lamb shanks are very filling.

Night after night Dragonfly is the best place to party in town, more so than the Parrot Club. Along with the latest gossip, you can enjoy live Latin jazz as background music.

Calle Fortaleza 364. © 787/977-3886. Reservations required. Main courses $10–$21. AE, MC, V. Mon–Wed 6–11pm; Thurs–Sat 6pm–midnight. Bus: Old Town Trolley.

Ostra Cosa *🎯🎯* *Finds* ECLECTIC/SEAFOOD This artfully promoted restaurant has a growing clientele that calls its ambience one of the most sensual and romantic in Old San Juan. Former advertising executive Alberto Nazario, a lifestyle guru who mingles New Age thinking with culinary techniques to promote love, devotion, and a heightened sexuality, created Ostra Cosa. Couples dine beneath a massive quenepe tree—waiters will tell you to hug the tree and make a wish—in a colonial courtyard surrounded by a 16th-century building that was once the home of the colony's governor. The atmosphere, enhanced by domesticated quail and chirping tree frogs, will remove you from the cares of the city. Foods are high in phosphorus, zinc, and flavor, designed to promote an "eat-up, dress-down experience." Try Alaskan king crab and grilled pork tenderloin in herb sauce.

Calle del Cristo 154. © 787/722-2672. Reservations recommended. Main courses $13–$35. AE, MC, V. Fri–Wed noon–11pm. Bus: Old Town Trolley.

Tantra *🎯* *Value* INDO-LATINO This is one of the most genuinely creative restaurants in San Juan, a one-of-a-kind luminary in a dining scene that sometimes relies merely on derivations of tried-and-true themes. Set in the heart of "restaurant row" on Calle Fortaleza, it has become famous for a sophisticated fusion of Latino with South Indian cuisine. Its chef and owner, Indian-born Ramesh Pillai, oversees a blend of slow-cooked tandoori cuisine from South India with Puerto Rico-derived spices, flavors, and ingredients. All of this occurs within a warm, candlelit environment that focuses on Indian handcrafts, Hindu and Buddhist symbols, intricately embroidered banners and batiks, and a terracotta and saffron color scheme that you might have expected in Rhajastan.

An appropriate way to begin a meal here is to order one of the best martinis we've ever had—a concoction flavored with cinnamon and cloves. Menu highlights include sesame masala-crusted sushi tuna with peanut sauce; fried coconut sesame jumbo shrimp with Indian noodles; chicken tikka masala with nan (flat bread); and rice and chicken rolls with passion-fruit sauce. One of the establishment's bestsellers is an absolutely brilliant version of tandoori chicken that combines the traditional Indian recipe with manchego and mozzarella cheese, guyaba fruit, guava-flavored dip, and nan. There are even curried versions of the most famous traditional dish in Puerto Rico—*mofongos* (meat-stuffed green plantains). Dessert might be a cardamon-flavored flan. Even if you've already had dinner, don't overlook this place as a nightlife option.

356 Calle Fortaleza. (C) 787/977-8141. Reservations recommended. Main courses $13–$17. AE, DC, MC, V. Sun–Thurs noon–11pm; Fri–Sat noon–midnight. Bus: T1 or 2.

Inexpensive
La Bombonera ⋆ *Value* PUERTO RICAN This place offers exceptional value in its homemade pastries, well-stuffed sandwiches, and endless cups of coffee, and has done so since 1902. Its atmosphere evokes turn-of-the-century Castile transplanted to the New World. The food is authentically Puerto Rican, homemade, and inexpensive, with regional dishes like rice with squid, roast leg of pork, and seafood *asopao* (stew). For dessert, you might select an apple, pineapple, or prune pie, or one of many types of flan. Service is polite, if a bit rushed, and the place fills up quickly at lunchtime.

Calle San Francisco 259. (C) 787/722-0658. Reservations recommended. American breakfast $4.50–$6.45; main courses $6–$18. DISC, MC, V. Daily 7:30am–8pm. Bus: M2 or M3.

IN CONDADO
Very Expensive
Pikayo ⋆⋆⋆ PUERTO RICAN/CAJUN This is an ideal place to go for the next generation of Puerto Rican fusion cuisine. Pikayo not only keeps up with the latest culinary trends, it often sets them, thanks to the inspired guidance of owner and celebrity chef Wilo Benet. Formal but not stuffy, and winner of more culinary awards than virtually any other restaurant in Puerto Rico, Pikayo is a specialist in the *criolla* cuisine of the colonial age (the starchy, down-home Creole cuisine that developed on the island a century ago), emphasizing the Spanish, Indian, and African elements in its unusual recipes. Appetizers include a dazzling array of taste explosions: witness shrimp spring rolls with a peanut-sofrito sauce; crab cake with aioli; or perhaps a ripe plantain, goat cheese, and onion tart. Our favorite main course is grilled shrimp with polenta and a barbecue sauce made with guava. Also recommended are charred rare yellowfin tuna with an onion *escabeche* (spicy vinegar sauce), and red snapper filet with sweet-potato purée and foie gras butter.

Museum of Art of Puerto Rico, 299 De Diego Ave. (C) 787/721-6194. Reservations recommended. Main courses $28–$40; tasting menus $65–$80. AE, DC, DISC, MC, V. Tues–Fri noon–3pm; Mon–Sat 6–11pm. Bus: M2, A7, or T1.

Ramiro's ☆ SPANISH/INTERNATIONAL   This restaurant boasts the most imaginative menu on the Condado. You might begin with breadfruit *mille-feuille* with local crabmeat and avocado. For your main course, any fresh fish or meat can be charcoal-grilled for you on request. Some of the latest specialties include grilled salmon on a bed of black rice and a Spanish prawn sauce, and a tantalizing roast duckling with a kumquat sauce. Among the many homemade desserts are caramelized mango on puff pastry with strawberry-and-guava sauce, and "four seasons" chocolate.

Ave. Magdalena 1106. ☎ 787/721-9056. Reservations required in winter, recommended off season. Main courses $27–$39. AE, DC, MC, V. Mon–Sat noon–3pm and 6–11pm; Sun noon–3pm and 6–10pm. Bus: A7, T1, or M2.

Expensive

Ajili Mojili ☆ *Kids* PUERTO RICAN/CREOLE   This restaurant is devoted exclusively to *la cucina criolla,* the starchy, down-home cuisine that developed on the island a century ago. It's set in the heart of the Condado tourist strip, across from the convention center. Though the building housing it is quite modern, look for replicas of the crumbling brick walls you find in Old San Juan, and a bar that evokes Old Spain. The staff will willingly describe menu items in colloquial English, and children will enjoy choosing from the featured kids' menu. Locals come here for a taste of the food they enjoyed at their mother's knee, like *mofongos* (green plantains stuffed with veal, chicken, shrimp, or pork), *arroz con pollo* (stewed chicken with saffron rice), *medallones de cerdo encebollado* (pork loin sautéed with onions), *carne mechada* (beef rib eye stuffed with ham), and *lechon asado con maposteado* (roast pork with rice and beans). Wash it all down with an ice-cold bottle of local beer.

1006 Ashford Ave. ☎ 787/725-9195. Reservations recommended. Main courses $13–$26 lunch; $17–$29 dinner; Sun buffet $24; children's menu $5.95. AE, DISC, MC, V. Mon–Fri noon–3pm; Mon–Sat 6–11pm; Sun 4–10pm. Bus: B21.

Chayote's ☆ PUERTO RICAN/INTERNATIONAL   Chayote's serves some of San Juan's most innovative cuisine. It attracts local business leaders, government officials, and the occasional celebrity. It's an artsy, modern, basement-level bistro in a surprisingly obscure hotel (the Olimpo). The restaurant changes its menu every 3 months, but you might find appetizers like a yucca turnover stuffed with crabmeat and served with a mango and papaya chutney, or a ripe plantain stuffed with chicken and served with a fresh tomato sauce. For a main dish, you might try a red snapper filet with a citrus vinaigrette made of passion fruit, orange, and lemon. An exotic touch appears in the pork filet seasoned with dried fruits and spices in a tamarind sauce and served with a green banana and taro root timbale. To finish off your meal, there's nothing better than the mango flan served with macerated strawberries.

In the Olimpo Court, Ave. Miramar 603. ☎ 787/722-9385. Reservations recommended. Main courses $21–$30. AE, MC, V. Tues–Fri noon–2:30pm; Tues–Sat 6:30–10:30pm. Bus: 5.

José José Restaurant ☆ *Finds* INTERNATIONAL   The imaginative and flavor-filled dishes at this elegant, colonial-styled restaurant next to the Convention Center come as a real surprise. The cooking is warm and generous, and some of the dishes appear on no other menu in San Juan. Try, for example, the loin of ostrich in a sweet cinnamon sauce served with plantain. The lobster-and–wild mushroom risotto tops anything we've ever sampled in San Juan. The chefs are equally adept at other seafood dishes, including a delectable broiled hake served with a tangy caper sauce. The meat dishes are imaginative as well, including beef cheeks with a garlic-laced linguini. Chef Josébreu is one of San Juan's finest chefs.

1110 Magdalena Ave. (🕐 **787/725-8546**. Reservations required. Main courses $23–$32; tasting menu $50–$70. AE, MC, V. Tues–Fri noon–3pm and 6:30–10pm; Sat 6:30–10:30pm; Sun noon–8pm. Bus: A7 or M2.

La Compostela 🍴 INTERNATIONAL   Established by a Galician-born family, this pine-trimmed restaurant has gained a reputation as one of the best in the capital. The chef made his name on the roast peppers stuffed with salmon mousse. Equally delectable is duck with orange and ginger sauce or baby rack of lamb with fresh herbs. Any shellfish grilled in a brandy sauce is a sure winner. The chef also makes two different versions of paella, both savory. The wine cellar, comprising some 10,000 bottles, is one of the most impressive in San Juan. A battalion of well-dressed waiters offers formal service.

Avenida Condado 106. (🕐 **787/724-6088**. Reservations required. Main courses $24–$39. AE, DC, MC, V. Mon–Fri noon–2:30pm; Mon–Sat 6:30–10pm. Bus: M2.

Zabó 🍴 INTERNATIONAL   This restaurant enjoys citywide fame thanks to its blend of bucolic charm and superb innovative food. It's set in a dignified villa that provides some low-rise dignity in a sea of skyscraping condos. The creative force here is owner and chef/culinary director Paul Carroll, who turned a simple deli into one of the most sought-after restaurants on the Condado. Menu items fuse the cuisines of the Mediterranean, the Pacific Rim, and the Caribbean into a collection that includes dishes like blinis stuffed with medallions of lobster with ginger, thyme, and beurre blanc; carpaccio of salmon with mesclun salad and balsamic vinegar; and baked chorizo stuffed with mushrooms, sherry, paprika, and cheddar. The black-bean soup is among the very best in Puerto Rico, served with parboiled cloves of garlic marinated in olive oil that melt in your mouth.

Calle Candina 14 (entrance is via an alleyway leading from Ashford Ave. between calles Washington and Cervantes). (🕐 **787/725-9494**. Reservations recommended. Main courses $12–$20 dinner. AE, MC, V. Tues–Thurs 6–10pm; Fri–Sat 7–11pm. Bus: A7.

IN SANTURCE

La Casona 🍴 SPANISH/INTERNATIONAL   In a turn-of-the-century mansion surrounded by gardens, La Casona offers the kind of dining usually found in Madrid, complete with a strolling guitarist. This charming place draws some of the most fashionable diners on Puerto Rico. Paella marinara, prepared for two or more, is a specialty, as is *zarzuela de mariscos* (seafood medley). Or you might select filet of grouper in Basque sauce, octopus vinaigrette, *osso buco* (veal shanks), or rack of lamb. Grilled red snapper is a specialty, and you can order it with almost any sauce you want, although the chef recommends one made from olive oil, herbs, lemon, and toasted garlic. The cuisine has both flair and flavor.

Calle San Jorge 609. (🕐 **787/727-2717**. Reservations required. Main courses $17–$48. AE, DC, MC, V. Mon–Fri noon–3pm; Mon–Sat 6–11pm. Bus: 1.

IN OCEAN PARK

Pamela's 🍴 CARIBBEAN FUSION   This restaurant's pronounced sense of style is somewhat surprising given its out-of-the-way location. Part of its allure derives from a sophisticated blend of Caribbean cuisines that combines local ingredients with Puerto Rican flair and New York style. Dishes include a salad that marries vine-ripened and oven-roasted tomatoes, each drizzled with a roasted garlic-and-cilantro vinaigrette; club sandwiches stuffed with barbecued shrimp and cilantro-flavored mayonnaise; plantain-encrusted crab cakes with a spicy tomato-herb emulsion; and grilled island-spiced pork loin served with guava glaze and fresh local fruits. Beer and a wide array of cocktails go well with this food.

In the Número Uno Guest House, Calle Santa Ana 1. © 787/726-5010. Reservations recommended. Sandwiches and salads at lunch $14–$17; main course platters $28–$35. AE, DC, MC, V. Daily noon–3pm and 7–10:30pm. Bus: A5.

IN ISLA VERDE
Very Expensive
The Vineyard 🔾🔾 CALIFORNIA/MEDITERRANEAN   Within the realm of haute cuisine served with impeccable European credentials, this is one of the finest restaurants in San Juan. The Vineyard duplicates the gourmet citadels of Italy and France more accurately than any other restaurant in Puerto Rico, thanks to a staff of culinary luminaries spearheaded by Philippe Trosch, a prize catch that Ritz-Carlton worked hard to get. The wait staff is the best trained in Puerto Rico. The wine-tasting menus, either four or five courses, are the best on the island. Try innovative appetizers like potato cannelloni filled with Caribbean lobster risotto, or a summer salad of cavaillon melon, serrano ham, mozzarella, and olive pesto with ciabatta toast. The main courses are equally appealing: Nantucket sea bass with a barley tapenade and a black-olive sabayon, or apple-smoked rabbit with a cannellini-bean mash. You might precede (or end) an experience here at the bar, where the dark paneling and deep leather seats emulate an Edwardian-era men's club in London.

In the Ritz-Carlton San Juan Spa & Casino, 6961 Ave. of the Governors. © 787/253-1700. Reservations required. Main courses $32–$38; fixed-price menus $45–$75. AE, DC, DISC, MC, V. Tues–Sat 6–10pm. Bus: A5, B40, or C45.

Expensive
La Piccola Fontana 🔾 NORTHERN ITALIAN   Right off the luxurious Palm Court in the El San Juan Hotel, this restaurant delivers plate after plate of delectable food nightly. From its white linen to its classically formal service, it enjoys a fine reputation. The food is straightforward, generous, and extremely well-prepared. You'll dine in one of two neo-Palladian rooms whose wall frescoes depict Italy's ruins and landscapes. Menu items range from the appealingly simple (grilled filets of fish or grilled veal chops) to more elaborate dishes such as *tortellini San Daniele,* made with veal, prosciutto, cream, and sage; or *linguine scogliere,* with shrimp, clams, and seafood. Grilled medallions of filet mignon are served with braised arugula, Parmesan cheese, and balsamic vinegar.

In the Wyndham El San Juan Hotel & Casino, 6063 Isla Verde Ave. © 787/791-0966. Reservations required. Main courses $17–$30. AE, DC, MC, V. Daily 6–11pm. Bus: A5.

Tangerine 🔾🔾 EURO-ASIAN   This is the ultimate in chic Isla Verde dining, and it just happens to lie adjacent to the street-level reception area of The Water Club (see "Accommodations"). Hailed by many international food critics, it glows in its much-deserved praise. Minimalist, postmodern, and angular, and outfitted in monochromatic colors that include steel gray and navy blue, it has a prominent bar area in back, bubbling waterfalls, big-windowed views of the tropical landscapes outside, and an occasional and rather whimsical reference to the orange-colored fruit that gave the place its name. Lighting radiates gently outward from the kind of ultraglam fixtures that makes ordinary-looking people look good and beautiful people look fabulous. Menu items include such appetizers (the restaurant rather coyly refers to them as "foreplay") as crispy Vietnamese lobster rolls with mango-based sweet chili and avocado-minted melon relish; or citrus-cured yellowfin tuna tartare. For a main course try the cassia-smoked breast of chicken with sweet-garlic potato purée or Asian-herbed crusted Colorado lamb chops with garlic-flavored mashed potatoes and a sauce made from goat cheese, pulverized cucumbers, plum-flavored sake, and yogurt. Dessert might be a lemon-lime crème brûlée.

Tartak St. 2. ℂ 787/728-3666. Reservations required. Main courses $21–$29. AE, DC, MC, V. Tues–Sat 6:30–11pm. Bus: T1 or A5.

Moderate

Ciao Mediterranean Café ⍟ MEDITERRANEAN   In its own informal and breezy way, this is Isla Verde's most charming restaurant. It's draped with bougainvillea and set directly on the sands, attracting both hotel guests and locals wandering in barefoot from the beach. Overall, the place is chic, charming, and popular—one of our enduring favorites. The visual centerpiece is an open-air kitchen set within the confines of an oval-shaped bar. Here, a crew of cheerfully animated chefs mingle good culinary technique with Latino theatricality. (Xandra Lopez is one of the few female head chefs in Puerto Rico.)

Pizzas and pastas are enduringly popular, but more appealing are such dishes as seafood salad, wherein shrimp, scallops, calamari, peppers, onions, and lime juice create something you might find in the south of Italy. Greek-style squid *(kalamarakia tiganita)* consists of battered and deep-fried squid served with ratatouille and spicy marinara sauce. Provençal-style rack of lamb, with ratatouille, polenta, and Provençal herbs, and a mixed seafood grill evoke Marseilles.

Intercontinental San Juan Resort & Casino, 5961 Isla Grande Ave. ℂ 787/791-5000. Reservations recommended for dinner. Pizzas and salads $8–$17; main courses $14–$26. AE, MC, V. Daily 11am–11pm. Bus: A7, M7, or T1.

Metropol CUBAN/PUERTO RICAN/INTERNATIONAL   Metropol is the happiest blend of Cuban and Puerto Rican cuisine we've ever had. This is part of a restaurant chain known for serving the island's best Cuban food, although the chefs prepare a much wider range of dishes. The black-bean soup is among the island's finest, served in the classic Havana style with a side dish of rice and chopped onions. Endless garlic bread accompanies most dinners, likely to include Cornish game hen stuffed with Cuban rice and beans or perhaps marinated steak topped with a fried egg (reportedly Castro's favorite). Smoked chicken or chicken fried steak are also heartily recommended. Plantains, yucca, and all that good stuff accompany most dishes and portions are huge. Finish with a choice of thin or firm custard. Most dishes are at the low end of the price scale.

Isla Verde Ave. ℂ 787/791-4046. Main courses $9.95–$36. AE, MC, V. Daily 11:30am–10:30pm. Bus: C41, B42, or A5.

IN MIRAMAR

Augusto's Cuisine ⍟ FRENCH/INTERNATIONAL   This is one of Puerto Rico's most elegant and glamorous restaurants. Austrian-born owner/chef Augusto Schreiner operates from a gray-and-green dining room set on the lobby level of a 15-story hotel in Miramar, a suburb near the island's main airport. Menu items use only fresh ingredients, and include such dishes as lobster risotto, rack of lamb with aromatic herbs and fresh garlic, an oft-changing cream-based soup of the day (one of the best is corn and fresh oyster soup), and a succulent version of medallions of veal Rossini style, prepared with foie gras and Madeira sauce. The wine list is one of the most extensive on the island.

In the Hotel Excelsior, 801 Ave. Ponce de León, Miramar. ℂ 787/725-7700. Reservations recommended. Main courses $24–$38. AE, MC, V. Tues–Fri noon–3pm; Tues–Sat 7–9:30pm. Bus: A5 or T1.

HITTING THE BEACH

Some public stretches of shoreline around San Juan are overcrowded, especially on Saturday and Sunday; others are practically deserted. If you find that secluded, hidden beach of your dreams, proceed with caution. Muggings have been known to occur on sparsely populated sands. For more information about the island's many beaches, call the **Department of Sports and Recreation** (© 787/771-8999).

All beaches on Puerto Rico, even those fronting the top hotels, are open to the public, although you will be charged for parking and for use of *balneario* facilities, such as lockers and showers. Beach hours are daily from 9am to 5pm in winter, to 6pm off season. Major public beaches in the San Juan area have changing rooms and showers; Luquillo Public Beach (see below) also has picnic tables.

Famous among beach buffs since the 1920s, **Condado Beach** put San Juan on the map as a tourist resort. Backed up by high-rise hotels, it seems more like Miami Beach than any other in the Caribbean. You can book all sorts of watersports at kiosks along the beach or at the activities desk of the various hotels. There are also plenty of outdoor bars and restaurants when you tire of the sands. Condado is especially busy wherever a high-rise resort is located. People-watching seems a favorite sport along these golden strands.

At the end of Puente Dos Hermanos, the westernmost corner of the Condado is the most popular strip. This section of the beach is small and shaded by palms, and a natural rock barrier calms the turbulence of the waters rushing in, making for protected, safe swimming in gin-clear waters. The lagoon on the other side of the beach is ideal for windsurfing and kayaking.

A favorite of San Juaneros themselves, golden-sand **Isla Verde Beach** is ideal for swimming, and it, too, is lined with high-rise resorts and luxury condos. Isla Verde has picnic tables, so you can pick up lunch and make it a day at the beach. This strip is also good for snorkeling because of its calm, clear waters; many kiosks will rent you equipment. Isla Verde Beach extends from the end of Ocean Park to the beginning of a section called Boca Cangrejos. The best beach at Isla Verde is in front of the Hotel El San Juan. Most sections of this long strip have separate names, such as El Alambique, which is often the site of beach parties, and Punta El Medio, bordering the new Ritz-Carlton, which is also a great beach and very popular even with the locals. If you go past the luxury hotels and expensive condos behind the Luís Muñoz Marín International Airport, you arrive at the major public beach at Isla Verde. Here you'll find a *balneario* with parking, showers, fast-food joints, and watersports equipment. The sands here are whiter than the golden sands of the Condado, and are lined with coconut palms, sea-grape trees, and even almond trees, all of which provide shade from the fierce noonday sun.

One of the most attractive beaches in the Greater San Juan area is **Ocean Park,** a mile of fine gold sand in a neighborhood east of Condado. This beach

---

⌒Warning Let the Swimmer Beware

You have to pick your spots carefully if you want to swim along Condado Beach. The waters along the Condado Plaza Hotel are calmer than in other areas because of a coral breakwater. However, the beach near the Marriott is not good for swimming because of rocks and an undertow. Proceed with caution.

attracts both young people and a big gay crowd. Access to the beach at Ocean Park has been limited recently, but the best place to enter is from a section called El Ultimo Trolley. This area is also ideal for volleyball, paddleball, and other games. The easternmost portion, known as Punta Las Marias, is best for windsurfing. The waters at Ocean Park are fine for swimming, although they can get rough at times.

Rivaling Condado and Isla Verde beaches, **Luquillo Public Beach** 𝆺𝅥 is the grandest in Puerto Rico and one of the most popular. It's 30 miles east of San Juan near the town of Luquillo. Here you'll find a mile-long half-moon bay set against a backdrop of coconut palms. Saturday and Sunday are the worst times to go, as hordes of San Juaneros head here for fun in the sun. Watersports kiosks are available, offering everything from windsurfing to sailing. Facilities include lifeguards, an emergency first-aid station, ample parking, showers, and toilets. You can easily grab lunch here at one of the beach shacks offering cod fritters and tacos.

SPORTS & OTHER OUTDOOR PURSUITS

CRUISES   For the best cruises of San Juan Bay, go to **Caribe Aquatic Adventures** (see "Scuba Diving," below). Bay cruises start at $25 per person.

DEEP-SEA FISHING   Deep-sea fishing here is top-notch. Allison tuna, white and blue marlin, sailfish, wahoo, mahimahi, mackerel, and tarpon are some of the fish inhabit Puerto Rican waters, where 30 world records have been broken. Charter arrangements can be made through most major hotels and resorts.

Capt. Mike Beñitez, who has chartered out of San Juan for more than 40 years, is one of the most qualified sport-fishing captains in the world. Past clients have included Jimmy Carter. Contact **Beñitez Fishing Charters** directly at P.O. Box 9066541, Puerto de Tierra, San Juan, PR 00906 (✆ **787/723-2292** until 6pm). The captain offers a 45-foot air-conditioned deluxe Hatteras, the *Sea Born*. Fishing tours for parties of up to six cost $490 for a half-day excursion and $850 for a full day, with beverages and all equipment included.

HORSE RACING   Great thoroughbreds and outstanding jockeys compete all year at **El Comandante,** Calle 65 Infantería, Route 3, km. 15.3, at Canovanas (✆ **787/876-2450**), Puerto Rico's only racetrack, a 20-minute drive east of the center of San Juan. Post time varies from 2:45 to 5:30pm on Monday, Wednesday, Friday, Saturday, and Sunday.

SCUBA DIVING   In San Juan, the best outfitter is **Caribe Aquatic Adventures** (✆ **787/281-8858**), which operates a dive shop in the rear lobby of the Radisson Normandie Hotel. The company offers diving certification from both PADI and NAUI as part of 40-hour courses priced at $465 each. A resort course for first-time divers costs $100. They have a variety of full-day diving expeditions to various reefs off the east coast of Puerto Rico. If your time is severely limited, you can take a half-day dive of sites near San Juan. But since the best dive sites are farther away, the serious scuba diver will want to take a full-day tour. They also offer windsurfing excursions (see below).

SNORKELING   Snorkeling is better in the outlying portions of the island than in overcrowded San Juan. But if you don't have time to explore greater Puerto Rico, you'll find that most of the popular beaches, such as Luquillo and Isla Verde, have pretty good visibility. One of the best places is the San Juan Bay marina near the Caribe Hilton. Snorkeling equipment generally costs $15 per day and is available from the kiosks on the public beaches. Watersports desks at the big San Juan hotels at Isla Verde and Condado can make arrangements for

(Finds A Side Trip to Mona Island

Known locally as "the Galápagos of the Caribbean," **Mona Island** enjoys many legends of pirate treasure and is known for its white-sand beaches and marine life. The island is virtually uninhabited, except for two police-men and the director of the Institute of Natural Resources. Although the island is closer to Mayagüez than to San Juan, most boat tours of the island leave from the capital.

The island attracts hunters seeking pigs and wild goats, along with big-game fishers. But mostly it's intriguing to anyone who wants to escape civilization. **Playa Sardinera** on Mona Island was a base for pirates. On one side of the island, at **Playa de Pajaros,** are caves where the Taíno people left their mysterious hieroglyphs. Everything needed, including water, must be brought in, and everything, including garbage, must be taken out. For further information, call the **Puerto Rico Department of Natural Resources** at © 787/721-5495.

Encantos Ecotours (© 787/272-0005 or 787/808-0005) offers bare-bones but ecologically sensitive tours to Mona Island at sporadic intervals that vary according to the demand. The experience includes ground transport to and from San Juan, sea transport departing from Cabo Rojo (a few miles south of Mayagüez), plus a half-day tour of the island. The approx-imately 4-hour tour costs $50 per person.

---

equipment rental and can also point you to the best places for snorkeling. If your hotel doesn't offer such services, you can contact **Caribe Aquatic Adventures** (see "Scuba Diving," above), which caters to both snorkelers and scuba divers. Other possibilities for equipment rentals are at **Caribbean School of Aquatics,** Taft No. 1, Suite 10F, in San Juan (© 787/728-6606).

TENNIS · There are 12 lighted public courts at **San Juan Central Municipal Park,** at Calle Cerra (exit on Route 2; © 787/722-1646). Fees are $3 an hour from 6am to 5pm, $4 per hour from 6 to 10pm. Most of the big resort hotels have their own tennis courts for the use of their guests.

WINDSURFING   The most savvy windsurfing advice and equipment rental is available at **Velauno,** Calle Loíza 2430, Punta Las Marías in San Juan (© 787/728-8716). A 1-day rental costs $75, 3 days $100, and 1 week $225. This is the second biggest, full-service headquarters for windsurfing in the United States. The staff here will guide you to the best windsurfing, which is likely to be the Punta Las Marías in the Greater San Juan metropolitan area. Other spots on the island for windsurfing include Santa Isabel, Guánica, and La Parguera in the south; Jobos & Shacks in the northwest, and the island of Culebra off the eastern coast.

STEPPING BACK IN TIME: EXPLORING THE HISTORIC SITES OF SAN JUAN

The Spanish moved to Old San Juan in 1521, and the city played an important role as Spain's bastion of defense in the Caribbean. Today, the streets are narrow and teeming with traffic, but a walk through Old San Juan (El Viejo San Juan) makes for a good stroll. Some visitors have likened it to a "Disney park with an old world theme." Fast food and junk stores mar a lot of the beauty. Nonetheless, it's the biggest and best collection of historic buildings, stretching back 5 centuries, in all the Caribbean. You can do it in less than a day. In a 7-square-block landmark area in the westernmost part of the city, you can see many of Puerto Rico's chief historical attractions, and do some shopping along the way.

CHURCHES

Capilla de Cristo

The chapel was built to commemorate what legend calls a miracle. In 1753, a young rider lost control of his horse in a race down this very street during the fiesta of St. John's Day, plunging over the precipice. Moved by the accident, the secretary of the city, Don Mateo Pratts, invoked Christ to save the youth, and had the chapel built when his prayers were answered. Today, it's a landmark in the old city and one of its best-known monuments. The chapel's gold-and-silver altar can be seen through its glass doors. Since the chapel is open only on Tuesdays and Wednesdays, most visitors have to settle for a view of its exterior.

Calle del Cristo (directly west of Paseo de la Princesa). © 787/722-0861. Free admission. Tues–Wed 9am–3:30pm. Bus: Old Town Trolley.

Catedral de San Juan

San Juan Cathedral was begun in 1540 and has had a rough life. Looting, a lack of funds, and hurricanes have continually hampered its construction and reconstruction. Over the years, a circular staircase and two adjoining vaulted Gothic chambers have been added. Many beautiful stained-glass windows escaped pillagers and natural disasters. In 1908, the body of Ponce de León was disinterred from the nearby Iglesia de San José and placed here in a marble tomb near the transept, where it remains. Since 1862, the cathedral has contained the wax-covered mummy of St. Pio, a Roman martyr persecuted and killed for his Christian faith. To the right of the mummy is a bizarre wooden statue of Mary with four swords stuck in her bosom. The cathedral faces Plaza de las Monjas (the Nuns' Square), a shady spot where you can rest and cool off.

Calle del Cristo 153 (at Caleta San Juan). © 787/722-0861. Free admission. Mon–Fri 8am–5pm; Sat 8am–3:30pm; Sun 7am–7pm. Bus: Old Town Trolley.

FORTS

Castillo San Felipe del Morro ⋆

Known as "El Morro," this fort stands on a rocky promontory dominating the entrance to San Juan Bay. Constructed in 1540, the original fort was a round tower, which can still be seen deep inside the lower levels of the castle. More walls and turrets were added, and by 1787, the fortification attained the complex design you see today. This fortress was attacked repeatedly by both the English and the Dutch.

The National Park Service protects the fortifications of Old San Juan, which have been declared a World Heritage Site by the United Nations. You'll find El Morro an intriguing labyrinth of dungeons, barracks, ramps, and vaults, with lookouts that provide some of the most dramatic views in the Caribbean. Historical information is provided in a video in English and Spanish. The nearest parking is the underground facility beneath the Quincentennial Plaza at the Ballajá barracks (Cuartel de Ballajá) on Calle Norzagaray. Sometimes park rangers lead hour-long tours for free, although you can also visit on your own. Your ticket here also entitles you to free admission to Fort San Cristóbal (see below) on the same day.

Before going into the citadel, you can visit the new $2 million **San Juan National Historic Site** (© 787/729-6960). The center is connected via two

⌒ *Moments* Jogger's Trail or Romantic Walk

El Morro Trail, a jogger's paradise, provides Old Town's most scenic views across the harbor. The first part of the trail extends to the San Juan Gate. The walk then goes by El Morro, a 16th-century fort, and eventually reaches a scenic area known as Bastion de Santa Barbara. The walk passes El Morro's well-preserved walls, and the trail ends at the entrance to the fortress. The walkway is designed to follow the undulating movement of the ocean, and sea grapes and tropical vegetation surround benches. The trail is romantic at night, when the walls of the fortress are illuminated. Stop in at the tourist office for a map and set off.

tunnels to **Fort San Cristóbal,** and was created from a strategic military base used in World War II. Visitors view a 12-minute film about the fortifications. A photo exhibit, a gift shop, and other exhibits are of interest.

At the end of Calle Norzagaray. ℂ **787/729-6960.** Admission $3 adults, $1 seniors and children age 13–17, free for children 12 and under. Daily 9am–5pm. Bus: A5, B21, or B40.

Fort San Cristóbal ⭐   This huge fortress, begun in 1634 and reengineered in the 1770s, is one of the largest the Spanish ever built in the Americas. Its walls rise more than 150 feet above the sea. Together San Cristóbal and El Morro, which are linked by a ½ mile of monumental walls and bastions filled with cannon-firing positions, protected San Juan against attackers coming by land. A complex system of tunnels and dry moats connects the center of San Cristóbal to its "outworks," defensive elements arranged layer after layer over a 27-acre site. You'll get the idea if you look at the scale model on display. The fort is administered and maintained by the National Park Service.

Be sure to see the **Garita del Diablo,** or the Devil's Sentry Box, one of the oldest parts of San Cristóbal's defenses, and famous in Puerto Rican legend. The devil himself, it is said, would snatch away sentinels at this lonely post at the edge of the sea. In 1898, the first shots of the Spanish-American War in Puerto Rico were fired by cannons on top of San Cristóbal during an artillery duel with a U.S. Navy fleet. Sometimes park rangers lead hour-long tours for free, although you can visit on your own.

In the northeast corner of Old San Juan (uphill from Plaza de Colón on Calle Norzagaray). ℂ **787/729-6960.** Admission $3 adults, $1 seniors and children age 13–17, free for children 12 and under. Daily 9am–5pm. Bus: A5, B21, or B40; then the free trolley from Covadonga station to the top of the hill.

OTHER HISTORIC SITES

The **city walls** around San Juan *(murallas de San Juan)* were built in 1630 to protect the town against both European invaders and Caribbean pirates, and indeed were part of one of the most impregnable fortresses in the New World. Even today, they're an engineering marvel. At their top, notice the balconied buildings that served for centuries as hospitals and also residences of the island's various governors. The thickness of the walls averages 20 feet at the base and 12 feet at the top, with an average height of 40 feet. Between Fort San Cristóbal and El Morro, bastions were erected at frequent intervals. The walls come into view as you approach from San Cristóbal on your way to El Morro. To get here, take the C45 and A5 bus.

San Juan Gate, Calle San Francisco and Calle Recinto Oeste, built around 1635, just north of La Fortaleza, several blocks downhill from the cathedral, was

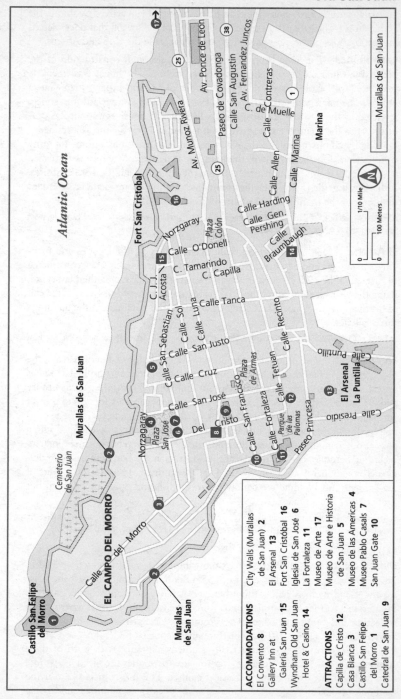

Old San Juan

Atlantic Ocean

Castillo San Felipe del Morro

EL CAMPO DEL MORRO

Cemeterio de San Juan

Murallas de San Juan

Murallas de San Juan

Calle del Morro

Murallas de San Juan

Fort San Cristobal

Norzgaray

Plaza Colón

Calle O'Donell

C. Tamarindo

C. Capilla

Calle Harding

Calle Gen. Pershing

Calle Braumbaugh

Av. Ponce de Leon

Paseo de Covadonga

Calle San Augustin

Av. Fernandez Juncos

Av. Contreras

C. de Muelle

Calle

Calle Allen

Calle Marina

Marina

Av. Munoz Rivera

C.J.I.

Acosta

Calle Tanca

Calle San Sebastian

Calle Sol

Calle Luna

Calle San Justo

Calle Cruz

Calle Recinto

Calle Tetuan

Calle San Francisco

Plaza de Armas

Calle Fortaleza

Calle San José

Norzagaray

Plaza San José

Del Cristo

Parque de las Palomas

Paseo Princesa

Calle Puntillo

El Arsenal La Puntilla

Calle Presidio

Murallas de San Juan

Murallas de San Juan

Murallas de San Juan

1/10 Mile
100 Meters

479

the main gate and entry point into San Juan—that is, if you arrived by ship in the 18th century. The gate is the only one remaining of the several that once pierced the fortifications of the old walled city. To get here, take the C45 and A5 bus.

Casa Blanca   Ponce de León never lived here, although construction of the house (built in 1521) is sometimes attributed to him. The house was erected 2 years after the explorer's death, by the order of his son-in-law, Juan García Troche. The parcel of land was given to Ponce de León as a reward for services rendered to the Crown. His descendants lived in the house for about 2½ centuries, until the Spanish government took it over in 1779 for use as a residence for military commanders. The U.S. government also used it as a home for army commanders. On the first floor, the Juan Ponce de León Museum is furnished with antiques, paintings, and artifacts from the 16th through the 18th centuries. In back is a garden with spraying fountains, offering an intimate and verdant respite from the monumental buildings of old San Juan.

Calle San Sebastián 1. ℂ 787/725-1454. Admission $2 adults, seniors and children under 12 $1. Tues–Sat 9am–noon and 1–4:30pm. Bus: 1 or 40.

El Arsenal   The Spaniards used shallow craft to patrol the lagoons and mangroves in and around San Juan. Needing a base for these vessels, they constructed El Arsenal in the 19th century. It was at this base that they staged their last stand, flying the Spanish colors until the final Spaniard was removed in 1898, at the end of the Spanish-American War. Changing art exhibitions are held in the building's three galleries.

La Puntilla. ℂ 787/723-3068. Free admission. Mon–Fri 10am–1pm and 2–5pm; Sat–Sun noon–5pm. Bus: B21.

La Fortaleza   The office and residence of the governor of Puerto Rico is the oldest executive mansion in continuous use in the Western Hemisphere, and has served as the island's seat of government for more than 3 centuries. Yet its history goes back even farther, to 1533, when construction began on a fortress to protect San Juan's Spanish settlers during raids by Carib tribesmen and pirates. The original medieval towers remain, but as the edifice was subsequently enlarged into a palace, other modes of architecture and ornamentation were also incorporated, including baroque, Gothic, neoclassical, and Arabian. La Fortaleza has been designated a national historic site by the U.S. government. Thirty-minute tours of the gardens and building are conducted in English and Spanish. Informal but proper attire is required.

Calle Fortaleza, overlooking San Juan Harbor. ℂ 787/721-7000, ext. 2211. Free admission. Tours Mon–Fri, every half-hour 9am–3:30pm. Closed on holidays and weekends. Bus: B21, then the Old Town Trolley.

MUSEUMS
Museo de Arte ⭐⭐   Puerto Rico's most important gallery, which opened in 2000 and was constructed at a cost of $55 million, is a state-of-the-art showcase for the island nation's rich cultural heritage as reflected mainly by its painters. Housed in a former city hospital in Santurce, the museum features a permanent collection and temporary exhibitions. Prominent local artists star—for example, Francisco Oller (1833–1917), who brought a touch of Cézanne or Camille Pissarro to Puerto Rico (Oller actually studied in France with both of these Impressionists). Another leading star of the permanent collection is José Campéche, a late 18th-century classical painter. The museum is like a living textbook of Puerto Rican art, beginning with its early development and going on to showcase camp aspects such as the poster art created here in the mid-20th century. All the important modern island artists are also represented, including

Moments **El Yunque Tropical Rainforest**

Some 25 miles east of San Juan lies the **Caribbean National Forest** ★★★, known as El Yunque, the only tropical forest in the U.S. National Forest Service system. It was given its status by former President Theodore Roosevelt. Within its 28,000 acres are some 240 tree species (only half a dozen of which are found on the mainland U.S.). In this world of cedars and satinwood, draped in tangles of vines, you'll hear chirping birds, see wild orchids, and perhaps hear the song of the tree frog, the *coquí*. The entire forest is a bird sanctuary and may be the last retreat of the rare Puerto Rican parrot.

El Yunque offers a number of **walking and hiking trails,** high above sea level. The most scenic is the rugged El Toro Trail, which passes through four different forest systems en route to the 3,523-foot Pico El Toro, the highest peak in the forest. The signposted El Yunque Trail leads to three of the recreation area's most spectacular lookouts, and the Big Tree Trail is an easy walk to panoramic La Mina Falls. Just off the main road is La Coca Falls, a sheet of water cascading down mossy cliffs. You can be fairly sure you'll encounter rain—more than 100 billion gallons of rain falls here annually—but showers are usually brief, and there are plenty of shelters in the park.

Nearby, the Sierra Palm Interpretive Service Center has maps and information and arranges for guided tours. A 45-minute drive southeast from San Juan (near the intersection of Route 3 and Route 191), El Yunque is a popular half-day or full-day outing. Major hotels provide guided tours.

El Portal Tropical Forest Center, Route 191, Rio Grande (© **787/888-1880**), an $18 million exhibition and information center, has 10,000 square feet of exhibition space. Three pavilions offer exhibits and bilingual displays. The actor Jimmy Smits narrates a documentary called *Understanding the Forest.* The center is open daily from 9am to 5pm, and it charges an admission of $3 for adults and $1.50 for children.

---

the best known, the late Angel Botello, but also such contemporaries as Rafael Tufiño and Arnaldo Roche Rabell.

299 Ave. Jose de Diego, Santurce. © **787/977-6277**. Admission $6 adults, $3 children under 12, seniors $2.50. Tues and Thurs–Sat 10am–5pm; Wed 10am–8pm; Sun 11am–6pm. Bus: A5 or B21.

Museo de Arte e Historia de San Juan   Located in a Spanish colonial building at the corner of Calle MacArthur, this cultural center was the city's main marketplace in the mid-19th century. Local art is displayed in several galleries, and audiovisual materials (in English and Spanish) explore the city's history (hourly from 9am–4pm Tues–Fri). Sometimes major cultural events are staged in the museum's large courtyard.

Calle Norzagaray 150. © **787/724-1875**. Free admission, but donations accepted. Tues–Fri 9am–4pm; Sat–Sun 10am–4pm. Bus: Old Town Trolley, then a short walk.

Museo de las Americas   Museo de las Americas showcases the artisans of North, South, and Central America, featuring everything from carved figureheads from New England whaling ships to dugout canoes carved by Carib Indians in Dominica. It is unique in Puerto Rico and well worth a visit. Also on display is a changing collection of paintings by artists from throughout the Spanish-speaking world, some of which are for sale, and a permanent collection called "Puerto Rican *Santos*," which includes a collection of carved wooden depictions of saints.

Cuartel de Ballajá. ℃ 787/724-5052. Free admission, but donations accepted. Tues–Sun 10am–4pm. Bus: Old Town Trolley.

Museo de Pablo Casals   Adjacent to Iglesia de San José, this museum is devoted to the memorabilia left to the people of Puerto Rico by the musician Pablo Casals. The maestro's cello is here, along with a library of videos (played upon request) of some of his festival concerts. This small 18th-century house also contains manuscripts and photographs of Casals. The annual Casals Festival draws worldwide interest and attracts some of the greatest performing artists; it's still held during the first 2 weeks of June.

Plaza San José, Calle San Sebastián 101. ℃ 787/723-9185. Admission $1 adults, 50¢ students and children. Tues–Sat 9:30am–4:30pm. Bus: Old Town Trolley.

SHOPPING 🐱🐱

U.S. citizens don't pay duty on items they purchase in Puerto Rico and bring back to the United States. And you can find great bargains on Puerto Rico, where the competition among shopkeepers is fierce.

The streets of **Old Town,** such as Calle San Francisco and Calle del Cristo, are the major venues for shopping. Note, however, that most stores in Old San Juan are closed on Sunday.

Local handcrafts can be good buys, including needlework, straw work, ceramics, hammocks, papier-mâché fruits and vegetables, and paintings and sculptures by Puerto Rican artists. Puerto Rican *santos* (saints) are sought by collectors. These carved wooden religious idols vary greatly in shape and size, and devout locals believe they have healing powers—often the ability to perform *milagros,* or miracles.

The biggest and most up-to-date shopping plaza in the Caribbean Basin is **Plaza Las Americas,** in the financial district of Hato Rey, right off the Las Americas Expressway. The complex, with its fountains and advanced architecture, has more than 200 mostly upscale shops. The stores (and their wares) are about what you'd find in a mall back home. Prices are comparable to those stateside.

Art

If you're interested in acquiring Puerto Rican art, there are many possibilities. **Galería Botello** 🐱, 314 Ave. Franklin D. Roosevelt at Hato Rey (℃ 787/754-7430), is a contemporary Latin American gallery, a living tribute to the late Angel Botello, one of Puerto Rico's most outstanding artists. His paintings and bronze sculptures, evocative of his colorful background, are done in a style uniquely his own. On display are his and other local artists' paintings and sculptures, as well as a large collection of antique Puerto Rican *santos*.

Galería Fosilarte, Calle del Cristo 200B (℃ 787/725-4252), is a specialty gallery, displaying unique art pieces from limestone and coral that may have existed at the time of the dinosaurs. The work is the creation of Radamés Rivera. One of the gallery's most noted artists is Yolanda Velasquez, who paints in an abstract style. The gallery also showcases the work of some 40 other artists.

Galería Palomas 🐱, Calle del Cristo 207 (℃ 787/724-8904), is another leading choice. Works range from $300 and include some of the leading painters of the Latin American world, and are rotated every 2 to 3 weeks. The setting is a 17th-century colonial house. Of special note are works by such local artists as Homer, Moya, and Alicea. **Galería San Juan,** at the Gallery Inn, Calle Norzagaray 204–206 (℗ **787/722-1808**), specializes in the sculpture and paintings of Jan D'Esopo, a Connecticut-born artist who has spent much of her time in Puerto Rico. Many of her fine pieces are in bronze.

Books

For travel guides, maps, and just something to read on the beach, there are two good bookstores. Try **Bell, Book & Candle,** 102 de Diego Ave., Santurce (℗ **787/728-5000**), a large general-interest bookstore that carries fiction and classics in both Spanish and English, plus a huge selection of postcards. **Librería Cronopios,** Calle San José 255 (℗ **787/724-1815**), is the leading choice in the old town. It sells a number of books on Puerto Rican culture as well as good maps of the island.

Coffee & Spices

Spicy Caribbee, Calle del Cristo 154 (℗ **787/725-4690**), offers the best selection of Puerto Rican coffee, which has a good reputation among aficionados. It also has the Old Town's best array of hot spicy sauces of the Caribbean.

Fashion

Nono Maldonado, 1051 Ashford Ave. (midway between the Condado Plaza and the Ramada Hotel, ℗ **787/721-0456**), is named after its owner, a Puerto Rican designer who worked for many years as the fashion editor of *Esquire* magazine. This is one of the most fashionable and upscale haberdashers in the Caribbean. Selling both men's and women's clothing, it has everything from socks to dinner jackets, as well as ready-to-wear versions of Maldonado's twice-a-year collections. **Polo Ralph Lauren Factory Store,** Calle del Cristo 201 (℗ **787/722-2136**), has prices that are often 35% to 40% less what you'd find on the U.S. mainland. You can find even greater discounts on irregular or slightly damaged garments. One upstairs room is devoted to home furnishings. **Speedo Authentic Fitness,** Calle Fortaleza 65 at the corner of Calle del Cristo (℗ **787/724-3089**), sells sportswear for women and men, specializing in shorts, jackets, and swimwear. There's also one of the town's best collections of sandals here.

Gifts, Arts & Crafts

Butterfly People 👤, Calle Fortaleza 152, Second Floor (℗ **787/723-2432**), is a gallery/cafe in a handsomely restored building in Old San Juan. Butterflies, preserved forever in artfully arranged boxes, range from $20 for a single mounting to thousands of dollars for whole-wall murals. Most of these butterflies come from farms around the world, some of the most beautiful from Indonesia, Malaysia, and New Guinea. Tucked away, on the same premises, is **Malula Antiques.** Specializing in tribal art from the Moroccan sub-Sahara and Syria, it contains a sometimes startling collection of primitive and timeless crafts and accessories.

   Barrachina's, Calle Fortaleza 104, between Calle del Cristo and Calle San José (℗ **787/725-7912**), is more than a jewelry store. This is also the birthplace, in 1963, of the piña colada. It's a favorite of cruise-ship passengers, offering one of the largest selections of jewelry, perfume, cigars, and gifts in San Juan. There's a patio for drinks, plus a Bacardi rum outlet selling bottles cheaper than stateside, but at the same prices as the Bacardi distillery. You'll also find a costume-jewelry department, a gift shop, a restaurant, and a section for authentic silver jewelry.

Xian Imports, Calle de la Cruz 153 (© 787/723-2214), is a jumbled, slightly claustrophobic shop where you'll find compactly arranged porcelain, sculptures, paintings, and Chinese furniture, much of it antique. It's favored by the island's decorators as a source for unusual art objects.

El Artesano, Calle Fortaleza 314 (© 787/721-6483), is a curiosity. You'll find Mexican and Peruvian icons of the Virgin Mary; charming depictions of fish and Latin American birds in terra cotta and brass; all kinds of woven goods; painted cupboards, chests, and boxes; and mirrors and Latin dolls.

Bóveda, Calle del Cristo 209 (© 787/725-0263), is a long narrow space crammed with exotic jewelry, clothing, greeting cards of images of life in Puerto Rico, some 100 handmade lamps, antiques, Mexican punched tin and glass, and art-nouveau reproductions, among other items.

Olé, Calle Fortaleza 105 (© 787/724-2445), deserves an olé. Browsing this store is a learning experience. Practically everything comes from Puerto Rico or Latin America. If you want a straw hat from Ecuador, hand-beaten Chilean silver, Christmas ornaments, or Puerto Rican *santos* (saints), this is the place.

Puerto Rican Arts & Crafts ☆, Calle Fortaleza 204 (© 787/725-5596), set in a 200-year-old colonial building, is one of the premier outlets on the island for authentic artifacts. Of particular interest are papier-mâché carnival masks from Ponce. Taíno designs inspired by ancient petroglyphs are incorporated into most of the sterling silver jewelry sold here. There's an art gallery in back, with silk-screened serigraphs by local artists, and a gourmet Puerto Rican food section with such items as coffee, rum, and hot sauces. The store also exhibits and sells small carved *santos* (saints), laboriously carved by artisans in private studios around the island.

Libreria y Tienda de Artesania del Instituto de Cultura Puertorriqueña, Calle Norzagaray 98 (© 787/721-6866), next to the Convento de los Dominicos, has not only a collection of books on Puerto Rico, but a good display of crafts in the Old Town, including *santos* (saints), Indian artifacts, carnival masks (many from Ponce), and baskets. All pieces are said to be made in Puerto Rico, and not in places such as Taiwan, as is so often the case.

Jewelry

Bared & Sons ☆, Calle Fortaleza 206 (at the corner of Calle San Justo; © 787/724-4811), now in its fourth decade, is the main outlet of a chain of at least 20 upscale jewelry stores on Puerto Rico. On the ground floor are gemstones, gold, diamonds, and watches. One floor up, there's a monumental collection of porcelain and crystal. It's a great source for hard-to-get and discontinued patterns discounted from Christofle, Royal Doulton, Wedgwood, Limoges, Royal Copenhagen, Lalique, Lladró, Herend, Baccarat, and Daum.

R. Kury, Calle Fortaleza 253 (© 787/977-4873), is a direct factory outlet for the oldest jewelry factory on Puerto Rico, the Kury Company. Don't expect a top-notch jeweler here: Many of the pieces are replicated in endless repetition. But don't overlook the place for 14-karat-gold ornaments. Some of the designs are charming, and prices are about 20% less than at retail stores in the U.S.

Joyería Riviera, Calle Fortaleza 257 (© 787/725-4000), is an emporium of 18-karat gold and diamonds, and the island's leading jeweler. Adjacent to Plaza de Armas, the shop has an impeccable reputation. This is the major distributor of Rolex watches on Puerto Rico.

Eduardo Barquet, Calle Fortaleza 200,at the corner of Calle La Cruz (© 787/723-1989), is known as a leading value-priced place to buy fine jewelry in Old San Juan. **Mounts and Gems,** Calle Fortaleza 205, sells convincing, glittering fake diamonds for those who don't want to wear or can't afford the real thing. It also stocks real diamond chips, emeralds, sapphires, and rubies, too.

Joseph Manchini, Calle Fortaleza 101 (© 787/722-7698), displays the works of its namesake and the shop's owner. He conceives almost anything you'd want in gold, silver, and bronze. Some of old town's most imaginative rings, bracelets, and chains are displayed here. If you don't like what's on sale, you can design your own, including pieces made with sapphire, emerald, and rubies.

Lace & Linens

Linen House, Calle Fortaleza 250 (© 787/721-4219), specializes in napery, bed linens, and lace, and has the island's best selection. Some of the more delicate pieces are expensive, but most are moderate in price. Inventories include embroidered shower curtains and lace doilies, bun warmers, placemats, and tablecloths that took workers weeks to complete. Some astonishingly lovely items are available for as little as $30. The aluminum/pewter serving dishes have beautiful Spanish-colonial designs. Prices here are sometimes 40% lower than those on the North American mainland.

SAN JUAN AFTER DARK
THE PERFORMING ARTS

Qué Pasa, the official visitor's guide to Puerto Rico, lists cultural events, including music, dance, theater, film, and art exhibits. It's distributed free by the tourist office.

A major cultural venue in San Juan is **Teatro Tapía,** Avenida Ponce de León (© 787/721-0169), across from Plaza de Colón, one of the oldest theaters in the Western Hemisphere (built around 1832). Much of Puerto Rican theater history is connected with the Tapía, named after the island's first prominent playwright, Alejandro Tapía y Rivera. Various productions, some musical, are staged here throughout the year and include drama, dance, and cultural events. You'll have to call the box office (open Mon–Fri 8am–4pm) for specific information. Tickets generally start at $20 to $30.

THE CLUB & MUSIC SCENE

San Juan Chateau, 9 Chardon Ave. in Hato Rey (© 787/751-2000), is the best venue in the city for reggae. The cover charge, ranging from $5 to $20, depends on what group is appearing. On Sunday night the club goes gay with drag shows and the like. The clientele is all ages, from late teens to the middle aged. The club has no set closing hours but opens on Friday and Saturday at 9pm, and Sunday at 8pm.

Another glitzy scene unfolds at the **Hacienda Country Club,** a 25-minute drive out of San Juan on the signposted road to Caguas (© 787/747-9692). You can't miss the club along the highway. Live musicians entertain here in an alfresco setting surrounded by mountains. A mainly 20- to 30-year-old crowd is attracted to a club evocative of one where Ricky Ricardo might have appeared in the '50s. The cover ranges from $10 to $30, depending on what's offered. Some of the hottest Latin groups in the Caribbean appear here. The club opens Saturday at 7:30pm and Sunday at noon, with no set closing hours.

Modeled after an artist's rendition of the once-notorious city of Mesopotamia, **Babylon,** in Wyndham El San Juan Hotel & Casino, 6063 Isla

Verde, Isla Verde (© 787/791-1000), is circular, with a central dance floor and a wraparound balcony where onlookers can scope out the action below. The crowd is usually in the 25-to-45 age group. This place has one of the best sound systems in the Caribbean. You might want to make a night of it, stopping into the El San Juan's bars and casino en route. The club is open from Thursday to Saturday from 10pm to 4am. Guests of the hotel enter free; otherwise, there's a $15 cover. Bus: A5.

Rumba, 152 Calle San Sebastian (© 787/365-1418), is small and cramped, but so photogenically hip that it was selected as the site for the filming of many of the crowd scenes within *Habana Nights.* (Scheduled for a release in early 2005, it was conceived by its producers as a Hispanic version of everybody's favorite tale of adolescent coming-of-age, *Dirty Dancing.*) Set immediately adjacent to the also-recommended restaurant Barú, with which it's not associated, it's known within San Juan's underground nightlife circuit as one of the places to hang. Expect beautiful people, a sense of cutting-edge Hispanic hip, and a cover charge of up to $15 whenever there's live music. Open Tuesday through Sunday 9pm to 4am. Bus: M2, M3, or A5.

Laser, Calle del Cruz 251 (© 787/725-7581), is set in the heart of the old town near the corner of Calle Fortaleza. This disco is especially crowded when cruise ships pull into town. Once inside, you can wander over the three floors, listening to whatever music happens to be hot, with lots of additional merengue and salsa thrown in as well. Depending on the night, the age of the crowd varies. It's open Thursday to Saturday from 9pm to 4am. It's also open on Monday and Tuesday when the cruise ships dock. Women enter free after midnight on Saturday. The cover ranges from $10 to $12. Bus: Old Town Trolley.

The Cabin, 2473 Loiza St., Punta Las Marias (no phone), is a local dive featuring food, fun, and rock 'n' roll near Ocean Park. It's like an Irish pub and draws an under-25 crowd to its simple precincts decorated in wood. It's mainly a bar, but the kitchen on-site serves food including *churrasco* (braised meat) with potatoes, chicken breast with mozzarella, and a selection of nachos, tapas, and burgers. When live music is featured on Saturday, there's a $6 cover. Open Tuesday to Sunday at 5pm (no set closing). Bus: B21.

Star Gate, Avenida Robert Todd, Santurce (no phone), is popular for dating couples. Most dress up to patronize this disco-bar, where they dance and drink until the late hours. Wednesday night is the most casual, Friday and Saturday the most formal nights. Cover charge is $15 to $25 (which includes drinks). Open Friday through Sunday 9:30pm to 4am. Some of the best live music along the Condado is played here. Bus: 1.

THE BAR SCENE

Two of the most dramatic bars in San Juan are at **Wyndham El San Juan Hotel & Casino,** 6063 Isla Verde Ave., Isla Verde (© 787/791-1000). There is no more beautiful bar in the Caribbean than the **Palm Court,** open daily 11am to 3am. Set in an oval wrapped around a sunken bar area, amid marble and burnished mahogany, it offers a view of one of the world's largest chandeliers. After 9pm Tuesday to Saturday, live music, often salsa and merengue, emanates from an adjoining room (the El Chico Bar). There's also the chic **Cigar Bar,** with a magnificent repository of the finest cigars in the world. Some of the most fashionable women in San Juan—and men, too—can be seen puffing away while sipping a cognac. It's open Thursday to Saturday from 6pm to 3am and Sunday to Wednesday from 6pm to 1am.

Ireland and its ales meet the Tropics at **Shannon's Irish Pub,** Calle Bori 496, Río Piedras (© **787/281-8466**). A sports bar, it's the regular watering hole of many university students, who come to play pool, listen to a constant supplier of high-energy rock 'n' roll, or watch one of the 10 TV monitors. There's live music Wednesday through Sunday—everything from rock to jazz to Latin. A simple cafe serves inexpensive food daily from 11:30am to 1am. A $3 cover is imposed after 7pm. It closes at 2:30am on Friday and at 3am on Saturday.

We're not so keen on the food served here any more (and neither are our readers), but we still like to visit old town's **El Patio de Sam,** Calle San Sebastian 102 (© **787/723-1149**), one of the most popular late-night joints with a good selection of beers. Live entertainment is presented here Monday to Saturday. This is one of the most enduring of the old town eateries and it remains a fun joint— that is, if you dine somewhere else before coming here.

HOT NIGHTS IN GAY SAN JUAN

The Beach Bar, on the ground floor of the Atlantic Beach Hotel, 1 Calle Vendig (© **787/721-6900**), is the site of a hugely popular Sunday afternoon gathering that gets really crowded beginning around 4pm, and which stretches into the wee hours. There's an occasional drag show on a dais at one end of the outdoor terrace. There's also an open-air rectangular bar. The Beach Bar is open daily from 10am to at least 2am. Bus: 21.

Cups, Calle San Mateo 1708, Santurce (© **787/268-3570**), is a Latin tavern, the only place in San Juan that caters almost exclusively to lesbians. Men (gay or straight) aren't particularly welcome. Although the club is open Wednesday through Saturday from 7pm to 4am, entertainment such as live music or cabaret is presented only on Wednesday at 9pm or Friday at 10pm.

A converted movie theater from the 1960s, **Teatro,** 1420 Ave. Ponce de León (© **787/722-1130**), is nicknamed "Asylum" by locals. One of the better gay and lesbian discos, it attracts with laser beams, artful lights, and a panoramic balcony. Dance music is committed to reggae, house, hip-hop, and garage. A cover of $6 to $25, depending on the night, is imposed after 11:30pm. Open Thursday 9am to 6am, Friday 9:30am to 6am, Saturday 10pm to 7am, and Sunday 9pm to 6am. Always take a taxi here.

Eros, 1257 Ave. Ponce de León, Santurce (© **787/722-1131**), is one of the town's most popular gay discos, with strippers and shows. Most of the crowd is in its late 20s. Rum-based drinks, merengue, and the latest dance tunes are on tap; the place really gets going after around 10:30pm. It's open Wednesday to Saturday from 10pm to 5am. The cover is $5.

CASINOS 🟊🟊

Gambling is big in Puerto Rico. Many people come here to do little more than that. As a result, there are plenty of options. Unlike European casinos, visitors don't need to flash passports or pay admission to enter.

The casino generating all the excitement today is the 18,500-square-foot gaming facility at **Ritz-Carlton San Juan Spa & Casino** 🟊, 6961 Ave. of Governors, Isla Verde (© **787/253-1700**), the largest in the whole Caribbean. It combines the elegant decor of the 1940s with tropical fabrics and patterns. This is one of the plushest and most exclusive entertainment complexes in the Caribbean. It features traditional games such as blackjack, roulette, baccarat, craps, and slot machines. It's open daily from 10am to 6am.

One of the splashiest of San Juan's casinos is at the **Wyndham Old San Juan Hotel & Casino,** Calle Brumbaugh 100 (© 787/721-5100). Five-card stud competes with some 240 slot machines and roulette tables. It's open daily from 10am to 2am.

You can also try your luck at **Wyndham El San Juan Hotel & Casino,** 6063 Isla Verde Ave. (© 787/791-1000), in Isla Verde (one of the most grand), and the **Wyndham Condado Plaza Hotel & Casino,** 999 Ashford Ave. (© 787/721-1000).

The oceanfront **Stellaris Casino** at the **San Juan Marriott Resort,** 1309 Ashford Ave. (© 787/722-7000), was recently remodeled but remains one of San Juan's minor casinos, with 10 tables for such games as craps, blackjack, and poker. There are also private "baccarat pits," plus 200 slot machines.

3 Dorado (★

Along the north shore of Puerto Rico, about a 40-minute (22-mile) drive west of San Juan, a luxury resort unfolds at the Hyatt Dorado Beach Hotel, which sits on a choice white-sand beach. Many guests of this hotel only pass through San Juan on arrival and departure, so if you're a first-time visitor you may want to spend a day or so sightseeing and shopping in San Juan before heading for this complete resort property, since, chances are, once you're at the resort you'll never leave the grounds.

GETTING THERE

If you don't have a car, call **Dorado Transport Corp.,** which is on the site shared by the Hyatt Resort (© 787/796-1234). It offers frequent shuttle service between the Hyatt and the San Juan airport every day between 9am and 10pm (every 20 minutes). The charge is $25 per person, but a minimum of three passengers must make the trip for the bus to operate.

ACCOMMODATIONS

Lodgings in Dorado are pretty much limited to the Hyatt, a good choice for families. It offers family getaway packages at Camp Coquí, the Puerto Rican version of Camp Hyatt, featuring professionally supervised day and evening programs for children age 3 to 12. Children also receive a 50% discount on meals.

Hyatt Dorado Beach Resort & Country Club ★★ *Kids*   Hyatt has spent millions on improvements here at what in the 1950s was Laurance Rockefeller's special getaway for presidents and the Hollywood elite, lying on 1,000 acres. The renovated guest rooms have marble bathrooms and terra-cotta floors throughout. Accommodations are available on the beach or in villas tucked in and around the lushly planted grounds. They're fairly spacious and bathrooms have everything from tubs to bathrobes, deluxe toiletries to power showers. The casitas are a series of private beach or poolside houses.

Dinner is served in a three-tiered main dining room where you can watch the surf. Hyatt Dorado chefs have won many awards, and the food at its restaurants is among the most appealing in Puerto Rico.

Hwy. 693, Dorado, PR 00646. © **800/233-1234** in the U.S., or 787/796-1234. Fax 787/796-6560. www.doradobeach.hyatt.com. 298 units, 17 casitas. Winter $415–$620 double, from $705 casita for 2; off season $206–$380 double, from $465 casita for 2. MAP (breakfast and dinner/mandatory in winter) $70 extra per day for adults, $35 extra per day for children. AE, DC, DISC, MC, V. **Amenities:** 5 restaurants; 3 bars; 2 outdoor pools; 2 18-hole championship golf courses; 7 all-weather tennis courts; spa; windsurfing school; children's camp; business center; 24-hr. room service; babysitting; laundry service; dry cleaning; nonsmoking rooms; rooms for those with limited mobility. *In room:* A/C, TV, minibar, hair dryer, iron/ironing board, safe.

DINING

El Malecón PUERTO RICAN   If you'd like an unpretentious local place serving good Puerto Rican cuisine, then head for El Malecón. It has a cozy family ambience and is especially popular on weekends. Some members of the staff speak English, and the chef is best with fresh seafood. Most of the dishes are at the lower end of the price scale; only the lobster is expensive. On Wednesday and Friday there's a live band and dancing.

Rte. 693, km. 8.2 Marginal Costa de Oro. © 787/796-1645. Main courses $8–$33. AE, MC, V. Daily 11am–11pm.

Su Casa Restaurant ₳₳₳ SPANISH/PUERTO RICAN   This is a restored version of the 19th-century Livingston family plantation home offering the finest dining at the Hyatt. It's an attractive setting, an old oceanfront hacienda with a red-tile roof, graceful staircases, and verandas in the Spanish style. Strolling musicians and candlelight add to the romantic ambience. The Rockefellers used to entertain their formally dressed guests at this posh hideaway, but today dress is casual (no shorts). The chef produces an innovative cuisine, using Puerto Rican fruits and vegetables whenever possible. Dining here is such an event patrons make an evening of it. For a refreshing starter, try the white gazpacho with grapes or a tropical green salad with papaya, avocado, and Caribbean spices. The kitchen whips up a delectable seafood and chicken paella, or you can order dorado (mahimahi) with a spicy corn sauce served with couscous and a spinach timbale. Meats are also savory, especially the roasted pork chops flavored with a tamarind sauce.

In the Hyatt Dorado Beach Resort. © 787/796-1234. Reservations required. Main courses $24–$30. AE, DC, MC, V. Daily 6:30–10pm.

SPORTS & OTHER OUTDOOR PURSUITS

GOLF   The Robert Trent Jones Sr.–designed courses at the **Hyatt Dorado Beach Resort & Country Club** ₳₳ match the finest anywhere. The two original courses, known as east and west (© 787/796-8961 for tee times), were carved out of a jungle and offer tight fairways bordered by trees and forests, with lots of ocean holes. The somewhat newer and less noted north and south courses (© 787/796-8915 for tee times) feature wide fairways with well-bunkered greens and an assortment of water traps and tricky wind factors. Each course has a 72 par. Guests of the Hyatt get preferred tee times and lower fees than nonguests. On the north and south courses, guests pay $65 to $85, with nonguests charged $80 to $110. On the east and west courses guests pay $89 to $130, with nonguests paying from $99 to $150. Golf carts at any of the courses are included in the greens fee. The north and south, and the east and west courses each maintain separate pro shops, each with a bar and snack-style restaurant. Both are open daily from 7am until dusk.

WINDSURFING & OTHER WATERSPORTS   The best place on the island's north shore is along the well-maintained beachfront of the Hyatt Dorado Beach Resort near the 10th hole of the east golf course. Here, **Penfield Island Adventures** (© 787/796-2188) offers 90-minute **windsurfing lessons** for $60 each; board rentals cost $60 per half-day and $20 per each extra hour. Well-supplied with a wide array of windsurfers, including some designed specifically for beginners and children, the school benefits from the almost uninterrupted flow of the north shore's strong, steady winds and an experienced crew of instructors.

4 Rincón ⭐

At the westernmost point of the island, Rincón, 6 miles north of Mayagüez and 100 miles west of San Juan, has one of the most exotic beaches on the island, drawing surfers from around the world. In and around this small fishing village are some unique accommodations.

GETTING THERE

If you rent a car at the San Juan airport, it will take approximately 2½ hours to drive here via the busy northern Route 2, or 3 hours via the scenic mountain route (no. 52) through Ponce to the south. We recommend the southern route.

In addition, there are two flights daily from San Juan to Mayagüez on **American Eagle** (📞 800/352-0714). These flights take 40 minutes, and round-trip fares range from $190 to $202. From the Mayagüez airport, Rincón is a 30-minute drive to the north on Route 2 (go left or west at the intersection with Route 115).

ACCOMMODATIONS

The Horned Dorset Primavera ⭐⭐⭐   This is the most sophisticated hotel on Puerto Rico and one of the most exclusive and elegant small properties anywhere in the Caribbean. Set on 8 acres, it opens onto a secluded semiprivate beach, and it was built on the massive breakwaters and seawalls erected by a local railroad many years ago. The hacienda evokes an aristocratic Spanish villa, with wicker armchairs, hand-painted tiles, ceiling fans, seaside terraces, and cascades of flowers. Accommodations are in a series of suites that ramble amid lush gardens. The decor is tasteful, with four-poster beds and brass-footed tubs in marble-sheathed bathrooms, with showers and tubs. Rooms are spacious and luxurious, with Persian rugs over tile floors, queen-size sofa beds in the sitting areas, and fine linen and tasteful fabrics on the elegant beds.

The eight-suite Casa Escondida villa, set at the edge of the property, adjacent to the sea, is decorated with an accent on teakwood and marble. Some of the units have private plunge pools; others offer private verandas or sundecks. Each contains high-quality reproductions of colonial furniture by Baker.

The hotel's restaurant, also called Horned Dorset Primavera, is one of the finest on Puerto Rico (see "Dining," below).

Rte. 429, km. 3.0 (P.O. Box 1132), Rincón, PR 00677. 📞 800/633-1857 or 787/823-4030. Fax 787/823-5580. www.horneddorset.com. 55 units. Winter $660–$1,000 double, $1,090–$1,490 suite for 2; off season $440–$890 double, $590–$999 suite for 2. MAP (breakfast and dinner) $82 per person extra. AE, MC, V. Children under age 12 not accepted. **Amenities:** 2 restaurants; bar; 3 outdoor pools; fitness center; room service (7am–10pm); massage; laundry service; library; 1 room for those with limited mobility. *In room:* A/C, minibar, hair dryer, iron/ironing board, safe.

Parador Villa Antonio *Kids*   Ilia and Hector Ruíz offer apartments by the sea in this privately owned and run *parador* (inn). The beach outside is nice, but the local authorities don't keep it as clean as they ought to. Surfing and fishing can be enjoyed just outside your front door, and you can bring your catch right into your cottage and prepare a fresh seafood dinner in your own kitchenette (there's no restaurant). This is a popular destination with families from Puerto Rico who crowd in on the weekends, occupying the motel-like rooms with balconies or terraces. Furnishings are well used but reasonably comfortable, and bathrooms are small with shower stalls.

Road 115, km. 12 (P.O. Box 68), Rincón, PR 00677. 📞 787/823-2645. Fax 787/823-3380. www.villa-antonio. com. 61 units. $96–$128 studio (up to 2 people); $123–$144 2-bedroom apt (holds up to 4 people);

$117 junior suite; $128 suite. AE, DISC, MC, V. **Amenities:** 2 outdoor pools; 2 tennis courts; children's center; babysitting; laundry service. *In room:* A/C, TV, dataport, kitchenette, beverage maker, iron, safe.

DINING

Horned Dorset Primavera *★★* FRENCH/CARIBBEAN   This is the finest restaurant in western Puerto Rico, so romantic that people sometimes come from San Juan just for an intimate dinner. A masonry staircase sweeps from the garden to the second floor, where soaring ceilings and an atmosphere similar to that within a private villa awaits you.

The menu, which changes virtually every night based on the inspiration of the chef, might include chilled parsnip soup, a fricassee of wahoo with wild mushrooms, grilled loin of beef with peppercorns, and medallions of lobster in an orange-flavored beurre-blanc sauce. The grilled breast of duckling with bay leaves and raspberry sauce is also delectable. Dorado (mahimahi) is grilled and served with a ginger-cream sauce on a bed of braised Chinese cabbage. It's delicious, as is the grilled squab with tarragon sauce.

In The Horned Dorset Primavera hotel, Rte. 429. ② 787/823-4030. Reservations recommended. Tasting menu $68 for 5-course, $92 for 8-course. AE, MC, V. Daily noon–2pm and 7–9:30pm.

HITTING THE BEACH & THE LINKS

One of Puerto Rico's most outstanding surfing beaches is at **Punta Higuero,** on Route 413 near Rincón. In the winter months especially, uninterrupted Atlantic swells with perfectly formed waves averaging 5 to 6 feet in height roll shoreward, and rideable swells sometimes reach 15 to 25 feet.

Punta Borinquén Golf Club, Route 107 (② 787/890-2987), 2 miles north of Aguadilla's center, across the highway from the city's airport, was originally built by the U.S. government as part of the Ramey Air Force Base. Today, its 18 holes function as a public golf course, open Monday to Friday 7am to 6pm and Saturday and Sunday 6am to 6pm. Greens fees are $18 to $20 for an all-day pass. Two-person golf carts can be rented for $30 for 18 holes. Clubs can be rented for $10. The clubhouse contains a bar and a simple restaurant.

5 Mayagüez

The port city Mayagüez, not architecturally remarkable, is the third-largest city on Puerto Rico; it lies 98 miles southwest of San Juan. It was once the needle-work capital of the island, and there are still craftspeople who sew fine embroidery. Mayagüez is also the honeymoon capital of Puerto Rico for certain tradition-minded Puerto Rican couples. If we were honeymooning, we'd rather stay in the Greater San Juan area or at one of the posh north-coast resorts, but this island tradition dates from the 16th century. It's said that when local fathers needed husbands for their daughters, they kidnapped young Spanish sailors who were en route to Latin America.

GETTING THERE

American Eagle (② 800/433-7300 or 787/832-1200) flies four times daily throughout the year between San Juan and Mayagüez. Flight time is 40 minutes, although there are often delays on the ground at either end of the itinerary. Depending on restrictions and the season you book your flight, round-trip fares range from $190 to $242 per person.

If you rent a car at the San Juan airport and want to **drive** to Mayagüez, it's fastest and most efficient to take the northern route that combines sections of the newly widened Route 22 with the older Route 2. Estimated driving time for a local resident is about 90 minutes, although newcomers usually take about 30 minutes longer. The southern route, which combines the modern Route 52 with a transit across the outskirts of historic Ponce, and a final access into Mayagüez via the southern section of Route 2, requires a total of about 3 hours and affords some worthwhile scenery across the island's mountainous interior.

ACCOMMODATIONS

Holiday Inn & Tropical Casino   This six-story hotel competes with the Mayagüez Resort & Casino, though we like the latter better. The Holiday Inn is well-maintained, contemporary, and comfortable. It has a marble-floored, high-ceilinged lobby, an outdoor pool with a waterside bar, and a big casino, but its lawn simply isn't as dramatically landscaped as the Mayagüez resort's surrounding acreage. Bedrooms here are comfortably but functionally outfitted in motel style; they've recently been refurbished. Each unit is equipped with a tiled bathroom with shower/tub combinations.

2701 Hwy. 2, km. 149.9, Mayagüez, PR 00680-6328. (800/HOLIDAY in the U.S. and Canada, or 787/833-1100. Fax 787/833-1300. www.holiday-inn.com. 142 units. Year-round $115–$162 double; $250 suite. Rates include breakfast. AE, DC, DISC, MC, V. **Amenities:** Restaurant; 2 bars; outdoor pool; casino; gym; business center; limited room service; laundry service; dry cleaning; nonsmoking rooms; rooms for those with limited mobility. *In room:* A/C, TV, beverage maker, hair dryer, iron/ironing board, safe.

Mayagüez Resort & Casino ⟨⟩   Except for the ritzy Horned Dorset Primavera (see above), this is the largest and best general hotel resort in western Puerto Rico, appealing equally to business travelers and vacationers. In 1995 local investors took over what was then a sagging Hilton and radically renovated it to the tune of $5 million. The hotel benefits from its redesigned casino, country-club format, and 20 acres of tropical gardens. The landscaped grounds have been designated an adjunct to the nearby Tropical Agriculture Research Station. Five species of palm trees, eight kinds of bougainvillea, and numerous species of rare flora are set adjacent to the institute's collection of tropical plants, which range from a pink torch ginger to a Sri Lankan cinnamon tree.

The hotel's well-designed bedrooms open onto views of the swimming pool, and many units have private balconies. Guest rooms tend to be small, but they have good beds. The restored bathrooms are well equipped with makeup mirrors, scales, and shower/tub combinations.

For details about El Castillo, the hotel's restaurant, see "Dining," below. The hotel is the major entertainment center of Mayagüez. Its casino has free admission and is open 24 hours a day. You can also drink and dance at the Victoria Lounge.

Rte. 104, km. 0.3 (P.O. Box 3781), Mayagüez, PR 00680. (888/689-3030 or 787/832-3030. Fax 787/834-3475. www.mayaguezresort.com. 140 units. Year-round $175–$235 double; $285 suite. AE, DC, DISC, MC, V. Parking $4.50. **Amenities:** Restaurant; 3 bars; Olympic-size pool; children's pool; casino; 3 tennis courts; small fitness room; Jacuzzi; scuba diving; snorkeling; surfing; playground; 24-hr. room service; babysitting; laundry service; nonsmoking rooms; rooms for those with limited mobility. *In room:* A/C, TV, dataport, minibar, beverage maker, iron/ironing board.

DINING

El Castillo INTERNATIONAL/PUERTO RICAN   This is the best-managed large-scale dining room in western Puerto Rico, as well as the main restaurant for the largest hotel and casino in the area. The food has real flavor and flair unlike the typical bland hotel fare so often dished up. Known for its generous lunch buffets, El Castillo serves only a la carte items at dinner, including seafood stew served on a bed of linguine with marinara sauce, grilled salmon with a mango-flavored Grand Marnier sauce, and filets of sea bass with a cilantro, white wine, and butter sauce. Steak and lobster are served on the same platter, if you want it.

In the Mayagüez Resort & Casino, Rte. 104, km. 0.3. (C) 787/832-3030. Breakfast buffet $12. Mon–Fri buffet lunch $15; Sat–Sun brunch buffet $23; main courses $14–$34. AE, MC, V. Daily 6:30am–midnight.

EXPLORING THE AREA: BEACHES & TROPICAL GARDENS

Along the western coastal bends of Route 2, north of Mayagüez, lie the best surfing **beaches** in the Caribbean. Surfers from as far away as New Zealand come to ride the waves. You can also check out panoramic **Punta Higuero** beach, nearby on Route 413, near Rincón (see above).

The chief sight in Mayagüez is the **Tropical Agriculture Research Station** ((C) 787/831-3435), located at the corner of roads 65 and 108, adjacent to the University of Puerto Rico at Mayagüez campus and across the street from the **Parque de los Próceres (Patriots' Park).** At the administration office, ask for a free map of the tropical gardens, which contain a huge collection of tropical species useful to people, including cacao, fruit trees, spices, timbers, and ornamentals. The grounds are open Monday to Friday from 7am to 5pm, and there is no admission charge.

6 San Germán

An hour's drive from Ponce or Mayagüez and the beaches of the southern coast, and just over 2 hours from San Juan, San Germán, Puerto Rico's second-oldest town, has been compared to a small-scale outdoor museum. It was founded in 1512 and destroyed by the French in 1528. Rebuilt in 1570, it was named after Germain de Foix, the second wife of King Ferdinand of Spain. Once the rival of San Juan, but without the benefit of Old San Juan's lavish restoration budgets, San Germán harbored many pirates, who pillaged the ships that sailed off the nearby coastline. Many of today's residents are descended from the smugglers, poets, priests, and politicians who lived here.

Although the pirates and sugar plantations are long gone and the city has settled into a slumber, it still retains some colorful reminders of the Spanish colonial era. Flowers brighten some of the patios here as they do in Seville. Also as in a small Spanish town, many of the inhabitants stroll through the small but choice historic zone in early evening. Nicknamed "Ciudad de las Lomas," or City of the Hills, San Germán boasts verdant scenery that provides a pleasant backdrop to a variety of architectural styles—Spanish colonial (1850s), creole (1880s), neoclassical (1910s), Art Deco (1930s), and international (1960s)— depicted in the gracious old world–style buildings that line some of its streets. So significant are these buildings that San Germán is the only city other than San Juan to be included in the National Register of Historic Places.

ACCOMMODATIONS

Parador El Oasis   Although it's not state-of-the-art, this hotel evokes some appealing doses of Spanish colonial charm. If you'd like to anchor into this quaint old town, far removed from the beaches, the El Oasis is a decent place to stay. A three-story building constructed around a pool and patio area, the hotel originated in the late 1700s as a privately owned mansion. The older rooms, positioned close to the lobby, show the wear and tear of the years. The more modern rooms, located in the back, are without character, but are cleaner and more spacious than the older units. Three of the units have private balconies, and each of the accommodations come with a tiled, shower-only bathroom. The hotel sits on the town's overcrowded main street, about 2 blocks from the historic churches of San Germán. The in-house restaurant is not the most imaginative choice in town, but it emerges year after year as the most reliable and consistent of those within the town center.

Calle Luna 72, San Germán, PR 00683. (C) 787/892-1175. 52 units. Year-round $62–$70 double. Extra person $10. Children 12 and under stay free in parent's room. AE, DC, DISC, MC, V. **Amenities:** Restaurant; bar; outdoor pool; babysitting; limited room service; 1 room for those with limited mobility. *In room:* A/C, TV, hair dryer.

SEEING THE SIGHTS

The city's 249 noteworthy historical treasures are within easy walking distance of one another, though you'll only see most of them from the outside. If some of them are actually open, count yourself fortunate, as they have no phones, keep no regular hours, and are staffed by volunteers who rarely show up. Also, be aware that most of the city's architectural treasures lie uphill from the impossibly congested main thoroughfare (Calle Luna), that streets in the old town tend to run only one-way (usually the way you don't want to go), and that you're likely to be confused by the bad signs and dilapidated condition of many of the historic buildings. We usually try to park on the town's main street (Carretera 102, which changes its name within the border of San Germán to Calle Luna), and then proceed on foot through the city's grimy-looking commercial core before reaching the architectural highlights described below.

One of the most noteworthy churches in Puerto Rico is **Iglesia Porta Coeli (Gate to Heaven)** ⟨ ((C) 787/892-0160), which sits atop a knoll at the eastern end of a cobble-covered square, the Parque de Santo Domingo. Dating from 1606, in a form inspired by the Romanesque architecture of northern Spain, this is the oldest church in the New World. Restored by the Institute of Puerto Rican Culture, and sheathed in a layer of salmon-colored stucco, it contains a museum of religious art with a collection of ancient *santos,* the carved figures of saints that have long been a major branch of Puerto Rican folk art. Look for the 17th-century portrait of St. Nicholas de Bari, the French Santa Claus. Inside, the original palm-wood ceiling and tough, brown ausobo-wood beams draw the eyes upward. Other treasures include early choral books from Santo Domingo, a primitive carving of Jesus, and 19th-century Señora de Monserrate (Black Madonna and Child) statues. Admission costs $1; free for children age 12 and under. It's open Wednesday through Sunday from 8:30am to noon and 1 to 4:30pm.

Less than 100 feet downhill from the church, at the bottom of the steps that lead from its front door down to the plaza below, is the **Casa Morales,** San Germán's most popular and widely recognized house. (It's also known as the **Tomás Vivoni House,** after its architect), Edwardian style, with wraparound porches, elaborate gables, and elements that might remind you of a Swiss chalet, it was built in 1913, reflecting the region's turn-of-the-century agrarian prosperity.

The long, narrow, gently sloping plaza that prefaces the Iglesia Porta Coeli is the **Parque de Santo Domingo,** one of San Germán's two main plazas. Street signs also identify the plaza as the Calle Ruiz Belvis. Originally a marketplace, the plaza is paved with red and black cobblestones, and bordered with cast-iron benches and portrait busts of some of the prominent figures in the town's history. This plaza merges gracefully with an equivalently shaped, identically sized twin, which street signs and maps identify simultaneously as the **Plaza**

Francisco Mariano Quiñones, the Calle José Julian Acosta, or the Plaza Principal. Separating the two plazas is the unused, gray-and-white bulk of San Germán's **Viejo Alcaldia (Old Town Hall).** Built late in the 19th century, and awaiting a new vision, perhaps as a museum or public building, it's closed to the public.

San Germán's most impressive church—and the most monumental building in the region—is **San Germán de Auxerre** ((C) **787/892-1027**), which rises majestically above the western end of the Plaza Francisco Mariano Quiñones. Designed in the Spanish baroque style, it was founded in 1573 in the form of a simple chapel with a low-slung thatch roof. Much of what you'll see today is the result of a rebuilding in 1688 and a restoration in 1737 that followed a disastrous earthquake. Inside, you'll find three naves, 10 altars, three chapels, and a belfry that was rebuilt in 1939 following the collapse of the original during another earthquake in 1918. The central chandelier, made from rock crystal and imported from Barcelona in 1866, is the largest in the Caribbean. The pride of the church is the *trompe l'oeil* ceiling, which was elaborately restored in 1993. The building's restoration was completed in 1999 with the insertion of a series of stained glass windows with contemporary designs. The church can be visited daily 7am or 7:30pm at either mass.

7 Ponce (★

Puerto Rico's second-largest city, Ponce ("The Pearl of the South"), was named after Loíza Ponce de León, grandson of Ponce de León. Today it's Puerto Rico's principal shipping port on the Caribbean Sea, located 75 miles southwest of San Juan. The city is well kept and attractive, with many plazas, parks, and public buildings. It has the air of a provincial Mediterranean town. Look for the *rejas* (framed balconies) of the handsome colonial mansions. Ponce is a city, not a beach resort, and should be visited mainly for its sights.

ESSENTIALS
GETTING THERE   Ponce is reached by Route 52. Allow at least 1½ hours if you **drive. Cape Air** ((C) **800/352-0714**) offers five daily flights between San Juan and Ponce (flight time is approximately 35 minutes) for $124 round-trip.

VISITOR INFORMATION   Maps and information can be found at the **tourist office,** Paseo del Sur Plaza, Suite 3 ((C) **787/843-0465**). Open Monday to Friday 8am to noon and 1 to 5pm; Saturday and Sunday 8:30am to noon and 1 to 5pm.

ACCOMMODATIONS
Meliá   A city hotel with southern hospitality, the Meliá, which has no connection with the international hotel chain, attracts businesspeople. The location is a few steps away from the Cathedral of Our Lady of Guadalupe and from the Parque de Bombas (the red-and-black firehouse). Although this old and somewhat tattered hotel was long ago outclassed by the more expensive Hilton, many people who can afford more upscale accommodations still prefer to stay here for its old-time atmosphere. The lobby floor and all stairs are covered with Spanish tiles of Moorish design. The desk clerks speak English. The small rooms are comfortably furnished and pleasant enough, and most have a balcony facing either busy Calle Cristina or the old plaza. Bathrooms are tiny, each with a shower stall. Breakfast is served on a rooftop terrace with a good view of Ponce,

and Mark's at the Meliá thrives under separate management (see "Dining," below). You can park your car in the lot nearby. There's no pool here.

Calle Cristina 75, Ponce, PR 00731. © 800/448-8355 in the U.S., or 787/842-0260. Fax 787/841-3602. 73 units. Year-round $80–$120 double. Rates include continental breakfast. AE, MC, V. Parking $3. **Amenities:** Restaurant; bar; limited room service; rooms for those with limited mobility. *In room:* A/C, TV, dataport, hair dryer, iron/ironing board.

Ponce Hilton & Casino 𝕣𝕣   On a 80-acre tract of land right on the beach, this is the most glamorous hotel in southern Puerto Rico. At the western end of Avenida Santiago de los Caballeros, it's about a 10-minute drive from the center of Ponce. Designed like a miniature village, with turquoise-blue roofs, white walls, and lots of tropical plants, ornamental waterfalls, and gardens, it welcomes both conventioneers and individual travelers. Accommodations contain tropically inspired furnishings, ceiling fans, and terraces or balconies. All the rooms are medium to spacious, with adequate desk and storage place, tasteful fabrics, good upholstery, and fine linen. The ground-floor rooms are the most expensive. Each is equipped with a generous tiled bathroom with shower/tub combinations.

The food is the most sophisticated and refined on the south coast of Puerto Rico. All the waiters seem to have an extensive knowledge of the menu and will guide you through some exotic dishes—of course, you'll find familiar fare, too.

1150 Ave. Caribe (P.O. Box 7419), Ponce, PR 00732-7419. © 800/HILTONS in the U.S. and Canada, or 787/259-7676. Fax 787/259-7674. www.ponce.hilton.com. 153 units. Year-round $200–$260 double; $475 suite. AE, DC, DISC, MC, V. Self-parking $5; valet parking $10. **Amenities:** 2 restaurants; 3 bars; lagoon-shaped pool ringed with gardens; casino; nightclub; 4 tennis courts; fitness center; basketball court; volleyball; bike rentals; children's center and summer camp; business center; room service (7am–midnight); babysitting; laundry service; dry cleaning; nonsmoking rooms; rooms for those with limited mobility. *In room:* A/C, TV, dataport, minibar, beverage maker, hair dryer, iron/board, safe.

DINING

El Ancla 𝕣 PUERTO RICAN/SEAFOOD   This is one of Ponce's best restaurants, with a lovely location 2 miles south of the city center, on soaring piers that extend from the rocky coastline out over the surf. As you dine, the sound of the sea rises literally from beneath your feet.

Menu items are prepared with real Puerto Rican zest and flavor. A favorite here is red snapper stuffed with lobster and shrimp, served either with fried plantain or mashed potatoes. Other specialties are filet of salmon in caper sauce, and a seafood medley of lobster, shrimp, octopus, and conch. Most of the dishes are reasonably priced, especially the chicken and conch. Lobster tops the price scale. The side orders, including crabmeat rice and yucca in garlic, are delectable.

805 Hostos Ave., Playa Ponce. © 787/840-2450. Main courses $12–$32. AE, DC, MC, V. Sun–Thurs 11am–9:30pm; Fri–Sat 11am–11pm.

La Cava 𝕣𝕣 INTERNATIONAL   This hive of venerable rooms within a 19th-century coffee plantation is the most appealing and elaborate restaurant in Ponce. There's a well-trained staff, old-fashioned charm, well-prepared cuisine, and a champagne-and-cigar bar where the bubbly sells for around $6 a glass. Menu items change every 6 weeks, but might include duck foie gras with toasted brioche, Parma ham with mango, cold poached scallops with mustard sauce, a fricassee of lobster and mushrooms in a pastry shell, and grilled lamb sausage with mustard sauce on a bed of couscous. Dessert could be a black-and-white soufflé or a trio of tropical sorbets.

In the Ponce Hilton, 1150 Ave. Caribe. © 787/259-7676. Reservations recommended. Main courses $26–$30. AE, DC, DISC, MC, V. Mon–Sat 6:30–10:30pm.

La Montserrate PUERTO RICAN/SEAFOOD Beside the seafront, in a residential area about 4 miles west of the town center, this restaurant draws a loyal following from the surrounding neighborhood. A culinary institution in Ponce since it was established 20 years ago, it occupies a large, airy, modern building divided into two different dining areas. The first of these is slightly more formal than the next. Most visitors head for the large room in back, where windows on three sides take in a view of some offshore islands. Specialties, concocted from the catch of the day, might include octopus salad, four different kinds of *asopao* (gumbo), a whole red snapper in Creole sauce, or a selection of steaks and grills. Nothing is innovative, but the cuisine is typical of the south of Puerto Rico, and it's a family favorite. Fish dishes are better than the meat selections.

Sector Las Cucharas, Rte. 2. ✆ 787/841-2740. Main courses $13–$35. AE, DC, DISC, MC, V. Daily 11am–10pm.

Mark's at the Meliá ✫✫✫ INTERNATIONAL Chef Mark French elevates Puerto Rican dishes to haute cuisine. With his constantly changing menus, and his insistence that everything be fresh, he's a winner. You'll fall in love with this guy when you taste his tamarind barbecued lamb with yucca mojo. Go on to sample his lobster *pionono* (cooked in plantain "shells") with tomato and chive salad or his freshly made sausage with pumpkin, cilantro, and chicken. All over Puerto Rico you get fried green plantains, but here they come topped with sour cream and a dollop of caviar. The corn-crusted red snapper with yucca purée and tempura jumbo shrimp with Asian salad are signature dishes. The desserts are spectacular, notably the vanilla flan layered with rum sponge cake and topped with a caramelized banana, and the award-winning bread pudding soufflé with coconut vanilla sauce.

In the Meliá Hotel, Calle Cristina. ✆ 787/284-6275. Reservations recommended. Main courses $16–$30. AE, MC, V. Wed–Sat noon–3pm and 6–10:30pm; Sun noon–5pm.

BEACHES & OTHER OUTDOOR PURSUITS

A 10-minute drive west of Ponce will take you to **Playa de Ponce,** a long strip of white sand opening onto the tranquil waters of the Caribbean. This beach is usually better for swimming than the Condado in San Juan. There's little in the way of organized sports here, however.

The city owns two **tennis complexes,** one at Poly Deportivos, with nine hard courts, and another at Rambla, with six courts. Both are open from 9am to 10pm and are lit for night play. You can play for free. For more information and for directions, call the Secretary of Sports at ✆ 787/840-4400.

Golfers have their choice of two nine-hole courses, one 30 miles east of Ponce, the other 30 miles west. The one to the east is **Aguirre Golf Club,** Route 705, Aguirre (✆ 787/853-4052); head east from Ponce on Highway 52. It's open from 7am to 5pm daily, and charges greens fees of $10 Tuesday to Friday, going up to $18 on weekends and holidays. The one to the west is **Club Deportivo,** Carretera 102, km. 15.4, Barrio Jogudas, Cabo Rojo (✆ 787/254-3748), open daily from 7am to 6pm. Greens fees range from $30 to 35 (including carts).

SEEING THE SIGHTS

A $40 million project has restored more than 1,000 buildings in town to their original turn-of-the-century charm. Architectural styles that combine neoclassical with "Ponce Creole" and Art Deco give the town a distinctive ambience.

Any Ponceño will direct you to their **Museo de Arte de Ponce** ⊛, Ave. de las Americas 23–25 (© 787/848-0505), which has a fine collection of European and Latin American art, the best on the island. Among the nearly 400 paintings, sculptures, and artworks on display are exceptional pre-Raphaelite and Italian baroque paintings. The building was designed by Edward Durell Stone and has been called the "Parthenon of the Caribbean." It's open daily from 10am to 5pm. Adults pay $4; children age 11 and under are charged $2.

Most visitors head for the **Parque de Bombas,** Plaza de las Delicias (© 787/284-4141), the main plaza of Ponce. This fantastic old black-and-red firehouse was built for a fair in 1883. It's open daily 9am to 6pm; admission is free.

Around the corner from the firehouse, a trail will lead you to the **Cathedral of Our Lady of Guadalupe,** Calle Concordia/Calle Union, Plaza de las Delicias (© 787/842-0134). Designed by architects Francisco Porrata Doría and Francisco Trublard in 1931, and featuring a pipe organ installed in 1934, it remains an important place for prayer. It's open Monday to Friday from 6am to 1pm, Saturday from 6 to 11:45am and 3 to 8pm, and Sunday 6am to 12:15pm and 3 to 8pm.

El Museo Castillo Serrallés, El Vigía 17 (© 787/259-1774), the largest and most imposing building in Ponce, was constructed high on a hilltop above town by the Serrallés family (owners of a local rum distillery) in the 1930s. This is one of the architectural gems of Puerto Rico and the best evidence of the wealth produced by the turn-of-the-century sugar boom. Guides will escort you through the Spanish Revival house, where Moorish and Andalusian details include panoramic courtyards, a baronial dining room, and a small cafe and souvenir shop. Hours are Tuesday to Sunday 9:30am to 5pm. Admission is $6 for adults, $3 for seniors over age 62 and children age 15 and under. From the Plaza las Delicias de Ponce, a free trolley bus runs frequently throughout the day, taking visitors to the museum.

The oldest cemetery in the Antilles, excavated in 1975, is near Ponce on Route 503 at km. 2.7. The **Tibes Indian Ceremonial Center** (© 787/840-2255) contains some 186 skeletons, dating from A.D. 300, as well as pre-Taíno plazas from A.D. 700. Guided tours in English and Spanish are conducted through the grounds. Shaded by trees are seven rectangular ball courts and two dance areas. The arrangements of stone points on the dance grounds, in line with the solstices and equinoxes, suggest a pre-Columbian Stonehenge. A re-created Taíno village includes not only the museum but also an exhibition hall where you can see a documentary about Tibes; you can also visit the cafeteria and souvenir shop. The museum is open Tuesday to Sunday from 9am to 4pm. Admission is $2 for adults and $1 for children.

Hacienda Buena Vista, Route 10, km. 16.8 (© 787/284-7020 or 787/722-5882), is a 30-minute drive north of Ponce. Built in 1833, it preserves an old way of life, with its whirring waterwheels and artifacts of 19th-century farm production. Once it was one of the most successful plantations on Puerto Rico, producing coffee, corn, and citrus. It was a working coffee plantation until the 1950s, and 86 acres of the original 500 acres are still part of the estate. The rooms of the hacienda have been furnished with authentic pieces from the 1850s. Tours, lasting 1½ hours, are conducted in Spanish Wednesday to Sunday at 8:30am, 10:30am, 1:30pm, and 3:30pm, and in English at 1:30pm. Reservations are required. Tours cost $7 for adults, $4 for seniors and children. The hacienda lies in the town of Barrio Magüeyes, on Route 123 (km. 16.8) between Ponce and Adjuntas.

If you feel a yen for **shopping,** head for the **Fox Delicias Mall,** at the intersection of Calle Reina Isabel and Plaza de Las Delicias de Ponce, the city's most innovative shopping center.

8 Las Croabas & Luquillo Beach ★★

From San Juan, Route 3 leads east toward the fishing town of Fajardo, where you'll turn north to Las Croabas, about 31 miles from the capital.

You'll be near **Luquillo Beach,** one of the island's best and most popular public stretches of sand. From here, you can also easily explore **El Yunque Rainforest.** See the section "San Juan," earlier in this chapter, for details on both.

GETTING THERE

The two big resort hotels in this area run buses to and from the San Juan airport, based on the arrival times of incoming flights. It's $25 per person each way to the Westin Rio Mar Beach, and $28 per person to the Wyndham El Conquistador. The trips takes from 45 minutes to an hour. A taxi from the airport will cost approximately $70 to either hotel. Private limousine service costs $225 per carload.

If you are driving from San Juan, go past the San Juan airport, following the signs to Carolina, which will lead to Route 3 going east. To reach the El Conquistador hotel, follow the signs to Fajardo, then to Las Croabas. To reach the Westin, follow signs to El Yunque, then signs to the Westin.

ACCOMMODATIONS

Westin Rio Mar Beach Resort & Casino ★★★   Marking Westin's debut in the Caribbean, this $180 million, 481-acre resort lies on relatively uncrowded Rio Mar Beach, a 5-minute drive from massively popular Luquillo Beach. It was designed to compete with the Hyatt hotel at Dorado and the El Conquistador, with which it's frequently compared. It's the best property in the area.

Landscaping includes several artificial lakes situated amid tropical gardens. More than 60% of the guest rooms look out over palm trees to the Atlantic. Other units open onto the mountains and forests of nearby El Yunque National Park (just a 15-minute drive away). The style is Spanish hacienda with nods to the surrounding jungle; unusual art and sculpture alternate with dark woods, deep colors, rounded archways, big windows, and tile floors. In the bedrooms, muted earth tones, wicker, rattan, and painted wood furniture add to the ambience. Bedrooms are spacious, with balconies or terraces, and good mattresses, plus shower/tub combinations in the large bathrooms.

The resort encompasses the **Rio Mar Country Club,** site of two important golf courses. The older of the two, the Ocean Course, was designed by George and Tom Fazio as part of the original resort, and has been a staple on Puerto Rico's professional golf circuit since the 1960s. In 1997, Westin opened the property's second 18-holer, the slightly more challenging River Course, the first Greg Norman–designed course in the Caribbean. The resort also has a 6,500-square-foot casino.

The only hotel in Puerto Rico with more diverse cuisine is Wyndham's El Conquistador (see below).

6000 Rio Mar Blvd. (19 miles east of Luís Muñoz Marín International Airport, with entrance off Puerto Rico Hwy. 3), Rio Grande, PR 00745. ✆ 800/WESTIN-1 or 787/888-6000. Fax 787/888-6600. www.westinriomar. com. 600 units. Winter $329 double, $1,200 suite; off season $215 double, $625 suite. Children age 5–17 staying in parent's room $85, including meals and activities. Free for 4 and under. AE, DC, DISC, MC, V. **Amenities:** 8 restaurants; 4 bars; outdoor pool; casino; 13 tennis courts; health club and spa; deep-sea fishing; sailing; horseback riding nearby; children's programs; 24-hr. room service; laundry; dry cleaning; non-smoking rooms; rooms for those with limited mobility. *In room:* A/C, TV, dataport, beverage maker, hair dryer, iron/ironing board, safe.

Wyndham El Conquistador Resort & Golden Door Spa ✿ *Kids*   El Conquistador is a destination unto itself. Its array of facilities sits on 500 acres of forested hills sloping down to the sea. Accommodations are divided into five separate sections united by their Mediterranean architecture and lush landscaping. Most lie several hundred feet above the sea. At the same altitude, a bit off to the side, is a replica of an Andalusian hamlet, Las Casitas Village, which seems straight out of the south of Spain. These pricey units, each with a full kitchen, form a self-contained enclave.

A short walk downhill takes you to a circular cluster of tastefully modern accommodations, Las Olas Village. And at sea level, adjacent to an armada of pleasure craft bobbing at anchor, is La Marina Village, whose balconies seem to hang directly over the water. The accommodations are outfitted with comfortable furniture, tropical colors, and robes. All the far-flung elements of the resort are connected by serpentine, landscaped walkways, and by a railroad-style funicular that makes frequent trips up and down the hillside.

One of the most comprehensive spas in the Caribbean, the Golden Door, maintains a branch in this resort. The hotel is sole owner of a "fantasy island" (Palomino Island), with caverns, nature trails, horseback riding, and watersports such as scuba diving, windsurfing, and snorkeling. About a half mile offshore, the island is connected by free private ferries to the main hotel at frequent intervals. There's also a 25-slip marina. The hotel operates an excellently run Westin Kids Club with activities planned daily.

1000 Conquistador Ave., Fajardo, PR 00738. (C) 800/468-5228 in the U.S., or 787/863-1000. Fax 787/ 863-6500. www.wyndham.com. 915 units. Winter $359–$769 double, from $1,445 suite for 1–4, from $715 casita for 1–6; off season $299–$529 double, from $1,095 suite for 1–4, $1,205 casita for 1–6. MAP (breakfast and dinner) $90 extra per adult per day, $45 extra per child age 12 and under. Children 15 and under stay free in parent's room. AE, DC, DISC, MC, V. Parking $10 per day. **Amenities:** 6 restaurants; 7 bars; 6 pools; casino; night club; golf course; 6 tennis courts; health club and spa; dive shop; fishing; sailing; snorkeling; windsurfing; horseback riding; children's programs; 24-hr. room service; massage; laundry service; dry cleaning; nonsmoking rooms; rooms for those with limited mobility. *In room:* A/C, TV, dataport, minibar, beverage maker, hair dryer, iron/ironing board, safe.

DINING

Isabela's Grill ✿ AMERICAN STEAKHOUSE   Of all the restaurants in El Conquistador Resort, this is the most American. If Ike were to miraculously return, he'd feel comfortable with this 1950s menu. The severely dignified baroque room was inspired by an aristocratic monastery in Spain. The massive gates are among the most impressive pieces of wrought iron on Puerto Rico. The service is impeccable, the steaks tender, and the seafood fresh.

Special care is taken with the beef dishes, even though the meat is imported frozen. You can begin with the lobster bisque or French soup, then move on to the thick cut of veal chop or the perfectly prepared rack of lamb. Prime rib of beef is a feature, as are the succulent steaks; try the New York strip or the porterhouse.

In the Wyndham El Conquistador Resort. (C) 787/863-1000. Reservations recommended. Main courses $22–$36. Parking $10–$15. AE, DISC, MC, V. Daily 6–11pm.

Otello's ✿ NORTHERN ITALIAN   Here you can dine by candlelight either indoors or out. The decor is neo-Palladian. You might begin with one of the soups, perhaps pasta fagioli, or select one of the zesty Italian appetizers, such as an excellently prepared clams Posillipo. Pastas can be ordered as a half-portion appetizer or as a main dish, and they include homemade gnocchi and fettuccine with shrimp. The chef is known for his superb veal dishes. A selection of poultry and vegetarian food is offered nightly, along with several shrimp and fish dishes. The salmon filet in champagne sauce has beautiful accents, as does the veal chop in an aromatic herb sauce.

In the Wyndham El Conquistador Resort. ℂ **787/863-1000.** Reservations required in winter, recommended off season. Main courses $20–$37. AE, DISC, MC, V. Daily 6–11pm.

TO THE LIGHTHOUSE: EXPLORING LAS CABEZAS DE SAN JUAN NATURE RESERVE ⟨⟩

Better known as El Faro or "The Lighthouse," this preserve in the northeastern corner of the island, north of Fajardo off Route 987, is one of the most beautiful and important areas on Puerto Rico. A number of different ecosystems flourish in the vicinity. Surrounded on three sides by the Atlantic Ocean, the 316-acre site encompasses forestland, mangroves, lagoons, beaches, cliffs, offshore cays, and coral reefs. El Faro serves as a research center for the scientific community. It's home to a vast array of flora and fauna, including sea turtles and other endangered species.

The nature reserve is open Wednesday to Sunday; reservations are required, so call before going. For reservations throughout the week, call ℂ **787/722-5882;** for reservations on Saturday and Sunday, call ℂ **787/860-2560** (reservations on weekends can be made only on the day of your intended visit). Admission is $7 for adults, $4 for seniors and children age 12 and under. Guided tours are conducted at 9:30am, 10am, 10:30am, and in English at 2pm.

18

Saba

An extinct volcano with no beaches or flat land, cone-shaped Saba is 13 sq. km (5 sq. miles) of rock carpeted with lush foliage like orchids, giant elephant ears, and Eucharist lilies. At its zenith, Mount Scenery, it measures 870m (2,853 ft.). Under the sea, the volcanic walls continue a sheer drop to great depths, making for some of the most panoramic diving in the Caribbean.

Unless you're a serious hiker or diver, you might confine your look at Saba to a day trip from St. Maarten. If you're a self-sufficient type who demands almost no artificial amusement, then sleepy Saba might be your hideaway.

One of the smallest islands of the Netherlands Antilles, Saba is 242km (150 miles) east of Puerto Rico and 145km (90 miles) east of St. Croix. Most visitors fly from St. Maarten, 45km (28 miles) to the north.

The official language of Saba is Dutch, but because so many English missionaries and Scottish seamen from the Shetland Islands settled here, Saba has always been English-speaking. All those European settlers have resulted in a population that is 60% Caucasian, many with red hair and freckled fair skin.

1 Essentials

VISITOR INFORMATION

The **Saba Tourist Board** is located in the heart of Windwardside (© 599/416-2231). It's open Monday through Friday from 8am to noon and 1 to 5pm.

Saba is on the Web at **www.sabatourism.com**.

GETTING THERE

BY PLANE   You'll have to get to St. Maarten before you can get to Saba. **American Airlines** (© 800/433-7300 in the U.S.; www.aa.com) offers direct flights from New York's JFK; **Continental Airlines** (© 800/231-0856 in the U.S.; www.continental.com) flies out of Newark, New Jersey. From Queen Juliana Airport on St. Maarten, you can take the 12-minute hop to Saba on **Winair** (Windward Islands Airways International; © 599/545-4237 or 800/634-4907). There are at least five flights per day, depending on volume; fares are $145 round-trip in the winter, $84 round-trip in the summer.

Saba's **Juancho Yrausquin Airport** (© 599/416-2255) is one of the shortest landing strips in the world, stretching only 394m (1,292 ft.) along the aptly named Flat Point, one of the few level areas on the island.

Many guests at hotels on St. Maarten fly over to Saba on the morning flight, spend the day sightseeing, and then return to St. Maarten on the afternoon flight. Winair connections can also be made on Saba to both St. Kitts and St. Eustatius.

BY BOAT   You can also take a high-speed ferry from St. Maarten's Pelican Marina at Simpson Bay to Fort Bay on Saba; you'll arrive in about an hour.

ATLANTIC OCEAN

Great Point
Saba Marine Park
Flat Point

Diamond Rock
Torrens Bay
Torrens Point

Juancho Yrausquin Airport
Cove Bay
Spring Bay

Well's Bay Beach
Well's Bay

1
Hell's Gate

Mount Scenery

2

Rendezvous

The Gap

Windwardside

7
6
5

3
The Road

The Bottom

St. John's

4
Booby Hill

Tent Point

Fort Bay
Fort Bay
Saba Marine Park

Caribbean Sea

Airport ✈ Beach 🏖 Mountain ▲▲

Cottage Club **7**
Cranston's Antique Inn **3**
The Gate House **1**
Juliana's **6**
Queen's Gardens Resort **2**
Scout's Place **5**
Willards of Saba **4**

The Edge (© **599/544-2640**) departs Wednesday, Thursday, Friday, Saturday, and Sunday at 9am, returning at 4pm, making a day trip to Saba possible. Sometimes the waters are turbulent, making passengers seasick. The round-trip fare is $60 per person. Bigger than the ferry and with smoother rides are *Voyager I,* a 150-passenger catamaran, and *Voyager II,* a 100-passenger powerboat. *Voyager I* sails from Marigot in French St. Martin for Fort Bay on Thursday at 8:45am, returning at 4:30pm. The cost is $57 round-trip. There are no trips in the winter months. For information and bookings, call © **599/542-4096.**

GETTING AROUND

BY TAXI Taxis meet every flight. Up to four people are allowed to share a cab. The fare from the airport to Windwardside is $8, or $13 to The Bottom. A taxi from Windwardside to The Bottom costs $6.50. There is no central number to call for service.

BY RENTAL CAR None of the major U.S. firms operates on Saba, partly because most visitors opt to get around by taxi. In the unlikely event that you should dare to drive a car on Saba, locally operated companies include **Kenny's Rental,** Windwardside (© **599/416-2388**), starting at $40 per day and including a full tank of gas and unlimited mileage. Some insurance is included in the rates, but you might be held partly responsible in the event of an accident. Because of the very narrow roads and dozens of cliffs, it's crucial to exercise caution when driving on Saba. Note that traffic moves on the right.

BY HITCHHIKING   Hitchhiking has long been an acceptable means of transport on Saba, where everybody seemingly knows everybody else. And if you hitchhike, you'll probably get to know everybody else, too. On our most recent sightseeing tour, our taxi rushed a sick child to the plane and picked up an old man to take him up the hill because he'd fallen and hurt himself.

ON FOOT   The traditional means of getting around on Saba—walking—is still much in evidence. But we suggest that only the sturdy in heart and limb walk from The Bottom up to Windwardside. Many do, but you'd better have some shoes with good traction, particularly after a recent rain.

FAST FACTS: Saba

Banks The main bank on the island is **First Caribbean International,** Windwardside (© **599/416-2216**), open Monday to Friday from 8:30am to 3:30pm. The **Royal Bank of Trinidad and Tobago** is another option. It's located at Windwardside (© **599/416-2454**), and is open Monday to Friday 8:30am to 3:30pm.

Currency Saba, like the other islands of the Netherlands Antilles, uses the **Netherlands Antilles guilder (NAf),** valued at 1.77 NAf to US$1 (1 Naf = US56¢). *However, rates in this chapter are quoted in U.S. dollars,* since U.S. money is accepted by almost everybody here.

Customs You don't have to go through Customs in Saba; it's a free port.

Documents The government requires that all U.S. and Canadian citizens show proof of citizenship, such as a passport or a birth certificate with a raised seal, along with a government-issued photo ID. A return or ongoing ticket must also be provided. United Kingdom citizens must have a valid passport.

Electricity Saba uses 110-volt AC (60 cycles), so most U.S.-made appliances don't need transformers or adapters.

Emergencies Call © **599/416-2410** in case of fire and © **599/416-3289** for an ambulance. The police can be reached by calling © **599/416-3237**.

Hospital Saba's hospital complex is the **A. M. Edwards Medical Centre,** The Bottom (© **599/416-3289**).

Language The official language on Saba is Dutch, but English is widely spoken.

Pharmacies Try **The Pharmacy,** The Bottom (© **599/416-3289**), open Monday through Friday from 7:30am to 5:30pm.

Safety Crime on this island, where everyone knows everyone else, is practically nonexistent. But who knows? A tourist might rob you. It is always wise to safeguard your valuables.

Taxes The government imposes an 5% tourist tax on hotel rooms. If you're returning to St. Maarten or flying over to Statia, you must pay a $5 departure tax. If you're going anywhere else, however, a $20 tax is imposed. A service charge of 10% to 15% will be added to your restaurant bill.

Telephone You can make international phone calls at **Saten,** The Bottom (© **599/416-1032**). To call Saba from the United States, dial **011** (the international access code), then **599** (the country code for the Netherlands

Antilles), and finally **416** (the area code for all of Saba) and the four-digit local number. To make a call within Saba, only the four-digit local number is necessary.

Time Saba is on Atlantic Standard Time year-round, 1 hour earlier than Eastern Standard Time. When the United States is on daylight savings time, clocks on Saba and the U.S. East Coast read the same.

Water The water on Saba is generally safe to drink.

Weather Winter temperatures from January to April 1 average 69°F to 83°F (21°C–28°C). The rest of the year temperatures range from 70°F to 88°F (21°C–31°C).

2 Accommodations

If you're looking for a hotel on the beach, you've come to the wrong island. Saba's only beach, Well's Bay Beach, is tiny and can be reached from most hotels only via a $10 taxi ride.

The Cottage Club ⭐ Small, intimate, and immersed in the architectural and aesthetic traditions of Saba, this hotel complex occupies about .2 hectares (½ acre) of steeply sloping and carefully landscaped terrain, a 2-minute walk from the center of the island's capital. Only its lobby evokes a historic setting: Designed of local stone, and set at an altitude above the other buildings of the complex, it's filled with a collection of island antiques and lace curtains.

Each medium-size studio apartment has a semiprivate patio, a living-room area, and a queen-size bed. Bathrooms have showers and are well maintained. These units are housed in clapboard replicas of antique cottages—two studios per cottage—with red roofs, green shutters, white walls, and yellow trim. The interiors are breezy, airy, and comfortable. If you'd like a room with an ocean view, request nos. 1 or 2. There's no bar or restaurant on the premises, but a nearby supermarket will deliver supplies on request. The owners of the establishment are three Saban brothers (Gary, Mark, and Dean) whose families all seem to help out.

Windwardside, Saba, N.A. ⓒ **599/416-2486.** Fax 599/416-2476. www.cottage-club.com. 10 cottages. Winter $118 studio apt for 2; off season $105 studio apt for 2. 3rd and 4th person $25 each. Children 12 and under stay free in parent's room. Dive packages available. AE, MC, V. **Amenities:** Outdoor pool; coin-operated laundry. *In room:* Ceiling fan, TV, kitchenette, beverage maker.

Cranston's Antique Inn ⭐ *(Finds* Come here for the old-time atmosphere and the cheap prices, not for any grand style. Everyone congregates for rum drinks and gossip on the front terrace of this inn near the village roadway, on the west coast north of Fort Bay. It's an old-fashioned house, more than 100 years old, with antique four-poster beds in all the rooms. Mr. Cranston, the owner, will gladly rent you the same bedroom where Queen Juliana once spent a holiday in 1955. Aside from the impressive wooden beds, the furnishings are mostly hit or miss, and not much has changed since the queen checked in oh-so-long ago. The bedrooms are quite tiny, although the floral spreads jazz them up a bit. All the rooms have private—but extremely cramped—shower-only bathrooms.

Mr. Cranston has a good island cook, who makes use of locally grown spices. Island dishes include goat meat, roast pork from Saba pigs, red snapper, and broiled grouper.

The Bottom, Saba, N.A. © **599/416-3203.** Fax 599/416-3469. 6 units. Winter $130 double; off season $99 double. MC, V. **Amenities:** Restaurant; bar; outdoor pool; babysitting. *In room:* A/C, TV.

The Gate House ⭐ *Finds*

In an amusingly named village, Hell's Gate, Lyliane and Michel Job welcome you to their bright little guesthome. All of their comfortably and tastefully furnished rooms are in a bright West Indian motif, each with a well-maintained private bath. Families may prefer the Gate House Cottage, which can house a couple with a child and even includes a fully equipped kitchen and its own pool. Balconies surrounding the house open onto scenic views. Yet another rental is a luxurious four-bedroom villa with spacious rooms, three bathrooms, a fully equipped kitchen, and a private pool along with deck, balconies, and patios galore. The Gate House also has one of the finest chefs on island.

Hell's Gate, Saba, N.A. © **599/416-2416.** Fax 599/416-2550. www.sabagatehouse.com. 7 units. Winter $130 double, $150 cottage, $315 villa (up to 4 people); off season $120 double, $140 cottage, $295 villa (up to 4 people). Rates include continental breakfast. DISC, MC, V. **Amenities:** Restaurant; 2 outdoor pools; laundry service. *In room:* Ceiling fans, TV (in villa), kitchen/kitchenette (in some), hair dryer, no phone.

Juliana's

This hostelry is set on a hillside and each guest room is modern, immaculate, and simply but comfortably furnished. All have access to a sun deck and balconies opening onto beautiful views of the Caribbean, except nos. 1, 2, and 3, which are in the rear. Opt for one of the upper-level rooms (nos. 7, 8, or 9), as they offer the best views. The shower-only bathrooms are small but adequate, and housekeeping wins high marks here. Also available are a 2½-room apartment, complete with kitchenette; and a renovated original Saban cottage, with two bedrooms, a spacious living room, a dining room, a TV, and a fully equipped kitchen.

Windwardside, Saba, N.A. © **599/416-2269.** Fax 599/416-2389. www.julianas-hotel.com. 12 units. Winter $90–$125 double, $150 apt, $165 cottage; off season $75–$110 double, $125 apt, $145 cottage. Extra person $30. Dive packages available. DISC, MC, V. **Amenities:** Restaurant; bar; outdoor pool; recreation room; babysitting. *In room:* Ceiling fan, TV, kitchen/kitchenette (in some), fridge, minibar, beverage maker (in some), hair dryer, iron/ironing board (in some), no phone.

Queen's Gardens Resort ⭐

It's still outclassed by Willard's of Saba (see below), but this is a classy joint as well. One of the most massive engineering projects in Saba's recent memory included the placement of a rock-sided terrace on this plot of forested, steeply sloping land 360m (1,181 ft.) above the sea. The result is a well-conceived cluster of white-walled, red-roofed bungalows angled for sweeping views, and clustered around the semicircular edges of the largest pool on Saba, with north-facing views over the island's capital and the sea. From a distance, the compound evokes a fortified village in Iberia; close-up, it's charming and comfortable. Accommodations are simple, modern, airy, and clean, with dark-wood furniture. Most units are split-level, with large living rooms; all have kitchenettes and fine king or queen beds. Bathrooms are large but have showers only, with the exception of a few suites that have their own Jacuzzi overlooking the coast and sea. On the premises is a restaurant, the Mango Royale (see "Dining," below).

Troy Hill, Drive 1 (P.O. Box 4), The Bottom, Saba, N.A. © **599/416-3494.** Fax 599/416-3495. www.queensaba. com. 12 units. Winter $285 double, $335 1-bedroom suite for 2, $435 2-bedroom suite for up to 4; off season $195 double, $250 1-bedroom suite for 2, $350 2-bedroom suite for up to 4. AE, MC, V. **Amenities:** Restaurant; bar; outdoor pool; dive shop; babysitting; laundry service. *In room:* TV, kitchen, minibar, beverage maker, hair dryer, safe.

Scout's Place

Right in the center of Windwardside, funky Scout's Place is hidden from the street and set on the ledge of a hill. With only 13 rooms, it's still the second-largest inn on the island. The old house has a large, covered, open-air dining room, where every table has a view of the sea. It's informal, with a decor ranging from Surinam hand-carvings to red-and-black wicker peacock chairs to silver samovars. Guest rooms open onto an interior courtyard filled with flowers, and each has a view of the sea. The rooms are small and rather plain, except for the four-poster beds; many have linoleum floors and tiny TVs. The best units are on the lower floor, as they have French doors opening onto balconies fronting the ocean. Furniture is haphazard. Bathrooms are small, with showers only. The apartment with kitchenette is suitable for up to four.

Windwardside, Saba, N.A. © 599/416-2740. Fax 599/416-2741. www.sabadivers.com. 13 units. Winter $75–$99 double; $112 cottage; off season $75–$89 double, $102 cottage. Extra person $43. Rates include continental breakfast. MC, V. **Amenities:** Restaurant; bar; outdoor pool; dive shop; laundry service. *In room:* Ceiling fan, TV, dataport, fridge, beverage maker (in some).

Willard's of Saba ✦✦ This is Saba's only pocket of posh. Until Brad Willard arrived, Saba never had anything remotely comparable. The hotel opened in 1994 and became an immediate sellout, attracting visitors, often celebrities, who might not have set foot on the island before. Guest rooms have *Casablanca*-like ceiling fans; furnishings are not of the highest standard, but are still comfortable. Because of the hotel is in a garden high on a hill overlooking the island's southwestern coastline, each room has sweeping views and almost constant ocean breezes. Much care went into the design, making use of everything from cedar from the U.S. Northwest to original island paintings.

The least expensive units are the two rooms in the main building, which are quite spacious. The other five units are in a concrete building designed in the island's distinctive style, with red roofs, white walls, and green shutters. For the most luxurious living, ask for the VIP Room overlooking the pool, with its own large balcony. Lower Cliffside units are the smallest, but have good views from their private balconies. Honeymooners prefer the Room in the Sky. Bathrooms are small, shower-only affairs.

The Corazon restaurant and its bar are recommended in "Dining," below.

Booby Hill, Saba, N.A. © 800/504-9861 or 599/416-2498. Fax 599/416-2482. www.willardsofsaba.com. 7 units. Winter $400 double; $700 honeymoon suite or VIP room; off season $350 double, $500 honeymoon suite or VIP room. Extra person $50. AE, DISC, MC, V. Children 12 and under not accepted. **Amenities:** Restaurant; bar; outdoor pool; tennis court; Jacuzzi; limited room service; laundry service. *In room:* Ceiling fan, no phone.

3 Dining

Brigadoon Pub & Eatery ✦ CARIBBEAN/AMERICAN This is the island's best restaurant. An array of Caribbean, American, and other international flavors combine to form a savory cuisine in this century-old colonial building with an open front. Whenever possible, fresh local ingredients are used, including herbs, spices, fruits, and farm-fresh vegetables. Fresh local fish is generally the preferred course, or you can order live local lobster (prices vary). Steaks are flown in weekly. Other recommended dishes include mahimahi (dolphin) with citrus-butter sauce (justifiably very popular) and Thai shrimp in a coconut-curry sauce.

Windwardside. © 599/416-2380. Main courses $12–$25. AE, MC, V. Wed–Mon 6:30–9:30pm.

Corazon ✦ ANTILLEAN/ASIAN/INTERNATIONAL This restaurant features a breezy island decor, a sweeping high-altitude view of Saba's southeastern coastline, and some of the freshest fish and lobster on the island. Most of the catch featured on the "island-inspired" menu comes from the boats of local fisherfolk. Entrees change with the availability of the ingredients, although grouper, snapper Florentine, and lobster thermidor are usually featured, as are pork loin with a champagne-and-caper sauce, and Chinese-style beef with oyster sauce. You can cool down with a crepe stuffed with banana and jackfruit, then fried and served with homemade ice cream. The restaurant takes its name from Corazon de Johnson, manager and chef. Although born in the Philippines, she doesn't limit her inspiration to her homeland, but roams the world for ideas for her fusion cuisine. There's a pleasant bar where you can enjoy a round of before-dinner drinks.

In the Willard's of Saba hotel, Booby Hill. (C) 599/416-2498. Reservations required. Main courses $23–$35. AE, DISC, MC, V. Daily 11:30am–3pm and 6:30–9:30pm.

The Gate House Café ★ Finds FRENCH/SABAN

Saba has never been known for its cuisine, but the chefs who run this place are masters of flavor. Michel Job, a self-taught cook, obtains fresh vegetables and seafood from local vendors, but 90% of the food items are imported from France, especially the chicken, duck, and pork, which comes from southwest France. The menu changes regularly but you might delight in such appetizers as a bisque made from fresh Saban lobster and flambéed with cognac. A classic French soup is served with Swiss cheese or you can delight in the coconut soup made from onions, leeks, and tania (a locally grown root vegetable). Seafood gets top priority here, especially the grilled mahimahi and the tuna steak coated in mild pepper. Savory meat offerings include sausage of chicken breast in a mushroom sauce and aged beef tenderloin generously coated with Jamaican cracked black pepper and flambéed in cognac. Ask about the freshly made dessert of the day. There is also an impressive wine list.

Hell's Gate. (C) 599/416-2416. Reservations recommended. Main courses $18–$28. MC, V. Daily 6:30–9:30pm.

Mango Royale INTERNATIONAL

Part of this restaurant's allure has to do with its location beside the largest pool on Saba, its high-altitude views that sweep northward over the sea, and the flaming torches that add a flickering glamour to the site during the dinner hour. You can dine on an indoor/outdoor terrace, or—for more privacy—within a lattice-covered structure inspired by a gazebo. Lunch includes salads, sandwiches, and relatively simple versions of grilled fish. Dinners are more elaborate, with offerings such as goat meat with mint sauce, duck breast in a guavaberry liqueur, grilled chicken with tropical herbs, barbecued beef kabobs, and fettuccine with cream sauce.

In the Queen's Gardens Resort, Troy Hill, The Bottom. (C) 599/416-3623. Reservations recommended. Lunch platters $10–$16; dinner main courses $16–$27. AE, MC, V. Daily 7am–3pm and 6:30–10pm.

Saba Chinese Bar & Restaurant (Moo Goo Gai Pan) CANTONESE/INDONESIAN

Amid a cluster of residential buildings on a hillside above Windwardside, this place is operated by a family from Hong Kong. It offers some 120 dishes, an unpretentious decor of plastic tablecloths and folding chairs, and food so popular that many residents claim this is their most frequented restaurant. Meals include an array of Cantonese and Indonesian specialties—lobster Cantonese, Chinese chicken with mushrooms, sweet-and-sour fish, conch chop suey, several curry dishes, roast duck, and *nasi goreng* (fried rice with vegetables and meat). It doesn't rank with the great Chinese restaurants of New York, San Francisco, and Hong Kong, but it's good, change-of-pace fare.

Windwardside. (C) 599/416-2353. Main courses $8–$20. V. Tues–Sun 11am–10pm.

Scout's Place INTERNATIONAL/CARIBBEAN

This is a popular dining spot among day-trippers to the island, so you should have your driver stop by early to make a reservation for you. Lunch is simple, good, and filling, and the prices are low. The sandwiches are the island's best, made with fresh-baked bread. Locals come from all over the island to sample them. Dinner is more elaborate, with tables placed on an open-sided terrace, the ideal spot for a drink at sundown. Fresh seafood is a specialty, as is curried goat. Each day, a selection of homemade soups is also offered, perhaps pumpkin or pigeon pea. Scout's chef is proud of his ribs as well. Fresh local fruits and vegetables are used whenever possible. Even if you don't like the food, it's the best place on the island to catch up on the latest gossip.

In the Scout's Place hotel, Windwardside. C 599/416-2740. Reservations recommended. Lunch $10–$15; fixed-price dinner $10–$25. MC, V. Daily 7am–11pm.

YIIK *Finds* INTERNATIONAL   Near the office of Saba Divers in the center of Windwardside, this rooftop restaurant prepares and serves food with considerable skill. The atmosphere alone is one of the more inviting on island, with its tropical plants, "Tequila Sunrise tablecloths," and a rustic deck overlooking the valley, the vegetable garden, a gazebo, and the mountains in the distance. A bakery is attached, and many islanders patronize the place during the day for coffee and some of the more delectable baked goods in Saba. At night, tasty dishes emerge from the kitchen's grills, ovens, and pots, including pastas, chicken, steaks, and burgers. Our favorite starter is the plate of grilled chicken strips in a mandarin orange–and–ginger sauce with honey mustard. This might be followed with a pasta stir-fry—actually penne with fresh vegetables—or you might delight in the spicy grilled shrimp.

Windwardside. C 533/416-2539. Reservations suggested. Main courses $7.50–$30. MC, V. Mon–Sat 11am–2:30pm and 6:30–8:30pm. Closed mid-June to mid-July.

4 Sports & Other Outdoor Pursuits

If it's beaches you're seeking, forget it: It's better to remain on the sands of St. Maarten. Sports here are limited primarily to diving and hiking.

DIVING & SNORKELING

Circling the entire island and including four offshore underwater mountains (seamounts), the **Saba Marine Park,** Fort Bay (C **599/416-3295**), preserves the island's coral reefs and marine life. The park is zoned for various pursuits. The all-purpose recreational zone includes **Well's Bay Beach,** Saba's only beach, but it's seasonal—it disappears with the winter seas, only to reappear in late spring. There are two anchorage zones for visiting yachts and Saba's only harbor. The five dive zones include a coastal area and four seamounts, 2km (1¼ miles) offshore. In these zones are more than two dozen marked and buoyed dive sites and a snorkeling trail. You plunge into a world of coral and sponges, swimming with parrot fish, doctorfish, and damselfish.

The **snorkel trail** is not for the neophyte. It can be approached from Well's Bay Beach but only from May to October. Depths of more than 450m (1,476 ft.) are found between the island and the seamounts, which reach a minimum depth of 27m (89 ft.). There's a $3 per dive visitor fee. Funds are also raised through souvenir sales and donations. The park office at Fort Bay is open Monday to Friday from 8am to 4pm, Saturday from 8am to noon, and Sunday from 10am to 2pm. There's a fully operational decompression chamber/hyperbaric facility in the Fort Bay harbor.

Sea Saba Dive Center, Windwardside (C **599/416-2246**), has nine experienced instructors eager to share their knowledge of Saba Marine Park and its famous deep and medium-depth pinnacles, walls, spur-and-groove formations, and giant boulder gardens. Their two 12m (39-ft.), uncrowded boats are best suited for a comfortable day on Saba's waters. Daily boat dives are made between

9:30am and 1:30pm, allowing a relaxing interval for snorkeling. Courses range from resort through dive master. Extra day and night dives can be arranged. A one-tank dive costs $50, a two-tank dive $90.

Saba Deep Dive Center, P.O. Box 22, Fort Bay, Saba, N.A. (© **599/416-3347**), is a full-service dive center that offers scuba diving, snorkeling, equipment rental/repair, and tank fills. Mike Myers and his staff of NAUI and PADI instructors and dive masters make an effort to provide personalized service and great diving, whether you're an old pro or a first-timer. A certification course goes for $400. A single-tank dive costs $50; a two-tank dive, $90. Night dives are $65. The center is open daily from 8am to 6pm. On the same property, the **In Two Deep Restaurant** and the **Deep Boutique** offer air-conditioned comfort, a view of the harbor area and the Caribbean Sea, good food and drink, and a wide selection of clothes, swimwear, lotions, and sunglasses. The restaurant is open for breakfast and lunch.

HIKING 🔍

Saba is as beautiful above the water as it is below. It offers many trails, both for beginners and more experienced hikers, all reached by paths leading off from "The Road." There's nothing more dramatic than the hike to the top of **Mount Scenery,** a volcano that erupted 5,000 years ago. Allow at least 3 hours and take your time climbing the 1,064 sometimes-slippery chiseled-rock and concrete steps up to the cloud-reefed, 857m (2,811-ft.) mountain. You'll pass through a lush rainforest of palms, bromeliads, elephant ears, heliconia, mountain raspberries, lianas, and tree ferns. Queen Beatrix of the Netherlands climbed these steps in her pumps and, upon reaching the summit, declared: "This is the smallest and highest place in my kingdom." On a clear day, you can see the neighboring islands of St. Kitts, St. Eustatius, St. Maarten, and even St. Barts. Ask your inn to pack you a picnic lunch, and bring water. The higher you climb, the cooler it grows, about a drop of about 1°F (.5°C) every 98m (321 ft.); on a hot day this can be an incentive.

One of our favorite hikes—with some of Saba's most panoramic views—is the **Crispeen Track,** reached from Windwardside as the main road descends to the hamlet of St. John's. Once at St. John's, the track heads northeast going through a narrow but dramatic gorge covered in thick tropical foliage. The vegetation grows lusher and lusher, taking in banana and citrus fields. As you reach the higher points of a section of the island called **Rendezvous,** the fields are no longer cultivated and begin to resemble a rainforest, covered with such flora as

---

⎛Moments A Roller-Coaster Road

Regardless of what road you travel in the Caribbean, there's nothing to compare with 31km-long (19-mile) **"The Road."** Its hairpin curves climb from the little airport up the steep, steep hillside to the lush interior of Saba. In days of yore, engineer after engineer came to the island and told Sabans they'd have to forget ever having a road on their volcanic mountain. Josephus Lambert Hassell, a local, had high hopes. In the 1930s he began to take a correspondence course in engineering while he plotted and planned The Road. Under his guidance, his fellow islanders built The Road over the next 2 decades or so. In recent years, it's been necessary to reconstruct The Road, but it's there waiting to thrill you. At the top of The Road stands Windwardside at 541m (1,774 ft.), Saba's second-largest settlement and the island's midpoint.

philodendron, anthurium, and the wild mammee. Hiking time to Rendezvous is about an hour.

If you don't want to explore the natural attractions of the island on your own, the **Saba Tourist Office,** P.O. Box 527, Windwardside (© **599/416-2231**), can arrange tours of the tropical rainforests. Jim Johnson (© **599/416-3307**), a fit, 40-ish Saban guide, conducts most of these tours, and knows the terrain better than anyone else on the island (he's sometimes difficult to reach, however). Johnson will point out orchids, golden heliconia, and other flora and fauna, as well as the rock formations and bromeliads you're likely to see. Tours can accommodate one to eight hikers and usually last about half a day; depending on your particular route and number of participants, the cost can be anywhere from $50 to $90. Actual prices, of course, are negotiated.

5 Exploring the Island

Tidy white houses cling to the mountainside, and small family cemeteries adjoin each dwelling. Lace-curtained, gingerbread-trimmed cottages give a Disneyland aura.

The first jeep arrived on Saba in 1947. Before that, Sabans went about on foot, climbing from village to village. Hundreds of steps had been chiseled out of the rock by the early Dutch settlers in the 1640s.

Past storybook villages, "The Road" goes over the crest to **The Bottom.** Derived from the Dutch word *botte,* which means "bowl-shaped," this village is nestled on a plateau 240m (787 ft.) above the sea, which is surrounded by rocky volcanic domes. It's also the official capital of Saba, a charming Dutch village of chimneys, gabled roofs, and gardens.

From The Bottom, you can take a taxi up the hill to the mountain village of **Windwardside,** perched on the crest of two ravines about 450m (1,476 ft.) above sea level. This village of red-roofed houses, the second most important on Saba, is the site of the two biggest inns and most of the shops.

From Windwardside, you can climb steep steps cut in the rock to yet another village, **Hell's Gate,** teetering on the edge of a mountain. There's also a serpentine road from the airport to Hell's Gate, where you'll find the island's largest church. Only the most athletic climb from here to the lip of the volcanic crater.

6 Saba After Dark

If you want to do a lot of partying on your vacation, you might want to consider another island. Saba is known for its tucked-away, relaxed, and calm atmosphere. However, don't be too dismayed; there's still something to do at night.

Scout's Place, Windwardside (© **599/416-2740**), is the place to hang out if you want to relax, enjoy a drink, and have a laugh, especially on weeknights. A hotel and restaurant, Scout's Place moonlights as a local watering hole, entertaining tourists and locals with a distinct Saban/Caribbean atmosphere. You won't do much dancing (well, that actually depends on how much you've had to drink), but it's much better than the weeknight alternative: nothing. It's open daily from 7am to around 11pm (but actual closing hours depend on business or the lack thereof). There's no cover.

If you'd like to combine the ambience of a British pub with a saloon that might have been found in the Arizona Badlands, head for **Swinging Doors,** Windwardside (© **599/416-2506**). Saba's good ol' boy watering hole, where locals start consuming the brew at 9am and keep drinking until late at night (no set closing hour). If you get hungry along the way, go for the jalapeño poppers.

19

St. Barthélemy

For luxury with minimum hassle, albeit at a high price tag, St. Barts is rivaled only by Anguilla. It's the ultimate in sophistication in the tropics: chic, rich, and very Parisian. Forget historic sites or ambitious watersports programs. You go to St. Barts for the relaxation, the French cuisine, the white-sand beaches, and the ultimate in comfort.

New friends call it "St. Barts," while old-time visitors prefer "St. Barths." Either way, it's short for St. Barthélemy (San Bar-te-le-*mee*), named by its discoverer Columbus in 1493. For the most part, St. Bartians are descendants of Breton and Norman fisherfolk. Many are of French and Swedish ancestry, the latter evident in their fair skin, blond hair, and blue eyes. The mostly Caucasian population is small, about 3,500 living in some 21 sq. km (8¼ sq. miles), 24km (15 miles) southeast of St. Martin and 225km (140 miles) north of Guadeloupe.

Occasionally you'll see St. Bartians dressed in the provincial costumes of Normandy and speaking Norman French. In little **Corossol,** more than anywhere else, people sometimes follow customs brought from 17th-century France. You might see elderly women wearing the traditional starched white bonnets, at least on special occasions. The bonnets, known as *quichenottes* (a corruption of "kiss-me-not"), served as protection from the close attentions of English or Swedish men on the island. The bonneted women can also be spotted at local celebrations, particularly on August 25, **St. Louis's Day.** Many of these women are camera-shy, but they offer their homemade baskets and hats for sale to visitors.

For a long time, the island was a paradise for a few millionaires, such as David Rockefeller, who had a hideaway on the northwest shore, and Edmond de Rothschild, who occupies some fabulous acres at the "other end" of the island. Nowadays, however, St. Barts is developing a broader base of tourism as it opens more hotels. Nevertheless, the island continues to be a favorite of celebrities, attracting the likes of Tom Cruise, Harrison Ford, and Mikhail Baryshnikov.

St. Barts also attracts a lot of star-seeking paparazzi, who stalk celebrities not only at their private villas, but also at the beach, including Grand Saline beach, where the late John F. Kennedy Jr. was photographed bathing in the nude (which is common and legal at this beach). On another occasion, the paparazzi caught Brad Pitt sunning in the nude at his private villa, with then-girlfriend Gwyneth Paltrow. In February, the island guest list reads like a roster from *Lifestyles of the Rich and Famous.*

The island's capital is **Gustavia,** named after a Swedish king. It's St. Barts's only town and seaport. A sheltered harbor, it has the appearance of a little dollhouse-scale port.

1 Essentials

VISITOR INFORMATION

For information before you go, contact the **French Government Tourist Office** (© **202/659-7779;** www.francetourism.com). There are offices at 444 Madison Ave., New York, NY 10022 (© **212/838-7800**); 9454 Wilshire Blvd., Suite 715, Beverly Hills, CA 90212 (© **310/271-6665**); or 676 N. Michigan Ave., Suite 3360, Chicago, IL 60611 (© **312/751-7800**).

On the island, go to the **Office du Tourisme,** in the commercial heart of Gustavia, adjacent to La Capitanerie (the Port Authority Headquarters), quai du Général-de-Gaulle (© **590/27-87-27;** www.stbarth.fr).

GETTING THERE

BY PLANE   Before you book your own airfare, read the section on "Packages for the Independent Traveler" in chapter 2—it can save you a bundle!

The makeshift landing strip on St. Barts has been the butt of many jokes. It's short and accommodates only small aircraft; the biggest plane it can land is a 19-seater. And even on these small planes, landing on St. Barts has often been compared (and not favorably) to touching down on an aircraft carrier. No landings or departures are permitted after dark.

There are no nonstop flights from North America. From the United States, the principal gateways are St. Maarten, St. Thomas, and Guadeloupe (see the individual chapters on these islands). At any of these islands, you can connect to St. Barts via interisland carriers.

From St. Maarten, your best bet is **Windward Islands Airways International** (known by everybody as **Winair;** © **800/634-4907** in the U.S., or 590/27-61-01 in St. Barts), which usually offers 18 daily flights to St. Barts. Round-trip passage costs 170€ ($213); flight duration is a mere 10 minutes.

Air Caraïbes (© **877/772-1005** in the U.S., or 590/82-47-00; www.air-caraibes.com) flights depart four or five times a day from Pointe-à-Pitre's Le Raizet Airport. One-way passage from Guadeloupe to St. Barts costs 135€ ($169); trip time is 45 minutes.

Air St. Thomas (© **800/522-3084** in the U.S. or 590/27-71-76) offers two flights a day to St. Barts from both San Juan and St. Thomas. However, customers have complained that the airline's schedule is unpredictable. The fare from either San Juan or St. Thomas to St. Barts is 355€ ($444) round-trip.

BY BOAT   The *Voyager* vessels (© **590/27-77-24**), which operate from a base in Gustavia harbor, make frequent (usually daily) runs between St. Barts and either side of St. Maarten/St. Martin. The schedule varies according to the season and the whim of the proprietors, but the *Voyager II* (a catamaran with room

---

Tips Flying Tips

Always reconfirm your return flight from St. Barts with your interisland airline. If you don't, your reservation will be canceled. Also, don't check your luggage all the way through to St. Barts, or you may not see it for a few days. Instead, check your bags to your gateway destination (whatever island you're connecting through, most often St. Maarten), then take your luggage to your interisland carrier and recheck your bags to St. Barts.

for 150 passengers) usually departs Marigot Harbor for St. Barts every morning at 9am, arriving in Gustavia at 10:30am. *Voyager I,* a single-hulled sailboat with room for 110 passengers, travels from Oyster Pond to Gustavia every Wednesday and Sunday at approximately 9am, arriving 45 minutes later in Gustavia. Both vessels charge around 58€ ($73) round-trip, or one-way for 40€ ($50). Advance reservations are a good idea, particularly since the schedule is so iffy.

GETTING AROUND

BY TAXI   Taxis meet all flights and are not superexpensive, mostly because destinations aren't far from one another. Dial ⓒ **590/27-66-31** for taxi service. A typical rate, St-Jean to Cul-de-Sac, is 15€ ($19). Night fares between 6:30pm and midnight are 50% higher. Except under rare circumstances, taxi service isn't available between midnight and 7am.

Virtually every cab driver is aware of the official prices that the island government imposes on **tours by taxi.** Many travelers simply approach a likely looking taxi driver and ask him to show them around. The official rates for one to three passengers are 40€ ($50) for 45 minutes, 44€ ($55) for 60 minutes, and 60€ ($75) for 90 minutes. For four or more passengers, add 8€ ($10) to each of the above-mentioned prices.

BY RENTAL CAR   Nowhere will you see so many open-sided Mitsubishi Mini-Mokes and Suzuki Samurais as on St. Barts. You'll enjoy driving one, too, as long as you're handy with a stick shift and don't care about your coiffure.

Budget (ⓒ **800/472-3325** in the U.S., or 590/27-67-43; www.budget rentacar.com) offers the least stringent terms for its midwinter rentals, and some of the most favorable rates. It rents Suzuki Samurais and Mitsubishis for 60€ ($75) a day or 390€ ($489) a week, with unlimited mileage. A collision-damage waiver (CDW; in French, *une assurance tous-risques*), absolving renters of all but 430€ ($538) of responsibility in the event of an accident, costs 11€ ($14) a day. For the lowest rate, you should reserve at least 3 business days before your arrival.

Hertz (ⓒ **800/654-3001** in the U.S.; www.hertz.com) operates on St. Barts through a local dealership, **Henry's Car Rental,** with branches at the airport and in St-Jean (ⓒ **590/27-71-14**). It offers open-sided Suzuki Samurais for 55€ ($69) a day, and more substantial Suzuki Sidekicks for 60€ ($75) per day. The CDW is about 10€ ($13) per day (with a 534€/$668 deductible).

At **Avis** (ⓒ **800/331-1212** in the U.S., or 590/27-71-43; www.avis.com or www.avis-stbarth.com), you'll need a reservation a full month in advance during high season. In the winter, cars range from 70€ to 115€ ($88–$144) a day, with weekly rentals in high season only. In the off season, rentals are 55€ to 98€ ($69–$123) a day, with weekly rentals from 370€ to 488€ ($463–$610). The CDW costs 10€ to 16€ ($13–$20) extra per day (with a 500€–1,000€/ $625–$1,250 deductible).

Driving is on the right. Never drive with less than half a tank of gas on St. Barts. There are only two gas stations on the island, and they're closed on Sunday and open only from 7:30am to noon and 2 to 5:30pm on other days of the week. (Remarkably, though, you can pay at the pump during business hours if you have a Visa card.) One gas station is near the airport; the other is near L'Orient. All valid foreign driver's licenses are honored. Honk your horn furiously while going around the island's blind corners to avoid having your fenders sideswiped.

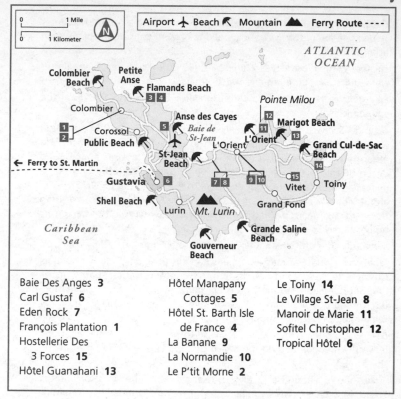

Airport ✈ Beach 🏖 Mountain ▲ Ferry Route - - - -

ATLANTIC OCEAN

Colombier Beach 🏖
Petite Anse
Flamands Beach **3** **4**
Colombier
Anse des Cayes
Baie de St-Jean
Pointe Milou
Marigot Beach **12**
Corossol
Public Beach
1 **2**
5
L'Orient **11**
L'Orient **13**
Grand Cul-de-Sac Beach
← Ferry to St. Martin
St-Jean Beach
14
Gustavia **6**
7 **8**
9 **10**
Vitet **15**
Toiny
Shell Beach 🏖
Lurin *Mt. Lurin*
Grand Fond
Caribbean Sea
Grande Saline Beach
Gouverneur Beach

Baie Des Anges **3**	Hôtel Manapany Cottages **5**	Le Toiny **14**
Carl Gustaf **6**	Hôtel St. Barth Isle de France **4**	Le Village St-Jean **8**
Eden Rock **7**		Manoir de Marie **11**
François Plantation **1**	La Banane **9**	Sofitel Christopher **12**
Hostellerie Des 3 Forces **15**	La Normandie **10**	Tropical Hôtel **6**
Hôtel Guanahani **13**	Le P'tit Morne **2**	

BY MOTORBIKE & SCOOTER **Denis Dufau** operates two affiliates (© 590/ 27-70-59 and © 590/27-54-83). Call either number to make arrangements for rentals. A helmet is provided, and renters must either leave an imprint of a valid credit card or pay a 500€ ($625) deposit. Rental fees vary from 24€ to 28€ ($30–$35) per day, depending on the size of the bike. For all but the smallest models, presentation of a valid driver's license is required.

FAST FACTS: St. Barthélemy

Banks The two main banks are both in Gustavia. The **Banque Francaise Commerciale**, rue du General-de-Gaulle (© 590/27-62-62), is open Monday through Friday from 8am to 12:30pm and 2 to 4pm; it's closed Wednesday afternoon. The **Banque Nationale de Paris**, rue du Bord-de-Mer (© 590/ 27-63-70), is open Monday through Friday from 8am to noon and 2 to 3:30pm; closes at noon on Wednesday.

Currency In 2002, St. Barts, as a political part of mainland France, abandoned its historic French franc and joined the **euro** umbrella. The current rate of exchange is .80€ to US$1. *Rates in this chapter are quoted in U.S. dollars.* Just before you leave home, you can check the current exchange rate on the Web at **www.x-rates.com**.

Documents U.S., British, and Canadian citizens need a passport to enter St. Barts. If you're flying in, you'll need to present your return or ongoing ticket.

Electricity The electricity is 220-volt AC (50 cycles); U.S.-made appliances will require adapter plugs and transformers.

Emergencies Dial 🕿 **16** for **police** or **medical** emergencies, 🕿 **18** for **fire** emergencies.

Hospital St. Barts is not the greatest place to find yourself in a medical emergency. Except for vacationing doctors escaping their own practices in other parts of the world, it has only seven resident doctors and about a dozen on-call specialists. The island's only hospital, with the only emergency facilities, is the **Hôpital de Bruyn,** rue Jean-Bart (🕿 **590/27-60-35**), about .4km (¼ mile) north of Gustavia. Serious medical cases are often flown to St. Maarten, Martinique, Miami, or wherever the person or his/her family specifies.

Language The official language is French, but English is widely spoken.

Pharmacies The **Pharmacie de Saint-Barth** is on quai de la Republique, Gustavia (🕿 **590/27-61-82**). Its only competitor is the **Pharmacie de l'Aeroport,** adjacent to the airport (🕿 590/27-66-61). Both are open Monday through Saturday from 8am to 8pm; on Sunday, one or the other remains open for at least part of the day.

Safety Although crime is rare, it's wise to protect your valuables. Don't leave them unguarded on the beach or in parked cars, even if locked in the trunk.

Taxes You're assessed a $5 departure tax if you're heading for another French island. Otherwise, you'll pay $10. Taxes are included in your airline ticket.

Telephone St. Barts is linked to the Guadeloupe telephone system. To call St. Barts from the United States, dial **011** (the international access code), then **590** (the country code for Guadeloupe), then **590** again, and finally the six-digit local number. To make a call to anywhere in St. Barts from within St. Barts, dial only the six-digit local number, and ignore the prefix 590. To reach an AT&T operator from anywhere on the island, dial 🕿 **0800-99-00-11.** To reach **MCI,** dial 🕿 **0800-99-00-19,** and to reach **Sprint,** dial 🕿 **0800-99-00-87.**

Time When standard time is in effect in the United States and Canada, St. Barts is 1 hour ahead of the U.S. East Coast. When daylight savings time is in effect in the United States (Apr–Oct), clocks in New York and St. Barts show the same time.

Tipping Hotels usually add a service charge of 10% to 15%; always ask if this is included in the price you're quoted. Restaurants typically add a service charge, too. Taxi drivers expect a tip of 10% of the fare.

Water The water on St. Barts is generally safe to drink.

Weather The climate of St. Barts is ideal: dry with an average temperature of 72°F to 86°F (22°C–30°C).

2 Accommodations

With the exception of a few of the really expensive hotels, most places here are homey, comfortable, and casual. Everything is small, as tiny St. Barts is hardly in the mainstream of tourism. In March, it's often hard to stay on St. Barts unless you've made reservations far in advance. Accommodations throughout the island, with some exceptions, tend to be exceptionally expensive, and a service charge of between 10% and 15% is usually added to your bill.

St. Barts has a sizable number of villas, beach houses, and apartments for rent by the week or month. Villas are dotted around the island's hills—very few are on the beach. Instead of an oceanfront bedroom, you get a panoramic view. One of the best agencies to contact for villa, apartment, or condo rentals is **St. Barth Properties,** 693 East Central St., Suite 201, Franklin, MA 02038 (© **800/ 421-3396** or 508/528-7727 in the U.S. and Canada; www.stbarth.com). Peg Walsh, a longtime aficionado of St. Barts, and her capable son, Tom Smyth, will let you know what's available. She can also make arrangements for car rentals and air travel to St. Barts. When you arrive, she can book babysitters and restaurant reservations. Rentals can range from a one-room "studio" villa away from the beach, for $980 per week off season, up to $40,000 per week for a mini-palace at Christmas. Yes, that $40,000 is right, but it's for a very unusual, antique-furnished luxury home. Most rentals average between $2,500 and $4,000 a week between mid-December and mid-April, with discounts of 30% to 50% the rest of the year. In addition to villas, Ms. Walsh can also arrange accommodations in all categories of St. Barts's hotels.

VERY EXPENSIVE

Carl Gustaf ✿✿✿   The most glamorous hotel in Gustavia rises above the town's harbor from a steep hillside. Each state-of-the-art unit is in one of a dozen pink or green, red-roofed villas whose facilities include a private kitchenette, two phones, a fax machine, a stereo system, a private terrace, a private plunge pool, two TVs, and comfortably plush rattan furniture. Access to each building is via a central staircase, which tests the stamina of even the most active guests. The wood-frame units are angled for maximum views of the boats bobbing far below in the bay and panoramic sunsets. Bedrooms aren't as large as might be expected at such prices, but they are exceedingly well furnished, especially suites nos. 30 through 33. You'll walk across Italian marble floors under a pitched ceiling to reach your luxurious bed fitted with elegant fabrics. Bathrooms are also well equipped, with mosaic-clad showers (no tubs), and makeup mirrors. Beach facilities are within a 10-minute walk. The mood is French, not unlike what you'd find on the coast of Provence.

The cuisine is French and Creole. Often a well-known chef from Paris appears in winter.

Rue des Normands, 97099 Gustavia, St. Barthélemy, F.W.I. © **800/322-2223** in the U.S., or 590/29-79-00. Fax 590/27-82-37. www.carlgustaf.com. 14 units. Winter 1,250€ ($1,563) 1-bedroom suite, 1,630€ ($2,038) 2-bedroom suite; off season 570€ ($713) 1-bedroom suite, 730€ ($913) 2-bedroom suite. Rates include continental breakfast. AE, MC, V. **Amenities:** Restaurant; piano bar; outdoor pool; health club; sauna; deep-sea fishing; sailing; scuba diving; water-skiing; windsurfing; 24-hr. room service; massage; laundry service; dry cleaning; helicopter rides. In room: A/C, TV, fax, dataport, kitchenette, minibar, fridge, hair dryer, iron/ironing board, safe.

Eden Rock ✿   Greta Garbo checked out long ago, but this legendary hotel still occupies the most spectacular site on St. Barts, flanked by two perfect beaches.

Years ago, when the island's former mayor, Remy de Haenen, bought the quartzite promontory this hotel sits on from an old woman, she laughed at him for paying too much. Today, the story is part of island lore. Offering the best panoramas on the island, it's surrounded on three sides by the waters of St. Jean Bay.

The building atop the pinnacle looks like an idealized version of a Provençal farmhouse. The stone house contains a collection of French antiques and paintings left over from the de Haenen family, plus English antiques and paintings imported by new owners. The decor in each guest room includes a stylish mixture of tasteful antiques and reproductions, and fabrics and accessories pulled together with flair. Some are right on the beach, with their own access to the sand. The best and most expensive are the ocean suites with private balconies. The least expensive are the small and cozy cabins. Bathrooms are compact and have showers.

There's great emphasis on the quality and elegance of the cuisine at Eden Rock's three restaurants. There's a casual beachfront bar for lunch and dinners are served at Le Tapas Bar and at Le Rock, a stylish and swank French restaurant.

97133 St-Jean, St. Barthélemy, F.W.I. **(C)** **877/563-7105** or 590/29-79-99. Fax 590/27-88-37. www. edenrockhotel.com. 16 units. Winter 615€–1,750€ ($769–$2,188) double; off season 475€–1,555€ ($594–$1,944) double. Rates include buffet breakfast. AE, MC, V. **Amenities:** 3 restaurants; 2 bars; outdoor pool; snorkeling; windsurfing; limited room service; laundry service; dry cleaning; babysitting; nonsmoking rooms. *In room:* A/C, TV, dataport, minibar, hair dryer, safe.

François Plantation ★★
On a steep hill with panoramic views of the beach below, this complex re-creates the plantation era. Twelve bungalows, each decorated in an elegant West Indian style, surround a tropical garden. Eight of the units have sea views, and the others look out over a garden. Spacious bedrooms contain mahogany four-posters, ceiling fans, and Moroccan rugs on marble or tile floors that make the places extra cozy. Marble bathrooms come with bidets, open showers, and dual basins. The owners are Françoise and François (you read it right) Beret, longtime residents of St. Barts.

The hotel has an exceptional restaurant, Wine and Dinner Club (see "Dining," later in this chapter).

Colombier, 97133 St. Barthélemy, F.W.I. **(C)** **590/29-80-22.** Fax 800/207-8071 in the U.S. or 590/27-61-26. www.francois-plantation.com. 12 units. Winter 430€–660€ ($538–$825) bungalow for 2; off season 280€–320€ ($350–$400) bungalow for 2. Rates include continental breakfast. AE, MC, V. Closed June 1–Oct 31. **Amenities:** Restaurant; bar; outdoor pool; health club; babysitting; room service (breakfast only); laundry service; dry cleaning. *In room:* A/C, TV, minibar, hair dryer, safe.

Hôtel Guanahani ★★ *Kids*
Better equipped than its nearest rival, Hôtel Manapany Cottages (see below), this is the largest hotel on St. Barts, opening onto two scenic beaches. It, along with the Sofitel Christopher (see below), are the most commercial properties on island. Isolated in the northeast part of the island, the hotel is spread over 6.4 steeply sloping hectares (16 acres) on its own peninsula, dotted with a network of 75 Lilliputian cottages trimmed in gingerbread and painted in bold, tropical colors. Don't consider this place if you have mobility problems or just don't relish the idea of huffing up and down steep slopes. But if that's not a problem, the views over the sea from each unit are broad and sweeping. Most units, at least those on the resort's upper slopes, are self-contained in their own individual cottages. Some of the bungalows closest to the beach, a private white-sand strip on a reef-protected bay, contain two units each. Every accommodation has a minibar, ceiling fans, and a private patio or balcony. Traditional and contemporary-style desks and tables, tasteful upholstery, and four-poster king-size beds spell deluxe living, as do the fine linen and comfortable beds. Bathrooms are brightly tiled with showers only.

Light lunches are served at Indigo, an airy venue positioned between the swimming pool and the sea. More formal dinners are available at Bartoloméo Restaurant. In summertime both lunch and dinner are served at Indigo.

Grand Cul-de-Sac, 97133 St. Barthélemy, F.W.I. 🕾 **800/223-6800** in the U.S., or 590/27-66-60. Fax 590/27-70-70. www.leguanahani.com. 75 units. Winter 518€–844€ ($648–$1,055) double, 944€–1,516€ ($1,180–$1,895) suite; off season 316€–530€ ($395–$663) double, 636€–840€ ($795–$1,050) suite. Rates include American breakfast and round-trip airport transfers. AE, MC, V. **Amenities:** 2 restaurants; 2 bars; 2 outdoor pools; 2 tennis courts; fitness center; Jacuzzi; boat rental; windsurfing; children's programs (ages 2–6); car rental; salon; 24-hr. room service; massage; babysitting; laundry service; dry cleaning. *In room:* A/C, ceiling fan, TV, dataport, minibar, hair dryer, safe.

Hôtel Manapany Cottages ⊛

This resort climbs a steep, well-landscaped hillside on the northwestern side of the island, a 10-minute taxi ride north of the airport. This is one of the most stylish hotels on St. Barts, although not in the league of Carl Gustaf (see above) or Sofitel Christopher (see below). It's small, intimate, and accommodating; the name, translated from Malagese, means "small paradise." The place was designed as a minivillage of gingerbread-trimmed Antillean cottages, set either on a steeply sloping hillside or beside the water. The rambling verandas and open-sided living rooms allow you to enjoy the trade winds, while the bedrooms have air-conditioning in case it gets too hot. The furnishings include both white rattan and Caribbean colonial pieces carved from mahogany and imported from the Dominican Republic. Mosquito netting covers most of the four-poster beds for a romantic touch. Rooms come with large-screen TVs with in-house videos, and kitchenettes. Bathrooms are quite luxurious, most with shower/tub combinations.

Le Fellini serves well-prepared Italian and French food at lunch and dinner.

Anse des Cayes, 97098 St. Barthélemy, F.W.I. 🕾 **800/847-4249** in the U.S., or 590/27-66-55. Fax 590/27-75-28. www.lemanapany.com. 46 units. Winter 372€–412€ ($465–$515) double, 584€–760€ ($730–$950) junior suite, 736€–840€ ($920–$1,050) cottage; off season 216€–240€ ($270–$300) double, 340€–432€ ($425–$540) junior suite, 424€–480€ ($530–$600) cottage. MC, V. **Amenities:** Restaurant; bar; outdoor pool; tennis court; gym; small spa; 24-hr. room service; babysitting; laundry service; dry cleaning. *In room:* A/C, TV, fridge, hair dryer, safe.

Hôtel St. Barth Isle de France ⊛

Like François Plantation (see above), this resort evokes colonial era charm, but François does it more elegantly. This small, family-run hotel has unusually spacious guest rooms for St. Barts. Each top-notch unit contains a private patio or terrace, and an individual decor with antique mahogany and rattan furniture and engravings collected from neighboring islands. Beds are luxurious, fitted with fine linen. Clad in marble, bathrooms are spacious and well equipped with dual basins, large tubs (in some cases with whirlpool jets) and showers.

Meals are charming and sophisticated (with strong French overtones), despite their informality.

97098 Baie des Flamands, St. Barthélemy, F.W.I. 🕾 **800/810-4691** in the U.S., or 590/27-61-81. Fax 590/27-86-83. www.isle-de-france.com. 33 units. Winter 690€ ($863) double, 980€ ($1,225) suite, 1,890€ ($2,363) bungalow; off season 455€ ($569) double, 635€–930€ ($794–$1,163) suite, 1,100€ ($1,375) bungalow. Rates include continental breakfast. AE, MC, V. **Amenities:** Restaurant; bar; 2 outdoor pools; tennis court; exercise room; car rental; limited room service; babysitting; laundry service; dry cleaning. *In room:* A/C, TV, kitchenette (in some), minibar, fridge, beverage maker, hair dryer, safe.

Le Toiny ⊛⊛⊛

This posh retreat is in a dead heat with Carl Gustaf (see above). One of the most glamorous and chillingly expensive resorts on St. Barts, it contains only a dozen suites, scattered among a half-dozen buildings clinging to a gently sloping hillside near Plage des Gouverneurs. The nearest swimming beach is a 5-minute drive away at Grande Saline, the only sanctioned nude beach on the island. All the suites have floors made of wide planks or terra-cotta tiles, kitchenettes, bathrooms with shower/tub combinations, and mahogany four-posters draped with mosquito netting. Each provides plenty of privacy, with lots of space and shrubbery between units. The hotel restaurant is reviewed below in "Dining," later in this chapter.

Anse de Toiny, 97133 St. Barthélemy, F.W.I. ⓒ **800/278-6469** or 590/27-88-88. Fax 590/27-89-30. www.hotelletoiny.com. 12 units. Winter 1,600€ ($2,000) 1-bedroom suite for 2, 2,900€ ($3,625) 3-bedroom suite for up to 6; off season 750€ ($938) 1-bedroom suite, 1,400€ ($1,750) 3-bedroom suite. AE, DC, MC, V. Closed Sept 1–Oct 25. No children under 10. **Amenities:** Restaurant; bar; outdoor pool; bike rental; car rental; 24-hr. room service; babysitting; laundry service; dry cleaning; rooms for those with limited mobility. *In room:* A/C, TV, dataport, kitchenette, minibar, beverage maker, hair dryer, safe.

Sofitel Christopher 🌟🌟🌟 Set on a dramatic promontory above the ocean, this full-service hotel offers views of St. Martin and nearby islets. Built and managed by Sofitel, it has a French-colonial decor and a low-rise design that incorporates four slate-roofed, white-sided buildings arranged in a semicircle above a rocky coastline. The hotel is not adjacent to the water; guests must drive about 10 minutes to reach a good beach, Plage de l'Orient. Most of the resort's activities revolve around the swimming pool. The roomy accommodations, with king-size and twin beds, fall into two categories: deluxe oceanfront with patio or deluxe ocean view with terrace. All are furnished in a Creole style and have ceiling fans. The differences between the two categories of rooms are most pronounced in the bathrooms. The oceanfront rooms have separate shower/tub combinations, while the rooms opening onto the gardens contain showers only. The resort's pool, a 405 sq. m (4,359-sq.-ft.) pair of interconnected ovals with a bridge, is the largest on the island.

Le Mango, a poolside daytime restaurant, specializes in barbecues. In the evening, more formal French and Creole meals are served at L'Orchidée. There's a barbecue every Thursday.

9 Pointe Milou (B.P. 571), 97133 St. Barthélemy, F.W.I. ⓒ **800/221-4542** in the U.S., or 590/27-63-63. Fax 590/27-92-92. www.accorhotels.com. 42 units. Winter 490€–590€ ($613–$738) double, from 990€ ($1,238) suite; off season 310€–380€ ($388–$475) double, 650€ ($813) suite. Rates include American breakfast. 1 child under age 12 can stay free in parent's room. AE, DC, MC, V. Closed Sept–Oct 25. **Amenities:** 2 restaurants; 2 bars; outdoor pool; gym; room service (noon–9:30pm); massage; babysitting; laundry service; dry cleaning; nonsmoking rooms; rooms for those with limited mobility. *In room:* A/C, ceiling fan, TV, dataport, minibar, beverage maker, hair dryer, iron/ironing board, safe.

EXPENSIVE

Baie des Anges 🌟 Opening right onto the white sands of Flamands beach, this retreat is cooled by trade winds and has a laid-back, carefree atmosphere, as opposed to the more snooty and pricey French inns on the island. Surrounded by gardens, the two-story, ocean-fronting property is relatively simple but has its own style and charm. You can opt for a room opening onto the sea or the courtyard with its pool, where guests can be found when the Atlantic waves get too rough for swimming. Some units have a kitchenette, plus a balcony with chaise longues. Newly redecorated, the accommodations are in sea colors of blue and green. For such a small place, the inn has a sophisticated, first-class restaurant, La Langouste, where nonguests are invited to drop in for lunch and dinner, feasting off the Creole or French specialties such as Caribbean lobsters selected from a tank.

Baie des Anges, Flamands, 97133 St. Barthélemy, FWI. ⓒ **590/27-63-61.** Fax 590/27-83-44. www.hotel baiedesanges.com. 10 units. Winter 276€–384€ ($345–$480) double, 308€–416€ ($385–$520) triple; off season 160€–228€ ($200–$285) double, 192€–264€ ($240–$330) triple. **Amenities:** Restaurant; bar;

outdoor pool; limited room service; laundry service; dry cleaning; babysitting. *In room:* A/C, ceiling fan, TV, kitchenette (in some), hair dryer, safe.

La Banane ⟨ᴙ⟩ On the outskirts of the village of L'Orient lies this intimate and well-furnished hotel. Because of La Banane's small size and carefully restricted access, it seems like a private hideaway. The Brussels-born owner, De Nys Philippe, uses such accents as Artemide lighting, Casa Milano canopy beds, and Belgian linens to effect a change of pace from Creole designs.

The hotel is elegant and harmonious. Nine bungalows are scattered around a minimalist two-tiered pool. Bathrooms open onto patios or private gardens so that taking a shower becomes a perfumed ritual in a setting of such plants as frangipani, jasmine, and hibiscus. Set on flat, low-lying grounds, the gardens are richly planted with bananas, flowering shrubs, and palms, and are just a 3-minute walk from the beach.

L'Orient, 97133 St. Barthélemy, F.W.I. ℂ 590/52-03-00. Fax 590/27-68-44. www.labanane.com. 9 units. Winter 450€–800€ ($563–$1,000) double; off season 310€ ($388) double. Rates include breakfast. AE, MC, V. **Amenities:** Bar; 2 outdoor pools; reading room; limited room service; babysitting; laundry service; dry cleaning. *In room:* A/C, ceiling fan, TV, dataport, minibar, hair dryer, safe.

MODERATE (FOR ST. BARTS)

Hostellerie des Trois Forces ⟨ᴙ⟩ *(Finds* The domain of St. Barts's astrologer emeritus might be called a New Age holistic retreat, but it's much more than that. It welcomes all patrons of whatever persuasion to one of its gingerbread cottages or its fine restaurant (see "Dining," later in this chapter). The heart and soul of the place is Hubert Delamotte, who arrived from Brittany with his wife to create a hotel where happiness, good food, comfort, and conversation are a way of life. Cottages are decorated in the color scheme of their astrological chart, such as red for the sign of Leo. Holistic services include massage therapy, osteopathy, and yoga. High on a hilltop, the inn occupies panoramic grounds in Vitet, above the freshwater ponds of Cul-de-Sac and about a 5-minute drive from the Cul-de-Sac beaches and L'Orient. As for the view, Hubert says, "There's not a soul between us and Africa."

Morne Viet, 97133 St. Barthélemy, F.W.I. ℂ 590/27-61-25. Fax 590/27-81-30. www.3forces.net. 7 cottages. Winter 160€ ($200) double; off season 120€ ($150) double. AE, MC, V. **Amenities:** Restaurant; outdoor pool; room service (8–10am); laundry service. *In room:* A/C, kitchenette (in 2 units), minibar, safe.

Le Village St-Jean ⟨ᴙ⟩ *(Value* This family-owned cottage colony hideaway, 2km (1¼ miles) from the airport toward St.-Jean, attracts a distinguished clientele. Lying in the center of St. Barts, a 5-minute drive uphill from Saint-Jean Beach, it offers one of the best values on this high-priced resort island. Despite that, you may see a media headliner here; after all, some of them like to save money, too. The cottages contain kitchens, sun decks or gardens, terraced living rooms, balconies, and ceiling fans. Furnishings are modest but comfortable, and the living space is generous. The tiled shower-only bathrooms are compact, and some have bidets. The complex has a well-managed restaurant and bar, La Terrazza, with a sprawling terrace on a platform above the sloping terrain (see "Dining," below).

Baie de Saint-Jean (B.P. 623), 97098 St. Barthélemy, F.W.I. ℂ 590/27-61-39. Fax 590/27-77-96. www. villagestjeanhotel.com. 20 units. Winter 185€ ($231) double, 215€–290€ ($269–$363) 1-bedroom cottage, 340€–450€ ($425–$563) 2-bedroom cottage, 560€ ($700) suite; off season 105€ ($131) double, 145€–185€ ($181–$231) 1-bedroom cottage, 220€–305€ ($275–$381) 2-bedroom cottage, 330€ ($413) suite. Extra person 40€–65€ ($50–$81). AE, MC, V. **Amenities:** Restaurant; bar; outdoor pool; Jacuzzi; car rental; limited room service; babysitting; laundry service; dry cleaning. *In room:* A/C, fridge, minibar, hair dryer.

Tropical Hôtel   The facade of this small, unpretentious hotel looks like a pic-ture-postcard Caribbean colonial inn. Originally built in 1981 and restored in 1997, it's perched on a hillside about 46m (151 ft.) above St-Jean Beach. Each room contains a private shower-only bathroom, a king-size bed with a good mattress, tile floors, and a fridge. Nine units have sea views and balconies; no. 11 has a porch that opens onto a garden that's so lush it looks like a miniature jungle.

The hotel has a hospitality center where guests read, listen to music, or order drinks and snacks at a paneled bar surrounded by antiques. The pool is small, but watersports are available on the beach.

St-Jean (B.P. 147), 97095 St. Barthélemy, F.W.I. © 800/223-9815 in the U.S., or 590/27-64-87. Fax 590/27-81-74. www.tropical-hotel.com. 21 units. Winter 198€–246€ ($248–$308); off season 116€–144€ ($145–$180). Rates include continental breakfast. AE, MC, V. Closed Jun to mid-July. **Amenities:** Outdoor pool; car rental; babysitting; laundry service. *In room:* A/C, TV, dataport, fridge, hair dryer.

INEXPENSIVE (RELATIVELY, ANYWAY)

La Normandie   This modest, unassuming, family-owned hotel offers no facil-ities other than the clean but somewhat dreary accommodations. But what do you expect for this kind of money on St. Barts? This is what the French call an *auberge antillaise* (Antillean inn). Set near the intersection of two major roads, about 91m (298 ft.) from L'Orient Beach, it offers motel-inspired bedrooms of casual comfort. The more expensive units are larger, lie adjacent to the hotel's modest pool, and contain TVs. The less expensive, smaller rooms are next to the highway. The shower-only bathrooms are really too small, but they're well-kept.

97133 L'Orient, St. Barthélemy, F.W.I. © 590/27-61-66. Fax 590/27-98-83. 8 units. Winter 60€ ($75) dou-ble, 70€ ($88) triple; off season 53€ ($66) double, 58€ ($73) triple. DC, MC, V. **Amenities:** Outdoor pool. *In room:* A/C, TV, dataport, fridge, beverage maker.

Le P'tit Morne ⭐ *Finds*   This is hardly the most luxurious or stylish lodging on an island that's legendary for its glamour and its five-star hotels. But the hotel's three-star format, its relatively low rates, and the warm welcome extended by its island-born owner, Marie-Joëlle, make it a worthy vacation site. It's a 10-minute drive from the beach. The colonial-designed guest rooms are filled with completely unpretentious furniture and comfortable king-size beds. There's plenty of elbowroom and units were built to catch the trade winds. Bathrooms are compact and have shower stalls.

Colombier (P.O. Box 14), 97098 St. Barthélemy, F.W.I. © 590/52-95-50. Fax 590/27-84-63. www.timorne.com. 14 units. Winter 163€–230€ ($204–$288) double; off season 75€–150€ ($94–$188) double. Off-season rates include daily breakfast and unlimited use of a car. AE, MC, V. Closed June. **Amenities:** Limited room serv-ice; babysitting; laundry service. *In room:* A/C, TV, dataport, kitchen, fridge, beverage maker, iron/ironing board.

Manoir de Marie *Value*   If this place looks as though it was built in Normandy, it was. Originally constructed as the centerpiece of a large farm in 1610, it was disassembled and rebuilt a minute's walk from the sands of Plage de L'Orient in the 1970s. Shortly thereafter, eight half-timbered bungalows, each in an ersatz Norman style, were erected in the garden, each facing a reflect-ing pool accented with water lilies, a fountain, and nearby palms and bougainvillea. Guests of the property won't have a lot to do with the main house, other than to check in and chitchat from time to time with the on-site managers. But each will probably construct a beach-going life that's private, isolated, and cost-efficient, thanks to the presence of kitchens within most of the units. Accommodations are Antillean rustic, with brown, white, and pink color schemes, white-linen hassocks, and beds draped in tulle. Each unit has a small, shower-only bathroom. Six of the accommodations have their own kitchens, and two are equipped with refrigerators. Usually, meals are not served on the premises, although with advance notification, something can be arranged.

Route de Saline, L'Orient, 97133 St. Barthélemy, F.W.I. ⓒ 590/27-79-27. Fax 590/27-65-75. http://lemanoirstbarth.com. 8 units. Winter 130€–300€ ($163–$375) double; off season 100€–240€ ($125–$300) double. 30€ ($38) per extra person. AE, MC, V. **Amenities:** Bar; outdoor pool; babysitting; laundry service; dry cleaning. In-room: A/C, ceiling fan, TV, dataport, kitchen (in most), minibar, beverage maker, hair dryer, no phone.

3 Dining

IN GUSTAVIA

Au Port FRENCH/CREOLE   This restaurant is one of the culinary staples of the island, having survived for many years, thanks to a straightforward and unpretentious ambience that focuses on good cooking, generous portions, and an utter lack of snobbery. Set one floor above street level, in the center of town, it features a neocolonial decor with models of sailboats, antique accessories, and flavorful cuisine. Appetizers are a delight, featuring such treats as creamy Caribbean pumpkin soup with a vanilla flavor or a goat-cheese salad with lavender honey. A homemade duck foie gras adds an elegant touch. Fresh seafood is always a good choice; specialties include sliced scallops and sweet potatoes in a red-pepper sauce and filet of sautéed shrimp with green curry. Meat and poultry are also treated with tender loving care, especially the breast of honey-roasted duck and the very typical island dish—goat stew with bananas au gratin.

Rue Sadi-Carnot. ⓒ 590/27-62-36. Reservations recommended, especially for veranda tables. Main courses 16€–30€ ($20–$38); menu Creole 33€ ($41). AE, MC, V. Mon–Sat 6:30–10pm. Closed June 15–July 31.

L'Arbre du Voyageur ⚘ (Finds) ITALIAN/FRENCH   Some villa owners cite this bistro, a sometimes raucous and always irreverent hangout for the wealthy, as their favorite restaurant on the island. It's set in a simple, industrial-looking building on the relatively unglamorous south side of Gustavia's harbor, adjacent to dozens of moored yachts. You can dine lightly and moderately here, but you can also spend a lot of money. Typical fare might include one of about a half-dozen meal-size salads, as well as such pastas as lasagna, *penne a l'arrabiata* (a hot, spicy, tomato sauce with hot peppers), or any of several gnocchis. Also available are fish terrine, terrine of roe fish, and a wide roster of grilled meats and fish such as a whole snapper, grilled and served with Creole sauce and rondelles of lemon. The chefs prepare an astonishing 99 different kinds of pizzas from their wood-fired ovens. The dessert specialty is the island's most theatrical version of flambéed bananas: Lights are dimmed and the shooting flames from the burning rum illuminate the entire restaurant.

Rue Jeanne-d'Arc, La Pointe. ⓒ 590/27-81-06. Reservations required in winter. Main courses 16€–27€ ($20–$34); pizza 7€–22€ ($8.75–$28). AE, DC, MC, V. Daily 11:30am–3pm and 5–11pm.

La Mandala ⚘⚘ THAI/EUROPEAN   This is one of the most exciting restaurants on St. Barts. It occupies a house on the steepest street in Gustavia, high above the harbor, with a dining deck overlooking a swimming pool. If you drive your car up to the entrance, a valet will park it for you. The owners and chefs are partners Kiki and Boubou (Christophe Barjetta and Olivier Megnin), whose nicknames belie their formidable training at some of the grandest restaurants of France. Some recommended dishes are tempura of snapper or mahimahi with mango salad and coriander sauce; a traditional Thai dish, *tataki*, composed of deliberately undercooked fish with a ginger-flavored vinaigrette, shallots, and sesame oil; grilled beef with saki sauce; or rack of lamb with soy sauce and caramel. Try the warm chocolate tart for dessert.

Rue Courbet. © 590/27-96-96. Reservations recommended. Main courses 22€–30€ ($28–$38). AE, MC, V. Daily 5–11pm; tapas and cocktails 5–7pm.

La Route des Boucaniers ✿ *Finds* FRENCH/CREOLE   What a discovery! Near the harbor, this bistro is the domain of Francis Delage, who is the definitive authority on Creole cuisine, having written a five-volume primer. Wonderful ingredients turn up here, and they are concocted into a medley of local dishes whose flavors are not found elsewhere on this island. The decor evokes a rum shack—there's even a boat wreck—but these artifacts belie the sophistication of the cuisine. Our avocado salad was reason to return the following night. It was given added zest by chewy flakes of dried cod in a hot Creole sauce. For the main course, the chef's pride and joy is a large bowl of fresh fish, shellfish, and octopus huddled together in red-bean purée, everything blended into a smooth texture that is properly seasoned and delicious. Other surprises await, especially the Cajun mahimahi with coin-shaped sautéed yucca. What makes everything taste so good? Maybe you don't want to know. It's *beurre rouge* (lobster butter) and *lardons* (strips of salt pork) that have been heavily spiced. Not what your doctor ordered, but irresistible.

Rue de Bord de Mer, Gustavia. © 590/27-73-00. Reservations required. Main courses 19€–30€ ($24–$38). MC, V. Daily 9am–11pm.

Le Rivage ✿ FRENCH/CARIBBEAN   This restaurant offers the kind of offhanded charm and oversize Gallic egos that you'd expect in a chic but somewhat disorganized beach resort in the south of France. It's set on a covered veranda built on piers above the waters of the lagoon. About half the tables are open to views of the stars. During the day, no one objects to bathing suits at the table; at night, fashionably casual is the preferred dress. With a rapidly changing menu, items that merit raves include carpaccio of beef and a tempting roster of "supersalads," the most popular of which combines shrimp with smoked salmon and melted goat cheese. There's also a seafood platter of raw shellfish (scallops, clams, and crayfish), artfully arranged on a bed of seaweed; grilled crayfish, *daurade* (bream), snapper, and tuna; and a full complement of such Creole specialties as *boudin noir* (blood sausage), *accras de morue* (beignets of codfish), and *court bouillon* of fish.

In the St. Barth Beach Hotel, Grand Cul-de-Sac. © 590/27-82-42. Reservations recommended. Main courses 15€–25€ ($19–$31). AE, MC, V. Daily noon–5:30pm and 7–10pm.

Le Sapotillier ✿✿ FRENCH/SEAFOOD   Le Sapotillier is near the top of the list for every visiting gourmet. This West Indian house beside the less frequented part of the harbor is the domain of Austrian-born Adam Rajner, who runs one of the best-known restaurants in Gustavia. Dine outside on the candlelit patio or inside the clapboard-covered Antillean bungalow that was transported from the outlying village of Corossol.

Chef Rajner pays strict attention to the quality and presentation of his food. Your meal might begin with snails in lasagna with a Provençal sauce, or a slice of fried duck liver served with caramelized pineapples and a zesty sprinkling of Szechuan pepper. From here, you can proceed to such perfectly prepared main courses as sole meunière with spinach. Two French specialties you'd be hard pressed to find anywhere else on St. Barts are based on chicken and pigeon flown in fresh from Bresse, a city known throughout Europe for its poultry. The chicken is served *en cocotte* (in a stew) and the pigeon with braised red cabbage and spaetzle (egg noodles).

Rue Sadi-Carnot. ⓒ 590/27-60-28. Reservations required. Main courses 26€–36€ ($33–$45). DISC, MC, V. Tues–Sun 6:30–10:30pm; Christmas–Easter daily 6:30–10pm. Closed Mar to mid-May and Oct to mid-Dec.

Le Toiny ⚝ FRENCH   This restaurant opens its doors to folks who want to dine among the rich and jaded at St. Barts's most upscale and expensive hotel, but aren't willing to mortgage their future for a room. Guests dine in an open-air pavilion adjacent to the resort's pool, with a view that sweeps out over the wide blue sea. The emphasis is French, casually stylish, and offhanded in a way that might remind you of a particularly rich version of bohemian Paris. At lunchtime, menu items might include eggplant ravioli with tomato coulis and Parmesan, a *tarte fine* with tomatoes and feta, or prawns in "an Oriental nest" with sage and onion sauce. After dark, choices are even more exquisite. The best examples include rack and saddle of lamb, Chilean sea bass, or ravioli of crayfish with foie gras. The cuisine, the setting, and the first-rate ingredients make for a memorable meal.

In Le Toiny hotel, Anse de Toiny. ⓒ 590/27-88-88. Reservations required. Main courses 17€–33€ ($21–$41) lunch; 28€–56€ ($35–$70) dinner. AE, MC, V. Daily noon–2:30pm and 7–9:30pm. Closed Sept 1–Oct 23.

L'Iguane JAPANESE/INTERNATIONAL   Set adjacent to three upscale shops, this restaurant and cafe serves sushi, American breakfasts, California-style sandwiches and salads, and more. The walls are ocher and blue, and the lighting flatters even the most weather-beaten skin. The ambience grows more Asian as the evening progresses. Sushi, imported twice a week from suppliers in Miami and served according to time-honored Japanese techniques, is the main allure here, with special emphasis on tuna, snapper, salmon, and eel.

Carre d'Or, quai de la Republique. ⓒ 590/27-88-46. Reservations recommended for dinner. Sushi 3.25€–3.75€ ($4.05–$4.70) per piece; main courses 17€–33€ ($21–$41). AE, MC, V. Mid-Nov to Aug, cafe daily 8–11am, restaurant daily 11am–midnight; off season cafe Mon–Sat 8–11am, restaurant Mon–Sat 11am–3pm and daily 7–midnight.

IN THE ST-JEAN BEACH AREA

La Terrazza ⟨Value⟩ ITALIAN/INTERNATIONAL   Proudly positioned as the centerpiece of a charming and not particularly expensive hotel (see "Accommodations," earlier in this chapter), La Terrazza has a deserved reputation for well-conceived food, such as a bowl of fish soup, based on the catch of the day, with

---

⟨Finds⟩ Picnic Fare on St. Barts

St. Barts is so expensive that many visitors opt to buy at least one of their meals (perhaps a "gourmet lunch to go" package) from a takeout deli. The most centrally located of the island's epicurean delis is **La Rôtisserie**, rue Oskar-II (ⓒ **590/27-63-13**), which is proud of its endorsement by Fauchon, the world-famous food store in Paris. On display are bottles of wine, crocks of mustard, pâté, herbs, caviar, chocolate, and exotic oils and vinegars, as well as takeout (and very French) platters sold by the gram. *Plats du jour* cost around 8€ to 18€ ($10–$23) for a portion suitable for one. Set on a narrow street behind the eastern edge of Gustavia's harbor, the place is open Monday through Saturday from 7am to 7pm, Sunday from 7am to 1pm. American Express, MasterCard, and Visa are accepted.

pesto and homemade croutons. Other examples include spaghetti with squid ink and eggplant, ravioli stuffed with spiny crayfish meat, *saltimbocca* (veal and ham) alla Romana, an unusual version of spaghetti *en papillote* (cooked in parchment paper) with fresh vegetable sauce, and one of our personal favorites, chicken breast with rosemary potatoes. There's a rotating choice of unusual pizzas as well, including versions that feature asparagus or freshwater crayfish with parsley. Desserts usually include a homemade tiramisu.

In Le Village St-Jean hotel, St-Jean Hill. ℂ 590/27-70-67. Reservations required. Main courses 16€–30€ ($20–$38). AE, MC, V. Thurs–Tues 6:30–10:30pm.

AT MORNE LURIN

Santa Fe AMERICAN/FRENCH/CREOLE   Set inland atop one of the highest points on the island, this burger house and sports bar occupies a enviable niche with the island's English-speaking clientele. Its wide-screen TVs allow as many as 450 fans to watch events like the Super Bowl. After the hurricanes of 1995, Santa Fe's roof, wraparound decks, and bar tops were completely rebuilt of teakwood, and a more nautical flair was introduced. You can take in the view of the surrounding landscapes while enjoying one of the well-recommended hamburgers or steak, shrimp, or barbecued-chicken dishes. This place has earned a reputation for its burgers and fresh-made fries, which some compare to the best available in the United States. You can also order more substantial dishes like lobster medallions in Creole sauce or the grilled catch of the day.

Morne Lurin. ℂ 590/27-61-04. Burgers 4€–8€ ($5–$10); platters 12€–20€ ($15–$25). MC, V. Tues–Sun noon–2pm and 5–10pm.

Wine and Dinner Club 𝄐𝄐 *Finds* FRENCH   Since 1995, Françoise and François Beret have been promoting food that many diners consider an enjoyable departure from the ubiquitous French/Creole. Their dining room, adapted from part of the old plantation that stood here, makes a point of flavoring many dishes with spices not usually seen in the French repertoire. Exact components change frequently but might include a crisp fried goat or a carpaccio of tuna. Refined and sunny tastes appear in such dishes as crayfish with a warm mango-flavored vinaigrette or a brochette of magret of duckling with roasted pineapple. For something truly divine, order the kumquat soufflé. The food is as cerebral as it is satisfying. The wine, the service, and the quality of ingredients used in the dishes presented are top-notch.

In the François Plantation, Colombier. ℂ 590/29-80-22. Reservations required. Main courses 12€–32€ ($15–$40). AE, MC, V. Daily 5–10pm. Closed May 31–Oct 30.

IN THE GRANDE SALINE BEACH AREA

Le Tamarin 𝄐 FRENCH/CREOLE   One of the island's genuinely offbeat restaurants is Le Tamarin, a deliberately informal bistro that caters to a clientele from the nearby Plage de Saline. It's isolated amid rocky hills and forests east of Gustavia, in a low-slung cottage whose eaves are accented with gingerbread. Inside, a teak-and-bamboo motif prevails. Lunch is the more popular and animated meal here, with most customers dining in T-shirts and bathing suits. If you have to wait, you can order an aperitif in one of the hammocks stretched under a tamarind tree. The menu focuses on light, summery meals that go well with the streaming sunlight and tropical heat. Examples include gazpacho, Cajun-style tuna with Creole sauce and baby vegetables, a carpaccio of fish that includes very fresh portions of marinated salmon and tuna, and chicken roasted with lemon and ginger. There's a broadly based wine list, plus a chocolate cake dessert specialty that appeals to dyed-in-the-wool chocoholics. Service can be erratic, but if you're in a rush, you shouldn't be here. It's the perfect place for a lazy afternoon on the beach.

Plage de Saline. ⓒ 590/27-72-12. Reservations required for dinner. Main courses 25€–35€ ($31–$44). AE, MC, V. Nov 1–May 15 daily noon–5pm, Fri–Sun 7–9:30pm. Closed May 16–Oct 31.

IN THE GRAND CUL-DE-SAC BEACH AREA

Bartoloméo ⚜ FRENCH/MEDITERRANEAN   Although this deluxe dining choice is at one of the island's most exclusive and expensive hotels, Bartoloméo works hard to be unthreatening, informally sophisticated, and gracefully upscale. A pianist plays soothing music while diners choose from a frequently changing menu. Appetizers are generally a delight, including on our last visit duck foie gras with caramelized mangoes and a hint of balsamic vinegar. Main courses are prepared with skill and flair, as evidenced by the Chilean sea bass with ratatouille or magret of duckling with orange sauce; Chinese-style sole with ginger; and filet of lamb with hummus and couscous grains. Wednesday features a sweeping array of cold antipasti, and the chef will prepare any pasta you want from an artfully arranged display of seafoods, meats, herbs, wines, and cream.

In the Hôtel Guanahani, Grand Cul-de-Sac. ⓒ 590/27-66-60. Reservations required, especially for nonguests. Main courses 35€–55€ ($44–$69). AE, DC, MC, V. Daily 7–11pm. Closed Sept.

Club Lafayette FRENCH/INTERNATIONAL   This is no fast-food beach joint. Lunching in the sun here, at a cove on the eastern end of the island, is like taking a meal at your own private beach club—and a very expensive one at that. After a dip in the ocean or pool, you can order a Planter's Punch in the shade of a sea grape, and later proceed to lunch itself. You might begin with a *tarte fine aux tomates, mozzarelle, et herbes de Provence* that's lighter and more flavorful than most pizzas. (The congenial owners and chefs, Toulouse-born Nadine and Georges Labau, would be horrified to hear it compared to a pizza.) There's also warm foie gras served with apples; veal with mushroom sauce; lobster served with basil-flavored pasta; Chinese mahimahi in ginger, soy, and sesame oil; and one of the best meal-size king crab salads on the island. Desserts include everything from simple, refreshing citrus-flavored sherbet to rich, crisp (and definitely fattening) *croustillant au chocolate* (phyllo dough filled with chocolate).

Grand Cul-de-Sac. ⓒ 590/27-62-51. Reservations recommended. Main courses 35€–65€ ($44–$81). AE, MC, V. Daily noon–4pm. Closed May–Oct.

IN VITET

Hostellerie des Trois Forces ⚜ *Finds* FRENCH/CREOLE/VEGETARIAN Isolated from the bulk of St. Barts's tourism, this restaurant lies midway up the island's highest mountain (Morne Vitet). The place has a resident astrologer, French provincial decor, terraces accented with gingerbread, and food that won its owner/chef an award from France's prestigious *Confrérie de la Marmite d'Or* in 1995. Although the same menu is available throughout the day and evening, dinners are more formal than lunches, and might include quenneles of fish, crayfish grilled over charcoal and served with a basil-flavored butter, filet of beef in pepper sauce, or magret of duckling with red berries and ginger. "Each dish takes time," in the words of the owner, as it's prepared fresh. Count on a leisurely meal and a well-informed host who has spent years studying astrology.

Vitet. ⓒ 590/27-61-25. Reservations required. Main courses 31€–52€ ($39–$65); fixed-price menu 41€ ($51). AE, MC, V. Mon–Sat noon–3pm and 6–10:30pm.

IN THE PUBLIC BEACH AREA

Maya's 👨 *Finds* CREOLE/THAI/FRENCH This is the most surprising restaurant on St. Barts, thanks to its artful simplicity and glamorous clients. This much-rebuilt Antillean house with almost no architectural charm attracts crowds of luminaries from the worlds of media, fashion, and entertainment. It's the kind of place you might find on Martinique, where its French Creole chef, Maya Beuzelin-Gurley, grew up. Maya's stresses "clean, simple" food with few adornments other than a sprinkling of island herbs and lime juice. You might begin with the salad of tomatoes, arugula, and endive, then follow with grilled fish in sauce *chien* (hot), or a grilled filet of beef. Maya also prepares what she calls "sailor's chicken," a marinated version made with fresh chives, lime juice, and hot peppers. Almost no cream is used in any dish, a fact that makes the place beloved by the fashion models and actors who hang out here. You'll find the place directly west of Gustavia, close to the island's densest collection of factories and warehouses. Views face west and south, ensuring glorious sunset-watching.

Public Beach. ℰ 590/27-75-73. Reservations required. Main courses 30€–36€ ($38–$45). AE, MC, V. Mon–Sat 6–10pm. Closed Sept–Oct.

AT POINTE MILOU

Le Ti St. Barth FRENCH/CARIBBEAN You'll either love or hate this place, depending on how you fit into an environment that manages to be frenetic, stylishly permissive, and Franco-chauvinistic all at the same time. Its personalized style is defined by Thierry de Badereau, who assists his partner, Carole Gruson, in its service rituals and cuisine. From a point near the summit of a low-rise hill, its decor is gussied up with Indian-print upholsteries and low banquettes. After dark, light from blazing torches illuminates an outdoor terrace. Menu items range from the affordable and practical (platters of locally smoked fish, barbecued ribs, grilled beefsteaks and filet mignons, wahoo or red snapper in Creole sauce, grilled filet of duck with cranberry sauce) to the overpriced. An example includes local lobster garnished with truffles—definitely not a bargain. Events that can, however, be a lot of fun here involve erratically scheduled late-night parties, some of them held in honor of the full moon or high tides.

Pointe Milou. ℰ 590/27-97-71. Reservations recommended. Main courses 11€–55€ ($14–$69). AE, MC, V. Daily 7:30pm to around midnight or later, depending on business.

4 Beaches

St. Barts has 14 white-sand beaches. Few are ever crowded, even in winter; all are public and free. Topless sunbathing is quite common. The best known is **St-Jean Beach** 👨👨, which is actually two beaches divided by the Eden Rock promontory. It offers watersports, restaurants, and a few hotels, as well as some shady areas. **Flamands Beach,** to the west, is a very wide, long beach with a few small hotels and some areas shaded by lantana palms. In winter, the surf here can be a bit rough, although it is rarely hazardous. **L'Orient Beach,** on the north shore, is quiet and calm, with shady areas. It's popular with surfers and swimmers who like rolling waves. **Marigot Beach,** also on the north shore, is narrow but offers good swimming and snorkeling.

For a beach with hotels, restaurants, and watersports, **Grand Cul-de-Sac Beach,** on the northeast shore, fits the bill. It's narrow and protected by a reef.

North of the commercial port at Gustavia, the rather unromantic-sounding **Public Beach** is a combination of sand and pebbles. This beach is more popular with boaters than swimmers—it's the location of the St. Barts Sailing School.

There is no more beautiful place on the island, however, to watch the boats at sunset. Located near a small fishing village, **Corossol Beach** offers a typical glimpse of French life, St. Barts style. This is a calm, protected beach, with a charming little **seashell museum.**

South of Gustavia, **Shell Beach** or **Grand Galet** is awash with seashells. Rocky outcroppings protect this beach from strong waves. It's also the scene of many a weekend party.

Gouverneurs Beach, on the southern coast, can be reached by driving south from Gustavia to Lurin. Turn at the Santa Fe restaurant (see "Dining," above) and head down a narrow road. The beach is gorgeous and completely uncrowded, but there's no shade. **Grande Saline Beach,** to the east of Gouverneurs Beach, is reached by driving up the road from the commercial center in St-Jean; a short walk over the sand dune and you're here. Like Gouverneurs Beach, Saline Beach offers some waves but no shade. This beach is full of beautiful sunbathers, all nude.

Colombier Beach is difficult to get to but well worth the effort. It can only be reached by boat or by taking a rugged goat path from Petite Anse past Flamands Beach, a 30-minute walk. Shade and snorkeling are found here, and you can pack a lunch and spend the day. Locals call it Rockefeller's Beach because for many years David Rockefeller owned the property surrounding it.

5 Sports & Other Outdoor Pursuits

FISHING   Anglers are fond of the waters around St. Barts. From March to July, they catch mahimahi; in September, wahoo. Atlantic bonito, barracuda, and marlin also turn up frequently. **Marine Service,** quai du Yacht-Club, Gustavia (© 590/27-70-34), rents a 9m (30-ft.) Phoenix specifically outfitted for big-game fishing. A half-day for four costs 537€ ($671), which includes a captain and first mate. The outfitter also offers shore fishing on a 6m (20-ft.) day cruiser, which tends to remain close to the island's shoreline, searching for tuna, barracuda, and other fish. A full-day excursion, with fishing for up to four, costs 587€ ($734).

SCUBA DIVING   **Marine Service,** quai du Yacht-Club, in Gustavia (© 590/27-70-34), is the most complete watersports facility on the island. It operates from a one-story building set directly on the water at the edge of a marina, on the opposite side of the harbor from the more congested part of Gustavia. Tailoring its dives for both beginners and advanced divers, the outfit is familiar with at least 20 unusual sites scattered at various points offshore. The most interesting of these include the **Grouper,** a remote reef west of St. Barts, close to the rich reef life surrounding the uninhabited cay known as Ile Forchue. The island has only one relatively safe wreck dive, the rusting hulk of *Kayali,* a trawler that sank offshore in 1994. Set in deep waters, it's recommended only for experienced divers. A resort course, including two open-water dives, costs 90€ ($113). A "scuba review," for certified divers who are out of practice, goes for 65€ ($81), while a one-tank dive for certified divers begins at 50€ ($63). Multidive packages are available.

SNORKELING   You can test your luck at hundreds of points offshore, simply by donning a mask, fins, and a snorkel. **Marine Services,** quai du Yacht-Club, Gustavia (© 590/27-70-34), runs daily snorkeling expeditions. A 7-hour excursion (9am–4pm), including a full French-style picnic, all equipment, and exploration of two separate snorkeling sites, costs 98€ ($123). They can also rent you snorkeling gear and tell you where to go on your own.

WINDSURFING Windsurfing is one of the most popular sports here. Try **Wind Wave Power,** Grand Cul-de-Sac (© **590/27-82-57**), open daily from 9:30am to 5pm. Windsurfing costs 25€ ($31) per hour, and professional instructors are on hand.

6 Shopping

You don't pay any duty on St. Barts, so it's a good place to buy liquor and French perfumes, at some of the lowest prices in the Caribbean—often cheaper than in France itself. You'll find good buys in sportswear, crystal, porcelain, watches, and other luxuries. The only trouble is that selections are limited. If you're in the market for **island crafts,** try to find the fine straw hats St. Bartians like to wear. You may also see some interesting block-printed resort clothing in cotton.

Diamond Genesis/Kornerupine, 12 rue du General-de-Gaulle/Les Suites du Roi-Oskar-II (© **590/27-66-94**), a well-respected gold, gemstone, and diamond shop, maintains an inventory of designs strongly influenced by European tastes. Although the prices can go as high as 65,000€ ($81,250), a particularly appealing and more affordable bestseller is an 18-karat-gold depiction of St. Barts, which sells for around 30€ ($38). It's one of the few shops on the island where jewelry is handcrafted on the premises. You can also peruse the selection of watches by Jaeger Lecoultre, available only through this store, as well as Breitling, Chanel, and Tag Heuer.

For handcrafts, **Made in St-Barth,** Villa Creole (© **590/27-56-57**), is the best place to shop. The women of the hamlet of Corossol sell their intricate straw work, including those ever-so-fashionable wide-brim beach hats at this outlet. Other crafts include local paintings and decorative ornaments.

Gold Fingers, rue de la France (© **590/27-64-66**), is the largest purveyor of luxury goods on St. Barts. The entire second floor is devoted to perfumes and crystal, the street level to jewelry and watches. Prices are usually 15% to 20% less than equivalent retail goods sold stateside. Ask about sales when you visit.

The elegant, upscale **Le Comptoir du Cigare,** 6 rue du Général-de-Gaulle (© **590/27-50-62**), caters to the December-to-April crowd of villa and yacht owners. It's sheathed in exotic hardwood, and enhanced with a glass-sided, walk-in humidor for the storage of thousands of cigars from Cuba and the Dominican Republic. Smoke the Cubans on the island—it's illegal to bring them back to the United States. There's also a worthy collection of silver ornaments suitable for adorning the desk of a CEO, artisan-quality Panama hats from Ecuador, and the most beautiful collection of cigar boxes and humidors in the Caribbean.

Laurent Eiffel, rue du Général-de-Gaulle (© **590/27-54-02**), is faux fashion. Despite the elegance of this store and the tact of its employees, nothing sold here is original—everything is either "inspired by" or crafted "in imitation of" designer models that usually cost 10 times as much. Look for belts, bags, and accessories that are copies of Versace, Prada, Hermès, Gucci, and Chanel, sold at prices much lower than what you'd pay in Paris.

St. Barts Style, rue Lafayette, near rue du Port (© **590/27-76-17**), offers racks of beachwear by such makers as Jams World and Vicidomine in citrus colors of lemon, lime, grapefruit, and orange, and psychedelic-looking T-shirts from about a dozen different manufacturers.

Sud, Sud, Galerie du Commerce (adjacent to the airport), St-Jean (© **590/27-98-75**), is known for its stylish clothing, both day and evening wear. Most of the inventory is for women, although a selection of swim trunks and

Bermuda shorts are stocked for men. If you're a high-fashion model, or an heiress who's trying to look like one, chances are this boutique will have something that might appeal.

7 St. Barts After Dark

Most visitors consider a French Creole dinner under the stars enough of a nocturnal adventure. Beyond that, there isn't a lot of excitement here.

In Gustavia, the most popular gathering place is **Le Select,** rue de la France (© 590/27-86-87), apparently named after its more famous granddaddy in the Montparnasse section of Paris. It's utterly simple: Tables are set on the gravel in the open-air garden, near the port, and a game of dominoes might be under way as you walk in. You never know who might show up here—perhaps Mick Jagger. Beer begins at 2€ to 4€ ($2.50–$5), and the place is open Monday to Saturday from 10am to 11pm. There is live entertainment weekly. The locals like it a lot; they allow outsiders, but don't necessarily embrace you until they get to know you a bit. If you want to start a rumor and have it travel fast across the island, do so here.

La Cantina, rue du Bord-de-Mer (© 590/27-55-66), is one of the more charming watering holes in Gustavia. It's set along the waterfront, with a decor that includes artifacts from Mexico. The mood is "Cote d'Azur in the 1970s" (before it was ruined by tour operators). The menu is set up like something aboard a cruise ship, and is very, very simple, featuring only sandwiches, salads, and drinks. Come to check out the people and the scenery from this portside perch in the heart of Gustavia. Salads and platters range from 8€ to 21€ ($10–$26); this place opens daily from 7am to 11pm.

Bar de l'Oubli, 5 rue de la Republique (© 590/27-70-06), occupies the most prominent corner in Gustavia, at the intersection of streets that are so well known that most local residents don't even know their names—they refer to it simply as "Centre-Ville." The setting is hip and Gallic, the color scheme is marine blue and white, and the background music might be the Rolling Stones. Sandwiches and salads are served. It's open daily from 7am (when breakfast is served to clients recovering from various stages of their hangovers) to 10 or 11pm, depending on business.

20

St. Eustatius

Called "Statia," this Dutch-held island, a mere 21 sq. km (8-sq.-mile) pinpoint in the Netherlands Antilles, still basks in its 18th-century heritage as the "Golden Rock." One of the true backwaters of the West Indies, it's just awakening to tourism.

You might want to visit first on a day trip from St. Maarten to see if you'd like it for an extended stay. The volcanic, black-sand beaches aren't especially alluring, and as Caribbean islands go, it's rather dull here, with no nightlife. Some pleasant strips of beach exist on the Atlantic side, but the surf is dangerous for swimming.

If you're a hiker or a diver, the outlook on Statia improves considerably. You can hike around the base of the Quill, an extinct volcano on the southern end of the island. Wandering through a tropical forest, you'll encounter wild orchids, philodendron, heliconia, anthurium, fruit trees, ferns, wildlife, and birds, along with the inevitable oleander, hibiscus, and bougainvillea.

The island's reefs are covered with corals and enveloped by marine life. At one dive site, known as Crack in the Wall, or sometimes "the Grand Canyon," pinnacle coral shoots up from the floor of the ocean. Darting among the reefs are barracudas, eagle rays, black-tip sharks, and other large fish.

Statia is 242 km (150 miles) east of Puerto Rico, 61km (38 miles) south of St. Maarten, and 27km (17 miles) southeast of Saba. The two extinct volcanoes, the Quill and "Little Mountain," are linked by a sloping agricultural plain known as De Cultuurvlakte, where yams and sweet potatoes grow.

Overlooking the Caribbean on the western edge of the plain, **Oranjestad (Orange City)** is the capital and the only village, consisting of both an Upper and Lower town, connected by stone-paved, dogleg Fort Road.

Columbus sighted Statia in 1493, on his second voyage, and Jan Snouck claimed the island for the Netherlands in 1640. The island's history was turbulent before it settled down to peaceful slumber under Dutch protection; from 1650 to 1816, Statia changed flags 22 times! Once the trading hub of the Caribbean, Statia was a thriving market, both for goods and for slaves.

Before the American Revolution, the population of Statia did not exceed 1,200, most of whom were slaves engaged in raising sugar cane. When war came and Britain blockaded the North American coast, Europe's trade was diverted to the Caribbean. Dutch neutrality lured many traders, leading to the construction of 2km (1¾ miles) of warehouses in Lower Town. The American revolutionaries obtained gunpowder and ammunition through Statia—perhaps one of the first places anywhere to recognize the United States of America as a new nation.

1 Essentials

VISITOR INFORMATION

On the island, the **Tourist Bureau** is located at 3 Fort Oranjestrat (© **599/ 318-2433**), open Monday through Friday from 8am to noon and 1 to 5pm (4:30 on Fri). The Internet address for Statia is **www.turq.com/statia**.

GETTING THERE

St. Eustatius can be reached from Dutch St. Maarten's Queen Juliana Airport via the 20-seat planes of **Windward Islands Airways International (Winair)** (© **599/545-4237**). The little airline, launched in 1961, has an excellent safety record. Always reconfirm your return passage once you're on Statia. The five flights a day take only 16 minutes to hop the waters to Statia's Franklin Delano Roosevelt Airport (© **599/318-2887**). There are usually three flights a day between Statia and Saba, and two per week between Statia and St. Kitts, but schedules are irregular. To be sure of getting to another island from Statia, you'll want to go to St. Maarten first.

GETTING AROUND

BY TAXI   Taxis meet all incoming flights. Taxi rates are low, probably no more than $3.50 to $5 from the airport to your hotel. On the way to the hotel your driver may offer himself as a guide. If you book a 2- to 3-hour tour (long enough to cover all the sights on Statia), the cost is about $40 per vehicle. To summon a taxi, call **Rainbow Taxis** (© **599/318-2811**) or **Josser Daniel** (© **599/318-2358**).

BY RENTAL CAR   **Rainbow Car Rental** (© **599/318-2811**) or **Walters** (© **599/318-2719**) are your best bets if you want to reserve a car in advance. Drivers must be 21 years old and present a valid license and credit or charge card. Walter's rents both cars and jeeps.

FAST FACTS: St. Eustatius

Banks **First Caribbean National Bank**, Wilhelminastraat, Oranjestad (© **599/318-2392**), the only bank on the island, is open Monday to Friday from 8:30am to 3:30pm. On weekends, most hotels will exchange money. There are no ATMs.

Currency The official unit of currency is the **Netherlands Antilles guilder (NAf)**, at NAf 1.77 to each US$1 (1 Naf = US56¢), but nearly all places will quote you prices in U.S. dollars. *Rates in this chapter are quoted in U.S. dollars.*

Customs There are no Customs duties since the island is a free port.

Documents U.S. and Canadian citizens need proof of citizenship, such as a passport or a birth certificate with a raised seal and a government-authorized photo ID, along with an ongoing ticket. British subjects need valid passports.

Electricity It's 100-volt AC (60 cycles), the same as in the United States.

Emergencies For the police call © **111**, for an ambulance © **140**, in case of fire call © **120**.

Hospital A licensed physician is on duty at the **Queen Beatrix Medical Center, 25** Princessweg, in Oranjestad (© **599/318-2211**).

Language Dutch is the official language, but English is commonly spoken.

Safety Although crime is rare, it's wise to secure your valuables and take the kind of discreet precautions you would anywhere. Don't leave valuables unguarded on the beach.

Taxes & Service Charges There's a $5.65 tax if you're returning to the Dutch-held islands of St. Maarten or Saba; if you're going elsewhere, the tax is $12. Hotels on Statia collect a 7% government tax, plus a 3% turnover tax. Most hotels, guesthouses, and restaurants add a 10% to 15% service charge.

Telephone St. Eustatius maintains a 24-hour-per-day telephone service—and sometimes it takes about that much time to get a call through! To access **AT&T Direct** for calls to the United States from Statia, call © **001-800-872-2881**.

To call Statia from the U.S., dial **011** (the international access code), then **599** (the country code for the Netherlands Antilles), and finally **318** (the area code for Statia) and the four-digit local number. To make a call within Statia, only the four-digit local number is necessary.

Time St. Eustatius operates on Atlantic Standard Time year-round. Between November and March, when it's 6pm in Oranjestad it's 5pm in New York. During daylight saving time (Apr–Oct) the island keeps the same time as the U.S. East Coast.

Water The water here is safe to drink.

Weather The average daytime temperature ranges from 78°F to 82°F (26°C–28°C). The annual rainfall is 45 inches.

2 Accommodations

Don't expect deluxe hotels or high-rises—Statia is strictly for escapists. Guests are sometimes placed in private homes. A 10% to 15% service charge and 7% government tax are added to hotel bills.

Golden Era Hotel   Set directly on the water, this 1960s hotel is clean, serviceable, and comfortable. Twelve units offer full or partial sea views (the most stunning panorama is from no. 205). All accommodations are spacious, with king-size or queen-size beds, although the look is that of a rather dated motel room. Regrettably, the shower-only bathrooms are so tiny that it's hard to maneuver. You can, if you wish, sit on the toilet and wash your face at the same time. Lunch and dinner are served daily in the simply decorated bar and dining room.

Lower Town, Oranjestad, St. Eustatius, N.A. © **800/223-9815** or 599/318-2345. Fax 599/318-2445. goldera@goldenrock.net. 20 units. Winter $85–$100 single, $90–$120 double; off season $75–$85 single, $90–$100 double. AE, DISC, MC, V. **Amenities:** Restaurant; bar; outdoor pool; laundry service. *In room:* A/C, TV, fridge.

Kings Well Resort ⊛   This small resort is the best address on Statia, surpassing The Old Gin House (see below). Set on the Caribbean side of the island, about .8km (½ mile) north of Oranjestad, this secluded choice occupies about .3 hectare

Map legend:
- Venus Bay
- Zeelandia Beach
- ATLANTIC OCEAN
- Jenkins Bay
- Little Mountain
- Concordia Bay
- Zeelandia
- Signal Hill
- Franklin D. Roosevelt Airport
- Compagnie Bay
- Golden Rock
- Lynch Plantation Museum
- Lynch Bay Beach
- Corre Corre Bay
- Orange Beach
- Upper Town
- Oranjestad
- Lower Town
- Fort Oranje
- Crooks Castle Beach
- The Quill
- Caribbean Sea
- Key Bay
- Buccaneers Bay

Golden Era Hotel **3**
Kings Well Resort **1**
The Old Gin House **2**

Airport ✈ Beach ☚ Mountain ▲▲▲

(¾ acre) on an oceanfront cliff, 18m (59 ft.) above the surf. Construction on the hotel started in 1994 and has progressed slowly ever since. If you're looking for a laid-back, escapist vacation, this is your place. (Your nearest neighbors are in the local cemetery.) Most views look to the southwest, ensuring colorful sunsets that tend to be enhanced by drinks served from the bar at the Kings Well Restaurant (see "Dining," below). Just below the hotel is a breeding bay for fish and octopus.

There are no room keys, so don't expect much security. The accommodations are small and rather sparsely furnished, and each is unique. Room 4 contains a waterbed. The rooms in the rear are larger and face the sea, and those in front open onto a shared seaview balcony. Bathrooms are small, with showers only. This resort might not be suitable for very young children, as there is no guard around the pool.

Oranje Bay Rd-1, Oranjestad, St. Eustatius, N.A. © and fax **599/318-2538**. 14 units. Winter $70–$105 double; off season $70–$100 double. Rates include breakfast. DISC, MC, V. **Amenities:** Restaurant; outdoor pool; boating; fishing; babysitting; laundry service. *In room:* Ceiling fans, TV, fridge.

The Old Gin House ⭐

For years the premier resort of Statia, The Old Gin House is a historic landmark. The inn is a faithful reconstruction of an 18th-century building that once housed a cotton gin. The bricks that went into the construction were once used by sailing ships as ballast. Surrounded by tropical gardens, including palms and bougainvillea, the hotel enjoys a central but tranquil location. All the good-size bedrooms are comfortably furnished, with queen-size beds, direct-dial phones, and restored shower-only bathrooms.

Oranjebaai 1, St. Eustatius, N.A. ℂ 599/318-2319. Fax 599/318-2135. www.oldginhouse.com. 18 units. Year-round $135–$165 double; $275 suite. Rates include breakfast. AE, MC, V. **Amenities:** 2 restaurants; 2 bars; outdoor pool; dive shop (across the street); babysitting; laundry service. *In room:* A/C, TV, dataport.

3 Dining

Chinese Bar & Restaurant CHINESE   This place caters to locals and offers standard Chinese-restaurant fare with a bit of local flavor—the curried shrimp, for example. The atmosphere is very laid-back. For instance, even though the terrace isn't set up for dining, you can request to have your table moved there for an alfresco meal. The portions are hearty and range from the typical sweet-and-sour pork and a variety of shrimp dishes to chop suey and chow mein. This is the best place on the island for vegetarian food.

Princessweg, Oranjestad. ℂ 599/318-2389. Main courses $8–$12. No credit cards. Mon–Sat 11am–3pm and 7:30–11pm.

Kings Well Restaurant INTERNATIONAL   The restaurant here is more successful than the simple hotel in which it's housed (see "Accommodations," above). Set about .8km (½ mile) north of Oranjestad, and perched on a cliff about 18m (59 ft.) above the surf, it features an open kitchen and great sunset panoramas. Enjoy a fruity drink from the rustic bar before your meal. Lunches feature deli-style sandwiches and a selection of platters from the dinner menu, which is more elaborate. Dishes might include veal *cordon bleu* (thin slices of ham and Swiss cheese sandwiched between scallops of veal, then breaded and sautéed), fresh lobster, pan-fried grouper or snapper with parsley-butter sauce, plus a few German dishes like Jaeger schnitzel (veal sautéed in burgundy with mushrooms). Finish off with the homemade apple strudel.

Oranje Bay Rd., Oranjestad. ℂ 599/318-2538. Reservations recommended. Lunch platters $6–$12; dinner main courses $10–$20. DISC, MC, V. Daily 6–8:30pm.

L'Etoile CREOLE   Caren Henriquez's simple second-floor restaurant is well known on Statia for its local cuisine, but you won't run into many tourists. Favored main dishes include the ubiquitous "goatwater" (a stew), mountain crab, stewed whelks, tasty spareribs, and Caribbean-style lobster. Caren is also known for her *pastechis*—deep-fried turnovers stuffed with meat. Expect a complete and very filling meal.

6 Van Rheeweg, northeast of Upper Town. ℂ 599/318-2299. Reservations required. Main courses $7–$20. No credit cards. Daily 8am–10pm.

Ocean View Terrace ✦ (Finds) CARIBBEAN/SEAFOOD   This pleasant restaurant is set within a billowing, open-sided tent, inside the courtyard of the government's guesthouse, part of historic Fort Oranje. Diners sit amidst dozens of hanging plants and historical artifacts and get a sweeping view of the sea. Menu items are firmly grounded in local culinary traditions, but usually include well-prepared versions of local seafood, especially dishes made from shrimp and lobster. Specific examples, based on the whim of the chef, might include shrimp in either a garlic- or a curry-flavored sauce; teriyaki fish; a medley of chicken dishes, and if you want to go native, several versions of goat and oxtail, including curried and stewed. Lunches, which include a range of salads and sandwiches, tend to be simpler than the more elaborate food featured at dinner.

In Fort Oranje. ℂ 599/318-2934. Reservations recommended. Lunch main courses $4.50–$8; dinner main courses $16–$27. DISC, MC, V. Mon–Sat 8am–2pm and 6:30–9pm.

The Old Gin House Restaurant ✿ INTERNATIONAL/FRENCH/ASIAN
Escape here for some of the more imaginative, exotic dishes on an island that tends to be devoted to a basic Antillean cuisine. It's a popular spot for divers, who can usually be found at the bar (Mooshay Pub) watching Winston prepare their favorite drinks. This beautiful old bar is in the main building, a former warehouse that once housed sugar, cotton, and indigo. The dining room and kitchen are also here. You can enjoy a candlelit dinner by the pool if the weather cooperates. Fresh lobster appears almost daily on the menu in winter, and the catch of the day, which can be grilled, typically includes red snapper, mahimahi, and kingfish. Fishermen bring their catch right to the door of the kitchen to sell.

Oranjebaai 1. ⓒ 599/318-2319. Reservations required. Main courses $8–$24; 3-course set-price $35–$45. AE, MC, V. Daily 7–10:30am, 11:30am–2pm, and 6:30–9pm.

4 Beaches

Most of the beaches of Statia are small, narrow strips of sand, either volcanic black or a dull mudlike gray. Regrettably, the best beaches are not on the tranquil Caribbean side, but on the turbulent Atlantic side, where the waters are often too rough for swimming.

Beachcombers delight, however, in their search for the fabled **blue-glass beads,** which were manufactured in the 1600s by a Dutch West Indies Company. They were used as money for the trading of such products as tobacco, cotton, rum—and even slaves. These beads, which are real collector's items, are often unearthed after a heavy rainfall or tropical storm.

Orange Beach, also called Smoke Alley Beach, lies on the Caribbean side of the island directly off Lower Town. This is one of the small volcanic beaches on the southwest shore, with beige or black sands and waters suitable for a leisurely swim. You virtually have the beach to yourself until late afternoon, when locals start to arrive for a dip.

Also on the leeward, or Caribbean, side is **Crooks Castle Beach,** south of Oranjestad. The waters, filled with giant yellow sea fans, sea whips, and pillar coral, attract snorkelers, while beachcombers are drawn to the many blue beads that have been unearthed here.

On the southeast Atlantic side of the island, **Corre Corre Bay** has a strip of dark golden sand. It's about half an hour down Mountain Road and is worth the trip to get here, although the waters are often too churned up for comfortable swimming. Two bends north of this beach, the light-brown-sand **Lynch Bay Beach** is more sheltered from the wild swells of the Atlantic. Nonetheless, the surf here is still almost always rough, plus there's a dangerous undertow; this beach is better for sunbathing than swimming.

Also on the Atlantic side, **Zeelandia Beach** is 3km (2 miles) long and filled with dark, dark beige and volcanic-black sand. One tourist promotion speaks of its "exciting Atlantic surf and invigorating trade winds," but fails to warn of the dangerous undertow. Only one small, designated section is safe for swimming. The beach is suitable, however, for wading, hiking, and sunbathing. It's almost always deserted.

5 Sports & Other Outdoor Pursuits

HIKING   Hiking is the most popular outdoor activity on the island. Those with enough stamina can climb the slopes of the **Quill,** the highest point on Statia. Its extinct volcanic cone harbors a crater filled with a dense tropical rainforest, containing towering kapok trees and a dozen or more species of wild

---

Moments **Catching Crabs Means Something Different Here**

We're perfectly serious: If you're interested, you can join Statians in a crab hunt. The Quill's crater is the breeding ground for these large crustaceans. At night they emerge from their holes to forage, and that's when they're caught. Either with flashlights or relying on moonlight, crab hunters climb the Quill, catch a crab, and take the local delicacy home to prepare stuffed crab-back. Your hotel can usually hook you up with this activity.

---

orchids, some quite rare. It's also home to at least 50 species of bird life, including the rare blue pigeon, known to frequent the breadfruit and cottonwood trees here. Islanders once grew cocoa, coffee, and cinnamon in the crater's soil, but today bananas are the only crop. The **tourist office** (© 599/318-2433) will supply you with a list of a dozen trails of varying degrees of difficulty and can also arrange for a guide. You'll have to negotiate the fee; it's usually $10 and up.

WATERSPORTS **Dive Statia** is a full PADI diving center on Fishermen's Beach in Lower Town (© 599/318-2435), offering everything from beginning instruction to dive master certification, costing $350. Its professional staff guides divers of all experience levels to spectacular walls, untouched coral reefs, and historic shipwrecks. Dive Statia offers one- and two-tank boat dives, costing $40 to $75. Equipment is $10 extra. Night dives and snorkel trips are also available.

Statia is mostly a divers' island, but there is some decent **snorkeling** on the Caribbean side. You can explore the remnants of an 18th-century man-of-war and the walls of warehouses, taverns, and ships that sank below the surface of Oranje Bay more than 200 years ago. The best place to go is **Crooks Castle Beach,** southwest of Lower Town. Any dive shop can rent you snorkeling gear.

Water-skiing is expensive on Statia. **Dive Statia,** Bay Road, Lower Town (© 599/318-2435), will hook you up for around $90 per hour.

TENNIS Statia maintains tennis courts at the **Community Center,** Rosemary Laan in Upper Town (© 599/318-2249), costing only $2 per hour. You'll have to bring your own rackets and balls, but there is a changing room.

6 Exploring the Island

Oranjestad stands on a cliff looking out on a beach and the island's calm anchorage, where in the 18th century you might have seen 200 vessels offshore. **Fort Oranje** was built in 1636 and restored in honor of the U.S. bicentennial celebration of 1976. Perched atop the cliffs, its terraced rampart is lined with the old cannons.

St. Eustatius Historical Foundation Museum, Upper Town (© 599/318-2288), is also called the Donker House in honor of its former tenant, Simon Donker. After British Admiral Rodney sacked Statia for cooperating with the United States, he installed his own headquarters here. Today, the 18th-century house and museum stands in a garden, with a 20th-century wing crafted from 17th-century bricks. There are exhibits on the process of sugar refining and shipping and commerce, a section devoted to the pre-Columbian period, archaeological artifacts from the colonial period, and a pair of beautiful rooms furnished with 18th-century antiques. In the annex is a massive piece of needlework by

American Catherine Mary Williams, showing the flowers of Statia. The museum is open Monday to Friday from 9am to 5pm, and Saturday and Sunday from 9am to noon; admission is $2 for adults, $1 for children.

A few steps away, a cluster of 18th-century buildings surrounding a quiet courtyard is called **Three Widows' Corner.**

Nearby are the ruins of the first **Dutch Reformed church,** on Kerkweg ("Church Way"). To reach it, turn west from Three Widows' Corner onto Kerkweg. Tilting headstones record the names of the characters in the island's past. The St. Eustatius Historical Foundation recently completed restoration of the church. Visitors may climb to the top level of the tower and see the bay as lookouts did many years before.

Statia once had a large colony of Jewish traders, and you can explore the ruins of **Honen Dalim,** the second oldest Jewish synagogue in the Western Hemisphere. Built around 1740 and damaged by a hurricane in 1772, the synagogue stands beside Synagogpad, a narrow lane whose entrance faces Madam Theatre on the square.

The walls of a *mikvah* (ritual bath) rise beside the **Jewish burial ground** on the edge of town. Most poignant is the memorial of David Haim Hezeciah de Lion, who died in 1760 at the age of 2 years, 8 months, 26 days; carved into the baroque surface is an angel releasing a tiny songbird from its cage.

You can also visit **Lynch Plantation Museum** at Lynch Bay (© **599/318-2338**), but you'll have to call to arrange a tour. Donations are accepted; otherwise, admission is free. Locals still call this place the Berkel Family Plantation, although today it's a museum depicting life on Statia a century ago, through antiques, fishing and farming equipment, pictures, and old Bibles. Usually Ismael Berkel is on hand to show you around. This is still very much a residence, rather than some dead, dull museum.

7 Shopping

At **Mazinga Giftshop,** Fort Oranje Straat, Upper Town (© **599/318-2245**), you'll find an array of souvenirs—T-shirts, liquor, costume jewelry, 14-karat-gold jewelry, cards, drugstore items, beachwear, office supplies, children's books, handbags, and paperback romances. You may have seen more exciting stores in your life, but this is without parallel for Statia. You can buy books, magazines, office supplies and stationery at the **Paper Corner,** Van Tonningenweg, Upper Town (© **599/318-2208**).

8 St. Eustatius After Dark

As for after-dark fun on Statia, Las Vegas it ain't. Nightlife pickings here are among the slimmest in the Caribbean. Weekends are the best—maybe the only—time to go out. **Smoke Alley Bar & Grill,** Lower Town, Gallows Bay (© **599/318-2002**), is an open-air beach bar with live music on Friday and Saturday nights. Open Monday to Saturday 6 to 10pm. **The Stone Oven,** 16A Feaschweg, Upper Town, Oranjestad (© **599/318-2543**), often has dancing and local bands on weekends; you can also enjoy simple West Indian fare. For local flavor, try **Cool Corner** (© **599/318-2523**), across from the St. Eustatius Historical Foundation Museum, in the center of town. Another option is **Largo Heights,** Chapel Piece (© **599/318-2811**).

21

St. Kitts & Nevis

The two islands of St. Kitts and Nevis (*Nee*-vis) were British possessions until 1983, when they became a tiny, independent two-island nation (a ministate, really), complete with U.N. membership. But British traditions remain in evidence. Cricket is still fiercely popular, and motorists drive on the left.

For decades St. Kitts and Nevis slumbered as backwaters of the Caribbean. The country's economy was dependent entirely on sugar cane, making it especially vulnerable to the ravages of hurricanes (Hurricane Hugo, in 1990, caused particularly serious damage). But in recent years, tourists, especially celebrities, have discovered the islands' average year-round temperature of 79°F (26°C), low humidity, white-sand beaches, and unspoiled natural beauty.

This doesn't mean that St. Kitts and Nevis are playgrounds for the rich and famous—not yet. But people who can go anywhere have been spotted here in the near past: Oprah Winfrey, Sylvester Stallone, Danny Glover, Robert De Niro, Michael J. Fox, and Gerald and Betty Ford, to name a few.

Of the two islands, Nevis is the sleepier. It has fewer direct flights from North America, fewer luxury hotels, and almost no nightlife to speak of. It also has a reputation as being a money-laundering haven for drug traffickers and other suspicious businesses (despite righteous denials by Nevis officials). The tiny island has some 9,000 offshore businesses—about one business per inhabitant—registered and operating under strict secrecy laws.

In fact, disagreements about controls over offshore banking activities triggered a rift between the two islands that almost led to Nevis's secession. In the most recent referendum on the issue, in 1998, a majority of Nevisians (but not the two-thirds required) voted for independence from St. Kitts.

1 St. Kitts & Nevis Essentials

VISITOR INFORMATION

Information is available from the tourist board's **stateside** offices at 414 E. 75th St., New York, NY 10021 (© **800/582-6208** or 212/535-1234).

In **Canada,** an office is located at 133 Richmond St., Suite 311, Toronto, ON, M5H 2L3 (© **416/368-6707**), and in the **United Kingdom** at 10 Kensington Court, London, W8 5DL (© **020/7376-0881**).

The website for both St. Kitts and Nevis is **www.stkittsnevis.com**.

FAST FACTS: St. Kitts & Nevis

Banks The most convenient bank, with ATM services, is the **St. Kitts-Nevis-Anguilla National Bank** on Central Street in Basseterre (© **869/465-2204**).

Currency The local currency is the **Eastern Caribbean dollar (EC$)**, pegged at $2.70 to the U.S. dollar (EC$1 = US37¢). Many prices, however, including those of hotels, are quoted in U.S. dollars. *Unless otherwise specified, rates in this chapter are quoted in U.S. dollars.* Always determine which "dollar" locals are talking about.

Customs You are allowed in duty-free with your personal belongings. Sometimes luggage is subjected to a drug check. If you clear customs in one of the islands, you don't have to do it again if you visit the other.

Documents U.S. and Canadian citizens can enter with proof of citizenship, such as a passport or birth certificate with a raised seal accompanied by a government-issued photo ID. British subjects need a passport, but not a visa.

Electricity Electricity on St. Kitts is 220-volt AC (60 cycles), so you'll need an adapter and a transformer for U.S.-made appliances. However, most hotels on the islands have outlets that will accept North American appliances. Check with your hotel to see if it has converted its voltage and outlets.

Emergencies Dial © **911** for emergencies.

Language English is the language of both islands, and it is spoken with a decided West Indian lilt; patois is commonly spoken as well.

Safety This is still a fairly safe place to travel. Most crimes against tourists—and there aren't a lot—are robberies on Conaree Beach on St. Kitts, so exercise the usual precautions. It's wise to safeguard your valuables, and women should not go jogging alone along deserted roads. Crime is rare on Nevis.

Taxes The government imposes a 7% tax on rooms and meals, plus another US$18 airport departure tax. (You don't pay the departure tax when you travel between the islands.)

Telephone The area code for St. Kitts and Nevis is **869**. You can make calls to or from the United States as you would for any other area code in North America. To access **AT&T Direct**, call © **800/225-5288** and to reach **MCI** dial © **800/888-8000**.

Time St. Kitts and Nevis are on Atlantic Standard Time year-round. This means that in winter, when it's 6am in Basseterre, it's 5am in New York. When the United States goes on daylight savings time, St. Kitts and Nevis are on the same time as the East Coast of the United States.

Tipping Most hotels and restaurants add a service charge of 10% to cover tipping. If not, tip 10% to 15%.

Water The water on St. Kitts and Nevis is so good that Baron de Rothschild's chemists selected St. Kitts as their only site in the Caribbean to distill and produce CSR (Cane Sugar Rothschild), a pure sugar-cane liqueur. In the

1700s, Lord Nelson regularly brought his fleet to Nevis just to collect water, and Nevis still boasts of having Nelson spring water.

Weather St. Kitts and Nevis are tropical, and the warm climate is tempered by the trade winds. The average air temperature is 79°F (26°C); the average water temperature, 80°F (27°C). Dry, mild weather is usually experienced from November to April; May to October it's hotter and rainier.

2 St. Kitts

St. Kitts has become a resort mecca in recent years. Its major crop is sugar, a tradition dating from the 17th century. But tourism may overwhelm it in the years to come, as its southeastern peninsula, site of the best white-sand beaches, has been set aside for massive resort development. Most of the island's other beaches are of gray or black volcanic sand.

The Caribs, the early settlers, called the island Liamuiga, or "fertile isle." Its mountain ranges reach up to nearly 1,200m (4,000 ft.), and its interior contains virgin rainforests, alive with hummingbirds and wild green vervet monkeys. The monkeys were brought in as pets by the early French settlers but were set free when the British took control of the island in 1783. These native African animals have proliferated and can be seen at the Estridge Estate Behavioral Research Institute. The British brought in mongooses to control rats in the sugar-cane fields, only to discover that the predators slept during the rats' most active forays. Wild deer are found in the mountains.

The capital of St. Kitts, **Basseterre**, lies on the Caribbean shore near the southern end of the island, about 2km (1¼ miles) from the airport. With its white colonial houses with toothpick balconies, it looks like a Hollywood version of a West Indian port.

ST. KITTS ESSENTIALS
GETTING THERE   There is only one nonstop flight a week to St. Kitts from North America: **US Airways** (© **800/428-4322;** www.usairways.com) flies every Saturday from Philadelphia to St. Kitts. Typically you have to connect through Antigua, St. Maarten, or Puerto Rico. **American Airlines** (© **800/ 433-7300** in the U.S.; www.aa.com) has dozens of daily flights to San Juan. From here, American's commuter partner, **American Eagle,** makes four daily nonstop flights into St. Kitts.

Windward Islands Airways International (known to everybody as **Winair;** © **800/634-4907** in the U.S., or 869/465-8010 in St. Kitts; www.fly-winair.com) flies to St. Kitts from St. Maarten. The Antigua-based carrier, **LIAT**

Moments Sweet Treat
At some point during your visit you should eat sugar directly from the cane—any farmer will sell you a huge stalk. Ask your taxi driver to take you to one of the sugar-cane plantations that dot the island. Strip off the hard exterior of the stalk, bite into it, chew on the tasty reeds, and swallow the juice. It's best with a glass of rum.

Airport ✈ Beach ⚑ Ferry Route --- Mountain ▲▲

0 — 5 Miles
0 — 5 Kilometers

Dieppe Bay

St. Paul's

Sandy Bay

Sadlers

Newton Ground

ATLANTIC OCEAN

Ottle

Hermitage Bay

Mount Liamuiga

Sandy Point Town

Brimstone Hill Fortress

Cayon

Keys

Half-Way Tree

Middle Island

Carib Rock Drawings

Old Road Town

St. Peter's

Challengers

Conaree Bay

Basseterre

North Frigate Bay

North Friar's Bay

Frigate Bay

Turtle Beach

South Friar's Bay

Sand Bank Bay

White House Bay

Great Salt Pond

Booby Shoals

St. Anthony's Peak

Caribbean Sea

Cockleshell Bay

Banana Bay

Nag's Head

To Nevis ↘

Bird Rock Beach Hotel **6**
Coconut Beach Club **8**
Frigate Bay Resort **7**
Golden Lemon Inn & Villas **2**
Morgan Heights Condo Resort **4**
Ocean Terrace Inn **5**
Ottley's Plantation Inn **3**
Rawlins Plantation Inn **1**
St. Kitts Marriott Royal Beach
  Resort & Spa **9**

(© **868/624-4727;** www.liatairline.com), flies to St. Kitts from Antigua, San Juan, and St. Maarten. Winair has two daily flights between Nevis and St. Kitts.

Air Canada (© **514/422-5000** in Canada, or 888/247-2262 in the U.S.; www.aircanada.ca) flies from Toronto to Antigua, and **British Airways** (© **800/ 247-9297** in the U.S.; www.britishairways.com) flies from London to Antigua. From Antigua, you can make connections on LIAT or Winair (see above).

You can also use the **interisland ferry service** between St. Kitts and Nevis. Ferry schedules are subject to change without notice, and follow no obvious patterns. The **MV *Sea Hustler*** makes at least three trips per day, and sometimes four. There is usually one morning crossing and one afternoon crossing from each island. Travel time is 1 hour. The **MV *Caribe Queen*** makes the crossing in 45 minutes, but it doesn't run on Thursdays or Sundays. Its schedule is also different every day—it generally makes one round-trip in the morning (usually 7 or 7:30am) and at least one trip each way in the afternoon (at 4, 5, or 6pm, depending on the island). The fare is US$8 round-trip for either ferry. The best vessel of all is the air-conditioned 110-passenger ferry **MV *Caribe Breeze,*** which makes the run in only 30 minutes. The regular fare is US$12 per passenger one-way (or US$15 in first class). There are only two runs per day on Thursday and Sunday but more frequent runs on other days, depending on demand. Contact the tourist office on either island for exact schedules.

> **Fun Fact Party Times in St. Kitts**
>
> Carnival in St. Kitts is celebrated not in the days leading up to Ash Wednesday, but from Christmas Eve to January 2. The festivities include parties, dancing, talent shows, and the crowning of the Carnival Queen. The final day of the celebration is known as "Last Lap," and features a repeat of many of the activities, including a multitude of bands jamming in the streets of Basseterre.
>
> Another popular party time is the **St. Kitts Music Festival,** held the last weekend in June (Thurs–Sun). The Soca/Calypso night is usually the festival's opening event, and its most popular. You can also hear reggae, jazz, rhythm and blues, and gospel performances over the 4 days. For more information, call the Department of Tourism at © **869/465-1999.**

GETTING AROUND   Since most **taxi** drivers are also guides, this is the best means of getting around. You don't even have to find a driver at the airport— one will find you. Drivers also wait outside the major hotels. First, however, you must agree on the price, since taxis aren't metered. Also, ask if the rates quoted to you are in U.S. or Eastern Caribbean dollars. The fare from the airport to Basseterre is about EC$18 (US$6.65); to Sandy Point, EC$40 (US$15) and up. For more information, call the **St. Kitts Taxi Association** (© **869/465-8487**).

Avis, South Independence Square, Bay Road (© **800/331-1212** in the U.S., or 869/465-6507), charges from US$40 to US$80 per day, US$240 to US$480 per week, plus US$15 per day for collision damage, with a US$950 deductible and a US$1.50 per day surcharge. Tax is 5% extra. The company offers free delivery service to either the airport or to any of the island's hotels; drivers must be between ages 25 and 75. Avis will arrange for a rental exchange if you also go to Nevis.

Delisle Walwyn & Co., Liverpool Row, Basseterre (© **869/465-8449**), is a local company offering cars and jeeps starting at US$30 to US$60 per day. Tax and insurance are extra (US$10 per day for collision damage, US$750 deductible). This might be your best deal on the island. You can also check the other local company: **G&L** (© **869/466-8040**), located at the airport.

Remember: Driving is on the left! You'll need a local driver's license, which can be obtained at the **Traffic Department,** on Cayon Street in Basseterre, for US$25. Usually a member of the staff at your car-rental agency will drive you to the Traffic Department to get one.

FAST FACTS   **Banks** on St. Kitts are open Monday to Thursday from 8am to 2pm and on Friday from 8am to 4pm. You can place **international telephone calls,** including collect calls, at **Cable and Wireless,** Cayon Street, Basseterre (© **869/465-1000**), Monday to Friday from 8am to 5pm, Saturday from 8am to noon.

The most centrally located pharmacy is **City Drug,** Fort Street in Basseterre (© **869/465-2156**), open Monday to Wednesday and Friday to Saturday from 8am to 7pm, Thursday from 8am to 5pm, and Sunday from 8 to 11am.

There's a 24-hour **emergency room** in Basseterre at **Joseph N. France General Hospital,** Buckley's Site (© **869/465-2551**).

The **St. Kitts tourist board** operates at Pelican Mall, Bay Road in Basseterre (© **869/465-4040**). It's open Monday through Friday from 7am to 6pm.

ACCOMMODATIONS
VERY EXPENSIVE

Golden Lemon Inn & Villas ☆☆☆   Sophisticated and elegant describe both the Golden Lemon and its clientele. Arthur Leaman, one-time decorating editor of *House & Garden* magazine, used his taste and background to create a hotel of great charm in this once-busy shipping port. The 1610 French manor house with an 18th-century Georgian upper story is set back from a coconut grove and a black volcanic-sand beach, on the northwest coast of St. Kitts. Flanking the great house are the Lemon Court and Lemon Grove Condominiums, where you can rent luxuriously furnished suites surrounded by manicured gardens; most have private pools.

The spacious rooms are furnished with antiques and always contain fresh flowers, but are not air-conditioned. Bedrooms were recently redecorated with new fabrics, rugs, and accessories. Many beds are raised four-posters draped in mosquito netting in the old plantation style; each is equipped with fine linen. Most of the tiled bathrooms are huge; they contain deluxe toiletries, shower/tub combinations, and dressing areas. The larger villas even have sunken tubs, kitchens, and dishwashers. The Golden Lemon restaurant serves fine Continental and Caribbean cuisine (see "Dining," below).

Dieppe Bay, St. Kitts, W.I. ℂ 800/633-7411 in the U.S., or 869/465-7260. Fax 869/465-4019. www.golden lemon.com. 26 units. Winter US$325–US$425 double, US$495–US$820 suite; off season US$240–US$325 double, US$420–US$685 suite. Rates include American breakfast. Extra person US$145. 4-night minimum stay required in winter. Honeymoon packages available. AE, MC, V. Closed Sept to mid-Oct. Children 18 and under not usually accepted. **Amenities:** Restaurant; outdoor pool; tennis court; catamarans; scuba diving; snorkeling; horseback riding; island tours; car rental; room service (7am–midnight); massage; laundry; rooms for those with limited mobility. *In room:* A/C (in 2); ceiling fan, dataport, kitchenette, fridge, hair dryer.

Ottley's Plantation Inn ☆☆☆   This is the island's finest place to stay, outdoing even the more mellow and time-seasoned Golden Lemon. Ten kilometers (6¼ miles) north of the airport, and near a rainforest, it occupies a 14-hectare (35-acre) site on a former 17th-century West Indian plantation. Those seeking charm and tranquillity will like the nine rooms in an 1832 great house. Other units are divided among three cottages, with air-conditioning and overhead fans. In winter 1997, two cottages with four new suites were constructed, each with modern amenities, including private pools and panoramic views. The suites are truly deluxe, with their own Jacuzzis. Rooms are elegantly appointed and very spacious with queen- or king-size beds; the bathrooms have shower/tub combinations and deluxe toiletries. The inn also rents a grand villa with a large wraparound patio and a private plunge pool with a full kitchen and sitting area. The villa can be rented as a two-bedroom unit for up to four guests for US$810 year-round, or as a three-bedroom unit for up to six guests for US$1,080.

The plantation operates one of the best restaurants on the island, The Royal Palm (see "Dining," below), which serves a Sunday champagne brunch.

Ottley's Village (P.O. Box 345), St. Kitts, W.I. ℂ 800/772-3039 in the U.S., or 869/465-7234. Fax 869/465-4760. www.ottleys.com. 24 units. Winter US$280–US$475 double, US$730 suite; off season US$225–US$365 double, US$530 suite. US$65 per person daily for half-board (breakfast and dinner). Wedding, honeymoon, and other packages available. AE, DISC, MC, V. Children under 10 discouraged. **Amenities:** Restaurant; 2 bars; outdoor pool; tennis court; croquet; spa; bikes; shuttle to beach; room service (8am–9pm); massage; babysitting; laundry service. *In room:* A/C, ceiling fans, TV (by advance request), dataport, minibar, beverage maker, hair dryer, iron/ironing board, safe.

Rawlins Plantation Inn ☆☆   This hotel near Dieppe Bay is situated among the remains of a muscovado sugar factory on the northeast coast, with a good sandy beach just a short drive away. The rather isolated former plantation is 105m (344 ft.) above sea level and enjoys cool breezes from both ocean and mountains. Behind the 5 hectares (12 acres) of manicured grounds, the land rises to a rainforest and Mount Liamuiga.

A 17th-century windmill has been converted into a charming accommodation, complete with private bathroom and sitting room; the boiling houses, formerly used to distill cauldrons of molasses, have been turned into a cool courtyard, where guests dine amid flowers and tropical birds. Other accommodations are in pleasantly decorated cottages equipped with modern facilities. There's no air-conditioning, but ceiling fans and cross-ventilation keep the place comfortable. Each unit, generous in size, is decorated in a Caribbean country-house style with antiques, stone or white walls, floral prints, local art, and rattan furnishings. Many bedrooms have mahogany four-posters; all have fine linen. Bathrooms are superb, with plenty of shelf space, toiletries, and shower/tub combinations.

Mount Pleasant (P.O. Box 340), St. Kitts, W.I. ⓒ **800/346-5358** in the U.S., 0208/874-9534 in London, or 869/465-6221. Fax 869/465-4954. www.rawlinsplantation.com. 10 units. Winter US$460 double; off season US$330 double. Rates include breakfast, dinner, afternoon tea, and laundry service. AE, MC, V. Closed Aug–Oct. No children under 12. **Amenities:** Restaurant; bar; outdoor pool; tennis court; croquet; laundry service. *In room:* Ceiling fan, hair dryer, no phone.

EXPENSIVE
St. Kitts Marriott Royal Beach Resort & Spa ★★★ *Kids*   At last St. Kitts has a resort to compete with the swanky Four Seasons Hotel on neighboring Nevis. The sprawling resort evokes the Mediterranean with its tile roofs and lush landscaping. In the center is a replica of Columbus's *Santa Maria,* complete with waterfalls. The location, with its adjacent Royal Beach Casino, is near the narrowest part of St. Kitts, close to Atlantic-fronting beaches. Its 9 hectares (22 acres) include an 18-hole golf course designed by Canadian-born Tom McBroom and one of the largest casinos in the Caribbean Basin. Architectural surprises include a ceiling in the casino that reflects the heavens, the stars, and meteors in electronic patterns.

The decor is self-tabbed as "Euro-Caribbean," with vague references to the Italian Renaissance within its pastel-colored compound of artfully landscaped buildings. Most of the tasteful, comfortable, and superelegant accommodations are within a five-story central core. Bubbling Jacuzzis, a lagoon-shaped pool, sprawling gardens, deluxe bathrooms, and a bevy of restaurants and bars ensure you'll never have to leave the grounds.

858 Frigate Bay Rd., Frigate Bay, St. Kitts, W.I. ⓒ **800/228-9290** in the U.S., or 869/466-1200. Fax 869/466-1201. www.marriott.com. 648 units. Winter US$249 double, US$524–US$674 suite; off season US$129 double, US$359–US$524 suite. AE, DC, DISC, MC, V. **Amenities:** 6 restaurants; 8 bars; 3 outdoor pools; casino; night club; 18-hole golf course; 4 tennis courts; health club; full-service spa; sauna; whirlpool; children's programs; business center; salon; 24-hr. room service; babysitting; laundry service (also self-serve); nonsmoking rooms; rooms for those with limited mobility. *In room:* A/C, TV, dataport, fridge, beverage maker, hair dryer, iron/ironing board, safe.

MODERATE
Bird Rock Beach Hotel   Set on a secluded, half-moon-shaped beach 3km (2 miles) southeast of Basseterre, this small resort is uncomplicated and easy-going. Views from most bedroom balconies are of either the Bay of Basseterre and the capital, or of the water stretching toward Nevis. All units have private patios or balconies and rather bland furniture inspired by the Tropics. Bedrooms

carry out the Caribbean motif with flowery fabrics and paintings of birds. The shower/tub combination bathrooms are small but adequate. Each superior room has one king-size or two double beds, and each studio suite offers a queen-size bed plus a sofa bed and a kitchenette. Apartments have full kitchens.

P.O. Box 227, Basseterre, St. Kitts, W.I. © 800/621-1270 in the U.S., or 869/465-8914. Fax 869/465-1675. www.birdrockbeach.com. 46 units. Winter US$110 double, US$160 studio suite for 2, US$220 2-bedroom apt, US$290 3-bedroom apt; off season US$85 double, US$100 studio suite for 2, US$135 2-bedroom apt, US$180 3-bedroom apt. AE, MC, V. **Amenities:** 2 restaurants; 2 bars; outdoor pool; dive shop; snorkeling; limited room service; laundry service; nonsmoking rooms. *In room:* A/C, TV, dataport, kitchenette (in some), fridge (in some), beverage maker (in some), hair dryer.

Frigate Bay Resort   On a verdant hillside east of Basseterre, Frigate Bay has standard rooms and condo suites administered as hotel units for their absentee owners. The older units are more spacious than the newer accommodations. Rooms are nicely furnished to the taste of the owners and painted in cool colors. Nautical prints, tile floors, flowery prints, and private terraces or balconies make the place alluring. The small shower/tub bathrooms are well maintained. Many units contain fully equipped kitchens with breakfast bars. The central core of the resort has a large pool and a swim-up bar.

Frigate Bay (P.O. Box 137), Basseterre, St. Kitts, W.I. © 869/465-8935. Fax 869/465-7050. www.frigatebay. com. 64 units. Winter double US$105–US$135, US$190–US$295 suite; off season US$85–US$105 double, US$160–US$225 suite. Breakfast and dinner US$50 per person extra. Packages available. AE, DC, MC, V. **Amenities:** Restaurant; swim-up bar; outdoor pool; babysitting; laundry service; nonsmoking rooms; rooms for those with limited mobility. *In room:* A/C, ceiling fans, TV, dataport, kitchenette (in some), fridge, beverage maker, hair dryer, iron/ironing board.

Ocean Terrace Inn ⚄   This inn is affectionately known as the "OTI" by its mainly business clients. If you want to be near Basseterre, it's the best hotel around the port, with oceanfront verandas and a view of the harbor and the capital. It's so compact that a stay here is like a house party on a great liner. Terraced into a landscaped hillside above the edge of Basseterre, the hotel also has gardens and well-kept grounds. All the handsomely decorated rooms have a light, tropical feel and overlook a well-planted terrace. Bedrooms are a wide variety of sizes, and bathrooms, with shower/tub combinations, are small and tidily maintained. The hotel also offers apartments at the Fisherman's Wharf and Village, a few steps from the nearby harbor. These units are filled with most of the comforts of home.

Wigley Ave. (P.O. Box 65), Fortlands, St. Kitts, W.I. © 869/465-2754. Fax 869/465-1057. www.oceanterraceinn. com. 78 units. Winter US$190–US$450 double; off season US$160–US$380 double. Dive, honeymoon, and eco-safari packages available. AE, DC, MC, V. Go west along Basseterre Bay Rd. past the Cenotaph. **Amenities:** 3 restaurants; 4 bars; 3 outdoor pools; fitness center; Jacuzzi; sauna; water-skiing; windsurfing; business center; limited room service; laundry service; nonsmoking rooms. *In room:* A/C, ceiling fans (in some), TV, dataport, kitchenette (in some), fridge, beverage maker, hair dryer, safe.

INEXPENSIVE

Coconut Beach Club 🄺ids   Located at the foot of a green mountain, 5km (3 miles) east of Basseterre, this condo resort is a family favorite. Though short on atmosphere, it's on one of St. Kitts' finest beaches. Naturally, the most sought-after units are those opening directly onto the beach, which offers swimming, sailing, and watersports. There's also a pool, and an 18-hole golf course is just a short drive away. The rooms are furnished in a Caribbean motif, and the larger accommodations have kitchens. Units here are timeshares, so there are no routine extras. All rooms have medium-size bathrooms with shower/tub combinations.

Frigate Bay (P.O. Box 1198), Basseterre, St. Kitts, W.I. ✆ 869/465-8597. Fax 869/466-7085. 60 units. Winter US$120–US$170 double, US$180 studio suite, US$200 1-bedroom apt, US$300 2-bedroom apt for up to 4; off season US$90–US$120 double, US$130 studio suite, US$145 1-bedroom apt, US$210 2-bedroom apt for up to 4. AE, MC, V. **Amenities:** Restaurant; bar; outdoor pool; golf (nearby); babysitting; laundry service; non-smoking rooms; rooms for those with limited mobility. *In room:* A/C, TV, dataport, kitchenette (in some), fridge, beverage maker, hair dryer, safe.

Morgan Heights Condo Resort Morgan Heights is more of a condo complex than a resort, and its staff is of minimal assistance. But each of the small to medium-size units is well maintained and fairly inviting. Most units have good beds and shower/tub combination bathrooms. The two-bedroom condos have wicker furniture, covered patios overlooking the Atlantic Ocean, and a kitchen. The suites are a more recent addition. Although there's a view of the water, the beach is a 10-minute drive away.

Canada Estate (P.O. Box 735), Basseterre, St. Kitts, W.I. ✆ 869/465-8633. Fax 869/465-9272. 20 units. Winter US$125 1-bedroom condo, US$175 2-bedroom condo; off season US$95 1-bedroom condo, US$105 2-bedroom condo. Extra person US$20 in winter, US$15 off season. AE, DC, MC, V. **Amenities:** Restaurant; outdoor pool; laundry service; babysitting; all nonsmoking rooms. *In room:* A/C, TV, kitchenette, beverage maker, iron/ironing board.

DINING
VERY EXPENSIVE
The Royal Palm ✿✿ CARIBBEAN FUSION On the grounds of Ottley's Plantation Inn, the Royal Palm is a local favorite, serving St. Kitts's most creative and best cuisine. It also has a colorful setting: Gaze through the ancient stone arches to the ocean on one side, and Mount Liamuiga and the inn's great house on the other. The menu changes daily. If they're available, you might start with roasted vegetable torte or chile-flavored shrimp corn cakes. The lobster quesadillas, made with local lobster, are worth crossing the island to sample. Main courses are impeccably prepared, especially the French roast of lamb and the breast of chicken Molyneux with almonds, country ham, mozzarella, and mushroom stuffing.

In Ottley's Plantation Inn, north of Basseterre, on the east coast. ✆ 869/465-7234. Reservations required. Lunch main courses US$10–US$27; Sun champagne brunch US$30; fixed-price dinner from US$65. AE, MC, V. Mon–Sat 8am–3pm; Sun brunch 11am–2pm; daily dinner seating 7–10pm.

EXPENSIVE
Ballahoo Restaurant ✿ CARIBBEAN Overlooking the town center's Circus Clock, the Ballahoo is about a block from the sea, on the second story of a traditional stone building. Its open-air dining area is one of the coolest places in town on a hot afternoon, thanks to the sea breezes. One of the best and most reliable dishes is blue parrotfish filet, but the house special is sexy, succulent conch in garlic butter. The chef also makes some of the best chile and baby back ribs in town. Seafood platters, such as chile shrimp or fresh lobster, are served with a coconut salad and rice. For more elegant fare, there's Italian-style chicken breast topped with pesto, tomatoes, and cheese and served with pasta and salad or the salad Niçoise (anchovies, eggs, and potatoes topped with fresh fish). The service is casual. Because of its central location, this restaurant draws the cruise-ship crowd.

The Circus, Fort St., Basseterre. ✆ 869/465-4197. Reservations recommended. Main courses US$9–US$27. MC, V. Mon–Sat 8am–10pm.

Fisherman's Wharf Seafood Restaurant and Bar ✿ SEAFOOD/ CARIBBEAN At the west end of Basseterre Bay Road, the Fisherman's Wharf is between the sea and the white picket fence of the Ocean Terrace Inn. Near the busy buffet grill, hardworking chefs prepare fresh seafood. An employee will take your drink order, but you personally place your food order at the grill. It's a bit like eating at picnic tables, but the fresh-fish selection is excellent, caught locally and grilled to order over St. Kitts charcoal. Spicy conch chowder is a good starter; grilled lobster is an elegant main course choice, or you may prefer the grilled catch of the day, often snapper. Grilled swordfish is always good, as is the combination platter, which includes lobster, barbecued shrimp kabob, and calypso chicken breast.

Fortlands, Basseterre. ☎ 869/465-2754. Reservations recommended. Main courses US$6–US$33. AE, DISC, MC, V. Daily 7–11pm.

The Golden Lemon ✦ CONTINENTAL/CREOLE
The food is very good, and the service polite in this fine hotel on the northern coast (see "Accommodations," earlier in this chapter). It makes a great lunch stop on a tour of the island. Dinner is served in an elegant, candlelit dining room, in the garden, or on the gallery. The hotel's sophisticated owner created many of the recipes. The menu changes daily, but is likely to include baked Cornish hen with ginger, fresh fish of the day, and Creole sirloin steak with a spicy rum sauce. Vegetarian dishes are also available. Dress is casually chic.

In the Golden Lemon Inn, Dieppe Bay. ☎ 869/465-7260. Reservations usually required; walk-ins accepted if space available. Lunch main courses US$8.50–US$25; fixed-price dinner US$35–US$60; Sun brunch US$15–US$30. AE, MC, V. Mon–Sat 7:30–10am, noon–3pm, and 7–10pm; Sun noon–3pm and 7–10pm.

Manhattan Gardens ✦ CARIBBEAN/INTERNATIONAL
This 18th-century island home is painted in flamboyant colors and extends a hearty welcome. Try to eat in the rear garden, which opens onto a view of the water. Chef/owner Rosalind Warner has some real local dishes such as conch fritters or curried mutton, although you might opt for the fresh catch of the day, which might be mahimahi in a lemon-and-thyme sauce. We're fond of her shrimp with white wine or garlic butter. Her boneless chicken stuffed with spinach is another winner, as are her homemade soups, especially the pumpkin.

Main Street, Old Road Town. ☎ 869/465-9121. Reservations required. Main courses EC$35–EC$65 (US$13–US$24). No credit cards. Mon–Sat 11am–3pm and 7–11pm.

Ocean Terrace Inn ✦ CARIBBEAN/INTERNATIONAL
Some of the finest cuisine in Basseterre is found here. The views from the open-air veranda, especially at night when the harbor is lit up, are also some of the best around. The kitchen is best at the real down-home island dishes—international specialties tend to be blander. Dinner might include tasty fish cakes, accompanied by breaded carrot slices, creamed spinach, a stuffed potato, a cornmeal dumpling known as johnnycake, and a green banana in a lime-butter sauce, topped off by a tropical fruit pie and coffee. The less daring can stick with chateaubriand. Friday night is Caribbean night with an all-you-can-eat buffet and a steel band at a cost of EC$65 (US$24).

Fortlands. ☎ 869/465-2754. Reservations recommended. Main courses EC$51–EC$78 (US$19–US$29); fixed-price lunch EC$24–EC$41 (US$8.90–US$15); fixed-price dinner EC$89 (US$33). AE, DISC, MC, V. Daily 7–10am, noon–2pm, and 7–11pm. Drive west on Basseterre Bay Rd. to Fortlands.

Rawlins Plantation Restaurant ✦ WEST INDIAN/CARIBBEAN
This previously recommended plantation inn serves some of the finest regional cuisine in the area, dishes with real West Indian flavor. It is especially known for its buffet lunch, and is just a 10-minute drive from Brimstone Hill. For diners tired of so-called international menus, this is an ideal choice. In an elegant setting, you can

order a rum punch and immerse yourself in the old Caribbean lifestyle, later enjoying a meal with locally farmed or fished ingredients. The lunchtime buffet is especially delightful, beginning with such appetizers as shrimp fritters in a mango salsa, or plantains baked with pecans. For a main dish, try pork with pineapple and hot chile peppers, or the lobster and spinach crepes. The dinner menu is limited but good, and often features such dishes as rack of lamb with a spicy herb crust, followed by local stewed guavas with a Grand Marnier cream sauce.

Mount Pleasant. ⑦ **869/465-6221.** Reservations recommended. No shorts at dinner. Lunch buffet US$26; set dinner US$50. AE, MC, V. Lunch daily 12:30–2pm; dinner nightly at 8pm.

Stonewalls ⑆ *Finds* CARIBBEAN/INTERNATIONAL   This casual, open-air bar in a tropical garden in Basseterre's historical zone is cozy and casual. It's the type of Caribbean bar that you hope exists but can rarely find. In a garden setting of banana, plantain, and bamboo trees, Wendy and Garry Steckles present an innovative and constantly changing menu. The fare might be Caribbean, with fresh kingfish or tuna and a zesty gumbo, or an authentic, spicy Dhansak-style curry. Hot-off-the-wok stir-fries are served along with sizzling grilled chicken breast in a teriyaki glaze. Appetizers might include piquant conch fritters. A small but carefully chosen wine list is available. The bar here is one of the most convivial places on the island for a drink.

Princes St. ⑦ **869/465-5248.** Reservations recommended. Main courses EC$51–EC$68 (US$19–US$25). AE, MC, V. Mon–Fri 5–11pm.

Turtle Beach Bar & Grill ⑆ SEAFOOD/INTERNATIONAL   Set directly on the sands above Turtle Beach, this airy, sun-flooded restaurant is one of the most popular lunch stops for those doing the whirlwind tour of St. Kitts. Many guests spend the hour before their meal swimming or snorkeling beside the off-shore reef; others simply relax on the verandas or in hammocks under the shade trees, perhaps with a drink in hand. Scuba diving, ocean kayaking, windsurfing, and volleyball are available, and a flotilla of rental sailboats is moored nearby. Menu specialties are familiar, but extremely flavorful. Typical dishes are stuffed broiled lobster, conch fritters, grilled fish, pasta salads, and barbecued honey-mustard spareribs.

Southeastern Peninsula. ⑦ **869/469-9086.** Main courses EC$27–EC$78 (US$10–US$29). AE, MC, V. Daily 10am–6pm. Follow the Kennedy Simmonds Hwy. over Basseterre's Southeastern Peninsula; then follow the signs.

INEXPENSIVE

The Atlantic Club SEAFOOD/WEST INDIAN   Nevisian Genford Gumbs worked at the deluxe Golden Lemon for 15 years before striking out on his own and opening this restaurant. On St. Kitts's east coast, a 5-minute drive from the Basseterre or the airport, this restaurant overlooks—what else?—the Atlantic Ocean. The cuisine is West Indian, with seafood like fresh fish, conch, and lobster usually available as well. The atmosphere is relaxed and casual, and the portions are large. A lot of locals show up on Saturday for the special: goat water (goat stew) and *souse* (pickled pigs' feet, ear, and head, sometimes compressed into a loaf similar to a terrine). Less adventurous visitors may want to skip this treat and instead order the burgers, soups, salads, and sandwiches, or even a Black Angus steak.

At the Morgan Heights Condominiums, Canada Estate. ⑦ **869/465-8633.** Reservations required for dinner. Main courses EC$25–EC$76 (US$9.25–US$28). AE, MC, V. Mon–Sat noon–11pm.

Glimbara Diner CARIBBEAN   Don't expect grand cuisine from this worka-day eatery. Established in 1998 in a simple family-run guesthouse in the heart of Basseterre, it has become a local favorite, thanks to the hardworking staff and down-to-earth food. Small and cozy, and painted in shades of blue, white, and gray, it serves Creole cuisine that varies with the mood and inspiration of the cook. Examples might include large or small portions of the stewlike goat water, pumpkin or bean soup, and several kinds of fried or grilled fish, which might be accompanied by coleslaw or green salad. American-style platters, including hamburgers and hot dogs, are usually served with fries and soda. Ask for a local fruit punch known as *fairling* or the bottled sugary grapefruit drink called Ting.

In the Glimbara Guesthouse, Cayon St., Basseterre. © 869/465-1786. Main courses EC$14–EC$20 (US$5.20–US$7.40). AE, MC, V. Daily 7am–11pm.

BEACHES

Beaches are the primary concern of most St. Kitts visitors. The narrow peninsula in the southeast that contains the island's salt ponds also boasts the best white-sand beaches. All beaches, even those that border hotels, are open to the public. However, to use the beach facilities of a hotel, you must first obtain permission and will probably have to pay a small fee.

Until the Dr. Kennedy Simmonds Highway (named for the nation's first prime minister), a 10km (6¼-mile) road beginning in the Frigate Bay area, opened to the public in 1989, it was necessary to take a boat to enjoy the beautiful, unspoiled beaches of the southeast peninsula. To travel this road is one of the pleasures of a visit to St. Kitts. Not only will you take in some of the island's most beautiful scenery, but you'll also pass lagoonlike coves and fields of tall guinea grass. If the day is clear (and it usually is), you'll have a panoramic vista of Nevis. The best beaches along the peninsula are **Frigate Bay, Friar's Bay, Sand Bank Bay, White House Bay, Cockleshell Bay,** and **Banana Bay.** Of all these, **Sand Bank Bay** ⚸ gets our nod as the finest strip of sand.

Both **Cockleshell Bay** and **Banana Bay** also have their devotees. Together these two beaches run a distance of 3km (2 miles), all with powder-white sands. So far, in spite of several attempts, this area hasn't filled with high-rise resorts.

A live steel band plays on Sundays from 12:30 to 3pm at the **Turtle Beach Bar and Grill,** Turtle Bay, making this the place for afternoon cocktails on the beach.

For excellent **snorkeling,** head to somewhat rocky **White House Bay,** which opens onto reefs. Schools of rainbow-hued fish swim around a tugboat sunken long ago—a stunning sight.

South Friar's Bay is lovely, although its pristine qualities may be forever disturbed by the construction of a new Hyatt. Friar's has powder-fine sand as well, and many locals consider it their favorite. **Frigate Bay,** with its powder-white sand, is ideal for swimming as well as windsurfing and water-skiing.

As a curiosity, you may want to visit **Great Salt Pond** at the southeastern end of St. Kitts. This is an inland beach of soft white sand, opening onto the Atlantic Ocean in the north and the more tranquil Caribbean Sea in the south.

The beaches in the north of St. Kitts are numerous but are of gray volcanic sand and much less frequented than those of the southeast peninsula. Beachcombers like to visit them, and they can be ideal for sunbathing, but swimming is much better in the southeast, as waters in the north, sweeping in from the Atlantic, can often be turbulent.

The best beach on the Atlantic side is **Conaree Bay,** with a narrow strip of gray-black sand. Bodysurfing is popular here. **Dieppe Bay,** another black-sand beach on the north coast, is good for snorkeling and windsurfing but not for swimming. This is the site of the island's most famous inn, the Golden Lemon, which you might want to visit for lunch. If you should be on this beach during a tropical shower, do not seek shelter under the dreaded manchineel trees, which are poisonous. Rain falling off the leaves will feel like acid on your skin.

SPORTS & OTHER OUTDOOR PURSUITS

GOLF   The **Royal St. Kitts Golf Course,** Frigate Bay (© **869/466-2700**), is an 18-hole championship course that covers 64 hectares (158 acres). It features 10 water hazards, not including the Caribbean Sea and the Atlantic Ocean, which border it. It's open daily from 7am to 6pm. Greens fees are US$115 for 18 holes. Carts are free for 18 holes, but US$50 for clubs. A bar and an on-site restaurant open daily at 7am.

HIKING   Kris Tours (© **869/465-4042**) takes small groups into the crater of Mount Liamuiga (see "Into the Volcano," below), through a rainforest to enjoy the lushness of the island. A full-day tour costs US$60 per person and includes lunch and drinks.

HORSEBACK RIDING   **Trinity Stables** (© **869/465-3226**) charges US$55 for a half-day tour through a rainforest. You might also get to see the wild lushness of the North Frigate Bay area and the rather desolate Conaree Beach. You must call for a reservation; you'll then be told where to meet and offered any advice, including what to wear.

SCUBA DIVING, SNORKELING & OTHER WATERSPORTS   Some of the best dive spots include **Nag's Head,** at the south tip of St. Kitts. This is an excellent shallow-water dive starting at 3m (10 ft.) and extending to 21m (69 ft.). A variety of tropical fish, eagle rays, and lobster are found here. The site is ideal for certified divers. Another good spot for diving is **Booby Shoals,** off the Southeast Atlantic coast near Cockleshell Bay. Booby Shoals has abundant sea life, including nurse sharks, lobster, and stingrays. Dives are up to 9m (30 ft.) in depth, ideal for both certified and resort divers.

A variety of activities are offered by **Pro-Divers,** at Turtle Beach (© **869/466-3483**). You can swim, float, paddle, or go on scuba-diving and snorkeling expeditions from here. A two-tank dive costs US$80; night dives are US$65. A PADI certification is available for US$375, and a resort course costs US$95. Three-hour snorkeling trips are US$35.

Pro-Divers also rents snorkeling gear and can tell you the best places to go **snorkeling.** We like **Dieppe Bay,** at the northern tip of St. Kitts.

EXPLORING THE ISLAND

The British colonial town of **Basseterre** is built around a so-called **Circus,** the town's round square. A tall green Victorian clock stands in the center of the Circus. After Brimstone Hill Fortress, **Berkeley Memorial Clock** is the most photographed landmark of St. Kitts. In the old days, wealthy plantation owners and their families used to promenade here.

At some point, try to visit the **marketplace,** especially on a Saturday morning. Here, country people bring baskets brimming with mangos, guavas, soursop, mammee apples, and wild strawberries and cherries just picked in the fields. Tropical flowers abound.

Another major landmark is **Independence Square.** Once an active slave market, it's surrounded by private homes of Georgian architecture.

You can negotiate with a taxi driver to take you on a tour of the island for about US$60 for a 3-hour trip; most drivers are well versed in the lore of the island. You might want to make lunch reservations at either the Rawlins Plantation Inn or the

Golden Lemon. For more information, call the **St. Kitts Taxi Association,** the Circus, Basseterre (𝄢 **869/465-8487** until 10pm).

The island's latest attraction is **The St. Kitts Scenic Railway** ⚔ (𝄢 **869/ 465-7263**). In double-decker and air-conditioned railcars, you're taken on a panoramic tour of the most spectacular scenery the island has to offer. The upper level features a spacious, open-air observation deck. The narrow gauge railway follows the old sugar-cane train tracks, taking in the best vistas of mountains and the Caribbean Sea. There is a service bar, and passengers can also enjoy live musical entertainment. The train is boarded at Needsmust Station. This is certainly the quickest and easiest way to see "St. Kitts in a nutshell," especially if you're a cruise-ship passenger with limited time. The 48km (30-mile) ride costs US$89 for adults, half price for children, and lasts 3½ hours. The first departure is daily at 8:10am. Sometimes a second tour, if demand warrants it, leaves at 11:50am.

Brimstone Hill Fortress ⚔ (𝄢 **869/465-6211**), 14km (8¾ miles) west of Basseterre, is a major stop. This historic monument, among the largest and best preserved in the Caribbean, is a complex of bastions, barracks, and other structures ingeniously adapted to the top and upper slopes of a steep-sided 240m (787-ft.) hill. The fortress dates from 1690, when the British attempted to recapture Fort Charles from the French. Admission is US$5 for adults, US$2.50 for children.

Today, the fortress is the centerpiece of a national park with nature trails and a diverse range of plant and animal life, including the **green vervet monkey.** It's also a photographer's paradise, with views of mountains, fields, and the Caribbean Sea. On a clear day, you can see six neighboring islands.

Visitors can enjoy self-guided tours among many ruins and restored structures, including the barrack rooms at Fort George, which contain an interesting museum. The gift shop stocks prints of rare maps and paintings of the Caribbean. Admission is US$5, half price for children. The Brimstone Hill Fortress National Park is open daily from 9:30am to 5:30pm.

You can visit the site where a large tamarind tree in the hamlet of **Half-Way Tree** once marked the boundary between the British- and French-held sectors.

It was near the hamlet of **Old Road Town** that Sir Thomas Warner landed with the first band of settlers and established the first permanent colony to the northwest at Sandy Point. Sir Thomas's grave is in the cemetery of St. Thomas Church.

A sign in the middle of Old Road Town points the way to **Carib Rock Drawings,** all the evidence that remains of the former inhabitants. The markings are on black boulders, and the pictographs date from prehistoric days.

INTO THE VOLCANO

Mount Liamuiga was dubbed "Mount Misery" long ago, but it sputtered its last gasp around 1692. This dormant volcano on the northeast coast is today one of the major highlights for hikers on St. Kitts. The peak of the mountain often lies under cloud cover.

The ascent to the volcano is usually made from the north end of St. Kitts at Belmont Estate. The trail winds through a rainforest and travels along deep ravines up to the rim of the crater at 788m (2,585 ft.). The actual peak is at 1,138m (3,733 ft.). Figure on 5 hours of rigorous hiking to complete the round-trip walk.

The caldera itself is some 120m (394 ft.) from its rim to the crater floor. Many hikers climb or crawl down into the dormant volcano. However, the trail is steep and slippery, so be careful. At the crater floor is a tiny lake along with volcanic rocks and various vegetation.

Greg's Safaris, P.O. Box Basseterre (© 869/465-4121), offers guided hikes to the crater, including breakfast and a picnic at the crater's rim, for US$85 per person with a minimum of six people. The same outfit also offers half-day rainforest explorations for US$50 per person. **Kris Tours** (© 869/465-4042) offers similar tours for US$60, but with no breakfast and a far less luxurious picnic spread.

SHOPPING

The good buys here are in local handcrafts, including leather (goatskin) items, baskets, and coconut shells. Some good values can also be found in clothing and fabrics, especially Sea Island cottons. Store hours vary, but are likely to be Monday to Saturday from 8am to noon and 1 to 4pm.

If your time is limited, head first for the **Pelican Shopping Mall,** Bay Road, which contains some two dozen shops. Opened in 1991, it also offers banking services, a restaurant, and a philatelic bureau. Some major retail outlets in the Caribbean, including Little Switzerland, have branches here. Also check out the offerings along the quaintly named **Liverpool Row,** which has some unusual merchandise, and **Fort Street.**

Linen and Gold Shop, in the Pelican Mall (© 869/465-9766), offers a limited selection of gold and silver jewelry, usually in bold modern designs. But the real appeal of this shop is the tablecloths, doilies, and napkins, laboriously handcrafted in China from cotton, linen, and polyester. The workmanship is as intricate as anything you'll find in the Caribbean.

Ashburry's, the Circus/Liverpool Row, Basseterre (© 869/465-8175), is a local branch of a chain of luxury-goods stores based on St. Maarten. This well-respected emporium sells fragrances, fine porcelain, Baccarat crystal, Fendi handbags, watches, and jewelry, at prices 25% to 30% below what you might pay in retail stores in North America; the selection is similar to dozens of equivalent stores throughout the Caribbean.

Cameron Gallery, 10 N. Independence Sq., Basseterre (© 869/465-1617), is a leading art gallery. On display are scenes of St. Kitts and Nevis by Brit Rosey Cameron-Smith, along with works by 10 to 15 other artists. Rosey is well known on the island for her paintings of Kittitian Carnival clowns, monkeys, and figurative work, and she also produces greeting cards, postcards, calendars, and lithographs.

The finest gallery on St. Kitts is **Kate Design,** Mount Pleasant (© 869/465-7740), set in an impeccably restored West Indian house, on a hillside below the Rawlins Plantation. Virtually all the works on display are by English-born Kate Spencer, who is well known throughout North America and Europe. Her paintings of island scenes range in price from US$200 to US$3,000 and have received critical acclaim. Also for sale is a series of Ms. Spencer's silk-screened scarves, each crafted from extra-heavy stonewashed silk.

Island Fever, in the Palms Arcade, Basseterre (© 869/465-2599), specializes in island things, including handcrafts, amber jewelry, West Indies spices, teas, and perfumes. Also available are some tropical clothing, and a wealth of souvenirs.

Island Hopper (known as "The Big Shop of the Little Island"), the Circus, below the popular Ballahoo Restaurant, Basseterre (© 869/465-1640), is one of St. Kitts's most patronized shops, with the biggest inventory of any store on the island. Notice the all-silk, shift-style dresses from China and the array of batiks made on St. Kitts. About half of the merchandise is from the islands.

Romney Manor, Old Road, 16km (10 miles) west of Basseterre (© **869/ 465-6253**), is the most unusual factory in St. Kitts. It was built around 1625 as a manor house for sugar baron Lord Romney. For years, it has been used as the headquarters and manufacturing center for a local clothier, Caribelle Batik, whose tropical cottons sell widely to cruise-ship passengers and tourists from at least three outlets in the eastern Caribbean. The merchandise ranges from scarves to dresses, along with an extensive collection of wall hangings and cushions. In 1995, a tragic fire and hurricane completely gutted the historic building. The manor has now been rebuilt and extended. Consider a stopover here if only to admire the 2 hectares (5 acres) of lavish gardens, where 30 varieties of hibiscus, rare orchids, huge ferns, and a 250-year-old saman tree still draw horticultural enthusiasts. Entrance to the gardens is free.

ST. KITTS AFTER DARK

The **Ocean Terrace Inn's Fisherman's Wharf,** Fortlands (© **869/465-2754**), has a live band every Friday from 8 to 10pm. It's not "after dark," but the **Turtle Beach Bar and Grill,** Turtle Bay (© **869/465-9086**), on the southeast peninsula, offers a live steel band daily from 12:30 to 3pm; on Saturday, it's beach disco time. There's no cover at either place.

A favorite watering hole is **Bambu's,** Bank St., right off the Circus in Basseterre (© **869/466-5280**), which is filled with lots of bamboo and bright colors. There's a big screen TV for those who want to watch the games, but also spaces for those who want to retreat. On Friday happy hour is from 5 to 7pm.

A few other nightspots come and go (mostly go). Currently, islanders hang out at **Bobsy's,** Bay Road (© **869/466-6133**) in Basseterre. A DJ often spins the latest and sometimes karaoke is staged. **Club Atmosphere,** Canada Estate (© **869/465-3655**), is the showcase for "Ronnie Rascal," the island's most popular DJ. Friday and Saturday nights are the time to go. Another local dive, **Henry's Night Spot,** Dunn's Cottage, Main Street, Cayon (© **869/465-3508**), has a loyal following.

3 Nevis

A local once said that the best reason to go to Nevis was to practice the fine art of *limin'*. To him, that meant doing nothing in particular. Limin' might still be the best reason to venture over to Nevis. Once here, you can relax and experience this small, calm volcanic island. If you want to lie out in the sun, head for reef-protected Pinney's Beach, a 5km (3-mile) strip of dark-gold sand set against a backdrop of palm trees, with panoramic views of St. Kitts.

Columbus sighted Nevis in 1493. He called it Las Nieves, Spanish for *snows,* because its mountains reminded him of the snow-capped range in the Pyrenees. From St. Kitts, the island appears to be a perfect cone, rising gradually to a height of 970m (3,181 ft.). A saddle joins the tallest mountain to two smaller peaks, Saddle Hill (375m/1,230 ft.) in the south and Hurricane Hill (only 75m/246 ft.) in the north.

Nevis' beauty has remained relatively unspoiled. Coral reefs rim the shoreline, and there's mile after mile of palm-shaded white-sand beaches. Natives of Nevis, for the most part, are descendants of African slaves.

Settled by the British in 1628, the volcanic island is famous as the birthplace of Alexander Hamilton, the American statesman who wrote many of the articles contained in *The Federalist Papers* and was George Washington's treasury secretary.

Nevis is also the island on which Admiral Horatio Lord Nelson married Frances Nisbet, a local woman, in 1787, an episode described in James Michener's *Caribbean* (the historical facts are romanticized, of course).

In the 18th century, Nevis's hot mineral springs made it the leading spa of the West Indies. The island was also once peppered with prosperous sugar-cane estates, but they're gone now—many have been converted into some of the most intriguing hotels in the Caribbean. Sea Island cotton is the chief crop today.

On the Caribbean side, **Charlestown,** the capital of Nevis, was fashionable in the 18th century, when sugar planters were carried around in carriages and sedan chairs. A town of wide, quiet streets, this port only gets busy when its major link to the world, the ferry from St. Kitts, docks at the harbor.

NEVIS ESSENTIALS

GETTING THERE   There are no nonstop flights to Nevis from North America. To get here, you'll have to stop or change planes in Antigua, St. Maarten, or Puerto Rico. **American Airlines** (© 800/433-7300 in the U.S.; www.aa.com) has dozens of daily flights to San Juan. From here, you can catch a propeller plane to Nevis. The Antigua-based carrier, **LIAT** (© 868/624-4727), flies to Nevis from Antigua, San Juan, and St. Maarten. The only island-to-island (St. Kitts to Nevis or vice versa) flights are on **Winair** (© 869/465-8010), a one-way fare costs EC$181 (US$67). There are two flights per day.

You can also use the **interisland ferry service** between St. Kitts and Nevis. Ferry schedules are subject to change without notice, and follow no obvious patterns. The **MV** *Sea Hustler* makes at least three trips per day, and sometimes four. There is usually one morning crossing and one afternoon crossing from each island. The duration of the crossing is 1 hour. The **MV** *Caribe Queen* makes the crossing in 45 minutes, but it doesn't run on Thursdays or Sundays. Its schedule is also different every day—it generally makes one round-trip in the morning (usually 7 or 7:30am) and at least one trip each way in the afternoon (at 4, 5, or 6pm, depending on the island). Fare is US$8 round-trip for either ferry. The vest vessel of all is the air-conditioned 110-passenger ferry, **MV** *Caribe Breeze,* which makes the run in only 30 minutes. The regular fare is US$12 per passenger one-way (or US$15 in first class). There are only two runs per day on Thursday and Sunday but more frequent runs on other days, depending on demand. Call © 869/446-INFO or contact the tourist office on either island for exact schedules.

GETTING AROUND   Taxi drivers double as guides, and you'll find them waiting at the airport or the ferry dock. The fare between Newcastle Airport and Charlestown is EC$41 (US$15); between Charlestown and Old Manor Estate, EC$32 (US$12); and from Charlestown to Pinney's Beach, EC$13 (US$4.80). Between 10pm and 6am, 50% is added to the prices. Call © 869/469-1042 for more information.

If you're prepared to face the winding, rocky, potholed roads of Nevis, you can arrange for a **rental car** from a local firm through your hotel. Or you can check with **Skeete's Car Rental,** Newcastle Village, near the airport (© 869/469-9458). To drive on Nevis, you must obtain a permit from the traffic department, which costs EC$66 (US$25) and is valid for a year. Car-rental companies will handle this for you. *Remember:* Drive on the left side of the road.

FAST FACTS   Banks are usually open Monday to Wednesday from 8am to 3pm, Thursday 8 to 11:30am, and some on Saturday 8am to noon. Normal **store**

Four Seasons Resort Nevis **1**
Golden Rock Plantation Inn **6**
Hermitage Plantation **8**
Hurricane Cove Bungalows **3**
Montpelier Plantation Inn **9**

Mount Nevis Hotel & Beach Club **4**
Nisbet Plantation Beach Club **5**
Old Manor Estate & Hotel **7**
Oualie Beach Hotel **2**

hours are Monday to Friday from 8am to noon and 1 to 4pm. On Thursday some places close in the afternoon, and on Saturday some stay open to 8pm. Most are closed Sunday.

The **post office** is on Main Street in Charlestown. It's open Monday to Friday from 8am to 3pm (it closes at 11am on Thurs), and Saturday from 8am to noon. You can make **international phone calls,** including collect calls, from the **Cable & Wireless office,** Main Street, Charlestown (© **869/469-5000**). It's open Monday to Friday from 8am to 5pm, Saturday from 8am to noon.

If you need a pharmacy, try **Evelyn's Drugstore,** Charlestown (© **869/469-5278**), open Monday to Friday from 8am to 6pm, Saturday from 8am to 7pm, and Sunday for only 1 hour, from 7 to 8pm, to serve emergency needs.

There's a 24-hour **emergency room** at **Alexandra Hospital,** Government Road, in Charlestown (© **869/469-5473**).

The **Nevis Tourist Bureau** is on Main Street in Charlestown (© **866/55-NEVIS** from the U.S., or 869/469-7550).

ACCOMMODATIONS
VERY EXPENSIVE

Four Seasons Resort Nevis ★★★ *Kids*   This hotel is one of the Caribbean's world-class properties and hands-down the best choice on the island. Located on Nevis's west coast, it's set in a palm grove beside Pinney's Beach, the finest sandy beach on Nevis. On an island known for its small and intimate inns, this 1991 low-rise resort stands out as the largest and best-managed hotel, with the most complete sports facilities (including a fabulous golf course), and even the best children's program. Designed in harmony with the surrounding landscape, the accommodations offer rich but conservative mahogany furniture, touches of marble, carpeting, and wide patios or verandas overlooking the beach, the golf course, or Mount Nevis. The spacious guest rooms have generous closet space, full-length mirrors, luxurious upholstery and fabrics, and king-size or double beds. The roomy bathrooms have shower/tub combinations, double sinks, makeup mirrors, and Bulgari toiletries. The public areas include rooms inspired by paneled libraries in London, complete with one of the few working fireplaces on Nevis.

Guests have the largest choice of bars and dining venues on Nevis. The resort's centerpiece is the plantation-inspired great house, which contains the most formal restaurant, the Dining Room (see "Dining," below). In 2003 the resort became even more "this side of paradise" with the addition of an elegant spa, featuring beachside massages and hydrotherapy. Ever had a mango-seasalt exfoliation and a heavenly hot-stone massage?

Pinney's Beach (P.O. Box 585), Charlestown, Nevis, W.I. © **800/332-3442** in the U.S., 800/268-6282 in Canada, or 869/469-1111. Fax 869/469-1112. www.fourseasons.com. 196 units. Winter US$595–US$835 double, from US$1,725 suite; off season US$245–US$450 double, from US$600 suite. MAP (breakfast and dinner) US$95 per person extra. Up to 2 children under 18 stay free in parent's room. AE, DC, MC, V. **Amenities:** 3 restaurants; 2 bars; 2 pools; 18-hole golf course; 10 tennis courts; health club; spa; Jacuzzi; sauna; fishing; scuba diving; horseback riding; children's programs; business services; 24-hr. room service; massage; babysitting; laundry service; dry cleaning; nonsmoking rooms; rooms for those with limited mobility. *In room:* A/C, TV, dataport, minibar, beverage maker, hair dryer, iron/ironing board, safe.

Hermitage Plantation ★★
This much-photographed, frequently copied historians' delight is said to be the oldest all-wood house in the Antilles, and was built amid the high-altitude plantations of Gingerland in 1740. Some say it once hosted Alexander Hamilton and Horatio Nelson. Today, former Philadelphian Richard Lupinacci and his wife, Maureen, have assembled one of the best collections of antiques on Nevis here. Wide-plank floors, intricate latticework, and high ceilings add to the hotel's beauty. The accommodations are in 12 glamorous buildings designed like small plantation houses. Many contain huge four-poster beds, antique accessories, and colonial louvered windows. The spotlessly maintained private bathrooms contain shower/tub combinations. The most luxurious and expensive unit is a yellow manor house on a .2 hectares (½ acre) of private gardens with its own ceramic-tile pool, three large bedrooms furnished with antique canopy beds, oversize bathrooms with dressing rooms, a comfortable living room, dining room, and a full kitchen.

Complimentary beach transportation is provided because the best nearby beach is a 15-minute drive away. The on-site restaurant is one of the finest hotel dining rooms on island (see "Dining," below).

St. John's Parish, Nevis, W.I. © **800/682-4025** in the U.S., or 869/469-3477. Fax 869/469-2481. www.hermitage nevis.com. 16 units. Winter US$325–US$450 double, US$790 manor house double; off season US$170–US$265 double, US$650 manor house double. AE, MC, V. Take the main island road 6km (3¾ miles) from Charlestown. **Amenities:** Restaurant; bar; outdoor pool; tennis court; stables; limited room service; laundry service. *In room:* Ceiling fans, TV, kitchen or kitchenette, fridge, beverage maker, hair dryer, iron/ironing board, safe.

Montpelier Plantation Inn ★★
One of the Plantation Inns of Nevis, the Montpelier stands in the hills, 210m (689 ft.) high, with grandstand views of the ocean. The 18th-century plantation is in the center of its own 12-hectare (30-acre) estate, which contains 4 hectares (10 acres) of ornamental gardens surrounding the cottage units. Accommodations are generally spacious and

brightened with fresh flowers and luxuries like comfortable chairs and dressing tables. Bathrooms, with glass-enclosed shower/tub combinations, are sparkling clean. New owners took over in 2003 and got rid of that colonial country house stuffiness. Out with the chintz and in with the camel and coral linen and toile. Today the look is one of minimalist chic as befits the 21st century. Most of the elegant bedrooms have four-posters.

Montpelier prides itself on its food, wine, and service. At the restaurant that shares the name of the resort, much use is made of fresh local produce (see "Dining," below).

St. John Figtree (P.O. Box 474), Montpelier, Nevis, W.I. ℂ 869/469-3462. Fax 869/469-2932. www.montpelier nevis.com. 17 units. Winter US$430 premier room, US$505 suite, US$613 2-bedroom suite; off season US$260 premier room, US$335 suite, US$400 2-bedroom suite. Rates include breakfast and afternoon tea. AE, MC, V. Closed Aug–Sept. Children under 8 not accepted. **Amenities:** Restaurant; 2 bars; outdoor pool; tennis court; spa; windsurfing; horseback riding; library; transport to private beach; room service (breakfast only); laundry service; babysitting. *In room:* A/C (in some), ceiling fan, fridge (in some), beverage maker, hair dryer, safe.

Nisbet Plantation Beach Club ★★   A respect for fine living prevails in this gracious estate house on a coconut plantation, which is the only plantation-style house that lives up to the grace notes of Montpellier Plantation Inn. This is the former home of Frances Nisbet, who, at the age of 22, married Lord Nelson. Although enamored of Miss Nisbet when he married her, Lord Nelson later fell in love with Lady Hamilton (as detailed in the classic film *That Hamilton Woman*). This is the only plantation hotel in Nevis that opens directly onto the beach—a half mile of pulverized coral sand against a backdrop of palm trees.

The present main building was rebuilt on the foundations of the original 18th-century great house. The ruins of a circular sugar mill stand at the entrance, covered with bougainvillea, hibiscus, and poinciana. Guest cottages are set in the palm grove. All rooms are brightly decorated and beautifully appointed, with king-size beds and firm mattresses. The bathrooms, with shower/tub combinations, are tidily maintained.

In addition to two casual beachfront eateries, the Great House Restaurant serves some of the most elegant and best dinners on the island, a delightful combination of Caribbean and international cuisine.

Newcastle, St. James's Parish, Nevis, W.I. ℂ 800/742-6008 in the U.S. and Canada, or 869/469-9325. Fax 869/469-9864. www.nisbetplantation.com. 38 units. Winter US$475–US$625 double, from US$645 suite; off season US$290–US$370 double, from US$390 suite. Rates include MAP (breakfast and dinner) and afternoon tea. AE, MC, V. Turn left out of the airport and go 2km (1¼ miles). **Amenities:** 3 restaurants; 2 bars; outdoor pool; golf at Four Seasons; tennis court; snorkeling; horseback riding; babysitting; laundry service; nonsmoking rooms. *In room:* A/C, dataport, minibar, beverage maker, hair dryer, iron/ironing board, safe.

EXPENSIVE

Golden Rock Plantation Inn ★   This place doesn't have the polish and glaze of such choices as the Hermitage (see above), but it has down-home qualities and quiet charm. This former sugar estate, built in 1815, is set in the lush hills only a 15-minute drive east of Charlestown. Set on 40 tropical hectares (99 acres), it fronts a 10-hectare (25-acre) garden. Guests live in fairly spacious surroundings, in a setting of pineapple friezes, island crafts, family heirlooms, and tile flowers. Fabrics are island-made, with tropical flower designs. The shower-only bathrooms are a bit small. Cottages are scattered about the garden, and each has a four-poster king-size bed made of bamboo or mahogany. Rooms have large porches with views of the sea as well. The original stone tower windmill has been turned into a duplex honeymoon suite (or accommodations for a family of four).

The hotel lies at the beginning of a rainforest walk; it takes about 3 to 4 hours to follow the trail round-trip (the hotel provides a map). For the equestrian, horseback riding can be arranged. If you want to go to the beach, the complimentary hotel shuttle will take you to either Pinney's Beach (on the leeward side) or White Bay Beach (aka Windward Beach), which has good surfing. The shuttle also stops in Charlestown if requested. Caribbean-style meals are served at the 175-year-old "long house."

P.O. Box 493, Gingerland, Nevis, W.I. ✆ 869/469-3346. Fax 869/469-2113. www.golden-rock.com. 14 units. Winter US$210 double, US$275 suite; off season US$140 double, US$175 suite. Children under age 2 stay free in parent's room. MC, V. **Amenities:** Restaurant; bar; outdoor pool; tennis court; sailing; scuba diving; snorkeling; windsurfing; horseback riding; beach shuttle; babysitting; laundry service. *In room:* Ceiling fans, hair dryer, no phone.

Mount Nevis Hotel & Beach Club ⚘ *Kids*   This family-owned and -run resort is on the slopes of Mount Nevis, a 5-minute drive southwest of the Vance Amori International Airport. It's known for the quality of its accommodations, for its panoramic views, and for serving some of the best food on Nevis. Near the historic fishing village of Newcastle, it offers standard rooms, junior suites, and supervisor suites—the latter with fully equipped kitchens and enough space for at least four guests, making it an ideal family choice. The rooms have such amenities as VCRs and ceiling fans, and are furnished in a tropical motif, with wicker and colorful island prints. The tidily maintained private bathrooms are well equipped and contain shower stalls.

See "Dining," below, for a review of the hotel's main restaurant, Mount Nevis Hotel Restaurant. The Mount Nevis Beach Club offers a site on Newcastle Bay and features a beach pavilion, bar, and restaurant. It pretty much introduced pizza to the island.

Newcastle (P.O. Box 494), Charlestown, Nevis, W.I. ✆ **800/75-NEVIS** in the U.S. and Canada, 212/679-7526 in New York City, or 869/469-9373. Fax 869/469-9375. www.mountnevishotel.com. 32 units. Winter US$235 double, US$300 suite, US$535 2-bedroom; off season US$165 double, US$210 suite, US$375 2-bedroom. Extra person US$35. AE, MC, V. **Amenities:** 2 restaurants; bar; outdoor pool; tennis court; exercise room; beach shuttle; business services; limited room service; laundry service; nonsmoking rooms. *In room:* A/C, ceiling fans, TV/VCR, dataport, kitchen (in some), fridge (in some), beverage maker (in some), hair dryer, iron/ironing board.

Old Manor Estate & Hotel ⚘   The least elaborate of the plantation-style inns of Nevis, this hotel is the most evocative of a *Gone with the Wind* Nevisian life. East of Charlestown and north of Gingerland, at a cool and comfortable elevation of 240m (787 ft.), the Old Manor Estate & Hotel has an old-world grace. The forested plot of land on which the hotel sits was granted to the Croney family in 1690 by the king of England. The estate thrived as a working sugar plantation until 1936. Today, the stately ruins of its great house, once described by British historians as "the best example of Georgian domestic architecture in the Caribbean," complement the hotel's outbuildings.

Since its acquisition by new owners in 1995, the hotel has been renovated and now has a far more cheerful, tropical appearance. Accommodations contain wide-plank floors of tropical hardwoods, reproduction furniture, and high ceilings. Bathrooms come neat and tidy; some are shower-only.

The Old Manor runs a complimentary shuttle to Pinney's Beach, 15 to 20 minutes away.

Gingerland, Nevis, W.I. ✆ **800/892-7093** in the U.S., or 869/469-3445. Fax 869/469-3388. www.oldmanor nevis.com. 13 units. Winter US$250–US$320 double; off season US$170–US$220 double. Rates include full breakfast. AE, MC, V. Closed Sept. **Amenities:** Restaurant; bar; outdoor pool; Jacuzzi; sauna; beach shuttle; babysitting; laundry service. *In room:* Ceiling fan, kitchenette (in some), minibar, beverage maker, hair dryer, iron/ironing board.

MODERATE

Hurricane Cove Bungalows   This cluster of self-contained bungalows is set on a hillside with a world-class ocean view, a far better sight than the complex's rather ramshackle facade. It's located on the northernmost point of Nevis, a 5-minute drive west of the airport. Each bungalow is wood-sided and vaguely Scandinavian in design, with a tile roof and a massive foundation that anchors it into the rocky hillside. No meals are served, but each unit has a full kitchen and there's a poolside barbecue grill. Each bungalow has a queen-size bed, a covered porch, and a ceiling fan. The small, compact bathrooms are efficiently organized, with adequate shelf space and a shower stall. A freshwater pool is built into the foundation of a 250-year-old fortification, and the beach lies at the bottom of a steep hillside. The three-bedroom villa has its own small, but private, pool.

Oualie Beach, Nevis, W.I. © and fax **869/469-9462.** www.hurricanecove.com. 12 units. Winter US$190–US$295 1-bedroom bungalow, US$295–US$345 2-bedroom bungalow, US$495 3-bedroom villa; off season US$135–US$195 1-bedroom bungalow, US$215–US$265 2-bedroom bungalow, US$325 3-bedroom villa. MC, V. **Amenities:** Outdoor pool; babysitting; laundry service; nonsmoking rooms. *In room:* Ceiling fan, kitchen, fridge, beverage maker, no phone.

Oualie Beach Hotel   This place is often fully booked several months in advance by European sun-worshipers. The Oualie Beach Hotel is set on flatlands adjacent to the white sands of its namesake, the island's second-most-famous beach. Each medium-size unit is clean and simple, with tiled floors and small fridges; a few have kitchenettes. Extras include full-length mirrors, mahogany furnishings, and double or four-poster queen-size beds. Bathrooms are small and have showers only. The resort's centerpiece is its well-recommended restaurant and bar, where doors open directly onto a view of the beach (see "Dining," below).

Oualie Beach, Nevis, W.I. © **869/469-9735.** Fax 869/469-9176. www.oualiebeach.com. 32 units. Winter US$245 double, US$255–US$305 studio; off season US$195–US$245 double, US$205 studio. Children under 12 stay free in parent's room. AE, DISC, MC, V. **Amenities:** Restaurant; bar; dive shop; fishing; kayaks; sailing; snorkeling; windsurfing; bikes; limited room service; massage; babysitting; laundry service; all nonsmoking rooms. *In room:* A/C, TV, kitchen (in studios), fridge, beverage maker, hair dryer, iron/ironing board, safe.

DINING
VERY EXPENSIVE

Four Seasons Dining Room ☆☆ INTERNATIONAL/CARIBBEAN/ASIAN   Set beneath a soaring, elaborately trussed ceiling, this is the largest and most formal dining room on Nevis, and the island's best and most expensive restaurant. Decorated in a Caribbean interpretation of French Empire design, it offers rows of beveled-glass windows on three sides, massive bouquets of flowers, hurricane lamps with candles, a fireplace, a collection of unusual paintings, and impeccable service.

The fusion cuisine, with lots of nouvelle touches, roams the world for inspiration. Only quality ingredients are used, and some dishes are low in fat and calories. The menu changes nightly, but appearing frequently are savory seafood gumbo, or Cuban black-bean soup with applewood-smoked bacon. The pan-seared salmon with a curried fruit relish is incomparably fragrant, although the grilled mahimahi with wasabi-mango sauce is equally tempting. Vegetarians also have options here, perhaps vegetable cannelloni gratinée with a purple basil–tomato sauce. Dessert might be a coconut or mango soufflé. The service and the wine selection are the island's best.

In the Four Seasons Resort Nevis, Pinney's Beach. ✆ **869/469-1111.** Reservations required. Main courses US$35–US$55. AE, DC, DISC, MC, V. Daily 6–10pm.

Hermitage Plantation 🖈 INTERNATIONAL At this restaurant, you can combine an excellent dinner with a visit to the oldest house on Nevis, now one of the island's most unusual hotels (see "Accommodations," above). Meals are served on the latticed porch of the main house, amid candles and good cheer. Maureen Lupinacci, who runs the place with her husband, Richard, combines Continental recipes with local ingredients. Enjoy a before-dinner drink in the colonial-style living room, then move on to the likes of snapper steamed in banana leaves, carrot-and-tarragon soup, brown-bread ice cream, and a delectable version of Grand Marnier soufflé. Many people turn up on Wednesday for the roast-pig dinner (in season).

In the Hermitage Plantation hotel, St. John's Parish. ✆ **869/469-3477.** Reservations required. Lunch US$8–US$15; dinner US$55. AE, MC, V. Daily 8–10am, noon–3pm, and 8pm–midnight. Go south on the main island road from Charlestown.

Miss June's 🖈🖈 *Finds* CARIBBEAN/INTERNATIONAL This charming venue, midway between the Four Seasons Resort and the airport, is the private home of June Mestier, a Trinidad-born grande dame, and probably wouldn't exist if it had not been for Oprah Winfrey's enthusiasm. While visiting Nevis, Oprah heard that Ms. Mestier was the finest cook on the island and arranged a private dinner; after being served an excellent meal, Oprah urged her to open a restaurant.

A dinner in Mestier's West Indian house, which is adorned with latticework, requires advance reservations; some visitors call before they even arrive on Nevis. Guests at these dinner parties assemble for canapés and drinks in an airy living room, then sit down for soup and sherry. The tables hold from four to eight diners, and the silver and porcelain are quaintly elegant and charmingly mismatched. Fish and wine follow. All this is followed with samples of about 20 to 40 buffet dishes that hail from Trinidad, New Orleans, India, and the French isles. Mestier's comments on the food are one of the evening's most delightful aspects. After dinner, guests retire to a lounge for coffee, chocolates, and port. Many visitors find a meal here to be one of the highlights of their visit to Nevis.

Jones Bay. ✆ **869/469-5330.** Reservations required. Fixed-price meal US$65. MC, V. 3–5 evenings a week, depending on business, beginning around 7:30pm. Dinner served at 8:30pm.

Montpelier Plantation Inn 🖈 INTERNATIONAL This hotel (see "Accommodations," above), 2km (1¼ miles) off the main island road to Gingerland, provides some of the finest dining on the island. You sit by candlelight on the verandas of a grand old West Indian mansion, overlooking floodlit gardens, the lights of Charlestown, and the ocean. Lobster and fish are served the day the catch comes in, and the foreign and Nevisian chefs conspire to produce delectable tropical dishes. The best menu items include Cajun prawns, fresh tuna salad, curried ackee, suckling pig, and soursop-and-orange mousse for dessert. There's limited seating for dinner, so try to show up on time. An excellent and well-balanced wine list is available.

In the Montpelier Plantation Inn, Montpelier. ✆ **869/469-3462.** Reservations recommended for lunch, required for dinner. Lunch main courses US$8–US$22; fixed-price dinner US$49. AE, MC, V. Daily 8:15–10:30am, 12:30–2pm, dinner at 7:45–8:15pm. Closed Aug–Sept.

EXPENSIVE

The Cooperage ✿ INTERNATIONAL/CARIBBEAN Directly east of Charlestown and north of Gingerland, The Cooperage is set in a reconstructed 17th-century building where coopers once made barrels for the sugar mill. The dining room has a high, raftered ceiling and stonewalls. The food doesn't even try to compete with that at the Four Seasons, but it's good and reliable. Some of the appetizers are those 1950s favorites: green-pepper soup or shrimp cocktail. For a main course, you can order a 12-ounce New York strip steak or charcoal-grilled filet mignon with a mushroom sauce. The grilled Caribbean lobster is also appealing, as is the jerk pork. Main dishes are served with fresh vegetables of the day and your choice of twice-baked potato, rice, or pasta. Few leave hungry, especially after finishing with Old Manor's cheesecake, which has been sampled by all the movers and shakers on the island. The ginger pudding is also recommended.

In the Old Manor Estate, Gingerland. ℂ **869/469-3445.** Reservations recommended, especially for nonguests. Main courses US$22–US$32. AE, MC, V. Daily 8am–3pm and 5–9pm.

Mount Nevis Hotel Restaurant ✿ CARIBBEAN/CONTINENTAL This hotel restaurant is a discovery, serving some of the finest cuisine on Nevis, with menus that change every night. The chef has done a wonderful job of combining local flavors with a big-city gourmet twist. Just steps above the pool, the restaurant offers vistas of palm groves and the Caribbean Sea from its bar and dining terrace. You never know what will be featured: A very smooth and spicy conch chowder, or an equally delectable coconut-fried lobster with grilled pineapple and green-chile salsa might appear on the appetizer menu. Standard filets of grouper, snapper, or mahimahi are served, as is a delectable lamb shank with an array of local vegetables. The duck confit salad is also worth a try. The lunch menu is more limited but has some surprises—*tannia* (a yam-like root) fritters (instead of conch), for example.

In the Mount Nevis Hotel & Beach Club, Newcastle. ℂ **869/469-9373.** Reservations recommended for dinner. Main courses US$7–US$16 lunch, US$15–US$62 dinner. AE, MC, V. Daily 8–10am, 11:30am–2:30pm, and 6:30–9pm.

Oualie Beach Hotel INTERNATIONAL/NEVISIAN This restaurant is the centerpiece of the Oualie Beach Hotel (see "Accommodations," above), the only lodging adjacent to Oualie Beach. The airy building contains a bar area and a screened-in veranda just a few steps from the ocean. Every day the chef prepares a creative menu with real Caribbean flair, so you may want to study it closely before ordering. The pleasant staff can also make recommendations. The chef also prepares several lobster dishes, and the Creole conch stew is the island's best. Pastas appear frequently, along with some fairly bland international dishes such as chicken breast with rice, fries, or salad. An array of brightly colored rum drinks is available, and you can get a reasonably priced breakfast or lunch here, too.

In the Oualie Beach Hotel. ℂ **869/469-9735.** Reservations recommended for dinner. Breakfast US$6.50–US$12; lunch US$6–US$14; dinner main courses US$15–US$30. AE, MC, V. Daily 7–10am, noon–3pm, and 6:30–10pm.

Pizza Beach INTERNATIONAL This open-air restaurant on the water, housed in a concrete-block building with cathedral ceilings, is part of the Mount Nevis Beach Club. From the deck, you can take in a panoramic sea view. The informal cuisine is usually prepared with flair by the hardworking chef. Examples are a roster of meal-size pizzas big enough for two (try the version with seafood) as well as chicken parmigiana with pasta, shrimp with salsa verde, and Mexican platters piled high with quesadillas, tacos, flautas, and spicy beef. The best way to begin a meal is with one of the colorful margaritas.

Newcastle Marina, Charlestown. © 869/469-9395. Reservations recommended. Main courses US$15–US$25; pizzas for 2 US$10–US$20. AE, MC, V. Thurs–Tues 6–10pm.

Tequila Sheila's WEST INDIAN/INTERNATIONAL   This restaurant is on the premises of the Inn at Cades Bay, set on a wooden platform less than 18m (59 ft.) from the seafront, with a covered parapet but without walls. It offers panoramic views as far away as St. Kitts, and a menu that incorporates West Indian, Mexican, and international cuisine. Lunchtime brings dishes such as *roti*, enchiladas, grilled or jerk chicken, and lobster quesadillas. Dinner platters include vegetable-stuffed chicken, lobster, filet mignon with horseradish sauce or béarnaise sauce, and fish. Flying fish, wahoo, and mahimahi are very fresh here, and prepared as simply as possible—usually grilled with nothing more than lemon juice and herbs. The bar, fashioned from an overturned fishing boat, offers margaritas, various brands of tequila, and all the usual party-colored drinks you'd expect.

Cades Bay. © 869/469-8139. Reservations recommended. Main courses US$10–US$20 lunch, US$12–US$23 dinner. AE, MC, V. Mon–Sat 11:30am–3pm and 6:30–10pm; Sun 11:30am–4pm.

INEXPENSIVE
Le Bistro INTERNATIONAL   This is one of the tiniest restaurants on island, but its Friday night happy hour makes it the most popular. Locals call this place "Matt's," for Matt Lloyd, who sharpened his skills cooking at Montpelier. All the dishes are familiar but full of flavor, including the ground beef lasagna, coconut chicken, and the spicy curried chicken. In the British tradition, you can also order fish and chips. A savory kettle of mussels flavored with lemon butter is another good choice. The fish is especially recommended, as Matt catches them himself in his boat, *Deep Venture*. The chef's specialty is lobster served in a coconut sauce.

Chapel St. © 869/469-5110. Reservations recommended. Main courses EC$18–EC$55 (US$6.65–US$20). No credit cards. Daily 11am–3pm and 6–10pm.

BEACHES
Most hotels in Nevis have their own private beaches that nonguests may be able to use for a fee. But there are several fabulous public beaches on the island as well. The best one—in fact, one of the best in the Caribbean—is the reef-protected **Pinney's Beach** 𝕣𝕣, which has crystal-clear water, golden sands, and a gradual slope. It's no accident that the Four Seasons chose this location for its chic and superexpensive Nevis Resort.

Pinney's is just a short walk north of Charlestown on the west coast. You'll have 5km (3 miles) of sand (often virtually to yourself) that culminates in a sleepy lagoon, set against a backdrop of coconut palms. It's almost never crowded, and its calm, shallow waters are perfect for swimming and wading, which makes it a family favorite. It's best to bring your own sports equipment; the hotels along this beach have only limited gear that may be in use by its guests. You can go snorkeling or scuba diving here among damselfish, tangs, grunts, blue-headed wrasses, and parrot fish, and other species. The beach is especially beautiful in the late afternoon, when flocks of cattle egrets fly into its north end to roost at the freshwater pond at **Nelson's Spring.**

If you're going to be around for a few days you might want to search out the other beaches as well, notably beige-sand **Oualie Beach,** known especially for its diving and snorkeling. The location is north of Pinney's and just south of Mosquito Bay. The beach is well maintained and rarely crowded; you can purchase food and drink, as well as rent watersports equipment, at the Oualie Beach Hotel.

Indian Castle Beach, at the southern end of Nevis, has active surf and a swath of fine-gray sand. Indian Castle is definitely for escapists—chances are you'll have the beach all to yourself except for an indigenous goat or two, who may be very social and interested in sharing your picnic lunch.

Newcastle Beach is by the Nisbet Plantation, at the northernmost tip of the island on the channel that separates St. Kitts and Nevis. Snorkelers flock to this strip of soft, beige sand set against a backdrop of coconut palms.

The beaches along the east coast aren't desirable. They front Long Haul Bay in the north and White Bay in the south. These bays spill into the Atlantic Ocean and are rocky and too rough for swimming, although they're rather dramatic to visit if you're sightseeing. Of them all, **White Bay Beach** (sometimes called Windward Beach), in the southeastern section, east of Gingerland, is the best (especially for surfers). But be careful, as the waters can become turbulent suddenly.

SPORTS & OTHER OUTDOOR PURSUITS

BOATING   Scuba Safaris, an outfit that operates independently on the premises of the Oualie Beach Hotel (© **869/469-9518**), offers boat charters to Turtle Beach, which can make for a great day's outing; it costs US$50 round-trip (minimum of two people).

FISHING   Nevis Water Sports (© **869/469-9060**) offers the best deep-sea fishing aboard its custom 9m (30-ft.) fishing boat. The boat holds up to six; a 4-hour trip costs US$350, while an 8-hour trip is US$700. Snorkeling trips are available for US$35 per person, including equipment.

GOLF   The **Four Seasons Resort Nevis** ★★★, Pinney's Beach (© **869/469-1111**), has one of the most challenging and visually dramatic golf courses in the world. Designed by Robert Trent Jones Jr. (who called it "the most scenic golf course I've ever designed"), this 18-hole championship course wraps around the resort and offers panoramic ocean and mountain views at every turn. From the first tee (which begins just steps from the sports pavilion), through the 660-yard, par-5 18th green at the ocean's edge, the course is, in the words of one avid golfer, "reason enough to go to Nevis." Both guests and nonguests of the hotel pay US$175 for 18 holes. Rental clubs are available at US$55 for 18 holes.

HIKING & MOUNTAIN CLIMBING   Hikers can climb **Mount Nevis,** 970m (3,182 ft.) up to the extinct volcanic crater, and enjoy a trek to the rainforest to watch for wild monkeys. This hike is strenuous and is recommended only for those in good shape. Ask your hotel to pack a picnic lunch and arrange a guide (who will charge about US$35 per person). The hike takes about 5 hours; at the summit you'll be rewarded with views of Antigua, Saba, Statia, St. Kitts, Guadeloupe, and Montserrat. Reaching the summit means scrambling up near-vertical sections of the trail requiring handholds on not-always-reliable vines and roots. It's definitely not for acrophobes! Information on guides can also be obtained at the **Nevis Historical and Conservation Society,** based at the Museum of Nevis History, Main Street, Charlestown (© **869/469-5786**).

You can also contact **Sunrise Tours** (© **869/469-2758**) for a 1½-hour tour of **Historic Charlestown,** which takes you through the charming, Victorian-era capital to explore its rich and turbulent past: 300 years of fire, earthquake, hurricanes, and warfare. The cost is US$15.

HORSEBACK RIDING You can ride English saddle at the **Nisbet Plantation Beach Club,** Newcastle (© **869/469-9325** or 869/469-8118). A guide takes you along mountain trails to visit sites of long-forgotten plantations. The cost is US$75 per adult for 2 hours, US$50 for children.

SCUBA DIVING & SNORKELING Some of the best dive sites on Nevis include **Monkey Shoals,** 3km (2 miles) west of the Four Seasons. This is a beautiful reef, starting at 12m (39 ft.), with dives up to 30m (98 ft.) in depth. Angelfish, turtles, nurse sharks, and extensive soft coral can be found here. **The Caves** are on the south tip of Nevis, a 20-minute boat ride from the Four Seasons. A series of coral grottoes with numerous squirrelfish, turtles, and needlefish make this ideal for both certified and resort divers. **Champagne Garden,** a 5-minute boat ride from the Four Seasons, gets its name from bubbles created from an underwater sulfur vent. Because of the warm water temperature, large numbers of tropical fish are found here. Finally, **Coral Garden,** 3km (2 miles) west of the Four Seasons, is another beautiful coral reef with schools of Atlantic spadefish and large sea fans. The reef is at a maximum depth of 21m (69 ft.) and is suitable for both certified and resort divers.

Snorkelers should head for Pinney's Beach. You might also try the waters of Fort Ashby, where the settlement of Jamestown is said to have slid into the sea; legend has it that the church bells can still be heard, and the underwater town can still be seen when conditions are just right. So far, no diver, to our knowledge, has ever found the conditions just right.

Scuba Safaris, Oualie Beach (© **869/469-9518**), on the island's north end, offers PADI scuba diving and snorkeling in an area rich in dive sites. It also offers resort and certification courses, dive packages, and equipment rental. A one-tank scuba dive costs US$45; a two-tank dive, US$80. Full certification courses cost US$450 per person. Snorkeling trips cost US$35 per person.

TENNIS There are no public courts on Nevis. Guests at the big hotels play on their courts for free. Nonguests can play on the courts at the **Hermitage Plantation** (© **869/469-3477**) for free.

WINDSURFING The waters here are often ideal for this sport, especially for beginners and intermediates. **Windsurfing Nevis** at the Oualie Beach Hotel (© **869/469-9682**) offers the best equipment, costing US$20 for 1 hour.

EXPLORING THE ISLAND

It's a good idea to negotiate with a taxi driver to take you around Nevis. The distance is only 58km (36 miles), but you may find yourself taking a long time if you stop to see specific sights and talk to all the people who will want to chat with you. A 3-hour sightseeing tour around the island will cost US$64; the average taxi holds up to four people. No sightseeing bus companies operate on Nevis, but a number of individuals own buses that they use for taxi service. Call **John's Taxis** (© 869/469-7357) for information.

The major attraction is the **Museum of Nevis History,** in the house where Alexander Hamilton was born, on Main Street in Charlestown (© **869/469-5786**), overlooking the bay. The lava-stone house by the shore has been restored. The museum, dedicated to the history and culture of Nevis, houses the island's archives. Hours are Monday to Friday from 9am to 4pm, Saturday from 9am to noon. Admission is US$5 for adults, US$2 for children.

Eden Brown Estate, about 2km (1¼ miles) from New River, is said to be haunted. It was once the home of a wealthy planter whose daughter was to be married, but her husband-to-be was killed in a duel at the prenuptial feast. The mansion was then closed forever and left to the ravages of nature. Only the most adventurous come here on a moonlit night.

At one time, Sephardic Jews from Brazil made up a quarter of the island's population, and it's believed that Jews introduced sugar production to the Leeward Islands. Outside the center of Charlestown, at the lower end of Government Road, the **Jewish Cemetery** has been restored and is the resting place of many of the early shopkeepers of Nevis. Most of the tombstones date from 1690 to 1710.

An archaeological team from the United States believes that an old stone building in partial ruin on Nevis is probably the oldest **Jewish synagogue** in the Caribbean. Preliminary findings in 1993 traced the building's history to one of the two oldest Jewish settlements in the West Indies, and current work at the site plus historic documents in England establish its existence before 1650. The site is adjacent to the government administration building in Charlestown.

One of the island's best attractions is the 4-hectare (10-acre) **Botanical Garden of Nevis** (© 869/469-3399), 5km (3 miles) south of Charlestown on the Montpelier Estate. Rainforest plants grow in re-created Mayan ruins on a hillside site overlooking the Caribbean. The on-site restaurant, **Martha's Tea House,** serves an English tea with scones and double Devon cream. You can also order a ploughman's lunch (French bread, pickled onions, and cheese), barbecue chicken breast, mahimahi, or tuna salad. If you patronize the restaurant and gift shop, you don't have to pay the admission of US$9 adults, US$6 children, to the gardens. The garden is open Monday to Saturday from 9am to 4pm.

Nevis Jockey Club organizes and sponsors thoroughbred races every month. Local horses as well as some brought over from other islands fill out a typical five-race card. If you want to have a glimpse at what horse racing must have been like a century or more ago, you'll find the Nevis races a memorable experience. For information, contact Richard Lupinacci, a Jockey Club officer and owner and operator of the Hermitage Plantation (© 869/469-3477).

Nevisian Heritage Village, Fothergill's Estate (© 869/469-5521), is a collection of historic structures moved to this site, with an old sugar mill as its centerpiece. Among the attractions are a blacksmith's workshop, a rum store, and a cobbler's outpost, along with replicas of buildings ranging from African-styled slave huts to thatched shelters once inhabited by the Caribs. Open Monday to Saturday 9am to 3:30pm, charging an admission of US$3 for adults and US$1 for children.

SHOPPING

For original art, visit **Eva Wilkins's Studio,** Clay Ghaut, Gingerland (© 869/469-2673). Wilkins was the island's most famous artist; even Prince Charles showed up to look at her work. Until her death in 1989, she painted island people, local flowers, and scenes of Nevis life. Prints are available in some of the local shops, but originals sell for US$100 and up. You can visit her former atelier, on the grounds of an old sugar-mill plantation near Montpelier.

In a stone building about 60m (197 ft.) from the wharf, near the marketplace, **Nevis Handicraft Cooperative Society,** Cotton House, Charlestown (© 869/469-1746), contains locally made gift items, including unusual objects of goatskin, local wines made from a variety of fruits grown on the island, hot-pepper sauce, guava cheese, jams, and jellies.

Hand-painted, tie-dyed, and batik clothing are featured at **Island Hopper,** in the TDC Shopping Mall, Main Street, Charlestown (© **869/469-0893**), which also has locations on St. Kitts and Antigua. From beach wraps to souvenirs, a wide selection of products is available.

The toniest boutique on island is **Island Fever,** Main Street in Charlestown (© **869/469-9613**), with a tasteful and varied selection of items that might range from puppets and batiks from Indonesia to caftans, informal ware, steel drums, painted fish, or handmade jewelry. Closed September.

Those interested in stamp collecting can see a wide range of colorful stamps at the **Nevis Philatelic Bureau,** Head Post Office, Market Street (next to the public market), Charlestown (© **869/469-5535**). It features butterflies, shells, birds, flowers, and fish.

NEVIS AFTER DARK

Nightlife is not the reason to visit Nevis. Summer nights are quiet, but there's organized entertainment in winter, often steel bands performing at the major hotels.

Most action takes place at the **Four Seasons Resort,** Pinney's Beach (© **869/469-1111**), on Friday and Saturday nights. The **Old Manor Estate,** Gingerland (© **869/469-3445**), often brings in a steel band on Friday nights.

Oualie Beach Hotel, Oualie Beach (© **869/469-9735**), offers a Saturday buffet with a live string band entertaining guests. Disco reigns supreme at **Tequila Sheila's** at Cades Bay (p. 564) on Saturday night.

If you're on Nevis on a Friday night, the place to be for happy hour (5–7pm) is **Le Bistro** (p. 564). Islanders flock here for the reduced drink prices, the good company, and the fun atmosphere.

Another Friday night "jump-up" is at **The Water Department Barbecue,** Pump Road, Charlestown (no phone), to help raise money for the department. Tents go up in the late afternoon, and meat goes on the grill. Some of the best barbecue chicken and ribs on island are served here.

On Saturday night, head over to **Bananas,** Tamarind Bay (© **869/469-1891**), where dance music is the best after dinner. Wednesday night is all the rage at **Eddy's Bar & Restaurant,** Main Street in Charlestown (© **869/469-5958**), which serves the best conch fritters in town. Karaoke and dancing to music by an island DJ lasts way past midnight.

22

St. Lucia

St. Lucia (*Loo*-sha) is one of the most popular destinations in the Caribbean, with some of its finest resorts. The heaviest tourist development is concentrated in the northwest, between the capital, Castries, and the northern end of the island, where there's a string of white-sand beaches.

The rest of St. Lucia remains relatively unspoiled, a checkerboard of green-mantled mountains, valleys, banana plantations, a bubbling volcano, wild orchids, and fishing villages. The island has a mixed French and British heritage, but there's a hint of the South Pacific about it as well.

A mountainous island of some 623 sq. km (243 sq. miles), St. Lucia has about 120,000 inhabitants. The capital, Castries, is built on the southern shore of a large harbor surrounded by hills.

Writer Derek Walcott was born in Castries. His father was an unpublished poet who died when Walcott was just a year old, and his mother was a former headmistress at the Methodist school on St. Lucia. In 1992, Walcott won the Nobel Prize for literature. He prefers, however, not to tout the charms of St. Lucia, telling the press, "I don't want everyone to go there and overrun the place." Alas, his warning has come too late.

1 Essentials

VISITOR INFORMATION

In the **United States,** the St. Lucia Tourist Board office is located at 800 Second Ave., Suite 910, New York, NY 10017 (© **800/456-3984** or 212/867-2950). In the **United Kingdom,** contact the tourist office at 421A Finchley Rd., London NW3 6HJ (© **0870/900-7697**). In **Canada,** information is provided at the tourist board at 8 King St. East, Suite 700, Toronto, Ontario M5V 1B5 (© **416/362-4242**).

On the island, the main tourist office is at Sureline Building, Vive Boutielle, Castries (© **758/452-4094**). In **Soufrière,** there's a branch on Bay Street (© **758/459-7419**). St. Lucia information is on the Web at **www.stlucia.org**.

GETTING THERE

Before you book your own airfare, read the section "Packages for the Independent Traveler" in chapter 2—it can save you a bundle.

The island maintains two separate airports, whose different locations cause endless confusion to many newcomers. Most international long-distance flights land at **Hewanorra International Airport** (© **758/454-6355**) in the south, 72km (45 miles) from Castries. If you arrive here and you're booked into a hotel in the north, you'll spend about an hour and a half traveling along the potholed East Coast Highway. Many hotels arrange transfers to and from the airport, but if not, taxis are available; the average fare is US$65 for up to four passengers.

Many visitors now prefer to take helicopter flights from Hewanorra International Airport to their resorts rather than endure the long, stomach-churning car ride. **St. Lucia Helicopters** (© 758/453-6950; www.stluciahelicopters.com), offers flights between Castries and Hewanorra Airport or Soufrière, costing US$100 per person one way. Flights can also be arranged to Jalousie Hilton Resort & Spa (p. 574), which has its own helicopter pad.

Flights from other parts of the Caribbean usually land at the smaller, somewhat antiquated **George F. L. Charles Airport** (formerly known as Vigie) (© 758/452-1156), in the northeast. Its location just outside Castries affords much more convenient access to the capital and many of the island's hotels. It's a long (about an hour and a half), twisting drive to lodging in and around Soufrière, however, but you pass through beautiful terrain and quaint fishing villages.

You'll probably have to change planes somewhere else in the Caribbean to get to St. Lucia. **American Eagle** (© 800/433-7300 in the U.S., or 758/452-6777; www.aa.com) serves George F. L. Charles Airport with nonstop flights from San Juan. Connections from all parts of the North American mainland to the airline's enormous hub in San Juan are frequent and convenient. American also offers some good package deals.

US Airways (© 800/428-4322, or 758/454-8186; www.usairways.com) flies two times a week from Philadelphia to St. Lucia's Hewanorra Airport.

Air Canada (© 888/247-2262 or 758/454-6038; www.aircanada.ca) has two nonstop weekly flights to St. Lucia's Hewanorra Airport that departs from Toronto.

British Airways (© 800/247-9297 in the U.S., or 0870/850-9850 in England; www.britishairways.com) offers three flights a week from London's Gatwick Airport to St. Lucia's Hewanorra Airport.

LIAT (© 888/844-5428 in the Caribbean or 868/624-4727; www.liat airline.com) has small planes flying from many points throughout the Caribbean into George F. L. Charles Airport. Points of origin include such islands as Barbados, Antigua, St. Thomas, St. Maarten, and Martinique. On some LIAT flights, you may visit all these islands before arriving in St. Lucia.

Air Jamaica (© 800/523-5585 in the U.S., or 758/453-6611; www.air jamaica.com) serves the Hewanorra Airport with nonstop service from either New York's JFK or Newark, New Jersey, five days a week.

Another option is **BWIA** (© 800/538-2942 in the U.S.; www.bwee.com), which offers two weekly flights on Sunday and Tuesday from London's Heathrow to St. Lucia's Hewanorra Airport. All flights make a quick stopover in Barbados. At least, we hope it's quick.

GETTING AROUND

BY TAXI Since driving St. Lucia's unmarked, bad roads is rather difficult, a taxi is recommended for all but the most adventurous. Taxis are ubiquitous and most drivers are eager to please. The drivers have special training that allows them to serve as guides. Their cabs are unmetered, but the government fixes tariffs for all standard trips. From Castries, the fare to Marigot Bay should be US$25 to US$30; to Rodney Bay, the fare is US$18 to US$20. Always ask if the driver is quoting a rate in U.S. dollars or Eastern Caribbean dollars (EC$).

Most day tours of the island cost US$132 per carload; you can also negotiate a half-day rate. One company that specializes in these tours is **Toucan Travel**, The Marina in Castries (© 758/452-9963).

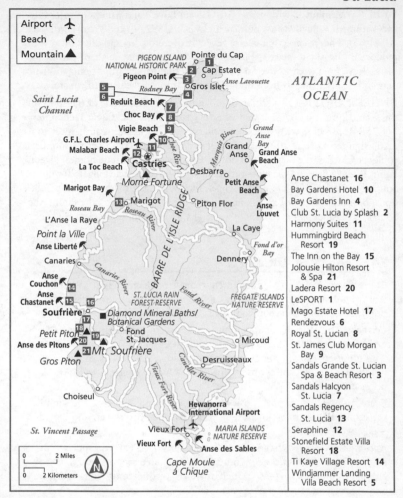

Airport ✈
Beach 🏖
Mountain ▲

PIGEON ISLAND — Pointe du Cap
NATIONAL HISTORIC PARK — **1**
Cap Estate
Pigeon Point — **3** — Gros Islet
Anse Lavouette

ATLANTIC OCEAN

Saint Lucia Channel

Rodney Bay — **5** **6**
Reduit Beach — **7**
Choc Bay — **8**
Vigie Beach — **9**
G.F.L. Charles Airport — **10**
Malabar Beach — **12** **11**
La Toc Beach
Castries

Grand Anse Bay
Grand Anse
Grand Anse Beach

Desbarra

Morne Fortune
Marigot Bay
Petit Anse Beach

13 — Marigot
Roseau Bay
L'Anse la Raye
Point la Ville
Anse Liberté
Canaries

Piton Flor
Anse Louvet

La Caye
Fond d'or Bay

Dennery

Anse Couchon — **14**
Anse Chastanet — **15** — **16**
Soufrière
17
Petit Piton — **18** ▲
Anse des Pitons — **20** **19**
Gros Piton — **21** ▲ Mt. Soufrière

ST. LUCIA RAIN FOREST RESERVE
Diamond Mineral Baths/ Botanical Gardens
Fond St. Jacques

FREGATE ISLANDS NATURE RESERVE

Micoud

Desruisseaux

Choiseul

Hewanorra International Airport

St. Vincent Passage

Vieux Fort
Vieux Fort 🏖
Anse des Sables

MARIA ISLANDS NATURE RESERVE

Cape Moule à Chique

0 — 2 Miles
0 — 2 Kilometers

Anse Chastanet	**16**
Bay Gardens Hotel	**10**
Bay Gardens Inn	**4**
Club St. Lucia by Splash	**2**
Harmony Suites	**11**
Hummingbird Beach Resort	**19**
The Inn on the Bay	**15**
Jolousie Hilton Resort & Spa	**21**
Ladera Resort	**20**
LeSPORT	**1**
Mago Estate Hotel	**17**
Rendezvous	**6**
Royal St. Lucian	**8**
St. James Club Morgan Bay	**9**
Sandals Grande St. Lucian Spa & Beach Resort	**3**
Sandals Halcyon St. Lucia	**7**
Sandals Regency St. Lucia	**13**
Seraphine	**12**
Stonefield Estate Villa Resort	**18**
Ti Kaye Village Resort	**14**
Windjammer Landing Villa Beach Resort	**5**

BY RENTAL CAR *Remember:* Drive on the left, and try to avoid some of the island's more obvious potholes. Drive carefully and honk your horn while going around the blind hairpin turns. You'll need a St. Lucia driver's license (US$21), which you can purchase at either airport when you pick up your rental car.

Avis (© **800/331-1212** in the U.S., or 758/452-2046 or 758/454-6325; www.avis.com), **Traders Auto Rentals** (© **758/452-0233;** www.alcorentacar. com), and **Hertz** (© **800/654-3131** in the U.S., or 758/454-9636; www.hertz. com) have offices at (or will deliver cars to) both of the island's airports. Each also has an office in Castries and, in some cases, at some of the island's major hotels.

You can sometimes save money by booking through one of the local car-rental agencies, where rates begin at US$45 to US$50 per day, depending on size. Try **C.T.L. Rent-a-Car,** Grosislet Highway, Rodney Bay Marina (© **758/452-0732**). **Cool Breeze Car Rental,** New Development, Soufrière (© **758/459-7729**), is also a good bet if you're staying in the south. Prices are US$45 and up.

BY BUS **Minibuses** (with names like "Lucian Love") and **jitneys** connect Castries with such main towns as Soufrière for EC$7 (US$2.60) and Vieux Fort EC$5 (US$1.85). They're cheap but they're generally overcrowded and often filled with produce on its way to market. Buses for Cap Estate, in the northern part of the island, leave from Jeremy Street in Castries, near the market. Buses going to Vieux Fort and Soufrière depart from Bridge Street in front of the department store.

BY HELICOPTER In addition to providing the fastest mode of transport on this island (preferred by such visitors as Harrison Ford) **St. Lucia Helicopters** (② 758/453-6950; www.stluciahelicopters.com) offers the islands most dramatic sightseeing. The 10-minute North Trip, costing US$55 per person, flies you over Castries, the major resort hotels, the elegant Cap Estate homes, Pigeon Point, Rodney Bay, and the more turbulent Atlantic coast. The longer 20-minute South Tour, costing US$95 per passenger, flies over Castries, the banana plantations, beautiful Marigot Bay, fishing villages, the lush rain forest, the Pitons, the Soufrière volcano, and even remote waterfalls, rivers, and lush valleys.

FAST FACTS: St. Lucia

Banks Banks are open Monday to Thursday from 8am to 3pm and on Friday from 8am to 5pm. ATMs can be found at all bank branches, transportation centers, and shopping malls.

Currency The official monetary unit is the **Eastern Caribbean dollar (EC$)**, which is pegged at EC$2.70 per U.S. dollar (EC$1 = US37¢). *Unless otherwise specified, rates in this chapter are quoted in U.S. dollars,* as nearly all hotels, restaurants, and shops accept them. Always ascertain which dollar prices are listed in.

Customs At either airport, Customs may be a hassle if there's the slightest suspicion, regardless of how ill-founded, that you're carrying illegal drugs.

Documents U.S., British, and Canadian citizens need valid passports, plus an ongoing or return ticket. If your stay is less than 6 months, you can also enter with proof of citizenship such as a birth certificate with a raised seal and a government-issued photo ID.

Electricity St. Lucia runs on 220- to 230-volt AC (50 cycles), so bring an adapter if you plan to use U.S. appliances. Some hotels are wired for U.S. appliances. Ask when you book.

Emergencies Call the police at ② **999**. For an ambulance or in case of fire call ② **911**.

Hospitals There are 24-hour emergency rooms at **St. Jude's Hospital,** Vieux Fort (② **758/454-6041**), and **Victoria Hospital,** Hospital Road, Castries (② **758/452-2421**).

Language Although English is the official tongue, St. Lucians probably don't speak it the way you do. Islanders also speak a French-Creole patois, similar to that heard on Martinique.

Pharmacies The best is **M&C Drugstore**, Bridge Street, in Castries (② **758/ 458-8147**), open Monday through Friday from 8am to 5pm, and Saturday from 8am to 1pm.

Safety St. Lucia has its share of crime, like every other place these days. Use common sense and protect yourself and your valuables. If you've got it, don't flaunt it! Don't pick up hitchhikers if you're driving around the island. The use of narcotic drugs is illegal, and their possession or sale could lead to stiff fines or jail.

Taxes The government imposes an 8% occupancy tax on hotel rooms, and there's a US$21 departure tax for both airports. Children under 12 don't pay departure tax.

Telephone The area code for St. Lucia is **758**. Make calls to or from St. Lucia just as you would with any other area code in North America. On the island, dial all seven digits of the local number. If your hotel won't send a fax for you, try **Cable & Wireless,** in the SMC Building on the waterfront in Castries (℅ **758/452-3301**). To access **AT&T Direct,** call ℅ **800/225-5288**; to reach **MCI,** dial ℅ **800/888-8000**.

Time St. Lucia is on Atlantic Standard Time year-round, placing it 1 hour ahead of New York. However, when the United States is on daylight savings time (Apr–Oct), St. Lucia matches the clocks of the U.S. East Coast.

Tipping Most hotels and restaurants add a 10% service charge (ask if it's been included in the initial hotel rate you're quoted). If you're pleased with the service in a restaurant, by all means, supplement with an extra 5%. Taxi drivers expect 10% of the fare.

Water Water here is generally considered safe to drink; if you're unsure or have a delicate constitution, stick to bottled water.

Weather This little island, lying in the path of the trade winds, has year-round temperatures of 70°F to 90°F (21°C–32°C).

2 Accommodations

Most of the leading hotels on this island are pretty pricey; you have to really search for the bargains. However, many of the big resorts here are frequently featured in packages (see the section "Packages for the Independent Traveler," in chapter 2). Once you reach your hotel, chances are you'll feel pretty isolated, which is exactly what most guests want. Many St. Lucian hostelries have kitchenettes where you can prepare simple meals. Prices are usually quoted in U.S. dollars. An 8% hotel tax is added to your bill. Most hotels also add a 10% service charge (ask if it's been included in the initial hotel rate you're quoted).

VERY EXPENSIVE

Anse Chastanet 🌟🌟🌟   One of the few places that merits the cliché "tropical paradise," this is not only St. Lucia's premier dive resort, but also an exceptional Caribbean inn. It offers warm service, excellent food, a beach location, and first-class facilities. It lies 29km (18 miles) north of Hewanorra International Airport (a 50-min. taxi ride), 3km (2 miles) north of Soufrière on a forested hill, and a 103-step climb above palm-fringed Anse Chastanet Beach. You're surrounded by coffee trees, mangos, papayas, banana plants, breadfruit, grapefruit, coconut palms, and hibiscus. The main building is decorated in a typical island style, with a relaxing bar and dining room. Guest can book first-rate spa treatments at the onsite Kai Belte Spa.

Guests can stay on the beach in spacious accommodations styled like West Indian plantation villas. Other units, constructed like octagonal gazebos and cooled by ceiling fans, have views of the Pitons. The spacious rooms are comfortably appointed with locally made furniture crafted from island woods. They have tropical hardwood floors, wooden jalousie louvers, king-size beds, and roomy private bathrooms with shower stalls and dual sinks. In the summer of 2004, the hotel planned to open two dozen deluxe suites that are among the finest places to stay on island. The cluster of suites have their own concierge desk and a communication room with phones and computers. The suites are spacious, each with one wall missing and opening onto a private pool the length of the suite. Also in the works is a terraced, freshwater pool on the resort's 18th-century French Colonial plantation, along the Jungle Biking trail.

You can dine or drink on a wind-cooled terrace, built like a tree house over the tropical landscape, in the Pitons Bar and Restaurant. Even if you're not a guest of the hotel, consider stopping at the beachside restaurant, Trou au Diable, which offers West Indian cuisine and a grill, plus a twice-weekly Creole dinner buffet. The resort's excellent staff has few equals in the Caribbean.

Anse Chastanet Beach (P.O. Box 7000), Soufrière, St. Lucia, W.I. ⓒ 800/223-1108 in the U.S., or 758/459-7000. Fax 758/459-7700. www.ansechastanet.com. 73 units. Winter US$445–US$795 double, from US$795 suite; off season US$255–US$450 double, from US$550 suite. Winter rates include breakfast and dinner. AE, MC, V. **Amenities:** 2 restaurants; 2 bars; tennis court; gym; spa; dive shop; kayaks; sailboat rentals; snorkeling; windsurfing; bikes; airport transfers; laundry service; nonsmoking rooms. *In room:* Ceiling fan, minibar, fridge, beverage maker, hair dryer, iron/ironing board (in some), safe, no phone.

Jalousie Hilton Resort & Spa ⁂ñ⁂
This unusual and elegant resort is for visitors to St. Lucia's southwest coast who are looking for privacy, a sense of isolation, and greater degrees of luxury than what's available at Ladera or Anse Chastanet. It originated in the late 1990s, when an already-existing hotel, positioned on the fertile tropical plain midway between the two Pitons, was radically upgraded with an infusion more than US$6 million in cash. Today, the ownership of this elegant hotel is divided between a group of Iranian investors, the St. Lucian government, and representatives of Hilton International. Sprawling across one of the best building sites in St. Lucia, the property is so large (130 hectares/321 acres) that vans constantly circulate to shuttle guests around. Most of the resort's accommodations are in individual villas or villa suites (slightly larger, with separate sitting rooms) that dot the hillside. All the tile-floored villa rooms have four-star luxuries, including remote-controlled air-conditioning, fold-out sofas, and shower/tub combinations. All villas and suites also have private plunge pools. Our only complaint is that the degree of privacy is not always enough to allow, say, nude sunbathing. In addition to the villas, 12 Sugar Mill double rooms are in two buildings; they're slightly smaller than the other rooms, but they still have private terraces. The staff here is especially friendly and helpful.

The chef's inventive cuisine is ambitious but best when it concentrates on flavorful, local ingredients.

P.O. Box 251, Soufrière, St. Lucia, W.I. ⓒ 888/744-5256 in the U.S. for reservations only, or 758/456-8000. Fax 758/459-7667. www.hilton.com. 112 units. Winter US$460 double, US$515 villa, US$730 villa suite; off season US$275–US$330 double, US$420 villa, US$520 villa suite. MAP (breakfast and dinner) US$70 per person extra. Honeymoon, dive, and spa packages available. AE, DC, DISC, MC, V. Small pets allowed. **Amenities:** 4 restaurants; 4 bars; outdoor pool; night club; par-3 executive golf course; 4 lit Laykold tennis courts; squash court; health club and spa; fitness classes; Jacuzzi; sauna; dive shop; fishing; scuba diving; snorkeling; water-skiing; children's activities; tour desk; car rental; business center; salon; 24-hr. room service; babysitting; laundry service; dry cleaning; nonsmoking rooms. *In room:* A/C, TV/VCR, dataport, minibar, iron/ironing board, coffeemaker, hair dryer, safe, bathrobes.

Ladera Resort ✰✰✰   The Ladera is an exercise in luxurious simplicity on St. Lucia's southwest end, frequently a retreat for the rich and famous who seek total privacy from the outside world: There are no phones or TVs in the rooms. Outside the town of Soufrière, this hideaway is perched on a hillside 330m (1,082 ft.) above sea level. Sandwiched between the Pitons, the resort has views of Jalousie Bay—perhaps the most stunning vistas you'll find on St. Lucia. The villas and suites are completely open to the views of the Pitons. You don't come here for the beach—it's a 15- to 20-minute complimentary shuttle ride away—but for the lovely setting, gracious service, and privacy.

Accommodations are constructed of tropical hardwoods, stone, and tile, and are furnished with 19th-century French furniture, wicker, and accessories built by local craftspeople. You'll find interesting touches in all the rooms: sinks made of shells, or open, rock-walled showers. All units afford total privacy and have indoor gardens and plunge pools, plus showers. Many rooms have four-poster queen-size beds draped in mosquito netting, and all have fridges. Breezes cool the rooms, which are not air-conditioned. To get in here in winter, reserve 4 months in advance. We're not kidding.

The Dasheene Restaurant & Bar offers fine dining and specializes in Creole and Continental cuisine. The seafood is caught fresh daily. Guests enjoy high tea in Ladera's botanical garden.

P.O. Box 225, Soufrière, St. Lucia, W.I. ℂ 800/738-4752 in the U.S. and Canada, or 758/459-7323. Fax 758/459-5156. www.ladera-stlucia.com. 33 units. Winter US$395–US$560 1- or 2-bedroom suite, US$600–US$820 villa; off season US$240–US$330 1- or 2-bedroom suite, US$375–US$565 villa. Extra person US$20–US$35. MAP (breakfast and dinner) US$65 per person extra (3-night minimum for meal plan). 7-night minimum stay Dec 25–Jan 4. AE, MC, V. Closed mid-Sept to mid-Oct. **Amenities:** Restaurant; bar; outdoor pool; fishing charters; sailing; scuba diving; snorkeling; horseback riding; shuttle service to the beach; limited room service; laundry service. *In room:* Fridge, hair dryer, safe, plunge pool, no phone.

LeSPORT ✰✰✰   Following a multimillion-dollar renovation and expansion, this luxury all-inclusive spa resort, now officially called The Body Holiday at LeSPORT, is better than ever. It's all the way at the northernmost tip of the island, a 13km (8-mile) drive from Castries. Guests seem to enjoy the isolation.

The resort faithfully keeps its promise that everything you "do, see, enjoy, drink, eat, and feel" is included in the price—that means not only accommodations, three meals a day, all refreshments, and bar drinks, but also use of sports equipment, facilities, and instruction, and most (though not all) of the spa treatments. Units are in a four-story building on a hill site fronting a long palm-fringed beach. Bedrooms are roomy and beautifully appointed, with fridges, wicker furnishings, and king-size or paired twin beds. Bathrooms are spacious, with tubs and showers and dual basins. To cater to the rapidly growing singles market, the resort has created rooms especially for solo travelers.

Meals are served in an open-air restaurant overlooking the Caribbean. Breakfast and lunch are buffet style; dinner offers a choice between light meals and heartier options. Tao, an East/West fusion restaurant is open to both guests and nonguests only at dinner with advance reservations. The food is arguably the best of that offered by the all-inclusive resorts. There's live entertainment, including a piano bar that's popular until late at night.

Cariblue Beach (P.O. Box 437), St. Lucia, W.I. ℂ 800/544-2883 in the U.S. and Canada, or 758/450-8551. Fax 758/450-0368. www.thebodyholiday.com. 154 units. Winter US$726–US$812 double, US$912 suite; off season US$526–US$612 double, US$712 suite. Rates are all-inclusive. AE, DISC, MC, V. Children age 12 and over allowed June 27–Sept. 25; otherwise, the minimum age is 16 years. **Amenities:** 3 restaurants; 3 bars (1 piano bar); 3 pools; tennis court; health club and spa; archery; fencing; sailing; scuba diving; snorkeling; water-skiing; windsurfing; airport transfers; room service (breakfast only); babysitting; laundry. *In room:* A/C, hair dryer, safe.

Moments Soft Adventures in the Wild

LeSPORT at Cariblue Beach (© 800/544-2883) has introduced several "soft adventures" costing from US$85 to US$90 per person, that include scenic walks, mountain climbing, turtle-watching, and hikes through the rainforest. Two river walks, with wading, go deep into the rainforest. One is along the River Doree in the southern part of St. Lucia and the other is along Anse la Raye River, which is midisland. Mountain climbing takes you to Gros Piton, one of the island's two dramatic sugarloaf peaks, where overnights are often arranged so you can wake up to a spectacular sunrise from a lofty vantage point.

These excursions often pass waterfalls, allowing hikers to swim in the pools below. Many tropical birds can be observed, including the St. Lucia parrot, which once was nearly extinct. During turtle-watching season, (March to July), LeSPORT guests can camp overnight at Grand Anse beach in order to watch the huge leatherback turtles lay eggs. Escorts from the hotel set up Arabian-like tents and serve a barbecue dinner.

Rendezvous 🌴🌴   On Malabar Beach, Rendezvous is an all-inclusive hotel for heterosexual couples only (no children, singles, or gay couples allowed). This is the down-market version of LeSPORT (see above) and suffers from its location at the end of the airport runway. Most guests are between the ages of 25 and 40, but you'll occasionally see some older folks. There are several price categories, depending on the season and the accommodation; top rates are charged for oceanfront luxury suites for two. Many beds are four-poster king-sizes draped in mosquito netting. The bathrooms are small but have combination shower/tubs, lighted makeup mirrors, and dual basins. Balconies and terraces are common to all units. The resort is north of George F. L. Charles Airport, near Castries, set within a 3-hectare (7½-acre) tropical garden on the edge of a large, sandy beach.

Polished brass chandeliers highlight the Trysting Place, a classical colonial-style dining room. The informal, open-air Terrace Restaurant features pastas and other classics. For live entertainment 6 nights a week, guests frequent the piano bar.

Malabar Beach (P.O. Box 190), St. Lucia, W.I. © 800/544-2883 in the U.S., or 758/452-4211. Fax 758/452-7419. www.rendezvous.com.lc. 100 units. Winter US$476–US$538 double, US$550 suite for 2; off season US$390 double, US$502 suite for 2. Rates are all-inclusive. AE, DISC, MC, V. **Amenities:** 2 restaurants; 2 bars (1 piano bar); 2 outdoor pools; 2 tennis courts; fitness center; archery; sauna; 2 whirlpools; scuba-diving facilities; water-skiing; windsurfing; bicycle tours; laundry service. *In room:* A/C, beverage maker, hair dryer, iron/ironing board, safe.

Royal St. Lucian 🌴🌴   A fine resort with a new spa, the Royal St. Lucian lies north of Castries. Standing in its own gardens of royal palms and tropical foliage, it opens onto a dramatic lobby. All the accommodations are luxury suites, the best of which have sea views and balconies. There are eight even more spacious suites right at beachfront, each with a private terrace. Some of the units are split-level, with spacious bathrooms containing tubs and jet showers, cream-colored tile floors, rattan furniture, and woven rugs. Everywhere you look, the setting is lush. The food is among the best hotel cuisine on the island, and candlelit beach dinners are featured. The chefs are also known for West Indian and Italian buffets. Jazz can be heard in the chic cocktail lounge, and the spa offers everything from hydrotherapy to herbal body wraps.

Rodney Bay (P.O. Box 977), Castries, St. Lucia, W.I. ℂ **800/255-5859** in the U.S., or 758/452-9999. Fax 758/452-9639. www.rexcaribbean.com. 96 units. Winter US$500–US$760 double; off season US$390–US$630 double. AE, DC, DISC, MC, V. **Amenities:** 3 restaurants; 2 bars; outdoor pool; 2 tennis courts; health club and spa; sauna; dive shop; fishing; snorkeling; Sunfish sailboats; water-skiing; windsurfing; children's programs; business services; room service (7am–midnight); babysitting; laundry service; rooms for those with limited mobility. *In room:* A/C, TV, minibar, beverage maker (in some), hair dryer, safe.

Sandals Grande St. Lucian Spa & Beach Resort 𝄞𝄞𝄞

The popular chain, Sandals, is leaving its footprints all over the sands of the island. In the summer of 2002, Jamaican hotelier Butch Stewart opened his third couples-only (male/female) all-inclusive on St. Lucia. This one is the best of the lot. The luxury resort lies at the causeway on the northern tip of St. Lucia, linking the "mainland" with Pigeon Island, with the tranquil Caribbean Sea on one side and the often more turbulent Atlantic Ocean on the other side. Set on a landscaped 1-hectare (2½-acre) lagoon, the megaresort took over an already existing property, Hyatt Regency, at a point 10km (6¼ miles) northwest of Castries at Rodney Bay. With a private golden sandy beach, the most lavish lagoon-style swimming pool on the island, a state-of-the-art spa, and a choice of restaurants, many find it hard to tear themselves away from the grounds.

Even the standard bedrooms are spacious, with antique reproductions in a plantation style. Local art brightens the walls, and the bathrooms are full and luxurious. The fourth-floor rooms have better views, service, and space, and are more comfortable. For the ultimate in luxury, ask for one of the two dozen "swim-up" units with their own free-form pools and terraces. Inquire about the "stay at one, play at three" program where you stay at one Sandals and are able to use facilities at other properties as well.

Pigeon Island Causeway, Gros Islet, St. Lucia. W.I. ℂ **800/SANDALS** or 758/455-2000. Fax 758/455-2001. www.sandals.com. 284 units. Winter US$370–US$540 double, from US$630 suite; off season US$340–US$500 double, from US$630 suite. Rates are per person and all-inclusive. AE, MC, V. Children not accepted. **Amenities:** 5 restaurants; 3 bars; 5 outdoor pools; night club; golf privileges; 4 tennis courts; health club and spa; sauna; deep-sea fishing; dive shop; kayaks; sailing; snorkeling; water-skiing; windsurfing; airport shuttle; business services; limited room service; laundry service; nonsmoking rooms; rooms for those with limited mobility. *In room:* A/C, TV, beverage maker, hair dryer, iron/ironing board, safe.

Sandals Halcyon Beach St. Lucia 𝄞

Within walking distance of Palm Beach and a 15-minute drive northeast of Castries, this is the smaller of the three Sandals properties on St. Lucia, and it has fewer facilities. But you can always take the free 15-minute minibus ride to Sandals Regency St. Lucia if you want to use the nine-hole golf course. Sandals "stay at one, play at three" program allows you to use the extensive facilities at Sandals Grande St. Lucian or Sandals regency St. Lucia. Guest rooms come in a wide range of categories, usually with a king-size mahogany four-poster bed. Each room has a full bathroom with a tub and shower. The food is copious but not of the highest quality. The best place to dine is the Pier Restaurant, a West Indian–style restaurant atop a 45m (148-ft.) pier. Children, singles, and gay and lesbian couples are not permitted.

Choc Bay (P.O. Box GM 910), Castries, St. Lucia, W.I. ℂ **800/SANDALS** or 758/453-0222. Fax 758/451-8435. www.sandals.com. 170 units. All-inclusive rates per person for 3 nights: winter US$660–US$940 double; off season US$590–US$860 double. AE, MC, V. Children not accepted. **Amenities:** 3 restaurants; 3 bars (2 swim-up); 2 pools; night club; golf privileges; 2 lit tennis courts; fitness center; 3 Jacuzzis; kayaks; sailing; scuba diving; snorkeling; windsurfing; transfers to airport; laundry service. *In room:* A/C, TV, beverage maker, hair dryer, iron/ironing board, safe.

Sandals Regency St. Lucia 𝄞𝄞

The Jamaica-based Sandals chain opened this clone on a forested 62-hectare (153-acre) site that slopes steeply down to the sea. This is larger and more upscale than the Sandals Halcyon, but not as spiffy as the newest Sandals Grande St. Lucian Beach Resort. However, the male-female couples thing is just as strongly emphasized here. The hotel is near Castries, on the island's northwestern coast. The center of the resort is a gazebo-capped pool that incorporates two waterfalls, a swim-up bar, and a dining pavilion. Larger-than-expected guest rooms contain king-size four-poster beds with mahogany headboards, balconies or patios, and a pastel tropical decor. Bathrooms are spacious, with shower/tub combinations.

The resort's six restaurants are infinitely superior to the cuisine served at Sandals Halcyon (see above). The most upscale, La Toc, features French cuisine. Kimonos offers Japanese food cooked on a heated table top, Teppanyaki style. The Arizona Restaurant, as befits its name, features the cuisine of the U.S. Southwest. After dark, guests gravitate to Jaime's, the nightclub/disco, or to Herbie's Piano Bar. Inquire about the "stay at one, play at three" program where you stay at one Sandals property but are able to use the other properties as well.

La Toc Rd. (P.O. Box 399), Castries, St. Lucia, W.I. ✆ **800/SANDALS** in the U.S. and Canada, or 758/452-3081. Fax 758/452-1012. www.sandals.com. 328 units. All-inclusive rates for 2 for 3 nights: winter US$2,100–US$3,000 double, US$3,200–US$4,950 suite; off season US$1,920–US$2,610 double, US$2,760–US$4,560 suite. AE, MC, V. Children not accepted. **Amenities:** 6 restaurants; 10 bars (1 swim-up); 3 outdoor pools; night club; 9-hole golf course; 5 lit tennis courts; health club and spa; 4 Jacuzzis; dive shop; kayaks; sailing; snorkeling; windsurfing; business services; salon; limited room service; massage; laundry service. *In room:* A/C, TV, beverage maker, hair dryer, iron/ironing board, safe.

St. James Club Morgan Bay 🎾 *Kids*   Set a 10-minute drive north of Castries, on 9 landscaped hectares (22 acres) partially shaded with trees and flowering shrubs, this all-inclusive resort draws more Europeans than Americans. It offers guest rooms in six different annexes. Standard features include patios or verandas, rattan and wicker furnishings, fridges, and queen-size or paired twin beds. The spacious marble-trimmed bathrooms contain shower/tub combinations. Unlike some other all-inclusive hostelries on the island, this one welcomes children. The beach here is small, with murky water. You can dine elegantly by candlelight at the resort's premier restaurant, the Trade Winds, overlooking the garden. The cuisine is resort standard, nothing more. Local musicians, steel bands, and calypso singers often perform live in the Sundowner Bar.

Choc Bay (P.O. Box 2167), Gros Islet, St. Lucia, W.I. ✆ **800/345-0356** in the U.S., or 758/450-2511. Fax 758/450-1050. www.eliteislandvacations.com. 240 units. Winter US$460–US$496 double; off season US$364–US$408 double; year-round US$660 suite for 2. Rates are all-inclusive. Winter, children age 13–18 staying in parent's room US$100, age 3–12 US$60, under age 2 free; off season, children 12 and under stay free in parent's room. AE, DC, DISC, MC, V. **Amenities:** 2 restaurants; 3 bars; 2 outdoor pools; 4 lit tennis courts; fitness center; spa; Jacuzzi; sauna/steam room; kayaks; sailing; snorkeling; children's center; airport shuttle; babysitting; laundry service; rooms for those with limited mobility. *In room:* A/C, TV, beverage maker, hair dryer, iron/ironing board, safe.

EXPENSIVE

Club St. Lucia by Splash 🎾 *Kids*   Beefed up by a US$6 million renovation, this all-inclusive resort sits in Cap Estate on a 26-hectare (64-acre) site, with two beaches in an area near LeSPORT. It's 13km (8 miles) north of George F. L. Charles Airport at the northern tip of the island. Very sports- and entertainment-oriented, with a well-organized children's club, the hotel opens onto a curved bay where smugglers used to bring in brandies, cognacs, and cigars from Martinique. The club's core is a wooden building with decks overlooking a free-form pool. The accommodations are in simple bungalows scattered over landscaped grounds. Each features one king-size or two twin beds, air-conditioning and/or

ceiling fans, and patios or terraces. Bathrooms have recently been upgraded, with makeup mirrors, marble vanities, and excellent shower/tub combinations.

The inclusive package is impressive, offering all meals, even snacks, along with unlimited beer, wine, and mixed drinks, both day and night. The food is standard resort fare, but you'll never go hungry. To break the monotony, guests are often transported to the Great House, a restaurant at Cap Estate, where they receive a discount on meals.

Cap Estate (P.O. Box 915), St. Lucia, W.I. ℭ **877/92-SPLASH** or 758/450-0551. Fax 758/450-0281. www.splash resorts.com. 369 units. Winter US$330–US$380 double; off season US$270–US$320 double. Rates are all-inclusive. AE, DC, MC, V. **Amenities:** 4 restaurants; 4 bars; 5 pools; dance club; 9 lit tennis courts; fitness center; squash court; kayaks; sailing; scuba lessons; snorkeling; water-skiing; windsurfing; children's club; airport shuttle; Internet cafe; babysitting; laundry service. *In room:* A/C, TV, beverage maker, hair dryer, iron/ironing board (on request), safe.

Stonefield Estate Villa Resort ℛ *Finds*

Nestled at the base of Petit Piton, this place is for escapists. In the southwestern part of the island, it stands on its own 10 hectares (2½ acres), complete with a nature trail and some of the island's most striking panoramas. Removed from the overrun resort areas, it lies near the little fishing village of Soufrière and close enough to the Jalousie Hilton that Stonefield guests can use the beach there, a free 5-minute shuttle ride away. The estate's plantation houses are surrounded by tropical greenery, and each of the cottages available for rent has its own character and privacy. The estate here has one of the island's oldest sites, a well-preserved petroglyph dating from pre-Columbian times. All the accommodations come with antiques, high ceilings, verandas, bedrooms, full bathrooms with intimate outdoor garden showers, and fully furnished kitchens. Villas range in size from one to three bedrooms.

Stonefield Villas (P.O. Box 228), Soufrière, St. Lucia, W.I. ℭ **758/459-5648.** Fax 758/459-5550. www.stonefieldvillas.com. 16 units. Winter US$190–US$330 1-bedroom villa, US$242–US$480 2-bedroom villa, US$535–US$600 3-bedroom villa; off season US$140–US$250 1-bedroom villa, US$160–US$330 2-bedroom villa, US$347–US$400 3-bedroom villa. AE, MC, V. **Amenities:** Restaurant; bar; outdoor pool; snorkeling; library; car rental; Internet service; babysitting; laundry service; nonsmoking rooms. *In room:* Ceiling fan, kitchen, beverage maker, iron/ironing board, safe, no phone.

Ti Kaye Village Resort ℛℛ

It's special, it's fun, and there's nothing like it on St. Lucia. An elite retreat, it sprawls across a cliff overlooking the Caribbean and evokes a little laid-back village. A hideaway for those seeking a tranquil getaway, it was designed by Wayne Brown, one of the founders of Anse Chastanet. Standing on 6.4 hectares (16 acres) of lushly planted grounds, it offers beautifully furnished and comfortable bedrooms in individual cottages trimmed in gingerbread or else a dozen units in duplex cottages. Each accommodation comes with a spacious porch with a hammock. Bedrooms are furnished with four-posters along with a private open-air garden shower, and some have their own plunge pool. You take a wooden staircase 166 steps down to a secluded cove of white sands. An on-site restaurant, House of Food (Kai M'jame, in Creole patois) serves excellent fresh meals overlooking the sea.

Anse Cochon, St. Lucia, W.I. ℭ **758/456-8101.** Fax 758/456-8105. www.tikaye.com. 33 units. Winter US$180–US$320 double; off season US$150–US$250 double. Rates include full breakfast. AE, DC, MC, V. **Amenities:** Restaurant; bar; outdoor pool; fitness center; kayaks; scuba diving; snorkeling; massage; laundry service. *In room:* A/C, fridge, beverage maker, hair dryer, iron/ironing board, safe.

Windjammer Landing Villa Beach Resort ℛℛℛ *Kids*

Windjammer, set on 22 tropical hectares (54 acres) north of Reduit Beach, about a 15-minute drive from Castries, is a quiet, luxurious retreat, one of the most glamorous in the West Indies. The resort was designed with a vaguely Moorish motif, heavily influenced by Caribbean themes; tropical colors predominate. It's composed of a cluster of white villas climbing a forested hillside above a desirable beach. This is an all-suite/villa resort (the larger villas have private plunge pools), making it a good choice for families or anyone who likes a lot of space. Standard features include ceiling fans, fridges, and queen-size, king-size, or paired twin beds. The roomy villas offer separate living and dining rooms, full kitchens, cassette players, and VCRs upon request. All bedrooms adjoin private bathrooms and open onto sun terraces. Some bathrooms have showers only.

The resort contains more restaurants per capita than most of its competitors. Papa Don's is an Italian trattoria specializing in pizza and pasta. Jammer's restaurant and bar is a nautically styled, informal bar/steakhouse/grill. Dragonfly serves Asian and West Indian food.

Labrelotte Bay (P.O. Box 1504), Castries, St. Lucia, W.I. (℃) **800/958-7376** in the U.S., or 758/456-9000. Fax 758/452-9454. www.windjammer-landing.com. 234 units. Winter US$200 double, US$395–US$485 1-bedroom villa for 2, US$640 2-bedroom villa for 4; off season US$190 double, US$225–US$325 1-bedroom villa for 2, US$420 2-bedroom villa for 4. Winter rates are 15%–20% higher Dec 20–Jan 3. Up to 2 extra occupants are allowed in the villas (but not in the double rooms) at US$45 each per night. MAP (breakfast and dinner) for US$55 per person extra. AE, DC, DISC, MC, V. **Amenities:** 5 restaurants; 3 bars; 4 outdoor pools; 2 lit tennis courts; fitness center; Jacuzzi; dive shop; sailing; snorkeling; water-skiing; windsurfing; children's programs; car rental; limited room service; massage; babysitting; laundry service; nonsmoking rooms; rooms for those with limited mobility. *In room:* A/C, ceiling fan, TV, dataport, kitchen, minibar, fridge, beverage maker, hair dryer, iron/ironing board, safe.

MODERATE

Bay Gardens Hotel *(Value) (Kids)* This hotel offers one of the best values, as well as some of the best service, on the island. It's not right on the sands, but Reduit Beach, one of St. Lucia's finest, is a 5-minute walk or a complimentary 2-minute shuttle ride away. One of the newest and most up-to-date hotels on the island, Bay Gardens opens onto a large atrium lobby with a designer fountain pool and bamboo furnishings. Joyce and Desmond Destang are among the most hospitable hosts on the island. Their medium-size bedrooms in vivid florals contain a terrace or balcony, and tropical art and accessories. Bathrooms are tiled with a combination tub and shower. Families might want to consider one of the eight apartments, each a self-contained unit with a kitchenette. One child is accommodated without charge. Its international restaurant, Spices, serves some of the island's best hotel food. Look for weekly rum punches, barbecues, Caribbean buffets, and live music on occasion. Did we mention the ice-cream shop?

Rodney Bay (P.O. Box 1892), Castries, St. Lucia. W.I. (℃) **877/434-1212** in the U.S., or 758/452-8060. Fax 758/ 452-8059. www.baygardenshotel.com. 71 units, 8 apts. Winter US$100–US$150 double; off season US$95–US$140 double. 1 child free in parent's room. AE, MC, V. **Amenities:** Restaurant; 2 bars; 2 outdoor pools; Jacuzzi; library; car rental; shuttle to beach; business services; room service (7:30am–10pm); babysitting; laundry service; dry cleaning; nonsmoking rooms; rooms for those with limited mobility. *In room:* A/C, TV, dataport, kitchenette, minibar, fridge, beverage maker, hair dryer, iron/ironing board, safe.

Harmony Suites *(Finds)* This complex of two-story buildings offers well-maintained accommodations at reasonable rates, a short walk from one of the island's finest beaches at Reduit. The suites, decorated in rattan, wicker, and florals, sit adjacent to a saltwater lagoon. Each unit offers a patio or balcony with views of moored yachts, the lagoon, and surrounding hills. Those on the top floor have more privacy. All suites, except the VIP/honeymoon units, have sofa beds. Each VIP suite features a double Jacuzzi, a four-poster queen-size bed on a pedestal, a sun deck, white rattan furnishings, and a bidet. Eight of the suites contain kitchenettes, complete with coffeemakers, fridges, and wet bars—ideal for families on a budget. Shower/tub combination bathrooms are small, of the routine motel variety, but are tidily maintained. The Mortar and Pestle Restaurant serves Caribbean fare.

Rodney Bay Lagoon (P.O. Box 155), Castries, St. Lucia, W.I. © **758/452-0336.** Fax 758/452-8677. www. harmonysuites.com. 30 units. Winter US$150–US$205 double; off season US$110–US$140 double. AE, MC, V. **Amenities:** Restaurant; bar; outdoor pool; limited room service; laundry service; rooms for those with limited mobility. *In room:* A/C, TV, kitchenette (in some), minibar, hair dryer, iron/ironing board, safe.

The Inn on the Bay

This small-scale inn perched 90m (295 ft.) above the waters of Marigot Bay makes for a great romantic escape. It's the creative statement of Montreal-born Normand Viau and his wife, Louise Boucher. Abandoning careers as a lawyer and social worker, respectively, they designed the hotel themselves, modeling its blue roof and veranda-ringed style on the island's plantation-house tradition. Today, the centerpiece of their establishment is an open-air terrace, site of a small pool and semiprivate dinners available only to hotel guests. Bedrooms, with 3m (10-ft.) ceilings, are spacious, comfortably furnished, and airy. Each has a ceiling fan and ample windows for cross-ventilation. Some bathrooms are shower only.

Seaview Ave., Marigot Bay (P.O. Box RB2377), Castries, St. Lucia, W.I. © **758/451-4260.** Fax 928/438-3828. www.saint-lucia.com. 5 units. Winter US$145 double; off season US$120 double. Rates include breakfast. MC, V. Children under 18 not accepted. **Amenities:** Breakfast room; outdoor pool; limited room service; non-smoking rooms. *In room:* Ceiling fan, kitchenette, fridge, hair dryer, iron/ironing board, no phone.

Mago Estate Hotel ★ (Finds)

This is a true Caribbean Shangri-La, ideal for a honeymoon. Just above the fishing village of Soufrière and overlooking the Pitons, German-born Peter Gloger runs this glamorous little inn. A 5-minute walk from the beach, this property is surrounded by tropical trees, including mango (*mago* is patois for mango), mahogany, papaya, *maracuya* (passion fruit), and banana. Each accommodation has only three walls; the other side of the room is open to a view of the mountains and sea. Guests sleep in four-poster beds underneath ceilings of painted clouds, with mosquito netting for protection from insects. Each unit comes with a small shower-only bathroom and a spacious private terrace. The most recently built units are four large bedrooms with teakwood furnishings or handcrafted antiques along with plunge pools, hammocks, and large sliding doors opening to the terrace and pool. The food is excellent, and it's served at communal tables surrounded by carved African chairs.

Palm Mist, Soufrière, St. Lucia, W.I. © **758/459-5880.** Fax 758/459-7352. www.mago-hotel.com. 10 units. Winter US$200–US$500 double; off season US$150–US$300 double. Rates include breakfast and beach shuttle service. MAP (Caribbean breakfast and dinner) US$40 per person extra. MC, V. **Amenities:** Dining room; bar; outdoor pool; limited room service; massage; laundry service. *In room:* A/C, ceiling fan, minibar, fridge, beverage maker, iron/ironing board, no phone.

Seraphine

This two-story concrete-sided building painted cerulean blue and white is a 15-minute walk from Vigie Beach, overlooking the marina and the harbor of Castries. Owned and operated by the St. Lucia–born Joseph family, whose hotel skills were honed during a long sojourn in England, the hotel offers well-maintained but very simple accommodations. They're generally spacious and decorated with bright colors, often tropical prints. The bathrooms, though small, are clean and have tiled showers. Most activities surround an open terrace whose surface is sheathed with terra-cotta tiles ringing a small round-sided pool. Don't expect too many extras, as the place's charm derives from its simplicity.

Vigie Cove (Box 390), Castries, St. Lucia, W.I. © **758/453-2073.** Fax 758/451-7001. 28 units. Year-round US$110 double; US$130 suite for 2. AE, MC, V. **Amenities:** Restaurant; bar; outdoor pool; limited room service; babysitting; laundry service; nonsmoking rooms. *In room:* A/C, TV, dataport, beverage maker, hair dryer, iron/ironing board.

INEXPENSIVE

The Green Parrot (see "Dining," below) also offers inexpensive rooms.

Bay Gardens Inn *(Value)*   In the heart of Rodney Bay, near Reduit Beach, this inn enjoys a prime location. Its proximity to Rodney Bay Marina puts it at the heart of the action. The inn is small and modern, with a 1.2m-deep (4-ft.) freshwater pool. Rooms are divided into four categories across two floors. The most desirable are called Bay View Superior, each with a spacious queen-size bed. Rooms open onto a private balcony or terrace, and each comes with a tiled bathroom with shower.

Rodney Bay, St. Lucia, W.I. © **758/452-8200.** Fax 758/452-8002. www.baygardensinn.com. 20 units. Winter US$95–US$120 double; off season US$90–US$112 double. **Amenities:** Restaurant; bar; outdoor pool; car rental; beach shuttle; Internet cafe; business services; salon; babysitting; laundry service; rooms for those with limited mobility. *In room:* A/C, TV, dataport, fridge, beverage maker, hair dryer, iron/ironing board.

Hummingbird Beach Resort *(Finds)*   Set on .3 hectare (¾ acre) of verdantly landscaped grounds, this is a small, charming, and carefully maintained inn that enjoys direct access to a sandy strip of beachfront, on the northern edge of Soufrière on St. Lucia's southwest coast. Bedrooms are sheathed in white stucco and accented with varnished hardwoods like mahogany. Views are of the water or the soaring nearby heights of Petit Titon and the rugged landscape of southern St. Lucia. Each has a ceiling fan and mosquito netting that's artfully draped over the sometimes elaborately carved bedsteads. Regrettably, the low wattage in the bedside lamps makes nighttime reading difficult. Bathrooms are very compact but have shower/tub combinations and adequate shelf space. There's a restaurant, The Hummingbird, on the premises (see "Dining," below).

P.O. Box 280, Soufrière, St. Lucia, W.I. © **800/795-7261** or 758/459-7232. Fax 758/459-7033. www. istlucia.co.uk. 10 units. Winter US$70 double, US$160 suite, US$285 cottage for 2–4; off season US$50 double, US$110 suite, US$175 cottage for 2–4. AE, DISC, MC, V. **Amenities:** Restaurant; 2 bars; outdoor pool; access to nearby health club; car rental; room service (7am–10pm); babysitting; laundry service; nonsmoking rooms; rooms for those with limited mobility. *In room:* A/C, ceiling fan, TV, safe.

3 Dining

IN CASTRIES

Green Parrot *(* CONTINENTAL/CARIBBEAN   About 2km (1¼ miles) east of the center of town, Green Parrot overlooks Castries Harbour and remains the local hot spot for visitors, expatriates, and locals. It takes about 12 minutes to walk here from downtown, but the effort is worth it. Chef Harry, who runs this elegant place, had many years of training in prestigious restaurants and hotels in London, including Claridge's. Guests take their time and make an evening of it; many enjoying a before-dinner drink in the Victorian-style salon. Try a Grass Parrot (made from coconut cream, crème de menthe, bananas, and white rum). An evening in the English-colonial dining room usually includes free entertainment on Wednesday and Saturday nights, which might be a limbo contest or a fire-eating show.

All this may sound gimmicky, but the food doesn't suffer. There's an emphasis on St. Lucian specialties and homegrown produce. Try the *christophene* au gratin (a Caribbean squash with cheese) or the Creole soup made with callaloo and pumpkin. There are five kinds of curry with chutney, as well as a selection of omelets and sandwiches at lunch.

Green Parrot also offers some of the island's least expensive lodging; rooms have air-conditioning and phones. In winter, doubles are US$100; in off season, US$80. Rates include breakfast.

Chef Harry Drive, Morne Fortune. © **758/452-3399.** Reservations recommended. Lunch main courses EC$46–EC$59 (US$17–US$22); fixed-price dinner EC$95–EC$124 (US$35–US$46). AE, MC, V. Daily 7am–midnight.

IN THE SOUFRIERE AREA

Camilla's Restaurant & Bar WEST INDIAN/CREOLE   Set a block inland from the waterfront, one floor above street level, this is a decent Caribbean-style restaurant with simple, unpretentious food. Local matriarch Camilla Alcindor will welcome you for coffee, a soda, or Perrier. The food is straightforward but flavorful. Opt for the fish and shellfish (Caribbean fish Creole or lobster thermidor) rather than the beef; chicken curry is another savory choice. Lunches are considerably less elaborate and include an array of sandwiches, salads, omelets, and burgers. Our favorite tables are the pair sitting on a balcony overlooking the energetic activities in the street below. The inside tables can get a bit steamy on a hot night as there's no air-conditioning.

7 Bridge St., Soufrière. © **758/459-5379.** Main courses EC$27–EC$89 (US$10–US$33). AE, DISC, MC, V. Daily 8am–11pm.

Dasheene Restaurant & Bar ♠ CARIBBEAN/INTERNATIONAL   This is one of the most widely heralded restaurants on St. Lucia and it has the most dramatic setting. Inspired by the best of the Caribbean/Creole kitchen and the innovations of California, this mountaintop hideaway offers some of the island's most refined and creative cuisine. Start with a garden salad of locally grown greens or the *christophene* (Caribbean squash) and coconut soup. We're especially fond of the chilled gazpacho. Moving on to main dishes, the chef has a special flair for seafood pasta or marinated sirloin steak, and chicken appears stuffed with breadcrumbs, sweet peppers, and onions. But the best bet is the catch of the day, usually kingfish or red snapper, grilled to perfection. The chocolate soufflé flambé for dessert makes the night out all the more festive.

In the Ladera Resort, between Gros and Petit Piton. © **758/459-7323.** Reservations recommended. Main courses EC$59–EC$81 (US$22–US$30). AE, MC, V. Daily 7:30–10am, noon–2:30pm, and 6:30–9:30pm.

The Hummingbird CARIBBEAN/INTERNATIONAL   This restaurant is the best part of the Hummingbird Beach Resort complex. Tables are set on a stylish veranda adjacent to the sands of Hummingbird Beach. The cuisine focuses on such West Indian dishes as Creole-style conch, lobster, burgers, steaks, and filets of both snapper and grouper, punctuated with such American staples as burgers and BLTs. A tiny gift shop on the premises sells batik items crafted by staff members.

At the Hummingbird Beach Resort, on the waterfront just north of the main wharf at Soufrière. © **758/459-7232.** Platters EC$46–EC$119 (US$17–US$44). AE, DISC, MC, V. Daily 6:30am–11pm.

The Still ♠ *Finds* CREOLE   This is the most authentic and atmospheric place for lunch in the southern Soufrière area. The first thing you'll see as you drive up the hill from the harbor is a very old rum distillery set on a platform of thick timbers. The site is a working cocoa and citrus plantation that has been in the same St. Lucian family for four generations. The front blossoms with avocado and breadfruit trees, and a few steps away is a mahogany forest. The bar near the front veranda is furnished with tables cut from cross-sections of mahogany tree trunks. In the more formal and spacious dining room, you can feast on excellently prepared St. Lucian specialties, depending on what's fresh at the market that day. Try to avoid the place when it's overrun with cruise-ship passengers or tour groups.

Soufrière. © **758/459-7224.** Main courses EC$57–EC$159 (US$21–US$59). AE, DC, DISC, MC, V. Daily 8am–5pm.

IN RODNEY BAY

Capone's ✿ ITALIAN/CARIBBEAN   This trattoria looks like a 1930s-era Miami Beach speakeasy. It could have been inspired by *Some Like It Hot.* North of Reduit Beach, near the lagoon, it's brightly lit at night. Make an evening of it and begin with a drink, perhaps Prohibition Punch or a St. Valentine's Day Massacre. A player piano enlivens the mood. If you feel that the atmosphere is a little too cute and gimmicky, rest assured that the dishes are well prepared, with fresh, quality ingredients. The Little Caesar salad leads off many a meal, and the creamy lasagna is a special favorite. The best bet is the fresh local grilled fish or some of the best steaks on the island.

Reduit Beach, Rodney Bay. © **758/452-0284.** Reservations recommended. Main courses EC$49–EC$119 (US$18–US$44). AE, MC, V. Tues–Sun 3pm–midnight.

The Charthouse AMERICAN/CREOLE   In a large building with a sky-lit ceiling and a mahogany bar, The Charthouse is one of the oldest restaurants in the area and one of the island's most popular. It was built several feet above the bobbing yachts of the lagoon, without walls, to allow an optimal view of the water. The helpful staff serves simple, honest, good food in large portions. The specialties might include pumpkin soup, St. Lucian crab backs, baby back ribs, and fresh local lobster (from Sept–Apr, you can often witness the live lobster being delivered from the boat at around 5pm). If you fancy a well-cooked charcoal-broiled steak, you'll see why this dish made the restaurant famous. Of course, traditionalists visit The Charthouse for one reason—its roast prime rib of beef, which is good, but never better here than in the U.S.

Reduit Beach, Rodney Bay. © **758/452-8115.** Reservations recommended. Main courses EC$51–EC$89 (US$19–US$33). AE, MC, V. Daily 6–10:30pm.

The Lime ✿ AMERICAN/CREOLE   This bistro stands north of Reduit Beach in an area that's known as restaurant row. Some of these places are rather expensive, but The Lime continues to keep its prices low, its food good and plentiful, and its service among the finest on the island. Both locals and visitors come here for *limin',* or hanging out. West Indian in feeling and open-air in setting, the restaurant features a "lime special" drink. Specialties include grilled lobster, and fish steak Creole, as well as shrimp, steaks, lamb and pork chops, and *rotis* (Caribbean burritos). The steaks are done over a charcoal grill. Nothing is fancy, nothing is innovative, and nothing is nouvelle—just like the savvy local foodies like it. It's less expensive than more touristy Capone's.

Rodney Bay. © **758/452-0761.** Reservations recommended for dinner. Main courses EC$35–EC$84 (US$13–US$31). MC, V. Wed–Mon 8am–1am.

The Mortar & Pestle CARIBBEAN/INTERNATIONAL   Set on the waterfront of Rodney Bay Lagoon, this restaurant offers indoor-outdoor dining with a view of the boats moored at the nearby marina. The menu includes select recipes from the various islands of the southern Caribbean, with their rich medley of African, British, French, Spanish, Portuguese, Dutch, Indian, Chinese, and even Amerindian influences. To start, try the rich and creamy conch chowder, followed by crab *farci* (a delicious stuffed crab in the shell). To sample something truly regional, try the local *souse,* with marinated pieces of lean cooked pork. A steel band or some other local band sometimes accompanies the meals.

In the Harmony Suites, Rodney Bay Lagoon. ⓒ 758/452-8711. Reservations recommended. Main courses EC$41–EC$95 (US$15–US$35). DISC, MC, V. Daily 7am–11pm.

Razmataz! INDIAN   Across from the Royal St. Lucian Hotel, this welcome entry into the island cuisine features delectable tandoori dishes. It's in an original Caribbean colonial timbered building with lots of gingerbread, decorated in a medley of colors and set in a garden, a 2-minute walk from the beach. A tempting array of starters ranges from fresh local fish marinated in spicy yogurt and cooked in the tandoor to mulligatawny soup (made with lentils, herbs, and spices). Tandoori delights include shrimp, fresh fish such as snapper or mahimahi, chicken, and mixed grill, not to mention the best assortment of vegetarian dishes on the island. There's live music on weekends, often performed by the owner.

Reduit Beach Marina. ⓒ 758/452-9800. Reservations recommended. Main courses EC$20–EC$41 (US$7.40–US$15). MC, V. Fri–Wed 4–11pm.

IN GROS ISLET

Great House ⓕ FRENCH/CREOLE/INTERNATIONAL   Built on the foundation stones of the original plantation house of Cap Estate, this restaurant lies under a canopy of cedar trees. The inviting ambience extends to the formal dining room, which opens onto a tranquil patio overlooking the sea. French cuisine is served here with Caribbean flair. The service, food, and wine are first rate. The menu is adjusted frequently to take advantage of the freshest ingredients. Begin with an appetizer such as shrimp and scallop gratinée (with a cheese sauce) and proceed to sample the delectable duck breast in a honey-and–balsamic vinegar sauce, a pork pepper pot, savory chicken, or a St. Lucian beef dish. You can finish off with velvety smooth passion fruit cheesecake.

Cap Estate. ⓒ 758/450-0450. Reservations recommended. Main courses EC$57–EC$100 (US$21–US$37). AE, DC, DISC, MC, V. Tues–Sun 6:30–10pm.

4 Beaches

Since most of the island hotels are built right on the beach, you won't have to go far to swim. All beaches are open to the public, even those along hotel properties. However, if you use any of the hotel's beach equipment, you must pay for it. We prefer the beaches along the western coast, as the rough surf on the windward (east) side makes swimming potentially dangerous. The best hotels are all on the western coast for a reason.

Top beaches include **Pigeon Point Beach** ⓕ off the north shore, part of the **Pigeon Island National Historic Park** (see below). The small beach here has white sand and is an ideal place for a picnic. Pigeon Island is joined to the mainland of St. Lucia by a causeway, so it's easy to reach.

The most frequented beach is **Reduit Beach** ⓕⓕ at Rodney Bay, 2km (1¼ miles) of soft beige sand fronting very clear waters. Many watersports kiosks can be found along the strip bordering Royal St. Lucian Hotel. With all its restaurants and bars, you'll find plenty of refueling stops.

Choc Bay is a long stretch of sand and palm trees on the northwestern coast, convenient to Castries and the big resorts. Its tranquil waters lure swimmers and especially families (including locals) with small children.

The 3km (2-mile) white-sand **Malabar Beach** runs parallel to the George F. L. Charles Airport runway, in Castries, to the Rendezvous resort. **Vigie Beach,** north of Castries Harbour, is also popular. It has fine beige sands, sloping gently into crystalline water. **La Toc Beach,** just south of Castries, opens onto a crescent-shaped bay containing golden sand.

Marigot Bay is the quintessential Caribbean cove, framed on three sides by steep emerald hills and skirted by palm trees. There are some small but secluded beaches here. Some of the Caribbean's most expensive yachts anchor in this bay.

One of the most charming and hidden beaches of St. Lucia is the idyllic cove of **Anse Chastanet,** north of Soufrière. This is a beach connoisseur's delight. Towering palms provide shade from the fierce noonday sun, and lush hills are a refreshing contrast to the dark sandy strip.

The dramatic crescent-shaped bay of **Anse des Pitons** is at the foot of and between the twin peaks of the Pitons, south of Soufrière. The Jalousie Hilton transformed the natural black-sand beach by covering it with white sand; you walk through the resort to get to it. It's popular with divers and snorkelers. While here, you can ask about a very special beach reached only by boat, the black volcanic sands and tranquil waters of **Anse Couchon.** With its shallow reefs, excellent snorkeling, and picture-postcard charm, this beach has become a hideaway for lovers. It's south of Anse-le-Raye.

You'll discover miles of white sand at the beach at **Vieux Fort,** at the southern end of the island. Reefs protect the crystal-clear waters here, rendering them tranquil and ideal for swimming. At the southern end of the windward side of the island is **Anse des Sables,** which opens onto a shallow bay swept by trade winds that are great for windsurfing.

5 Sports & Other Outdoor Pursuits

BOATING   The most dramatic trip offered is aboard the 42m (138-ft.) **brig** *Unicorn* (© 758/452-8644), used in the filming of the TV miniseries, *Roots.* Passengers sail from Rodney Bay in Castries to Soufrière and the twin peaks of the Pitons, among other natural attractions of the island. A full-day sail costs US$90.

CAMPING   Camping is now possible on St. Lucia courtesy of the **Environmental Educational Centre,** a division of the St. Lucia National Trust (© 758/452-5005). This reserve features 12 campsites (with more to be added) along a beautiful stretch of beach on historic Anse Liberté, in the fishing town of Canaries, 40km (25 miles) southwest of Castries and 13km (8 miles) north of Soufrière. Beachfront campsites, available for around US$25 per night (advance notice required), offer a view of the harbor and of Martinique on a clear day. There are nearby community bathrooms and community cooking areas. The reserve has 8km (5 miles) of hiking trails; staff members give tours of the area and explain the rich history of the Anse Liberté, which literally translated means "freedom harbor." Camping equipment is available for rent.

DEEP-SEA FISHING   The waters around St. Lucia are known for their game fish, including blue marlin, sailfish, mako sharks, and barracuda, with tuna and kingfish among the edible catches. Most hotels can arrange fishing expeditions. Call **Mako Watersports** (© 758/452-0412), which offers half-day fishing trips for US$360 for four people or full-day trips for US$720. **Captain Mike's** (© 758/452-7044) also conducts fishing trips, renting boats by the half-day for US$400 to US$500, or a whole day in the US$750 to US$900 price range.

GOLF   St. Lucia has an 18-hole golf course (6,815 yd., par 71) at the **St. Lucia's Golf and Country Club,** at the northern end of the island (© 758/ 450-9905). Greens fees are US$95 for 18 holes, US$70 for nine holes; there are no caddies. Carts are included, and clubs can be rented for US$20. Hours are from 7am to 6pm daily. Reservations are needed.

HIKING   A tropical rainforest covers a large area in the southern half of St. Lucia, and the St. Lucia Forest and Lands Department manages it wisely. This forest reserve divides the western and eastern halves of the island. There are several trails, the most popular of which is the **Barre de l'Isle Trail,** located almost in the center of St. Lucia, southeast of Marigot Bay; it's a fairly easy trail that even children can handle. There are four panoramic lookout points with dramatic views of the sea where the Atlantic and the Caribbean meet. It takes about an hour to walk this 2km-long (1.2-mile) trail, which lies about a 30-minute ride from Castries. Guided hikes can usually be arranged through the major hotels or through the **Forest and Lands Department** (© 758/450-2231 or 758/450-2375, ext. 316 or 317).

HORSEBACK RIDING   North of Castries, you can ride at **Cas-En-Bas. Trim's National Riding Stable,** Cas-en-Bas, Gros Islet ([tel **758/450-8273**), St. Lucia's oldest riding establishment. Its activities range from trail rides to beach tours, even horse-drawn carriage tours of Pigeon Island. Rides are US$35 for an hour, US$45 for 2 hours, or US$60 for a 3-hour beach ride with a picnic.

SCUBA DIVING   In Soufrière, **Scuba St. Lucia,** in the Anse Chastanet Hotel (© **758/459-7000**), offers one of the world's top dive locations at a five-star PADI dive center. At the southern end of Anse Chastanet's .4km-long (¼-mile), secluded beach, it features premier diving and comprehensive facilities for divers of all levels. Some of the most spectacular coral reefs of St. Lucia, many only 3m to 6m (10 ft.–20 ft.) below the surface, lie a short distance from the beach.

Many PADI instructors offer five dive programs a day. Photographic equipment is available for rent (film can be processed on the premises), and instruction is offered in picture taking. Experienced divers can rent any equipment they need. PADI certification courses are available for US$535. A 2- to 3-hour introductory lesson costs US$85 and includes a short theory session, equipment familiarization, development of skills in shallow water, a tour of the reef, and all equipment. Single dives cost US$50. Hours are from 8am to 6pm daily.

Another full-service scuba center is available on St. Lucia's southwest coast at the **Jalousie Hilton,** at Soufrière (© **758/456-8000**). The PADI center offers dives in St. Lucia's National Marine Park; there are numerous shallow reefs near the shore. The diver certification program is available to hotel guests and other visitors age 12 and up. Prices range from a single dive for US$65 to a certification course for US$535. There's a daily resort course for noncertified divers that includes a supervised dive from the beach; it costs US$83. A 10-dive package is US$347; a six-dive package is US$237. All prices include equipment, tax, service charges.

TENNIS   The best place for tennis on the island is the **St. Lucia Racquet Club,** adjacent to Club St. Lucia (© **758/450-0551**). It's one of the finest tennis facilities in the Lesser Antilles. Its seven illuminated courts are maintained in state-of-the-art condition, and there's also a good pro shop on-site. You must reserve 24 hours in advance. Guests of the hotel play for free; nonguests are charged EC$54 (US$20) for a full-day pass. Tennis racquets rent for EC$20 (US$7.40) per hour.

The **Jalousie Hilton,** at Soufrière (© **758/459-7666**) has a good program. Vernon Lewis, the top-ranked player in St. Lucia, is the pro. You'll find four brand-new Laykold tennis courts (three lit for night play). Hotel guests play for free (though they pay for lessons). Nonguests can play for US$20 per hour.

OTHER WATERSPORTS   The best all-around watersports center is **St. Lucian Watersports,** at the Rex St. Lucian Hotel (© **758/452-8351**). Water-skiing costs US$15 for a 10- to 15-minute ride. Windsurfers can be rented for US$20 for half an hour or US$40 an hour. Snorkeling is free for guests of the hotel; nonguests pay US$10 per hour for equipment.

6 Exploring the Island

Lovely little towns, beautiful beaches and bays, mineral baths, banana plantations—St. Lucia has all this and more. You can even visit a volcano.

Most hotel front desks will make arrangements for tours that take in all the major sights of St. Lucia. For example, **Sunlink Tours,** Reduit Beach Avenue (© **758/456-9100** or 758/452-8232), offers many island tours, including full-day boat trips along the west coast of Soufrière, the Pitons, and the volcano; the cost is US$90 per person. Jeep safaris can be arranged for US$85 to US$120 apiece, depending on the tour. One of the most popular jaunts is a rainforest ramble for US$60 by bus or US$85 by jeep. There's also a daily shopping tour for US$25. The company has tour desks and/or representatives at most of the major hotels.

CASTRIES

The capital city has grown up around its **harbor,** which occupies the crater of an extinct volcano. Charter captains and the yachting set drift in here, and large cruise-ship wharves welcome vessels from around the world. Because several devastating fires (most recently in 1948) destroyed almost all the old buildings, the town today looks new, with glass-and-concrete (or steel) buildings rather than the French colonial or Victorian look typical of many West Indian capitals.

Castries may be architecturally dull, but its **public market** is one of the most fascinating in the West Indies, and our favorite people-watching site on the island. It goes full blast every day of the week except Sunday, and is most active on Friday and Saturday mornings. The market stalls are a block from Columbus Square along Peynier Street, running down toward the water. The country women dress traditionally, with cotton headdresses; the number of knotted points on top reveals their marital status (ask one of the locals to explain it to you). The luscious fruits and vegetables of St. Lucia may be new to you; the array of color alone is astonishing. Sample one of the numerous varieties of bananas: on St. Lucia, they're allowed to ripen on the tree, and taste completely different from those picked green and sold at supermarkets in the United States. You can also pick up St. Lucian handcrafts such as baskets and unglazed pottery here.

To the south of Castries looms **Morne Fortune,** the inappropriately named "Hill of Good Luck." In the 18th century, some of the most savage battles between the French and the British took place here. You can visit the military cemetery, a small museum, the old powder magazine, and the "Four Apostles Battery" (a quartet of grim muzzle-loading cannons). Government House, now the official residence of the governor-general of St. Lucia, is one of the few examples of Victorian architecture that escaped destruction by fire. The private gardens are beautifully planted, aflame with scarlet and purple bougainvillea. Morne Fortune also offers what many consider the most **scenic lookout** perch in the Caribbean. The view of the harbor of Castries is panoramic: You can see north to Pigeon Island or south to the Pitons; on a clear day, you may even spot Martinique. To reach Morne Fortune, head east on Bridge Street.

PIGEON ISLAND NATIONAL HISTORIC PARK ⟨★⟩

St. Lucia's first **national park** is joined to the mainland by a causeway. On its west coast are two white-sand beaches (see "Beaches," above). There's also a restaurant, Jambe de Bois, named after a wooden-legged pirate who once used the island as a hideout.

Pigeon Island offers an **Interpretation Centre,** equipped with artifacts and a multimedia display on local history, ranging from the Amerindian occupation of A.D. 1000 to the Battle of the Saints, when Admiral Rodney's fleet set out from Pigeon Island and defeated Admiral De Grasse in 1782. The Captain's Cellar Olde English Pub lies under the center and is evocative of an 18th-century English bar.

Pigeon Island, only 18 hectares (44 acres), got its name from the red-neck pigeon, or ramier, that once colonized this island in huge numbers. Now the site of a Sandals Hotel and interconnected to the St. Lucian "mainland" with a causeway, the island offers pleasant panoramas but no longer the sense of isolated privacy that reigned here prior to its development. Parts of it, those far from the hotel on the premises, seem appropriate for nature walks. For more information, call ⟨©⟩ **758/452-2231.**

RODNEY BAY ⟨★⟩

This scenic bay is a 15-minute drive north of Castries. Set on a man-made lagoon, it has become a chic center for nightlife, hotels, and restaurants—in fact, it's the most active place on the island at night. Its marina is one of the top watersports centers in the Caribbean, and a destination every December for the Atlantic Rally for Cruisers, when yachties cross the Atlantic to meet and compare stories.

MARIGOT BAY ⟨★⟩

Movie crews, including those for Sophia Loren's *Fire Power,* have used this bay, one of the most beautiful in the Caribbean, for background shots. Thirteen kilometers (8 miles) south of Castries, it's narrow yet navigable by yachts of any size. Here Admiral Rodney camouflaged his ships with palm leaves while lying in wait for French frigates. The shore, lined with palm trees, remains relatively unspoiled, although some building sites have been sold. It's a delightful spot for a picnic. A 24-hour ferry connects the bay's two sides.

SOUFRIERE

This little fishing port, St. Lucia's second-largest settlement, is dominated by two pointed hills called **Petit Piton** and **Gros Piton** ⟨★★★⟩. The Pitons, two volcanic cones rising to 738m and 696m (2,421 ft. and 2,283 ft.), have become the very symbol of St. Lucia. Formed of lava and rock, and once actively volcanic, they are now covered in green vegetation. Their sheer rise from the sea makes them a landmark visible for miles around, and waves crash at their bases. It's recommended that you attempt to climb only Gros Piton, but doing so requires the permission of the **Forest and Lands Department** (⟨©⟩ **758/450-2231** or 758/450-2375, ext. 316 or 317) and the company of a knowledgeable guide.

Near Soufrière lies the famous "drive-in" volcano, **Mount Soufrière** ⟨★★⟩, a rocky lunar landscape of bubbling mud and craters seething with sulfur. You literally drive your car into a millions-of-years-old crater and walk between the sulfur springs and pools of hissing steam. Entrance costs EC$7.55 (US$2.80) per person and includes the services of your guide, who will point out the blackened waters, among the few of their kind in the Caribbean. Hours are daily from 9am to 5pm; for more information, call ✆ 758/459-7200.

Nearby are the **Diamond Mineral Baths** (✆ 758/452-4759) in the **Diamond Botanical Gardens** ✿. Deep in the lush tropical gardens is the Diamond Waterfall, one of the geological attractions of the island. Created from water bubbling up from sulfur springs, the waterfall changes colors (from yellow to black to green to gray) several times a day. The baths were constructed in 1784 on the orders of Louis XVI, whose doctors told him these waters were similar in mineral content to the waters at Aix-les-Bains; they were intended to provide recuperative effects for French soldiers fighting in the West Indies. The baths have an average temperature of 106°F (41°C). For between EC$10 (US$3.70) and EC$15 (US$5.55), depending on the degree of privacy, you can bathe and try out the recuperative effects for yourself.

From Soufrière in the southwest, the road winds toward Fond St-Jacques, where you'll have a good view of mountains and villages as you cut through St. Lucia's Cape Moule-Chique tropical rainforest. You'll also see the Barre de l'Isle divide.

NATURE RESERVES

The fertile volcanic soil of St. Lucia sustains a rich diversity of bird and animal life. Some of the richest troves for ornithologists are in protected precincts off the St. Lucian coast, in either of two national parks, Fregate Islands Nature Reserve and the Maria Islands Nature Reserve.

The **Fregate Islands** are a cluster of rocks a short distance offshore from Praslin Bay, midway up St. Lucia's eastern coastline. Barren except for tall grasses that seem to thrive in the salt spray, the islands were named after the scissor-tailed frigate birds *(Fregata magnificens)* that breed here. Between May and July, large colonies of the graceful birds fly in well-choreographed formations over islands that you can only visit under the closely supervised permission of government authorities. Many visitors believe that the best way to admire the Fregate Islands (and to respect their fragile ecosystems) is to walk along the nature trail that the St. Lucian government has hacked along the cliff top of the St. Lucian mainland, about 45m (148 ft.) inland from the shoreline. Even without

---

⟨Finds⟩ Discovering "Forgotten" Grande Anse

The northeast coast is the least visited and least accessible part of St. Lucia, but it contains dramatic rockbound shores interspersed with secret sandy coves. The government has set Grand Anse aside as a **nature reserve** so that it will never be developed. The terrain is arid and can be unwelcoming, but it is fascinating nonetheless. Grande Anse is home to some **rare bird** species, notably the white-breasted thrasher, as well as the fer-de-lance, the only poisonous snake on the island (but visitors report rarely seeing them). Its beaches—Grande Anse, Petite Anse, and Anse Louvet—are nesting grounds for **endangered sea turtles,** including the hawksbill, the green turtle, the leatherback, and the loggerhead. Nesting season lasts from February to October. Many locals tackle the poor road in a four-wheel-drive vehicle, especially the bumpiest part from Desbarra to Grande Anse.

binoculars, you'll be able to see the frigates wheeling overhead. You'll also enjoy eagle's-eye views of the unusual geology of the St. Lucian coast, which includes sea caves, dry ravines, a waterfall (during the rainy season), and a strip of mangrove swamp.

The **Maria Islands** are larger and more arid and are almost constantly exposed to salt-laden winds blowing up from the equator. Set to the east of St. Lucia's southernmost tip, off the town of Vieux Fort, their biodiversity is strictly protected. The approximately 12 hectares (30 acres) of cactus-dotted land that make up the two largest islands (Maria Major and Maria Minor) are home to more than 120 species of plants, lizards, butterflies, and snakes that are believed to be extinct in other parts of the world. These include the large ground lizard *(Zandolite)* and the nocturnal, nonvenomous kouwes snake *(Dromicus ornatus)*.

The Marias are also a bird refuge, populated by such species as the sooty tern, the bridled tern, the Caribbean martin, the red-billed tropicbird, and the brown noddy, which usually nests under the protective thorns of prickly pear cactus.

Tours to either island must be arranged through the staff of the **St. Lucia National Trust** (© 758/454-5014). Full-day excursions, including the boat ride to the refuge and the guided tour, cost US$70 for the Fregates and US$85 for the Marias (the Marias jaunt includes lunch).

7 Shopping

Most of the shopping is in **Castries,** where the principal streets are William Peter Boulevard and Bridge Street. Many stores will sell you goods at duty-free prices (providing you don't take the merchandise with you but have it delivered to the airport or cruise dock). There are some good (but not remarkable) buys in bone china, jewelry, perfume, watches, liquor, and crystal.

Built for the cruise-ship passenger, **Pointe Seraphine,** in Castries, has the best collection of shops on the island, along with offices for car rentals, organized taxi service (for sightseeing), a bureau de change, a philatelic bureau, an information center, and international phones. Cruise ships berth right at the shopping center. Under red roofs in a Spanish-style setting, the complex requires that you present a cruise pass or an airline ticket to the shopkeeper when purchasing goods. Visitors can take away their purchases, except liquor and tobacco, which will be delivered to the airport. The center is open in winter Monday to Friday from 8am to 5pm and Saturday from 8am to 2pm; off season, Monday to Saturday from 9am to 4pm. It has extended hours when cruise ships are in port.

On Gros Islet Highway, 3km (2 miles) north of Castries, **Gablewoods Mall** contains three restaurants and one of the island's densest concentrations of shops.

8 St. Lucia After Dark

There isn't much nightlife in St. Lucia besides the entertainment offered by hotels. In the winter, at least one hotel has a steel band or calypso music every night of the week. Otherwise, check to see what's happening at **Capone's** (© 758/452-0284) or the **Green Parrot** (© 758/452-3399), both in Castries.

One of the island's most action-packed dance clubs is **Folley,** Rodney Bay (©758/450-0022), adjoining La Creole Restaurant. Patrons age 21 and up can enjoy an array of music from reggae to rock. Entrance is EC$18 (US$7.40).

If you'd like to go barhopping, begin at **Shamrocks Pub,** Rodney Bay (© 758/452-8725). This Irish-style pub is especially popular among boaters and gets really lively on weekends.

Among the dance clubs, islanders and visitors favor **Late Lime,** Reduit Beach (© **758/452-0761**). A DJ plays dance music on Saturday. **The Chalet,** Rodney Bay (© **758/450-0022**), near La Creole Restaurant, lies at Rodney Bay marina, luring dancing feet to its wild disco nights. Some of the best *zouk* and salsa are played here.

At Marigot Bay, where the 1967 version of *Doctor Doolittle* starring Rex Harrison was filmed, the memory is perpetuated at **Doolittle's,** part of the Marigot Beach Club Hotel (© **758/451-4974**), lying 14km (9 miles) south of Castries. The Marigot Bay ferry takes you to the palm-studded peninsula of the resort, tickets cost EC$5 (US$1.85). On Saturday nights, this is the best place to be on the island as there is a lavish seafood and barbeque buffet and a steel band. You can come here for drinks (try the Singapore Slings) or dishes like chunky pumpkin soup, jerk chicken, or lobster and coconut shrimp Creole.

In the center of Rodney Bay is **Charlie's** (© **758/458-0565**), which opened in 2004. It has an imported Italian chef, and brings in piano players from both Britain and the States to entertain the crowd.

23

St. Maarten/St. Martin

For an island with a big reputation for restaurants, hotels, and energetic nightlife, St. Maarten is small—only 96 sq. km (37 sq. miles), about half the area of Washington, D.C. An island divided between the Netherlands and France, St. Maarten (Sint Maarten) is the Dutch half, and St. Martin is French. Legend has it that a gin-drinking Dutchman and a wine-guzzling Frenchman walked around the island to see how much territory each could earmark for his country in a day; the Frenchman walked farther, but the canny Dutchman got the more valuable piece of property.

The divided island is the smallest territory in the world shared by two sovereign states. The only way you'll know you're crossing an international border is when you see the sign BIEN-VENUE PARTIE FRANCAISE, attesting to the peaceful coexistence between the two nations. The island was officially split in 1648, and many visitors still ascend Mount Concordia, near the border, where the agreement was reached. Even so, St. Maarten changed hands 16 times before it became permanently Dutch.

Returning visitors who haven't been to the island for a while are often shocked when they see today's St. Maarten. No longer a sleepy Caribbean backwater, now it's a boomtown. Duty-free shopping has turned the island into a virtual mall, and the Dutch capital, Philipsburg, is often bustling with cruise-ship hordes.

Although the island's 39 white-sand beaches remain unspoiled, much has been lost to the bulldozer on St. Maarten. This is not a place for people who don't like crowds, so if you want to get away from it all, head to the nearby Dutch islands of St. Eustatius (Statia) and Saba (or choose another getaway, such as the British Virgin Islands). Even the French side of the island would suit you better. Nevertheless, despite problems like crime, occasional storms, traffic congestion, and corruption, St. Maarten continues to attract massive numbers of visitors who want a Caribbean island vacation with a splash of Las Vegas.

The Dutch capital, **Philipsburg,** curves like a toy village along Great Bay. The town lies on a narrow sand isthmus separating Great Bay and the Great Salt Pond. Commander John Philips, a Scot in Dutch employ, founded the capital in 1763. To protect Great Bay, Fort Amsterdam was built in 1737.

The French side of the island has a slightly different character. It's been undergoing a building boom of late, with lots of new hotels opening, but for now at least, it's still sleepier than the Dutch side. Most hotels tend to be quieter and more secluded than their Dutch counterparts, and you won't be overwhelmed with cruise-ship crowds. There are no dazzling sights; there's no spectacular nightlife. Even the sports scene on St. Martin isn't as well organized as on many Caribbean islands (though the Dutch side has golf and other diversions). Most people come to St. Martin to relax on its many white-sand beaches and to experience "France in the Tropics."

French St. Martin has a distinctly French air. Police officers, for example, wear *képis*. The towns have names like Colombier and Orléans, the streets are *rues*, and the French flag flies over the *gendarmerie* in **Marigot**, the capital. It also boasts some of the best cuisine in the Caribbean, with an extraordinary number of good bistros and restaurants. Advocates cite French St. Martin as distinctly more sophisticated, prosperous, stylish, and cosmopolitan than its neighboring *départements d'outre-mer*, Guadeloupe and Martinique.

French St. Martin is governed from Guadeloupe and has direct representation in the government in Paris. The principal town on the French side is Marigot, the seat of the subprefect and municipal council.

Marigot is not quite the same size as its counterpart, Philipsburg, in the Dutch sector. It has none of the frenzied pace of Philipsburg, which is often overrun with cruise-ship passengers. In fact, Marigot looks like a French village transplanted to the Caribbean. If you climb the hill over this tiny port, you'll be rewarded with a view from the old fort.

About 20 minutes by car beyond Marigot is **Grand-Case,** a small fishing village that's an outpost of French civilization, with many good restaurants and a few places to stay.

1 Essentials

VISITOR INFORMATION

If you're going to either **Dutch St. Maarten** or **French St. Martin,** contact the St. Maarten/St. Martin Tourist Office, 675 Third Ave., Suite 1807, New York, NY 10017 (© **800/786-2278** or 212/953-2084 for the department servicing the Dutch side, and © **877/956-1234** or 212/475-8970 for the department servicing the French side). In Canada, the office for information about the Dutch side of the island is located at 703 Evans Ave., Suite 106, Toronto, Ontario M9C 5E9 (© **416/622-4300**). For information about the French side of the island, contact 1981 Ave. McGill College, Suite 490, in Montreal (© **514/288-4264**). Once on the island, go to the **Tourist Information Bureau,** Vineyard Park, 33 W. G. Buncamper Rd., Philipsburg, St. Maarten, N.A. (© **599/54-22337**), open Monday to Friday from 8am to noon and 1 to 5pm.

The tourist board on French St. Martin, called the **Office du Tourisme,** is at Route de Sandy Ground, Marigot, 97150 St. Martin (© **590/ 87-57-21**), open Monday to Friday from 8:30am to 1pm and 2:30 to 5:30pm and Saturday from 8am to noon.

For information on the Web about the French side, go to **www.st-martin. org**. For information about the island's Dutch side, search out **www.st-maarten. com**.

GETTING THERE

There are two airports on the island. St. Maarten's **Queen Juliana International Airport** (© **599/54-54211**) is the second-busiest airport in the Caribbean, topped only by San Juan, Puerto Rico. You can also fly to the smaller **L'Espérance Airport,** in Grand-Case on French St. Martin (© **590/87-53-03**).

American Airlines (© **800/433-7300** in the U.S.; www.aa.com) offers more options and more frequent service into St. Maarten than any other airline—two daily nonstop flights from both New York's JFK and Miami. Additional nonstop daily flights into St. Maarten are offered by American and its local affiliate, **American Eagle** (© **800/433-7300** in the U.S.; www.aa.com), from San Juan. Ask about American's package tours, which can save you a bundle.

Continental Airlines (© 800/231-0856 in the U.S.; www.flycontinental.com) has daily nonstop flights out of its hub in Newark, New Jersey, during the winter months. However, in low season flight times vary.

US Airways (© 800/428-4322) offers nonstop service from Philadelphia and Charlotte, North Carolina, to St. Maarten. BWIA (© 800/538-2942 or 599/545-4646 on St. Maarten) flies from Trinidad, Antigua, and Jamaica to St. Maarten.

LIAT (© 868/624-4727; www.liatairline.com) has one flight out of San Juan. Other flights stop first at Tortola in the British Virgin Islands before going on to St. Maarten. Even so, the trip usually takes only 90 minutes. From St. Martin, LIAT, often with connections, offers ongoing service to Anguilla, Antigua, St. Croix, San Juan, St. Kitts, St. Thomas, and Dominica.

Air DCA (Dutch Caribbean Airlines; © 800/327-7230 in the U.S.; www.flydca.net) offers nonstop daily service from the airline's home base on Curaçao.

If you're coming from St. Barts, there's at least one airline serving the short route directly to French-speaking St. Martin. Winair (© 800/634-4907 in the U.S., or 599/545-4237) offers 15 flights daily between St. Maarten and St. Barts.

GETTING AROUND

BY TAXI Most visitors use taxis to get around. Since they are unmetered on both sides of the island, always agree on the rate before getting into a cab.

Rates are slightly different depending on which side of the island the taxi is based, though both Dutch and French cabs service the entire island. St. Maarten taxis have minimum fares for two passengers, and each additional passenger pays $4 extra. One piece of luggage per person is allowed free; each additional piece is $1 extra. Fares are 25% higher between 10pm and midnight, and 50% higher between midnight and 6am. Typical fares around the island are as follows: Queen Juliana Airport to Grand-Case: $20 for up to two passengers and all their luggage; Marigot to Grand Case, $18; Queen Juliana airport to anywhere in Marigot, $12 to $15; Queen Juliana Airport to the Maho Beach Hotel, $6; and from Queen Juliana Airport to Philipsburg, about $12.

St. Martin taxi fares are also for two passengers, but you should plan to add about $1 for each suitcase or valise. These fares are in effect from 7am to 10pm; after that, they go up by 25% until midnight, rising by 50% after midnight. On the French side, the fare from Marigot to Grand-Case is $10, from Queen Juliana Airport to Marigot and from Queen Juliana Airport to La Samanna, $15.

For late-night cab service on St. Maarten, call © 599/54-54317. Taxi Service & Information Center operates at the port of Marigot (© 590/87-56-54) on the French side of the island.

BY RENTAL CAR Especially if you want to experience both the Dutch and the French sides of the island, you might want to rent a car. The taxi drivers' union strictly enforces a law that forbids anyone from picking up a car at the airport. As a result, every rental agency delivers cars directly to your hotel, where an employee will complete the paperwork. If you prefer to rent a car on arrival, head for one of the tiny rental kiosks across the road from the airport, but beware of long lines.

Hertz (© 800/654-3131 in the U.S., 599/54-54314 on the Dutch side, or 590/87-83-71 on the French side; www.hertz.com), and Avis (© 800/331-1212 in the U.S., 599/54-52847 on the Dutch side, or 590/87-50-60 on the French side; www.avis.com) both maintain offices on both sides of the island.

St. Maarten/St. Martin

ST. MAARTEN

ACCOMMODATIONS
Belair Beach Hotel **21**
Caravanserai Beach Resort **12**
Divi Little Bay Beach Resort **20**
The Horny Toad Guesthouse **14**
La Vista **19**
Maho Beach Hotel & Casino **10**
Mary's Boon Beach Plantation **16**
Oyster Bay Beach Resort **27**
Pasanggrahan Royal Inn **23**
The Pelican **18**

DINING
Antoine's **25**
The Boathouse **17**
Cheri's Café **11**
Da Livio Ristorante **26**
The Greenhouse **22**
Kangaroo Court **24**
Saratoga **15**
Turtle Pier Bar & Restaurant **13**

ST. MARTIN

ACCOMMODATIONS
Captain Oliver's Resort Hotel **28**
Club Orient Naturist Resort **41**
Esmeralda Resort **38**
Hôtel Beach Plaza **6**
Hotel L'Esplanade Caraïbe **29**
Hotel Mont Vernon **42**
Hôtel St-Tropez des Caraïbes **40**
La Plantation Orient Bay Resort **43**
La Résidence **1**
La Samanna **9**
Le Méridien L'Habitation/
  Le Domaine **37**
Le Petit Hotel **30**
Le Royale Louisiana **2**
Mercure Coralia Simson Beach **7**
Nettlé Bay Beach Club **8**

DINING
Claude Mini-Club **5**
Il Nettuno **31**
Kakao **39**
La Vie en Rose **4**
Le Cottage **33**
Le Jasmin **32**
Le Pressoir **34**
L'Oizeau Rare **3**
Rainbow Café **35**
Sunset Café **36**

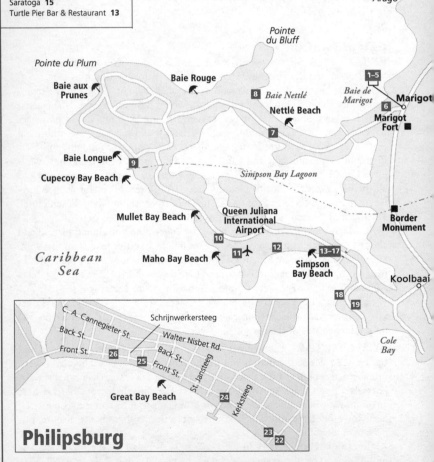

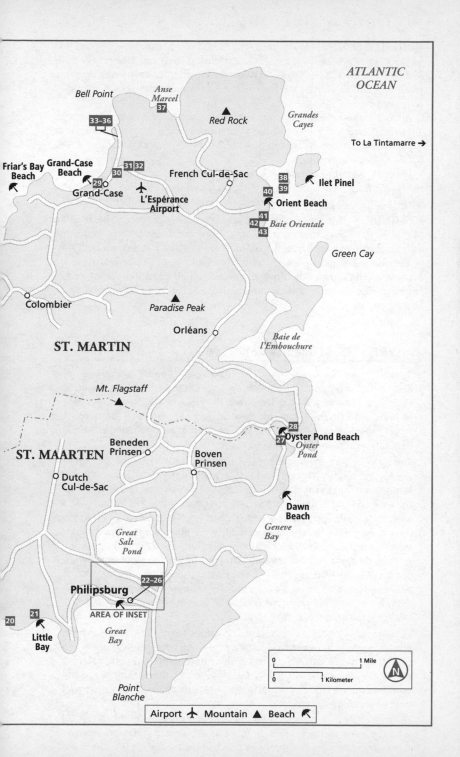

ATLANTIC
OCEAN

Bell Point

Anse
Marcel
37

Red Rock

Grandes
Cayes

To La Tintamarre →

33–36

Friar's Bay
Beach

Grand-Case
Beach

31 32

French Cul-de-Sac

**38
39**

Ilet Pinel

29

30

Grand-Case

L'Espérance
Airport

40

Orient Beach

41

42

43

Baie Orientale

Green Cay

Colombier

Paradise Peak

Orléans

Baie de
l'Embouchure

ST. MARTIN

Mt. Flagstaff

28

Oyster Pond Beach

ST. MAARTEN

Beneden
Prinsen

Boven
Prinsen

27

Oyster
Pond

Dutch
Cul-de-Sac

Dawn
Beach

Geneve
Bay

Great
Salt
Pond

22–26

Philipsburg

AREA OF INSET

20

21

Little
Bay

Great Bay

Point
Blanche

| 0 | | 1 Mile |
| 0 | | 1 Kilometer |

N

Airport ✈ Mountain ▲ Beach ☂

National (© **800/328-4567** in the U.S., 599/54-55552 downtown, or 599/54-54415 at Queen Juliana Airport; www.nationalcar.com) and **Budget** (© **800/472-3325** in the U.S., 599/54-54030 on the Dutch side; www.budgetrentacar.com); have offices only on the Dutch side. All these companies charge roughly equivalent rates.

All four major car-rental agencies require that renters be at least 25 years old. Your credit card issuer may provide insurance coverage, so check before your trip; otherwise, it may be wise to buy the fairly cheap collision-damage waiver (CDW) when you rent.

Drive on the right-hand side of both the French and Dutch roads, and expect traffic jams near the major towns. International road signs are observed, and there are no Customs formalities at the border between the two sides of the island.

BY MINIBUS   Minibus is a reasonable means of transport on St. Maarten/St. Martin if you don't mind some inconvenience and overcrowding. Buses run daily from 6am to midnight and serve most of the major locations on both sides of the island. The most popular run is from Philipsburg on the Dutch side to Marigot on the French side. Privately owned and operated, minibuses tend to follow specific routes, with fares ranging from $1.50 to $2.50, depending on how far you travel.

FAST FACTS: St. Maarten/St. Martin

Banks   On the Dutch side, most banks are open Monday to Friday from 8am to 4:30pm, Saturday from 9am to 1pm. On the French side, they are usually open every weekday from 8am to 1pm and 2:30 to 4pm. It's easy to find ATMs. On the Dutch side, several banks are clustered along Front Street in Philipsburg. On the French side, most banks are along rue de la République in Marigot.

Currency   Despite the dominance of the euro since January 2002 within the mother country, Holland, the legal tender on the Dutch side is still the **Netherlands Antilles guilder (NAf);** the official exchange rate is NAf 1.77 for each US$1. U.S. dollars are widely accepted, and prices in hotels and most restaurants and shops are widely designated in dollars as well. On the French side, the official monetary unit is the **euro,** with most establishments widely quoting and accepting either dollars or NAf guilders as well. At press time, the U.S. dollar was trading at $1.25 to the euro. (Just before you leave home, you can check the current exchange rates on the Web at **www.x-rates.com**.) *Prices throughout this chapter are given in U.S. currency for establishments on the Dutch side, and in either euros or U.S. dollars for establishments on the French side.*

Documents   U.S., British, and Canadian citizens should have a passport, plus an ongoing or return ticket and a confirmed hotel reservation. In lieu of a passport, U.S. citizens can get away with presenting an original birth certificate and a photo ID, but frankly, we get the feeling that local authorities prefer to see passports. We always recommend that you travel with your passport.

Electricity   Dutch St. Maarten uses the same voltage (110-volt AC, 60 cycles) with the same electrical configurations as the United States, so adapters and transformers are not necessary. However, on French St. Martin, you'll usually need transformers and adapters. To simplify things, many hotels on both sides of the island have installed sockets suitable for both European and North American appliances.

Emergencies On the **Dutch** side, call the **police** at ✆ **599/54-22222** or an **ambulance** at ✆ **599/54-22111;** to report a **fire,** call ✆ **911** or ✆ **111.** On the **French** side, you can reach the **police** by dialing ✆ **17** or 590/87-88-33. In case of **fire,** dial ✆ **18.** For an **ambulance** dial ✆15.

Hospitals On the Dutch side, go to the **Medical Center,** Welegen Road, Cay Hill (✆ **599/54-31111**). On the French side, the local hospital is **Hôpital Concordia Mont Accords,** near Marigot in Concordia (✆ **590/52-25-25**).

Language The language on the St. Maarten side is officially Dutch, and it's officially French on St. Martin. But most people speak English. A French-based patois is spoken by a small segment of the local populace, as is French Creole, Spanish, and Papiamento.

Liquor Laws On both sides of the island, liquor is sold in grocery and liquor stores on any day of the week. It's legal to have an open container in public, though the authorities are very strict with any littering, disorderly behavior, or drunk driving.

Safety If possible, avoid night driving—it's particularly unwise to drive on remote, unlit, back roads at night. Also, let that deserted, isolated beach remain so. You're safer in a crowd, although under no circumstances should you ever leave anything unguarded on the beach.

Taxes & Service Charges There is no departure tax for departures from Espérance Airport on the French side. However, for departures from Queen Juliana Airport on the Dutch side, there's a departure tax of $20 ($6 if you're leaving the island for St. Eustatius or Saba).

On the Dutch side, a government tax of between 5% and 8%, depending on the category of hotel you stay in, is added to hotel bills. On the French side, hotels must levy a *taxe de séjour* (hotel tax); this differs from hotel to hotel, depending on its classification, but is often 5% a day. In addition to these taxes, most hotels add a (mandatory) service charge of around 10% to 15% to your hotel bill.

Telephone To call Dutch St. Maarten from the United States, dial **011** (the international access code), then **599** (the country code for the Netherlands Antilles), followed by **54** and then the five-digit local number. To make a local call on Dutch St. Maarten, dial **54,** then the five-digit local number. But if you're calling "long distance" from the Dutch side of the island to the French side of the island, dial **00,** followed by **590590** (the most prevalent international access code for French St. Martin) or for cellular phones **590690,** followed by the six-digit local number.

If you're on the French side of the island and want to call anyone on the Dutch side, dial **00,** followed by **599,** then **54** and the five-digit local number. Know in advance that calls between the French and Dutch sides are considered long-distance calls and are much, much more expensive than you might have imagined, considering the relatively short distance.

French St. Martin is linked to the Guadeloupe telephone system. To call French St. Martin from the United States, dial **011** (the international access code), then **590** (the country code for Guadeloupe), then **590** again, and the six-digit local number. To make a call from French St. Martin to any point within French St. Martin, no codes are necessary; just dial the local six-digit French number.

To call the United States from the island, dial **AT&T Direct** at ✆ 001-800-872-28881. To reach **MCI**, dial ✆ 0800/99-00-19, and to reach **Sprint**, dial ✆ 0800/99-00-87. On the Dutch side there are facilities for overseas calls, but from the French side you cannot make collect calls to the States and there are no coin-operated phones. At the Marigot post office you can purchase a *Telecarte*, giving you 40 units. A typical 5-minute call to the States takes up to 120 units. There is only one public phone at the Marigot tourist office from which it's possible to make credit card calls.

Time   St. Maarten and St. Martin operate on Atlantic Standard Time year-round. Thus in winter, if it's 6pm in Philipsburg, it's 5pm in New York. During daylight savings time in the United States, the island and the U.S. East Coast are on the same time.

Tipping   Most hotels on both sides on the island add a 10% or 15% service charge to your bill; make sure you understand whether or not it's already included in the original price quoted to you. Most restaurants automatically add a service charge to your bill. If service has not been added (unlikely), it's customary to tip around 15% in restaurants. Taxi drivers also expect a 15% tip.

Water   The water on the island is safe to drink. In fact, most hotels serve desalinated water.

Weather   The island has a year-round temperature of about 80°F (27°C).

2 Accommodations

IN DUTCH ST. MAARTEN

Remember, a government tax of between 5% and 8%, plus a service charge of 10% to 15% will be added to your hotel bill. Ask whether it's included in the original rates you're quoted to save yourself a shock when you check out.

VERY EXPENSIVE/EXPENSIVE

Belair Beach Hotel ⓡ *Kids*   Families, who appreciate the kitchens and the fact that children stay free, find this timeshare a good value. Originally built in 1980, a 10-minute drive from the airport, this hotel has lasted because of excellent management, good maintenance, and a reputation for quality and good value. The resort rises above a smallish swimming pool and beach. The units are one- and two-bedroom suites, each with a rather large master bedroom, two full bathrooms with shower/tub combinations, a fully equipped kitchenette (there's an on-site grocery store), and a 6m (20-ft.) terrace with a sweeping view of the sea. The suites are either timeshares or privately owned condos that are rented to visitors when their owners are not on the island.

Belair (P.O. Box 940), Philipsburg, St. Maarten, N.A. ✆ 800/480-8555 in the U.S., or 599/54-23362. Fax 599/54-25295. www.sxmhotels.com. 72 units. Winter $275 1-bedroom suite, $319–$499 2-bedroom suite; off season $229 1-bedroom suite, $269–$409 2-bedroom suite. Children 17 and under stay free in parent's suite (subject to availability). AE, DC, DISC, MC, V. **Amenities:** Restaurant; bar; outdoor pool; tennis court; jet skis; kayaks; sailing; scuba diving; snorkeling; water-skiing; windsurfing; tour desk; car rental; babysitting; laundry service and coin-operated laundry; rooms for those with limited mobility. *In room:* A/C, TV/VCR, kitchen, beverage maker, hair dryer, iron/ironing board, safe.

Caravanserai Beach Resort ★   This long-time favorite at the airport keeps getting blown away by hurricanes, but it always bounces back to reclaim its place as one of the island's leading hostelries. It fronts a small beach where the hotel has erected a sea wall for protection. Grounds feature palms, waterfalls, and rock pools. Accommodations are spacious and tastefully furnished, with shower/tub combinations, a mixture of pastel colors and dark-stained wood trim, and much comfort. You can choose between seaview rooms and units opening onto the gardens.

2 Beacon Hill Rd., St. Maarten, N.A. © **877/796-1002** in the U.S., or 599/54-54000. Fax 599/54-54001. www.caravanseraibeachresort.com. 75 units. Winter $210–$270 double, $395 1-bedroom apt; off season $160–$220 double, $350 1-bedroom apt. AE, MC, V. **Amenities:** 3 restaurants; 3 bars; 3 outdoor pools; casino; 2 tennis courts; fitness center; babysitting; laundry service; nonsmoking rooms; rooms for those with limited mobility. *In room:* A/C, TV/VCR, fax, fridge, hair dryer, iron/ironing board, safe.

Divi Little Bay Beach Resort ★   Built on a desirable peninsula about a 10-minute drive east of the airport, this hotel sits on a sandy beach that's rocky in places. It originated as a simple guesthouse in 1955, and it soon became famous as the vacation home of the Netherlands' Queen Juliana, Prince Bernhard, and Queen Beatrix. It was severely damaged during the hurricanes of the early 1990s, and then it was rebuilt in 1997 as the flagship of the Divi chain. Its design evokes a European seaside village, with pastel stucco walls and terra-cotta roofs, with some Dutch colonial touches. In the upper reaches of the property are the ruins of Fort Amsterdam, once Dutch St. Maarten's most prized military stronghold and today a decorative historical site. Gardens are carefully landscaped, and Divi improved the nearby beach after it suffered massive erosion.

This hotel development is larger than its 235 units imply, since part of it is devoted to the maintenance and marketing of timeshare units. It evokes a large residential apartment complex that's enhanced with hotel-style amenities and services. Accommodations are airy, accented with ceramic tiles and pastel colors; deluxe units have kitchenettes. Bathrooms tend to be small and compact, but have adequate shelf space and a shower/tub combination.

Little Bay (P.O. Box 961), Philipsburg, St. Maarten, N.A. © **800/367-3484** in the U.S., or 599/54-22333. Fax 599/54-24336. www.diviresorts.com. 235 units. Winter $183–$229 double, $298–$308 1-bedroom apt, $405 2-bedroom apt; off season $150–$188 double, $244–$250 1-bedroom apt, $330 2-bedroom apt. MAP (breakfast and dinner) $40 per day adult, $24 per day child. Children under 15 stay free in parent's room. AE, DC, MC, V. **Amenities:** 3 restaurants; bar; 3 outdoor pools; 3 lit tennis courts; gym; dive shop; jet skis; kayaks; sailing; snorkeling; water-skiing; windsurfing; car rental; salon; laundry service and coin-operated laundry; nonsmoking rooms. *In room:* A/C, TV, kitchenette (in some), beverage maker, hair dryer, iron/ironing board, safe.

The Horny Toad Guesthouse ★ *Value*   This homey, welcoming place is run by an expatriate from Maine, Betty Vaughan. Unfortunately, the hotel is near the airport, but the roar of jumbo jets is heard only a few times a day for a few moments. Children age 7 and under are not allowed, but families with older children often come here to avoid the megaresorts, and second-timers quickly become "part of the family."

Seven well-maintained units are in an amply proportioned beachside house originally built in the 1950s as a private home by the island's former governor. The eighth room is in half of an octagonal "round house," with large windows and views of the sea. Guest rooms range from medium size to spacious, and each has a kitchenette, a good-quality mattress, and a small but well-kept shower-only bathroom. There's no pool, no restaurant, and no organized activities of any kind, However, the beach is a few steps away, and there are often impromptu get-togethers around the pair of gas-fired barbecues.

2 Vlaun Dr., Simpson Bay, St. Maarten, N.A. © **800/417-9361** in the U.S., or 599/54-54323. Fax 599/54-53316. www.thehornytoadguesthouse.com. 8 units. Winter $198 double; off season $107 double. Extra person $40 in winter; $25 off season. MC, V. No children under age 7. **Amenities:** Laundry service. *In room:* Ceiling fan, kitchen, fridge, safe, no phone.

La Vista 🍸   This small West Antillean–style complex lies at the foot of Pelican Cay. Guests often stay at here, but use the more elaborate facilities of the nearby Pelican Resort (for a charge), with its casino and restaurant, The Hideaway. A good, sandy beach lies only a 2-minute walk from La Vista. Rooms with a view come in seven different categories, including a junior suite, deluxe suite, penthouse, or cottage. Accommodations feature fully equipped kitchenettes and medium-size bathrooms with shower. Our preference is the one-bedroom Antillean cottage with its front porch (suitable for occupancy by four).

The Hideaway serves well-prepared international cuisine adjacent to the pool.

53 Billy Folly Rd., Pelican Cay (P.O. Box 2086), Simpson Bay, St. Maarten, NA © **599/54-43005.** Fax 599/54-43010. www.lavistaresort.com. 32 suites. Winter $180 double, $210–$330 for 4; off season $140 double, $160–$225 for 4. Children under 12 free when sharing with 2 adults. AE, DISC, MC, V. **Amenities:** Restaurant; 2 bars; large pool; coin-operated laundry. *In room:* A/C, TV, kitchenette, fridge, hair dryer, safe.

Maho Beach Hotel & Casino 🍸   Separated into three distinct sections, each built over an 8-year period beginning in the mid-1980s, this megaresort, with its sprawling convention facilities, is the largest hotel on the island. Even with its failings, it's the closest thing on either side of the island to a Las Vegas–style blockbuster resort. It has a rather anonymous feeling (it's always full of conventioneers and giant tour groups), but it is completely modern and up-to-date, with lots of facilities that were enhanced after a $30 million upgrade that was completed in 2001. Set on a 4-hectare (10-acre) tract that straddles the busy, and often congested, coastal road adjacent to the crescent-shaped Maho Beach, the hotel's scattered structures are all painted a trademark cream and white.

The rooms are fairly spacious and conservatively but comfortably furnished. Each has wicker furniture, Italian tiles, a large TV, comfortable upholstered pieces, a walk-in closet, and good soundproofing (which is important, since you hear the thundering noise of planes landing at the nearby airport several times a day when you're on the hotel's beach). Bathrooms are spacious, with bidets and shower/tub combinations.

Because of its size, the hotel contains three separate restaurants that are managed directly by the hotel, with another half-dozen on-site that are independently managed. The Casino Royale, across the street from the hotel's accommodations, is the largest casino on the island, with a recently enlarged cabaret theater for glittery shows loaded with girls, razzmatazz, and glitter. The Q-Club, attached to the Casino Royale, is the island's splashiest, most electronically sophisticated late-night spot for drinking and dancing, complete with light shows and cat-walks looking down on the action below.

Maho Bay, 1 Rhine Rd., St. Maarten, N.A. © **800/223-0757** in the U.S., or 599/54-52115. Fax 599/54-53180. www.mahobeach.com. 600 units. Winter $235–$330 double, $390–$575 suite, from $845 2-bedroom unit; off season $190–$260 double, $330–$400 suite, from $660 2-bedroom unit. AE, DC, MC, V. **Amenities:** 9 restaurants; 4 bars; 3 outdoor pools; casino; dance club; golf (nearby); 4 tennis courts; fitness center; spa; business services; babysitting; laundry service; rooms for those with limited mobility. *In room:* A/C, TV, dataport, beverage maker (in some), hair dryer, safe.

Oyster Bay Beach Resort 🍸   At the end of a twisting, scenic road, a 1-minute walk from Dawn Beach, this elegant retreat was originally designed for vacationers who don't like overly commercialized megaresorts, like Maho Beach Hotel. Once an intimate inn, it's been growing by leaps and bounds, having witnessed a five-fold increase in size since it was established as an isolated inn in the 1960s. It can't be considered intimate anymore, but it's still not overwhelming. On a circular harbor on the eastern shore, near the French border, the fortresslike structure stands guard over a 14-hectare (35-acre) protected marina. There's a central courtyard and an alfresco lobby, with brown wicker and fine paintings. There's an intense focus here on marketing some of the units as timeshares.

More than half the units have kitchens, and most have West Indian decor with lots of rattan and wicker. The bedrooms offer balconies overlooking the pond or sea; the deluxe and superior rooms are preferable to the tower suites. Rooms are airy and fairly spacious, and suites have a bathroom with a tub and a shower.

The resort's only restaurant, Jade, serves international and Asian (mostly Indonesian) food at lunch and dinner.

10 Emerald Merit Rd., Oyster Pond (P.O. Box 239), Philipsburg, St. Maarten, N.A. © **877/478-6669** in the U.S., or 599/54-36040. Fax 599/54-36695. www.oysterbaybeachresort.com. 173 units (of those, 157 are timeshares). Winter $200–$290 double, $310–$600 suite; off season $120–$190 double, $200–$400 suite. Extra person $40. Children under 12 stay free in parent's room. AE, DISC, MC, V. **Amenities:** Restaurant; bar; outdoor pool; fitness center; car rental; coin-operated laundry; 1 room for those with limited mobility. *In room:* A/C, TV, dataport, kitchenette (in some), beverage maker, hair dryer, iron/ironing board, safe.

MODERATE/INEXPENSIVE
Mary's Boon Beach Plantation ⭐ (Finds)   This is the most charming and well-managed small inn on Dutch St. Maarten. It's very near the airport (so you do get the sounds of jets taking off and landing a few times a day), but it's also only minutes from casinos, shops, and restaurants. Mary's Boon draws a loyal repeat clientele that appreciates its sense of intimacy and understated elegance. Everything's relaxed and informal, though the service is alert and attentive.

Accommodations have verandas or terraces, but each varies architecturally. Those facing the sea directly are breezy, high-ceilinged, and comfortably unpretentious, with furnishings like what you'd expect in a 1970s-era Florida motel. Try to get one of the newer units, set within the garden; they're very stylish, showing the deft touch of a professional decorator. Done in jewel tones, they usually contain four-poster cherrywood beds and Balinese woodcarvings. Regardless of their age, most units have king-size beds. The inn enjoys direct access to one of the best beaches on St. Maarten, with white sands. The family-style restaurant offers good-value fixed-price dinners (with seconds included).

117 Simpson Bay Rd., St. Maarten, N.A. (or P.O. Box 523882, Miami, FL 33152). © **599/54-54235.** Fax 599/54-57000. www.marysboon.com. 28 units. Winter $175–$275 double; off season $75–$175 double. MC, V. Take the first right-hand turn as you head from the airport toward Philipsburg, then follow the signs to Mary's Boon. **Amenities:** Restaurant; bar; outdoor pool; gym; babysitting. *In room:* A/C, ceiling fans, TV, dataport, kitchenette, fridge, beverage maker, hair dryer, iron/ironing board, safe.

Pasanggrahan Royal Inn ⭐ (Value   *Pasanggrahan* is the Indonesian word for guesthouse, and this West Indian–style guesthouse lies 15m (49 ft.) from a private beach. A small, informal place, it's right on the busy, narrow main street of Philipsburg, toward the end of the mountainside of Front Street. It's set back under tall trees, with a white wooden veranda. The interior has peacock bamboo chairs, Indian spool tables, and a gilt-framed oil portrait of Queen Wilhelmina. The small- to medium-size renovated bedrooms have queen-size, double, or king-size beds with good mattresses and four-poster designs; some are in the main building and others are in an adjoining annex. Bathrooms are small but tidy, and all have shower/tub combinations. Set among the wild jungle of palms and shrubbery is the Pasanggrahan Restaurant.

15 Front St. (P.O. Box 151), Philipsburg, St. Maarten, N.A. ℂ 599/54-23588. Fax 599/54-22885. 31 units. Winter $148–$175 double; off season $88–$125 double. MC, V. Closed Sept. **Amenities:** Restaurant; bar; laundry service. *In room:* A/C, ceiling fan, TV, dataport, kitchenette (in some), fridge, beverage maker (in some), safe (in some).

The Pelican *Kids*   This resort, built in 1979 on 5 hectares (12 acres) of land near the airport, is the largest timeshare facility on St. Maarten, and the staff appears at times more interested in hawking these properties than in running a hotel. Nevertheless, it's a good value, with lots of amenities, and it's a good backup choice if the other resorts are full. Although many of the suites are leased for predesignated periods throughout the year, others are rented by the on-site managers as they become available. Accommodations, which contain ceiling fans, shower and tub bathrooms, and full kitchens, are arranged into village-style clusters separated from other units by lattices, hibiscus hedges, and bougainvillea. Each unit is fairly spacious, equipped with straightforward furnishings and comfortable king-size or double beds and most units have patios or verandas. Scattered around the property are many small waterways, and an orchid garden, not to mention the beachfront.

Simpson Bay (P.O. Box 431), Philipsburg, St. Maarten, N.A. ℂ 800/550-7088 in the U.S., or 599/54-42503. Fax 599/54-42133. www.pelicanresort.com. 342 units. Winter $125–$145 studio for 2–4, $200 1-bedroom suite for up to 4, $300 2-bedroom suite for up to 6, $360 3-bedroom suite for up to 8; off season $85–$110 studio for 2–4, $140 1-bedroom suite for 4, $215 2-bedroom suite for 6, $260 3-bedroom suite for 8. Holiday rates higher. AE, DISC, MC, V. **Amenities:** 2 restaurants; 5 bars; 5 outdoor pools; casino; 4 tennis courts (3 lit); gym; spa; dive shop; windsurfing; children's center; car rental; babysitting; laundry service. *In room:* A/C, ceiling fans, TV, kitchen, fridge, beverage maker, hair dryer (in some), safe.

IN FRENCH ST. MARTIN

Hotels on French St. Martin add a 10% service charge and a *taxe de séjour.* This visitors' tax on rooms differs from hotel to hotel, depending on its classification, but is often $4 a day.

VERY EXPENSIVE

Esmeralda Resort *⟨✦⟩*   Originally conceived as a site for a single private villa, and then for a semiprivate club, this hillside housing development gives the appearance of a well-maintained compound of Creole-inspired villas on sloping terrain that's interspersed with lush gardens. It lies within a 25-minute taxi ride northeast of Queen Juliana Airport. Opening onto Orient Beach, the Esmeralda blossomed into a full-scale resort in the early 1990s, offering views over Orient Bay and a decidedly French focus. Each of the 18 Spanish mission–style, tile-roofed villas can be configured into four separate units by locking or unlocking the doors between rooms. Each individual unit contains a king-size or two double beds, a kitchenette, a shower or tub bathroom, a terrace, and a private entrance. Each villa has a communal pool, which creates the feeling of a private club.

L'Astrolabe serves French food at breakfast and dinner daily. At lunch, the hotel issues an ID card that can be used at any of a half-dozen restaurants along the nearby beach.

Parc de la Baie Orientale (B.P. 5141), 97071 St. Martin, F.W.I. ℂ 590/87-36-36. Fax 590/87-35-18. www. esmeralda-resort.com. 65 units. Winter $300–$450 double, $550–$800 suite; off season $200–$270 double, from $320–$420 suite. AE, MC, V. **Amenities:** 2 restaurants; bar; 17 outdoor pools; 2 tennis courts; scuba diving; snorkeling; water-skiing; horseback riding (nearby); limited room service; massage; babysitting; laundry service. *In room:* A/C, TV, dataport, kitchenette (in some), fridge, beverage maker, hair dryer, safe.

Hotel Mont Vernon *⟨✦⟩ ⟨Kids⟩*   George Washington never slept here, but you might want to. Last renovated in 2004, this 1989 structure stands in a secluded corner of the 3km-long (2-mile) Orient Bay Beach with its white sands. One of the largest hotels on island, it offers spacious and tropically furnished junior suites with one king or two twin beds. Each suite can accommodate a maximum of four guests (the hotel allows three adults, or two adults and two children). The resort offers the largest freshwater pool on island and well-organized activities for children ages 5 to 12. All of the bedrooms have balconies, but those facing the ocean are more spacious. With its Creole-inspired architecture, the sprawling complex stands in a manicured setting of 28 hectares (69 acres). It has some of the best sports on island, including even *Petangue* (French Boce). There are plenty of complimentary activities for guests, including live entertainment, watersports, and a hotel shuttle that carries guests to the casinos at night.

French Cul de Sac, Baie Orientale, 97070 St. Martin, F.W.I. © **590/87-62-00.** Fax 590/87-37-25. www. mont-vernon.com. 390 units. Winter 370€–553€ ($463–$691) for up to 4; off season 281€–481€ ($351–$601) for up to 4. AE, DC, MC, V. **Amenities:** 2 restaurants; 2 bars; outdoor pool; 2 tennis courts; exercise room; kayaks; snorkeling; windsurfing; kids' programs (age 5–12); car rental; babysitting; laundry service/dry cleaning. *In room:* A/C, TV, fridge, safe.

La Samanna ☆☆☆   Luxurious, sybaritic, and spectacularly expensive, this world-class resort features Mediterranean-style architecture on a 2km (1¼-mile) stretch of one of St. Martin's finest beaches. The resort was acquired by Orient Express Hotels and made especially competitive with regular and massive infusions of cash. Since then, the resort has earned a reputation as a sleek, sexy, and stylish complex where celebrities sometimes come to hide out and unwind. Despite the price tag, La Samanna isn't stuffy, and in fact reminds us at times of the French Riviera.

Rows of mature royal palms enhance the 22-hectare (54-acre) property's front entrance. As you enter, you see lavish art objects from Morocco and Thailand. Regardless of their size, most units have private terraces. Suites and villas have spacious bedrooms with luxurious beds, fully equipped kitchens, living and dining rooms, and large patios. The bathrooms are simpler than might be expected, but they're well designed nonetheless, with bidets, hand-painted Mexican tiles, and shower/tub combinations. The fourth floor of the main building is the site of one of the grandest suites in the Caribbean.

Guests enjoy superb French cuisine alfresco, on a candlelit terrace overlooking Baie Longue. After dinner, the bar becomes a disco. At the poolside grill, waiters serve food, St-Tropez style, on the beach.

Baie Longue (B.P. 4077), 97064 St. Martin CEDEX, F.W.I. © **800/854-2252** or 590/87-64-00. Fax 590/87-87-86. www.orient-expresshotels.com. 81 units. Winter $765–$960 double, from $1,350 suite or villa; off season $405–$600 double, from $960 suite or villa. Rates include breakfast. AE, MC, V. Closed late Aug to late Oct. **Amenities:** Restaurant; 2 bars; outdoor pool; 3 tennis courts; fitness center; spa; sailing; snorkeling; water-skiing; windsurfing; library; 24-hr. room service; babysitting; laundry service; dry cleaning; nonsmoking rooms. *In room:* A/C, TV, minibar, beverage maker, hair dryer, iron/ironing board, safe.

Le Méridien L'Habitation/Le Domaine ☆☆ *Kids*   This, the largest resort on the French side of the island, is often packed with French-speaking tour groups. It's tucked under Pigeon Pea Hill, opening onto a beautiful white-sand beach. The older section (L'Habitation), with less panoramic bedroom views, is on a 60-hectare (148-acre) tract of rugged scrubland nestled between the sea and a mountain ridge. In the early 1990s, work began on Le Domaine, a few steps to the west of the original complex. Today, both resorts are fully integrated, sharing all entertainment, dining, drinking, and recreational facilities.

Accommodations at both resorts are in a string of neo-Victorian two- and three-story buildings ringed with lattices, gingerbread, and verandas. Most of the rooms in Le Domaine overlook the ocean, and are thus more expensive. The rooms in L'Habitation mostly open onto a 120-slip marina and a garden. All rooms and suites are comfortably and stylishly furnished, each with quality beds, soundproofing, a balcony or terrace, a two-sink bathroom with a shower/tub combo, an airy, tropical decor, and in many cases, kitchens. Thanks to some special children's programs that combine activities for children with limited child-minding services, this is an ideal place for families.

Anse Marcel (B.P. 581), Marigot, 97150 St. Martin, F.W.I. ℂ **800/253-0861** in the U.S., or 590/87-67-67. Fax 590/87-67-88. www.lemeridien-ledomaine.com. 377 units. Winter $370–$440 double, $500–$850 suite; off season $260–$290 double, $350–$550 suite. AE, DC, DISC, MC, V. Closed late Aug to early Oct. **Amenities:** 4 restaurants; 3 bars; 2 outdoor pools; 6 tennis courts; health club and spa; 120-slip marina; children's programs; room service (7am–10:30pm); babysitting; laundry service; dry cleaning; nonsmoking rooms; rooms for those with limited mobility. *In room:* A/C, TV, dataport, kitchen (in some), minibar, fridge, beverage maker, hair dryer, iron/ironing board, safe.

EXPENSIVE

Captain Oliver's Resort Hotel 𝕣 *(Kids* A quiet, intimate place, this is one of French St. Martin's most appealing, upper-middle-bracket hotels. It's similar to the Esmeralda Resort (see above). At the French-Dutch border 16km (10 miles) east of Queen Juliana Airport, this hotel is near the Dutch side's Oyster Bay Beach Hotel. The pink bungalows, with a bit of gingerbread, are set in a labyrinth and connected by boardwalks. High on a hill, they command panoramic views, and from the large terraces you can gaze over to St. Barts. On-site is a little zoo with monkeys, toucans, iguanas, an alligator or two, and many tropical birds. The resort is also a rehabilitation center for injured turtles. The accommodations, which are clustered three to a bungalow, are furnished in white rattan and decorated with local prints, and have marble-trimmed full bathrooms with double sinks, large double closets, and many amenities. Each junior suite has two beds and a sofa bed, which makes them perfect for families.

Oyster Pond, 97150 St. Martin, F.W.I. ℂ **590/87-40-26.** Fax 590/87-40-84. www.captainolivers.com. 50 units. Winter $175–$205 junior suite for 2; off season $120–$150 junior suite for 2. Rates include buffet breakfast. AE, MC, V. **Amenities:** 2 restaurants; 2 bars; outdoor pool; scuba diving; private taxi boat to beach; room service (7am–10:30pm); babysitting; laundry service; nonsmoking rooms; rooms for those with limited mobility. *In room:* A/C, TV, minibar, beverage maker, hair dryer, safe.

Club Orient Naturist Resort 𝕣 *(Finds* Occupying an isolated spot, this is the only true nudist resort in the French West Indies. Established in the late 1970s by a Dutch-born family, it welcomes a European and North American clientele. This is definitely *not* a wild, swinging, party place. It's very clean, decent, middle-class, and even family friendly. Very few single guests check in, so if you're looking for partners to play with, don't think that you'll meet someone here. Despite their lack of clothing, many of the guests are very conservative—looking for a quiet, reclusive getaway with like-minded nudists. There's no pool on the premises, but the chalets are right on an excellent beach. Accommodations, set in red-pine chalets imported from Finland, are utterly plain and simple; all have outside showers and most have both front and back porches. At Papagayo you can dine alfresco (literally). However, most guests opt to cook their own meals, as each unit has a kitchenette and there's a minimarket on-site.

Baie Orientale, 97150 St. Martin, F.W.I. ℂ **800/452-9016** in the U.S., or 590/87-33-85. Fax 590/87-33-76. www.cluborient.com. 136 units. Winter $235 studio, $276–$299 minisuite, $351–$391 chalet; off season $127 studio, $138–$150 minisuite, $167–$178 chalet. AE, DC, DISC, MC, V. **Amenities:** Restaurant; 2 bars; gym; library; laundry service and coin-operated laundry; 1 room for those with limited mobility. *In room:* A/C, ceiling fan, kitchen, beverage maker, safe.

Hotel Beach Plaza ✿ This is our favorite hotel within a reasonable distance of Marigot's commercial center. A three-story hotel that's centered on a soaring atrium festooned with live banana trees and climbing vines, it's within a cluster of buildings mostly composed of condominiums. Built in 1996, and painted in shades of blue and white, it's set midway between the open sea and the lagoon, giving all rooms water views. Inside, the decor is pure white, accented with varnished, dark-tinted woods and an inviting tropical motif. Each room contains a balcony, tile floors, native art, and simple hardwood furniture, including a writing desk and comfortable beds. Bathrooms have shower/tub combinations and generous shelf space.

The hotel's restaurant, Le Corsaire, serves French food except for all-you-can-eat buffets on Tuesday and Friday nights, which feature Creole and seafood, respectively.

Baie de Marigot, 97150 St. Martin, F.W.I. ✆ **590/87-87-00.** Fax 590/87-18-87. www.hotelbeachplazasxm. com. 144 units. Winter $203–$284 double, from $464 suite; off season $160–$224 double, from $359 suite. Rates higher between Christmas and New Year's. Rates include buffet breakfast. MAP (breakfast and dinner) $33 per person per day. AE, MC, V. **Amenities:** Restaurant; 2 bars; outdoor pool; kayaks; jet skis; scuba diving; snorkeling; water-skiing; bike rental; car rental; room service; babysitting; laundry service; nonsmoking rooms; rooms for those with limited mobility. In room: A/C, TV, minibar, hair dryer, safe.

Hôtel L'Esplanade Caraïbe ✿ This elegant collection of suites lies on a steeply sloping hillside above the road leading into the village of Grand-Case from Marigot. Covered with cascades of bougainvillea, and accented with a vaguely Hispanic overlay of white walls, hand-painted tiles, and light blue-colored roofs, the resort's various elements are connected by a network of concrete steps that add to the layout's drama. There's a pool, a series of gorgeous terraced gardens, and access to a beach via a 6-minute walk on a winding, stair-dotted pathway. There's no restaurant (only a bar that's open in midwinter), but the village of Grand-Case is known for its restaurants.

All views from the guest rooms and their terraces are angled out toward the sea and the sunset. Each unit contains a kitchen with a large fridge, up-to-date cookware, mahogany and wicker furniture, and very comfortable queen-size or king-size beds. Bathrooms are beautifully equipped right down to elegant toiletries baskets, bidets, and showers. The loft suites on the upper floors are worth the extra charge, as they include a sofa bed that can sleep extra guests, an upstairs master bedroom with a king-size bed, and a partial bathroom downstairs.

Grand-Case (B.P. 5007), 97150 St. Martin, F.W.I. ✆ **866/596-8365** or 590/87-06-55. Fax 590/87-29-15. www.lesplanade.com. 24 units. Winter $280–$320 double studio, $380 suite; off season $180–$220 double studio, $280 suite. AE, MC, V. **Amenities:** Bar (winter season); outdoor pool; car rental; babysitting; laundry service; rooms for those with limited mobility. In room: A/C, ceiling fan, TV, dataport, kitchen, fridge, beverage maker, hair dryer, safe.

Le Petit Hotel ✿ This is a stylish, well-managed, thoughtfully designed hotel, set on a small parcel of property that's squeezed between other buildings, with direct access to the sands of Grand-Case Beach. Much of its appeal derives from its hard-working manager, Kristin Petrelluzi, who offers advice on any of two dozen restaurants in nearby Grand-Case (since there's no restaurant on-site). Nine of the spacious units are studios, while the 10th is a one-bedroom apartment. Each has a well-equipped kitchenette with a microwave, fridge, and a two-burner stove, but no oven. All units have balconies or outdoor terraces, plus durable, comfortable furniture. The small bathrooms come with shower stalls.

248 Blvd. de Grand-Case, Grand-Case, 97150 St. Martin, F.W.I. ✆ **590/29-09-65.** Fax 590/87-09-19. www.l epetithotel.com. 10 units. Winter $290–$330 studio for 2, $390 1-bedroom apt for up to 4; off season

$190–$230 studio for 2, $290 1-bedroom apt for up to 4. Children under 7 stay free in parent's room. AE, MC, V. **Amenities:** Babysitting; laundry service; 1 room for those with limited mobility. *In room:* A/C, TV, kitchenette, fridge, beverage maker, hair dryer, iron/ironing board, safe.

MODERATE/INEXPENSIVE

Hôtel St.-Tropez des Caraïbes   In the early 1990s, a much larger hotel on this spot split up after its managers dissolved their partnership. This hotel is one of the two separate entities, and the background explains why it's flanked on either side by very similar-looking properties. The St.-Tropez des Caraïbes is the best maintained of the two. Don't expect too many hotel-style amenities here, as there's no bar, and very little to do on-site—but with the sweeping sands of Orient Beach at your disposal, you may not care. Three of the units have a kitchen, but many bars and restaurants are within walking distance. Seven units lie within each of eight neo-Romanesque buff- and pink-colored buildings. Rooms are genuinely appealing, each with bright but soft tones of pink and green, floral upholsteries, a balcony, and a bathroom with a shower/tub combination. The best accommodations, with the highest ceilings and the greatest sense of space, lie on the top (third) floor of each of the eight buildings.

Baie Orientale (B.P. 5137), 97070 St. Martin, F.W.I. © **590/87-42-01.** Fax 590/87-42-14. www.st-tropez-caraibes.com. 28 units. Winter $211–$259 double; off season $172–$211 double. AE, DISC, MC, V. **Amenities:** Laundry service; outdoor pool; 1 room for those with limited mobility. *In room:* A/C, TV, kitchenette (in some), fridge, beverage maker, hair dryer, safe.

La Plantation Orient Bay Resort ⊛   Although it requires a few minutes' walk to reach the gorgeous white-sand beach, this is one of the most attractive and appealing hotels at Orient Bay. It's set on a steep, carefully landscaped slope, and designed like an upscale and rather charming condo complex. Seventeen colonial-style villas are scattered around the tropically landscaped grounds and pool; each villa contains a suite and two studios, which can be rented separately or combined. The spacious units are stylishly furnished in a South Seas/Polynesian/Creole theme, complete with hand-painted or hand-stenciled murals, and each sports its own oceanview terrace. Studios have kitchenettes and queen-size or twin beds; the suites have separate bedrooms with king-size beds, spacious living rooms, full kitchens, and beautifully tiled full bathrooms.

Café Plantation serves French and Creole dinners. At lunch, clients use an in-house ID card to buy French/Creole/international meals at any of five beach-front restaurants loosely associated with the resort.

C 5 Parc de la Baie Orientale, Orient Bay, 97150 St. Martin, F.W.I. © **590/29-58-00.** Fax 590/29-58-08. www.la-plantation.com. 52 units. Winter $165 studio for 2, $230 suite; off season $131 studio, $190 suite. Rates include breakfast. DISC, MC, V. Closed Sept 1 to mid-Oct. **Amenities:** 2 restaurants; beach bar and grill; outdoor pool; health club; diving; windsurfing; bike rental; horseback riding; massage. *In room:* A/C, TV, kitchen, fridge, beverage maker, hair dryer, safe.

La Résidence   In the commercial center of Marigot (and favored by business travelers for its location), La Résidence's concrete facade is enlivened with neo-Victorian gingerbread fretwork. A bar with a soaring tent serves drinks to guests relaxing on wicker and bentwood furniture. The small bedrooms are arranged around a landscaped central courtyard with a fish-shaped fountain. Each room is minimally decorated, and all but a few are duplexes with mahogany-trimmed stairs climbing to a sleeping loft. Bathrooms are also small, with shower stalls.

The simple restaurant serves dinner only. The staff rather arrogantly defines meals as French *cuisine gastronomique,* but we think they're more prosaic than that.

Rue du Général-de-Gaulle (B.P. 679), Marigot, 97150 St. Martin, F.W.I. © **590/87-70-37.** Fax 590/87-90-44. laresidence@wanadoo.fr. 15 units. Year-round $86 double. Rates include continental breakfast. AE, MC, V. **Amenities:** Restaurant. *In room:* A/C, TV, minibar, safe.

Le Royale Louisiana   Occupying a prominent position in the center of Marigot, 16km (10 miles) north of Queen Juliana Airport, this hotel is designed in a hip-roofed French-colonial Louisiana style; its rambling balconies are graced with ornate balustrades. It's about a 10-minute drive to the nearest good beach; you'll want a car if you stay here. Each small- to medium-size guest room contains big sunny windows and modern furniture. Standard rooms have queen-size beds, and in many cases, small verandas. Duplexes, ideal for families, have a sitting room with a sofa bed on the lower floor, with a bedroom and bathroom on the upper level. Note that duplex rates are not based on the number of occupants. Bathrooms are well maintained but a bit cramped, with shower and tubs.

The in-house restaurant is much more popular at lunch than it is at dinner, charging as little as $10 for a simple set menu. Dinners are a bit more formal, but limited to 2 nights a week at most, usually Monday and Friday.

Rue du Général-de-Gaulle, Marigot, 97150 St. Martin, F.W.I. © **590/87-86-51.** Fax 590/87-96-49. louisiana @top-saint-martin.com. 33 units. Winter $74 double, $100 duplex; off season $69 double, $89 duplex. Rates include continental breakfast. AE, MC, V. **Amenities:** Restaurant; bar; babysitting. *In room:* A/C, TV, fridge.

Mercure Coralia Simson Beach *(Value*   This is one of the most stylish hotels in its price bracket on the French side of the island. It's good value for the money, especially since each unit contains a kitchenette. The complex occupies a flat, sandy stretch of land between a saltwater lagoon and the beach, 8km (5 miles) west of Queen Juliana Airport. Decorated throughout in ocean-inspired pastels, its five three-story buildings are each evocative of a large, many-balconied Antillean house. In its center, a pool serves as the focal point for a bar built out over the lagoon, an indoor/outdoor restaurant, and a flagstone terrace that hosts steel bands and evening cocktail parties. Each unit, in addition to the kitchenette, offers ceiling fans and simple, durable wicker furniture, plus a tiled, shower-only bathroom. The most desirable accommodations, on the third (top) floor, contain sloping ceilings sheltering sleeping lofts and two bathrooms.

Baie Nettlé (B.P. 172), Marigot, 97150 St. Martin, F.W.I. © **800/221-4542** in the U.S., or 590/87-54-54. Fax 590/87-92-11. 168 units. Winter 124€–241€ ($155–$301) studio for 2, from 146€–265€ ($183–$331) duplex; off season 105€ ($131) studio for 2, 124€ ($155) duplex. Rates include buffet breakfast. AE, DC, MC, V. **Amenities:** Restaurant; bar; outdoor pool; tennis court; dive shop; snorkeling; windsurfing; bikes; car rental; babysitting; laundry service; dry cleaning; rooms for those with limited mobility. *In room:* A/C, ceiling fan, TV, dataport, kitchenette, beverage maker (in some), safe.

Nettlé Bay Beach Club   This is a stylish and appealing colony of villas scattered across a landscaped garden that opens onto four bays, each fronted with its own swimming pool. Each villa is a two-story Creole-style cottage set with some degree of privacy into its own garden. Villas can be rented as a complete two-story, two-bedroom house that's very comfortable for four occupants, or either the upper floor or the lower floor can be rented as a self-contained studio or one-bedroom apartment, respectively. If your plan is to rent just one floor of any of these cottages, try to book the lower floors, which are larger and more comfortable. Regardless of their size, each unit has terra-cotta floors, wicker furniture, shower-only bathrooms, and a veranda or terrace. All the apartments have kitchens, as do some of the studios.

Baie Nettlé, (B.P. 4081), 97064 St. Martin, F.W.I. © **590/87-68-68.** Fax 590/87-21-51. reservation@hotel nettlebay. 68 units. Winter 144€–162€ ($180–$203) studio, 159€–183€ ($199–$229) 1-bedroom villa;

summer 95€ ($119) studio, 105€ ($131) 1-bedroom villa. AE, MC, V. **Amenities:** 2 restaurants; bar; 4 outdoor pools; 3 lit Laykold tennis courts; babysitting; laundry service; dry cleaning. *In room:* A/C, TV, data-port, kitchen/kitchenette (in most), beverage maker, hair dryer, safe.

3 Dining

IN DUTCH ST. MAARTEN
EXPENSIVE

Antoine's ⚑ FRENCH/CREOLE/ITALIAN   In a lovely setting by the sea, Antoine's serves fine food with sophistication and style. The service is first-class and the wine list impressive. Start off with a cocktail in the bar while you peruse the menu. The Gallic specialties with Creole overtones are among the best on the island, and as good as those in the better restaurants in the French zone. However, Da Livio (see below) serves better Italian food. We always start with the chef's savory kettle of fish soup or his homemade pâté. If it's featured, try the baked red snapper fillet delicately flavored with white wine, lemon, shallots, and a butter sauce, or lobster thermidor. Although the veal and beef are shipped in frozen, they're used in some rather good dishes—try the veal scaloppini with a smooth, perfectly balanced mustard-and-cream sauce.

119 Front St., Philipsburg. ⓒ 599/54-22964. Reservations recommended, especially in winter. Lunch main courses $10–$16; dinner main courses $20–$37. AE, DISC, MC, V. Daily 11am–10pm.

The Boathouse AMERICAN/INTERNATIONAL   Funky, irreverent, and friendly, this is one of the Dutch side's most enduringly popular bars and restaurants. The seafaring theme of the interior includes a soaring network of heavy timbers accented with soft yellows, blues, greens, and lots of nautical accessories. Come here for the bar, a wraparound affair that attracts good-natured expatriates and locals alike, and for the generous portions dished up by the hardworking kitchen staff. Lunches consist of sandwiches, pastas, and salads. (Especially good are the shrimp salad and the grilled chicken Caesar salad.) Main courses at dinner are more substantial, including filet mignon, pepper steak, surf and turf, and red snapper that's either charcoal-grilled or stuffed with shrimp and crabmeat and served with a white-wine cream sauce.

74 Airport Rd., Simpson Bay. ⓒ 599/54-45409. Reservations recommended for dinner. Lunch main courses $10–$15; dinner main courses $16–$35. MC, V. Mon–Sat 11:30am–4pm; daily 5:30–10:30pm.

Da Livio Ristorante ⚑ ITALIAN   This is the finest Italian dining on the Dutch side of St. Maarten, though Il Nettuno (see below) on the French side is better. The place is as Italian as they come, and the staff is graciousness itself. Owner Bergamasco Livio hails from near Venice, and he purchases most of his ingredients from the finest suppliers in his home country. At the western edge of Front Street, with a panoramic view of the Great Bay, the restaurant sets a romantic mood in the evening with background music. We love the homemade manicotti della casa, filled with ricotta, spinach, and a zesty tomato sauce, as well as the lasagna. For a main course, we suggest the tender and juicy veal chop with sage-flavored butter. Tony Bennett and even Eddie Murphy have sung the praises of these dishes. The kitchen staff goes as far as to grow tomatoes in their own garden.

189 Front St., Philipsburg. ⓒ 599/54-22690. Reservations recommended for dinner. Main courses $17–$36. MC, V. Mon–Fri noon–2pm; Mon–Sat 6–10pm.

Saratoga ⚑ INTERNATIONAL   This is the most creative and cutting-edge restaurant in St. Maarten; it's laid-back and intensely choreographed at the same time. It's a beautiful setting, resembling a Spanish colonial structure from the outside, and lined with rich mahogany inside. You might like a predinner drink ("ultrapremium margaritas" and vodka martinis are the house specialties) in the bar. Seating is either indoors or on a marina-side veranda. The menu changes every 2 days, but there's always an artfully contrived low-fat selection like onion-crusted salmon served on a compote of lentils and sweet corn. Yellowfin tuna might be grilled with basmati rice or wasabi-flavored butter and daikon leaves. Another dish is crispy-fried black sea bass with an Asian-style sauce of fermented black beans and scallions. Rack of venison is often featured with port sauce or some other sauce concocted by owner/chef John Jackson, who hails from Saratoga Springs, New York.

Simpson Bay Yacht Club, Airport Rd. ℭ 599/54-42421. Reservations recommended. Main courses $20–$35. AE, MC, V. Mon–Sat 6:30–10:30pm. Closed Aug to mid-Oct.

MODERATE/INEXPENSIVE

Cheri's Café ℛ AMERICAN   American expatriate Cheri Batson's island hot spot is the best bar on the island. Touristy but fun and sassy, a great place to meet people, it's outfitted in an irrepressible color scheme of hot pink and white. This open-air cafe, serving some 400 meals a night, is really only a roof without walls, and it's not even on a beach. But people flock to it anyway, devouring 18-ounce steaks, ever-popular burgers, and grilled fresh-fish platters. The clientele covers everybody from rock bands to movie stars, high rollers at the casino to beach bums. Some come for the cheap eats, others for the potent drinks, many to dance and flirt. The bartender's special is a frozen Straw Hat made with vodka, coconut, tequila, pineapple and orange juices, and strawberry liqueur. Maybe even one more ingredient, we suspect—although nobody's talking. There's live music every night beginning at 8pm, and ending around 10:15pm.

45 Cinnamon Grove Shopping Centre, Maho Beach. ℭ 599/54-53361. Reservations not accepted. Main courses $10–$26. DISC, MC, V. Wed–Mon 11am–10pm (until midnight Fri–Sat). Closed Sept.

The Greenhouse AMERICAN   Breezes filter through this plant-filled, open-air eatery with a view of the harbor. The menu features the catch of the day as well as burgers, pizza, and salads. Dinner specials might include fresh lobster thermidor, Jamaican jerk pork, or salmon in light dill sauce. Some of the island's best steaks are served here, each cut certified Angus beef, including New York strip, T-bone, porterhouse, or filet mignon. The chef specializes in chicken, ranging from mango chicken to chicken parmigiana. Happy hour is daily 4:30 to 7pm and features half-price appetizers and two-for-one drinks. If entertainment is what you're after, then show up on Tuesday nights, when a DJ not only spins out tunes but also gives prizes to bingo champs and trivia experts. Other nights, you can occupy yourself with pool tables and video games.

Bobby's Marina (off Front St.), Philipsburg. ℭ 599/54-22941. Main courses $5.95–$29. AE, MC, V. Daily 11am–10pm (2am on Tues).

Kangaroo Court SANDWICHES/SALADS   Simple and unpretentious, this cafe and sandwich shop is set on a side street between Front and Back streets, adjacent to the courthouse. The thick 200-year-old walls that shelter it are among the oldest in town, crafted of black stone that has withstood many a hurricane. Within an interior that's brightly painted in vibrant Creole colors, you'll find display racks loaded with fresh-baked pastries and espresso machines that chug out endless cups of caffeine. Salads (including versions with sesame chicken, or shrimp, avocado, and papaya) and sandwiches (beef, turkey, tuna, and grilled chicken) are sold at a roaring pace, mostly to passengers from the nearby cruise-ship docks, throughout the day.

Hendrick's Straat 6, Philipsburg. © 599/54-27557. Sandwiches and salads $7.25–$11. AE, DISC, MC, V. Mon–Fri 7:30am–5pm; Sat 8am–4pm.

Turtle Pier Bar & Restaurant AMERICAN/SEAFOOD 🍴 *Finds*   Although turtles swim in a large protected pool in the nearby lagoon, they're not destined for the stew pot, but are released when they become adults. This restaurant does, however, offer one of the island's best menus of fresh seafood, much of which is caught in waters off neighboring islands. The location across from the Juliana airport is not its greatest asset, but once inside, you forget all about jets. Located on a pier beside the water, the place evokes a small zoo, with chattering parrots, macaws, cockatoos, even rabbits, and monkeys. On Wednesday, lobster prepared many different ways is the specialty. Because they're shipped in containers of seawater by air or sea, they're the freshest-tasting on the island. At night, you can start with the Creole-style conch soup. Fish such as mahimahi, tuna, or grouper can be grilled, poached, served meunière, or blackened. Duck is also a specialty. Our favorite is pan-seared duck breast in a sauce made from local guavaberry liqueur. Chops and steaks round out the menu.

Turtle Pier, Simpson Bay. 114 Airport Rd. © 599/54-52562. Main courses $12–$18 lunch, $16–$22 dinner. AE, DISC, MC, V. Daily 7:30am–10pm.

IN FRENCH ST. MARTIN

No other town in the Caribbean features as many restaurants, per capita, as the village of Grand-Case, set near French St. Martin's northernmost tip. Don't be put off by the town's ramshackle appearance: Behind the slowly decaying clapboards are French-, Italian-, and American-style restaurants managed by some extremely canny entrepreneurs, many of whom are extremely sophisticated cooks. If you're a real foodie and you want a decadent vacation, check into one of Grand-Case's hotels, go to a topless beach every day, and dine at a different restaurant every night.

EXPENSIVE

La Vie en Rose 🍴🍴 FRENCH   The dining room in this balconied second-floor restaurant evokes a tropical version of Paris in the 1920s, thanks to ceiling fans, candlelight, and some well-developed culinary showmanship. The menu is classic French, although Caribbean flavors and overtones often creep in. Lunches are relatively simple affairs, with an emphasis on fresh, meal-size salads, simple grills like beefsteak with shallot sauce, brochettes of fresh fish, pastas, sandwiches, and salads. Dinners are more elaborate, and might begin with sautéed fresh foie gras. Main courses include grilled fillet of red snapper in puff pastry with fresh basil sauce; breast of duck with an orange-walnut sauce; fresh medallions of smoked lobster with fresh-made pasta and herbs; boneless breast of duck with raspberry sauce and fried bananas; and an unusual version of roasted rack of lamb with mushrooms. A particularly worthwhile beginner at either lunch or dinner is the house version of lobster bisque.

Blvd. de France at rue de la République, Marigot. © 590/87-54-42. Reservations recommended, especially in winter and as far in advance as possible. Main courses 10€–18€ ($13–$23) lunch, 19€–35€ ($24–$44) dinner. AE, MC, V. Mon–Sat 11am–2:30pm; daily 6:30–10pm.

Le Pressoir 🍴 FRENCH   This bistro occupies a charming, old-fashioned Creole house painted yellow and blue. Favored by locals, it presents a combination of old and new French cuisine that includes sliced foie gras terrine, smoked salmon with rosemary and pepper, filet of snapper in vanilla sauce, and roasted rack of lamb with sweet clove and garlic. Fresh products are deftly handled, their natural flavors enhanced by the use of imaginative flavorings. The restaurant's signature dish combines very fresh grilled shellfish and fish in a stew pot with beurre blanc.

30 Blvd. de Grand-Case, Grand-Case. ℂ 590/87-76-62. Reservations recommended. Main courses 23€–34€ ($29–$43). AE, MC, V. Daily 6–10:30pm.

Rainbow Café FRENCH/INTERNATIONAL   Set on the northeastern end of the row of restaurants that line Grand-Case's main road, this little bistro thrives under the direction of Dutch-born Fleur Radd, and Buffalo, New York–born David Hendricks. The house containing the cafe opens onto views over the sea. Meals are served in an artfully simple dining room outfitted in shades of dark blue and white. Menu items evolve almost every evening—we've enjoyed chopped lamb with mashed potatoes and an onion-garlic marmalade; snapper in Parmesan-onion crust with tomato-flavored vinaigrette, and chicken breast marinated in lemon grass and ginger, with grilled balsamic-glazed vegetables. There's also salmon in puff pastry with spinach and citrus-dill butter sauce, and fricassee of scallops and shrimp served with Caribbean pineapple chutney.

176 Blvd. de Grand-Case, Grand-Case. ℂ 590/87-55-80. Reservations recommended. Main courses 22€–32€ ($28–$40). MC, V. Mon–Sat 6:30–10:30pm.

MODERATE

Il Nettuno ⭐ ITALIAN   This is the most elaborate, best-managed, and most appealing Italian restaurant on either side of the island, coping gracefully with a cosmopolitan, international crowd. It was established by a seasoned Italian restaurateur, Raymond Losito, whose career included a 25-year stint at a French restaurant in Washington, D.C., where he developed a deep attachment to the Washington Redskins football team, whose banners and memorabilia decorate the walls of the restaurant's bar. It's a great watering hole, outfitted in the colors of the Italian flag, and drawing a fervent crowd of fans for U.S. football games.

Meals are served on a large, rambling wooden veranda that the owners bravely refurbish after hurricanes. It serves the best blackened tuna we've ever had, as well as grilled portobello mushrooms, mussels in white-wine sauce, fresh Chilean sea bass or fillet of sea wolf cooked in parchment, fillet of grouper with prosciutto, and a worthy version of lobster risotto. The pastas are superb. There's an especially worthwhile version of sea bass baked in rock salt, prepared for a minimum of two diners.

70 Blvd. de Grand-Case, Grand-Case. ℂ 590/87-77-38. Reservations recommended. Main courses 18€–28€ ($23–$35). AE, DISC, MC, V. Daily noon–2:30pm and 6–10:30pm. Closed for lunch Apr–Oct; closed entirely Sept.

Le Cottage ⭐ FRENCH/CREOLE   One of our favorite restaurants in a town that's loaded with worthy contenders is set in what looks like a private house on the inland side of the main road running through Grand-Case. Its atmosphere is at least partly influenced by Burgundy-born wine steward, Stephane Émorine, who shows a canny ability to recommend the perfect wine by the glass to complement the French and Caribbean cuisine. Meals tend to begin dramatically with such dishes as a casserole of crayfish and avocados with a citrus sauce, or foie gras. Mains include both rustic *cuisine du terroir* (such as roasted rack of lamb with either a rosemary or a cream-based *pistou* sauce) and Creole dishes, including a filet of local dorado (mahimahi) served with a reduction of crayfish.

97 Blvd. de Grand-Case, Grand-Case. (© 590/29-03-30. Reservations recommended. Main courses 20€–24€ ($25–$30). AE, DC, MC, V. Daily 6:30–10pm.

Le Jasmin 🅰 *(Finds* FRENCH Many other restaurants have occupied this blue-and-white clapboard-sided house that's set on the seaward side of the main road running through Grand-Case. Under its current management, it's one of the most laid-back restaurants in town, with the kind of insouciance you might associate with the French Riviera, and an otherwise charming staff that's sometimes a wee bit distracted. If you happen to just walk into this place, you'll be offered a roster of well-prepared but relatively uncomplicated food. These will include at least three kinds of fish fast-frozen and flown in from the French mainland, including sole, tuna, and hake, each prepared as grills or "in the French style" *(à la meunière).* There are also lamb cutlets, beefsteaks, and chicken. Many locals who find this menu too limited phone in their orders a day or two in advance. If you have a hankering for duck with cocoa-and-black-pepper sauce, or fresh local fish, it's wise to do likewise. (You might be asked to pay a deposit if your gastronomic demands are too esoteric.)

158 Blvd de Grand-Case, Grand-Case. (© 590/87-02-31. Reservations recommended. Main courses 16€–30€ ($20–$38). AE, DC, MC, V. Daily 6–10:30pm.

INEXPENSIVE

Claude Mini-Club 🅰 *(Finds* CREOLE/FRENCH For a real Caribbean aura, head for this little discovery overlooking the harbor at Marigot. For more than 3 decades, this has been a long-enduring favorite with in-the-know locals as well as discerning visitors. The setting has a certain charm as it was constructed to resemble a tree house around the trunks of old palms. The decor is Haitian, capturing much of the vibrancy of that troubled island. A big terrace opens onto the sea.

The cuisine features a judicious treatment of fine products, including crab *farci* (stuffed) served with a Creole sauce. The grilled crayfish is succulent and tender. One of our favorite dishes, and certainly one of the most authentic Creole offerings, is a *lambi* (conch) stew in a zesty tomato sauce with hot spices. Other more classical dishes include a filet of beef in a green-peppercorn sauce, and veal escalope with fresh morels. Such classic desserts as banana flambé or crème brûlée are offered. This place is busiest on Wednesday and Saturday nights, as the restaurant stages the island's best buffets, featuring such party delights as roast suckling pig, roast beef, and Caribbean lobster.

Blvd. de la Mer, Marigot. (© 590/87-50-69. Reservations required. Main courses 10€–20€ ($13–$25); fixed-price menu 23€ ($29); buffet 40€ ($50). AE, MC, V. Mon–Sat 11am–3pm and 6–10pm. Closed Sept.

Kakao *(Finds* *(Kids* INTERNATIONAL This French Polynesian–style open-air pavilion beside the sands of Orient Beach is always hopping. Amid dark-stained timbers, thatch-covered roofs, and nautical pieces that include the artifacts from several demolished or sunken yachts, you can drink, eat, sun, lie on lounge chairs, or simply gossip with the Euro-Caribbean crowd that hangs out here. If you're hungry, a menu lists pizzas, grilled steaks and fish, burgers, ice cream, and banana splits. This place is a bit more family friendly, and a bit less irreverent and raunchy, than the Kon Tiki next door.

Orient Beach. (© 590/87-43-26. Pizzas 10€–15€ ($13–$19); main courses 14€–23€ ($18–$29). AE, DISC, MC, V. Daily 8am–6pm.

L'Oizeau Rare 🅰 *(Value* FRENCH/INTERNATIONAL This rather grand, upscale restaurant is reminiscent of a stylish eatery along the Côte d'Azur. French cuisine is served in a blue-and-ivory-colored antique house with a view of three artfully landscaped waterfalls in the garden. The tables are dressed with snowy cloths and Limogès china. At lunch, served on the covered terrace, you can choose from a number of salads as well as fish and meat courses. Dinner choices include fresh fish, such as snapper, salmon, or fresh-caught mahimahi with lemon-flavored coconut sauce; ostrich steak with wild mushroom fricassee; and fillets of lamb with Provençal herbs. Duck with mango or raspberries has always been a specialty, as has bouillabaisse. The cooking is grounded firmly in France, but there are Caribbean twists and flavors, which come as delightful surprises. The wine list has an extensive selection of imported French options at moderate prices. Many guests come here at sundown to enjoy the harbor view.

Blvd. de France, Marigot. ℂ 590/87-56-38. Reservations recommended. Main courses 10€–25€ ($13–$31) lunch, 20€–25€ ($25–$31) dinner. AE, DISC, MC, V. Mon–Sat noon–2:30pm and 6–10pm. Closed June.

Sunset Café INTERNATIONAL   Set on the sands at the Grand-Case Beach Club, this open-air restaurant and bar wraps around the rocky peninsula that divides Grand-Case Beach from Petite Plage. Tables are strewn along a narrow veranda-style terrace that affords sweeping views of the setting sun. A planter's punch will make the fish soup, locally smoked fish, snails with Roquefort sauce, or red snapper fillet with vanilla sauce taste even better. Lunch items are simpler, with emphasis on sandwiches, burgers, melon with slices of Parma ham, pastas, and salads. The hotel here tends to be a little staid, so this place is better suited to a quiet and romantic dinner than a wild party.

In the Grand-Case Beach Club, rue de Petit-Plage, Grand-Case. ℂ 590/87-51-87. Reservations recommended for weekend dinners in winter. Main courses 9€–14€ ($11–$18) lunch, 18€–25€ ($23–$31) dinner. AE, MC, V. Daily 7:30am–10pm.

4 Beaches ⟨★⟨★

The island has 37 beautiful white-sand beaches, so it's fairly easy to find a place to park your towel. Most beaches have recovered from the erosion caused by the 1995 hurricane. *Warning:* If it's too secluded, be careful. It's unwise to carry valuables to the beach; there have been robberies on some remote strips.

Regardless of where you stay, you're never far from the water. If you're a beach sampler, you can often use the changing facilities at some of the bigger resorts for a small fee. Nudists should head for the French side of the island, although the Dutch side is getting more liberal about such things. Here's a rundown of the best, starting on the Dutch side of the island.

Popular **Cupecoy Bay Beach** is very close to the Dutch-French border, on the western side of the island. It's a string of three white-sand beaches set against a backdrop of caves, beautiful rock formations, and cliffs that provide morning shade. There are no restaurants, bars, or other facilities, but locals come around with coolers of cold beer and soda for sale. The beach has two parking lots, one near Cupecoy and Sapphire beach clubs, the other a short distance to the west. Parking costs $2. You must descend stone-carved steps to reach the sands. Cupecoy is also the island's major gay beach.

Also on the west side of the island, west of the airport, white-sand **Mullet Bay Beach** is shaded by palm trees. Once it was the most crowded beach on the island, but St. Maarten's largest resort, Mullet Bay, remained closed at press time, so the crowds aren't so bad anymore. Weekdays are best, as many locals flock here on weekends. Watersports equipment can be rented at a local kiosk.

Another lovely spot near the airport, **Maho Bay Beach,** at the Maho Beach Hotel and Casino, is shaded by palms and is ideal in many ways, if you don't mind the planes taking off and landing nearby. This is one of the island's busiest beaches, buzzing with windsurfers. Food and drink can be purchased at the hotel.

Stretching the length of Simpson Bay Village are the 2km-long (1¼-mile) white sands of crescent-shaped **Simpson Bay Beach,** west of Philipsburg before you reach the airport. This beach is popular with windsurfers, and it's an ideal place for a stroll or a swim. Watersports equipment rentals are available, but there are no changing rooms or other facilities.

Great Bay Beach 𝒜 is best if you're staying along Front Street in Philipsburg. This 2km-long (1¼-mile) beach is sandy, but since it borders the busy capital, it may not be as clean as some of the more remote choices. On a clear day, you'll have a view of Saba. Immediately to the west, at the foot of Fort Amsterdam, is picturesque **Little Bay Beach,** but it, too, can be overrun with tourists. When you tire of the sands here, you can climb up to the site of Fort Amsterdam itself. Built in 1631, it was the first Dutch military outpost in the Caribbean. The Spanish captured it two years later, making it their most important bastion east of Puerto Rico. Only a few of the fort's walls remain, but the view is panoramic.

On the east side of the island, **Dawn Beach** is noted for its underwater life, with some of the island's most beautiful reefs immediately offshore. Visitors talk ecstatically of its incredible sunrises. Dawn is suitable for swimming and offers year-round activities such as sand-castle-building contests and crab races. There's plenty of wave action for both surfers and windsurfers. The road to this beach is bumpy, but worth the effort. Nearby are the pearly white sands of **Oyster Pond Beach,** near the Oyster Bay Beach Resort. Bodysurfers like the rolling waves here.

Top rating on French St. Martin goes to **Baie Longue** 𝒜 on the west side of the island, a beautiful beach that's rarely overcrowded. Chic, expensive La Samanna opens onto this beachfront. Its reef-protected waters are ideal for snorkeling, but there is a strong undertow. Baie Longue is to the north of Cupecoy Bay Beach, reached via the Lowlands Road. Don't leave any valuables in your car, as many break-ins have been reported along this occasionally dangerous stretch of highway.

Isolated **Friar's Bay Beach** lies at the end of a winding country road; its clearly signposted entrance intersects with the main highway between Grand-Case and Marigot. Although you certainly won't be alone here, this is a less-visited beach with ample parking. There's some topless sunbathing, depending on who happens to show up.

White-sand **Grand-Case Beach** is right in the middle of Grand-Case and is likely to be crowded, especially on weekends. The waters are very calm, so swimming is excellent and it's a good choice for kids. A small but select beach, it has its own charm, with none of the carnival-like atmosphere found elsewhere.

On the eastern side of the island, **Orient Beach** is the island's only official nudist beach. There's steady action here: bouncy Caribbean bands, refreshments of all kinds, watersports, and clothing, crafts, and jewelry vendors. Everyone comes to enjoy this stretch of velvety white sands. The coral reef off the beach teems with marine life, making for great snorkeling. Club Orient, the nude resort, is at the end of the beach; voyeurs from cruise ships can always be spotted here. This is also a haven for windsurfers.

Finally, for the most isolated and secluded beach of all, you have to leave St. Martin. **Ilet Pinel,** off the coast at Cul-de-Sac, is reached by a boat ride off the northeast coast (you can hire a local boatman to take you from Cul-de-Sac for about $5 one-way). The island has no residents (except wild goats), phones, or electricity. You will find fine white-sand beaches, idyllic reefs with great snorkeling, and waters great for bodysurfing. There are even two beach bars that rent lounge chairs and serve dishes such as lobster, ribs, and grilled chicken.

5 Sports & Other Outdoor Pursuits

DEEP-SEA FISHING   Pelican Watersports, on the Dutch side, at the Pelican Resort and Casino, Simpson Bay (② **599/54-42640**), is part of one of the island's most comprehensive resorts. Their 12m (39-ft.) *Kratuna* is available for deep-sea-fishing expeditions priced at $500 for a half-day (7:30–11am) or $950 for a full day (7:30am–3pm) excursion.

GOLF   The **Mullet Bay Resort** (② **599/54-53069**), on the Dutch side, has the island's only golf course. It's a slightly battered, slightly dusty 18-hole Joseph Lee–designed course, whose fate has hung in the balance, based on some ongoing court battles, for years. Although the resort itself is closed, the golf course is still operational. Mullet Pond and Simpson Bay Lagoon provide both beauty and hazards. Greens fees are $40 for 9 holes or $70 for 18 holes, for players who opt to walk instead of ride. Renting a two-person electric cart will cost an additional $30 to $36, depending on how many holes you play. Club rentals cost $21 for 9 holes or $26 for 18 holes.

HORSEBACK RIDING   Horseback riding is available at **Bayside Riding Club,** Route Galion Beach, Orientale (② **590/87-36-64**). Beach rides are a highlight, and prices start at $60 for 2 hours per person.

SCUBA DIVING   Scuba diving is excellent around **St. Martin,** with reef, wreck, night, cave, and drift diving; the depth of dives is 6m to 21m (20 ft.– 69 ft.). Off the northeastern coast on the French side, dive sites include Ilet Pinel, for shallow diving; Green Key, a barrier reef; and Tintamarre, for sheltered coves and geologic faults. To the north, Anse Marcel and neighboring Anguilla are good choices. Most hotels will arrange scuba excursions on request.

The island's premier dive operation is **Scuba Fun,** whose offices are immediately adjacent to the West Indies Mall, Chemin du Port, Marigot (② **590/87-36-13**). Operated by Englishman Philip Baumann, it offers morning and afternoon dives in deep and shallow water, wreck dives, and reef dives, at a cost of $45 per dive. A resort course for first-time divers with reasonable swimming skills costs $75 and includes 60 to 90 minutes of instruction in a swimming pool and a one-tank dive above a coral reef. Full PADI certification costs $350, an experience that requires 5 days and includes classroom training, sessions with a scuba tank within the safety of a swimming pool, and three open-water dives. Snorkeling trips cost $30 for a half-day, plus $10 for equipment rental.

St. Maarten's crystal-clear bays and countless coves make for good scuba diving as well as snorkeling. Underwater visibility runs from 23m to 38m (75 ft.–125 ft.). The biggest attraction for divers is the 1801 British man-of-war, **HMS *Proselyte,*** which came to a watery grave on a reef 2km (1¼ miles) off the coast. Most of the big resorts have facilities for scuba diving and can provide information about underwater tours, photography, and night diving.

SNORKELING ☆☆   The calm waters ringing the shallow reefs and tiny coves found throughout the island make it a snorkeler's heaven. The waters off the northeastern shores of French St. Martin have been classified as a regional underwater nature reserve, **Réserve Sous-Marine Régionale,** which protects the area around Flat Island (also known as Tintamarre), Ilet Pinel, Green Key, Proselyte, and Petite Clef. Equipment can be rented at almost any hotel, and most beaches have watersports kiosks.

One of St. Martin's best sources for snorkeling and other beach diversions is **Carib Watersports** (© 590/87-51-87), a clothing store, art gallery, and watersports kiosk on the beachfront of the Grand-Case Beach Club. Its French and U.S. staff provides information on island activities and rents kayaks for $20 an hour, paddleboats for $25 an hour, and snorkeling equipment for $12 a day. The main allure, however, are the guided snorkeling trips to St. Martin's teeming offshore reefs, including Creole Rock, an offshore clump of reef-ringed boulders rich in underwater fauna. The 1½-hour trips depart daily at 10am, noon, and 2pm, and cost $30, with all equipment included. Reservations are recommended.

TENNIS   You can try the courts at most of the large resorts, but you must call first for a reservation. Preference, of course, is given to hotel guests.

On the Dutch side, there are four courts at the **Maho Beach Hotel,** Maho Bay (© 599/54-52115). **The Pelican,** Simpson Bay (© 599/54-42503) and the **Divi Little Bay Beach Resort,** Little Bay Road (© 599/54-22333), each offer three lit courts, but they are for guest play only. On the French side, the **Privilège Resort & Spa,** Anse Marcel (© 590/87-46-15), offers four lit tennis courts and two squash courts; the **Hotel Mont Vernon,** Baie Orientale (© 590/87-62-00), has two courts; and the **Nettlé Bay Beach Club,** Baie Nettlé (© 590/87-68-68), has three lit Laykold courts.

WATER-SKIING & PARASAILING   Most of French St. Martin's large beachfront hotels maintain facilities for water-skiing and parasailing, often from kiosks that operate on the beach.

Two independent operators on Orient Bay, close to the cluster of hotels near the Esmeralda Hotel, include **Kon Tiki Watersports** (© 590/87-46-89) and **Bikini Beach Watersports** (© 590/87-43-25). They both rent jet skis for around $40 to $45 per half-hour; parasailing costs $50 for 10 minutes or $80 if two go together.

Jet-skiing and water-skiing are also especially popular in Dutch St. Maarten. The unruffled waters of Simpson Bay Lagoon, the largest lagoon in the West Indies, are ideal for these sports, and outfitters have facilities right on the sands.

WINDSURFING   Most windsurfers gravitate to the eastern part of the island, most notably Coconut Grove Beach, Orient Beach, and to a lesser extent, Dawn Beach, all in French St. Martin. The best of the several outfitters here is **Tropical Wave,** Coconut Grove, Le Galion Beach, Baie de l'Embouchure (© 590/87-37-25). Set midway between Orient Beach and Oyster Pond, it has an ideal combination of wind and calm waters. Tropical Wave is the island's leading sales agent for Mistral windsurfers. They rent for $25 an hour, with instruction offered at $56 an hour.

In St. Maarten, visitors usually head to Simpson Bay Lagoon for windsurfing.

7 Shopping ⟨★⟨★⟨★

IN DUTCH ST. MAARTEN

Not only is St. Maarten a free port, but it has no local sales taxes. Prices are sometimes lower here than anywhere else in the Caribbean, except possibly St. Thomas. On some items (fine liqueurs, cigarettes, Irish linen, German cameras, French perfumes), we've found prices 30% to 50% lower than in the United States or Canada. Many well-known shops on Curaçao have branches here.

Except for the boutiques at resort hotels, the main shopping area is in the center of **Philipsburg.** Most of the shops are on **Front Street** (called Voorstraat in Dutch), which stretches for about 2km (1¼ miles) and is lined with stores. More shops are along the little lanes, known as *steegijes,* that connect Front Street with **Back Street (Achterstraat),** another shoppers' haven.

In general, the prices marked on the merchandise are firm, though at some small, very personally run shops, where the owner is on-site, some bargaining might be in order.

Antillean Liquors, Queen Juliana Airport (© **599/54-54267**), has a complete assortment of liquor and liqueurs, cigarettes, and cigars. Prices are generally lower here than in other stores on the island, and the selection is larger. Guavaberry island liqueur is made on island.

Del Sol St-Maarten, 23 Front St. (© **599/54-28784**), sells men's and women's sportswear. Embedded into the mostly black-and-white designs are organic crystals that react to ultraviolet light, which transforms the fabric into a rainbow of colors. Step back into the shadows, and your T-shirt will revert to its original black-and-white design. The same technology is applied to yo-yos, which shimmer psychedelically when you bob them up and down.

Colombian Emeralds International, Old Street Shopping Center (© **599/ 54-23933**), sells unmounted emeralds from Colombia, as well as emerald, gold, diamond, ruby, and sapphire jewelry. Prices are approximately the same as in other outlets of this famous Caribbean chain. There are some huckster vendors around the island pawning fakes off on unsuspecting tourists; if you're seriously shopping for emerald, this is the place.

Belgian Chocolate Shop, 109 Old St. (© **599/54-28863**), is the best of its kind on island. Contrary to popular rumor, only *some* of the velvety chocolates sold in this upscale shop are pornographic, portraying parts of the human anatomy. It's always busy here, especially when cruise ships are berthed at the nearby piers.

Guavaberry Company, 8–10 Front St. (© **599/54-22965**), sells the rare "island folk liqueur" of St. Maarten, which for centuries was made only in private homes. Sold in square bottles, this rum-based liqueur is flavored with rare guavaberries, usually grown on the hills in the center of the island. (Don't confuse guavaberries with guavas—they're very different.) The liqueur has a fruity, woody, almost bittersweet flavor. You can blend it with coconut for a guavaberry colada or pour a splash into a glass of icy champagne. They also sell gift items and various types of hot sauces.

Greenwich Galleries, 20 Front St. (© **599/54-23842**), is the most interesting and sophisticated art gallery on either side of the island, with Bajan pottery in tones of sea greens and blues, replicas of Taíno artifacts from the Dominican Republic, enameled metal cutouts that are both quirky and perplexing, and a range of paintings and lithographs from artists as far away as Holland and Britain.

Nanette Bearden Fine Arts Gallery, 44 Front St. (© **599/54-31540**), is the legacy of the late American artist Romare Bearden, some of whose work hangs in such galleries as New York's Metropolitan and the Smithsonian. Known for his images of black culture in the Caribbean, the Manhattan artist created this gallery to exhibit the work of island artists. A different artist is showcased every month.

Little Switzerland, 52 Front St. (© **599/54-22523**), is part of a chain of stores spread throughout the Caribbean. These fine-quality European imports are made even more attractive by the prices, often 25% (or more) lower than stateside. Elegant famous-name watches, china, crystal, and jewelry are for sale, plus perfume and accessories. Little Switzerland has the best overall selection of these items of any shop on the Dutch side.

IN FRENCH ST. MARTIN

Many day-trippers come over to Marigot from the Dutch side of the island just to visit the French-inspired boutiques and shopping arcades. Because St. Martin is also a duty-free port, you'll find some of the best shopping in the Caribbean here as well. There's a wide selection of European merchandise, much of it luxury items such as crystal, fashions, fine liqueurs, and cigars, sometimes at 25% to 50% less than in the United States and Canada. Whether you're seeking jewelry, perfume, or St. Tropez bikinis, you'll find it in one of the boutiques along **rue de la République** and **rue de la Liberté** in Marigot. Look especially for French luxury items, such as Lalique crystal, Vuitton bags, and Chanel perfume.

Prices are often quoted in U.S. dollars, and salespeople frequently speak English. Credit cards and traveler's checks are generally accepted. When cruise ships are in port on Sundays and holidays, some of the larger shops stay open.

At harborside in Marigot, there's a lively **morning market** with vendors selling spices, fruit, shells, and handcrafts. Shops here tend to be rather upscale, catering to passengers of the small but choice cruise ships that dock offshore.

At bustling **Port La Royale,** mornings are even more active: Schooners unload produce from the neighboring islands, boats board guests for picnics on deserted beaches, a brigantine sets out on a sightseeing sail, and a dozen different little restaurants are readying for the lunch crowd. The largest shopping arcade on St. Martin, it has lots of boutiques.

Havane Boutique, 50 Marina Port La Royale (ⓒ **590/87-70-39**), is a hyperstylish menswear store, more couture than ready-to-wear. **Serge Blanco "15" Boutique,** Marina Port La Royale (ⓒ **590/29-65-49**), is a relatively unknown name in North America, but in France Blanco is revered as one of the most successful rugby players of all time. His menswear is sporty, fun, and elegant. Clothes include polo shirts, shorts, shoes, and truly wonderful latex jackets.

Gingerbread & Mahogany Gallery, 4–14 Marina Royale (ⓒ **590/87-73-21**), is among the finest galleries on the island. Owner Simone Seitre is one of the most knowledgeable purveyors of Haitian art in the Caribbean. Even if you're not in the market for an expensive piece, you'll find dozens of charming and inexpensive handcrafts. The little gallery is a bit hard to find (on a narrow alleyway at the marina), but it's worth the search.

Another complex, the **Galerie Périgourdine,** facing the post office, also has a cluster of boutiques. Here you might pick up designer wear for both men and women, including items from the collection of Ted Lapidus.

Act III, 3 rue du Général-de-Gaulle (ⓒ **590/29-28-43**), is perhaps the most glamorous women's boutique in St. Martin. It prides itself on its evening gowns and chic cocktail dresses. If you've been invited to a reception aboard a private yacht, this is the place to find the right outfit. Designers include Alaïa, Thierry Mugler, Gianni Versace, Christian Lacroix, Cerruti, Lanvin, and Gaultier. The bilingual staff is accommodating, tactful, and charming.

La Romana, 12 rue de la République (ⓒ **590/87-88-16**), specializes in chic women's clothing that's a bit less pretentious and more fun and lighthearted than the selection at Act III. Italian rather than French designers are emphasized, including lines such as Anna Club, plus La Perla swimwear, handbags, and perfumes. A small collection of menswear is also available.

Roland Richardson Paintings and Prints, 6 rue de la République (ⓒ **590/87-84-08**), has a beautiful gallery. A native of St. Martin, Mr. Richardson is one of the Caribbean's premier artists, working in oil, watercolors, pastels, and charcoal. Called a "modern-day Gauguin," he is known for his landscapes, portraits, and colorful still lifes. His work has been exhibited in more than 70 one-man and group exhibitions in museums and galleries around the world.

A charming roadside Creole cottage is home to **Gloria Lynn Studio,** 83 Blvd. de Grand-Case (© **590/87-77-24**), which offers some of the most interesting paintings in Grand-Case. Inside, you'll find artworks by four members of the Lynn family (Gloria, Marty, Peter, and Robert). Their shared theme is island life and island sociology.

8 St. Maarten/St. Martin After Dark ★★

After-dark activities begin early here, as guests start off with a sundowner, perhaps on the garden patio of **Pasanggrahan Royal Inn** (p. 603). The most popular bar on the island is **Cheri's Café** (p. 611).

Many hotels sponsor **beachside barbecues** (particularly in season) with steel bands, native music, and folk dancing. Outsiders are welcomed at most of these events, but call ahead to see if it's a private affair.

One of the island's most visited **casinos,** the **Dolphin,** is at the Caravanserai on Beacon Hill Road (© **599/54-54000**). Gamblers start pouring in here at 3pm daily, some staying until 4 the next morning.

Pelican Resort Club, Simpson Bay (© **599/54-42503**), has a popular Vegas-style casino with a panoramic view of the bay. It offers two craps tables, three roulette tables, nine blackjack tables, two stud-poker tables, and 120 slot machines. The Pelican also features horse racing, bingo, and sports nights with events broadcast via satellite, plus nightly dancing on the Pelican Reef Terrace and island shows featuring Caribbean bands. It's open daily from 2pm to 4am.

Right in the heart of Philipsburg's shopping-crazed Front Street, **Rouge et Noir** (© **599/54-22952**) has a futuristic design. It offers slot machines, a Sigma Derby horse machine, video keno, and video poker. It opens Monday to Saturday at 9am and Sunday at 11am to snag cruise-ship passengers.

Casino Royale, at the Maho Beach Hotel on Maho Bay (© **599/54-52115**), has 16 blackjack tables, six roulette wheels, and three craps and three Caribbean stud-poker tables. The casino offers baccarat, minibaccarat, and more than 340 slot machines. It's open daily from 2pm to 4am. The **Showroom Royale** is the largest and most technologically sophisticated theater on either side of St Maarten/St. Martin; its glittery shows change according to whatever act has been booked. Within the same building is the island's loudest disco, the **Q-Club.** Containing wraparound catwalks that look down on the dance floor, multiple bars, and colored lights, it's open nightly from around 10pm, attracting dancers from both sides of the island. A cover charge of between $5 and $10 is sometimes imposed, depending on the season and the night of the week.

Sunset Beach Bar, 2 Beacon Hill Rd., Airport Beach (© **599/54-53998**), is directly on the sands of the beach, and resembles an oversize gazebo. This place is mobbed most afternoons and evenings with office workers, off-duty airline pilots, beach people, and occasional celebs like Sandra Bullock. No one seems to

---

Moments **Spectacular Sunsets**

Each evening, visitors watch for the legendary **green flash,** an atmospheric phenomenon described by Hemingway that sometimes occurs in these latitudes just as the sun drops below the horizon.

mind the whine of airplane engines, or the fumes that filter down from aircraft that seem to fly just a few dozen feet overhead. Drinks are cheap, and you can order burgers, sandwiches, steaks, fish, chicken, and hot dogs from an outdoor charcoal grill. Many local residents time their arrival here for sundown (usually beginning around 6:30pm), when "shooters of the day" cost only $1 each.

Indiana Beach Restaurant & Bar and Indy's Bar, Kimshore, Simpson Bay (© 599/54-42797), are immediately adjacent to one another and set beside the sands of Simpson's Bay. They jointly reign as queen (or king) of the night every Thursday after 8:30pm, when they're mobbed with singles, who enjoy the two-for-one frozen margaritas and other drink specials. Daily happy hour is 4 to 6pm. The decor combines aspects of Harrison Ford's *Indiana Jones and the Temple of Doom* (theme-ish looking flaming torches, statues of Polynesian demigods, caged alligators, and so on) with thatch-covered huts set directly on the sands of the beach. If you want a full-fledged meal, Indiana Beach serves lunch and dinner daily.

On the French side, **Le Bar de la Mer,** Market Square, Marigot (© 590/87-81-79), fills up at twilight, and remains active throughout the evening, often until the wee hours. The Friday soca and salsa sessions are big at **L'Atmo,** Marina Royale (© 590/87-98-41), in the heart of Marigot. Another marina hot spot is **Club One,** Marina Royale, Marigot Bay (© 590/87-98-41), whose big nights are Sunday and Monday.

In Grand-Case, **Calmos Café,** Blvd. du Grand-Case no. 4 (© 590/29-01-85), is funky and low-key. This beachfront shack draws a young, hip crowd, with an occasional pop icon like Linda Evangelista dropping in. Management posts a sign that says NO SNOBS near the entrance. In winter, there's sometimes live music after 9:30pm. Most people come just to flirt, gossip, and drink, but there's also good, affordable food, such as a Greek salad, a tuna salad, and "New Wave burgers" that are slathered with goat cheese. There is also jazz and lounge music to accompany your food. Also popular is the Ocean Salad, combining salad greens with three kinds of grilled fish plus shrimp. The house special drink is a Ti Punch that's a local variation on an old-fashioned rum punch. It's open daily from 10am to 1am.

From the Orient Beach parking lot, **Kon Tiki** (© 590/87-43-27) is the most distant of the several bars that flank the sands of Orient Bay. Inside, you'll find everything you'll need to amuse yourself for a day at the beach. Facilities include three bars, a watersports facility, volleyball courts, and a bandstand where there's often live music. On Saturday and Sunday there is a beach party. Chaise longues with mattresses rent for 4.80€ ($6) for a full day's use, and there's a staff member who'll bring you drinks like Sex on the Beach (4€/$5). If you opt to spend part of a day here, you won't be alone: Previous clients have included the late John F. Kennedy, Jr. and Diana Ross. Sundays are particularly animated, thanks to a live band that plays between 2pm and around midnight, and a mousse machine that spits out dozens of gallons of foam onto the partyers gathered on the outdoor deck. Open daily 9am to 9pm November through May, and until 6pm off season. The party goes until 1am Sunday, year-round.

24

St. Vincent & The Grenadines

One of the major British Windward Islands, sleepy St. Vincent is just beginning to awaken to tourism. Sailors and the yachting set have long known of St. Vincent and the Grenadines, and until recently it was a well-kept vacation secret.

You visit St. Vincent for its lush beauty, and the Grenadines for the best sailing waters in the Caribbean. Don't come for nightlife, grand cuisine, or spectacular beaches. There are some white-sand beaches near Kingstown on St. Vincent, but most of the other beaches ringing the island are black sand. The yachting crowd seems to view St. Vincent merely as a launching pad for the 64km (40-plus-mile) string of the Grenadines, but the island still has a few attractions that make it worth exploring on its own.

Unspoiled by the fallout that mass tourism sometimes brings, islanders treat visitors courteously. British customs predominate, along with traces of Gallic cultural influences, but all with a distinct West Indian flair.

South of St. Vincent, the small chain of islands called the Grenadines extends for more than 64km (40 miles). The islands have such romantic-sounding names as Bequia, Mustique, Canouan, and Petit St. Vincent. We'll explore Union and Palm Islands, and Mayreau as well. A few of the islands have accommodations, but many are so small and undeveloped that they attract only beachcombers and stray boaters.

Populated by the descendants of African slaves and administered by St. Vincent, the Grenadines collectively add up to a landmass of 78 sq. km (30 sq. miles). These specks of land may lack natural resources, but they're blessed with white-sand beaches, coral reefs, and their own sleepy beauty. If you don't stay overnight in the Grenadines, at least try to visit one on a day trip, and enjoy a picnic lunch (which your hotel will pack for you) on your own quiet stretch of sand.

1 St. Vincent & The Grenadines Essentials

VISITOR INFORMATION

In the United States, you can get information at the **St. Vincent and Grenadines Tourist Office,** 801 Second Ave., 21st Floor, New York, NY 10017 (© **800/729-1726** or 212/687-4981).

The website for St. Vincent and the Grenadines is **www.svgtourism.com.**

On St. Vincent, the local **Department of Tourism** is on Upper Bay Street, Government Administrative Centre, Kingstown (© **784/457-1502**). Hours are Monday to Friday from 8am to 4:15pm.

GETTING THERE

In the eastern Caribbean, St. Vincent—the "gateway to the Grenadines" (the individual islands are discussed later in this chapter)—lies 161km (100 miles) west of Barbados. There are no direct flights. The best connections are through Barbados and Antigua. From Barbados you can take **LIAT** (© **868/624-4727** in the U.S., or 888/844-5428 in the St. Vincent), which flies five times daily to St. Vincent. From Antigua, **Caribbean Star** (© **866/864-6272** in the U.S., or 268/GO1-STAR) flies twice daily to St. Vincent.

There are also other links as well. **Air Caraïbe** (© **784/458-4528**) flies from Martinique to St. Vincent, with ongoing connections to Union and Canouan islands. **BWee Express,** under the auspices of BWIA (© **784/627-6222**), flies to St. Vincent from both Trinidad and Barbados. For details on getting to Barbados from North America, see chapter 6.

Dependable **Mustique Airways** (© **784/458-4380;** www.mustique.com) makes daily shuttle runs from St. Vincent to the satellite islands of Mustique, Union, and Canouan, with per person fares ranging from US$40 to US$60. With advance warning, Mustique Airways will arrange reasonably priced special charters to and from many of the surrounding islands and inner islands (including Grenada, Aruba, St. Lucia, Antigua, Barbados, Trinidad, and any others in the southern Caribbean). The price of these chartered flights is less than you might expect and often matches the fares on conventional Caribbean airlines. The airline currently owns four small aircraft, none of which carries more than nine passengers.

GETTING AROUND ST. VINCENT

BY TAXI   Because of the bad roads, most visitors use taxis to get around. The government sets the rates, but taxis are unmetered, so be sure to agree on the fare before getting in. Figure on spending US$10 or more to go from the airport to your hotel. You should tip about 12% of the fare.

You can also hire taxis to take you to the island's major attractions. Most drivers seem to be well-informed guides (it won't take you long to learn everything you need to know about St. Vincent). You'll spend from US$20 per hour for a car holding two to four passengers.

BY RENTAL CAR   Driving on St. Vincent is a bit of an adventure because of the narrow, twisting roads (sound your horn as you make the sharp hairpin turns). *Most importantly:* Drive on the left. If you present your valid driver's license from home at the police department, on Bay Street in Kingstown, and pay an EC$76 (US$28) fee, you'll get a temporary permit to drive.

Avis (© **800/331-1212** in the U.S., or 784/456-2929 locally; www.avis.com) has a branch at the airport. One local rental firm is **Star Garage,** on Grenville Street in Kingstown (© **784/456-1743**). Make sure your car has a spare tire because the roads are full of potholes.

BY BUS   Flamboyantly painted "alfresco" buses travel the principal roads of St. Vincent, linking the major towns and villages. The price is low, depending

---

> **Fun Fact** **Special Events**
>
> Late June brings St. Vincent's weeklong **Carnival,** one of the largest such celebrations in the eastern Caribbean. The festivities include steel-band and calypso competitions, parades, costumes, and the crowning of the king and queen of the carnival. The fun extends through the first two weeks in July, culminating in a huge street party.

on where you're going, and the experience will connect you with the locals. The central departure point is the bus terminal at the New Kingstown Fish Market. Fares range from EC95¢ to EC$5.95 (US35¢–US$2.20).

FAST FACTS: St. Vincent & The Grenadines

Banks Most banks are open Monday to Thursday from 8am to either 1 or 3pm, and Friday from either 8am to 5pm or 8am to 1pm and 3 to 5pm. There are a few banks with ATMs on Halifax Street in Kingstown on St. Vincent (plus one at the airport), and there are also a few on Bequia and Union Island.

Currency The official currency of St. Vincent is the **Eastern Caribbean dollar (EC$)**, pegged at about $2.70 per U.S. dollar (EC$1 = US37¢). *Unless otherwise specified, rates in this chapter are quoted in U.S. dollars.* Most restaurants, shops, and hotels will accept payment in U.S. dollars or traveler's checks.

Documents British, Canadian, and U.S. citizens should have a passport and a return or ongoing airplane ticket. A birth certificate with a raised seal is often accepted with a photo ID, but we always recommend traveling with your passport overseas.

Electricity Electricity is 220-volt AC (50 cycles), so if you're traveling with U.S. appliances, you'll need an adapter and a transformer. Some hotels have transformers, but it's best to bring your own.

Emergencies In an emergency, dial ⓒ **999.**

Hospitals There is one hospital on St. Vincent in Kingstown: **Miton Cato Memorial General Hospital (ⓒ 784/456-1185).**

Language English is the official language.

Liquor Laws Liquor can be sold on any day of the week. It's legal to have an open container on the beach as long as you don't get rowdy or litter.

Pharmacies On St. Vincent, try **Deane's Pharmacy,** Halifax Street, Kingstown (ⓒ **784/457-2056**), open Monday to Friday from 8:30am to 4:30pm. There are a few other drugstores in Kingstown as well.

Post Office The **General Post Office,** on Halifax Street in Kingstown (ⓒ **784/456-1111**), is open Monday to Friday from 8:30am to 3pm and Saturday from 8:30 to 11:30am. There are smaller post offices in 56 districts throughout the country, including offices on the Grenadine islands of Bequia, Mustique, Canouan, Mayreau, and Union Island.

Safety St. Vincent and its neighboring islands of the Grenadines are quite safe. Even in Kingstown, the capital of St. Vincent, chances are you'll encounter little serious crime. However, take the usual precautions and never leave valuables unguarded.

Taxes & Service Charges The government imposes an airport departure tax of EC$41 (US$15) per person. A 10% government occupancy tax is charged for all hotel accommodations. Hotels and restaurants almost always add a 10% to 15% service charge. Ask whether or not it's included in the initial hotel rates you're quoted. If it's not already added at a restaurant, tip at that rate.

Telephone To call St. Vincent from the United States, dial **1**, then **784** (the area code for St. Vincent) and the local seven-digit number. Once on St. Vincent, you can access **AT&T Direct** at ℭ **800/225-5288**. To reach **MCI**, dial ℭ **800/888-8000**.

Time Both St. Vincent and the Grenadines operate on Atlantic Standard Time year-round: When it's 6am on St. Vincent, it's 5am in New York. During daylight savings time in the United States, St. Vincent keeps the same time as the U.S. East Coast.

Water In St. Vincent and the Grenadines, stick to bottled water.

Weather The climate of St. Vincent and the Grenadines is pleasantly cooled by the trade winds year-round. The tropical temperature is in the 78°F to 82°F (26°C–28°C) range. The rainy season is July to October.

2 St. Vincent Accommodations

Don't expect high-rise resorts here. The places are small and comfortable, not fancy, and you usually get a lot of personal attention from the staff.

If you want a luxurious resort, head for the Grenadines. Except for Young Island, most resorts here are fairly simple affairs, and since most people are only in St. Vincent for a night or two, you may prefer to be located directly in the center in the capital of Kingstown.

VERY EXPENSIVE

Young Island Resort ⟨⟨⟨   On its own private island off Villa Beach, this resort is as good as it gets in St. Vincent. It's far more stylish and comfortable than its nearest competitor, Grand View Beach Hotel. This 14-hectare (35-acre) resort, its grounds full of lush fruit trees, white ginger, hibiscus, and ferns, is supposedly where a Carib tribal chieftain kept his harem. It lies just 182m (597 ft.) off the south shore of St. Vincent; a ferry makes the 5-minute run from the pier right on Villa Beach. Hammocks are hung under thatched roofs, and the beach has brilliant white sand. Set in a tropical garden are romantic wood-and-stone Tahitian cottages (all for couples), with bamboo decor and outdoor showers in little rock grottoes (open but hidden from public view). Floors are of tile and terrazzo, covered with rush rugs. The spacious accommodations come with queen- or king-size beds (rarely a twin) and generous storage. Some units open onto the beach; others are on a hillside. Some guests have complained of hearing noises from the rooms adjoining them.

Food and service are not always of a high standard. Dining is by candlelight, and dress is informal. Sometimes a steel band plays for after-dinner dancing, and strolling singers serenade diners.

Young Island (P.O. Box 211), St. Vincent, W.I. ℭ **800/223-1108** in the U.S. and Canada, or 784/458-4826. Fax 784/457-4567. www.youngisland.com. 30 units. Winter US$475–US$710 cottage for 2; off season US$390–US$655 cottage for 2. Extra person US$100. Rates include breakfast and dinner. Ask about packages. AE, MC, V. **Amenities:** Restaurant; 2 bars; outdoor pool; tennis court; access to nearby health club; boating; snorkeling; windsurfing; car rental; airport shuttle; room service (7:30am–9:30pm); babysitting; laundry service; dry cleaning. *In room:* Ceiling fan; kitchenettes (in some), fridge, beverage maker (in some), hair dryer, safe.

EXPENSIVE

Grand View Beach Hotel ⟨   Owner/manager F. A. (Tony) Sardine named this place well: The "grand view" promised is of islets, bays, yachts, Young

Map legend:

Airport ✈
Beach ⚲
Mountain ▲

Beachcombers Hotel **9**
The Cobblestone Inn **2**
Coconut Beach Hotel **6**
Grand View Beach Hotel **8**
Heron Hotel **4**
Lagoon Marina & Hotel **10**
New Montrose Hotel **3**
Petit Byahaut **1**
Villa Lodge Hotel **7**
Young Island Resort **5**

Map labels: Fancy, Falls of Baleine, La Soufrière, Crater Lake, Kearton's Bay, Morne Garu Mountains, Wallibou Beach, Richmond Beach, Wallibou River, Rabacca Dry River, Windward Hwy., Chateaubelair Islet, Richmond, Troumaka, Chateaubelair, Richmond Peak, Georgetown, Mt. Brisbane, Wallilabou Bay, Leeward Hwy., Barrouallie, Colonarie, Peter's Hope, Sans Souci, Greiggs, ATLANTIC OCEAN, Vermont Nature Trails, Jackson's Point, Layou, Mt. St. Andrew, Biabou, Windward Hwy., Buccament Bay Beach, Mesopotamia, Questelle's Bay Beach, Marriqua Valley, E. T. Joshua Airport, Belmont, Argyle Beach, KINGSTOWN, Vigie Hwy., Stubbs, Bequia Channel, Caribbean Sea, Indian Bay Beach, Villa Beach, Young Island, Blue Lagoon, 0 5 Miles, 0 5 Kilometers, N

Island, headlands, lagoons, and sailing craft. On well-manicured grounds, this resort is set on 3 hectares (8 acres) of gardens, just steps from the beach. The 19th-century plantation house is a large, white, two-story mansion. Most bedrooms are medium-size and comfortable, opening onto views. The most luxurious and spacious rooms, some of which have wide terraces and faraway views of the Grenadines, are in the Mediterranean-style modern wing. The other units are on the upper level of a former great house and have a B&B feel. Most of the bathrooms have showers only. The West Indian fare served here is average.

Villa Point (P.O. Box 173), St. Vincent, W.I. ✆ **800/223-6510** in the U.S., or 784/458-4811. Fax 784/457-4174. www.grandviewhotel.com. 19 units. Winter US$150–US$215 double; off season US$130–US$170 double. MAP (breakfast and dinner) US$55 per person extra. AE, MC, V. **Amenities:** 2 restaurants; 2 bars; outdoor pool; tennis court; squash court; fitness center; sauna; bike rental; car rental; limited room service; massage; laundry service; dry cleaning. *In room:* A/C, TV, dataport, hair dryer, safe.

Petit Byahaut ✪ *(Finds)*   This ecologically sensitive place attracts snorkelers, scuba divers, and anyone who truly wants to get away from it all and get back to nature. (All that simplicity is awfully expensive, though.) Lying 7km (4½ miles) north of Kingstown on the leeward coast and accessible only by boat, Petit Byahaut accepts no more than 14 guests at a time. Guests are housed in roomy tents with queen-size beds, screened windows and doors, and large covered decks with hammocks. In various nooks and crannies built into the hills are your outdoor freshwater shower, sink, and toilet. Lush foliage between the tents provides privacy; hummingbirds and other winged creatures often visit the tropical flowers blooming on the grounds. Opening onto a horseshoe-shaped bay, where more hammocks await on the sands, the complex stands in a 20-hectare (50-acre) private valley. A seaside bar and restaurant offers wholesome, healthy meals, picnics are prepared during the day, and dinner is served by candlelight. The reef right off the beach has excellent snorkeling and scuba diving, and watersports equipment is available. Rainforest trips, boating, and guided snorkeling and scuba trips can be arranged.

Petit Byahaut Bay, St. Vincent, W.I. ©/fax 784/457-7008. www.petitbyahaut.com. 4 units: 3 tents, 1 patio dwelling. Year-round US$175 double. Rates are all-inclusive. Scuba packages available. 3-night minimum stay. MC, V. **Amenities:** Restaurant; bar; boating; dive shop; snorkeling; airport shuttle. *In room:* No phone.

MODERATE

Lagoon Marina & Hotel   A two-story group of rambling modern buildings crafted from local wood and stone, this hotel lies 6km (3¾ miles) from the airport on the main island road, opening onto a narrow, curved, black-sand beach. There's a pleasantly breezy bar that's often filled with sailors and yachties. As you relax, you'll overlook a moored armada of boats tied up at a nearby marina. A lagoon-shaped pool is terraced into a nearby hillside. Snorkeling, windsurfing, and daily departures on sailboats to Mustique and Bequia can be arranged through the hotel. Each of the recently refurbished medium-size, high-ceilinged guest rooms has a balcony. The bedrooms have ceramic-tile floors and good furnishings. Bathrooms are in the standard motel style, with shower/tub combinations. The simple, airy ground-floor restaurant serves international and West Indian food.

Blue Lagoon (P.O. Box 133), St. Vincent, W.I. ©/fax 784/458-4308. www.lagoonmarina.com. 19 units. Winter US$120 double; off season US$95 double. AE, MC, V. **Amenities:** Restaurant; bar; outdoor pool; boating; snorkeling; bike rental; car rental; room service (7:30am–10pm); laundry service. *In room:* A/C, TV, hair dryer.

Villa Lodge Hotel   Set on a residential hillside a few minutes southeast of the center of Kingstown and the airport, this place is a favorite of visiting business-people. Because of its access to a beach and its well-mannered staff, it evokes the feeling of a modern villa. It's ringed with tropical, flowering trees and shrubs growing in the gardens. The air-conditioned rooms have ceiling fans, king-size beds, comfortable rattan and local mahogany furniture, and small bathrooms equipped with a shower/tub combination. The hotel also rents eight apartments in its Breezeville Apartments complex next door, charging US$145 for a double in winter and US$130 for a double in summer.

The restaurant serves straightforward West Indian and international dishes.

Indian Bay (P.O. Box 1191), St. Vincent, W.I. © 800/742-4276 or 784/458-4641. Fax 784/457-4468. www.villalodge.com. 10 units. Year-round US$110 double; US$140 triple; US$220 apt for 4. MAP (breakfast and dinner) US$30 per person extra. AE, DISC, MC, V. **Amenities:** Restaurant; bar; outdoor pool; limited room service; babysitting; laundry service. *In room:* A/C, ceiling fan, TV, dataport, kitchenette (in some), fridge, hair dryer, safe.

INEXPENSIVE

Beachcombers Hotel 🎇 *Value*   Richard and Flora Gunn operate this B&B in a tropical garden right on the beach. Three chaletlike buildings house the small to medium-size accommodations, all with private bathrooms and tasteful decor. All have ceiling fans; a few rooms have air-conditioning as well. The rooms are spotless and well maintained. Try for no. 1, 2, or 3, as they open onto the water. Two units have small kitchenettes. Bathrooms are a bit cramped, with showers only. The hotel has a health spa (Mrs. Gunn is a massage and beauty therapist) with a steam room, sauna, facials, and aromatherapy. The Beachbar & Restaurant, a favorite gathering place for locals, fronts an open terrace and has excellent food. Curtis Chas, who mastered his cooking skills in the Caribbean, is the chef.

Villa Beach (P.O. Box 126), Kingstown, St. Vincent, W.I. ⓒ 784/458-4283. Fax 784/458-4385. www.beach combershotel.com. 20 units. Year-round US$90–US$99 double. AE, MC, V. **Amenities:** Restaurant; bar; outdoor pool; spa; sauna; library; limited room service; babysitting; laundry service. *In room:* A/C, ceiling fan, TV, dataport, kitchenette (in some), fridge (in some), beverage maker (in some).

The Cobblestone Inn
Originally built as a warehouse for sugar and arrowroot in 1814, the core of this historic hotel is made of stone and brick. Today, it's one of the most famous hotels on St. Vincent, known for its labyrinth of passages, arches, and upper hallways. To reach the high-ceilinged reception area, you pass from the waterfront through a stone tunnel into a chiseled courtyard. At the top of a massive sloping stone staircase, you're shown to one of the simple, old-fashioned bedrooms. Most of the small units contain TVs, and some have windows opening over the rooftops of town. The most spacious is no. 5, but it opens onto a noisy street. Furnishings are comfortable, but bathrooms are tiny, with shower/tub combinations. Meals are served on a third-floor aerie, high above the hotel's central courtyard. The bar here is one of the most popular in town. The hotel is convenient to town, but it's a 5km (3-mile) drive to the nearest beach.

Bax St. (P.O. Box 867), Kingstown, St. Vincent, W.I. ⓒ 784/456-1937. Fax 784/456-1938. www.the cobblestoneinn.com. 19 units. Year-round US$65 double; US$75 triple. AE, MC, V. **Amenities:** Restaurant; bar; laundry service. *In room:* A/C, TV (in most).

Coconut Beach Hotel
This inn, restaurant, and bar is 5 minutes south of the airport and 5 minutes from Kingstown. It grew out of a villa constructed in the 1930s by one of the region's noted eccentrics, and it lies across the channel from the much more expensive Young Island. Its seaside setting makes it good for swimming and sunbathing. Island tours, such as sailing the Grenadines, can be arranged, as can diving, snorkeling, and mountain climbing. There's minimum comfort here: Each small guest room is straightforward and modern and has a tiny shower-only bathroom. The restaurant is a simple, laid-back affair specializing in West Indian food.

Indian Bay (P.O. Box 355), Kingstown, St. Vincent, W.I. ⓒ/fax 784/457-4900. 11 units. Year-round US$65 double. AE, MC, V. **Amenities:** Restaurant; bar; laundry service. *In room:* Ceiling fan, no phone.

Heron Hotel
This recently renovated hotel is in one of St. Vincent's historic buildings. It exudes a sense of old-fashioned timelessness you simply won't find in modern resorts. Built of local stone and tropical hardwoods, it served as a warehouse in the late 18th century, then later provided lodgings for colonial planters doing business along the wharves of Kingstown. Some of the simple and rather small rooms overlook an inner courtyard; others face the street. Room no. 15 is the largest. Accommodations have renewed furnishings, single beds, and cramped bathrooms with shower stalls. Although you don't get grand comfort here, the price is hard to beat, and the staff is hospitable. The hotel attracts a clientele of moderately eccentric guests: Some conduct business in the heart of the island's capital, others want to be near the docks for early-morning departures. The on-site restaurant is busiest at lunch (it may close after dusk, so dinner reservations are important).

Upper Middle St. (P.O. Box 226), Kingstown, St. Vincent, W.I. ⓒ 784/457-1631. Fax 784/457-1189. 8 units. Year-round US$70 double. Rates include full breakfast. AE, MC, V. **Amenities:** Restaurant; bar. *In room:* A/C, TV, fridge, beverage maker, iron/ironing board.

New Montrose Hotel ⭐ *Finds* A real discovery, this bright, sunflower-yellow hotel lies on the northern fringe of town. The beach is a short ride away and there is no on-site pool, but what you will find is a handsomely furnished and comfortable room at an affordable price in a tranquil location. Accommodations have such extras as a full-length mirror closet, smoke detector, and good lighting. Some of the units have refrigerators or even a fully equipped kitchenette. The best rooms, even more expensive than the two-bedroom family apartments, are the deluxe executive suites with a complete kitchen and a vista balcony. The Caribbean/International dishes are good so you can eat in if you don't want to wander the streets of Kingstown at night.

New Montrose (P.O. Box 215), Kingstown, St. Vincent, W.I. © **784/457-0172.** Fax 784/457-0213. www. newmontrosehotel.com. 23 units. Year-round US$60–US$95 double; US$80 2-bedroom family apt. AE, MC, V. **Amenities:** Restaurant; bar; room service (7am–10pm); laundry service. *In room:* A/C, kitchenette (in some), refrigerator (in some), beverage maker (in some).

3 St. Vincent Dining

Most guests eat at their hotels on the Modified American Plan (breakfast and dinner), and many Vincentian hostelries serve authentic West Indian cuisine. There are also a few independent restaurants, but not many.

Basil's Bar & Restaurant ⭐ SEAFOOD/INTERNATIONAL This enclave is set beneath the previously recommended Cobblestone Inn, a former sugar warehouse. The air-conditioned interior is accented with exposed stone and brick, soaring arches, and a rambling mahogany bar, which remains open throughout the day. The food is quite acceptable, but nowhere near as good as that enjoyed by Princess Margaret or Mick Jagger at Basil's more famous bar on Mustique. The menu might include lobster salad, shrimp in garlic butter, sandwiches, hamburgers, and barbecued chicken. Dinners feature grilled lobster, shrimp cocktail, grilled red snapper, and grilled filet mignon, all fairly standard dishes of the international repertoire. You can order meals here throughout the day and late into the evening.

Bay St., Kingstown. © **784/457-2713.** Reservations recommended. Main courses EC$38–EC$65 (US$14–US$24). AE, MC, V. Mon–Sat 8am–10:30pm.

Bounty AMERICAN/WEST INDIAN In the redbrick Troutman Building in the center of Kingstown, you'll find the extremely affordable Bounty serving the local workers (the true power-lunch venue is Basil's, recommended above). Fill up on pastries, *rotis* (Caribbean burrito), sandwiches, homemade soups, pastas, quiche, and pizza. The cooking is as simple as the surroundings. An interesting collection of juices includes passion fruit. An on-site gallery and gift shop sells works by local artists.

Egmont St., Kingstown. © **784/456-1776.** Snacks and sandwiches EC$7–EC$8 (US$2.60–US$2.95); main courses EC$8.10–EC$20 (US$3–US$7.50). No credit cards. Mon–Fri 7:30am–4:30pm; Sat 7:30am–1:30pm.

Juliette's Restaurant WEST INDIAN Set amid the capital's cluster of administrative buildings, across from the National Commercial Bank, this restaurant caters to office workers on their lunch breaks. Meals are served in a clean and respectable dining area headed by a veteran of the restaurant trade, Juliette Campbell. (Campbell's husband is the island's well-known attorney general.) Menu items include soups, curried mutton, an array of fish, stewed chicken, stewed beef, and sandwiches. Many of the platters are garnished with fried plantains and rice. Although Juliette's opens early, it doesn't serve breakfast, offering only snacks and lunch-type items in the morning.

Egmont St., Kingstown. ℭ **784/457-1645**. Rotis and sandwiches EC$7.95–EC$12 (US$2.95–US$4.45); fixed-price menu EC$10–EC$15 (US$3.70–US$5.55). No credit cards. Mon–Fri 8am–6pm; Sat 8am–3pm.

L'Aubergine des Grenadines ☆ FRENCH/CARIBBEAN

On the waterfront opening onto Admiralty Bay, this expat operation is popular with yachties, locals, and visitors alike. With its wood tables and high ceilings, it offers as a special feature a lobster tank. With your guaranteed fresh catch, the lobster can be grilled to your specifications. The couple who runs the place consistently turn out excellent fare, including appetizers such as salads made with fresh conch or goat cheese. The mussels came all the way from New Zealand, and they are awash in garlic and butter. For a main course, we go for the lobster flamed with old dark rum or the seafood platter with the likes of shrimp, mussels, fresh white fish, and lobster. The seafood curry has mussels, shrimp, and lobster cooked delectably in coconut milk.

Belmont Walkway, Belmont. ℭ **784/458-3201**. Reservations required in winter. Main courses EC$49–EC$108 (US$18–US$40). MC, V. Nov to mid-May daily 11:30am–9:30pm; off season Mon–Sat 11:30am–9:30pm.

Lime N' Pub Restaurant ☆ _Value_ WEST CARIBBEAN/INDIAN/INTER-NATIONAL

Opposite superexpensive Young Island Hotel on Young Island Channel sits one of the island's most popular restaurants. It's the most congenial pub on St. Vincent, with a wide selection of pub grub, including pizza. In the more formal section of this indoor and alfresco restaurant, you can partake of some good West Indian food, along with dishes from India or the international kitchen. The _rotis_ win high praise, but we always order fresh fish and lobster (from the live lobster pond). The coconut shrimp is usually excellent. Service is among the most hospitable on the island and a local band livens things up a few times a week in winter.

Opposite Young Island at Villa Beach. ℭ **784/458-4227**. Main courses EC$25–EC$251 (US$9.25–US$93). AE, DISC, MC, V. Daily 9am–midnight.

Ocean Allegro MEDITERRANEAN

In a clapboard waterfront house 3km (2 miles) from the airport, near the pier where the ferry from Young Island docks, this is one of the most consistently good restaurants on the island. It offers a long, semi-shadowed bar, which you pass on your way to the rear veranda. While overlooking moored yachts off the coast of Young Island, you can order well-seasoned appetizers like spicy garlic prawns or a freshly made Greek salad. Delectable main courses we sampled recently include beef tenderloin in a peppercorn-brandy cream and mushroom sauce and a very tropical-tasting coconut curry snapper. The chef is also known for his cheesecakes, including Key lime and raspberry.

Villa Beach. ℭ **784/458-4972**. EC$30–EC$103 (US$11–US$38). MC, V. Wed–Mon 9am–1 or 2am.

Rooftop Restaurant & Bar WEST INDIAN/INTERNATIONAL

This restaurant does a thriving business, thanks to its well-prepared food and its location three stories above the center of Kingstown. After you climb some flights of stairs, you'll see a bar near the entrance, an indoor area decorated in earth tones, and a patio open to the prevailing breezes. Lunches stress traditional Creole recipes using fresh fish, chicken, mutton, beef, and goat. Dinners are more international, and may include lobster, excellent snapper with lemon-butter and garlic sauce, steaks with onions and mushrooms, and several savory preparations of pork. Every Wednesday and Friday, there's a karaoke sing-along; Saturday is family night, with a barbecue and a steel band after 6pm. In addition, 60 different drinks are featured at the bar.

Bay St., Kingstown. ✆ **784/457-2845.** Reservations recommended for dinner. Lunch platters EC$26 (US$9.60); dinner main courses EC$10–EC$41 (US$3.70–US$15). AE, MC, V. Mon–Wed 9am–10pm; Thurs–Fri 9am–1am; Sat 10am–1am.

Young Island Resort Restaurant 🐷🐷 CARIBBEAN/CONTINENTAL St. Vincent's best dining is on this 14-hectare (35-acre) private island lying off Villa Beach that's reached by a 5-minute scenic ride on the hotel's launch. Even if you're not staying here we recommend one dinner. The restaurant, under thatched kiosks near the beach and surrounded by tropical gardens, will be your most romantic night on St. Vincent. If you drop in for a predinner drink, try one of the exotic rum punches. Patrons are treated to lavish and elegant buffets twice a week.

Whenever possible, fresh local fish, fruit, and vegetables are served. We always enjoy their freshly baked bread—banana, raisin, cinnamon, wheat, coconut, or just plain white with lots of butter. The lunch menu changes frequently but is likely to feature the catch of the day served on rice with roasted garlic and thyme sauce.

Go in the evening for the most glamorous experience and order the five-course dinner, which changes nightly. On our most recent visit we were enthralled by the roasted-red-pepper soup dusted with Parmesan, followed by oven-roasted baby quail on a tropical sweet-potato purée or grilled local lobster with a timbale of pine-nut couscous. A delightful memory lingers of the chocolate espresso torte with caramel sauce.

Young Island. ✆ **784/458-4826.** Reservations required. Lunch main courses EC$22–EC$27 (US$8–US$10); 5-course fixed-price dinner EC$108 (US$40); Sun lunch buffet EC$54 (US$20); Sat barbecue buffet EC$122 (US$45). AE, MC, V. Daily 12:30–2:30pm and 7:30–9:30pm.

4 Exploring St. Vincent

BEACHES

All beaches on St. Vincent are public, and many of the best border hotels, where you can order drinks or lunch. Most of the resorts are in the south, where the beaches have golden-yellow sand. The only real white-sand beach on St. Vincent is Young Island, which is private (see "St. Vincent Accommodations," earlier in this chapter, for a review of this resort). Many of the beaches in the north have sands of a lava-ash color. The safest swimming is on the leeward beaches; the surf on the windward or eastern beaches is often rough and can be quite dangerous.

The island's most popular strip is narrow **Villa Beach,** only a 10-minute drive from Kingstown. Its tranquil waters make swimming safe, and there are numerous simple cafes and watersports stands. Unfortunately this beach can barely accommodate the crowds who flock here; weekends can be particularly bad.

Nearby **Indian Bay Beach** is similar to Villa Beach and also attracts lots of Vincentians on weekends. Monday through Thursday, however, you'll probably have plenty of room on this narrow strip. The sand is slightly golden, but tends to be rocky. The reef-protected tranquil waters are ideal for both swimming and snorkeling. You'll find both bars and restaurants here.

Heading north from Kingstown, you'll reach **Buccament Bay Beach,** where the waters are clean, clear, and tranquil enough for swimming. This beach is very tiny, however, and it has black volcanic sand. In the same area, **Questelle's Bay Beach** (pronounced keet-*ells*) is also on the leeward, tranquil Caribbean side of the island. This black-sand beach, next to Camden Park, is very similar to Buccament Bay.

Only die-hards head for the beaches on the east coast, or windward side, where the big breakers roll in from the Atlantic. Don't plan to go swimming in these rough waters; you might just enjoy a beach picnic instead. The best beaches, all with black volcanic sand, are found at **Kearton's Bay, Richmond Beach,** and **Peter's Hope,** all reached along the leeward highway running up the west coast of St. Vincent.

SPORTS & OTHER OUTDOOR PURSUITS

FISHING   It's best to go to a local fisherman for advice, but your hotel can also arrange a trip for you. It's sometimes possible to accompany a fisherman on a trip, perhaps 6 or 8km (4 or 5 miles) from shore. A modest fee should suffice. The fishing fleet leaves from the leeward coast at Barrouallie. People have been known to return to shore with everything from a 6-inch redfish to a 6m (20-ft.) pilot whale. Visitors don't need a fishing license.

HIKING   Exploring St. Vincent's hot volcano, **La Soufrière,** is an intriguing adventure. As you travel the island, you can't miss its cloud-capped splendor. The most recent eruption was in 1979, when it spewed ashes, lava, and hot mud that covered the vegetation on its slopes. Belching rocks and black curling smoke filled the blue Caribbean sky. About 17,000 people were evacuated from a 16km (10-mile) ring around the volcano.

At the rim of the crater, you'll be rewarded with one of the most panoramic views in the Caribbean—that is, if the wind doesn't blow too hard and make you topple over into the crater itself! *Please:* Use extreme caution. Looking inside, you can see the steam rising from the crater.

Even if you're an experienced hiker, don't attempt to explore the volcano without a guide. Wear suitable hiking clothes and be sure that you're in the best of health before making the arduous journey. The easiest route is the 5km-long (3-mile) eastern approach from Rabacca. The more arduous trail, longer by 2km (1¼ miles), is the western trail from Chateaubelair. The round-trip to the crater takes about 5 hours.

St. Vincent Forestry Headquarters, in the village of Campden Park, about 5km (3 miles) from Kingstown along the west coast (© 784/457-8594), offers a pamphlet on hiking to La Soufrière. It's open Monday to Friday from 8am to noon and 1 to 4pm. **HazEco Tours** (© 784/457-8634) offers guided hikes up to La Soufrière, costing US$120 per couple, including lunch, snacks, and rain gear.

If you don't want to face Soufrière, the best hikes are the **Vermont Nature Trails.** These marked trails (get a map at the tourist office) take you through a rainforest and pass long-ago plantations reclaimed by nature. If it's your lucky day, you might even see the rare St. Vincent parrot with its flamboyant plumage. Wear good hiking shoes and lots of mosquito repellent.

SAILING & YACHTING ⭐⭐   St. Vincent and the Grenadines are one of the great sailing centers of the Caribbean. If you want to go bareboating, you can obtain a fully provisioned yacht. If you're a well-heeled novice, you can hire a captain and a crew. Rentals are available for a half-day, a full day, overnight, or even longer.

The longest established yacht-chartering company in St. Vincent, **Barefoot Yacht Charters,** Blue Lagoon (© 784/456-9526; www.barefootyachts.com), is better than ever, and is now granting substantial discounts for last-minute or walk-in bookings, notably US$105 to US$260 per day for a 10m (33-ft.) yacht in off season. The outfitter has a fleet of 25 yachts run by the American Sailing Association and offers charters with or without a crew. Its operation is at its own custom-built marina with docks and moorings, along with a restaurant opening onto a panoramic vista of Bequia. There's even an Internet cafe.

We'd also suggest **Nicholson Yacht Charters** ⚓⚓ (© **800/662-6066** in the U.S.) and the **Lagoon Marina and Hotel,** in the Blue Lagoon area (© **800/ 327-2276** in the U.S., or 784/458-4308). The latter offers 13m (44-ft.) crewed sloops for US$300 per person per day (maximum of six people). Prices at Nicholson are roughly comparable to those at Barefoot Yacht Charters.

SNORKELING & SCUBA DIVING ⚓⚓ St. Vincent's 30 or so dive sites are sprinkled along its leeward shore, where you might spot seahorses and frogfish. The best area for snorkeling and scuba diving is the Villa/Young Island section on the southern end of the island.

Dive St. Vincent, on the Young Island Cut (© **784/457-4928;** www.divest vincent.com), has been owned and operated by a transplanted Texan, Bill Tewes, for more than a decade. St. Vincent's oldest and best dive company, it now has two additional shops: **Dive Canouan,** at the Tamarind Beach Hotel on Canouan Island (© **784/458-8044**), and **Grenadines Dive,** at the Sunny Grenadines Hotel on Union Island (© **784/458-8138**). The shops have a total of one instructor and four dive masters, as well as three dive boats. They offer dive/ snorkel trips as well as sightseeing day-trips and dive instruction. Single-tank dives cost US$55 and two-tank dives go for US$100, including all equipment and instructors and/or dive master guides. Dive packages are also available.

EXPLORING KINGSTOWN

Though lush and tropical, the capital isn't as architecturally significant as Grenada's St. George's. There are some English-style houses, many of which look as though they belonged in Penzance or Cornwall rather than the Caribbean. This is a chief port and gateway to the Grenadines, and you can see the small boats and yachts that have dropped anchor here. On Saturday morning, the **market** at the south end of town is at its most active.

At the top of a winding road on the north side of Kingstown, **Fort Charlotte** (© **784/456-1165**) was built on Johnson Point around the time of the American Revolution. The ruins aren't much—the reason to come here is the view. The fort sits atop a steep promontory some 192m (630 ft.) above the sea. From its citadel, you'll have a sweeping view of the leeward shores to the north, Kingstown to the south, and the Grenadines beyond. On a clear day, you can even see Grenada. Three cannons used to fight off French troops are still in place and there's a series of oil murals depicting the history of black Caribs. Admission is free, and the fort is open daily 6am to 6pm.

The second major sight is the **Botanic Gardens** ⚓, on the north side of Kingstown at Montrose (© **784/457-1003**). Founded in 1765 by Gov. George Melville, these are the oldest botanic gardens in the West Indies. You'll see 8 hectares (20 acres) of such tropical exotics as teak, almond, cinnamon, nutmeg, cannonball, and mahogany; some of the trees are more than 200 years old. One of the breadfruit trees was reputedly among those original seedlings brought to this island by Captain Bligh in 1793. There's also a large *Spachea perforata* (the Soufrière tree), a species believed to be unique to St. Vincent and not found in the wild since 1812. The gardens are open daily from 6am to 6pm; admission is free.

THE LEEWARD HIGHWAY ⚓⚓

The leeward, or sheltered, west side of the island has the most dramatic scenery. North of Kingstown, you rise into lofty terrain before descending to the water again. There are views in all directions. Here you can see one of the finest petroglyphs in the Caribbean: the massive **Carib Rock,** with a human face carving dating from A.D. 600.

Continuing north, you reach **Barrouallie,** where there's a Carib stone altar. Even if you're not into fishing, you might want to spend some time in this village, where whalers still occasionally set out in brightly painted boats armed with harpoons. While Barrouallie may be one of the few outposts in the world where whaling is legal, Vincentians claim that it doesn't endanger an already endangered species, as so few are caught each year. If one is caught, it's an occasion for festivities.

The highway continues to **Chateaubelair,** the end of the line. Here you can swim at attractive **Richmond Beach** before heading back to Kingstown. In the distance, the volcano, La Soufrière, looms menacingly.

The adventurous set out from here to see the **Falls of Baleine,** 12km (7½ miles) north of Richmond Beach on the northern tip of the island, accessible only by boat. Baleine is a freshwater falls that comes from a stream in the volcanic hills. If you're interested in making the trip, check with the tourist office in Kingstown for tour information.

MARRIQUA VALLEY 🐠

Sometimes known as the Mesopotamia Valley, the Marriqua Valley is one of the lushest cultivated valleys in the eastern Caribbean. Surrounded by mountain ridges, the drive takes you through a landscape planted with nutmeg, cocoa, coconut, breadfruit, and bananas. The road begins at the Vigie Highway, east of the airport. Surrounded by mountain ridges, it opens onto a panoramic view of Grand Bonhomme Mountain, rising 954m (3,129 ft.). At Montréal, you'll come upon natural mineral springs where you can have lunch and take a dip. Only rugged vehicles should make this trip.

Around Kingstown, you can also enjoy the **Queen's Drive,** a scenic loop into the high hills to the east of the capital. From here, the view is panoramic over Kingstown and its yacht-clogged harbor to the Grenadines in the distance.

SHOPPING

St. Vincent isn't a shopping destination, but while you're here, you might pick up some of the Sea Island cotton fabrics and clothing that are local specialties. Vincentian artisans also make pottery, jewelry, and baskets.

Since Kingstown consists of about 12 small blocks, you can walk, browse, and see about everything in a single morning. Try to be in town for the colorful, noisy **Friday-morning market.** You might not purchase anything, but you'll enjoy the riot of color.

At **Sprott Brothers,** Homeworks, Bay Street (© **784/457-1121**), you can buy clothing designed by Vincentians, along with an array of fabrics, linens, and silk-screened T-shirts, and even Caribbean-made furniture.

St. Vincent Philatelic Services, Dee's Service Building, Bay Street (© **784/ 457-1911**), is the largest operating bureau in the Caribbean, and its issues are highly acclaimed by stamp collectors around the world.

ST. VINCENT AFTER DARK

Most nightlife centers on the hotels, where activities usually include barbecues and dancing to steel bands. In season, at least one hotel seems to have something planned every night. Beer is extremely cheap at all the places noted.

Aquatic Club, adjacent to the departure point of the ferryboat from St. Vincent to Young Island (© **784/458-4205**), is the loudest and most raucous nightspot on St. Vincent; it often features live reggae, soca, or calypso. It's a source of giddy fun to its fans and a bone of contention to nearby hotel guests, who claim they can't sleep because of the noise. On Friday and Saturday nights, things heat up by 11pm and continue to the wee hours. Other nights of the week the place functions as a bar. Centered on an open-sided veranda and an outdoor deck, it's open every night from 10pm to 2 or 3am. There's no cover.

The hotel with the best entertainment is predictably **Young Island Resort,** Young Island (© 784/458-4825), which in winter hosts live musical entertainment on Wednesday nights. A West Indian band is brought in on Friday night for the manager's sunset cocktail party. Local musicians play on instruments made of bottles, gourds, and bamboo. The week's events are climaxed on Saturday with steel band music and a barbecue dinner.

Vee Jay's Rooftop Diner & Pub, Upper Bay Street in Kingstown (© 784/457-2845), across from the Cobblestone Inn. Come here for vegetable *rotis* and curried goat, consumed with the bittersweet *mauby,* a local drink made from tree bark. Come here on a Wednesday or Friday night, and you're treated to karaoke along with a panoramic view of the harbor.

Emerald Valley Casino, Peniston Valley (© 784/456-7824), is not one of the Caribbean's glamorous casinos. This "down-home" spot offers a trio of roulette tables, three blackjack tables, and one Caribbean stud poker table. You can also play craps. There's a bar, and you can order food. Hours are Wednesday through Monday from 8pm to 4am.

5 The Grenadines

GETTING THERE

BY PLANE Four of the Grenadines—Bequia, Mustique, Union Island, and Canouan—have small airports. Service from St. Vincent is by small interisland carriers including **Mustique Airways** (© 784/458-4380), which serves Canouan and Mustique. **SVG Air** (© 784/457-5124), one of the longest-established airlines in the region, will fly you in modern five- to nine-seaters to any island within the Eastern Caribbean. The one-way fare from E. T. Joshua Airport on St. Vincent is EC$62 (US$23) per person to Mustique, and EC$86 (US$32) per person to Canouan or Union Island.

BY BOAT The ideal way to go, of course, is to hire your own yacht, as many wealthy visitors do. A far less expensive option is to take a mail, cargo, or passenger boat, as the locals do, but you'll need time and patience. The **government mail boat,** MV *Barracuda* (© 784/457-1502, St. Vincent's tourist office), leaves on Monday, Wednesday, and Friday at 10:30am, stops at Bequia, Canouan, and Mayreau, and arrives at Union Island at about 3:45pm. On Tuesday, the boat leaves Union Island at about 6:30am, stops at Mayreau and Canouan, reaches Bequia at about 10:45am, and makes port at St. Vincent at noon. One-way fares from St. Vincent to Bequia are EC$15 (US$5.55). To Canouan, it's EC$20 (US$7.50); Mayreau; EC$25 (US$9.40); and Union Island, EC$30 (US$11).

You can also reach Bequia daily on the *Admiral I* and *Admiral II* for EC$25 (US$9.40). For information on these sea trips, inquire at the **Tourist Board,** Upper Bay Street, in Kingstown (© 784/457-1502).

BEQUIA ⋆⋆

Only 18 sq. km (7 sq. miles) of land, Bequia (*Beck*-wee) is the largest of the Grenadines. It's the northernmost island in the chain (only 14km/8¾ miles south

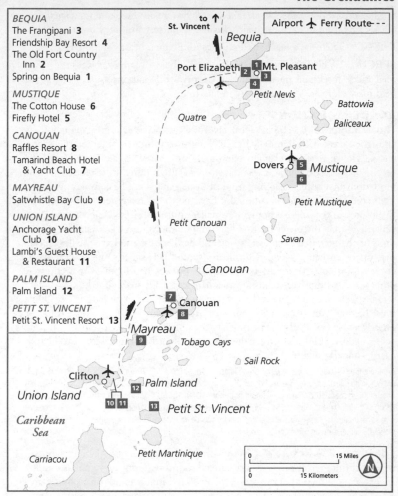

BEQUIA
The Frangipani **3**
Friendship Bay Resort **4**
The Old Fort Country
Inn **2**
Spring on Bequia **1**

MUSTIQUE
The Cotton House **6**
Firefly Hotel **5**

CANOUAN
Raffles Resort **8**
Tamarind Beach Hotel
& Yacht Club **7**

MAYREAU
Saltwhistle Bay Club **9**

UNION ISLAND
Anchorage Yacht
Club **10**
Lambi's Guest House
& Restaurant **11**

PALM ISLAND
Palm Island **12**

PETIT ST. VINCENT
Petit St. Vincent Resort **13**

Airport ✈ Ferry Route- - -

to ↑
St. Vincent

Bequia
Port Elizabeth — **1** Mt. Pleasant
2 ○ **3**
4
Petit Nevis
Quatre
Battowia
Baliceaux
Dovers ○✈ **5** Mustique
6
Petit Mustique
Petit Canouan
Savan
Canouan
7
○ Canouan
✈ **8**
Mayreau
9 Tobago Cays
Sail Rock
Clifton ✈
12 Palm Island
Union Island **10** **11**
13 Petit St. Vincent
Caribbean
Sea
Carriacou
Petit Martinique

0 ——————— 15 Miles
0 ——————— 15 Kilometers
N

of St. Vincent), offering quiet lagoons, reefs, and long stretches of nearly deserted beaches. Its friendly population of some 6,000 is descended from seafarers and other early adventurers. Some 10% are of Scottish ancestry, living mostly in the Mount Pleasant region. A feeling of relaxation and informality prevails.

ESSENTIALS
VISITOR INFORMATION   The **Tourist Information Centre,** is at Port Elizabeth (② **784/458-3286;** www.bequiatourism.com).

GETTING AROUND   Most visitors find it unnecessary to rent a car as roads are atrocious. Those wanting to see more of the island might consider a taxi guide. Before going to your hotel, drop in at the **Tourist Information Centre** and ask for a driver who's familiar with the attractions of the island (all of them are). You should negotiate the fare in advance. **Rental cars,** owned by locals, are available at the port, or you can hire a **taxi** at the dock to take you around the island or to your hotel. Taxis are reasonably priced, but an even better bet are the so-called **dollar cabs,** which take you anywhere on the island for a small fee. They don't seem to have a regular schedule—you just flag one down.

BANKS   There are a few bank branches on Bequia, mostly in Port Elizabeth.

SPECIAL EVENTS   The **Easter Regatta** is held over Easter weekend, with boat races, food, and music. Bequia's **Carnival** celebrations are a 4-day affair, held just before St. Vincent's party in late June.

ACCOMMODATIONS

The Frangipani 🌺🌺   This local favorite of yachties is a great hangout, its ambience created by James Mitchell, longtime prime minister of the island chain. The core of this pleasant guesthouse originated as the home of a 19th-century sea captain. Since it was transformed into a hotel, it has added accommodations that border a sloping tropical garden in back. The complex overlooks the island's historic harbor, Admiralty Bay, and draws many return visitors. The five rooms in the original house are smaller and much less glamorous (and less expensive) than the better-outfitted accommodations in the garden. The garden units are handcrafted from local stone and hardwoods, and have tile floors, carpets of woven hemp, wooden furniture (some made on St. Vincent), and balconies. Most of the rooms have a small private bathroom with a shower; otherwise, corridor bathrooms are adequate and tidily maintained.

The open-sided restaurant, Frangipani, overlooks the yacht harbor (see "Dining," below). Guests can play tennis or arrange scuba dives, sailboat rides, or other watersports nearby. (The nearest scuba outfitter, Dive Adventures, is fully accredited by PADI.) In winter there is an outdoor barbecue, with a steel band, every Thursday night.

Admiralty Bay (P.O. Box 1), Bequia, The Grenadines, St. Vincent, W.I. ℂ 784/458-3255. Fax 784/458-3824. www.frangipanibequia.com. 15 units. Winter US$55 double without bathroom, US$150–US$175 double with bathroom; off season US$40 double without bathroom, US$90–US$120 double with bathroom. Extra person US$25. Children 12 and under US$15. AE, MC, V. **Amenities:** Restaurant; bar; tennis court; boating; nearby dive shop; limited room service; babysitting; laundry service. *In room:* Ceiling fan, fridge (in some), beverage maker (in some), safe (in some), no phone.

Friendship Bay Resort 🌺   More comfortable and stylish than Frangipani, this beachfront resort offers well-decorated rooms with private verandas, nestled in 5 hectares (12 acres) of tropical gardens. The complex stands on a sloping hillside above one of the best white-sand beaches on the island, at Friendship Cove. Guests have a view of the sea and neighboring islands. Brightly colored curtains, handmade wall hangings, and grass rugs decorate the rooms, which are cooled by the trade winds and ceiling fans (in lieu of air-conditioning). Driftwood and various flotsam art, along with sponge-painted walls, evoke the sea. The accommodations have generous storage space, beds draped in mosquito netting, and small, shower-only bathrooms. The most requested units are those set directly on the ocean. The owners have added a beach bar and offer a local string band on Wednesday and every other Sunday. The food is good, and the menu features many island specialties.

Friendship Cove (P.O. Box 9), Bequia, The Grenadines, St. Vincent, W.I. ℂ 784/458-3222. Fax 784/458-3840. www.friendshipbayresort.com. 27 units. Winter US$165–US$210 double, US$225–US$335 suite; off season US$125–US$185 double, US$225 suite. Rates include continental breakfast. MC, V. **Amenities:** 2 restaurants; 2 bars; tennis court; boating; dive shop; water-skiing; windsurfing; babysitting; laundry service. *In room:* A/C (in some), ceiling fan, no phone.

The Old Fort Country Inn 🌺   This special hideaway was built from the ruins of a French-built plantation house commanding the best views on Bequia. Set on 12 tropical hectares (30 acres) at a point 135m (443 ft.) above the sea, the climate is excellent, with no mosquitoes. The property dates from at least 1756 (it may be older), and the .9m-thick (3-ft.) walls are made from cobblestones. In the reconstruction, the owner matched the original style by using the old stones with exposed ceiling beams and rafters, creating a medieval feel. The views from the spacious bedrooms are the best of any hotel on the island. Each unit has modern Scandinavian-style furnishings, a private balcony or terrace (in only two rooms), and a shower-only bathroom. An unstocked fridge can be supplied upon request. The rooms aren't air-conditioned, but trade winds seem to suffice.

The atmospheric restaurant holds eight tables and serves Creole and Mediterranean specialties, including a whole barbecued fish. On special occasions they present fine four- or five-course dinners. On the property are nature trails, a beach that's a 10-minute hike from the hotel, and a 5m by 9m (16-ft. by 30-ft.) pool, with views of the ocean on three sides.

Mount Pleasant, Bequia, The Grenadines, St. Vincent, W.I. © 784/458-3440. Fax 784/457-3340. www. theoldfort.com. 6 units. Winter US$140 double; off season US$95 double. MC, V. **Amenities:** Restaurant; outdoor pool; babysitting; laundry service. *In room:* Ceiling fan, no phone.

Spring on Bequia ⚐ *(Finds* In the late 1960s, the Frank Lloyd Wright design of this hotel won an award from the American Institute of Architects. Fashioned from beautifully textured honey-colored stone, it has a flattened hip roof inspired by the old plantation houses of Martinique. Constructed on the 18th-century foundations of a West Indian homestead, it sits in the middle of 11 hectares (27 acres) of hillside orchards, producing oranges, grapefruit, bananas, breadfruit, plums, and mangos. Thanks to the almost constant blossoming of one crop or another, it always feels like spring (hence the name). From the main building's stone bar and open-air dining room, you might hear the lowing of a herd of cows.

All rooms have terraces; the three units in the main building are smaller and darker than the others. Each room is ringed with stone and contains Japanese-style screens to filter the sun. The high pyramidal ceilings and the constant trade winds keep things cool. The king or double platform beds are draped in mosquito netting, and the bathrooms have stone-grotto-like showers that use solar-heated water. The overall feeling is quiet and tranquil. The sandy beach is a 3-minute walk away through a coconut grove, but it's too shallow for good swimming.

Spring Bay, Bequia, The Grenadines, St. Vincent, W.I. © 784/458-3414, or 612/823-1202 in the U.S. Fax 784/ 457-3305. www.springonbequia.com. 9 units. Winter US$130–US$220 double; off season US$70–US$140 double. Extra person US$50. MAP (breakfast and dinner) US$45 per person extra. AE, DISC, MC, V. Closed end of June–Oct. **Amenities:** Restaurant; bar; outdoor pool; tennis court; snorkeling; laundry service. *In room:* Ceiling fan, fridge, no phone.

DINING

The food here is good and healthy—lobster, chicken, and steaks from such fish as mahimahi, kingfish, and grouper, plus tropical fruits, fried plantains, and coconut and guava puddings made fresh daily. Even the beach bars are kept spotless.

Frangipani ⚐ CARIBBEAN/INTERNATIONAL This waterside dining room, always full of yachties, is one of the best restaurants on the island. With the exception of the juicy steaks imported for barbecues, only local food is used in the specialties. Lunches, served throughout the day, include sandwiches, salads, and seafood platters. Dinner specialties include homemade soup, conch chowder, baked chicken with rice-and-coconut stuffing, lobster, and an array of fresh fish. A Thursday-night barbecue with live entertainment is an island event.

In the Frangipani Hotel, Port Elizabeth. ✆ 784/458-3255. Reservations required for dinner. Breakfast EC$8.10–EC$27 (US$3–US$10); lunch EC$27–EC$108 (US$10–US$40); dinner main courses EC$27–EC$135 (US$10–US$50); fixed-price dinner EC$46–EC$135 (US$17–US$50). AE, MC, V. Daily 7:30am–3pm and 6:30–10pm. Closed Sept.

Friendship Bay Resort INTERNATIONAL/WEST INDIAN   Guests dine in a candlelit room high above a sweeping expanse of seafront on a hillside rich with the scent of frangipani and hibiscus. Lunch is served at the Spicy 'n Herby beach bar, but dinner is more elaborate. Meals, based on fresh ingredients, might include grilled lobster in season, curried beef, grilled or broiled fish (served Creole style with a spicy sauce), shrimp curry, and charcoal-grilled steak flambé. Dishes are flavorful and well prepared. Special barbecues are held on Wednesday and Sunday nights.

Port Elizabeth. ✆ 784/458-3222. Reservations required for dinner. Main courses EC$15–EC$41 (US$5.55–US$15) lunch, EC$35–EC$76 (US$13–US$28) dinner. MC, V. Daily 10am–10pm. Closed Sept to mid-Oct.

Le Petit Jardin 🦀 INTERNATIONAL   Set in a varnished wooden house behind the post office, this restaurant is the slow-moving but likable creation of the Belmar family, who use as many fresh ingredients as the vagaries of the local fishing fleet will allow. You'll dine within view of a garden, in a likable ambience inspired by both the British and French West Indies. Menu items include grilled swordfish with lemon sauce; grilled lobster; shrimp and vegetable kabobs; chipped steak in cream sauce; and conventional grilled sirloin.

Backstreet, Port Elizabeth. ✆ 784/458-3318. Reservations recommended. Main courses EC$60–EC$86 (US$22–US$32). AE, DC, MC, V. Daily 11:30am–2pm and 6:30–9:30pm.

Whaleboner Inn WEST INDIAN/SEAFOOD/INTERNATIONAL   An enduring favorite, the Whaleboner is still going strong, serving Bequia's most authentic local dishes. Inside, the bar is carved from the jawbone of a giant whale, and the barstools are made from the vertebrae. The owners serve the best pizza on the island, along with a selection of fish and chips and well-made sandwiches for lunch. At night, you choose among lobster, fish, chicken, or steak. We prefer the curried-conch dinner beginning with the callaloo soup. The bar often stays open later than 10:30pm, depending on the crowd. On Monday, Friday, and Saturday there is live music.

Next to the Frangipani Hotel, Port Elizabeth. ✆ 784/458-3233. Reservations required for dinner. Main courses EC$54–EC$89 (US$20–US$33). MC, V. Daily 8am until closing (8:30 pm dinner; around 10:30 pm bar).

EXPLORING BEQUIA

Obviously, the secluded beaches are at the top of everyone's list of Bequia's attractions. As you walk along the beaches, especially near Port Elizabeth, you'll see craftspeople building boats by hand, a method passed on by their ancestors. Whalers sometimes still set out from here in wooden boats with harpoons. Some beaches require a taxi ride. You might check out the uncrowded, pristine white sands at **Friendship Bay,** where you can rent watersports equipment or order a drink from the bar at the hotel. **Industry Bay** and **Lower Bay** are both gorgeous beaches shaded by palm trees, offering good swimming and snorkeling.

Dive Bequia, Gingerbread House, Admiralty Bay (P.O. Box 199), Bequia (✆ 784/458-3504), specializes in diving and snorkeling on the lush reefs of Bequia, where you might spot manta rays. Scuba dives cost US$55 for one, US$70 for two in the same day, and US$225 for a five-dive package. A four-dive open-water certification course is US$450. Snorkeling trips are US$20 per person, and these prices include all the necessary equipment.

The main harbor village, **Port Elizabeth,** is known for its safe anchorage, Admiralty Bay. The bay was a haven in the 17th century for the British, French, and Spanish navies, as well as for pirates. Descendants of Captain Kydd (or Kidd) still live on the island. Today, the yachting set anchors here.

SHOPPING

The **Crab Hole,** next door to the Plantation House, Admiralty Bay (© 784/ 458-3290), is the best of the shops scattered along the water, selling sterling-silver and 14-karat-gold jewelry.

Anyone on the island can show you the way to the workshops of **Sargeant's Model Boatshop Bequia,** Front Street, Port Elizabeth (© 784/458-3344), west of the pier past the oil-storage facility. Sought out by yacht owners looking for a scale-model reproduction of their favorite vessel, Lawson Sargeant is the self-taught wood carver who established this business. The models are carved from white pine and mahogany, and then painted brilliant colors. When a scale model of the royal family's yacht, *Britannia,* was commissioned in 1985, it required 5 weeks of work and cost US$10,000. You can pick up a model of a Bequia whaling boat for much less.

MUSTIQUE 🌟🌟🌟

This island of luxury villas, which someone once called "Georgian West Indian," is so remote and small that it would be unknown—if it didn't attract the likes of Princess Margaret, Paul Newman, Mick Jagger, Raquel Welch, Richard Avedon, Tommy Hilfiger, and Prince Andrew, many of whom have cottages here.

The island, privately owned by a consortium of businesspeople, is only 5km-long (3 miles) and 2km-wide (1¼-mile), and it has only one major hotel. It's located 24km (15 miles) south of St. Vincent. After settling in, you'll find many good white-sand beaches against a backdrop of luxuriant foliage. Our favorite is **Macaroni Beach,** where the water is turquoise, the sands are pure white, and a few trees shade the picnic tables. If you've come over on a day trip, you might go to **Britannia Bay,** which is next to the jetty and close to Basil's Bar.

On the northern reef of Mustique lies the wreck of the French liner *Antilles,* which ran aground on the Pillories in 1971. Its massive hulk, now gutted, can be seen cracked and rusting a few yards offshore—an eerie sight.

If you want to tour the small island, you can rent a **Mini-Moke** (a small golf cart–like car) to see some of the most elegant homes in the Caribbean, includ-ing the late Princess Margaret's place, **Les Jolies Eaux (Pretty Waters).**

GETTING THERE & GETTING AROUND

Mustique Airways (© 784/458-4380 in St. Vincent) runs one daily commuter flight between St. Vincent and Mustique. The flight departs St. Vincent daily at 9:30am, landing on Mustique 8 minutes later, then heading immediately back to St. Vincent. The airport closes at dusk.

Once here, you can call **Pecky's** taxi (© 784/488-8000, ext. 448), but chances are someone at the Cotton House will already have seen you land.

ACCOMMODATIONS

The Cotton House 🌟🌟🌟   The Caribbean's most exclusive hotel is as casually elegant and sophisticated as its clientele. The 18th-century main house is built of coral and stone, and it was painstakingly restored, reconstructed, and redeco-rated by Oliver Messel, uncle by marriage to Princess Margaret. The antique log-gia, arched louvered doors, and cedar shutters set the style. The decor includes everything from Lady Bateman's steamer trunks to a scallop-shell fountain on a quartz base, where guests sit and enjoy their sundowners, perhaps after an afternoon on the tennis court or in the pool. Guests go between two beaches, each only a couple of minutes away on foot—Endeavour Bay, on the leeward side, with calmer waters, and L'Ansecoy, on the other side.

Guest rooms are in five fully restored Georgian houses, a trio of cottages, a newer block of four rooms, and a five-room beach house, all of which open onto windswept balconies or patios. Extras include king-size beds dressed in Egyptian cotton and swathed in netted canopies, robes, slippers, and toiletries from Floris in London. Some of the more romantic units have wrought-iron four-posters, and some of the bathrooms offer private outdoor showers. The Tower Suite is the most luxurious accommodation, filling the entire second floor.

The hotel enjoys an outstanding reputation for its Caribbean/Continental food and service. Nonguests are welcome to dine here but must make reservations. The hotel also has three bars—you might find Mick Jagger at one of them.

Endeavour Bay, Mustique (P.O. Box 349), The Grenadines, St. Vincent, W.I. © **784/456-4777.** Fax 784/456-5887. www.cottonhouse.net. 20 units. Winter US$750–US$1,150 double; off season US$510–US$850 double. Rates include MAP (breakfast and dinner). AE, MC, V. **Amenities:** 2 restaurants; 2 bars; outdoor pool; 2 tennis courts; spa; boating; deep-sea fishing; dive shop; snorkeling; windsurfing; horseback riding; limited room service; massage; babysitting; laundry service. *In room:* A/C, ceiling fan, dataport, minibar, beverage maker (in some), hair dryer, safe.

Firefly Hotel 🌟 *Finds* This stone house, constructed in 1972, is one of the first homes ever built by an expatriate English or North American on Mustique. It functioned as a simple, not particularly glamorous B&B until the late 1990s, when Sussex-born Elizabeth Clayton spent huge sums of money to upgrade and enlarge the hotel and its restaurant. Although it contains only four bedrooms, it thrives as one of the most consistently popular and animated bars and restaurants (see "Dining," below) on an island where lots of the expatriate residents enjoy partying 'til the wee hours. Each of the rooms has Caribbean decor, ceiling fans, mahogany furniture, an antique four-poster bed, and a bathroom with a plunge pool, plus showers and countertops crafted from smooth-worn pebbles set into beds of mortar. The ambience is more like a private home than a hotel.

Britannia Bay (P.O. Box 349), Mustique, The Grenadines, W.I. © **784/488-8414.** Fax 784/488-8514. www.fireflymustique.com. 4 units. Winter US$675–US$775 double; off season US$575–US$600 double. Rates are all-inclusive. AE, MC, V. Children under 12 are not allowed. **Amenities:** Restaurant; bar; 2 outdoor pools; tennis (nearby); snorkeling; limited room service; laundry service; nonsmoking rooms. *In room:* Ceiling fan, minibar, hair dryer, safe.

DINING

Basil's Beach Bar 🌟 SEAFOOD/CARIBBEAN Nobody ever visits this island of indigenous farmers and fisherfolk without spending a night at Basil's, which looks straight out of the South Seas with its wooden deck, open-air dance floor, and thatched roof. Built on piers above the sea, the beach bar is a popular gathering place for yachties sailing the Grenadines. Some people come for drinks and the panoramic view, but Basil's also has a reputation as one of the finest seafood restaurants in the Caribbean. Everything is simple, but well prepared. You can dine under the open-air sunscreens or in the sun. On Wednesday night in winter you can "jump-up" at a barbecue, and there's live music on Mondays. A boutique is also on the premises.

13 Britannia Bay. © **784/488-8000.** Reservations recommended. Main courses EC$59–EC$89 (US$22–US$33). AE, MC, V. Daily 8am–10:30pm. Bar daily 8am "until very late."

The Restaurant at Firefly 🌟 FRENCH/INTERNATIONAL This is one of the island's most consistently popular restaurants, characterized by its bright tropical colors and open-air terraces, a busy bar area where you're likely to see Mustique's glitterati at play, and a menu that's the byproduct of a European-trained chef whose earlier venues were very grand and very prestigious. Some of the establishment's tried-and-true dishes include spicy Caribbean crab cakes and pineapple-shrimp curry with rice. Other entrees change with the season and the inspiration of the chef. The drink associated with this place is the Firefly Special, made with coconut cream, two kinds of rum, fresh papaya, and nutmeg. Don't miss the banana flambé.

In the Firefly Hotel, Britannia Bay. ⓒ 784/488-8414. Reservations recommended for dinner. Main courses EC$76–EC$95 (US$28–US$35). AE, MC, V. Daily 8:30am–10pm. Bar daily 8am–midnight.

CANOUAN ⭐⭐
In the shape of a half circle, Canouan rises from its sandy beaches to the 240m (787-ft.) high peak of Mount Royal in the north, where you'll find unspoiled forests of white cedar. Twenty-three kilometers (14 miles) south of St. Vincent and 32km (20 miles) north of Grenada, Canouan has a population of fewer than 2,000 people, many of whom fish for a living and live in **Retreat Village,** the island's only village.

Only 6km by 2km (3¾ by 1¼ miles), Canouan is surrounded by long ribbons of absolutely gorgeous powdery white-sand beaches and blue lagoons. The surrounding coral reefs teem with life, making for great snorkeling and diving. **Canovan Dive Center,** in the Grand Bay (ⓒ **784/458-8888**), offers resort courses, equipment rentals, and all kinds of dive and snorkel trips.

GETTING THERE
Reaching Canouan by air is slightly different from traveling to the other islands of the Grenadines. **Mustique Airways** (ⓒ **784/458-4380**) flies twice from St. Vincent on Monday, Wednesday, and Friday. The cost is EC$154 (US$57) round-trip. **SVG Air** in St. Vincent (ⓒ **784/457-5124**) makes two daily flights on Monday, Wednesday, and Friday to Canouan at a cost of EC$154 (US$57) round-trip.

ACCOMMODATIONS & DINING
Raffles Resort ⭐⭐   Named after the famous hotel of Singapore, this villa-studded resort opens onto a beautiful white-sand beach set on 121 hectares (300 acres). It is the latest reincarnation of the Carenage Bay Club, which was once hailed as one of the grandest and most luxurious resorts in the southern Caribbean. The Raffles incarnation has even better facilities and more comfortable bedrooms. Opening onto Carenage Bay, each accommodation is a villa suite set near the beach. The golf course has been extended to a full 18 holes, and a deluxe European-style casino has been added. Each suite comes with its own private terrace. Decorated in pastels, the bedrooms have a light, airy, tropical feel. Rooms come in a variety of categories from deluxe through luxurious suites. The Caribbean's largest hotel pool is one of the allures, lying at the edge of the beach. Top chefs, often Italian, have been imported to turn out a first-rate cuisine that begins with an opulent breakfast buffet and ends with late night Continental dining.

Carenage Bay, Canouan, St. Vincent, W.I. ⓒ 784/458-8000. Fax 784/458-8885. www.raffles-canouanisland. com. 156 units. Winter from US$625 double; off season from US$345 double. AE, DC, MC, V. **Amenities:** 4 restaurants; 4 bars; giant outdoor pool; children's pool; casino; 18-hole golf course; 4 tennis courts; fitness center; spa; boat excursions; limited room service; laundry service. *In room:* A/C, TV, dataport, kitchenette (in some), minibar, hair dryer, safe.

Tamarind Beach Hotel & Yacht Club ⭐ Italian owned and managed, this idyllic inn opens onto the long white sands of Grand Bay Beach. Thatched-roof bungalow-style hideaways, each enveloped by tropical gardens, are called seaside hideaways here—and so they are. Rooms have private balconies or patios, wicker furnishings, louvered wooden doors, and wood walls. Whirling ceiling fans go night and day. The staff provides several thoughtful touches, such as leaving a tropical fruit basket in your bedroom. The staff will help you arrange "island safaris" to such neighboring sandy strips as the Tobago Cays. Although everything is imported, the food is good and is served at water's edge on an open terrace with a view of the boats.

Charlestown, Canouan, St. Vincent, W.I. © 784/458-8044. Fax 784/458-8851. www.tamarindbeachhotel. com. 42 units. Winter US$265–US$305 double, US$460–US$590 suite; off season US$195–US$240 double, US$360–US$460 suite. MAP (breakfast and dinner) US$60 per person extra. Children under 12 stay free in parent's room. AE, MC, V. **Amenities:** 2 restaurants; 2 bars; dive shop; sailing; scuba diving; windsurfing; travel services; car rental; babysitting; laundry service; nonsmoking rooms. *In room:* A/C (in suites), ceiling fans, kitchenette (in suites), minibar, fridge, beverage maker, hair dryer, iron/ironing board, safe.

MAYREAU ⭐

A tiny cay, 4 sq. km (1½ sq. miles) of land, Mayreau is a privately owned island shared by a hotel and a little hilltop village of about 170 inhabitants. It's on the route of the mail boat that plies the seas to and from St. Vincent (see "Getting There" at the beginning of this section). It's completely sleepy unless a cruise ship anchors offshore and hustles its passengers over for a lobster barbecue on the beach.

ACCOMMODATIONS & DINING

Saltwhistle Bay Club ⭐ *Finds* Slightly less formal and expensive than the Petit St. Vincent Resort on Petit St. Vincent (see below), to which it's frequently compared, Saltwhistle Bay Club caters to escapists with money. You can spend your days lolling in one of the hammocks strung among the trees in the 8-hectare (20-acre) tropical garden, perhaps taking a swim off the expanse of white-sand beaches that curve along both the leeward and windward sides of the island, or the staff will take you to a little uninhabited island nearby for a Robinson Crusoe–style picnic.

Set back from the beach, the accommodations were built by local craftspeople, using local stone and tropical woods like purpleheart and greenheart. All units have ceiling fans. Inside, the spacious cottages have an almost medieval feel, with thick stone walls and dark wood furnishings. Bathrooms are large, with cylindrical stone showers.

The dining room is made up of circular stone booths topped by thatch canopies, where you can enjoy seafood fresh from the waters around Mayreau: lobster, curried conch, and grouper.

Mayreau, The Grenadines, St. Vincent, W.I. © 784/458-8444. Fax 784/458-8944. www.saltwhistlebay.com. 10 units. Winter US$480 double; off season US$360 double. Children under 18 pay half. Rates include MAP (breakfast and dinner). AE, MC, V. Closed Sept–Oct. Take the private hotel launch from the airport on Union Island (US$50 per person round-trip). **Amenities:** Restaurant; bar; boating; scuba diving; snorkeling; limited room service; babysitting; laundry service; rooms for those with limited mobility. *In room:* Ceiling fan, hair dryer, no phone.

UNION ISLAND

Midway between Grenada and St. Vincent, Union Island is one of the southernmost of the Grenadines. It's known for its dramatic 270m (886-ft.) peak, Mount Parnassus, which yachters can see from miles away. For those cruising in the area, Union is the port of entry for St. Vincent. Yachters are required to check in with Customs upon entry.

ESSENTIALS
GETTING THERE   The island is reached by chartered or scheduled aircraft, cargo boat, private yacht, or mail boat (see "Getting There" at the beginning of this section). **Mustique Airways** (© 784/458-4380 on St. Vincent) makes two flights per day Monday to Friday and one flight a day on Saturday and Sunday; the fare is US$40 one-way.

SPECIAL EVENTS   Over Easter weekend, **Easterval** features boat races, a calypso competition, and the Big Drum Dance, a festive cultural show that highlights the islanders' African heritage.

ACCOMMODATIONS & DINING
Anchorage Yacht Club   Although at least two other hotels are nearby, this club is the best. It has a threefold function as a hotel, a restaurant, and a bar, with a busy marine-service facility in the same compound under different management.

It occupies a prominent position a few steps from the bumpy landing strip that services at least two nearby resorts (Petit St. Vincent and Palm Island) and about a half dozen small islands nearby. Something of an airline-hub aura permeates the place, as passengers shuttle between their planes, boats, and the yacht club's bar and restaurant.

Each of the small guest rooms, set between a pair of airy verandas, has white-tile floors and simple, somewhat sun-bleached modern furniture. Shower-only bathrooms are very small and the towels a bit thin, but in this remote part of the world, you're grateful for hot water. The better units are the bungalows and cabanas beside the beach.

The yachting set meets in the wood-and-stone bar, which serves breakfast, lunch, and dinner daily.

Clifton, Union Island, The Grenadines, St. Vincent, W.I. © 784/458-8221. Fax 784/458-8365. www.ayc-hotel-grenadines.com. 15 units. Winter US$110 double, US$130 bungalow or apt, US$180 cabana; off season US$70 double, US$80 bungalow or apt, US$130 cabana. Extra person US$40. Rates include continental breakfast. MC, V. **Amenities:** Restaurant; bar; marina; snorkeling; babysitting; laundry service. *In room:* A/C (in some), ceiling fans, beverage (in some).

Lambi's Guest House & Restaurant *(Value* CREOLE/SEAFOOD   *Lambi* means conch in Creole patois, and if you've never tried this shellfish before, this is a good place to do so. Built partially on stilts on the waterfront in Clifton, this is also the best place to sample the local cuisine. You can order various fresh fish platters depending on the catch of the day, and lobster is frequently available. You can also order chicken, steak, lamb, or pork chops, but all this is shipped in frozen. Fresh vegetables are used whenever possible. In winter a steel band entertains nightly in the bar. Other entertainment includes limbo dancers or fire dancing.

Upstairs are 41 dormitory-style rooms for rent, each with two double beds, ceiling fans, and a tiny, tiny bathroom. Year-round, they go for EC$62 (US$23) single, EC$81 (US$30) double, and EC$100 (US$37) triple.

Clifton Harbour, Union Island, The Grenadines, St. Vincent, W.I. © 784/458-8549. Fax 784/458-8395. Main courses EC$30–EC$59 (US$11–US$22); 50-dish buffet EC$46 (US$17). MC, V. Daily 7am–11pm.

PALM ISLAND 🐫
Is this island a resort or is the resort the island? Casual elegance prevails on these 52 hectares (129 acres) in the southern Grenadines. Surrounded by five

white-sand beaches, this private island is sometimes called "Prune," so we can easily understand the more appealing name change. This little islet offers complete peace and quiet with plenty of sea, sand, sun, and sailing.

To get to Palm Island, you must first fly to Union Island. From Union Island, a hotel launch will take you to Palm Island.

ACCOMMODATIONS

Palm Island 𝕲𝕲𝕲 Tranquillity reigns at this all-inclusive resort with its five white-sand beaches. The old Palm Island Beach Club was completely razed to the ground and rebuilt in 1999. This exclusive and remote retreat has come a long way since its founder, John Caldwell ("Coconut Johnny"), began planting palms here to give the island a lush, tropical look. Now under new developers, the posh retreat consists of a cluster of 40 units contained in 22 Caribbean cottages. Bedrooms capture the spirit of the Grenadines, occupying both standard guest rooms and "tree houses," each with ceiling fans, custom-designed bamboo and rattan furnishings, colorful balconies or patios opening onto the view, shower and tub bathrooms, and bathrobes. The romantic tree houses have high-peaked ceilings, breezy balconies, and four-poster bamboo beds. In addition to the regular accommodations, the Plantation House boasts four bedrooms, each with queen-size beds.

Good-quality cuisine is served in the Grenadines Restaurant and the Royal Palm Restaurant with specialties from the Caribbean, the U.S., and Europe. One guest wrote, "If you don't dig the vittles here, you can rent a boat for the night to take you over to Union Island or else crack open a coconut." Chances are you won't have to do either, as the cuisine is great. From the pink grapefruit with honey-rum sauce that begins breakfast to the coconut mousse that completes dinner, you dine "high on the hog," as the chef says.

Palm Island, The Grenadines, St. Vincent, W.I. ℭ 800/345-0356 or 784/458-8824. Fax 784/458-8804. www. eliteislandresorts.com. 37 units. Winter US$800–US$1,000 double; off season US$560–US$780 double. Rates are all-inclusive. AE, MC, V. **Amenities:** 2 restaurants; 2 bars; outdoor pool; tennis court; fishing; marina; snorkeling; windsurfing; bikes; laundry service; nonsmoking rooms. *In room:* A/C, minibar, beverage maker, hair dryer, safe, no phone.

PETIT ST. VINCENT 𝕲

A private island 6km (3¾ miles) from Union Island in the southern Grenadines, this speck of land is rimmed with white-sand beaches. On 45 hectares (111 acres), it's an out-of-this-world corner of the Caribbean that's only for self-sufficient types who want to escape just about everything.

The easiest way to get to Petit St. Vincent is to fly to Union Island via St. Vincent. Make arrangements with the hotel to have its "PSV boat" pick you up on Union Island. This is the southernmost of St. Vincent's Grenadines.

ACCOMMODATIONS

Petit St. Vincent Resort 𝕲𝕲𝕲 This nautical-chic resort was conceived by Hazen K. Richardson, who did everything from planting trees to laying cables on the 45-hectare (111-acre) property. It's the only place to stay on the island. Open to the trade winds, this self-contained cottage colony was designed by a Swedish architect, Arne Hasselquist, who used purpleheart wood and the local stone, blue bitch (yes, that's right), for the walls.

Some cottages are built on a hillside, with great views, and some are set conveniently close to the beach. Cottages open onto big outdoor patios and are cooled by trade winds and ceiling fans. Each spacious accommodation has an ample living area, two daybeds, a good-size bedroom with two queen-size beds, a shower-only bathroom, a dressing room, Caribbean-style wicker and rattan furnishings, and a large patio with a hammock for lying back and taking it easy. For payment, personal checks are accepted and preferred. When you need something (perhaps a picnic lunch made up for your day on the beach), you simply write out your request, place it in a slot in a bamboo flagpole, and run up the yellow flag. A staff member will arrive on a motorized cart to take your order.

This resort has a top-notch chef, and menus are changed daily. Although the food has to be shipped in, the fine U.S. and Continental dishes taste fresh and are very well prepared. The chefs are sensitive to special requests and special diets.

Petit St. Vincent, The Grenadines, St. Vincent, W.I. © **800/654-9326** or 784/458-8801. Fax 784/458-8428. www.psvresort.com. 22 units. Winter US$910 cottage for 2; off season US$740 cottage for 2. Rates are all-inclusive. AE, MC, V. Closed Sept–Oct. **Amenities:** Dining room; bar; tennis court; fitness trail; kayaks; sailing; snorkeling; windsurfing; 24-hr. room service; laundry service; babysitting. *In room:* Ceiling fan, minibar, hair dryer, iron/ironing board, no phone.

25

Trinidad & Tobago

Trinidad, which is about the size of Delaware, and even tinier Tobago, 32km (20 miles) to the northeast, form a nation popularly known as "T&T." South African Bishop Desmond Tutu once dubbed it "The Rainbow Country," for its abundance of floral growth and the diversity of its population. The islands are the southernmost outposts of the West Indies. Trinidad lies only 11km (6¾ miles) from the Paria Peninsula of Venezuela, to which it was physically connected in prehistoric times.

Trinidad, birthplace of calypso, steel drum music, and the limbo, used to be visited only by business travelers in Port-of-Spain. The island was more interested in its oil, natural gas, and steel industries than in tourism. But that has changed. Trinidad is now a serious vacation destination, with a spruced-up capital and a renovated airport. The island's sophistication and cultural mélange, far greater than that of any other island in the southern Caribbean, is also a factor in increased tourism.

Conversely, Tobago, its sibling island, is just as drowsy as ever, and that's its charm. Through the years, immigrants from almost every corner of the world have come here, and today the island is a fascinating mixture of cultures, races, and creeds.

The Spanish founded Trinidad in 1592 and held it longer than they did any of their other real estate in the Caribbean. The English settled Tobago in 1642, and captured Trinidad in 1797. Both islands remained in British hands until the two-island nation declared its independence in 1962. The British influence is still clearly visible today, from the strong presence of the British dialect to the islanders' fondness for cricket.

1 Trinidad & Tobago Essentials

VISITOR INFORMATION

There is no Trinidadian tourism office that can be visited in the U.S., but you can call the **Trinidad & Tobago Tourism Office** (© **800/748-4224** or 888/595-4TNT) for information. There are also three government offices of the two-island nation within the U.S. that provide information and pamphlets on Trinidad and Tobago: 733 3rd Ave., Suite 1716, New York, NY 10017 (© **212/697-7620**); 1000 Brickell Ave., Suite 800, Miami, FL 33131 (© **305/374-2199**); and 1708 Massachusetts Ave. NW, Washington, DC 20036 (© **202/476-6490**). The islands are also on the Web at **www.visittnt.com.**

Canadians can get information from **RMR Group,** 512 Duplex Ave., Toronto, Ontario M4R 2E3 (© **888/535-5617** or 416/485-7827).

There's also an office in **England** at **Morris Kevan International,** 66 Abbey Road, Bush Hill Park, Enfield, Middlesex EN1 2QE (© **020/8350-1009**).

Once you're on Trinidad, you can stop by **TIDCO,** 10–14 Phillips St., Port-of-Spain (© **868/623-6022** or -6023). There's also an information desk at Piarco Airport (© **868/669-5196**).

On Tobago, go to the **Tobago Division of Tourism,** Mt. Marie, Scarborough (© **868/639-2125**), or the information desk at Crown Point Airport (© **868/639-0509**).

FAST FACTS: Trinidad & Tobago

Currency The official currency is the **Trinidad and Tobago dollar (TT$),** which has an exchange rate of about US$1 = TT$6.28 (TT$1 = US16¢). Ask what currency is being referred to when rates are quoted. We've used both in this chapter, depending on the establishment. U.S. and Canadian dollars are often accepted, particularly in Port-of-Spain. However, you'll usually do better by converting your Canadian or U.S. dollars into local currency. British pounds should be converted into the local currency. *Unless otherwise specified, rates in this chapter are quoted in U.S. dollars.* The most convenient bank is one of the many branches of **First Citizens Bank** (© **868/623-2576**), which are found at Piarco airport and elsewhere throughout Port-of-Spain, including at many shopping malls. A good choice in Port-of-Spain is **Scotiabank,** 56-58 Richmond St. (© **868/625-3566**).

Customs Readers have reported long delays in clearing Customs on Trinidad. Visitors may bring in 200 cigarettes or 50 cigars plus 1 quart of spirits.

Documents Citizens of the United States, Britain, and Canada need passports and an ongoing or return ticket to enter Trinidad and Tobago. A visa is not required for tourist/business stays shorter than 6 weeks. Save the carbon copy of the immigration card you fill out when you arrive: you'll have to return it to immigration officials when you depart.

Electricity The electricity is either 110- or 230-volt AC (60 cycles), so ask when making your hotel reservations if you'll need transformers and/or adapters.

Embassies & High Commissions In Port-of-Spain on Trinidad, the **U.S. Embassy** is at 7–9 Marli St., 15 Queen's Park West (© **868/622-6371**; Mon–Fri 7:30am–noon and 1–4pm); the **Canadian High Commission** is situated at Maple House, 3 Sweet Briar Rd., St. Clair (© **868/622-6232**); and the **British High Commission** is found at 19 St. Clair Ave., St. Clair (© **868/622-2748**).

Emergencies On either Trinidad or Tobago, call the **police** at © **999**; to report a **fire** or summon an **ambulance,** dial © **990.**

Language English is the official language, although you'll hear it spoken with many different accents, especially British. Chinese, French, Spanish, Hindi, and a local dialect, Trinibagianese, are also spoken.

Safety As a general rule, Tobago is safer than Trinidad. Crime does exist on Tobago, but it's not of raging dimensions. If you can, avoid the downtown streets of Port-of-Spain at night, especially those around Independence Square, where muggings have been reported. Evening jaunts down Wilson Street and the Market of Scarborough are also discouraged. Visitors are open prey for pickpockets during Carnival, so be alert during large street parties. It is wise to safeguard your valuables; never leave them unattended at the beach or even in a locked car.

Taxes & Service Charges The government imposes a 10% value-added tax (VAT) on room rates. It also imposes a departure tax of TT$100 (US$16) on every passenger over 5 years old. The big hotels and restaurants add a 10% to 15% service charge to your final tab.

Telephone The area code for Trinidad and Tobago is **868**. Make calls to or from the islands as you would to any other area code in North America. On either island, just dial the local seven-digit number. For **MCI** call ℂ **800-888-8000**, for **Sprint** ℂ **800-877-8000**, and for **AT&T** ℂ **800-225-5288**.

Time Trinidad and Tobago are in the Eastern Time zone; from November through March, time here is the same as the U.S. East Coast. From April through October (daylight savings time in the United States), when it's 6am on the East Coast, it's 5am in T&T.

Tipping Tip taxi drivers 10% to 15% of the fare, and tip waiters 10% to 15% of the cost of a meal. Tip skycaps and bellboys US$1 per bag.

Water On Trinidad and Tobago, stick to bottled water.

Weather Trinidad has a tropical climate all year, with constant trade winds maintaining mean temperatures of 84°F (29°C) during the day and 74°F (23°C) at night. It rarely gets above 90°F (32°C) or below 70°F (21°C). The rainy season runs from May to November, but it shouldn't deter you from visiting; the rain usually lasts no more than 2 hours before the sun comes out again. However, carry along plenty of insect repellent if you visit then.

2 Trinidad

Trinidad is completely different from the other Caribbean islands, which is part of its charm and appeal. It's not for everyone, though. Because **Port-of-Spain,** the capital, is one of the most bustling commercial centers in the Caribbean, more business travelers than tourists are drawn here. The island, 81km-long (50-miles) and 64km-wide (40-miles), does have beaches, but the best of them are far away from the capital. The city itself, with a population of about 120,000, is hot, humid, and somewhat dirty. With the opening of its US$2 million cruise-ship complex, Port-of-Spain has become a major port of call for Caribbean cruise lines.

Although Port-of-Spain, with its shopping centers, fast-food joints, modern hotels, and active nightlife, draws mixed reviews, the countryside is calmer. Far removed from the traffic jams of the capital, you can explore the fauna and flora of the island. It's estimated that there are some 700 varieties of orchids alone, plus 400 species of birds.

Prices on Trinidad are often lower than on many other islands in the West Indies. Port-of-Spain abounds in inexpensive inns and guesthouses. Since most of the restaurants cater to locals, dining prices reflect the low wages.

The people are part of the attraction on Trinidad, the most cosmopolitan island in the Caribbean. The island's polyglot population includes Syrians, Chinese, Americans, Europeans, East Indians, Parsees, Madrasis, Venezuelans, and the last of the original Amerindian settlers of the island. You'll also find Hindustanis, Javanese, Lebanese, African descendants, and Creole mixes. The main religions are Christianity, Hinduism, and Islam. In all, there are about 1.2 million

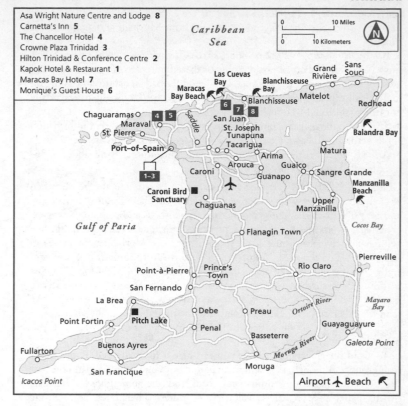

Asa Wright Nature Centre and Lodge **8**
Carnetta's Inn **5**
The Chancellor Hotel **4**
Crowne Plaza Trinidad **3**
Hilton Trinidad & Conference Centre **2**
Kapok Hotel & Restaurant **1**
Maracas Bay Hotel **7**
Monique's Guest House **6**

inhabitants, whose language is English, although you may also hear the local dialect, Trinibagianese.

One of the most industrialized nations in the Caribbean, and one of the biggest exporters of oil in the Western Hemisphere, Trinidad is also blessed with huge 46-hectare (114-acre) Pitch Lake, the source of most of the world's asphalt. It's also the home of Angostura Bitters, the recipe for which is a closely guarded secret.

TRINIDAD ESSENTIALS

GETTING THERE From North America, Trinidad is one of the most distant islands in the Caribbean. **Caribbean Star** (© 800/744-7827) services Trinidad from Antigua, Barbados, Dominica, Grenada, St. Kitts, St. Lucia, and St. Vincent. **Air DCA** (© 800/327-7230 or 868/623-6522; www.flydca.net) has direct flights from Curaçao to Trinidad Wednesday to Monday.

In addition, **Air Canada** (© 888/247-2262 or 868/664-4065; www.air canada.ca) flies daily nonstop from Toronto to Trinidad, and **British Airways** (© 800/247-9297; www.britishairways.com) has three flights a week (Mon, Thurs, and Sat), leaving year-round from London's Gatwick Airport. **Monarch Airlines** (© 868/639-0484) also offers two flights weekly from London's Gatwick Airport. Because of the legendary toughness of Trinidadian Customs, it's preferable to arrive during the day (presumably when your stamina is at its peak) if you can schedule it. Most passengers from eastern North America fly

American Airlines (© 800/433-7300 in the U.S., or 868/627-7013; www. aa.com), which has one daily nonstop flight from San Juan and another from Miami.

BWIA (© 800/538-2942 or 868/625-1010; www.bwee.com) offers service from New York to Port-of-Spain. Some of these flights are direct and nonstop; most of them touch down en route, usually on Barbados, before continuing on to Trinidad, the airline's home base. From Miami, BWIA usually offers a daily nonstop flight to Port-of-Spain.

Trinidad is the transfer point for many passengers to Tobago. For information about getting to Tobago, see the section "Tobago," later in this chapter.

Arrivals are at Trinidad's Piarco International Airport, lying about a 30-minute ride east of Port-of-Spain.

GETTING AROUND   Trinidad **taxis** are unmetered, and they're identified by their license plates, which begin with the letter *H*. There are also "pirate taxis" as well: private cars that cruise around like regular taxis and pick up passengers. Whether you take an official taxi or a pirate taxi, make sure you agree on the fare beforehand, otherwise you're likely to get ripped off. Maxi Taxis, or vans, can also be hailed on the street. A fare from Piarco Airport into Port-of-Spain generally costs US$20 (US$30 after 10pm). Call © 868/628-8294 for taxi information. A 50% surcharge is added to fares after 10pm. The most reliable service is found by calling © 868/628-TAXI, which we have found to be less expensive than the other cabbies. Also, this company doesn't impose a night surcharge. If you call them, a taxi will be sent to the airport for you or anywhere else you might be within the area.

To avoid the anxiety of driving, you can **hire a local driver** for your sightseeing jaunts. Although it costs more than doing it yourself, it alleviates the hassles of badly marked (or unmarked) roads and the sometimes-bizarre local driving patterns. Most drivers will serve as guides. Their rates, however, are based on route distances, so get an overall quotation and agree on the actual fare before setting off.

If you're brave enough to set out via **rental car,** arm yourself with a good map and *never forget:* Drive on the left. Visitors with a valid international driver's license or a license from the United States, Canada, France, or the United Kingdom may drive without extra documentation for up to 3 months.

Since the island is one of the world's largest exporters of asphalt, Trinidad's some 7,245km (4,494 miles) of roads are well paved. However, outback roads should be avoided during the rainy season, as they're often narrow, twisting, and prone to washouts. Inquire about conditions, particularly if you're headed for the north coast. The fierce traffic jams of Port-of-Spain are legendary, and night driving anywhere on the island is rather hazardous.

The major U.S.-based car-rental firms currently have no franchises on the island, so you'll have to make arrangements with a local firm (go over the terms and insurance agreements carefully). Count on spending about US$40 to US$60 per day or more, with unlimited mileage included. Your best bet is one of the firms maintaining offices at Piarco Airport. These include **Econo-Car Rentals** (© 868/669-2342), **Thrifty** (© 868/669-0602), and the simply named **Auto Rentals** (© 868/669-2277). *A word of warning:* Although these local car-rental firms technically accept reservations, a car may not be waiting for you even if you reserve ahead of time.

All the towns of Trinidad are linked by regular **bus service** from Port-of-Spain. Fares are low (about US$1 for runs within the capital). However, the old

Fun Fact **The Carnival of Trinidad**

Called "the world's most colorful festival," the **Carnival of Trinidad** is a spectacle of dazzling costumes and gaiety. Hundreds of bands of masqueraders parade through the cities on the Monday and Tuesday preceding Ash Wednesday, bringing traffic to a standstill. The island seems to explode with music, fun, and dancing.

Some of the **Carnival costumes** cost hundreds of dollars. "Bands" might depict the birds of Trinidad, such as the scarlet ibis and the keskidee, or a bevy of women might come out in the streets dressed as cats. Costumes are also satirical and comical.

Trinidad, of course, is the land of **calypso,** which grew out of the folk songs of the African–West Indian immigrants. The lyrics command great attention, as they're rich in satire and innuendo. The calypsonian is a poet-musician, and lyrics have often toppled politicians from office. In banter and bravado, the calypsonian gives voice to the sufferings and aspirations of his people. At Carnival time, the artist sings his compositions to spectators in tents. There's one show a night at each of the calypso tents around town, from 8pm to midnight. Tickets for these are sold in the afternoon at most record shops.

You can attend rehearsals of **steel bands** at their headquarters, called panyards, beginning about 7pm. Preliminary band competitions are held at the grandstand of Queen's Park Savannah in Port-of-Spain and at Skinner Park in San Fernando, beginning 2 weeks before Carnival.

Carnival parties, or fetes, with three or four orchestras at each one, are public and are advertised in the newspaper. For a really wild time, attend a party on Sunday night before Carnival Monday. To reserve tickets, contact the **National Carnival Committee,** Queen's Park Savannah, Port-of-Spain, Trinidad (© **868/627-1358**). Hotels are booked months in advance, and most inns raise their prices—often considerably—over Carnival.

buses are likely to be very overcrowded. Try to avoid them at rush hours, and beware of pickpockets.

FAST FACTS   Most **banks** are open Monday to Thursday from 8am to 2pm and Friday from 9am to noon and 3 to 5pm. **Citibank** has offices at 12 Queen's Park East, Port-of-Spain (© **868/625-1046** or 868/625-1049), and 18–30 High St., San Fernando (© **868/652-3691**). **Republic Bank Ltd.** (9–17 Park St.; © **868/625-4411**) and **Royal Bank of Trinidad & Tobago Ltd.** (Royal Court, 19–21 Park St.; © **868/623-1322**) are two of the many banks in Port-of-Spain with ATMs. You'll also find ATMs at some big supermarkets.

There is no 24-hour **pharmacy** on either island. In Port-of-Spain, **Star Lite Drugs** at Four Roads (© **868/632-0516**) is open Monday to Saturday from 8:30am to 9:30pm.

The **Port-of-Spain General Hospital** is located at 169 Charlotte St. (© **868/623-2951**). Medical care is sometimes limited, and physicians and health-care facilities expect immediate cash payment for services.

The main **post office** (℅ **868/625-4784**) is on Wrightson Road, Port-of-Spain, and is open Monday to Friday from 7am to 5pm.

If your hotel can't send or receive faxes for you, try **TSTT Communications,** Caroline Wilson Street, Port-of-Spain (℅ **868/639-1195**).

ACCOMMODATIONS

The number of hotels on Trinidad is limited, and you shouldn't expect your Port-of-Spain room to open directly onto a white-sand beach. The nearest beach is a long, costly taxi ride away. Hotels are booked months in advance of Carnival (the week before Ash Wednesday) and they raise their rates, often considerably, at this time.

EXPENSIVE

Asa Wright Nature Centre & Lodge 🏕 *Finds* There really isn't anything else like this in the Caribbean. Known to bird-watchers throughout the world, this center sits on 74 remote hectares (183 acres) of protected land at an elevation of 360m (1,180 ft.) in the rain-forested northern mountain range of Trinidad, 16km (10 miles) north of Arima, beside Blanchisseuse Road. Hummingbirds, toucans, bellbirds, manakins, several varieties of tanagers, and the rare oilbird are all on the property. Back-to-basics accommodations are available in the lodge, in the 1908 Edwardian main house, and in the cottages on elevated ground above the main house. Even though they offer less privacy, we prefer the two rooms in the main house, which are more atmospheric and are outfitted with dark-wood antiques and two king-size beds each. Furnishings in the cottages are rather plain but comfortable. Shower-only bathrooms are a bit cramped, but you generally get hot water—count yourself lucky.

Guided tours are available on the nature center's grounds, which contain several well-maintained trails and a natural waterfall with a pool in which guests can swim (getting to the beach involves a 90-min. drive to the coast).

The kitchen prepares Caribbean food, based for the most part on the catch of the day. Some regional meat dishes, such as stewed goat, are also offered.

Spring Hill Estate, Arima, Trinidad, W.I. (For information or reservations, call the toll-free number or write Caligo Ventures, 156 Bedford Rd., Armonk, NY 10504.) ℅ **800/426-7781** in the U.S., or 868/667-4655. Fax 868/667-4540. www.asawright.org. 24 units. Winter US$260 double; off season US$180 double. Rates include all meals, afternoon tea, and a welcoming rum punch on arrival. MC, V. Children 8 and over accepted if accompanied by an adult, or 17 if unaccompanied. **Amenities:** Dining room; bar; swimming pond; laundry service; rooms for those with limited mobility. *In room:* Ceiling fan, no phone.

Crowne Plaza Trinidad 🏕 This bland but modern inn is a favorite with business travelers who tolerate the noise and congestion for the convenient location, a 5-minute walk from the city center. The recently renovated bedrooms, tastefully decorated in pastels, contain private balconies and two double beds. The hotel has added two executive floors and such luxuries as trouser presses, magnifying mirrors, mahogany furniture, and brass lamps. The bathrooms have shower/tub combinations and dual basins in faux marble or granite.

The Olympia Restaurant, adorned with Roman-style pillars, cascading plants, and French decor, is the only revolving restaurant in the Caribbean and serves standard international cuisine.

Wrightson Rd. at London Rd. (P.O. Box 1017), Port-of-Spain, Trinidad, W.I. ℅ **800/2-CROWNE** in the U.S. and Canada, or 868/625-3366. Fax 868/625-4166. www.crowneplaza.com. 245 units. Year-round US$130–US$185 double; US$245–US$600 suite. AE, MC, V. **Amenities:** 2 restaurants; bar; pool; fitness center; business center; 24-hr. room service; babysitting; laundry service; dry cleaning; nonsmoking rooms; rooms for those with limited mobility. *In room:* A/C, TV, dataport, beverage maker, hair dryer, iron/ironing board, safe.

Hilton Trinidad & Conference Centre ★★ *(Kids)* This is the most dramatic and architecturally sophisticated hotel on Trinidad. The lobby is on the uppermost floor, while the guest rooms are staggered in rocky but verdant terraces that sweep down the steep hillside. The location just above Queen's Park Savannah affords most of its rooms a view of the sea and mountains. The higher rooms are cheaper than lower ones. This is not the greatest Hilton in the world, or even in the Caribbean, but all rooms still meet international first-class standards, with queen-size or twin beds, balconies, generous closet space, and modern tiled bathrooms with combination shower/tubs. Accommodations in the main wing are the most sought after, as they have good views over Queen's Park Savannah. Executive Floor rooms have upgraded services and amenities.

The main dining room, La Boucan (see "Dining," below), contains museum-quality murals by Geoffrey Holder, one of the island's best-known artists.

Lady Young Rd. (P.O. Box 442), Port-of-Spain, Trinidad, W.I. ⓒ 800/HILTONS in the U.S. and Canada, or 868/624-3211. Fax 868/624-4485. www.hilton.com. 380 units. Year-round US$125–US$229 double; US$250–US$300 suite. AE, DC, MC, V. **Amenities:** 2 restaurants; 3 bars; outdoor pool; 2 tennis courts; fitness center; sauna; car rental; salon; massage; babysitting; children's activities; laundry service. *In room:* A/C, TV, dataport, minibar, hair dryer, safe.

MODERATE

Kapok Hotel & Restaurant ★ *(Value)* This modern but unpretentious nine-floor hotel, in the residential suburb of St. Clair, is an efficient, well-maintained operation run by the Chan family. It's located away from the worst traffic of the city, near the zoo, the Presidential Palace, and just north of Queen's Park Savannah. From its lounge, you'll have panoramic views of the Savannah and the Gulf of Paria. The comfortably appointed, spacious rooms have wicker furnishings and private bathrooms with combination shower/tubs. For a hotel of this price range, it comes as a surprise to find phones with voice mail and dataports, and even room service until 10pm. The rooftop restaurant, Tiki Village, serves Chinese and Polynesian food. In the back is an expanded pool area with a bistro/bar, waterfall, garden, menagerie, and sun deck.

16–18 Cotton Hill, St. Clair, Trinidad, W.I. ⓒ 868/622-6441. Fax 868/622-9677. www.kapokhotel.com. 94 units. Year-round US$142–US$172 double; US$205 suite. Additional person US$25 per night. Rates include continental breakfast. AE, MC, V. **Amenities:** 2 restaurants; outdoor pool; fitness center; business services; room service (7am–10pm); babysitting; laundry service; self-service laundry; nonsmoking rooms; rooms for those with limited mobility. *In room:* A/C, TV, dataport, kitchenette (in some), beverage maker, hair dryer.

Maracas Bay Hotel If you'd like to sightsee in Trinidad and also be on the beach, Maracas Bay Hotel is a decent choice. It's the only beachfront hotel in all of Trinidad, and even here, you'll have to walk across the coastal road to reach the sands. Owned and operated by a local family, it's nestled in a valley on sloping terrain across the road from Maracas Bay. As the crow flies, it's only 11km (6¾ miles) north of Port-of-Spain. But dense traffic and a winding road mean at least a 45-minute drive from the commercial center of the capital. There's a bar/lounge accented with Hindu art, and an unpretentious dining room. Bedrooms contain simple furnishings, white-and-blue walls, and terra-cotta tile floors. Each unit has two queen-size beds and a tiled bathroom with a shower/tub combination. The beach, a wide strip of white sand bordered by palm trees, is a lovely oasis from the bustle of Port-of-Spain. The inn provides chaises and beach umbrellas for its guests, though nobody will be taking your drink order on the sands.

Maracas Bay, Trinidad, W.I. ⓒ 868/669-1914. Fax 868/669-1643. www.maracasbay.com. 32 units. Year-round US$75–US$120 double. Extra person US$13. AE, MC, V. **Amenities:** Restaurant; bar; room service (8am–9pm); rooms for those with limited mobility. *In room:* A/C, safe, no phone.

INEXPENSIVE

Carnetta's Inn ✦ _Finds_   This home is in the suburb of Andalusia in the cool and scenic Maraval neighborhood, about a 15-minute ride from the central business district and a 45-minute ride to Maracas Beach, the most popular sand strip on island. It's owned by Winston and Carnetta Borrell—both have a wealth of information about touring the island (he was a former director of tourism) and both are keen naturalists. Winston is a gardener, filling his property with orchids, ginger lilies, and anthuriums, among other plant life. Carnetta grows her own herbs to produce some of the finest meals around. The rooms have floral themes and are furnished in a tropical style. For the most privacy, request a guest room on the upper floor. Our preferred nest is Le Flamboyant, opening onto the little inn's patio. Most of the rooms are medium in size, and each has a small and immaculately maintained bathroom with shower.

99 Saddle Rd., Maraval, Trinidad, W.I. ✆ 868/628-2732. Fax 868/628-7717. www.carnettasinn.com. 14 units. Year-round US$55–US$60 double; US$70 triple. Dinner US$13 extra. AE, MC, V. **Amenities:** Restaurant; bar; car rental; limited room service; laundry service; nonsmoking rooms. _In room:_ A/C, TV, kitchenette (in some), safe.

The Chancellor Hotel _Value_   Designed for the business traveler, this lovely little inn is also ideal for vacationers. In the valley of St. Ann's, the hotel sits in lush landscaped gardens studded with palms. An Iberian-style courtyard filled with sculptures and a cascading waterfall emptying into a swimming pool is one of the hotel's more attractive features. Each of the accommodations is tastefully and comfortably furnished with batik quilts, wall hangings, and teakwood desks. All units come with a small tiled bathroom with shower. The beds are Victorian style.

The chef prepares both Caribbean and international dishes, and locals often come here for the fresh fish of the day. The chef is known for game specials such as stewed deer. More standard meats like grilled lamb chops or grilled pork chops are also served.

5A St. Ann's Ave., St. Ann's, Trinidad. ✆ 868/623-0883. Fax 868/623-0883. www.thechancellorhotel.com. 22 units. Year-round US$95–US$105 double; US$135 suite; US$150 family suite. AE, MC, V. **Amenities:** Restaurant; bar; outdoor pool; limited room service; laundry service; nonsmoking rooms; rooms for those with limited mobility. _In room:_ A/C, TV, dataport, fridge (in some), hair dryer, iron/ironing board.

Monique's Guest House _Kids_   In the lush Maraval Valley just an 8-minute (5km/3-mile) drive north of the center of Port-of-Spain, Monique's offers 20 bungalow-style rooms. Some are large enough to accommodate up to four people, and 10 rooms offer kitchenettes with their own porches. The biggest are units 25 and 26, which can sleep up to six, though that would be a bit crowded. Families are fond of booking rooms here because of the kitchenettes. Accommodations have open balconies so you can enjoy the tropical breezes and scenic hills. The bathrooms are well organized and spotless, each with a shower. The air-conditioned dining room and bar offers a medley of local and international dishes, and Maracas Beach is only a 25-minute drive away.

114–116 Saddle Rd., Maraval, Trinidad, W.I. ✆ 868/628-3334. Fax 868/622-3232. www.moniquestrinidad. com. 20 units. Year-round US$72–US$84 double. AE, DC, MC, V. **Amenities:** Restaurant; bar; limited room service; babysitting; laundry service; nonsmoking rooms; rooms for those with limited mobility. _In room:_ A/C, TV, dataport, hair dryer, iron/ironing board.

DINING

The food in Trinidad should be better, considering all the different culinary backgrounds that shaped the island. As it is, we recommend sticking to local specials like stuffed crabs and _chip-chip_ (tiny clamlike shellfish), but skip the armadillo and opossum stews. Spicy *rotis* filled with vegetables or ground meat seems to be everyone's favorite lunch, and the drink of choice is a fresh rum punch flavored with Angostura Bitters. Except for a few fancy places, dress tends to be very casual.

EXPENSIVE

Apsara ✵ NORTHERN INDIAN   Marie Kavanagh welcomes you graciously to her restaurant, whose name translates as "heavenly dancer." An island painter, Sarah Beckett, has decorated the place with her contemporary take on Moghul art. The skilled chefs are from India, bringing with them their exotic palette of spices. The menu is widely varied—almost too large—but the dishes are a delight, especially tandoori specialties like jumbo shrimp marinated in yogurt, fresh lime juice, and Indian spices. We're also fond of the tender lamb cooked in a rich curry sauce. Many dishes will please vegetarians. Some of the main courses emerge from the oven on a sizzling platter—try *machi masala,* a hot and spicy fish cooked in a rich and aromatic sauce. Most meals end with the masala tea flavored with clove, cardamom, and cinnamon.

13 Queen's Park East, Port-of-Spain. ℂ 868/623-7659. Reservations required. Main courses TT$28–TT$185 (US$4.50–US$30). AE, MC, V. Mon–Sat 11am–3pm and 6–11pm.

Battimamzelle ✵ *Finds* *Kids* CARIBBEAN/INTERNATIONAL   The name of this restaurant, which means "dragonfly" in local dialect, sets the whimsical tone for this joint, whose decor is often called "Mexicanish"—its red and yellow walls are adorned with flower paintings and the lamps have red shades with imprints of *battimamzelles* on them. In addition to his jazzy decor, the talented chef, Khalid Mohammed, operates this slightly hidden little spot in the small Coblentz Inn. For his inspiration, the chef roams the world, offering Greek-style lamb (but stuffed with Moroccan sausage) and served with fruits, nuts, and couscous. The barbecued kingfish is brushed with fresh guava and served with pumpkin. The delightful Cornish hens come with a fricassee of wild mushrooms, and the 22-ounce "cowboy" rib-eye steak is tantalizingly provided with hash browns and sizzling onions. A kiddie menu is also offered on request. Most dishes are priced at the lower end of the scale.

In the Coblentz Inn, 44 Coblentz Ave., Cascade. ℂ 868/621-0591. Reservations recommended. Main courses US$14–US$40. AE, MC, V. Mon–Fri 7am–11pm; Sat 6–11pm. Closed Dec 22–29.

La Boucan ✵ INTERNATIONAL   The finest hotel restaurant on Trinidad, this establishment satisfies the eye and the palate, though not all dishes reflect the nurturing and refinement they should. Taking its name from the smoking process by which pirates and buccaneers used to preserve meat for long voyages, La Boucan incorporates this smoky flavor into many of its West Indian dishes. Against one of its longest walls stretches a graceful mural by Geoffrey Holder, one of the most famous artists and dancers in the Caribbean. Typical choices include lobster (grilled or thermidor); a daily selection of fish (usually grouper or snapper), which is grilled, poached, or pan-fried and served with herb-butter sauce; and prime rib of beef. The desserts are sumptuous, especially the chocolate crème brûlée and a rich, creamy cheesecake. A pianist provides entertainment on Monday and Wednesday and on weekends there's a dance band.

In the Hilton Trinidad, Lady Young Rd., Port-of-Spain. ℂ 868/624-3211. Reservations required. Main courses US$20–US$47. AE, MC, V. Daily 7–11:30pm.

Plantation House Restaurant ✵ CARIBBEAN   This 1920s gingerbread colonial building makes an elegant setting for the excellent cuisine here. The chefs search for quality ingredients and allow their natural flavors to shine. One of our favorite dishes is red snapper stuffed with crabmeat in ginger sauce. For real island taste, however, we suggest grilled chicken in a Cajun sauce and Shirley pepper gravy or a kabob of fresh shrimp and scallops. Only the most adventurous will try the game specialties like stewed agouti that sometimes appear on the menu. Agouti is a Trinidad-based rodent—and a big one at that. A spicy and refreshing appetizer is strips of conch marinated in a mixture of lime juice and red peppers.

38 Ariapita Ave., Woodbrook. © 868/628-5551. Reservations recommended. Main courses US$12–US$35. AE, MC, V. Mon–Fri 11:30am–2:30pm and 6:30–10:30pm; Sat 6:30–10:30pm.

Solimar ⚜ INTERNATIONAL   Some think this restaurant offers the most creative cuisine in Trinidad and Tobago. Established by Joe Brown, an English-born chef who worked for many years in the kitchens of Hilton hotels around the world, it occupies a garden-style building cooled by open walls and ceiling fans. As you dine, you'll hear the sound of an artificial waterfall that cascades into a series of fishponds.

The menu, which changes every 3 months, presents local ingredients inspired by the cuisines of the world. The results are usually very convincing. Dishes might include an English-inspired combination of grilled breast of chicken and jumbo shrimp dressed with a lobster sauce, and a Sri Lankan dish of herb-flavored chicken vindaloo. The restaurant's double-chocolate mousse is the highlight of any meal here.

6 Nook Ave. (next to the Normandie Hotel, 6km/3¾ miles northwest of the city center), St. Ann's. © 868/624-6267. Reservations recommended. Main courses TT$110–TT$325 (US$18–US$52). AE, MC, V. Mon–Sat 6–10:30pm, Fri opening at noon. Closed 2 weeks in mid-Aug (exact dates vary).

Tamnak Thai ⚜⚜ THAI   In the landmark center at Queen's Park Savannah, this upmarket restaurant lies in a restored colonial home and is the island nation's finest Asian restaurant, specializing in the regional fare of Thailand. In an elegant, tasteful setting evocative of old Saigon, refined dishes are beautifully served in luxuriant surroundings, especially if you select a table on the patio. The kitchen makes the most of excellent ingredients, fashioning them into subtle dishes like red-curry chicken in coconut milk or stir-fried lobster with spring onions. Our favorite dish is the steamed mussels in a clay pot with fresh herbs such as lemon grass. If you're with a large party, you can order a selection of hors d'oeuvres that are full of zest and flavor. Many dishes are very spicy, filled with fiery chiles, but there are also milder choices.

13 Queen's Park East, Port-of-Spain. © 868/625-9715. Reservations required. Main courses TT$85–TT$185 (US$14–US$30); set lunch TT$75 ($12). AE, MC, V. Mon–Fri 11am–11pm; Sat–Sun 6–11pm.

MODERATE

Restaurant Singho CHINESE   This restaurant, with an almost mystically illuminated bar and aquarium, is on the second floor of one of the capital's largest shopping malls, midway between the commercial center of Port-of-Spain and the Queen's Park Savannah. For Trinidad, the food isn't bad: It's better than your typical chop suey and chow mein joint, and many of its dishes are quite tasty and spicy. A la carte choices include shrimp with oyster sauce, stewed or curried beef, almond pork, and spareribs with black-bean sauce. The to-go service is one of the best in town. The Wednesday-night buffet offers an enormous selection of main dishes, along with heaps of rice and fresh vegetables, and dessert.

Long Circular Mall, Level 3, Port-of-Spain. © 868/628-2077. Main courses TT$50–TT$246 (US$8–US$39); Wed night buffet TT$125 (US$20). AE, MC, V. Daily 11am–10pm.

Veni Mangé ★★ *Finds* CREOLE/INTERNATIONAL   Originally built in the 1930s and set about 2km (1¼ mile) west of Port-of-Spain's center, Veni Mangé (whose name means "come and eat") is painted in coral tones and has louvered windows on hinges that ventilate the masses of potted plants. It was established by two of the best-known women in Trinidad, Allyson Hennessy and her sister, Rosemary Hezekiah. Allyson, the Julia Child of Trinidad, hosts a daily TV talk show that's broadcast throughout the island.

Start with the bartender's special, a coral-colored fruit punch that's a rich, luscious mixture of papaya, guava, orange, and passion fruit juices. The authentic callaloo soup, according to Trinidadian legend, can make a man propose marriage. With a menu that changes daily, the main courses might be curried crab or West Indian hot pot (a variety of meats cooked Creole style), or perhaps a vegetable lentil loaf. The helpings are large, but if you still have room, order the pineapple upside-down cake. On Friday, the bar buzzes, but the only foods served are snacks known as "cutters" because they cut the appetite so you can drink more punch.

67A Ariapita Ave., Port-of-Spain. © **868/624-4597**. Reservations recommended. Main courses TT$60–TT$82 (US$9.60–US$13). AE, MC, V. Mon–Fri 11:30am–3pm; Wed 7–10pm; Fri open for bar service only 11:30am–3pm and 7–10pm.

HITTING THE BEACH

Trinidad isn't thought of as beach country, yet it has more beach frontage than any other island in the West Indies. The only problem is that most of its beaches are undeveloped and in distant, remote places, far removed from Port-of-Spain. The closest of the better beaches, **Maracas Bay,** is a full 29km (18 miles) from Port-of-Spain on the North Coast Road. It's a delight to visitors, with its protected cove and quaint fishing village. The only drawbacks are the crowds and the strong current. Facilities include restrooms and snack bars.

Farther up the North Coast Road is **Las Cuevas Bay,** which is far less crowded. The narrow beach is set against a backdrop of palm trees. There are changing rooms and vendors selling luscious tropical fruit juices.

To reach the other beaches, you'll have to range farther afield, perhaps to **Blanchisseuse Bay** on the North Coast Road. This narrow strip of sand set against palms is excellent for a picnic, although there are no facilities.

Bodysurfers frequent **Balandra Bay** on the northeast coast, but the waters generally aren't good for more pedestrian swimming.

Manzanilla Beach, along the east coast of Trinidad, north of Cocos Bay and south of Matura Bay, is not ideal for swimming. Nonetheless, it has some picnic facilities, and the view of the water is dramatic.

SPORTS & OTHER OUTDOOR PURSUITS

For serious golf and tennis, we recommend that you try another island.

DEEP-SEA FISHING   Some of the best fishing in the Caribbean is possible in the waters off the northwest coast of Trinidad—or at least Franklin D. Roosevelt used to think so. Try **Hard Play Fishing Charters,** 13 The Evergreen, Auchenskeoch, Buccoo (© **868/639-7108** or 868/682-3474). Your skipper is "Frothy" De Silva, who charges US$350 for 4-hour trips on his 12m (41-ft.) vessel, *Hard Play.* Another good possibility is **Dillon's Fishing Charter,** Crown Point (© **868/639-8765**), offering 4-hour trips costing US$350 or full-day trips for US$500. Along with record catches in blue marlin, fishermen also pursue wahoo, mahimahi, kingfish, and barracuda.

GOLF   The oldest golf club on the island, **St. Andrew's Golf Course,** Moka Estate (© **868/629-2314**), is in Maraval, about 3km (2 miles) from Port-of-Spain. This 18-hole course has been internationally acclaimed ever since it hosted the 1976 Hoerman Cup Golf Tournament. There's a full-service clubhouse on the premises. Greens fees are TT$100 to TT$185 (US$16–US$30) for 18 holes. Club rental costs TT$100 (US$16). Hours are daily 6am to 6pm.

TENNIS   At the **Trinidad Country Club,** Champs-Elysées, Maraval (© **868/622-3470**), six courts are lit at night. You must purchase a day pass for TT$25 (US$4) and pay an additional TT$5 (US80¢) per hour of play during the day or TT$22 (US$3.50) per hour at night. Visitors can also obtain a temporary pass for 1 month at the cost of TT$233 (US$37). There are public courts in Port-of-Spain on the grounds of the Prince's Building (ask at your hotel for directions).

EXPLORING TRINIDAD
ORGANIZED TOURS
Sightseeing tours are offered by **Trinidad & Tobago Sightseeing Tours,** 12 Western Main Rd., St. James (© **868/628-1051**), in late-model sedans with a trained driver/guide. Several different tours are offered, including a daily city tour that takes you past (but not inside) the main points of interest of Port-of-Spain. The 2½-hour tour costs US$25 per person for two, or US$20 per person for three or more.

You'll see tropical splendor at its best on a Port-of-Spain/Maracas Bay/Saddle Road jaunt leaving at 9am or 1pm daily, lasting 4 hours. The tour begins with a drive around Port-of-Spain, passing the main points of interest in town and then going on through mountain scenery. The cost is US$30 per person.

PORT-OF-SPAIN ✦
One of the busiest harbors in the Caribbean, Trinidad's capital, Port-of-Spain, can be explored on foot. Start out at **Queen's Park Savannah** ✦, on the northern edge of the city. "The Savannah" consists of 80 hectares (198 acres), complete with soccer, cricket, and rugby fields, and vendors hawking coconut water and *rotis.* This was once a sugar plantation, until it was swept by a fire in 1808 that destroyed hundreds of homes.

Among the Savannah's outstanding buildings is pink-and-blue **Queen's Royal College** ✦, containing a clock tower with Westminster chimes. Today a school for boys, it stands on Maraval Road at the corner of St. Clair Avenue. On the same road, the family home of the Roodal clan is affectionately called **"the gingerbread house"** by Trinidadians. It was built in the baroque style of the French Second Empire.

Nearby stands **Whitehall,** which was once a private mansion but today has been turned into the office of the prime minister of Trinidad and Tobago. In the Moorish style, it was erected in 1905 and served as the U.S. Army headquarters here during World War II. These houses, including Hayes Court, the residence of the Anglican bishop of Trinidad, and others, form what is known as the **"Magnificent Seven"** ✦ big mansions standing in a row.

On the south side of Memorial Park, a short distance from the Savannah and within walking distance of the major hotels, stands the **National Museum and Art Gallery,** 117 Frederick St. (© **868/623-5941**), open Tuesday to Saturday from 10am to 6pm, Sunday from 2 to 6pm. The free museum contains a representative exhibition of Trinidad artists, including an entire gallery devoted to Jean Michel Cazabon (1813–88), permanent collections of artifacts giving a general overview of the island's history and culture, Amerindian archaeology, British historical documents, and a small natural-history exhibition including geology, corals, and insect collections. There's also a large display filled with costumes dedicated to the colorful culture of Carnival.

At the southern end of Frederick Street, the main artery of Port-of-Spain's shopping district, stands **Woodford Square.** The gaudy **Red House,** a large neo-Renaissance structure built in 1906, is the seat of the government of Trinidad and Tobago. Nearby stands **Holy Trinity Cathedral,** whose Gothic look may remind you of the churches of England.

Another of the town's important landmarks is **Independence Square,** dating from Spanish days. Now mainly a parking lot, it stretches across the southern part of the capital from Wrightson Road to the **Cathedral of the Immaculate Conception.** This Roman Catholic church was built in 1815 in the neo-Gothic style and consecrated in 1832.

The cathedral has an outlet that leads to the **Central Market,** on Beetham Highway on the outskirts of Port-of-Spain. Here you can see all the spices and fruits for which Trinidad is known. It's one of the island's most colorful sights, made all the more so by the wide diversity of people who sell their wares here.

North of the Savannah, the **Royal Botanical Gardens** (© 868/622-4221) cover 28 hectares (69 acres) and are open daily from 6am to 6pm; admission is free. The park is filled with flowering plants, shrubs, and rare and beautiful trees, including an orchid house. Seek out the raw beef tree: An incision made in its bark is said to resemble rare, bleeding roast beef. Guides will take you through and explain the luxuriant foliage. In the gardens is the **President's House,** official residence of the president of Trinidad and Tobago. Victorian in style, it was built in 1875.

Part of the gardens is the **Emperor Valley Zoo** (© 868/622-3530), in St. Clair, which shows a good selection of the fauna of Trinidad as well as some exotic animals from around the world. The star attractions are a family of mandrills, a reptile house, and open bird parks. You can take shady jungle walks through tropical vegetation. Admission is TT$4 (US65¢) for adults, TT$2 (US30¢) for children age 3 to 12, and free for children under 3. It's open daily from 9:30am to 6pm.

AROUND THE ISLAND

One of the most popular attractions in the area is the **Asa Wright Nature Centre** (© 800/426-7781 in the U.S. or 868/667-4655; www.asawright.org; see "Accommodations," earlier in this chapter). If you're not a guest of the hotel, you can call and reserve a space for its noonday lunch for US$9. It's also possible to reserve one of the daily guided tours of the sanctuary at 10:30am or 1:30pm, which costs US$12.

On a peak 330m (1,082 ft.) above Port-of-Spain, **Fort George** was built by Governor Sir Thomas Hislop in 1804 as a signal station in the days of the sailing ships. Once reached only by hikers, today it's accessible by an asphalt road. From its citadel, you can see the mountains of Venezuela. Locals refer to the climb up the winding road as "traveling up to heaven." The drive is only 16km (10 miles), but to play it safe, allow about 2 hours.

Pointe-à-Pierre Wild Fowl Trust, Le Riene Town House, Flagstaff Hill, Long Circular Road (© 868/658-4230, ext. 2512), is a 10-hectare (25-acre) bird sanctuary, 2 hours by car south of Port-of-Spain. The setting is unlikely, near an industrial area of the state-owned Petrotrin oil refinery, with flames spouting from flare stacks in the sky. However, in this seemingly inhospitable clime, wildfowl flourish amid such luxuriant vegetation as crape myrtle, flamboyant soursop and mango trees, even black sage bushes said to be good for high blood pressure. You can spot the yellow-billed jacana, plenty of Muscovies, and, if you're lucky, such endangered species as the toucan or the purple gallinule. Admission is TT$8 (US$1.30) or TT$3 (US50¢) for kids under age 12. Hours are Monday to Friday from 8am to 5pm, Saturday and Sunday by appointment only from 10am to 4pm.

Enhanced by the blue and purple hues of the sky at sunset, clouds of scarlet ibis, the national bird of Trinidad and Tobago, fly in from their feeding grounds to roost at the 104 sq. km (41-sq.-mile) **Caroni Bird Sanctuary** (© 868/645-1305), a big mangrove swamp interlaced with waterways. The setting couldn't be more idyllic, with blue, mauve, and white lilies; oysters growing on mangrove roots; and caimans resting on mud banks. Visitors are taken on a launch through these swamps to see the birds (bring along insect repellent). The most reliable tour operator is **James Meddoo,** Bamboo Grove Settlement, 1 Butler Hwy. (© 868/662-7356), who has toured the swamps for some 25 years. His 3-hour tour leaves daily at 3pm and costs US$10 per person, or US$5 for kids. The sanctuary is about a half-hour drive (11km/6¾ miles) south of Port-of-Spain.

Pitch Lake is on the west coast of Trinidad, with the village of Le Brea on its north shore. To reach it from Port-of-Spain, take the Solomon Hocoy Highway. It's about a 2-hour drive, depending on traffic. One of the wonders of the world, with a surface like elephant skin, the lake is 90m (295 ft.) deep at its center. It's possible to walk on its rough side, but we don't recommend that you proceed far. Legend has it that the lake devoured a tribe of Chayma Amerindians, punishing them for eating hummingbirds in which the souls of their ancestors reposed. The lake was formed millions of years ago, and it's believed that at one time it was a huge mud volcano into which muddy asphaltic oil seeped. Churned up and down by underground gases, the oil and mud eventually formed asphalt. According to legend, Sir Walter Raleigh discovered the lake in

---

Finds Evocative of India

It's like taking a shopping trip to India to visit the little town of Chaguanas, lying south of Port-of-Spain and the Parco International Airport. To get here, drive out Uriah Butler Highway and look for the turn-off sign to **Chaguanas.** This was the birthplace of the Nobel Prize–winning novelist V. S. Naipaul.

As you come in on Main Road you'll think you've miraculously arrived in Calcutta. A hodgepodge of shops sell Indian clothing, jars of spicy chutney, and Bollywood music. The gem of shops is **Radika's Pottery,** 183 Edinburgh Village (© 868/665-4267), run for three generations by the Pickal family, who are acclaimed around the world for their exquisite pottery—jugs, pots, candle holders, whatever. Even Naipaul is a fan of this pottery, which is exhibited at international art fairs.

If you're in town for lunch, head for the very simple but good **Indo-Chinese Vegetarian Restaurant** on Main Road (© 868/665-6928). Main courses cost from US$1 to US$3 (anyone old enough to remember the prices of the 1950s?).

1595 and used the asphalt to caulk his ships. Today, the bitumen mined here is used to pave highways throughout the world. You can tour Pitch Lake on your own, paying an admission of US$5 per person. **Trinidad & Tobago Tours** (© **868/628-1051**) runs guided tours of the lake for US$60 per person. You'll find some bars and restaurants at Le Brea.

The **Saddle** ⚑ is a humped pass on a ridge dividing the Maraval and the Santa Cruz valleys. Along this circular run, you'll see luxuriant grapefruit, papaya, cassava, and cocoa trees. Leaving Port-of-Spain by Saddle Road, going past the Trinidad Country Club, you pass through Maraval Village and St. Andrew's Golf Course. The road rises to cross the ridge at the spot from which the Saddle gets its name. After going over the hump, you descend through Santa Cruz Valley (rich with giant bamboo), into San Juan, and back to the capital along Eastern Main Road or Beetham Highway. You'll see panoramic views in every direction; the 29km (18-mile) tour takes about 2 hours.

Nearly all cruise-ship passengers are hauled along Trinidad's "Skyline Highway," the **North Coast Road.** Starting at the Saddle, it winds for 11km (6¾ miles) across the Northern Range and down to Maracas Bay. At one point, 30m (98 ft.) above the Caribbean, you'll see on a clear day as far as Venezuela to the west or Tobago in the east, a sweep of some 161km (100 miles).

Most visitors take this route to the beach at **Maracas Bay,** the most splendid beach on Trinidad. Enclosed by mountains, it has the charm of a Caribbean fantasy: white sands, swaying coconut palms, and crystal-clear water (see "Hitting the Beach," above).

SHOPPING

One of the largest bazaars of the Caribbean, Port-of-Spain has luxury items from all over the globe, including Irish linens, English china, Scandinavian crystal, French perfumes, Swiss watches, and Japanese cameras. Even more interesting are the Asian bazaars, where you can pick up items in brass. Reflecting the island's culture are calypso shirts, sisal goods, woodwork, cascadura bracelets (made from the scales of the cascadura fish), silver jewelry in local motifs, and saris. For souvenirs, visitors often like to bring back figurines of limbo dancers, carnival masqueraders, or calypso singers.

Stecher's, Gulf City (© **868/657-6993**), is the best bet for luxury items—crystal, watches, jewelry, perfumes, Georg Jensen silver, Lladró, Wedgwood, Royal Doulton, Limoges, and Royal Albert. You can find other branches at Long Circular Mall and West Mall. You can also pay a last-minute call at their tax-free airport branches or at the cruise-ship complex at the Port-of-Spain docks.

Y. De Lima, 83 Queen St. (© **868/623-1364**), is a good store for watches, but the main focus is local jewelry. Its third-floor workroom will make whatever you want in jewelry or bronze. You might emerge with anything from steel drum earrings to a hibiscus-blossom brooch.

Art Creators and Suppliers, Apt. 402, Aldegonda Park, 7 St. Ann's Rd., St. Ann's (© **868/624-4369**), is in a banal apartment complex, but the paintings and sculptures here are among the finest in the Caribbean. Among the artistic giants displayed are Glasgow, Sundiata, Keith Ward, Jackie Hinkson, and many others.

Lovers of Caribbean art also flock to the **101 Art Gallery,** 101 Tragarete Rd. (© **868/628-4081**), in Port-of-Spain. This is the best showcase for the hottest local talent. Some of local artist Sarah Beckett's work is viewed so highly that her abstract oils appear on regional stamps. Often you can meet some of the artists here, especially on Tuesday evenings during openings. The gallery is closed on Sunday and Monday.

Gallery 1-2-3-4, in the Normandie Hotel, 10 Nook Ave., St. Ann's Village (© **868/625-5502**), is more iconoclastic and less conservative than any other gallery on the island. Since it opened in 1985, it has attracted the attention of the art world for its wide selection of Caribbean artists.

The Market, 10 Nook Ave., St. Ann's (© **868/624-1181**), is one of the most fashionable shopping complexes on Trinidad. Some 20 boutiques represent the best jewelers, designers, and art dealers on the island. You'll find a wide assortment of clothing, cosmetics, bags, shoes, china, tableware, handcrafts, and accessories. The complex forms an interconnected bridge among the Normandie Hotel and Restaurant, the restaurant Vidalia, and Gallery 1-2-3-4.

The Boutique, 43 Syndeham Ave., St. Ann's (© **868/624-3274**), is a notable handcrafts outlet and a showcase for batik silks created by Althea Bastien, one of Trinidad's finest artisans. Her fabric art is highly prized but reasonably priced. She also sells shirts, scarves, and ties.

If you'd like to go home with some music of Trinidad, head for **Rhyner's Record Shop,** 54 Prince St. (© **868/623-5673**), which has the best selection of soca and calypso, plus other types of music. There's another branch at the airport (© **868/669-3064**).

TRINIDAD AFTER DARK

The most popular spot on the weekends, although busy any night, is **Trotters,** at Maraval and Sweet Briar roads, St. Clair (© **868/627-8768**), a rustic, earthy, and multilevel English-style sports bar and pub. There's an eatery on the upper level. The bartenders stock more than 25 beers from around the world, and the pub has 30 TV monitors blaring at all times. There's pub grub, of course, such as barbecue ribs and chicken. Friday night a DJ is brought in for your listening pleasure, at which time a US$7 cover is imposed after 10pm.

Known for its pop-rock nights, **HiRpm,** Gulf City Mall, South Trunk Road, La Romain (© **868/652-3760**), lies slightly out of town, reached by heading south of Port-of-Spain, following the South Trunk Road to the mall. Attracting mostly a 21-to-35 age group, it features different entertainment on different nights—for example, techno night on Tuesday, rock bands on Wednesday. Club nights are on weekends when there is a great mix of music and a gyrating dance party. On Saturday the action begins at noon and doesn't stop until Sunday morning.

You can catch us having a beer at **Mas Camp Pub,** corner of French Street and Avenue Ariapata in Woodbrook (© **868/627-4042**). This place has a big stage where some of the best live bands in Trinidad frequently appear (or a DJ rules the night). There's also a reliable kitchen dishing up local specialties.

Local joints come and go with alarming frequency, but locals continue to flock to the live music at **The Base,** Main Street (no phone), at Chaguaramas, a 20-minute drive or taxi ride west of Port-of-Spain. This nightclub takes its name from its former role as a World War II air base. Open Friday and Saturday night (no set hours). Also on this former airfield is The Base's competitor, **Anchorage,** Point Gourde Road (© **868/634-4334**), a popular gathering spot for "sundowners." Later on groups head across the base to **Pier 1,** Williams Bay (© **868/634-4426**), for dancing. Back in town, British pub–style **Pelican,** 2–4 Coblentz Ave., St. Ann's (© **868/624-7486**), is a hot drinking spot, especially on the weekend. It draws a very mixed crowd, including singles and businessmen (who wish they were single, at least for the night), plus a colony of Trinidadian gays.

3 Tobago

Tobago lies 32km (20 miles) northeast of Trinidad, to which it's connected by frequent flights. Long known as a honeymooner's paradise, Tobago's idyllic natural beauty makes it one of the greatest escapes in the Caribbean. It has forests of breadfruit, mango, cocoa, and citrus through which a chartreuse-colored iguana will suddenly dart. It's for those who like a generous dose of sand, sun, and solitude, in a mellow atmosphere. Snorkelers especially will find plenty to entertain them.

Unlike bustling Trinidad, Tobago is sleepy, and Trinidadians come here, especially on weekends, to enjoy the wide, sandy beaches. The legendary home of Daniel Defoe's Robinson Crusoe, Tobago is only 43km-long (27-miles) and 12km-wide (7½-miles). The people are hospitable, and their villages are so tiny that they seem to blend in with the landscape.

The island's village-like capital and main port, **Scarborough,** lies on the southern coast. Surrounded by mountains, its bay provides a scenic setting, but the town itself is rather plain. Most of the shops are clustered in streets around the local market.

TOBAGO ESSENTIALS

GETTING THERE   Combining services with BWIA, **LIAT** (© 868/624-4727) has two daily flights from Trinidad to Tobago. If you'd like to skip Trinidad completely, you can book a LIAT flight with direct service to Tobago from either Barbados or Grenada. There are also regular flights from Trinidad to Tobago on **Tobago Express** (© 868/625-1010) and **Caribbean Star** (© 800/744-7827).

Tobago's small **airport** lies at Crown Point (© 868/639-8531 or 868/639-0509), near the island's southwestern tip.

It's possible to travel between Trinidad and Tobago by **ferry service,** although the trip takes 5½ to 6 hours. Call the **Port Authority of Trinidad and Tobago** (© 868/639-2416 in Scarborough, Tobago, or 868/625-3055 in Port-of-Spain) for departure times. The round-trip fare is TT$160 (US$26) in economy or TT$61 (US$9.75) in tourist class.

GETTING AROUND   From the airport to your accommodations, you can take a **taxi,** which will cost US$8 to US$36, depending on the location of your hotel (taxis are unmetered). You can also arrange (or have your hotel do it for you) a **sightseeing tour** by taxi. Rates must be negotiated on an individual basis.

If you want to do extensive touring, we recommend a car as attractions are very spread out. To **rent a car** you have to rely on local companies—no international car rental agencies are here as of yet. Options include **Rattan's Car Rentals** at Crown Point Airport (© 868/639-8271), and **Singh's Auto Rentals,** Grafton Beach Resort (© 868/639-0191). One final possibility is **Thrifty,** at the airport or at the Rex Turtle Beach Hotel, Courtland Bay, Black Rock (© 868/639-8507). Charges range from US$40 to US$60 a day.

Inexpensive **public buses** travel from one end of the island to the other several times a day. Expect an unscheduled stop at any passenger's doorstep, and never, never be in a hurry. Fares are TT$6 (US95¢).

FAST FACTS   Most **banks** are open Monday to Thursday from 8am to 2pm and Friday from 8am to 1pm and 3 to 5pm. **RBTT Bank Limited** (Main St. in Scarborough; © 868/639-2404) and **Republic Bank Ltd.** (Carrington St., Scarborough; © 868/639-2811) both have **ATMs.**

You can send mail from the island post offices: **Tobago Post Office,** Scarborough Wilser Road ((C) **868/639-2412**), and the **TT Post Office,** Cruise Ship Complex, Milford Road, Scarborough ((C) **868/660-7377**).

The **TSTT Phone Company** ((C) **868/639-1759**) lies at the end of Wilson Street in Scarborough.

For **tourist information,** contact the Tourism Division of the Tobago House of Assembly at the airport office ((C) **868/639-0509**), or at the main office on Mount Marie Road in Scarborough ((C) **868/639-2125**). Also dispensing tourism information is the **TIDCO** at IDC Mall, Sangsters Hill, Scarborough ((C) **868/639-4333**).

Scarborough Regional Hospital is on Fort George Street, Scarborough ((C) **868/639-2551**). Medical care is sometimes limited, and physicians and health-care facilities expect immediate cash payment for services.

ACCOMMODATIONS

To save money, it may be best to take the breakfast and dinner (MAP) plan when reserving a room. There's a 10% value-added tax (VAT) on all hotel bills, and often a service charge of about 10%. In addition, there is a 15% service charge on other hotel charges (other than the room rate) and on restaurant bills. Don't forget to ask if the VAT and service charge are included in the prices quoted to you.

VERY EXPENSIVE

Blue Haven Hotel (F) *Finds* It's made a comeback. In the 1950s, it was the hottest ticket in town. Rita Hayworth and Robert Mitchum stayed here when they made *Fire Down Below* in 1957. Allowed to fall into ruins, the hotel was recently restored, and, of course, it still opens onto its secluded beach of fine white sands. In romantic legend, the inn stands at the place where Robinson Crusoe was stranded in 1659 in the Defoe novel. Elegantly furnished bedrooms open onto panoramic views of the water—the inn, is in fact, surrounded on three sides by the sea. Guests walk on wooden floors, and there's a glass wall separating the bedrooms from the sleekly modern bathrooms. Guests have several options for lodging, ranging from standard doubles to deluxe, even superposh suites and villas. All accommodations come with private balconies with ocean views. Even the pool overlooks the ocean. Honeymooners take special delight in this little charmer. In winter live entertainment is brought in to amuse the guests—folklore shows, calypso soca, and steel bands.

Bacolet Bay, Scarborough, Tobago, W.I. (C) 868/660-7400. www.bluehavenhotel.com. 51 units. Winter US$238–US$275 double, US$355 suite, US$585 villa; off season US$181–US$215 double, US$270 suite, US$425 villa. AE, DISC, MC, V. **Amenities:** Restaurant; 2 bars; outdoor pool; tennis court; gym; sauna; watersports by special arrangement; children's playground; room service (7am–10pm); babysitting; laundry service; nonsmoking rooms; units for those with limited mobility. *In room:* A/C, ceiling fan, TV, dataport, minibar, hair dryer, iron/ironing board, safe.

Hilton Tobago (F)(F)(F) On an 8-hectare (20-acre) site 4km (2½ miles) east of the airport is Tobago's first international hotel and the island's market leader. This five-star luxury resort lies on a 1,500m (4,920-ft.) beach with a mangrove forest in the background. The hotel is on the island's southwest coast and is part of a 300-hectare (741-acre) development that embraces a 36-hectare (89-acre) lagoon.

With an 18-hole, par-72 championship PGA golf course, the hotel lures golfers from Mount Irvine Bay (see review below). The Hilton also lies in the heart of some of the best scuba-diving waters in the southern Caribbean. Rooms

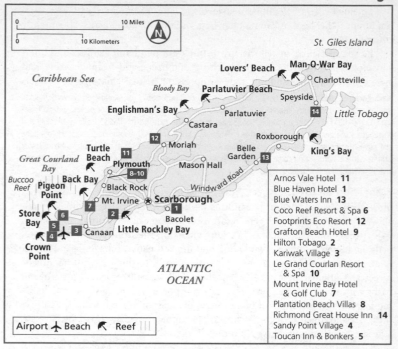

Arnos Vale Hotel	11
Blue Haven Hotel	1
Blue Waters Inn	13
Coco Reef Resort & Spa	6
Footprints Eco Resort	12
Grafton Beach Hotel	9
Hilton Tobago	2
Kariwak Village	3
Le Grand Courlan Resort & Spa	10
Mount Irvine Bay Hotel & Golf Club	7
Plantation Beach Villas	8
Richmond Great House Inn	14
Sandy Point Village	4
Toucan Inn & Bonkers	5

are tastefully and luxuriously furnished, and every suite has a Jacuzzi. Each unit opens onto ocean views and has a shower/tub combination.

The food is the finest on the island in terms of quality, although we still prefer our favorite local eateries, some mere dives. The best local bands are brought in, and the Hilton has more activities than all its rivals.

Lowlands, Scarborough, Tobago, W.I. © 800/HILTONS in the U.S., or 868/660-8500. Fax 868/660-8503. www.hilton.com. 200 units. Winter US$155–US$300 double, US$310–US$400 suite; off season US$105–US$300 double; US$230–US$330 suite. Ask about discount rates and promotional rates. AE, DC, MC, V. **Amenities:** 3 restaurants; 2 bars; 3 pools; 18-hole golf course; 2 tennis courts; gym; sauna; deep-sea fishing; glass-bottom boat tours; scuba diving; snorkeling; children's learning center; limited room service; massage; babysitting; laundry service; dry cleaning; nonsmoking rooms; rooms for those with limited mobility. *In room:* A/C, TV, minibar, beverage maker, hair dryer, iron/ironing board, safe.

Le Grand Courlan Resort & Spa 🏵🏵🏵
Operated by the same owners as the Grafton Beach Resort (see below), this pricey hotel is definitely 5-star and definitely deluxe. For those who want to live in style but don't want a megaresort like the Hilton, the Courlan is a good choice. It's named for the bay on the western edge of the island on which it sits. A soft, sandy beach is at its door, and everything is set against a backdrop of bougainvillea, white frangipani, and hibiscus. Constructed to fit in with its natural surroundings, the hotel was built of stone and teak harvested from farms on Trinidad, then furnished with handcrafted mahogany pieces and decorated with original artwork. The floors are covered in Italian porcelain tile, and the ceilings are made from Guyanan hardwood. The bedrooms are handsomely tropical in decor, with two phones, king-size beds, and large balconies. Bathrooms are small, but equipped with robes, scales, phones, and shower/tub combinations.

The hotel offers a Caribbean-style bistro and an international a la carte restaurant. The food is among the best on the island. There's also nightly entertainment.

The spa specializes in cell therapy. It has a koi pond and aerobics and offers consultations in nutrition, fitness coaching, and ozone-and-steam detoxing, and even fresh-fruit facials and full-body compression "release" massages.

Black Rock (P.O. Box 25), Scarborough, Tobago, W.I. © 868/639-9667. Fax 868/639-9292. www.legrand courlan-resort.com. 85 units. Winter US$205–US$325 per person double, US$325 per person suite; off season US$160–US$172 per person double, US$355 per person suite. Extra person US$50. Includes all meals and beverages, 1 spa treatment, and 1 scuba dive daily. AE, MC, V. **Amenities:** 2 restaurants; 2 bars; outdoor pool; golf privileges; 2 tennis courts; spa; sauna; steam room; dive shop; fishing; bikes; car rental; salon; massage; laundry service; nonsmoking rooms; rooms for those with limited mobility. *In room:* A/C, TV, minibar, hair dryer, iron/ironing board, safe.

Plantation Beach Villas ✦

At the edge of a tropical rainforest, between a bird sanctuary and the Caribbean, this pink-and-white cottage complex stands above a palm-fringed beach. The resort is reminiscent of the plantation era, with its British colonial architecture, rocking chairs on the front porch, four-poster beds, and louvered doors. Two sailing buddies and native Tobagonians, Jennifer Avey and Brenda Farfan, created this little gem, furnishing it with handmade pieces and original art work. Each spacious villa has three bedrooms, a trio of baths with showers, and a teak-covered front porch with a sea view. It's like living in your own private vacation retreat. A member of the staff will even prepare breakfast and lunch or come back to make dinner, but that costs US$20 extra. The site is a 15-minute drive from the airport.

Stonehaven Bay Rd., Black Rock (P.O. Box 435), Scarborough, Tobago, W.I. © 800/633-7411 in the U.S. or 868/639-9377. Fax 868/639-0455. www.plantationbeachvillas.com. 6 units. Winter US$545–US$660 up to 4 persons, US$620–US$715 up to 6 persons; off season US$375 up to 4 persons, US$420–US$465 up to 6 persons. AE, MC, V. **Amenities:** Restaurant; bar; outdoor pool; babysitting; laundry service; rooms for those with limited mobility. *In room:* A/C, TV, kitchenette, beverage maker, hair dryer, iron/ironing board.

EXPENSIVE

Arnos Vale Hotel ✦

This inn—one of the first hotels of Tobago's modern tourist age—sprawls over 180 hectares (445 acres) of very private land. It's named after a township in England, although tour groups from Italy often fill up its chambers. This place was once a closely guarded secret, but it was a long time ago that the late Princess Margaret honeymooned here. The other celebs who used to flock here are off in Anguilla these days. Rooms, each with a private patio or veranda, are furnished with a wide spectrum of furniture, including some pieces dating back to the early 1960s, retained because many clients appreciate their slightly battered charm. Only a few of the units are actually on the beach. Suites are in a handful of individual bungalows. Not all bathrooms have tubs. Most of the socializing occurs at the likable bar, where you'll find a TV, strong drinks, and a loyal clientele that returns year after year.

Arnos Vale Rd. (P.O. Box 2081), Plymouth, Tobago, W.I. © 868/639-2881. Fax 868/639-4629. www.arnos valehotel.com. 29 units. Winter US$125–US$170 double, US$140–US$260 suite; off season US$80–US$105 double, US$140–US$175 suite. AE, MC, V. **Amenities:** Restaurant; 2 bars (1 swim-up); outdoor pool; tennis court; babysitting; laundry service; nonsmoking rooms; rooms for those with limited mobility. *In room:* A/C, minibar, kitchenettes (in some), beverage maker.

Coco Reef Resort & Spa ✦✦

This is one of the largest beachfront hotels on the island and has a certain South Florida pizzazz. It's on Tobago's northern shore, near the airport. Most accommodations are in the two- and three-story main building, although about a half dozen villas are scattered over the surrounding acreage. The designer incorporated a number of environmentally friendly features and used some recycled materials. The bedrooms are spacious and airy, filled with wicker furniture, the big bathrooms are tiled in white and have shower/tub combinations. Most rooms have an intricately trimmed balcony. In 1998, the hotel added 15 new suites with large balconies and patios overlooking the Caribbean and lush tropical gardens. These suites contain marble bathrooms equipped with shower/tub combinations and are embellished with hand-painted murals and custom-designed wicker furniture. The complex is near a trio of the island's best beaches—Store Bay, Pigeon Point, and Coconut Beach itself, which is just steps from your room.

Tamara's, the resort's most formal restaurant, offers some of the most sophisticated food in Trinidad and Tobago (see "Dining," below).

Coconut Bay (P.O. Box 434), Tobago, W.I. © **800/221-1294** in the U.S., or 868/639-8571. Fax 868/639-8574. www.cocoreef.com. 137 units. Winter US$280–US$320 double, from US$522 suite or villa; off season US$213–US$272 double, from US$432 suite or villa. MAP (breakfast and dinner) US$66 per person extra, US$46 for children age 5–12. Extra person US$60 per day. AE, MC, V. **Amenities:** 2 restaurants; 2 bars; outdoor pool; tennis court; health club and spa; dive shop; snorkeling; car rental; salon; 24-hr. room service; babysitting; laundry service; nonsmoking rooms. *In room:* A/C, TV, dataport, fridge, minibar, hair dryer.

Footprints Eco Resort ✭ *(Finds)*　The island's first "eco-resort" sprawls across some 24 hectares (59 acres) on Culloden Bay. A local doctor and his daughter carved this "environmentally responsible" resort out of a dense forest of cocoa and fruit trees in 1997. The result is a rustic and charming compound of wood-sided, thatch-roofed cottages. Each unit is artfully built of recycled lumber with an emphasis on native termite-resistant hardwoods such as wallaba and teak. Accommodations are rough-hewn but comfortable, with a hammock for classic island lounging, wooden floors, and a lot of idiosyncratic charm.

Rooms range from standard doubles to king superior units with fridges. Some rooms have garden showers, and others have two full bathrooms with shower/tub combinations, as well as a small private pool and Jacuzzi. On-site luxuries include the excellent Cocoa House restaurant (see "Dining," below), a network of nature trails that fan out across the nearby hills, and a minimuseum that contains Amerindian artifacts uncovered during the excavations on the property. You can practice your yoga here with on-site instruction, and there's a library to satisfy your cravings for the written word. Most guests opt to swim in the resort's pool, although good beaches, including Courland Bay and Castara Bay, are a 15-minute drive away.

Golden Lane, Culloden Bay Rd., Tobago, W.I. © **800/814-1396** in the U.S., or 868/660-0118. Fax 868/660-0027. www.footprintseco-resort.com. 7 units. Winter US$169–US$272 double, US$363 villa; off season US$139–US$223 double, US$302 villa. MAP (breakfast and dinner) US$30 per person extra. AE, MC, V. **Amenities:** Restaurant; bar; 2 pools; yoga; Jacuzzi; rainforest tours; massage; babysitting; laundry service; nonsmoking rooms. *In room:* A/C, ceiling fan, fridge, beverage maker.

Grafton Beach Resort ✭　Still going strong although it's now outclassed by many others, this complex sprawls across a beach shoreline set against a backdrop of palms. It draws the most European clientele on the island, and is under the same ownership as the neighboring and superior Le Grand Courlan Resort (Grafton guests can use Courlan's spa). Rooms are in three- and four-story buildings scattered over 2 hectares (5 acres) descending to a nice white-sand beach. The well-furnished units contain ceiling fans, sliding-glass doors opening onto balconies, and handcrafted teak furniture. Most bathrooms are small but well appointed, with combination shower/tubs, mirrored closets, and retractable laundry lines.

The resort's pool is ringed with cafe/restaurant tables, and there is a swim-up bar. Both a fine regional and international cuisine are served in the Ocean View and Neptunes restaurants. Limbo dancing and calypso, or some other form of entertainment, is featured nightly.

Black Rock (P.O. Box 25), Scarborough, Tobago, W.I. © 868/639-0191. Fax 868/639-0030. www.grafton-resort.com. 106 units. Winter US$168 per person; off season US$140 per person. Suite supplement US$70 per person. Rates are all-inclusive. AE, MC, V. **Amenities:** 2 restaurants; 3 bars (1 swim-up); outdoor pool; golf privileges; boating; dive shop; snorkeling; windsurfing; car rental; Internet cafe; babysitting; laundry service; nonsmoking rooms; rooms for those with limited mobility. *In room:* A/C, ceiling fan, TV, fridge, hair dryer, safe.

Mount Irvine Bay Hotel & Golf Club ✿✿

This 6-hectare (15-acre) resort, established in 1972, stands on the site of an 18th-century sugar plantation. The surrounding Mount Irvine Golf Course is one of the finest courses in the Caribbean. Although Mount Irvine retains a loyal clientele, Le Grand Courlan Resort and the Hilton surpassed it long ago. The center of the resort is a luxurious oval pool and the ruins of a stone sugar mill. The grounds slope down to a good sandy beach. On the hill leading to the beach are the newer and better-maintained cottage suites, covered with heliconia. Most accommodations are in the main building, a two-story, hacienda-inspired wing of rather large but standard guest rooms, each with a view of green lawns and flowering shrubbery. Some of the better units have Queen Anne–style furniture with two- and four-posters. Bathrooms have shower/tub combinations.

The hotel serves good international food. There's dancing almost every evening, and often calypso singers. There is also a resident piano player.

Mount Irvine (P.O. Box 222), Scarborough, Tobago, W.I. © **868/639-8871.** Fax 868/639-8800. www.mtirvine.com. 105 units. Winter US$235 double, US$363 cottage, US$566 1-bedroom suite, US$690 2-bedroom suite; off season US$124 double, US$207 cottage, US$380 1-bedroom suite, US$570 2-bedroom suite. AE, MC, V. An 8km (5-mile) drive northwest of the airport. **Amenities:** 3 restaurants; 5 bars; outdoor pool; 18-hole golf course; 2 tennis courts; fitness center; sauna; fishing; snorkeling; water-skiing; windsurfing; Internet cafe; salon; room service (7am–10pm); massage; babysitting; laundry service; rooms for those with limited mobility. *In room:* A/C, TV, hair dryer, safe.

MODERATE

Blue Waters Inn ✿ *Kids* Attracting nature lovers, this family-run property on the northeastern coast of Tobago is nestled along the shore of Batteaux Bay, where a private 300m-long (984-ft.) beach beckons guests. This charming and rustic retreat extends onto acres of tropical rainforest with myriad exotic birds, butterflies, and other wildlife. The building's entrance almost appears to drop over a cliff, and birds may actually fly through the open windows of the driftwood-adorned dining room. It's a very informal place, so leave your fancy resort wear at home. The inn now offers several units with kitchenettes, suitable for families. A few are wheelchair accessible, and all of the basic, no-frills accommodations have ceiling fans and small private showers; all are air-conditioned as well. The second-floor rooms open onto lovely views of the water. The inn is about 39km (24 miles) from the airport, a 75-minute drive along narrow, winding country roads.

The food is a mix of Tobago and international dishes. The emphasis in on fresh fish caught daily, and the chef also offers leaner dishes with reduced fats.

Batteaux Bay, Speyside, Tobago, W.I. © 800/448-8355 in the U.S., or 868/660-4341. Fax 868/660-5195. www.bluewatersinn.com. 38 units. Winter US$160 double, US$190 efficiency, US$330 1-bedroom suite, US$490 2-bedroom suite; off season US$100 double, US$130 efficiency, US$205 1-bedroom suite, US$305 2-bedroom suite. Additional person US$20 per day. Children age 5–12 US$15. MAP (breakfast and dinner) US$36 per person extra. AE, MC, V. **Amenities:** Restaurant; bar; tennis court; boating; dive shop; kayaks; snorkeling; windsurfing; car rental; limited room service; babysitting; nonsmoking rooms; rooms for those with limited mobility. *In room:* A/C, ceiling fan, hair dryer.

Kariwak Village ☆ (*Finds*)   This cluster of cottages evoking the South Pacific is about a 6-minute walk from the beach on the island's west end and a 2-minute drive from the airport. The name is a combination of the two native tribes that originally inhabited Tobago, the Caribs and the Arawaks. In this "village" Cynthia and Allan Clovis run a "holistic" haven as well as an inn. Come here, among other reasons, for Hatha Yoga, Qi Gong, and various stretching and relaxing exercises. Two on-site massage therapists give you all your favorite massages. If you're a vegetarian headed for Tobago, this is the place for you. You can even walk through Cynthia's garden, where she grows fresh herbs and vegetables for the meals served here. Nine of the accommodations are hexagonal cabanas with two rooms each, opening onto the pool. The units are quite spacious, with king-size beds, and the shower-only bathrooms are bright and well-maintained.

Live entertainment is provided on Friday and Saturday year-round. The food served in the Kariwak Village Restaurant (see "Dining," below) is among the best on the island, and you may want to come by for a bite even if you aren't staying here.

Local Rd., Store Bay (P.O. Box 27), Scarborough, Tobago, W.I. © **868/639-8545**. Fax 868/639-8441. www. kariwak.co.tt. 24 units. Winter US$150 double; off season US$108 double. Children 12 and under stay free in parent's room. AE, MC, V. **Amenities:** Restaurant; bar; outdoor pool; yoga; Jacuzzi; limited room service; massage; laundry service; nonsmoking rooms; rooms for those with limited mobility. *In room:* A/C, safe.

Richmond Great House Inn ☆ (*Value*)   One of the most charming accommodations on the island is this 18th-century home set on 2 hectares (5 acres) 45 minutes from the airport. Dr. Hollis R. Lynch, a Tobago-born professor of African history at Columbia University, owns this inn near Richmond Beach, on the southern (windward) coast. Dr. Lynch has decorated the mansion with African art and island antiques. Guests are free to explore the garden and grounds and to enjoy the pool and the barbecue. Most rooms have hardwood floors, country estate–style furnishings, and tasteful, colorful fabrics. Shower-only bathrooms are small and strictly functional, with somewhat dated plumbing; suites have tubs. Families might want to consider one of the three small, basic family units in the extension to the main house. On the premises are two 19th-century tombs containing the remains of the original English founders of the plantation.

Both regional and international cuisine are served. Because it's such a small place, the cook asks guests about their culinary preferences.

Belle Garden, Tobago, W.I. ©/fax **868/660-4467**. 10 units. Winter US$125 double, US$185 suite for 2, US$180 family unit; off season US$105 double, US$135 suite for 2, US$160 family unit. Room and suite rates include breakfast. MC, V. **Amenities:** Dining room; outdoor pool; tennis court; limited room service; laundry service. *In room:* Ceiling fan, no phone.

INEXPENSIVE

Sandy Point Village   This miniature vacation village resembles a Riviera condominium complex. It's just a 5-minute ride from the airport, but its shoreside position on the island's southwestern coast makes it seem remote. Airport noise, however, can be a problem. The little village of peaked and gabled roofs is landscaped all the way down to the sandy beach, where the rustic Steak and Lobster Grill serves meals throughout the day and evening. The fully equipped accommodations have patios that open toward the sea, living and dining areas with Jamaican wicker furniture, and satellite TV. All but six of the units (those at poolside) contain kitchenettes, and each has a shower-only bathroom. Some of the studios have a rustic open stairway leading to a loft with bunk beds, with a twin-bedded room on the lower level as well.

Crown Point, Tobago, W.I. © 868/639-8533. Fax 868/639-8496. www.sandypt.net. 54 units. Winter US$66 double studio, US$77 double suite, US$88 2-bedroom apt; off season US$44 double studio, US$55 double suite, US$66 2-bedroom apt. Extra adult US$15. Children age 11 and under US$15 extra. MAP (breakfast and dinner) US$20 per person extra. AE, MC, V. **Amenities:** Restaurant; bar; 2 outdoor pools; fitness center; Jacuzzi; sauna; car rental; bike rental; limited room service; babysitting; rooms for those with limited mobility. *In room:* A/C, TV, kitchenette (in most), hair dryer, iron/ironing board.

Toucan Inn & Bonkers ⭐ (Value)   This combination restaurant and hotel is one of Tobago's best values. An inn of charm and grace, it lies close to the airport surrounded by attractively landscaped gardens. If you stay here, you'll be just a short drive from some of the island's best sandy beaches. The staff is helpful in directing you. Bedrooms are done in a modern style with comfortable though streamlined furniture; rooms come in various shapes and sizes, each with a queen-size or two twins and a small but efficiently organized private bathroom with shower. The hotel offers an option of well-furnished bedrooms with tiled shower bathrooms. The cluster of rooms facing the garden are more secluded, but even so, many guests prefer the cabanas around the pool. Teak furnishings predominate in the bedrooms. On-site Bonkers is one of the most frequented restaurants and bars in Tobago. Live entertainment is presented about 4 nights a week, and savory regional fare includes the likes of sweet curried lamb or sizzling blackened shrimp.

Store Bay Local Rd. (Box 452), Crown Point, Tobago, W.I. © **868/639-7173.** Fax 868/639-8933. www.toucan-inn.com. 20 units. Winter US$80 double; off season US$60 double. AE, MC, V. **Amenities:** Restaurant; bar; outdoor pool; babysitting; laundry service; dry cleaning; nonsmoking rooms. *In room:* A/C, dataport, hair dryer, iron/ironing board, safe.

DINING
EXPENSIVE

Dillon's ⭐ INTERNATIONAL   Set in a simple house near the Coco Reef Resort and the airport, this restaurant is run by one of Tobago's leading operators of a deep-sea-fishing boat. Consequently, the fish is sure to be fresh. There's both an indoor, air-conditioned room with framed memorabilia of the island's tradition of steel-pan music, and an outdoor terrace with views over the garden. Menu items include fresh snapper with lemon-butter sauce; tenderloin steak with a spinach-bacon ragout; pan-fried or grilled shrimp served with grilled Parmesan polenta, basmati rice, and a tomato/basil sauce; curried shrimp in coconut sauce and mango chutney, and a lobster crepe with white-wine sauce and fresh herbs.

Milford Rd., near Crown Point. © **868/639-8765.** Reservations recommended. Main courses TT$60–TT$160 (US$9.60–US$26). AE, MC, V. Mon–Sat 6–10pm. Closed 6 weeks May–June.

Tamara's ⭐ INTERNATIONAL   One of the most appealing restaurants on Tobago occupies a two-tiered, stone-and-timber gazebo whose curved edges are open on all sides for maximum exposure to cool breezes and views of the nearby sea. It serves some of Trinidad and Tobago's most sophisticated food, based on West Indian traditions with lots of international touches. Start, perhaps, with homemade veal and bacon terrine or pan-fried shrimp with wilted greens and wasabi sauce. Try the lamb loin on couscous, the charcoal-grilled ocean snapper with a cream mushroom and lemongrass sauce, or most definitely the pork tenderloin garnished with a lima-bean ragout. The menu changes every 2 days.

In the Coco Reef Resort, Coconut Beach. © **868/639-8571.** Reservations recommended. Fixed-price dinner TT$166–TT$338 (US$27–US$54). AE, MC, V. Daily 7–10pm.

MODERATE

The Blue Crab ★ (Finds) CARIBBEAN/INTERNATIONAL   One of our

favorite restaurants in the capital, this family-run spot occupies an Edwardian-era house with an oversize veranda. The menu makes the most of local ingredients and regional spices, and is dictated by whatever is available that day in the marketplace. The good, homemade food includes fresh conch, stuffed crab backs, an array of Creole meat dishes grilled over coconut husks, flying fish in a mild curry-flavored batter, shrimp with garlic butter or cream, and a vegetable rice dish of the day. Lobster sometimes appears on the menu.

Robinson St., Scarborough. ℂ 868/639-2737. Reservations required for dinner. Lunch TT$44–TT$50 (US$7.05–US$8); dinner main courses TT$115–TT$150 (US$18–US$24). AE, MC, V. Mon–Fri 11:30am–3pm and 7–10pm (but call first to be sure).

The Cocoa House ★ WEST INDIAN/TOBAGONIAN   Proud of its eco-

sensitivity (waste water and paper trash are recycled here), this restaurant is a worthy choice for its allegiance to tried-and-true Tobagonian food that's prepared in a style endorsed by many of the island's matriarchs and grandmothers. Its name comes from its unusual roof, made from the fronds of the Timit palm. On balmy evenings, the roof retracts (just as it might at an old-fashioned cocoa pod drying room), allowing views of the setting sun and, a bit later, of the moon and stars. Well-flavored dishes include jerk versions of shrimp, chicken, and pork; duck with either orange or pineapple sauce; and *pelau,* a French-inspired dish that combines chicken and beef bound together with rice. For a dish that many Tobagans remember from their childhood, try pork and dumplings.

In Footprints Eco Resort, Golden Lane, Culloden Bay Rd. ℂ 868/657-05891. Reservations required for dinner before 1pm on the day of your intended arrival. Main courses TT$17–TT$40 (US$2.70–US$6.40) lunch, TT$50–TT$100 (US$8–US$16) dinner. AE, MC, V. Daily 7am–8pm.

Jemma's Seaview Kitchen ★ (Finds) TOBAGONIAN   A short walk north of

the hamlet of Speyside, on Tobago's northeastern coast, this is one of the very few restaurants in the Caribbean designed as a tree house. Although the simple kitchen is firmly anchored to the shoreline, the dining area is set on a platform nailed to the massive branches of a 200-year-old almond tree that leans out over the water. Some 50 tables are available on a wooden deck that provides a rooflike structure for shelter from the rain. The charming staff serves up good main courses that come with soup or salad. Lunch platters include shrimp, fish, and chicken, while dinners feature more elaborate portions of each, as well as steaks, curried lamb, grilled or curried kingfish, lamb chops, and lobster served grilled or thermidor style. No liquor is served.

Speyside. ℂ 868/660-4066. Reservations recommended. Lunch main courses TT$60–TT$200 (US$9.60–US$32); dinner main courses TT$80–TT$200 (US$13–US$32). MC, V. Sun–Thurs 9am–9pm; Fri 9am–4pm.

Kariwak Village Restaurant ★ (Value) CARIBBEAN   Even if you're not a

guest here, consider visiting at dinnertime. The chefs prepare one of the choicest menus on the island, a four-course repast that changes nightly, based on what's best and freshest at the market. On our latest rounds, we began with creamy breadfruit soup, followed by freshly grilled fish, rice, stuffed butternut pumpkin, and *christophene* (Caribbean squash). The price even included dessert and coffee. In an open-air setting, you can enjoy recorded music from Trinidadian steel bands. The owner, Cynthia Clovis, grows herbs and vegetables in an on-site organic garden. The Friday or Saturday evening buffet is one of the best spreads on the island, with live music to boot. Shrimp and steak are favorites, but save room for the green-banana salad seasoned with fresh herbs.

In the Kariwak Village hotel, Local Rd., Store Bay. © 868/639-8442. Reservations recommended. Breakfast US$10; lunch US$5–US$15; 4-course dinner US$28. AE, MC, V. Daily 7am–11pm.

La Belle Creole 𝒦 *Finds* CAJUN/INTERNATIONAL   This unusual and noteworthy restaurant occupies an Edwardian house .8km (½ mile) south of Scarborough. Its owner, Gloria Jones-Knapp, was once a fashion model in Europe. "Born, bred, and dragged up" on Tobago, she is today the island's leading authority on select European wines. Her restaurant also serves freshly made fruit drinks laced with the local rum. We highly recommend the delectable "mammy's golden apple chutney," and the locally caught crayfish shaped into cakes and served with a tangy sauce. The kitchen also prepares Cajun dishes such as blackened chicken and shrimp jambalaya along with seared tuna. To begin your meal, you can do no better than the callaloo soup with tender crab meat (the secret is in the tender, young dasheen leaves). A house specialty is piña colada mahimahi marinated in herbs and coconut milk along with a honey-pineapple purée.

In the Half-Moon Blue Hotel, Bacolet St., Scarborough. © 868/639-3551. Fax 868/639-6124. Reservations required. Main courses TT$100–TT$200 (US$16–US$32). MC, V. Sat–Thurs 8am–11pm; Fri 7am–3pm.

INEXPENSIVE

Arnos Vale Water Wheel Restaurant INTERNATIONAL   This restaurant occupies the weathered premises of a former 19th-century water mill used to crush sugar cane. You'll dine in the wheelhouse, with an antique oven and the wheel's original machinery still in place, while overlooking the verdant banks of the Franklin River. Menu items include Cornish hen, shaved pear and Parmesan salad, deviled chicken, honey-roasted duck breast, caramelized breast of chicken with polenta and callaloo sauce, grilled fish served with a medley of sauces, and at least three different shrimp and lobster dishes. Three times a week, there's a performance of live Trinidadian/Tobagan music and dance; the animated sounds perk up the otherwise calm and quiet landscape of chirping tree frogs and splashing water.

Arnos Vale Rd., Plymouth. © 868/660-0815 or 868/639-2881. Reservations recommended. Main courses TT$45–TT$172 (US$7.20–US$28). MC, V. Daily 7:30–10pm. The restaurant is a 5-min. drive from the Arnos Vale Hotel.

First Historical Café/Bar 𝒦 *Finds* TRINIDADIAN/INTERNATIONAL   A sign in the dining room reads, "Trinidad hustles and bustles/Tobago takes its time." Expect a laid-back, slightly funky atmosphere at this traditional local structure in Studley Park on the way to the settlement at Charlotte. The Washington family is on hand to welcome you to this brightly painted and atmospheric little dive. As you peruse the menu, glance up at the decorative wall postings with tidbits about Tobago's history and culture. The food is hearty and filling, and you can drop in for lunch or snacks throughout the day, filling up on well-stuffed sandwiches, hot dogs, burgers, fruit plates, even a veggie salad. By all means, try their freshly baked coconut bread.

8 Mile Mark Windward Rd. © 868/660-2233. Prices TT$10–TT$15 (US$1.60–US$2.40). No credit cards. Mon–Fri 10am–7pm.

HITTING THE BEACH 𝒦𝒦

On Tobago, you can still feel like Robinson Crusoe in a solitary sandy cove—at least until Saturday, when the Trinidadians fly over for a weekend on the beach.

  Pigeon Point, on the northwestern shore, is the best-known bathing area, with a long coral beach. It's public, but to reach it you must enter a former coconut estate, which charges a fee of TT$10 (US$1.60). Set against a backdrop of royal palms, this beach is becoming increasingly commercial. Facilities include food kiosks, crafts shops, a diving concession, paddleboat rentals, changing rooms in thatched shelters, and picnic tables. Pigeon Point is also the jumping off point for snorkeling cruises to **Buccoo Reef.**

Another good beach, **Back Bay,** is an 8-minute walk from the Mount Irvine Bay Hotel on Mount Irvine Bay. Along the way, you'll pass a coconut plantation and an old cannon emplacement. Snorkeling is generally excellent, even in winter. There are sometimes dangerous currents, but you can always explore Rocky Point Beach and its brilliantly colored parrotfish. In July and August, the surfing is the finest in Tobago; it's also likely to be good in January and April. Stop in Scarborough for picnic fixings, which you can enjoy at the picnic tables here; a snack bar sells cold beer and drinks.

Great Courland Bay is known for its calm, gin-clear waters, and is flanked by **Turtle Beach,** named for the turtles that nest here. Near Fort Bennett and south of Plymouth, Great Courland Bay is one of the longest sandy beaches on the island and the site of several hotels and a marina.

The locals and the fishing boats make the setting at half-moon-shaped **Parlatuvier Beach** (on the north side of the island) more bucolic than the swimming. If you can't stand crowds, head for **Englishman's Bay,** on the north coast just west of Parlatuvier. We don't know why this beach is virtually deserted: It's charming, secluded, and good for swimming.

Near the little fishing village of Charlotteville, **Man-O-War Bay** is one of the finest natural harbors in the West Indies. It has a long sandy beach and a government-run rest house. Sometimes local fishermen will hawk the day's catch (and clean it for you as well). Nearby **Lovers' Beach** is accessible only by boat and is famous for its pink sand, formed long ago from crushed sea shells. Negotiate a fee with one of the local boatmen; expect to pay around US$25.

The true beach buff will head for **King's Bay** in the northeast, south of the town of Speyside near Delaford. Against a backdrop of towering green hills, the crescent-shaped grayish-sand beach is one of the best places for swimming.

SPORTS & OTHER OUTDOOR PURSUITS

GOLF Tobago is the proud possessor of an 18-hole, 6,800-yard course at Mount Irvine. Called the **Tobago Golf Club** at the Mount Irvine Estates (② 868/639-8871), it covers 60 breeze-swept hectares (148 acres) and was featured in the *Wonderful World of Golf* TV series. Even beginners agree the course is friendly to duffers. Guests of the Mount Irvine Bay Hotel are granted temporary membership, use of the clubhouse and facilities, and a 15% discount on greens fees. The course is also open to nonguests, who pay US$53 for 18 holes or US$35 for nine holes. Cart rentals are US$42 for 18 holes or US$23 for nine holes; clubs cost US$17 for 18 holes or US$11 for nine holes. **Tobago Plantations Golf & Country Club,** Hampden Road, Lowlands (② 868/631-0875), lies on a 303-hectare (748-acre) estate that was previously a sugar-cane plantation. It adjoins the grounds of the Hilton Tobago. Some holes on this on this par-72, 7,000-yard course follow the coastline. Greens fees, including golf cart, are US$85 for 18 holes, US$60 for nine holes.

SCUBA DIVING, SNORKELING ✿✿ & OTHER WATERSPORTS The unspoiled reefs off Tobago teem with a great variety of marine life. Divers can swim through rocky canyons 18m to 39m (59 ft.–128 ft.) deep, underwater photographers can shoot pictures they won't find anywhere else, and snorkelers can explore the celebrated **Buccoo Reef** (off Pigeon Point), which teems with gardens of coral and hundreds of fish in the waist-deep water. Even nonswimmers can wade knee-deep in the waters. Remember to protect your head and body from the sun and to guard your feet against the sharp coral. Nearly all the major hotels arrange boat trips here. After about half an hour at the reef, passengers reboard their boats and go over to **Nylon Pool,** with its crystal-clear waters. Here in this white-sand-bottom spot, about 2km (1¼ mile) offshore, you can enjoy a dip in water only 1m (3 ft.–4 ft.) deep.

Wreck divers have a new adventure to enjoy with the sinking of the former ferryboat *Maverick,* in 30m (98 ft.) of water near Mount Irvine Bay Hotel on Tobago's southwest coast.

Dive Tobago, Pigeon Point (© **868/639-0202**), is the oldest and most established operation on Tobago, operated by Jay Young, a certified PADI instructor. It offers easy resort courses, single dives, and dive packages, along with equipment rentals. A basic resort course costs US$55, although for certification you must pay US$300. A one-tank dive goes for US$40.

Tobago Dive Experience, at the Manta Lodge, Speyside (© **868/660-4888**), offers scuba dives, snorkeling, and boat trips. All dives are guided, with a boat following. Exciting drift dives are available for experienced divers. A one-tank dive costs US$39 without equipment; a two-tank dive starts at US$70; and a resort course costs US$65.

Man Friday Diving, Charlotteville (© **868/660-4676**), is a Danish-owned dive center with certified PADI instructors and dive masters. It's right on the beach of Man-O-War Bay at the northernmost tip of Tobago. With more than 40 different dive sites, it's always able to find suitable locations, no matter what the water conditions. Guided boat trips for certified divers go out Monday to Saturday at 9:30am and 1pm. A resort course costs US$75; a PADI open-water certification, US$375; a one-tank dive, US$35 (US$43 with equipment); and a night dive, US$50.

Frank's Glass Bottom Boat Tours, Blue Waters Inn, Bateaux Bay, Speyside (© **868/660-5438**), takes visitors on trips to Angel Reef to see a collection of the largest brain coral in the world. Combined with a snorkeling trip, the cost is US$15 per person. A glass bottom boat tour and snorkeling tour plus a guided tour of the Little Tobago Bird Sanctuary, costs only US$20, and is the most popular jaunt.

TENNIS   The best courts on the island are at the **Mount Irvine Bay Hotel** (© **868/639-8871**). Nonguests may use the two courts here for TT$12 (US$1.90) per half-hour or TT$23 (US$3.70) per hour. There is an additional TT$23 (US$3.70) light fee on request.

EXPLORING TOBAGO

If you'd like a close-up view of Tobago's many rare and exotic tropical birds, as well as a range of other island wildlife and lush tropical flora, naturalist-led field trips are the answer. Each 5-hour trip leads you to forest trails and coconut plantations, along rivers and past waterfalls; one excursion even goes to two nearby islands. Trips cost US$40 to US$50. For details, contact **Newton George,** Speyside, Charlotteville (© **868/660-5463** or 868/754-7881 cell).

Tobago's capital, **Scarborough,** need claim your attention only briefly before you climb up the hill to **Fort King George,** about 129m (423 ft.) above the town. Built by the English in 1779, it was later captured by the French, then was tossed back and forth among various conquerors until nature decided to end it all in 1847, blowing off the roofs of its buildings. You can view the ruins of a military hospital, and also see artifacts displayed at the **Tobago Museum** (C **868/639-3970**), in the fort's old barracks.

From Scarborough, you can drive northwest to **Plymouth,** Tobago's other town. Perched on a point at Plymouth is **Fort James,** which dates from 1768. Now it's mainly in ruins.

From Speyside in the north, you can make arrangements with a local fisher to go to **Little Tobago** ☆, a 180-hectare (445-acre) offshore island whose bird sanctuary attracts ornithologists. The 20-minute crossing is likely to be rough, but the effort is worth it. Threatened with extinction in New Guinea, many birds, perhaps 50 species in all, were brought over to this little island in the early part of last century. The islet is arid and hilly, with a network of marked trails.

Off Pigeon Point in the south lies **Buccoo Reef** ☆☆, where sea gardens of coral and hundreds of fish can be seen in waist-deep water (see "Scuba Diving, Snorkeling, & Other Watersports" above). This is the natural aquarium of Tobago, offering the island's best **snorkeling** and **scuba diving.** Nearly all the major hotels arrange boat trips here.

SHOPPING

In Tobago's capital, Scarborough, you can visit the local **market** Monday to Saturday mornings. Scarborough's stores have a limited range of merchandise, more to tempt the browser than the serious shopper.

Farro's, Wilson Road (no phone), across from the marketplace, offers the tastiest condiments on the island, packed into little straw baskets for you to carry back home. Sample the delectable lime marmalade, any of the hot sauces, the guava jelly, and most definitely the homemade tamarind chutney.

If you're seeking handcrafts, especially straw baskets, head for the **Souvenir & Gift Shop,** Port Mall (C **868/660-1000**), also in Scarborough.

Cotton House Fashion Studio, Old Windward Road, in Bacolet (C **868/ 639-2727**), is the island's best choice for "hands-on" appreciation of the fine art of batik. In the Indonesian tradition, melted wax is brushed onto fabric, resisting dyes and creating unusual colors and designs. This outlet contains the largest collection of batik clothing and wall hangings on Tobago. Dying techniques are demonstrated to visitors, who can then try their skills.

The Art Gallery, Hibiscus Drive, Lowlands (C **868/639-0457**), across from the Tobago Hilton, features the works of at least 10 artists. On permanent exhibit upstairs is a collection of island watercolors by Rachel Superville and her husband, Martin. Sculptures and a number of handcrafts are also sold here.

TOBAGO AFTER DARK

Your best bet for entertainment is at the **Mount Irvine Bay Hotel** at Mount Irvine Bay (C **868/639-8871**), where you might find some disco action or a steel band performing by the beach or pool.

Grafton Beach Resort at Black Road owns one of the island's most charming bars, **Buccaneer's Beach Bar** (C **868/639-0191**), across from the resort. Here you'll find a wide wood terrace sheltered by a grove of almond trees. Daily specials written up on a surfboard include burgers, fried fish, and the like (don't expect the elegant beachside Creole cooking of Martinique). The resort itself offers cabaretlike entertainment nightly. Try to catch the local troupe, Les Couteaux Cultural Group, which performs a version of Tobagonian history set to dance.

Want some local action? Try **Bonkers,** Store Bay Road at Crown Point (© **868/639-7173**), a lively bar where you'll hear the best soca, reggae, or jazz. If you've been "bad," the DJ might order you to walk the gangplank into the pool. An enduringly popular hangout site with what might be the most amusing name on Tobago is **Lush,** Shirvan Road in Mount Irvine (© **868/639-9087**). Friendly, outgoing, and set upon a covered veranda with open sides, it's the kind of place where the staff at the island's resort hotels might hang out after hours, sometimes with any client of those hotels looking for local flavor. Admission is free unless there's live music at the time of your arrival, which could cost you TT$60 (US$9.60) per person. Here, beer seems to be the universal drink of choice.

26

Turks & Caicos

The Turks and Caicos (*Kayk*-us) Islands (or "Turks and Who?" as they're often called) have long been dubbed the "forgotten islands." Sun worshippers discovered them in the early 1990s, however, and now there's talk of a "second Bahamas" in the making. Although they are actually part of the Bahamian archipelago, they are tucked away to the east of the southernmost islands of the Bahamas and governed separately.

Directly north of Haiti and the Dominican Republic, the islands lie a the crossroads of the Caribbean and the Americas. Technically, however, this obscure outpost is not in Caribbean waters, but on the fringe of the Atlantic.

Grand Turk and Salt Cay (which constitute the Turks Islands) and Cockburn Harbour (South Caicos) are ports of entry, while the major island to visit is Provo.

Many of the islanders today work in the salt-raking industry; others export lobsters (crayfish), conch, and conch shells. But more and more, the citizens of this little country feed off the tourist industry. It's the kind of place where you still greet people as you encounter them walking along the roads.

The Turks and Caicos Islands (TCI) are a coral-reef paradise, largely shut off from the world, free of pollution and crowds. Even with the advent of real tourist development and the bustle of construction, particularly in Provo, the beauty and tranquillity of this little island chain remain intact. They're still off the beaten track, and they're not right for travelers who want lots of glitzy facilities or nightlife. You won't find the highly refined tourist infrastructure that exists in the Bahamas, but that's the appeal for some travelers.

What's beginning to put Turks and Caicos on the map is an incredible array of beaches—362km (224 miles) worth, to be precise. Some stretches of soft white sand run for miles; others are small, hidden in secluded coves. The islands are also home to some of the world's most magnificent underwater life. For years, divers and snorkelers have enjoyed the countless varieties of brilliant coral and colorful fish that thrive within TCI's nearly 805km (499-mile) pristine reef system.

Turks and Caicos are mainly self-governing today. Queen Elizabeth selects a governor to be her representative in island affairs, and this governor appoints the chief minister who, in turn, appoints minor ministers.

1 Turks & Caicos Essentials

VISITOR INFORMATION

The Turks & Caicos Sales and Information Office, Front Street, Cockburn Town, Grand Turk, B.W.I. (© **800/241-0824** in the U.S., or 649/946-2322),

The Turks & Caicos Islands

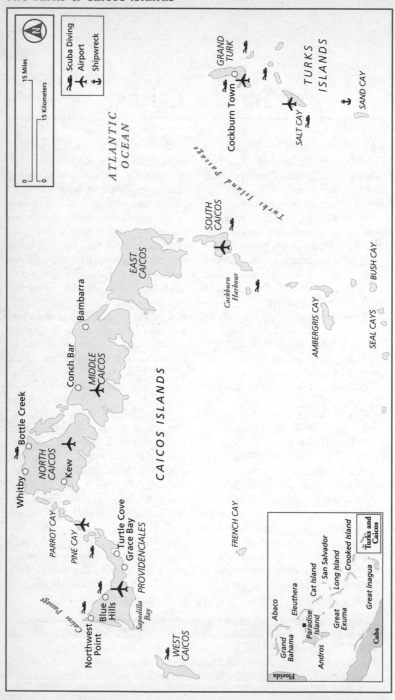

is open Monday through Friday from 8:30am to 4:30pm. The website for Turks and Caicos is **www.turksandcaicostourism.com**.

FAST FACTS: Turks & Caicos Islands

Currency The **U.S. dollar** is the official currency. Branches of **Barclays Bank** (© **649/946-4245**) and **Scotiabank** (© **649/946-4750**) are at convenient and central locations on both Provo and Grand Turk.

Customs On arriving, you may bring in 1 quart of liquor, 200 cigarettes, 50 cigars, or 8 ounces of tobacco duty-free. There are no restrictions on cameras, film, sports equipment, or personal items, provided they aren't for resale. Absolutely no spear guns are allowed, and the importation of firearms without a permit is also prohibited. Illegal imported drugs bring heavy fines and lengthy terms of imprisonment.

Electricity The electric current on the islands is 120 volts, 60 cycles, AC. European appliances will need adapters.

Emergencies Call © **911** for an **ambulance** or to report a **fire**.

Entry Requirements U.S. and Canadian citizens must have a passport or a combination of a birth certificate and photo ID, plus a return or ongoing ticket, to enter the country. These entry requirements are subject to change, so always confirm what the latest entry requirements are before heading for a foreign country. Citizens of the United Kingdom, Commonwealth countries of the Caribbean, the Republic of Ireland, and EU countries must have a current passport.

Hospitals The islands are served by medical practitioners and a qualified nursing staff. Anyone critically ill is transferred to Grand Turk for hospital treatment or evacuated to Nassau, Miami, or Jamaica for specialist treatment. Should you become ill, your hotel will locate the nearest medical facility.

Language The official language is English.

Safety Although crime is minimal in the islands, petty theft does take place, so protect your valuables, money, and cameras. Don't leave luggage or parcels in an unattended car. Beaches are also vulnerable to thievery.

Taxes There is a departure tax of $23, payable when you leave the islands. Also, the government collects a 10% occupancy tax, applicable to all hotels, guesthouses, and restaurants in the 40-island chain. Hotels add a 10% to 15% service charge on top of the government tax.

Telephone To call Turks and Caicos, dial **1** and then the number. To call U.S. and to call a phone carrier, dial **0**, then **1**, and then the number. The international-operator telephone service is available 24 hours a day.

Time The islands are in the Eastern Standard Time zone, and daylight savings time is observed.

Tipping Hotels usually add 10% to 15% to your bill automatically, to cover service. If individual staff members perform various services for you, it is customary to tip them something extra. In restaurants, 10% to 15% is appropriate unless a service charge has already been added. If in doubt, ask. Taxi drivers like at least a 10% tip.

Water Government officials insist that the water in the Turks & Caicos is safe to drink. Nonetheless, stick to bottled water, especially if you have a delicate stomach.

Weather The average temperature here is 82°F (28°C), dropping to 77°F (25°C) at night. The cooling breezes of the prevailing trade winds prevent the climate from being oppressive. The islands receive approximately 21 inches of rainfall annually.

2 Providenciales (Provo) ★★★

Affectionately known as **Provo,** Providenciales has white-sand beaches that stretch for 19km (12 miles) along the northeast coast. It also has peaceful rolling hills, flowering cactus, clear water, a natural deep harbor, and a barrier reef that attracts swimmers, divers, and boaters. The island is served by an airport (capable of handling wide-body jets), four marinas, and diving facilities.

Provo is the most developed island in the Turks and Caicos chain. Once known mainly to a group of millionaires headed by Dick du Pont, Provo has now developed a broader base of tourism.

The island is undergoing a major growth spurt, and you're sure to see lots of construction around the island from the minute you land at the airport. New resorts are being built, and the real-estate market is booming. Once you reach your hotel, however, it's easy to feel that you've gotten away from it all.

ESSENTIALS

GETTING THERE Provo is the most easily reached island in the nation because of frequency of flights. **American Airlines** (© 800/433-7300; www.aa.com) flies twice daily from Miami to Provo and Tuesday to Sunday direct from New York's JFK. There is also a Saturday flight from Boston. **U.S. Airways** (© 800/428-4322; www.usairways.com) flies from Boston to Provo daily. **Delta Airlines** (© 800/241-4141; www.delta.com) flies daily from Charlotte, North Carolina, to Provo and from Atlanta every Saturday. **Air Canada** (© 888/247-2262; www.aircanada.ca) flies from Toronto to Provo on Saturday and **British Airways** (© 800/247-9297 in the U.S., or 0870/850-9850 in the U.K.; www.britishairways.com) flies Sunday from Heathrow to Provo with a drop-off in Nassau. **Bahamasair** (© 800/222-4262; www.bahamasair.com) flies from Nassau twice weekly to Provo.

GETTING AROUND Taxis meet arriving flights; otherwise, call the Provo Taxi Association (© **649/946-5481**). Cabs are metered and rates set by the government.

Because the island is so large and its hotels and restaurants are so far-flung, you might find a car useful on Providenciales. A major U.S.-based car-rental agency with a franchise in the Turks and Caicos Islands is **Budget Rent-a-Car** on Providenciales. It's located in Butterfield Square, near the airport (© **800/472-3325** in the U.S., or 649/946-4079; www.budgetrentacar.com). Cars rent for $350 to $474 per week; collision-damage insurance costs $10 to $12 a day. The local government will collect a $15 tax for each rental contract, regardless of the number of days you keep the car. Because the company's main office lies in the commercial center of the island, a short drive from the airport, a representative will come to meet your flight at the airport if you notify them in advance of your arrival.

Charging comparable prices, **Avis Rent-a-Car** (© 800/331-1084 or 649/946-4705; www.avis.com) has also moved into the island, with a branch at the airport.

If you'd like to try your chance with a local agency, call one of the following: **Rent A Buggy** (© 649/946-4158), **Turks & Caicos National** (© 649/946-4701), or **Provo Rent-a-Car** (© 649/946-4404). Rates average from $37 to $89 per day, plus a $15 government tax.

Note: In the British tradition, cars throughout the country drive on the left.

VISITOR INFORMATION   There's a branch of the **Turks & Caicos Islands Tourist Board** at Stubbs Diamond Place, The Bite, Providenciales (© 649/946-4970), open Monday to Thursday 8am to 4:30pm and Friday 8am to 4pm.

FAST FACTS   Head for First Caribbean International Bank, Butterfield Town Square (© 649/946-4245), for cashing traveler's checks and other banking services on Provo. **The Bank of Nova Scotia** is also at Leeward Highway, Cherokee Road (© 649/946-4752).

Myrtle Rigby Health Complex, Leeward Highway and Airport Road (© 649/941-3000), can help if you have a medical problem. Anyone critically ill is transferred to Grand Turk for hospital treatment or evacuated to Nassau, Miami, or Jamaica for specialist treatment.

Call © 649/946-4259 if you need the **police.**

There's a **post office** in the Town Square (© 649/946-4676), open Monday through Thursday from 8am to 4pm, Friday from 8am to 3:30pm.

ACCOMODATIONS
VERY EXPENSIVE
Beaches Turks and Caicos Resort and Spa ☆ *(Kids)*   This resort is part of the Sandals chain of all-inclusive hotels, though unlike most Sandals, families with kids are welcome here. This is a luxurious, pampering place, opening onto the luscious sands of 19km-long (12-mile) Grace Bay Beach. The $30 million resort's Bermuda-style bungalows, with lovely pink and yellow exteriors, are gorgeous. The price tag is high, but you get a lot for your money; there's a fine spa, excellent watersports, and good service.

Catering to travelers from Europe and North America, the property features guest rooms that are finely decorated, though they could use more warmth; the one- and two-bedroom villa suites are veritable pockets of posh. All accommodations have panoramic ocean views from private balconies, king-size or double beds, individual climate control, and full bathrooms. Villa suites also have a spacious living room, a kitchenette, and two bathrooms (one with a Roman tub and separate shower).

The restaurant Reflections offers casual fare for breakfast, lunch, and dinner. Its weekend breakfast buffet is the island's best. Otherwise, it serves burgers and fries and other basics. Other restaurants offer seafood, Southwestern cuisine, and Japanese food. The Turtles and Iguanas is the spot for an after-dinner drink, and there's another bar and lounge at poolside. The resort's showcase restaurant, Sapodilla's, features Caribbean-influenced international cuisine.

Lower Bight Rd. (P.O. Box 186), Providenciales, Turks and Caicos, B.W.I. © 800/BEACHES or 649/946-8000. Fax 649/946-8001. www.beaches.com. 453 units. Winter $400–$500 double, $540–$675 1-bedroom suite, $643–$698 2-bedroom for 4, $875 3-bedroom family suite; off season $370–$435 double, $475–$660 1-bedroom suite, $595–$620 2-bedroom suite for 4, $805 3-bedroom family suite. Rates are all-inclusive. AE, MC, V.

Provo

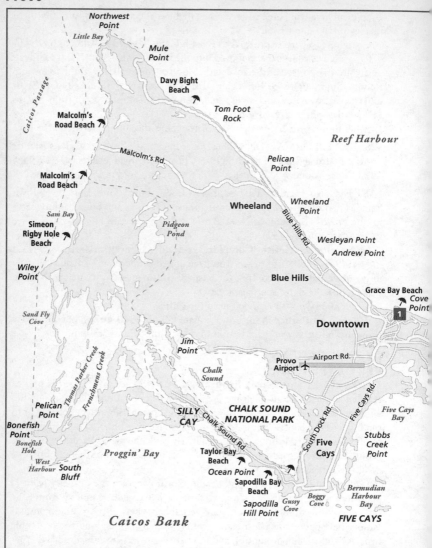

ACCOMMODATIONS ◼

Beaches Turks and Caicos
    Resort and Spa **6**
Caribbean Paradise Inn **12**
Club Med Turkoise **13**
Comfort Suites **5**
Grace Bay Club **11**

Ocean Club **14**
Parrot Cay Resort **16**
Point Grace **9**
Royal West Indies Resort **1**
Sibonné Beach Hotel **7**
Turtle Cove Inn **4**

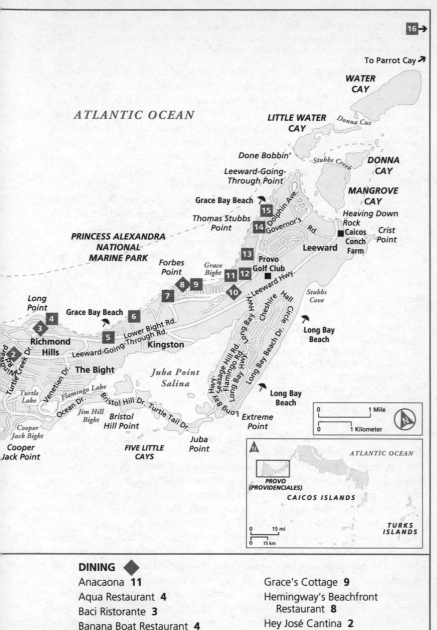

To Parrot Cay ↗

WATER CAY

ATLANTIC OCEAN

LITTLE WATER CAY

Donna Cut

Done Bobbin'

Stubbs Creek

DONNA CAY

Leeward-Going-Through Point

Grace Bay Beach ↗

15

Thomas Stubbs Point

14

Dolphin Ave.

Governor's Rd.

MANGROVE CAY

Heaving Down Rock

■ Caicos Conch Farm

Crist Point

Leeward

PRINCESS ALEXANDRA NATIONAL MARINE PARK

Forbes Point

Grace Bight

13

Provo Golf Club ■

12

Stubbs Cove

11

Long Point

10

Grace Bay Beach ↗

6

Cheshire Hall Circle

Leeward Hwy.

4

8 9

7

5

3

Richmond Hills

Leeward-Going-Through Rd.

Lower Bight Rd.

Long Bay Hwy.

Flamingo Rd.

Seasage Hill Rd.

Long Bay Hwy.

Long Bay Beach Dr.

Long Bay Beach ↗

2

Turtle Creek Dr.

Kingston

The Bight

Venetian Dr.

Flamingo Lake

Ocean Dr.

Bristol Hill Dr.

Turtle Tail Dr.

Juba Point Salina

Long Bay Beach ↗

Turtle Lake

Jim Hill Bight

Bristol Hill Point

Extreme Point

Cooper Jack Bight

FIVE LITTLE CAYS

Juba Point

Cooper Jack Point

0   1 Mile

0   1 Kilometer

N

ATLANTIC OCEAN

N

PROVO (PROVIDENCIALES)

CAICOS ISLANDS

TURKS ISLANDS

0   15 mi

0   15 km

DINING ◆

Anacaona **11**

Aqua Restaurant **4**

Baci Ristorante **3**

Banana Boat Restaurant **4**

Coco Bistro **10**

Coyaba Restaurant **15**

Grace's Cottage **9**

Hemingway's Beachfront Restaurant **8**

Hey José Cantina **2**

Amenities: 9 restaurants; 12 bars; 5 pools; disco; golf course (nearby); 4 lit tennis courts; fitness center; spa; 3 saunas; kayaks; parasailing; children's center; game room; 24-hr. room service; massage; babysitting; laundry service; dry cleaning; nonsmoking rooms; rooms for those with limited mobility. *In room:* A/C, TV, dataport, kitchenettes (in some), minibar, beverage maker, hair dryer, safe.

Club Med Turkoise ⭒

Set on 28 hectares (69 acres) of sun-blasted scrubland, on a white strip of beachfront overlooking Grace Bay, 18km (11 miles) from the airport, this is one of the most popular and successful Club Meds in the Americas. This was the first major resort built on Provo, and although more recent newcomers have pulled out in front, it remains an appealing oasis of charm and communal fun. Unlike some Club Meds, this one does not allow children under 18. Its ambience is also among the most casual of any Club Med, a fact that seems to appeal to the laid-back French and North American clientele.

The village-style cluster of two- and three-story, basic accommodations are painted a pastel pink and capped with cedar shingles imported from Sweden. The resort contains simple rooms with twin or king-size beds, all designed with beachfront living in mind. Each has a midsize, shower-only bathroom.

Most meals are served buffet-style and consumed at long communal tables. Table wine and beer are free at mealtime. Two specialty restaurants have waiter/waitress service and include a pizzeria and a beachfront eatery (the Grill) that specializes in late breakfasts, late lunches, and late suppers. A disco keeps residents active, if they wish, from 11:30pm to at least 3am nightly. All meals are included; drinks, which cost extra, are paid for with bar tickets.

Grace Bay, Providenciales, Turks and Caicos, B.W.I. ⓒ **800/CLUB-MED** in the U.S., or 649/946-5591. Fax 649/946-5500. www.clubmed.com. 291 units. Winter $1,200–$1,540 per person weekly; off season $1,064–$1,260 per person weekly. Rates include all meals, wine and beer at meals, and most activities except for scuba diving. AE, MC, V. No children under 18. **Amenities:** 2 restaurants; 3 bars; pool; nightclub; 8 lit tennis courts; gym; sailing; snorkeling; windsurfing; laundry service and coin-operated laundry; nonsmoking rooms. *In room:* A/C, TV, hair dryer, iron/ironing board, safe.

Grace Bay Club ⭒⭒⭒

This tasteful American-owned and -managed development is the island's top hotel, sitting in a desirable spot on a white-sand beach. Ringed with about 200 palm trees imported from Florida and Nevis, it lies on 2 landscaped hectares (5 acres) of what used to be sun-blasted and barren scrubland on Provo's North Shore. Designed in the spirit of a Spanish seaside village at the edge of a white-sand beach, the hotel is capped with terra-cotta tiles and partially sheathed in sculpted coral stone, and it was built around a courtyard with a splashing fountain in the center. The price is high, but if you can afford it, you'll get a lot of pampering and superb food for your money.

Each accommodation has an eclectic kind of elegance and can be configured as an individual room or as an extended suite simply by opening or closing inner doors. The bedrooms contain king-size beds with carved headboards imported from Mexico, carpets from Turkey or India, tables and armoires from Mexico or Guatemala, and artwork from Haiti or Brazil. Suites and penthouses each have their own kitchens, washing machines, and dryers. Full-size bathrooms throughout the resort contain shower-tub combinations, hand-painted Mexican tiles, and lots of mirrors.

The hotel's restaurant, Anacaona, is recommended in "Dining," below. The gracefully furnished bar area contains its own artificial waterfall and meandering stream, and a wide selection of tropical drinks. Live music is presented several times a week.

Grace Bay Rd. (P.O. Box 128), Providenciales, Turks and Caicos, B.W.I. ℭ **800/946-5757** in the U.S., or 649/946-5050. Fax 649/946-5758. www.gracebayclub.com. 21 units. Winter $705–$725 junior suite, $745–$1,195 1-bedroom suite, $1,095–$1,295 2-bedroom suite, $1,495 penthouse; off season $395–$425 junior suite, $435–$735 1-bedroom suite, $765–$835 2-bedroom suite, $995 penthouse. Rates include continental breakfast. MAP (full breakfast and dinner) $65 per person extra. AE, MC, V. Closed Sept. No children under 12. **Amenities:** Restaurant; bar; 2 pools; 2 lit tennis courts; Jacuzzi; sauna; boating excursions; deep-sea fishing; kayaks; sailing; windsurfing; bikes; car rental; business services; room service (7am–9pm daily); massage; laundry service; 1 room for those with limited mobility. *In room:* A/C, ceiling fan, TV/DVD, dataport, washer/dryer, hair dryer, safe.

Parrot Cay Resort ✸✸

This laid-back hideaway is on an isolated and very private 400-hectare (988-acre) island with a white-sand beach that lies north of Provo. The compound features 10 white- or peach-colored buildings, each with a terra-cotta roof and a design by Keith Hobbs, creator of such London landmarks as the Clarence Hotel and the Metropolitan Hotel. What he's created is a leave-your-jewelry-at-home kind of place, where a mostly neutral decor enhances the intense sunlight, turquoise waters, sands, and greenery.

Spacious rooms have louvered doors that open onto private terraces or verandas, stark white walls with dark wooden trim, terra-cotta tiles, and mosquito netting artfully draped over four-poster beds. The large tiled bathrooms are beautifully appointed with tub and shower combos and deluxe toiletries.

There's a rectangular swimming pool—the largest in the Turks and Caicos—on-site. Watersports facilities include access to scuba diving, Hobie Cats, snorkeling, canoes, and water-skiing. A holistic spa has a trio of pavilions with treatment salons where Eastern-influenced healing and rejuvenating therapies are applied, everything from yoga to meditation. The resort is riddled with nature trails, which guests can explore at their leisure. However, the beach is the real draw. There's a shuttle that will take you to the restaurants and diversions on the "mainland" of Provo.

The kitchen produces elegant and wholesome meals; they are served in the stylish main dining room or your room.

Parrot Cay (P.O. Box 164), Providenciales, Turks and Caicos, B.W.I. ℭ **877/754-0726** in the U.S., or 649/946-7788. Fax 649/946-7789. www.parrot-cay.com. 60 units. Winter $575–$730 double, $1,300 1-bedroom suite, from $1,670 1-bedroom beach house; off season $450–$590 double, $1,050 1-bedroom suite, from $1,370 1-bedroom beach house. Rates include breakfast and round-trip airport transfers by car and hotel boat. AE, MC, V. Reached by a 30-min. private boat ride north from Provo. **Amenities:** 2 restaurants; 2 bars; outdoor pool; 2 tennis courts; health club; yoga; spa; Jacuzzi; sauna; kayaks; sailing; snorkeling; bikes; limited room service; babysitting; laundry service; all nonsmoking rooms. *In room:* A/C, TV, dataport, kitchenette (in some), minibar, beverage maker, hair dryer, safe.

Point Grace ✸✸✸

This boutique hotel, the most charming and atmospheric on the island, opened in March 2000 on one of the best beaches in the Western Hemisphere. From exceptional suites to panoramic penthouses, its accommodations are the finest in the country. The motif is British colonial–inspired, and the services and amenities are first-rate, ranging from complimentary Indonesian sarongs to scented oil lamps. The complex features one-, two-, and three-bedroom suites, furnished with Indonesian hardwood and teak, and brightened by Indonesian silk fabrics. Hand-painted tile and mahogany grace the bedrooms and each suite has a full kitchen. Point Grace is set in the Princess Alexandra Park, a protected marine reserve on the north coast. The hotel is named for Grace Hutchings, who spent her honeymoon here in a small cottage a century ago. Four replicas of Grace's original honeymoon cottage sit poolside.

A very contemporary Caribbean cuisine with Asian touches is served here.

Grace Bay, (P.O. Box 158), Providenciales, Turks and Caicos, B.W.I. © 866/92-GRACE in the U.S., or 649/946-5096. Fax 649/946-5097. www.pointgrace.com. 26 units. Winter $525–$795 double, $895–$1,120 2-bedroom suite, from $1,410 3-bedroom suite; off season $395–$695 double, $625–$795 2-bedroom suite, from $970 3-bedroom suite. AE, DISC, MC, V. **Amenities:** Restaurant; bar; outdoor pool; golf (nearby); oceanfront spa facility; fishing; kayaks; sailing; limited room service; babysitting; nonsmoking rooms. *In room:* A/C, TV, dataport, kitchenette, washer/dryer, minibar, beverage maker, hair dryer, iron/ironing board, safe.

EXPENSIVE

Ocean Club 🐝🐝   Across from the Provo Golf Club, this luxury condo complex—the best of its type on the island—opens onto Grace Bay, site of the finest beach. This resort community has accommodations available for sale or rent, all spread across a 3-hectare (7½-acre) piece of landscaped property.

The resort consists of studio suites, deluxe studio suites, and one-, two-, or three-bedroom deluxe suites, all with ocean views and shower-tub combination bathrooms, plus fully equipped kitchens (studios have kitchenettes only). Each suite is equipped with both ceiling fans and central air-conditioning. A series of buildings surrounds gardens and a courtyard. Except for the studio suite (the cheapest rental), accommodations are spacious and comfortable, with large screened balconies.

The hotel has a grill restaurant that serves international food, plus a cabana bar. There is a dive shop that is an annex for Art Pickering's Provo Turtle Divers Ltd. (see the section "Snorkeling and Scuba Diving," later in the chapter). Dive classes are available at the hotel, but for diving and rental equipment, you'll have to take a shuttle bus to the company's headquarters in Turtle Cove. There's also a daily shuttle-bus service for dining in the evenings and a part-time shuttle bus for daytime shopping, both for a small fee.

Grace Bay Beach (P.O. Box 240), Providenciales, Turks and Caicos, B.W.I. © 800/457-8787 or 649/946-5880. Fax 649/946-5845. www.oceanclubresorts.com. 88 units. Winter $225–$280 studio suite, $425–$525 1-bedroom suite, $630–$685 2-bedroom suite, $835–$910 3-bedroom suite; off season $180–$225 studio suite, $315–$335 1-bedroom suite, $415–$485 2-bedroom suite, $550–$600 3-bedroom suite. AE, MC, V. **Amenities:** 2 restaurants; 2 bars; 2 outdoor pools; tennis court; fitness room; sauna; dive shop; babysitting. *In room:* A/C, ceiling fan, TV, dataport, kitchen or kitchenette, washer/dryer, fridge, beverage maker, hair dryer, iron/ironing board, safe.

Royal West Indies Resort 🐝🐝   This is one of the most luxurious condo resorts along Grace Bay, offering first-class style and a hint of British colonial architecture. Lying on one of the best parts of the sandy beach, this elegant retreat is between Grace Bay Club and Club Med. Surrounding the property are well-manicured gardens, the centerpiece of which is a 24m-long (79-ft.) pool set against a backdrop of tropical fruit trees. Guests have a choice of oceanfront, oceanview, studio, or gardenview one- and two-bedroom suites. Suites are large and have balconies and kitchenettes with different bedding configurations to suit various groups or families. Two-bedroom suites can be subdivided into one-bedroom accommodations or self-sufficient units. The interiors are furnished in an eclectic blend of woods and fabrics from South America and other locales. Even if you're not a guest, consider a meal at Mango Reef, the on-site Caribbean restaurant.

Grace Bay (P.O. Box 482), Providenciales, Turks and Caicos, B.W.I. © 800/332-4203 in U.S. or 649/946-5004. Fax 649/946-5008. www.royalwestindies.com. 99 units. Winter $225–$340 studio, $295–$445 1-bedroom, $425–$595 2-bedroom suite; off season $160–$235 studio, $225–$350 1-bedroom, $320–$425 2-bedroom suite. AE, MC, V. **Amenities:** Restaurant; bar; 2 outdoor pools; sauna; kayaks; sailing; scuba diving; snorkeling; scooter and bike rental; massage; babysitting. *In room:* A/C, ceiling fan, TV, kitchenette, fridge, hair dryer, iron/ironing board, safe.

MODERATE

Caribbean Paradise Inn This intimate, cozy inn is a short walk to Grace Bays Beach, which is visible from the balconies of the second-floor units. All the midsize units are furnished like a high-grade motel and have a combination bedroom and living area. The small bathrooms have showers only.

The swimming pool and sun deck are accessible from each unit, and divers are given lockable open-air closets to store their gear.

Grace Bay (P.O. Box 673), Providenciales, Turks and Caicos, B.W.I. ✆ **649/946-5020.** Fax 649/946-5022. www.paradise.tc. 16 units. Winter $145–$169 double; off season $135–$149 double. Extra person $30. MC, V. Rates include breakfast. **Amenities:** Bar; outdoor pool; babysitting; laundry service. *In room:* A/C, ceiling fan, TV, dataport, minibar, beverage maker, hair dryer, safe.

Comfort Suites This is the first franchise hotel ever to open on Provo. As a Comfort Suites hotel, it is far superior to the standard format, and the welcome and hospitality provided by the staff is exceptional. The handsomely landscaped property lies across the road from Grace Bay Beach, and is within an easy walk of many attractions, including the casino. Guests live here in one of the spacious junior suites, with either a king-size or two double beds, or else in one of the so-called honeymoon suites (you don't have to be a honeymooner to book one of these). Accommodations are spread across two three-floor structures, enveloping an Olympic-size swimming pool and courtyard.

Grace Bay, Providenciales, Turks and Caicos, B.W.I. ✆ **888/678-3483** or 649/946-8888. Fax 649/946-5444. www.comfortsuitestci.com. 100 suites. Winter $150–$160 double, $170 suite; off season $135–$150 double, $160 suite. AE, DISC, MC, V. **Amenities:** Bar; outdoor pool; babysitting; nonsmoking rooms. *In room:* A/C, TV, dataport, beverage maker, safe.

Sibonné Beach Hotel ✦ *Value* This was the first hotel constructed on the fabulous sands of Grace Bay Beach. If you prefer an intimate inn of charm and a certain grace, this is a good bet. The hotel is informal and laid-back, and its courtyard gardens are especially alluring. Each accommodation has a light, breezy decor with an emphasis on comfort. Their best accommodation here is a beach-bordering one-bedroom suite, detached from the actual hotel. Even if you're not a guest, consider a visit to the Grace Bay Bistro, one of only a few on the beach itself. The restaurant excels at offering a creative menu that features fresh local seafood along with a selection of international dishes. Honeymooners like the seclusion of the place, as do more mature visitors. For shopping, spas, casino action, or nightlife, several options lie a short walk away at one of the larger resorts.

Grace Bay (P.O. Box 144), Providenciales, Turks and Caicos, B.W.I. ✆ **800/528-1905** in the U.S., or 649/946-5547. Fax 649/946-5770. www.sibonne.com. 27 units. $175–$200 double; $225 suite; off season $125–$170 double, $200 suite. AE, MC, V. **Amenities:** Restaurant; bar; outdoor pool; kayaks; snorkeling; babysitting; laundry service. *In room:* A/C, ceiling fans, TV, dataport, fridge, beverage maker, hair dryer, iron/ironing board, safe.

Turtle Cove Inn ✦ This two-story hotel, built in a U shape around a freshwater swimming pool, is a favorite with divers and boaters. A few feet away, boats dock directly at the hotel's pier, which juts into Seller's Pond amid the many yachts floating at anchor. Each bedroom is simply but comfortably furnished, with views over either the pool or the marina. All units are equipped with a small bathroom containing a shower stall. The on-site Aqua Restaurant is reviewed in "Dining" below.

Turtle Cove Marina, Suzie Turn Rd. (P.O. Box 131), Providenciales, Turks and Caicos, B.W.I. © 800/887-0477 in the U.S., or 649/946-4203. Fax 649/946-4141. www.turtlecoveinn.com. 28 units. Winter $118–$145 double; off season $98–$120 double. AE, MC, V. **Amenities:** Restaurant; bar; outdoor pool; scooter and bike rental; car rental; babysitting; laundry service; all nonsmoking rooms. *In room:* A/C, TV, fridge.

DINING

In addition to the restaurants below, you may want to check out the options at Beaches Turks and Caicos Resort and Spa (recommended above). The resort's showcase restaurant, **Sapodilla's** (© **649/946-8000**), can be visited by outsiders who purchase a day pass for $85 or an evening pass for $80 valid from 6pm to 2am. The price of the pass allows you to dine and drink anywhere at the resort.

Be aware that the island is undergoing many changes, and the restaurants do come and go. Have your hotel call ahead for you if you're venturing off the beaten path.

EXPENSIVE

Anacaona 𝘊 MEDITERRANEAN/CARIBBEAN   Set in three thatched-roof outbuildings at the Grace Bay Club, this place is lighthearted, fun, and elegant. It's as good as hotel restaurants get in Provo. You might enjoy a frothy drink in the bar before crossing over a fountain stream to the restaurant. French recipes are combined effectively with Caribbean produce—not always an easy marriage, but here the result is successful. In the evening the atmosphere becomes more romantic, with flickering light from the torches and candlelight on the tables. The chef's grilled lobster is among the island's finest dishes. He also does fresh fish dishes extremely well. A local specialty is the conch chowder flavored with dark rum. Creative dishes with successful flavor combinations include roast herb-crusted rack of lamb with eggplant chips and sun-dried tomatoes, and the grilled filet of beef tenderloin on a bed of French beans. Try also the grilled filet of grouper tantalizingly served with mango flavoring.

In the Grace Bay Club, Grace Bay Rd. © 649/946-5050. Reservations recommended. Lunch salads, sandwiches, and platters $9–$20; dinner main courses $26–$36. AE, MC, V. Daily noon–3pm and 7–9pm.

Aqua Restaurant 𝘊 CARIBBEAN/INTERNATIONAL   Divers, boaters, and couples have turned this convivial place into Provo's trendiest spot. Trendy would mean little if the food weren't good; fortunately, it is. The setting, an enclosed outdoor bar and terrace overlooking the marina, also helps. The menu changes weekly. The chef's classic, home-smoked conch, appears with a wasabi-laced mayonnaise. The best of the signature dishes include pan-seared wahoo on a bed of sweet coconut hummus with mango salsa and grilled local lobster with lemon-garlic butter. One of the most enticing conch dishes sampled in the islands is pecan-encrusted conch with a spicy orange-butter sauce.

In the Turtle Cove Inn, Suzie Turn Rd., North Shore. © 649/946-4763. Reservations recommended for dinner. Main courses $17–$32. AE, MC, V. Daily 7am–10pm.

Baci Ristorante 𝘊 ITALIAN   At a waterside table here you can imagine you're dining on the Mediterranean. The affordable and tasty cuisine, the romantic patio, the stone floors and wrought iron, and the whirling *Casablanca*-style overhead fans conspire to make this an agreeable stopover. Since 1999, this has been one of the preferred dining choices at Provo. The chef specializes in veal, serving it five different ways that include fork-tender filets in a zesty lemon-butter sauce. Pasta dishes are usually superb, and we also like the well-flavored breast of chicken with shrimp. If you want a particular dish that's not on the limited but varied menu, the chef will often prepare it for you if he has the ingredients. For dessert, we recommend the tiramisu, the best on island.

Turtle Cove Marina, Harbour Town. 🕿 **649/941-3044.** Reservations recommended. Lunch main courses $8–$12; dinner main courses $15–$25. AE, MC, V. Mon–Fri noon–2:30pm; daily 6–10pm.

Coyaba Restaurant 🟆🟆🟆 CONTINENTAL/CARIBBEAN   Chef Paul Newman (no, not that one) shows off his culinary flair in the tropical garden setting of this gazebolike restaurant. A helpful staff serves some of the island's freshest and best seafood against a background of pleasant music. Many local recipes have a strong Continental influence. Start your meal with tempura shrimp in Barcelo honey–rum sauce, a freshly made ceviche, or a platter of smoked fish. The truffle mousse with sherry and the New England–style fish chowder are also delightful. For a main course, try the French-trimmed rack of lamb or *osso buco* with a porcini risotto. A first for many diners is the baked spiny lobster (with vanilla extract, chèvre, toasted coconut, and threads of saffron). For dessert, nothing tops the made-to-order upside-down apple pie accompanied by Blue Mountain coffee from Jamaica.

Penns Rd. 🕿 **649/946-5186.** Reservations required. Main courses $23–$39. AE, MC, V. Winter Wed–Mon 6–10pm; off season Wed–Mon 6:30–10pm. From Leeward Highway, turn left on Pratt Rd. and then right on Lower Bight Rd.; take the second left (Penns Rd.) to Coral Gardens Beach Resort at the end of the road.

Grace's Cottage 🟆🟆 CARIBBEAN/ASIAN   An elegant restaurant seating 62, Grace's Cottage is a little architectural gem with bright white gingerbread trim that features outdoor seating under gazebos on a terrace. Inside you can enjoy an aperitif at the mahogany bar before taking a chair at one of the teak tables covered with Egyptian cotton tablecloths set with Villeroy Boch china, Italian glasses, and Sambonet cutlery. The light, sophisticated cuisine changes daily, taking advantage of exotic ingredients. Begin with the West Indian pumpkin-and-coconut soup with toasted macadamias, or wrapped seared tuna with sweet-yam mash. For a main course, you might want to order pan-fried jerk wahoo with a ginger-plum sauce, or chargrilled filet of beef beautifully accented with roast shallots, onion rings, and sautéed mushrooms. Desserts are also sumptuous and include chargrilled peppered pineapple and Swiss chocolate fondue with fruits and a vanilla-cream sauce.

In the Point Grace Hotel, Grace Bay. 🕿 **649/946-5096.** Main courses $28–$54. AE, MC, V. Daily 6:30–10:30pm.

MODERATE

Banana Boat Restaurant INTERNATIONAL   The Banana Boat is the most popular restaurant on the island that's not in a hotel. It's not the best, but it's certainly the most convivial. Since 1981, there's not a yachtie on Provo who hasn't moored here to enjoy an island meal and a potent tropical drink. For a main course, you might try T-bone steak, cracked conch, or some freshly caught local fish. At lunch, favorites include lobster salad or a half-pound burger. Dessert might be cheesecake or Key lime pie. No one in the kitchen fusses too much with these dishes, but they are good and flavorful. A choice seat is on the timber-and-plank veranda that juts out over piers on Turtle Cove.

Turtle Cove Marina. 🕿 **649/941-5706.** Reservations recommended. Main courses $16–$35; lunch $6–$12. AE, MC, V. Daily 11am–11pm.

Coco Bistro ★ *Finds* FRENCH/MEDITERRANEAN   The most attractive and appealing French restaurant on Provo lies on a plot of land that was a plant nursery in the 1980s, which has since grown into the largest palm grove on the island. The vaguely Mexican/vaguely Moroccan-looking restaurant is run by a husband-and-wife team from Provence, Yves Coutisson and Dominique Rousset (he tends bar; she cooks). Most meals are enjoyed in the garden, under the palms. Menu items, often Mediterranean in origin, include penne pasta with chicken and basil-infused sun-dried tomatoes; spaghetti in a lobster-flavored cream sauce; grouper in puff pastry; *tagine* (stew) of lamb or lamb kabobs; or snapper baked in a crust of sea salt, served with a sauce of olive oil, basil, and sage. Desserts are all French and homemade. We especially recommend the crème brûlée.

Grace Bay Rd. ⓒ 649/946-5369. Reservations recommended. Main courses $6–$30. DISC, MC, V. Mon–Sat 6–9:30pm.

Hemingway's Beachfront Restaurant CARIBBEAN/INTERNATIONAL An instant island hot spot, Hemingway's beachside locale attracts international travelers as well as locals. The selections are inviting. Fresh grouper is lightly spiced and pan-seared, served with a tequila-spiked veggie salsa with charred onions, black beans, corn, red and green peppers, and carrots. Shrimp is lightly sautéed with a scrumptious pesto cream over penne, and filet mignon is exquisitely grilled with a fragrant red wine mushroom sauce. Hemingway's is also a good lunch choice, serving gourmet sandwiches, hearty salads, soft fish tacos, or fresh vegetable pitas. Finish with crème brûlée or deep-fried ice cream. At night torches and candlelight lend a hint of romance.

At The Sands at Grace Bay. ⓒ 649/946-5199. Reservations required. Main courses $10–$30. AE, MC, V. Daily 8am–10pm.

INEXPENSIVE

Hey José Cantina MEXICAN/PIZZA/AMERICAN   One of the focal points of a small shopping center in the center of the island, this lighthearted place is run by Steve and Marilyn Mull. Surrounded by burnt orange, green, and yellow hues, you can enjoy the best margaritas in Provo. The parade of burritos, tacos, quesadillas, chimichangas, and grilled steaks and chicken will make you think you've been transplanted to some fiery little eatery along the Tex-Mex border. Also popular, especially with expatriate North Americans who have had their fill of grouper and cracked conch, are the richly topped pizzas. Available in three sizes, they culminate with a variety known as "the kitchen sink," with virtually everything you can think of thrown into the mix.

Central Square, Leeward Hwy. ⓒ 649/946-4812. Lunch platters $7–$12; pizzas $7–$21; dinner main courses $12–$20. MC, V. Mon–Sat noon–10pm. Bar Mon–Sat noon–midnight.

HITTING THE BEACH

Starting at Leeward and running all the way to Thompson Cove, **Grace Bay Beach** ★★★ is Provo's finest beach, stretching for 19km (12 miles) of spectacular, powdery-soft white sand. The gin-clear, crystal-blue waters are extremely tranquil and there are no rocks, making it ideal for kids. Many resorts, such as Club Med, have developed along its edge, so you won't have these sands all to yourself. Though there are no public facilities on the beach, the hotels themselves come in handy, because all of them have rest rooms and bars serving tropical drinks. The folks at *Condé Nast* rated Grace Bay the "number one beach on the planet."

Grace Bay Beach is so stunning that you might not want to venture anywhere else, but there are a few other beaches on the island. They're less spectacular, but also less crowded. In the east, **Long Bay Beach** lies on the opposite shore from Grace Bay, opening onto Long Bay itself. It begins around Juba Point and extends east to Stubbs Cove, and is virtually free of hotels. The sand here isn't as powdery fine as that of Grace Bay, but you'll have more privacy. The waters here are very sheltered and there are virtually no waves.

If you want to flee the hordes, you can rent a four-wheel-drive vehicle, following Malcolm's Road west to **Malcolm's Road Beach.** Figure a 30-minute drive to reach this beach from Grace Bay, and the last 5km (3 miles) of the road are very rocky. But once you reach this beach, it is stunningly lovely, with fine white sands, and nearly always empty. There's good snorkeling, though you'll have to bring your own gear. There are no facilities.

A final choice worth exploring is **Sapodilla Bay Beach** in the west, opening on Proggin's Bay, south of the airport. It's a gem of a white-sand beach with crystal-clear waters. It lies between two 9m (30-ft.) cliffs at Gussy Cove, stretching all the way west to Ocean Point. This is such a well-protected beach, with fine sands and clear shallow water (even 30m/98 ft. out), that the locals often refer to it as "the children's beach."

WATERSPORTS & OTHER OUTDOOR PURSUITS

FISHING   Silver Deep (© 649/941-5441) offers the best fishing excursions, with both half- and full-day expeditions, usually for bonefishing or bottom fishing. Tackle and bait are thrown in.

For those who'd like to venture farther afield—and pay a lot more money— half- and full-day deep-sea fishing expeditions are available, with all equipment included. Catches turn up wahoo, tuna, kingfish, marlin, and even shark.

GOLF   **Provo Golf Club** ⚐ at Grace Bay Road (© 649/946-5991), is the only golf course in the country. It was rated as one of the top-10 golf courses in the Caribbean by *Caribbean Travel and Life.* The 6,560-yard, par-72, 18-hole course was designed by Karl Litten of Boca Raton, Florida, and is owned by the Turks and Caicos Water Company. It is powerfully green and takes an extraordinary amount of water to keep it so, because Provo is one of the driest spots on the globe. Young palms and bougainvillea, as well as rocky outcroppings and powdery sand traps, help make the course a challenge to the serious golfer or a lovely day on the links for the beginner or novice. Four sets of tees allow golfers to tailor a game to their level of expertise. A driving range and putting greens are also available. The clubhouse contains a bar and a restaurant open daily from 7am to 10pm. Greens fees are $130 per person for 18 holes. The price includes the use of a golf cart, which is mandatory. Golf clubs can be rented for $20 to $40 per set.

PARASAILING   This increasingly popular sport is offered by **J&B Tours,** Leeward Marina (© 649/946-5047). A 15-minute flight costs around $70.

SAILING & KAYAKING   Boating in the hard-to-reach islands has become a popular pastime. Sailing craft, even with a private captain for half- or full-day excursions, are available from **J&B Tours** (© 649/946-5047).

SNORKELING & SCUBA DIVING   Dive experts, including the late Jacques Cousteau, have cited Provo as one of the 10 best sites in the world, because of a barrier reef that runs the full length of the island's 27km (17-mile) north coast. At Northwest Point there is a vertical drop-off to 2,100m (6,888 ft.).

From the shore at **Grace Bay** ⟨ℛ⟩, visitors can see where the sea breaks along 23km (14 miles) of barrier reef, the teeming undersea home to sea life that ranges from swarms of colorful schools of fish to barracuda to rotund grouper.

Off the northwest corner of the island of Provo is **Smith's Reef** ⟨ℛ⟩, a walk-in dive to a seascape of brain and fan corals, purple gorgonians, anemones, sea cucumbers, sergeant majors, green parrot fish, long-nosed trumpet fish, the ominous-looking green moray, an occasional southern ray, and a visiting hawks-bill turtle or two. Smith's Reef has a total of 13 underwater signs that describe the coral reef ecosystem and the diversity of life that thrives there. Snorkelers can learn about the various creatures camouflaged within the reef, the importance of sea-grass beds, and the ways that parrotfish contribute to the environment. The trail follows the perimeter of the reef starting inshore in about 1m to 2m (3¼–6½ ft.) of water, increasing to 7m to 9m (23 ft.–30 ft.) deep. The depth marks a spectacular display of coral creations, colorful schooling fish, and spotted eagle rays; even resident turtles can be found.

Bight Reef is located in the Grace Bay area known as the Bight, just offshore from a large white house. A public footpath leads to the beach, and two marker buoys indicate both ends of the snorkel trail. The Bight Reef Snorkel Trail has a total of 11 underwater trail signs that describe corals and how they grow. Water depth ranges from 1m to 5m (3¼ ft.–16 ft.), and visitors can view mobile species like yellow-tailed snappers, big jolthead porgies, and sand-sifting mojarras.

If you'd like to take a snorkel cruise, consider **Ocean Outback** (© **649/941-5810**). A 21m (69-ft.) motor cruiser will take you to neighboring, uninhabited islands for snorkeling. For $99 per person, you are taken to your own private island for the day (9am–4pm). The cost includes the boat shuttle to the island (pickup is at 4pm), snorkel gear, a beach umbrella, a picnic lunch, and plenty of cold drinks.

Art Pickering's Provo Turtle Divers Ltd., Turtle Cove (© **649/946-4232; 800/833-1341** for reservations), with headquarters directly in front of the Miramar Resort on the water, is the oldest and best dive operation in the islands, offering personalized service. There are scuba tanks for rent, plus ample backpacks and weight belts. A single-tank dive costs $55, a night dive goes for $65, and a morning two-tank dive is $80 to $90. Prices include all equipment. Provo Turtle is a PADI training facility, with full instruction and resort courses. An open-water PADI referral course goes for $325. A PADI open-water certification course is $500.

TENNIS   The best courts are at the all-inclusive **Club Med Turkoise** (see "Accommodations" above), but these are usually set aside for guests. Nonguests can play at many other courts, however, including **Miramar Resort** (© **649/946-4240**), for a per-hour fee.

EXPLORING THE ISLAND

Chalk Sound, a landlocked lagoon west of Five Cays Settlement, has been turned into a public park. The hamlet of Five Cays itself boasts a small harbor and a modern airport.

Caicos Conch Farm, Leeward Highway (© 649/946-5330), is located on the isolated eastern end of the island, amid a flat and sun-baked terrain of scrub and sand. This is the only place in the West Indies where the conch is commercially produced. Though its techniques are not economically viable, this conch farm could spark breeding techniques that could change the way conch is cultivated worldwide. Its staff will give visitors a walking tour of the breeding basins. Admission of $6 for adults and $3 for children includes a tour of the hatchery and the laboratories. In the gift shop, you can buy rare conch pearls, shell jewelry, and T-shirts. Open Monday through Friday 9am to 4pm, Saturday 9am to 2pm.

SHOPPING

You might enjoy browsing through the Bamboo Gallery, Leeward Highway (© 649/946-4748), one of the island's leading art galleries. Its inventories include woodcarvings, ceramic sculptures, and the kinds of colorful oil paintings that, if they don't come directly from Haiti, were at least inspired by that island's traditions. The most unusual pieces—to look at if not to buy—are some of the locally made metal sculptures, sometimes created from oil drums or old car wrecks.

Paradise Gifts & Art, Central Square (© 649/946-4748), owned by the Bamboo Galley, specializes in local art, and handcrafts. It also carries a line of souvenir and gift items.

For the best duty-free shopping, head to Royal Jewels, Leeward Highway (© 649/946-4699). It has good stocks in gold jewelry and designer watches, and French and international perfumes—all that standard showcase stuff found on other islands in the Caribbean.

PROVO AFTER DARK

The major center for after-dark diversion on Provo is the American Casino, Grace Bay (© 649/946-5555), which is one of the few to operate in any British Dependent Territory. It's generally packed every night with gamblers playing blackjack, Caribbean stud, roulette, and poker. There are also about 80 slot machines. Fans whirl overhead as waiters serve frosty drinks. Hours are daily from 7pm until 1am.

Many hotels stage entertainment for their guests. If yours doesn't, you can seek some action at Stardust and Ashes, Leeward Highway (© 649/941-5475), which often offers live music such as reggae, soca, and a steel band. Open Tuesday to Thursday 9:30pm to 2am, Friday 9:30pm to 3am, and Saturday 7:30pm to midnight.

The bar at the lovely Gecko Grille, Ocean Plaza, in the Ocean Club, Grace Bay Beach (© 649/946-5880), stays open until 10pm.

Dora's, Leeward Highway (© 649/946-4558), is an island hot spot, with casual dining, cold beer and island-style drinks, and a good jukebox. On Thursday and Friday nights, you might catch a local band.

3 Grand Turk ✸

Grand Turk is the capital of the Turks and Caicos Islands, although it is no longer the financial and business hub of the island nation, having lost that position to Provo. It is no longer the transportation hub either, as Provo receives

95% of the international airplane landings. The island is rather barren and windswept, and there is little vegetation. Don't come here looking for lush tropical foliage. Do consider Grand Turk, however, if you want a real bargain destination that's excellent for snorkeling and diving, with luscious white-sand beaches.

Many scholars believe that Grand Turk was the site of Columbus's first landfall in 1492. They maintain he set foot on the western shores of the island late on the day of October 12. The native Arawaks were here to welcome him to their island of "Guanahani," although they were later to pay a terrible price for that hospitality, because they were sold into slavery in the Caribbean.

Cockburn Town (*Coe*-burn) is the financial and business hub of this tiny island. You'll find **Governor's Beach** near—you guessed it—the governor's residence on the west coast of the island. It's the best place for swimming. If you are on your way to another island, at least take time to tour Cockburn Town's **historic section,** particularly Duke and Front streets, where some houses built of wood and limestone stand along the waterfront. The 12-sq.-km (4¾-sq.-mile) island of Grand Turk has several protected historical buildings, one of which is a hotel, Turks Head Inn. The other landmark buildings include the police station and Government House.

ESSENTIALS

GETTING THERE   Once on Provo (see "Getting There" in section 2, earlier in this chapter), you can fly **Sky King Airlines** (© **649/941-5464**) to Grand Turk. Sky King has seven daily flights from Providenciales to South Caicos and Grand Turk. The fare to Grand Turk is $74 one-way or $133 round-trip.

VISITOR INFORMATION   The **Turks & Caicos Islands Tourist Board Information Office,** Front Street, Cockburn Town, Grand Turk, B.W.I. (© **800/241-0824** in the U.S., or 649/946-2322), is open Monday through Friday from 8:30am to 4:30pm. At this office, the National Parks of Turks and Caicos produces a guide to the marine parks, nature reserves, sanctuaries, and historic sites of the island nation.

GETTING AROUND   Many visitors walk where they are going, or check with **Yellow Man Car Rental** (© **649/231-0167**) if they need a car. Rental prices start at $65 per day. *Remember:* Drive on the left.

Used mainly by the islanders themselves, a new public **bus** system was launched, but service is patchy, with fares costing 50¢ one-way.

Taxis are available, but there is no central agency to call. Your hotel can to summon you one, or you can find them at the airport when you arrive. The fare is $10 to $12 from the airport to most major hotels.

Another way to get around is by bike. Along Duke Street in Grand Turk, the **Osprey Beach Hotel** (© **649/946-1453**) rents bikes for $10 per day or $60 per week.

FAST FACTS   For cashing traveler's checks and other transactions, try **First Caribbean International,** Front Street (© **649/946-2831**), or the **Bank of Nova Scotia,** also on Front Street (© **649/946-2506**). Both banks have ATMs.

Grand Turk Hospital, Hospital Road (© **649/946-2040**), can fill prescriptions and provide simple medical assistance. The hospital itself has 35 beds, X-ray facilities, an operating theater, and a pathology laboratory.

Call © **649/946-2299** if you need the **police.**

The **General Post Office** (© **649/946-1334**) is open Monday through Thursday from 8am to 12:30pm and from 2 to 4pm, Friday from 8am to 3:30pm. There's also a Philatelic Bureau, operated separately from the post office, but with the same hours.

ACCOMODATIONS

Hotels add a 10% to 15% service charge, plus a 10% government occupancy tax, to the rates quoted below.

EXPENSIVE

The Arches of Grand Turk Island *Kids*   Atop the island's North Ridge, these modern town houses—a short walk from beautiful beaches—are the most deluxe way to live on Grand Turk. Bedrooms open onto island or ocean views. At Arches you find two-story town house units, each linked together and containing two bedrooms with two baths with shower-tub combinations and balconies for taking in those sunsets. Families and couples are especially fond of the complex, and accommodations contain two double beds or queen-size bed. Two-bedroom units are suitable for six guests who make use of a fully equipped kitchen. Maid service is available upon request.

Lighthouse Road (P.O. Box 226), Grand Turk, Turks and Caicos, B.W.I. © 649/946-2941. Fax 649/946-1312. www.grandturkarches.com. 4 units. Winter $180 double, $240 2-bedroom; off season $160 double, $220 2-bedroom. DISC, MC, V. **Amenities:** Outdoor pool; bikes; coin-operated laundry; all nonsmoking rooms. *In room:* A/C, ceiling fans, kitchen, fridge, beverage maker, hair dryer, iron/ironing board, no phone.

Island House *Finds*   On a breezy site overlooking North Creek, this inn is the creation of Colin Brooker, an English expat, and his Grand Turk–born wife, Lucy. The complex's architectural style evokes the Mediterranean, with rooms opening onto water views. The studios and one-bedroom suites all have kitchens, bathrooms with tub and shower, and balconies overlooking the water and the well-planted gardens. The location is 2km (1¼ miles) from the center of town, which can be reached by a gas-powered golf cart. The idyllic spot here is a pool set against a backdrop of palms. Activities such as fishing and scuba diving can be arranged. Divers often book here because of the inn's location near fabulous reefs and "walls" only minutes from shore. The hotel offers its own dock on North Creek, featuring sailing, canoeing, and windsurfing.

Lighthouse Rd. (P.O. Box 36), Grand Turk, Turks and Caicos, B.W.I. © 649/946-1388. Fax 649/946-2646. www.islandhouse-tci.com. 8 units. Winter $168–$198 per person nondiver, $228–$259 per person diver; off season $150–$180 per person nondiver, $210–$240 per person diver. Dive rates include 2 morning boat dives. Children under 12 stay free in parent's room. AE, MC, V. **Amenities:** Outdoor pool; dock; fishing; sailing; snorkeling; windsurfing; bikes; babysitting; coin-operated laundry. *In room:* A/C, ceiling fans, TV, dataport, kitchen, fridge, hair dryer, beverage maker, safe.

MODERATE

Arawak Inn and Beach Club   Set near the extreme southern tip of Grand Turk, this two-story apartment complex was built in 1996 on a sugar-white strip of beachfront. It's largely geared to divers, many of whom book here on dive packages. Each spacious unit has a separate bedroom and living room, as well as a kitchenette and a private veranda or patio, plus a full-size bathroom with a shower unit.

There's a full bar on the premises, as well as a simple indoor-outdoor restaurant serving moderately priced American food, including a lunch menu of burgers, club sandwiches, and salads. Although there aren't a lot of luxuries and diversions on-site, the staff is able to arrange all manner of tours and sports for you, if you want to rouse yourself off those white sands.

Harbour Sands Condominium (P.O. Box 290), Cockburn Town, Grand Turk, Turks and Caicos, B.W.I. © 649/ 946-2277. Fax 649/946-2279. www.fortmyers.com/turks/arawak.htm. 14 apts. Winter $165 double; off season $150 double. Children under 5 stay free in parent's room. MC, V. **Amenities:** Restaurant; bar; outdoor pool; kayak rental; laundry service; nonsmoking rooms; rooms for those with limited mobility. *In room:* A/C, TV, dataport, kitchenette, fridge, beverage maker, iron/ironing board.

Osprey Beach Hotel *(Kids*   This landmark hotel has a white-sand beach that offers good swimming and snorkeling. A family favorite, its bedrooms occupy modern two-story town houses, each with a ceiling crafted from varnished pine. Some rooms have kitchenettes, but all contain ceiling fans and verandas with a view of the sea, plus small bathrooms with shower-tub combinations. The rooms on the upper floors are larger and have higher ceilings. Across the street in the older wing of the hotel is The Courtyard Café, open for breakfast and lunch. Dinner is served at the Osprey Pool bar.

Duke St., P.O. Box 216, Grand Turk, Turks and Caicos, B.W.I. © **649/946-1453.** Fax 649/946-2817. www. ospreybeachhotel.com. 27 units. Winter $165–$190 double; off season $153–$200 double. Children under 12 stay free in parent's room. Dive packages available. AE, MC, V. **Amenities:** Restaurant/cafe; bar; outdoor pool; laundry service; rooms for those with limited mobility. *In room:* A/C, TV, dataport, kitchenettes (in some), fridge.

Turks Head Inn *(Finds*   As charming as anything you'll find on the island, this old-fashioned hotel was built in 1840 by Bermudan shipwrights as a private home. Thoroughly overhauled in 2004, it has a more European flavor than any other inn on the island and doesn't really offer resort-style facilities, although a sandy beach is nearby. Most business comes from its bar and restaurant (see "Dining," below), and that's where most of the staff's attention is focused. However, behind a two-level veranda with ornate balustrades painted in bright tropical colors, a handful of bedrooms can be rented. Two of the bedrooms have access to an open second-floor veranda in front; four have access to the somewhat-more-private enclosed veranda overlooking the back. Each has a private bathroom with a shower unit, a ceiling fan, high ceilings, and antique or period furnishings. All contain queen-size beds, two of which are four-posters. The inn lies in a mature garden with towering trees and a shady terrace with outdoor tables.

Duke St. (P.O. Box 58), Grand Turk, Turks and Caicos, B.W.I. © **649/946-2466.** Fax 649/946-1716. www. grand-turk.com. 8 units. $125–$175 double. MAP (breakfast and dinner) $45 per person extra. MC, V. **Amenities:** Restaurant; bar; car rental; babysitting; laundry service. *In room:* A/C, ceiling fans, TV, minibar, beverage maker, hair dryer.

DINING

Regal Beagal CARIBBEAN   Located about a 3-minute drive from the center of Cockburn Town, this is one of the simplest and least pretentious restaurants on the island. There's a bar as well as a handful of plain tables where you can order lobster salad, several variations of conch, chicken or fish with chips, pork, or burgers.

Hospital St. © **649/946-2274.** Sandwiches and salads $5–$8; platters $9–$23. No credit cards. Mon–Sat 11am–3pm and 6:30pm–midnight.

Turk's Head Restaurant *(* INTERNATIONAL/CARIBBEAN   This is the island's oldest and busiest pub, a landmark for the many divers, dock workers, writers, and eccentrics living on Grand Turk. Set within the Turks Head Inn, it has a funky tropical indoor dining room, and a thatched-roof annex so you can catch the breezes.

The food is served informally, in large portions, and uses whatever happens to have arrived from mainland suppliers that week. You might find chargrilled sirloin steak, traditional baked grouper in Cajun spices, or smoked chicken and mango with a raspberry coulis. Desserts are the best on the island, especially the chocolate mousse or the mango and peach Romanoff. The bar is open every day throughout the afternoon until 11pm.

Duke St. © **649/946-2466.** Reservations recommended. Lunch platters $9–$15; dinner main courses $19–$28. MC, V. Daily 7:30am–9:30pm.

Water's Edge BAHAMIAN/AMERICAN   Set directly on the sands, close to the center of town, this newly renovated and enlarged restaurant manages to transform the simple conch into a surprising number of dishes. Come here for views of the sea, an engaging informality, a short list of standard fish and chicken dishes, as well as "conch burgers," pizzas, curried conch platters, and overstuffed sandwiches.

Duke St. © **649/946-1680.** Main courses $10–$25. MC, V. Daily 11am–midnight.

SCUBA DIVING & SNORKELING 👓

Some of the finest diving in the archipelago is around Grand Turk. Here you can enjoy one of the underwater world's great experiences: a night dive on a wall where, due to bioluminescence, the colors of the day become the phosphorescent illumination of the night.

Divers can explore the wreck of the **HMS *Endymion*** 👓 off **Salt Cay,** which went down in a storm in 1790. Two centuries later, Brian Sheedy, a local diver and inn operator, discovered the wreck. Today, while the reef has reclaimed the hull and all else that was biodegradable, divers can still get a close-up look at its cannons and four huge anchors lying about.

But Salt Cay is more than the resting place of a ghost ship. Between January and March, humpback whales come here to play. Visitors can watch their antics from shore, boat out among them, or don dive equipment and go below.

The dive shops below all also rent snorkel gear.

Blue Water Diver, Front Street (© and fax **649/946-1226**), offers single dives, PADI registration, dive packages, and even runs trips to Salt Cay. These people are top rate and will tell you many facts and legends about diving in their country (like the fact that the highest mountain in the Turks and Caicos is 2,400m/7,872 ft. tall, but only the top 42m/138 ft. are above sea level!). Scuba divers flock here to enjoy panoramic "wall dives" on the vertical sides of the reefs. A single-tank dive costs $40, with a two-tank dive going for $60; a night dive costs $45. A PADI-instruction resort course is priced at $110. Full PADI certification is $400.

Sea Eye Diving, Duke Street or Front Street (© **649/946-1407**), is convenient to most hotels in town. It offers two-tank morning dives at $60. An afternoon single-tank dive costs $35, and a single-tank night dive goes for $40. Rental equipment is also available. NAUI and PADI courses at all levels are offered. A full-certification course goes for $400, including training equipment and boat checkout dives. Dive packages that include accommodations can be arranged at a hotel of your choice. Snorkeling and cay trips are available for nondivers. The owners and operators are among the more experienced divers on the island, and they know where to find marine life in a kaleidoscope of colors.

EXPLORING THE ISLAND

People go to Grand Turk mainly to swim, snorkel, dive, or do nothing but soak up the sun. Other activities include bird-watching, horseback riding, heritage walks, and golf. You might also want to stroll over to the lighthouse which was brought in pieces from the United Kingdom, where it had been constructed in 1852. It has been restored and still works, guarding the northern tip of the island.

Turks & Caicos National Museum ⊕ This is the country's first (and only) museum. It occupies a 150-year-old residence, Guinep House, originally built by Bermudan wreckers from timbers they salvaged from ships that crashed on nearby reefs. Today, about half of its display areas are devoted to the remains of the most complete archaeological excavation ever performed in the West Indies, the wreck of a Spanish caravel (sailing ship) that sank in shallow offshore water sometime before 1513. Used to transport local Arawaks who had been enslaved, the boat was designed solely for exploration purposes and is similar to vessels built in Spain and Portugal during the 1400s.

Treasure hunters found the wreck and announced that it was Columbus's *Pinta,* in order to attract financial backers for their salvage—to guarantee a value to the otherwise-valueless iron artifacts, in case there proved to be no gold on board. There is no proof, however, that the *Pinta* ever came back to the New World after returning to Spain from the first voyage. Researchers from the Institute of Nautical Archaeology at Texas A&M University began excavations in 1982, although staff members never assumed that the wreck was the *Pinta.* Today, the remains are referred to simply as the Wreck of Molasses Reef.

Today, although only 2% of the hull remains intact, the exhibits contain a rich legacy of the everyday (nonbiodegradable) objects used by the crews and officers.

The remainder of the museum is devoted to exhibits about the island's salt industries, its plantation economy, the pre-Columbian inhabitants of the island, and its natural history. The natural-history exhibit features a 2m-by-6m (6½-ft.-by-20-ft.), three-dimensional reproduction of a section of the Grand Turk Wall, the famous vertical reef. You'll also find displays on the geology of the islands and information on the reef and coral growth.

Guinep House, Front St., Cockburn Town, Grand Turk. ℂ 649/946-2160. www.tcmuseum.org. Admission $5 nonresidents, free for full-time island residents. Mon–Tues and Thurs–Fri 9am–4pm; Wed 9am–5pm; Sat 9am–1pm.

GRAND TURK AFTER DARK

At night, people mainly hang out and drink. Sing-alongs often burst out at the **Turks Head Inn,** on Duke Street (ℂ **649/946-2466**). Still in search of action? **Nookie Hill Club,** Nookie Hill (no phone), offers occasional dancing.

The U.S. Virgin Islands

The U.S. Virgin Islands are known for their sugar-white beaches, among the finest in the world, and also for duty-free shopping. The most developed island in the chain is **St. Thomas,** whose capital, Charlotte Amalie, is the shopping mecca of the Caribbean. With a population of some 50,000 and thousands more cruise-ship passengers arriving on any given day, tiny St. Thomas isn't exactly a secluded tropical retreat; you won't have its beautiful beaches to yourself. It abounds in bars and restaurants, including fast-food joints, and has a vast selection of hotels at all prices.

St. Croix is bigger, but more tranquil, than St. Thomas. A favorite with cruise-ship passengers (as is St. Thomas), St. Croix touts its shopping and has more stores than most islands in the Caribbean, especially in and around Christiansted, although it's not as dense with stores as Charlotte

Amalie. Its major attraction is Buck Island, a U.S. National Park that lies offshore. St. Croix is peppered with inns and hotels and is condo heaven.

St. John, the smallest of the three islands, is also the most beautiful and the least developed. It has only two big hotels. Some two-thirds of this island is set aside as a U.S. National Park. Even if you visit only for the day while based on St. Thomas, you'll want to sample the island's dreamy beach, Trunk Bay.

The U.S. Virgin Islands lie in two bodies of water: St. John is entirely in the Atlantic Ocean, St. Croix is entirely in the Caribbean Sea, and St. Thomas separates the Atlantic and the Caribbean. Directly in the belt of the subtropical, easterly trade winds, these islands enjoy one of the most perfect year-round climates in the world. The U.S. Virgins are some 60 miles east of Puerto Rico and 1,100 miles southeast of Miami.

1 U.S. Virgin Islands Essentials

VISITOR INFORMATION

Before you go, contact the **U.S. Virgin Islands Division of Tourism,** at 1270 Ave. of the Americas (Suite 2108), **New York, NY** 10020 (© 212/332-2222). Branch offices are located at: 225 Peachtree St. NE, Suite 260, **Atlanta, GA** 30303 (© 404/688-0906); 500 N. Michigan Ave., Suite 2030, **Chicago, IL** 60611 (© 312/670-8784); 2655 Le Jeune Rd., Suite 907, **Coral Gables, FL** 33134 (© 305/442-7200); 3460 Wilshire Blvd., Suite 412, **Los Angeles, CA** 90010 (© 213/739-0138); and 900 17th St. NW, Suite 500, **Washington, D.C.** 20006 (© 202/624-3590).

In **Canada,** there's an office at 703 Evan Ave., Suite 106, Toronto, ON M9C 5E9, Canada (© 416/622-7600). In **Britain,** contact the office at 114 Power Rd., Chiswick, London W45PY (© 020/7978-5262).

On the Web, you can get information at **www.usvi.net**.

GETTING THERE

Before you book your airline ticket, refer to the section "Packages for the Independent Traveler," in chapter 2. You might save a bundle.

It's possible to fly from the mainland of the U.S. directly to St. Thomas and St. Croix, but the only way to get to St. John is by a ferry from St. Thomas, or from Jost Van Dyke or Tortola in the British Virgin Islands.

TO ST. THOMAS OR ST. CROIX   American Airlines (© 800/433-7300 in the U.S.; www.aa.com) offers frequent service to St. Thomas and St. Croix from the U.S. mainland, with five daily flights from New York to St. Thomas in high season. Passengers originating in other parts of the world are usually routed to St. Thomas through American's hubs in Miami or San Juan, both of which offer nonstop service (often several times a day) to St. Thomas. (American Eagle has 11 nonstop flights daily from San Juan to St. Thomas.)

Delta (© 800/241-4141 in the U.S.; www.delta.com) offers two daily nonstop flights between Atlanta and St. Thomas in winter. **US Airways** (© 800/428-4322 in the U.S.; www.usairways.com) has one nonstop daily flight from Philadelphia to St. Thomas, and an additional flight on Saturday.

Cape Air (© 800/352-0714 in the U.S.; www.flycapeair.com) has service between St. Thomas and Puerto Rico. This Massachusetts-based airline offers 12 flights daily. Cape Air has expanded its service to include flights from San Juan to St. Croix and flights between St. Croix and St. Thomas.

United Airlines (© 800/538-2929 in the U.S.; www.united.com) has nonstop service on Saturday and Sunday to St. Thomas from Chicago and Washington, D.C.

Continental Airlines (© 800/231-0856 in the U.S.; www.continental.com) has flights from Newark International Airport in New Jersey to St. Thomas.

A **ferry** service between Charlotte Amalie in St. Thomas and Puerto Rico, with a stop in St. John, is available about once every 2 weeks (sometimes more often in high season). The trip takes about 2 hours, costing $60 one-way or $100 round-trip. Children pay $60 round-trip. For more information, call © 340/776-6282.

TO ST. CROIX FROM ST. THOMAS   It's now easier than ever before to travel between St. Thomas and St. Croix. **American Eagle** (© 800/433-7300 in the U.S.) has 9 to 10 flights a day, costing $90 to $259 one-way. In addition, **Seaborne Airlines** (© 888/FLYTOUR or 340/773-6442; www.seaborne airlines.com) offers 10 to 17 round-trip flights daily, going for $75 one-way and $135 round-trip. Flight time is 25 minutes.

TO ST. JOHN   The easiest and most common way to get to St. John is by **ferry** (© 340/776-6282), which leaves from the Red Hook landing pier on St. Thomas's eastern tip; the trip takes about 20 minutes each way. Beginning at 6:30am, boats depart more or less every hour. The last ferry back to Red Hook departs from St. John's Cruz Bay at midnight. The service is frequent and efficient enough that even cruise-ship passengers temporarily anchored in Charlotte Amalie can visit St. John for a quick island tour. The one-way fare is $3 for adults, $1 for children age 12 and under. Schedules change without notice, so call in advance.

To reach the ferry, take the **Vitran** bus from a point near Market Square (in Charlotte Amalie) directly to Red Hook. The cost is $1 per person each way. In addition, privately owned taxis will negotiate a price to carry you from virtually anywhere to the docks at Red Hook.

If you've just landed on St. Thomas and want to go straight to the ferry dock, your best bet is to take a cab from the airport (Vitran buses run from Charlotte Amalie but don't serve the airport area). After disembarking from the ferry on St. John, you'll have to get another cab to your hotel. Depending on the traffic, the cab ride on St. Thomas could take 30 to 45 minutes, at a fare of about $14.

It's also possible to board a **boat** for St. John directly at the Charlotte Amalie waterfront for a cost of $7 each way. The ride takes 45 minutes. The boats depart from Charlotte Amalie at 9am and continue at intervals of between 1 and 2 hours, until the last boat departs around 5:30pm. (The last boat to leave St. John's Cruz Bay for Charlotte Amalie departs at 3:45pm.) Call © **340/776-6282** for more information.

FAST FACTS: The U.S. Virgin Islands

Banks Banks are generally open Monday to Thursday from 9am to 3pm, and Friday from 9am to 4pm. It's not hard to find a bank with an ATM on St. Thomas or St. Croix. Chase Manhattan Bank has branches, with ATMs, on all three islands.

Currency The **U.S. dollar** is the unit of currency in the Virgin Islands.

Customs Every U.S. resident can bring home $1,400 worth of duty-free purchases, including 5 liters of liquor per adult. If you go over the $1,400 limit, you pay a flat 5% duty, up to $1,000. You can also mail home gifts valued at up to $100 per day, which you don't have to declare. (At other spots in the Caribbean, U.S. citizens are limited to $400 or $600 worth of merchandise and a single bottle of liquor.)

Documents U.S. and Canadian citizens are required to present some proof of citizenship to enter the Virgin Islands, such as a birth certificate with a raised seal along with a government-issued photo ID. A passport is not strictly required, but carrying one is a good idea. The requirements for other citizens are the same as for foreigners entering the U.S. mainland; travelers from the United Kingdom, Australia, and New Zealand need valid passports, but not visas.

Electricity It's the same as on the U.S. mainland: 120-volt AC (60 cycles). No transformer, adapter, or converter is needed for U.S. appliances.

Emergencies In an emergency, dial © **911.**

Liquor Laws Liquor is sold 7 days a week, and it is not permitted on beaches.

Safety The U.S. Virgin Islands have more than their share of crime. Travelers should exercise extreme caution both day and night, especially in the back streets of Charlotte Amalie on St. Thomas, and in Christiansted and Frederiksted on St. Croix. Muggings are commonplace. Avoid strolling at night, especially on the beaches.

Taxes There is no departure tax for the U.S. Virgin Islands. Hotels add on an 8% tax (always ask if it's included in the original price you're quoted).

Telephone The phone system for the U.S. Virgin Islands is the same as on the U.S. mainland. The area code is **340.** To reach **Sprint** dial © **800/999-9000,** and to reach **MCI** dial © **800/950-5555.**

Time The U.S. Virgins are on Atlantic Standard Time, which is 1 hour ahead of Eastern Standard Time. However, the islands do not observe daylight saving time, so in the summer during daylight savings time, the Virgin Islands and the U.S. East Coast are on the same time. In winter, when it's 6am in Charlotte Amalie, it's 5am in Miami.

Tipping Tip as you would on the U.S. mainland (15% in restaurants, 10%–15% to taxi drivers, $1 or $2 per round to bartenders, at least $1 or $2 per day for chambermaids). Some hotels add a 10% to 15% surcharge to cover service, so check before you wind up paying twice.

Water Most visitors drink the local tap water with no harmful aftereffects. Those with more delicate stomachs might want to stick to bottled water.

Weather From November to February, temperatures average about 77°F (25°C). Sometimes in August the temperature peaks in the high 90s (mid-30s Celsius), but the subtropical breezes keep it comfortably cool in the shade. The temperature in winter may drop into the low 60s (mid-teens Celsius), but this rarely happens.

2 St. Thomas ★★★

St. Thomas, the busiest cruise-ship destination in the West Indies, is not the largest of the U.S. Virgins (St. Croix holds that distinction). But bustling Charlotte Amalie is the capital of the U.S. Virgin Islands, and the shopping hub of the Caribbean. The beaches on this island are renowned for their white sand and calm, turquoise waters, including the very best of them all, **Magens Bay.** Despite all the development, *National Geographic* rated St. Thomas as one of the top destinations in the world for sailing, scuba diving, and fishing.

Charlotte Amalie, with its white houses and bright red roofs glistening in the sun, is one of the most beautiful towns in the Caribbean. It's most famous for its shopping, but the town is also filled with historic sights, like Fort Christian, an intriguing 17th-century building constructed by the Danes. The town's architecture reflects the island's culturally diverse past. You'll pass Dutch doors, Danish red-tile roofs, French iron grillwork, and Spanish-style patios.

Because of St. Thomas's thriving commercial activity, as well as its lingering drug and crime problems, the island is often referred to as the most "unvirgin" of the Virgin Islands. Charlotte Amalie's Main Street is virtually a 3- to 4-block-long shopping center. But while this area tends to be overcrowded, for the most

Fun Fact Carnival

The annual **Carnival** celebration, held after Easter, is a spectacular event, with echoes of the islanders' African heritage. "Mocko Jumbies," people dressed as spirits, parade through the streets on stilts nearly 20 feet high. Steel and fungi bands, "jump-ups" (Caribbean hoedowns), and parades bring the event to life. Events take place islandwide, but most of the action is on the streets of Charlotte Amalie. Contact the visitor center in St. Thomas for a schedule of events.

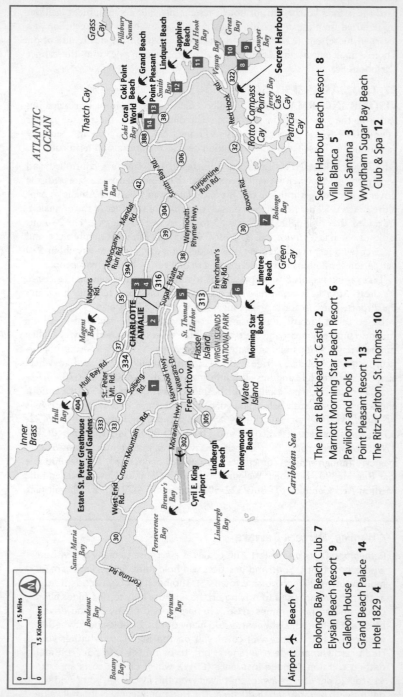

St. Thomas

ATLANTIC OCEAN

Grass Cay

Pillsbury Sound

Thatch Cay

Inner Brass

Santa Maria Bay

Bordeaux Bay

Botany Bay

Fortuna Rd.

Fortuna Bay

Lindbergh Bay

Brewer's Bay

Perseverance Bay

West-End Rd.

Crown Mountain Rd.

Hull Bay Rd.

Hull Bay

Estate St. Peter Greathouse Botanical Gardens

Magens Bay

Tutu Bay

Mandal Run Rd.

Mahogany Run Rd.

Magens Rd.

St. Peter Mt. Rd.

Solberg Rd.

Moravian Hwy.

Harwood Hwy.

Veterans Dr.

CHARLOTTE AMALIE

Frenchtown

Sugar Estate Rd.

Weymouth Rhymer Hwy.

Turpentine Run Rd.

Smith Bay Rd.

St. Thomas Harbor

Hassel Island

Water Island

VIRGIN ISLANDS NATIONAL PARK

Caribbean Sea

Green Cay

Bolongo Bay

Bovoni Rd.

Limetree Beach

Frenchman's Bay Rd.

Morning Star Beach

Honeymoon Beach

Lindbergh Beach

Cyril E. King Airport

Coki Coral Bay World

Coki Point Beach

Grand Beach

Lindquist Beach

Point Pleasant

Sapphire Beach

Red Hook Bay

Vessup Bay

Great Bay

Coupet Bay

Secret Harbour

Jersey Bay

Cas Cay

Patricia Cay

Rotto Compass Point

Red Hook Rd.

Smith Bay

Botanical

1.5 Miles

1.5 Kilometers

Airport ✈   Beach ⌐

Bolongo Bay Beach Club **7**
Elysian Beach Resort **9**
Galleon House **1**
Grand Beach Palace **14**
Hotel 1829 **4**

The Inn at Blackbeard's Castle **2**
Marriott Morning Star Beach Resort **6**
Pavilions and Pools **11**
Point Pleasant Resort **13**
The Ritz-Carlton, St. Thomas **10**

Secret Harbour Beach Resort **8**
Villa Blanca **5**
Villa Santana **3**
Wyndham Sugar Bay Beach Club & Spa **12**

part, the island's beaches, major hotels, restaurants, and entertainment facilities are removed from the cruise-ship chaos. And you can always find seclusion at a resort in more remote sections of the island. Hotels on the north side of St. Thomas look out at the Atlantic; those on the south side front the calmer Caribbean Sea.

ST. THOMAS ESSENTIALS

VISITOR INFORMATION At Tolbod Gade 1, across from Emancipation Park, on the waterfront in downtown Charlotte Amalie, the **visitor center** (© 340/774-8784) is open Monday to Friday from 8am to 5pm and Saturday 9am to noon. There's also an information desk at the cruise-ship terminal.

GETTING AROUND Taxis are unmetered, but fares are controlled and widely posted; however, we still recommend that you negotiate a fare with the driver before you get into the car. A typical fare from Charlotte Amalie to Sapphire Beach is $9 per person. Surcharges, one-third of the price of the excursion, are added after midnight. You'll pay $1 to $4 per bag for luggage. For 24-hour radio-dispatch taxi service, call © 340/774-7457. If you want to hire a taxi and a driver (who just may be a great tour guide) for a day, expect to pay about $20 per person for 2 hours of sightseeing in a shared car, or $50 for two people.

Taxi vans transport 8 to 12 passengers to multiple destinations on the island. It's cheaper to take a van instead of a taxi if you're going between your hotel and the airport. The cost for luggage ranges from 50¢ to $1 per bag.

Buses, called **Vitrans,** leave from street-side stops in the center of Charlotte Amalie, fanning out east and west along all the most important highways. They run between 5:30am and 8pm daily, but waits can be very long and this is a difficult way to get about. A ride within Charlotte Amalie is 75¢, and anywhere else, $1. For schedule and bus-stop information, call © 340/774-5678.

St. Thomas has many leading North American **car-rental firms** at the airport, and competition is stiff. Before you go, compare the rates of the "big three": **Avis** (© 800/331-1084 or 340/774-1468; www.avis.com), **Budget** (© 800/472-3325; www.budgetrentacar.com), and **Hertz** (© 800/654-3131 or 340/774-1789; www.hertz.com). You can often save money by renting from a local agency, although vehicles sometimes aren't as well maintained. Try **Dependable Car Rental,** 3901 B Altona, Welgunst, behind the Bank of Nova Scotia and the Medical Arts Complex (© 800/522-3076 or 340/774-2253), which will pick

---

⟨Warning **Drivers Beware**

Remember: Drive on the left. This comes as a surprise to many U.S. visitors who expect that U.S. driving practices will hold here. Speed limits are 20 mph in towns, 35 mph outside towns. St. Thomas has a high accident rate, as tourists are not used to driving on the left, the hilly terrain hides blind curves and entrance ramps, roads are narrow and poorly lit, and drivers often get behind the wheel after too many drinks. Double-check whether your own car insurance will cover you on the island, or whether your credit card will provide coverage. If not, to be on the safe side, consider getting **collision-damage insurance (CDW),** which usually costs an extra $13 to $20 per day. Be aware that even with this insurance, you could still get hit with a whopping deductible: The Hertz deductible is the full value of the car; at Avis and Budget, it's $500.

up renters at the airport or their hotel; or the aptly named **Discount Car Rental,** 14 Harwood Hwy., outside the airport on the main highway (© **340/776-4858**), which grants drivers a 12% discount on rivals' rates. There is no tax on car rentals in the Virgin Islands.

FAST FACTS   The local **American Express** representative on St. Thomas is **Caribbean Travel Agency/Tropic Tours,** 14AB The Guardian Building (© **800/524-4334** or 340/774-1855), a 5-minute drive east of Charlotte Amalie's center, opposite Havensight shopping mall; it's open Monday to Friday from 8:30am to 5pm and Saturday from 10:30am to 2pm.

Roy Lester Schneider Hospital, 9048 Sugar Estate, Charlotte Amalie (© **340/776-8311**), a 5-minute drive east of the town's commercial center, is the largest hospital with the best-equipped emergency room.

ACCOMMODATIONS

Nearly every beach on St. Thomas has its own hotel, and the island also has more quaint inns than anyplace else in the Caribbean. If you want to stay here on the cheap, consider one of the guesthouses in the Charlotte Amalie area. All the glittering, expensive properties lie in the east end.

Remember that hotels in the Virgin Islands slash their prices in summer by 20% to 60%. Unless otherwise noted, the rates listed below do *not* include the 8% government tax.

VERY EXPENSIVE

Marriott Morning Star Beach Resort ★★★   Built right on white sands, the Marriott Morning Star is next to and better than the Marriott Frenchman's Reef Beach Resort (not reviewed). Guests can wander between the two, which allows a broader range of restaurants and facilities than any other hotel on the island can offer. This beachside enclave has a striking Caribbean decor; both its public areas and its plushly outfitted accommodations are among the best on the island. Its five cottage-style buildings each contain between 16 and 24 units. Guests have the amenities and attractions of the large hotel nearby, yet maintain the privacy of this more intimate property. Each unit has rattan furniture and views of the garden, beach, or the lights of Charlotte Amalie from your own veranda. Bedrooms are roomy and spacious, with fine furnishings and tasteful fabrics, plus extras such as phones with voice mail and dataports; tiled bathrooms have shower/tub combinations.

No. 5 Estate Bakkeroe, Flamboyant Point (P.O. Box 7100), St. Thomas, U.S.V.I. 00801. © 800/524-2000 or 340/776-8500. Fax 340/716-6623. www.marriott.com. 96 units. Winter $350–$680 double; off season $160–$250 double. AE, DC, DISC, MC, V. **Amenities:** 5 restaurants; 9 bars; dance club; 2 pools; 2 tennis courts; business center; health club and spa; sauna; steam room; watersports; children's program; car rental; 24-hr. room service; babysitting; laundry service/dry cleaning; nonsmoking rooms; rooms for those with limited mobility. *In room:* A/C, TV, dataport, minibar, beverage maker, hair dryer, safe.

The Ritz-Carlton, St. Thomas ★★★   Fronted by white-sand beaches, this is the toniest resort in all the U.S. Virgin Islands, its architecture evoking a *palazzo* in Venice. To the other luxury hotels on the island, it can say, "Eat my dust." Guests arriving in winter 2003 found it even better, as it took over more land for a total of 30 acres of an oceanfront estate at the island's southeastern tip, 4 miles from Charlotte Amalie. The Ritz is set amid landscaped gardens, blending European elegance with Caribbean style. Bubbling fountains and hidden courtyards evoke the feel of a sprawling villa.

Most of the accommodations are in half a dozen three-story villas designed with Italian Renaissance motifs and the sunny colors of the Mediterranean.

Recently added to this roster are 48 new guest rooms and suites. The finest are a series of luxuriously furnished club-level units. Guests register in a palacelike reception area. Once shown to their rooms, guests find more amenities and luxuries than at any other hotel on the island; each room features a private balcony and excellent quality linens. The least desirable units are those on the ground floor with only partial views.

The elegant dining room, The Great Bay Grill, captures the best of scenic views of Great Bay and St. John and serves a refined and deluxe cuisine that's complimented by a first-rate wine list.

6900 Great Bay, St. Thomas, U.S.V.I. 00802. ℂ 800/241-3333 or 340/775-3333. Fax 340/775-4444. www.ritz carlton.com. 200 units. Winter $549–$599 double, $1,500 suite; off season $319–$489 double, $799 suite. AE, DC, DISC, MC, V. **Amenities:** 4 restaurants; 4 bars; 3 outdoor pools; 3 tennis courts; health club; spa; Jacuzzi; nonmotorized watersports equipment rental; children's programs; salon; 24-hr. room service; massage; babysitting; laundry service; dry cleaning; club-level rooms. In room: A/C, TV, minibar, beverage maker, hair dryer, safe.

Wyndham Sugar Bay Beach Club & Spa 𝕂𝕂   At the east end of the island, a 5-minute ride from Red Hook, this all-inclusive hotel is much improved but still lags behind the Marriotts. It has panoramic views, although its secluded beach is really too small for a resort of this size. Many of the attractive rooms are decorated with rattan pieces and pastels, and they have roomy marble bathrooms with shower stalls. After a recent $5 million renovation, guest rooms have new carpeting, furnishings, electronics, wall treatments, and plumbing. The hotel's spa, Journeys, is the largest full-service spa in the U.S. Virgins, and the first to offer hydrotherapy treatments. The spa is also open to nonvisitors who call for an appointment.

6500 Estate Smith Bay, St. Thomas, U.S.V.I. 00802. ℂ 800/WYNDHAM in the U.S., or 340/777-7100. Fax 340/777-7200. www.wyndham.com. 297 units. Winter $540–$640 double, $850–$1,200 suite; off season $350–$440 double, $850–$1,200 suite. Rates are all-inclusive. AE, DC, DISC, MC, V. **Amenities:** 3 restaurants; 2 bars; 3 outdoor pools; 4 lit Laykold tennis courts; fitness center; spa; sauna; dive shop; kayaks; sailing; snorkeling; windsurfing; children's club; secretarial services; babysitting; laundry service; dry cleaning; nonsmoking rooms; rooms for those with limited mobility. In room: A/C, TV, dataport, fridge, minibar, beverage maker, iron/ironing board, hair dryer, safe.

EXPENSIVE

Bolongo Bay Beach Club 𝕂 (Value)   This is an unpretentious, barefoot kind of place. You'll find a half-moon-shaped, 1,000-foot white-sand beach and a cluster of pink two- and three-story buildings, plus some motel-like units closer to the sands. There's also a social center consisting of a smallish pool and a beachfront bar, replete with palm fronds. It's a relatively small property, but it offers all the facilities of a big resort. Many guests check in on the continental plan, which includes breakfast; others opt for all-inclusive plans that include all meals, drinks, a sailboat excursion to St. John, and use of scuba equipment. Rooms are simple, summery, and filled with unremarkable but comfortable furniture. Each unit has its own balcony or patio, a refrigerator, and one king-size or two double beds, plus tiled, shower-only bathrooms. Some of the units on the beach come with kitchenettes. Villas, in a three-story building, are apartment-style condos with full kitchens.

The best dining, and most formal, is at the Beach House, known especially for its fresh seafood. Iggies Beach Bar and Grill is more fun and casual.

7150 Bolongo, St. Thomas, U.S.V.I. 00802. ℂ 800/524-4746 or 340/775-1800. Fax 340/775-3208. www. bolongobay.com. 95 units. Winter $245 double with continental breakfast, $450 all-inclusive double, $245 studio villa, $345 2-bedroom villa; off season $195 double with no meals, $400 all-inclusive double, $175 studio villa, $245 2-bedroom villa. Ask about packages and various meal plans. AE, MC, V. **Amenities:**

2 restaurants; 2 bars; 3 outdoor pools; 2 tennis courts; fitness center; basketball courts; sauna; boating; deep-sea fishing; dive shop; scuba diving; snorkeling; windsurfing; children's programs (ages 4–12); babysitting. *In room:* A/C, TV; kitchenette (in some), fridge, beverage maker, hair dryer, iron/ironing board, safe.

Elysian Beach Resort ⟨Я⟩

This timeshare resort on Cowpet Bay in the east end, a 30-minute drive from Charlotte Amalie, is imbued with a certain European resort chic. The beautiful white-sand beach is the most compelling reason to stay, but you should also stay here if you're looking for tranquillity and seclusion without the razzle-dazzle of other east-end resorts. The thoughtfully planned bedrooms contain balconies, and 14 offer sleeping lofts that are reached by a spiral staircase. The decor is tropical, with rattan and bamboo furnishings, ceiling fans, and natural-wood ceilings. The rooms are in a bevy of four-story buildings connected to landscaped gardens. Of the various units, 43 can be converted into one-bedroom suites, 43 into two-bedroom suites, and 11 into three-bedroom suites. Designer fabrics and white ceramic-tile floors make the tropical living quite grand. Try to avoid rooms in buildings V through Z, as they are some distance from the beach. Each unit has a full, tiled bathroom.

Robert's American Grill serves American food, while less formal Barney's By The Sea features cocktails and West Indian and international food.

6800 Estate Nazareth, Cowpet Bay, St. Thomas, U.S.V.I. 00802. ⟨Ⓒ⟩ **800/225-3522** or 340/775-1000. Fax 340/776-0910. www.equivest.com. 180 units. Winter $169–$199 double, $269 suite; off season $120–$159 double, $209 suite. AE, DC, DISC, MC, V. **Amenities:** 2 restaurants; 2 bars; outdoor pool; tennis court; fitness center; sauna; canoes; snorkeling gear; Sunfish sailboats; open-air shuttle to town; massage; laundry service; dry cleaning; nonsmoking rooms; rooms for those with limited mobility. *In room:* A/C, TV, dataport, kitchenette, beverage maker, hair dryer, iron/ironing board, safe.

Grand Beach Palace ⟨ЯЯЯ⟩ ⟨Kids⟩

This four-story resort, which occupies 34 acres on the northeast shore of St. Thomas, is perched on a steep hillside above a beautiful, small white-sand beach. The Ritz-Carlton (see above) is more luxurious, but Grand Beach has a friendlier layout and design than another major competitor, the Wyndham Sugar Bay Beach Club (see above). The accommodations, all stylishly outfitted, are in seven two-story buildings designed like beach houses and staggered so that each unit has a view. The Bougainvillea section is adjacent to the beach, while the units in the Hibiscus section are literally carved into the hillside. All rooms have quality mattresses, marble foyers, wall-to-wall carpeting, marble bathrooms with tubs and showers, private safes, minibars, robes, and private patios or balconies with views of the Caribbean. The two-story town house suites and one- or two-bedroom suites have whirlpool spas. This is a good family resort; trained counselors operate a children's program on holidays for ages 3 to 14.

The Smugglers is known for its seafood and steaks, and Baywinds is especially popular on Thursday night when it features a $40 Caribbean buffet.

Rte. 38, Smith Bay Rd. (P.O. Box 8267), St. Thomas, U.S.V.I. 00801. ⟨Ⓒ⟩ **800/635-1836** or 800/346-8225 in the U.S., or 340/775-1510. Fax 340/775-2185. www.palaceresorts.com. 290 units. Winter $240–$267 double; off season $216–$240 double. Ask about packages. AE, DC, DISC, MC, V. **Amenities:** 3 restaurants; 2 bars; outdoor pool; 6 lit tennis courts; health club and spa; sauna; steam room; kayaks; sailing; snorkeling; windsurfing; children's program; salon; babysitting; laundry service; dry cleaning; nonsmoking rooms; rooms for those with limited mobility. *In room:* A/C, TV, dataport, minibar, beverage maker, hair dryer, iron/ironing board, safe.

The Inn at Blackbeard's Castle ⟨Я⟩

Once a private residence, this is now one of the most charming and atmospheric inns in the Virgin Islands. Perched high on a hillside above the town, it lies at the site of a 1679 tower of chiseled stone that the Danish governor ordered erected. The tower served as a lookout for unfriendly ships, and legend says that Blackbeard himself lived in the tower half

---

Tips **Renting a Condo, an Apartment, or a Villa**

Sometimes you can get a deal on a moderately priced condo, apartment, or villa. We've found that **Calypso Realty** (© 800/747-4858 or 340/774-1620; www.calypsorealty.com) has the best offers, especially on rentals from April to mid-December. A condo overlooking St. John often goes for $1,400 and up per week.

Another source to check is **McLaughlin Anderson Vacations Ltd.** (© 800/666-6246 or 340/776-0635; www.mclaughlinanderson.com), which has rentals not only on St. Thomas, but on St. John and St. Croix as well. A two-bedroom villa begins at $1,800 per week in winter, with off-season rates at $1,600.

You can also contact **Paradise Properties of St. Thomas** (© 800/524-2038 or 340/779-1540; fax 340/779-6109; www.st-thomas.com/paradise properties), which currently represents five condo complexes. Rental units range from studio apartments to two-bedroom villas suitable for up to eight people; each has a fully equipped kitchen. A minimum stay of 3 days is required in any season, and 7 nights around Christmas. The prices range from $150 to $535 per day in winter and from $125 to $445 per day in the off season.

---

a century later. It's not on the sand, and the nearest beach is a 10-minute shuttle ride away. Most of the well-furnished bedrooms and all the suites are spacious. The garden rooms are much smaller than other rooms and have no balconies, though they're located near a private pool area; travelers on a budget might choose these. Accommodations are decorated with tile floors or dark wood, with much use made of Caribbean mahogany furnishings. Each unit is equipped with a well-maintained, shower-only bathroom. Blackbeard's is also the site of one of the most romantic restaurants in St. Thomas (see "Dining," below).

Blackbeard's Hill (P.O. Box 6227), Charlotte Amalie, St. Thomas, U.S.V.I. 00801. © 800/344-5771 in the U.S., or 340/776-1234. Fax 340/776-4321. www.blackbeardscastle.com. 13 units. Winter $110 garden room, $165–$195 balcony or junior suite; off season $80 garden room, $120–$155 balcony or junior suite. Rates include breakfast. AE, DISC, MC, V. **Amenities:** Restaurant; bar; 3 outdoor pools; nonsmoking rooms. *In room:* A/C, TV, fridge, safe.

Pavilions and Pools *Finds* Ideal for a honeymoon, at this resort you stay in your own villa with floor-to-ceiling glass doors that open onto a private swimming pool. It's ideal for those who want to run around nude as Adam and Eve, Eve and Eve, or Adam and Adam. The resort, 7 miles east of Charlotte Amalie, is a string of condominium units, tastefully rebuilt and furnished. After checking in and following a wooden pathway to your attached villa, you don't have to see another soul until you leave, if you so wish—the fence and gate around your space are that high. Your swimming pool is encircled by a deck and plenty of tropical greenery. Inside, a room divider screens a full, well-equipped kitchen. The place is not posh, and an average good motel in the States will have better-quality furniture. The bathroom has an outdoor garden shower where you can rinse off after a swim or trip to the beach. The resort adjoins Sapphire Bay, which boasts one of the island's best beaches and many watersports concessions. Honeymooning couples should ask about packages.

Clients can head for any of a half-dozen lunch (independently operated) kiosks on the nearby beach. Dinners are simple and focus on steaks and seafood.

6400 Estate Smith Bay, St. Thomas, U.S.V.I. 00802. © **800/524-2001** or 340/775-6110. Fax 340/775-6110. www.pavilionsandpools.com. 25 units. Winter $270–$295 double; off season $180–$195. Rates include continental breakfast. AE, MC, V. **Amenities:** Restaurant; outdoor pool; day sails; snorkeling gear; laundry service; nonsmoking rooms; rooms for those with limited mobility. *In room:* A/C, TV, dataport, kitchen, fridge, beverage maker, hair dryer, iron/ironing board, safe.

Point Pleasant Resort ⋇   This is a very private, unique resort on Water Bay, on the northeastern tip of St. Thomas, just a 5-minute walk from lovely Stouffer's Beach. These condo units, which are rented when their owners are not in residence, are set on a 15-acre bluff with flowering shrubbery, century plants, frangipani trees, secluded nature trails, old rock formations, and lookout points. The villa-style accommodations have light and airy furnishings, mostly rattan and floral fabrics. They all have full kitchens with microwaves and full bathrooms. Beds are very comfortable with fine linen. From your living room, you'll have a gorgeous view over Tortola, St. John, and Jost Van Dyke.

The restaurant, Agavé Terrace (see review later in this chapter), is one of the finest on the island. The cuisine, featuring seafood, is a blend of nouvelle American dishes and Caribbean specialties. Local entertainment is provided Tuesday and Thursday night, and you can brush up on your samba with a complimentary lesson.

6600 Estate Smith Bay, St. Thomas, U.S.V.I. 00802. © **800/524-2300** or 340/775-7200. Fax 340/776-5694. www.pointpleasantresort.com. 128 units. Winter $255–$275 junior or superior suite, $355 deluxe suite, $525 2-bedroom suite; off season $180–$195 junior or superior suite, $255 deluxe suite, $355 2-bedroom suite. Ask about package deals. Children under 12 stay free in parent's room. AE, DC, DISC, MC, V. **Amenities:** 2 restaurants; 2 bars; 3 outdoor pools; fitness center; coin-operated laundry; nonsmoking rooms. *In room:* A/C, ceiling fan, TV, beverage maker, hair dryer, iron/ironing board, safe.

Secret Harbour Beach Resort ⋇   This all-suites combo resort is on the stunning white-sand beach at Nazareth Bay, just outside Red Hook Marina. All four contemporary buildings have southwestern exposure (great for sunsets), and each unit has a private deck or patio. You'll be just steps from the sand, and great snorkeling is right offshore. There are three types of accommodations: studio apartments, one-bedroom suites, and two-bedroom suites. Each studio apartment has a bedroom/sitting-room area, patio, and dressing-room area; each one-bedroom suite has a living/dining area, a separate bedroom, and a sun deck; and each luxurious two-bedroom suite has two bathrooms with shower/tub combinations and a private living room. Honeymooners are likely to show up in the winter months.

The Blue Moon Café (see "Dining," below) serves simple American dishes at lunch. At dinner look for some of the best steaks on the island and the fresh catch of the day.

6280 Estate Nazareth, Charlotte Amalie, St. Thomas, U.S.V.I. 00802-1104. © **800/524-2250** or 340/775-6550. Fax 340/775-1501. www.secretharbourvi.com. 60 units. Winter $255–$295 studio double, $275–$345 1-bedroom suite, $455–$555 2-bedroom suite; off season $149–$189 studio double, $179–$219 1-bedroom suite, $279–$329 2-bedroom suite. Children under 12 stay free in parent's room. AE, MC, V. **Amenities:** Restaurant; bar; outdoor pool; 3 tennis courts; fitness center; Jacuzzi; dive shop; snorkeling; windsurfing; massage; babysitting; rooms for those with limited mobility. *In room:* A/C, TV, kitchen, fridge, beverage maker, hair dryer, safe.

MODERATE/INEXPENSIVE
Galleon House   The rates at Galleon House are among the most competitive around. You walk up a long flight of stairs to reach a concrete terrace that

doubles as the reception area. The small rooms are in scattered hillside buildings, each with a ceiling fan and air-conditioning, plus a well-maintained shower-only bath. The best accommodations have panoramic views from private verandas. Breakfast is served on a veranda overlooking the harbor, and Magens Beach is a 15-minute drive from the hotel.

Government Hill (P.O. Box 6577), Charlotte Amalie, St. Thomas, U.S.V.I. 00804. © **800/524-2052** in the U.S., or 340/774-6952. Fax 340/774-6952. www.galleonhouse.com. 12 units, 11 with bathroom. Winter $79 double without bathroom, $89–$139 double with bathroom; off season $59 double without bathroom, $99 double with bathroom. Extra person $15 each. Rates include full breakfast. AE, MC, V. **Amenities:** Outdoor pool; snorkeling equipment. *In room:* A/C, TV, dataport, beverage maker, hair dryer.

Hotel 1829 ☆

This national historic site is one of the leading small hotels in the Caribbean. It was designed by an Italian architect in a Spanish motif, with French grillwork, Danish bricks, and sturdy Dutch doors. Danish and African labor completed the structure in 1829 (hence the name), and since then it has entertained the likes of Edna St. Vincent Millay and Mikhail Baryshnikov. The place stands right in the heart of town, on a hillside 3 minutes from Government House. Magens Bay Beach is about a 10-minute drive away. It's a bit of a climb to the top of this multitiered structure—there are many steps, but no elevator. Amid a cascade of flowering bougainvillea are the upper rooms, which overlook a central courtyard with a miniature pool. The rooms in the main house are well designed and attractive, and most face the water. All have wood beams and stone walls. The smallest units, in the former slave quarters, are the least comfortable. Each unit has a small, tiled bathroom with a shower stall. One of the most historic restaurants on St. Thomas, **Hervé Restaurant & Wine Bar,** is located here (see "Dining," below).

Kongens Gade (P.O. Box 1567), Charlotte Amalie, St. Thomas, U.S.V.I. 00804. © **800/524-2002** in the U.S., or 340/776-1829. Fax 340/776-4313. www.hotel1829.com. 15 units. Winter $105–$180 double, from $220 suite; off season $75–$135 double, from $160 suite. Rates include continental breakfast. AE, DISC, MC, V. **Amenities:** Bar; small outdoor pool; laundry service; nonsmoking rooms. *In room:* A/C, TV, fridge, hair dryer, iron/ironing board.

Villa Blanca ☆ *Value*

Small, intimate, and charming, this hotel lies east of Charlotte Amalie on 3 secluded acres of hilltop land, among the most panoramic areas on the island, with views over the harbor and the green rolling hills. The hotel's main building served as the private home of its present owner, Blanca Terrasa Smith, between 1973 and 1985. After the death of her husband, Mrs. Smith added a 12-room annex in the garden and opened her grounds to paying guests. Today, a homey, caring ambience prevails. Each room contains tile floors, a ceiling fan and/or air-conditioning, a shower-only tiled bathroom, a well-equipped kitchenette, and a private balcony or terrace with sweeping views either eastward to St. John or westward to Puerto Rico and the harbor of Charlotte Amalie. On the premises are a freshwater pool and a large covered patio where you can enjoy the sunset. The closest beach is Morning Star Bay, about a 4-mile drive away. Other than a continental breakfast, no meals are served.

4 Raphune Hill, Rte. 38, Charlotte Amalie, St. Thomas, U.S.V.I. 00801. © **800/231-0034** in the U.S., or 340/776-0749. Fax 340/779-2661. www.villablancahotel.com. 14 units. Winter $125–$145 double; off season $85–$115 double. Rates include continental breakfast. AE, DISC, MC, V. **Amenities:** Outdoor pool; sportfishing; nonsmoking rooms; rooms for those with limited mobility. *In room:* A/C and/or ceiling fan, TV, kitchenette, beverage maker, hair dryer, iron/ironing board.

Villa Santana ☆

This unique country villa is an all-suites property. It was originally built by Gen. Antonio Lopez de Santa Anna of Mexico in the 1850s, and has a panoramic view of Charlotte Amalie and the St. Thomas harbor. The shopping district in Charlotte Amalie is just a 5-minute walk away, and Magens Beach is a 15-minute drive. Guest rooms are at La Mansion, the former library of the general; La Terraza, originally the wine cellar; La Cocina de Santa Anna, once the central kitchen for the entire estate; La Casa de Piedra, once the bedroom of the general's most trusted attaché; and La Torre, the old pump house that has been converted into a modern lookout tower. All rooms have fully equipped kitchens and tiled shower-only bathrooms. The Mexican decor features clay tiles, rattan furniture, and stonework. The property has a pool, sun deck, and small garden with hibiscus and bougainvillea.

Denmark Hill, Charlotte Amalie, St. Thomas, U.S.V.I. 00802. ©/fax 340/776-1311. www.st-thomas.com/villasantana. 6 units. Winter $125–$195 suite for 2; off season $85–$135 suite for 2. AE, MC, V. **Amenities:** Outdoor pool. *In room:* Ceiling fan, TV, kitchen, beverage maker, hair dryer, iron/ironing board, no phone.

DINING

The St. Thomas dining scene these days is among the best in the West Indies, but it has its drawbacks. Meals tend to be expensive, and the best spots (with a few exceptions) are outside Charlotte Amalie, and can only be reached by taxi or car.

IN CHARLOTTE AMALIE

If you must go, the local branch of the **Hard Rock Cafe** chain is at the International Plaza, the Waterfront (© **340/777-5555**). It features live music on Saturday nights.

Banana Tree Grille INTERNATIONAL   This place serves up candlelit dinners, sweeping views over the busy harbor, and a decor that includes genuine banana plants artfully scattered through the two dining rooms. The cuisine is creative, the patrons are often hip and laid-back. Start with one of the aptly named "fabulous firsts," such as bacon-wrapped horseradish shrimp grilled and dancing over mango glaze. The house specialties, lobster tail tempura with orange-sambal sauce and mango-mustard-glazed salmon, are particularly good. Try the aioli lamb shank, another specialty, if it's offered: The meat is slowly braised in chianti and served with aioli sauce over vegetables and garlic mashed potatoes. The desserts are truly decadent. Happy hour is 5:30 to 6:30pm.

In Bluebeard's Castle, Bluebeard's Hill. © **340/776-4050.** Reservations recommended. Main courses $17–$36. AE, MC, V. Tues–Sun 6–9:30pm.

Beni Iguana's Sushi Bar JAPANESE   The only sushi restaurant on St. Thomas makes a nice change of pace from the Caribbean, steak, and seafood choices nearby. Along with a handful of shops, it occupies the sheltered courtyard and an old cistern across from Emancipation Square Park. You can eat outside or pass through wide Danish colonial doors into a red-and-black-lacquered interior devoted to a sushi bar and a handful of simple tables. A perennial favorite is the "13" roll, stuffed with spicy crabmeat, salmon, lettuce, cucumbers, and scallions.

In the Grand Hotel Court, Veteran's Dr. © **340/777-8744.** Reservations recommended. Sushi $4–$18 per portion (2 pieces); main courses $8–$17; combo plates for 4 to 5 diners $26–$36 each. AE, DC, DISC, MC, V. Mon–Sat 11:30am–3pm and 5–9pm.

Blackbeard Castle's Restaurant ✺✺   CONTINENTAL/ASIAN   In the castle's open-air tower, you can enjoy a romantic, gourmet meal while taking in a stunning view of the port of Charlotte Amalie. Chefs roam the world for inspiration, and pack a lot of flavor into every dish while still allowing natural flavors to shine through. Try the salmon and polenta, or dig into the grilled tuna ancho with chile and tomatillo sauces. Other additions include blackened mahimahi on a roasted red pepper and cilantro-flavored polenta topped with curried mango butter, and pan-seared scallops with a spicy coconut-and-mango salsa.

In Blackbeard's Castle, Blackbeard's Hill. (C) 340/776-1234. Reservations recommended. Main courses $19–$28. AE, DISC, MC, V. Mon–Sat 5:30–9pm.

Blue Moon Café CREATIVE AMERICAN   For idyllic dining in an open-air setting under the Caribbean moon, this beachfront restaurant claims, with some degree of accuracy, one of the most memorable settings for panoramic sunset views. *The Wine Spectator* acclaimed the restaurant for having the most romantic setting in St. Thomas. In winter, there is piano bar music on Wednesday night with a steel drum band on Friday. The menu, based on market-fresh ingredients, is changed twice seasonally. The list of food is geared to appeal to a wide range of palates, beginning with such tropical starters as coconut-honey shrimp with a guava dipping sauce or a portobello mushroom–and–goat cheese tart with field onions. Tip-top foodstuffs are handled with imagination and given zestful combinations such as mahimahi with pecans, bananas, and a coconut-rum sauce, and grilled scallops with a tomato-basil risotto with fresh asparagus. For lunch, you may want to confine yourself to burgers, wraps, salads, and sandwiches.

In the Secret Harbour Beach Resort, 6280 Estate Nazareth Bay. (C) 340/779-2262. Reservations required. Main courses $14–$35. AE, DC, DISC, MC, V. Daily 8am–3pm and 6–10pm.

Hervé Restaurant & Wine Bar ⊕ AMERICAN/CARIBBEAN/FRENCH This is the hottest restaurant on St. Thomas. A panoramic view of Charlotte Amalie and a historic setting are minor benefits—it's the cuisine that matters. Hervé P. Chassin is a restaurateur with a vast classical background. Here in an unpretentious setting, he offers high-quality food at reasonable prices. There are two dining areas: a large open-air terrace and a more intimate wine room. Start with the pistachio-encrusted brie, shrimp in a stuffed crab shell, or conch fritters with mango chutney. For a main course, try the house special bouillabaisse, or a delectable black-sesame-crusted tuna with a ginger/raspberry sauce. There are also nightly specials of game, fish, and pasta. Desserts are divine—you'll rarely taste a creamier crème caramel or a lighter, fluffier mango or raspberry cheesecake.

Next to Hotel 1829, Government Hill. (C) 340/777-9703. Reservations requested. Main courses $5.50–$17 lunch, $19–$28 dinner. AE, MC, V. Daily 11am–3pm and 6–10pm.

Tavern on the Waterfront ⊕ *Finds* CARIBBEAN/FRENCH   Celebrities visiting the island often come here. The setting is relatively simple but elegant, with African mahogany vaulted ceilings. Original artwork hangs on the white walls. The chefs present their inventive dishes attractively. Start with the St. Thomas conch fritters or the coconut shrimp with mango chutney. Main dishes include award-winning barbecue pork ribs that take 120 hours—from marinade to cooking—to prepare. We also enjoy the exotic pork platter, with espresso and cinnamon-encrusted pork medallions with a passion fruit demi-glace. The blackened seafood linguini, another winner, comes with mahimahi, jumbo sea scallops, New Zealand mussels, and shrimp blended with a Cajun cream sauce. There's often live reggae entertainment on Saturday, which you can enjoy while taking in harbor views. There's a happy hour, plus a children's menu.

Waterfront at Royal Dane Mall. (C) 340/776-4328. Reservations required. Main courses $19–$42. AE, DISC, MC, V. Mon–Sat 11am–3pm and 5:30–10pm.

Virgilio's ⊕ NORTHERN ITALIAN   Virgilio's is the best northern Italian restaurant in the Virgin Islands. Its neobaroque interior is sheltered under heavy ceiling beams and brick vaulting. A well-trained staff serves meals against a backdrop of stained-glass windows, crystal chandeliers, and soft Italian music. The *cinco peche* (clams, mussels, scallops, oysters, and crayfish simmered in a saffron broth) is delicious, and the alfredo fettuccine is the best there is. Classic dishes are served with a distinctive flair—the lamb shank, for example, is filled with a porcini-mushroom stuffing and glazed with a roasted garlic aioli. The marinated grilled duck is served chilled. You can even order an individual margherita pizza.

18 Dronningens Gade (entrance on a narrow alley running between Main and Back sts.). ℭ 340/776-4920. Reservations recommended. Main courses $11–$23 lunch, $16–$35 dinner. AE, MC, V. Mon–Sat 11am–10:30pm.

IN FRENCHTOWN

Bella Blue ℛ MEDITERRANEAN/SEAFOOD   West of Charlotte Amalie, this restaurant's 12 tables overlook the harbor. For years this restaurant enjoyed fame throughout the Caribbean when it was called Alexander's and served a rather heavy (for the Tropics) Austrian cuisine. Under its new owners, the fare is much lighter and focuses on the sunny flavors of the Mediterranean. To begin with, you might try the tuna tartare or even a Moroccan dish. The cooks are a whiz at concocting superb creations from lamb, veal, and seafood. The menu changes based on seasonal shopping and what's good and fresh at the marketplace.

French Town Mall. ℭ 340/774-4349. Reservations recommended. Main courses $8–$20 lunch, $16–$25 dinner. AE, MC, V. Mon–Sat 11:30am–3pm and 5:30–10pm.

Craig & Sally's ℛ ECLECTIC/INTERNATIONAL   This Caribbean cafe is set in an airy, open-sided pavilion in Frenchtown, with views of the sea and sky. Dishes range from pasta to seafood, with influences from Europe and Asia. You can try such light dishes as filet of salmon with a lemon grass–flavored mayonnaise or perhaps the pan-seared trout with fresh mushrooms. The lobster-stuffed, twice-baked potatoes are inspired, and the wine list is the most extensive and sophisticated on St. Thomas.

3525 Honduras. ℭ 340/777-9949. Reservations recommended. Main courses $15–$31. AE, MC, V. Wed–Fri 11:30am–3pm; Wed–Sun 5–10pm.

Oceana INTERNATIONAL/SEAFOOD   Upscale and sought after as a hip and stylish enclave, especially for local residents, this restaurant occupies what functioned during the Danish occupation of the island as the Russian consulate. Outfitted with slabs of carefully oiled paneling, and painted in bright blues and greens inspired by the colors of the ocean from which the restaurant took its name, it offers two distinctly different venues. The street level has a wine bar–cum–singles bar where small platters of food (blinis, crostinis, and cheese platters) specifically designed to go with the changing array of wine help to foster convivial after-work chitchat. Upstairs, within a relaxed but relatively formal dining room, candles and oil lamps flicker amid bouquets of flowers. Menu items focus mainly on fish dishes, with a healthy roster of beef and lamb dishes as well. Expect a list of food that includes spicy shrimp served with a cup of Andalusian-style gazpacho; house-marinated salmon (gravlax); mussels in white-wine sauce; pan-fried freshwater trout from Idaho; oven-roasted sea bass with a white wine, thyme, and olive oil sauce; grilled sirloin of lamb; several different preparations of Caribbean lobster; and filets of Midwestern beef with bacon, pepper, and a port-wine sauce. If the ambience and conviviality of the wine bar appeal to you more than the relative formality of the upstairs dining room, the staff will set up a dining table there for you as well.

In the Villa Olga, 8 Honduras. ℭ 340/774-4262. Reservations recommended. Appetizers in the wine bar $8–$15; main courses $20–$32. AE, DC, MC, V. Bar Mon–Sat 5pm–midnight; restaurant Mon–Sat 6–10pm.

ON THE NORTH COAST

The Old Stone Farmhouse AMERICAN/INTERNATIONAL Set in a wooded valley close to the 11th hole of the Mahogany Run Golf Course, this restaurant dates from the 1750s. Once it was a stable for a nearby Danish sugar plantation, with walls more than 2 feet thick. Ceiling fans and breezes blowing through the valley keep the place cool. For more than a quarter of a century, it has been feeding golfers and those who love them from an eclectic menu that takes advantage of the best seasonal produce. The fresh fish dishes are always the best option. Begin, perhaps, with grilled portobello mushrooms with Asian duck. Many regulars come here for the well-prepared steak.

Mahogany Run. ⓒ 340/777-6277. Reservations recommended. Main courses $19–$31. AE, MC, V. Tues–Sun 5:30–9:30pm.

Romanos Restaurant ITALIAN Located near Coral World, this hideaway is owned by New Jersey chef Tony Romano, who specializes in a flavorful and herb-laden cuisine that makes a nice change from Caribbean food. House favorites include *linguine con pesto,* four-cheese lasagna, a tender and well-flavored *osso buco* (veal shanks), scaloppini Marsala, and broiled salmon. All desserts are made on the premises. With exposed brick and well-stocked wine racks, this restaurant always seems full of happy, lively diners.

66–97 Smith Bay Rd. ⓒ 340/775-0045. Reservations recommended. Main courses $19–$30; pastas $18–$22. AE, MC, V. Mon–Sat. 6–10:30pm. Closed Sept and 4 days in Apr for Carnival.

IN & AROUND RED HOOK BAY (THE EAST END)

Agavé Terrace ⓡ CARIBBEAN Perched high above a steep and heavily forested hillside on the eastern tip of St. Thomas, one of the island's best restaurants offers a sweeping panorama and unparalleled romance. The house drink is Desmond Delight, a combination of Midori, rum, pineapple juice, and a secret ingredient. After a few Delights, try the house appetizer, an Agavé sampler for two, which includes portions of crabmeat, conch fritters, and shrimp cocktail. The catch of the day features three different fish, which can be prepared in any of seven different ways with a choice of nine sauces. Some of our favorite meals here include pan-roasted breast of chicken with black beans, and mango and coconut fried shrimp with banana fritters and dark-rum butter sauce. There are also vegetarian selections. The wine list is extensive. A live steel drum band draws listeners Tuesday and Thursday nights.

In the Point Pleasant Resort, 6600 Estate Smith Bay. ⓒ 340/775-4142. Reservations recommended. Main courses $18–$36. AE, MC, V. Daily 6–10pm.

Duffy's Love Shack ⓡ *Finds* AMERICAN/CARIBBEAN You can mingle with locals at this fun, happening place. As the evening wears on, the customers become the entertainment, often dancing on tables or forming conga lines. Yes, Duffy's also serves food, standard American cuisine with Caribbean flavors. The restaurant is open-air, with lots of bamboo and a thatched roof over the bar. Even the menu appears on a bamboo stick, like an old-fashioned fan. Start with honey-barbecued ribs, then move on to cowboy steak or pork Cuban. After 10pm, a late-night menu of mostly sandwiches appears. The bar business is huge, and the bartender is known for his lethal rum drinks.

650 Red Hook Plaza, Rte. 38. ⓒ 340/779-2080. Main courses $8–$16. No credit cards. Daily 11:30am–2am.

Fungi's on the Beach CARIBBEAN This funky native bar opens onto Pineapple Beach. It's a lot of fun and the burgers are some of the juiciest on the island. You can also order Caribbean specialties like conch in butter sauce, roast suckling pig, johnnycakes, plantains, rice and beans, and callaloo soup. Stewed chicken is a local favorite. The place has an outdoorsy atmosphere with a reggae theme. Nightly entertainment—reggae and more reggae—is also a feature.

Point Pleasant. ℂ 340/775-4142. Main courses $8–$20. AE, MC, V. Daily 11:30am–10pm.

Molly Malone's IRISH/CARIBBEAN At the Red Hook American Yacht Harbor, you can join the good ol' boys and dig into the best baby back ribs on the island. No one can drink more brew than the boisterous crowd that assembles here every night to let the good times roll. If you're nostalgic for the Emerald Isle, go for the shepherd's pie. The conch fritters are the best in the east end, and an Irish/Caribbean stew is a nightly feature. You can dine outdoors under a canopy on the dock at the eastern end of Red Hook where the ferry from St. John pulls in. The only time the place closes is when a hurricane comes along and blows it away.

6100 Red Hook Quarters. ℂ 340/775-1270. Main courses $15–$25. AE, MC, V. Daily 6:30am–1am.

Off the Hook ℱ ASIAN/CARIBBEAN Using some of the West Indies' freshest and finest ingredients, the chefs here concoct an eclectic medley of Asian-inspired dishes. In an open-air dining room near the American Yacht Harbor, close to the departure point for the ferry to St. John, the fresh catch of the day— hauled off the little fishing boats just pulling in—is delivered to the kitchen, where it's grilled to perfection. The yellowfin tuna keeps us coming back and the tuna and salmon sushi platter is also excellent. The Black Angus steak is always a pure delight. The decor is rustic, with outdoor dining and wooden tables.

6300 Estate Smith Bay. ℂ 340/775-6350. Reservations required. Main courses $16–$25. AE, MC, V. Daily 6–10pm. Closed Sept 15–Oct 15.

HITTING THE BEACH

Chances are your hotel will be right on the beach, or very close to one. All the beaches in the Virgin Islands are public, and most lie anywhere from 2 to 5 miles from Charlotte Amalie.

THE NORTH SIDE The gorgeous white sands of **Magens Bay** ℱℱ lie between two mountains 3 miles north of the capital. *Condé Nast Traveler* named this beach one of the world's 10 most beautiful. The turquoise waters here are

---

Moments **Two Great Escapes**

Water Island, ¾ mile off the coast from the harbor of Charlotte Amalie, is the fourth-largest island of the U.S. Virgins, with 500 acres of land. At palm-shaded **Honeymoon Beach,** you can swim, snorkel, sail, water-ski, or sunbathe, then order lunch or a drink from the beach bar (on Saturday and Sunday only). A ferry runs between Crown Bay Marina and Water Island several times a day. (Crown Bay Marina, ℂ 340/774-2255, is part of the St. Thomas submarine base.)

In the same bay, and even closer to shore, is **Hassel Island.** It's almost completely deserted, and it is protected as part of a U.S. National Park. There are no hotels or services of any kind here, and swimming is limited to narrow, rocky beaches. Even so, many visitors hire a boat to drop them off for an hour or two. A hike along part of the shoreline is a welcome relief from the cruise-ship congestion of Charlotte Amalie. Bring water and food if you plan to spend more than 3 hours here.

Finds Hidden Beach Discoveries

At this point you'd think all the beaches of overrun St. Thomas had been destroyed. But there are two less trampled strands of sand we recently came upon. A sparkling beach of white sand, **Vessup Bay,** is found at the end of Bluebeard's Road (Route 322) as it branches off Route 30 near the hamlet of Red Hook. Against a rocky backdrop, the beach curves around a pristine bay studded with vegetation including cacti, agave plants, and sea grape. One end of the beach is less populated than the other. A watersports concessionaire operates here. Another find is **Hull Bay,** on the north shore, just west of overcrowded Magens Bay. Surfers are attracted to the waves along the western tip of Hull Bay, and local St. Thomas fishermen anchor in the more tranquil strands. Part of the beach is in shade. Don't expect much in the way of watersports, but there is a combined restaurant and open-air bar.

---

calm and ideal for swimming, and the snorkeling is also good. The beach is no secret, and it's usually terribly overcrowded, though it gets better in the midafternoon. Changing facilities, snorkeling gear, lounge chairs, paddleboats, and kayaks are available. There is no public transportation to get here (though some hotels provide shuttle buses); from Charlotte Amalie, take Route 35 north all the way. The gates to the beach are open daily from 5am to 6pm (after 4pm, you'll need insect repellent). Admission is $3 per person. Don't bring valuables, and certainly don't leave anything of value in your parked car.

A marked trail leads to **Little Magens Bay,** a separate, clothing-optional beach that is especially popular with gay and lesbian visitors. This is also former President Clinton's preferred beach on St. Thomas (no, he doesn't go nude).

Coki Point Beach, in the northeast near Coral World, is good but often very crowded. It's noted for its warm, crystal-clear water, ideal for swimming and snorkeling (you'll see thousands of rainbow-hued fish swimming among the beautiful corals). Locals even sell small bags of fish food, so you can feed the sea creatures while you're snorkeling. From the beach, there's a panoramic view of offshore Thatch Cay. Concessions can arrange everything from water-skiing to parasailing. An east-end bus runs to Smith Bay and lets you off at the gate to Coral World and Coki. Watch out for pickpockets.

Also on the north side is luscious **Grand Beach,** one of the island's most beautiful. It opens onto Smith Bay and is near Coral World. Many watersports are available here. The beach is right off Route 38.

THE EAST END Small and special, **Secret Harbour** is near a collection of condos. With its white sand and coconut palms, it's the epitome of Caribbean charm. The snorkeling near the rocks is some of the best on the island. No public transportation stops here, but it's an easy taxi ride east of Charlotte Amalie heading toward Red Hook.

Sapphire Beach is set against the backdrop of the Doubletree Sapphire Beach Resort and Marina, where you can have lunch or order drinks. There are good views of offshore cays and St. John, a large reef is close to the shore, and windsurfers enjoy this beach. Snorkeling gear and lounge chairs can be rented. Take the east end bus from Charlotte Amalie, going via Red Hook. Ask to be let off at the entrance to Sapphire Bay; it's not too far to walk from here to the water.

White-sand **Lindquist Beach** isn't a long strip, but it's one of the island's prettiest. It's between Wyndham Sugar Bay Beach Club and the Sapphire Beach Resort. Many films and TV commercials have used this photogenic beach as a backdrop. It's not likely to be crowded, as it's not very well-known.

THE SOUTH SIDE   Morning Star Beach (also known as Frenchman's Bay Beach) is near the Marriott Frenchman's Reef Beach Resort, about 2 miles east of Charlotte Amalie. Here, among the often-young crowds (many of whom are gay), you can don your skimpiest bikini. Sailboats, snorkeling equipment, and lounge chairs are available for rent. The beach is easily reached by a cliff-front elevator at Frenchman's Reef.

Limetree Beach, set against a backdrop of sea-grape trees and shady palms, lures those who want a serene spread of sand where they can bask in the sun and even feed hibiscus blossoms to iguanas. Snorkeling gear, lounge and beach chairs, towels, and drinks are available. There's no public transportation, but the beach can easily be reached by taxi from Charlotte Amalie.

WEST OF CHARLOTTE AMALIE   Near the University of the Virgin Islands in the southwest, **Brewer's Bay is one of the island's most popular beaches. The strip of white coral sand is almost as long as the beach at Magens Bay. Unfortunately, this isn't the place for snorkeling. Vendors sell light meals and drinks. From Charlotte Amalie, take the Fortuna bus heading west; get off at the edge of Brewer's Bay, across from the Reichhold Center.

Lindbergh Beach, which has a lifeguard, restrooms, and a bathhouse, lies at the Island Beachcomber Hotel and is used almost exclusively by locals, who sometimes stage political rallies here, as well as Carnival parties. It's not good for snorkeling. Drinks are served on the beach. Take the Fortuna bus route west from Charlotte Amalie.

SPORTS & OTHER OUTDOOR PURSUITS

**DEEP-SEA FISHING   The U.S. Virgins have excellent deep-sea fishing—some 19 world records (8 for blue marlin) have been set in these waters. Outfitters abound at the major marinas like Red Hook. We recommend angling off the *Fish Hawk* (© 340/775-9058), which Captain Al Petrosky sails out of Fish Hawk Marina Lagoon on the east end. His 48-foot diesel-powered craft is fully equipped with rods and reels. For all equipment (but not meals) you'll pay $550 per half-day for up to six passengers. Full-day excursions start at $1,100.

⌢Moments Bringing Out the Sir Francis Drake in You

Tired of escorted tours? **Nauti Nymph Powerboat Rentals,** American Yacht Harbor, Red Hook (© **800/734-7345** in the U.S., or **340/775-5066**), reaches out to the independent traveler and adventurer. The knowing staff assists in designing a personal itinerary for a bareboat rental, or can hook you up with a captained day trip. A choice of Coast Guard–approved and fully equipped vessels ranging in size from 25 feet to 29 feet are available. Boats are kept in top-of-the-line condition. On your own you can explore the British Virgin Islands, including such little-known islands as Jost van Dyke and Norman Island, in the tradition of Sir Francis Drake. Norman Island, incidentally, was the inspiration for Robert Louis Stevenson's *Treasure Island*.

GOLF Mahogany Run, on the north shore at Mahogany Run Road (℡ 800/ 253-7103), is an 18-hole, par-70 course. This beautiful course rises and drops like a roller coaster on its journey to the sea; cliffs and crashing sea waves are the ultimate hazards at the 13th and 14th holes. Former President Clinton pronounced this course very challenging. Greens fees are $130 for 18 holes, reduced to $105 in the late afternoon. Carts are included. Club rental costs $35.

SAILING 🎿 **American Yacht Harbor** 🎿, Red Hook (℡ 340/775-6454), can refer both bareboat and fully crewed charters. It leaves from the east end of St. Thomas in Vessup Bay. The harbor is home to numerous boat companies, including day-trippers, fishing boats, and sailing charters. There are also five restaurants on the property, serving everything from Continental to Caribbean cuisine. Another reliable outfitter is **Charteryacht League** 🎿, at Gregory East (℡ 800/524-2061 in the U.S., or 340/774-3944).

Sailors may want to check out the *Yachtsman's Guide to the Virgin Islands,* available at major marine outlets, at bookstores, through catalog merchandisers, or directly from **Tropic Isle Publishers,** P.O. Box 610938, North Miami, FL 33261-0938 (℡ 877/923-9653; www.yachtsmansguide.com). This annual guide, which costs $11, is supplemented by sketch charts, photographs, and landfall sketches and charts showing harbors and harbor entrances, anchorages, channels, and landmarks, plus information on preparations necessary for cruising the islands.

SCUBA DIVING The best scuba diving site off St. Thomas, especially for novices, has to be **Cow and Calf Rocks,** off the southeast end (45 minutes from Charlotte Amalie by boat); here you'll discover a network of coral tunnels riddled with caves, reefs, and ancient boulders encrusted with coral. The *Cartanser Sr.,* a sunken World War II cargo ship that lies in about 35 feet of water, is beautifully encrusted with coral and now home to a myriad of colorful resident fish. Another popular wreck dive is the *Maj. General Rogers,* the stripped-down hull of a former Coast Guard cutter.

Experienced divers may want to dive at exposed sheer rock pinnacles like **Sail Rock** and **French Cap Pinnacle,** which are encrusted with hard and soft corals and frequented by lobsters and green and hawksbill turtles. They are also exposed to open-ocean currents that can make these very challenging dives.

⸢Tips Getting to the Bottom of It

The air-conditioned *Atlantis* submarine will take you on a 1-hour voyage (the whole experience is really 2 hours, when you include transportation to and from the sub) to depths of 90 feet, where an amazing world of exotic marine life unfolds. You'll have up-close views of coral reefs and sponge gardens through the sub's 2-foot windows. On some voyages, *Atlantis* divers swim with the fish and bring them close to the windows for photos.

Passengers take a surface boat from the West Indies Dock, right outside Charlotte Amalie, to the submarine, which is near Buck Island (the St. Thomas version, not the more famous Buck Island near St. Croix). The fare is $79 for adults, $39 for children age 4 to 17; children 3 and under are not allowed. The *Atlantis* operates daily. Reservations are a must (the sub carries only 48 passengers). For tickets, go to the Havensight shopping mall, building 6, or call ℡ 340/776-5650.

St. Thomas Diving Club, 7147 Bolongo Bay (© **877/538-8734** in the U.S., or 340/776-2381), is a full-service, PADI five-star IDC center, the best on the island. An open-water certification course, including four scuba dives, costs $385. An advanced open-water certification course, including five dives that can be accomplished in 2 days, goes for $275. On request, participants are taken on an all-day scuba excursion that includes a two-tank dive to the wreck of the **HMS *Rhone*** in the British Virgin Islands; the trip costs $130. A scuba tour of the 350-foot wreck of the *Witshoal* is offered for experienced divers only; the cost is $88. You can also enjoy local snorkeling for $30.

DIVE IN!, in the Sapphire Beach Resort & Marina, Smith Bay Road, Route 36 (© **866/434-8346,** ext. 2144, in the U.S., or 340/777-5255), is a well-recommended, complete diving center that offers some of the finest services in the U.S. Virgin Islands, including professional instruction (beginner to advanced), daily beach and boat dives, custom dive packages, snorkeling trips, and a full-service PADI dive center. An introductory resort course costs $65, with a one-tank dive going for $55 and two-tank dives for $75. A six-dive pass costs $203.

SEA KAYAKING   Virgin Island Ecotours/Mangrove Adventures (© **340/ 779-2155**) offers half-day kayak trips through a mangrove lagoon on the southern coastline. The cost is $75 per person. The tour is led by professional naturalists who allow for 45 minutes of snorkeling.

SNORKELING ⋆⋆   With 30 spectacular reefs just off St. Thomas, this is a spectacular destination for snorkeling. We like the waters off **Coki Point** ⋆⋆, on the northeast shore of St. Thomas; especially enticing are the coral ledges near Coral World's underwater tower. **Magens Bay** also has great snorkeling year-round. If your hotel doesn't provide snorkel gear, it's easy to rent on most of the island's popular beaches.

You may also want to take a snorkeling cruise. Many leave from the Red Hook and Yacht Haven marinas. The 50-foot yacht *Nightwind,* Sapphire Marina (© **340/775-4110,** 24 hr. a day), offers full-day sails to St. John and the outer islands. The $110 price includes free snorkeling equipment and instruction, plus a continental breakfast, a champagne buffet lunch, and an open bar.

New Horizons, 6501 Red Hook Plaza, Suite 16, Red Hook (© **340/775- 1171**), offers wind-borne excursions amid the cays and reefs of the Virgin Islands. The two-masted, 65-foot sloop has circumnavigated the globe and has been used as a design prototype for other boats. Owned and operated by Canadian Tim Krygsveld, it contains a hot-water shower, serves a specialty drink called a New Horizons Nooner (with a melon-liqueur base), and carries a complete line of snorkeling equipment for adults and children. A full-day excursion, with continental breakfast, an Italian buffet lunch, and an open bar, costs $110 per person. Children age 2 to 12, when accompanied by an adult, pay $55. Excursions depart daily, weather permitting, from the Sapphire Beach Resort & Marina. Call ahead for reservations and information. Another vessel, *New Horizons II,* a 44-foot custom-made speedboat, runs full-day trips to some of the most scenic highlights of the British Virgin Islands, costing $120 for adults or $95 for children age 2 to 12.

You can avoid the crowds by sailing aboard the *Fantasy,* 6700 Sapphire Village, no. 253 (© **340/775-5652;** fax 340/775-6256), which departs from the American Yacht Harbor at Red Hook at 9:30am daily. It takes a maximum of six passengers to St. John and nearby islands for swimming, snorkeling, beachcombing, and trolling. Snorkel gear with expert instruction is provided, as is a champagne lunch; an underwater camera is available. The full-day trip costs $120 per person in the summer. A half-day sail, morning or afternoon, lasts 3 hours and costs $85. Sunset tours are also popular, with an open bar and hors d'oeuvres, costing $350 for a group.

TENNIS   The best tennis on the island is at the **Wyndham Sugar Bay Beach Club & Spa** 🕉🕉, 6500 Estate Smith Bay (© **340/777-7100**), with four Laykold courts lit at night. Nonguests pay $10 per hour. There's also a pro shop.

Another good resort for tennis is the **Bolongo Bay Beach Resort,** Bolongo Bay (© **340/775-1800**), which has two courts that are lit until 6pm. They're free to members and hotel guests, but cost $12 for nonguests.

Marriott Frenchman's Reef Tennis Courts, Flamboyant Point (© **340/776-8500**), has two courts. Again, nonguests are charged $10 per hour per court. Lights stay on until 10pm.

WINDSURFING   Windsurfing is available through the major resorts and at some public beaches, including Morning Star Beach and Limetree Beach. The **Grand Beach Palace,** Smith Bay Road, Route 38 (© **340/775-1510**), is the major hotel offering windsurfing. It's available to guests at no charge and to nonguests at $20 per hour. Sapphire Beach is also a popular spot.

EXPLORING ST. THOMAS
CHARLOTTE AMALIE 🕉

The capital, Charlotte Amalie, where most visitors begin their sightseeing, has all the color and charm of an authentic Caribbean waterfront town. In days of yore, seafarers from all over the globe flocked here, as did pirates and members of the Confederacy, who used the port during the American Civil War. (Sadly, St. Thomas was the biggest slave market in the world.)

The old warehouses once used for storing pirate goods still stand, and today, many of them house shops. In fact, the main streets are now a virtual shopping mall and are usually packed. (See "Shopping," below, for our specific recommendations.) Sandwiched among these shops are a few historic buildings, most of which can be seen on foot in about 2 hours.

Fort Christian   This imposing structure, which dates from 1671, dominates the center of town. It was named after the Danish king Christian V and has been everything from a fort to a governor's residence to a jail. It became a national historic landmark in 1977, but still functioned as a police station, court, and jail until 1983. Now a museum, the fort houses displays on the island's history and culture. Cultural workshops and turn-of-the-20th-century furnishings are just some of the exhibits. A museum shop features local crafts, maps, and prints.

In the town center. © 340/776-4566. Adults $3, children 12 and under free. Mon–Fri 8:30am–4pm.

St. Thomas Skyride   This contraption affords visitors a dramatic view of Charlotte Amalie harbor, with a ride to a 700-foot peak. The tramway, similar to those used at ski resorts, operates six cars, each with a 12-person capacity, for the 15-minute round-trip ride. It transports customers from the Havensight area to Paradise Point, where they can disembark to visit shops and the popular restaurant and bar.

© 340/774-9809. Round-trip $15 adults, $7.50 children age 6–12. Thurs–Tues 9am–5pm; Wed 9am–9pm.

Seven Arches Museum   Browsers love checking out the private home of longtime residents Philibert Fluck and Barbara Demaras. This is an 18th-century Danish house, restored to its original condition and furnished with

West Indian antiques. You can walk through the yellow ballast arches and visit the great room, with its wonderful view of the busiest harbor in the Caribbean. Night-blooming cacti and iguanas are on the roof of some of the quarters.

Government Hill. ℂ 340/774-9295. Admission $5. Daily 10am–4pm.

Synagogue of Beracha Veshalom Vegmiluth Hasidim ⋒ This is the oldest synagogue in continuous use under the American flag. It was erected in 1833 by Sephardic Jews, and it maintains the tradition of having sand on the floor, commemorating the exodus from Egypt. The structure was built of local stone, along with ballast brick from Denmark and mortar made of molasses and sand. Next door, the **Weibel Museum** showcases 300 years of Jewish history. It keeps the same hours as the synagogue.

16 Crystal Gade. ℂ 340/774-4312. Free admission. Mon–Fri 10am–4pm.

ELSEWHERE ON THE ISLAND

Route 30 (Veterans Drive) will take you west of Charlotte Amalie to **Frenchtown.** (Turn left at the sign to the Admiral's Inn.) Early French-speaking settlers arrived on St. Thomas from St. Bart's after they were uprooted by the Swedes. Some island residents today are the direct descendants of those long-ago immigrants, who were known for speaking a distinctive French patois. This colorful village contains a number of restaurants and taverns and a reputation as a night-clubbing destination. Because Charlotte Amalie has become somewhat dangerous at night, Frenchtown has picked up its after-dark business and is the best spot for dancing and other local entertainment.

Coral World Marine Park & Underwater Observatory ⋒ This marine complex features a three-story underwater observation tower 100 feet offshore. Inside, you'll see sponges, fish, coral, and other aquatic creatures in their natural state. An 80,000-gallon reef tank features exotic marine life of the Caribbean; another tank is devoted to sea predators, with circling sharks and giant moray eels. Activities include daily fish and shark feedings. The latest attraction is a Nautilus semisubmarine going 6 feet below the surface of the water. On board, passengers can enjoy close encounters with a sea of coral gardens and rainbow-hued fish outside their portholes.

Coral World's guests can take advantage of adjacent **Coki Beach** for snorkel rentals, scuba lessons, or simply swimming and relaxing. Lockers and showers are available. Also at the marine park are a bar and a nature trail.

6450 Estates Smith Bay, a 20-min. drive from Charlotte Amalie off Route 38. ℂ 340/775-1555. Admission $18 adults, $9 children age 3–12. Daily 9am–5pm.

Estate St. Peter Greathouse Botanical Gardens ⋒ This estate consists of 11 acres at the foot of volcanic peaks on the northern rim of the island. The grounds are laced with self-guided nature walks that identify some 200 varieties of West Indian plants and trees, including an umbrella plant from Madagascar. From a panoramic deck in the gardens, you can see some 20 of the Virgin Islands, including Hans Lollick, an uninhabited island between Thatched Cay and Madahl Point. The house itself, filled with local art, is worth a visit.

At the corner of Rte. 40 (6A St. Peter Mountain Rd.) and Barrett Hill Rd. ℂ 340/774-4999. Admission $10 adults, $5 children age 4–12. Daily 8am–4pm.

SHOPPING ⋒⋒⋒

The discounted, duty-free shopping in the Virgin Islands makes St. Thomas a shopping mecca. It's possible to find well-known brand names here at savings of

---

Moments Into the Deep for Nondivers

Nondivers can get some of the thrill known to scuba aficionados by participating in **Sea Trek at the Coral World Marine Park & Underwater Observatory** (© **340/775-1555**). For $68 you get a full immersion undersea. No experience is needed. Participants are given a helmet and a tube to breathe through. The tube is attached to an air source at the observatory tower. You then enjoy a 600-foot, 30-minute stroll in water 18 feet deep. You're on the sea floor taking in the rainbow-hued tropical fish and the coral reefs as you go along. It's a marvelous way to experience the world through the eyes of a fish.

---

up to 60% off mainland U.S. prices. But be warned—not all savings are so good. Before you leave home, check prices in your local stores if you think you might want to make a major purchase, so you can be sure that you are in fact getting a good deal. Having said that, we'll recommend some shops where we have found really good buys.

The best deals include china, crystal, perfume, jewelry (especially emeralds), Haitian art, fashion, watches, and items made of wood. Cameras and electronic items, based on our experience, are not the good buys they're reputed to be. St. Thomas is also the best place in the Caribbean for discounts on porcelain, but remember that U.S. brands may often be purchased for 25% off the retail price on the U.S. mainland. Look for the imported patterns for the biggest savings.

Most shops, some of which occupy former pirate warehouses, are open Monday to Saturday from 9am to 5pm. Some stores open Sunday and holidays if a cruise ship is in port. *Note:* Friday is the biggest cruise-ship day at Charlotte Amalie (we once counted eight ships in port at once), so try to avoid shopping then. It's a zoo.

Nearly all the major shopping is along the harbor of Charlotte Amalie. Cruise-ship passengers mainly shop at the **Havensight Mall** at the eastern edge of town. The principal shopping street is **Main Street,** or Dronningens Gade (its old Danish name). To the north is another merchandise-loaded street called **Back Street,** or Vimmelskaft. Many shops are also spread along the **Waterfront Highway** (Kyst Vejen). Between these major streets is a series of side streets, walkways, and alleys, all filled with shops. You might also browse along Tolbod Gade, Raadets Gade, Royal Dane Mall, Palm Passage, Storetvaer Gade, and Strand Gade.

It's illegal for most street vendors (food vendors are about the only exception) to ply their trades outside the designated area called **Vendors Plaza,** at the corner of Veterans Drive and Tolbod Gade. Hundreds of vendors converge here at 8am; they usually pack up around 5pm, Monday to Saturday.

When you completely tire of French perfumes and Swiss watches, head for **Market Square,** also called Rothschild Francis Square. Under a Victorian tin roof, locals with machetes slice open fresh coconuts, while women wearing bandanas sell akee, cassava, and breadfruit.

All the major stores in St. Thomas are located by number on an excellent map in the publication *St. Thomas This Week,* distributed free to all arriving plane and boat passengers and at the visitor center. A lot of the stores on the island don't have street numbers, or don't display them, so look for their signs instead.

Diamonds International ☆, 31 Main St. (© **340/775-2010**), boasts the biggest inventory of diamonds in the Virgin Islands. A wide selection of loose diamonds and fine jewelry are on display, although not necessarily living up to the outlet's boast of "the best deals on the planet." Appraisals accompany sales over $500.

Caribbean Chocolate, 15 Main St. (© **340/774-6675**), boasts a tantalizing collection of fresh chocolates, many of which are made fresh daily. The claim here is that the outlet sells "anything under the sun with chocolate." What a delight to tuck into some of their homemade fudge.

Crystal Shoppe ⊛, 14 Main St. (© **340/777-9835**). This family-run store offers a dazzling array of crystal from around the world. All the big names in glass—Wedgwood, Hummel, Royal Copenhagen, Swarovski, and Rosenthal—are on parade, along with some particularly good pieces from the Swedish firm of Kosta Boda. Their porcelain Lladró figurines from Spain are also a fast-moving item.

Fabric in Motion, Storetvaer Gade (© **340/774-2006**), culls the globe for fabrics, and has a wonderful selection of silklike cottons from Liberty's of London, the best Italian linens, and flamboyant batiks from Indonesia. There are many tempting items, including leather handbags and fun beach bags.

Boolchand's ⊛⊛, 31 Main St. (© **340/776-0794**), is the place to go when you're in the market for a camera. Famous throughout the Caribbean, this is the major retailer of not only cameras but electronics and digital products throughout the West Indies. Now into its 8th decade, it sells all the big names from Kodak to Leica, from Nikon to Fuji. In the electronics divisions are the latest in DVDs, minidiscs, and other items. There is also a jewelry department and a wide selection of watches.

Bernard K. Passman ⊛⊛⊛, 38A Main St. (© **340/777-4580**), is the world's leading sculptor of black-coral art and jewelry. He's famous for his *Can Can Girl* and his four statues of Charlie Chaplin. After being polished and embellished with gold and diamonds, some of Passman's work has been treasured by royalty. There are also simpler and more affordable pieces for sale.

Gallery Camille Pissarro, 14 Main St. (© **340/774-4621**), is located in the house where Pissarro was born in 1830. In three high-ceilinged and airy rooms, you can view many prints of local artists, and the gallery also sells original batiks, alive in vibrant colors.

Mango Tango Art Gallery, Al Cohen's Plaza, Raphune Hill, Route 38 (© **340/777-3060**), is one of the largest galleries on island, closely connected with a half-dozen internationally recognized artists who spend at least part of the year in the Virgin Islands. Original works begin at $300; prints and posters are cheaper.

Gallery St. Thomas, Government Hill (© **877/797-6363** or 340/774-9440), showcases the works of Virgin Island painters, notably Lucinda Schutt, best known for her Caribbean land and seascapes. At this gallery, to the west of Hotel 1829, Schutt sells artwork beginning at $125 and prints for $18, and teaches painting with watercolors.

Native Arts and Crafts Cooperative ⊛, Tarbor Gade 1 (© **340/777-1153**), is the largest arts-and-crafts emporium in the U.S. Virgin Islands, offering the output of 90 different artisans. It specializes in items small enough to be packed into a suitcase or trunk, such as spice racks, lamps crafted from conch shells, salad bowls, crocheted goods, and straw goods.

Caribbean Marketplace, Havensight Mall, building 3 (© **340/776-5400**), carries a selection of spices including the Sunny Caribbee line, a vast array of condiments, and botanical products. (Don't expect very attentive service.)

Aromatic **Down Island Traders,** Waterfront (© **340/776-4641**), has Charlotte Amalie's most attractive array of spices, teas, candies, jellies, jams, and condiments, most of which are packaged in natural Caribbean products. There are also local cookbooks, and silk-screened T-shirts and bags.

The clutter and eclecticism of **Carson Company Antiques,** Royal Dane Mall, off Main Street (© **340/774-6175**), may appeal to you. The shop is loaded with merchandise, tasteless and otherwise, from virtually everywhere. Bakelite jewelry is cheap and cheerful, and the African artifacts are often interesting.

A. H. Riise Gift ✱, 37 Main St. (© **800/524-2037** or 340/776-2303), is St. Thomas's oldest outlet for luxury items, and offers the best liquor selection on the island. The store carries fine jewelry and watches from Europe's leading craftspeople, including Bulgari, Omega, Rolex, and Gucci, as well as a wide selection of gold, platinum, and precious gemstone jewelry. Imported cigars are stored in a climate-controlled walk-in humidor. Waterford, Lalique, Baccarat, and Rosenthal are featured in the china and crystal department. Specialty shops in the complex sell Caribbean gifts, books, T-shirts, food, prints, note cards, and designer sunglasses.

One of the island's most famous outlets, **Al Cohen's Discount Liquors,** Havensight Mall (© **340/774-3690**), occupies a big warehouse at Havensight with a huge selection of liquor and wine. The wine department is especially impressive. You can also purchase T-shirts and souvenirs.

Royal Caribbean ✱, 33 Main St. (© **340/776-4110**), is the largest camera and electronics store in the Caribbean. It carries Nikon, Minolta, Pentax, Canon, and Panasonic products, plus watches by Seiko, Movado, Corum, Fendi, Philippe Charriol, and Zodiac. There are also leather bags, Mikimoto pearls, 14- and 18-karat jewelry, and Lladró figurines. Another branch is located at the Havensight Mall (© **340/776-8890**).

Often called the Tiffany's of the Caribbean, **Cardow Jewelers** ✱✱, 39 Main St. (© **340/776-1140**), boasts the largest selection of fine jewelry in the world. This fabulous shop, where more than 20,000 rings are displayed, offers savings because of its worldwide direct buying, large turnover, and duty-free prices. Unusual and traditional designs are offered in diamonds, emeralds, rubies, sapphires, and pearls. The Treasure Cove has cases of fine gold jewelry priced under $300.

Cardow's leading competitor is **H. Stern Jewellers,** Havensight Mall (© **800/ 524-2024** or 340/776-1223), the international chain with some 175 outlets. Besides this branch, there are two more on Main Street. Stern gives worldwide guaranteed service, including a 1-year exchange privilege.

Colombian Emeralds International, Havensight Mall (© **340/774-2442**), is renowned throughout the Caribbean for its collection of Colombian emeralds, both set and unset. Here you buy direct from the source, which can mean significant savings. The shop also stocks fine watches. There's another outlet on Main Street.

Another good place to browse for gemstones is **Pierre's,** 24 Palm Passage (© **800/300-0634** or 340/776-5130), one of the most impressive repositories of collector's items in the Caribbean. Look for alexandrites (garnets in three shades of green); spinels (pink and red); sphenes, yellow-green sparklers from Madagascar that are as reflective as high-quality diamonds; and tsavorites, green stones from Tanzania.

Cosmopolitan, Drakes Passage and the waterfront (© **340/776-2040**), carries Bruno Magli shoes; women's and men's swimwear by Gottex, Hom, Lahco, and Sunflair; ties by Brioni and Pancaldi (at least 30% less than the U.S. mainland price); and Timberland sportswear for men (discounted 10%).

The most comprehensive and the best showcase for Caribbean music in all the Virgin Islands is found at **Parrot Fish Music,** Back Street at Store Tvaer Gade (© 340/776-4514). With the selection available here, you can dance all night to the sounds of calypso, reggae, soca, and the music of steel bands.

Among stores that have vastly upgraded their stock is **Amsterdam Sauer,** 1 Main St. (© 340/774-2222), where the Sauer family still remains a leader in jewelry and gems. They stock their store with works by some of the most world-renowned designers of jewelry. The Sauers also offer one of the largest selections of unset gems in the Caribbean. Hot on their trail is the vastly improved stock at **Artistic Jewelers,** 32 Main St. (© 800/653-3113), which carries exclusive designer jewelry lines, including Judith Ripka silver and gold designs.

Mr. Tablecloth, 6 Main St. (© 340/774-4343), receives shipments of top-quality linen from the Republic of China. It has the best selection of tablecloths, doilies, place mats, aprons, and runners in Charlotte Amalie.

Since 1974, **Arts and Jewels,** Havensight Mall (© 340/776-1557), has been flourishing here at this outlet near the pier where cruise ships dock. The store boasts the biggest array of Chopard Happy Diamond watches and jewelry in the Virgin Islands. Nothing is more stunning than the black diamond jewelry by famed designer Barry Kronen. Many prices are 30% below what they are sold for in the States.

Instead of serious purchases, many short-term visitors are shopping for a souvenir. If so, **Captain's Corner,** Main Street (© 340/774-8435) across from H. Stern, is the oldest and also the biggest souvenir outlet in town. Its most popular item is the Caribbean "map watch," but there is countless other merchandise, including voodoo masks and other island crafts such as handmade items crafted from wood.

Virgin Islands Brewing Company, across from Happy Buzzard at Royal Dane Mall (© 340/714-1683), was founded on St. Croix but has invaded St. Thomas with two local beers, Blackbeard Ale and Foxy's Lager. At the company store, you're given free samples and can purchase six-packs of the home-brewed suds along with T-shirts, caps, and polo shirts.

Outside of Charlotte Amalie, another noteworthy destination is **Tillett Gardens,** a virtual oasis of arts and crafts—pottery, silk-screened fabrics, candles, watercolors, jewelry, and more. It's on the highway across from Four Winds Shopping Center (take Route 38 east from Charlotte Amalie). A major island attraction is the **Jim Tillett Art Gallery and Silk Screen Print Studio** ☆☆ (© 340/775-1929), which displays the best work of local artists, including originals in oils, watercolors, and acrylics. The prints are all one of a kind, and prices start as low as $15. The famous Tillett maps on fine canvas are priced from $30.

ST. THOMAS AFTER DARK ☆☆

St. Thomas has more nightlife than any other island in the Virgins, U.S. and British, but not as much as you might think. Charlotte Amalie is no longer the swinging town it used to be. Many of the streets are dangerous after dark, so visitors have abandoned all but a few places in town. Most of the action is in **Frenchtown,** which has some great restaurants and bars. However, just as in Charlotte Amalie, some of these little hot spots are along dark, badly lit roads.

Note: Sexual harassment can be a problem in certain bars in Charlotte Amalie, where few single women would want to be alone at night anyway. Any of the major resort hotels are generally safe.

The big hotels, such as Marriott's Frenchman's Reef Beach Resort and Blue-beard's, have the liveliest after-dark scenes. After a day of sightseeing and shop-ping in the hot West Indies sun, sometimes your best bet is just to stay at your hotel in the evening, perhaps listening to a local calypso band. You might also call the **Reichhold Center for the Arts,** University of the Virgin Islands, 2 John Brewer's Bay (© 340/693-1559), or check with the tourist office to see what's on during your visit. Its Japanese-inspired amphitheater is set into a natural val-ley, with seating for 1,196. Several different repertory companies of music, dance, and drama perform here. Performances usually begin at 8pm. Tickets range from $7.50 to $60.

In Charlotte Amalie, head to the **Bar at Paradise Point** (© 340/777-4540) at sunset. It's located 700 feet above sea level, across from the cruise-ship dock, and provides excellent photo ops and panoramic views. A tram takes you up the hill (see St. Thomas Skyride in "Exploring St. Thomas," above). Get the bar-tender to serve you his specialty, a Bushwacker. Sometimes a one-man steel band is on hand to serenade the sunset watchers. You can also order inexpensive food, such as pizza, hot dogs, and hamburgers. Happy hour, with discounted drinks, begins at 5pm.

We recommend only a few other places in Charlotte Amalie. They include **Greenhouse,** Veterans Drive (© 340/774-7998), a bar/restaurant that's directly on the waterfront and features live entertainment Friday night, ranging from reggae to disco. There's a $5 charge.

Attracting a wide age group, **Happy Buzzard,** 26A Royal Dane Mall (© 340/777-8676), once known as Fat Tuesday, is also along the waterfront in the cen-ter of Charlotte Amalie. The bartenders offer a wide variety of beer, highballs, and shooters, including the Head Butt, which contains Jagermeister, Bailey's, and amaretto. Special events are often presented here, such as live music on Tuesday night. Open daily from 10am to 11pm, later on Friday and Saturday.

The scenic **Dungeon Bar,** Bluebeard's Hill (© 340/774-1600), overlooking the yacht harbor, offers piano-bar entertainment nightly. It's a popular gathering spot for both locals and visitors. You can dance from 6pm to midnight on Thursday and from 5pm to 11pm on Saturday. Entertainment varies from month to month, but a steel band comes in some nights, while others are devoted to karaoke or jazz. It's open Tuesday to Friday from 5pm to midnight and Saturday to Monday from 5pm to 11pm. There's no cover.

During the day **Iggie's Bolongo,** in the Bolongo Beach Resort, 7150 Bolongo (© 340/775-1800), is an informal, open-air restaurant, serving hamburgers, sandwiches, and salads. After dark, it presents karaoke and offers night volley-ball. It's also one of the most active sports bars on island.

West of Charlotte Amalie, in Frenchtown, **Epernay,** rue de St. Barthélemy (© 340/774-5348), next to Bella Blu, is a stylish watering hole with an ocean view. You can order vintage wines and at least six different brands of champagne by the glass. Also available are appetizers, including sushi, main courses ($18–$25), and tempting desserts like chocolate-dipped strawberries.

Latitude 18, Vessup Lane, Vessup Point Marina (© 340/779-2495), is the hot spot on the east coast, where the ferryboats depart for St. John. The ceiling is adorned with boat sails. This casual place is both a restaurant and bar, with live entertainment almost nightly and a crowd that includes some locals.

The popular **Turtle Rock Bar,** in the Mangrove Restaurant at the Wyndham Sugar Bay Beach Club, 6500 Estate Smith Bay (© 340/777-7100), presents live music, steel bands, and karaoke. There's space to dance, but most folks just sway and listen to the steel-pan bands that play from 1pm to 2am. Sunday night is karaoke. Burgers, salads, steaks, and grilled fish are available at the Iguana Grill a few steps away. There's no cover.

Near Coki Beach on the northeast shore, posh **Baywinds,** at the Renaissance Grand Beach Resort, Smith Bay Road (© **340/775-1510**), is a romantic place for an evening. Couples dance at the side of the luxurious pool as moonlight glitters off the ocean in the background. Music ranges from jazz to pop. It's open nightly, with live music and dinner from 6pm to midnight (10pm on Thurs).

The Sugar Mill, 193 Contant (© **340/776-3004**), is the largest and newest entertainment complex to open on island. On the grounds of a restored 18th-century historic sugar mill, big plans were afoot as we went to press. This was being turned into the most all-inclusive, most comprehensive, and hippest night-club and restaurant complex in St. Thomas. Bars and dance clubs announced include the Roots Bar, the Spice Restaurant (with a Sun jazz brunch and a Sun blues evening), the rooftop Grove Garden, and a disco with the largest sound system—imported from London—in the Caribbean. Call for more details before striking out here.

3 St. Croix ✦✦✦

At 84 sq. miles, St. Croix is the largest of the U.S. Virgin Islands. At the east end (actually the easternmost point of the United States), the terrain is rocky and arid. The west end is lusher, and even includes a small "Rain Forest" of mango, mahogany, tree ferns, and dangling lianas. Between the two extremes are beautiful beaches, rolling hills, pastures, and, increasingly, miles of condos.

Columbus named the island *Santa Cruz* (Holy Cross) when he landed here on November 14, 1493. He anchored his ship off the north shore but was quickly driven away by the spears, arrows, and axes of the Carib Indians. The French laid claim to the island in 1650, and the Danes purchased it from them in 1773. Under Danish rule, slave labor and sugar-cane fields proliferated during a golden era for both planters and pirates, which came to an end in the latter half of the 19th century. Danish influence still permeates the island today.

ESSENTIALS
See "Getting There" at the beginning of the chapter for details on flights to St. Croix.

VISITOR INFORMATION   You can begin your explorations at the **visitors bureau,** 53A Company Street, in Christiansted (© **340/773-0495**), a yellow building across from the open-air market. It's open Monday to Friday 8am to 5pm.

GETTING AROUND   At Henry E. Rohlsen International Airport, official taxi rates are posted. From the airport, expect to pay about $20 to Christiansted and about $10 to Frederiksted. Cabs are unmetered, so agree on the rate before you get in. The **St. Croix Taxicab Association** (© **340/778-1088**) offers door-to-door service.

Air-conditioned **buses** run between Christiansted and Frederiksted about every 45 minutes daily between 5:30am and 9pm. They start at Tide Village, to the east of Christiansted, and go along Route 75 to the Golden Rock Shopping Center. They transfer along Route 70, with stopovers at the Sunny Isle Shopping Center, La Reine Shopping Center, St. George Village Botanical Garden, and Whim Plantation Museum, before reaching Frederiksted. The fare is $1, or 55¢ for seniors. For more information, call © **340/778-0898**.

Fun Fact **Special Holiday Events**

Christmas is celebrated in a big way on St. Croix. A 12-day celebration includes Christmas Day, the legal holiday on December 26, New Year's Eve (called "Old Year's Day"), and New Year's Day. It ends January 6, the Feast of the Three Kings, with a parade of flamboyantly attired merrymakers. For information, call the **tourism office** in Christiansted (© **340/773-0495**).

If your hotel is in Christiansted, and you don't plan to do extensive touting around the island, you can manage without a car. But if you plan to get out and explore, a car is the way to go. Many of the roads are quite good. St. Croix offers moderately priced car rentals, even on cars with automatic transmission and air-conditioning. However, because of the island's higher-than-normal accident rate, insurance costs are a bit higher than usual. If you're not covered under your existing insurance policies or by your credit card, you should consider paying for the collision damage waiver.

Avis (© **800/331-1212** or 340/778-9355; www.avis.com), **Budget** (© **800/472-3325** or 340/778-9636; www.budgetrentacar.com), and **Hertz** (© **800/654-3131** or 340/778-9744; www.hertz.com) all maintain headquarters at the airport; look for their kiosks near the baggage-claim areas. In most rural areas, the speed limit is 35 mph; certain parts of the major artery, Route 66, are 55 mph. In towns and urban areas, the speed limit is 20 mph. If you're going into the "bush country," you'll find the roads very difficult. Sometimes the government smoothes the roads out before the rainy season begins (often in Oct or Nov), but they deteriorate rapidly. *Be warned:* Driving is on the left.

FAST FACTS   The local **American Express** representative is Southerland, Queens Cross Street, Carvelle Arcade Building. (© **800/260-2603** or 340/773-9500).

If you need medical assistance, go to the **Governor Juan F. Luis Hospital & Medical Center,** 4007 Diamond Ruby, Christiansted (© **340/778-6311**).

ACCOMMODATIONS

All rooms are subject to an 8% hotel room tax, which is not included in the rates below.

If you're interested in a villa or condo rental, contact the places reviewed below or **Island Villas,** Property Management Rentals, 53B Company St., Christiansted, St. Croix, U.S.V.I. 00820 (© **800/626-4512** or 340/773-8821; fax 340/719-5553), which offers some of the best accommodations on the island. Some are private residences with pools; many are on the beach. They range from one-bedroom units to seven-bedroom villas, with prices from $1,500 to $6,500 per week year-round.

VERY EXPENSIVE

The Buccaneer 🏛🏛🏛 *Kids*   This large, luxurious, family-owned resort boasts three of the island's best beaches, and the best sports program on St. Croix. The property was once a cattle ranch and a sugar plantation; its first estate house, which dates from the mid–17th century, stands near a freshwater pool. Accommodations are either in the main building or in one of the beachside properties. The baronially arched main building has a lobby opening onto landscaped terraces, with a sea vista on two sides and Christiansted to the west. The rooms are fresh and comfortable, though some of the standard units are a bit small. All

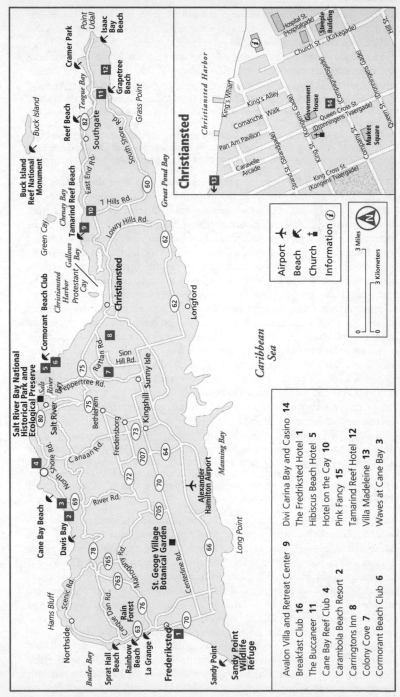

St. Croix

Point Udall

Isaac Bay Beach

Cramer Park

Teague Bay

12

Grapetree Beach

11

Grass Point

Reef Beach

82

Southgate

South Shore Rd.

Buck Island

Buck Island

Buck Island Reef National Monument

East End Rd.

Chenay Bay

Tamarind Reef Beach

10

Great Pond Bay

9

60

7 Hills Rd.

Lowry Hills Rd.

Green Cay

Gallows Bay

62

Christiansted Harbor

Protestant Cay

Christiansted

62

Longford

Cormorant Beach Club

5 **6**

8

Sion Hill Rd.

Rattan Rd.

75

7

Sunny Isle

Salt River Bay National Historical Park and Ecological Preserve

Salt River

Peppertree Rd.

Kingshill

80

Salt River

75

Bethlehem

73

Manning Bay

4

North Shore Rd.

Canaan Rd.

Fredensborg

707

64

72

70

Alexander Hamilton Airport

Cane Bay Beach

3

69

River Rd.

705

Davis Bay

2

Long Point

78

765

St. George Village Botanical Garden

763

Centerline Rd.

66

Harris Bluff

Mahogany Rd.

76

Rain Forest

63

Scenic Rd.

Creque Dan Rd.

70

1

Sprat Hall Beach

Northside

Butler Bay

Rainbow Beach

La Grange

Frederiksted

Sandy Point

Sandy Point Wildlife Refuge

Caribbean Sea

Christiansted

Hospital St. (Hospitalgade)

Church St. (Kirkegade)

Steeple Building

Hill St.

Christiansted Harbor

King's Wharf

King's Alley

Government House

Queen Cross St. (Compagniesgade)

14

Company St.

Queen St. (Dronningens Gade)

Comanche Walk

King St. (Kongens Gade)

Pan Am Pavilion

Strand St. (Strandgade)

Queen Cross St. (Dronningens Tvaergade)

Market Square

Caravelle Arcade

13

King Cross St. (Kongens Tvaergade)

Airport ✈

Beach ⚓

Church ⛪

Information ℹ

3 Miles

3 Kilometers

Avalon Villa and Retreat Center **9**

Breakfast Club **16**

The Buccaneer **11**

Cane Bay Reef Club **4**

Carambola Beach Resort **2**

Carringtons Inn **8**

Colony Cove **7**

Cormorant Beach Club **6**

Divi Carina Bay and Casino **14**

The Fredriksted Hotel **1**

Hibiscus Beach Hotel **5**

Hotel on the Cay **10**

Pink Fancy **15**

Tamarind Reef Hotel **12**

Villa Madeleine **13**

Waves at Cane Bay **3**

have wicker or mahogany furnishings and full bathrooms. The best bathrooms are in the Beachside Doubloons, and come complete with whirlpool tubs. A free Kid's Camp is available year-round.

This resort serves the best cuisine of any hotel on the island—a Caribbean and international repertoire of first-class dishes.

P.O. Box 25200, Gallows Bay (2 miles east of Christiansted on Rte. 82), Christiansted, St. Croix, U.S.V.I. 00824. ℭ 800/255-3881 in the U.S., or 340/773-2100. Fax 340/712-2104. www.thebuccaneer.com. 138 units. Winter $295–$550 double, $500–$800 suite; off season $215–$360 double, $345–$550 suite. Rates include American breakfast. AE, DISC, MC, V. **Amenities:** 4 restaurants; bar; 3 outdoor pools; 18-hole golf course; 8 tennis courts (2 lit); fitness center; spa; kayaks; snorkeling; Sunfish sailboats; children's program; limited room service; massage; babysitting; laundry service, nonsmoking rooms; rooms for those with limited mobility. *In room:* A/C, TV, dataport, fridge, beverage maker, hair dryer, iron/ironing board, safe.

Carambola Beach Resort ⍟

This hotel is set on 28 acres above Davis Bay, about a 30-minute drive from Christiansted. It's one of the largest hotels on St. Croix, and it lies adjacent to an outstanding golf course, in a lovely, lush setting on a white-sand beach whose turquoise waters boast fine snorkeling. Despite its spectacular physical location, this resort doesn't match The Buccaneer's class and style. Originally built as a Rock Resort, it has suffered hurricanes and management changes, and today is hot on the trail of the timeshare market. Guests are housed in red-roofed, two-story buildings, each of which contains six units. The accommodations are furnished in mahogany, with Danish design; each has a balcony partially concealed from outside view, overlooking either the garden or the sea. Rooms have an upscale flair, with louvered doors, tile floors, mahogany trim, and sometimes extras like screened-in porches with rocking chairs. Bathrooms are luxurious and roomy, with oversize showers (with seats) and tiled vanities. If you want the very finest room, ask for the Davis Bay Suite, which was a former Rockefeller private beach home. Its veranda alone is capable of entertaining 50 people, should that many drop in.

The resort is known for its excellent cuisine, especially the Caribbean and international dishes served at the formal Mahogany Restaurant.

Estate Davis Bay (P.O. Box 3031), Kingshill, St. Croix, U.S.V.I. 00851. ℭ 888/503-8760 in the U.S., or 340/778-3800. Fax 340/778-1682. www.carambolabeach.com. 151 units. Winter $240–$340 suite; off season $175–$240 suite. AE, DC, DISC, MC, V. **Amenities:** 3 restaurants; bar; outdoor pool; golf course; 4 tennis courts; fitness center; dive shop; fishing; snorkeling; library; car rental; massage; babysitting; laundry service; dry cleaning; nonsmoking rooms; rooms for those with limited mobility. *In room:* A/C, TV, kitchenette, fridge, beverage maker, hair dryer, iron/ironing board, safe.

Villa Madeleine ⍟⍟

This deluxe 6½-acre property has some of the island's poshest rooms. When it first opened, the Villa showed great promise of overtaking The Buccaneer. That never happened. The place remains distinguished, but service has fallen off greatly and The Buccaneer is far superior. The Villa is very independent of everything else on St. Croix—guests check in and never leave the grounds. Many of the well-heeled occupants are retirees who live here full-time. The focal point is the great house, whose Chippendale balconies and proportions emulate the Danish colonial era. Inside, a splendidly conceived decor incorporates masses of English chintz and mahogany paneling.

Each stylish one- or two-bedroom villa has its own kitchen, privacy wall, and plunge pool. The marble bathrooms have double dressing areas and oversize shower/tub combinations. The villas within the resort are handled by different management companies; therefore, standards can vary greatly, depending on which one you're assigned. Beach lovers willingly travel ⅓ mile to the nearest beaches, Duggan's Reef.

The Villa employs top chefs and is known for its steaks and its rack of lamb.

P.O. Box 26160, Teague Bay (8 miles east of Christiansted), St. Croix, U.S.V.I. 00824. © **800/496-7379** or 340/778-8782. Fax 340/773-2150. www.teaguebayproperties.com. 45 units. Winter $275 1-bedroom villa, $350 2-bedroom villa; off season $200 1-bedroom villa, $275 2-bedroom villa. MC, V. Children 11 and under discouraged. **Amenities:** Restaurant; bar; outdoor pool; golf course nearby; tennis court; car rental; nonsmoking rooms; rooms for those with limited mobility. *In room:* A/C, TV, kitchen, fridge, beverage maker.

EXPENSIVE

Cormorant Beach Club ✿   This is the poshest gay resort in the Caribbean Basin. About 70% of its clients are gay males, mostly from the eastern United States and California. The 6-acre property is designed in a boxy, modern-looking series of rectangles, with strong horizontal lines and outcroppings of exposed natural stone. It strikes a pleasant balance between seclusion and accessibility. Long Reef lies a few hundred feet offshore from the resort's sandy beachfront. Bedrooms contain a restrained decor of cane and wicker furniture, spacious bathrooms with tubs and showers, and sliding-glass doors that flood the interior with sunlight.

The social life revolves around an open-air clubhouse, with views of the sea. Off the central core is a bar (see "St. Croix After Dark," later in this chapter) and an airy dining room. The restaurant is St. Croix's leading gay eatery (see "Dining," below).

4126 La Grande Princesse (about 3 miles northwest of Christiansted, beside Rte. 75), St. Croix, U.S.V.I. 00820. © **800/548-4460** in the U.S., or 340/778-8920. Fax 340/778-9218. www.cormorantbeachclub.com. 40 units. Winter $170–$210 double, $265 suite; off season $130–$160 double, $225 suite. Extra bed $20. AE, DC, DISC, MC, V. Dive, golf, scuba, and "commitment ceremony" packages available. **Amenities:** Restaurant; bar; outdoor pool; 2 tennis courts; health club; snorkeling; Internet cafe; massage; nonsmoking rooms; rooms for those with limited mobility. *In room:* A/C, ceiling fan, TV, beverage maker, safe.

Divi Carina Bay Resort and Casino ✿   Opening onto 1,000 feet of sugar-white beach, this resort brought gambling to the U.S. Virgin Islands. That fact seems to obscure its success as a place of barefoot elegance and a top resort property. The complex was built on the ruins of the former Grapetree Shores, which was wiped away by Hurricane Hugo. Accommodations feature oceanfront guest rooms and villa suites with views of the Caribbean. Rooms are good size and well equipped with computer/fax lines, VCRs, a small kitchen, full bathrooms, and balconies. We prefer the accommodations on the ground floor as they are closer to the water's edge. The 20 villas across the street are about a 3-minute walk from the sands.

The kitchen is strong on fresh seafood and serves the island's best Sunday brunch ($25) in its Starlite Grille.

25 Estate Turner Hole, Christiansted, St. Croix, U.S.V.I. 00820. © **800/823-9352** in the U.S., or 340/773-9700. Fax 340/773-6802. www.diviresorts.com. 146 units. Winter $190–$250 double, $350–$395 suite; off season $143 double, $250–$275 suite. AE, DC, MC, V. **Amenities:** 3 restaurants; 2 bars; 2 pools; casino; lit tennis court, health club; spa services; 2 outdoor whirlpools; dive center; snorkeling; game room; salon; limited room service; massage; laundry service; nonsmoking rooms; rooms for those with limited mobility. *In room:* A/C, TV, fax, dataport, kitchen, fridge, hair dryer, safe.

Hibiscus Beach Hotel ✿   This hotel, on one of the island's best beaches, attracts a lively clientele. The accommodations are in five two-story pink buildings. Each guest room is a retreat unto itself, with a private patio or balcony and a view of the Caribbean, plus tasteful Caribbean furnishings and floral prints. Shower-only bathrooms are small but well maintained. The on-site restaurant serves standard American food—competent, but nothing exciting.

4131 La Grande Princesse (about 3 miles northwest of Christiansted, beside Rte. 75, next to the Cormorant), St. Croix, U.S.V.I. 08820. © **800/442-0121** or 340/773-4042. Fax 340/773-7668. www.1hibiscus.com. 37 units. Winter $180–$190 double, $290 efficiency; off season $130–$140 double, $220 efficiency. Honeymoon, dive, and golf packages available. AE, DISC, MC, V. **Amenities:** Restaurant; bar; outdoor pool; snorkeling; laundry service; nonsmoking rooms. *In room:* A/C, ceiling fan, TV, dataport, minibar, beverage maker, hair dryer, iron/ironing board, safe.

Tamarind Reef Hotel   There's a sandy beach at the Tamarind Reef's doorstep and good snorkeling along the reef. Each motel-style room features a garden patio or private balcony, affording guests a view of the blue Caribbean. In addition, 19 of the suites provide fully equipped kitchenettes and accommodate up to four people. All units have well maintained bathrooms with shower stalls. Guests can relax by the pool and enjoy cocktails, light lunches, and snacks from the poolside bar and grill. For those who want to explore St. Croix underwater, the hotel offers complimentary watersports equipment. Adjoining the hotel is the Green Cay Marina, where guests can charter boats for deep-sea fishing or sailing expeditions.

On-site a restaurant serves burgers, sandwiches, fries, and pasta. For more formal dining, the hotel's restaurant, Galleon, at the adjacent Green Cay Marina, serves French and northern Italian cuisine.

5001 Tamarind Reef, St. Croix, U.S.V.I. 00820. © **800/619-0014** in the U.S., or 340/773-4455. Fax 340/773-3989. www.usvi.net/hotel/tamarind. 46 units. Winter $195–$245 double; off season $145–$160 double. Includes daily continental breakfast. Extra person $30. Children under 6 stay free in parent's room. Ask about dive, golf, and honeymoon packages. AE, DC, MC, V. **Amenities:** 2 restaurants; bar; outdoor pool; 4 lit tennis courts; kayaks; snorkeling; windsurfing; coin-operated laundry; nonsmoking rooms; rooms for those with limited mobility. *In room:* A/C, TV, dataport, kitchenette (in some), minibar, fridge, beverage maker, hair dryer, iron/ironing board, safe.

MODERATE

Avalon Villa and Retreat Center ⊘⊘   This tranquil B&B perches on a 2-acre hilltop surrounded by mountains, west of Christiansted, a 15-minute ride from the airport. The place is housed in a 200-year-old building that was once a rum distillery. Upon arriving, guests pass through a shaded courtyard to a set of iron gates that lead to the inn's gardens. The beautifully appointed plantation-style house has a high-ceilinged living room and an enormous fireplace. Accommodations are generous in size, containing fine beds and small but beautifully kept shower-only bathrooms. Two self-catering cottages are also available for rental. The Danish Kitchen, one of the cottages, has a covered porch, TV, and phone. The overall atmosphere here is very homelike and warm.

Questa Verde Rd. (P.O. Box 25193), Gallows Bay, St. Croix, U.S.V.I. 00824. © **340/773-0694.** Fax 340/719-4906. 7 units. Winter $120 double, $145 cottage; off season $95 double, $115 cottage. 3-night minimum stay in cottages. Extra person $25. Room rates include continental breakfast. No credit cards. No children under 12. **Amenities:** Outdoor pool; spa services. *In room:* A/C (in most), ceiling fan, no phone.

Cane Bay Reef Club ⊘ *Finds*   This is one of the little gems of the island, offering large suites, each with a living room, a full kitchen, and a balcony overlooking the water. It's on the north shore, about a 20-minute taxi ride from Christiansted, fronting the rocky Cane Bay Beach near the Waves at Cane Bay. Sunsets are beautiful, and the snorkeling's great. The decor is breezily tropical, with cathedral ceilings, overhead fans, and Chilean tiles. Bedrooms are spacious, cool, and airy, with comfortable beds; living rooms also contain futons. The shower-only bathrooms are medium in size and excellently maintained. There's a golf course nearby, and there's a dive shop within walking distance. You can cook in your own kitchen, barbecue, or dine at the in-house restaurant, Bogey's.

P.O. Box 1407, Kingshill, St. Croix, U.S.V.I. 00851. © **800/253-8534** in the U.S., or 340/778-2966. Fax 340/778-2966. www.canebay.com. 9 units. Winter double $150–$250 daily; $970–$1,600 weekly; off season double $110–$160 daily, $700–$990 weekly. Extra person $20. AE, DC, DISC, MC, V. **Amenities:** Restaurant; bar; outdoor pool; laundry service; nonsmoking rooms; rooms for those with limited mobility. *In room:* A/C, ceiling fan, TV, dataport, kitchenette, minibar, fridge, beverage maker, hair dryer, iron/ironing board, no phone.

Carringtons Inn *Finds*   If you've read all those magazine stories about celebrities, such as screen legend Maureen O'Hara, who own villas on St. Croix, and you wonder what life is like in them, here's your chance to experience one first hand. This grandly elegant B&B was once the home of a wealthy family who spent winters here. Much evidence of their former lifestyle remains. This is an intimate B&B with personalized attention and five spacious and beautifully furnished guest rooms with first-class private bathrooms. Some rooms have a king-size canopy bed, and wicker furnishings are in tasteful abundance. When guests gather around the pool, a house party atmosphere prevails. Even your breakfast of such delights as rum-flavored French toast can be served poolside. The staff delivers thoughtful touches such as a full concierge service, bathrobes, and even freshly baked cookies in the evening.

4001 Estate Hermon Hill (1 mile west of Christiansted), St. Croix U.S.V.I. 00820. © 877/658-0508 or 340/713-0508. Fax 340/719-0841. www.carringtonsinn.com. 5 units. Winter $120–$150 double; off season $100–$120 double. Rates include breakfast. AE, MC, V. **Amenities:** Breakfast room; outdoor pool; tennis courts (nearby); health club (nearby); rooms for those with limited mobility. *In room:* A/C, ceiling fans, kitchenette (in some), hair dryer, iron/ironing board.

Waves at Cane Bay   This intimate and tasteful condo property is about 8 miles from the airport, midway between the island's two biggest towns. It's set on a well-landscaped plot of oceanfront property on Cane Bay, the heart of the best scuba and snorkeling at Cane Bay Beach, though the beach here is rocky and tends to disappear at high tide. There's a PADI dive shop on the property. Accommodations are within a pair or two-story cement-sided buildings, each directly on the beach. Each accommodation is high-ceilinged and relatively large, with a well-equipped kitchenette, a selection of reading material, tiled floors, a shower-only bathroom, and a very private screened-in veranda that's partially or fully concealed from the views of any of the other verandas. Attached to one of the buildings is an open-sided pavilion that functions as a bar and restaurant, open every Monday to Saturday for dinner. A short walk from this condo complex, and owned by the same investors, is a two-bedroom free-standing cottage that's available for rental whenever the owners aren't on location.

Cane Bay (P.O. Box 1749), Kingshill, St. Croix, U.S.V.I. 00851. © 800/545-0603 in the U.S., or 340/778-1805. Fax 340/778-4945. www.canebaystcroix.com. 12 units. Winter $140–$155 double, $195 2-room cottage, extra person $20; off season $75–$105 double, $140 2-room cottage, extra person $10. AE, DC, DISC, MC, V. From the airport, go left on Rte. 64; after 1 mile, turn right on Rte. 70; after another mile, go left at the junction with Rte. 75; after 2 miles, turn left at the junction with Rte. 80; follow for 5 miles. **Amenities:** Restaurant; bar; outdoor pool; dive shop; snorkeling; nonsmoking rooms. *In room:* A/C (in some), TV, dataport, kitchenette, beverage maker, safe.

INEXPENSIVE

Breakfast Club *Value*   Here you'll get the best value of any bed-and-breakfast on St. Croix. This comfortable place combines a 1950s compound of efficiency apartments with a traditional-looking stone house that was rebuilt from a ruin in the 1930s. Each of the units has a kitchenette, a cypress-sheathed ceiling, white walls, a beige-tile floor, and simple, summery furniture. Shower-only bathrooms are small and adequately maintained. Toby Chapin, the Ohio-born owner, cooks one of the most generous and appealing breakfasts on the island; try the banana pancakes or the chile rellenos. A three-piece band plays twice a month.

18 Queen Cross St., Christiansted, St. Croix, U.S.V.I. 00820. © 340/773-7383. www.nav.to/thebreakfastclub. 6 units. Year-round $75 double. Rates include breakfast. AE, MC, V. *In room:* A/C (in some), kitchen, fridge, beverage maker, iron/ironing board, no phone.

The Frederiksted Hotel　This contemporary four-story inn is a good choice for the heart of historic Frederiksted. It's located in the center of town, about a 10-minute ride from the airport. Much of the activity takes place in the outdoor tiled courtyard, where guests enjoy drinks. The cheery rooms are like those of a motel on the U.S. mainland, perhaps showing a bit of wear, and with good ventilation but bad lighting. They're done in a tropical motif of pastels and are equipped with small fridges. The best (and most expensive) rooms are those with ocean views; they're subject to street noise but have the best light. Accommodations come with a small, tiled shower-only bathroom. The nearest beach is Fort Frederik, a 3-minute walk away.

442 Strand St., Frederiksted, St. Croix, U.S.V.I. 00840. © **800/595-9519** in the U.S., or 340/772-0500. Fax 340/772-0500. www.frederikstedhotel.com. 40 units. Winter $100–$110 double; off season $90–$100 double. Extra person $10. AE, DISC, MC, V. **Amenities:** Restaurant; bar; outdoor pool; laundry service; rooms for those with limited mobility. *In room:* A/C, TV, fridge, beverage maker, iron/ironing board.

Pink Fancy ⋒ *Finds*　This small, unique hotel is a block from the Annapolis Sailing School. You get more atmosphere here than anywhere else in town. The oldest part of the four-building complex is a historic 1780 Danish town house. In the 1950s, the hotel became a mecca for writers and artists, including Noël Coward. The owners have made major renovations, installing more antiques and fine furnishings. Guest rooms have a bright, tropical feel, with ceiling fans, floral prints, and rattan furnishings. The deluxe rooms are furnished with canopy or iron beds, as well as antiques and artwork. The medium-size bathrooms have combination shower/tubs. A 3-minute launch ride takes guests to the beach on the Cay, a sandy islet in Christiansted's harbor.

27 Prince St., Christiansted, St. Croix, U.S.V.I. 00820. © **800/524-2045** in the U.S., or 340/773-8460. Fax 340/773-6448. www.pinkfancy.com. 12 units. Winter $95–$150 double; off season $85–$150 double. Extra person $20. Ask about packages and weekly rates. AE, DC, MC, V. **Amenities:** Outdoor pool; nonsmoking rooms. *In room:* A/C, ceiling fan, TV, dataport, kitchenette, fridge, beverage maker, iron/ironing board.

DINING
IN CHRISTIANSTED

Bacchus ⋒ STEAKHOUSE/CONTINENTAL　In a restaurant dedicated to the god of wine, the wine *carte* receives as much attention as the regular menu. Their cellar has been praised by both *Spectator* and *Food and Wine*. The decor, the fine service, and the presentation of the dishes make for a fine evening out. The kitchen uses first-class ingredients, many imported, to craft a number of dishes that combine flavor and finesse. You're sure to delight in the lobster Bacchus or the rib-eye steak Florentine, a local favorite. One tantalizing dish is the apple-smoked bacon wrapped around a filet mignon. To finish, it doesn't get any better than the rum-infused sourdough bread pudding. Most dishes, except lobster, are at the lower end of the price scale.

Queen Cross St., off King St. © 340/692-9922. Reservations recommended. Main courses $16–$28. AE, DC, MC, V. Tues–Sun 6–10pm.

Comanche Club CARIBBEAN/CONTINENTAL　Relaxed yet elegant, Comanche is one of the island's most popular restaurants. It's not the best, but the specialties are eclectic—everything from fish and conch chowder to shark cakes. Each night, a different special and a different local dish are featured. Other choices include salads, curries, fish sautéed with lemon butter and capers, and typical West Indian dishes such as conch Creole with fungi. There are also standard international dishes like a New York strip.

1 Strand St. ⓒ **340/773-0210.** Reservations recommended. Main courses $13–$35; lunch from $7–$12. AE, MC, V. Mon–Sat 11:30am–2:30pm and 5:30–9:30pm. Open on Sun for special holidays.

Kendricks 🏵🏵 FRENCH/CONTINENTAL   Kendricks, the island's toniest restaurant, lies in the historic Quin House complex at King Cross and Company streets. Some of its recipes have been featured in *Bon Appétit,* and deservedly so. You'll immediately warm to such specialties as pan-seared Thai shrimp with cucumber relish and coconut-infused rice, and grilled filet mignon with a port-wine demi-glace and red-onion confit. The signature appetizer is king-crab cakes with lemon-pepper aioli. Another great choice is the pecan-crusted roast pork loin with ginger mayonnaise.

2132 Company St. ⓒ **340/773-9199.** Main courses $23–$33. AE, MC, V. Mon–Sat 6–10pm.

Luncheria Mexican Food *Value* MEXICAN/CUBAN/PUERTO RICAN   This Mexican restaurant is a bargain. You get the usual tacos, tostadas, burritos, nachos, and enchiladas, as well as chicken fajitas, enchiladas verde, and *arroz con pollo* (spiced chicken with brown rice). Daily specials feature both low-calorie and vegetarian choices (the chef's refried beans are lard-free), and whole-wheat tortillas are offered. The complimentary salsa bar has mild to hot sauces, plus jalapeños. Some Cuban and Puerto Rican dishes appear on the menu, these include a zesty chicken curry, black-bean soup, and roast pork. The bartender makes the island's best margaritas.

In the historic Apothecary Hall Courtyard, 2111 Company St. ⓒ **340/773-4247.** Main courses $3–$9. No credit cards. Mon–Sat 11am–9pm.

Nolan's Tavern *Value* INTERNATIONAL/WEST INDIAN   This warm, cozy tavern has no pretensions. It's across from the capital's most prominent elementary school, the Pearl B. Larsen School. Your host is Nolan Joseph, a Trinidad-born chef who makes a special point of welcoming guests and offering "tasty food and good service." No one will mind if you stop in just for a drink. Mr. Joseph, referred to by some diners as "King Conch," prepares that mollusk in at least half a dozen ways, including versions with curry, Creole sauce, and garlic-pineapple sauce. He reportedly experimented for 3 months to perfect a means of tenderizing the conch without artificial chemicals. His ribs are also excellent.

5A Estate St. Peter (2 miles east of Christiansted's harbor), Christiansted East. ⓒ **340/773-6660.** Reservations recommended only for groups of 6 or more. Burgers $7–$10; main courses $13–$18. AE, MC, V. Kitchen Mon–Sun 3:30–8:30pm. Bar from 3pm.

Paradise Café *Value* DELI/AMERICAN   This neighborhood favorite draws locals seeking good food and great value. Its brick walls and beamed ceiling were originally part of an 18th-century great house. New York–style deli fare is served during the day. Enjoy the savory homemade soups or freshly made salads, to which you can add grilled chicken or fish. At breakfast, you can select from an assortment of omelets, or try the steak and eggs. Dinners are more elaborate. The 12-ounce New York strip steak and the freshly made pasta specialties are good choices. Appetizers include mango chicken quesadillas and crab cakes.

53B Company St. (at Queen Cross St., across from Government House). ⓒ **340/773-2985.** Breakfast $4–$9.50; lunch $5–$10; dinner $14–$20. No credit cards. Mon–Sat 7:30am–10pm.

Savant 🏵 *Finds* CARIBBEAN/THAI/MEXICAN   The spicy fusion cuisine here provides a marvelous burst of palate-awakening flavors. The bistro atmosphere is stylish, yet fun and laid-back. Black-and-white photos and other original artwork line the walls of the restaurant. Fresh fish is deftly handled to enhance its natural goodness. We gravitate to the tantalizing Thai curries, most of which are mildly spiced. You can ask the chef "to go nuclear" if you prefer hotter food. The red-coconut-curry sauce is one of the best we've ever had on the island. If you're craving an enchilada, try the one stuffed with seafood. The maple-teriyaki pork tenderloin, one of the chef's specialties, is terrific. There are only 10 candlelit tables, so call for a reservation as far in advance as you can.

4C Hospital St. ℂ 340/713-8666. Reservations required. Main courses $14–$25. AE, MC, V. Mon–Sat 6–10pm.

Tivoli Gardens INTERNATIONAL   The large second-floor porch festooned with lights affords the same view of Christiansted Harbor that a sea captain might have. This well-known local gathering spot has white beams, trellises, and hanging plants that evoke its namesake, the pleasure gardens of Copenhagen. Ingredients are fresh and deftly handled. Begin with the house special soup, Tivolienne, made with onions and cabbage in a hearty beef broth, with added flavor from Swiss cheese. There's also a West Indian pea soup made with ham and island spices. Main courses come with garlic bread and include succulent pastas, such as linguine with Italian sausage or penne with chicken and broccoli. Other choices are the Thai seafood curry and the fresh grilled fish of the day—perhaps wahoo, tuna, or mahimahi. If you still have room left, opt for the peanut butter pie with chocolate frosting or the local favorite, guava cream pie. The kitchen is also known for its homemade ice creams, especially the lemon cheesecake ice cream.

39 Strand St. (upstairs in the Pan Am Pavilion). ℂ 340/773-6782. Reservations recommended after 7pm. Main courses $12–$24. AE, MC, V. Mon–Fri 11am–2:30pm; daily 5:30–9:30pm.

IN FREDERIKSTED

Blue Moon INTERNATIONAL/CAJUN   The best little bistro in Frederiksted becomes a hot, hip spot during Sunday brunch and on Friday nights, when it offers entertainment. The 200-year-old stone house on the waterfront is a favorite of visiting jazz musicians, and tourists have discovered (but not ruined) it. It's decorated with funky, homemade art from the U.S., including a trash can–lid restaurant sign. The atmosphere is casual and cafelike. Begin with the "lunar pie," with feta, cream cheese, onions, mushrooms, and celery in phyllo pastry, or the artichoke-and-spinach dip. Main courses include the catch of the day and, on occasion, Maine lobster. The clams served in garlic sauce are also from Maine. Vegetarians opt for the spinach fettuccine. There's also the usual array of steak and chicken dishes. Save room for the yummy apple spice pie.

17 Strand St. ℂ 340/772-2222. Reservations recommended. Main courses $18–$25. AE, DISC, MC, V. Tues–Fri 11:30am–2pm and 6–9pm (Fri until 2am); Sat 6–9pm; Sun 11am–2pm. Closed Aug.

Le St. Tropez FRENCH/MEDITERRANEAN   This is the most popular bistro in Frederiksted. It's small, so call ahead for a table. If you're visiting for the day, make this bright little cafe your lunch stop, and enjoy crepes, quiches, soups, or salads in the sunlit courtyard. At night, the atmosphere glows with candlelight and becomes more festive. Try the pâté de champagne and escargots Provençal, or one of the freshly made soups. Main dishes are likely to include rack of lamb with mushrooms, the fish of the day, or a magret of duck. Ingredients are always fresh and well-prepared.

Limetree Court, 227 King St. ℂ 340/772-3000. Reservations recommended. Main courses $16–$29. AE, MC, V. Mon–Fri 11:30am–2:30pm; Mon–Sat 6–10pm.

Villa Morales PUERTO RICAN   This inland spot is one of the best Puerto Rican restaurants on St. Croix. You can choose between indoor and outdoor seating areas. No one will mind if you come here just to drink; the cozy bar is lined with the memorabilia collected by several generations of the family who maintain the place. Look for a broad cross-section of Hispanic dishes, including many that Puerto Ricans remember from their childhood. These include fried snapper with white rice and beans, stewed conch, roasted or stewed goat, and stewed beef. Meal platters are garnished with beans and rice. Most of the dishes are inexpensive. On special occasions, the owners transform the place into a dance hall, bringing in live salsa and merengue bands.

Plot 82C, Estate Whim (off Rte. 70 about 2 miles from Frederiksted). ℂ 340/772-0556. Reservations recommended. Main courses $6–$14 lunch, $8–$15 dinner. MC, V. Thurs–Sat 10am–10pm.

AROUND THE ISLAND

Cormorant Beach Club Restaurant 𝒦 INTERNATIONAL   This is the premier gay restaurant on St. Croix. Both the restaurant and its bar are a mecca for gay and gay-friendly people who appreciate its relaxed atmosphere, well-prepared food, and gracefully arched premises overlooking the sea. The menu changes nightly. Lunch specialties may include meal-size salads, club sandwiches, burgers, and fresh fish. To begin, sample the chef's classic Caesar salad. In the evening expect such dishes as roast rack of lamb served with a pecan-and-Parmesan-herb crust or grilled fresh local mahimahi, its flavor enhanced with fresh cilantro and lime-butter sauce. Desserts are sumptuous, especially the Cruzan rum cake with bananas, chocolate, or coconut and the chocolate rum torte with layers of mousse and rum cake sealed in chocolate.

In the Cormorant Beach Club, 4126 La Grande Princesse. ℂ 340/778-8920. Reservations recommended. Main courses $7–$12 lunch, $18–$26 dinner. AE, DC, DISC, MC, V. Daily 7:30am–9pm.

Duggan's Reef CONTINENTAL/CARIBBEAN   This is one of the most popular restaurants on St. Croix. It's only 10 feet from the still waters of Reef Beach and makes an ideal perch for watching windsurfers and Hobie Cats. At lunch, an array of salads, crepes, and sandwiches is offered. The more elaborate night menu features the popular house specialties: Duggan's Caribbean lobster pasta and Irish whiskey lobster. Begin with fried calamari or conch chowder. Main dishes include New York strip steak, fish, and pastas. The local catch of the day can be baked, grilled, blackened Cajun style, or served island style (with tomato, pepper, and onion sauce).

East End Rd., Teague Bay. ℂ 340/773-9800. Reservations required for dinner in winter. Main courses $17–$29; pastas $16–$23. MC, V. Mon–Fri noon–3pm and 6–9:30pm; Sun brunch 11am–3pm year-round. Closed for lunch in summer. Bar daily noon–11:30pm.

The Galleon FRENCH/NORTHERN ITALIAN   This restaurant, which overlooks the ocean, is a local favorite, and deservedly so. It serves northern Italian and French cuisine, including *osso buco,* just as good as that dished up in Milan. Freshly baked bread, two fresh vegetables, and rice or potatoes accompany main dishes. The menu always includes at least one local fish, such as wahoo, tuna, swordfish, mahimahi, or even fresh Caribbean lobster. You can order a perfectly done rack of lamb, which will be carved right at your table. There's an extensive wine list, including many sold by the glass. Music from a baby grand accompanies your dinner on weekends.

East End Rd., Green Cay Marina, 5000 Estate Southgate. ℂ 340/773-9949. Reservations recommended. Main courses $17–$40; lunch main courses $9–$10. MC, V. Daily 11am–5pm and 6–10pm. Go east on Rte. 82 from Christiansted for 5 min.; after going 1 mile past The Buccaneer, turn left into Green Cay Marina.

Sunset Grill 𝒦 *Finds* CARIBBEAN/AMERICAN   This informal spot is on the west coast, near Sprat Hall Plantation. It's the best place on the island to combine lunch and a swim. The restaurant has been in business since 1948, feeding both locals and visitors. Try such local dishes as seafood chowder and the fried fish of the day. These dishes have authentic island flavor, perhaps more so than any other place on St. Croix. You can also get salads and burgers. The bread is baked fresh daily. The owners allow free use of the showers and changing rooms.

Rte. 63 (1 mile north of Frederiksted). (C) 340/772-5855. Lunch $7–$9; main courses $18–$27. Tues–Sun 11:30am–2:30pm and 5:30–9pm; Sun brunch 11:30am–3pm.

HITTING THE BEACH

The most celebrated beach is offshore **Buck Island,** part of the U.S. National Park Service network. Buck Island is actually a volcanic islet surrounded by some of the most stunning underwater coral gardens in the Caribbean. The white-sand beaches on the southwest and west coasts are beautiful, but the snorkeling is even better. The islet's interior is filled with such plants as cactus, wild frangipani, and pigeonwood. There are picnic areas for those who want to make a day of it. Boat departures are from Kings Wharf in Christiansted; the ride takes half an hour. For more information, see the section "Buck Island," later in this chapter.

Your best choice for a beach in Christiansted is the one at the **Hotel on the Cay.** This white-sand strip is on a palm-shaded island. To get here, take the ferry from the fort at Christiansted; it runs daily from 7am to midnight. The 4-minute trip costs $3, free for guests of the Hotel on the Cay. Five miles west of Christiansted is the **Cormorant Beach Club,** where some 1,200 feet of white sand shaded by palm trees attracts a gay crowd. Since a reef lies just off the shore, snorkeling conditions are ideal.

We highly recommend **Davis Bay** and **Cane Bay,** with swaying palms, white sand, and good swimming. Because they're on the north shore, these beaches are often windy, and their waters are not always tranquil. The snorkeling at Cane Bay is truly spectacular; you'll see elkhorn and brain corals, all some 750 feet off the "Cane Bay Wall." Cane Bay adjoins Route 80 on the north shore. Davis Beach doesn't have a reef; it's more popular among bodysurfers than snorkelers. There are no changing facilities. It's near Carambola Beach Resort.

On Route 63, a short ride north of Frederiksted, lies **Rainbow Beach,** which has white sand and ideal snorkeling conditions. Nearby, also on Route 63, about 5 minutes north of Frederiksted, is another good beach, called **La Grange.** Lounge chairs can be rented here, and there's a bar nearby.

Sandy Point, directly south of Frederiksted, is the largest beach in all the U.S. Virgin Islands. Its waters are shallow and calm, perfect for swimming. Try to concentrate on the sands and not the unattractive zigzagging fences that line the beach. Continue west from the western terminus of the Melvin Evans Highway (Rte. 66).

There's an array of beaches at the east end of the island; they're somewhat difficult to get to, but much less crowded. The best choice here is **Isaac Bay Beach,** ideal for snorkeling, swimming, or sunbathing. Windsurfers like **Reef Beach,** which opens onto Teague Bay along Route 82, East End Road, a half-hour ride from Christiansted. You can get food at Duggan's Reef (see recommendation, above). **Cramer Park** is a special public park operated by the Department of Agriculture. It's lined with sea-grape trees and has a picnic area, a restaurant, and a bar. **Grapetree Beach** is off Route 60 (the South Shore Rd.). Watersports are popular here.

SPORTS & OTHER OUTDOOR PURSUITS

Some of the best snorkeling, diving, and hiking are found on Buck Island. See the section "Buck Island," below.

FISHING   The fishing grounds at **Lang Bank** are about 10 miles from St. Croix. Here you'll find kingfish, dolphin fish, and wahoo. Using light-tackle boats to glide along the reef, you'll probably turn up jack or bonefish. At **Clover Crest,** in Frederiksted, local anglers fish right from the rocks.

Serious sportfishers can board the *Fantasy,* a 38-foot Bertram special. It's anchored at King's Alley Hotel at 59 Kings Wharf in Christiansted. Reservations can be made by calling © 340/773-2628 during the day, or 340/773-0917 at night. The cost for up to six passengers is $450 for 4 hours, $600 for 6 hours, and $800 for 8 hours with bait and tackle included.

GOLF   St. Croix has the best golf in the U.S. Virgins. Guests staying on St. John and St. Thomas often fly over for a round on one of the island's three courses.

Carambola Golf Course, on the northeast side of St. Croix (© 340/778-5638), was created by Robert Trent Jones Sr., who called it "the loveliest course I ever designed." It's been likened to a botanical garden. The par-3 holes here are known to golfing authorities as the best in the Tropics. The greens fee of $132 in winter, or $85 in summer, allows you to play as many holes as you like. Carts are included.

The Buccaneer, Gallows Bay (© 340/773-2100, ext. 738), 3 miles east of Christiansted, has a challenging 5,685-yard, 18-hole course with panoramic vistas. Nonguests of this deluxe resort pay $70 in winter or $45 off season, plus $16 for use of a cart.

The **Reef,** on the east end of the island at Teague Bay (© 340/773-8844), is a 3,100-yard, 9-hole course, charging greens fees of $22 including carts. The longest hole here is a 465-yard par 5.

HIKING   Scrub-covered hills make up much of St. Croix's landscape. The island's western district, however, includes a dense, 15-acre forest known as the **"Rain Forest"** (though it's not a real one). The network of footpaths here offer some of the best nature walks in the Caribbean. For more details on hiking in this area, see the section, "The 'Rain Forest,'" below. **Buck Island** (see the section "Buck Island," below), just off St. Croix, also offers some wonderful nature trails.

The **St. Croix Environmental Association,** Arawak Building, Suite 3, Gallows Bay (© 340/773-1989; www.stxenvironmental.org), has regularly scheduled hikes during the weekend from December to March and by request Monday to Friday. A minimum of four people are required, costing $30 per person, $15 for children under 12.

HORSEBACK RIDING   **Paul and Jill's Equestrian Stables,** 2 Sprat Hall Estate, Route 58 (© 340/772-2880), the largest equestrian stable in the Virgin Islands, is known throughout the Caribbean for its horses. It's set on the sprawling grounds of the island's oldest plantation great house. The operators lead scenic trail rides through the forests, along the beach, and past ruins of abandoned 18th-century plantations and sugar mills, to the tops of the hills of St. Croix's western end. Beginners and experienced riders alike are welcome. A 2-hour trail ride costs $50. Tours usually depart daily in winter at 10:30am and 3pm, and in the off season at 4pm, with slight variations according to demand. Reserve at least a day in advance.

KAYAKING The beauty of St. Croix is best seen on a kayak tour offered by **Caribbean Adventure Tours** (© 340/778-1522). You use stable, sit-on-top ocean kayaks, which are a blast. These enable you to traverse the tranquil waters of Salt River of Columbus landfall fame and enjoy the park's ecology and wildlife. You also go into secluded estuaries and mangrove groves. Some of the landscape was used as ancient Indian burial grounds. Highlights of are snorkeling on a pristine beach and paddling to where Christopher Columbus and his crew came ashore some 500 years ago. The tour, lasting 3 hours, costs $45 per person and includes water and a light snack.

SAFARI TOURS The best are offered by **St. Croix Safari Tours** (© 340/773-6700) in a 25-passenger open-air bus tour run by a hip tour guide who knows all about the botany, cuisine, and history of the island. Tours crisscross the island with stops at plantation houses, historic Frederiksted, the Salt River landfall of Columbus, and a drive through the rainforest, with a stop for lunch. There are lots of photo ops. The cost of the tour is $38 per person, including admission fees to the botanical garden, rum factory, and museum.

SNORKELING & SCUBA DIVING ⟨⟨⟨⟨ Sponge life, black coral (the finest in the West Indies), and steep drop-offs near the shoreline make St. Croix a snorkeling and diving paradise. The island is home to the largest living reef in the Caribbean, including the fabled north-shore wall that begins in 25 feet to 30 feet of water and drops to 13,200 feet, sometimes straight down. See "Hitting the Beach," above, for information on good snorkeling beaches. The **St. Croix Water Sports Center** (see "Windsurfing," below) rents snorkeling equipment for $20 per day if your hotel doesn't supply it.

Buck Island ⟨⟨⟨⟨ is a major scuba-diving site, with a visibility of some 100 feet. It also has an underwater snorkeling trail. All the outfitters offer scuba and snorkeling tours to Buck Island. See the section "Buck Island," below.

Other favorite dive sites include the historic **Salt River Canyon** (northwest of Christiansted at Salt River Bay), which is for advanced divers. Submerged canyon walls are covered with purple tube sponges, deep-water gorgonians, and black coral saplings. You'll see schools of yellowtail snapper, turtles, and spotted eagle rays. We also like the gorgeous coral gardens of **Scotch Banks** (north of Christiansted), and **Eagle Ray** (also north of Christiansted), the latter so named because of the rays that cruise along the wall there. **Cane Bay** ⟨⟨⟨⟨ is known for its coral canyons.

Davis Bay is the site of the 12,000-foot-deep Puerto Rico Trench. **Northstar Reef,** at the east end of Davis Bay, is a spectacular wall dive, recommended for intermediate or experienced divers only. The wall here is covered with stunning brain corals and staghorn thickets. At some 50 feet down, a sandy shelf leads to a cave where giant green moray eels hang out.

The ultimate night dive is at the **Frederiksted Pier.** The old pier was damaged by Hurricane Hugo and torn down to make way for a new one. The heavily encrusted rubble from the old pier remains beneath the new one, carpeted with rainbow-hued sponges and both hard and soft coral, preserving a fantastic night dive where you're virtually guaranteed to see seahorses and moray eels.

At **Butler Bay,** to the north of the pier on the west shore, three ships were wrecked: the *Suffolk Maid,* the *Northwind,* and the *Rosaomaira,* the latter sitting in 100 feet of water. These wrecks form the major part of an artificial reef system that also contains abandoned trucks and cars. This site is recommended for intermediate or experienced divers.

Anchor Dive, Salt River National Park (© **800/523-DIVE** in the U.S., or 340/778-1522), is located within the most popular dive destination in St. Croix. It operates three boats, including the 27-foot dive boat *Queen Bee*. The staff offers complete instruction, from resort courses through full certification, as well as night dives. A resort course is $90, with a two-tank dive going for $80. Dive packages begin at $215 for six dives.

Another recommended outfitter is the **Cane Bay Dive Shop** (© **340/773-9913**).

TENNIS   Some authorities rate the tennis at **The Buccaneer** 🟊🟊, Gallows Bay (© **340/773-2100,** ext. 736), as the best in the Caribbean. This resort offers a choice of eight courts, two lit for night play, all open to the public. Nonguests pay $8 daytime, $10 nighttime per person per hour; you must call to reserve a court. A tennis pro is available for lessons, and there's also a pro shop.

WINDSURFING   Head for the **St. Croix Water Sports Center** (© **340/773-7060**), on a small offshore island in Christiansted Harbor and part of the Hotel on the Cay. It's open daily from 11am to 3pm. Windsurfing rentals are $25 per hour. Lessons are available. The center also offers parasailing for $65 per person and rents snorkeling equipment for $20 per day and Sea Doos that seat two for $45 per half-hour.

EXPLORING ST. CROIX

Taxi tours are the ideal way to explore the island. The cost is around $70 for 2 hours or $75 for 3 hours for one or two passengers. All prices should be negotiated in advance. For more information, call the **St. Croix Taxi Association** at © **340/778-1088.**

CHRISTIANSTED 🟊🟊

One of the most picturesque towns in the Caribbean, **Christiansted** is an old, handsomely restored (or at least in the process of being restored) Danish port. On the northeastern shore of the island, on a coral-bound bay, the town is filled with Danish buildings erected by prosperous merchants in the booming 18th century. These red-roofed structures are often washed in pink, ocher, or yellow. Arcades over the sidewalks provide shade for shoppers. The whole area around the harbor front has been designated a historic site, including **Government House** (© **340/773-1404**), which is looked after by the U.S. National Park Service.

Fort Christiansvaern   This fortress overlooking the harbor is the best-preserved colonial fortification in the Virgin Islands. It's maintained as a historic monument by the U.S. National Park Service. Its original four-pronged, star-shaped design was in accordance with the most advanced military planning of its era. The fort is now the site of a military museum, which has exhibits on local Danish military history on the island from the late 1800s to the present.

On the waterfront. © 340/773-1460. Admission $3 (also includes admission to the Steeple Building). Daily 8am–4:30pm.

Steeple Building   This building's full name is the Church of Lord God of Sabaoth. It was built in 1753 as St. Croix's first Lutheran church, and it was deconsecrated in 1831; the building subsequently served as a bakery, a hospital, and a school. Today, it houses exhibits relating to island history and culture.

On the waterfront off Hospital St. © 340/773-1460. Admission $3 (also includes admission to Fort Christiansvaern). Daily 8:30am–4:30pm.

FREDERIKSTED ☆

This former Danish settlement at the western end of the island, about 17 miles from Christiansted, is a sleepy port town that comes to life only when a cruise ship docks at its shoreline. Frederiksted was destroyed by a fire in 1879. Its citizens subsequently rebuilt it with wood frames and clapboards on top of the old Danish stone and yellow-brick foundations.

Most visitors begin their tour at russet-colored **Fort Frederik,** at the northern end of Frederiksted next to the cruise-ship pier (© **340/772-2021**). This fort, completed in 1760, is said to have been the first to salute the flag of the new United States. When a U.S. brigantine anchored at port in Frederiksted hoisted a homemade Old Glory, the fort returned the salute with cannon fire, violating the rules of neutrality. It was also here on July 3, 1848, that Governor-General Peter von Scholten emancipated the slaves in the Danish West Indies in response to a slave uprising led by a young man named Moses "Buddhoe" Gottlieb. A bust of Buddhoe now stands here. The fort has been restored to its 1840 appearance and is today a national historic landmark. You can explore the courtyard and stables. A **local history museum** has been installed in what was once the Garrison Room. Admission is free. It's open Monday to Friday from 8:30am to 4pm.

The **Customs House,** just east of the fort, is an 18th-century building with a 19th-century two-story gallery. On the ground floor is the **visitor bureau** (© **340/772-0357**), where you can pick up a free map of the town.

BUCK ISLAND ☆☆☆

The crystal-clear water and white coral sand of **Buck Island,** a satellite of St. Croix, are legendary. Some call this island the single most important attraction of the Caribbean. Only ⅓ mile wide and 1 mile long, Buck Island lies 1½ miles off the northeastern coast of St. Croix. A barrier reef here shelters many reef fish, including queen angelfish and smooth trunkfish. In years past, Morgan, Blackbeard, and Captain Kidd frequented the island.

Buck Island's greatest attraction is its **underwater snorkeling trails,** which ring part of the island and provide some of the most beautiful underwater views in the Caribbean. Plan on spending at least two-thirds of a day at this famous ecological site maintained by the U.S. National Park Service. There are also many **labyrinths and grottoes for scuba divers.** The sandy **beach** has picnic tables and barbecue pits, as well as restrooms and a small changing room.

You can follow **hiking trails** through the tropical vegetation that covers the island. Circumnavigating the island on foot takes about 2 hours. Buck Island's trails meander from several points along its coastline to its sunny summit, affording views over nearby St. Croix. *A couple of warnings:* Wear lots of sunscreen. Even more important, don't touch every plant you see. The island's

---

Moments Exploring Underwater Without Getting Wet

St. Croix Water Sports Center (© 340/773-7060), features the *Oceanique,* a semisubmersible vessel that acts as part submarine and part cruiser. It takes visitors on 1-hour excursions through Christiansted harbor and along Protestant Cay. The inch-thick windows lining the vessel's underwater observation room provide views of St. Croix's colorful marine life, in a cool and dry environment. This trip is especially popular with children and nonswimmers. Day and night excursions are available for $45 for adults and $25 for children. Call for reservations.

The St. Croix Heritage Trail

A trail that leads into the past, **St. Croix Heritage Trail,** launched at the millennium, helps visitors relive the Danish colonial past of the island. All you need are a brochure and map, available at the tourist office in Christiansted (p. 729). This 72-mile itinerary includes a combination of asphalt-covered roadway, suitable for driving, and narrow woodland trails which must be navigated on foot. Many aficionados opt to drive along the route whenever practical, descending onto the footpaths wherever indicated, then returning to their cars for the continuation of the tour. En route, you'll be exposed to one of the Caribbean's densest concentrations of historical and cultural sites.

The route connects the two major towns of Christiansted and Frederiksted, going past the sites of former sugar plantations.

The trail traverses the entire 28-mile length of St. Croix, passing cattle farms, suburban communities, even industrial complexes and resorts. It's not all manicured and pretty, but much is scenic and worth the drive. Allow at least a day for this trail, with stops along the way.

Nearly everyone gets out of the car at **Point Udall,** the easternmost point under the U.S. flag in the Caribbean. You'll pass an eclectic mix of churches and even a prison. The route consists mainly of existing roadways; the brochure will identify everything you're seeing.

The highlight of the trail is the **Estate Mount Washington** (p. 747), a strikingly well-preserved sugar plantation. Another highlight is **Estate Whim Plantation** (p. 747), one of the best of the restored great houses with a museum and gift shop. Another stop is along **Salt River Bay,** which cuts into the northern shoreline. This is the site of Columbus's landfall in 1493.

Of course, you'll want to stop and get to know the locals. We recommend a refreshment break at **Smithens Market.** Lying off Queen Mary Highway, vendors here offer freshly squeezed sugar-cane juice and sell locally grown fruits and homemade chutneys.

western edge has groves of poisonous manchineel trees, whose leaves, bark, and fruit cause extreme irritation to human skin that comes into contact with them.

Small boats run between St. Croix and Buck Island. Nearly all charters provide snorkeling equipment and allow for 1½ hours of snorkeling and swimming. **Mile Mark Watersports,** in the King Christian Hotel, 59 King's Wharf, Christiansted (© **340/773-2628**), conducts two different types of tours. The first option is a half-day tour aboard a glass-bottom boat departing from the King Christian Hotel, daily from 9:30am to 1pm and 1:30 to 5pm; it costs $40 per person. The second is a full-day tour, offered daily from 10am to 4pm on a 40-foot trimaran for $85. Included in this excursion is a small picnic on Buck Island's beach.

Captain Heinz (© **340/773-3161** or 340/773-4041) is an Austrian-born skipper with more than 25 years of sailing experience. His trimaran, *Teroro II,* leaves the Green Cay Marina "H" Dock at 9am and 2pm, never filled with more than 23 passengers. This snorkeling trip costs $50 for adults, $30 for children

10 and under. The captain is not only a skilled sailor but also a considerate host. He will even take you around the outer reef, which the other guides do not, for an unforgettable underwater experience.

THE "RAIN FOREST" ⊛

The island's western district contains a dense, 15-acre forest, called the "Rain Forest" (though it's not a real one). The area is thick with mahogany trees, *kapok* (silk-cotton) trees, turpentine (red-birch) trees, *samaan* (rain) trees, and all kinds of ferns and vines. Sweet limes, mangoes, hog plums, and breadfruit trees, all of which have grown in the wild since the days of the plantations, are also interspersed among the larger trees. Crested hummingbirds, pearly eyed thrashers, green-throated caribs, yellow warblers, and perky but drably camouflaged banana quits nest here. The 150-foot-high Creque Dam is the major man-made sight in the area.

The "Rain Forest" is private property, but the owner lets visitors go inside to explore. To experience its charm, some people opt to drive along Route 76 (also known as Mahogany Road), stopping beside the footpaths that meander off on either side of the highway into dry riverbeds and glens. Stick to the most worn footpaths. You can also hike along some of the little-traveled four-wheel-drive roads in the area. Three of the best for hiking are the **Creque Dam Road** (routes 58/78), the **Scenic Road** (Rte. 78), and the **Western Scenic Road** (routes 63/78).

Our favorite trail in this area takes about 2½ hours one-way. From Frederiksted, drive north on Route 63 until you reach Creque Dam Road, where you turn right, park the car, and start walking. About a mile past the Creque Dam, you'll be deep within the forest's magnificent flora and fauna. Continue along the trail until you come to the Western Scenic Road. Eventually, you reach Mahogany Road (Rte. 76), near St. Croix Leap Project. Hikers rate this trail moderate in difficulty.

You could also begin near the junction of Creque Dam Road and Scenic Road. From here, your trek will cover a broad triangular swath, heading north and then west along Scenic Road. First, the road will rise, and then descend toward the coastal lighthouse of the island's extreme northwestern tip, **Hams Bluff.** Most trekkers decide to retrace their steps after about 45 minutes of northwesterly hiking. Real die-hards, however, will continue all the way to the coastline, then head south along the coastal road (Butler Bay Rd.), and finally head east along Creque Dam Road to their starting point at the junction of Creque Dam Road and Scenic Road. Embark on this longer expedition only if you're really prepared for a hike lasting about 5 hours.

SANDY POINT WILDLIFE REFUGE ⊛

St. Croix's rarely visited southwestern tip is composed of salt marshes, tidal pools, and low vegetation inhabited by birds, turtles, and other wildlife. More than 3 miles of ecologically protected coastline lie between Sandy Point (the island's westernmost tip) and the shallow waters of the Westend Saltpond. The area is home to colonies of green, leatherback, and hawksbill turtles. It's one of only two such places in U.S. waters. It's also home to thousands of birds, including herons, brown pelicans, Caribbean martins, black-necked stilts, and whitecrowned pigeons. As for flora, Sandy Point gave its name to a rare form of orchids, a brown/purple variety.

This wildlife refuge is only open on Saturday and Sunday from 8am to 6pm. To get here, drive to the end of Route 66 (Melvin Evans hwy.) and continue down a gravel road. For guided weekend visits, call © **340/773-4554.**

AROUND THE ISLAND

North of Frederiksted, you can drop in at **Sprat Hall,** the island's oldest plantation, or continue along to the "Rain Forest" (see above). Most visitors come to
the area to see the jagged estuary of the northern coastline's **Salt River.** The Salt
River was where Columbus landed on November 14, 1493. Marking the 500th
anniversary of Columbus's arrival, former President George H. W. Bush signed a
bill creating the 912-acre **Salt River Bay National Historical Park and Ecological Preserve.** The park contains the site of the original Carib village explored by
Columbus and his men, including the only ceremonial ball court ever discovered
in the Lesser Antilles. Also within the park is the largest mangrove forest in the
Virgin Islands, sheltering many endangered animals and plants, plus an underwater canyon attracting divers from around the world. Call the **St. Croix Environmental Association,** 3 Arawak Building, Gallows Bay (© **340/773-1989**), for
information on tours of the area. Tours cost $30 for adults, $15 for children
under age 12.

Estate Mount Washington Plantation is the island's best-preserved sugar
plantation and a highlight along the St. Croix Heritage Trail. It flourished from
1780 to 1820 when St. Croix was the second-largest producer of sugar in the
West Indies. The on-site private residence is closed to the public, but you can
arrange to go on a self-guided tour of the 13 acres (there is no admission charge,
although donations are appreciated). Know in advance that this is one of the
more loosely organized cultural attractions of St. Croix, but if you phone in
advance (© **340/772-1026**), someone might give you permission. The plantation site lies at the very southwestern tip of the island, off Route 63, 1 mile
inland from the highway that runs along the Frederiksted coast.

Cruzan Rum Factory   This factory distills the famous Virgin Islands rum,
which some consider the finest in the world. Guided tours depart from the visitors' pavilion; call for reservations and information. There's also a gift shop.

Estate Diamond W. Airport Rd., Rte. 64, Frederiksted. © **340/692-2280.** Admission $4. Tours given Mon–Fri
9–11:30am and 1–4:15pm.

Estate Whim Plantation Museum   This restored great house is unique
among those of the many sugar plantations whose ruins dot the island. It's composed of only three rooms. With 3-foot-thick walls made of stone, coral, and
molasses, the house resembles a luxurious European château. A division of Baker
Furniture Company used the Whim Plantation's collection of models for one of
its most successful reproductions, the "Whim Museum–West Indies Collection."
Upscale reproductions of some of the furniture on display within the Whim
Plantation, plus others from the Caribbean, are for sale on-site. Slightly different

---

Moments **The Easternmost Point of the Caribbean**

The rocky promontory of **Point Udall,** jutting into the Caribbean Sea, is the
easternmost point under the U.S flag in the Caribbean. Die-hards go out
to see the sun rise, but considering the climb is via a rutted dirt road, you
may want to wait until there's more light before heading here. Once at
the top, you'll be rewarded with one of the best views in the U.S. Virgin
Islands. On the way to the lookout point, you'll see **"The Castle,"** a local
architectural oddity, owned by the island's most prominent socialite, the
Contessa Nadia Farbo Navarro. Point Udall is signposted along Route 82.

inventories are available from an associated store in downtown Christiansted: **The St. Croix Landmarks Museum Store,** 58 Queen St. (© **340/713-8102**). For more information, refer to "Shopping" later in this section.

The ruins of the plantation's sugar-processing plant, complete with a restored windmill, also remain.

Centerline Rd. (2 miles east of Frederiksted). © **340/772-0598**. Admission $6 adults, $3 children. June–Oct Mon, Wed, Fri, and Sat 10am–4pm.

St. George Village Botanical Garden

This is a 16-acre Eden of tropical trees, shrubs, vines, and flowers. The garden is a feast for the eye and the camera, from the entrance drive bordered by royal palms and bougainvillea to the towering kapok and tamarind trees. It was built around the ruins of a 19th-century sugar-cane workers' village. Self-guided walking-tour maps are available at the entrance to the garden's great hall. Facilities include restrooms and a gift shop.

127 Estate St., 1 St. George, Frederiksted (just north of Centerline Rd., 4 miles east of Frederiksted). © **340/692-2874**. Admission $6 adults, $1 children 12 and under; donations welcome. Daily 9am–5pm.

SHOPPING ✸✸✸

In **Christiansted,** the emphasis is on hole-in-the-wall boutiques selling one-of-a-kind merchandise; the selection of handmade items is especially strong. Knowing that it can't compete with the volume of Charlotte Amalie on St. Thomas, Christiansted has forged its own identity as the chic spot for merchandise in the Caribbean. All its shops are within about a half mile of each other. The relatively new **King's Alley Complex** (© **340/778-8135**) is a pink-sided compound filled with the densest concentration of shops on St. Croix.

In recent years, **Frederiksted** has also become a popular shopping destination. Its urban mall appeals to cruise-ship passengers arriving at Frederiksted Pier. The mall is on a 50-foot strip of land between Strand and King streets, the town's bustling main thoroughfare.

The casual visitor to Frederiksted might want to visit **Island WeBe,** 210 Strand St. (© **340/772-2555**), which offers some unusual West Indian products, or "Caribbean memories," as the store puts it. A wide selection of art, crafts, and rainforest products from the Virgin Islands, along with delicacies such as jams, spices, and other items are available. Mocko jumbie dolls, inspired by Africa, are also sold. These dolls are said to represent the souls of the ancestors of slaves brought over from Africa.

Below are our favorite shops in Christiansted.

The operators of **Folk Art Traders** ✸, Strand Street (© **340/773-1900**), travel throughout the Caribbean ("in the bush") to add to their unique collection of local art and folk-art treasures: Carnival masks, pottery, ceramics, original paintings, and hand-wrought jewelry. There's nothing else like it in the Virgin Islands.

At the hip and eclectic **From the Gecko,** 1233 Queen Cross St. (© **340/778-9433**), you can find anything from hand-painted local cottons and silks to that old West Indian staple, batiks. We found the Indonesian collection here among the most imaginative in the U.S. Virgin Islands—everything from glass jewelry to hemp linens.

Many Hands, in the Pan Am Pavilion, Strand Street (© **340/773-1990**), sells locally made pottery, art, and handmade jewelry. The collection of local paintings is intriguing, as is the year-round "Christmas tree."

For an upscale insight into the 19th-century aesthetics of plantation life on St. Croix, head to the well-organized and genteel **St. Croix Landmarks**

Museum Store 𝒜, 58 Queen St. (© **340/713-8102**). It focuses on reproductions of some of the antiques on display at the Whim Plantation, recommended earlier in this section. Also available are framed engravings of the kind of botany you'd expect on St. Croix, paperweights, books, brass candlesticks, and gift items redolent with memories and references to the West Indies.

Purple Papaya, 39 Strand St., Pan Am Pavilion (© **340/713-9412**), is the best place to go for inexpensive island gifts. It has the biggest array of embroidered T-shirts and sweatshirts on island. Although you're in the Caribbean and not Hawaii, there is a large selection of Hawaiian shirts and dresses, along with beachwear for the whole family, plus island souvenirs.

Royal Poinciana, 1111 Strand St. (© **340/773-9892**), looks like an antique apothecary. You'll find hot sauces, seasoning blends for gumbos, island herbal teas, Antillean coffees, and a scented array of soaps, toiletries, lotions, and shampoos. There's also a selection of museum-reproduction greeting cards and calendars, plus educational but fun gifts for children.

About 60% of the merchandise at **Gone Tropical,** 5 Company St. (© **340/773-4696**), is made in Indonesia (usually Bali). Prices of new, semiantique, or antique sofas, beds, chests, tables, mirrors, and decorative carvings are the same as (and sometimes less than) those of new furniture in conventional stores. Gone Tropical also sells art objects, jewelry, batiks, candles, and baskets.

The small West Indian cottage of **Crucian Gold,** 59 Kings Wharf (© **877/773-5241**), holds the gold and silver creations of island-born Brian Bishop. His most popular item is the Crucian bracelet, which contains a "True Lovers' Knot" in its design. The shop also sells hand-tied knots (bound in gold wire), rings, pendants, and earrings.

Elegant Illusions Copy Jewelry, 55 King St. (© **340/773-2727**), a branch of a hugely successful chain based in California, sells convincing fake jewelry. The look-alikes range in price from $15 to $2,000, and include credible copies of the baroque and antique jewelry your great-grandmother might have worn. If you want the real thing, you can go next door to **King Alley Jewelry** (© **340/773-4746**), which is owned by the same company and specializes in fine designer jewelry, including Tiffany and Cartier.

Sonya Hough of **Sonya Ltd.,** 1 Company St. (© **340/778-8605**), has a group of loyal local fans who wouldn't leave home without wearing one of her bracelets. She's most famous for the sterling-silver and gold versions of her C-clasp bracelet. Locals say that if the cup of the "C" is turned toward your heart, you're taken; if the cup is turned outward, you're available. Prices range from $30 to $2,000.

Everything sold at **Waterfront Larimar Mines,** the Boardwalk/King's Walk (© **340/692-9000**), is produced by the largest manufacturer of gold settings for larimar in the world. Discovered in the 1970s, larimar is a pale-blue pectolite prized for its color. It comes from a single mountain located on the southwestern edge of the Dominican Republic. Prices range from $25 to $1,000. Although other shops sell the stone as well, this place has the widest selection.

Coconut Vine, Strand Street (© **340/773-1991**), is one of the most colorful and popular little boutiques on the island. Hand-painted batiks for both men and women are the specialty.

Urban Threadz, 52C Company St. (© **340/773-2883**), is the most comprehensive clothing store in Christiansted's historic core, with a two-story, big-city scale and appeal. It's where island residents shop for hip, urban styles. Men's items are on the street level, women's upstairs. The inventory includes everything from

Bermuda shorts to lightweight summer blazers and men's suits. The store carries Calvin Klein, Polo, and Oakley, among other brands.

ST. CROIX AFTER DARK

St. Croix doesn't have the nightlife of St. Thomas. To find the action, you might have to consult the publication *St. Croix This Week,* which is distributed free to cruise-ship and air passengers and is also available at the tourist office.

It's advisable, if it's available, to try to catch a performance of one of the **Quadrille Dances** 🎭 which are performed by either of two independent, part-time dance troupes based on St. Croix. Hours, performance details, and organization of these dance groups vary widely from season to season, but the basic steps associated with *La Quadrille* have changed little since the plantation days. The women wear long dresses, white gloves, and turbans, while the men wear flamboyant shirts, sashes, and tight black trousers. At one of these performances, after you've learned the (relatively basic) steps, you might be invited to join the dancers on the floor. Ask at your hotel if and when one of these loosely organized dance troupes might be performing, if at all, during your visit.

If you enjoy gambling, visit the **Divi Carina Bay Casino,** 25 Estate Turner Hole (© **340/773-7529**). Set on the grounds of the Divi Carina Bay Resort, with which its management is not associated, it's sheltered from the glaring Caribbean sunlight with a glistening white dome inspired by the architecture of the North African desert. Inside, within a decor inspired by the Moroccan casbah, you'll find the only casino in the U.S. Virgin Islands, with 10,000 feet of gaming space, a cafe-style bistro and bar, at least 20 gaming tables, and 300 jangling slot machines. Entrance is free. It's open Monday to Thursday from noon to 4am; from Friday to Sunday, 24 hours a day.

If you're looking to hear some live music, try **Blue Moon,** 17 Strand St. (© **340/772-2222**), a hip little dive and a good bistro. It's currently the hottest spot in Frederiksted on Fridays, when a five-piece ensemble entertains. On Sunday a live jazz trio performs. There's no cover.

The **Terrace Lounge,** in The Buccaneer, Route 82, Estate Shoys (© **340/773-2100**), off the main dining room of one of St. Croix's most upscale hotels, welcomes some of the Caribbean's finest entertainers every night, often including a full band.

2 Plus 2 Disco, at the La Grande Princess (© **340/773-3710**), is a real Caribbean disco. It features the regional sounds of the islands, not only calypso and reggae but also salsa and soca (a hybrid of calypso and reggae). Usually there's a DJ, except on weekends when local bands are brought in. The place isn't fancy or large. Come here for *Saturday Night Fever.* Hours are Thursday and Sunday from 8:30pm to 2am and Friday and Saturday from 9pm to either 5 or 6am. The cover is $15 when there's a live band.

For a sunset cocktail, head to the **Marina Bar,** in the King's Alley Hotel, King's Alley/The Waterfront (© **340/773-0103**). It has a great position on the waterfront, on a shaded terrace overlooking the deep-blue sea and Protestant Cay. It's open throughout the day, but the most appealing activities begin right after the last seaplane departs for St. Thomas, around 5:30pm, and continue until 8:30pm. Cocktails made with rum, mango, banana, papaya, and grenadine are the drinks of choice. You can stave off hunger with burgers, sandwiches, and West Indian–style platters. There's live entertainment most nights, usually street bands. On Monday, you can bet on crab races.

Cormorant Beach Club Bar, 4126 La Grande Princesse (© **340/778-8920**), is set in a predominantly gay resort about 3 miles northwest of Christiansted. It caters both to resort guests and to gay men and women from other parts of the island. You can sit at tables overlooking the ocean or around an open-centered mahogany bar, adjacent to a gazebo. Excellent tropical drinks are mixed here, including the house specialty, a Cormorant Cooler, made with champagne, pineapple juice, and Triple Sec. It opened daily from 7am till the last customer leaves.

4 St. John ★★★

A few miles east of St. Thomas, across a glistening, turquoise channel known as Pillsbury Sound, lies St. John, the smallest and least densely populated of the three main U.S. Virgin Islands.

St. John is a wonder of unspoiled beauty. Along its rocky coastline are beautiful crescent-shaped bays and white-sand beaches, and the interior is no less impressive. The variety of wildlife here is the envy of naturalists around the world. And there are miles of serpentine hiking trails, leading past the ruins of 18th-century Danish plantations to magnificent panoramic views. At scattered intervals along the trails, you can even find mysteriously geometric petroglyphs, of unknown age and origin, incised into boulders and cliffs.

Today, St. John (unlike the other U.S. islands) remains truly pristine, its preservation rigidly enforced by the U.S. Park Service. Thanks to the efforts of Laurance Rockefeller, who purchased acres of land here and donated them to the United States, the island's shoreline waters, as well as more than half its surface area, make up the **Virgin Islands National Park.** The hundreds of coral gardens that surround St. John are protected rigorously—any attempt to damage or remove coral from the water is punishable with large and strictly enforced fines.

Despite the unspoiled beauty of much of St. John, the island manages to provide visitors with modern amenities and travel services, including a sampling of restaurants, car-rental kiosks, yacht-supply facilities, hotels, and campgrounds. **Cinnamon Bay,** founded by the U.S. National Park Service in 1964, is the most famous campsite in the Caribbean. In addition, the roads are well maintained, and there's even a small commercial center, **Cruz Bay,** on the island's western tip. Don't come here for nightlife; St. John is sleepy, and that's why people love it.

To get to St. John, you take a ferry from St. Thomas. (There are also ferries from the British Virgin Islands.) See the "Getting There" section at the beginning of this chapter for information on how to get to St. Thomas.

ST. JOHN ESSENTIALS

VISITOR INFORMATION   The **tourist office** (© 340/776-6450) is located near the Battery, a 1735 fort that's a short walk from the St. Thomas ferry dock. It's open Monday to Friday from 8am to 1pm and 2 to 5pm. A **National Park visitor center** (© 340/776-6201) is also found at Cruz Bay, offering two floors of information and wall-mounted wildlife displays, plus a video presentation about the culture of the Virgin Islands.

GETTING AROUND   The most popular way to get around is by the local **Vitran** service, the same company that runs the buses on St. Thomas. Buses run between Cruz Bay and Coral Bay, costing $1 for adults and 75¢ for children.

An open-air **surrey-style taxi** is more fun, however. Typical fares are $4 to Trunk Bay, $5.50 to Cinnamon Bay, or $5 to Maho Bay. Between midnight and 6am, fares are increased by 50%. Call © 340/693-7530 for more information.

The island's undeveloped roads offer some of the best views anywhere. Because of this, many people opt to rent a vehicle (sometimes with four-wheel drive) to tour the island. Most visitors need a car for only a day or two. **Remember:** Drive on the left and follow posted speed limits, which are generally very low.

Unless you need to carry luggage, which should probably be locked away in a trunk, you might consider one of the sturdy, open-sided, jeeplike vehicles that offer the best view of the surroundings and are the most fun way to tour St. John. Note that most of these vehicles have manual transmission, which can be especially tricky in a car built to drive on the left side of the road. They cost $76 to $84 a day.

The largest car-rental agency on St. John is **Hertz** (© **800/654-3131** in the U.S., or 340/693-7580 or 340/776-6171; www.hertz.com). If you want a local firm, try **St. John Car Rental,** across from the Catholic church in Cruz Bay (© **340/776-6103**).

FAST FACTS   If you need a **pharmacy,** or want to purchase film, books, and other daily necessities, try **St. John Drugcenter,** in the Boulon Shopping Center, Cruz Bay (© **340/776-6353**). It's open Monday to Saturday from 9am to 6pm.

If you need a **hospital,** go to **St. John Myrah Keating Smith Community Health Clinic,** 38 Sussanaberg (© **340/693-8900**), which can be reached along Route 10, 2 miles east of Cruz Bay.

ACCOMMODATIONS

There are actually more villa and condo beds available on St. John than there are hotel beds. These units offer spaciousness and comfort, as well as privacy and freedom, and they often come with fully equipped kitchens, dining areas, bedrooms, and such amenities as VCRs and patio grills. Rentals range from large multiroom resort homes to simply decorated one-bedroom condos. In addition to the condo and villa complexes reviewed below, **Caribbean Villas & Resorts** (© **800/338-0987,** fax 207/871-1673 in the U.S., or 340/776-6152), the island's biggest real-estate agency, is an excellent choice. Most condos go for around $225 per night, though private homes are more expensive.

VERY EXPENSIVE

Caneel Bay 🐟🐟🐟   Conceived by megamillionaire Laurance S. Rockefeller in 1956, this is the Caribbean's first eco-resort. Though long one of the Caribbean's premier resorts, Caneel Bay is definitely not one of the most luxurious. A devoted fan once told us, "It's like living at summer camp." That means no phones or TVs in the rooms. Nevertheless, the movers and shakers of the world continue to come here, though younger people tend to head elsewhere. To attract more families, young children are now allowed. Go to Westin St. John Resort (see below) for the glitz and glitter; head here for a touch of class.

The resort lies on a 170-acre portion of the National Park, offering a choice of seven beaches. Surrounded by lush greenery, the main buildings are strung along the bays, with a Caribbean lounge and dining room at the core. Other buildings housing guest rooms stand along the beaches. Try to get one of the five rooms in cottage no. 7, overlooking two of the most idyllic beaches, Scott and Paradise. This was the former beach house owned and occupied by Laurence R. himself. Now it's a cluster of five different accommodations, the most upscale at the entire resort. Most rooms, however, are set back on low cliffs or headlands. The decor within is understated, with Indonesian wicker furniture, hand-woven fabrics, sisal mats, and plantation fans. All have neatly kept bathrooms with showers.

The resort has consistently maintained a high level of cuisine, often quite formal for the laid-back Caribbean. See "Dining," below for more information on the Equator.

St. John

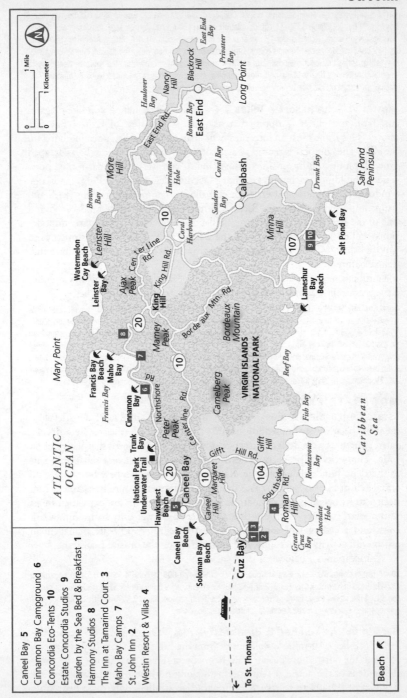

Beach ⤦

Legend (keyed numbers):

Caneel Bay **5**
Cinnamon Bay Campground **6**
Concordia Eco-Tents **10**
Estate Concordia Studios **9**
Garden by the Sea Bed & Breakfast **1**
Harmony Studios **8**
The Inn at Tamarind Court **3**
Maho Bay Camps **7**
St. John Inn **2**
Westin Resort & Villas **4**

Map labels:

ATLANTIC OCEAN

Caribbean Sea

VIRGIN ISLANDS NATIONAL PARK

Mary Point

To St. Thomas

Cruz Bay

Soloman Bay Beach
Caneel Bay Beach
Hawksnest Beach
National Park Underwater Trail
Trunk Bay
Cinnamon Bay
Francis Bay Beach
Maho Bay
Leinster Bay
Watermelon Cay Beach

East End
East End Bay
Privateer Bay
Long Point
Blackrock Hill
Nancy Hill
Haulover Bay
Brown Bay
More Hill
Leinster Hill
Round Bay
East End Rd.
Hurricane Hole
Coral Harbour
Calabash
Sanders Bay
Coral Bay
Drunk Bay
Salt Pond Peninsula
Salt Pond Bay
Minna Hill
Lameshur Bay Beach
Reef Bay
Bordeaux Mountain
Bor de aux Mtn. Rd.
Camelberg Peak
Fish Bay
Mamey Peak
King Hill
Ajax Peak
Center line Rd.
King Hill Rd.
Peter Peak
Northshore Rd.
Centerline Rd.
Gifft Hill Rd.
Gifft Hill
Margaret Hill
Caneel Hill
Southside Rd.
Roman Hill
Rendezvous Bay
Chocolate Hole
Great Cruz Bay
Francis Bay Rd.

Roads: 10, 20, 7, 104, 107

753

Virgin Islands National Park, St. John, U.S.V.I. 00831. ℂ 340/776-6111. Fax 340/693-8280. www.caneel bay.com. 166 units. Winter $450–$1,100 double; off season $300–$700 double. MAP (breakfast and dinner) $80 per person extra. 1 child under 17 can stay free in parent's room. AE, DC, MC, V. **Amenities:** 3 restaurants; 2 bars; outdoor pool; 11 tennis courts; fitness center; spa; boating; deep-sea fishing; dive shop; kayaks; snorkeling; Sunfish sailboats; windsurfing; children's center; business center; limited room service; babysitting; laundry service; dry cleaning; nonsmoking rooms; rooms for those with limited mobility. *In room:* A/C, minibar, beverage maker, hair dryer, iron/ironing board, safe, no phone.

Westin St. John Resort & Villas ★★★ *Kids* Come here if you like megaresort flash and glitter as opposed to the "old-school ties" of Caneel Bay (see above). This is the most architecturally dramatic and visually appealing hotel on St. John. The complex is set on 34 acres of gently sloping, intricately landscaped grounds on the southwest side of the island. It consists of 13 cedar-roofed postmodern buildings, each with ziggurat-shaped angles, soaring ceilings, and large windows. Herringbone-patterned brick walkways connect the gardens (with 400 palms imported from Puerto Rico) with the 1,200-foot white-sand beach and one of the largest pools in the Virgin Islands. Some of the stylish accommodations contain fan-shaped windows and curved ceilings. Most units open onto private balconies, and some have their own whirlpools. All bedrooms have full, deluxe bathrooms.

Cuisine is more versatile here than at Caneel Bay, but it's not always as good. Expect nouvelle cuisine, buffets, and even New York–deli sandwiches.

Great Cruz Bay, St. John, U.S.V.I. 00831. ℂ 800/808-5020 in the U.S., or 340/693-8000. Fax 340/779-4985. www.westinresortstjohn.com. 349 units. Winter $406–$679 double, $939–$1,589 suite; off season $299–$500 double, $739–$1,189 suite. AE, DC, DISC, MC, V. Round-trip shuttle and private ferryboat transfers from St. Thomas airport $65 per adult, $45 per child. **Amenities:** 3 restaurants; 3 bars; outdoor pool; 6 lit tennis courts; fitness center; sauna; dive shop; fishing; sailboats; snorkeling; windsurfing; children's programs, 24-hr. room service; babysitting; laundry service; nonsmoking rooms; rooms for those with limited mobility. *In room:* A/C, TV, dataport, minibar, kitchenette (in some), beverage maker, hair dryer, iron/ironing board, safe.

MODERATE/EXPENSIVE

Estate Concordia Studios This environmentally sensitive 51-acre development has been widely praised for its integration with the local ecosystem. Its elevated structures were designed to coexist with the stunning southern edge of St. John. The secluded property is nestled on a low cliff above a salt pond, surrounded by hundreds of pristine National Park acres. It's best for those with rental vehicles. Each building was designed to protect mature trees and is connected to its neighbors with boardwalks. The nine studios are contained in six postmodern cottages. Each unit has a kitchen, a shower-only bathroom, a balcony, and a ceiling fan; some have an extra bedroom. On-site management assists with activity suggestions. For information on the on-site **Eco-Tents,** refer to "Campgrounds," below.

20–27 Estate Concordia, Coral Bay, St. John, U.S.V.I. 00830. ℂ 800/392-9004 in the U.S. and Canada, or 212/472-9453 in New York City. Fax 212/861-6210. www.maho.org. 9 units. Winter $200 studio for 2; off season $95–$150 studio for 2. Extra person $25 winter, $15 off season. AE, MC, V. **Amenities:** Outdoor pool; coin-operated laundry. *In room:* Ceiling fan, kitchenette, no phone.

Garden by the Sea Bed & Breakfast ★ *Finds* Overlooking the ocean, this little B&B lies a 10-minute walk south from the little port Cruz Bay. It has easy access to the north shore beaches and lies between Frank and Turner Bays. From the gardens of the house, a 1-minute path along Audubon Pond leads to Frank Bay Beach. Be sure to reserve a room ahead, as it offers only three bedrooms. Artifacts from around the world have been used to furnish the units. Each bedroom features elephant bamboo canopy beds, Japanese fountains, hardwood

floors, and well-kept bathrooms with shower stalls. Don't expect phones or TVs, as this is a getaway, not a communications center. The 1970s house is designed in a Caribbean gingerbread style with cathedral beamed ceilings. Breakfast is served on the veranda (try the homemade muffins and quiche).

P.O. Box 37, Cruz Bay, St. John, U.S.V.I. 00831. ℂ 340/779-4731. www.gardenbythesea.com. 3 units. Winter $200–$215 double; off season $125–$150 double. No credit cards. **Amenities:** Nonsmoking rooms. *In room:* Ceiling fan, iron/ironing board, no phone.

Harmony Studios ⟨ᴋ⟩ Built on a hillside above the Maho Bay Camps, this is a small-scale cluster of 12 luxury studios in six two-story houses with views sweeping down to the sea. The complex is designed to combine both ecological technology and comfort; it's one of the few resorts in the Caribbean to operate exclusively on sun and wind power. Most of the building materials are derived from recycled materials, including reconstituted plastic and glass containers, newsprint, old tires, and scrap lumber. The managers and staff are committed to offering educational experiences, as well as the services of a small-scale resort. The studios contain tiled shower-only bathrooms, kitchenettes, dining areas, and outdoor terraces. Guests can walk a short distance downhill to use the restaurant, grocery store, and watersports facilities at the Maho Bay Camps.

P.O. Box 310, Cruz Bay, St. John, U.S.V.I. 00831. ℂ 800/392-9004 in the U.S. and Canada, 212/472-9453 in New York City, or 340/776-6226. Fax 340/776-6504, or 212/861-6210 in New York City. www.maho.org. 12 units. Winter $195–$210 studio for 2; off season $110–$145 studio for 2. Extra person $25. AE, MC, V. **Amenities:** Sailing; snorkeling; windsurfing. *In room:* Ceiling fan, no phone.

INEXPENSIVE

The following places offer just the basics, but they're fine if you're not too finicky.

The Inn at Tamarind Court Right outside Cruz Bay but still within walking distance of the ferryboat dock, this modest place consists of a small hotel and an even simpler West Indian inn. Bedrooms are small, evoking those in a little country motel. Most have twin beds. Shower-only bathrooms in the inn are shared among the single rooms; units in the hotel have small private bathrooms. The social life here revolves around its courtyard bar and the in-house restaurant under the same name. From the hotel, you can walk to shuttles that take you to the beaches.

South Shore Rd. (P.O. Box 350), Cruz Bay, St. John, U.S.V.I. 00831. ℂ 800/221-1637 or 340/776-6378. Fax 340/776-6722. www.tamarindcourt.com. 20 units, 14 with bathroom. Winter $75 single without bathroom, $148 double with bathroom, $240 apt, $240 suite; off season $60–$65 single without bathroom, $110-$120 double with bathroom, $170-$190 apt, $190 suite. Rates include continental breakfast. AE, DISC, MC, V. **Amenities:** Restaurant; bar. *In room:* A/C, ceiling fan, TV, fridge, no phone.

St. John Inn *⟨Value⟩* The old Cruz Inn, once the budget staple of the island, enjoys a new lease on life. Although its rates have gone up, it has also been much improved. The inn overlooks Enighed Pond, only a few blocks from the Cruz Bay dock area. Accommodations have a light, airy, California feel. The small to medium-size bedrooms have wrought-iron or mahogany beds, handcrafted pine armoires, and a touch of Ralph Lauren flair to make for an inviting nest. The junior suites have full sofa beds, kitchenettes, and sitting areas. Shower-only bathrooms are small.

P.O. Box 37, Cruz Bay, St. John, U.S.V.I. 00831. ℂ 800/666-7688 in the U.S., or 340/693-8688. Fax 340/693-9900. www.stjohninn.com. 11 units. Winter $140–$225 double; off season $80–$150 double. Extra person $15. Rates include continental breakfast. AE, MC, V. **Amenities:** Bar; outdoor pool; babysitting; nonsmoking rooms. *In room:* A/C, TV, dataport, kitchenette, fridge, beverage maker, hair dryer, iron/ironing board.

CAMPGROUNDS

Cinnamon Bay Campground ⚔ This National Park Service campground is the most complete in the Caribbean. The site is directly on the beach, surrounded by thousands of acres of tropical vegetation. Life is simple here: You have a choice of a tent, a cottage, or a bare site. At the bare campsites, you get just the site, with no fancy extras. Each canvas tent is 10 feet by 14 feet and has a floor as well as a number of extras, including all cooking equipment; your linen is even changed weekly. Each cottage is 15 feet by 15 feet, consisting of a room with two concrete walls and two screen walls. Each cottage contains cooking facilities and four twin beds with thin mattresses; one cot can be added. Lavatories and cool-water showers are in separate buildings nearby. Camping is limited to a 2-week period in winter in any given year.

P.O. Box 720, Cruz Bay, St. John, U.S.V.I. 00831. © 340/776-6330. Fax 340/776-6458. www.cinnamonbay. com. 126 units, none with bathroom. Winter $110 cottage for 2, $80 tent site, $27 bare site; off season $70 cottage for 2, $58 tent site, $25 bare site. Extra person $17. AE, MC, V. **Amenities:** Restaurant; sailing; snorkeling; windsurfing; grocery store. *In room:* Fridge (in some), beverage maker (in some), no phone.

Concordia Eco-Tents This is the newest addition to Stanley Selengut's celebrated Concordia development project on the southern tip of St. John, overlooking Salt Pond Bay and Ram Head Point. These solar- and wind-powered tent-cottages combine sustainable technology with some of the most spectacular views on the island. The light framing, fabric walls, and large screened-in windows lend a tree-house atmosphere to guests' experience. Set on the windward side of the island, the tent-cottages enjoy natural ventilation from the cooling trade winds. Inside, each has two twin beds with rather thin mattresses in each bedroom, one or two twin mattresses on a loft platform, and a queen-size futon in the living-room area (each unit can sleep up to six people comfortably). Each kitchen is equipped with a running-water sink, propane stove, and cooler. In addition, each Eco-Tent has a small private shower, rather meager towels, and a composting toilet. The secluded hillside location, surrounded by hundreds of acres of pristine National Park land, requires guests to arrange for a rental vehicle. Beaches, hikes, and the shops and restaurants of Coral Bay are only a 10-minute drive from the property. (If you're interested in regular on-site studios, see Estate Concordia Studios, above.)

20–27 Estate Concordia, Coral Bay, St. John, U.S.V.I. 00830. © 800/392-9004, or 212/472-9453 for reservations. Fax 212/861-6210. www.maho.org. 11 tent-cottages. Winter $125 tent for 2; off season $85 tent for 2. Extra person $25 winter, $15 off season. AE, MC, V. **Amenities:** Outdoor pool. *In room:* No phone.

Maho Bay Camps ⚔ Right on Maho Bay, this is an interesting concept in ecology vacationing, where you camp close to nature, but with considerable comfort. It's set on a hillside above the beach surrounded by the Virgin Islands National Park. To preserve the existing ground cover, all 114 tent-cottages are on platforms, above a thickly wooded slope. Utility lines and pipes are hidden under wooden boardwalks and stairs. Each tent-cottage, covered with canvas and screens, has two twin beds with thin mattresses, a couch, electric lamps and outlets, a dining table, chairs, a propane stove, an ice chest (cooler), linen, thin towels, and cooking and eating utensils. Guests share communal bathhouses. Maho Bay Camps is more intimate and slightly more luxurious than its nearest competitor, Cinnamon Bay.

P.O. Box 310, Cruz Bay, St. John, U.S.V.I. 00831. © 800/392-9004, 212/472-9453 in New York City, or 340/776-6226. Fax 340/776-6504, or 212/861-6210 in New York City. www.maho.org. 114 tent-cottages, none with bathroom. Winter $110–$115 tent-cottage for 2 (minimum stay of 7 nights); off season $75 tent-cottage for 2. Extra person $15. AE, MC, V. **Amenities:** Restaurant; sailing; snorkeling; windsurfing. *In room:* No phone.

DINING

St. John has some posh dining, particularly at the luxury resorts like Caneel Bay, but it also has West Indian establishments with plenty of local color and flavor. Many of the restaurants here command high prices, but you can lunch almost anywhere more reasonably. Dinner is often an event on St. John, since it's about the only form of nightlife the island has.

EXPENSIVE

Asolare ✦ INTERNATIONAL/ASIAN   This is the most beautiful and elegant restaurant on St. John, with the hippest and best-looking staff. It sits on a hill overlooking Cruz Bay and some of the British Virgin Islands. *Asolare* translates as "the leisurely passing of time without purpose," and that's what many diners do here. The chef uses some of the best and freshest ingredients available on island. To begin, try the grilled Asian barbecued shrimp or the squid-and-shrimp medley. For a main course, you might be tempted by ginger lamb or the peppercorn-dusted filet of beef. Two truly excellent dishes are the chicken Kiev and sashimi tuna on a sizzling plate with plum-passion fruit-sake vinaigrette. For dessert, try the fresh berry dishes, or chocolate pyramid cake.

Cruz Bay. © 340/779-4747. Reservations required. Main courses $30–$50. AE, MC, V. Daily 5:30–9pm.

Equator ✦ CARIBBEAN/INTERNATIONAL   This restaurant lies behind the tower of an 18th-century sugar mill, where ponds with water lilies fill former crystallization pits for hot molasses. A flight of stairs leads to a monumental circular dining room, with a wraparound veranda and sweeping views of a park. In the center rises the stone column that horses and mules once circled to crush sugar-cane stalks. In its center the restaurant grows a giant poincianalike Asian tree of the *Albizia lebbeck* species. Islanders call it "woman's tongue tree."

The cuisine is the most daring on the island, and for the most part, the chefs pull off their transcultural dishes. A spicy and tantalizing opener is lemon grass–and-ginger-cured salmon salad. A classic Caribbean callaloo soup is offered, and the salads use fresh ingredients such as Roma tomatoes and endive. Daily Caribbean selections are offered, or you can opt for such fine dishes as seared Caribbean tuna, or penne pasta with shiitake mushrooms and roasted tomatoes in an herb-garlic-cream sauce. There's always a dry, aged Angus steak or a grilled veal chop for the more traditional palate.

In the Caneel Bay hotel, Caneel Bay. © 340/776-6111. Reservations required. Main courses $22–$39. Year-round Tues–Sun 6:30–9pm.

Le Château de Bordeaux ✦ MEDITERRANEAN   This restaurant is 5 miles east of Cruz Bay, near the geographical center of the island and close to one of its highest points. It's known for having some of the best views on St. John. A lunch grill on the patio serves burgers and drinks daily from 11am to 4pm. In the evening, amid the Victorian decor and lace tablecloths, you can begin with a house-smoked chicken spring roll or velvety carrot soup. After that, move on to one of the saffron-flavored pastas or savory West Indian seafood chowder. The well-flavored Dijon mustard and pecan-crusted roast rack of lamb with shallot-port reduction is a good choice. For dessert, there's a changing array of cheesecakes, among other options.

Junction 10, Bordeaux Mountain. © 340/776-6611. Reservations recommended. Main courses $28–$34. AE, MC, V. Daily 6–9pm.

Paradiso ✦✦ CONTEMPORARY/AMERICAN   This is the most talked-about restaurant on St. John, other than Asolare (see above), and it's the only one that's air-conditioned. The interior has lots of brass, glowing hardwoods, and nautical antiques, not to mention the most beautiful bar on the island, crafted from mahogany, purpleheart, and angelique.

Try such appetizers as grilled chicken spring rolls with roasted sweet peppers. Roasted garlic Caesar salad with sun-dried tomatoes and Parmesan grissini is a new twist on this classic dish. But the main dishes truly shine, especially a pan-seared local yellowfin tuna with baby arugula, fennel, pear, and radicchio, and a grilled Kansas City sirloin marinated in garlic and fresh herbs. Another enticing choice is oven-roasted free-range chicken breast with roasted potatoes, carrots, and butternut squash.

Mongoose Junction. ℂ **340/693-8899.** Reservations recommended. Main courses $24–$32. AE, MC, V. Daily 5:30–9:30pm. Bar daily 5–10:30pm.

Zozo's Ristorante ITALIAN An in-the-know crowd of locals and visitors flocks to this charming Italian trattoria, with an open-air terrace and a sweeping panoramic view over the sea. It's the kind of place that locals would book to the rafters on holidays such as New Year's Eve or private celebrations such as birthdays or anniversaries. First-rate ingredients, style, and fresh seasonings contribute to such winning dishes as an eggplant tower (layers of eggplant, fontina, and ricotta and red peppers); little neck clams in white wine, garlic, and plum tomatoes; and lump crab cakes with a roasted-pepper aioli. The pastas are the island's best, especially the lobster ravioli with wild mushrooms and toasted pine nuts, and the basil-infused linguine. Tuck into such fish dishes as a grilled sea bass with an eggplant tapenade in a roasted garlic–shrimp sauce or pan-seared black grouper with a sauce flavored with orange and fresh basil. Their veal shank *(osso buco)* is slowly simmered in red wine, tomato, and veal stock and is a tasty main course.

Gallows Point. ℂ **340/693-9200.** Reservations recommended. Main courses $27–$36. AE, MC, V. Daily 5:30–10pm.

MODERATE

Café Roma ITALIAN This restaurant in the center of Cruz Bay is not a place for great cooking finesse, but it's a longtime favorite, and has pleased many who just want a casual meal. To enter, you have to climb a flight of stairs. You might arrive early and have a strawberry colada, then enjoy a standard pasta, veal, seafood, or chicken dish. There are usually 30 to 40 vegetarian items on the menu. The owner claims, with justification, that his pizzas are the best on the island; try the white pizza. Italian wines are sold by the glass or bottle, and you can end the evening with an espresso.

Cruz Bay. ℂ **340/776-6524.** Main courses $12–$24. MC, V. Daily 5–10pm.

La Tapa INTERNATIONAL/MEDITERRANEAN At one of our favorite restaurants in Cruz Bay you can sample tapas, Spanish-inspired bite-size morsels of fish, meat, or marinated vegetables, accompanied by pitchers of sangria. There's a tiny bar with no more than five stools, a two-tiered dining room, and lots of original paintings (the establishment doubles as an art gallery). Menu items are thoughtful and well conceived, and include fast-seared tuna with a Basque-inspired relish of onions, peppers, garlic, and herbs; filet *poivre,* a steak soaked with rum and served with a cracked-pepper sauce and mashed potatoes; and linguine with shrimp, red peppers, and leeks in peanut sauce. Live jazz is offered on Mondays, and on Wednesdays, Spanish meringue and salsa music is played.

Centerline Rd. (across from Scotia Bank), Cruz Bay. ℂ 340/693-7755. Reservations recommended. Tapas from $4; main courses $19–$45. AE, MC, V. Daily 5:30–10pm.

Morgan's Mango CARIBBEAN   The chefs here roam the Caribbean for tantalizing flavors, which they adapt for their ever-changing menu. The restaurant is easy to spot, with its big canopy, the only protection from the elements. The bar wraps around the main dining room and offers some 30 frozen drinks. Some think the kitchen tries to do too much with the nightly menu, but it does produce some zesty fare—everything from Anegada lobster cakes to spicy Jamaican pickapepper steak. Try flying fish served as an appetizer, followed by Haitian voodoo snapper pressed in Cajun spices, then grilled and served with fresh-fruit salsa. Equally delectable is mahimahi in Cruzan rum-and-mango sauce. The knockout dessert is the mango-banana pie.

Cruz Bay (across from the National Park dock). ℂ 340/693-8141. Reservations recommended. Main courses $9–$24. AE, MC, V. Daily 5–10pm.

Shipwreck Landing SEAFOOD/CONTINENTAL   Eight miles east of Cruz Bay on the road to Salt Pond Beach, Shipwreck Landing has palms and tropical plants on a veranda overlooking the sea. The intimate bar specializes in tropical frozen drinks. Lunch features a lot more than sandwiches, salads, and burgers—try pan-seared blackened snapper in Cajun spices, or the conch fritters. The chef shines at night, offering a pasta of the day along with such specialties as tantalizing Caribbean blackened shrimp. A lot of the fare is routine, including New York strip steak and fish and chips, but the grilled mahimahi in lime butter is worth the trip. Entertainment, including jazz and rock, is featured Wednesday and Saturday or Sunday nights, with no cover.

34 Freeman's Ground, Rte. 107, Coral Bay. ℂ 340/693-5640. Reservations requested. Main courses $6–$25; lunch from $6–$12. AE, DISC, MC, V. Daily 11am–10pm. Bar until 11pm.

INEXPENSIVE

Vie's Snack Shack ★ *Finds* WEST INDIAN   Vie's looks like little more than a plywood-sided hut, but its charming and gregarious owner is known as one of the best local chefs on St. John. Her garlic chicken is famous. She also serves conch fritters, johnnycakes, island-style beans and rice with meat sauce, and coconut and pineapple tarts. Don't leave without a glass of homemade limeade. The place is open most days, but as Vie says, "Some days, we might not be here at all"—so you'd better call before you head out.

East End Rd., Rte. 10 (13 miles east of Cruz Bay). ℂ 340/693-5033. Main courses $5–$6. No credit cards. Tues–Sat 10am–5pm (but call first!).

HITTING THE BEACH

The best beach, hands down, is **Trunk Bay** ★★, the biggest attraction on St. John. To miss its picture-perfect shoreline of white sand would be like touring Paris and skipping the Eiffel Tower. One of the loveliest beaches in the Caribbean, it offers ideal conditions for diving, snorkeling, swimming, and sailing. The only drawback is the crowds (watch for pickpockets). Beginning snorkelers in particular are attracted to the underwater trail near the shore (see "Sports & Other Outdoor Pursuits," below); you can rent snorkeling gear here. Lifeguards are on duty. Admission is $4 per person for those over age 16. If you're coming from St. Thomas, both taxis and safari buses to Trunk Bay meet the ferry from Red Hook when it docks at Cruz Bay.

Caneel Bay, the stamping ground of the rich and famous, has seven beautiful beaches on its 170 acres, and all are open to the public. **Caneel Bay Beach**

is easy to reach from the main entrance of the Caneel Bay resort. A staff member at the gatehouse will provide directions. **Hawksnest Beach** is one of the most beautiful beaches near the Caneel Bay properties. It's not wide, but it's choice. Since it's near Cruz Bay, where the ferry docks, it is the most crowded, especially when cruise-ship passengers come over from St. Thomas. Safari buses and taxis from Cruz Bay will take you along Northshore Road.

The campgrounds of **Cinnamon Bay** have their own beach, where forest rangers sometimes have to remind visitors to put their swim trunks back on. This is our particular favorite, a beautiful strip of white sand with hiking trails, great windsurfing, ruins, and wild donkeys (don't feed or pet them!). Changing rooms and showers are available, and you can rent watersports equipment. Snorkeling is especially popular; you'll often see big schools of purple triggerfish. This beach is best in the morning and at midday, as afternoons are likely to be windy. A marked **nature trail,** with signs identifying the flora, loops through a tropical forest on even turf before leading up to Centerline Road.

Maho Bay Beach is immediately to the east of Cinnamon Bay, and it also borders campgrounds. As you lie on the sand, you can see a whole hillside of pitched tents. This is also a popular beach, often with the campers themselves.

Francis Bay Beach and **Watermelon Cay Beach** are just a few more of the beaches you'll encounter traveling eastward along St. John's gently curving coastline. The beach at **Leinster Bay** is another haven for those seeking the solace of a private sunny retreat. You can swim in the bay's shallow water or snorkel over the spectacular and colorful coral reef, perhaps in the company of an occasional turtle or stingray.

The remote **Salt Pond Bay** is known to locals but often missed by visitors. It's on the beautiful coast in the southeast, adjacent to **Coral Bay.** The bay is tranquil, but the beach is somewhat rocky. It's a short walk down the hill from a parking lot (*Beware:* A few cars have recently been broken into). The snorkeling is good, and the bay has some fascinating tidal pools. The Ram Head Trail begins here and, winding for a mile, leads to a belvedere overlooking the bay. Facilities are meager but include an outhouse and a few tattered picnic tables.

If you want to escape the crowds, head for **Lameshur Bay Beach,** along the rugged south coast, west of Salt Pond Bay and accessible only via a bumpy dirt road. The sands are beautiful and the snorkeling is excellent. You can also take a 5-minute stroll down the road past the beach to explore the nearby ruins of an old plantation estate that was destroyed in a slave revolt.

Does St. John have a nude beach? Not officially, but lovely **Solomon Bay Beach** is a contender, although park rangers of late have sometimes asked people to put their swimwear back on. Leave Cruz Bay on Route 20 and turn left at the park service sign, about a ¼ mile past the visitor center. Park at the end of a cul-de-sac, then walk along the trail for about 15 minutes. Go early, and you'll practically have the beach to yourself.

SPORTS & OTHER OUTDOOR PURSUITS 🏝🏝

St. John offers some of the best snorkeling, scuba diving, swimming, fishing, hiking, sailing, and underwater photography in the Caribbean. The island is known for the Virgin Islands National Park, as well as for its coral-sand beaches, winding mountain roads, hidden coves, and trails that lead past old, bush-covered sugar-cane plantations. Just don't visit St. John expecting to play golf.

The most complete line of watersports equipment available, including rentals for windsurfing, snorkeling, kayaking, and sailing, is offered at the **Cinnamon Bay Watersports Center,** on Cinnamon Bay Beach (© **340/776-6330**).

One- and two-person sit-on-top kayaks rent for $15 to $20 per hour. You can also sail away in a 14-foot or 16-foot Hobie monohull **sailboat,** for $45 to $55 per hour.

BOAT EXCURSIONS   You can take half- and full-day boat trips, including a full-day excursion to The Baths at Virgin Gorda, for $95. A snorkel excursion on St. John costs $60 per person. Call **Vacation Vistas and Motor Yachts** (© **340/776-6462**) for details. **Cruz Bay Watersports** (© **340/776-6234**) offers trips to the British Virgin Islands (bring your passport) for $90, including food and beverages. British Customs fees are another $20.

FISHING   Outfitters located on St. Thomas offer sport-fishing trips here—they'll come over and pick you up. Call the **Charter Boat Center** (© **340/775-7990**) at Red Hook. Count on spending from $400 to $600 per party for a half-day of fishing.

HIKING   St. John has the most rewarding hiking in the Virgin Islands. The terrain ranges from arid and dry (in the east) to moist and semitropical (in the northwest). The island boasts more than 800 species of plants, 160 species of birds, and more than 20 trails maintained in fine form by the island's crew of park rangers. Much of the land on the island is designated as **Virgin Islands National Park.** Visitors must stop by the **Cruz Bay Visitor Center,** where you can pick up the park brochure, which includes a map of the park, and the *Virgin Islands National Park News,* which has the latest information on park activities. It's important to carry a lot of water and wear sunscreen and insect repellent when you hike.

St. John is laced with a wide choice of clearly marked walking paths. At least 20 of these originate from Northshore Road (Rte. 20) or from the island's main east–west artery, Centerline Road (Rte. 10). Each is marked at its starting point with a preplanned itinerary; the walks can last anywhere from 10 minutes to 2 hours. Maps are available from the national park headquarters at Cruz Bay.

One of our favorite hikes, the **Annaberg Historic Trail** (identified by the U.S. National Park Service as trail no. 10), requires only about a half-mile stroll. It departs from a clearly marked point along the island's north coast, near the junction of routes 10 and 20. This self-guided tour passes the partially restored ruins of a manor house built during the 1700s. Signs along the way give historical and botanical data. Visiting the ruins costs $4 per person for those over age 16. If you want to prolong your hiking experience, take the **Leinster Bay Trail** (trail no. 11), which begins near the point where trail no. 10 ends. It leads past mangrove swamps and coral inlets rich with plant and marine life; markers identify some of the plants and animals.

Near the beach at **Cinnamon Bay,** there's a marked nature trail, with signs identifying the flora. It's a relatively flat walk through a tropical forest, eventually leading straight up to Centerline Road.

The **National Park Service** (© **340/776-6201**) provides a number of ranger-led activities. One of the most popular is the guided 2½-mile **Reef Bay Hike.** Included is a stop at the only known petroglyphs on the island and a tour of the sugar-mill ruins. A park ranger discusses the area's natural and cultural history along the way. The hike starts at 9:30am on Monday, Tuesday, Thursday, and Friday and costs $20 per person. Reservations are required and can be made by phone.

SCUBA DIVING & SNORKELING 🤿🤿   **Cruz Bay Watersports,** P.O. Box 252, Cruz Bay, St. John (© **340/776-6234**), is a PADI and NAUI five-star

---

Moments Underwater Wonderful

At Trunk Bay, divers and snorkelers can follow the **National Park Underwater Trail** (© 340/776-6201), which stretches for 650 feet and helps you identify what you see—everything from false coral to colonial anemones. You'll pass lavender sea fans and schools of silversides. Rangers are on hand to provide information. There is a $4 admission fee to access the beach.

---

diving center. Certifications can be arranged through a dive master, for $350. Beginner scuba lessons start at $95. Two-tank reef dives with all dive gear cost $85, and wreck dives, night dives, and dive packages are available. In addition, snorkel tours are offered daily.

Divers can ask about scuba packages at **Low Key Watersports,** Wharfside Village (© 800/835-7718 in the U.S., or 340/693-8999). All wreck dives offered are two-tank/two-location dives and cost $83. One-tank dives cost $58 per person, with night dives going for $70. Snorkel tours are also available at $35 to $120 per person. The center also rents watersports gear, including masks, fins, snorkels, and dive skins, and arranges day sailing trips, kayaking tours, and deepsea fishing. Parasailing costs $65 per person.

The best place for snorkeling is **Trunk Bay** (see "Hitting the Beach," above). Snorkeling gear can be rented from the Cinnamon Bay Watersports Center (see above) for $5, plus a $25 deposit. Two of the best **snorkeling spots** around St. John are **Leinster Bay** 🐟🐟 and **Haulover Bay** 🐟🐟. Usually uncrowded Leinster Bay offers some of the best snorkeling in the U.S. Virgins. The water is calm, clear, and filled with brilliantly hued tropical fish. Haulover Bay is a favorite among locals. It's often deserted, and the waters are often clearer than in other spots around St. John. The ledges, walls, and nooks here are set very close together, making the bay a lot of fun for anyone with a little bit of experience.

SEA KAYAKING   Arawak Expeditions, based in Cruz Bay (© 800/238-8687 in the U.S., or 340/693-8312), provides kayaking gear, healthful meals, and experienced guides for full- and half-day outings. Trips cost $90 and $50, respectively. Multiday excursions with camping are also available; call their toll-free number if you'd like to arrange an entire vacation with them. These 5-day trips range in price from $995 to $1,295.

WINDSURFING   The windsurfing at Cinnamon Bay is some of the best anywhere, for either the beginner or the expert. The **Cinnamon Bay Watersports Center** (see above) rents high-quality equipment for all levels, even for kids. Boards cost $25 an hour; a 2-hour introductory lesson costs $80.

EXPLORING ST. JOHN

The best way to see St. John quickly, especially if you're on a cruise-ship layover, is to take a 2-hour **taxi tour.** The cost is $45 for one or two passengers, or $16 per person for three or more. Almost any taxi at Cruz Bay will take you on these tours, or you can call the **St. John Taxi Association** (© 340/693-7530).

Many visitors spend time at **Cruz Bay,** where the ferry docks. This village has interesting bars, restaurants, boutiques, and pastel-painted houses. It's a bit sleepy, but relaxing after the fast pace of St. Thomas.

Most cruise-ship passengers dart through Cruz Bay and head for the island's biggest attraction, **Virgin Islands National Park** 🐟🐟 (© 340/776-6201). The park totals 12,624 acres, including submerged lands and water adjacent to

St. John, and has more than 20 miles of hiking trails to explore. See "Sports & Other Outdoor Pursuits," above, for information on trails and organized park activities.

Other major sights on the island include **Trunk Bay** (see "Hitting the Beach," above), one of the world's most beautiful beaches, and **Fort Berg** (also called Fortsberg), at Coral Bay, which served as the base for the soldiers who brutally crushed the 1733 slave revolt. Finally, try to make time for the **Annaberg Ruins** on Leinster Bay Road, where the Danes maintained a thriving plantation and sugar mill after 1718. It's located off Northshore Road, east of Trunk Bay. Admission is $4 for those over age 16. On certain days of the week (dates vary), guided walks of the area are given by park rangers. For information on the **Annaberg Historic Trail,** see "Sports & Other Outdoor Pursuits," above.

SHOPPING 🖈🖈

Compared to St. Thomas, St. John's shopping isn't much, but what's here is interesting. The boutiques and shops of Cruz Bay are individualized and quite special. Most of the shops are clustered at **Mongoose Junction,** in a woodsy area beside the roadway, about a 5-minute walk from the ferry dock.

Before you leave the island, you'll want to visit the recently expanded **Wharfside Village,** just a few steps from the ferry-departure point. In this complex of courtyards, alleys, and shady patios is a mishmash of all sorts of boutiques, along with some restaurants, fast-food joints, and bars.

Bamboula, Mongoose Junction (© 340/693-8699), has an exotic and very appealing collection of gifts from St. John, the Caribbean, India, Indonesia, and Central Africa. The store also has clothing for both men and women under its own label—hand-batiked soft cottons and rayons made for comfort in a hot climate.

Clothing Studio, Mongoose Junction (© 340/776-6585), is the Caribbean's oldest hand-painted-clothing studio. Here you can watch talented artists create original designs on fine tropical clothing, including swimwear and daytime and evening clothing, mainly for women and children, with shirts for men.

Coconut Coast Studios, Frank Bay (© 340/776-6944), is the studio of Elaine Estern, best known for her Caribbean landscapes. It's 5 minutes from Cruz Bay; walk along the waterfront, bypassing Gallows Point. The outlet also sells calendars, gifts, limited edition prints, and lithographs. From December to May, the studio hosts a free sunset cocktail party Wednesday 5:30 to 7pm.

At the **Donald Schnell Studio,** Mongoose Junction (© 340/776-6420), Mr. Schnell and his assistants have created one of the finest collections of handmade pottery, sculpture, and blown glass in the Caribbean. The staff can be seen working daily. They're known for their rough-textured coral work. Water fountains are a specialty item, as are house signs and coral-pottery dinnerware.

The **Fabric Mill,** Mongoose Junction (© 340/776-6194), features silkscreened and batik fabrics from around the world. Vibrant rugs and bed, bathroom, and table linens, sarongs, scarves, and handbags are all made here.

R and I Patton Goldsmithing, Mongoose Junction (© 340/776-6548), is one of the oldest businesses on the island. Three-quarters of the merchandise here is made on St. John. There's a large selection of jewelry in sterling silver, gold, and precious stones. Also featured are the works of goldsmiths from outstanding American studios, as well as Spanish coins.

ST. JOHN AFTER DARK

Bring a good book. When it comes to nightlife, St. John is no St. Thomas. Most people are content to have a leisurely dinner and then head for bed.

Woody's Seafood Saloon, Cruz Bay (© **340/779-4625**), is the local dive and hangout at Cruz Bay, 150 feet from the ferry dock. It draws both visitors and a cross-section of island life from ex-pats to villa owners. You can come here to eat or drink. The place is particularly popular during happy hour from 3 to 6pm. It's about the only place on island you can order food at 10pm. Try the blackened-fish sandwich. The joint jumps Sunday to Thursday 11am to 1am, Friday and Saturday 11am to 2am.

The **Caneel Bay Bar,** at the Caneel Bay resort (© **340/776-6111**), has live music Thursday to Saturday 8 to 10:30pm. The most popular drinks are the Cool Caneel (local rum with sugar, lime, and anisette) and the trademark Plantation Punch (lime and orange juice with three different kinds of rum, bitters, and nutmeg).

The two places above are very touristy. If you'd like to drink and gossip with the locals, try **JJ's Texas Coast Café,** Cruz Bay (© **340/776-6908**), a real dive, across the park from the ferry dock. The margaritas here are lethal. Also at Cruz Bay, check out the action at **Fred's** (© **340/776-6363**), across from the Lime Inn. Fred's brings in bands and has dancing on Wednesday and Friday nights. It's just a little hole-in-the-wall and can get crowded fast.

The best sports bar on the island is **Skinny Legs,** Emmaus, Coral Bay, beyond the fire station (© **340/779-4982**). This shack made of tin and wood happens to have the best burgers in St. John. (The chili dogs aren't bad, either.) The yachting crowd likes to hang out here, though you wouldn't know it at first glance—it often seems that the richer they are, the poorer they dress. The bar has a satellite dish, dartboard, and horseshoe pits. Live music is presented on Saturday nights.

Morgan's Mango (© **340/693-8141**), a restaurant, is also one of the hottest watering holes on the island. It's in Cruz Bay, across from the National Park dock. Count yourself lucky if you get in on a crowded night in winter. The place became famous locally when it turned away Harrison Ford, who was vacationing at Caneel Bay. Thursday is Margarita Night, and Tuesday night is Lobster Night.

Index

Great Trips Like Great Days Begin with a Plan

FranklinCovey and Frommer's Bring You *Frommer's Favorite Places*® Planner

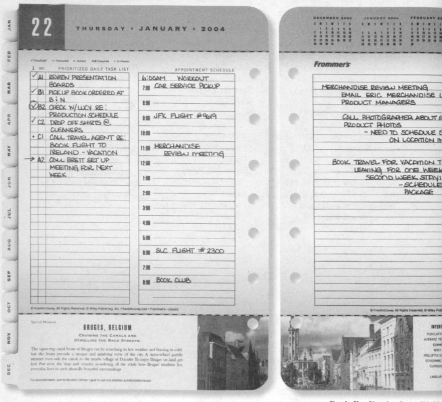

Classic Size Planning Pages $39.95

The planning experts at FranklinCovey have teamed up with the travel experts at Frommer's. The result is a full-year travel-themed planner filled with rich images and travel tips covering fifty-two of Frommer's Favorite Places.

- Each week will make you an expert about an intriguing corner of the world
- New facts and tips every day
- Beautiful, full-color photos of some of the most beautiful places on earth
- Proven planning tools from FranklinCovey for keeping track of tasks, appointments, notes, address/phone numbers, and more

Save 15%

when you purchase Frommer's Favorite Places travel-themed planner and a binder.

Order today before your next big trip.

www.franklincovey.com/frommers
Enter promo code 12252 at checkout for discount. Offer expires June 1, 2005.

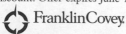

FROMMER'S® COMPLETE TRAVEL GUIDES

Alaska
Alaska Cruises & Ports of Call
American Southwest
Amsterdam
Argentina & Chile
Arizona
Atlanta
Australia
Austria
Bahamas
Barcelona, Madrid & Seville
Beijing
Belgium, Holland & Luxembourg
Bermuda
Boston
Brazil
British Columbia & the Canadian Rockies
Brussels & Bruges
Budapest & the Best of Hungary
Calgary
California
Canada
Cancún, Cozumel & the Yucatán
Cape Cod, Nantucket & Martha's Vineyard
Caribbean
Caribbean Cruises & Ports of Call
Caribbean Ports of Call
Carolinas & Georgia
Chicago
China
Colorado
Costa Rica
Cuba
Denmark
Denver, Boulder & Colorado Springs
England
Europe
Europe by Rail
European Cruises & Ports of Call

Florence, Tuscany & Umbria
Florida
France
Germany
Great Britain
Greece
Greek Islands
Halifax
Hawaii
Hong Kong
Honolulu, Waikiki & Oahu
India
Ireland
Israel
Italy
Jamaica
Japan
Kauai
Las Vegas
London
Los Angeles
Maryland & Delaware
Maui
Mexico
Montana & Wyoming
Montréal & Québec City
Munich & the Bavarian Alps
Nashville & Memphis
Newfoundland & Labrador
New England
New Mexico
New Orleans
New York City
New York State
New Zealand
Northern Italy
Norway
Nova Scotia, New Brunswick & Prince Edward Island
Oregon
Ottawa
Paris

Peru
Philadelphia & the Amish Country
Portugal
Prague & the Best of the Czech Republic
Provence & the Riviera
Puerto Rico
Rome
San Antonio & Austin
San Diego
San Francisco
Santa Fe, Taos & Albuquerque
Scandinavia
Scotland
Seattle
Shanghai
Sicily
Singapore & Malaysia
South Africa
South America
South Florida
South Pacific
Southeast Asia
Spain
Sweden
Switzerland
Texas
Thailand
Tokyo
Toronto
USA
Utah
Vancouver & Victoria
Vermont, New Hampshire & Maine
Vienna & the Danube Valley
Virgin Islands
Virginia
Walt Disney World® & Orlando
Washington, D.C.
Washington State

FROMMER'S® DOLLAR-A-DAY GUIDES

Australia from $50 a Day
California from $70 a Day
England from $75 a Day
Europe from $70 a Day
Florida from $70 a Day
Hawaii from $80 a Day

Ireland from $80 a Day
Italy from $70 a Day
London from $90 a Day
New York from $90 a Day
Paris from $90 a Day
San Francisco from $70 a Day

Washington, D.C. from $80 a Day
Portable London from $90 a Day
Portable New York City from $90 a Day
Portable Paris from $90 a Day

FROMMER'S® PORTABLE GUIDES

Acapulco, Ixtapa & Zihuatanejo
Amsterdam
Aruba
Australia's Great Barrier Reef
Bahamas
Berlin
Big Island of Hawaii
Boston
California Wine Country
Cancún
Cayman Islands
Charleston
Chicago
Disneyland®
Dominican Republic
Dublin

Florence
Frankfurt
Hong Kong
Las Vegas
Las Vegas for Non-Gamblers
London
Los Angeles
Los Cabos & Baja
Maine Coast
Maui
Miami
Nantucket & Martha's Vineyard
New Orleans
New York City
Paris

Phoenix & Scottsdale
Portland
Puerto Rico
Puerto Vallarta, Manzanillo & Guadalajara
Rio de Janeiro
San Diego
San Francisco
Savannah
Vancouver
Vancouver Island
Venice
Virgin Islands
Washington, D.C.
Whistler

FROMMER'S® NATIONAL PARK GUIDES

Algonquin Provincial Park
Banff & Jasper
Family Vacations in the National
  Parks

Grand Canyon
National Parks of the American
  West
Rocky Mountain

Yellowstone & Grand Teton
Yosemite & Sequoia/Kings
  Canyon
Zion & Bryce Canyon

FROMMER'S® MEMORABLE WALKS

Chicago
London

New York
Paris

San Francisco

FROMMER'S® WITH KIDS GUIDES

Chicago
Las Vegas
New York City

Ottawa
San Francisco
Toronto

Vancouver
Walt Disney World® & Orlando
Washington, D.C.

SUZY GERSHMAN'S BORN TO SHOP GUIDES

Born to Shop: France
Born to Shop: Hong Kong,
  Shanghai & Beijing

Born to Shop: Italy
Born to Shop: London

Born to Shop: New York
Born to Shop: Paris

FROMMER'S® IRREVERENT GUIDES

Amsterdam
Boston
Chicago
Las Vegas
London

Los Angeles
Manhattan
New Orleans
Paris
Rome

San Francisco
Seattle & Portland
Vancouver
Walt Disney World®
Washington, D.C.

FROMMER'S® BEST-LOVED DRIVING TOURS

Austria
Britain
California
France

Germany
Ireland
Italy
New England

Northern Italy
Scotland
Spain
Tuscany & Umbria

THE UNOFFICIAL GUIDES®

Beyond Disney
Central Italy
Chicago
Cruises
Disneyland®
England
Florida
Florida with Kids
Inside Disney

Hawaii
Las Vegas
London
Maui
Mexico's Best Beach Resorts
Mini Las Vegas
Mini-Mickey
New Orleans
New York City

Paris
San Francisco
Skiing & Snowboarding in the
  West
Walt Disney World®
Walt Disney World® for
  Grown-ups
Walt Disney World® with Kids
Washington, D.C.

SPECIAL-INTEREST TITLES

Athens Past & Present
Cities Ranked & Rated
Frommer's Best Day Trips from London
Frommer's Caribbean Hideaways
Frommer's China: The 50 Most Memorable Trips
Frommer's Exploring America by RV
Frommer's Gay & Lesbian Europe
Frommer's Best RV and Tent Campgrounds
  in the U.S.A.

Frommer's Road Atlas Europe
Frommer's Road Atlas France
Frommer's Road Atlas Ireland
Frommer's Wonderful Weekends from
  New York City
The New York Times' Guide to Unforgettable
  Weekends
Retirement Places Rated
Rome Past & Present

Travel Tip: He who finds the best hotel deal has more to spend on facials involving knobbly vegetables.

Hello, the Roaming Gnome here. I've been nabbed from the garden and taken round the world. The people who took me are so terribly clever. They find the best offerings on Travelocity. For very little cha-ching. And that means I get to be pampered and exfoliated till I'm pink as a bunny's doodah.

*** travelocity®

Travel Tip: Make sure there's customer service for any change of plans — involving friendly natives, for example.

One can plan and plan, but if you don't book with the right people you can't seize le moment and canoodle with the poodle named Pansy. I, for one, am all for fraternizing with the locals. Better yet, if I need to extend my stay and my gnome nappers are willing, it can all be arranged through the 800 number at, oh look, how convenient, the lovely company coat of arms.

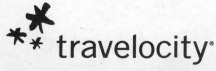